Annual Abstract of Statistics

No 156
2020 Edition
Volume 2 of 2
Compiled by: Dandy Booksellers

Contacts

For information about the content of this publication, contact
Dandy Booksellers: Tel 020 7624 2993
Email: enquiries@dandybooksellers.com

Publications orders

To obtain the print version of this publication, please contact
Dandy Booksellers
Tel: 0207 624 2993
Fax: 0207 624 5049
Email: enquiries@dandybooksellers.com
Post: 15 Hoopers Yard, Kimberley Road, London, NW6 7EJ
Web: www.dandybooksellers.com

Annual Abstract of Statistics 2020

Contents	Page No.

Annual Abstract of Statistics 2020

Contents		Page No.

Annual Abstract of Statistics 2020

Contents		Page No.

Annual Abstract of Statistics 2020

Contents	Page No.

Annual Abstract of Statistics 2020

Contents	Page No.

Annual Abstract of Statistics 2020

Contents	Page No.

Annual Abstract of Statistics 2020

Contents	Page No.

Units of measurement

Length

1 millimetre (mm)	= 0.03937 inch	
1 centimetre (cm)	= 10 millimetres	= 0.3937 inch
1 metre (m)	= 1,000 millimetres	= 1.094 yards
1 kilometre (km)	= 1,000 metres	= 0.6214 mile
1 inch (in.)		= 25.40 millimetres or 2.540 centimetres
1 foot (ft.)	= 12 inches	= 0.3048 metre
1 yard (yd.)	= 3 feet	= 0.9144 metre
1 mile	= 1,760 yards	= 1.609 kilometres

Area

1 square millimetre (mm2)		= 0.001550 square inch
1 square metre (m2)	= one million square millimetres	= 1.196 square yards
1 hectare (ha)	= 10,000 square metres	= 2.471 acres
1 square kilometre (km2)	= one million square metres	= 247.1 acres
1 square inch (sq. in.)		= 645.2 square millimetres or 6.452 square centimetres
1 square foot (sq. ft.)	= 144 square inches	= 0.09290 square metre or 929.0 square centimetres
1 square yard (sq. yd.)	= 9 square feet	= 0.8361 square metre
1 acre	= 4,840 square yards	= 4,046 square metres or 0.4047 hectare
1 square mile (sq. mile)	= 640 acres	= 2.590 square kilometres or 259.0 hectares

Volume

1 cubic centimetre (cm3)		= 0.06102 cubic inch
1 cubic decimetre (dm3)	= 1,000 cubic centimetres	= 0.03531 cubic foot
1 cubic metre (m3)	= one million cubic centimetres	= 1.308 cubic yards
1 cubic inch (cu.in.)		=16.39 cubic centimetres
1 cubic foot (cu. ft.)	= 1,728 cubic inches	= 0.02832 cubic metre or 28.32 cubic decimetres
1 cubic yard (cu. yd.)	= 27 cubic feet	= 0.7646 cubic metre

Capacity

1 litre (l)	= 1 cubic decimetre	= 0.2200 gallon
1 hectolitre (hl)	= 100 litres	= 22.00 gallons
1 pint		= 0.5682 litre
1 quart	= 2 pints	= 1.137 litres
1 gallon	= 8 pints	= 4.546 litres
1 bulk barrel	= 36 gallons (gal.)	= 1.637 hectolitres

Weight

1 gram (g)		= 0.03527 ounce avoirdupois
1 hectogram (hg)	= 100 grams	= 3.527 ounces or 0.2205 pound
1 kilogram (kg)	= 1,000 grams or 10 hectograms	= 2.205 pounds
1 tonne (t)	= 1,000 kilograms	= 1.102 short tons or 0.9842 long ton
1 ounce avoirdupois (oz.)	= 437.5 grains	= 28.35 grams
1 pound avoirdupois (lb.)	= 16 ounces	= 0.4536 kilogram
1 hundredweight (cwt.)	= 112 pounds	= 50.80 kilograms
1 short ton	= 2,000 pounds	= 907.2 kilograms or 0.9072 tonne
1 long ton (referred to as ton)	= 2,240 pounds	= 1,016 kilograms or 1.016 tonnes
1 ounce troy	= 480 grains	= 31.10 grams

Energy

British thermal unit (Btu)	= 0.2520 kilocalorie (kcal) = 1.055 kilojoule (kj)
Therm	= 105 British thermal units = 25,200 kcal = 105,506 kj
Megawatt hour (MWh)	= 106 watt hours (Wh)
Gigawatt hour (GWh)	= 106 kilowatt hours = 34,121 therms

Food and drink

Butter	23,310 litres milk	= 1 tonne butter (average)
Cheese	10,070 litres milk	= 1 tonne cheese
Condensed milk	2,550 litres milk	= 1 tonne full cream condensed milk
	2,953 litres skimmed milk	= 1 tonne skimmed condensed milk
Milk	1 million litres	= 1,030 tonnes
Milk powder	8,054 litres milk	= 1 tonne full cream milk powder
	10,740 litres skimmed milk	= 1 tonne skimmed milk powder
Eggs	17,126 eggs	= 1 tonne (approximate)
Sugar	100 tonnes sugar beet	= 92 tonnes refined sugar
	100 tonnes cane sugar	= 96 tonnes refined sugar

Shipping

Gross tonnage	= The total volume of all the enclosed spaces of a vessel, the unit of measurement being a 'ton' of 100 cubic feet.
Deadweight tonnage	= Deadweight tonnage is the total weight in tons of 2,240 lb. that a ship can legally carry, that is the total weight of cargo, bunkers, stores and crew.

Introduction

Welcome to the 2020 edition of the Annual Abstract of Statistics. This compendium draws together statistics from a wide range of official and other authoritative sources.

Dandy Booksellers have sourced and formatted these tables under instruction from various government departments/ organisations

Current data for many of the series appearing in this Annual Abstract are contained in other ONS publications, such as Economic & Labour Market Review, Population Trends, Health Statistics Quarterly and Financial Statistics. These titles can be purchased through Dandy Booksellers.

The name (and telephone number, where this is available) of the organisation providing the statistics are shown under each table. In addition, a list of Sources is given at the back of the book, which sets out the official publications or other sources to which further reference can be made.

Identification codes

The four-letter identification code at the top of each data column, or at the side of each row is the ONS reference for this series of data on their database. Please quote the relevant code if you contact them requiring any further information about the data. On some tables it is not possible to include these codes, so please quote the table number in these cases.

Definitions and classification

Time series
So far as possible annual totals are given throughout, but quarterly or monthly figures are given where these are more suitable to the type of series.

Standard Industrial Classification

A Standard Industrial Classification (SIC) was first introduced into the UK in 1948 for use in classifying business establishments and other statistical units by the type of economic activity in which they are engaged. The classification provides a framework for the collection, tabulation, presentation and analysis of data about economic activities. In addition, it can be used for administrative purposes and by non-government bodies as a convenient way of classifying industrial activities into a common structure.

Classification changes

Since 1948 the classification has been revised in 1958, 1968, 1980, 1992, 1997, and 2003. One of the principal objectives of the 1980 revision was to eliminate differences from the activity classification issued by the Statistical Office of the European Communities (Eurostat) and entitled 'Nomenclature générale des activités économiques dans les Communautés Européennes', usually abbreviated to NACE.

EC regulation

A European Community regulation is directly applicable in all member states. In 1990 the European Communities introduced a new statistical classification of economic activities (NACE Rev 1) by regulation. The regulation made it obligatory for the UK to introduce a new Standard Industrial Classification SIC(92), based on NACE Rev 1. UK SIC(92) was based exactly on NACE Rev 1 but, where it was thought necessary or helpful, a fifth digit was added to form subclasses of the NACE 1 four digit system. Classification systems need to be revised periodically because, over time, new products, processes and industries emerge. In January 2003 a minor revision of NACE Rev 1, known as NACE Rev 1.1, was published in the Official Journal of the European Communities.

Consequently, the UK was obliged to introduce a new Standard Industrial Classification, SIC(2003) consistent with NACE Rev 1.1. The UK took the opportunity of the 2003 revision also to update the national Subclasses. Full details are available in UK Standard Industrial Classification of Economic Activities 2003 and the Indexes to the UK Standard Industrial Classification of Economic Activities 2003.

Following a major revision to NACE in 2007 (NACE Rev. 2) an updated UK SIC was published. The current UK Standard Industrial Classification of Economic activities is SIC2007 and was effective from 1 January 2008.

As already indicated, NACE was originally an acronym but now all countries use 'NACE' to describe the European Community classification of Economic Activities.

UK SIC structure

The UK SIC is based exactly on NACE but, where it was thought necessary or helpful, a fifth digit has been added to form subclasses of the NACE four digit classes. Thus, the UK SIC is a hierarchical five digit system. UK SIC (2007) is divided into 21 sections, each denoted by a single letter from A to U. The letters of the sections can be uniquely defined by the next breakdown, the divisions (denoted by two digits). The divisions are then broken down into groups (three digits), then into classes (four digits) and, in several cases, again into subclasses (five digits).

As with previous versions of the SIC, there is a separate publication containing detailed lists of activities and, in some cases, the products of those activities, contained in UK SIC (2007) at: www.statistics.gov.uk/ statbase/Product.asp?vlnk=14012

Related classifications

There are other classifications, both national and international, which may be used in conjunction with the industrial classification. These include, for example, the classification of occupations, which relates to the jobs performed by individual workers rather than to the industry in which they work. The workers classified to a particular industry will fall into a number of different categories of an occupational classification and similarly the workers in some occupations may be found in many different industries. The UK uses the Standard Occupational Classification (SOC).

A second classification is by sector. In the UK this is the Sector Classification for the National Accounts. The economy is split up into institutional sectors with each economic unit allocated to one of these sectors. The sectors are: General government, Financial corporations, Non-financial corporations (private and public), Non-profit institutions serving households and the 'Rest of the world' sector. In principle, the classification embraces all economic units engaging in transactions in goods and services and financial assets.

Symbols and conventions used

Change of basis
Where consecutive figures have been compiled on different bases and are not strictly comparable, a footnote is added indicating the nature of the difference.

Geographic coverage
Statistics relate mainly to the UK. Where figures relate to other areas, this is indicated on the table.

Units of measurement
The various units of measurement used are listed after the Contents.

Rounding of figures
In tables where figures have been rounded to the nearest final digit, the constituent items may not add up exactly to the total.

Symbols
The following symbols have been used throughout:

.. = not available or not applicable (also information supressed to avoid disclosure)

- = nil or less than half the final digit shown

Office for National Statistics online:
www.ons.gov.uk
Web-based access to time series, cross-sectional data and metadata from across the Government Statistical Service (GSS), is available using the site search function from the homepage. Download many datasets, in whole or in part, or consult directory information for all GSS statistical resources, including censuses, surveys, periodicals and enquiry services. Information is posted as PDF electronic documents or in XLS and CSV formats, compatible with most spreadsheet packages.

Contact point
Dandy Booksellers welcomes any feedback on the content of the Annual Abstract, including comments on the format of the data and the selection of topics. Comments and requests for general information should be addressed to:

Dandy Booksellers Ltd.
15 Hoopers Yard
Kimberley Road
London, NW6 7EJ
Tel: 020 7624 2993
Fax: 020 7624 5049

www.dandybooksellers.com
www.publicinformationonline.com
www.civilserviceyearbook.com
@dandybookseller
or
enquiries@dandybooksellers.com

Defence

Chapter 14

Defence

This section includes figures on Defence expenditure, on the size and role of the Armed Forces and on related support activities. Much of the material used in this section can be found in UK Defence Statistics.

Rounding of the figures in these tables is used both as a means of disclosure control and to improve the clarity of outputs and convey appropriate levels of precision to users. For more details on the MOD statistical disclosure plicy see: https://www.gov.uk/government/publications/defence-statistics-policies/ministry-of-defence-disclosure-control-and-rounding-policy

Table 14.1 United Kingdom Defence Expenditure by Commodity Block

This table shows a breakdown of Resource & Capital DEL and AME by Commodity Block. Under Clear Line of Sight (CLoS), the main MOD expenditure categories are now presented as Commodity Blocks. This provides a more meaningful description of the Department's planned and actual spend, and enables a clearer understanding of the MOD's plans and expenditure over the Spending Review period.

These statistics are produced using data from the MOD's Financial Management Information Systems (FMIS). This data is also used to produce the MOD Annual Report and Accounts, is subject to international standards and is audited by the NAO. The R&D figures provided in are not Frascati compliant, and are based on a wider, accounting definition of R&D.

There are some differences between these figures and government transparency data. This is because this table includes all MOD spend as recorded in the accounts, whereas some transactions have been redacted from the transaction data (which is at a lower level of granularity) for national security reasons. This divergence between data published in UK Defence Statistics and that released under transparency will continue for the foreseeable future. UK Defence Statistics does not display data at a level that could be considered sensitive, disclosive or impact on contractual confidentiality.

Further information on these statistics please contact Defence Economics by email: DefStrat-Stat-Enquiries-Mailbox@mod.gov.uk or visit their website: www.gov.uk/government/organisations/ministry-of-defence/about/statistics

Table 14.2 Intake to UK Regular Forces by gender

Intake to UK Regular Forces Comprises new entrants, re-entrants, direct trained entrants (including Professionally Qualified Officers) and intake from the reserves. It excludes all movements within the Regular Forces; including flows from the untrained to trained strength, transfers between Services and flows from Ranks to Officer due to promotion. **UK Regulars** are Full-time Service personnel, including Nursing Services, but excluding FTRS personnel, Gurkhas, mobilised Reservists, MPGS, LEP and NRPS.

Personnel statistics are derived from the Department's Joint Personnel Administration (JPA) system, which is used for the administration of all Armed Forces personnel. All personnel in the Regular Armed Forces must be recorded on JPA in order for them to receive their pay. Therefore the overall intake figures are accurate.

Table 14.3abc - UK Armed Forces Equipment and Formations

These tables provide information on the numbers and types of formations, vessels, aircraft and selected land equipment of the UK Armed Forces. Data are received annually via data suppliers from Navy Command, Army HQ, Air Command and Joint Helicopter Command. For more details see: https://www.gov.uk/government/collections/uk-armed-forces-equipment-and-formations.

Table 14.3a - Data on numbers of Naval ships and submarines, aircraft and formations are provided by associated 1* Divisional areas within Navy Command Headquarters and from across the wider Royal Navy. These numbers are collated and crossed checked internally by each area before submission.

Table 14.3b - Data on Army formations are provided by the Army HQ Organisation Branch, which is responsible for the structure of the Army and the supporting Management Information Systems. The data held on these systems is cross-checked by Organisation Branch staff with the Army HQ's Planning and Military Strategy branches.

Table 14.3c - Data on RAF aircraft numbers are provided by Air Command and are cross-checked against numbers planned in the relevant Annual Budgeting Cycle. Information on RAF squadrons and formations has been incrementally generated from planned force structure changes.

Table 14.4 Outflow from UK Regular Forces, trained and untrained

Outflow from UK Regular Forces, both trained and untrained, include personnel leaving the Services, deaths, recalled reservists on release and outflow to the Home Service battalions of the Royal Irish Regiment (which disbanded on 31 March 2008). They do not include promotion from Ranks to Officers or flows between Services. Prior to year ending 31 March 2009, Army Outflow included the net flow of personnel from the Regular Armed Forces to LTA. After year ending 31 March 2009 outflow does not include this flow to LTA.

Trained Strength comprises military personnel who have completed Phase 1 and 2 training for Royal Navy/Royal Marines, the Army (prior to 1 October 2016) and the Royal Air Force. Following the change in definition of trained strength from 1 October 2016 trained strength for the Army comprises of personnel who have completed Phase 1 training.

UK Regulars are Full-time Service personnel, including Nursing Services, but excluding FTRS personnel, Gurkhas, mobilised Reservists, MPGS, LEP and NRPS.

Table 14.5 UK Armed Forces Full-time trained strength (FTTS) and workforce requirement

The Full-Time Trained Strength of the UK Armed Forces is defined as comprising of trained UK Regular Forces, trained Gurkhas and elements of the FTRS (Full Time Reserve Service) personnel. It does not include mobilised reservists.

Workforce Requirement is the number of Service personnel needed, based on the Defence Planning Round, set for each of the three Services.

Table 14.6 Trends in Service and civilian personnel strengths

All UK Forces Service Personnel comprises UK Regular Forces, Gurkhas, Military Provost Guard Service (MPGS), Locally Engaged Personnel (LEP), Volunteer Reserve, Serving Regular Reserve, Sponsored Reserve, and FTRS of unknown origin. University Officer Cadets are excluded. Unless otherwise stated, includes trained and untrained personnel.

Volunteer Reserves are members of society who voluntarily accept a liability to attend training with the Armed Forces on a part-time basis (usually conducted during evenings and weekends) and to be mobilised to deploy on operations alongside the Regular Force.

Locally Engaged Personnel (LEP) are personnel recruited overseas exclusively for employment in support of the UK Armed Forces deployed in a particular overseas location and on terms and conditions of service applicable only to that overseas location or Administration. In this publication, LEP equates to those members of the Royal Gibraltar Permanent Cadre only and therefore exclude UK Regular Army Officers and Royal Gibraltar Volunteer Reserve.

Civilian Level 0 contains all those at Level 1 plus DE&S Trading Entity, Trading Funds and Locally Engaged Civilians. This is used for external reporting, including National Statistics publications, Strategic Defence and Security Review Baseline, UKDS and Parliamentary Business.

Civilian Level 1 includes permanent and casual civilian personnel, Royal Fleet Auxiliary, but excludes DE&S Trading Entity, Trading Funds and Locally engaged civilians. This is generally used for MOD internal reporting and planning.

Top Level Budgetary Area (TLB) are the major organisational groupings of the MOD directly responsible for the planning, management and delivery of departmental capability.

DE&S Trading Entity: Defence Equipment and Support (DE&S) has been reported as a bespoke trading entity from 1 July 2015.

Locally engaged civilians: MOD employs a number of civilian personnel overseas, known as Locally engaged civilians (LECs). They have not been recruited through fair and open competition in the UK under the Civil Service Order in Council and they are not therefore members of the Home Civil Service or the Diplomatic Service.

Table 14.7a Land holdings by parent service and type of ownership

The Ministry of Defence (MOD) is one of the largest landowners in the country, with an estate nearly equal to 2% of the UK land mass. MOD sites are used for training, accommodation and provides a base from which operations can be instigated. The estate is currently managed by the Defence Infrastructure Organisation (DIO), who have a remit to ensure the safety, sustainability and rationalisation of the estate. The MOD has published land holdings and building statistics since 1981.

There are several ways that land can be held by organisations, DIO manages land through the following three ways:

1. Freehold – land which has been bought on a permanent basis

2. Leasehold – land which is held by an organisation for a definitive period of time

3. Rights Held – land which is held on a (most usually) short term and contractual basis or through grants for a specific purpose. MOD holds a lot of land in this way because it is a more cost effective and flexible way to meet the changing operational requirements for defence.

The figures in this table have been taken from the Infrastructure Management System (IMS). IMS was implemented by DIO in 2014 as a mechanism to more effectively manage the defence infrastructure

Table 14.7b Service Family Accommodation in the United Kingdom

The provision of good quality living accommodation for Service personnel and their families is managed by the MOD's Defence Infrastructure Organisation (DIO), and should meet the aims set out in the Armed Forces Covenant. DIO manages these properties in the UK (and some overseas locations), including planning targeted improvement programmes and future requirements.

For further information see: https://www.gov.uk/government/collections/service-family-accommodation-bulletin-index

Table 14.8ab National and international locations of UK Regular Forces and civilian personnel

There are a number of planned modifications to the structure and way each of the Services would operate, with a focus on creating a versatile Force. The modifications include the decisions to reconfigure the Army by reducing it from six to five multirole brigades. The Royal Air Force (RAF) structure will focus around fewer Fast Jet platforms with increasing numbers of Unmanned Air Vehicles and an improved strategic Air Transport Fleet. Additionally, the British Forces personnel currently based in Germany will be relocated back in the UK. These changes are planned to come into effect by 2020 and will consequently impact on basing both overseas and in the UK.

Figures are for UK Regular Forces (including both Trained and Untrained personnel), and therefore exclude Gurkhas, Full Time Reserve Service personnel and mobilised reservists. MOD Civilian figures are reported as Full Time Equivalent (FTE). FTE is a measure of the size of the workforce taking into account that some people work part-time. Part-time staff are counted according to the number of hours they work per week as a proportion of normal hours for their grade and location.

Table 14.9ab UK Regular Armed Forces Mortality rates

The data is presented for Tri-Service and separately for each of the services; Naval Service (Royal Navy and Royal Marines), Army (including Gurkhas) and Royal Air Force (RAF). UK Armed Forces Reservists who died whilst deployed on operations are included in the data presented since they are classed as 'Regulars' whilst on deployment. Figures include suicides in line with the definition used by the Office for National Statistics (ONS) in the publication of National Statistics.

Standardised Mortality Ratios (SMR) - To make comparisons between death rates in the UK Armed Forces and the UK general population, an SMR is calculated which takes account of the different age and gender structure in the two populations. The SMR is the ratio of the number of deaths observed in the Armed Forces to the number of deaths expected if the Armed Forces population had the same age and gender specific rates as the UK general population in each year. An SMR over (or under) 100 indicates a higher (or lower) number of observed deaths than expected compared to the UK general population and represents whether the Armed Forces are at an increased or decreased risk of death compared to the UK population. An SMR of 100 implies there is no difference in rates when comparing the UK Regular Armed Forces population with the UK population. An SMR where the 95% confidence interval does not encompass 100 implies there is a statistically significant difference in rates when comparing the UK regular Armed Forces population with the UK general population.

14.10 Strength of United Kingdom Medical Staff

The figures shown in 14.10 are for regular personnel only and therefore do not represent the strength of either Reserve or veterinarian personnel.

14.1 Defence Expenditure by Commodity Block

Inclusive of non-recoverable VAT at Current Prices (£ million)

	Outturn 2012/13	Outturn 2013/14	Outturn 2014/15	Outturn 2015/16	Outturn 2016/17	Outturn 2017/18	Outturn 2018/19
Defence Spending	**34 260**	**34 559**	**34 365** [1]	**35 100** [1]	**35 283** [1]	**36 605** [1]	**38 026**
Departmental Expenditure Limits (DEL)	**43 718**	**44 020**	**42 891**	**42 826**	**44 111**	**43 902**	**44 866**
Cash Resource DEL	**35 874**	**36 448**	**35 105**	**35 253**	**35 423**	**34 199**	**34 571**
Personnel Costs	11 921	11 473	10 903	11 009	11 377	11 417	11 654
of which: Service Personnel Costs[2]	9 598	9 156	8 588	9 319	9 623	9 684	9 785
Civilian Personnel Costs[3]	2 323	2 318	2 315	1 690	1 753	1 733	1 869
Infrastructure Costs[4]	4 594	4 707	4 664	4 177	4 153	4 114	4 322
Inventory Consumption[5]	2 312	2 161	1 822	1 515	1 280	1 283	1 254
Equipment Support Costs[6]	5 588	6 411	6 528	6 452	6 674	6 831	7 064
Other Costs & Services[7]	1 923	2 027	2 395	2 197	1 662	1 803	1 943
Receipts & Other Income[8]	-1 277	-1 196	-1 133	-1 001	-1 018	-1 082	-1 091
Depreciation & Impairment[9]	9 458	9 462	8 510	7 711	8 819	7 287	6 830
Cash Release of Provisions[10]	239	178	219	256	265	303	395
Research & Development Costs[11]	944	988	1 012	894 ||	164	223	229
Conflict Stability and Security Fund	44	50	56	53	87	91	89
Arm's Length Bodies[1,12]	127	187	130	165	153	165	204
DE&S Bespoke Trading Entity[13]	*	*	*	1 028	1 044	1 041	981
War Pension Benefits[14]	*	*	*	795	765	723	697
Capital DEL[15]	**7 843**	**7 572**	**7 786**	**7 574**	**8 689**	**9 704**	**10 294**
Single Use Military Equipment[16]	4 768	4 528	4 889	5 290	5 304	5 708	5 893
Other Capital (Fiscal)[17]	3 141	3 091	3 202	2 621	2 283	2 950	3 272
Research & Development Costs[11]	*	*	*	*	1 104	1 008	1 110
Fixed Asset/Estate Disposal Costs	- 64	- 44	- 251	- 423	- 37	- 33	- 43
New Loans and Loan Repayments	- 6	- 6	- 57	- 3	- 63	-	9
Arm's Length Bodies[12]	3	3	2	2	2	2	3
DE&S Bespoke Trading Entity[13]	*	*	*	87	95	64	51
Conflict Stability and Security Fund	-	-	-	-	-	4	-
Annually Managed Expenditure (AME)	**1 831**	**835**	**1 915**	**6 132**	**- 211**	**9 735**	**-7 883**
Resource AME	**1 867**	**963**	**1 864**	**6 103**	**- 211**	**9 690**	**-7 883**
Depreciation & Impairment	1 062	- 208	461	563	142	861	71
Provisions	318	148	742	6 096	501	8 548	-7 377
Cash Release of Provisions	- 239	- 203	- 219	- 256	- 265	- 303	- 395
Movement on Fair Value of Financial Instruments	- 183	368	43	- 300	- 589	584	- 181
War Pension Benefits[14]	908	859	838	*	*	*	*
Capital AME	**- 35**	**- 129**	**51**	**29**	**-**	**44**	**-**
Provision Costs	- 35	- 129	51	29	-	44	-

|| discontinuity in time series

Source: Defence Economics (Defence Expenditure Analysis) and Defence Resources

1. Since 2014/15 a small amount of Depreciation from the Arm's Length Bodies Resource DEL Total (£17m in 2015/16), has been included in the calculation of Defence Spending.
2. Military and other ranks pay and other allowances; SCAPE; Employer's National Insurance Contributions (ERNIC).
3. Civilian pay and other allowances; pension contributions; Employer's National Insurance Contributions (ERNIC).
4. Property management; service charges; IT & communications costs; utilities costs.
5. Munitions; stores; fuel (marine & aviation); clothing; other materials consumed e.g. stationary, sundries, general stores etc.
6. Equipment support costs, including leases & hire charges for plant, machinery and transport.
7. Travel & subsistence; professional services & fees; training.
8. Receipts from various sources; costs recoveries; dividends; interest.
9. Depreciation & impairments on Non-Current Assets (Property, SUME, dual purpose).
10. Nuclear and non nuclear provisions e.g. staff redundancies, legal costs, environmental, etc.
11. Research and Development expenditure is incurred mainly for the future benefit of the Department. Such expenditure is primarily incurred on the development of new Single Use Military Equipment (SUME) and on the improvement of the effectiveness and capability of existing SUME.
12. Council of Reserve Forces and Cadet Associations; Royal Hospital Chelsea; National Army Museum; RAF Museum; National Museum of the Royal Navy; Commonwealth War Graves Commission; Single Source Regulations Office.
13. The Defence Equipment & Support Bespoke Trading Entity (DE&S BTE) became an arms-length body of the MOD on 01 April 2014. DE&S BTE has a distinct operating cost cap as a financial control and reporting mechanism. This is to reflect its Arm's Length management from the MOD Head Office and exclusion from the MOD's Administration targets. The DE&S BTE is an Executive Agency in terms of classification by the ONS but will still be part of the MOD Vote and will publish separate plans and annual accounts at the end of FY 2015-16
14. In 2015/16 War Pensions Benefits was reclassified from AME to Cash Resource DEL.
15. Expenditure on the acquisition of Non-Current Assets.
16. Single Use Military Equipment (SUME) are assets which only have a military use, such as tanks and fighter aircraft. Dual use items i.e. those that also have a civilian use are recorded under the other category.
17. Expenditure on Property, Plant and dual use military equipment that could be used by civilian organisations for the production of goods and services.

14.2 Intake to UK Regular Forces by gender

12 Months Ending:

	2015 31 Mar		2015 30 Sep		2016 31 Mar		2016 30 Sep		2017 31 Mar		2017 30 Sep		2018 31 Mar		2018 30 Sep		2019 31 Mar		2019 30 Sep	
	Number	%	Number	%	Number	%	Number	%	Number	%	Number	%	Number	%	Number	%	Number	%	Number	%
All Services	**12 980**		**13 580**		**13 800**		**13 650**		**13 380**		**12 260**		**12 360**		**12 130**		**12 480**		**14 880**	
Female	1 400	10.8	1 330	9.8	1 340	9.7	1 340	9.8	1 260	9.4	1 270	10.4	1 320	10.7	1 320	10.9	1 300	10.4	1 600	10.8
Male	11 580	89.2	12 250	90.2	12 450	90.3	12 310	90.2	12 130	90.6	10 990	89.6	11 040	89.3	10 820	89.1	11 180	89.6	13 280	89.2
Officers	**1 130**		**1 220**		**1 220**		**1 350**		**1 400**		**1 410**		**1 420**		**1 440**		**1 420**		**1 340**	
Female	180	15.5	170	14.0	180	14.7	220	16.5	230	16.3	210	15.0	210	15.0	260	17.8	250	17.8	240	17.8
Male	960	84.5	1 050	86.0	1 040	85.3	1 120	83.5	1 170	83.7	1 200	85.0	1 210	85.0	1 180	82.2	1 160	82.2	1 100	82.2
Other Ranks	**11 850**		**12 360**		**12 580**		**12 300**		**11 990**		**10 860**		**10 940**		**10 700**		**11 070**		**13 540**	
Female	1 220	10.3	1 160	9.4	1 160	9.2	1 190	9.0	1 030	8.6	1 060	9.8	1 110	10.1	1 060	9.9	1 050	9.5	1 370	10.1
Male	10 630	89.7	11 210	90.6	11 420	90.8	11 190	91.0	10 960	91.4	9 800	90.2	9 830	89.9	9 640	90.1	10 020	90.5	12 180	89.9
Royal Navy / Royal Marines	**2 930**		**2 980**		**3 000**		**3 150**		**3 040**		**2 880**		**3 040**		**3 200**		**3 140**		**3 290**	
Female	310	10.6	310	10.4	270	9.1	270	8.7	280	9.0	250	8.7	270	8.8	300	9.4	280	8.9	350	10.6
Male	2 620	89.4	2 670	89.6	2 720	90.9	2 880	91.3	2 770	91.0	2 620	91.3	2 770	91.2	2 900	90.6	2 860	91.1	2 940	89.4
Officers	**360**		**400**		**360**		**360**		**350**		**380**		**370**		**360**		**340**		**380**	
Female	50	13.6	50	13.3	50	12.9	60	16.1	60	16.2	50	13.9	50	14.6	60	15.4	40	11.4	50	13.8
Male	310	86.4	350	86.7	320	87.1	300	83.9	290	83.8	320	86.1	320	85.4	300	84.6	300	88.6	320	86.2
Other Ranks	**2 570**		**2 580**		**2 630**		**2 790**		**2 690**		**2 500**		**2 670**		**2 840**		**2 800**		**2 920**	
Female	260	10.1	260	9.9	230	8.6	220	7.7	220	8.1	200	8.0	210	8.0	250	8.6	240	8.6	300	10.2
Male	2 310	89.9	2 320	90.1	2 410	91.4	2 580	92.3	2 480	91.9	2 300	92.0	2 460	92.0	2 600	91.4	2 560	91.4	2 620	89.8
Army	**8 160**		**8 580**		**8 600**		**8 350**		**8 290**		**7 440**		**7 220**		**6 720**		**6 980**		**9 080**	
Female	800	9.8	720	8.4	730	8.5	740	8.9	660	8.0	700	9.4	740	10.2	680	10.1	640	9.1	820	9.0
Male	7 360	90.2	7 850	91.6	7 870	91.5	7 610	91.1	7 630	92.0	6 740	90.6	6 480	89.8	6 040	89.9	6 350	90.9	8 260	91.0
Officers	**520**		**560**		**580**		**640**		**690**		**720**		**670**		**660**		**670**		**620**	
Female	80	15.5	70	12.7	70	12.6	90	13.8	90	13.5	100	13.6	90	13.8	110	16.8	110	16.3	90	15.2
Male	440	84.5	490	87.3	510	87.4	550	86.2	600	86.5	620	86.4	580	86.2	550	83.2	560	83.7	520	84.8
Other Ranks	**7 650**		**8 010**		**8 020**		**7 710**		**7 600**		**6 720**		**6 540**		**6 060**		**6 320**		**8 460**	
Female	720	9.4	650	8.1	650	8.2	660	8.5	570	7.5	600	8.9	640	9.8	570	9.4	530	8.3	730	8.6
Male	6 930	90.6	7 360	91.9	7 370	91.8	7 060	91.5	7 030	92.5	6 120	91.1	5 900	90.2	5 490	90.6	5 790	91.7	7 740	91.4
Royal Air Force	**1 880**		**2 020**		**2 200**		**2 140**		**2 040**		**1 950**		**2 100**		**2 210**		**2 360**		**2 510**	
Female	290	15.2	300	14.6	340	15.6	320	14.8	320	15.4	320	16.6	320	15.2	340	15.2	390	16.5	440	17.3
Male	1 600	84.8	1 730	85.4	1 860	84.4	1 820	85.2	1 730	84.6	1 620	83.4	1 780	84.8	1 880	84.8	1 970	83.5	2 080	82.7
Officers	**250**		**250**		**270**		**350**		**350**		**310**		**380**		**420**		**400**		**350**	
Female	50	18.2	40	18.1	60	21.8	80	22.0	80	22.1	60	19.5	70	17.4	90	21.5	100	25.9	90	26.8
Male	210	81.8	200	81.9	210	78.2	270	78.0	280	77.9	250	80.5	310	82.6	330	78.5	300	74.1	250	73.2
Other Ranks	**1 630**		**1 780**		**1 930**		**1 790**		**1 690**		**1 640**		**1 720**		**1 800**		**1 960**		**2 160**	
Female	240	14.7	240	14.1	280	14.7	240	13.4	240	14.0	260	16.0	250	14.7	250	13.8	280	14.6	340	15.8
Male	1 390	85.3	1 530	85.9	1 640	85.3	1 550	86.6	1 450	86.0	1 370	84.0	1 470	85.3	1 550	86.2	1 670	85.4	1 820	84.2

Source: Defence Statistics (Tri-Service)

Intake - Comprises all personnel joining the Armed Forces either as new entrants or re-entrants.

UK Regulars - Full-time Service personnel, including Nursing Services, but excluding FTRS personnel, Gurkhas, mobilised Reservists, MPGS, LEP and NRPS.

Glossary of terms: https://assets.publishing.service.gov.uk/government/uploads/system/uploads/attachment_data/file/569187/Tri-Service_Glossary_-_Nov16.pdf

14.3a Number of vessels in the Royal Navy and Royal Fleet Auxiliary, as at 1 April each year.

This table is a National Statistic.

Number

	2016		2017		2018		2019		2020	
	In Service[1]	Total	In Service[1]	Total	In Service[1]	Total	In Service[1]	Total	In Service[1]	Total
Royal Navy Submarine Service	**11**	**11**	**11**	**11**	**10**	**10**	**10**	**10**	**10**	**10**
Ballistic Nuclear Submarine	4	**4**	4	**4**	4	**4**	4	**4**	4	**4**
Nuclear Submarine	7	**7**	7	**7**	6	**6**	6	**6**	6	**6**
Royal Navy Surface Fleet	**64**	**64**	**64**	**64**	**60**	**60**	**60**	**60**	**66**	**66**
Aircraft Carriers	-	**-**	-	**-**	1	**1**	1	**1**	2	**2**
Landing Platform Docks/Helicopters	3	**3**	3	**3**	2	**2**	2	**2**	2	**2**
Destroyers	6	**6**	6	**6**	6	**6**	6	**6**	6	**6**
Frigates	13	**13**	13	**13**	13	**13**	13	**13**	13	**13**
Mine Countermeasures Vessels (MCMV)	15	**15**	15	**15**	13	**13**	13	**13**	13	**13**
Inshore Patrol Vessels	18	**18**	18	**18**	18	**18**	18	**18**	18	**18**
Offshore Patrol Vessels	4	**4**	4	**4**	3	**3**	3	**3**	7	**7**
Survey Ships	4	**4**	4	**4**	3	**3**	3	**3**	4	**4**
Ice Patrol Ship	1	**1**	1	**1**	1	**1**	1	**1**	1	**1**
Royal Fleet Auxiliary	**12**	**12**	**9**	**9**	**10**	**10**	**13**	**13**	**13**	**13**
Fleet Tanker	2	**2**	2	**2**	3	**3**	6	**6**	6	**6**
Small Fleet Tanker	2	**2**	-	**-**	-	**-**	-	**-**	-	**-**
Fleet Replenishment Ship	3	**3**	3	**3**	3	**3**	3	**3**	3	**3**
Landing Ship Dock	3	**3**	3	**3**	3	**3**	3	**3**	3	**3**
Primary Casualty Receiving Ship	1	**1**	1	**1**	1	**1**	1	**1**	1	**1**
Forward Repair Ship	1	**1**	-	**-**	-	**-**	-	**-**	-	**-**

Source: Navy Command

1. 'In service' here is defined as any element held at a state of "Readiness". Readiness time is the period required for an element to be ready to deploy form their home base (or current location) to undertake specific tasks, with appropriate Manpower, Equipment, Training and Sustainability (METS) criteria, to conduct the allocated task.

*   not applicable

..   not available

-      zero

Data as at 1 April each year

14.3b Land Formations of the UK Armed Forces

The number of formations, which are all or primarily land-based, in the Army.
Note: Hybrid (Regular and Reserve) units are counted as Regular Army units.

This table is a National Statistic.

Number

		2016	2017	2018	2019	2020
Combat Forces						
Infantry						
Regular Army	Battalions	32	32	32	32	32
Army Reserves	Battalions	14	14	16	16	16
Royal Armoured Corps						
Regular Army	Regiments	11	11	11	11	11
Army Reserves	Regiments	4	4	4	4	4
Combat Support Forces						
Royal Artillery						
Regular Army	Regiments	14	14	14	14	14
Army Reserves	Regiments	5	6	6	6	6
Royal Engineers						
Regular Army	Regiments	14	14	14	14	14
Army Reserves	Regiments	4	3	3	4	4
Royal Signals						
Regular Army	Regiments	12	12	12	12	13
Army Reserves	Regiments	4	4	4	4	4
Intelligence Corps						
Regular Army	Regiments	4 [r]	4 [r]	4 [r]	4 [r]	4
Army Reserves	Regiments	5	5	5	5	5
Combat Service Support						
Royal Electrical and Mechanical Engineers						
Regular Army	Battalions	8	8	8	8	8
Army Reserves	Battalions	6	6	6	3	3
Royal Logistic Corps						
Regular Army	Regiments	13	13	13	13	13
Army Reserves	Regiments	12	12	12	12	12
Royal Army Medical Corps						
Regular Army	Regiments	11	11	11	9	9
Army Reserves	Regiments	15	15	15	15	15
Royal Military Police						
Regular Army	Regiments	6	6	6	6	6
Army Reserves	Regiments	-	-	-	-	-
Corps, Division & Brigade HQ						
NATO Corps HQ	HQs	1	1	1	1	1
Division / District HQ						
Deployable	HQs	2	2	2	2	2
Non-deployable	HQs	4	4	4	4	4
Brigade HQ[1]						
Deployable	HQs	7	7	7	7	7
Non-deployable	HQs	4	3	3	3	3

Source: Army Org Branch

1. Includes Commando Logistic Regiment (Navy).

2. Brigade HQ figures do not include Logistics or Specialist Brigades.

r The previously published figure for the number of Intelligence Corps Regiments has been revised. This is due to an administrative error.

- zero

14.3c Numbers of formations in the Royal Air Force and Royal Auxiliary Air Force, and in the air components of the Royal Navy and the Army, as at 1 April each year.

This table is a National Statistic.

Number

		2016	2017	2018	2019	2020
Royal Navy Fleet Air Arm						
Battlefield Helicopter	Squadrons	1	1	1	1	1
Flying Training & Operational Support [1]	Squadrons	4	4	4	5	5
Maritime Helicopter	Squadrons	6	6	6	6 [r]	6
Remotely Piloted Air Systems	Squadrons	1	1	1	1	1
Support	Squadrons	2	2	2	2	2
Support Helicopter	Squadrons	2	2	2	2	2
Test and Evaluation	Squadrons	-	-	-	1 [r]	1
Commando Helicopter Force	HQ	1	1	1	1	1
Fixed Wing Force	HQ	1	1	1	1	1
Wildcat Maritime Force [2]	HQ	1	1	1	1	1
Merlin Helicopter Force	HQ	1	1	1	1	1
Sea King Force	HQ	1	1	1	-	-
Army Air Corps						
Regular Army [3]	Regiments	6	6	6	6	7
Army Reserves	Regiments	1	1	1	1	1
Royal Air Force						
Flying Support						
Air Transport & Air-to-Air Refuelling	Squadrons	8	7	7	7	7
Airborne Command and Control	Squadrons	1	1	1	1	1
Combat Air	Squadrons	8	8	9	7	8
Flying Training & Operational Training Support	Squadrons	12	12	12	12	10
Intelligence, Surveillance and Reconnaissance	Squadrons	3	3	3	3	4
Operational Conversion and Evaluation Units	Squadrons	9	8	2	5	9
Remotely Piloted Aircraft Systems	Squadrons	2	2	2	2	2
Search and Rescue	Squadrons	1	-	-	-	-
Support Helicopter	Squadrons	5	5	5	5	5
Combat Support - Force Protection						
RAF Force Protection Wing	HQs	6	6	6	6	6
RAF Regiment Field	Squadrons	6	6	6	6	6
RAF Police Wing	HQs	3	3	1	1	1
RAF Police	Squadrons	5	5	5	5	5
Defence CBRN Wing	HQ	1	1	1	0*	-
Defence CBRN Wing	Squadrons	2	2	1	0*	-
Combat Support - Communications						
Operational Information Services Wing	Squadrons	3	3	4	3	3
Tactical Communications Wing	Squadrons	3	3	3	3	3
Technical Information Assurance [4]	Squadrons	1	*	*	*	*
Combat Support - Engineering and Logistics						
Air Mobility Wing	Squadrons	2	2	3	3	3
Engineering Support Wing	Squadrons	4	4	4	5	5
Expeditionary Logistics Wing	Squadrons	5	5	5	4	4
Combat Support - Medical						
Aeromedical Evacuation & Medical Support [5]	Squadrons	*	5	5	6	6
Royal Auxiliary Air Force						
Aeromedical Evacuation & Medical Support	Squadrons	2	2	2	2	2
Air Operations & Aerospace Battle Management	Squadrons	1	1	0	0	0
Air Transport & Air-to-Air Refuelling	Squadrons	1	1	1	1	1
Reserves Expeditionary Logistics Wing	Squadrons	5	5	4	3	3
Air Mobility Wing (Aux Movements Sqn)	Squadrons	-	-	1	1	1
Force Protection	Squadrons	7	7	8	8	8
General Operations Support	Squadrons	5	5	7	7	7
Intelligence and Imagery Analyst Support	Squadrons	3	3	3	3	3
Musical & Ceremonial Support	HQ	1	1	1	1	1
Provost Wing	Wing	1	1	-	0	0
Public Relations	Squadrons	1	1	1	1	1
Support Helicopter	Squadrons	1	1	1	1	1
Intelligence, Surveillance and Reconnaissance	Squadrons	-	-	-	1	1
RAF Reserve - Sponsored Reserves	**Units/Squadrons**	**3**	**4**	**5**	**5**	**5**

Sources: Navy Command; Army Org Branch; Air Command

1. Formerly Flying Training

2. Formerly Lynx Wildcat Maritime Force. The title changed as Lynx are now out of service.

3. Includes two training regiments.

4. Post-2016 data for the Technical Information Assurance squadron is no longer available. This squadron was formerly an old RAF Support Unit role but has now transformed into a Joint Forces Command Unit.

5. Previously categorised under Combat Support - Engineering & Logistics. Total comprises three Pre-Hospital Care (PHC) Squadrons and three Deployed Aeromed Squadrons (DAS), one of which is now an Enhanced DAS.

r The previously published figures for the number of Maritime Helicopter Squadrons and Test and Evaluation Squadrons have been revised. This is due to an administrative error leading to the miscategorisation of some squadrons.

* not applicable

14.4 Outflow from the UK Regular Forces, trained or untrained

	2018				2019			
	31 Mar	30 Jun	30 Sep	31 Dec	31 Mar	30 Jun	30 Sep	31 Dec
Tri Service Outflow	**15 172**	**14 861**	**14 759**	**14 698**	**14 633**	**14 875**	**15 122**	**15 233**
Trained	12 455	12 218	12 242	12 323	12 315	12 359	12 279	11 996
Untrained	2 717	2 643	2 517	2 375	2 318	2 516	2 843	3 237
Officers	**1 858**	**1 824**	**1 779**	**1 778**	**1 773**	**1 790**	**1 823**	**1 818**
Trained	1 713	1 685	1 638	1 622	1 607	1 622	1 637	1 657
Untrained	145	139	141	156	166	168	186	161
Other Ranks	**13 314**	**13 037**	**12 980**	**12 920**	**12 860**	**13 085**	**13 299**	**13 415**
Trained	10 742	10 533	10 604	10 701	10 708	10 737	10 642	10 339
Untrained	2 572	2 504	2 376	2 219	2 152	2 348	2 657	3 076
Royal Navy/ Royal Marines	**3 088**	**3 116**	**3 066**	**3 139**	**3 092**	**3 163**	**3 235**	**3 215**
Trained	2 428	2 429	2 410	2 500	2 460	2 506	2 498	2 392
Untrained	660	687	656	639	632	657	737	823
Officer	**460**	**468**	**431**	**439**	**440**	**442**	**457**	**447**
Trained	390	396	357	359	355	354	365	365
Untrained	70	72	74	80	85	88	92	82
Other Ranks	**2 628**	**2 648**	**2 635**	**2 700**	**2 652**	**2 721**	**2 778**	**2 768**
Trained	2 038	2 033	2 053	2 141	2 105	2 152	2 133	2 027
Untrained	590	615	582	559	547	569	645	741
Army	**9 650**	**9 397**	**9 268**	**9 102**	**9 046**	**9 174**	**9 344**	**9 439**
Trained	8 329	8 119	8 027	7 965	7 985	7 952	7 965	7 828
Trade Trained	7 804	7 668	7 648	7 626	7 632	7 603	7 579	7 377
Untrained	1 321	1 278	1 241	1 137	1 061	1 222	1 379	1 611
Officers	**906**	**905**	**907**	**902**	**904**	**896**	**908**	**917**
Trained	848	859	861	848	854	848	861	885
Trade Trained	845	856	858	844	843	836	838	860
Untrained	58	46	46	54	50	48	47	32
Other Ranks	**8 744**	**8 492**	**8 361**	**8 200**	**8 142**	**8 278**	**8 436**	**8 522**
Trained	7 481	7 260	7 166	7 117	7 131	7 104	7 104	6 943
Trade Trained	6 959	6 812	6 790	6 782	6 789	6 767	6 741	6 517
Untrained	1 263	1 232	1 195	1 083	1 011	1 174	1 332	1 579
Royal Air Force	**2 434**	**2 348**	**2 425**	**2 457**	**2 495**	**2 538**	**2 543**	**2 579**
Trained	2 223	2 121	2 184	2 197	2 223	2 250	2 202	2 227
Untrained	211	227	241	260	272	288	341	352
Officers	**492**	**451**	**441**	**437**	**429**	**452**	**458**	**454**
Trained	478	433	423	419	409	432	434	432
Untrained	14	18	18	18	20	20	24	22
Other Ranks	**1 942**	**1 897**	**1 984**	**2 020**	**2 066**	**2 086**	**2 085**	**2 125**
Trained	1 745	1 688	1 761	1 778	1 814	1 818	1 768	1 795
Untrained	197	209	223	242	252	268	317	330

Source: Defence Statistics (Tri-Service)
Email: Analysis-Tri-Service@mod.gov.uk

Notes

|| discontinuity in time series

1. Due to the change in definition for Trained Strength for Army in October 2016, 12 month ending untrained intake figures have been changed to reflect the new definition.

2. Figures show outflow from UK Regular Forces, both trained and untrained, including personnel leaving the Services, deaths and recalled reservists on release. They do not include promotion from Ranks to Officers or flows between Services.

3. Figures are not comparable with gains to trained strength figures which include promotion from Ranks to Officers.

4 From 2018 onwards, UK armed forces personnel statistics changed from monthly to quarterly release.

A full set of definitions and abbreviations can be found in the glossary of terms available online at:
https://www.gov.uk/government/publications/armed-forces-monthly-service-personnel-statistics-supplementary-documents

14.5 Full-Time Trained Strength (FTTS)[1], Liability[2] and Surplus/Deficit of the UK Armed Forces, at 1 April each year

Number of personnel

	2012	2013	2014	2015	2016	2017	2018	2019
All Services	**170 012**	**160 712**	**150 891**	**144 102**	**140 432**	**138 844**	**136 769**	**134 304**
Liability	**174 840**	**162 942**	**159 644**	**150 697**	**146 186**	**145 303**	**145 573**	**144 423**
Surplus / Deficit	*-4 828*	*-2 230*	*-8 753*	*-6 595*	*-5 754*	*-6 459*	*-8 804*	*-10 119*
% Surplus / Deficit	*-2.8%*	*-1.4%*	*-5.5%*	*-4.4%*	*-3.9%*	*-4.4%*	*-6.0%*	*-7.0%*
By service								
Royal Navy/Royal Marines	**33 287**	**31 423**	**30 509**	**30 058**	**29 702**	**29 584**	**29 299**	**29 224**
Liability	**34 800**	**30 533**	**30 345**	**30 285**	**30 100**	**30 249**	**30 451**	**30 584**
Surplus / Deficit	*-1 513*	*890*	*164*	*- 227*	*- 398*	*- 665*	*-1 152*	*-1 360*
% Surplus / Deficit	*-4.3%*	*2.9%*	*0.5%*	*-0.7%*	*-1.3%*	*-2.2%*	*-3.8%*	*-4.4%*
Army[3]	**98 600**	**93 939**	**87 176**	**82 216**	**79 746**	**78 407**	**77 119**	**75 070**
Liability	**101 210**	**96 790**	**94 103**	**86 535**	**82 638**	**82 645**	**82 646**	**82 018**
Surplus / Deficit	*-2 610*	*-2 851*	*-6 927*	*-4 319*	*-2 892*	*-4 238*	*-5 527*	*-6 948*
% Surplus / Deficit	*-2.6%*	*-2.9%*	*-7.4%*	*-5.0%*	*-3.5%*	*-5.1%*	*-6.7%*	*-8.5%*
Royal Air Force (FTTS)	**38 125**	**35 350**	**33 206**	**31 828**	**30 984**	**30 853**	**30 351**	**30 010**
Liability	**38 830**	**35 619**	**35 196**	**33 877**	**33 448**	**32 409**	**32 476**	**31 821**
Surplus / Deficit	*- 705*	*- 269*	*-1 990*	*-2 049*	*-2 464*	*-1 556*	*-2 125*	*-1 811*
% Surplus / Deficit	*-1.8%*	*-0.8%*	*-5.7%*	*-6.0%*	*-7.4%*	*-4.8%*	*-6.5%*	*-5.7%*

Source: Defence Statistics (Tri-Service)

1. Full-Time Trained Strength (FTTS) - The element of the UK Armed Forces comprised of trained UK Regular Forces, trained Gurkhas and a number of Reserve Forces personnel filling Regular posts whilst serving on FTRS. It does not include mobilised reservists. Following the change in definition of trained strength for Army, from 1 October 2016 this includes UK Regular Forces and Gurkhas who have passed Phase 1 training for the Army; these figures should not be compared to previous years. For Royal Navy/Royal Marines and Royal Air Force, this includes personnel who have passed Phase 2 training.

2. Liability is the number of Service personnel needed, based on the Defence Planning Round, set for each of the three Services.

3. Full-time Trade Trained Strength (FTTTS) - This relates to Army only and includes Full-time personnel who have passed Phase 2 training, including: UK Regular Forces, Gurkhas and a number of Reserve Forces personnel filling Regular posts whilst serving on FTRS. It does not include mobilised reservists.

Please note: Please note: Approximately 400 FTRS personnel reported in this table to be serving against the UK Full-time Trained Workforce Requirement, are also reported against the Future Reserves 2020 (FR20) targets.

Trained Strength comprises military personnel who have completed Phase 1 and 2 training for Royal Navy/Royal Marines, the Army (prior to 1 October 2016) and the Royal Air Force. Following the change in definition of trained strength for Army, from 1 October 2016, trained strength for the Army comprises of personnel who have completed Phase 1 training.

14.6a Trends in service and civilian personnel strengths, at 1 April each year

	2015 1 Apr	2016 1 Apr	2017 1 Apr	2018 1 Apr	2019 1 Apr	2020 1 Apr
UK Forces Service Personnel[1]	**195 686**	**197 089**	**197 041**	**194 112**	**192 160**	**193 977**
Full-time Trained Strength (RN/RM & RAF) & Full-time Trade Trained Strength (Army)	*144 117*	*140 432*	*138 844*	*136 769*	*134 304*	*132 634*
Trained Future Reserve 2020	*24 627*	*27 268*	*31 364*	*32 196*	*32 556*	*32 919*
UK Regular Forces	153 724	150 996	149 366	146 556	144 428	145 317
Gurkhas	2 866	2 855	2 992	3 150	3 429	3 757
Volunteer Reserve[2]	31 260	35 068	36 459	36 447	36 502	37 058
Serving Regular Reserve[4]	2 581	3 043	3 232	3 220	3 204	3 323
Sponsored Reserve[5]	2 047	2 019	2 039	2 034	2 037	2 029
Military Provost Guard Service	2 937	2 872	2 724	2 535	2 378	2 332
Locally Engaged Personnel	225	200	188	170	182	161
FTRS (of unknown origin)[3,6]	46	36	41	-	-	-
Civilian (Level 0)[9]	**58 161**	**56 243**	**56,676**	**56,865**	**57,760**	**58,253**
Civilian (Level 1)[10]	48 648	37 656	37,303	36,366	36,885	36,814
DE&S Trading Entity[11]	*	9 836	10,671	10,243	10,050	10,560
Trading Funds & Executive Agencies	4 495	4 405	4,456	6,032	6,574	7,291
Locally engaged civilians	5 018	4 347	4,246	4,224	4,252	3,588

Source: Defence Statistics (Tri-Service)

Notes

1. All UK Forces Service Personnel comprises UK Regular Forces, Gurkhas, Military Provost Guard Service (MPGS), Locally Engaged Personnel (LEP), Volunteer Reserve, Serving Regular Reserve, Sponsored Reserve, and FTRS of unknown origin. University Officer Cadets are excluded. Unless otherwise stated, includes trained and untrained personnel.

2. Volunteer Reserve comprises the Royal Naval Reserve, Royal Marine Reserve, Army Reserve, and Royal Air Force Reserves.

3. For information on the FTRS, and an explanation of the different commitments, please see the Glossary. The Army has a number of Full Time Reserve Service (FTRS) personnel for whom they are unable to identify whether they are from the Volunteer or the Regular Reserve. These personnel are reported at the foot of this table, and hence all FTRS figures are reported as estimates.

4. The Regular Reserve comprises ex-Regular service personnel who retain a liability to be called up for military service in times of need. The serving component identified here comprises ex-Regular personnel who have applied to return to military service, on a fixed term reserve commitment.

5. A JPA data cleansing exercise to the Army Sponsored Reserve data resulted in a decrease to the strength. Figures reported from July 2014 are correct, however it has not been possible to revise the data prior to this time, therefore all figures reported before July 2014 are believed to be overestimated by up to approximately 30 personnel.

6. These personnel are serving on FTRS, however, at the time extracted, the Army was unable to identify whether they were Volunteer or Regular Reserve personnel.

7 There has been an "step change" increase in the number of Locally Engaged Personnel (LEP) as at 1st December 2016. This is due to a change in the data source. The previous source included only those members of the Gibraltar Regiment serving in Gibraltar, whereas the latest data includes all LEP Gibraltar Regiment personnel regardless of where there are serving e.g. those on secondment. LEP figures exclude the Gibraltar Regiment Reserves.

8 There has been a change in the methodology used to produce Reserves statistics from 1 April 2017. This has resulted in some minor revisions - seldom affecting greater than 10 personnel in a month - to historic data, in particular to flows. This aligns our methodology with that used to produce Regulars statistics. All historic Reserves data affected have been revised to reflect this.

9 Civilian Personnel data have been provided on a Full Time Equivalent (FTE) basis as it enables a fair comparison with Service figures. Full Time Equivalent (FTE) is a measure of the size of the workforce that takes account of the fact that some Civilian personnel work part-time. These data have been provided to the nearest whole number, therefore adding individual components together may not match the sub-total.

10 Civilian Level 1 includes: Top Level Budgetary Areas (TLBs) and Royal Fleet Auxiliary (RFA).

11 From July 2015 Defence Equipment & Support (DE&S) has been reported in a separate row as 'DE&S Trading Entity' outside of Level 1.

12 Future Reserves 2020 includes volunteer reserves who are mobilised, HRR and volunteer reserve personnel serving on ADC or FTRS contracts. Sponsored Reserves who provide a more cost effective solution than volunteer reserve are also included in the Army Reserve FR20. Non Regular Permanent Staff (NRPS), Expeditionary Forces Institute (EFI) and University Officer Cadets and Regular Reservists are excluded.

14.6b Civilian personnel by Top Level Budgetary Area (Full Time Equivalent)

	2015 1 April	2016 1 April	2017 1 April	2018 1 April	2019 1 April	FTE 2020 1 April
Top Level Budgetary areas (TLBs)	**36,149**	**35,704**	**35,375**	**34,448**	**36,288**	**34,984**
Navy Command	2,524	2,562	2,525	2,592	2,779	2,653
Army TLB	10,693	10,360	9,991	9,604	9,655	8,703
HQ Air Command	5,039	4,814	4,509	4,367	4,443	4,251
Head Office & Corporate Services	7,843	7,827	7,966	7,249	8,050	7,660
Joint Forces Command / UK StratCom[1]	5,868	5,938	6,045	6,149	6,721	6,924
Defence Infrastructure Organisation[1]	4,165	4,200	4,335	4,477	4,635	4,788
Unallocated	17	3	5	9	5	5
Royal Fleet Auxiliary (RFA)	**1,893**	**1,952**	**1,928**	**1,918**	**1,880**	**1,830**
Apprentices	..	81	117	113	114	115
Cadets	76	84	76	68	66	79
Civilians	181	170	152	156	170	122
Sponsored Reserves	1636	1,617	1,583	1,581	1,530	1,514
Civilian Level 1 Total	**48,648**	**37,656**	**37,303**	**36,366**	**38,168**	**36,814**
DE&S Trading Entity	..	**9,836**	**10,671**	**10,243**	**10,346**	**10,560**
Trading Funds & Executive Agencies	**4,495**	**4,405**	**4,456**	**6,032**	**6,810**	**7,291**
UK Hydrographic Office	943	900	842	836	865	792
Defence Science & Technology Laboratory	3,552	3,505	3,614	3,557	3,989	4,303
Defence Electronics Components Agency[2]	*	*	*	397	420	406
Defence Nuclear Organisation[3]	*	*	*	1,242	1,536	1,790
Locally engaged civilians (LEC)	**5,018**	**4,347**	**4,246**	**4,224**	**4,390**	**3,588**
Civilian Level 0 Total	**58,161**	**56,243**	**56,676**	**56,865**	**59,714**	**58,253**

Source: Defence Statistics (Civilian)

To note: There have been a number of changes to the structure of TLBs and Trading Funds which affect the direct comparability of data across the time-period. Details are given in the background notes and glossary supporting publication (https://www.gov.uk/government/statistics/mod-biannual-civilian-personnel-report-2020/biannual-civilian-personnel-report-bcpr-1-april-2020-background-notes-and-glossary).

1. Prior to 2020, reported as Joint Forces Command (JFC).

2. As at 1 April 2018, approximately 400 posts forming the Defence Electronics Components Agency (DECA) previously reported in Head Office & Corporate Services (HO&Cs) within Level 1 were reported separately as an Executive Agency within level 0, for improved consistency and transparency of data reporting.

3. As at 1 April 2018 approximately 1,160 posts transferred out of DE&S Trading Entity to form Defence Nuclear Organisation (DNO) as an Executive Agency, additionally approximately 80 personnel within DG Nuclear also transferred to DNO, moving from Level 1 to Level 0 reporting.

14.6c Civilian personnel by grade equivalence[1] (Full Time Equivalent)

	2015 1 Jul	2016 1 Jul	2017 1 Jul	2018 1 Jul	2019 1 Jul	FTE 2020 1 Jul
Civilian Level 0 Total	58,203	56,145	56,689	56,925	58,143	58,439
Non Industrial Total	30,455	30,363	30,371	30,115	31,085	31,721
Senior Civil Service & Equivalent[2]	186	200	200	205	230	261
Band B1 & Equivalent	408	435	465	464	515	556
Band B2 & Equivalent	1,207	1,299	1,345	1,443	1,556	1,736
Band C1 & Equivalent	3,277	3,356	3,377	3,409	3,803	4,133
Band C2 & Equivalent	6,444	6,345	6,375	6,419	6,626	6,524
Band D & Equivalent	6,302	6,253	6,232	6,172	6,310	6,374
Band E1 & Equivalent	9,141	9,182	9,154	8,788	8,775	8,727
Band E2 & Equivalent	3,426	3,218	3,149	3,151	3,075	3,039
Other[3]	62	75	73	64	195	370
Industrial Total	5,672	5,241	4,846	4,227	4,029	3,443
Firefighter	798	739	731	731	689	168
Skill Zone 4	405	378	363	267	287	300
Skill Zone 3	1,634	1,478	1,329	1,216	1,168	1,156
Skill Zone 2	1,748	1,670	1,566	1,408	1,316	1,293
Skill Zone 1	1,082	974	852	600	557	516
Apprentice	5	2	5	6	10	9
Royal Fleet Auxiliary [4]	1,912	1,955	1,942	1,922	1,878	1,845
DE&S Trading Entity	10,531	9,815	10,818	10,173	10,186	10,483
Trading Funds & Executive Agenies [4]	4,560	4,383	4,413	6,279	6,752	7,360
Locally engaged civilians [4]	5,073	4,388	4,299	4,209	4,213	3,587

Source: Defence Statistics (Civilian)

1. Grade equivalence is shown in terms of the broader banding structure and is based on paid grade.

2. Includes personnel outside the Senior Civil Service but of equivalent grade, primarily Senior Medical Specialists.

3. 'Other' represents core civilian personnel for whom no grade information is available.

4. Data by grade are not available for Royal Fleet Auxiliary, Trading Funds, Executive Agencies and
Locally engaged civilians (LECs).

14.7a Land holdings by parent Service area and whether owned, leased or with legal rights, at 1 April each year

These holdings include land declared as surplus to defence requirements.
A thousand hectares is 3.86 square miles.
This table is a National Statistic.

Thousand hectares

	2000 [1]		2011 [2,3]	2012	2013	2014 [4]		2015	2016		2017		2018		2019
Total land & foreshore holdings and Rights held[5]	363.3	‖	435.3	434.1	432.9	‖	449.3	439.6	434.6	‖	437.4	r	431.5	r	431.4
Land and foreshore holdings	238.5	‖	230.4	229.1	228.0		227.3	‖	222.6	221.1	‖	223.5	r	224.1	r	223.9
Freehold	219.9	‖	209.8	208.8	207.7		207.0		207.1	205.8	‖	208.1	r	207.8	r	207.5
Leasehold	18.6	‖	20.6	20.3	20.3		20.3	‖	15.5	15.3	‖	15.4		16.3		16.4
Rights held[6]	124.8	‖	204.9	204.9	204.9	‖	222.0	‖	217.0	213.5	‖	213.9	r	207.4		207.4

Of which:

	2000		2011	2012	2013	2014		2015	2016		2017		2018		2019
Naval Service	39.3	‖	2.3	2.3	2.3		2.3		3.8	3.8	‖	3.8		3.7		3.7
Land and foreshore holdings	13.1	‖	2.2	2.3	2.3		2.2		3.7	3.7	‖	3.7		3.7		3.7
Freehold	10.7	‖	2.1	2.1	2.1		2.0		3.5	3.5	‖	3.5		3.4		3.4
Leasehold	2.4	‖	0.1	0.2	0.2		0.2		0.2	0.2	‖	0.2		0.2		0.2
Rights held[6]	26.2	‖	0.1	0.1	0.1		0.1		0.1	0.1	‖	0.1		0.1		0.1
Army	243.9	‖	15.1	15.1	14.7		14.6		13.6	14.5	‖	14.2		14.1	r	13.9
Land and foreshore holdings	155.9	‖	14.7	14.6	14.3		14.2		13.2	14.0	‖	13.5		13.7	r	13.5
Freehold	152.1	‖	14.2	14.1	13.8		13.7		12.7	13.6	‖	13.1		13.2	r	12.9
Leasehold	3.8	‖	0.5	0.5	0.5		0.5		0.5	0.5	‖	0.5		0.5		0.5
Rights held[6]	88.0	‖	0.5	0.5	0.4		0.4		0.4	0.4	‖	0.7		0.4		0.4
Royal Air Force	48.6	‖	21.7	21.7	21.7		21.4		20.7	20.2	‖	20.1	r	19.1	r	19.2
Land and foreshore holdings	39.3	‖	21.7	21.6	21.6		21.4		20.7	20.2	‖	20.1	r	19.1	r	19.1
Freehold	30.9	‖	17.8	17.7	17.7		17.5		17.0	16.5	‖	16.4	r	15.4	r	15.4
Leasehold	8.4	‖	3.9	3.9	3.9		3.9		3.7	3.7	‖	3.7		3.7		3.7
Rights held[6]	9.3	‖	-	-	-		-		-	-	‖	-		-		-
The Centre[7]	27.4	‖	392.8	391.8	391.1	‖	406.6		396.6	391.3	‖	394.0	r	389.3	r	389.3
Land and foreshore holdings	26.1	‖	188.6	187.4	186.8		185.2	‖	180.1	178.3	‖	181.0	r	182.4	r	182.4
Freehold	25.1	‖	172.7	171.9	171.2		169.7		169.2	167.6	‖	170.1	r	170.6	r	170.6
Leasehold	1.0	‖	15.9	15.5	15.6		15.5	‖	10.9	10.7	‖	10.9	r	11.8		11.8
Rights held[6]	1.3	‖	204.3	204.4	204.4	‖	221.4	‖	216.5	213.0	‖	213.0		206.9		206.9
Other[8]	4.1	‖	3.3	3.2	3.1		4.3		4.9	4.9	‖	5.2	r	5.2		5.3
Land and foreshore holdings	4.1	‖	3.3	3.1	3.1		4.3		4.8	4.8	‖	5.2	r	5.2		5.3
Freehold	1.0	‖	3.2	3.0	3.0		4.1		4.7	4.7	‖	5.0	r	5.0		5.1
Leasehold	3.1	‖	0.1	0.1	0.1		0.2		0.1	0.1	‖	0.1		0.1		0.3
Rights held[6]	-	‖	-	-	-		-		-	-	‖	-		-		-

Source: MOD Defence Infrastructure Organisation (DIO)

1. The figures presented for years 2009 and 2010 were rounded to the nearest thousand hectares.
2. Data from 2011 has been compiled using a new spatial dataset which allows for greater accuracy in the measurement of the estate. Because of this new dataset, comparable figures for earlier years are not available. Figures have been rounded to the nearest hundred hectares.
3. The large changes in the allocations to parent service areas between 2010 and 2011 reflect the outcome of the Defence Estate Training Review, with the Training Estate now transferred to the Defence Infrastructure Organisation, part of the Centre.
4. Part of the Kinlochleven Training Area in Scotland, over which MOD holds rights, is included from 2014 onwards, having been omitted from figures previously reported. It was highlighted by data quality improvement work as a result of the introduction of the DIO's Infrastructure Management System.
5. Balduff Training Area (2,000 hectares), which was shown as leasehold in 2014, has been updated to rights held in 2015.
6. Rights held are land and foreshore that are not owned by, or leased to MOD, but over which the Department has limited rights under grants and rights.
7. The Centre includes Defence Equipment & Support, Defence Infrastructure Organisation (including former Defence Training Estate (hence marked increase in values from 2011) and Service family quarters leased from Annington Property Ltd.) and Centre TLBs.
8. Includes Permanent Joint Headquarters and Trading Funds.
9. From 2017 Service Family Accommodation is included in total Land Holdings figures.
10. Several small amendments made to 2018 Freehold figures in Army, Royal Air Force, and The Centre.
‖ discontinuity in time series
.. not available
- zero or rounded to zero

14.7b Service Family Accommodation in the United Kingdom at 31 March each year

This table is a National Statistic.

Numbers of dwellings are rounded to the nearest thousand

Thousands of dwellings

	2000	2009	2010	2011	2012	2013	2014	2015	2016	2017	2018	2019
Permanent holdings	**64.8**	**49.9**	**49.1**	**49.2**	**49.0**	**49.4**	**49.4**	**49.6**	**49.7**	**49.5**	**49.8**	**49.6**
By country:												
England & Wales	55.9	44.9	44.1	44.2	44.0	44.5	44.5	44.7	44.8	44.7	45.0	45.0
Scotland	5.7	3.2	3.2	3.2	3.3	3.3	3.3	3.3	3.3	3.3	3.3	3.3
Northern Ireland	3.2	1.8	1.8	1.7	1.7	1.6	1.6	1.6	1.6	1.5	1.5	1.4
Vacant properties	**14.7**	**8.4**	**7.3**	**6.0**	**6.5**	**7.7**	**9.3**	**10.4**	**10.0**	**10.4**	**11.3**	**11.6**
By country:												
England & Wales	12.6	7.3	6.1	5.0	5.0	6.1	7.5	8.4	8.0	8.3	9.2	9.6
Scotland	1.7	0.6	0.6	0.5	0.7	0.7	0.8	1.0	0.9	1.1	1.1	1.1
Northern Ireland	0.4	0.5	0.6	0.5	0.8	0.9	1.0	1.0	1.1	1.0	1.0	0.9
Vacant properties as a percentage of all dwellings	*23*	*17*	*15*	*12*	*13*	*16*	*19*	*21*	*20*	*21*	*23*	*23*
By country:												
England & Wales	*23*	*16*	*14*	*11*	*11*	*14*	*17*	*19*	*18*	*19*	*21*	*21*
Scotland	*30*	*19*	*18*	*16*	*21*	*21*	*23*	*30*	*27*	*34*	*35*	*33*
Northern Ireland	*13*	*28*	*34*	*29*	*47*	*56*	*63*	*62*	*69*	*64*	*64*	*64*

Source: Defence Infrastructure Organisation

14.8a Location of service and civilian personnel[1,2] in the United Kingdom, at 1st April each year

FTE

	2000[3]	2010	2011	2012	2013	2014	2015	2016	2017	2018	2019
United Kingdom	267,700	236,710	229,400	214,310	203,480	192,970	187,820	189,020	189,350	187,040	186,540
Service	170,300	166,100	161,790	156,970	150,310	141,180	138,130	140,410	140,080	137,490	136,190
Civilians	97,410	70,610	67,610	57,340	53,170	51,780	49,690	48,610	49,270	49,550	50,360
England	222,560	207,890	201,320	188,810	180,080	170,680	167,400	168,230	168,940	166,910	166,500
Service	143,040	146,950	142,860	139,260	133,810	125,640	124,070	125,980	126,060	123,620	122,390
Civilians	79,520	60,940	58,450	49,560	46,270	45,040	43,330	42,250	42,880	43,290	44,100
Wales	8,260	4,900	4,580	4,150	3,910	3,810	3,550	3,450	3,310	3,270	3,230
Service	3,220	2,930	2,820	2,780	2,650	2,600	2,400	2,300	2,210	2,210	2,190
Civilians	5,040	1,970	1,760	1,370	1,260	1,210	1,160	1,150	1,100	1,050	1,040
Scotland	24,680	17,840	17,630	15,880	15,340	14,510	13,230	13,800	13,760	13,700	13,700
Service	15,080	12,080	12,090	11,190	11,310	10,600	9,460	10,000	9,770	9,680	9,690
Civilians	9,600	5,760	5,540	4,690	4,020	3,910	3,760	3,800	3,990	4,010	4,010
Northern Ireland	11,640	6,080	5,870	5,350	4,030	3,790	3,470	3,350	3,150	2,930	2,840
Service	8,390	4,140	4,010	3,740	2,530	2,340	2,190	2,120	2,030	1,980	1,910
Civilians	3,250	1,930	1,850	1,610	1,500	1,450	1,280	1,240	1,120	950	930

Source: Defence Statistics

Service and Civilian[1,2] personnel by region

FTE

	Service			Civilian		
	2018	2019	% change	2018	2019	% change
United Kingdom	137,490	136,190	-1	49,550	50,360	2
England	123,620	122,390	-1	43,290	44,100	2
East of England	13,450	13,040	-3	3,600	3,530	-2
East Midlands	8,790	8,760	0	1,490	1,670	12
London	4,430	4,450	0	3,340	3,470	4
North East	1,120	1,260	13	250	250	0
North West	1,820	1,850	2	1,670	1,720	3
South East	37,500	38,000	1	9,640	9,490	-2
South West	36,450	35,080	-4	18,610	19,260	3
West Midlands	7,840	7,620	-3	2,380	2,410	1
Yorkshire and The Humber	12,200	12,320	1	2,330	2,300	-1
Wales	2,210	2,190	-1	1,050	1,040	-1
Scotland	9,680	9,690	0	4,010	4,010	0
Northern Ireland	1,980	1,910	-4	950	930	-2

Source: Defence Statistics

1. UK Regular Forces - Figures are for UK Regular Forces (including both Trained and Untrained personnel), and therefore exclude Gurkhas, Full Time Reserve Service personnel and mobilised reservists. Royal Navy / Royal Marines personnel on sea service are included against the local authority containing the home port of their ship. RAF Other Ranks serving in the South Atlantic are shown against the location containing their home base.

2. MOD Civilian Personnel - Civilian figures are reported as Full Time Equivalent (FTE). FTE is a measure of the size of the workforce taking into account that some people work part-time. Part-time staff are counted according to the number of hours they work per week as a proportion of normal hours for their grade and location.

3. 2000 figures are at 1 July.

4

466

14.8b Global locations of service[1,2] and civilian personnel[3,4], at 1st April each year

Number:FTE

		2000[5]	2010	2011	2012	2013	2014	2015	2016	2017	2018	2019
Global Total		333,960	277,560	269,420	250,800	236,110	222,130	211,890	207,240	206,040	203,420	202,190
	Service	213,220	191,710	186,360	179,790	170,710	159,630	153,720	151,000	149,370	146,560	144,430
	Civilian	120,740	85,850	83,060	71,010	65,390	62,500	58,160	56,240	56,680	56,870	57,760
United Kingdom		26,700	236,710	229,390	214,310	203,480	192,970	187,820	189,060	189,350	187,040	186,540
	Service	170,300	161,790	156,970	156,970	150,310	141,180	138,130	140,450	140,080	137,490	136,190
	Civilian	97,410	70,610	67,610	57,340	53,170	51,780	49,690	48,610	49,270	49,550	50,360
Overseas Total		54,000	37,650	36,910	33,700	30,050	26,660	21,720	16,050	14,620	14,340	13,510
	Service	37,200	25,260	24,230	22,430	20,060	18,070	15,300	10,500	9,260	9,040	8,220
	Civilian	16,800	12,400	12,680	11,270	9,990	8,590	6,420	5,550	5,350	5,300	5,290
EUROPE (exc. UK)		--	33,000	31,300	29,050	25,610	22,570	18,190	12,360	10,640	10,280	9,460
of which:												
Germany	Service	--	19,100	18,240	16,990	14,840	12,960	10,020	5,290	3,870	3,580	2,850
	Civilian	--	7,020	6,470	5,800	5,300	4,250	2,850	1,920	1,710	1,660	1,560
Cyprus	Service	3,510	2,880	2,830	2,590	2,400	2,340	2,400	2,240	2,250	2,160	2,150
	Civilian	--	1,610	1,570	1,670	1,380	1,330	1,180	1,210	1,140	1,210	1,220
Belgium	Service	--	410	340	330	330	320	310	290	290	280	290
	Civilian	--	140	100	100	40	60	70	60	80	90	90
Gibraltar	Service	550	270	260	230	200	180	160	160	160	170	160
	Civilian	--	730	750	650	530	550	600	560	530	500	510
Italy	Service	--	250	210	170	140	140	180	180	180	190	180
	Civilian	--	60	50	50	20	30	20	20	30	20	20
Netherlands	Service				170	200	120	130	120	120	120	120
	Civilian				40	10	10	10	10	20	20	20
ASIA (EXC. MIDDLE EAST)		--	1,920	2,080	2,110	2,020	1,710	1,070	1,070	1,070	1,010	1,000
	Service	970	260	280	260	260	260	260	260	280	280	290
	Civilian	--	1,660	1,800	1,860	1,760	1,450	810	800	800	730	710
NORTH AFRICA / MIDDLE EAST		--	460	500	430	420	440	460	480	470	500	520
	Service	1,300	380	420	340	330	350	370	370	360	380	390
	Civilian	--	80	80	90	90	90	100	100	110	120	140
SUB SAHARAN AFRICA		--	690	1,540	870	730	670	670	800	830	830	890
of which:												
Kenya	Service	--	90	140	180	180	200	200	260	250	250	260
	Civilian	--	360	1,190	640	480	420	400	470	500	510	560
Sierra Leone	Service	--	30	30	20	20	10	10	10	10	~	~
	Civilian	--	150	130	~	~	~	~	~	~	~	~
NORTH AMERICA		--	990	980	990	1,000	1,010	1,070	1,090	1,290	1,370	1,290
of which:												
United States	Service	910	520	550	560	560	570	610	660	820	920	790
	Civilian	--	160	150	150	150	160	160	160	170	170	170
Canada	Service	1,610	270	270	270	280	270	280	250	290	280	310
	Civilian	--	50	10	10	10	10	10	10	10	10	20
CENTRAL AMERICA / CARIBBEAN		--	240	240	70	70	70	70	70	140	160	180
	Service	--	70	70	10	10	10	10	10	20	30	40
	Civilian	--	170	160	60	60	60	60	60	120	130	140
SOUTH AMERICA		--	20	20	20	20	20	20	20	20	20	20
	Service	--	10	10	10	10	10	10	10	10	10	10
	Civilian	--	10	10	10	10	10	10	10	10	10	10

Continued on the next page

14.8b Global locations of service[1,2] and civilian personnel[3,4] , at 1st April each year

Number:FTE

		2000[5]	2010	2011	2012	2013	2014	2015	2016	2017	2018	2019
SOUTH ATLANTIC		--	270	180	80	110	100	100	110	80	90	80
of which:												
Falkland Islands	Service	780	220	120	50	70	70	70	80	60	60	40
	Civilian	--	40	40	20	30	30	30	30	30	30	30
OCEANIA		--	60	70	70	70	70	60	60	70	70	70
	Service	20	50	50	60	60	60	50	50	60	60	60
	Civilian	--	10	20	10	10	10	10	10	10	20	20
UNALLOCATED		--	860	760	790	680	690	460	180	140	130	250
	Service	5,720	350	340	390	350	370	300	50	20	20	10
	Civilian	4,080	520	420	400	330	320	160	130	120	100	240

Source: Defence Statistics (Tri Service) :e: Defence Statistics

1. UK Regular Forces - Figures are for UK Regular Forces (including both Trained and Untrained personnel), and therefore exclude Gurkhas, Full Time Reserve Service personnel and mobilised reservists. Royal Navy / Royal Marines personnel on sea service are included against the local authority containing the home port of their ship. RAF Other Ranks serving in the South Atlantic are shown against the location containing their home base.

2. Personnel deployed on operations and temporary assignments are shown against their permanent stationed location. As such figures for locations such as North Africa / Middle East & South Atlantic exclude large numbers of personnel deployed in those locations.

3. MOD Civilian Personnel - Civilian figures are reported as Full Time Equivalent (FTE). FTE is a measure of the size of the workforce taking into account that some people work part-time. Part-time staff are counted according to the number of hours they work per week as a proportion of normal hours for their grade and location.

4. The Royal Fleet Auxiliary (RFA) are included in the Civilians Grand Total but excluded from all Location breakdowns. This is because location data is not available for RFAs.

5. Detailed break down of LEC data for 2000 are not available. The "Overseas Total" for year 2000 subsumes the total LEC figure. 2000 figures as at 1 July.

14.9a UK Regular Armed Forces deaths by Service, by year of registration, numbers, age and gender standardised rates[1].

1 January 2007 to 31 December 2019

Year	All		Naval Service[2]		Army		RAF	
	number	*rate*	number	*rate*	number	*rate*	number	*rate*
2007	204	*106*	27	*73*	145	*127*	32	*75*
2008	137	*74*	40	*108*	79	*75*	18	*37*
2009	205	*105*	23	*58*	158	*131*	24	*55*
2010	187	*94*	30	*73*	136	*113*	21	*49*
2011	132	*69*	19	*51*	98	*87*	15	*35*
2012	130	*73*	20	*66*	95	*91*	15	*43*
2013	86	*51*	13	*45*	63	*66*	10	*22*
2014	68	*43*	12	*36*	40	*43*	16	*41*
2015	60	*39*	11	*33*	39	*45*	10	*28*
2016	74	*51*	17	*66*	43	*51*	14	*36*
2017	63	*42*	12	*34*	40	*50*	11	*29*
2018	61	*41*	12	*34*	38	*46*	11	*29*
2019	**66**	***45***	**9**	***27***	**40**	***54***	**17**	***43***

Source: Defence Statistics (Health)

[1] Rates have been age and gender standardised to the 2019 Regular Armed Forces population, expressed per 100,000 personnel at risk.

[2] Naval Service includes Royal Navy and Royal Marines.

14.9b UK Regular Armed Forces deaths by Service[1], Standardised Mortality Ratios[2,3] (SMR) (95% confidence intervals (CI)).

1 January 2007 to 31 December 2019

Year	All			Naval Service			Army			RAF		
	Number	SMR	(95% CI)	Number	SMR	(95% CI)	Number	SMR	(95% CI)	Number	SMR	(95% CI)
2007	204	96	(84-110)	27	61	(40-89)	145	132	(112-155)	32	55	(39-78)
2008	137	65	(55-76)	40	89	(65-122)	79	72	(58-90)	18	32	(19-50)
2009	205	99	(86-113)	23	53	(33-79)	158	146	(125-170)	24	43	(28-64)
2010	187	94	(81-108)	30	71	(50-102)	136	131	(111-155)	21	39	(24-60)
2011	132	71	(60-84)	19	48	(29-76)	98	100	(82-122)	15	30	(17-50)
2012	130	76	(64-90)	20	56	(34-86)	95	105	(86-128)	15	34	(19-56)
2013	86	52	(42-65)	13	37	(20-63)	63	73	(57-93)	10	24	(11-44)
2014	68	44	(35-56)	12	35	(18-61)	40	50	(37-68)	16	40	(23-65)
2015	60	40	(31-51)	11	32	(16-57)	39	50	(37-68)	10	25	(12-47)
2016	74	48	(38-60)	17	47	(28-76)	43	54	(40-73)	14	35	(19-59)
2017	63	41	(32-53)	12	34	(18-59)	40	52	(38-70)	11	28	(14-50)
2018	61	38	(30-49)	12	32	(17-56)	38	47	(34-64)	11	27	(13-48)
2019	**66**	**41**	**(32-53)**	**9**	**24**	**(11-45)**	**40**	**50**	**(36-67)**	**17**	**41**	**(24-66)**

Source: Defence Statistics (Health)

[1] Naval Service includes Royal Navy and Royal Marines.

[2] Standardised mortality ratios have been age and gender standardised.

[3] An SMR below, equal to, or above 100 indicates that the rate for the armed forces or the Service is respectively below, equal to, or higher than the rate in the general UK population.

14.10 Strength of Uniformed United Kingdom Medical Staff , 2011-2019

	2011	2012	2013	2014	2015	2016	2017	2018	2019
Qualified Doctors	588	575	578	604	616	595	584	559	595
Qualified Dentists	245	244	226	207	183	182	178	168	164
Nursing Services	1,329	1,461	1,286	1,298	1,262	1,222	1,219	1,207	1,233
Support Staff	4,038	4,000	4,127	4,125	3,838	3,863	3,663	3,786	3,919
Total	**6,200**	**6,280**	**6,217**	**6,234**	**5,899**	**5,862**	**5,644**	**5,720**	**5,911**

Source: Joint Medical Group

this page is intentionally blank

Population and vital statistics

Chapter 15

Population and Vital Statistics

This section begins with a summary of population figures for the United Kingdom and constituent countries for 1851 to 2066 and for Great Britain from 1801 (Table 15.1). Table 15.2 analyses the components of population change. Table 15.3 gives details of the national sex and age structures for years up to the present date, and with projected figures. Legal marital condition of the population is shown in Table 15.4. The distribution of population at regional and local levels is summarised in Table 15.5.

In the main, historical series relate to census information, while mid-year estimates, which make allowance for under-enumeration in the census, are given for the recent past and the present (from 1961 onwards).

Population (Tables 15.1 - 15.3)

Population estimates provide statistics on the current size and age structure of the population in the UK. Figures shown in these tables relate to the population enumerated at successive censuses, mid-year estimates and population projections.

Population estimates are produced using a well-established demographic approach called the cohort component method, combining information from several data sources including the previous census, survey data and administrative registers. They are released 12 months after the reference date to which they relate, consequently, these estimates pre-date the appearance of the coronavirus (COVID-19).

Population estimates refer to the **usually resident population**. This can mean that estimates of population do not necessarily coincide with the number of people to be found in an area at a particular time. For most people, defining where they usually live - for the purposes of the census, for example - is straightforward. For a minority of people, the concept of usual residence is more difficult to define, for example, for students, members of the armed forces, prisoners and international migrants.

Specific rules are used for these groups:

- higher education students and schoolchildren studying away from home are resident at their term-time address

- members of the armed forces are usually resident at the address where they spend most of their time

- prisoners are usually resident in the prison estate if they have a sentence of six months or more

- international migrants are usually resident if they intend to stay in England and Wales for more than 12 months

Further information can be found on the National Statistics website: https://www.ons.gov.uk/peoplepopulationandcommunity/populationandmigration/populationestimates/

Marital condition (de jure): estimated population (Table 15.4)

This table shows population estimates by marital status. The figures are produced using the April to June quarter of the Labour Force Survey (LFS), a large-scale UK household survey we carry out that interviews approximately 40,000 households per quarter.

A family is a married, civil partnered or cohabiting couple with or without children, or a lone parent, with at least one child, who live at the same address. Children may be dependent or non-dependent.

Dependent children are those aged under 16 years living with at least one parent, or aged 16 to 18 years in full-time education, excluding all children who have a spouse, partner or child living in the household.

Non-dependent children are those living with their parent(s), and either (a) aged 19 years or over, or (b) aged 16 to 18 years who are not in full-time education or who have a spouse, partner or child living in the household. Non-dependent children are sometimes called adult children.

A household is one person living alone, or a group of people (not necessarily related) living at the same address who share cooking facilities and share a living room, sitting room or dining area. A household can consist of a single family, more than one family, or no families in the case of a group of unrelated people.

For further information see: https://www.ons.gov.uk/peoplepopulationandcommunity/birthsdeathsandmarriages/families/methodologies/familiesandhouseholdsqmi

Geographical distribution of the population (Table 15.5)

The mid-year population estimates are provided for standard regions of the United Kingdom, for metropolitan areas, for broad groupings of local authority districts by type within England and Wales, and for some of the larger cities.

Population of the UK by country of birth / nationality (Table 15.6)

Estimates of the population of the UK by country of birth and nationality are based upon data from the Annual Population Survey (APS). The APS is a survey of households in the UK, so does not include most communal establishments. The APS, which began in 2004, is a continuous survey, comprising the Labour Force Survey (LFS), supplemented by sample boosts in England, Wales and Scotland to ensure small areas are sufficiently sampled.

Country of birth refers to the country that a person was born in and cannot change. Nationality refers to the nationality stated by the respondent when they are interviewed and is subject to change.

Long-Term International Migration (Tables 15.7 - 15.8)

Long Term International Migration (LTIM) estimates are the most comprehensive estimates of immigration, emigration and net migration flows to and from the UK. LTIM estimates are based on data from the International Passenger Survey (IPS) with adjustments made using administrative data.

Approximately 800,000 IPS interviews are conducted each year for migration purposes and of these around 3,000 interviewees are identified as long-term international migrants. Given the sample size many variables can only be disaggregated to a certain level before being subject to unacceptable margins of error, for example, migration from individual countries by single year.

ONS is currently transforming the way these statistics on migration are produced and as such they have been reclassified as "Experimental Statistics" in line with Office for Statistics Regulation guidance.

A long-term international migrant is defined as a person who changes his or her country of usual residence for a period of at least a year,so that the country of destination effectively becomes the country of usual residence.

For further information on LTIM statistics see: https://www.ons.gov.uk/peoplepopulationandcommunity/populationandmigration/populationestimates/methodologies/longterminternationalmigrationqmi

Grants for settlement in the United Kingdom (Table 15.9)

The settlement figures comprise people granted settlement on arrival (also known as 'indefinite leave to enter'), and people who have applied for settlement having lived in the UK for a certain length of time (also known as 'on removal of time limit' or 'indefinite leave to remain). Settlement generally occurs after a period of five or more years of residency in the UK. Following changes in immigration legislation in the 1980s, the majority of grants are to people already in the country.

Prior to the 1st January 2021, Swiss and EEA nationals were not subject to immigration control so were not included in the figures. Historically landing cards were used as a data source for grants of settlement until their discontinuation in May 2019.

Asylum applications and initial decisions in the UK (Table 15.10ab)

The asylum applications and resettlements data tables, produced by the Home Office as part of the Immigration Statistics release, have been remapped to present new collections of information. This change is reflected in the new tables 15.10a and 15.10b in this edition of AOS. Further details can be found in the 'publishing detailed datasets in Immigration Statistics' document (https://www.gov.uk/government/publications/publishingdetailed-datasets-in-immigration-statistics). The majority of asylum and resettlement data are extracted from the Home Office's Case Information Database (CID).

A refugee is someone who meets the definition under the 1951 United Nations Convention relating to the Status of Refugees or 'Refugee Convention', having been forced to flee his or her country because of a well-founded fear of persecution for reasons of race, religion, nationality, political opinion or membership in a particular social group.

An asylum applicant (also referred to as 'asylum seeker') is someone who makes a claim to be recognised as a refugee under the Refugee Convention. The core principle of the Convention is that a refugee should not be returned to a country where they face serious threats to their life or freedom. The Convention outlines the definition of the term 'refugee', the rights of refugees and the kind of legal protection, other assistance and social rights they should receive from the countries who have signed the document. An individual seeking international protection is expected to claim asylum in the first safe country they reach, or by approaching the United Nations High Commissioner for Refugees (UNHCR). Asylum applicants will receive a decision on their application, which may be a grant of refugee status (or 'asylum'), humanitarian protection, or another form of permission to stay, or a refusal.

The UK Immigration Rules (paragraph 334) outlines the criteria an asylum applicant must meet to be granted asylum in the UK. An application which does not meet these criteria will be refused. In certain circumstances an applicant may be refused asylum but granted other forms of protection or leave. Table 15.10a shows the number of people granted protection, resettlement, or an alternative form of leave annually since 2010.

Asylum-related grants:
- Discretionary leave (DL) is granted to an individual who does not qualify for international protection (asylum or Humanitarian Protection) but who is able to demonstrate particularly compelling reasons why removal would not be appropriate.

- Humanitarian Protection (HP) is leave granted to a person who does not require protection for reasons covered by the Refugee Convention but who would, if removed, face a real risk to life or person in the country of origin or country of former habitual residence. These risks include a threat to life (for example from the death penalty, unlawful killing), torture, inhuman or degrading treatment; or serious threat by reason of indiscriminate violence in situations of international or internal armed conflict.

- UASC leave is granted to UASC who do not qualify for refugee status or Humanitarian Protection, if they are under 17.5 years old and cannot be returned because there are no adequate reception arrangements in the country to which they would be returned.

Resettlement is the transfer of refugees from the country in which they have sought refuge to another State that has agreed to admit them. The UK currently has four resettlement schemes that it operates in partnership with the United Nations High Commission for Refugees (UNHCR) and the International Organization for Migration (IOM). Resettlement is provided as a durable solution when integration in the host country or a safe return to a person's country of origin is not possible.

Table 15.10b provides the number of asylum applications (from main applicants only) lodged in the UK by the top 20 nationalities claiming asylum in the period 2010 - 2020.

Marriages (Table 15.11)

This table shows the number of marriages by type of ceremony and denomination. The figures are derived from information recorded when marriages are registered as part of civil registration, a legal requirement.

The popularity of religious ceremonies has steadily declined over time compared with civil ceremonies. In 1900, religious ceremonies accounted for 85% of all marriages; by the late 1970s this had fallen to less than half (49%) and then to 23% in 2017. Civil marriages have outnumbered religious marriages every year since 1992.

Figures represent civil and religious marriages that took place in England and Wales only. Following the implementation of the Marriage Same Sex Couples Act 2013, the first marriages of same-sex couples took place on 29 March 2014. Not all religious organisations conduct marriages of same-sex couples.

A civil marriage can take place at a register office or other buildings approved for civil marriage. The bride and bridegroom must personally give a formal notice of their intention to marry to the superintendent registrar of the district(s) where they have resided for the previous seven days.

Births (Tables 15.14 - 15.15)

Birth statistics for England and Wales are produced by the Office for National Statistics (ONS). They are derived from information recorded when live births and stillbirths are registered as part of civil registration, a legal requirement; these data represent the most complete data source available. Birth registration is a legal requirement under the Births and Deaths Registration Act 1836.

Local authorities and other government departments use birth statistics for planning and resource allocation. For example, local authorities use birth statistics to decide how many school places will be needed in a given area. The Department for Work and Pensions uses detailed birth statistics to feed into statistical models for pensions and benefits. The Department of Health and Social Care uses the data to plan maternity services and inform policy decisions.

A birth to a mother whose usual residence is outside England and Wales is included in total figures for "England, Wales and elsewhere " but are excluded from any sub-divisions of England and Wales. The England and Wales and elsewhere figures correspond to figures published at the national level for England and Wales not based on area of usual residence.

For more informationn on birth statistics see: https://www.ons.gov.uk/peoplepopulationandcommunity/birthsdeathsandmarriages

Abortions (Table 15.16)

The Abortion Act 1967, as amended by the Human Fertilisation and Embryology Act 1990, permits termination of a pregnancy by a registered medical practitioner subject to certain conditions. Legal requirements apply to the certification and notification of abortion procedures. Within the terms of the Abortion Act, only a registered practitioner can terminate a pregnancy. The doctor taking responsibility for the procedure is legally required to notify the Chief Medical Officer (CMO) of the abortion within 14 days of the termination. Ground E abortions are those performed because of fetal abnormality at any gestation.

For further information on abortion statistics see: https://www.gov.uk/health-and-social-care/abortion

Death rates (Tables 15.17)

The Births and Deaths Registration Act (1836) made it a legal requirement for all deaths to be registered from 1 July 1837. Mortality statistics in England and Wales are based on the details collected when deaths are certified and registered.

The death rates in this table are derived from total deaths registered in England and Wales in the specific calendar year and corresponding mid-year population estimates. The death rates provided are Age-standardised mortality rates (ASMRs). ASMRs allow for differences in the age structure of populations and therefore allow valid comparisons to be made between geographic areas, over time and between sexes.

Still births and infant deaths (Table 15.18)

This table shows perinatal mortality statistics published by ONS. They are based on all births and deaths registered via the General Register Office regardless of gestational age, and all stillbirths registered at 24 weeks or more gestation in line with the Stillbirth (Definition) Act 1992.

Stillbirth - A baby born after 24 or more weeks completed gestation and which did not, at any time, breathe or show signs of life.

Early neonatal - The death of an infant aged under 7 days.

Perinatal - A baby who was recorded as either a stillbirth or early neonatal death.

Neonatal - The death of an infant aged under 28 days.

Postneonatal - The death of an infant aged between 28 days and 1 year.

Infant - The death of those aged under 1 year.

Childhood - The death of those aged between 1 and 15 years. The overall decline in infant mortality rates in recent decades is likely to reflect general improvements in healthcare and more specific improvements in midwifery and neonatal intensive care.

National life tables (Table 15.19)

National life tables (previously called interim life tables) have been produced annually for the UK and its constituent countries since 1980 to 1982. They provide period expectation of life statistics. Period life expectancy is the average number of additional years a person can be expected to live for if he or she experiences the age-specific mortality rates of the given area and time period for the rest of his or her life.

Each life table is based on the population estimates and deaths by date of registration data for a period of 3 consecutive years.

Adoptions (Table 15.20)

Please note that adoption figures for England & Wales, Northern Ireland and Scotland may not always be on exactly the same basis. There can be differences in the coverage of what at first sight appear to be the same statistics.

England and Wales - From 2016-17, looked after children data is now collected during the year through the 'Looked after children' census which is carried out by Department for Education. These tables present the number of children who were adopted from the care of the local authorities during the year.

Scotland - The Registrar General for Scotland registers adoptions under the Adoption and Children (Scotland) Act 2007. The registration of adopted children, and the number of adoptions registered has been recorded for each year since the introduction of the Adoption of Children (Scotland) Act 1930.

Northern Ireland - Registers of children adopted under the provisions of the Adoption (NI) Order 1987 and Adoption (Hague Convention) Act (NI) 1969 and of previous adoption Acts of 1929, 1950 and 1967 are kept by the General Register Office.

15.1 Population summary: by country and sex

Thousands

	UK			England and Wales[1]			Wales			Scotland			Northern Ireland		
	Persons	Males	Females	Persons	Males	Females	Persons	Males	Females	Persons	Males	Females	Persons	Males	Females
Enumerated population: census figures															
1801	..	..	..	8,893	4,255	4,638	587	..	..	1,608	739	869	..	..	..
1851	22,259	10,855	11,404	17,928	8,781	9,146	1,163	..	..	2,889	1,376	1,513	1,442	698	745
1901	38,237	18,492	19,745	32,528	15,729	16,799	2,013	..	..	4,472	2,174	2,298	1,237	590	647
1911	42,082	20,357	21,725	36,070	17,446	18,625	2,421	..	..	4,761	2,309	2,452	1,251	603	648
1921	44,027	21,033	22,994	37,887	18,075	19,811	2,656	..	..	4,882	2,348	2,535	1,258	610	648
1931	46,038	22,060	23,978	39,952	19,133	20,819	2,593	..	..	4,843	2,326	2,517	1,243	601	642
1951	50,225	24,118	26,107	43,758	21,016	22,742	2,599	..	..	5,096	2,434	2,662	1,371	668	703
1961	52,709	25,481	27,228	46,105	22,304	23,801	2,644	..	..	5,179	2,483	2,697	1,425	694	731
Resident population: year estimates															
1973	56,223	27,332	28,891	49,459	24,061	25,399	2,773	1,345	1,428	5,234	2,515	2,718	1,530	756	774
1974	56,236	27,349	28,887	49,468	24,075	25,393	2,785	1,352	1,433	5,241	2,519	2,722	1,527	755	772
1975	56,226	27,361	28,865	49,470	24,091	25,378	2,795	1,359	1,437	5,232	2,516	2,716	1,524	753	770
1976	56,216	27,360	28,856	49,459	24,089	25,370	2,799	1,361	1,438	5,233	2,517	2,716	1,524	754	769
1977	56,190	27,345	28,845	49,440	24,076	25,364	2,801	1,361	1,439	5,226	2,515	2,711	1,523	754	769
1978	56,178	27,330	28,848	49,443	24,067	25,375	2,804	1,362	1,442	5,212	2,509	2,704	1,523	754	770
1979	56,240	27,373	28,867	49,508	24,113	25,395	2,810	1,365	1,445	5,204	2,505	2,699	1,528	755	773
1980	56,330	27,411	28,919	49,603	24,156	25,448	2,816	1,367	1,449	5,194	2,501	2,693	1,533	755	778
1981	56,357	27,412	28,946	49,634	24,160	25,474	2,813	1,365	1,448	5,180	2,495	2,685	1,543	757	786
1982	56,291	27,364	28,927	49,582	24,119	25,462	2,804	1,358	1,446	5,165	2,487	2,677	1,545	757	788
1983	56,316	27,371	28,944	49,617	24,133	25,484	2,803	1,358	1,446	5,148	2,479	2,669	1,551	759	792
1984	56,409	27,421	28,989	49,713	24,185	25,528	2,801	1,357	1,444	5,139	2,475	2,664	1,557	761	796
1985	56,554	27,489	29,065	49,861	24,254	25,606	2,803	1,358	1,445	5,128	2,470	2,658	1,565	765	800
1986	56,684	27,542	29,142	49,999	24,311	25,687	2,811	1,362	1,449	5,112	2,462	2,649	1,574	768	805
1987	56,804	27,599	29,205	50,123	24,371	25,752	2,823	1,368	1,454	5,099	2,455	2,644	1,582	773	809
1988	56,916	27,652	29,265	50,254	24,434	25,820	2,841	1,376	1,465	5,077	2,444	2,633	1,585	774	812
1989	57,076	27,729	29,348	50,408	24,510	25,898	2,855	1,382	1,473	5,078	2,443	2,635	1,590	776	814
1990	57,237	27,819	29,419	50,561	24,597	25,964	2,862	1,385	1,477	5,081	2,444	2,637	1,596	778	818
1991	57,439	27,909	29,530	50,748	24,681	26,067	2,873	1,391	1,482	5,083	2,445	2,639	1,607	783	824
1992	57,585	27,977	29,608	50,876	24,739	26,136	2,878	1,392	1,485	5,086	2,445	2,640	1,623	792	831
1993	57,714	28,039	29,675	50,986	24,793	26,193	2,884	1,396	1,488	5,092	2,448	2,644	1,636	798	837
1994	57,862	28,108	29,754	51,116	24,853	26,263	2,887	1,399	1,489	5,102	2,453	2,649	1,644	802	842
1995	58,025	28,204	29,821	51,272	24,946	26,326	2,889	1,400	1,488	5,104	2,453	2,650	1,649	804	845
1996	58,164	28,287	29,877	51,410	25,030	26,381	2,891	1,401	1,490	5,092	2,447	2,645	1,662	810	851
1997	58,314	28,371	29,943	51,560	25,113	26,446	2,895	1,404	1,491	5,083	2,442	2,641	1,671	816	856
1998	58,475	28,458	30,017	51,720	25,201	26,519	2,900	1,407	1,492	5,077	2,439	2,638	1,678	819	859
1999	58,684	28,578	30,106	51,933	25,323	26,610	2,901	1,408	1,493	5,072	2,437	2,635	1,679	818	861
2000	58,886	28,690	30,196	52,140	25,438	26,702	2,907	1,408	1,499	5,063	2,432	2,631	1,683	820	862
2001	59,113	28,832	30,281	52,360	25,574	26,786	2,910	1,409	1,502	5,064	2,434	2,630	1,689	824	865
2002	59,366	28,973	30,393	52,602	25,708	26,894	2,923	1,415	1,508	5,066	2,436	2,630	1,698	829	869
2003	59,637	29,125	30,511	52,863	25,854	27,009	2,938	1,426	1,511	5,069	2,438	2,630	1,705	833	872
2004	59,950	29,297	30,653	53,152	26,012	27,140	2,957	1,439	1,519	5,084	2,447	2,638	1,714	838	876
2005	60,413	29,541	30,872	53,575	26,234	27,341	2,969	1,448	1,522	5,110	2,461	2,649	1,728	845	882
2006	60,827	29,762	31,065	53,951	26,433	27,518	2,986	1,456	1,530	5,133	2,475	2,658	1,743	853	890
2007	61,319	30,028	31,291	54,387	26,669	27,718	3,006	1,469	1,538	5,170	2,497	2,673	1,762	862	899
2008	61,824	30,301	31,523	54,842	26,914	27,927	3,026	1,479	1,546	5,203	2,515	2,688	1,779	871	908
2009	62,260	30,532	31,728	55,235	27,122	28,114	3,039	1,488	1,551	5,232	2,532	2,700	1,793	879	915
2010	62,759	30,805	31,954	55,692	27,373	28,320	3,050	1,495	1,554	5,262	2,548	2,714	1,805	885	920
2011	63,285	31,097	32,188	56,171	27,638	28,533	3,064	1,504	1,559	5,300	2,570	2,730	1,814	889	925
2012	63,705	31,315	32,390	56,568	27,843	28,724	3,074	1,510	1,564	5,314	2,577	2,736	1,824	895	929
2013	64,106	31,533	32,573	56,948	28,049	28,899	3,082	1,515	1,567	5,328	2,587	2,741	1,830	897	933
2014	64,597	31,794	32,803	57,409	28,295	29,114	3,092	1,521	1,571	5,348	2,597	2,751	1,840	903	938
2015	65,110	32,074	33,036	57,885	28,555	29,331	3,099	1,526	1,574	5,373	2,610	2,763	1,852	909	942
2016	65,648	32,378	33,270	58,381	28,835	29,546	3,113	1,534	1,579	5,405	2,628	2,777	1,862	915	947
2017	66,040	32,582	33,458	58,745	29,021	29,723	3,125	1,540	1,585	5,425	2,640	2,785	1,871	920	951
2018	66,436	32,790	33,645	59,116	29,215	29,901	3,139	1,547	1,591	5,438	2,649	2,789	1,882	926	955
2019	66,797	32,978	33,819	59,440	29,383	30,057	3,153	1,555	1,598	5,463	2,663	2,800	1,894	933	961
2020	67,081	33,146	33,936	59,720	29,546	30,173	3,170	1,564	1,606	5,466	2,665	2,801	1,896	934	961

15.1 Population summary: by country and sex

Thousands

	UK			England and Wales[1]			Wales			Scotland			Northern Ireland		
	Persons	Males	Females	Persons	Males	Females	Persons	Males	Females	Persons	Males	Females	Persons	Males	Females
Resident population: projections (year)[2]															
2021	67,531	33,373	34,157	60,144	29,760	30,384	3,175	1,567	1,608	5,476	2,671	2,805	1,911	942	968
2026	68,921	34,111	34,810	61,456	30,451	31,005	3,212	1,586	1,625	5,522	2,699	2,823	1,943	961	982
2031	70,057	34,707	35,351	62,540	31,016	31,525	3,235	1,599	1,636	5,555	2,719	2,836	1,962	972	990
2036	71,059	35,235	35,824	63,514	31,525	31,989	3,247	1,606	1,641	5,570	2,730	2,841	1,974	980	994
2041	72,032	35,758	36,274	64,472	32,035	32,436	3,253	1,610	1,643	5,575	2,736	2,839	1,985	987	998
2046	72,971	36,271	36,700	65,406	32,539	32,866	3,258	1,614	1,643	5,571	2,739	2,833	1,994	993	1,001
2051	73,754	36,712	37,042	66,204	32,980	33,224	3,257	1,617	1,641	5,554	2,736	2,819	1,996	996	1,000
2056	74,338	37,062	37,276	66,822	33,338	33,485	3,251	1,617	1,634	5,526	2,729	2,797	1,990	996	994
2061	74,835	37,379	37,457	67,360	33,664	33,696	3,244	1,617	1,627	5,497	2,722	2,775	1,978	993	985
2066	75,393	37,727	37,667	67,954	34,020	33,934	3,240	1,619	1,621	5,474	2,717	2,757	1,965	990	975

Notes

Source: Office for National Statistics

1. The population of England and Wales is exclusive of the Population of the Islands in the Britsh Seas, and of the portions of the Armed Forces and Merchant Service Abroad.

2. 2018-based princial projections.

Figures may not add exactly due to rounding

15.2a Population projections by the Office for National Statistics
United Kingdom, PERSONS, thousands

Components of change (mid-year to mid-year), total fertility rate
and expectation of life at birth (EOLB) based on the mortality rates for the year

	2020-2021	2021-2022	2022-2023	2023-2024	2024-2025	2025-2026	2026-2027	2027-2028	2028-2029	2029-2030	2030-2031	2031-2032	2032-2033	2033-2034	2034-2035	2035-2036	2036-2037	2037-2038	2038-2039	2039-2040
Population at start	67,081	67,351	67,596	67,844	68,082	68,305	68,512	68,702	68,881	69,049	69,207	69,355	69,494	69,624	69,747	69,863	69,975	70,086	70,196	70,307
Births	671	663	659	662	663	660	657	655	652	651	650	649	650	649	652	656	662	668	675	681
Deaths	646	655	642	649	656	664	672	681	689	698	707	715	724	733	741	749	756	763	769	775
Natural change	25	8	17	13	6	-4	-15	-26	-37	-47	-57	-66	-75	-82	-89	-93	-94	-95	-94	-94
International migration inflows	611	598	585	572	559	546	533	533	533	533	533	533	533	533	533	533	533	533	533	533
Cross border migration inflows	-	-	-	-	-	-	-	-	-	-	-	-	-	-	-	-	-	-	-	-
International migration outflows	366	361	354	348	342	334	328	328	328	328	328	328	328	328	328	328	328	328	328	328
Cross border migration outflows	-	-	-	-	-	-	-	-	-	-	-	-	-	-	-	-	-	-	-	-
Net international migration	244	237	231	224	217	212	205	205	205	205	205	205	205	205	205	205	205	205	205	205
Net cross border migration	-	-	-	-	-	-	-	-	-	-	-	-	-	-	-	-	-	-	-	-
Net migration	244	237	231	224	217	212	205	205	205	205	205	205	205	205	205	205	205	205	205	205
Total change	269	245	248	237	223	207	190	179	168	158	148	139	130	123	116	112	111	110	111	111
Population at end	67,351	67,596	67,844	68,082	68,305	68,512	68,702	68,881	69,049	69,207	69,355	69,494	69,624	69,747	69,863	69,975	70,086	70,196	70,307	70,418
Annual growth rate	0.40%	0.36%	0.37%	0.35%	0.33%	0.30%	0.28%	0.26%	0.24%	0.23%	0.21%	0.20%	0.19%	0.18%	0.17%	0.16%	0.16%	0.16%	0.16%	0.16%
Total fertility rate (TFR)	1.54	1.52	1.52	1.53	1.53	1.53	1.53	1.53	1.53	1.53	1.53	1.54	1.54	1.54	1.54	1.54	1.55	1.55	1.56	1.57
EOLB Males	79.2	79.3	79.8	79.9	80.0	80.1	80.2	80.3	80.4	80.5	80.6	80.7	80.8	80.9	81.0	81.1	81.2	81.3	81.4	81.6
Females	83.1	83.0	83.4	83.4	83.5	83.6	83.7	83.8	83.8	83.9	84.0	84.1	84.2	84.2	84.3	84.4	84.5	84.6	84.7	84.8

	2040-2041	2041-2042	2042-2043	2043-2044	2044-2045	2045-2046	2046-2047	2047-2048	2048-2049	2049-2050	2050-2051	2051-2052	2052-2053	2053-2054	2054-2055	2055-2056	2056-2057	2057-2058	2058-2059	2059-2060
Population at start	70,418	70,530	70,642	70,752	70,862	70,968	71,070	71,165	71,253	71,332	71,402	71,461	71,511	71,550	71,580	71,601	71,614	71,620	71,621	71,619
Births	687	691	695	698	698	697	695	691	687	681	675	669	663	656	650	645	640	636	632	630
Deaths	780	785	789	793	797	801	805	809	813	817	821	825	828	832	835	837	839	840	840	840
Natural change	-93	-94	-94	-96	-99	-104	-110	-117	-126	-135	-145	-155	-166	-175	-184	-192	-199	-204	-208	-210
International migration inflows	533	533	533	533	533	533	533	533	533	533	533	533	533	533	533	533	533	533	533	533
Cross border migration inflows	-	-	-	-	-	-	-	-	-	-	-	-	-	-	-	-	-	-	-	-
International migration outflows	328	328	328	328	328	328	328	328	328	328	328	328	328	328	328	328	328	328	328	328
Cross border migration outflows	-	-	-	-	-	-	-	-	-	-	-	-	-	-	-	-	-	-	-	-
Net international migration	205	205	205	205	205	205	205	205	205	205	205	205	205	205	205	205	205	205	205	205
Net cross border migration	-	-	-	-	-	-	-	-	-	-	-	-	-	-	-	-	-	-	-	-
Net migration	205	205	205	205	205	205	205	205	205	205	205	205	205	205	205	205	205	205	205	205
Total change	112	111	110	110	106	101	95	88	79	70	60	50	39	30	21	13	6	1	-3	-5
Population at end	70,530	70,642	70,752	70,862	70,968	71,070	71,165	71,253	71,332	71,402	71,461	71,511	71,550	71,580	71,601	71,614	71,620	71,621	71,619	71,614
Annual growth rate	0.16%	0.16%	0.16%	0.15%	0.15%	0.14%	0.13%	0.12%	0.11%	0.10%	0.08%	0.07%	0.06%	0.04%	0.03%	0.02%	0.01%	0.00%	0.00%	-0.01%
Total fertility rate (TFR)	1.57	1.58	1.58	1.59	1.59	1.59	1.59	1.59	1.59	1.59	1.59	1.59	1.59	1.59	1.59	1.59	1.59	1.59	1.59	1.59
EOLB Males	81.7	81.8	81.9	82.0	82.1	82.2	82.4	82.5	82.6	82.7	82.8	83.0	83.1	83.2	83.3	83.4	83.5	83.6	83.8	83.9
Females	84.9	85.0	85.1	85.2	85.3	85.4	85.5	85.6	85.7	85.8	85.9	86.0	86.1	86.2	86.3	86.5	86.6	86.7	86.8	86.9

15.2a Population projections by the Office for National Statistics
United Kingdom, PERSONS, thousands

Components of change (mid-year to mid-year), total fertility rate
and expectation of life at birth (EOLB) based on the mortality rates for the year

	2060 -2061	2061 -2062	2062 -2063	2063 -2064	2064 -2065	2065 -2066	2066 -2067	2067 -2068	2068 -2069	2069 -2070	2070 -2071	2071 -2072	2072 -2073	2073 -2074	2074 -2075	2075 -2076	2076 -2077	2077 -2078	2078 -2079	2079 -2080
Population at start	71,614	71,607	71,601	71,595	71,591	71,589	71,590	71,594	71,601	71,610	71,623	71,637	71,653	71,669	71,686	71,702	71,716	71,729	71,740	71,748
Births	627	626	625	625	626	626	628	629	631	633	635	637	639	640	641	642	642	642	641	640
Deaths	839	838	836	834	832	830	829	827	826	826	826	826	827	828	830	832	834	836	838	840
Natural change	-211	-212	-211	-209	-207	-204	-201	-198	-195	-193	-191	-189	-189	-188	-189	-190	-192	-194	-197	-200
International migration inflows	533	533	533	533	533	533	533	533	533	533	533	533	533	533	533	533	533	533	533	533
Cross border migration inflows	-	-	-	-	-	-	-	-	-	-	-	-	-	-	-	-	-	-	-	-
International migration outflows	328	328	328	328	328	328	328	328	328	328	328	328	328	328	328	328	328	328	328	328
Cross border migration outflows	-	-	-	-	-	-	-	-	-	-	-	-	-	-	-	-	-	-	-	-
Net international migration	205	205	205	205	205	205	205	205	205	205	205	205	205	205	205	205	205	205	205	205
Net cross border migration	-	-	-	-	-	-	-	-	-	-	-	-	-	-	-	-	-	-	-	-
Net migration	205	205	205	205	205	205	205	205	205	205	205	205	205	205	205	205	205	205	205	205
Total change	-6	-7	-6	-4	-2	1	4	7	10	12	14	16	16	17	16	15	13	11	8	5
Population at end	71,607	71,601	71,595	71,591	71,589	71,590	71,594	71,601	71,610	71,623	71,637	71,653	71,669	71,686	71,702	71,716	71,729	71,740	71,748	71,754
Annual growth rate	-0.01%	-0.01%	-0.01%	-0.01%	0.00%	0.00%	0.01%	0.01%	0.01%	0.02%	0.02%	0.02%	0.02%	0.02%	0.02%	0.02%	0.02%	0.01%	0.01%	0.01%
Total fertility rate (TFR)	1.59	1.59	1.59	1.59	1.59	1.59	1.59	1.59	1.59	1.59	1.59	1.59	1.59	1.59	1.59	1.59	1.59	1.59	1.59	1.59
EOLB Males	84.0	84.1	84.2	84.3	84.4	84.6	84.7	84.8	84.9	85.0	85.1	85.2	85.3	85.5	85.6	85.7	85.8	85.9	86.0	86.1
Females	87.0	87.1	87.2	87.3	87.4	87.5	87.6	87.7	87.8	87.9	88.0	88.1	88.2	88.2	88.3	88.4	88.5	88.6	88.7	88.8

	2080 -2081	2081 -2082	2082 -2083	2083 -2084	2084 -2085	2085 -2086	2086 -2087	2087 -2088	2088 -2089	2089 -2090	2090 -2091	2091 -2092	2092 -2093	2093 -2094	2094 -2095	2095 -2096	2096 -2097	2097 -2098	2098 -2099	2099 -2100
Population at start	71,754	71,756	71,755	71,752	71,745	71,736	71,724	71,710	71,694	71,675	71,656	71,635	71,612	71,589	71,566	71,542	71,517	71,491	71,465	71,438
Births	639	637	634	632	629	626	623	620	618	615	613	611	609	608	607	606	606	605	606	606
Deaths	841	842	843	843	843	843	842	842	841	840	839	838	837	836	836	836	836	837	838	839
Natural change	-203	-206	-209	-212	-214	-217	-219	-221	-223	-225	-226	-227	-228	-229	-229	-230	-230	-231	-232	-233
International migration inflows	533	533	533	533	533	533	533	533	533	533	533	533	533	533	533	533	533	533	533	533
Cross border migration inflows	-	-	-	-	-	-	-	-	-	-	-	-	-	-	-	-	-	-	-	-
International migration outflows	328	328	328	328	328	328	328	328	328	328	328	328	328	328	328	328	328	328	328	328
Cross border migration outflows	-	-	-	-	-	-	-	-	-	-	-	-	-	-	-	-	-	-	-	-
Net international migration	205	205	205	205	205	205	205	205	205	205	205	205	205	205	205	205	205	205	205	205
Net cross border migration	-	-	-	-	-	-	-	-	-	-	-	-	-	-	-	-	-	-	-	-
Net migration	205	205	205	205	205	205	205	205	205	205	205	205	205	205	205	205	205	205	205	205
Total change	2	-1	-4	-7	-9	-12	-14	-16	-18	-20	-21	-22	-23	-24	-24	-25	-25	-26	-27	-28
Population at end	71,756	71,755	71,752	71,745	71,736	71,724	71,710	71,694	71,675	71,656	71,635	71,612	71,589	71,566	71,542	71,517	71,491	71,465	71,438	71,410
Annual growth rate	0.00%	-0.01%	-0.01%	-0.01%	-0.01%	-0.02%	-0.02%	-0.02%	-0.03%	-0.03%	-0.03%	-0.03%	-0.03%	-0.03%	-0.03%	-0.03%	-0.04%	-0.04%	-0.04%	-0.04%
Total fertility rate (TFR)	1.59	1.59	1.59	1.59	1.59	1.59	1.59	1.59	1.59	1.59	1.59	1.59	1.59	1.59	1.59	1.59	1.59	1.59	1.59	1.59
EOLB Males	86.2	86.3	86.4	86.5	86.6	86.8	86.9	87.0	87.1	87.2	87.3	87.4	87.5	87.6	87.7	87.8	87.9	88.0	88.1	88.2
Females	88.9	89.0	89.1	89.2	89.3	89.4	89.5	89.6	89.7	89.8	89.9	90.0	90.0	90.1	90.2	90.3	90.4	90.5	90.6	90.7

15.2a Population projections by the Office for National Statistics
United Kingdom, PERSONS, thousands

2020-based
Principal projection

Components of change (mid-year to mid-year), total fertility rate
and expectation of life at birth (EOLB) based on the mortality rates for the year

	2100 -2101	2101 -2102	2102 -2103	2103 -2104	2104 -2105	2105 -2106	2106 -2107	2107 -2108	2108 -2109	2109 -2110	2110 -2111	2111 -2112	2112 -2113	2113 -2114	2114 -2115	2115 -2116	2116 -2117	2117 -2118	2118 -2119	2119 -2120
Population at start	71,410	71,381	71,351	71,319	71,286	71,253	71,219	71,184	71,150	71,118	71,086	71,058	71,032	71,009	70,991	70,976	70,965	70,958	70,954	70,954
Births	606	607	607	608	608	609	609	609	609	609	609	608	608	607	606	604	603	602	600	599
Deaths	840	842	844	846	847	848	849	848	847	845	843	839	835	831	825	820	815	810	806	801
Natural change	-234	-235	-237	-238	-239	-239	-239	-239	-238	-236	-234	-231	-228	-224	-220	-216	-212	-208	-205	-202
International migration inflows	533	533	533	533	533	533	533	533	533	533	533	533	533	533	533	533	533	533	533	533
Cross border migration inflows	-	-	-	-	-	-	-	-	-	-	-	-	-	-	-	-	-	-	-	-
International migration outflows	328	328	328	328	328	328	328	328	328	328	328	328	328	328	328	328	328	328	328	328
Cross border migration outflows	-	-	-	-	-	-	-	-	-	-	-	-	-	-	-	-	-	-	-	-
Net international migration	205	205	205	205	205	205	205	205	205	205	205	205	205	205	205	205	205	205	205	205
Net cross border migration	-	-	-	-	-	-	-	-	-	-	-	-	-	-	-	-	-	-	-	-
Net migration	205	205	205	205	205	205	205	205	205	205	205	205	205	205	205	205	205	205	205	205
Total change	-29	-30	-32	-33	-34	-34	-34	-34	-33	-31	-29	-26	-22	-19	-15	-11	-7	-3	0	3
Population at end	71,381	71,351	71,319	71,286	71,253	71,219	71,184	71,150	71,118	71,086	71,058	71,032	71,009	70,991	70,976	70,965	70,958	70,954	70,954	70,957
Annual growth rate	-0.04%	-0.04%	-0.04%	-0.05%	-0.05%	-0.05%	-0.05%	-0.05%	-0.05%	-0.04%	-0.04%	-0.04%	-0.03%	-0.03%	-0.02%	-0.02%	-0.01%	0.00%	0.00%	0.00%
Total fertility rate (TFR)	1.59	1.59	1.59	1.59	1.59	1.59	1.59	1.59	1.59	1.59	1.59	1.59	1.59	1.59	1.59	1.59	1.59	1.59	1.59	1.59
EOLB Males	88.3	88.4	88.5	88.6	88.7	88.8	88.9	89.0	89.1	89.2	89.3	89.4	89.5	89.6	89.7	89.8	89.9	90.0	90.1	90.2
Females	90.8	90.9	90.9	91.0	91.1	91.2	91.3	91.4	91.5	91.6	91.6	91.7	91.8	91.9	92.0	92.1	92.1	92.2	92.3	92.4

Source: Office for National Statistics

Note: Figures may not add exactly due to rounding.

481

15.2b Population projections by the Office for National Statistics
England and Wales, PERSONS, thousands

2020-based
Principal projection

Components of change (mid-year to mid-year), total fertility rate
and expectation of life at birth (EOLB) based on the mortality rates for the year

	2020 -2021	2021 -2022	2022 -2023	2023 -2024	2024 -2025	2025 -2026	2026 -2027	2027 -2028	2028 -2029	2029 -2030	2030 -2031	2031 -2032	2032 -2033	2033 -2034	2034 -2035	2035 -2036	2036 -2037	2037 -2038	2038 -2039	2039 -2040
Population at start	59,720	59,980	60,219	60,460	60,690	60,906	61,108	61,293	61,468	61,635	61,792	61,941	62,081	62,215	62,342	62,464	62,582	62,699	62,817	62,935
Births	604	598	594	597	598	595	593	591	589	588	587	587	588	589	591	595	600	606	613	619
Deaths	568	576	564	571	577	584	591	599	606	614	622	630	638	646	653	660	667	673	679	684
Natural change	35	22	30	27	20	11	2	-8	-17	-26	-35	-43	-50	-57	-62	-66	-67	-67	-66	-65
International migration inflows	560	548	536	524	512	500	488	488	488	488	488	488	488	488	488	488	488	488	488	488
Cross border migration inflows	43	43	42	42	42	42	42	42	42	42	42	42	42	42	42	42	42	42	42	42
International migration outflows	325	320	315	311	306	300	295	295	295	295	295	295	295	295	295	295	295	295	295	295
Cross border migration outflows	53	52	52	52	52	52	52	52	52	52	52	52	52	52	52	51	51	51	51	51
Net international migration	234	228	220	213	206	200	193	193	193	193	193	193	193	193	193	193	193	193	193	193
Net cross border migration	-10	-10	-10	-10	-10	-10	-10	-10	-10	-10	-9	-9	-9	-9	-9	-9	-9	-9	-9	-9
Net migration	225	218	211	203	196	190	183	183	183	183	184	184	184	184	184	184	184	184	184	184
Total change	260	239	241	230	217	201	185	176	166	157	149	141	134	127	122	118	117	117	118	119
Population at end	59,980	60,219	60,460	60,690	60,906	61,108	61,293	61,468	61,635	61,792	61,941	62,081	62,215	62,342	62,464	62,582	62,699	62,817	62,935	63,054
Annual growth rate	0.44%	0.40%	0.40%	0.38%	0.36%	0.33%	0.30%	0.29%	0.27%	0.26%	0.24%	0.23%	0.22%	0.20%	0.20%	0.19%	0.19%	0.19%	0.19%	0.19%
Total fertility rate (TFR)	1.56	1.54	1.54	1.55	1.55	1.55	1.55	1.55	1.55	1.55	1.55	1.56	1.56	1.56	1.56	1.56	1.57	1.57	1.58	1.59
EOLB Males	79.4	79.5	80.0	80.1	80.2	80.3	80.4	80.5	80.6	80.7	80.8	80.9	81.0	81.1	81.2	81.3	81.4	81.6	81.7	81.8
Females	83.3	83.2	83.6	83.6	83.7	83.8	83.9	84.0	84.0	84.1	84.2	84.3	84.4	84.5	84.5	84.6	84.7	84.8	84.9	85.0

	2040 -2041	2041 -2042	2042 -2043	2043 -2044	2044 -2045	2045 -2046	2046 -2047	2047 -2048	2048 -2049	2049 -2050	2050 -2051	2051 -2052	2052 -2053	2053 -2054	2054 -2055	2055 -2056	2056 -2057	2057 -2058	2058 -2059	2059 -2060
Population at start	63,054	63,173	63,292	63,411	63,529	63,645	63,756	63,861	63,960	64,052	64,135	64,209	64,273	64,329	64,376	64,415	64,447	64,472	64,493	64,510
Births	624	628	632	634	635	635	633	630	626	621	616	611	605	599	594	589	585	582	579	576
Deaths	689	693	697	700	704	707	711	714	718	722	726	729	733	736	739	742	744	745	746	746
Natural change	-65	-65	-65	-66	-68	-73	-78	-85	-92	-101	-110	-119	-128	-137	-145	-152	-158	-163	-167	-169
International migration inflows	488	488	488	488	488	488	488	488	488	488	488	488	488	488	488	488	488	488	488	488
Cross border migration inflows	41	41	41	40	40	40	40	39	39	39	39	38	38	38	38	38	37	37	37	37
International migration outflows	295	295	295	295	295	295	295	295	295	295	295	295	295	295	295	295	295	295	295	295
Cross border migration outflows	50	50	50	49	49	49	49	49	48	48	48	48	47	47	47	47	46	46	46	46
Net international migration	193	193	193	193	193	193	193	193	193	193	193	193	193	193	193	193	193	193	193	193
Net cross border migration	-9	-9	-9	-9	-9	-9	-9	-9	-9	-9	-9	-9	-9	-9	-9	-9	-9	-9	-9	-9
Net migration	184	184	184	184	184	184	184	184	184	184	184	184	184	184	184	184	184	184	184	184
Total change	119	119	119	118	115	111	106	99	91	83	74	65	56	47	39	32	26	21	17	15
Population at end	63,173	63,292	63,411	63,529	63,645	63,756	63,861	63,960	64,052	64,135	64,209	64,273	64,329	64,376	64,415	64,447	64,472	64,493	64,510	64,525
Annual growth rate	0.19%	0.19%	0.19%	0.19%	0.18%	0.17%	0.17%	0.16%	0.14%	0.13%	0.12%	0.10%	0.09%	0.07%	0.06%	0.05%	0.04%	0.03%	0.03%	0.02%
Total fertility rate (TFR)	1.59	1.60	1.60	1.61	1.61	1.61	1.61	1.61	1.61	1.61	1.61	1.61	1.61	1.61	1.61	1.61	1.61	1.61	1.61	1.61
EOLB Males	81.9	82.0	82.1	82.2	82.3	82.5	82.6	82.7	82.8	82.9	83.0	83.1	83.3	83.4	83.5	83.6	83.7	83.8	83.9	84.1
Females	85.1	85.2	85.3	85.4	85.5	85.6	85.7	85.8	85.9	86.0	86.1	86.2	86.3	86.4	86.5	86.6	86.7	86.8	86.9	87.0

15.2b Population projections by the Office for National Statistics
England and Wales, PERSONS, thousands

Components of change (mid-year to mid-year), total fertility rate
and expectation of life at birth (EOLB) based on the mortality rates for the year

	2060 -2061	2061 -2062	2062 -2063	2063 -2064	2064 -2065	2065 -2066	2066 -2067	2067 -2068	2068 -2069	2069 -2070	2070 -2071	2071 -2072	2072 -2073	2073 -2074	2074 -2075	2075 -2076	2076 -2077	2077 -2078	2078 -2079	2079 -2080
Population at start	64,525	64,539	64,553	64,567	64,582	64,600	64,621	64,644	64,671	64,700	64,731	64,764	64,799	64,835	64,871	64,907	64,942	64,975	65,007	65,036
Births	575	573	573	573	574	575	576	578	580	581	583	585	587	589	590	591	591	591	591	590
Deaths	745	744	743	742	740	739	737	736	735	735	735	735	736	737	739	741	743	744	746	748
Natural change	-171	-171	-170	-169	-167	-164	-161	-159	-156	-153	-151	-150	-149	-149	-149	-150	-152	-153	-156	-158
International migration inflows	488	488	488	488	488	488	488	488	488	488	488	488	488	488	488	488	488	488	488	488
Cross border migration inflows	37	37	37	37	37	37	37	36	36	36	36	36	36	36	35	35	35	35	35	34
International migration outflows	295	295	295	295	295	295	295	295	295	295	295	295	295	295	295	295	295	295	295	295
Cross border migration outflows	46	45	45	45	45	45	45	45	45	44	44	44	44	44	43	43	43	43	43	42
Net international migration	193	193	193	193	193	193	193	193	193	193	193	193	193	193	193	193	193	193	193	193
Net cross border migration	-9	-9	-9	-8	-8	-8	-8	-8	-8	-8	-8	-8	-8	-8	-8	-8	-8	-8	-8	-8
Net migration	184	184	184	185	185	185	185	185	185	185	185	185	185	185	185	185	185	185	185	185
Total change	14	13	14	16	18	21	23	26	29	31	33	35	36	36	36	35	33	32	29	27
Population at end	64,539	64,553	64,567	64,582	64,600	64,621	64,644	64,671	64,700	64,731	64,764	64,799	64,835	64,871	64,907	64,942	64,975	65,007	65,036	65,063
Annual growth rate	0.02%	0.02%	0.02%	0.02%	0.03%	0.03%	0.04%	0.04%	0.04%	0.05%	0.05%	0.05%	0.06%	0.06%	0.06%	0.05%	0.05%	0.05%	0.05%	0.04%
Total fertility rate (TFR)	1.61	1.61	1.61	1.61	1.61	1.61	1.61	1.61	1.61	1.61	1.61	1.61	1.61	1.61	1.61	1.61	1.61	1.61	1.61	1.61
EOLB Males	84.2	84.3	84.4	84.5	84.6	84.7	84.8	85.0	85.1	85.2	85.3	85.4	85.5	85.6	85.7	85.8	85.9	86.0	86.2	86.3
Females	87.1	87.2	87.3	87.4	87.5	87.6	87.7	87.8	87.9	88.0	88.1	88.2	88.3	88.4	88.5	88.6	88.7	88.8	88.9	89.0

	2080 -2081	2081 -2082	2082 -2083	2083 -2084	2084 -2085	2085 -2086	2086 -2087	2087 -2088	2088 -2089	2089 -2090	2090 -2091	2091 -2092	2092 -2093	2093 -2094	2094 -2095	2095 -2096	2096 -2097	2097 -2098	2098 -2099	2099 -2100
Population at start	65,063	65,088	65,109	65,129	65,145	65,159	65,171	65,180	65,187	65,193	65,197	65,200	65,201	65,202	65,202	65,201	65,199	65,197	65,194	65,190
Births	588	587	585	583	580	578	575	573	571	568	566	565	563	562	562	561	561	561	561	561
Deaths	749	750	751	751	752	751	751	751	750	750	749	749	748	748	748	748	749	750	751	752
Natural change	-161	-163	-166	-169	-171	-174	-176	-178	-180	-181	-183	-184	-185	-186	-187	-187	-188	-189	-190	-191
International migration inflows	488	488	488	488	488	488	488	488	488	488	488	488	488	488	488	488	488	488	488	488
Cross border migration inflows	34	34	34	34	33	33	33	33	33	33	33	32	32	32	32	32	32	32	32	32
International migration outflows	295	295	295	295	295	295	295	295	295	295	295	295	295	295	295	295	295	295	295	295
Cross border migration outflows	42	42	42	41	41	41	41	41	40	40	40	40	40	40	39	39	39	39	39	39
Net international migration	193	193	193	193	193	193	193	193	193	193	193	193	193	193	193	193	193	193	193	193
Net cross border migration	-8	-8	-8	-8	-8	-8	-8	-8	-8	-8	-8	-7	-7	-7	-7	-7	-7	-7	-7	-7
Net migration	185	185	185	185	185	185	185	185	185	185	186	186	186	186	186	186	186	186	186	186
Total change	24	22	19	16	14	12	9	7	6	4	3	2	1	0	-1	-2	-2	-3	-4	-5
Population at end	65,088	65,109	65,129	65,145	65,159	65,171	65,180	65,187	65,193	65,197	65,200	65,201	65,202	65,202	65,201	65,199	65,197	65,194	65,190	65,185
Annual growth rate	0.04%	0.03%	0.03%	0.03%	0.02%	0.02%	0.01%	0.01%	0.01%	0.01%	0.00%	0.00%	0.00%	0.00%	0.00%	0.00%	0.00%	0.00%	-0.01%	-0.01%
Total fertility rate (TFR)	1.61	1.61	1.61	1.61	1.61	1.61	1.61	1.61	1.61	1.61	1.61	1.61	1.61	1.61	1.61	1.61	1.61	1.61	1.61	1.61
EOLB Males	86.4	86.5	86.6	86.7	86.8	86.9	87.0	87.1	87.2	87.3	87.4	87.5	87.6	87.7	87.8	87.9	88.0	88.1	88.2	88.3
Females	89.1	89.2	89.3	89.4	89.5	89.5	89.6	89.7	89.8	89.9	90.0	90.1	90.2	90.3	90.4	90.5	90.5	90.6	90.7	90.8

15.2b Population projections by the Office for National Statistics
England and Wales, PERSONS, thousands

2020-based
Principal projection

Components of change (mid-year to mid-year), total fertility rate and expectation of life at birth (EOLB) based on the mortality rates for the year

	2100 -2101	2101 -2102	2102 -2103	2103 -2104	2104 -2105	2105 -2106	2106 -2107	2107 -2108	2108 -2109	2109 -2110	2110 -2111	2111 -2112	2112 -2113	2113 -2114	2114 -2115	2115 -2116	2116 -2117	2117 -2118	2118 -2119	2119 -2120
Population at start	65,185	65,179	65,172	65,163	65,153	65,142	65,131	65,119	65,107	65,096	65,086	65,079	65,073	65,071	65,071	65,075	65,083	65,094	65,108	65,124
Births	562	562	563	564	564	565	565	566	566	566	566	565	565	564	563	562	561	560	559	557
Deaths	754	756	758	760	761	763	763	763	763	761	759	757	753	749	745	741	736	732	728	725
Natural change	-192	-193	-195	-196	-197	-198	-198	-198	-197	-196	-194	-191	-189	-185	-182	-179	-175	-172	-170	-167
International migration inflows	488	488	488	488	488	488	488	488	488	488	488	488	488	488	488	488	488	488	488	488
Cross border migration inflows	31	31	31	31	31	31	31	31	30	30	30	30	30	30	30	30	29	29	29	29
International migration outflows	295	295	295	295	295	295	295	295	295	295	295	295	295	295	295	295	295	295	295	295
Cross border migration outflows	39	38	38	38	38	38	38	38	37	37	37	37	37	37	36	36	36	36	36	36
Net international migration	193	193	193	193	193	193	193	193	193	193	193	193	193	193	193	193	193	193	193	193
Net cross border migration	-7	-7	-7	-7	-7	-7	-7	-7	-7	-7	-7	-7	-7	-7	-7	-7	-7	-7	-7	-7
Net migration	186	186	186	186	186	186	186	186	186	186	186	186	186	186	186	186	186	186	186	186
Total change	-6	-7	-9	-10	-11	-12	-12	-12	-11	-10	-8	-5	-3	1	4	7	11	14	17	19
Population at end	65,179	65,172	65,163	65,153	65,142	65,131	65,119	65,107	65,096	65,086	65,079	65,073	65,071	65,075	65,075	65,083	65,094	65,108	65,124	65,143
Annual growth rate	-0.01%	-0.01%	-0.01%	-0.02%	-0.02%	-0.02%	-0.02%	-0.02%	-0.01%	-0.01%	-0.01%	0.00%	0.00%	0.01%	0.01%	0.01%	0.02%	0.02%	0.03%	0.03%
Total fertility rate (TFR)	1.61	1.61	1.61	1.61	1.61	1.61	1.61	1.61	1.61	1.61	1.61	1.61	1.61	1.61	1.61	1.61	1.61	1.61	1.61	1.61
EOLB Males	88.4	88.5	88.6	88.7	88.8	88.9	89.0	89.1	89.2	89.3	89.4	89.5	89.6	89.7	89.8	89.9	90.0	90.1	90.2	90.3
Females	90.9	91.0	91.1	91.2	91.2	91.3	91.4	91.5	91.6	91.7	91.8	91.8	91.9	92.0	92.1	92.2	92.3	92.3	92.4	92.5

Note: Figures may not add exactly due to rounding.

Source: Office for National Statistics

15.2c Population projections by the Office for National Statistics
Scotland, PERSONS, thousands

2020-based
Principal projection

Components of change (mid-year to mid-year), total fertility rate
and expectation of life at birth (EOLB) based on the mortality rates for the year

	2020 -2021	2021 -2022	2022 -2023	2023 -2024	2024 -2025	2025 -2026	2026 -2027	2027 -2028	2028 -2029	2029 -2030	2030 -2031	2031 -2032	2032 -2033	2033 -2034	2034 -2035	2035 -2036	2036 -2037	2037 -2038	2038 -2039	2039 -2040
Population at start	5,466	5,469	5,471	5,474	5,477	5,479	5,481	5,482	5,483	5,483	5,482	5,479	5,476	5,472	5,468	5,462	5,456	5,449	5,442	5,435
Births	47	46	45	45	45	45	45	45	44	44	44	43	43	43	43	43	43	43	43	43
Deaths	61	62	61	61	62	62	63	64	64	65	65	66	67	67	68	68	69	69	69	70
Natural change	-15	-16	-15	-16	-16	-17	-18	-19	-20	-21	-22	-23	-24	-24	-25	-26	-26	-26	-26	-27
International migration inflows	39	38	37	36	35	34	33	33	33	33	33	33	33	33	33	33	33	33	33	33
Cross border migration inflows	46	46	46	45	45	45	45	45	45	45	45	45	45	45	45	45	45	44	44	44
International migration outflows	30	30	28	27	26	24	23	23	23	23	23	23	23	23	23	23	23	23	23	23
Cross border migration outflows	36	36	36	36	36	36	35	35	35	35	35	36	36	36	36	35	35	35	35	35
Net international migration	9	8	9	9	9	10	10	10	10	10	10	10	10	10	10	10	10	10	10	10
Net cross border migration	10	10	10	10	10	10	10	10	10	10	10	10	10	9	9	9	9	9	9	9
Net migration	18	18	19	19	19	19	20	20	20	20	20	20	20	19	19	19	19	19	19	19
Total change	3	1	3	3	2	2	2	1	0	-1	-2	-3	-4	-5	-6	-6	-7	-7	-7	-8
Population at end	5,469	5,471	5,474	5,477	5,479	5,481	5,482	5,483	5,483	5,482	5,479	5,476	5,472	5,468	5,462	5,456	5,449	5,442	5,435	5,427
Annual growth rate	0.06%	0.03%	0.06%	0.05%	0.04%	0.03%	0.03%	0.01%	0.00%	-0.02%	-0.04%	-0.06%	-0.07%	-0.09%	-0.10%	-0.11%	-0.12%	-0.13%	-0.13%	-0.14%
Total fertility rate (TFR)	1.28	1.25	1.25	1.26	1.26	1.26	1.26	1.26	1.26	1.26	1.26	1.26	1.26	1.26	1.26	1.26	1.27	1.27	1.28	1.29
EOLB Males	77.0	77.2	77.6	77.7	77.8	77.9	78.0	78.1	78.2	78.3	78.4	78.5	78.6	78.7	78.8	79.0	79.1	79.2	79.3	79.4
Females	81.3	81.2	81.5	81.5	81.6	81.6	81.7	81.8	81.9	81.9	82.0	82.1	82.2	82.2	82.3	82.4	82.5	82.6	82.7	82.8

	2040 -2041	2041 -2042	2042 -2043	2043 -2044	2044 -2045	2045 -2046	2046 -2047	2047 -2048	2048 -2049	2049 -2050	2050 -2051	2051 -2052	2052 -2053	2053 -2054	2054 -2055	2055 -2056	2056 -2057	2057 -2058	2058 -2059	2059 -2060
Population at start	5,427	5,419	5,411	5,403	5,394	5,385	5,376	5,366	5,355	5,344	5,332	5,320	5,307	5,293	5,279	5,264	5,250	5,234	5,219	5,204
Births	43	43	43	43	43	43	43	42	42	41	41	40	39	39	38	38	38	37	37	37
Deaths	70	70	71	71	71	71	71	72	72	72	72	72	72	72	72	72	71	71	71	70
Natural change	-27	-27	-27	-28	-28	-28	-29	-30	-30	-31	-31	-32	-32	-33	-33	-34	-34	-34	-34	-34
International migration inflows	33	33	33	33	33	33	33	33	33	33	33	33	33	33	33	33	33	33	33	33
Cross border migration inflows	44	43	43	43	43	43	42	42	42	42	42	41	41	41	41	40	40	40	40	40
International migration outflows	23	23	23	23	23	23	23	23	23	23	23	23	23	23	23	23	23	23	23	23
Cross border migration outflows	35	34	34	34	34	34	33	33	33	33	33	32	32	32	32	32	32	31	31	31
Net international migration	10	10	10	10	10	10	10	10	10	10	10	10	10	10	10	10	10	10	10	10
Net cross border migration	9	9	9	9	9	9	9	9	9	9	9	9	9	9	9	9	9	9	9	9
Net migration	19	19	19	19	19	19	19	19	19	19	19	19	19	19	19	19	19	19	19	19
Total change	-8	-8	-8	-9	-9	-9	-10	-11	-11	-12	-12	-13	-14	-14	-15	-15	-15	-15	-15	-15
Population at end	5,419	5,411	5,403	5,394	5,385	5,376	5,366	5,355	5,344	5,332	5,320	5,307	5,293	5,279	5,264	5,250	5,234	5,219	5,204	5,188
Annual growth rate	-0.15%	-0.15%	-0.16%	-0.16%	-0.17%	-0.18%	-0.19%	-0.20%	-0.21%	-0.22%	-0.23%	-0.24%	-0.26%	-0.27%	-0.28%	-0.28%	-0.29%	-0.29%	-0.29%	-0.29%
Total fertility rate (TFR)	1.29	1.29	1.30	1.30	1.30	1.30	1.30	1.30	1.30	1.30	1.30	1.30	1.30	1.30	1.30	1.30	1.30	1.30	1.30	1.30
EOLB Males	79.6	79.7	79.8	79.9	80.1	80.2	80.3	80.4	80.6	80.7	80.8	81.0	81.1	81.2	81.3	81.5	81.6	81.7	81.8	82.0
Females	82.9	83.0	83.1	83.2	83.4	83.5	83.6	83.7	83.8	83.9	84.0	84.1	84.3	84.4	84.5	84.6	84.7	84.8	84.9	85.0

15.2c Population projections by the Office for National Statistics
Scotland, PERSONS, thousands

Components of change (mid-year to mid-year), total fertility rate
and expectation of life at birth (EOLB) based on the mortality rates for the year

	2060 -2061	2061 -2062	2062 -2063	2063 -2064	2064 -2065	2065 -2066	2066 -2067	2067 -2068	2068 -2069	2069 -2070	2070 -2071	2071 -2072	2072 -2073	2073 -2074	2074 -2075	2075 -2076	2076 -2077	2077 -2078	2078 -2079	2079 -2080
Population at start	5,188	5,173	5,158	5,143	5,128	5,113	5,099	5,085	5,070	5,056	5,042	5,027	5,013	4,998	4,983	4,967	4,952	4,936	4,919	4,902
Births	36	36	36	36	36	35	35	35	35	35	35	35	35	35	35	35	35	34	34	34
Deaths	70	70	69	69	69	68	68	68	68	68	68	68	68	68	68	68	69	69	69	69
Natural change	-34	-34	-33	-33	-33	-33	-33	-33	-33	-32	-33	-33	-33	-33	-33	-34	-34	-34	-35	-35
International migration inflows	33	33	33	33	33	33	33	33	33	33	33	33	33	33	33	33	33	33	33	33
Cross border migration inflows	39	39	39	39	39	39	39	39	38	38	38	38	38	38	37	37	37	37	37	36
International migration outflows	23	23	23	23	23	23	23	23	23	23	23	23	23	23	23	23	23	23	23	23
Cross border migration outflows	31	31	31	31	31	30	30	30	30	30	30	30	30	30	29	29	29	29	29	29
Net international migration	10	10	10	10	10	10	10	10	10	10	10	10	10	10	10	10	10	10	10	10
Net cross border migration	9	9	8	8	8	8	8	8	8	8	8	8	8	8	8	8	8	8	8	8
Net migration	19	19	18	18	18	18	18	18	18	18	18	18	18	18	18	18	18	18	18	18
Total change	-15	-15	-15	-15	-15	-15	-14	-14	-14	-14	-14	-15	-15	-15	-15	-16	-16	-16	-17	-17
Population at end	5,173	5,158	5,143	5,128	5,113	5,099	5,085	5,070	5,056	5,042	5,027	5,013	4,998	4,983	4,967	4,952	4,936	4,919	4,902	4,885
Annual growth rate	-0.29%	-0.29%	-0.29%	-0.29%	-0.29%	-0.28%	-0.28%	-0.28%	-0.28%	-0.28%	-0.29%	-0.29%	-0.30%	-0.30%	-0.31%	-0.32%	-0.32%	-0.33%	-0.34%	-0.35%
Total fertility rate (TFR)	1.30	1.30	1.30	1.30	1.30	1.30	1.30	1.30	1.30	1.30	1.30	1.30	1.30	1.30	1.30	1.30	1.30	1.30	1.30	1.30
EOLB Males	82.1	82.2	82.3	82.5	82.6	82.7	82.8	83.0	83.1	83.2	83.3	83.4	83.6	83.7	83.8	83.9	84.0	84.2	84.3	84.4
Females	85.1	85.2	85.4	85.5	85.6	85.7	85.8	85.9	86.0	86.1	86.2	86.3	86.4	86.5	86.6	86.7	86.9	87.0	87.1	87.2

	2080 -2081	2081 -2082	2082 -2083	2083 -2084	2084 -2085	2085 -2086	2086 -2087	2087 -2088	2088 -2089	2089 -2090	2090 -2091	2091 -2092	2092 -2093	2093 -2094	2094 -2095	2095 -2096	2096 -2097	2097 -2098	2098 -2099	2099 -2100
Population at start	4,885	4,868	4,850	4,832	4,813	4,795	4,776	4,758	4,739	4,720	4,701	4,682	4,664	4,645	4,627	4,609	4,591	4,573	4,555	4,537
Births	34	34	33	33	33	33	32	32	32	32	31	31	31	31	31	31	30	30	30	30
Deaths	69	69	69	69	69	69	69	68	68	68	67	67	67	66	66	66	65	65	65	65
Natural change	-35	-35	-36	-36	-36	-36	-36	-36	-36	-36	-36	-36	-36	-36	-35	-35	-35	-35	-35	-35
International migration inflows	33	33	33	33	33	33	33	33	33	33	33	33	33	33	33	33	33	33	33	33
Cross border migration inflows	36	36	35	35	35	35	35	35	35	34	34	34	34	34	33	33	33	33	33	33
International migration outflows	23	23	23	23	23	23	23	23	23	23	23	23	23	23	23	23	23	23	23	23
Cross border migration outflows	28	28	28	28	28	28	28	27	27	27	27	27	27	27	26	26	26	26	26	26
Net international migration	10	10	10	10	10	10	10	10	10	10	10	10	10	10	10	10	10	10	10	10
Net cross border migration	8	8	8	8	8	7	7	7	7	7	7	7	7	7	7	7	7	7	7	7
Net migration	18	18	18	18	18	17	17	17	17	17	17	17	17	17	17	17	17	17	17	17
Total change	-17	-18	-18	-18	-18	-19	-19	-19	-19	-19	-19	-19	-18	-18	-18	-18	-18	-18	-18	-18
Population at end	4,868	4,850	4,832	4,813	4,795	4,776	4,758	4,739	4,720	4,701	4,682	4,664	4,645	4,627	4,609	4,591	4,573	4,555	4,537	4,520
Annual growth rate	-0.36%	-0.37%	-0.37%	-0.38%	-0.38%	-0.39%	-0.39%	-0.40%	-0.40%	-0.40%	-0.40%	-0.40%	-0.40%	-0.39%	-0.39%	-0.39%	-0.39%	-0.39%	-0.39%	-0.39%
Total fertility rate (TFR)	1.30	1.30	1.30	1.30	1.30	1.30	1.30	1.30	1.30	1.30	1.30	1.30	1.30	1.30	1.30	1.30	1.30	1.30	1.30	1.30
EOLB Males	84.5	84.6	84.8	84.9	85.0	85.1	85.2	85.3	85.4	85.6	85.7	85.8	85.9	86.0	86.1	86.2	86.4	86.5	86.6	86.7
Females	87.3	87.4	87.5	87.6	87.7	87.8	87.9	88.0	88.1	88.2	88.3	88.4	88.5	88.6	88.7	88.8	88.9	89.0	89.1	89.2

15.2c Population projections by the Office for National Statistics
Scotland, PERSONS, thousands

Components of change (mid-year to mid-year), total fertility rate
and expectation of life at birth (EOLB) based on the mortality rates for the year

	2100 -2101	2101 -2102	2102 -2103	2103 -2104	2104 -2105	2105 -2106	2106 -2107	2107 -2108	2108 -2109	2109 -2110	2110 -2111	2111 -2112	2112 -2113	2113 -2114	2114 -2115	2115 -2116	2116 -2117	2117 -2118	2118 -2119	2119 -2120
Population at start	4,520	4,502	4,485	4,467	4,450	4,433	4,416	4,399	4,382	4,366	4,349	4,333	4,318	4,303	4,288	4,274	4,260	4,247	4,234	4,221
Births	30	30	30	30	30	30	30	29	29	29	29	29	29	29	29	29	28	28	28	28
Deaths	65	64	64	64	64	64	63	63	63	62	62	61	61	60	59	59	58	58	57	57
Natural change	-35	-34	-34	-34	-34	-34	-34	-34	-33	-33	-33	-32	-32	-31	-31	-30	-30	-30	-29	-29
International migration inflows	33	33	33	33	33	33	33	33	33	33	33	33	33	33	33	33	33	33	33	33
Cross border migration inflows	33	33	33	32	32	32	32	32	32	32	32	31	31	31	31	31	31	31	31	30
International migration outflows	23	23	23	23	23	23	23	23	23	23	23	23	23	23	23	23	23	23	23	23
Cross border migration outflows	26	26	26	26	26	25	25	25	25	25	25	25	25	25	24	24	24	24	24	24
Net international migration	10	10	10	10	10	10	10	10	10	10	10	10	10	10	10	10	10	10	10	10
Net cross border migration	7	7	7	7	7	7	7	7	7	7	7	7	7	7	7	7	7	7	6	6
Net migration	17	17	17	17	17	17	17	17	17	17	17	17	17	17	17	17	17	17	16	16
Total change	-18	-17	-17	-17	-17	-17	-17	-16	-16	-16	-16	-15	-15	-14	-14	-13	-13	-13	-13	-12
Population at end	4,502	4,485	4,467	4,450	4,433	4,416	4,399	4,382	4,366	4,349	4,333	4,318	4,303	4,288	4,274	4,260	4,247	4,234	4,221	4,208
Annual growth rate	-0.39%	-0.39%	-0.39%	-0.39%	-0.39%	-0.39%	-0.38%	-0.38%	-0.38%	-0.37%	-0.37%	-0.36%	-0.35%	-0.34%	-0.33%	-0.32%	-0.32%	-0.31%	-0.30%	-0.29%
Total fertility rate (TFR)	1.30	1.30	1.30	1.30	1.30	1.30	1.30	1.30	1.30	1.30	1.30	1.30	1.30	1.30	1.30	1.30	1.30	1.30	1.30	1.30
EOLB Males	86.8	86.9	87.0	87.1	87.2	87.4	87.5	87.6	87.7	87.8	87.9	88.0	88.1	88.2	88.3	88.4	88.5	88.6	88.7	88.8
Females	89.3	89.4	89.5	89.6	89.7	89.7	89.8	89.9	90.0	90.1	90.2	90.3	90.4	90.5	90.6	90.7	90.8	90.9	91.0	91.0

Source: Office for National Statistics

Note: Figures may not add exactly due to rounding.

15.2d Population projections by the Office for National Statistics
Northern Ireland, PERSONS, thousands

2020-based
Principal projection

Components of change (mid-year to mid-year), total fertility rate and expectation of life at birth (EOLB) based on the mortality rates for the year

	2020-2021	2021-2022	2022-2023	2023-2024	2024-2025	2025-2026	2026-2027	2027-2028	2028-2029	2029-2030	2030-2031	2031-2032	2032-2033	2033-2034	2034-2035	2035-2036	2036-2037	2037-2038	2038-2039	2039-2040
Population at start	1,896	1,902	1,906	1,910	1,915	1,920	1,924	1,927	1,930	1,932	1,934	1,935	1,936	1,937	1,937	1,937	1,937	1,937	1,937	1,938
Births	21	20	20	20	20	19	19	19	19	19	19	19	18	18	18	19	19	19	19	19
Deaths	17	18	17	17	17	18	18	18	18	19	19	19	19	20	20	20	20	21	21	21
Natural change	4	3	3	3	2	2	1	1	1	0	0	-1	-1	-1	-2	-2	-2	-2	-2	-2
International migration inflows	13	13	12	12	12	12	12	12	12	12	12	12	12	12	12	12	12	12	12	12
Cross border migration inflows	11	10	10	10	10	10	10	10	10	10	10	10	10	10	10	10	10	10	10	10
International migration outflows	11	11	10	10	10	9	9	9	9	9	9	9	9	9	9	9	9	9	9	9
Cross border migration outflows	10	10	10	10	10	10	10	10	11	11	11	11	11	11	11	11	11	11	10	10
Net international migration	1	1	2	2	2	2	2	2	2	2	2	2	2	2	2	2	2	2	2	2
Net cross border migration	0	0	0	0	0	0	0	0	0	0	0	0	0	0	0	0	0	0	0	0
Net migration	2	2	2	2	2	2	2	2	2	2	2	2	2	2	2	2	2	2	2	2
Total change	6	4	5	5	4	4	3	3	2	2	1	1	1	0	0	0	0	0	0	0
Population at end	1,902	1,906	1,910	1,915	1,920	1,924	1,927	1,930	1,932	1,934	1,935	1,936	1,937	1,937	1,937	1,937	1,937	1,937	1,938	1,938
Annual growth rate	0.32%	0.22%	0.24%	0.25%	0.23%	0.20%	0.17%	0.14%	0.12%	0.09%	0.07%	0.05%	0.03%	0.02%	0.01%	0.00%	####	0.00%	0.00%	0.01%
Total fertility rate (TFR)	1.74	1.66	1.66	1.67	1.68	1.68	1.68	1.68	1.68	1.68	1.68	1.68	1.68	1.68	1.68	1.69	1.70	1.71	1.71	1.71
EOLB Males	78.9	78.6	79.2	79.3	79.4	79.5	79.6	79.7	79.8	79.9	80.1	80.2	80.3	80.4	80.5	80.6	80.7	80.8	80.9	81.0
Females	82.7	82.4	82.8	82.9	83.0	83.1	83.2	83.3	83.3	83.4	83.5	83.6	83.7	83.8	83.9	84.0	84.0	84.1	84.2	84.3

	2040-2041	2041-2042	2042-2043	2043-2044	2044-2045	2045-2046	2046-2047	2047-2048	2048-2049	2049-2050	2050-2051	2051-2052	2052-2053	2053-2054	2054-2055	2055-2056	2056-2057	2057-2058	2058-2059	2059-2060
Population at start	1,938	1,938	1,938	1,938	1,939	1,939	1,938	1,938	1,937	1,936	1,935	1,933	1,931	1,928	1,925	1,921	1,918	1,914	1,909	1,905
Births	19	20	20	20	20	20	20	19	19	19	19	19	18	18	18	18	17	17	17	17
Deaths	21	21	22	22	22	22	22	23	23	23	23	23	23	23	24	24	24	24	24	24
Natural change	-2	-2	-2	-2	-2	-2	-3	-3	-3	-4	-4	-5	-5	-5	-6	-6	-6	-7	-7	-7
International migration inflows	12	12	12	12	12	12	12	12	12	12	12	12	12	12	12	12	12	12	12	12
Cross border migration inflows	10	10	10	10	10	10	10	10	10	10	10	10	10	9	9	9	9	9	9	9
International migration outflows	9	9	9	9	9	9	9	9	9	9	9	9	9	9	9	9	9	9	9	9
Cross border migration outflows	10	10	10	10	10	10	10	10	10	9	9	9	9	9	9	9	9	9	9	9
Net international migration	2	2	2	2	2	2	2	2	2	2	2	2	2	2	2	2	2	2	2	2
Net cross border migration	0	0	0	0	0	0	0	0	0	0	0	0	0	0	0	0	0	0	0	0
Net migration	2	2	2	2	2	2	2	2	2	2	2	2	2	2	2	2	2	2	2	2
Total change	0	0	0	0	0	0	0	-1	-1	-1	-2	-2	-3	-3	-3	-4	-4	-4	-5	-5
Population at end	1,938	1,938	1,939	1,939	1,939	1,938	1,938	1,937	1,936	1,935	1,933	1,931	1,928	1,925	1,921	1,918	1,914	1,909	1,905	1,900
Annual growth rate	0.01%	0.01%	0.01%	0.01%	####	-0.01%	-0.02%	-0.04%	-0.06%	-0.08%	-0.10%	-0.12%	-0.14%	-0.16%	-0.18%	-0.20%	-0.21%	-0.23%	-0.24%	-0.25%
Total fertility rate (TFR)	1.72	1.73	1.73	1.73	1.74	1.74	1.74	1.74	1.74	1.74	1.74	1.74	1.74	1.74	1.74	1.74	1.74	1.74	1.74	1.74
EOLB Males	81.1	81.2	81.4	81.5	81.6	81.7	81.8	82.0	82.1	82.2	82.3	82.4	82.6	82.7	82.8	82.9	83.0	83.1	83.3	83.4
Females	84.4	84.5	84.6	84.7	84.9	85.0	85.1	85.2	85.3	85.4	85.5	85.6	85.7	85.8	85.9	86.0	86.1	86.2	86.3	86.4

15.2d Population projections by the Office for National Statistics
Northern Ireland, PERSONS, thousands

2020-based
Principal projection

Components of change (mid-year to mid-year), total fertility rate
and expectation of life at birth (EOLB) based on the mortality rates for the year

	2060-2061	2061-2062	2062-2063	2063-2064	2064-2065	2065-2066	2066-2067	2067-2068	2068-2069	2069-2070	2070-2071	2071-2072	2072-2073	2073-2074	2074-2075	2075-2076	2076-2077	2077-2078	2078-2079	2079-2080
Population at start	1,900	1,895	1,890	1,885	1,880	1,875	1,870	1,865	1,860	1,855	1,850	1,845	1,841	1,836	1,832	1,827	1,823	1,818	1,814	1,810
Births	17	16	16	16	16	16	16	16	16	16	16	16	16	16	16	17	17	17	16	16
Deaths	24	24	23	23	23	23	23	23	23	23	23	23	23	23	23	23	23	23	23	23
Natural change	-7	-7	-7	-7	-7	-7	-7	-7	-7	-7	-7	-7	-7	-7	-7	-7	-7	-7	-7	-7
International migration inflows	12	12	12	12	12	12	12	12	12	12	12	12	12	12	12	12	12	12	12	12
Cross border migration inflows	9	9	9	9	9	9	9	9	9	9	9	9	9	9	9	9	9	9	9	9
International migration outflows	9	9	9	9	9	9	9	9	9	9	9	9	9	9	9	9	9	9	9	9
Cross border migration outflows	9	9	9	9	9	9	9	9	9	9	9	9	9	9	9	9	9	9	8	8
Net international migration	2	2	2	2	2	2	2	2	2	2	2	2	2	2	2	2	2	2	2	2
Net cross border migration	0	0	0	0	0	0	0	0	0	0	0	0	0	0	0	0	0	0	0	0
Net migration	2	2	2	2	2	2	2	2	2	2	2	2	2	2	2	2	2	2	2	2
Total change	-5	-5	-5	-5	-5	-5	-5	-5	-5	-5	-5	-5	-5	-5	-4	-4	-4	-4	-4	-4
Population at end	1,895	1,890	1,885	1,880	1,875	1,870	1,865	1,860	1,855	1,850	1,845	1,841	1,836	1,832	1,827	1,823	1,818	1,814	1,810	1,805
Annual growth rate	-0.26%	-0.26%	-0.27%	-0.27%	-0.27%	-0.27%	-0.27%	-0.26%	-0.26%	-0.26%	-0.26%	-0.25%	-0.25%	-0.25%	-0.24%	-0.24%	-0.24%	-0.24%	-0.24%	-0.25%
Total fertility rate (TFR)	1.74	1.74	1.74	1.74	1.74	1.74	1.74	1.74	1.74	1.74	1.74	1.74	1.74	1.74	1.74	1.74	1.74	1.74	1.74	1.74
EOLB Males	83.5	83.6	83.7	83.8	83.9	84.1	84.2	84.3	84.4	84.5	84.6	84.7	84.8	85.0	85.1	85.2	85.3	85.4	85.5	85.6
Females	86.5	86.6	86.7	86.8	86.9	87.0	87.1	87.2	87.3	87.4	87.5	87.6	87.7	87.8	87.9	88.0	88.1	88.2	88.3	88.4

	2080-2081	2081-2082	2082-2083	2083-2084	2084-2085	2085-2086	2086-2087	2087-2088	2088-2089	2089-2090	2090-2091	2091-2092	2092-2093	2093-2094	2094-2095	2095-2096	2096-2097	2097-2098	2098-2099	2099-2100
Population at start	1,805	1,801	1,796	1,791	1,787	1,782	1,777	1,772	1,767	1,762	1,757	1,752	1,747	1,742	1,737	1,732	1,726	1,721	1,716	1,711
Births	16	16	16	16	16	16	16	15	15	15	15	15	15	15	15	15	14	14	14	14
Deaths	23	23	23	23	23	23	23	23	22	22	22	22	22	22	22	22	22	22	22	22
Natural change	-7	-7	-7	-7	-7	-7	-7	-7	-7	-7	-7	-7	-7	-7	-7	-7	-7	-7	-7	-8
International migration inflows	12	12	12	12	12	12	12	12	12	12	12	12	12	12	12	12	12	12	12	12
Cross border migration inflows	9	9	9	9	9	9	9	9	8	8	8	8	8	8	8	8	8	8	8	8
International migration outflows	9	9	9	9	9	9	9	9	9	9	9	9	9	9	9	9	9	9	9	9
Cross border migration outflows	8	8	8	8	8	8	8	8	8	8	8	8	8	8	8	8	8	8	8	8
Net international migration	2	2	2	2	2	2	2	2	2	2	2	2	2	2	2	2	2	2	2	2
Net cross border migration	0	0	0	0	0	0	0	0	0	0	0	0	0	0	0	0	0	0	0	0
Net migration	2	2	2	2	2	2	2	2	2	2	2	2	2	2	2	2	2	2	2	2
Total change	-4	-5	-5	-5	-5	-5	-5	-5	-5	-5	-5	-5	-5	-5	-5	-5	-5	-5	-5	-5
Population at end	1,801	1,796	1,791	1,787	1,782	1,777	1,772	1,767	1,762	1,757	1,752	1,747	1,742	1,737	1,732	1,726	1,721	1,716	1,711	1,705
Annual growth rate	-0.25%	-0.25%	-0.26%	-0.26%	-0.27%	-0.27%	-0.27%	-0.28%	-0.28%	-0.29%	-0.29%	-0.29%	-0.29%	-0.30%	-0.30%	-0.30%	-0.31%	-0.31%	-0.31%	-0.31%
Total fertility rate (TFR)	1.74	1.74	1.74	1.74	1.74	1.74	1.74	1.74	1.74	1.74	1.74	1.74	1.74	1.74	1.74	1.74	1.74	1.74	1.74	1.74
EOLB Males	85.7	85.8	86.0	86.1	86.2	86.3	86.4	86.5	86.6	86.7	86.8	86.9	87.0	87.1	87.2	87.3	87.4	87.6	87.7	87.8
Females	88.5	88.6	88.7	88.8	88.9	89.0	89.1	89.2	89.3	89.4	89.5	89.6	89.7	89.8	89.9	90.0	90.0	90.1	90.2	90.3

15.2d Population projections by the Office for National Statistics
Northern Ireland, PERSONS, thousands

**Components of change (mid-year to mid-year), total fertility rate
and expectation of life at birth (EOLB) based on the mortality rates for the year**

	2100 -2101	2101 -2102	2102 -2103	2103 -2104	2104 -2105	2105 -2106	2106 -2107	2107 -2108	2108 -2109	2109 -2110	2110 -2111	2111 -2112	2112 -2113	2113 -2114	2114 -2115	2115 -2116	2116 -2117	2117 -2118	2118 -2119	2119 -2120
Population at start	1,705	1,700	1,694	1,689	1,683	1,678	1,672	1,667	1,661	1,656	1,651	1,646	1,641	1,636	1,631	1,626	1,622	1,618	1,613	1,609
Births	14	14	14	14	14	14	14	14	14	14	14	14	14	14	14	14	14	14	14	14
Deaths	22	22	22	22	22	22	22	22	22	22	22	21	21	21	21	21	20	20	20	20
Natural change	-8	-8	-8	-8	-8	-8	-8	-8	-8	-7	-7	-7	-7	-7	-7	-7	-7	-6	-6	-6
International migration inflows	12	12	12	12	12	12	12	12	12	12	12	12	12	12	12	12	12	12	12	12
Cross border migration inflows	8	8	8	8	8	8	8	8	8	8	8	8	7	7	7	7	7	7	7	7
International migration outflows	9	9	9	9	9	9	9	9	9	9	9	9	9	9	9	9	9	9	9	9
Cross border migration outflows	8	8	8	8	8	8	8	7	7	7	7	7	7	7	7	7	7	7	7	7
Net international migration	2	2	2	2	2	2	2	2	2	2	2	2	2	2	2	2	2	2	2	2
Net cross border migration	0	0	0	0	0	0	0	0	0	0	0	0	0	0	0	0	0	0	0	0
Net migration	2	2	2	2	2	2	2	2	2	2	2	2	2	2	2	2	2	2	2	2
Total change	-5	-5	-5	-5	-5	-5	-5	-5	-5	-5	-5	-5	-5	-5	-5	-4	-4	-4	-4	-4
Population at end	1,700	1,694	1,689	1,683	1,678	1,672	1,667	1,661	1,656	1,651	1,646	1,641	1,636	1,631	1,626	1,622	1,618	1,613	1,609	1,605
Annual growth rate	-0.32%	-0.32%	-0.32%	-0.32%	-0.33%	-0.33%	-0.33%	-0.33%	-0.32%	-0.32%	-0.31%	-0.31%	-0.30%	-0.29%	-0.28%	-0.27%	-0.27%	-0.26%	-0.25%	-0.25%
Total fertility rate (TFR)	1.74	1.74	1.74	1.74	1.74	1.74	1.74	1.74	1.74	1.74	1.74	1.74	1.74	1.74	1.74	1.74	1.74	1.74	1.74	1.74
EOLB Males	87.9	88.0	88.1	88.2	88.3	88.4	88.5	88.6	88.7	88.8	88.9	89.0	89.1	89.2	89.3	89.4	89.5	89.6	89.7	89.8
Females	90.4	90.5	90.6	90.7	90.8	90.9	90.9	91.0	91.1	91.2	91.3	91.4	91.5	91.6	91.7	91.8	91.8	91.9	92.0	92.1

Source: Office for National Statistics

Note: Figures may not add exactly due to rounding.

15.3a Mid-2019 Population estimates for United Kingdom by sex and single year of age

Ages	Persons	Males	Females	Ages	Persons	Males	Females
All ages	66,796,807	32,978,229	33,818,578	45	822,075	406,788	415,287
0	722,881	371,576	351,305	46	858,311	424,886	433,425
1	752,554	386,072	366,482	47	895,065	442,944	452,121
2	777,309	398,693	378,616	48	924,065	453,979	470,086
3	802,334	411,883	390,451	49	902,606	443,759	458,847
4	802,185	411,576	390,609	50	924,754	454,492	470,262
5	809,152	414,890	394,262	51	924,666	454,552	470,114
6	827,149	423,939	403,210	52	936,289	462,402	473,887
7	852,059	436,175	415,884	53	934,335	458,869	475,466
8	838,680	429,626	409,054	54	940,971	462,400	478,571
9	822,812	420,942	401,870	55	930,783	457,484	473,299
10	813,774	416,804	396,970	56	909,684	447,432	462,252
11	820,269	420,435	399,834	57	888,131	437,699	450,432
12	793,405	407,426	385,979	58	856,779	421,755	435,024
13	777,849	398,281	379,568	59	820,531	403,136	417,395
14	748,569	383,486	365,083	60	801,220	393,200	408,020
15	736,855	377,844	359,011	61	782,729	384,208	398,521
16	717,056	368,405	348,651	62	752,215	368,698	383,517
17	708,482	364,437	344,045	63	723,647	354,603	369,044
18	733,067	375,939	357,128	64	695,374	339,429	355,945
19	761,508	392,588	368,920	65	694,374	337,661	356,713
20	797,247	409,863	387,384	66	682,311	331,841	350,470
21	811,223	417,910	393,313	67	659,691	319,092	340,599
22	842,201	432,740	409,461	68	661,251	319,137	342,114
23	850,411	438,189	412,222	69	670,572	322,371	348,201
24	851,998	436,369	415,629	70	683,532	329,074	354,458
25	879,406	450,326	429,080	71	714,929	342,943	371,986
26	882,616	448,552	434,064	72	768,023	368,417	399,606
27	911,206	459,046	452,160	73	588,245	280,126	308,119
28	928,979	471,462	457,517	74	564,138	267,180	296,958
29	912,042	462,714	449,328	75	556,173	262,739	293,434
30	903,442	453,849	449,593	76	511,519	238,533	272,986
31	912,000	454,817	457,183	77	451,509	208,283	243,226
32	889,687	439,802	449,885	78	400,077	182,487	217,590
33	896,728	447,789	448,939	79	406,018	184,443	221,575
34	895,275	446,085	449,190	80	393,605	177,139	216,466
35	872,653	432,076	440,577	81	372,612	166,187	206,425
36	879,070	434,413	444,657	82	344,104	150,863	193,241
37	877,449	432,853	444,596	83	316,201	136,325	179,876
38	883,170	437,060	446,110	84	288,806	122,828	165,978
39	883,325	437,482	445,843	85	255,542	106,041	149,501
40	848,120	421,790	426,330	86	230,667	93,770	136,897
41	790,679	393,363	397,316	87	210,077	83,112	126,965
42	778,814	387,840	390,974	88	186,163	71,405	114,758
43	793,909	393,401	400,508	89	159,641	58,821	100,820
44	808,017	400,472	407,545	90	605,181	193,416	411,765

Source: Office for National Statistics

1. Estimates are presented both rounded to the nearest hundred and unrounded. Unrounded estimates are published to enable and encourage further calculations and analysis. However, the estimates should not be taken to be accurate to the level of detail provided. More information on the accuracy of the estimates is available in the Quality and Methodology document (QMI):

https://www.ons.gov.uk/peoplepopulationandcommunity/populationandmigration/
populationestimates/methodologies/annualmidyearpopulationestimatesqmi

2. The estimates are produced using a variety of data sources and statistical models, including some statistical disclosure control methods, and small estimates should not be taken to refer to particular individuals.

3. The estimated resident population of an area includes all those people who usually live there, regardless of nationality. Arriving international migrants are included in the usually resident population if they remain in the UK for at least a year. Emigrants are excluded if they remain outside the UK for at least a year. This is consistent with the United Nations definition of a long-term migrant. Armed forces stationed outside of the UK are excluded. Students are taken to be usually resident at their term time address.

4. Where data appears for age 90 please note this is for ages 90 and above.

15.3b Population projections by the Office for National Statistics
United Kingdom, PERSONS, thousands

Projected populations at mid-years by age last birthday

Ages	2020	2021	2022	2023	2024	2025	2026	2027	2028	2029	2030	2031	2032	2033	2034	2035	2036	2037	2038	2039	2040
Thousands																					
0-14	11,975	11,924	11,844	11,729	11,618	11,494	11,348	11,182	11,034	10,900	10,766	10,626	10,506	10,404	10,326	10,274	10,257	10,254	10,263	10,275	10,294
15-29	12,293	12,263	12,261	12,311	12,353	12,425	12,504	12,591	12,675	12,749	12,841	12,953	13,069	13,155	13,197	13,200	13,141	13,055	12,934	12,820	12,695
30-44	13,018	13,165	13,312	13,423	13,477	13,475	13,479	13,495	13,492	13,488	13,443	13,380	13,299	13,206	13,141	13,081	13,033	13,018	13,056	13,090	13,157
45-59	13,431	13,348	13,222	13,092	13,001	12,936	12,880	12,817	12,768	12,715	12,706	12,681	12,679	12,737	12,822	12,931	13,073	13,215	13,320	13,373	13,371
60-74	10,575	10,731	10,755	10,865	11,033	11,228	11,429	11,637	11,817	11,989	12,142	12,293	12,394	12,437	12,432	12,401	12,329	12,220	12,108	12,036	11,992
75 & over	5,789	5,920	6,202	6,424	6,599	6,747	6,871	6,980	7,095	7,208	7,309	7,422	7,547	7,686	7,828	7,976	8,142	8,325	8,515	8,713	8,911
All ages	67,081	67,351	67,596	67,844	68,082	68,305	68,512	68,702	68,881	69,049	69,207	69,355	69,494	69,624	69,747	69,863	69,975	70,086	70,196	70,307	70,418
Percentages																					
0-14	17.9	17.7	17.5	17.3	17.1	16.8	16.6	16.3	16.0	15.8	15.6	15.3	15.1	14.9	14.8	14.7	14.7	14.6	14.6	14.6	14.6
15-29	18.3	18.2	18.1	18.1	18.1	18.2	18.3	18.3	18.4	18.5	18.6	18.7	18.8	18.9	18.9	18.9	18.8	18.6	18.4	18.2	18.0
30-44	19.4	19.5	19.7	19.8	19.8	19.7	19.7	19.6	19.6	19.5	19.4	19.3	19.1	19.0	18.8	18.7	18.6	18.6	18.6	18.6	18.7
45-59	20.0	19.8	19.6	19.3	19.1	18.9	18.8	18.7	18.5	18.4	18.4	18.3	18.2	18.3	18.4	18.5	18.7	18.9	19.0	19.0	19.0
60-74	15.8	15.9	15.9	16.0	16.2	16.4	16.7	16.9	17.2	17.4	17.5	17.7	17.8	17.9	17.8	17.8	17.6	17.4	17.2	17.1	17.0
75 & over	8.6	8.8	9.2	9.5	9.7	9.9	10.0	10.2	10.3	10.4	10.6	10.7	10.9	11.0	11.2	11.4	11.6	11.9	12.1	12.4	12.7
All ages	100.0	100.0	100.0	100.0	100.0	100.0	100.0	100.0	100.0	100.0	100.0	100.0	100.0	100.0	100.0	100.0	100.0	100.0	100.0	100.0	100.0
Mean age	41.0	41.2	41.4	41.5	41.7	41.9	42.1	42.3	42.4	42.6	42.8	42.9	43.1	43.3	43.4	43.6	43.7	43.8	43.9	44.0	44.1
Median age	40.4	40.6	40.8	40.9	41.1	41.3	41.5	41.7	41.9	42.1	42.3	42.5	42.7	42.9	43.1	43.3	43.4	43.6	43.7	43.8	43.9

Ages	2041	2042	2043	2044	2045	2046	2047	2048	2049	2050	2051	2052	2053	2054	2055	2056	2057	2058	2059	2060
Thousands																				
0-14	10,321	10,355	10,396	10,442	10,490	10,537	10,583	10,626	10,662	10,692	10,711	10,719	10,714	10,696	10,666	10,624	10,573	10,515	10,450	10,382
15-29	12,548	12,382	12,236	12,102	11,969	11,829	11,709	11,608	11,530	11,479	11,462	11,460	11,468	11,481	11,500	11,527	11,562	11,603	11,649	11,697
30-44	13,234	13,322	13,407	13,482	13,575	13,687	13,803	13,889	13,932	13,935	13,877	13,792	13,673	13,561	13,437	13,291	13,128	12,984	12,852	12,720
45-59	13,377	13,395	13,394	13,393	13,351	13,292	13,216	13,128	13,067	13,013	12,971	12,960	13,003	13,041	13,110	13,191	13,282	13,368	13,446	13,540
60-74	11,955	11,913	11,885	11,852	11,860	11,854	11,869	11,937	12,029	12,140	12,281	12,420	12,524	12,582	12,590	12,606	12,632	12,640	12,646	12,616
75 & over	9,095	9,273	9,435	9,591	9,724	9,869	9,985	10,065	10,112	10,143	10,159	10,160	10,168	10,220	10,298	10,374	10,443	10,512	10,576	10,659
All ages	70,530	70,642	70,752	70,862	70,968	71,070	71,165	71,253	71,332	71,402	71,461	71,511	71,550	71,580	71,601	71,614	71,620	71,621	71,619	71,614
Percentages																				
0-14	14.6	14.7	14.7	14.7	14.8	14.8	14.9	14.9	14.9	15.0	15.0	15.0	15.0	14.9	14.9	14.8	14.8	14.7	14.6	14.5
15-29	17.8	17.5	17.3	17.1	16.9	16.6	16.5	16.3	16.2	16.1	16.0	16.0	16.0	16.0	16.1	16.1	16.1	16.2	16.3	16.3
30-44	18.8	18.9	18.9	19.0	19.1	19.3	19.4	19.5	19.5	19.5	19.4	19.3	19.1	18.9	18.8	18.6	18.3	18.1	17.9	17.8
45-59	19.0	19.0	18.9	19.0	18.8	18.7	18.6	18.4	18.3	18.2	18.2	18.1	18.2	18.2	18.3	18.4	18.5	18.7	18.8	18.9
60-74	17.0	16.9	16.8	16.7	16.7	16.7	16.7	16.8	16.9	17.0	17.2	17.4	17.5	17.6	17.6	17.6	17.6	17.6	17.7	17.6
75 & over	12.9	13.1	13.3	13.5	13.7	13.9	14.0	14.1	14.2	14.2	14.2	14.2	14.2	14.3	14.4	14.5	14.6	14.7	14.8	14.9
All ages	100.0	100.0	100.0	100.0	100.0	100.0	100.0	100.0	100.0	100.0	100.0	100.0	100.0	100.0	100.0	100.0	100.0	100.0	100.0	100.0
Mean age	44.2	44.3	44.4	44.5	44.6	44.7	44.7	44.8	44.9	45.0	45.0	45.1	45.2	45.3	45.3	45.4	45.5	45.6	45.7	45.7
Median age	44.1	44.2	44.2	44.3	44.3	44.4	44.4	44.4	44.5	44.5	44.6	44.8	44.9	45.1	45.2	45.4	45.6	45.7	45.9	46.1

15.3b Population projections by the Office for National Statistics
United Kingdom, PERSONS, thousands

2020-based
Principal projection

Projected populations at mid-years by age last birthday

Ages	2061	2062	2063	2064	2065	2066	2067	2068	2069	2070	2071	2072	2073	2074	2075	2076	2077	2078	2079	2080
Thousands																				
0-14	10,312	10,244	10,178	10,117	10,062	10,013	9,972	9,939	9,914	9,897	9,888	9,885	9,888	9,896	9,908	9,922	9,939	9,956	9,972	9,987
15-29	11,745	11,791	11,833	11,870	11,900	11,919	11,927	11,922	11,905	11,874	11,833	11,782	11,724	11,660	11,591	11,522	11,454	11,389	11,328	11,272
30-44	12,583	12,465	12,366	12,289	12,239	12,223	12,222	12,231	12,245	12,264	12,293	12,328	12,369	12,416	12,464	12,513	12,559	12,602	12,640	12,670
45-59	13,653	13,769	13,856	13,900	13,905	13,850	13,768	13,654	13,546	13,427	13,288	13,131	12,992	12,866	12,740	12,609	12,496	12,401	12,330	12,283
60-74	12,569	12,504	12,431	12,384	12,344	12,317	12,321	12,373	12,422	12,499	12,588	12,687	12,780	12,864	12,962	13,077	13,192	13,279	13,325	13,335
75 & over	10,745	10,827	10,931	11,031	11,140	11,267	11,383	11,480	11,579	11,660	11,748	11,840	11,915	11,985	12,036	12,073	12,088	12,112	12,153	12,206
All ages	71,607	71,601	71,595	71,591	71,589	71,590	71,594	71,601	71,610	71,623	71,637	71,653	71,669	71,686	71,702	71,716	71,729	71,740	71,748	71,754
Percentages																				
0-14	14.4	14.3	14.2	14.1	14.1	14.0	13.9	13.9	13.8	13.8	13.8	13.8	13.8	13.8	13.8	13.8	13.9	13.9	13.9	13.9
15-29	16.4	16.5	16.5	16.6	16.6	16.6	16.7	16.7	16.6	16.6	16.5	16.4	16.4	16.3	16.2	16.1	16.0	15.9	15.8	15.7
30-44	17.6	17.4	17.3	17.2	17.1	17.1	17.1	17.1	17.1	17.1	17.2	17.2	17.3	17.3	17.4	17.4	17.5	17.6	17.6	17.7
45-59	19.1	19.2	19.4	19.4	19.4	19.3	19.2	19.1	18.9	18.7	18.5	18.3	18.1	17.9	17.8	17.6	17.4	17.3	17.2	17.1
60-74	17.6	17.5	17.4	17.3	17.2	17.2	17.2	17.3	17.3	17.5	17.6	17.7	17.8	17.9	18.1	18.2	18.4	18.5	18.6	18.6
75 & over	15.0	15.1	15.3	15.4	15.6	15.7	15.9	16.0	16.2	16.3	16.4	16.5	16.6	16.7	16.8	16.8	16.9	16.9	16.9	17.0
All ages	100.0	100.0	100.0	100.0	100.0	100.0	100.0	100.0	100.0	100.0	100.0	100.0	100.0	100.0	100.0	100.0	100.0	100.0	100.0	100.0
Mean age	45.8	45.9	46.0	46.1	46.1	46.2	46.3	46.4	46.5	46.5	46.6	46.7	46.7	46.8	46.9	46.9	47.0	47.0	47.1	47.2
Median age	46.2	46.4	46.5	46.7	46.8	46.9	47.0	47.1	47.1	47.2	47.2	47.2	47.3	47.3	47.3	47.3	47.4	47.4	47.4	47.4

Ages	2081	2082	2083	2084	2085	2086	2087	2088	2089	2090	2091	2092	2093	2094	2095	2096	2097	2098	2099	2100
Thousands																				
0-14	10,000	10,009	10,014	10,015	10,011	10,002	9,989	9,971	9,949	9,923	9,895	9,864	9,831	9,798	9,764	9,732	9,701	9,673	9,647	9,624
15-29	11,224	11,184	11,151	11,126	11,109	11,100	11,097	11,100	11,120	11,120	11,135	11,152	11,169	11,186	11,201	11,213	11,222	11,228	11,229	11,225
30-44	12,690	12,698	12,694	12,677	12,647	12,607	12,557	12,500	12,436	12,369	12,301	12,233	12,169	12,108	12,054	12,007	11,967	11,935	11,911	11,895
45-59	12,270	12,271	12,283	12,299	12,321	12,351	12,389	12,432	12,480	12,530	12,580	12,628	12,673	12,712	12,743	12,765	12,775	12,773	12,758	12,730
60-74	13,287	13,215	13,114	13,018	12,912	12,788	12,648	12,525	12,413	12,303	12,188	12,090	12,009	11,949	11,913	11,908	11,916	11,934	11,957	11,985
75 & over	12,285	12,378	12,496	12,611	12,735	12,876	13,030	13,165	13,289	13,410	13,536	13,646	13,739	13,813	13,866	13,892	13,910	13,923	13,938	13,952
All ages	71,756	71,755	71,752	71,745	71,736	71,724	71,710	71,694	71,675	71,656	71,635	71,612	71,589	71,566	71,542	71,517	71,491	71,465	71,438	71,410
Percentages																				
0-14	13.9	13.9	14.0	14.0	14.0	13.9	13.9	13.9	13.9	13.8	13.8	13.8	13.7	13.7	13.6	13.6	13.6	13.5	13.5	13.5
15-29	15.6	15.6	15.5	15.5	15.5	15.5	15.5	15.5	15.5	15.5	15.5	15.6	15.6	15.6	15.7	15.7	15.7	15.7	15.7	15.7
30-44	17.7	17.7	17.7	17.7	17.6	17.6	17.5	17.4	17.4	17.3	17.2	17.1	17.0	16.9	16.8	16.8	16.7	16.7	16.7	16.7
45-59	17.1	17.1	17.1	17.1	17.2	17.2	17.3	17.3	17.4	17.5	17.6	17.6	17.7	17.8	17.8	17.8	17.9	17.9	17.9	17.8
60-74	18.5	18.4	18.3	18.1	18.0	17.8	17.6	17.5	17.3	17.2	17.0	16.9	16.8	16.7	16.7	16.7	16.7	16.7	16.7	16.8
75 & over	17.1	17.3	17.4	17.6	17.8	18.0	18.2	18.4	18.5	18.7	18.9	19.1	19.2	19.3	19.4	19.4	19.5	19.5	19.5	19.5
All ages	100.0	100.0	100.0	100.0	100.0	100.0	100.0	100.0	100.0	100.0	100.0	100.0	100.0	100.0	100.0	100.0	100.0	100.0	100.0	100.0
Mean age	47.2	47.2	47.3	47.3	47.4	47.4	47.5	47.5	47.6	47.6	47.7	47.8	47.8	47.9	47.9	48.0	48.0	48.1	48.1	48.2
Median age	47.4	47.4	47.4	47.5	47.5	47.5	47.6	47.7	47.7	47.8	47.9	48.0	48.1	48.1	48.2	48.3	48.4	48.5	48.5	48.6

15.3b Population projections by the Office for National Statistics
United Kingdom, PERSONS, thousands

2020-based
Principal projection

Projected populations at mid-years by age last birthday

Ages	2101	2102	2103	2104	2105	2106	2107	2108	2109	2110	2111	2112	2113	2114	2115	2116	2117	2118	2119	2120
Thousands																				
0-14	9,604	9,587	9,575	9,565	9,558	9,555	9,553	9,553	9,555	9,558	9,561	9,564	9,566	9,568	9,568	9,566	9,563	9,557	9,550	9,540
15-29	11,216	11,203	11,185	11,163	11,138	11,109	11,078	11,046	11,013	10,980	10,947	10,917	10,888	10,862	10,839	10,820	10,803	10,791	10,781	10,775
30-44	11,886	11,884	11,887	11,896	11,908	11,924	11,941	11,958	11,975	11,991	12,004	12,013	12,019	12,020	12,017	12,009	11,996	11,979	11,957	11,932
45-59	12,692	12,645	12,590	12,529	12,464	12,399	12,334	12,272	12,214	12,162	12,117	12,080	12,050	12,028	12,014	12,007	12,006	12,011	12,021	12,035
60-74	12,021	12,064	12,112	12,165	12,220	12,274	12,326	12,374	12,417	12,453	12,479	12,493	12,496	12,486	12,464	12,432	12,391	12,343	12,290	12,232
75 & over	13,962	13,968	13,970	13,969	13,965	13,959	13,952	13,947	13,943	13,943	13,950	13,965	13,991	14,027	14,074	14,131	14,198	14,273	14,355	14,442
All ages	71,381	71,351	71,319	71,286	71,253	71,219	71,184	71,150	71,118	71,086	71,058	71,032	71,009	70,991	70,976	70,965	70,958	70,954	70,954	70,957
Percentages																				
0-14	13.5	13.4	13.4	13.4	13.4	13.4	13.4	13.4	13.4	13.4	13.5	13.5	13.5	13.5	13.5	13.5	13.5	13.5	13.5	13.4
15-29	15.7	15.7	15.7	15.7	15.6	15.6	15.6	15.5	15.5	15.4	15.4	15.4	15.3	15.3	15.3	15.2	15.2	15.2	15.2	15.2
30-44	16.7	16.7	16.7	16.7	16.7	16.7	16.8	16.8	16.8	16.9	16.9	16.9	16.9	16.9	16.9	16.9	16.9	16.9	16.9	16.8
45-59	17.8	17.7	17.7	17.6	17.5	17.4	17.3	17.2	17.2	17.1	17.1	17.0	17.0	16.9	16.9	16.9	16.9	16.9	16.9	17.0
60-74	16.8	16.9	17.0	17.1	17.1	17.2	17.3	17.4	17.5	17.5	17.6	17.6	17.6	17.6	17.6	17.5	17.5	17.4	17.3	17.2
75 & over	19.6	19.6	19.6	19.6	19.6	19.6	19.6	19.6	19.6	19.6	19.6	19.7	19.7	19.8	19.8	19.9	20.0	20.1	20.2	20.4
All ages	100.0	100.0	100.0	100.0	100.0	100.0	100.0	100.0	100.0	100.0	100.0	100.0	100.0	100.0	100.0	100.0	100.0	100.0	100.0	100.0
Mean age	48.2	48.2	48.3	48.3	48.3	48.4	48.4	48.4	48.4	48.5	48.5	48.5	48.5	48.5	48.6	48.6	48.6	48.7	48.7	48.7
Median age	48.6	48.7	48.7	48.8	48.8	48.8	48.8	48.8	48.8	48.8	48.8	48.8	48.8	48.8	48.8	48.9	48.9	48.9	49.0	49.0

Note: Figures may not add exactly due to rounding.

Source: Office for National Statistics

15.3b Population projections by the Office for National Statistics
United Kingdom, MALES, thousands

Principal projection

Projected populations at mid-years by age last birthday

Ages	2020	2021	2022	2023	2024	2025	2026	2027	2028	2029	2030	2031	2032	2033	2034	2035	2036	2037	2038	2039	2040
Thousands																					
0-14	6,141	6,115	6,074	6,015	5,959	5,896	5,821	5,736	5,661	5,591	5,522	5,450	5,387	5,334	5,293	5,266	5,257	5,256	5,260	5,266	5,276
15-29	6,306	6,297	6,308	6,340	6,365	6,404	6,446	6,493	6,536	6,575	6,621	6,681	6,741	6,786	6,809	6,811	6,782	6,737	6,676	6,618	6,554
30-44	6,475	6,555	6,630	6,691	6,728	6,738	6,756	6,779	6,793	6,807	6,800	6,780	6,758	6,726	6,704	6,680	6,663	6,666	6,692	6,713	6,750
45-59	6,613	6,571	6,509	6,447	6,404	6,373	6,345	6,310	6,285	6,259	6,257	6,248	6,242	6,270	6,315	6,375	6,452	6,524	6,582	6,618	6,629
60-74	5,120	5,192	5,202	5,255	5,334	5,428	5,523	5,623	5,707	5,788	5,858	5,927	5,974	5,993	5,990	5,974	5,940	5,889	5,837	5,805	5,786
75 & over	2,491	2,557	2,696	2,806	2,892	2,963	3,022	3,073	3,128	3,180	3,227	3,280	3,338	3,402	3,468	3,535	3,612	3,696	3,783	3,874	3,964
All ages	33,146	33,288	33,420	33,554	33,682	33,802	33,913	34,015	34,110	34,201	34,285	34,365	34,440	34,511	34,578	34,643	34,705	34,768	34,831	34,894	34,958
Percentages																					
0-14	18.5	18.4	18.2	17.9	17.7	17.4	17.2	16.9	16.6	16.3	16.1	15.9	15.6	15.5	15.3	15.2	15.1	15.1	15.1	15.1	15.1
15-29	19.0	18.9	18.9	18.9	18.9	18.9	19.0	19.1	19.2	19.2	19.3	19.4	19.6	19.7	19.7	19.7	19.5	19.4	19.2	19.0	18.7
30-44	19.5	19.7	19.8	19.9	20.0	19.9	19.9	19.9	19.9	19.9	19.8	19.7	19.6	19.5	19.4	19.3	19.2	19.2	19.2	19.2	19.3
45-59	20.0	19.7	19.5	19.2	19.0	18.9	18.7	18.6	18.4	18.3	18.2	18.2	18.1	18.2	18.3	18.4	18.6	18.8	18.9	19.0	19.0
60-74	15.4	15.6	15.6	15.7	15.8	16.1	16.3	16.5	16.7	16.9	17.1	17.2	17.3	17.4	17.3	17.2	17.1	16.9	16.8	16.6	16.6
75 & over	7.5	7.7	8.1	8.4	8.6	8.8	8.9	9.0	9.2	9.3	9.4	9.5	9.7	9.9	10.0	10.2	10.4	10.6	10.9	11.1	11.3
All ages	100.0	100.0	100.0	100.0	100.0	100.0	100.0	100.0	100.0	100.0	100.0	100.0	100.0	100.0	100.0	100.0	100.0	100.0	100.0	100.0	100.0
Mean age	40.1	40.2	40.4	40.6	40.8	40.9	41.1	41.3	41.5	41.6	41.8	41.9	42.1	42.2	42.4	42.5	42.7	42.8	42.9	43.0	43.1
Median age	39.3	39.4	39.6	39.7	39.9	40.1	40.3	40.4	40.6	40.8	41.0	41.2	41.4	41.6	41.7	41.9	42.0	42.2	42.3	42.4	42.6

Ages	2041	2042	2043	2044	2045	2046	2047	2048	2049	2050	2051	2052	2053	2054	2055	2056	2057	2058	2059	2060
Thousands																				
0-14	5,290	5,308	5,329	5,352	5,377	5,401	5,425	5,446	5,465	5,480	5,490	5,494	5,492	5,482	5,467	5,446	5,420	5,390	5,357	5,322
15-29	6,479	6,394	6,319	6,250	6,181	6,109	6,047	5,994	5,953	5,926	5,918	5,917	5,921	5,928	5,937	5,952	5,969	5,990	6,014	6,038
30-44	6,790	6,838	6,882	6,921	6,968	7,028	7,088	7,133	7,156	7,159	7,130	7,087	7,026	6,969	6,906	6,832	6,749	6,675	6,607	6,540
45-59	6,647	6,671	6,686	6,702	6,696	6,679	6,659	6,629	6,610	6,590	6,575	6,581	6,609	6,633	6,671	6,714	6,763	6,809	6,850	6,897
60-74	5,770	5,748	5,734	5,720	5,727	5,729	5,733	5,767	5,815	5,877	5,953	6,023	6,080	6,119	6,135	6,158	6,186	6,205	6,224	6,224
75 & over	4,047	4,129	4,203	4,273	4,332	4,396	4,449	4,485	4,505	4,519	4,526	4,527	4,532	4,558	4,595	4,631	4,662	4,695	4,726	4,768
All ages	35,023	35,088	35,152	35,217	35,280	35,341	35,399	35,454	35,505	35,551	35,592	35,629	35,661	35,688	35,712	35,732	35,749	35,764	35,778	35,790
Percentages																				
0-14	15.1	15.1	15.2	15.2	15.2	15.3	15.3	15.4	15.4	15.4	15.4	15.4	15.4	15.4	15.3	15.2	15.2	15.1	15.0	14.9
15-29	18.5	18.2	18.0	17.7	17.5	17.3	17.1	16.9	16.8	16.7	16.6	16.6	16.6	16.6	16.6	16.7	16.7	16.7	16.8	16.9
30-44	19.4	19.5	19.6	19.7	19.8	19.9	20.0	20.1	20.2	20.1	20.0	19.9	19.7	19.5	19.3	19.1	18.9	18.7	18.5	18.3
45-59	19.0	19.0	19.0	19.0	19.0	18.9	18.8	18.7	18.6	18.5	18.5	18.5	18.5	18.6	18.7	18.8	18.9	19.0	19.1	19.3
60-74	16.5	16.4	16.3	16.2	16.2	16.2	16.2	16.3	16.4	16.5	16.7	16.9	17.1	17.1	17.2	17.2	17.3	17.4	17.4	17.4
75 & over	11.6	11.8	12.0	12.1	12.3	12.4	12.6	12.6	12.7	12.7	12.7	12.7	12.7	12.8	12.9	13.0	13.0	13.1	13.2	13.3
All ages	100.0	100.0	100.0	100.0	100.0	100.0	100.0	100.0	100.0	100.0	100.0	100.0	100.0	100.0	100.0	100.0	100.0	100.0	100.0	100.0
Mean age	43.2	43.3	43.4	43.4	43.5	43.6	43.7	43.7	43.8	43.9	44.0	44.1	44.1	44.2	44.3	44.4	44.5	44.6	44.7	44.7
Median age	42.7	42.8	42.8	42.9	42.9	42.9	43.0	43.1	43.2	43.3	43.4	43.6	43.7	43.9	44.1	44.3	44.5	44.6	44.8	45.0

15.3b Population projections by the Office for National Statistics
United Kingdom, MALES, thousands

Projected populations at mid-years by age last birthday

Ages	2061	2062	2063	2064	2065	2066	2067	2068	2069	2070	2071	2072	2073	2074	2075	2076	2077	2078	2079	2080
Thousands																				
0-14	5,286	5,251	5,217	5,186	5,158	5,133	5,112	5,095	5,082	5,074	5,069	5,067	5,069	5,073	5,079	5,086	5,095	5,104	5,112	5,120
15-29	6,063	6,087	6,108	6,127	6,142	6,153	6,157	6,154	6,145	6,130	6,109	6,083	6,053	6,020	5,985	5,950	5,915	5,881	5,850	5,822
30-44	6,469	6,408	6,357	6,317	6,291	6,283	6,282	6,287	6,294	6,305	6,319	6,337	6,359	6,383	6,408	6,433	6,456	6,479	6,498	6,513
45-59	6,958	7,018	7,063	7,087	7,091	7,064	7,023	6,965	6,911	6,851	6,781	6,702	6,631	6,567	6,503	6,436	6,379	6,330	6,293	6,269
60-74	6,213	6,199	6,176	6,165	6,152	6,147	6,160	6,193	6,223	6,266	6,313	6,366	6,416	6,461	6,511	6,572	6,632	6,677	6,702	6,709
75 & over	4,812	4,851	4,903	4,956	5,017	5,087	5,148	5,203	5,261	5,310	5,364	5,419	5,467	5,511	5,548	5,575	5,593	5,615	5,644	5,680
All ages	35,801	35,813	35,825	35,838	35,851	35,866	35,882	35,898	35,916	35,935	35,955	35,975	35,995	36,014	36,033	36,052	36,069	36,085	36,100	36,113
Percentages																				
0-14	14.8	14.7	14.6	14.5	14.4	14.3	14.2	14.2	14.2	14.1	14.1	14.1	14.1	14.1	14.1	14.1	14.1	14.1	14.2	14.2
15-29	16.9	17.0	17.1	17.1	17.1	17.2	17.2	17.1	17.1	17.1	17.0	16.9	16.8	16.7	16.6	16.5	16.4	16.3	16.2	16.1
30-44	18.1	17.9	17.7	17.6	17.5	17.5	17.5	17.5	17.5	17.5	17.6	17.6	17.7	17.7	17.8	17.8	17.9	18.0	18.0	18.0
45-59	19.4	19.6	19.7	19.8	19.8	19.7	19.6	19.4	19.2	19.1	18.9	18.6	18.4	18.2	18.0	17.9	17.7	17.5	17.4	17.4
60-74	17.4	17.3	17.2	17.2	17.2	17.1	17.2	17.3	17.3	17.4	17.6	17.7	17.8	17.9	18.1	18.2	18.4	18.5	18.6	18.6
75 & over	13.4	13.5	13.7	13.8	14.0	14.2	14.3	14.5	14.6	14.8	14.9	15.1	15.2	15.3	15.4	15.5	15.5	15.6	15.6	15.7
All ages	100.0	100.0	100.0	100.0	100.0	100.0	100.0	100.0	100.0	100.0	100.0	100.0	100.0	100.0	100.0	100.0	100.0	100.0	100.0	100.0
Mean age	44.8	44.9	45.0	45.1	45.2	45.3	45.4	45.5	45.6	45.7	45.7	45.8	45.9	46.0	46.0	46.1	46.2	46.2	46.3	46.4
Median age	45.2	45.3	45.5	45.6	45.8	45.9	45.9	46.0	46.0	46.1	46.1	46.2	46.2	46.3	46.3	46.3	46.4	46.4	46.4	46.4

Ages	2081	2082	2083	2084	2085	2086	2087	2088	2089	2090	2091	2092	2093	2094	2095	2096	2097	2098	2099	2100
Thousands																				
0-14	5,126	5,131	5,133	5,134	5,132	5,128	5,121	5,112	5,100	5,087	5,072	5,057	5,040	5,023	5,006	4,989	4,973	4,959	4,945	4,934
15-29	5,797	5,776	5,760	5,747	5,739	5,734	5,732	5,734	5,738	5,744	5,752	5,761	5,769	5,778	5,786	5,792	5,797	5,799	5,800	5,798
30-44	6,524	6,528	6,526	6,517	6,502	6,482	6,456	6,427	6,395	6,360	6,326	6,291	6,258	6,228	6,200	6,176	6,156	6,139	6,127	6,119
45-59	6,263	6,264	6,271	6,279	6,291	6,307	6,327	6,351	6,374	6,400	6,426	6,451	6,474	6,494	6,510	6,522	6,527	6,526	6,519	6,505
60-74	6,686	6,651	6,601	6,554	6,502	6,441	6,372	6,311	6,256	6,201	6,143	6,095	6,055	6,025	6,008	6,006	6,012	6,022	6,034	6,050
75 & over	5,727	5,783	5,850	5,916	5,985	6,062	6,145	6,219	6,287	6,353	6,421	6,480	6,530	6,571	6,601	6,616	6,627	6,635	6,645	6,653
All ages	36,124	36,134	36,141	36,147	36,151	36,153	36,153	36,152	36,149	36,145	36,140	36,134	36,127	36,119	36,111	36,101	36,092	36,082	36,071	36,060
Percentages																				
0-14	14.2	14.2	14.2	14.2	14.2	14.2	14.2	14.1	14.1	14.1	14.0	14.0	14.0	13.9	13.9	13.8	13.8	13.7	13.7	13.7
15-29	16.0	16.0	15.9	15.9	15.9	15.9	15.9	15.9	15.9	15.9	15.9	15.9	16.0	16.0	16.0	16.0	16.1	16.1	16.1	16.1
30-44	18.1	18.1	18.1	18.0	18.0	17.9	17.9	17.8	17.7	17.6	17.5	17.4	17.3	17.2	17.2	17.1	17.1	17.0	17.0	17.0
45-59	17.3	17.3	17.4	17.4	17.4	17.4	17.5	17.6	17.6	17.7	17.8	17.9	17.9	18.0	18.0	18.1	18.1	18.1	18.1	18.0
60-74	18.5	18.4	18.3	18.1	18.0	17.8	17.6	17.5	17.3	17.2	17.0	16.9	16.8	16.7	16.6	16.6	16.7	16.7	16.7	16.8
75 & over	15.9	16.0	16.2	16.4	16.6	16.8	17.0	17.2	17.4	17.6	17.8	17.9	18.1	18.2	18.3	18.3	18.4	18.4	18.4	18.5
All ages	100.0	100.0	100.0	100.0	100.0	100.0	100.0	100.0	100.0	100.0	100.0	100.0	100.0	100.0	100.0	100.0	100.0	100.0	100.0	100.0
Mean age	46.4	46.5	46.5	46.6	46.7	46.7	46.8	46.8	46.9	47.0	47.0	47.1	47.1	47.2	47.2	47.3	47.4	47.4	47.5	47.5
Median age	46.5	46.5	46.5	46.6	46.6	46.7	46.8	46.8	46.9	47.0	47.1	47.2	47.3	47.4	47.4	47.5	47.6	47.7	47.7	47.8

15.3b Population projections by the Office for National Statistics
United Kingdom, MALES, thousands

Projected populations at mid-years by age last birthday

Ages	2101	2102	2103	2104	2105	2106	2107	2108	2109	2110	2111	2112	2113	2114	2115	2116	2117	2118	2119	2120
Thousands																				
0-14	4,924	4,915	4,909	4,904	4,900	4,898	4,898	4,898	4,899	4,900	4,902	4,903	4,904	4,905	4,905	4,904	4,903	4,900	4,896	4,891
15-29	5,794	5,787	5,778	5,767	5,754	5,739	5,723	5,707	5,690	5,673	5,656	5,641	5,626	5,613	5,601	5,591	5,583	5,576	5,571	5,568
30-44	6,115	6,114	6,116	6,120	6,127	6,135	6,143	6,152	6,161	6,169	6,176	6,181	6,184	6,185	6,183	6,179	6,173	6,164	6,153	6,140
45-59	6,486	6,462	6,435	6,404	6,371	6,338	6,306	6,274	6,245	6,219	6,197	6,178	6,163	6,152	6,145	6,142	6,142	6,145	6,150	6,158
60-74	6,069	6,092	6,118	6,145	6,174	6,203	6,230	6,255	6,278	6,297	6,310	6,319	6,321	6,317	6,306	6,291	6,271	6,248	6,221	6,193
75 & over	6,660	6,665	6,668	6,670	6,670	6,670	6,670	6,671	6,673	6,677	6,685	6,697	6,714	6,736	6,764	6,797	6,835	6,876	6,921	6,968
All ages	36,048	36,036	36,023	36,010	35,997	35,983	35,970	35,958	35,946	35,935	35,926	35,918	35,912	35,907	35,905	35,904	35,906	35,908	35,913	35,918
Percentages																				
0-14	13.7	13.6	13.6	13.6	13.6	13.6	13.6	13.6	13.6	13.6	13.6	13.7	13.7	13.7	13.7	13.7	13.7	13.6	13.6	13.6
15-29	16.1	16.1	16.0	16.0	16.0	15.9	15.9	15.9	15.8	15.8	15.7	15.7	15.7	15.6	15.6	15.6	15.5	15.5	15.5	15.5
30-44	17.0	17.0	17.0	17.0	17.0	17.0	17.1	17.1	17.1	17.2	17.2	17.2	17.2	17.2	17.2	17.2	17.2	17.2	17.1	17.1
45-59	18.0	17.9	17.9	17.8	17.7	17.6	17.5	17.4	17.4	17.3	17.2	17.2	17.2	17.1	17.1	17.1	17.1	17.1	17.1	17.1
60-74	16.8	16.9	17.0	17.1	17.2	17.2	17.3	17.4	17.5	17.5	17.6	17.6	17.6	17.6	17.6	17.5	17.5	17.4	17.3	17.2
75 & over	18.5	18.5	18.5	18.5	18.5	18.5	18.5	18.6	18.6	18.6	18.6	18.6	18.7	18.8	18.8	18.9	19.0	19.1	19.3	19.4
All ages	100.0	100.0	100.0	100.0	100.0	100.0	100.0	100.0	100.0	100.0	100.0	100.0	100.0	100.0	100.0	100.0	100.0	100.0	100.0	100.0
Mean age	47.6	47.6	47.6	47.7	47.7	47.7	47.7	47.8	47.8	47.8	47.8	47.9	47.9	47.9	48.0	48.0	48.0	48.1	48.1	48.2
Median age	47.8	47.9	47.9	48.0	48.0	48.0	48.0	48.0	48.0	48.0	48.0	48.0	48.0	48.1	48.1	48.1	48.1	48.2	48.2	48.3

Note: Figures may not add exactly due to rounding.

Source: Office for National Statistics

15.3b Population projections by the Office for National Statistics
United Kingdom, FEMALES, thousands

2020-based
Principal projection

Projected populations at mid-years by age last birthday

Ages	2020	2021	2022	2023	2024	2025	2026	2027	2028	2029	2030	2031	2032	2033	2034	2035	2036	2037	2038	2039	2040
Thousands																					
0-14	5,834	5,808	5,770	5,713	5,659	5,598	5,526	5,445	5,374	5,309	5,244	5,177	5,119	5,070	5,033	5,008	5,000	4,998	5,002	5,008	5,018
15-29	5,987	5,965	5,953	5,971	5,988	6,020	6,058	6,099	6,138	6,174	6,220	6,272	6,328	6,370	6,388	6,401	6,359	6,318	6,259	6,203	6,141
30-44	6,543	6,610	6,682	6,732	6,750	6,737	6,724	6,716	6,699	6,681	6,643	6,599	6,541	6,480	6,437	6,401	6,370	6,352	6,364	6,377	6,407
45-59	6,818	6,777	6,713	6,645	6,597	6,563	6,535	6,507	6,483	6,456	6,450	6,433	6,437	6,467	6,508	6,556	6,621	6,691	6,738	6,755	6,742
60-74	5,455	5,539	5,552	5,610	5,699	5,801	5,907	6,014	6,109	6,201	6,284	6,367	6,420	6,443	6,442	6,427	6,389	6,331	6,271	6,231	6,206
75 & over	3,298	3,363	3,505	3,618	3,707	3,784	3,849	3,907	3,967	4,028	4,082	4,142	4,209	4,283	4,361	4,440	4,530	4,628	4,731	4,839	4,947
All ages	33,936	34,063	34,176	34,290	34,400	34,503	34,599	34,687	34,771	34,849	34,922	34,990	35,054	35,113	35,169	35,220	35,270	35,318	35,366	35,413	35,460
Percentages																					
0-14	17.2	17.1	16.9	16.7	16.5	16.2	16.0	15.7	15.5	15.2	15.0	14.8	14.6	14.4	14.3	14.2	14.2	14.2	14.1	14.1	14.1
15-29	17.6	17.5	17.4	17.4	17.4	17.4	17.5	17.6	17.7	17.7	17.8	17.9	18.1	18.1	18.2	18.1	18.0	17.9	17.7	17.5	17.3
30-44	19.3	19.4	19.6	19.6	19.6	19.5	19.4	19.4	19.3	19.2	19.0	18.9	18.7	18.5	18.3	18.2	18.1	18.0	18.0	18.0	18.1
45-59	20.1	19.9	19.6	19.4	19.2	19.0	18.9	18.8	18.6	18.5	18.5	18.4	18.4	18.4	18.5	18.6	18.8	18.9	19.1	19.1	19.0
60-74	16.1	16.3	16.2	16.4	16.6	16.8	17.1	17.3	17.6	17.8	18.0	18.2	18.3	18.4	18.3	18.2	18.1	17.9	17.7	17.6	17.5
75 & over	9.7	9.9	10.3	10.6	10.8	11.0	11.1	11.3	11.4	11.6	11.7	11.8	12.0	12.2	12.4	12.6	12.8	13.1	13.4	13.7	14.0
All ages	100.0	100.0	100.0	100.0	100.0	100.0	100.0	100.0	100.0	100.0	100.0	100.0	100.0	100.0	100.0	100.0	100.0	100.0	100.0	100.0	100.0
Mean age	42.0	42.1	42.3	42.5	42.7	42.9	43.0	43.2	43.4	43.6	43.8	43.9	44.1	44.2	44.4	44.6	44.7	44.8	45.0	45.1	45.2
Median age	41.5	41.7	41.9	42.1	42.3	42.5	42.7	42.9	43.2	43.4	43.6	43.8	44.0	44.2	44.4	44.6	44.8	45.0	45.1	45.3	45.4

Ages	2041	2042	2043	2044	2045	2046	2047	2048	2049	2050	2051	2052	2053	2054	2055	2056	2057	2058	2059	2060
Thousands																				
0-14	5,031	5,048	5,067	5,090	5,113	5,136	5,159	5,179	5,197	5,212	5,221	5,225	5,222	5,214	5,199	5,179	5,154	5,125	5,094	5,060
15-29	6,069	5,988	5,917	5,852	5,788	5,721	5,663	5,614	5,577	5,552	5,544	5,543	5,547	5,553	5,562	5,576	5,593	5,613	5,635	5,658
30-44	6,444	6,485	6,525	6,561	6,606	6,659	6,715	6,756	6,775	6,776	6,747	6,705	6,647	6,592	6,530	6,459	6,379	6,309	6,244	6,181
45-59	6,730	6,724	6,708	6,691	6,655	6,613	6,557	6,499	6,457	6,423	6,396	6,379	6,393	6,408	6,439	6,477	6,519	6,560	6,597	6,643
60-74	6,185	6,166	6,151	6,132	6,133	6,126	6,136	6,171	6,214	6,264	6,328	6,397	6,443	6,463	6,455	6,448	6,446	6,434	6,422	6,391
75 & over	5,048	5,143	5,232	5,319	5,393	5,473	5,536	5,580	5,607	5,624	5,633	5,633	5,636	5,662	5,703	5,743	5,781	5,817	5,850	5,891
All ages	35,507	35,554	35,600	35,645	35,688	35,728	35,766	35,799	35,827	35,851	35,869	35,882	35,889	35,892	35,889	35,882	35,871	35,857	35,841	35,824
Percentages																				
0-14	14.2	14.2	14.2	14.3	14.3	14.4	14.4	14.5	14.5	14.5	14.6	14.6	14.6	14.5	14.5	14.4	14.4	14.3	14.2	14.1
15-29	17.1	16.8	16.6	16.4	16.2	16.0	15.8	15.7	15.6	15.5	15.5	15.4	15.5	15.5	15.5	15.5	15.6	15.7	15.7	15.8
30-44	18.1	18.2	18.3	18.4	18.5	18.6	18.8	18.9	18.9	18.9	18.8	18.7	18.5	18.4	18.2	18.0	17.8	17.6	17.4	17.3
45-59	19.0	18.9	18.8	18.8	18.6	18.5	18.3	18.2	18.0	17.9	17.8	17.8	17.8	17.9	17.9	18.1	18.2	18.3	18.4	18.5
60-74	17.4	17.3	17.3	17.2	17.2	17.1	17.2	17.2	17.3	17.5	17.6	17.8	18.0	18.0	18.0	18.0	18.0	17.9	17.9	17.8
75 & over	14.2	14.5	14.7	14.9	15.1	15.3	15.5	15.6	15.6	15.7	15.7	15.7	15.7	15.8	15.9	16.0	16.1	16.2	16.3	16.4
All ages	100.0	100.0	100.0	100.0	100.0	100.0	100.0	100.0	100.0	100.0	100.0	100.0	100.0	100.0	100.0	100.0	100.0	100.0	100.0	100.0
Mean age	45.3	45.4	45.5	45.5	45.6	45.7	45.8	45.9	45.9	46.0	46.1	46.2	46.2	46.3	46.4	46.4	46.5	46.6	46.7	46.7
Median age	45.5	45.6	45.7	45.8	45.8	45.9	45.9	45.9	45.9	45.9	46.0	46.1	46.2	46.3	46.4	46.6	46.7	46.9	47.0	47.2

15.3b Population projections by the Office for National Statistics
United Kingdom, FEMALES, thousands

Projected populations at mid-years by age last birthday

Ages	2061	2062	2063	2064	2065	2066	2067	2068	2069	2070	2071	2072	2073	2074	2075	2076	2077	2078	2079	2080
Thousands																				
0-14	5,026	4,993	4,961	4,931	4,904	4,880	4,860	4,844	4,832	4,824	4,819	4,818	4,819	4,823	4,829	4,836	4,844	4,852	4,860	4,867
15-29	5,682	5,704	5,725	5,743	5,757	5,767	5,771	5,768	5,759	5,745	5,724	5,700	5,671	5,640	5,606	5,573	5,539	5,507	5,477	5,451
30-44	6,114	6,057	6,009	5,973	5,948	5,940	5,940	5,944	5,950	5,960	5,974	5,991	6,011	6,033	6,057	6,080	6,103	6,124	6,142	6,157
45-59	6,696	6,752	6,793	6,813	6,814	6,786	6,746	6,689	6,636	6,576	6,507	6,429	6,361	6,299	6,237	6,173	6,118	6,071	6,037	6,014
60-74	6,355	6,306	6,254	6,219	6,192	6,171	6,161	6,180	6,199	6,233	6,275	6,320	6,364	6,404	6,451	6,505	6,561	6,603	6,623	6,626
75 & over	5,932	5,976	6,028	6,075	6,123	6,180	6,235	6,277	6,318	6,350	6,383	6,421	6,449	6,473	6,488	6,498	6,496	6,498	6,509	6,527
All ages	35,806	35,788	35,770	35,753	35,738	35,724	35,712	35,702	35,694	35,687	35,682	35,678	35,675	35,671	35,668	35,664	35,660	35,655	35,648	35,641
Percentages																				
0-14	14.0	14.0	13.9	13.8	13.7	13.7	13.6	13.6	13.5	13.5	13.5	13.5	13.5	13.5	13.5	13.6	13.6	13.6	13.6	13.7
15-29	15.9	15.9	16.0	16.1	16.1	16.1	16.2	16.2	16.1	16.1	16.0	16.0	15.9	15.8	15.7	15.6	15.5	15.4	15.4	15.3
30-44	17.1	16.9	16.8	16.7	16.6	16.6	16.6	16.6	16.7	16.7	16.7	16.8	16.8	16.9	17.0	17.0	17.1	17.2	17.2	17.3
45-59	18.7	18.9	19.0	19.1	19.1	19.0	18.9	18.7	18.6	18.4	18.2	18.0	17.8	17.7	17.5	17.3	17.2	17.0	16.9	16.9
60-74	17.7	17.6	17.5	17.4	17.3	17.3	17.3	17.3	17.4	17.5	17.6	17.7	17.8	18.0	18.1	18.2	18.4	18.5	18.6	18.6
75 & over	16.6	16.7	16.9	17.0	17.1	17.3	17.5	17.6	17.7	17.8	17.9	18.0	18.1	18.1	18.2	18.2	18.2	18.2	18.3	18.3
All ages	100.0	100.0	100.0	100.0	100.0	100.0	100.0	100.0	100.0	100.0	100.0	100.0	100.0	100.0	100.0	100.0	100.0	100.0	100.0	100.0
Mean age	46.8	46.9	46.9	47.0	47.1	47.2	47.2	47.3	47.4	47.4	47.5	47.5	47.6	47.7	47.7	47.8	47.8	47.9	47.9	47.9
Median age	47.3	47.5	47.6	47.8	47.9	48.0	48.1	48.2	48.2	48.3	48.3	48.3	48.3	48.4	48.4	48.4	48.4	48.4	48.4	48.4

Ages	2081	2082	2083	2084	2085	2086	2087	2088	2089	2090	2091	2092	2093	2094	2095	2096	2097	2098	2099	2100
Thousands																				
0-14	4,873	4,878	4,880	4,881	4,879	4,875	4,868	4,860	4,849	4,836	4,822	4,807	4,791	4,775	4,759	4,743	4,728	4,714	4,701	4,690
15-29	5,427	5,407	5,391	5,379	5,371	5,366	5,365	5,366	5,370	5,376	5,383	5,391	5,400	5,408	5,415	5,421	5,426	5,428	5,429	5,427
30-44	6,166	6,170	6,168	6,160	6,145	6,125	6,101	6,073	6,041	6,008	5,975	5,942	5,910	5,881	5,854	5,831	5,811	5,795	5,783	5,775
45-59	6,007	6,007	6,012	6,020	6,030	6,044	6,062	6,083	6,106	6,130	6,154	6,178	6,199	6,218	6,233	6,243	6,248	6,246	6,239	6,225
60-74	6,601	6,565	6,513	6,464	6,410	6,347	6,276	6,214	6,158	6,102	6,044	5,995	5,954	5,924	5,905	5,902	5,904	5,912	5,922	5,935
75 & over	6,557	6,595	6,646	6,695	6,751	6,814	6,884	6,946	7,002	7,057	7,115	7,166	7,209	7,242	7,265	7,276	7,283	7,288	7,293	7,299
All ages	35,632	35,622	35,611	35,598	35,585	35,571	35,557	35,541	35,526	35,510	35,494	35,478	35,463	35,447	35,431	35,415	35,400	35,384	35,367	35,350
Percentages																				
0-14	13.7	13.7	13.7	13.7	13.7	13.7	13.7	13.7	13.6	13.6	13.6	13.5	13.5	13.5	13.4	13.4	13.4	13.3	13.3	13.3
15-29	15.2	15.2	15.1	15.1	15.1	15.1	15.1	15.1	15.1	15.1	15.2	15.2	15.2	15.3	15.3	15.3	15.3	15.3	15.3	15.4
30-44	17.3	17.3	17.3	17.3	17.3	17.2	17.2	17.1	17.0	16.9	16.8	16.7	16.7	16.6	16.5	16.5	16.4	16.4	16.4	16.3
45-59	16.9	16.9	16.9	16.9	16.9	17.0	17.0	17.1	17.2	17.3	17.3	17.4	17.5	17.5	17.6	17.6	17.6	17.7	17.6	16.8
60-74	18.5	18.4	18.3	18.2	18.0	17.8	17.7	17.5	17.3	17.2	17.0	16.9	16.8	16.7	16.7	16.7	16.7	16.7	16.7	16.8
75 & over	18.4	18.5	18.7	18.8	19.0	19.2	19.4	19.5	19.7	19.9	20.0	20.2	20.3	20.4	20.5	20.5	20.6	20.6	20.6	20.6
All ages	100.0	100.0	100.0	100.0	100.0	100.0	100.0	100.0	100.0	100.0	100.0	100.0	100.0	100.0	100.0	100.0	100.0	100.0	100.0	100.0
Mean age	48.0	48.0	48.1	48.1	48.1	48.2	48.2	48.3	48.3	48.4	48.4	48.5	48.5	48.6	48.6	48.7	48.7	48.8	48.8	48.8
Median age	48.4	48.4	48.4	48.4	48.4	48.4	48.5	48.5	48.6	48.7	48.7	48.8	48.9	49.0	49.0	49.1	49.2	49.3	49.4	49.4

15.3b Population projections by the Office for National Statistics
United Kingdom, FEMALES, thousands

Projected populations at mid-years by age last birthday

Ages	2101	2102	2103	2104	2105	2106	2107	2108	2109	2110	2111	2112	2113	2114	2115	2116	2117	2118	2119	2120
Thousands																				
0-14	4,680	4,672	4,666	4,661	4,658	4,656	4,655	4,656	4,657	4,658	4,659	4,661	4,662	4,662	4,662	4,662	4,660	4,657	4,654	4,649
15-29	5,423	5,416	5,407	5,397	5,384	5,370	5,355	5,339	5,323	5,307	5,291	5,276	5,262	5,250	5,238	5,229	5,221	5,215	5,210	5,207
30-44	5,771	5,770	5,772	5,776	5,782	5,789	5,797	5,806	5,814	5,821	5,828	5,832	5,835	5,836	5,834	5,830	5,824	5,815	5,805	5,792
45-59	6,206	6,182	6,155	6,125	6,093	6,060	6,028	5,997	5,969	5,943	5,921	5,902	5,887	5,876	5,869	5,865	5,864	5,867	5,871	5,878
60-74	5,952	5,972	5,995	6,020	6,046	6,071	6,096	6,119	6,139	6,156	6,168	6,174	6,175	6,169	6,158	6,141	6,120	6,096	6,068	6,039
75 & over	7,302	7,303	7,302	7,299	7,294	7,288	7,282	7,276	7,270	7,266	7,265	7,268	7,277	7,290	7,310	7,334	7,363	7,397	7,434	7,474
All ages	35,333	35,315	35,296	35,277	35,256	35,235	35,214	35,193	35,172	35,151	35,132	35,114	35,098	35,083	35,071	35,060	35,052	35,046	35,042	35,039
Percentages																				
0-14	13.2	13.2	13.2	13.2	13.2	13.2	13.2	13.2	13.2	13.3	13.3	13.3	13.3	13.3	13.3	13.3	13.3	13.3	13.3	13.3
15-29	15.3	15.3	15.3	15.3	15.3	15.2	15.2	15.2	15.1	15.1	15.1	15.0	15.0	15.0	14.9	14.9	14.9	14.9	14.9	14.9
30-44	16.3	16.3	16.4	16.4	16.4	16.4	16.5	16.5	16.5	16.6	16.6	16.6	16.6	16.6	16.6	16.6	16.6	16.6	16.6	16.5
45-59	17.6	17.5	17.4	17.4	17.3	17.2	17.1	17.0	17.0	16.9	16.9	16.8	16.8	16.7	16.7	16.7	16.7	16.7	16.8	16.8
60-74	16.8	16.9	17.0	17.1	17.1	17.2	17.3	17.4	17.5	17.5	17.6	17.6	17.6	17.6	17.5	17.5	17.5	17.4	17.3	17.2
75 & over	20.7	20.7	20.7	20.7	20.7	20.7	20.7	20.7	20.7	20.7	20.7	20.7	20.7	20.8	20.8	20.9	21.0	21.1	21.2	21.3
All ages	100.0	100.0	100.0	100.0	100.0	100.0	100.0	100.0	100.0	100.0	100.0	100.0	100.0	100.0	100.0	100.0	100.0	100.0	100.0	100.0
Mean age	48.9	48.9	49.0	49.0	49.0	49.0	49.1	49.1	49.1	49.1	49.1	49.1	49.1	49.2	49.2	49.2	49.2	49.3	49.3	49.3
Median age	49.5	49.5	49.6	49.6	49.6	49.6	49.6	49.6	49.6	49.6	49.6	49.6	49.6	49.6	49.6	49.6	49.7	49.7	49.7	49.8

Note: Figures may not add exactly due to rounding.

Source: Office for National Statistics

15.3c Mid-2019 Population estimates for England and Wales by sex and single year of age

Ages	Persons	Males	Females	Ages	Persons	Males	Females
All ages	59,439,840	29,382,509	30,057,331	45	732,367	362,929	369,438
0	649,388	333,765	315,623	46	763,688	378,695	384,993
1	676,412	347,033	329,379	47	795,939	394,915	401,024
2	698,837	358,209	340,628	48	821,630	404,794	416,836
3	720,721	369,596	351,125	49	801,260	394,940	406,320
4	719,821	369,309	350,512	50	820,123	404,023	416,100
5	726,317	372,325	353,992	51	818,248	403,097	415,151
6	742,744	380,825	361,919	52	829,626	410,430	419,196
7	765,225	391,546	373,679	53	828,203	407,359	420,844
8	750,173	384,456	365,717	54	831,741	409,311	422,430
9	737,531	377,526	360,005	55	823,099	405,400	417,699
10	726,528	372,267	354,261	56	802,885	395,372	407,513
11	733,267	376,082	357,185	57	784,119	386,992	397,127
12	709,958	364,655	345,303	58	755,249	372,260	382,989
13	696,722	356,851	339,871	59	722,779	355,455	367,324
14	668,590	342,314	326,276	60	705,065	346,521	358,544
15	658,280	337,364	320,916	61	689,075	338,742	350,333
16	640,608	329,348	311,260	62	661,702	324,648	337,054
17	632,385	325,550	306,835	63	636,452	312,135	324,317
18	653,732	335,493	318,239	64	612,394	299,092	313,302
19	677,608	349,262	328,346	65	612,894	297,830	315,064
20	708,336	364,369	343,967	66	602,897	293,332	309,565
21	720,698	371,626	349,072	67	583,460	282,145	301,315
22	748,254	385,032	363,222	68	585,085	282,360	302,725
23	755,826	389,905	365,921	69	594,546	285,697	308,849
24	757,151	388,132	369,019	70	606,965	292,274	314,691
25	782,598	401,477	381,121	71	637,206	305,799	331,407
26	784,090	399,460	384,630	72	686,169	329,666	356,503
27	807,248	407,271	399,977	73	524,406	249,941	274,465
28	824,760	419,256	405,504	74	503,866	239,106	264,760
29	810,973	412,201	398,772	75	496,130	234,760	261,370
30	802,809	403,707	399,102	76	455,010	212,840	242,170
31	810,906	404,660	406,246	77	400,818	185,570	215,248
32	790,832	391,092	399,740	78	354,441	162,379	192,062
33	798,415	399,077	399,338	79	361,072	164,663	196,409
34	797,946	398,283	399,663	80	350,455	158,350	192,105
35	777,820	385,617	392,203	81	332,255	148,761	183,494
36	783,817	387,931	395,886	82	306,983	135,371	171,612
37	781,425	386,129	395,296	83	282,197	122,422	159,775
38	787,003	389,897	397,106	84	257,792	110,254	147,538
39	788,497	390,952	397,545	85	228,197	95,281	132,916
40	756,871	376,940	379,931	86	206,177	84,226	121,951
41	705,441	351,931	353,510	87	188,071	74,839	113,232
42	694,855	346,480	348,375	88	167,219	64,453	102,766
43	706,616	350,755	355,861	89	143,992	53,447	90,545
44	720,070	357,752	362,318	90	547,789	175,925	371,864

Source: Office for National Statistics

1. Estimates are presented both rounded to the nearest hundred and unrounded. Unrounded estimates are published to enable and encourage further calculations and analysis. However, the estimates should not be taken to be accurate to the level of detail provided. More information on the accuracy of the estimates is available in the Quality and Methodology document (QMI):

https://www.ons.gov.uk/peoplepopulationandcommunity/populationandmigration/populationestimates/methodologies/annualmidyearpopulationestimatesqmi

2. The estimates are produced using a variety of data sources and statistical models, including some statistical disclosure control methods, and small estimates should not be taken to refer to particular individuals.

3. The estimated resident population of an area includes all those people who usually live there, regardless of nationality. Arriving international migrants are included in the usually resident population if they remain in the UK for at least a year. Emigrants are excluded if they remain outside the UK for at least a year. This is consistent with the United Nations definition of a long-term migrant. Armed forces stationed outside of the UK are excluded. Students are taken to be usually resident at their term time address.

4. Where data appears for age 90 please note this is for ages 90 and above.

15.3d Population projections by the Office for National Statistics
England, PERSONS, thousands

Projected populations at mid-years by age last birthday

Ages	2020	2021	2022	2023	2024	2025	2026	2027	2028	2029	2030	2031	2032	2033	2034	2035	2036	2037	2038	2039	2040
Thousands																					
0-14	10,214	10,178	10,117	10,027	9,941	9,842	9,724	9,585	9,463	9,351	9,241	9,125	9,025	8,941	8,877	8,835	8,824	8,825	8,837	8,852	8,872
15-29	10,360	10,345	10,357	10,409	10,453	10,522	10,595	10,679	10,760	10,833	10,921	11,027	11,134	11,215	11,258	11,269	11,225	11,160	11,065	10,977	10,876
30-44	11,039	11,155	11,269	11,352	11,389	11,380	11,379	11,387	11,378	11,369	11,327	11,269	11,202	11,127	11,077	11,032	11,001	10,999	11,041	11,076	11,140
45-59	11,276	11,219	11,125	11,030	10,965	10,923	10,882	10,836	10,803	10,765	10,761	10,742	10,739	10,786	10,852	10,936	11,046	11,153	11,231	11,266	11,258
60-74	8,795	8,923	8,939	9,030	9,172	9,337	9,511	9,689	9,844	9,995	10,131	10,267	10,361	10,407	10,416	10,402	10,353	10,273	10,191	10,142	10,115
75 & over	4,866	4,980	5,222	5,412	5,561	5,687	5,792	5,884	5,981	6,076	6,160	6,254	6,358	6,473	6,592	6,715	6,855	7,008	7,168	7,336	7,503
All ages	56,550	56,800	57,029	57,260	57,482	57,690	57,883	58,061	58,230	58,389	58,541	58,684	58,819	58,948	59,071	59,189	59,304	59,419	59,533	59,648	59,764
Percentages																					
0-14	18.1	17.9	17.7	17.5	17.3	17.1	16.8	16.5	16.3	16.0	15.8	15.5	15.3	15.2	15.0	14.9	14.9	14.9	14.8	14.8	14.8
15-29	18.3	18.2	18.2	18.2	18.2	18.2	18.3	18.4	18.5	18.6	18.7	18.8	18.9	19.0	19.1	19.0	18.9	18.8	18.6	18.4	18.2
30-44	19.5	19.6	19.8	19.8	19.8	19.7	19.7	19.6	19.5	19.5	19.3	19.2	19.0	18.9	18.8	18.6	18.6	18.5	18.5	18.6	18.6
45-59	19.9	19.8	19.5	19.3	19.1	18.9	18.8	18.7	18.6	18.4	18.4	18.3	18.3	18.3	18.4	18.5	18.6	18.8	18.9	18.9	18.8
60-74	15.6	15.7	15.7	15.8	16.0	16.2	16.4	16.7	16.9	17.1	17.3	17.5	17.6	17.7	17.6	17.6	17.5	17.3	17.1	17.0	16.9
75 & over	8.6	8.8	9.2	9.5	9.7	9.9	10.0	10.1	10.3	10.4	10.5	10.7	10.8	11.0	11.2	11.3	11.6	11.8	12.0	12.3	12.6
All ages	100.0	100.0	100.0	100.0	100.0	100.0	100.0	100.0	100.0	100.0	100.0	100.0	100.0	100.0	100.0	100.0	100.0	100.0	100.0	100.0	100.0
Mean age	40.9	41.0	41.2	41.4	41.6	41.7	41.9	42.1	42.3	42.4	42.6	42.8	42.9	43.1	43.2	43.4	43.5	43.6	43.7	43.9	44.0
Median age	40.2	40.4	40.5	40.7	40.9	41.1	41.3	41.5	41.7	41.9	42.1	42.3	42.5	42.7	42.8	43.0	43.2	43.3	43.4	43.5	43.7

Ages	2041	2042	2043	2044	2045	2046	2047	2048	2049	2050	2051	2052	2053	2054	2055	2056	2057	2058	2059	2060
Thousands																				
0-14	8,901	8,936	8,977	9,022	9,069	9,116	9,162	9,204	9,242	9,273	9,295	9,307	9,308	9,297	9,276	9,245	9,205	9,159	9,106	9,051
15-29	10,758	10,621	10,500	10,389	10,280	10,164	10,064	9,980	9,917	9,876	9,865	9,866	9,878	9,893	9,914	9,943	9,978	10,019	10,064	10,111
30-44	11,211	11,296	11,378	11,453	11,541	11,647	11,754	11,835	11,878	11,889	11,845	11,780	11,687	11,599	11,499	11,383	11,247	11,128	11,019	10,912
45-59	11,258	11,267	11,260	11,253	11,214	11,160	11,096	11,025	10,980	10,939	10,913	10,915	10,960	10,998	11,064	11,137	11,224	11,308	11,383	11,472
60-74	10,091	10,062	10,045	10,023	10,033	10,029	10,040	10,094	10,164	10,250	10,359	10,463	10,540	10,579	10,579	10,587	10,603	10,603	10,603	10,573
75 & over	7,661	7,815	7,954	8,089	8,206	8,333	8,437	8,512	8,559	8,595	8,616	8,625	8,641	8,693	8,766	8,835	8,898	8,960	9,018	9,090
All ages	59,880	59,997	60,113	60,229	60,341	60,450	60,553	60,650	60,739	60,821	60,893	60,957	61,012	61,059	61,098	61,129	61,155	61,176	61,194	61,209
Percentages																				
0-14	14.9	14.9	14.9	15.0	15.0	15.1	15.1	15.2	15.2	15.2	15.3	15.3	15.3	15.2	15.2	15.1	15.1	15.0	14.9	14.8
15-29	18.0	17.7	17.5	17.2	17.0	16.8	16.6	16.5	16.3	16.2	16.2	16.2	16.2	16.2	16.2	16.3	16.3	16.4	16.4	16.5
30-44	18.7	18.8	18.9	19.0	19.1	19.3	19.4	19.5	19.6	19.5	19.5	19.3	19.2	19.0	18.8	18.6	18.4	18.2	18.0	17.8
45-59	18.8	18.8	18.7	18.7	18.6	18.5	18.3	18.2	18.1	18.0	17.9	17.9	18.0	18.0	18.1	18.2	18.4	18.5	18.6	18.7
60-74	16.9	16.8	16.7	16.6	16.6	16.6	16.6	16.6	16.7	16.9	17.0	17.2	17.3	17.3	17.3	17.3	17.3	17.3	17.3	17.3
75 & over	12.8	13.0	13.2	13.4	13.6	13.8	13.9	14.0	14.1	14.1	14.1	14.1	14.2	14.2	14.3	14.5	14.5	14.6	14.7	14.9
All ages	100.0	100.0	100.0	100.0	100.0	100.0	100.0	100.0	100.0	100.0	100.0	100.0	100.0	100.0	100.0	100.0	100.0	100.0	100.0	100.0
Mean age	44.0	44.1	44.2	44.3	44.4	44.4	44.5	44.6	44.7	44.7	44.8	44.9	45.0	45.0	45.1	45.2	45.3	45.3	45.4	45.5
Median age	43.8	43.8	43.9	44.0	44.0	44.0	44.0	44.0	44.1	44.2	44.3	44.4	44.5	44.7	44.8	45.0	45.2	45.3	45.5	45.7

15.3d Population projections by the Office for National Statistics
England, PERSONS, thousands

Projected populations at mid-years by age last birthday

Ages	2061	2062	2063	2064	2065	2066	2067	2068	2069	2070	2071	2072	2073	2074	2075	2076	2077	2078	2079	2080
Thousands																				
0-14	8,995	8,939	8,885	8,835	8,790	8,751	8,719	8,693	8,675	8,663	8,658	8,659	8,665	8,676	8,689	8,706	8,724	8,743	8,761	8,778
15-29	10,158	10,204	10,246	10,284	10,315	10,338	10,350	10,352	10,342	10,321	10,290	10,251	10,205	10,153	10,098	10,042	9,987	9,934	9,884	9,840
30-44	10,798	10,700	10,619	10,557	10,517	10,507	10,509	10,521	10,537	10,559	10,588	10,624	10,665	10,711	10,759	10,807	10,853	10,896	10,934	10,965
45-59	11,579	11,685	11,765	11,809	11,821	11,780	11,718	11,629	11,546	11,451	11,340	11,211	11,097	10,993	10,891	10,783	10,690	10,613	10,556	10,519
60-74	10,530	10,476	10,417	10,383	10,354	10,341	10,354	10,406	10,452	10,524	10,603	10,695	10,783	10,863	10,954	11,061	11,166	11,246	11,291	11,306
75 & over	9,163	9,231	9,317	9,397	9,484	9,585	9,674	9,749	9,827	9,892	9,963	10,037	10,097	10,152	10,192	10,220	10,234	10,256	10,292	10,338
All ages	61,222	61,236	61,250	61,265	61,283	61,303	61,326	61,351	61,379	61,410	61,443	61,477	61,512	61,548	61,584	61,620	61,654	61,686	61,717	61,746
Percentages																				
0-14	14.7	14.6	14.5	14.4	14.3	14.3	14.2	14.2	14.1	14.1	14.1	14.1	14.1	14.1	14.1	14.1	14.1	14.2	14.2	14.2
15-29	16.6	16.7	16.7	16.8	16.8	16.9	16.9	16.9	16.8	16.8	16.7	16.7	16.6	16.5	16.4	16.3	16.2	16.1	16.0	15.9
30-44	17.6	17.5	17.3	17.2	17.2	17.1	17.1	17.1	17.2	17.2	17.2	17.3	17.3	17.4	17.5	17.5	17.6	17.7	17.7	17.8
45-59	18.9	19.1	19.2	19.3	19.3	19.2	19.1	19.0	18.8	18.6	18.5	18.2	18.0	17.9	17.7	17.5	17.3	17.2	17.1	17.0
60-74	17.2	17.1	17.0	16.9	16.9	16.9	16.9	17.0	17.0	17.1	17.3	17.4	17.5	17.6	17.8	18.0	18.1	18.2	18.3	18.3
75 & over	15.0	15.1	15.2	15.3	15.5	15.6	15.8	15.9	16.0	16.1	16.2	16.3	16.4	16.5	16.6	16.6	16.6	16.6	16.7	16.7
All ages	100.0	100.0	100.0	100.0	100.0	100.0	100.0	100.0	100.0	100.0	100.0	100.0	100.0	100.0	100.0	100.0	100.0	100.0	100.0	100.0
Mean age	45.6	45.6	45.7	45.8	45.9	45.9	46.0	46.1	46.2	46.2	46.3	46.4	46.4	46.5	46.5	46.6	46.7	46.7	46.8	46.8
Median age	45.8	46.0	46.1	46.3	46.4	46.5	46.5	46.6	46.6	46.6	46.7	46.7	46.7	46.8	46.8	46.8	46.8	46.8	46.8	46.8

Ages	2081	2082	2083	2084	2085	2086	2087	2088	2089	2090	2091	2092	2093	2094	2095	2096	2097	2098	2099	2100
Thousands																				
0-14	8,792	8,804	8,812	8,817	8,817	8,813	8,804	8,792	8,776	8,757	8,734	8,710	8,684	8,658	8,632	8,606	8,581	8,559	8,539	8,521
15-29	9,801	9,769	9,743	9,725	9,714	9,709	9,710	9,716	9,726	9,740	9,757	9,775	9,794	9,812	9,829	9,844	9,856	9,864	9,869	9,870
30-44	10,988	11,001	11,002	10,993	10,972	10,942	10,903	10,858	10,807	10,753	10,698	10,643	10,591	10,542	10,499	10,461	10,429	10,405	10,387	10,377
45-59	10,511	10,516	10,530	10,547	10,571	10,602	10,639	10,682	10,729	10,778	10,827	10,874	10,917	10,957	10,989	11,014	11,027	11,031	11,023	11,004
60-74	11,272	11,218	11,140	11,067	10,983	10,885	10,771	10,671	10,580	10,491	10,396	10,317	10,251	10,204	10,176	10,175	10,185	10,204	10,227	10,255
75 & over	10,408	10,490	10,593	10,691	10,801	10,923	11,060	11,181	11,291	11,400	11,514	11,614	11,701	11,771	11,823	11,852	11,875	11,894	11,913	11,931
All ages	61,773	61,798	61,820	61,840	61,858	61,874	61,887	61,899	61,910	61,919	61,927	61,933	61,939	61,944	61,948	61,952	61,954	61,956	61,957	61,957
Percentages																				
0-14	14.2	14.2	14.3	14.3	14.3	14.2	14.2	14.2	14.2	14.1	14.1	14.1	14.0	14.0	13.9	13.9	13.9	13.8	13.8	13.8
15-29	15.9	15.8	15.8	15.7	15.7	15.7	15.7	15.7	15.7	15.7	15.8	15.8	15.8	15.8	15.9	15.9	15.9	15.9	15.9	15.9
30-44	17.8	17.8	17.8	17.8	17.7	17.7	17.6	17.5	17.5	17.4	17.3	17.2	17.1	17.0	16.9	16.9	16.8	16.8	16.8	16.7
45-59	17.0	17.0	17.0	17.1	17.1	17.1	17.2	17.3	17.3	17.4	17.5	17.6	17.6	17.7	17.7	17.8	17.8	17.8	17.8	17.8
60-74	18.2	18.2	18.0	17.9	17.8	17.6	17.4	17.2	17.1	16.9	16.8	16.7	16.6	16.5	16.4	16.4	16.4	16.5	16.5	16.6
75 & over	16.8	17.0	17.1	17.3	17.5	17.7	17.9	18.1	18.2	18.4	18.6	18.8	18.9	19.0	19.1	19.1	19.2	19.2	19.2	19.3
All ages	100.0	100.0	100.0	100.0	100.0	100.0	100.0	100.0	100.0	100.0	100.0	100.0	100.0	100.0	100.0	100.0	100.0	100.0	100.0	100.0
Mean age	46.9	46.9	46.9	47.0	47.0	47.1	47.1	47.2	47.2	47.3	47.4	47.4	47.5	47.5	47.6	47.6	47.6	47.7	47.7	47.8
Median age	46.9	46.9	46.9	46.9	47.0	47.0	47.1	47.1	47.2	47.3	47.4	47.5	47.6	47.6	47.7	47.8	47.9	48.0	48.0	48.1

15.3d Population projections by the Office for National Statistics
England, PERSONS, thousands

Projected populations at mid-years by age last birthday

Ages	2101	2102	2103	2104	2105	2106	2107	2108	2109	2110	2111	2112	2113	2114	2115	2116	2117	2118	2119	2120
Thousands																				
0-14	8,506	8,494	8,485	8,479	8,476	8,475	8,477	8,480	8,484	8,489	8,494	8,499	8,504	8,507	8,510	8,511	8,511	8,508	8,504	8,498
15-29	9,866	9,858	9,846	9,830	9,811	9,789	9,765	9,739	9,713	9,687	9,662	9,637	9,615	9,595	9,577	9,562	9,551	9,542	9,536	9,533
30-44	10,372	10,374	10,380	10,391	10,406	10,423	10,441	10,461	10,479	10,497	10,512	10,524	10,533	10,538	10,538	10,535	10,527	10,516	10,500	10,481
45-59	10,976	10,940	10,897	10,849	10,797	10,745	10,693	10,643	10,596	10,555	10,520	10,490	10,468	10,452	10,443	10,440	10,443	10,451	10,463	10,479
60-74	10,291	10,332	10,379	10,429	10,482	10,534	10,584	10,631	10,673	10,708	10,736	10,754	10,761	10,757	10,744	10,721	10,691	10,654	10,612	10,567
75 & over	11,945	11,956	11,963	11,966	11,967	11,967	11,966	11,966	11,967	11,972	11,981	11,999	12,025	12,060	12,105	12,158	12,220	12,289	12,364	12,443
All ages	61,956	61,954	61,950	61,945	61,939	61,932	61,925	61,918	61,912	61,907	61,904	61,903	61,905	61,909	61,917	61,928	61,943	61,960	61,980	62,002
Percentages																				
0-14	13.7	13.7	13.7	13.7	13.7	13.7	13.7	13.7	13.7	13.7	13.7	13.7	13.7	13.7	13.7	13.7	13.7	13.7	13.7	13.7
15-29	15.9	15.9	15.9	15.9	15.8	15.8	15.8	15.7	15.7	15.6	15.6	15.6	15.5	15.5	15.5	15.4	15.4	15.4	15.4	15.4
30-44	16.7	16.7	16.8	16.8	16.8	16.8	16.9	16.9	16.9	17.0	17.0	17.0	17.0	17.0	17.0	17.0	17.0	17.0	16.9	16.9
45-59	17.7	17.7	17.6	17.5	17.4	17.3	17.3	17.2	17.1	17.0	17.0	16.9	16.9	16.9	16.9	16.9	16.9	16.9	16.9	16.9
60-74	16.6	16.7	16.8	16.8	16.9	17.0	17.1	17.2	17.2	17.3	17.3	17.4	17.4	17.4	17.4	17.3	17.3	17.2	17.1	17.0
75 & over	19.3	19.3	19.3	19.3	19.3	19.3	19.3	19.3	19.3	19.3	19.4	19.4	19.4	19.5	19.6	19.6	19.7	19.8	19.9	20.1
All ages	100.0	100.0	100.0	100.0	100.0	100.0	100.0	100.0	100.0	100.0	100.0	100.0	100.0	100.0	100.0	100.0	100.0	100.0	100.0	100.0
Mean age	47.9	47.9	48.0	48.0	48.0	48.0	48.1	48.1	48.1	48.1	48.2	48.2	48.2	48.2	48.2	48.3	48.3	48.3	48.4	48.4
Median age	48.1	48.2	48.2	48.3	48.3	48.3	48.3	48.3	48.3	48.3	48.3	48.3	48.3	48.3	48.3	48.4	48.4	48.4	48.5	48.5

Source: Office for National Statistics

Note: Figures may not add exactly due to rounding.

504

15.3d Population projections by the Office for National Statistics
England, MALES, thousands

Projected populations at mid-years by age last birthday

Ages	2020	2021	2022	2023	2024	2025	2026	2027	2028	2029	2030	2031	2032	2033	2034	2035	2036	2037	2038	2039	2040
Thousands																					
0-14	5,239	5,220	5,189	5,143	5,099	5,048	4,988	4,917	4,853	4,796	4,739	4,679	4,627	4,583	4,550	4,528	4,522	4,523	4,529	4,536	4,547
15-29	5,318	5,316	5,331	5,362	5,387	5,425	5,464	5,509	5,551	5,589	5,633	5,689	5,745	5,786	5,810	5,816	5,794	5,760	5,712	5,667	5,615
30-44	5,500	5,563	5,621	5,667	5,693	5,699	5,710	5,727	5,735	5,744	5,735	5,717	5,698	5,673	5,657	5,639	5,629	5,636	5,662	5,683	5,718
45-59	5,567	5,538	5,494	5,449	5,419	5,399	5,379	5,354	5,336	5,317	5,317	5,309	5,303	5,325	5,359	5,407	5,467	5,522	5,565	5,590	5,596
60-74	4,260	4,320	4,327	4,371	4,440	4,520	4,603	4,691	4,764	4,836	4,900	4,963	5,009	5,031	5,034	5,028	5,005	4,968	4,932	4,911	4,900
75 & over	2,100	2,157	2,277	2,370	2,442	2,502	2,551	2,594	2,640	2,683	2,722	2,766	2,814	2,868	2,923	2,979	3,044	3,115	3,188	3,265	3,342
All ages	27,983	28,114	28,237	28,362	28,481	28,592	28,696	28,791	28,881	28,966	29,047	29,123	29,196	29,266	29,332	29,397	29,460	29,524	29,587	29,652	29,717
Percentages																					
0-14	18.7	18.6	18.4	18.1	17.9	17.7	17.4	17.1	16.8	16.6	16.3	16.1	15.8	15.7	15.5	15.4	15.3	15.3	15.3	15.3	15.3
15-29	19.0	18.9	18.9	18.9	18.9	19.0	19.0	19.1	19.2	19.3	19.4	19.5	19.7	19.8	19.8	19.8	19.7	19.5	19.3	19.1	18.9
30-44	19.7	19.8	19.9	20.0	20.0	19.9	19.9	19.9	19.9	19.8	19.7	19.6	19.5	19.4	19.3	19.2	19.1	19.1	19.1	19.2	19.2
45-59	19.9	19.7	19.5	19.2	19.0	18.9	18.7	18.6	18.5	18.4	18.3	18.2	18.2	18.2	18.3	18.4	18.6	18.7	18.8	18.9	18.8
60-74	15.2	15.4	15.3	15.4	15.6	15.8	16.0	16.3	16.5	16.7	16.9	17.0	17.2	17.2	17.2	17.1	17.0	16.8	16.7	16.6	16.5
75 & over	7.5	7.7	8.1	8.4	8.6	8.7	8.9	9.0	9.1	9.3	9.4	9.5	9.6	9.8	10.0	10.1	10.3	10.5	10.8	11.0	11.2
All ages	100.0	100.0	100.0	100.0	100.0	100.0	100.0	100.0	100.0	100.0	100.0	100.0	100.0	100.0	100.0	100.0	100.0	100.0	100.0	100.0	100.0
Mean age	39.9	40.1	40.2	40.4	40.6	40.8	41.0	41.1	41.3	41.5	41.6	41.8	41.9	42.1	42.2	42.4	42.5	42.6	42.7	42.8	42.9
Median age	39.1	39.2	39.4	39.6	39.7	39.9	40.1	40.3	40.4	40.6	40.8	41.0	41.2	41.4	41.5	41.7	41.8	42.0	42.1	42.2	42.3

Ages	2041	2042	2043	2044	2045	2046	2047	2048	2049	2050	2051	2052	2053	2054	2055	2056	2057	2058	2059	2060
Thousands																				
0-14	4,562	4,580	4,600	4,624	4,648	4,672	4,695	4,717	4,736	4,752	4,764	4,770	4,770	4,765	4,754	4,738	4,718	4,694	4,667	4,639
15-29	5,555	5,485	5,422	5,365	5,309	5,249	5,198	5,154	5,121	5,099	5,094	5,095	5,100	5,108	5,119	5,134	5,152	5,173	5,196	5,220
30-44	5,756	5,801	5,845	5,883	5,928	5,984	6,039	6,081	6,104	6,111	6,089	6,056	6,008	5,963	5,912	5,853	5,784	5,722	5,667	5,611
45-59	5,608	5,625	5,634	5,644	5,637	5,620	5,603	5,580	5,566	5,551	5,543	5,553	5,580	5,603	5,640	5,679	5,725	5,769	5,808	5,854
60-74	4,889	4,874	4,866	4,856	4,863	4,864	4,866	4,893	4,930	4,978	5,037	5,090	5,134	5,161	5,170	5,187	5,207	5,220	5,233	5,230
75 & over	3,414	3,486	3,549	3,611	3,663	3,721	3,769	3,804	3,825	3,841	3,851	3,857	3,866	3,891	3,926	3,959	3,987	4,017	4,045	4,081
All ages	29,783	29,850	29,916	29,982	30,047	30,110	30,171	30,228	30,282	30,332	30,378	30,420	30,458	30,491	30,521	30,548	30,573	30,595	30,615	30,635
Percentages																				
0-14	15.3	15.3	15.4	15.4	15.5	15.5	15.6	15.6	15.6	15.7	15.7	15.7	15.7	15.6	15.6	15.5	15.4	15.3	15.2	15.1
15-29	18.7	18.4	18.1	17.9	17.7	17.4	17.2	17.1	16.9	16.8	16.8	16.7	16.7	16.8	16.8	16.8	16.9	16.9	17.0	17.0
30-44	19.3	19.4	19.5	19.6	19.7	19.9	20.0	20.1	20.2	20.1	20.0	19.9	19.7	19.6	19.4	19.2	18.9	18.7	18.5	18.3
45-59	18.8	18.8	18.8	18.8	18.8	18.7	18.6	18.5	18.4	18.3	18.2	18.3	18.3	18.4	18.5	18.6	18.7	18.9	19.0	19.1
60-74	16.4	16.3	16.3	16.2	16.2	16.2	16.1	16.2	16.3	16.4	16.6	16.7	16.9	16.9	16.9	17.0	17.0	17.1	17.1	17.1
75 & over	11.5	11.7	11.9	12.0	12.2	12.4	12.5	12.6	12.6	12.7	12.7	12.7	12.7	12.8	12.9	13.0	13.0	13.1	13.2	13.3
All ages	100.0	100.0	100.0	100.0	100.0	100.0	100.0	100.0	100.0	100.0	100.0	100.0	100.0	100.0	100.0	100.0	100.0	100.0	100.0	100.0
Mean age	43.0	43.1	43.2	43.3	43.3	43.4	43.5	43.6	43.6	43.7	43.8	43.9	43.9	44.0	44.1	44.2	44.3	44.3	44.4	44.5
Median age	42.4	42.5	42.5	42.6	42.6	42.6	42.7	42.7	42.8	43.0	43.1	43.3	43.4	43.6	43.8	43.9	44.1	44.3	44.5	44.6

15.3d Population projections by the Office for National Statistics
England, MALES, thousands

Projected populations at mid-years by age last birthday

Ages	2061	2062	2063	2064	2065	2066	2067	2068	2069	2070	2071	2072	2073	2074	2075	2076	2077	2078	2079	2080
Thousands																				
0-14	4,610	4,581	4,554	4,528	4,505	4,485	4,469	4,456	4,446	4,440	4,438	4,438	4,441	4,447	4,454	4,462	4,471	4,481	4,490	4,499
15-29	5,244	5,268	5,289	5,309	5,325	5,337	5,343	5,343	5,338	5,328	5,312	5,292	5,269	5,242	5,214	5,186	5,157	5,130	5,105	5,082
30-44	5,553	5,502	5,460	5,428	5,407	5,402	5,403	5,410	5,418	5,429	5,444	5,463	5,484	5,507	5,532	5,556	5,580	5,602	5,622	5,638
45-59	5,910	5,965	6,007	6,031	6,038	6,018	5,986	5,941	5,899	5,851	5,795	5,729	5,671	5,618	5,566	5,511	5,463	5,424	5,394	5,376
60-74	5,218	5,206	5,189	5,181	5,173	5,172	5,188	5,219	5,246	5,286	5,329	5,378	5,425	5,467	5,514	5,570	5,624	5,665	5,690	5,699
75 & over	4,118	4,150	4,192	4,235	4,284	4,340	4,388	4,432	4,478	4,517	4,560	4,605	4,643	4,679	4,708	4,729	4,744	4,763	4,789	4,820
All ages	30,654	30,673	30,692	30,711	30,732	30,754	30,776	30,800	30,825	30,851	30,878	30,905	30,932	30,960	30,987	31,014	31,040	31,066	31,090	31,113
Percentages																				
0-14	15.0	14.9	14.8	14.7	14.7	14.6	14.5	14.5	14.4	14.4	14.4	14.4	14.4	14.4	14.4	14.4	14.4	14.4	14.4	14.5
15-29	17.1	17.2	17.2	17.3	17.3	17.4	17.4	17.3	17.3	17.3	17.2	17.1	17.0	16.9	16.8	16.7	16.6	16.5	16.4	16.3
30-44	18.1	17.9	17.8	17.7	17.6	17.6	17.6	17.6	17.6	17.6	17.6	17.7	17.7	17.8	17.9	17.9	18.0	18.0	18.1	18.1
45-59	19.3	19.4	19.6	19.6	19.6	19.6	19.4	19.3	19.1	19.0	18.8	18.5	18.3	18.1	18.0	17.8	17.6	17.5	17.4	17.3
60-74	17.0	17.0	16.9	16.9	16.8	16.8	16.9	16.9	17.0	17.1	17.3	17.4	17.5	17.7	17.8	18.0	18.1	18.2	18.3	18.3
75 & over	13.4	13.5	13.7	13.8	13.9	14.1	14.3	14.4	14.5	14.6	14.8	14.9	15.0	15.1	15.2	15.2	15.3	15.3	15.4	15.5
All ages	100.0	100.0	100.0	100.0	100.0	100.0	100.0	100.0	100.0	100.0	100.0	100.0	100.0	100.0	100.0	100.0	100.0	100.0	100.0	100.0
Mean age	44.6	44.7	44.8	44.9	45.0	45.0	45.1	45.2	45.3	45.4	45.5	45.5	45.6	45.7	45.7	45.8	45.9	45.9	46.0	46.1
Median age	44.8	45.0	45.1	45.2	45.3	45.4	45.5	45.5	45.6	45.6	45.7	45.7	45.8	45.8	45.8	45.8	45.9	45.9	45.9	45.9

Ages	2081	2082	2083	2084	2085	2086	2087	2088	2089	2090	2091	2092	2093	2094	2095	2096	2097	2098	2099	2100
Thousands																				
0-14	4,506	4,512	4,517	4,519	4,519	4,517	4,513	4,506	4,498	4,488	4,477	4,464	4,451	4,438	4,424	4,411	4,399	4,387	4,377	4,368
15-29	5,062	5,046	5,033	5,024	5,018	5,015	5,016	5,019	5,024	5,031	5,040	5,049	5,059	5,068	5,077	5,085	5,091	5,095	5,098	5,098
30-44	5,650	5,656	5,657	5,652	5,642	5,627	5,607	5,584	5,558	5,530	5,502	5,474	5,448	5,423	5,401	5,381	5,365	5,353	5,344	5,339
45-59	5,372	5,375	5,382	5,392	5,404	5,420	5,439	5,462	5,486	5,511	5,536	5,561	5,583	5,604	5,620	5,633	5,640	5,642	5,639	5,629
60-74	5,683	5,656	5,617	5,581	5,540	5,491	5,435	5,385	5,340	5,295	5,249	5,209	5,177	5,153	5,140	5,140	5,146	5,157	5,169	5,185
75 & over	4,862	4,911	4,969	5,025	5,086	5,152	5,226	5,292	5,352	5,410	5,471	5,525	5,571	5,609	5,637	5,654	5,667	5,677	5,688	5,698
All ages	31,135	31,155	31,174	31,192	31,208	31,222	31,236	31,247	31,258	31,267	31,275	31,283	31,289	31,295	31,300	31,304	31,308	31,312	31,314	31,317
Percentages																				
0-14	14.5	14.5	14.5	14.5	14.5	14.5	14.4	14.4	14.4	14.4	14.3	14.3	14.2	14.2	14.1	14.1	14.0	14.0	14.0	13.9
15-29	16.3	16.2	16.1	16.1	16.1	16.1	16.1	16.1	16.1	16.1	16.1	16.1	16.2	16.2	16.2	16.2	16.3	16.3	16.3	16.3
30-44	18.1	18.2	18.1	18.1	18.1	18.0	18.0	17.9	17.8	17.7	17.6	17.5	17.4	17.3	17.3	17.2	17.1	17.1	17.1	17.0
45-59	17.3	17.3	17.3	17.3	17.3	17.4	17.4	17.5	17.6	17.6	17.7	17.8	17.8	17.9	18.0	18.0	18.0	18.0	18.0	18.0
60-74	18.3	18.2	18.0	17.9	17.8	17.6	17.4	17.2	17.1	16.9	16.8	16.7	16.5	16.5	16.4	16.4	16.4	16.5	16.5	16.6
75 & over	15.6	15.8	15.9	16.1	16.3	16.5	16.7	16.9	17.1	17.3	17.5	17.7	17.8	17.9	18.0	18.1	18.1	18.1	18.2	18.2
All ages	100.0	100.0	100.0	100.0	100.0	100.0	100.0	100.0	100.0	100.0	100.0	100.0	100.0	100.0	100.0	100.0	100.0	100.0	100.0	100.0
Mean age	46.1	46.2	46.2	46.3	46.3	46.4	46.5	46.5	46.6	46.6	46.7	46.8	46.8	46.9	46.9	47.0	47.0	47.1	47.1	47.2
Median age	46.0	46.0	46.0	46.1	46.1	46.2	46.3	46.4	46.4	46.5	46.6	46.7	46.8	46.9	47.0	47.1	47.1	47.2	47.3	47.3

15.3d Population projections by the Office for National Statistics
England, MALES, thousands

2020-based
Principal projection

Projected populations at mid-years by age last birthday

Ages	2101	2102	2103	2104	2105	2106	2107	2108	2109	2110	2111	2112	2113	2114	2115	2116	2117	2118	2119	2120
Thousands																				
0-14	4,360	4,354	4,349	4,346	4,345	4,344	4,345	4,346	4,349	4,351	4,354	4,356	4,359	4,361	4,362	4,363	4,362	4,361	4,359	4,356
15-29	5,096	5,092	5,086	5,078	5,068	5,057	5,044	5,031	5,018	5,005	4,992	4,979	4,968	4,957	4,949	4,941	4,935	4,931	4,928	4,926
30-44	5,337	5,337	5,341	5,347	5,354	5,363	5,372	5,382	5,392	5,401	5,409	5,415	5,419	5,422	5,423	5,421	5,417	5,411	5,403	5,394
45-59	5,615	5,597	5,575	5,551	5,525	5,498	5,472	5,447	5,424	5,403	5,385	5,370	5,359	5,351	5,347	5,346	5,347	5,352	5,358	5,366
60-74	5,204	5,226	5,250	5,277	5,304	5,331	5,357	5,382	5,404	5,422	5,437	5,447	5,451	5,450	5,443	5,433	5,418	5,400	5,379	5,357
75 & over	5,707	5,713	5,719	5,722	5,725	5,727	5,729	5,732	5,735	5,741	5,749	5,761	5,778	5,800	5,825	5,856	5,890	5,928	5,968	6,011
All ages	31,318	31,319	31,320	31,320	31,320	31,320	31,320	31,320	31,321	31,322	31,325	31,329	31,334	31,341	31,349	31,359	31,370	31,382	31,396	31,410
Percentages																				
0-14	13.9	13.9	13.9	13.9	13.9	13.9	13.9	13.9	13.9	13.9	13.9	13.9	13.9	13.9	13.9	13.9	13.9	13.9	13.9	13.9
15-29	16.3	16.3	16.2	16.2	16.2	16.1	16.1	16.1	16.0	16.0	15.9	15.9	15.9	15.8	15.8	15.8	15.7	15.7	15.7	15.7
30-44	17.0	17.0	17.1	17.1	17.1	17.1	17.2	17.2	17.2	17.2	17.3	17.3	17.3	17.3	17.3	17.3	17.3	17.2	17.2	17.2
45-59	17.9	17.9	17.8	17.7	17.6	17.6	17.5	17.4	17.3	17.2	17.2	17.1	17.1	17.1	17.1	17.0	17.0	17.1	17.1	17.1
60-74	16.6	16.7	16.8	16.8	16.9	17.0	17.1	17.2	17.3	17.3	17.4	17.4	17.4	17.4	17.4	17.3	17.3	17.2	17.1	17.1
75 & over	18.2	18.2	18.3	18.3	18.3	18.3	18.3	18.3	18.3	18.3	18.4	18.4	18.4	18.5	18.6	18.7	18.8	18.9	19.0	19.1
All ages	100.0	100.0	100.0	100.0	100.0	100.0	100.0	100.0	100.0	100.0	100.0	100.0	100.0	100.0	100.0	100.0	100.0	100.0	100.0	100.0
Mean age	47.2	47.3	47.3	47.4	47.4	47.4	47.4	47.5	47.5	47.5	47.5	47.6	47.6	47.6	47.7	47.7	47.7	47.8	47.8	47.9
Median age	47.4	47.4	47.5	47.5	47.5	47.5	47.5	47.5	47.6	47.6	47.6	47.6	47.6	47.6	47.6	47.7	47.7	47.7	47.8	47.8

Note: Figures may not add exactly due to rounding.

Source: Office for National Statistics

15.3d Population projections by the Office for National Statistics
England, FEMALES, thousands

Projected populations at mid-years by age last birthday

Ages	2020	2021	2022	2023	2024	2025	2026	2027	2028	2029	2030	2031	2032	2033	2034	2035	2036	2037	2038	2039	2040
Thousands																					
0-14	4,976	4,957	4,928	4,884	4,843	4,794	4,736	4,669	4,609	4,555	4,502	4,446	4,398	4,357	4,327	4,308	4,302	4,303	4,308	4,315	4,326
15-29	5,042	5,030	5,027	5,047	5,066	5,096	5,131	5,170	5,209	5,244	5,287	5,337	5,389	5,428	5,448	5,453	5,431	5,399	5,354	5,310	5,261
30-44	5,540	5,593	5,648	5,684	5,695	5,682	5,669	5,660	5,643	5,625	5,592	5,553	5,504	5,454	5,420	5,393	5,373	5,363	5,379	5,393	5,421
45-59	5,709	5,680	5,632	5,581	5,546	5,524	5,503	5,483	5,467	5,448	5,445	5,433	5,436	5,461	5,492	5,529	5,579	5,632	5,666	5,675	5,662
60-74	4,535	4,603	4,612	4,659	4,733	4,817	4,908	4,999	5,080	5,159	5,231	5,304	5,353	5,377	5,382	5,374	5,348	5,305	5,259	5,231	5,216
75 & over	2,766	2,823	2,945	3,043	3,119	3,185	3,240	3,290	3,341	3,393	3,438	3,488	3,543	3,605	3,669	3,736	3,811	3,893	3,980	4,071	4,161
All ages	28,567	28,686	28,792	28,898	29,001	29,098	29,188	29,270	29,349	29,424	29,494	29,560	29,623	29,683	29,739	29,792	29,844	29,895	29,945	29,996	30,047
Percentages																					
0-14	17.4	17.3	17.1	16.9	16.7	16.5	16.2	16.0	15.7	15.5	15.3	15.0	14.8	14.7	14.6	14.5	14.4	14.4	14.4	14.4	14.4
15-29	17.7	17.5	17.5	17.5	17.5	17.5	17.6	17.7	17.7	17.8	17.9	18.1	18.2	18.3	18.3	18.3	18.2	18.1	17.9	17.7	17.5
30-44	19.4	19.5	19.6	19.7	19.6	19.5	19.4	19.3	19.2	19.1	19.0	18.8	18.6	18.4	18.2	18.1	18.0	17.9	18.0	18.0	18.0
45-59	20.0	19.8	19.6	19.3	19.1	19.0	18.9	18.7	18.6	18.5	18.5	18.4	18.4	18.4	18.5	18.6	18.7	18.8	18.9	18.9	18.8
60-74	15.9	16.0	16.0	16.1	16.3	16.6	16.8	17.1	17.3	17.5	17.7	17.9	18.1	18.1	18.1	18.0	17.9	17.7	17.6	17.4	17.4
75 & over	9.7	9.8	10.2	10.5	10.8	10.9	11.1	11.2	11.4	11.5	11.7	11.8	12.0	12.1	12.3	12.5	12.8	13.0	13.3	13.6	13.8
All ages	100.0	100.0	100.0	100.0	100.0	100.0	100.0	100.0	100.0	100.0	100.0	100.0	100.0	100.0	100.0	100.0	100.0	100.0	100.0	100.0	100.0
Mean age	41.8	42.0	42.1	42.3	42.5	42.7	42.9	43.0	43.2	43.4	43.6	43.7	43.9	44.1	44.2	44.4	44.5	44.6	44.8	44.9	45.0
Median age	41.3	41.5	41.7	41.9	42.1	42.3	42.5	42.7	42.9	43.1	43.3	43.6	43.8	44.0	44.1	44.3	44.5	44.7	44.8	44.9	45.0

Ages	2041	2042	2043	2044	2045	2046	2047	2048	2049	2050	2051	2052	2053	2054	2055	2056	2057	2058	2059	2060
Thousands																				
0-14	4,339	4,357	4,376	4,398	4,421	4,444	4,467	4,487	4,505	4,521	4,532	4,537	4,538	4,533	4,522	4,507	4,488	4,465	4,439	4,412
15-29	5,203	5,136	5,077	5,024	4,971	4,915	4,867	4,826	4,796	4,777	4,771	4,772	4,777	4,785	4,795	4,809	4,826	4,846	4,868	4,891
30-44	5,455	5,495	5,534	5,570	5,613	5,663	5,715	5,754	5,773	5,778	5,756	5,724	5,679	5,636	5,587	5,530	5,464	5,405	5,352	5,300
45-59	5,650	5,642	5,626	5,609	5,577	5,540	5,493	5,445	5,413	5,388	5,370	5,362	5,379	5,395	5,424	5,458	5,499	5,538	5,575	5,618
60-74	5,202	5,188	5,179	5,167	5,170	5,164	5,173	5,201	5,234	5,272	5,322	5,373	5,406	5,418	5,408	5,400	5,396	5,384	5,371	5,343
75 & over	4,248	4,329	4,405	4,479	4,542	4,613	4,668	4,708	4,734	4,753	4,765	4,769	4,776	4,802	4,840	4,877	4,910	4,943	4,973	5,009
All ages	30,097	30,147	30,197	30,246	30,294	30,339	30,382	30,421	30,457	30,488	30,515	30,537	30,555	30,567	30,576	30,581	30,582	30,581	30,578	30,574
Percentages																				
0-14	14.4	14.5	14.5	14.5	14.6	14.6	14.7	14.8	14.8	14.8	14.9	14.9	14.9	14.8	14.8	14.7	14.7	14.6	14.5	14.4
15-29	17.3	17.0	16.8	16.6	16.4	16.2	16.0	15.9	15.7	15.7	15.6	15.6	15.6	15.7	15.7	15.7	15.8	15.8	15.9	16.0
30-44	18.1	18.2	18.3	18.4	18.5	18.7	18.8	18.9	19.0	18.9	18.9	18.7	18.6	18.4	18.3	18.1	17.9	17.7	17.5	17.3
45-59	18.8	18.7	18.6	18.5	18.4	18.3	18.1	17.9	17.8	17.7	17.6	17.6	17.6	17.6	17.7	17.8	18.0	18.1	18.2	18.4
60-74	17.3	17.2	17.2	17.1	17.1	17.0	17.0	17.1	17.2	17.3	17.4	17.6	17.7	17.7	17.7	17.7	17.6	17.6	17.6	17.5
75 & over	14.1	14.4	14.6	14.8	15.0	15.2	15.4	15.5	15.5	15.6	15.6	15.6	15.6	15.7	15.8	15.9	16.1	16.2	16.3	16.4
All ages	100.0	100.0	100.0	100.0	100.0	100.0	100.0	100.0	100.0	100.0	100.0	100.0	100.0	100.0	100.0	100.0	100.0	100.0	100.0	100.0
Mean age	45.1	45.2	45.2	45.3	45.4	45.5	45.5	45.6	45.7	45.8	45.8	45.9	46.0	46.0	46.1	46.2	46.2	46.3	46.4	46.4
Median age	45.1	45.2	45.3	45.4	45.4	45.4	45.4	45.4	45.4	45.5	45.5	45.6	45.7	45.9	46.0	46.1	46.3	46.4	46.6	46.7

15.3d Population projections by the Office for National Statistics
England, FEMALES, thousands

2020-based
Principal projection

Projected populations at mid-years by age last birthday

Ages	2061	2062	2063	2064	2065	2066	2067	2068	2069	2070	2071	2072	2073	2074	2075	2076	2077	2078	2079	2080
Thousands																				
0-14	4,385	4,358	4,331	4,307	4,285	4,266	4,250	4,238	4,229	4,223	4,221	4,221	4,224	4,229	4,236	4,244	4,253	4,262	4,271	4,279
15-29	4,914	4,936	4,957	4,975	4,991	5,002	5,008	5,008	5,003	4,993	4,978	4,959	4,936	4,911	4,884	4,857	4,830	4,804	4,779	4,758
30-44	5,246	5,198	5,159	5,129	5,110	5,105	5,106	5,112	5,119	5,130	5,144	5,162	5,182	5,204	5,227	5,250	5,273	5,293	5,312	5,327
45-59	5,668	5,720	5,759	5,778	5,783	5,763	5,732	5,689	5,648	5,600	5,546	5,482	5,426	5,375	5,325	5,272	5,227	5,189	5,161	5,143
60-74	5,311	5,270	5,228	5,202	5,181	5,169	5,166	5,187	5,206	5,237	5,274	5,317	5,358	5,396	5,441	5,491	5,542	5,581	5,601	5,608
75 & over	5,045	5,082	5,125	5,162	5,200	5,245	5,287	5,318	5,349	5,375	5,402	5,432	5,454	5,473	5,484	5,491	5,489	5,492	5,503	5,519
All ages	30,569	30,563	30,558	30,554	30,551	30,549	30,549	30,551	30,554	30,559	30,565	30,572	30,580	30,589	30,597	30,605	30,613	30,621	30,628	30,633
Percentages																				
0-14	14.3	14.3	14.2	14.1	14.0	14.0	13.9	13.9	13.8	13.8	13.8	13.8	13.8	13.8	13.8	13.9	13.9	13.9	13.9	14.0
15-29	16.1	16.2	16.2	16.3	16.3	16.4	16.4	16.4	16.4	16.3	16.3	16.2	16.1	16.1	16.0	15.9	15.8	15.7	15.6	15.5
30-44	17.2	17.0	16.9	16.8	16.7	16.7	16.7	16.7	16.8	16.8	16.8	16.9	16.9	17.0	17.1	17.2	17.2	17.3	17.3	17.4
45-59	18.5	18.7	18.8	18.9	18.9	18.9	18.8	18.6	18.5	18.3	18.1	17.9	17.7	17.6	17.4	17.2	17.1	16.9	16.9	16.8
60-74	17.4	17.2	17.1	17.0	17.0	16.9	16.9	17.0	17.0	17.1	17.3	17.4	17.5	17.6	17.8	17.9	18.1	18.2	18.3	18.3
75 & over	16.5	16.6	16.8	16.9	17.0	17.2	17.3	17.4	17.5	17.6	17.7	17.8	17.8	17.9	17.9	17.9	17.9	17.9	18.0	18.0
All ages	100.0	100.0	100.0	100.0	100.0	100.0	100.0	100.0	100.0	100.0	100.0	100.0	100.0	100.0	100.0	100.0	100.0	100.0	100.0	100.0
Mean age	46.5	46.6	46.6	46.7	46.8	46.8	46.9	47.0	47.0	47.1	47.1	47.2	47.3	47.3	47.4	47.4	47.4	47.5	47.5	47.6
Median age	46.9	47.0	47.2	47.3	47.4	47.5	47.6	47.7	47.7	47.7	47.7	47.8	47.8	47.8	47.8	47.8	47.8	47.8	47.8	47.8

Ages	2081	2082	2083	2084	2085	2086	2087	2088	2089	2090	2091	2092	2093	2094	2095	2096	2097	2098	2099	2100
Thousands																				
0-14	4,286	4,292	4,296	4,298	4,298	4,296	4,292	4,286	4,278	4,268	4,258	4,246	4,233	4,220	4,207	4,195	4,183	4,172	4,162	4,153
15-29	4,739	4,723	4,711	4,702	4,696	4,694	4,694	4,697	4,702	4,709	4,717	4,726	4,735	4,744	4,752	4,759	4,765	4,769	4,772	4,772
30-44	5,338	5,345	5,345	5,340	5,330	5,315	5,296	5,274	5,249	5,223	5,196	5,169	5,143	5,119	5,098	5,079	5,064	5,052	5,043	5,038
45-59	5,139	5,141	5,147	5,156	5,167	5,182	5,200	5,220	5,243	5,267	5,290	5,313	5,334	5,353	5,369	5,380	5,387	5,388	5,384	5,375
60-74	5,589	5,563	5,523	5,486	5,444	5,394	5,336	5,286	5,240	5,195	5,148	5,107	5,074	5,051	5,036	5,035	5,039	5,047	5,057	5,071
75 & over	5,546	5,580	5,624	5,667	5,715	5,770	5,834	5,889	5,940	5,990	6,043	6,090	6,130	6,162	6,186	6,199	6,209	6,216	6,225	6,232
All ages	30,638	30,642	30,646	30,648	30,650	30,651	30,652	30,652	30,652	30,652	30,651	30,651	30,650	30,649	30,648	30,647	30,646	30,645	30,643	30,641
Percentages																				
0-14	14.0	14.0	14.0	14.0	14.0	14.0	14.0	14.0	14.0	13.9	13.9	13.9	13.8	13.8	13.8	13.7	13.6	13.6	13.6	13.6
15-29	15.5	15.4	15.4	15.3	15.3	15.3	15.3	15.3	15.3	15.4	15.4	15.4	15.4	15.5	15.5	15.5	15.5	15.6	15.6	15.6
30-44	17.4	17.4	17.4	17.4	17.4	17.3	17.3	17.2	17.1	17.0	17.0	16.9	16.8	16.7	16.6	16.6	16.5	16.5	16.5	16.4
45-59	16.8	16.8	16.8	16.8	16.9	16.9	17.0	17.0	17.1	17.2	17.3	17.3	17.4	17.5	17.5	17.6	17.6	17.6	17.6	17.5
60-74	18.2	18.2	18.0	17.9	17.8	17.6	17.4	17.2	17.1	16.9	16.8	16.7	16.6	16.5	16.4	16.4	16.4	16.5	16.5	16.5
75 & over	18.1	18.2	18.4	18.5	18.6	18.8	19.0	19.2	19.4	19.5	19.7	19.9	20.0	20.1	20.2	20.2	20.3	20.3	20.3	20.3
All ages	100.0	100.0	100.0	100.0	100.0	100.0	100.0	100.0	100.0	100.0	100.0	100.0	100.0	100.0	100.0	100.0	100.0	100.0	100.0	100.0
Mean age	47.6	47.6	47.7	47.7	47.8	47.8	47.8	47.9	47.9	48.0	48.0	48.1	48.1	48.2	48.2	48.3	48.3	48.4	48.4	48.5
Median age	47.8	47.8	47.8	47.8	47.8	47.9	47.9	48.0	48.0	48.1	48.2	48.3	48.3	48.4	48.5	48.6	48.7	48.8	48.8	48.9

15.3d Population projections by the Office for National Statistics
England, FEMALES, thousands

2020-based
Principal projection

Projected populations at mid-years by age last birthday

Ages	2101	2102	2103	2104	2105	2106	2107	2108	2109	2110	2111	2112	2113	2114	2115	2116	2117	2118	2119	2120
Thousands																				
0-14	4,146	4,140	4,136	4,133	4,131	4,131	4,132	4,133	4,135	4,137	4,140	4,143	4,145	4,147	4,148	4,148	4,148	4,147	4,145	4,142
15-29	4,770	4,766	4,760	4,752	4,743	4,732	4,720	4,708	4,695	4,682	4,670	4,658	4,647	4,637	4,629	4,621	4,616	4,611	4,609	4,607
30-44	5,036	5,036	5,040	5,045	5,052	5,060	5,069	5,078	5,087	5,096	5,103	5,109	5,113	5,116	5,116	5,114	5,110	5,105	5,097	5,088
45-59	5,361	5,343	5,322	5,298	5,272	5,246	5,220	5,196	5,173	5,152	5,135	5,120	5,109	5,101	5,096	5,095	5,096	5,099	5,105	5,113
60-74	5,087	5,107	5,129	5,153	5,178	5,203	5,227	5,249	5,269	5,286	5,299	5,307	5,310	5,308	5,300	5,288	5,273	5,254	5,233	5,210
75 & over	6,238	6,242	6,244	6,244	6,243	6,240	6,237	6,234	6,232	6,231	6,232	6,237	6,247	6,261	6,279	6,303	6,330	6,361	6,395	6,432
All ages	30,638	30,634	30,630	30,625	30,619	30,612	30,606	30,598	30,592	30,585	30,579	30,574	30,571	30,569	30,568	30,570	30,573	30,577	30,584	30,591
Percentages																				
0-14	13.5	13.5	13.5	13.5	13.5	13.5	13.5	13.5	13.5	13.5	13.5	13.5	13.6	13.6	13.6	13.6	13.6	13.6	13.6	13.5
15-29	15.6	15.6	15.5	15.5	15.5	15.5	15.4	15.4	15.3	15.3	15.3	15.2	15.2	15.2	15.1	15.1	15.1	15.1	15.1	15.1
30-44	16.4	16.4	16.5	16.5	16.5	16.5	16.6	16.6	16.6	16.7	16.7	16.7	16.7	16.7	16.7	16.7	16.7	16.7	16.7	16.6
45-59	17.5	17.4	17.4	17.3	17.2	17.1	17.1	17.0	16.9	16.8	16.8	16.7	16.7	16.7	16.7	16.7	16.7	16.7	16.7	16.7
60-74	16.6	16.7	16.7	16.8	16.9	17.0	17.1	17.2	17.2	17.3	17.3	17.4	17.4	17.4	17.3	17.3	17.2	17.2	17.1	17.0
75 & over	20.4	20.4	20.4	20.4	20.4	20.4	20.4	20.4	20.4	20.4	20.4	20.4	20.4	20.5	20.5	20.6	20.7	20.8	20.9	21.0
All ages	100.0	100.0	100.0	100.0	100.0	100.0	100.0	100.0	100.0	100.0	100.0	100.0	100.0	100.0	100.0	100.0	100.0	100.0	100.0	100.0
Mean age	48.5	48.6	48.6	48.6	48.7	48.7	48.7	48.7	48.7	48.8	48.8	48.8	48.8	48.8	48.8	48.9	48.9	48.9	49.0	49.0
Median age	48.9	49.0	49.0	49.1	49.1	49.1	49.1	49.1	49.1	49.1	49.1	49.1	49.1	49.1	49.1	49.1	49.1	49.2	49.2	49.2

Source: Office for National Statistics

Note: Figures may not add exactly due to rounding.

15.3d Population projections by the Office for National Statistics
Wales, PERSONS, thousands

Projected populations at mid-years by age last birthday

Ages	2020	2021	2022	2023	2024	2025	2026	2027	2028	2029	2030	2031	2032	2033	2034	2035	2036	2037	2038	2039	2040
Thousands																					
0-14	528	523	518	511	505	498	491	484	478	472	467	462	457	453	451	450	451	451	452	452	453
15-29	588	588	588	589	589	592	595	597	598	598	598	599	601	603	603	600	594	589	581	575	568
30-44	555	567	579	590	599	602	607	613	619	625	629	633	633	631	629	627	625	624	624	624	626
45-59	632	623	614	603	595	588	582	576	571	565	562	559	558	561	567	575	587	598	609	618	623
60-74	559	566	565	568	574	582	589	597	603	609	615	621	624	623	619	614	606	596	586	578	572
75 & over	307	313	327	338	347	355	361	366	371	376	380	384	390	395	401	408	415	423	430	439	448
All ages	3,170	3,180	3,190	3,200	3,208	3,217	3,225	3,232	3,239	3,245	3,251	3,257	3,262	3,267	3,271	3,274	3,278	3,281	3,284	3,287	3,290
Percentages																					
0-14	16.7	16.4	16.2	16.0	15.7	15.5	15.2	15.0	14.7	14.6	14.4	14.2	14.0	13.9	13.8	13.7	13.8	13.8	13.8	13.8	13.8
15-29	18.6	18.5	18.4	18.4	18.4	18.4	18.5	18.5	18.5	18.4	18.4	18.4	18.4	18.5	18.4	18.3	18.1	17.9	17.7	17.5	17.3
30-44	17.5	17.8	18.1	18.4	18.7	18.7	18.8	19.0	19.1	19.3	19.3	19.4	19.4	19.3	19.2	19.2	19.1	19.0	19.0	19.0	19.0
45-59	19.9	19.6	19.2	18.9	18.5	18.3	18.1	17.8	17.6	17.4	17.3	17.2	17.1	17.2	17.3	17.6	17.9	18.2	18.6	18.8	18.9
60-74	17.6	17.8	17.7	17.7	17.9	18.1	18.3	18.5	18.6	18.8	18.9	19.1	19.1	19.1	18.9	18.7	18.5	18.2	17.9	17.6	17.4
75 & over	9.7	9.8	10.2	10.6	10.8	11.0	11.2	11.3	11.5	11.6	11.7	11.8	11.9	12.1	12.3	12.4	12.6	12.9	13.1	13.4	13.6
All ages	100.0	100.0	100.0	100.0	100.0	100.0	100.0	100.0	100.0	100.0	100.0	100.0	100.0	100.0	100.0	100.0	100.0	100.0	100.0	100.0	100.0
Mean age	42.4	42.6	42.7	42.9	43.0	43.2	43.4	43.5	43.7	43.8	43.9	44.1	44.2	44.3	44.5	44.6	44.7	44.8	44.9	45.0	45.1
Median age	42.4	42.4	42.5	42.6	42.7	42.8	42.8	42.9	43.0	43.1	43.3	43.4	43.5	43.7	43.9	44.1	44.3	44.5	44.6	44.8	44.9

Ages	2041	2042	2043	2044	2045	2046	2047	2048	2049	2050	2051	2052	2053	2054	2055	2056	2057	2058	2059	2060
Thousands																				
0-14	453	454	454	455	455	455	455	455	455	454	453	452	450	447	445	442	439	436	433	429
15-29	560	552	546	540	535	530	525	522	519	518	519	520	520	521	521	522	522	523	523	524
30-44	629	631	631	631	631	632	634	636	636	634	629	623	616	610	603	595	588	582	577	571
45-59	627	634	640	646	651	654	655	653	652	650	648	647	647	647	650	653	655	656	656	656
60-74	568	562	558	553	552	550	550	554	561	570	582	594	605	614	619	625	632	638	645	650
75 & over	455	462	469	475	480	485	489	490	490	488	485	482	478	478	479	481	481	483	484	487
All ages	3,292	3,295	3,298	3,301	3,303	3,306	3,308	3,311	3,312	3,314	3,315	3,316	3,317	3,317	3,317	3,317	3,317	3,317	3,317	3,317
Percentages																				
0-14	13.8	13.8	13.8	13.8	13.8	13.8	13.8	13.7	13.7	13.7	13.7	13.6	13.6	13.5	13.4	13.3	13.2	13.1	13.0	12.9
15-29	17.0	16.8	16.6	16.4	16.2	16.0	15.9	15.8	15.7	15.6	15.7	15.7	15.7	15.7	15.7	15.7	15.7	15.8	15.8	15.8
30-44	19.1	19.1	19.1	19.1	19.1	19.1	19.2	19.2	19.2	19.1	19.0	18.8	18.6	18.4	18.2	17.9	17.7	17.5	17.4	17.2
45-59	19.1	19.2	19.4	19.6	19.7	19.8	19.8	19.7	19.7	19.6	19.5	19.5	19.5	19.5	19.6	19.7	19.7	19.8	19.8	19.8
60-74	17.2	17.1	16.9	16.8	16.7	16.6	16.6	16.7	16.9	17.2	17.5	17.9	18.2	18.5	18.7	18.8	19.0	19.2	19.4	19.6
75 & over	13.8	14.0	14.2	14.4	14.5	14.7	14.8	14.8	14.8	14.7	14.6	14.5	14.4	14.4	14.4	14.5	14.5	14.5	14.6	14.7
All ages	100.0	100.0	100.0	100.0	100.0	100.0	100.0	100.0	100.0	100.0	100.0	100.0	100.0	100.0	100.0	100.0	100.0	100.0	100.0	100.0
Mean age	45.2	45.3	45.3	45.4	45.5	45.6	45.7	45.8	45.8	45.9	46.0	46.1	46.2	46.3	46.4	46.5	46.6	46.7	46.8	46.9
Median age	45.1	45.2	45.4	45.6	45.7	45.8	46.0	46.1	46.1	46.2	46.3	46.5	46.6	46.8	47.0	47.2	47.4	47.6	47.8	48.1

15.3d Population projections by the Office for National Statistics
Wales, PERSONS, thousands

Principal projection

Projected populations at mid-years by age last birthday

Ages	2061	2062	2063	2064	2065	2066	2067	2068	2069	2070	2071	2072	2073	2074	2075	2076	2077	2078	2079	2080
Thousands																				
0-14	426	424	421	419	416	415	413	412	411	410	410	410	409	409	409	409	409	408	408	407
15-29	524	524	524	524	523	522	520	518	516	513	510	507	504	500	497	494	491	488	486	484
30-44	566	561	557	555	554	555	556	556	557	557	558	558	559	559	560	560	560	560	560	559
45-59	657	660	662	662	660	655	649	642	636	629	622	614	608	602	597	592	587	583	581	580
60-74	654	654	653	652	651	649	649	650	651	654	658	661	662	663	664	666	669	672	672	671
75 & over	490	494	499	506	513	522	532	541	550	557	564	572	581	588	596	602	606	609	612	616
All ages	3,317	3,317	3,317	3,317	3,318	3,318	3,319	3,320	3,320	3,321	3,322	3,322	3,323	3,323	3,323	3,322	3,322	3,320	3,319	3,317
Percentages																				
0-14	12.9	12.8	12.7	12.6	12.6	12.5	12.5	12.4	12.4	12.4	12.3	12.3	12.3	12.3	12.3	12.3	12.3	12.3	12.3	12.3
15-29	15.8	15.8	15.8	15.8	15.8	15.7	15.7	15.6	15.5	15.4	15.4	15.3	15.2	15.1	15.0	14.9	14.8	14.7	14.6	14.6
30-44	17.1	16.9	16.8	16.7	16.7	16.7	16.7	16.8	16.8	16.8	16.8	16.8	16.8	16.8	16.9	16.9	16.9	16.9	16.9	16.9
45-59	19.8	19.9	20.0	20.0	19.9	19.7	19.6	19.4	19.2	19.0	18.7	18.5	18.3	18.1	18.0	17.8	17.7	17.6	17.5	17.5
60-74	19.7	19.7	19.7	19.6	19.6	19.6	19.5	19.6	19.6	19.7	19.8	19.9	19.9	20.0	20.0	20.0	20.1	20.2	20.3	20.2
75 & over	14.8	14.9	15.0	15.2	15.5	15.7	16.0	16.3	16.6	16.8	17.0	17.2	17.5	17.7	17.9	18.1	18.2	18.3	18.4	18.6
All ages	100.0	100.0	100.0	100.0	100.0	100.0	100.0	100.0	100.0	100.0	100.0	100.0	100.0	100.0	100.0	100.0	100.0	100.0	100.0	100.0
Mean age	47.0	47.1	47.3	47.4	47.5	47.6	47.7	47.8	47.9	48.1	48.2	48.3	48.4	48.5	48.6	48.7	48.8	48.9	49.0	49.1
Median age	48.3	48.5	48.6	48.8	49.0	49.2	49.4	49.5	49.7	49.8	49.8	49.9	50.0	50.0	50.1	50.2	50.3	50.3	50.4	50.5

Ages	2081	2082	2083	2084	2085	2086	2087	2088	2089	2090	2091	2092	2093	2094	2095	2096	2097	2098	2099	2100
Thousands																				
0-14	407	406	405	404	403	401	400	398	397	395	393	392	390	388	387	385	384	383	382	381
15-29	482	480	479	478	478	477	477	477	476	476	476	476	476	475	475	474	473	472	471	470
30-44	558	557	555	553	550	547	544	541	538	534	531	528	526	523	521	519	518	517	516	515
45-59	581	582	582	583	584	584	585	586	587	587	588	588	588	588	587	586	585	583	581	578
60-74	665	660	653	647	641	633	626	620	615	610	605	601	598	596	595	596	598	599	600	601
75 & over	622	627	634	640	647	654	661	666	671	676	680	684	687	688	688	687	685	684	684	683
All ages	3,314	3,312	3,308	3,305	3,301	3,297	3,293	3,288	3,283	3,278	3,273	3,268	3,263	3,258	3,253	3,248	3,243	3,238	3,233	3,228
Percentages																				
0-14	12.3	12.3	12.2	12.2	12.2	12.2	12.1	12.1	12.1	12.0	12.0	12.0	12.0	11.9	11.9	11.9	11.8	11.8	11.8	11.8
15-29	14.5	14.5	14.5	14.5	14.5	14.5	14.5	14.5	14.5	14.5	14.5	14.6	14.6	14.6	14.6	14.6	14.6	14.6	14.6	14.5
30-44	16.8	16.8	16.8	16.7	16.7	16.6	16.5	16.4	16.4	16.3	16.2	16.2	16.1	16.1	16.0	16.0	16.0	16.0	16.0	16.0
45-59	17.5	17.6	17.6	17.6	17.7	17.7	17.8	17.8	17.9	17.9	18.0	18.0	18.0	18.0	18.0	18.0	18.0	18.0	18.0	17.9
60-74	20.1	19.9	19.7	19.6	19.4	19.2	19.0	18.9	18.7	18.6	18.5	18.4	18.3	18.3	18.3	18.4	18.4	18.5	18.6	18.6
75 & over	18.8	18.9	19.2	19.4	19.6	19.8	20.1	20.3	20.4	20.6	20.8	20.9	21.0	21.1	21.2	21.1	21.1	21.1	21.1	21.2
All ages	100.0	100.0	100.0	100.0	100.0	100.0	100.0	100.0	100.0	100.0	100.0	100.0	100.0	100.0	100.0	100.0	100.0	100.0	100.0	100.0
Mean age	49.2	49.2	49.3	49.4	49.5	49.5	49.6	49.6	49.7	49.8	49.8	49.9	49.9	50.0	50.0	50.1	50.1	50.1	50.2	50.2
Median age	50.5	50.6	50.6	50.7	50.7	50.8	50.8	50.9	50.9	51.0	51.1	51.1	51.2	51.3	51.4	51.4	51.5	51.6	51.6	51.7

15.3d Population projections by the Office for National Statistics
Wales, PERSONS, thousands

2020-based
Principal projection

Projected populations at mid-years by age last birthday

Ages	2101	2102	2103	2104	2105	2106	2107	2108	2109	2110	2111	2112	2113	2114	2115	2116	2117	2118	2119	2120
Thousands																				
0-14	380	379	379	378	377	377	376	376	376	375	374	374	373	373	372	371	370	369	368	368
15-29	468	467	465	463	462	460	458	456	455	453	452	450	449	448	447	446	445	445	444	444
30-44	515	514	514	514	514	514	514	513	513	512	512	511	510	509	508	506	505	503	502	500
45-59	575	572	569	566	563	559	556	554	551	549	547	546	545	544	543	543	543	543	542	542
60-74	602	603	604	605	606	607	608	608	608	608	607	606	605	603	600	598	595	592	588	585
75 & over	683	682	682	682	681	681	681	681	681	681	682	683	684	686	688	690	693	696	700	703
All ages	3,223	3,218	3,213	3,208	3,203	3,198	3,193	3,188	3,184	3,179	3,174	3,170	3,166	3,162	3,158	3,155	3,151	3,148	3,145	3,142
Percentages																				
0-14	11.8	11.8	11.8	11.8	11.8	11.8	11.8	11.8	11.8	11.8	11.8	11.8	11.8	11.8	11.8	11.8	11.8	11.7	11.7	11.7
15-29	14.5	14.5	14.5	14.4	14.4	14.4	14.3	14.3	14.3	14.3	14.2	14.2	14.2	14.2	14.2	14.1	14.1	14.1	14.1	14.1
30-44	16.0	16.0	16.0	16.0	16.0	16.1	16.1	16.1	16.1	16.1	16.1	16.1	16.1	16.1	16.1	16.0	16.0	16.0	16.0	15.9
45-59	17.9	17.8	17.7	17.6	17.6	17.5	17.4	17.4	17.3	17.3	17.2	17.2	17.2	17.2	17.2	17.2	17.2	17.2	17.2	17.3
60-74	18.7	18.7	18.8	18.9	18.9	19.0	19.0	19.1	19.1	19.1	19.1	19.1	19.1	19.1	19.0	18.9	18.9	18.8	18.7	18.6
75 & over	21.2	21.2	21.2	21.2	21.3	21.3	21.3	21.4	21.4	21.4	21.5	21.5	21.6	21.7	21.8	21.9	22.0	22.1	22.2	22.4
All ages	100.0	100.0	100.0	100.0	100.0	100.0	100.0	100.0	100.0	100.0	100.0	100.0	100.0	100.0	100.0	100.0	100.0	100.0	100.0	100.0
Mean age	50.3	50.3	50.3	50.4	50.4	50.4	50.4	50.5	50.5	50.5	50.5	50.6	50.6	50.6	50.7	50.7	50.7	50.8	50.8	50.9
Median age	51.8	51.8	51.8	51.9	51.9	51.9	52.0	52.0	52.0	52.0	52.0	52.0	52.0	52.1	52.1	52.1	52.2	52.2	52.2	52.3

Source: Office for National Statistics

Note: Figures may not add exactly due to rounding.

15.3d Population projections by the Office for National Statistics
Wales, MALES, thousands

Projected populations at mid-years by age last birthday

Ages	2020	2021	2022	2023	2024	2025	2026	2027	2028	2029	2030	2031	2032	2033	2034	2035	2036	2037	2038	2039	2040
Thousands																					
0-14	271	268	265	262	259	256	252	248	245	242	240	237	235	233	232	231	232	232	232	233	233
15-29	305	306	306	307	307	309	310	311	312	312	312	312	313	314	314	313	310	307	304	300	297
30-44	276	282	287	293	298	300	303	307	310	314	317	319	320	320	320	319	318	318	319	319	320
45-59	307	303	298	292	288	284	281	277	275	272	271	269	268	270	273	277	283	288	294	298	301
60-74	271	274	273	274	276	279	282	286	288	291	292	295	296	294	292	289	285	280	275	271	268
75 & over	133	136	143	149	153	157	160	162	164	166	168	170	172	174	177	179	182	186	189	193	196
All ages	1,564	1,569	1,573	1,578	1,581	1,585	1,588	1,591	1,594	1,597	1,600	1,602	1,604	1,606	1,607	1,609	1,610	1,611	1,613	1,614	1,615
Percentages																					
0-14	17.3	17.1	16.9	16.6	16.4	16.1	15.9	15.6	15.4	15.2	15.0	14.8	14.6	14.5	14.4	14.4	14.4	14.4	14.4	14.4	14.4
15-29	19.5	19.5	19.5	19.5	19.4	19.5	19.5	19.6	19.5	19.5	19.5	19.5	19.5	19.6	19.6	19.5	19.3	19.1	18.8	18.6	18.4
30-44	17.6	18.0	18.3	18.6	18.8	18.9	19.1	19.3	19.5	19.7	19.8	19.9	20.0	19.9	19.9	19.8	19.8	19.8	19.8	19.8	19.8
45-59	19.7	19.3	18.9	18.5	18.2	17.9	17.7	17.4	17.2	17.0	16.9	16.8	16.7	16.8	17.0	17.2	17.6	17.9	18.2	18.5	18.6
60-74	17.3	17.5	17.4	17.4	17.5	17.6	17.8	18.0	18.1	18.2	18.3	18.4	18.4	18.3	18.2	18.0	17.7	17.4	17.0	16.8	16.6
75 & over	8.5	8.7	9.1	9.4	9.7	9.9	10.0	10.2	10.3	10.4	10.5	10.6	10.7	10.9	11.0	11.1	11.3	11.5	11.7	11.9	12.2
All ages	100.0	100.0	100.0	100.0	100.0	100.0	100.0	100.0	100.0	100.0	100.0	100.0	100.0	100.0	100.0	100.0	100.0	100.0	100.0	100.0	100.0
Mean age	41.4	41.5	41.7	41.8	42.0	42.1	42.2	42.4	42.5	42.6	42.7	42.9	43.0	43.1	43.2	43.3	43.4	43.5	43.6	43.6	43.7
Median age	40.8	40.9	40.9	41.0	41.0	41.1	41.1	41.2	41.3	41.4	41.5	41.7	41.8	42.0	42.1	42.3	42.5	42.6	42.8	42.9	43.1

Ages	2041	2042	2043	2044	2045	2046	2047	2048	2049	2050	2051	2052	2053	2054	2055	2056	2057	2058	2059	2060
Thousands																				
0-14	233	233	234	234	234	234	234	234	234	233	233	232	231	230	229	227	226	224	222	221
15-29	292	289	285	282	280	277	275	273	272	271	272	272	272	273	273	273	273	274	274	274
30-44	322	322	323	323	323	323	324	325	325	324	321	319	315	312	309	305	301	298	295	293
45-59	304	308	312	315	318	321	322	322	322	321	321	321	322	322	323	325	326	326	327	327
60-74	265	262	260	258	257	256	256	258	261	266	272	277	283	288	291	295	299	303	306	310
75 & over	199	202	205	207	209	211	212	212	212	210	208	207	205	204	205	206	206	206	207	208
All ages	1,616	1,617	1,618	1,620	1,621	1,622	1,623	1,624	1,625	1,626	1,627	1,628	1,628	1,629	1,629	1,630	1,630	1,631	1,631	1,632
Percentages																				
0-14	14.4	14.4	14.4	14.4	14.4	14.4	14.4	14.4	14.4	14.4	14.3	14.3	14.2	14.1	14.0	13.9	13.8	13.7	13.6	13.5
15-29	18.1	17.8	17.6	17.4	17.3	17.1	16.9	16.8	16.7	16.7	16.7	16.7	16.7	16.7	16.7	16.8	16.8	16.8	16.8	16.8
30-44	19.9	19.9	19.9	19.9	19.9	19.9	20.0	20.0	20.0	19.9	19.7	19.6	19.3	19.1	18.9	18.7	18.5	18.3	18.1	17.9
45-59	18.8	19.1	19.3	19.5	19.6	19.8	19.8	19.8	19.8	19.8	19.7	19.7	19.8	19.8	19.8	19.9	20.0	20.0	20.0	20.0
60-74	16.4	16.2	16.1	15.9	15.9	15.8	15.8	15.9	16.1	16.3	16.7	17.0	17.4	17.7	17.9	18.1	18.3	18.6	18.8	19.0
75 & over	12.3	12.5	12.6	12.8	12.9	13.0	13.1	13.1	13.0	12.9	12.8	12.7	12.6	12.6	12.6	12.6	12.6	12.6	12.7	12.7
All ages	100.0	100.0	100.0	100.0	100.0	100.0	100.0	100.0	100.0	100.0	100.0	100.0	100.0	100.0	100.0	100.0	100.0	100.0	100.0	100.0
Mean age	43.8	43.9	43.9	44.0	44.1	44.2	44.2	44.3	44.4	44.5	44.6	44.7	44.7	44.8	44.9	45.0	45.2	45.3	45.4	45.5
Median age	43.2	43.4	43.5	43.7	43.8	43.9	43.9	44.0	44.1	44.3	44.4	44.6	44.8	45.0	45.2	45.4	45.7	45.9	46.1	46.3

15.3d Population projections by the Office for National Statistics
Wales, MALES, thousands

Projected populations at mid-years by age last birthday

Ages	2061	2062	2063	2064	2065	2066	2067	2068	2069	2070	2071	2072	2073	2074	2075	2076	2077	2078	2079	2080
Thousands																				
0-14	219	218	216	215	214	213	213	212	211	211	211	211	211	210	210	210	210	210	210	209
15-29	274	274	274	274	274	273	272	271	270	269	267	265	264	262	260	259	257	256	254	253
30-44	290	288	286	285	284	285	285	285	286	286	286	287	287	287	287	287	288	287	287	287
45-59	327	328	329	330	329	326	323	320	317	313	310	306	303	300	298	295	293	291	290	289
60-74	313	314	314	314	314	314	314	315	316	318	320	321	322	323	323	324	325	326	327	326
75 & over	210	211	214	217	221	226	230	234	239	243	247	252	256	260	264	268	270	272	274	276
All ages	1,632	1,633	1,634	1,635	1,635	1,636	1,637	1,638	1,639	1,640	1,641	1,641	1,642	1,642	1,643	1,643	1,643	1,643	1,642	1,642
Percentages																				
0-14	13.4	13.3	13.2	13.2	13.1	13.0	13.0	12.9	12.9	12.9	12.9	12.8	12.8	12.8	12.8	12.8	12.8	12.8	12.8	12.8
15-29	16.8	16.8	16.8	16.8	16.7	16.7	16.6	16.6	16.5	16.4	16.3	16.2	16.1	16.0	15.8	15.7	15.7	15.6	15.5	15.4
30-44	17.8	17.6	17.5	17.4	17.4	17.4	17.4	17.4	17.4	17.4	17.4	17.5	17.5	17.5	17.5	17.5	17.5	17.5	17.5	17.5
45-59	20.0	20.1	20.1	20.2	20.1	19.9	19.7	19.5	19.3	19.1	18.9	18.6	18.5	18.3	18.1	18.0	17.8	17.7	17.6	17.6
60-74	19.1	19.2	19.2	19.2	19.2	19.2	19.2	19.3	19.3	19.4	19.5	19.6	19.6	19.6	19.7	19.7	19.8	19.9	19.9	19.9
75 & over	12.8	12.9	13.1	13.3	13.5	13.8	14.0	14.3	14.6	14.8	15.1	15.3	15.6	15.8	16.1	16.3	16.4	16.6	16.7	16.8
All ages	100.0	100.0	100.0	100.0	100.0	100.0	100.0	100.0	100.0	100.0	100.0	100.0	100.0	100.0	100.0	100.0	100.0	100.0	100.0	100.0
Mean age	45.6	45.7	45.8	46.0	46.1	46.2	46.3	46.5	46.6	46.7	46.8	47.0	47.1	47.2	47.3	47.4	47.5	47.6	47.7	47.8
Median age	46.5	46.7	46.9	47.1	47.3	47.4	47.6	47.7	47.7	47.8	47.9	48.0	48.1	48.2	48.3	48.4	48.5	48.5	48.6	48.7

Ages	2081	2082	2083	2084	2085	2086	2087	2088	2089	2090	2091	2092	2093	2094	2095	2096	2097	2098	2099	2100
Thousands																				
0-14	209	209	208	208	207	206	206	205	204	203	202	201	201	200	199	198	198	197	196	196
15-29	252	252	251	251	250	250	250	250	250	250	249	249	249	249	249	248	248	247	247	246
30-44	286	286	285	284	282	281	279	278	276	274	273	271	270	269	268	267	266	265	265	265
45-59	290	290	291	291	291	292	292	293	293	293	294	294	294	294	293	293	292	291	290	289
60-74	324	321	318	315	312	308	305	302	300	297	295	293	292	291	291	291	292	293	293	294
75 & over	279	282	286	289	292	296	300	303	305	308	310	312	314	314	315	314	314	313	313	313
All ages	1,641	1,640	1,638	1,637	1,635	1,634	1,632	1,630	1,628	1,625	1,623	1,621	1,619	1,616	1,614	1,611	1,609	1,607	1,604	1,602
Percentages																				
0-14	12.7	12.7	12.7	12.7	12.7	12.6	12.6	12.6	12.5	12.5	12.5	12.4	12.4	12.4	12.3	12.3	12.3	12.3	12.2	12.2
15-29	15.4	15.3	15.3	15.3	15.3	15.3	15.3	15.3	15.3	15.4	15.4	15.4	15.4	15.4	15.4	15.4	15.4	15.4	15.4	15.4
30-44	17.5	17.4	17.4	17.3	17.3	17.2	17.1	17.0	17.0	16.9	16.8	16.7	16.7	16.6	16.6	16.5	16.5	16.5	16.5	16.5
45-59	17.7	17.7	17.7	17.8	17.8	17.9	17.9	18.0	18.0	18.0	18.1	18.1	18.2	18.2	18.2	18.2	18.2	18.1	18.1	18.0
60-74	19.7	19.6	19.4	19.2	19.1	18.9	18.7	18.5	18.4	18.3	18.2	18.1	18.0	18.0	18.0	18.1	18.1	18.2	18.3	18.3
75 & over	17.0	17.2	17.4	17.7	17.9	18.1	18.4	18.6	18.8	18.9	19.1	19.2	19.4	19.5	19.5	19.5	19.5	19.5	19.5	19.5
All ages	100.0	100.0	100.0	100.0	100.0	100.0	100.0	100.0	100.0	100.0	100.0	100.0	100.0	100.0	100.0	100.0	100.0	100.0	100.0	100.0
Mean age	47.9	48.0	48.1	48.2	48.2	48.3	48.4	48.4	48.5	48.6	48.6	48.7	48.7	48.8	48.8	48.8	48.9	49.0	49.0	49.1
Median age	48.8	48.8	48.9	49.0	49.0	49.1	49.2	49.2	49.3	49.4	49.5	49.5	49.6	49.7	49.8	49.8	49.9	50.0	50.0	50.1

15.3d Population projections by the Office for National Statistics
Wales, MALES, thousands

Principal projection

Projected populations at mid-years by age last birthday

Ages	2101	2102	2103	2104	2105	2106	2107	2108	2109	2110	2111	2112	2113	2114	2115	2116	2117	2118	2119	2120
Thousands																				
0-14	196	195	195	194	194	194	194	193	193	193	193	192	192	192	191	191	190	190	190	189
15-29	245	245	244	243	242	241	240	239	238	238	237	236	236	235	234	234	234	233	233	233
30-44	264	264	264	264	264	264	264	264	263	263	263	262	262	261	261	260	259	259	258	257
45-59	288	286	284	283	281	280	278	277	276	275	274	273	272	272	272	271	271	271	271	271
60-74	294	295	296	296	297	297	298	298	298	298	298	297	296	295	294	293	291	290	288	287
75 & over	313	313	313	313	313	313	313	313	313	314	314	315	316	317	318	320	321	323	325	327
All ages	1,600	1,598	1,595	1,593	1,591	1,588	1,586	1,584	1,582	1,580	1,578	1,576	1,574	1,572	1,571	1,569	1,568	1,566	1,565	1,563
Percentages																				
0-14	12.2	12.2	12.2	12.2	12.2	12.2	12.2	12.2	12.2	12.2	12.2	12.2	12.2	12.2	12.2	12.2	12.2	12.1	12.1	12.1
15-29	15.3	15.3	15.3	15.2	15.2	15.2	15.1	15.1	15.1	15.0	15.0	15.0	15.0	14.9	14.9	14.9	14.9	14.9	14.9	14.9
30-44	16.5	16.5	16.6	16.6	16.6	16.6	16.6	16.6	16.6	16.7	16.7	16.7	16.6	16.6	16.6	16.6	16.5	16.5	16.5	16.4
45-59	18.0	17.9	17.8	17.7	17.7	17.6	17.5	17.5	17.4	17.4	17.3	17.3	17.3	17.3	17.3	17.3	17.3	17.3	17.3	17.4
60-74	18.4	18.5	18.5	18.6	18.7	18.7	18.8	18.8	18.8	18.9	18.9	18.9	18.8	18.8	18.7	18.7	18.6	18.5	18.4	18.4
75 & over	19.5	19.6	19.6	19.6	19.7	19.7	19.7	19.8	19.8	19.9	19.9	20.0	20.1	20.2	20.3	20.4	20.5	20.6	20.8	20.9
All ages	100.0	100.0	100.0	100.0	100.0	100.0	100.0	100.0	100.0	100.0	100.0	100.0	100.0	100.0	100.0	100.0	100.0	100.0	100.0	100.0
Mean age	49.1	49.1	49.2	49.2	49.2	49.3	49.3	49.3	49.4	49.4	49.4	49.4	49.5	49.5	49.6	49.6	49.6	49.7	49.7	49.8
Median age	50.1	50.2	50.2	50.3	50.3	50.3	50.3	50.3	50.4	50.4	50.4	50.4	50.4	50.5	50.5	50.5	50.6	50.6	50.7	50.7

Source: Office for National Statistics

Note: Figures may not add exactly due to rounding.

15.3d Population projections by the Office for National Statistics
Wales, FEMALES, thousands

2020-based
Principal projection

Projected populations at mid-years by age last birthday

Ages	2020	2021	2022	2023	2024	2025	2026	2027	2028	2029	2030	2031	2032	2033	2034	2035	2036	2037	2038	2039	2040
Thousands																					
0-14	257	255	252	249	246	243	239	235	232	230	227	224	222	220	219	219	219	219	220	220	220
15-29	283	283	282	282	282	283	285	286	286	286	286	287	288	289	289	287	284	282	278	275	271
30-44	280	285	292	297	301	302	304	306	309	311	312	313	313	311	309	308	307	305	305	305	306
45-59	324	321	316	311	307	304	301	298	296	293	292	290	289	291	294	298	304	310	316	320	321
60-74	288	292	292	294	298	302	307	311	315	319	322	326	328	328	327	324	321	316	312	307	305
75 & over	173	176	183	189	194	198	201	204	207	210	212	215	218	221	225	228	232	237	241	246	251
All ages	1,606	1,612	1,617	1,622	1,627	1,632	1,636	1,640	1,644	1,648	1,652	1,655	1,658	1,661	1,663	1,666	1,668	1,670	1,671	1,673	1,675
Percentages																					
0-14	16.0	15.8	15.6	15.3	15.1	14.9	14.6	14.3	14.1	13.9	13.8	13.6	13.4	13.3	13.2	13.1	13.1	13.1	13.1	13.1	13.1
15-29	17.6	17.5	17.4	17.4	17.3	17.4	17.4	17.4	17.4	17.3	17.3	17.3	17.4	17.4	17.4	17.2	17.1	16.9	16.6	16.4	16.2
30-44	17.4	17.7	18.0	18.3	18.5	18.5	18.6	18.7	18.8	18.9	18.9	18.9	18.8	18.7	18.6	18.5	18.4	18.3	18.3	18.2	18.3
45-59	20.2	19.9	19.5	19.2	18.9	18.6	18.4	18.2	18.0	17.8	17.7	17.5	17.5	17.5	17.7	17.9	18.2	18.6	18.9	19.1	19.2
60-74	17.9	18.1	18.1	18.1	18.3	18.5	18.7	19.0	19.1	19.3	19.5	19.7	19.8	19.8	19.7	19.5	19.2	18.9	18.6	18.4	18.2
75 & over	10.8	10.9	11.3	11.7	11.9	12.1	12.3	12.4	12.6	12.7	12.8	13.0	13.1	13.3	13.5	13.7	13.9	14.2	14.4	14.7	15.0
All ages	100.0	100.0	100.0	100.0	100.0	100.0	100.0	100.0	100.0	100.0	100.0	100.0	100.0	100.0	100.0	100.0	100.0	100.0	100.0	100.0	100.0
Mean age	43.4	43.6	43.7	43.9	44.1	44.3	44.4	44.6	44.8	44.9	45.1	45.2	45.4	45.5	45.7	45.8	45.9	46.1	46.2	46.3	46.4
Median age	44.0	44.0	44.0	44.1	44.2	44.4	44.5	44.6	44.7	44.9	45.0	45.2	45.3	45.5	45.7	45.8	46.0	46.2	46.5	46.7	46.9

Ages	2041	2042	2043	2044	2045	2046	2047	2048	2049	2050	2051	2052	2053	2054	2055	2056	2057	2058	2059	2060
Thousands																				
0-14	220	220	221	221	221	221	221	221	221	221	220	219	218	217	216	215	213	212	210	209
15-29	267	264	261	258	255	253	251	249	248	247	247	248	248	248	248	249	249	249	249	250
30-44	308	308	308	308	308	309	310	311	311	310	307	305	301	298	295	291	287	284	281	279
45-59	323	326	328	331	332	333	333	331	330	329	327	326	325	325	327	328	329	329	329	329
60-74	302	300	298	295	295	294	294	296	299	304	310	316	322	326	328	330	333	335	338	340
75 & over	256	260	264	268	271	274	277	278	278	277	276	275	274	273	274	275	276	277	277	279
All ages	1,676	1,678	1,680	1,681	1,683	1,684	1,685	1,686	1,687	1,688	1,688	1,688	1,688	1,688	1,688	1,687	1,687	1,686	1,686	1,685
Percentages																				
0-14	13.1	13.1	13.1	13.1	13.1	13.1	13.1	13.1	13.1	13.1	13.0	13.0	12.9	12.9	12.8	12.7	12.6	12.6	12.5	12.4
15-29	15.9	15.7	15.5	15.3	15.2	15.0	14.9	14.7	14.7	14.6	14.7	14.7	14.7	14.7	14.7	14.7	14.8	14.8	14.8	14.8
30-44	18.3	18.4	18.4	18.3	18.3	18.3	18.4	18.5	18.5	18.4	18.2	18.0	17.8	17.7	17.5	17.2	17.0	16.8	16.7	16.5
45-59	19.3	19.4	19.5	19.7	19.7	19.8	19.7	19.6	19.5	19.5	19.4	19.3	19.3	19.3	19.3	19.5	19.5	19.5	19.5	19.5
60-74	18.0	17.9	17.7	17.6	17.5	17.4	17.4	17.5	17.8	18.0	18.4	18.7	19.1	19.3	19.4	19.6	19.7	19.9	20.1	20.2
75 & over	15.3	15.5	15.7	15.9	16.1	16.3	16.4	16.5	16.5	16.4	16.4	16.3	16.2	16.2	16.2	16.3	16.3	16.4	16.4	16.5
All ages	100.0	100.0	100.0	100.0	100.0	100.0	100.0	100.0	100.0	100.0	100.0	100.0	100.0	100.0	100.0	100.0	100.0	100.0	100.0	100.0
Mean age	46.5	46.6	46.7	46.8	46.9	47.0	47.1	47.2	47.2	47.3	47.4	47.5	47.6	47.7	47.8	47.9	48.0	48.1	48.2	48.3
Median age	47.0	47.2	47.3	47.5	47.6	47.8	47.9	48.1	48.2	48.3	48.4	48.4	48.6	48.7	48.8	49.0	49.2	49.4	49.6	49.8

15.3d Population projections by the Office for National Statistics
Wales, FEMALES, thousands

Projected populations at mid-years by age last birthday

Ages	2061	2062	2063	2064	2065	2066	2067	2068	2069	2070	2071	2072	2073	2074	2075	2076	2077	2078	2079	2080
Thousands																				
0-14	207	206	204	203	202	201	201	200	200	199	199	199	199	199	199	199	198	198	198	198
15-29	250	250	250	249	249	249	248	247	246	244	243	241	240	238	237	235	234	232	231	230
30-44	276	274	272	270	270	270	271	271	271	271	272	272	272	272	273	273	273	273	273	272
45-59	330	332	333	333	332	329	326	323	320	316	312	308	305	302	300	297	294	292	291	290
60-74	341	341	339	338	337	336	335	335	335	337	339	340	340	341	341	342	344	345	345	344
75 & over	280	282	285	289	292	297	302	306	311	314	317	321	325	328	332	334	336	337	338	340
All ages	1,684	1,684	1,683	1,683	1,682	1,682	1,682	1,682	1,681	1,681	1,681	1,681	1,681	1,681	1,680	1,680	1,679	1,678	1,677	1,675
Percentages																				
0-14	12.3	12.2	12.1	12.1	12.0	12.0	11.9	11.9	11.9	11.9	11.8	11.8	11.8	11.8	11.8	11.8	11.8	11.8	11.8	11.8
15-29	14.8	14.8	14.8	14.8	14.8	14.8	14.7	14.7	14.6	14.5	14.5	14.4	14.3	14.2	14.1	14.0	13.9	13.9	13.8	13.7
30-44	16.4	16.2	16.1	16.1	16.0	16.1	16.1	16.1	16.1	16.1	16.2	16.2	16.2	16.2	16.2	16.2	16.2	16.3	16.3	16.2
45-59	19.6	19.7	19.8	19.8	19.7	19.6	19.4	19.2	19.0	18.8	18.6	18.3	18.1	18.0	17.8	17.7	17.5	17.4	17.4	17.3
60-74	20.3	20.2	20.2	20.1	20.0	20.0	19.9	19.9	19.9	20.0	20.1	20.2	20.3	20.3	20.3	20.4	20.5	20.6	20.6	20.5
75 & over	16.6	16.8	16.9	17.2	17.4	17.6	17.9	18.2	18.5	18.7	18.9	19.1	19.3	19.5	19.7	19.9	20.0	20.1	20.2	20.3
All ages	100.0	100.0	100.0	100.0	100.0	100.0	100.0	100.0	100.0	100.0	100.0	100.0	100.0	100.0	100.0	100.0	100.0	100.0	100.0	100.0
Mean age	48.4	48.5	48.6	48.7	48.8	48.9	49.0	49.1	49.2	49.4	49.5	49.6	49.7	49.8	49.9	50.0	50.1	50.2	50.2	50.3
Median age	50.0	50.2	50.4	50.6	50.8	50.9	51.1	51.3	51.5	51.6	51.7	51.8	51.8	51.9	51.9	52.0	52.1	52.1	52.2	52.2

Ages	2081	2082	2083	2084	2085	2086	2087	2088	2089	2090	2091	2092	2093	2094	2095	2096	2097	2098	2099	2100
Thousands																				
0-14	198	197	197	196	195	195	194	193	193	192	191	190	189	189	188	187	187	186	185	185
15-29	229	229	228	228	227	227	227	227	227	227	227	226	226	226	226	226	225	225	224	223
30-44	272	271	270	269	268	266	265	263	262	260	259	257	256	255	254	253	252	251	251	251
45-59	291	291	292	292	292	292	293	293	293	294	294	294	294	294	294	293	293	292	291	289
60-74	342	339	335	332	329	325	321	318	315	313	310	308	306	305	304	305	306	306	307	307
75 & over	343	345	348	351	354	358	361	364	366	368	370	372	373	374	374	373	372	371	371	370
All ages	1,674	1,672	1,670	1,668	1,666	1,663	1,661	1,658	1,656	1,653	1,650	1,647	1,645	1,642	1,639	1,636	1,634	1,631	1,628	1,626
Percentages																				
0-14	11.8	11.8	11.8	11.8	11.7	11.7	11.7	11.7	11.6	11.6	11.6	11.5	11.5	11.5	11.5	11.4	11.4	11.4	11.4	11.4
15-29	13.7	13.7	13.7	13.7	13.6	13.7	13.7	13.7	13.7	13.7	13.7	13.7	13.8	13.8	13.8	13.8	13.8	13.8	13.8	13.7
30-44	16.2	16.2	16.2	16.1	16.1	16.0	15.9	15.9	15.8	15.7	15.7	15.6	15.6	15.5	15.5	15.4	15.4	15.4	15.4	15.4
45-59	17.4	17.4	17.5	17.5	17.5	17.6	17.6	17.7	17.7	17.8	17.8	17.9	17.9	17.9	17.9	17.9	17.9	17.9	17.8	17.8
60-74	20.4	20.3	20.1	19.9	19.7	19.5	19.3	19.2	19.0	18.9	18.8	18.7	18.6	18.6	18.6	18.6	18.7	18.8	18.8	18.9
75 & over	20.5	20.7	20.9	21.1	21.3	21.5	21.7	21.9	22.1	22.3	22.4	22.6	22.7	22.8	22.8	22.8	22.8	22.8	22.8	22.8
All ages	100.0	100.0	100.0	100.0	100.0	100.0	100.0	100.0	100.0	100.0	100.0	100.0	100.0	100.0	100.0	100.0	100.0	100.0	100.0	100.0
Mean age	50.4	50.5	50.5	50.6	50.7	50.7	50.8	50.8	50.9	50.9	51.0	51.0	51.1	51.1	51.2	51.2	51.3	51.3	51.3	51.4
Median age	52.3	52.3	52.4	52.4	52.4	52.5	52.5	52.6	52.6	52.6	52.7	52.8	52.8	52.9	53.0	53.0	53.1	53.2	53.2	53.3

15.3d Population projections by the Office for National Statistics
Wales, FEMALES, thousands

2020-based
Principal projection

Projected populations at mid-years by age last birthday

Ages	2101	2102	2103	2104	2105	2106	2107	2108	2109	2110	2111	2112	2113	2114	2115	2116	2117	2118	2119	2120
Thousands																				
0-14	185	184	184	184	183	183	183	183	182	182	182	182	181	181	181	180	180	179	179	178
15-29	223	222	221	220	220	219	218	217	216	216	215	214	214	213	213	212	212	211	211	211
30-44	250	250	250	250	250	250	250	250	249	249	249	249	248	247	247	246	245	245	244	243
45-59	288	286	285	283	281	280	278	277	276	275	274	273	272	272	272	271	271	271	271	271
60-74	308	308	309	309	310	310	310	310	310	310	310	309	308	307	306	305	303	302	300	298
75 & over	370	370	369	369	369	368	368	368	367	367	367	368	368	369	370	371	372	373	375	376
All ages	1,623	1,620	1,618	1,615	1,612	1,610	1,607	1,604	1,602	1,599	1,597	1,594	1,592	1,590	1,588	1,585	1,584	1,582	1,580	1,578
Percentages																				
0-14	11.4	11.4	11.4	11.4	11.4	11.4	11.4	11.4	11.4	11.4	11.4	11.4	11.4	11.4	11.4	11.4	11.4	11.3	11.3	11.3
15-29	13.7	13.7	13.7	13.6	13.6	13.6	13.6	13.5	13.5	13.5	13.5	13.4	13.4	13.4	13.4	13.4	13.4	13.4	13.4	13.4
30-44	15.4	15.4	15.5	15.5	15.5	15.5	15.5	15.6	15.6	15.6	15.6	15.6	15.6	15.6	15.6	15.5	15.5	15.5	15.4	15.4
45-59	17.7	17.7	17.6	17.5	17.5	17.4	17.3	17.3	17.2	17.2	17.1	17.1	17.1	17.1	17.1	17.1	17.1	17.1	17.2	17.2
60-74	19.0	19.0	19.1	19.1	19.2	19.3	19.3	19.3	19.4	19.4	19.4	19.4	19.4	19.3	19.3	19.2	19.1	19.1	19.0	18.9
75 & over	22.8	22.8	22.8	22.8	22.9	22.9	22.9	22.9	22.9	23.0	23.0	23.1	23.1	23.2	23.3	23.4	23.5	23.6	23.7	23.8
All ages	100.0	100.0	100.0	100.0	100.0	100.0	100.0	100.0	100.0	100.0	100.0	100.0	100.0	100.0	100.0	100.0	100.0	100.0	100.0	100.0
Mean age	51.4	51.5	51.5	51.5	51.5	51.6	51.6	51.6	51.6	51.6	51.7	51.7	51.7	51.7	51.8	51.8	51.8	51.9	51.9	52.0
Median age	53.3	53.4	53.4	53.5	53.5	53.5	53.6	53.6	53.6	53.6	53.6	53.6	53.6	53.6	53.7	53.7	53.7	53.7	53.8	53.8

Note: Figures may not add exactly due to rounding.

Source: Office for National Statistics

519

15.3e Mid-2019 Population estimates for Scotland by sex and single year of age

Ages	Persons	Males	Females	Ages	Persons	Males	Females
All ages	5,463,300	2,663,003	2,800,297	45	65,725	32,217	33,508
0	50,772	26,138	24,634	46	69,677	34,006	35,671
1	52,734	27,059	25,675	47	73,842	35,622	38,220
2	54,266	28,045	26,221	48	76,666	36,697	39,969
3	56,539	29,267	27,272	49	75,548	36,270	39,278
4	57,404	29,473	27,931	50	78,567	37,782	40,785
5	57,837	29,750	28,087	51	79,919	38,446	41,473
6	59,032	30,203	28,829	52	80,362	39,141	41,221
7	60,560	31,168	29,392	53	79,788	38,547	41,241
8	62,408	31,913	30,495	54	82,454	40,024	42,430
9	59,479	30,263	29,216	55	81,429	39,184	42,245
10	61,119	31,119	30,000	56	81,224	39,315	41,909
11	60,860	30,969	29,891	57	79,062	38,548	40,514
12	58,512	29,924	28,588	58	77,036	37,472	39,564
13	57,366	29,231	28,135	59	74,372	36,256	38,116
14	56,817	29,244	27,573	60	73,504	35,533	37,971
15	55,692	28,678	27,014	61	71,388	34,534	36,854
16	54,052	27,624	26,428	62	69,244	33,646	35,598
17	53,713	27,457	26,256	63	66,867	32,428	34,439
18	56,834	28,903	27,931	64	63,690	30,711	32,979
19	61,667	31,510	30,157	65	62,599	30,358	32,241
20	65,838	33,412	32,426	66	60,993	29,455	31,538
21	67,735	34,303	33,432	67	58,595	28,260	30,335
22	70,870	35,814	35,056	68	58,657	28,175	30,482
23	71,430	36,286	35,144	69	58,600	28,212	30,388
24	71,583	36,251	35,332	70	59,394	28,497	30,897
25	73,182	36,890	36,292	71	60,782	29,071	31,711
26	74,857	37,228	37,629	72	65,059	30,844	34,215
27	79,127	39,349	39,778	73	48,394	22,913	25,481
28	79,100	39,702	39,398	74	45,227	21,014	24,213
29	75,989	37,976	38,013	75	45,388	21,118	24,270
30	75,648	37,656	37,992	76	42,595	19,268	23,327
31	75,743	37,555	38,188	77	38,406	17,046	21,360
32	73,301	36,029	37,272	78	34,798	15,232	19,566
33	72,691	36,090	36,601	79	34,764	15,222	19,542
34	72,080	35,305	36,775	80	33,039	14,311	18,728
35	69,835	34,205	35,630	81	31,191	13,403	17,788
36	70,584	34,472	36,112	82	28,436	11,771	16,665
37	71,428	34,755	36,673	83	26,237	10,682	15,555
38	70,962	34,853	36,109	84	23,904	9,681	14,223
39	69,713	34,339	35,374	85	21,126	8,261	12,865
40	67,127	33,353	33,774	86	18,701	7,296	11,405
41	62,229	30,309	31,920	87	17,001	6,384	10,617
42	61,101	30,279	30,822	88	14,569	5,356	9,213
43	64,358	31,511	32,847	89	12,032	4,185	7,847
44	64,617	31,338	33,279	90	43,658	13,411	30,247

Source: Office for National Statistics

1. Estimates are presented both rounded to the nearest hundred and unrounded. Unrounded estimates are published to enable and encourage further calculations and analysis. However, the estimates should not be taken to be accurate to the level of detail provided. More information on the accuracy of the estimates is available in the Quality and Methodology document (QMI):

https://www.ons.gov.uk/peoplepopulationandcommunity/populationandmigration/
populationestimates/methodologies/annualmidyearpopulationestimatesqmi

2. The estimates are produced using a variety of data sources and statistical models, including some statistical disclosure control methods, and small estimates should not be taken to refer to particular individuals.

3. The estimated resident population of an area includes all those people who usually live there, regardless of nationality. Arriving international migrants are included in the usually resident population if they remain in the UK for at least a year. Emigrants are excluded if they remain outside the UK for at least a year. This is consistent with the United Nations definition of a long-term migrant. Armed forces stationed outside of the UK are excluded. Students are taken to be usually resident at their term time address.

4. Where data appears for age 90 please note this is for ages 90 and above.

15.3f Population projections by the Office for National Statistics
Scotland, PERSONS, thousands

2020-based Principal projection

Projected populations at mid-years by age last birthday

Ages	2020	2021	2022	2023	2024	2025	2026	2027	2028	2029	2030	2031	2032	2033	2034	2035	2036	2037	2038	2039	2040
Thousands																					
0-14	860	852	841	828	814	802	786	772	759	746	733	721	711	701	693	687	683	681	678	676	674
15-29	1,001	989	977	972	970	968	969	968	968	968	970	971	974	975	973	968	959	948	935	921	908
30-44	1,054	1,071	1,090	1,105	1,113	1,117	1,120	1,122	1,124	1,124	1,121	1,116	1,108	1,096	1,086	1,077	1,067	1,054	1,050	1,048	1,047
45-59	1,142	1,127	1,107	1,086	1,071	1,057	1,048	1,039	1,030	1,022	1,019	1,016	1,017	1,025	1,036	1,050	1,067	1,087	1,102	1,110	1,114
60-74	939	955	958	969	982	997	1,011	1,025	1,038	1,048	1,054	1,060	1,061	1,056	1,047	1,036	1,022	1,005	987	974	964
75 & over	470	477	498	514	528	538	548	556	565	575	584	595	606	619	632	645	659	674	690	705	721
All ages	5,466	5,469	5,471	5,474	5,477	5,479	5,481	5,482	5,483	5,483	5,482	5,479	5,476	5,472	5,468	5,462	5,456	5,449	5,442	5,435	5,427
Percentages																					
0-14	15.7	15.6	15.4	15.1	14.9	14.6	14.3	14.1	13.8	13.6	13.4	13.2	13.0	12.8	12.7	12.6	12.5	12.5	12.5	12.4	12.4
15-29	18.3	18.1	17.9	17.8	17.7	17.7	17.7	17.7	17.7	17.7	17.7	17.7	17.8	17.8	17.8	17.7	17.6	17.4	17.2	16.9	16.7
30-44	19.3	19.6	19.9	20.2	20.3	20.4	20.4	20.5	20.5	20.5	20.5	20.4	20.2	20.0	19.9	19.7	19.5	19.3	19.3	19.3	19.3
45-59	20.9	20.6	20.2	19.8	19.5	19.3	19.1	19.0	18.8	18.6	18.6	18.6	18.6	18.7	19.0	19.2	19.6	19.9	20.2	20.4	20.5
60-74	17.2	17.5	17.5	17.7	17.9	18.2	18.4	18.7	18.9	19.1	19.2	19.3	19.4	19.3	19.1	19.0	18.7	18.4	18.1	17.9	17.8
75 & over	8.6	8.7	9.1	9.4	9.6	9.8	10.0	10.1	10.3	10.5	10.6	10.9	11.1	11.3	11.6	11.8	12.1	12.4	12.7	13.0	13.3
All ages	100.0	100.0	100.0	100.0	100.0	100.0	100.0	100.0	100.0	100.0	100.0	100.0	100.0	100.0	100.0	100.0	100.0	100.0	100.0	100.0	100.0
Mean age	42.2	42.4	42.6	42.8	43.0	43.2	43.4	43.6	43.8	44.0	44.2	44.3	44.5	44.7	44.9	45.0	45.2	45.3	45.5	45.6	45.7
Median age	42.1	42.2	42.4	42.6	42.8	42.9	43.1	43.3	43.5	43.7	43.9	44.1	44.3	44.5	44.8	45.0	45.3	45.5	45.8	46.0	46.2

Ages	2041	2042	2043	2044	2045	2046	2047	2048	2049	2050	2051	2052	2053	2054	2055	2056	2057	2058	2059	2060
Thousands																				
0-14	672	671	669	669	668	667	666	665	664	663	661	658	654	650	645	640	634	628	621	615
15-29	892	877	863	850	837	824	813	803	795	789	785	782	779	777	774	773	771	770	769	768
30-44	1,049	1,048	1,048	1,048	1,049	1,051	1,054	1,055	1,053	1,048	1,039	1,028	1,015	1,001	988	972	957	943	930	917
45-59	1,117	1,120	1,121	1,122	1,119	1,115	1,106	1,095	1,086	1,077	1,065	1,055	1,052	1,050	1,050	1,052	1,051	1,052	1,053	1,055
60-74	957	951	944	939	938	937	940	949	961	974	991	1,011	1,025	1,034	1,039	1,042	1,046	1,048	1,049	1,047
75 & over	733	746	757	767	774	782	786	788	785	782	779	773	768	767	768	771	775	778	782	787
All ages	5,419	5,411	5,403	5,394	5,385	5,376	5,366	5,355	5,344	5,332	5,320	5,307	5,293	5,279	5,264	5,250	5,234	5,219	5,204	5,188
Percentages																				
0-14	12.4	12.4	12.4	12.4	12.4	12.4	12.4	12.4	12.4	12.4	12.4	12.4	12.4	12.3	12.3	12.2	12.1	12.0	11.9	11.8
15-29	16.5	16.2	16.0	15.8	15.5	15.3	15.2	15.0	14.9	14.8	14.8	14.7	14.7	14.7	14.7	14.7	14.7	14.8	14.8	14.8
30-44	19.3	19.4	19.4	19.4	19.5	19.5	19.6	19.7	19.7	19.6	19.5	19.4	19.2	19.0	18.8	18.5	18.3	18.1	17.9	17.7
45-59	20.6	20.7	20.8	20.8	20.8	20.7	20.6	20.4	20.3	20.2	20.0	19.9	19.9	19.9	19.9	20.0	20.1	20.2	20.2	20.3
60-74	17.7	17.6	17.5	17.4	17.4	17.4	17.5	17.7	18.0	18.3	18.6	19.0	19.4	19.6	19.7	19.9	20.0	20.1	20.2	20.2
75 & over	13.5	13.8	14.0	14.2	14.4	14.5	14.7	14.7	14.7	14.7	14.6	14.6	14.5	14.5	14.6	14.7	14.8	14.9	15.0	15.2
All ages	100.0	100.0	100.0	100.0	100.0	100.0	100.0	100.0	100.0	100.0	100.0	100.0	100.0	100.0	100.0	100.0	100.0	100.0	100.0	100.0
Mean age	45.9	46.0	46.1	46.2	46.3	46.4	46.5	46.6	46.7	46.8	46.9	47.0	47.1	47.2	47.4	47.5	47.6	47.7	47.8	47.9
Median age	46.3	46.5	46.7	46.8	47.0	47.1	47.2	47.3	47.4	47.5	47.6	47.7	47.8	47.9	48.1	48.3	48.5	48.6	48.8	49.1

15.3f Population projections by the Office for National Statistics
Scotland, PERSONS, thousands

2020-based
Principal projection

Projected populations at mid-years by age last birthday

Ages	2061	2062	2063	2064	2065	2066	2067	2068	2069	2070	2071	2072	2073	2074	2075	2076	2077	2078	2079	2080
Thousands																				
0-14	608	601	595	589	583	578	574	569	566	562	560	557	555	553	551	550	548	547	546	544
15-29	768	767	766	765	763	761	758	755	751	746	740	734	727	720	713	706	700	693	687	681
30-44	904	893	883	875	869	864	862	859	857	855	853	851	850	850	849	848	848	847	846	844
45-59	1,056	1,059	1,061	1,060	1,054	1,046	1,036	1,022	1,009	996	980	966	952	940	927	915	904	894	886	880
60-74	1,044	1,036	1,026	1,018	1,011	1,001	993	991	991	992	995	996	998	1,000	1,002	1,005	1,008	1,011	1,010	1,005
75 & over	794	801	811	822	833	847	862	873	883	891	899	908	915	920	924	928	927	927	928	931
All ages	5,173	5,158	5,143	5,128	5,113	5,099	5,085	5,070	5,056	5,042	5,027	5,013	4,998	4,983	4,967	4,952	4,936	4,919	4,902	4,885
Percentages																				
0-14	11.7	11.7	11.6	11.5	11.4	11.3	11.3	11.2	11.2	11.2	11.1	11.1	11.1	11.1	11.1	11.1	11.1	11.1	11.1	11.1
15-29	14.8	14.9	14.9	14.9	14.9	14.9	14.9	14.9	14.8	14.8	14.7	14.6	14.6	14.5	14.4	14.3	14.2	14.1	14.0	13.9
30-44	17.5	17.3	17.2	17.1	17.0	17.0	16.9	16.9	16.9	17.0	17.0	17.0	17.0	17.1	17.1	17.1	17.2	17.2	17.2	17.3
45-59	20.4	20.5	20.6	20.7	20.6	20.5	20.4	20.2	19.9	19.8	19.5	19.3	19.1	18.9	18.7	18.5	18.3	18.2	18.1	18.0
60-74	20.2	20.1	20.0	19.9	19.8	19.6	19.5	19.5	19.6	19.7	19.8	19.9	20.0	20.1	20.2	20.3	20.4	20.5	20.6	20.6
75 & over	15.3	15.5	15.8	16.0	16.3	16.6	17.0	17.2	17.5	17.7	17.9	18.1	18.3	18.5	18.6	18.7	18.8	18.8	18.9	19.0
All ages	100.0	100.0	100.0	100.0	100.0	100.0	100.0	100.0	100.0	100.0	100.0	100.0	100.0	100.0	100.0	100.0	100.0	100.0	100.0	100.0
Mean age	48.0	48.1	48.2	48.4	48.5	48.6	48.7	48.8	48.9	49.1	49.2	49.3	49.4	49.5	49.6	49.7	49.7	49.8	49.9	50.0
Median age	49.3	49.5	49.7	49.9	50.1	50.3	50.5	50.6	50.8	50.9	51.0	51.1	51.2	51.2	51.3	51.3	51.4	51.4	51.4	51.5

Ages	2081	2082	2083	2084	2085	2086	2087	2088	2089	2090	2091	2092	2093	2094	2095	2096	2097	2098	2099	2100
Thousands																				
0-14	543	541	539	537	535	532	529	527	523	520	517	513	510	506	503	499	496	493	490	487
15-29	676	671	666	662	659	656	653	651	649	648	646	645	643	642	640	639	637	635	633	630
30-44	842	839	836	831	826	821	815	808	801	794	787	780	774	767	761	756	751	747	743	739
45-59	876	874	872	870	868	866	865	864	864	863	863	862	862	861	860	858	855	852	848	843
60-74	998	988	976	963	952	938	924	912	901	889	878	869	860	853	848	845	843	842	840	839
75 & over	933	937	943	950	956	964	971	977	982	987	991	995	997	998	997	994	991	987	984	981
All ages	4,868	4,850	4,832	4,813	4,795	4,776	4,758	4,739	4,720	4,701	4,682	4,664	4,645	4,627	4,609	4,591	4,573	4,555	4,537	4,520
Percentages																				
0-14	11.1	11.2	11.2	11.2	11.2	11.1	11.1	11.1	11.1	11.1	11.0	11.0	11.0	10.9	10.9	10.9	10.8	10.8	10.8	10.8
15-29	13.9	13.8	13.8	13.8	13.7	13.7	13.7	13.7	13.8	13.8	13.8	13.8	13.8	13.9	13.9	13.9	13.9	13.9	13.9	13.9
30-44	17.3	17.3	17.3	17.3	17.2	17.2	17.1	17.1	17.0	16.9	16.8	16.7	16.7	16.6	16.5	16.5	16.4	16.4	16.4	16.4
45-59	18.0	18.0	18.0	18.1	18.1	18.1	18.2	18.2	18.3	18.4	18.4	18.5	18.6	18.6	18.6	18.7	18.7	18.7	18.7	18.6
60-74	20.5	20.4	20.2	20.0	19.9	19.6	19.4	19.3	19.1	18.9	18.8	18.6	18.5	18.4	18.4	18.4	18.4	18.5	18.5	18.6
75 & over	19.2	19.3	19.5	19.7	19.9	20.2	20.4	20.6	20.8	21.0	21.2	21.3	21.5	21.6	21.6	21.7	21.7	21.7	21.7	21.7
All ages	100.0	100.0	100.0	100.0	100.0	100.0	100.0	100.0	100.0	100.0	100.0	100.0	100.0	100.0	100.0	100.0	100.0	100.0	100.0	100.0
Mean age	50.0	50.1	50.2	50.2	50.3	50.3	50.4	50.4	50.5	50.5	50.6	50.6	50.7	50.7	50.8	50.8	50.9	50.9	50.9	51.0
Median age	51.5	51.5	51.5	51.6	51.6	51.6	51.6	51.6	51.7	51.7	51.8	51.8	51.9	51.9	52.0	52.1	52.2	52.2	52.3	52.4

15.3f Population projections by the Office for National Statistics
Scotland, PERSONS, thousands

2020-based
Principal projection

Projected populations at mid-years by age last birthday

Ages	2101	2102	2103	2104	2105	2106	2107	2108	2109	2110	2111	2112	2113	2114	2115	2116	2117	2118	2119	2120
Thousands																				
0-14	484	482	479	477	475	474	472	470	469	467	466	465	463	462	460	459	457	456	454	452
15-29	628	625	622	619	615	612	608	604	601	597	594	590	587	584	581	578	575	573	571	569
30-44	736	734	732	730	728	726	725	724	722	721	719	717	715	713	711	708	705	702	699	696
45-59	837	831	825	818	811	804	797	791	785	779	774	769	765	761	758	755	752	750	748	747
60-74	838	838	838	838	838	838	838	838	838	837	835	833	830	827	822	817	812	806	800	793
75 & over	978	975	972	969	965	962	958	955	951	948	946	944	943	942	942	943	945	947	949	952
All ages	4,502	4,485	4,467	4,450	4,433	4,416	4,399	4,382	4,366	4,349	4,333	4,318	4,303	4,288	4,274	4,260	4,247	4,234	4,221	4,208
Percentages																				
0-14	10.8	10.7	10.7	10.7	10.7	10.7	10.7	10.7	10.7	10.7	10.8	10.8	10.8	10.8	10.8	10.8	10.8	10.8	10.8	10.7
15-29	13.9	13.9	13.9	13.9	13.9	13.9	13.8	13.8	13.8	13.7	13.7	13.7	13.6	13.6	13.6	13.6	13.5	13.5	13.5	13.5
30-44	16.4	16.4	16.4	16.4	16.4	16.5	16.5	16.5	16.5	16.6	16.6	16.6	16.6	16.6	16.6	16.6	16.6	16.6	16.6	16.5
45-59	18.6	18.5	18.5	18.4	18.3	18.2	18.1	18.0	18.0	17.9	17.9	17.8	17.8	17.7	17.7	17.7	17.7	17.7	17.7	17.7
60-74	18.6	18.7	18.7	18.8	18.9	19.0	19.1	19.1	19.2	19.2	19.3	19.3	19.3	19.3	19.2	19.2	19.1	19.0	18.9	18.9
75 & over	21.7	21.7	21.8	21.8	21.8	21.8	21.8	21.8	21.8	21.8	21.8	21.9	21.9	22.0	22.0	22.1	22.2	22.4	22.5	22.6
All ages	100.0	100.0	100.0	100.0	100.0	100.0	100.0	100.0	100.0	100.0	100.0	100.0	100.0	100.0	100.0	100.0	100.0	100.0	100.0	100.0
Mean age	51.0	51.1	51.1	51.1	51.2	51.2	51.2	51.2	51.2	51.2	51.3	51.3	51.3	51.3	51.4	51.4	51.4	51.5	51.5	51.5
Median age	52.4	52.5	52.6	52.6	52.6	52.7	52.7	52.7	52.7	52.7	52.7	52.7	52.7	52.7	52.7	52.8	52.8	52.8	52.8	52.8

Note: Figures may not add exactly due to rounding.

Source: Office for National Statistics

15.3f Population projections by the Office for National Statistics
Scotland, MALES, thousands

2020-based
Principal projection

Projected populations at mid-years by age last birthday

Ages	2020	2021	2022	2023	2024	2025	2026	2027	2028	2029	2030	2031	2032	2033	2034	2035	2036	2037	2038	2039	2040
Thousands																					
0-14	441	437	431	425	418	412	404	397	390	383	377	370	365	360	356	352	351	349	348	347	346
15-29	507	501	496	494	494	493	493	493	493	493	493	495	497	498	497	494	490	485	478	471	465
30-44	519	528	538	546	550	553	556	559	561	563	563	562	558	553	550	546	540	536	535	534	533
45-59	552	544	534	524	517	511	507	502	498	494	493	493	494	498	504	512	521	531	538	543	546
60-74	451	458	460	464	470	476	482	489	494	498	501	502	502	500	495	489	483	475	467	461	456
75 & over	195	200	210	219	226	231	236	241	245	250	255	260	266	271	277	284	290	297	305	311	318
All ages	2,665	2,668	2,669	2,672	2,674	2,676	2,678	2,680	2,681	2,682	2,682	2,682	2,681	2,680	2,679	2,677	2,675	2,672	2,670	2,667	2,664
Percentages																					
0-14	16.5	16.4	16.2	15.9	15.6	15.4	15.1	14.8	14.5	14.3	14.1	13.8	13.6	13.4	13.3	13.2	13.1	13.1	13.0	13.0	13.0
15-29	19.0	18.8	18.6	18.5	18.5	18.4	18.4	18.4	18.4	18.4	18.4	18.4	18.5	18.6	18.5	18.5	18.3	18.1	17.9	17.7	17.4
30-44	19.5	19.8	20.2	20.4	20.6	20.7	20.8	20.9	20.9	21.0	21.0	20.9	20.8	20.6	20.5	20.4	20.2	20.1	20.0	20.0	20.0
45-59	20.7	20.4	20.0	19.6	19.3	19.1	18.9	18.7	18.6	18.4	18.4	18.4	18.4	18.6	18.8	19.1	19.5	19.9	20.2	20.4	20.5
60-74	16.9	17.2	17.2	17.4	17.6	17.8	18.0	18.2	18.4	18.6	18.7	18.7	18.7	18.6	18.5	18.3	18.1	17.8	17.5	17.3	17.1
75 & over	7.3	7.5	7.9	8.2	8.4	8.6	8.8	9.0	9.2	9.3	9.5	9.7	9.9	10.1	10.4	10.6	10.9	11.1	11.4	11.7	11.9
All ages	100.0	100.0	100.0	100.0	100.0	100.0	100.0	100.0	100.0	100.0	100.0	100.0	100.0	100.0	100.0	100.0	100.0	100.0	100.0	100.0	100.0
Mean age	41.2	41.3	41.5	41.8	42.0	42.2	42.3	42.5	42.7	42.9	43.1	43.3	43.4	43.6	43.8	43.9	44.1	44.2	44.4	44.5	44.6
Median age	40.7	40.9	41.1	41.2	41.4	41.6	41.7	41.9	42.1	42.3	42.5	42.7	42.9	43.2	43.4	43.7	43.9	44.1	44.3	44.5	44.7

Ages	2041	2042	2043	2044	2045	2046	2047	2048	2049	2050	2051	2052	2053	2054	2055	2056	2057	2058	2059	2060
Thousands																				
0-14	345	344	343	343	343	342	342	341	341	340	339	337	336	334	331	328	325	322	319	315
15-29	456	449	442	435	428	421	416	411	406	403	401	399	398	397	396	395	394	393	393	393
30-44	534	534	534	534	535	536	538	539	538	536	532	526	519	512	506	498	490	483	477	470
45-59	549	552	554	556	556	555	552	547	544	540	535	531	530	530	530	531	531	532	532	533
60-74	454	451	448	446	446	447	449	453	459	467	476	486	493	498	501	505	508	510	513	513
75 & over	324	329	334	338	341	344	346	346	345	344	342	340	337	337	339	340	342	344	346	349
All ages	2,662	2,659	2,656	2,652	2,649	2,646	2,642	2,638	2,634	2,629	2,624	2,619	2,614	2,608	2,603	2,597	2,591	2,585	2,579	2,573
Percentages																				
0-14	12.9	12.9	12.9	12.9	12.9	12.9	12.9	12.9	12.9	12.9	12.9	12.9	12.8	12.8	12.7	12.6	12.6	12.5	12.4	12.3
15-29	17.1	16.9	16.6	16.4	16.2	15.9	15.7	15.6	15.4	15.3	15.3	15.2	15.2	15.2	15.2	15.2	15.2	15.2	15.2	15.3
30-44	20.1	20.1	20.1	20.1	20.2	20.3	20.4	20.4	20.4	20.4	20.3	20.1	19.9	19.6	19.5	19.2	18.9	18.7	18.5	18.3
45-59	20.6	20.8	20.9	21.0	21.0	21.0	20.9	20.7	20.6	20.5	20.4	20.3	20.3	20.3	20.4	20.4	20.5	20.6	20.6	20.7
60-74	17.0	16.9	16.9	16.8	16.8	16.9	17.0	17.2	17.4	17.8	18.1	18.5	18.9	19.1	19.3	19.4	19.6	19.7	19.9	19.9
75 & over	12.2	12.4	12.6	12.8	12.9	13.0	13.1	13.1	13.1	13.1	13.0	13.0	12.9	12.9	13.0	13.1	13.2	13.3	13.4	13.6
All ages	100.0	100.0	100.0	100.0	100.0	100.0	100.0	100.0	100.0	100.0	100.0	100.0	100.0	100.0	100.0	100.0	100.0	100.0	100.0	100.0
Mean age	44.8	44.9	45.0	45.1	45.2	45.3	45.4	45.5	45.6	45.7	45.8	45.9	46.0	46.2	46.3	46.4	46.5	46.6	46.8	46.9
Median age	44.9	45.1	45.2	45.4	45.5	45.7	45.8	45.8	45.9	46.0	46.2	46.3	46.5	46.6	46.9	47.1	47.3	47.5	47.7	48.0

15.3f Population projections by the Office for National Statistics
Scotland, MALES, thousands

Projected populations at mid-years by age last birthday

Ages	2061	2062	2063	2064	2065	2066	2067	2068	2069	2070	2071	2072	2073	2074	2075	2076	2077	2078	2079	2080
Thousands																				
0-14	312	308	305	302	299	297	294	292	290	289	287	286	285	284	283	282	281	281	280	279
15-29	392	392	391	391	390	389	387	386	383	381	378	375	372	368	365	361	358	354	351	348
30-44	463	457	452	448	445	443	441	440	439	438	437	436	436	435	435	435	434	434	433	433
45-59	535	537	538	537	535	531	526	519	513	507	499	491	485	478	472	465	460	455	451	448
60-74	512	510	506	503	500	496	493	493	494	494	496	497	498	499	501	503	505	506	506	504
75 & over	353	357	362	368	374	382	389	395	400	405	410	415	420	423	426	429	429	430	431	433
All ages	2,567	2,561	2,555	2,549	2,543	2,537	2,531	2,525	2,519	2,513	2,507	2,501	2,495	2,488	2,481	2,474	2,467	2,460	2,453	2,445
Percentages																				
0-14	12.1	12.0	11.9	11.9	11.8	11.7	11.6	11.6	11.5	11.5	11.5	11.4	11.4	11.4	11.4	11.4	11.4	11.4	11.4	11.4
15-29	15.3	15.3	15.3	15.3	15.3	15.3	15.3	15.3	15.2	15.2	15.1	15.0	14.9	14.8	14.7	14.6	14.5	14.4	14.3	14.2
30-44	18.1	17.9	17.7	17.6	17.5	17.5	17.4	17.4	17.4	17.4	17.4	17.4	17.5	17.5	17.5	17.6	17.6	17.6	17.7	17.7
45-59	20.8	21.0	21.1	21.1	21.0	20.9	20.8	20.6	20.3	20.2	19.9	19.7	19.4	19.2	19.0	18.8	18.6	18.5	18.4	18.3
60-74	20.0	19.9	19.8	19.7	19.7	19.6	19.5	19.5	19.6	19.7	19.8	19.9	20.0	20.1	20.2	20.3	20.5	20.6	20.6	20.6
75 & over	13.7	13.9	14.2	14.4	14.7	15.0	15.4	15.6	15.9	16.1	16.4	16.6	16.8	17.0	17.2	17.3	17.4	17.5	17.6	17.7
All ages	100.0	100.0	100.0	100.0	100.0	100.0	100.0	100.0	100.0	100.0	100.0	100.0	100.0	100.0	100.0	100.0	100.0	100.0	100.0	100.0
Mean age	47.0	47.2	47.3	47.4	47.5	47.7	47.8	47.9	48.1	48.2	48.3	48.4	48.5	48.7	48.8	48.9	48.9	49.0	49.1	49.2
Median age	48.2	48.4	48.6	48.8	49.1	49.3	49.4	49.6	49.8	49.9	50.0	50.0	50.1	50.2	50.3	50.3	50.4	50.4	50.5	50.5

Ages	2081	2082	2083	2084	2085	2086	2087	2088	2089	2090	2091	2092	2093	2094	2095	2096	2097	2098	2099	2100
Thousands																				
0-14	278	278	277	276	274	273	272	270	269	267	265	263	262	260	258	256	255	253	251	250
15-29	345	343	341	339	337	335	334	333	332	331	330	329	329	328	327	326	325	325	323	322
30-44	432	430	428	426	424	421	418	414	411	407	404	400	397	394	391	388	385	383	381	380
45-59	446	445	444	443	442	441	440	440	440	440	440	439	439	439	438	437	436	434	432	430
60-74	501	496	490	484	479	472	465	459	454	448	442	438	433	430	427	426	425	424	424	423
75 & over	436	438	442	446	449	454	458	461	465	468	471	473	475	476	476	475	473	472	471	470
All ages	2,437	2,429	2,421	2,413	2,404	2,396	2,387	2,378	2,370	2,361	2,352	2,343	2,335	2,326	2,317	2,309	2,300	2,291	2,283	2,274
Percentages																				
0-14	11.4	11.4	11.4	11.4	11.4	11.4	11.4	11.4	11.3	11.3	11.3	11.2	11.2	11.2	11.1	11.1	11.1	11.0	11.0	11.0
15-29	14.2	14.1	14.1	14.0	14.0	14.0	14.0	14.0	14.0	14.0	14.0	14.1	14.1	14.1	14.1	14.1	14.2	14.2	14.2	14.2
30-44	17.7	17.7	17.7	17.7	17.6	17.6	17.5	17.4	17.3	17.3	17.2	17.1	17.0	16.9	16.9	16.8	16.8	16.7	16.7	16.7
45-59	18.3	18.3	18.3	18.3	18.4	18.4	18.5	18.5	18.6	18.6	18.7	18.8	18.8	18.9	18.9	18.9	19.0	19.0	18.9	18.9
60-74	20.5	20.4	20.2	20.1	19.9	19.7	19.5	19.3	19.2	19.0	18.8	18.7	18.6	18.5	18.4	18.5	18.5	18.5	18.6	18.6
75 & over	17.9	18.0	18.2	18.5	18.7	18.9	19.2	19.4	19.6	19.8	20.0	20.2	20.3	20.5	20.5	20.6	20.6	20.6	20.6	20.7
All ages	100.0	100.0	100.0	100.0	100.0	100.0	100.0	100.0	100.0	100.0	100.0	100.0	100.0	100.0	100.0	100.0	100.0	100.0	100.0	100.0
Mean age	49.3	49.4	49.4	49.5	49.6	49.6	49.7	49.7	49.8	49.9	49.9	50.0	50.0	50.1	50.1	50.2	50.2	50.3	50.3	50.4
Median age	50.6	50.6	50.6	50.7	50.7	50.7	50.8	50.8	50.9	50.9	51.0	51.1	51.1	51.2	51.3	51.4	51.4	51.5	51.6	51.7

15.3f Population projections by the Office for National Statistics
Scotland, MALES, thousands

2020-based
Principal projection

Projected populations at mid-years by age last birthday

Ages	2101	2102	2103	2104	2105	2106	2107	2108	2109	2110	2111	2112	2113	2114	2115	2116	2117	2118	2119	2120
Thousands																				
0-14	249	247	246	245	244	243	242	241	241	240	239	239	238	237	236	236	235	234	233	232
15-29	321	319	318	316	315	313	311	309	307	305	303	302	300	298	297	295	294	293	292	291
30-44	378	377	376	375	374	373	372	372	371	370	369	368	367	366	365	364	362	361	359	357
45-59	427	424	421	417	414	410	407	404	401	398	395	393	391	389	387	386	385	384	383	382
60-74	423	423	423	423	423	423	424	424	423	423	422	421	420	418	416	414	411	408	405	402
75 & over	469	467	466	465	463	462	461	459	458	457	456	455	455	455	456	456	457	459	460	462
All ages	2,266	2,258	2,249	2,241	2,233	2,225	2,217	2,209	2,201	2,193	2,186	2,178	2,171	2,164	2,157	2,151	2,144	2,138	2,132	2,126
Percentages																				
0-14	11.0	11.0	10.9	10.9	10.9	10.9	10.9	10.9	10.9	10.9	10.9	10.9	11.0	11.0	11.0	11.0	10.9	10.9	10.9	10.9
15-29	14.2	14.1	14.1	14.1	14.1	14.1	14.0	14.0	14.0	13.9	13.9	13.9	13.8	13.8	13.8	13.7	13.7	13.7	13.7	13.7
30-44	16.7	16.7	16.7	16.7	16.7	16.8	16.8	16.8	16.9	16.9	16.9	16.9	16.9	16.9	16.9	16.9	16.9	16.9	16.8	16.8
45-59	18.8	18.8	18.7	18.6	18.5	18.5	18.4	18.3	18.2	18.1	18.1	18.0	18.0	18.0	17.9	17.9	17.9	17.9	17.9	18.0
60-74	18.7	18.7	18.8	18.9	19.0	19.0	19.1	19.2	19.2	19.3	19.3	19.3	19.4	19.3	19.3	19.2	19.2	19.1	19.0	18.9
75 & over	20.7	20.7	20.7	20.7	20.8	20.8	20.8	20.8	20.8	20.8	20.9	20.9	21.0	21.0	21.1	21.2	21.3	21.5	21.6	21.7
All ages	100.0	100.0	100.0	100.0	100.0	100.0	100.0	100.0	100.0	100.0	100.0	100.0	100.0	100.0	100.0	100.0	100.0	100.0	100.0	100.0
Mean age	50.4	50.5	50.5	50.5	50.6	50.6	50.6	50.6	50.7	50.7	50.7	50.7	50.8	50.8	50.8	50.9	50.9	50.9	51.0	51.0
Median age	51.7	51.8	51.8	51.9	51.9	52.0	52.0	52.0	52.0	52.0	52.0	52.0	52.1	52.1	52.1	52.1	52.1	52.2	52.2	52.2

Note: Figures may not add exactly due to rounding.

Source: Office for National Statistics

15.3f Population projections by the Office for National Statistics
Scotland, FEMALES, thousands

2020-based
Principal projection

Projected populations at mid-years by age last birthday

Ages	2020	2021	2022	2023	2024	2025	2026	2027	2028	2029	2030	2031	2032	2033	2034	2035	2036	2037	2038	2039	2040
Thousands																					
0-14	419	415	410	403	396	390	382	375	369	363	357	351	346	341	338	335	333	332	330	329	328
15-29	494	488	481	478	476	475	476	475	475	475	476	476	477	478	476	474	469	464	457	450	443
30-44	535	542	552	559	563	564	564	563	562	561	558	555	550	543	537	531	525	518	515	514	514
45-59	590	583	572	562	553	546	541	537	532	528	526	523	523	527	532	538	546	556	563	567	568
60-74	488	497	498	505	512	521	528	536	543	550	554	557	559	556	551	546	539	530	521	513	507
75 & over	274	277	288	296	302	307	312	315	320	324	329	335	341	347	354	361	369	377	385	394	402
All ages	2,801	2,802	2,802	2,802	2,802	2,802	2,802	2,802	2,802	2,801	2,799	2,797	2,795	2,792	2,789	2,785	2,781	2,777	2,772	2,768	2,763
Percentages																					
0-14	15.0	14.8	14.6	14.4	14.1	13.9	13.6	13.4	13.2	12.9	12.7	12.5	12.4	12.2	12.1	12.0	12.0	11.9	11.9	11.9	11.9
15-29	17.7	17.4	17.2	17.0	17.0	17.0	17.0	17.0	17.0	17.0	17.0	17.0	17.1	17.1	17.1	17.0	16.9	16.7	16.5	16.3	16.0
30-44	19.1	19.4	19.7	20.0	20.1	20.1	20.1	20.1	20.1	20.0	19.9	19.8	19.7	19.4	19.2	19.1	18.9	18.7	18.6	18.6	18.6
45-59	21.1	20.8	20.4	20.1	19.7	19.5	19.3	19.2	19.0	18.8	18.8	18.7	18.7	18.9	19.1	19.3	19.6	20.0	20.3	20.5	20.6
60-74	17.4	17.7	17.8	18.0	18.3	18.6	18.9	19.1	19.4	19.6	19.8	19.9	20.0	19.9	19.8	19.6	19.4	19.1	18.8	18.5	18.4
75 & over	9.8	9.9	10.3	10.5	10.8	11.0	11.1	11.3	11.4	11.6	11.8	12.0	12.2	12.4	12.7	13.0	13.3	13.6	13.9	14.2	14.6
All ages	100.0	100.0	100.0	100.0	100.0	100.0	100.0	100.0	100.0	100.0	100.0	100.0	100.0	100.0	100.0	100.0	100.0	100.0	100.0	100.0	100.0
Mean age	43.2	43.4	43.6	43.8	44.0	44.2	44.4	44.6	44.8	45.0	45.2	45.4	45.6	45.7	45.9	46.1	46.2	46.4	46.5	46.7	46.8
Median age	43.5	43.6	43.7	43.9	44.0	44.2	44.5	44.7	44.9	45.0	45.2	45.4	45.7	45.9	46.1	46.4	46.6	46.8	47.1	47.3	47.6

Ages	2041	2042	2043	2044	2045	2046	2047	2048	2049	2050	2051	2052	2053	2054	2055	2056	2057	2058	2059	2060
Thousands																				
0-14	327	327	326	326	325	325	325	324	324	323	322	320	319	317	314	312	309	306	303	299
15-29	435	428	421	415	408	403	397	393	389	386	384	382	381	380	379	378	377	377	376	376
30-44	514	514	514	514	514	514	515	516	515	512	508	502	495	488	482	474	466	459	453	447
45-59	568	568	567	566	563	560	554	548	542	536	530	524	521	520	520	521	520	521	521	522
60-74	503	500	496	493	492	491	491	495	501	507	515	525	532	536	537	538	538	537	536	534
75 & over	409	416	423	429	433	438	441	441	440	439	437	433	430	429	430	431	433	434	436	438
All ages	2,758	2,753	2,747	2,742	2,736	2,730	2,724	2,717	2,710	2,703	2,696	2,688	2,679	2,671	2,662	2,653	2,643	2,634	2,625	2,616
Percentages																				
0-14	11.9	11.9	11.9	11.9	11.9	11.9	11.9	11.9	11.9	11.9	11.9	11.9	11.9	11.9	11.8	11.8	11.7	11.6	11.5	11.4
15-29	15.8	15.6	15.3	15.1	14.9	14.7	14.6	14.5	14.3	14.3	14.2	14.2	14.2	14.2	14.2	14.2	14.3	14.3	14.3	14.4
30-44	18.7	18.7	18.7	18.7	18.8	18.8	18.9	19.0	19.0	18.9	18.8	18.7	18.5	18.3	18.1	17.9	17.6	17.4	17.3	17.1
45-59	20.6	20.6	20.6	20.6	20.6	20.5	20.4	20.2	20.0	19.8	19.7	19.5	19.5	19.5	19.5	19.6	19.7	19.8	19.9	19.9
60-74	18.3	18.2	18.1	18.0	18.0	18.0	18.0	18.2	18.5	18.8	19.1	19.5	19.9	20.1	20.2	20.3	20.3	20.4	20.4	20.4
75 & over	14.8	15.1	15.4	15.6	15.8	16.0	16.2	16.2	16.2	16.2	16.2	16.1	16.1	16.1	16.1	16.2	16.4	16.5	16.6	16.8
All ages	100.0	100.0	100.0	100.0	100.0	100.0	100.0	100.0	100.0	100.0	100.0	100.0	100.0	100.0	100.0	100.0	100.0	100.0	100.0	100.0
Mean age	46.9	47.1	47.2	47.3	47.4	47.5	47.6	47.7	47.8	47.9	48.0	48.1	48.2	48.3	48.4	48.5	48.6	48.7	48.8	48.9
Median age	47.8	48.0	48.1	48.3	48.4	48.6	48.7	48.8	48.9	49.0	49.0	49.1	49.2	49.3	49.4	49.5	49.7	49.8	50.0	50.2

15.3f Population projections by the Office for National Statistics
Scotland, FEMALES, thousands

Projected populations at mid-years by age last birthday

Ages	2061	2062	2063	2064	2065	2066	2067	2068	2069	2070	2071	2072	2073	2074	2075	2076	2077	2078	2079	2080
Thousands																				
0-14	296	293	290	287	284	282	279	277	275	274	272	271	270	269	268	268	267	266	266	265
15-29	376	375	375	374	373	372	371	369	367	365	362	359	356	352	349	345	342	339	336	333
30-44	441	435	431	427	424	422	420	419	418	417	416	415	415	414	414	414	413	413	412	411
45-59	522	523	523	522	520	516	510	503	496	490	482	475	468	461	455	449	444	439	435	432
60-74	532	527	521	515	510	505	500	498	497	498	499	499	500	501	502	502	503	504	503	501
75 & over	441	445	449	454	459	466	473	478	483	486	489	492	495	497	498	499	498	497	497	497
All ages	2,606	2,597	2,588	2,579	2,571	2,562	2,553	2,545	2,537	2,528	2,520	2,512	2,503	2,495	2,486	2,477	2,468	2,459	2,450	2,440
Percentages																				
0-14	11.4	11.3	11.2	11.1	11.1	11.0	10.9	10.9	10.9	10.8	10.8	10.8	10.8	10.8	10.8	10.8	10.8	10.8	10.8	10.9
15-29	14.4	14.4	14.5	14.5	14.5	14.5	14.5	14.5	14.5	14.4	14.4	14.3	14.2	14.1	14.0	13.9	13.9	13.8	13.7	13.6
30-44	16.9	16.8	16.6	16.5	16.5	16.5	16.5	16.5	16.5	16.5	16.5	16.5	16.6	16.6	16.7	16.7	16.7	16.8	16.8	16.9
45-59	20.0	20.1	20.2	20.3	20.2	20.1	20.0	19.8	19.6	19.4	19.1	18.9	18.7	18.5	18.3	18.1	18.0	17.9	17.8	17.7
60-74	20.4	20.3	20.1	20.0	19.9	19.7	19.6	19.6	19.6	19.7	19.8	19.9	20.0	20.1	20.2	20.3	20.4	20.5	20.6	20.5
75 & over	16.9	17.1	17.4	17.6	17.9	18.2	18.5	18.8	19.0	19.2	19.4	19.6	19.8	19.9	20.0	20.1	20.2	20.2	20.3	20.4
All ages	100.0	100.0	100.0	100.0	100.0	100.0	100.0	100.0	100.0	100.0	100.0	100.0	100.0	100.0	100.0	100.0	100.0	100.0	100.0	100.0
Mean age	49.0	49.1	49.2	49.3	49.4	49.5	49.6	49.7	49.8	49.9	50.0	50.1	50.2	50.3	50.4	50.5	50.5	50.6	50.7	50.7
Median age	50.4	50.6	50.8	51.0	51.2	51.3	51.5	51.7	51.8	52.0	52.1	52.2	52.2	52.3	52.3	52.3	52.4	52.4	52.4	52.4

Ages	2081	2082	2083	2084	2085	2086	2087	2088	2089	2090	2091	2092	2093	2094	2095	2096	2097	2098	2099	2100
Thousands																				
0-14	264	263	262	261	260	259	258	256	255	253	252	250	248	246	245	243	241	240	238	237
15-29	330	328	326	324	322	321	319	318	317	317	316	315	314	314	313	312	311	310	309	308
30-44	410	409	407	405	403	400	397	394	390	387	383	380	377	374	371	368	366	363	362	360
45-59	431	429	428	427	426	425	425	424	424	424	423	423	423	422	421	420	419	417	415	413
60-74	497	492	486	479	473	466	459	453	447	441	436	431	427	423	421	419	418	417	416	416
75 & over	498	499	502	504	507	510	513	515	517	519	521	521	522	522	521	519	517	515	513	512
All ages	2,430	2,421	2,411	2,401	2,391	2,381	2,370	2,360	2,350	2,340	2,330	2,321	2,311	2,301	2,292	2,282	2,273	2,264	2,254	2,245
Percentages																				
0-14	10.9	10.9	10.9	10.9	10.9	10.9	10.9	10.9	10.8	10.8	10.8	10.8	10.7	10.7	10.7	10.7	10.6	10.6	10.6	10.6
15-29	13.6	13.5	13.5	13.5	13.5	13.5	13.5	13.5	13.5	13.5	13.6	13.6	13.6	13.6	13.7	13.7	13.7	13.7	13.7	13.7
30-44	16.9	16.9	16.9	16.9	16.8	16.8	16.7	16.7	16.6	16.5	16.5	16.4	16.3	16.2	16.2	16.1	16.1	16.1	16.0	16.0
45-59	17.7	17.7	17.8	17.8	17.8	17.9	17.9	18.0	18.0	18.1	18.2	18.2	18.3	18.3	18.4	18.4	18.4	18.4	18.4	18.4
60-74	20.5	20.3	20.1	20.0	19.8	19.6	19.4	19.2	19.0	18.9	18.7	18.6	18.5	18.4	18.4	18.4	18.4	18.4	18.5	18.5
75 & over	20.5	20.6	20.8	21.0	21.2	21.4	21.6	21.8	22.0	22.2	22.3	22.5	22.6	22.7	22.7	22.8	22.8	22.8	22.8	22.8
All ages	100.0	100.0	100.0	100.0	100.0	100.0	100.0	100.0	100.0	100.0	100.0	100.0	100.0	100.0	100.0	100.0	100.0	100.0	100.0	100.0
Mean age	50.8	50.8	50.9	50.9	51.0	51.0	51.1	51.1	51.1	51.2	51.2	51.3	51.3	51.4	51.4	51.4	51.5	51.5	51.6	51.6
Median age	52.5	52.5	52.5	52.5	52.5	52.5	52.5	52.5	52.5	52.5	52.6	52.6	52.7	52.7	52.8	52.8	52.9	53.0	53.1	53.1

15.3f Population projections by the Office for National Statistics
Scotland, FEMALES, thousands

Projected populations at mid-years by age last birthday

Ages	2101	2102	2103	2104	2105	2106	2107	2108	2109	2110	2111	2112	2113	2114	2115	2116	2117	2118	2119	2120
Thousands																				
0-14	236	234	233	232	231	230	230	229	228	227	227	226	225	225	224	223	223	222	221	220
15-29	307	305	304	302	301	299	297	295	294	292	290	288	287	285	284	282	281	280	279	278
30-44	358	357	356	355	354	353	353	352	351	351	350	349	348	347	346	344	343	342	340	338
45-59	410	407	404	401	397	394	390	387	384	381	378	376	374	372	370	369	368	367	366	365
60-74	415	415	415	415	415	415	415	414	414	414	413	412	410	408	406	404	401	398	395	391
75 & over	510	508	506	504	502	500	498	495	493	492	490	488	487	487	487	487	487	488	489	490
All ages	2,236	2,227	2,218	2,209	2,200	2,191	2,182	2,173	2,165	2,156	2,148	2,140	2,132	2,124	2,117	2,109	2,102	2,095	2,089	2,082
Percentages																				
0-14	10.5	10.5	10.5	10.5	10.5	10.5	10.5	10.5	10.5	10.6	10.6	10.6	10.6	10.6	10.6	10.6	10.6	10.6	10.6	10.6
15-29	13.7	13.7	13.7	13.7	13.7	13.6	13.6	13.6	13.6	13.5	13.5	13.5	13.5	13.4	13.4	13.4	13.4	13.4	13.4	13.3
30-44	16.0	16.0	16.1	16.1	16.1	16.1	16.2	16.2	16.2	16.3	16.3	16.3	16.3	16.3	16.3	16.3	16.3	16.3	16.3	16.2
45-59	18.3	18.3	18.2	18.1	18.1	18.0	17.9	17.8	17.7	17.7	17.6	17.6	17.5	17.5	17.5	17.5	17.5	17.5	17.5	17.5
60-74	18.6	18.6	18.7	18.8	18.8	18.9	19.0	19.1	19.1	19.2	19.2	19.2	19.2	19.2	19.2	19.1	19.1	19.0	18.9	18.8
75 & over	22.8	22.8	22.8	22.8	22.8	22.8	22.8	22.8	22.8	22.8	22.8	22.8	22.9	22.9	23.0	23.1	23.2	23.3	23.4	23.5
All ages	100.0	100.0	100.0	100.0	100.0	100.0	100.0	100.0	100.0	100.0	100.0	100.0	100.0	100.0	100.0	100.0	100.0	100.0	100.0	100.0
Mean age	51.6	51.7	51.7	51.7	51.7	51.8	51.8	51.8	51.8	51.8	51.8	51.8	51.9	51.9	51.9	51.9	51.9	52.0	52.0	52.0
Median age	53.2	53.2	53.3	53.3	53.4	53.4	53.4	53.4	53.4	53.4	53.4	53.4	53.4	53.4	53.4	53.4	53.4	53.5	53.5	53.5

Note: Figures may not add exactly due to rounding.

Source: Office for National Statistics

15.3g Mid-2019 Population estimates for Northern Ireland by sex and single year of age

Ages	Persons	Males	Females	Ages	Persons	Males	Females
All ages	1,893,667	932,717	960,950	45	23,983	11,642	12,341
0	22,721	11,673	11,048	46	24,946	12,185	12,761
1	23,408	11,980	11,428	47	25,284	12,407	12,877
2	24,206	12,439	11,767	48	25,769	12,488	13,281
3	25,074	13,020	12,054	49	25,798	12,549	13,249
4	24,960	12,794	12,166	50	26,064	12,687	13,377
5	24,998	12,815	12,183	51	26,499	13,009	13,490
6	25,373	12,911	12,462	52	26,301	12,831	13,470
7	26,274	13,461	12,813	53	26,344	12,963	13,381
8	26,099	13,257	12,842	54	26,776	13,065	13,711
9	25,802	13,153	12,649	55	26,255	12,900	13,355
10	26,127	13,418	12,709	56	25,575	12,745	12,830
11	26,142	13,384	12,758	57	24,950	12,159	12,791
12	24,935	12,847	12,088	58	24,494	12,023	12,471
13	23,761	12,199	11,562	59	23,380	11,425	11,955
14	23,162	11,928	11,234	60	22,651	11,146	11,505
15	22,883	11,802	11,081	61	22,266	10,932	11,334
16	22,396	11,433	10,963	62	21,269	10,404	10,865
17	22,384	11,430	10,954	63	20,328	10,040	10,288
18	22,501	11,543	10,958	64	19,290	9,626	9,664
19	22,233	11,816	10,417	65	18,881	9,473	9,408
20	23,073	12,082	10,991	66	18,421	9,054	9,367
21	22,790	11,981	10,809	67	17,636	8,687	8,949
22	23,077	11,894	11,183	68	17,509	8,602	8,907
23	23,155	11,998	11,157	69	17,426	8,462	8,964
24	23,264	11,986	11,278	70	17,173	8,303	8,870
25	23,626	11,959	11,667	71	16,941	8,073	8,868
26	23,669	11,864	11,805	72	16,795	7,907	8,888
27	24,831	12,426	12,405	73	15,445	7,272	8,173
28	25,119	12,504	12,615	74	15,045	7,060	7,985
29	25,080	12,537	12,543	75	14,655	6,861	7,794
30	24,985	12,486	12,499	76	13,914	6,425	7,489
31	25,351	12,602	12,749	77	12,285	5,667	6,618
32	25,554	12,681	12,873	78	10,838	4,876	5,962
33	25,622	12,622	13,000	79	10,182	4,558	5,624
34	25,249	12,497	12,752	80	10,111	4,478	5,633
35	24,998	12,254	12,744	81	9,166	4,023	5,143
36	24,669	12,010	12,659	82	8,685	3,721	4,964
37	24,596	11,969	12,627	83	7,767	3,221	4,546
38	25,205	12,310	12,895	84	7,110	2,893	4,217
39	25,115	12,191	12,924	85	6,219	2,499	3,720
40	24,122	11,497	12,625	86	5,789	2,248	3,541
41	23,009	11,123	11,886	87	5,005	1,889	3,116
42	22,858	11,081	11,777	88	4,375	1,596	2,779
43	22,935	11,135	11,800	89	3,617	1,189	2,428
44	23,330	11,382	11,948	90	13,734	4,080	9,654

Source: Office for National Statistics

1. Estimates are presented both rounded to the nearest hundred and unrounded. Unrounded estimates are published to enable and encourage further calculations and analysis. However, the estimates should not be taken to be accurate to the level of detail provided. More information on the accuracy of the estimates is available in the Quality and Methodology document (QMI):

https://www.ons.gov.uk/peoplepopulationandcommunity/populationandmigration/
populationestimates/methodologies/annualmidyearpopulationestimatesqmi

2. The estimates are produced using a variety of data sources and statistical models, including some statistical disclosure control methods, and small estimates should not be taken to refer to particular individuals.

3. The estimated resident population of an area includes all those people who usually live there, regardless of nationality. Arriving international migrants are included in the usually resident population if they remain in the UK for at least a year. Emigrants are excluded if they remain outside the UK for at least a year. This is consistent with the United Nations definition of a long-term migrant. Armed forces stationed outside of the UK are excluded. Students are taken to be usually resident at their term time address.

4. Where data appears for age 90 please note this is for ages 90 and above.

15.3h Population projections by the Office for National Statistics
Northern Ireland, PERSONS, thousands

2020-based
Principal projection

Projected populations at mid-years by age last birthday

Ages	2020	2021	2022	2023	2024	2025	2026	2027	2028	2029	2030	2031	2032	2033	2034	2035	2036	2037	2038	2039	2040
Thousands																					
0-14	373	372	368	363	358	353	347	341	335	330	325	319	313	309	304	301	298	297	296	295	295
15-29	344	341	339	340	341	343	345	347	349	350	353	357	360	362	363	363	362	358	353	348	343
30-44	369	372	375	376	376	375	374	373	371	369	366	361	356	352	349	345	342	341	341	342	343
45-59	381	379	376	373	371	369	368	366	364	364	363	364	365	366	367	370	373	376	378	378	377
60-74	282	288	293	299	305	312	319	326	332	337	342	346	349	350	351	350	348	346	344	342	341
75 & over	147	151	155	159	163	167	171	174	178	181	185	189	193	198	203	208	214	220	226	232	239
All ages	1,896	1,902	1,906	1,910	1,915	1,920	1,924	1,927	1,930	1,932	1,934	1,935	1,936	1,937	1,937	1,937	1,937	1,937	1,937	1,938	1,938
Percentages																					
0-14	19.7	19.5	19.3	19.0	18.7	18.4	18.0	17.7	17.4	17.1	16.8	16.5	16.2	15.9	15.7	15.5	15.4	15.3	15.3	15.2	15.2
15-29	18.1	17.9	17.8	17.8	17.8	17.9	17.9	18.0	18.1	18.1	18.3	18.5	18.6	18.7	18.7	18.7	18.7	18.5	18.2	18.0	17.7
30-44	19.5	19.6	19.7	19.7	19.7	19.5	19.4	19.3	19.2	19.1	18.9	18.6	18.4	18.2	18.0	17.8	17.7	17.6	17.6	17.7	17.7
45-59	20.1	19.9	19.7	19.5	19.4	19.2	19.1	19.0	18.9	18.8	18.8	18.8	18.8	18.9	19.0	19.1	19.3	19.4	19.5	19.5	19.5
60-74	14.9	15.1	15.4	15.6	15.9	16.3	16.6	16.9	17.2	17.4	17.7	17.9	18.0	18.1	18.1	18.1	18.0	17.9	17.7	17.6	17.6
75 & over	7.8	7.9	8.1	8.3	8.5	8.7	8.9	9.0	9.2	9.4	9.6	9.8	10.0	10.2	10.5	10.8	11.1	11.4	11.7	12.0	12.3
All ages	100.0	100.0	100.0	100.0	100.0	100.0	100.0	100.0	100.0	100.0	100.0	100.0	100.0	100.0	100.0	100.0	100.0	100.0	100.0	100.0	100.0
Mean age	39.8	40.0	40.2	40.4	40.7	40.9	41.1	41.4	41.6	41.8	42.1	42.3	42.5	42.7	43.0	43.2	43.4	43.5	43.7	43.9	44.0
Median age	39.2	39.5	39.7	40.0	40.3	40.6	40.8	41.1	41.4	41.7	42.0	42.3	42.6	42.9	43.2	43.4	43.7	43.9	44.1	44.3	44.5

Ages	2041	2042	2043	2044	2045	2046	2047	2048	2049	2050	2051	2052	2053	2054	2055	2056	2057	2058	2059	2060
Thousands																				
0-14	295	295	295	296	297	299	300	301	302	302	303	303	302	301	300	298	295	293	290	287
15-29	338	332	327	322	317	312	307	303	299	296	293	292	291	291	290	290	291	292	292	294
30-44	345	347	349	351	353	358	361	363	364	365	364	361	356	351	347	341	336	331	326	321
45-59	375	375	373	371	368	363	358	354	351	348	345	343	344	345	347	349	351	353	354	357
60-74	340	339	338	337	338	338	340	341	343	346	349	352	354	354	354	352	352	351	349	346
75 & over	245	250	256	260	265	269	272	275	277	278	279	280	281	282	285	287	289	291	293	295
All ages	1,938	1,938	1,938	1,939	1,939	1,938	1,938	1,937	1,936	1,935	1,933	1,931	1,928	1,925	1,921	1,918	1,914	1,909	1,905	1,900
Percentages																				
0-14	15.2	15.2	15.2	15.3	15.3	15.4	15.5	15.5	15.6	15.6	15.7	15.7	15.7	15.6	15.6	15.5	15.4	15.3	15.2	15.1
15-29	17.4	17.1	16.9	16.6	16.4	16.1	15.8	15.6	15.4	15.3	15.2	15.1	15.1	15.1	15.1	15.1	15.2	15.3	15.4	15.5
30-44	17.8	17.9	18.0	18.1	18.2	18.5	18.6	18.7	18.8	18.9	18.8	18.7	18.5	18.2	18.0	17.8	17.5	17.3	17.1	16.9
45-59	19.4	19.3	19.3	19.2	19.0	18.7	18.5	18.3	18.1	18.0	17.8	17.8	17.9	17.9	18.0	18.2	18.3	18.5	18.6	18.8
60-74	17.5	17.5	17.4	17.4	17.4	17.5	17.5	17.6	17.7	17.9	18.1	18.2	18.3	18.4	18.4	18.4	18.4	18.4	18.3	18.2
75 & over	12.6	12.9	13.2	13.4	13.7	13.9	14.0	14.2	14.3	14.4	14.4	14.5	14.6	14.7	14.8	15.0	15.1	15.2	15.4	15.5
All ages	100.0	100.0	100.0	100.0	100.0	100.0	100.0	100.0	100.0	100.0	100.0	100.0	100.0	100.0	100.0	100.0	100.0	100.0	100.0	100.0
Mean age	44.2	44.3	44.4	44.6	44.7	44.8	44.9	45.0	45.1	45.2	45.3	45.3	45.4	45.5	45.6	45.7	45.8	45.9	46.0	46.1
Median age	44.6	44.8	44.9	45.0	45.1	45.0	45.1	45.1	45.1	45.2	45.3	45.4	45.6	45.8	46.0	46.1	46.3	46.6	46.8	47.0

15.3h Population projections by the Office for National Statistics
Northern Ireland, PERSONS, thousands

2020-based
Principal projection

Projected populations at mid-years by age last birthday

Ages	2061	2062	2063	2064	2065	2066	2067	2068	2069	2070	2071	2072	2073	2074	2075	2076	2077	2078	2079	2080
Thousands																				
0-14	284	280	277	274	271	269	266	264	263	261	260	259	258	258	258	258	258	258	258	258
15-29	295	296	297	298	298	298	298	298	297	295	293	291	288	286	283	280	277	274	271	268
30-44	315	311	306	302	299	297	295	295	294	294	294	294	295	295	297	298	299	300	301	301
45-59	362	365	367	368	369	368	365	360	355	351	346	340	335	330	325	320	315	311	307	304
60-74	342	338	334	331	328	326	325	326	328	329	332	334	336	338	341	346	349	351	352	353
75 & over	298	301	304	306	309	312	315	317	319	320	321	323	323	324	324	322	322	321	321	321
All ages	1,895	1,890	1,885	1,880	1,875	1,870	1,865	1,860	1,855	1,850	1,845	1,841	1,836	1,832	1,827	1,823	1,818	1,814	1,810	1,805
Percentages																				
0-14	15.0	14.8	14.7	14.6	14.5	14.4	14.3	14.2	14.2	14.1	14.1	14.1	14.1	14.1	14.1	14.1	14.2	14.2	14.3	14.3
15-29	15.5	15.6	15.7	15.8	15.9	16.0	16.0	16.0	16.0	15.9	15.9	15.8	15.7	15.6	15.5	15.3	15.2	15.1	15.0	14.9
30-44	16.6	16.4	16.2	16.1	15.9	15.9	15.8	15.8	15.8	15.9	15.9	16.0	16.0	16.1	16.2	16.3	16.4	16.5	16.6	16.7
45-59	19.1	19.3	19.5	19.6	19.7	19.7	19.6	19.4	19.2	19.0	18.7	18.5	18.3	18.0	17.8	17.6	17.3	17.1	17.0	16.8
60-74	18.0	17.9	17.7	17.6	17.5	17.4	17.4	17.5	17.7	17.8	18.0	18.2	18.3	18.5	18.7	19.0	19.2	19.3	19.5	19.5
75 & over	15.7	15.9	16.1	16.3	16.5	16.7	16.9	17.1	17.2	17.3	17.4	17.5	17.6	17.7	17.7	17.7	17.7	17.7	17.7	17.8
All ages	100.0	100.0	100.0	100.0	100.0	100.0	100.0	100.0	100.0	100.0	100.0	100.0	100.0	100.0	100.0	100.0	100.0	100.0	100.0	100.0
Mean age	46.2	46.4	46.5	46.6	46.7	46.8	46.9	47.0	47.1	47.1	47.2	47.3	47.4	47.4	47.5	47.6	47.6	47.7	47.7	47.8
Median age	47.2	47.4	47.6	47.8	48.0	48.1	48.3	48.4	48.5	48.6	48.7	48.7	48.8	48.8	48.8	48.8	48.8	48.8	48.8	48.8

Ages	2081	2082	2083	2084	2085	2086	2087	2088	2089	2090	2091	2092	2093	2094	2095	2096	2097	2098	2099	2100
Thousands																				
0-14	258	258	258	258	257	256	255	254	253	252	250	248	247	245	243	241	240	238	236	235
15-29	266	264	262	260	259	258	257	257	256	256	256	256	256	256	257	257	257	256	256	256
30-44	302	302	301	300	299	297	295	293	290	287	284	281	278	276	273	271	268	266	265	264
45-59	302	300	300	299	299	299	299	300	301	302	303	305	306	307	307	308	308	307	306	305
60-74	352	349	345	340	336	331	326	322	317	313	308	304	300	296	293	291	290	290	290	290
75 & over	321	323	326	329	332	335	339	342	344	347	351	353	355	357	358	359	359	358	357	357
All ages	1,801	1,796	1,791	1,787	1,782	1,777	1,772	1,767	1,762	1,757	1,752	1,747	1,742	1,737	1,732	1,726	1,721	1,716	1,711	1,705
Percentages																				
0-14	14.3	14.4	14.4	14.4	14.4	14.4	14.4	14.4	14.4	14.3	14.3	14.2	14.2	14.1	14.0	14.0	13.9	13.9	13.8	13.8
15-29	14.8	14.7	14.6	14.6	14.5	14.5	14.5	14.5	14.5	14.6	14.6	14.7	14.7	14.8	14.8	14.9	14.9	14.9	15.0	15.0
30-44	16.8	16.8	16.8	16.8	16.8	16.7	16.7	16.6	16.5	16.3	16.2	16.1	16.0	15.9	15.8	15.7	15.6	15.5	15.5	15.5
45-59	16.7	16.7	16.7	16.7	16.8	16.8	16.9	17.0	17.1	17.2	17.3	17.4	17.5	17.7	17.7	17.8	17.9	17.9	17.9	17.9
60-74	19.5	19.4	19.2	19.1	18.9	18.7	18.4	18.2	18.0	17.8	17.6	17.4	17.2	17.1	16.9	16.9	16.9	16.9	16.9	17.0
75 & over	17.8	18.0	18.2	18.4	18.6	18.9	19.1	19.3	19.5	19.8	20.0	20.2	20.4	20.6	20.7	20.8	20.8	20.9	20.9	20.9
All ages	100.0	100.0	100.0	100.0	100.0	100.0	100.0	100.0	100.0	100.0	100.0	100.0	100.0	100.0	100.0	100.0	100.0	100.0	100.0	100.0
Mean age	47.8	47.9	47.9	48.0	48.0	48.1	48.1	48.2	48.2	48.3	48.3	48.4	48.5	48.5	48.6	48.7	48.7	48.8	48.9	48.9
Median age	48.8	48.8	48.8	48.8	48.8	48.8	48.8	48.9	48.9	49.0	49.1	49.2	49.3	49.4	49.5	49.6	49.8	49.9	50.0	50.1

15.3h Population projections by the Office for National Statistics
Northern Ireland, PERSONS, thousands

2020-based
Principal projection

Projected populations at mid-years by age last birthday

Ages	2101	2102	2103	2104	2105	2106	2107	2108	2109	2110	2111	2112	2113	2114	2115	2116	2117	2118	2119	2120
Thousands																				
0-14	233	232	231	230	229	229	228	228	227	227	227	226	226	226	225	225	224	224	223	223
15-29	255	254	253	252	250	249	247	246	244	242	241	239	237	236	234	233	232	231	230	230
30-44	262	262	261	261	261	261	261	261	261	261	261	261	261	261	260	260	259	258	257	255
45-59	303	301	299	296	293	290	287	285	282	279	277	275	273	271	270	269	268	267	267	267
60-74	290	290	291	292	294	295	296	298	299	299	300	300	300	299	298	296	294	292	289	287
75 & over	356	355	354	352	351	349	347	345	344	342	341	340	339	339	339	339	340	341	343	344
All ages	1,700	1,694	1,689	1,683	1,678	1,672	1,667	1,661	1,656	1,651	1,646	1,641	1,636	1,631	1,626	1,622	1,618	1,613	1,609	1,605
Percentages																				
0-14	13.7	13.7	13.7	13.7	13.7	13.7	13.7	13.7	13.7	13.7	13.8	13.8	13.8	13.8	13.9	13.9	13.9	13.9	13.9	13.9
15-29	15.0	15.0	15.0	15.0	14.9	14.9	14.8	14.8	14.7	14.7	14.6	14.6	14.5	14.5	14.4	14.4	14.3	14.3	14.3	14.3
30-44	15.4	15.4	15.5	15.5	15.5	15.6	15.6	15.7	15.8	15.8	15.9	15.9	16.0	16.0	16.0	16.0	16.0	16.0	15.9	15.9
45-59	17.8	17.8	17.7	17.6	17.5	17.4	17.2	17.1	17.0	16.9	16.8	16.7	16.7	16.6	16.6	16.6	16.6	16.6	16.6	16.6
60-74	17.1	17.1	17.3	17.4	17.5	17.6	17.8	17.9	18.0	18.1	18.2	18.3	18.3	18.3	18.3	18.3	18.2	18.1	18.0	17.9
75 & over	20.9	20.9	20.9	20.9	20.9	20.9	20.8	20.8	20.8	20.7	20.7	20.7	20.7	20.8	20.8	20.9	21.0	21.1	21.3	21.4
All ages	100.0	100.0	100.0	100.0	100.0	100.0	100.0	100.0	100.0	100.0	100.0	100.0	100.0	100.0	100.0	100.0	100.0	100.0	100.0	100.0
Mean age	49.0	49.0	49.0	49.1	49.1	49.1	49.2	49.2	49.2	49.2	49.2	49.2	49.2	49.2	49.3	49.3	49.3	49.3	49.4	49.4
Median age	50.1	50.2	50.3	50.3	50.3	50.4	50.4	50.4	50.4	50.4	50.3	50.3	50.3	50.3	50.3	50.3	50.3	50.3	50.3	50.3

Note: Figures may not add exactly due to rounding.

Source: Office for National Statistics

15.3h Population projections by the Office for National Statistics
Northern Ireland, MALES, thousands

Projected populations at mid-years by age last birthday

Ages	2020	2021	2022	2023	2024	2025	2026	2027	2028	2029	2030	2031	2032	2033	2034	2035	2036	2037	2038	2039	2040
Thousands																					
0-14	191	191	189	186	183	181	178	175	172	169	167	163	161	158	156	154	153	152	151	151	151
15-29	177	175	175	176	177	177	178	180	181	182	183	185	186	187	188	188	187	185	183	180	178
30-44	181	182	184	185	186	186	186	186	186	186	185	183	181	179	178	177	176	175	176	177	178
45-59	186	185	183	182	180	179	178	177	176	176	176	176	177	177	178	180	182	184	185	186	186
60-74	137	140	143	146	149	152	155	158	161	163	165	167	168	168	168	168	167	166	164	163	162
75 & over	62	64	66	68	71	73	75	76	78	80	82	84	86	89	91	93	96	98	101	104	107
All ages	934	938	940	943	946	948	951	953	954	956	957	958	959	959	960	960	960	961	961	961	961
Percentages																					
0-14	20.5	20.3	20.1	19.7	19.4	19.1	18.7	18.4	18.0	17.7	17.4	17.1	16.8	16.5	16.3	16.0	15.9	15.8	15.8	15.7	15.7
15-29	18.9	18.7	18.6	18.7	18.7	18.7	18.8	18.9	18.9	19.0	19.1	19.3	19.4	19.5	19.6	19.6	19.5	19.3	19.0	18.7	18.5
30-44	19.3	19.4	19.6	19.6	19.7	19.6	19.6	19.5	19.5	19.4	19.3	19.1	18.9	18.7	18.6	18.4	18.3	18.3	18.3	18.4	18.5
45-59	19.9	19.7	19.5	19.3	19.0	18.9	18.7	18.6	18.5	18.4	18.4	18.4	18.4	18.5	18.6	18.8	18.9	19.1	19.2	19.3	19.3
60-74	14.7	15.0	15.2	15.5	15.7	16.0	16.3	16.6	16.9	17.1	17.2	17.4	17.5	17.6	17.5	17.5	17.4	17.3	17.1	17.0	16.9
75 & over	6.7	6.8	7.0	7.3	7.5	7.7	7.8	8.0	8.2	8.4	8.6	8.8	9.0	9.2	9.5	9.7	10.0	10.3	10.6	10.8	11.1
All ages	100.0	100.0	100.0	100.0	100.0	100.0	100.0	100.0	100.0	100.0	100.0	100.0	100.0	100.0	100.0	100.0	100.0	100.0	100.0	100.0	100.0
Mean age	38.8	39.0	39.2	39.5	39.7	39.9	40.2	40.4	40.6	40.9	41.1	41.3	41.5	41.7	41.9	42.1	42.3	42.5	42.7	42.8	43.0
Median age	38.0	38.2	38.4	38.7	39.0	39.3	39.5	39.8	40.1	40.4	40.6	40.9	41.2	41.5	41.7	41.9	42.2	42.4	42.6	42.8	42.9

Ages	2041	2042	2043	2044	2045	2046	2047	2048	2049	2050	2051	2052	2053	2054	2055	2056	2057	2058	2059	2060
Thousands																				
0-14	151	151	151	152	152	153	153	154	154	155	155	155	155	154	153	152	151	150	148	147
15-29	175	172	169	167	164	161	159	157	154	153	151	151	150	150	150	150	150	151	151	152
30-44	178	180	181	181	183	185	186	188	188	189	188	186	184	181	179	177	174	171	169	166
45-59	186	186	186	186	185	183	181	180	178	177	176	176	177	178	178	179	181	182	183	184
60-74	162	161	161	161	161	161	162	163	164	166	168	170	171	172	172	172	172	173	172	172
75 & over	110	112	115	117	118	120	121	123	123	124	124	124	124	125	125	126	127	128	129	130
All ages	962	962	962	963	963	963	963	963	963	963	962	962	961	960	958	957	955	954	952	950
Percentages																				
0-14	15.7	15.7	15.7	15.8	15.8	15.9	15.9	16.0	16.0	16.1	16.1	16.1	16.1	16.1	16.0	15.9	15.8	15.7	15.6	15.5
15-29	18.2	17.9	17.6	17.3	17.1	16.7	16.5	16.3	16.0	15.9	15.7	15.7	15.7	15.6	15.6	15.7	15.7	15.8	15.9	16.0
30-44	18.6	18.7	18.8	18.8	19.0	19.2	19.4	19.5	19.6	19.6	19.5	19.4	19.1	18.9	18.7	18.5	18.2	17.9	17.7	17.5
45-59	19.3	19.3	19.3	19.3	19.2	19.0	18.8	18.6	18.5	18.4	18.3	18.3	18.4	18.5	18.6	18.7	18.9	19.0	19.2	19.3
60-74	16.8	16.8	16.7	16.7	16.7	16.7	16.8	16.9	17.0	17.2	17.4	17.6	17.8	17.9	18.0	18.0	18.0	18.1	18.1	18.1
75 & over	11.4	11.7	11.9	12.1	12.3	12.5	12.6	12.7	12.8	12.8	12.9	12.9	12.9	13.0	13.1	13.2	13.3	13.4	13.6	13.7
All ages	100.0	100.0	100.0	100.0	100.0	100.0	100.0	100.0	100.0	100.0	100.0	100.0	100.0	100.0	100.0	100.0	100.0	100.0	100.0	100.0
Mean age	43.1	43.2	43.3	43.5	43.6	43.7	43.8	43.8	43.9	44.0	44.1	44.2	44.3	44.4	44.5	44.6	44.7	44.9	45.0	45.1
Median age	43.1	43.2	43.3	43.3	43.4	43.4	43.5	43.6	43.7	43.8	43.9	44.1	44.3	44.5	44.7	45.0	45.2	45.4	45.6	45.8

15.3h Population projections by the Office for National Statistics
Northern Ireland, MALES, thousands

Projected populations at mid-years by age last birthday

Ages	2061	2062	2063	2064	2065	2066	2067	2068	2069	2070	2071	2072	2073	2074	2075	2076	2077	2078	2079	2080
Thousands																				
0-14	145	144	142	140	139	138	136	135	134	134	133	133	132	132	132	132	132	132	132	132
15-29	152	153	153	154	154	154	154	154	153	152	151	150	149	148	146	144	143	141	140	139
30-44	163	161	158	156	155	153	153	152	152	152	152	152	152	153	153	154	154	155	155	156
45-59	186	188	189	190	190	189	188	185	183	181	178	175	173	170	168	165	162	160	158	157
60-74	170	169	167	166	165	165	165	166	167	168	169	170	171	172	174	176	177	179	179	180
75 & over	132	133	135	136	138	140	142	143	144	145	146	147	148	149	149	149	149	149	150	150
All ages	948	947	945	943	941	939	937	935	933	931	929	928	926	924	922	920	919	917	915	913
Percentages																				
0-14	15.3	15.2	15.0	14.9	14.8	14.7	14.6	14.5	14.4	14.4	14.3	14.3	14.3	14.3	14.3	14.3	14.4	14.4	14.4	14.5
15-29	16.0	16.1	16.2	16.3	16.4	16.4	16.4	16.4	16.4	16.4	16.3	16.2	16.1	16.0	15.8	15.7	15.6	15.4	15.3	15.2
30-44	17.2	17.0	16.8	16.6	16.4	16.3	16.3	16.3	16.3	16.3	16.3	16.4	16.5	16.5	16.6	16.7	16.8	16.9	17.0	17.1
45-59	19.6	19.8	20.0	20.1	20.2	20.2	20.0	19.8	19.6	19.4	19.2	18.9	18.7	18.4	18.2	17.9	17.7	17.5	17.3	17.1
60-74	17.9	17.8	17.7	17.6	17.6	17.5	17.6	17.7	17.9	18.0	18.1	18.3	18.5	18.6	18.8	19.1	19.3	19.5	19.6	19.7
75 & over	13.9	14.1	14.3	14.5	14.7	14.9	15.1	15.3	15.4	15.6	15.7	15.9	16.0	16.1	16.2	16.2	16.3	16.3	16.4	16.5
All ages	100.0	100.0	100.0	100.0	100.0	100.0	100.0	100.0	100.0	100.0	100.0	100.0	100.0	100.0	100.0	100.0	100.0	100.0	100.0	100.0
Mean age	45.2	45.3	45.4	45.6	45.7	45.8	45.9	46.0	46.1	46.2	46.4	46.4	46.5	46.6	46.7	46.8	46.9	46.9	47.0	47.1
Median age	46.0	46.3	46.5	46.7	46.9	47.1	47.3	47.4	47.5	47.6	47.7	47.7	47.8	47.9	47.9	47.9	47.9	48.0	48.0	48.0

Ages	2081	2082	2083	2084	2085	2086	2087	2088	2089	2090	2091	2092	2093	2094	2095	2096	2097	2098	2099	2100
Thousands																				
0-14	132	132	132	132	132	131	131	130	130	129	128	127	126	125	124	124	123	122	121	120
15-29	137	136	135	134	134	133	133	133	132	132	132	132	132	132	133	133	133	132	132	132
30-44	156	156	156	155	155	154	153	151	150	149	147	146	144	143	141	140	139	138	137	136
45-59	155	155	154	154	154	154	154	155	155	156	156	157	158	158	158	159	159	158	158	157
60-74	179	178	176	173	171	169	167	164	162	160	157	155	153	151	150	149	148	148	148	148
75 & over	151	152	154	156	158	160	162	163	165	167	169	170	171	172	173	173	173	173	173	172
All ages	911	909	907	905	903	901	899	897	894	892	890	887	885	882	880	877	874	872	869	866
Percentages																				
0-14	14.5	14.5	14.6	14.6	14.6	14.6	14.6	14.5	14.5	14.4	14.4	14.3	14.3	14.2	14.2	14.1	14.0	14.0	13.9	13.9
15-29	15.1	15.0	14.9	14.9	14.8	14.8	14.8	14.8	14.8	14.8	14.9	14.9	15.0	15.0	15.1	15.1	15.2	15.2	15.2	15.2
30-44	17.1	17.2	17.2	17.2	17.1	17.1	17.0	16.9	16.8	16.7	16.5	16.4	16.3	16.2	16.1	16.0	15.9	15.8	15.8	15.7
45-59	17.0	17.0	17.0	17.0	17.1	17.1	17.2	17.3	17.4	17.5	17.6	17.7	17.8	17.9	18.0	18.1	18.1	18.2	18.2	18.2
60-74	19.7	19.5	19.4	19.2	19.0	18.8	18.5	18.3	18.1	17.9	17.7	17.5	17.3	17.2	17.0	17.0	17.0	17.0	17.0	17.1
75 & over	16.6	16.8	17.0	17.2	17.5	17.7	18.0	18.2	18.5	18.7	18.9	19.2	19.4	19.5	19.7	19.8	19.8	19.8	19.9	19.9
All ages	100.0	100.0	100.0	100.0	100.0	100.0	100.0	100.0	100.0	100.0	100.0	100.0	100.0	100.0	100.0	100.0	100.0	100.0	100.0	100.0
Mean age	47.1	47.2	47.2	47.3	47.4	47.4	47.5	47.6	47.6	47.7	47.8	47.8	47.9	48.0	48.1	48.1	48.2	48.3	48.3	48.4
Median age	48.0	48.0	48.0	48.0	48.0	48.1	48.1	48.2	48.3	48.4	48.5	48.6	48.7	48.8	48.9	49.0	49.1	49.2	49.3	49.4

15.3h Population projections by the Office for National Statistics
Northern Ireland, MALES, thousands

2020-based
Principal projection

Projected populations at mid-years by age last birthday

Ages	2101	2102	2103	2104	2105	2106	2107	2108	2109	2110	2111	2112	2113	2114	2115	2116	2117	2118	2119	2120
Thousands																				
0-14	120	119	118	118	117	117	117	117	116	116	116	116	116	116	115	115	115	115	114	114
15-29	132	131	131	130	129	129	128	127	126	125	124	123	123	122	121	120	120	119	119	119
30-44	136	136	135	135	135	135	135	135	135	135	135	135	135	135	135	135	134	134	133	132
45-59	156	155	154	153	151	150	148	147	146	144	143	142	141	140	139	139	139	138	138	138
60-74	148	149	149	150	150	151	152	152	153	153	154	154	153	153	152	152	151	150	148	147
75 & over	172	172	171	170	170	169	168	167	167	166	165	165	165	165	165	165	166	166	167	168
All ages	864	861	858	856	853	850	848	845	842	840	837	835	833	830	828	826	824	822	820	818
Percentages																				
0-14	13.8	13.8	13.8	13.8	13.8	13.8	13.8	13.8	13.8	13.8	13.9	13.9	13.9	13.9	13.9	13.9	13.9	13.9	13.9	13.9
15-29	15.2	15.2	15.2	15.2	15.2	15.1	15.1	15.0	15.0	14.9	14.8	14.8	14.7	14.7	14.6	14.6	14.6	14.5	14.5	14.5
30-44	15.7	15.7	15.8	15.8	15.8	15.9	15.9	16.0	16.0	16.1	16.2	16.2	16.2	16.3	16.3	16.3	16.3	16.3	16.2	16.2
45-59	18.1	18.0	18.0	17.9	17.7	17.6	17.5	17.4	17.3	17.2	17.1	17.0	16.9	16.9	16.8	16.8	16.8	16.8	16.8	16.9
60-74	17.2	17.2	17.4	17.5	17.6	17.7	17.9	18.0	18.1	18.2	18.3	18.4	18.4	18.4	18.4	18.4	18.3	18.2	18.1	18.0
75 & over	19.9	19.9	19.9	19.9	19.9	19.9	19.8	19.8	19.8	19.7	19.7	19.8	19.8	19.8	19.9	20.0	20.1	20.3	20.4	20.6
All ages	100.0	100.0	100.0	100.0	100.0	100.0	100.0	100.0	100.0	100.0	100.0	100.0	100.0	100.0	100.0	100.0	100.0	100.0	100.0	100.0
Mean age	48.4	48.5	48.5	48.5	48.6	48.6	48.6	48.6	48.6	48.7	48.7	48.7	48.7	48.7	48.8	48.8	48.8	48.9	48.9	48.9
Median age	49.5	49.6	49.6	49.7	49.7	49.7	49.7	49.7	49.7	49.7	49.7	49.7	49.7	49.7	49.7	49.7	49.7	49.7	49.7	49.8

Source: Office for National Statistics

Note: Figures may not add exactly due to rounding.

15.3h Population projections by the Office for National Statistics
Northern Ireland, FEMALES, thousands

2020-based
Principal projection

Projected populations at mid-years by age last birthday

Ages	2020	2021	2022	2023	2024	2025	2026	2027	2028	2029	2030	2031	2032	2033	2034	2035	2036	2037	2038	2039	2040
Thousands																					
0-14	181	181	179	177	174	172	169	166	163	161	158	155	153	150	148	147	145	145	144	144	144
15-29	167	165	164	164	165	166	167	168	168	169	170	172	174	175	175	175	174	173	170	168	166
30-44	188	190	191	191	190	189	188	187	185	184	181	178	175	173	170	168	166	165	165	165	166
45-59	195	194	193	192	191	190	190	189	188	188	188	188	188	188	189	190	191	192	193	192	191
60-74	144	147	150	153	157	160	164	168	171	174	177	179	181	182	182	182	181	180	179	179	178
75 & over	85	87	89	91	93	95	96	98	99	101	103	105	107	110	112	115	118	122	125	128	132
All ages	961	964	966	968	970	971	973	974	975	976	977	977	977	977	977	977	977	977	977	976	976
Percentages																					
0-14	18.9	18.8	18.6	18.3	18.0	17.7	17.4	17.0	16.7	16.5	16.2	15.9	15.6	15.4	15.2	15.0	14.9	14.8	14.8	14.7	14.7
15-29	17.4	17.2	17.0	17.0	17.0	17.0	17.1	17.2	17.3	17.3	17.5	17.6	17.8	17.9	17.9	17.9	17.9	17.7	17.4	17.2	17.0
30-44	19.6	19.7	19.7	19.7	19.6	19.5	19.3	19.1	19.0	18.8	18.6	18.2	17.9	17.7	17.4	17.2	17.0	16.9	16.9	16.9	17.0
45-59	20.3	20.1	20.0	19.8	19.7	19.6	19.5	19.4	19.3	19.2	19.2	19.2	19.2	19.3	19.3	19.4	19.6	19.7	19.7	19.7	19.6
60-74	15.0	15.3	15.5	15.8	16.1	16.5	16.8	17.2	17.5	17.8	18.1	18.3	18.5	18.6	18.6	18.6	18.6	18.5	18.4	18.3	18.3
75 & over	8.8	9.0	9.2	9.4	9.6	9.7	9.9	10.0	10.2	10.3	10.5	10.7	11.0	11.2	11.5	11.8	12.1	12.4	12.8	13.1	13.5
All ages	100.0	100.0	100.0	100.0	100.0	100.0	100.0	100.0	100.0	100.0	100.0	100.0	100.0	100.0	100.0	100.0	100.0	100.0	100.0	100.0	100.0
Mean age	40.7	40.9	41.2	41.4	41.6	41.9	42.1	42.3	42.6	42.8	43.1	43.3	43.5	43.7	44.0	44.2	44.4	44.6	44.8	44.9	45.1
Median age	40.4	40.6	40.9	41.2	41.5	41.8	42.1	42.4	42.7	43.1	43.4	43.7	44.0	44.3	44.6	44.9	45.2	45.4	45.7	45.9	46.1

Ages	2041	2042	2043	2044	2045	2046	2047	2048	2049	2050	2051	2052	2053	2054	2055	2056	2057	2058	2059	2060
Thousands																				
0-14	144	144	144	145	145	146	146	147	147	148	148	148	147	147	146	145	144	143	141	140
15-29	163	160	158	155	153	151	148	146	144	143	142	141	141	140	140	140	141	141	141	142
30-44	167	168	169	169	171	173	174	175	176	176	176	174	172	170	167	165	162	160	157	155
45-59	190	189	187	186	183	180	177	175	172	170	169	167	167	168	168	169	170	171	172	174
60-74	178	178	177	177	177	177	178	178	179	180	181	183	183	183	182	180	179	178	177	175
75 & over	135	138	141	144	146	149	151	153	154	155	155	156	157	158	159	160	161	163	164	165
All ages	976	976	976	976	975	975	975	974	973	972	971	969	967	965	963	961	958	955	953	950
Percentages																				
0-14	14.7	14.7	14.8	14.8	14.9	14.9	15.0	15.1	15.1	15.2	15.2	15.2	15.2	15.2	15.2	15.1	15.0	15.0	14.8	14.7
15-29	16.7	16.4	16.2	15.9	15.7	15.4	15.2	15.0	14.8	14.7	14.6	14.6	14.6	14.6	14.6	14.6	14.7	14.8	14.8	14.9
30-44	17.1	17.2	17.3	17.3	17.5	17.7	17.9	18.0	18.1	18.1	18.1	18.0	17.8	17.6	17.4	17.2	16.9	16.7	16.5	16.3
45-59	19.4	19.3	19.2	19.0	18.8	18.5	18.2	17.9	17.7	17.5	17.4	17.3	17.3	17.4	17.5	17.6	17.8	17.9	18.1	18.3
60-74	18.2	18.2	18.1	18.1	18.1	18.2	18.2	18.3	18.4	18.5	18.7	18.8	18.9	18.9	18.8	18.8	18.7	18.6	18.6	18.4
75 & over	13.8	14.1	14.5	14.7	15.0	15.3	15.5	15.7	15.8	15.9	16.0	16.1	16.2	16.3	16.5	16.7	16.9	17.0	17.2	17.4
All ages	100.0	100.0	100.0	100.0	100.0	100.0	100.0	100.0	100.0	100.0	100.0	100.0	100.0	100.0	100.0	100.0	100.0	100.0	100.0	100.0
Mean age	45.2	45.4	45.5	45.6	45.7	45.9	46.0	46.1	46.2	46.3	46.4	46.5	46.6	46.6	46.7	46.8	46.9	47.0	47.1	47.2
Median age	46.3	46.4	46.5	46.6	46.7	46.8	46.8	46.8	46.8	46.8	46.8	46.9	46.9	47.1	47.2	47.4	47.6	47.7	47.9	48.1

15.3h Population projections by the Office for National Statistics
Northern Ireland, FEMALES, thousands

Projected populations at mid-years by age last birthday

Ages	2061	2062	2063	2064	2065	2066	2067	2068	2069	2070	2071	2072	2073	2074	2075	2076	2077	2078	2079	2080
Thousands																				
0-14	138	137	135	134	132	131	130	129	128	127	127	126	126	126	126	126	126	126	126	126
15-29	142	143	143	144	144	144	144	144	143	143	142	141	139	138	137	135	134	132	131	130
30-44	152	150	148	146	144	143	143	142	142	142	142	142	142	143	143	144	144	145	145	146
45-59	176	177	178	179	179	179	177	175	173	170	168	165	162	160	158	155	153	151	149	147
60-74	172	169	167	165	163	161	160	161	161	162	163	164	165	166	168	170	171	172	173	173
75 & over	166	168	169	170	171	173	174	174	175	175	175	175	175	175	174	173	172	171	171	170
All ages	947	944	940	937	934	931	928	925	922	919	916	913	910	908	905	902	900	897	895	892
Percentages																				
0-14	14.6	14.5	14.4	14.3	14.2	14.1	14.0	13.9	13.9	13.9	13.8	13.8	13.8	13.9	13.9	13.9	14.0	14.0	14.1	14.1
15-29	15.1	15.2	15.3	15.3	15.4	15.5	15.5	15.6	15.5	15.5	15.5	15.4	15.3	15.2	15.1	15.0	14.9	14.7	14.6	14.5
30-44	16.1	15.9	15.7	15.6	15.5	15.4	15.4	15.4	15.4	15.4	15.5	15.5	15.6	15.7	15.8	15.9	16.0	16.1	16.2	16.3
45-59	18.6	18.8	19.0	19.1	19.2	19.2	19.1	18.9	18.7	18.5	18.3	18.1	17.8	17.6	17.4	17.2	17.0	16.8	16.6	16.5
60-74	18.1	17.9	17.7	17.6	17.4	17.3	17.3	17.4	17.5	17.6	17.8	18.0	18.1	18.3	18.5	18.8	19.0	19.2	19.3	19.4
75 & over	17.6	17.8	18.0	18.1	18.3	18.5	18.7	18.9	19.0	19.1	19.1	19.2	19.2	19.3	19.3	19.2	19.1	19.1	19.1	19.1
All ages	100.0	100.0	100.0	100.0	100.0	100.0	100.0	100.0	100.0	100.0	100.0	100.0	100.0	100.0	100.0	100.0	100.0	100.0	100.0	100.0
Mean age	47.3	47.4	47.5	47.6	47.7	47.7	47.8	47.9	48.0	48.0	48.1	48.2	48.2	48.3	48.3	48.4	48.4	48.4	48.5	48.5
Median age	48.3	48.5	48.7	48.9	49.0	49.2	49.3	49.5	49.6	49.7	49.7	49.8	49.8	49.8	49.8	49.8	49.8	49.8	49.7	49.7

Ages	2081	2082	2083	2084	2085	2086	2087	2088	2089	2090	2091	2092	2093	2094	2095	2096	2097	2098	2099	2100
Thousands																				
0-14	126	126	126	126	125	125	125	124	124	123	122	121	120	120	119	118	117	116	115	115
15-29	129	127	127	126	125	125	124	124	124	124	124	124	124	124	124	124	124	124	124	124
30-44	146	146	146	145	144	144	143	141	140	139	137	136	134	133	132	130	129	128	128	127
45-59	146	146	145	145	145	145	145	145	146	146	147	148	148	149	149	149	149	149	148	148
60-74	173	171	169	167	165	162	160	157	155	153	151	149	147	145	144	143	142	142	142	142
75 & over	170	171	172	173	174	176	177	178	179	181	182	183	184	185	185	185	185	185	185	184
All ages	889	887	884	881	879	876	873	871	868	865	863	860	857	855	852	849	847	844	841	839
Percentages																				
0-14	14.2	14.2	14.2	14.3	14.3	14.3	14.3	14.3	14.2	14.2	14.1	14.1	14.0	14.0	13.9	13.9	13.8	13.8	13.7	13.7
15-29	14.5	14.4	14.3	14.3	14.2	14.2	14.2	14.2	14.3	14.3	14.4	14.4	14.5	14.5	14.6	14.6	14.6	14.7	14.7	14.7
30-44	16.4	16.4	16.5	16.5	16.4	16.4	16.3	16.2	16.1	16.0	15.9	15.8	15.7	15.6	15.5	15.4	15.3	15.2	15.2	15.2
45-59	16.4	16.4	16.4	16.4	16.5	16.5	16.6	16.7	16.8	16.9	17.0	17.2	17.3	17.4	17.5	17.6	17.6	17.6	17.6	17.6
60-74	19.4	19.3	19.1	18.9	18.8	18.5	18.3	18.1	17.9	17.7	17.5	17.3	17.1	17.0	16.9	16.8	16.8	16.8	16.8	16.9
75 & over	19.1	19.2	19.4	19.6	19.8	20.0	20.3	20.5	20.7	20.9	21.1	21.3	21.5	21.6	21.7	21.8	21.9	21.9	21.9	22.0
All ages	100.0	100.0	100.0	100.0	100.0	100.0	100.0	100.0	100.0	100.0	100.0	100.0	100.0	100.0	100.0	100.0	100.0	100.0	100.0	100.0
Mean age	48.5	48.6	48.6	48.6	48.7	48.7	48.7	48.8	48.8	48.9	48.9	49.0	49.0	49.1	49.2	49.2	49.3	49.4	49.4	49.5
Median age	49.7	49.6	49.6	49.6	49.6	49.6	49.6	49.6	49.6	49.7	49.8	49.9	50.0	50.1	50.2	50.3	50.4	50.5	50.6	50.7

15.3h Population projections by the Office for National Statistics
Northern Ireland, FEMALES, thousands

Projected populations at mid-years by age last birthday

Ages	2101	2102	2103	2104	2105	2106	2107	2108	2109	2110	2111	2112	2113	2114	2115	2116	2117	2118	2119	2120
Thousands																				
0-14	114	113	113	112	112	112	111	111	111	111	111	110	110	110	110	110	110	109	109	109
15-29	123	123	122	122	121	120	120	119	118	117	116	115	115	114	113	113	112	112	111	111
30-44	127	126	126	126	126	126	126	126	126	126	126	126	126	126	125	125	125	124	124	123
45-59	147	146	145	143	142	140	139	138	136	135	134	133	132	131	130	130	129	129	129	129
60-74	142	142	142	143	143	144	145	145	146	146	146	146	146	146	145	144	143	142	141	140
75 & over	184	183	183	182	181	180	179	178	177	176	176	175	174	174	174	174	174	175	175	176
All ages	836	833	830	828	825	822	819	817	814	811	808	806	803	801	798	796	794	791	789	787
Percentages																				
0-14	13.6	13.6	13.6	13.6	13.6	13.6	13.6	13.6	13.6	13.7	13.7	13.7	13.7	13.8	13.8	13.8	13.8	13.8	13.8	13.8
15-29	14.7	14.7	14.7	14.7	14.7	14.6	14.6	14.5	14.5	14.4	14.4	14.3	14.3	14.2	14.2	14.2	14.1	14.1	14.1	14.1
30-44	15.1	15.1	15.2	15.2	15.2	15.3	15.3	15.4	15.5	15.5	15.6	15.6	15.7	15.7	15.7	15.7	15.7	15.7	15.7	15.6
45-59	17.6	17.5	17.4	17.3	17.2	17.1	17.0	16.9	16.7	16.6	16.5	16.5	16.4	16.4	16.3	16.3	16.3	16.3	16.3	16.4
60-74	16.9	17.0	17.1	17.3	17.4	17.5	17.7	17.8	17.9	18.0	18.1	18.2	18.2	18.2	18.2	18.1	18.1	18.0	17.9	17.8
75 & over	22.0	22.0	22.0	22.0	21.9	21.9	21.9	21.8	21.8	21.7	21.7	21.7	21.7	21.7	21.8	21.9	22.0	22.1	22.2	22.3
All ages	100.0	100.0	100.0	100.0	100.0	100.0	100.0	100.0	100.0	100.0	100.0	100.0	100.0	100.0	100.0	100.0	100.0	100.0	100.0	100.0
Mean age	49.5	49.6	49.6	49.6	49.7	49.7	49.7	49.7	49.7	49.7	49.7	49.7	49.7	49.8	49.8	49.8	49.8	49.8	49.9	49.9
Median age	50.8	50.9	50.9	51.0	51.0	51.1	51.1	51.1	51.1	51.0	51.0	51.0	51.0	50.9	50.9	50.9	50.9	50.9	50.9	50.9

Note: Figures may not add exactly due to rounding.

Source: Office for National Statistics

15.4 Families by family type and presence of children

United Kingdom, 2003-2019

Number of families (thousands) [note 4]	2003 Est	CV	CI+/-	2004 Est	CV	CI+/-	2005 Est	CV	CI+/-	2006 Est	CV	CI+/-	2007 Est	CV	CI+/-	2008 Est	CV	CI+/-	2009 Est	CV	CI+/-	2010 Est	CV	CI+/-
Married couple family [note 2]	12,219	a	74	12,210	a	77	12,278	a	78	12,237	a	80	12,246	a	82	12,216	a	83	12,267	a	85	12,287	a	88
No children [note 7]	5,976	a	69	5,922	a	71	6,006	a	71	6,046	a	72	5,997	a	74	6,042	a	75	5,961	a	76	6,039	a	79
Dependent children [note 5]	4,746	a	56	4,689	a	57	4,732	a	58	4,682	a	59	4,689	a	60	4,642	a	61	4,709	a	63	4,701	a	65
Non-dependent children only [note 6]	1,497	a	45	1,599	a	47	1,539	a	47	1,509	a	47	1,560	a	48	1,532	a	49	1,597	a	50	1,548	a	51
Civil partner couple family [note 1]	[z]		[z]	[z]	[z]	[z]	[z]	[z]	[z]	13	c	5	33	c	9	40	c	9	41	c	9	45	c	10
No children or non-dependent children only [note 3]	[z]		[z]	[z]	[z]	[z]	[z]	[z]	[z]	13	d	5	29	c	8	37	c	9	37	c	9	43	c	10
Dependent children [note 5]	[z]		[z]	[z]	[z]	[z]	[z]	[z]	[z]	[u]		[u]	4	d	3	3	d	2	4	d	3	2	d	2
Opposite sex cohabiting couple family	2,242	a	58	2,298	a	60	2,392	a	62	2,457	a	63	2,549	a	65	2,653	a	67	2,689	a	69	2,749	a	71
No children [note 7]	1,354	a	47	1,331	a	48	1,409	a	49	1,419	a	50	1,480	a	52	1,522	a	53	1,564	a	55	1,556	a	56
Dependent children [note 5]	819	a	36	885	a	38	899	a	38	954	a	40	974	a	40	1,040	a	42	1,025	a	43	1,077	a	45
Non-dependent children only [note 6]	68	b	11	81	b	12	85	b	13	85	b	13	96	b	14	92	b	14	101	b	15	116	b	16
Same sex cohabiting couple family	53	b	10	61	b	11	57	b	11	68	b	12	52	c	11	61	b	11	54	c	11	51	c	11
No children or non-dependent children only [note 3]	52	b	10	60	b	11	54	c	11	65	b	12	48	c	10	58	b	11	51	c	11	48	c	11
Dependent children [note 5]	[u]		[u]	[u]	[u]	[u]	3	d	2	3	d	2	4	d	3	3	d	2	3	d	2	3	d	2
Lone parent family [note 8]	2,597	a	60	2,685	a	62	2,697	a	63	2,695	a	63	2,692	a	64	2,759	a	66	2,889	a	68	2,943	a	70
Dependent children [note 5]	1,804	a	47	1,869	a	49	1,883	a	49	1,870	a	50	1,880	a	50	1,905	a	52	1,989	a	54	2,002	a	54
Non-dependent children only [note 6]	793	a	37	817	a	38	814	a	39	825	a	39	812	a	39	854	a	41	901	a	43	942	a	44
Lone mother family [note 8]	2,250	a	53	2,320	a	55	2,352	a	56	2,347	a	57	2,339	a	57	2,414	a	59	2,512	a	61	2,562	a	63
Dependent children [note 5]	1,626	a	43	1,686	a	45	1,708	a	46	1,701	a	46	1,713	a	47	1,736	a	48	1,803	a	50	1,813	a	51
Non-dependent children only [note 6]	625	a	32	634	a	33	644	a	34	646	a	34	627	a	33	678	a	35	709	a	37	749	a	39
Lone father family [note 8]	347	a	24	366	a	26	345	a	25	347	a	26	353	a	26	345	a	26	377	a	28	381	a	28
Dependent children [note 5]	178	a	17	183	b	19	175	b	18	169	b	18	167	b	18	169	b	18	185	b	19	188	b	20
Non-dependent children only [note 6]	168	b	17	183	b	19	170	b	18	178	b	19	186	b	20	176	b	19	192	b	20	193	b	21
All families	17,110	a	65	17,254	a	67	17,424	a	67	17,470	a	69	17,571	a	71	17,729	a	72	17,940	a	73	18,075	a	75
No children [note 7]	7,383	a	78	7,314	a	80	7,469	a	81	7,542	a	82	7,553	a	84	7,657	a	85	7,612	a	87	7,686	a	90
Dependent children [note 5]	7,370	a	46	7,444	a	47	7,517	a	48	7,509	a	48	7,550	a	50	7,592	a	50	7,729	a	52	7,784	a	53
Non-dependent children only [note 6]	2,358	a	54	2,497	a	57	2,438	a	57	2,420	a	58	2,469	a	59	2,480	a	60	2,599	a	62	2,605	a	64

15.4 Families by family type and presence of children

United Kingdom, 2003-2019

Number of families (thousands) [note 4]	2011 Est	CV	CI+/-	2012 Est	CV	CI+/-	2013 Est	CV	CI+/-	2014 Est	CV	CI+/-	2015 Est	CV	CI+/-	2016 Est	CV	CI+/-	2017 Est	CV	CI+/-	2018 Est	CV	CI+/-	2019 Est	CV	CI+/-
Married couple family [note 2]	12,208	a	102	12,301	a	102	12,385	a	107	12,498	a	104	12,490	a	110	12,701	a	112	12,845	a	114	12,750	a	115	12,740	a	119
No children [note 7]	5,983	a	92	5,984	a	91	5,947	a	95	6,092	a	94	6,076	a	98	6,215	a	101	6,166	a	102	6,197	a	102	6,184	a	105
Dependent children [note 5]	4,641	a	67	4,698	a	67	4,756	a	69	4,767	a	68	4,730	a	70	4,829	a	72	4,963	a	74	4,892	a	75	4,935	a	77
Non-dependent children only [note 6]	1,584	a	52	1,619	a	53	1,681	a	55	1,638	a	54	1,684	a	56	1,657	a	58	1,716	a	60	1,661	a	60	1,622	a	61
Civil partner couple family [note 1]	60	c	12	67	b	13	64	c	14	61	c	12	48	c	11	45	c	11	54	c	13	47	c	11	46	c	13
No children or non-dependent children only [note 3]	54	c	12	61	b	12	55	c	13	49	c	11	44	c	11	36	c	10	47	c	12	40	c	10	41	c	12
Dependent children [note 5]	5	d	3	6	d	3	9	d	4	12	d	5	4	d	3	9	d	4	8	d	4	7	d	4	5	d	3
Opposite sex cohabiting couple family	2,863	a	76	2,879	a	75	2,823	a	77	2,971	a	78	3,089	a	82	3,170	a	86	3,182	a	87	3,297	a	88	3,406	a	92
No children [note 7]	1,632	a	60	1,618	a	60	1,521	a	60	1,663	a	63	1,692	a	64	1,736	a	68	1,773	a	69	1,829	a	70	1,915	a	72
Dependent children [note 5]	1,107	a	47	1,131	a	47	1,170	a	49	1,163	a	48	1,251	a	51	1,265	a	53	1,248	a	54	1,285	a	55	1,307	a	56
Non-dependent children only [note 6]	123	b	17	131	b	18	132	b	18	146	b	19	147	b	20	170	b	22	161	b	22	182	b	23	183	b	24
Same sex cohabiting couple family	63	c	13	70	b	13	89	b	16	84	b	15	90	b	18	87	b	16	100	b	18	117	b	20	109	c	22
No children or non-dependent children only [note 3]	61	c	13	64	c	13	84	b	16	75	b	14	88	c	18	78	c	16	96	b	18	111	b	20	107	c	21
Dependent children [note 5]	3	d	2	6	d	3	5	d	3	9	d	4	3	d	2	9	d	5	4	d	3	7	d	4	3	d	2
Lone parent family [note 8]	2,909	a	71	3,039	a	74	3,001	a	77	3,007	a	76	3,032	a	79	2,899	a	79	2,815	a	79	2,862	a	81	2,852	a	83
Dependent children [note 5]	1,991	a	56	2,055	a	57	1,975	a	58	1,986	a	58	1,973	a	60	1,873	a	59	1,784	a	59	1,823	a	62	1,793	a	62
Non-dependent children only [note 6]	918	a	45	984	a	47	1,026	a	49	1,021	a	49	1,058	a	52	1,026	a	52	1,032	a	53	1,039	a	53	1,058	a	55
Lone mother family [note 8]	2,565	a	65	2,634	a	66	2,594	a	69	2,613	a	68	2,594	a	71	2,495	a	71	2,429	a	71	2,475	a	73	2,452	a	74
Dependent children [note 5]	1,826	a	53	1,877	a	53	1,807	a	55	1,815	a	54	1,771	a	56	1,692	a	56	1,604	a	55	1,645	a	57	1,622	a	58
Non-dependent children only [note 6]	739	a	39	758	a	40	788	a	43	799	a	43	823	a	45	803	a	45	825	a	47	830	a	47	831	a	48
Lone father family [note 8]	344	a	28	405	a	31	406	a	31	394	a	31	437	a	33	405	a	33	386	a	33	387	a	33	400	a	35
Dependent children [note 5]	165	b	19	178	b	20	168	b	20	172	b	20	203	b	23	181	b	21	180	b	22	178	b	23	172	b	23
Non-dependent children only [note 6]	179	b	20	227	a	24	238	a	25	222	b	24	235	b	25	223	b	25	206	b	24	209	b	25	228	b	27
All families	18,102	a	90	18,356	a	88	18,362	a	95	18,620	a	93	18,749	a	97	18,901	a	99	18,997	a	101	19,072	a	101	19,153	a	104
No children [note 7]	7,730	a	103	7,724	a	102	7,605	a	106	7,878	a	106	7,898	a	109	8,064	a	113	8,080	a	115	8,173	a	117	8,247	a	120
Dependent children [note 5]	7,747	a	55	7,896	a	55	7,915	a	57	7,937	a	55	7,961	a	57	7,984	a	59	8,006	a	61	8,014	a	61	8,043	a	62
Non-dependent children only [note 6]	2,625	a	65	2,737	a	66	2,842	a	69	2,806	a	68	2,890	a	71	2,854	a	73	2,910	a	75	2,886	a	75	2,864	a	76

Source: Labour Force Survey (LFS), Office for National Statistics
Produced by Demographic Analysis Unit, Office for National Statistics
Email: pop.info@ons.gov.uk

This table contains estimates of the number of families by family type, including those with dependent and non-dependent children and those without, for the UK.

Totals may not sum due to rounding.

Symbols used within the tables

Est = estimate
CV = coefficient of variation indicates the robustness of each estimate.
CI+/- = the upper(+) and lower(-) 95% confidence interval. The confidence interval provides an estimated range of values in which an actual data value is likely to fall 95% of the time.
[z] = Not applicable.
[x] = Not available.
[w] = No people are estimated to be in this category, either because there were not any recorded by the survey or because none exist in the population.
[u] = Low reliability/unreliable. The estimate has been based on a sample of less than 3.
[low] = Rounds to 0.

15.4 Families by family type and presence of children

United Kingdom, 2003-2019

Notes:

1. Same-sex civil partnerships were introduced in the UK in December 2005. Opposite-sex civil partnerships became legal from 31 December 2019 in England and Wales, 13 January 2020 in Northern Ireland and 28 July 2020 in Scotland. A small number of opposite-sex civil partner (CP) couple families and households were sampled as part of the April to June 2020 Labour Force Survey so CP estimates for 2020 include some opposite-sex civil partner couple families and households.

2. Marriages of same sex couples were introduced in England and Wales in March 2014, in Scotland in December 2014 and in Northern Ireland in January 2020. Estimates relating to same sex married couples are presented along with opposite sex married couples within the 'Married couple family' category.

3. Families with no children and non-dependent children only have been added together for civil partner couple families and same sex cohabiting couple families to improve the robustness of the estimates.

4. A family is a married, civil partnered or cohabiting couple with or without children, or a lone parent with at least one child. Children may be dependent or non-dependent.

5. Dependent children are those living with their parent(s) and either (a) aged under 16, or (b) aged 16 to 18 in full-time education, excluding children aged 16 to 18 who have a spouse, partner or child living in the household.

6. Non-dependent children are those living with their parent(s), and either (a) aged 19 or over, or (b) aged 16 to 18 who are not in full-time education or who have a spouse, partner or child living in the household. Non-dependent children are sometimes called adult children.

7. Families with no children are families where there are no children currently living in the household. This does not necessarily indicate that the adult(s) in the household have never had children.

8. The definition of a lone parent does not make any distinction between situations where a child has regular contact and/or partly resides with their other parent and a child who solely resides with and is cared for by one parent. Only the parent living with their children is included in the estimated number of lone parent families and households.

9. For 1996 to 2010, a household is defined as a person living alone, or a group of people living at the same address who have the address as their only or main residence and either share one main meal a day or share living accommodation (or both). For 2011 onwards it is defined as one person living alone, or a group of people (not necessarily related) living at the same address who share cooking facilities and share a living room or sitting room or dining area.

10. Two or more unrelated adults households do not contain either a couple or a parent with their child. Typically such households may consist of a group of friends or students, but could consist of two siblings for example.

11. Multi-family households contain at least two families. The families may be related, for example a couple with their daughter and her child, or two brothers and their wives. Households where there is one family and one individual for example a married couple with their daughter and a lodger or a married couple with one elderly parent are classified as a one family household.

12. There is no confidence interval for all people in households because the latter is a known population estimate to which the sample has been weighted. In other words, this value would be the same regardless of the sample taken so there is no sampling variability.

Statistical Robustness

The robustness of an estimate is presented in two ways:

The coefficient of variation (CV) indicates the robustness of each estimate.

It is defined as **CV = (standard error ÷ estimate) * 100** where standard error is an estimate of the margin of error associated with a sample survey.

The coloured shading on the table indicates the precision of each estimate as follows:

CV Value	CV Category	Definition of Category
CV ≤ 5	a	Estimates are considered precise
CV > 5 and ≤ 10	b	Estimates are considered reasonably precise
CV > 10 and ≤ 20	c	Estimates are considered acceptable
CV > 20	d	Estimates are considered unreliable for practical purposes

Confidence intervals are also presented. CI+/- is the upper(+) and lower(−) 95% confidence interval. It is defined as **1.96 x standard error**.

The confidence interval provides an estimated range of values in which an actual data value is likely to fall 95% of the time.

For example, there were 12,280,000 married couple families in 2001. This estimate has a confidence interval of 71,000, meaning that there is 95 per cent confidence that the true value is in the interval 12,280,000 ± 71,000 or lies between 12,209,000 and 12,351,000.

Coronavirus and Families and Households Statistics

The coronavirus (COVID-19) pandemic has affected the data collection and weighting methodology of the Labour Force Survey (LFS). As a result, all face-to-face interviewing for the LFS was suspended and replaced with telephone interviewing. This change in the method for initial contact has changed the non-response bias of the survey, affecting interviews from March 2020 onwards.

To mitigate the impact of the change in non-response bias, in October 2020, we introduced housing tenure into the LFS weighting methodology for periods from January to March 2020 onwards. LFS responses are usually weighted to official population projections however LFS responses published from 15 July 2021 have been reweighted to new populations using growth rates from HM Revenue and Customs (HMRC) Real Time Information (RTI). This is to allow for different trends during the coronavirus pandemic. The reweighting gives improved estimates of both rates and levels. We plan to reweight LFS and Annual Population Survey (APS) datasets that include data from March 2020. We will provide further details on our plans including a timeline in our March Labour Market publication.

Further information can be found by following the links below:

1. Coronavirus and its impact on the LFS: https://www.ons.gov.uk/employmentandlabourmarket/peopleinwork/employmentandemployeetypes/articles/coronavirusanditsimpactonthelabourforcesurvey/2020-10-13

2. Measuring the labour market during the pandemic: https://blog.ons.gov.uk/2020/10/12/measuring-the-labour-market-during-the-pandemic/

3. Understanding the impact of COVID-19 on UK population: https://blog.ons.gov.uk/2021/01/25/understanding-how-the-pandemic-population/

4. The impact of the change in weighting on main LFS indicators published in October 2020:
https://www.ons.gov.uk/employmentandlabourmarket/peopleinwork/employmentandemployeetypes/datasets/x08impactofflfstenurereweightingonkeylabourforcesurveyindicators

15.5 Geographical distribution of the population

All persons

Name	Code	Mid-year population estimate	
		2018	2019
UNITED KINGDOM	K02000001	66,435,550	66,796,807
GREAT BRITAIN	K03000001	64,553,909	64,903,140
ENGLAND AND WALES	K04000001	59,115,809	59,439,840
ENGLAND	E92000001	55,977,178	56,286,961
NORTH EAST	E12000001	2,657,909	2,669,941
County Durham	E06000047	526,980	530,094
Darlington	E06000005	106,566	106,803
Hartlepool	E06000001	93,242	93,663
Middlesbrough	E06000002	140,545	140,980
Northumberland	E06000057	320,274	322,434
Redcar and Cleveland	E06000003	136,718	137,150
Stockton-on-Tees	E06000004	197,213	197,348
Tyne and Wear (Met County)	E11000007	1,136,371	1,141,469
Gateshead	E08000037	202,508	202,055
Newcastle upon Tyne	E08000021	300,196	302,820
North Tyneside	E08000022	205,985	207,913
South Tyneside	E08000023	150,265	150,976
Sunderland	E08000024	277,417	277,705
NORTH WEST	E12000002	7,292,093	7,341,196
Blackburn with Darwen	E06000008	148,942	149,696
Blackpool	E06000009	139,305	139,446
Cheshire East	E06000049	380,790	384,152
Cheshire West and Chester	E06000050	340,502	343,071
Halton	E06000006	128,432	129,410
Warrington	E06000007	209,547	210,014
Cumbria	E10000006	498,888	500,012
Allerdale	E07000026	97,527	97,761
Barrow-in-Furness	E07000027	67,137	67,049
Carlisle	E07000028	108,387	108,678
Copeland	E07000029	68,424	68,183
Eden	E07000030	52,881	53,253
South Lakeland	E07000031	104,532	105,088
Greater Manchester (Met County)	E11000001	2,812,569	2,835,686
Bolton	E08000001	285,372	287,550
Bury	E08000002	190,108	190,990
Manchester	E08000003	547,627	552,858
Oldham	E08000004	235,623	237,110
Rochdale	K08000005	220,001	222,412
Salford	E08000006	254,408	258,834
Stockport	E08000007	291,775	293,423
Tameside	E08000008	225,197	226,493
Trafford	E08000009	236,370	237,354
Wigan	E08000010	326,088	328,662
Lancashire	E10000017	1,210,053	1,219,799
Burnley	E07000117	88,527	88,920
Chorley	E07000118	116,821	118,216
Fylde	E07000119	79,770	80,780
Hyndburn	E07000120	80,815	81,043
Lancaster	E07000121	144,246	146,038
Pendle	E07000122	91,405	92,112
Preston	E07000123	141,818	143,135
Ribble Valley	E07000124	60,057	60,888
Rossendale	E07000125	70,895	71,482
South Ribble	E07000126	110,527	110,788
West Lancashire	E07000127	113,949	114,306

15.5 Geographical distribution of the population

All persons

Name	Code	Mid-year population estimate	
		2018	2019
Wyre	E07000128	111,223	112,091
Merseyside (Met County)	E11000002	1,423,065	1,429,910
Knowsley	E08000011	149,571	150,862
Liverpool	E08000012	494,814	498,042
Sefton	E08000014	275,396	276,410
St. Helens	E08000013	180,049	180,585
Wirral	E08000015	323,235	324,011
YORKSHIRE AND THE HUMBER	**E12000003**	**5,479,615**	**5,502,967**
East Riding of Yorkshire	E06000011	339,614	341,173
Kingston upon Hull, City of	E06000010	260,645	259,778
North East Lincolnshire	E06000012	159,821	159,563
North Lincolnshire	E06000013	172,005	172,292
York	E06000014	209,893	210,618
North Yorkshire	E10000023	614,505	618,054
Craven	E07000163	56,832	57,142
Hambleton	E07000164	91,134	91,594
Harrogate	E07000165	160,533	160,831
Richmondshire	E07000166	53,244	53,730
Ryedale	E07000167	54,920	55,380
Scarborough	E07000168	108,736	108,757
Selby	E07000169	89,106	90,620
South Yorkshire (Met County)	E11000003	1,402,918	1,409,020
Barnsley	E08000016	245,199	246,866
Doncaster	E08000017	310,542	311,890
Rotherham	E08000018	264,671	265,411
Sheffield	E08000019	582,506	584,853
West Yorkshire (Met County)	E11000006	2,320,214	2,332,469
Bradford	E08000032	537,173	539,776
Calderdale	E08000033	210,082	211,455
Kirklees	E08000034	438,727	439,787
Leeds	E08000035	789,194	793,139
Wakefield	E08000036	345,038	348,312
EAST MIDLANDS	**E12000004**	**4,804,149**	**4,835,928**
Derby	E06000015	257,174	257,302
Leicester	E06000016	355,218	354,224
Nottingham	E06000018	331,069	332,900
Rutland	E06000017	39,697	39,927
Derbyshire	E10000007	796,142	802,694
Amber Valley	E07000032	126,678	128,147
Bolsover	E07000033	79,530	80,562
Chesterfield	E07000034	104,628	104,900
Derbyshire Dales	E07000035	71,977	72,325
Erewash	E07000036	115,490	115,371
High Peak	E07000037	92,221	92,666
North East Derbyshire	E07000038	101,125	101,462
South Derbyshire	E07000039	104,493	107,261
Leicestershire	E10000018	698,268	706,155
Blaby	E07000129	100,421	101,526
Charnwood	E07000130	182,643	185,851
Harborough	E07000131	92,499	93,807
Hinckley and Bosworth	E07000132	112,423	113,136
Melton	E07000133	51,100	51,209
North West Leicestershire	E07000134	102,126	103,611
Oadby and Wigston	E07000135	57,056	57,015
Lincolnshire	E10000019	755,833	761,224
Boston	E07000136	69,366	70,173

15.5 Geographical distribution of the population

All persons

Name	Code	Mid-year population estimate	
		2018	2019
East Lindsey	E07000137	140,741	141,727
Lincoln	E07000138	99,039	99,299
North Kesteven	E07000139	115,985	116,915
South Holland	E07000140	93,980	95,019
South Kesteven	E07000141	141,853	142,424
West Lindsey	E07000142	94,869	95,667
Northamptonshire	E10000021	747,622	753,278
Corby	E07000150	70,827	72,218
Daventry	E07000151	84,484	85,950
East Northamptonshire	E07000152	93,906	94,527
Kettering	E07000153	101,266	101,776
Northampton	E07000154	225,146	224,610
South Northamptonshire	E07000155	92,515	94,490
Wellingborough	E07000156	79,478	79,707
Nottinghamshire	E10000024	823,126	828,224
Ashfield	E07000170	127,151	127,918
Bassetlaw	E07000171	116,839	117,459
Broxtowe	E07000172	113,272	114,033
Gedling	E07000173	117,786	117,896
Mansfield	E07000174	108,841	109,313
Newark and Sherwood	E07000175	121,566	122,421
Rushcliffe	E07000176	117,671	119,184
WEST MIDLANDS	**E12000005**	**5,900,757**	**5,934,037**
Herefordshire, County of	E06000019	192,107	192,801
Shropshire	E06000051	320,274	323,136
Stoke-on-Trent	E06000021	255,833	256,375
Telford and Wrekin	E06000020	177,799	179,854
Staffordshire	E10000028	875,219	879,560
Cannock Chase	E07000192	100,109	100,762
East Staffordshire	E07000193	118,574	119,754
Lichfield	E07000194	103,965	104,756
Newcastle-under-Lyme	E07000195	129,490	129,441
South Staffordshire	E07000196	112,126	112,436
Stafford	E07000197	135,880	137,280
Staffordshire Moorlands	E07000198	98,397	98,435
Tamworth	E07000199	76,678	76,696
Warwickshire	E10000031	571,010	577,933
North Warwickshire	E07000218	64,850	65,264
Nuneaton and Bedworth	E07000219	128,902	129,883
Rugby	E07000220	107,194	108,935
Stratford-on-Avon	E07000221	127,580	130,098
Warwick	E07000222	142,484	143,753
West Midlands (Met County)	E11000005	2,916,458	2,928,592
Birmingham	E08000025	1,141,374	1,141,816
Coventry	E08000026	366,785	371,521
Dudley	E08000027	320,626	321,596
Sandwell	E08000028	327,378	328,450
Solihull	E08000029	214,909	216,374
Walsall	E08000030	283,378	285,478
Wolverhampton	E08000031	262,008	263,357
Worcestershire	E10000034	592,057	595,786
Bromsgrove	E07000234	98,662	99,881
Malvern Hills	E07000235	78,113	78,698
Redditch	E07000236	84,989	85,261
Worcester	E07000237	101,891	101,222
Wychavon	E07000238	127,340	129,433
Wyre Forest	E07000239	101,062	101,291

15.5 Geographical distribution of the population

All persons

Name	Code	Mid-year population estimate 2018	Mid-year population estimate 2019
EAST	**E12000006**	**6,201,214**	**6,236,072**
Bedford	E06000055	171,623	173,292
Central Bedfordshire	E06000056	283,606	288,648
Luton	E06000032	214,109	213,052
Peterborough	E06000031	201,041	202,259
Southend-on-Sea	E06000033	182,463	183,125
Thurrock	E06000034	172,525	174,341
Cambridgeshire	E10000003	651,482	653,537
Cambridge	E07000008	125,758	124,798
East Cambridgeshire	E07000009	89,362	89,840
Fenland	E07000010	101,491	101,850
Huntingdonshire	E07000011	177,352	177,963
South Cambridgeshire	E07000012	157,519	159,086
Essex	E10000012	1,477,764	1,489,189
Basildon	E07000066	185,862	187,199
Braintree	E07000067	151,561	152,604
Brentwood	E07000068	76,550	77,021
Castle Point	E07000069	90,070	90,376
Chelmsford	E07000070	177,079	178,388
Colchester	E07000071	192,523	194,706
Epping Forest	E07000072	131,137	131,689
Harlow	E07000073	86,594	87,067
Maldon	E07000074	64,425	64,926
Rochford	E07000075	86,981	87,368
Tendring	E07000076	145,803	146,561
Uttlesford	E07000077	89,179	91,284
Hertfordshire	E10000015	1,184,365	1,189,519
Broxbourne	E07000095	96,876	97,279
Dacorum	E07000096	154,280	154,763
East Hertfordshire	E07000242	148,105	149,748
Hertsmere	E07000098	104,205	104,919
North Hertfordshire	E07000099	133,214	133,570
St Albans	E07000240	147,373	148,452
Stevenage	E07000243	87,754	87,845
Three Rivers	E07000102	93,045	93,323
Watford	E07000103	96,767	96,577
Welwyn Hatfield	E07000241	122,746	123,043
Norfolk	E10000020	903,680	907,760
Breckland	E07000143	139,329	139,968
Broadland	E07000144	129,464	130,783
Great Yarmouth	E07000145	99,370	99,336
King's Lynn and West Norfolk	E07000146	151,811	151,383
North Norfolk	E07000147	104,552	104,837
Norwich	E07000148	141,137	140,573
South Norfolk	E07000149	138,017	140,880
Suffolk	E10000029	758,556	761,350
Babergh	E07000200	91,401	92,036
East Suffolk	E07000244	248,249	249,461
Ipswich	E07000202	137,532	136,913
Mid Suffolk	E07000203	102,493	103,895
West Suffolk	E07000245	178,881	179,045
LONDON	**E12000007**	**8,908,081**	**8,961,989**
Camden	E09000007	262,226	270,029
City of London	E09000001	8,706	9,721
Hackney	E09000012	279,665	281,120
Hammersmith and Fulham	E09000013	185,426	185,143

15.5 Geographical distribution of the population

All persons

Name	Code	Mid-year population estimate	
		2018	2019
Haringey	E09000014	270,624	268,647
Islington	E09000019	239,142	242,467
Kensington and Chelsea	E09000020	156,197	156,129
Lambeth	E09000022	325,917	326,034
Lewisham	E09000023	303,536	305,842
Newham	E09000025	352,005	353,134
Southwark	E09000028	317,256	318,830
Tower Hamlets	E09000030	317,705	324,745
Wandsworth	E09000032	326,474	329,677
Westminster	E09000033	255,324	261,317
Barking and Dagenham	E09000002	211,998	212,906
Barnet	E09000003	392,140	395,869
Bexley	E09000004	247,258	248,287
Brent	E09000005	330,795	329,771
Bromley	E09000006	331,096	332,336
Croydon	E09000008	385,346	386,710
Ealing	E09000009	341,982	341,806
Enfield	E09000010	333,869	333,794
Greenwich	E09000011	286,186	287,942
Harrow	E09000015	250,149	251,160
Havering	E09000016	257,810	259,552
Hillingdon	E09000017	304,824	306,870
Hounslow	E09000018	270,782	271,523
Kingston upon Thames	E09000021	175,470	177,507
Merton	E09000024	206,186	206,548
Redbridge	E09000026	303,858	305,222
Richmond upon Thames	E09000027	196,904	198,019
Sutton	E09000029	204,525	206,349
Waltham Forest	E09000031	276,700	276,983
SOUTH EAST	**E12000008**	**9,133,625**	**9,180,135**
Bracknell Forest	E06000036	121,676	122,549
Brighton and Hove	E06000043	290,395	290,885
Isle of Wight	E06000046	141,538	141,771
Medway	E06000035	277,855	278,556
Milton Keynes	E06000042	268,607	269,457
Portsmouth	E06000044	215,133	214,905
Reading	E06000038	163,203	161,780
Slough	E06000039	149,112	149,539
Southampton	E06000045	252,796	252,520
West Berkshire	E06000037	158,527	158,450
Windsor and Maidenhead	E06000040	150,906	151,422
Wokingham	E06000041	167,979	171,119
Buckinghamshire	E06000060	540,059	543,973
East Sussex	E10000011	554,590	557,229
Eastbourne	E07000061	103,160	103,745
Hastings	E07000062	92,855	92,661
Lewes	E07000063	102,744	103,268
Rother	E07000064	95,656	96,080
Wealden	E07000065	160,175	161,475
Hampshire	E10000014	1,376,316	1,382,542
Basingstoke and Deane	E07000084	175,729	176,582
East Hampshire	E07000085	120,681	122,308
Eastleigh	E07000086	131,819	133,584
Fareham	E07000087	116,339	116,233
Gosport	E07000088	85,283	84,838
Hart	E07000089	96,293	97,073
Havant	E07000090	125,813	126,220

15.5 Geographical distribution of the population

All persons

Name	Code	Mid-year population estimate	
		2018	2019
New Forest	E07000091	179,753	180,086
Rushmoor	E07000092	95,142	94,599
Test Valley	E07000093	125,169	126,160
Winchester	E07000094	124,295	124,859
Kent	E10000016	1,568,623	1,581,555
Ashford	E07000105	129,281	130,032
Canterbury	E07000106	164,553	165,394
Dartford	E07000107	109,709	112,606
Dover	E07000108	116,969	118,131
Folkestone and Hythe	E07000112	112,578	112,996
Gravesham	E07000109	106,385	106,939
Maidstone	E07000110	169,955	171,826
Sevenoaks	E07000111	120,293	120,750
Swale	E07000113	148,519	150,082
Thanet	E07000114	141,819	141,922
Tonbridge and Malling	E07000115	130,508	132,153
Tunbridge Wells	E07000116	118,054	118,724
Oxfordshire	E10000025	687,524	691,667
Cherwell	E07000177	149,161	150,503
Oxford	E07000178	154,327	152,457
South Oxfordshire	E07000179	140,504	142,057
Vale of White Horse	E07000180	133,732	136,007
West Oxfordshire	E07000181	109,800	110,643
Surrey	E10000030	1,189,934	1,196,236
Elmbridge	E07000207	136,626	136,795
Epsom and Ewell	E07000208	79,928	80,627
Guildford	E07000209	147,889	148,998
Mole Valley	E07000210	87,253	87,245
Reigate and Banstead	E07000211	147,757	148,748
Runnymede	E07000212	88,000	89,424
Spelthorne	E07000213	99,334	99,844
Surrey Heath	E07000214	88,874	89,305
Tandridge	E07000215	87,496	88,129
Waverley	E07000216	125,610	126,328
Woking	E07000217	101,167	100,793
West Sussex	E10000032	858,852	863,980
Adur	E07000223	63,869	64,301
Arun	E07000224	159,827	160,758
Chichester	E07000225	120,750	121,129
Crawley	E07000226	112,448	112,409
Horsham	E07000227	142,217	143,791
Mid Sussex	E07000228	149,716	151,022
Worthing	E07000229	110,025	110,570
SOUTH WEST	**E12000009**	**5,599,735**	**5,624,696**
Bath and North East Somerset	E06000022	192,106	193,282
Bournemouth, Christchurch and Poole	E06000058	395,784	395,331
Bristol, City of	E06000023	463,405	463,377
Cornwall	E06000052	565,968	569,578
Dorset	E06000059	376,484	378,508
Isles of Scilly	E06000053	2,242	2,224
North Somerset	E06000024	213,919	215,052
Plymouth	E06000026	263,100	262,100
South Gloucestershire	E06000025	282,644	285,093
Swindon	E06000030	221,996	222,193
Torbay	E06000027	135,780	136,264
Wiltshire	E06000054	498,064	500,024
Devon	E10000008	795,286	802,375

15.5 Geographical distribution of the population

All persons

Name	Code	Mid-year population estimate	
		2018	2019
East Devon	E07000040	144,317	146,284
Exeter	E07000041	130,428	131,405
Mid Devon	E07000042	81,695	82,311
North Devon	E07000043	96,110	97,145
South Hams	E07000044	86,221	87,004
Teignbridge	E07000045	132,844	134,163
Torridge	E07000046	68,143	68,267
West Devon	E07000047	55,528	55,796
Gloucestershire	E10000013	633,558	637,070
Cheltenham	E07000078	117,090	116,306
Cotswold	E07000079	89,022	89,862
Forest of Dean	E07000080	86,543	86,791
Gloucester	E07000081	129,285	129,128
Stroud	E07000082	119,019	119,964
Tewkesbury	E07000083	92,599	95,019
Somerset	E10000027	559,399	562,225
Mendip	E07000187	114,881	115,587
Sedgemoor	E07000188	122,791	123,178
Somerset West and Taunton	E07000246	153,866	155,115
South Somerset	E07000189	167,861	168,345
WALES	**W92000004**	**3,138,631**	**3,152,879**
Isle of Anglesey	W06000001	69,961	70,043
Gwynedd	W06000002	124,178	124,560
Conwy	W06000003	117,181	117,203
Denbighshire	W06000004	95,330	95,696
Flintshire	W06000005	155,593	156,100
Wrexham	W06000006	136,126	135,957
Powys	W06000023	132,447	132,435
Ceredigion	W06000008	72,992	72,695
Pembrokeshire	W06000009	125,055	125,818
Carmarthenshire	W06000010	187,568	188,771
Swansea	W06000011	246,466	246,993
Neath Port Talbot	W06000012	142,906	143,315
Bridgend	W06000013	144,876	147,049
Vale of Glamorgan	W06000014	132,165	133,587
Cardiff	W06000015	364,248	366,903
Rhondda Cynon Taf	W06000016	240,131	241,264
Merthyr Tydfil	W06000024	60,183	60,326
Caerphilly	W06000018	181,019	181,075
Blaenau Gwent	W06000019	69,713	69,862
Torfaen	W06000020	93,049	93,961
Monmouthshire	W06000021	94,142	94,590
Newport	W06000022	153,302	154,676
SCOTLAND	**S92000003**	**5,438,100**	**5,463,300**
Aberdeen City	S12000033	227,560	228,670
Aberdeenshire	S12000034	261,470	261,210
Angus	S12000041	116,040	116,200
Argyll and Bute	S12000035	86,260	85,870
City of Edinburgh	S12000036	518,500	524,930
Clackmannanshire	S12000005	51,400	51,540
Dumfries and Galloway	S12000006	148,790	148,860
Dundee City	S12000042	148,750	149,320
East Ayrshire	S12000008	121,840	122,010
East Dunbartonshire	S12000045	108,330	108,640
East Lothian	S12000010	105,790	107,090
East Renfrewshire	S12000011	95,170	95,530

15.5 Geographical distribution of the population

All persons

Name	Code	Mid-year population estimate	
		2018	2019
Falkirk	S12000014	160,340	160,890
Fife	S12000047	371,910	373,550
Glasgow City	S12000049	626,410	633,120
Highland	S12000017	235,540	235,830
Inverclyde	S12000018	78,150	77,800
Midlothian	S12000019	91,340	92,460
Moray	S12000020	95,520	95,820
Na h-Eileanan Siar	S12000013	26,830	26,720
North Ayrshire	S12000021	135,280	134,740
North Lanarkshire	S12000050	340,180	341,370
Orkney Islands	S12000023	22,190	22,270
Perth and Kinross	S12000048	151,290	151,950
Renfrewshire	S12000038	177,790	179,100
Scottish Borders	S12000026	115,270	115,510
Shetland Islands	S12000027	22,990	22,920
South Ayrshire	S12000028	112,550	112,610
South Lanarkshire	S12000029	319,020	320,530
Stirling	S12000030	94,330	94,210
West Dunbartonshire	S12000039	89,130	88,930
West Lothian	S12000040	182,140	183,100
NORTHERN IRELAND	**N92000002**	**1,881,641**	**1,893,667**
Antrim and Newtownabbey	N09000001	142,492	143,504
Ards and North Down	N09000011	160,864	161,725
Armagh City, Banbridge and Craigavon	N09000002	214,090	216,205
Belfast	N09000003	341,877	343,542
Causeway Coast and Glens	N09000004	144,246	144,838
Derry City and Strabane	N09000005	150,679	151,284
Fermanagh and Omagh	N09000006	116,835	117,397
Lisburn and Castlereagh	N09000007	144,381	146,002
Mid and East Antrim	N09000008	138,773	139,274
Mid Ulster	N09000009	147,392	148,528
Newry, Mourne and Down	N09000010	180,012	181,368

Source: Office for National Statistics

15.6 Overseas-born population in the United Kingdom, excluding some residents in communal establishments, by sex, by country of birth[1,2,3] January 2018 to December 2018

United Kingdom

60 most common countries of birth — *thousands*

	Country	Total estimate	Total CI[4,5] +/-	Male estimate	Male CI +/-	Female estimate	Female CI +/-
1	Poland	832	44	395	30	437	32
2	India	832	44	420	31	412	31
3	Pakistan	535	35	282	25	253	24
4	Romania	392	30	207	22	185	21
5	Republic of Ireland	369	29	165	19	204	22
6	Germany	309	27	137	18	172	20
7	Italy	253	24	139	18	114	16
8	South Africa	246	24	125	17	122	17
9	Bangladesh	241	23	124	17	117	16
10	China	207	22	93	15	114	16
11	Nigeria	205	22	104	15	101	15
12	Lithuania	190	21	80	14	109	16
13	United States of America	170	20	76	13	94	15
14	France	170	20	73	13	96	15
15	Spain	150	19	70	13	80	13
16	Portugal	141	18	74	13	68	12
17	Philippines	141	18	49	11	92	15
18	Australia	140	18	69	13	70	13
19	Jamaica	134	17	55	11	79	13
20	Sri Lanka	128	17	68	12	60	12
21	Kenya	127	17	61	12	66	12
22	Zimbabwe	124	17	56	11	68	12
23	Ghana	120	17	56	11	64	12
24	Somalia	108	16	43	10	65	12
25	Bulgaria	103	15	49	11	54	11
26	Turkey	99	15	54	11	45	10
27	Brazil	87	14	40	10	47	10
28	Canada	87	14	41	10	45	10
29	Latvia	86	14	41	10	45	10
30	Hungary	82	14	40	10	42	10
31	Netherlands	81	14	34	9	47	10
32	Greece	75	13	47	10	28	8
33	Afghanistan	73	13	42	10	31	8
34	Iran	73	13	45	10	28	8
35	Iraq	73	13	39	9	33	9
36	Slovakia	72	13	34	9	38	9
37	Malaysia	69	13	30	8	39	9
38	Nepal	64	12	33	9	30	8
39	New Zealand	62	12	31	8	31	8
40	Taiwan	61	12	19	7	41	10
41	Uganda	58	11	27	8	31	8
42	Cyprus (European Union)	52	11	23	7	29	8
43	Singapore	52	11	21	7	31	8
44	Japan	48	10	18	6	30	8
45	Thailand	47	10	9	5	38	9
46	Russia	47	10	17	6	29	8
47	Czech Republic	45	10	15	6	31	8
48	Egypt	45	10	26	8	19	7
49	Syria	43	10	20	7	23	7
50	Sweden	40	10	14	6	27	8
51	Mauritius	39	9	20	7	19	7
52	Colombia	38	9	16	6	23	7
53	Ukraine	33	9	17	6	17	6
54	Albania	32	9	16	6	16	6
55	Sudan	32	8	19	7	13	5
56	Belgium	31	8	15	6	17	6
57	Eritrea	31	8	14	6	17	6
58	Malta	29	8	15	6	14	6
59	Zambia	27	8	13	5	14	6
60	Tanzania	27	8	15	6	12	5

Totals may not sum due to rounding

Source: Annual Population Survey (APS), ONS

. = no contact   : = not available   z = not applicable

c = not available due to disclosure control   0~ = rounded to zero

1. Estimates are based on the Annual Population Survey (APS) which is made up of wave 1 and wave 5 of the Labour Force Survey (LFS) plus annual sample boosts which are included primarily to enhance the geographical coverage. As some residents of communal establishments are excluded from the coverage of this survey the estimates in this table are different from the standard ONS mid-year population estimates, which cover all usual residents. For a more comprehensive estimate of the UK population, please refer to:

https://www.ons.gov.uk/peoplepopulationandcommunity/populationandmigration/populationestimates

2. It should be noted that the LFS :-

*   excludes students in halls who do not have a UK resident parent

*   excludes people in most other types of communal establishments (eg hotels, boarding houses, hostels, mobile home sites, etc)

*   is grossed to population estimates of those living in private households. An adjustment is made for those who live in some NHS accommodation and halls of residence whose parents live in the UK. For this reason the sum of those born in the UK and outside the UK may not agree with the published population estimate.

3. The LFS weighting does not adjust for non-response bias by the country of birth variable.

4. CI = confidence interval. CI is defined as: 1.96 x standard error. Estimate + CI and Estimate - CI are the upper and lower 95% confidence limits.

5. If the confidence interval is higher than the estimate, the estimate is not considered reliable for practical purposes. Where the lower confidence limit is below zero users should assume the estimate is above zero.

15.7 Long-Term International Migration 2004 - 2019
United Kingdom, England and Wales

thousands

Citizenship	All citizenships 2011 Census Revisions[1]		British (Including Overseas Territories)		Non-British		European Union[2]		European Union EU15		European Union EU8		European Union EU2		European Union Other		Non-European Union[3] All[3]		Other Europe[3]	
Year	Estimate	+/-CI	Estimate	+/-CI	Estimate	+/-CI	Estimate	+/-CI	Estimate	+/-CI	Estimate	+/-CI	Estimate	+/-CI	Estimate	+/-CI	Estimate	+/-CI	Estimate	+/-CI
United Kingdom																				
Inflow																				
2004	**589**	**40**	92	14	497	38	127	22	76	15	51	16	z	z	0~	1	370	30	17	5
2005	**567**	**37**	99	18	468	33	151	23	72	14	77	18	z	z	3	2	317	24	17	6
2006	**596**	**39**	83	17	513	35	170	26	74	13	93	22	z	z	4	3	343	24	17	6
2007	**574**	**40**	74	14	500	37	195	29	77	17	112	24	5	4	1	1	305	23	13	6
2008	**590**	**39**	85	16	505	36	198	28	90	19	89	19	15	9	3	3	307	22	12	5
2009	**567**	**30**	96	14	471	26	167	19	82	13	68	13	13	5	4	3	303	18	10	4
2010	**591**	**31**	93	15	498	27	176	21	76	13	86	16	10	3	4	3	322	17	10	4
2011	**566**	**28**	78	12	488	25	174	18	83	12	77	12	13	4	1	1	314	18	10	3
2012	**498**	**27**	80	12	418	25	158	18	85	12	60	13	11	4	2	2	260	17	14	4
2013	**526**	**29**	77	12	449	27	201	20	104	13	70	12	25	10	3	3	248	17	15	5
2014	**632**	**36**	81	14	551	34	264	25	129	17	80	15	49	10	5	3	287	22	15	6
2015	**631**	**33**	84	12	548	30	269	24	130	15	73	12	65	14	2	2	279	19	15	5
2016	**589**	**34**	74	14	515	31	249	24	132	17	48	10	67	13	3	3	265	20	16	5
2017	**644**	**40**	81	16	563	36	243	28	120	19	52	12	60	14	11	9	321	24	17	7
2018	**604**	**42**	77	18	527	37	202	28	113	23	35	10	48	11	6	5	325	25	17	10
2019	**681**	**45**	78	22	603	39	198	26	114	21	32	9	50	9	1	1	406	29	19	6
Outflow																				
2004	344	28	196	23	148	16	43	10	39	9	3	3	z	z	1	2	104	13	8	2
2005	361	31	186	22	175	21	55	13	40	11	15	8	z	z	1	1	119	17	11	4
2006	398	34	207	26	192	22	66	16	44	11	22	11	z	z	0~	1	126	15	13	6
2007	341	27	171	20	169	18	69	15	41	11	25	10	0~	0~	2	3	101	10	8	3
2008	427	41	173	22	255	34	134	32	54	15	69	21	12	19	0~	1	120	12	11	5
2009	368	22	140	11	228	18	109	16	53	11	52	12	3	1	1	1	119	9	5	2
2010	339	20	136	11	203	16	99	14	58	12	37	8	2	2	1	1	104	8	6	2
2011	351	22	149	13	202	17	92	14	49	10	37	9	5	3	1	1	110	10	8	6
2012	321	20	143	14	179	14	75	11	41	8	30	8	3	2	1	1	103	8	5	2
2013	317	19	134	12	183	15	78	12	47	10	26	7	3	2	2	2	105	9	7	3
2014	319	22	137	13	182	18	89	15	51	12	32	9	5	3	1	1	93	10	6	3
2015	299	20	124	13	175	16	86	13	50	10	27	7	7	5	1	1	90	9	4	2
2016	340	23	134	13	206	19	116	16	59	11	43	10	13	6	2	1	90	10	3	2
2017	360	26	129	13	231	23	144	20	75	15	47	11	20	7	3	2	87	11	7	3
2018	344	31	125	15	219	27	127	24	66	18	45	13	14	7	2	2	92	13	10	6
2019	368	32	138	17	230	28	148	24	69	18	44	12	32	11	2	3	82	13	6	4

15.7 Long-Term International Migration 2004 - 2019
United Kingdom, England and Wales

thousands

Citizenship / Year	All citizenships: 2011 Census Revisions[1] Estimate	+/-CI	British (Including Overseas Territories) Estimate	+/-CI	Non-British Estimate	+/-CI	European Union[2] Estimate	+/-CI	EU15 Estimate	+/-CI	EU8 Estimate	+/-CI	EU2 Estimate	+/-CI	EU Other Estimate	+/-CI	Non-EU[3] All[3] Estimate	+/-CI	Other Europe[3] Estimate	+/-CI
United Kingdom — Balance																				
2004	+ 268	:	- 104	27	+ 349	41	+ 84	24	+ 37	18	+ 47	17	z	z	- 1	2	+ 265	33	+ 9	5
2005	+ 267	:	- 88	29	+ 293	39	+ 96	27	+ 32	17	+ 62	20	z	z	+ 2	3	+ 197	29	+ 5	7
2006	+ 265	:	- 124	31	+ 322	41	+ 104	30	+ 30	17	+ 71	24	z	z	+ 3	3	+ 218	29	+ 4	8
2007	+ 273	:	- 97	24	+ 330	41	+ 127	33	+ 36	20	+ 87	26	4	4	- 1	3	+ 204	25	+ 5	7
2008	+ 229	:	- 87	28	+ 250	50	+ 63	43	+ 37	24	+ 20	28	4	4	+ 3	3	+ 187	25	+ 1	7
2009	+ 229	:	- 44	18	+ 242	32	+ 58	25	+ 29	17	+ 16	18	11	5	+ 2	3	+ 184	20	+ 5	4
2010	+ 256	:	- 43	18	+ 294	32	+ 77	25	+ 18	17	+ 49	18	7	4	+ 3	4	+ 217	19	+ 5	4
2011	+ 205	:	- 70	18	+ 286	31	+ 82	23	+ 34	16	+ 40	15	8	5	+ 0~	2	+ 204	20	+ 2	6
2012	+ 177	34	- 63	19	+ 239	28	+ 82	21	+ 44	14	+ 30	15	8	4	+ 1	2	+ 157	19	+ 9	5
2013	+ 209	35	- 57	17	+ 266	31	+ 123	24	+ 58	16	+ 44	14	21	10	+ 1	3	+ 142	19	+ 8	5
2014	+ 313	43	- 55	19	+ 368	38	+ 174	29	+ 79	21	+ 48	18	44	11	+ 4	4	+ 194	25	+ 9	7
2015	+ 332	38	- 40	18	+ 372	34	+ 184	27	+ 80	18	+ 46	14	58	15	+ 1	2	+ 189	20	+ 11	5
2016	+ 249	41	- 60	19	+ 308	37	+ 133	29	+ 73	20	+ 5	14	54	14	+ 1	3	+ 175	23	+ 13	5
2017	+ 285	48	- 48	21	+ 333	43	+ 99	34	+ 45	24	+ 6	16	40	16	+ 8	9	+ 234	26	+ 10	8
2018	+ 260	52	- 48	24	+ 308	46	+ 75	36	+ 48	29	- 10	17	34	13	+ 4	6	+ 233	28	+ 7	12
2019	+ 313	55	- 61	28	+ 373	47	+ 50	35	+ 45	28	- 12	15	18	15	- 1	3	+ 323	32	+ 13	7
England and Wales — Inflow																				
2004	549	38	84	13	464	36	119	21	71	14	48	16	z	z	0~	1	345	29	17	5
2005	523	36	88	17	435	32	142	22	65	13	74	18	z	z	3	2	293	22	16	6
2006	549	36	78	16	471	33	149	23	67	12	78	19	z	z	4	3	322	23	17	6
2007	524	38	65	13	460	35	175	28	68	16	101	23	5	4	1	1	285	21	12	6
2008	528	36	68	13	460	34	178	27	75	17	84	19	15	8	3	3	283	21	10	4
2009	507	28	83	13	424	25	142	18	69	12	58	13	12	5	4	3	282	17	10	4
2010	532	29	80	14	451	26	151	20	68	12	72	15	8	3	4	3	300	16	9	3
2011	515	26	71	12	445	24	153	17	74	12	67	12	11	3	1	1	291	17	10	3
2012	451	26	72	11	380	23	138	16	74	11	52	11	10	4	2	2	241	16	13	4
2013	484	28	71	11	412	26	183	19	94	12	63	12	23	10	3	3	229	17	12	4
2014	583	34	76	14	507	31	240	25	116	16	74	15	47	10	4	3	267	19	13	4
2015	581	31	73	11	508	29	248	23	122	15	63	11	61	14	2	2	260	17	13	4
2016	540	33	69	14	471	30	227	22	121	16	41	9	64	12	2	1	244	19	15	5
2017	596	38	74	16	523	35	224	26	108	17	48	11	58	14	10	9	298	23	16	7
2018	558	40	73	18	485	36	186	27	104	22	32	10	44	11	6	5	299	24	16	10
2019	622	41	68	16	554	37	179	25	102	20	29	9	47	11	1	1	375	27	18	6

15.7 Long-Term International Migration 2004 - 2019

United Kingdom, England and Wales

Citizenship

thousands

Year	All citizenships 2011 Census Revisions[1] Estimate	+/-CI	British (Including Overseas Territories) Estimate	+/-CI	Non-British Estimate	+/-CI	European Union[2] Estimate	+/-CI	European Union EU15 Estimate	+/-CI	European Union EU8 Estimate	+/-CI	European Union EU2 Estimate	+/-CI	European Union Other Estimate	+/-CI	Non-European Union[3] All[3] Estimate	+/-CI	Other Europe[3] Estimate	+/-CI
Outflow																				
2004	311	27	175	22	135	15	41	10	36	9	3	3	z	z	z	1	95	12	8	2
2005	328	29	171	22	157	19	50	13	35	10	8	8	z	z	z	1	107	15	11	4
2006	369	33	192	25	177	21	60	15	38	10	11	11	z	z	0~	1	117	15	12	6
2007	307	25	152	19	155	17	60	14	38	11	9	9	0~	0~	2	3	94	9	8	3
2008	393	40	157	21	235	34	126	32	49	15	20	20	12	19	0~	1	110	11	10	5
2009	328	20	123	10	205	18	98	16	49	11	11	11	2	2	1	1	107	8	5	2
2010	308	19	123	10	184	16	89	14	54	11	8	8	2	2	1	1	95	7	6	2
2011	312	20	134	12	178	16	78	13	42	9	9	9	4	3	1	1	100	9	8	6
2012	286	19	126	13	160	14	66	11	38	8	7	7	3	2	1	1	94	8	4	2
2013	280	18	118	11	163	14	68	12	42	9	7	7	2	1	2	2	95	8	6	3
2014	285	21	124	12	161	12	76	14	44	11	8	8	4	3	1	1	85	10	5	2
2015	272	20	114	12	158	15	75	13	47	10	7	7	6	5	1	1	83	8	3	2
2016	309	22	124	12	185	18	107	16	53	10	10	10	12	6	2	1	78	9	3	2
2017	329	24	120	13	209	21	134	19	69	14	10	10	19	7	2	2	75	9	6	3
2018	313	30	113	15	200	26	117	23	59	17	13	13	13	7	2	2	83	12	10	6
2019	340	32	129	17	211	27	139	24	66	18	12	12	31	11	3	3	72	12	5	4
Balance																				
2004	+ 238	47	− 91	26	+ 329	39	+ 79	23	+ 35	16	+ 44	17	z	z	z	2	+ 250	31	+ 9	5
2005	+ 195	46	− 83	27	+ 278	37	+ 92	26	+ 30	20	+ 60	16	z	z	z	3	+ 186	27	+ 6	7
2006	+ 180	49	− 114	30	+ 294	39	+ 89	27	+ 29	16	+ 57	22	z	z	+	3	+ 205	28	+ 5	8
2007	+ 217	45	− 88	23	+ 305	39	+ 115	32	+ 30	19	+ 81	25	4	4	−	3	+ 190	23	+ 4	7
2008	+ 135	54	− 90	25	+ 225	48	+ 52	42	+ 26	22	+ 19	28	3	21	+	3	+ 173	24	0~	6
2009	+ 179	35	− 40	17	+ 219	30	+ 44	24	+ 20	16	+ 12	17	10	5	+	3	+ 174	18	+ 5	4
2010	+ 224	35	− 43	17	+ 267	30	+ 62	24	+ 14	17	+ 39	17	6	3	+	3	+ 205	18	+ 4	4
2011	+ 203	33	− 64	17	+ 267	29	+ 75	21	+ 32	15	+ 37	15	6	4	+	2	+ 192	19	+ 2	6
2012	+ 165	32	− 54	18	+ 219	27	+ 73	19	+ 37	13	+ 28	13	8	4	+	2	+ 147	18	+ 8	4
2013	+ 203	33	− 46	15	+ 249	29	+ 115	23	+ 52	15	+ 40	15	22	10	+	3	+ 135	19	+ 5	5
2014	+ 298	40	− 49	18	+ 347	36	+ 165	28	+ 72	20	+ 47	17	43	11	+	3	+ 182	21	+ 8	5
2015	+ 309	37	− 42	17	+ 351	33	+ 173	26	+ 75	18	+ 43	13	55	14	+	2	+ 177	19	+ 10	5
2016	+ 231	39	− 55	19	+ 286	35	+ 120	27	+ 68	19	0~	13	52	14	0~	2	+ 166	21	+ 12	5
2017	+ 267	45	− 47	20	+ 314	41	+ 91	32	+ 38	22	+ 5	15	39	15	+ 8	9	+ 223	25	+ 9	8
2018	+ 244	50	− 40	23	+ 285	44	+ 69	36	+ 45	28	− 11	17	31	13	+ 4	6	+ 215	27	+ 7	12
2019	+ 281	51	− 61	23	+ 343	46	+ 41	35	+ 36	27	− 11	15	17	15	− 1	3	+ 302	30	+ 13	7

15.7 Long-Term International Migration 2004 - 2019

United Kingdom, England and Wales

Citizenship

| | Asia | | | | | | | | | | Non-European Union³ — Rest of the World | | | | | | | | | | | | | | All citizenships |
| | All | | Middle East and Central Asia | | East Asia | | South Asia | | South East Asia | | All | | Sub-Saharan Africa | | North Africa | | North America | | Central and South America | | Oceania | | Stateless | | Original Estimates¹ |
Year	Estimate	+/-CI	Estimate	+/-CI	Estimate	+/-CI	Estimate	+/-CI	Estimate	+/-CI	Estimate	+/-CI	Estimate	+/-CI	Estimate	+/-CI	Estimate	+/-CI	Estimate	+/-CI	Estimate	+/-CI	Estimate	+/-CI	Estimate +/-CI
United Kingdom																									
Inflow																									
2004	192	24	24	11	53	16	87	13	28	7	160	18	86	12	7	3	20	7	10	4	37	8	0~	0~	
2005	173	19	19	6	45	12	83	11	27	8	126	13	62	9	3	1	20	5	8	3	33	7	0~	0~	
2006	201	20	17	4	40	7	110	14	34	11	125	13	49	8	5	3	23	5	9	3	39	8	0~	0~	
2007	187	18	21	4	37	8	102	13	27	9	105	12	42	7	6	5	19	5	10	5	27	5	0~	0~	
2008	177	16	28	6	35	8	83	9	31	8	118	15	48	9	8	4	26	7	14	6	23	5	0~	0~	
2009	202	14	24	4	39	6	110	10	29	5	90	10	39	7	3	3	23	6	8	3	17	4	0~	0~	
2010	221	13	20	4	43	6	126	9	32	6	90	10	29	5	7	5	21	5	10	4	22	5	0~	0~	
2011	226	15	21	4	56	9	129	10	20	4	76	9	25	5	4	1	23	6	6	2	18	4	1	0~	
2012	165	13	17	3	55	8	71	8	22	5	81	11	24	5	6	4	23	6	7	3	21	5	0~	0~	
2013	156	14	20	4	64	11	53	6	20	5	77	10	20	4	14	7	19	5	8	3	15	3	0~	0~	
2014	168	17	26	5	53	10	67	12	23	6	104	13	25	5	9	3	31	8	17	7	22	4	0~	0~	
2015	168	14	29	4	62	9	55	8	23	5	95	11	28	5	8	1	25	6	12	6	22	6	1	0~	
2016	163	16	33	5	56	12	58	8	17	4	85	12	25	8	7	2	21	5	15	7	17	4	1	0~	
2017	204	17	27	5	77	11	77	10	23	6	100	15	31	7	7	4	25	8	7	3	29	10	0~	0~	
2018	222	19	34	6	77	11	78	11	33	8	86	13	27	7	7	3	28	8	10	4	13	5	1	0~	
2019	286	22	37	6	97	14	121	15	31	6	100	17	36	8	8	3	27	12	12	7	18	7	1	0~	
Outflow																									
2004	41	8	5	2	18	6	7	2	10	5	55	9	13	4	1	1	14	6	6	4	22	5	0~	0~	
2005	44	11	6	2	18	9	16	5	5	3	64	12	15	4	1	1	16	8	7	4	24	5	0~	0~	
2006	46	9	7	3	18	6	16	5	5	3	67	10	20	6	1	0~	16	6	5	3	26	6	0~	0~	
2007	43	7	4	1	15	4	18	5	6	2	50	6	15	3	1	1	8	2	5	3	21	3	0~	0~	
2008	47	7	5	1	16	4	20	5	6	1	62	8	14	5	2	2	13	4	7	3	25	4	0~	0~	
2009	55	5	6	1	19	3	23	3	7	2	59	7	13	3	1	1	16	4	4	2	26	4	0~	0~	
2010	53	5	7	2	19	4	21	3	6	2	46	5	12	3	1	1	12	3	5	2	16	3	0~	0~	
2011	61	6	6	2	17	3	29	4	9	2	41	6	9	3	1	1	12	3	3	2	16	3	0~	0~	
2012	63	6	5	2	21	4	26	4	11	3	36	5	8	2	1	1	11	3	4	2	12	3	0~	0~	
2013	59	6	5	2	21	4	26	4	8	2	39	6	8	2	2	1	13	4	4	2	13	3	0~	0~	
2014	59	9	5	2	27	8	21	3	7	3	27	4	6	2	1	1	9	3	1	1	10	3	0~	0~	
2015	53	6	4	2	20	4	20	4	9	3	33	5	7	2	2	1	10	3	5	2	9	3	0~	0~	
2016	51	7	7	4	18	4	18	4	8	3	36	7	5	3	2	2	16	5	4	2	9	3	0~	0~	
2017	49	7	9	4	21	4	12	3	6	3	31	7	5	3	2	1	11	5	4	3	9	3	0~	0~	
2018	49	8	4	3	24	5	13	4	8	3	34	9	5	3	1	1	14	6	5	3	9	4	0~	0~	
2019	47	8	6	3	23	5	13	4	5	2	30	9	4	3	0~	0~	8	4	8	5	10	6	0~	0~	

15.7 Long-Term International Migration 2004 - 2019
United Kingdom, England and Wales

thousands

Citizenship	Asia		Middle East and Central Asia		East Asia		South Asia		South East Asia		Non-European Union³ Rest of the World		Sub-Saharan Africa		North Africa		North America		Central and South America		Oceania		Stateless		All citizenships Original Estimates¹	
	All										All															
Year	Estimate	+/-CI	Estimate	+/-CI	Estimate	+/-CI	Estimate	+/-CI	Estimate	+/-CI	Estimate	+/-CI	Estimate	+/-CI	Estimate	+/-CI	Estimate	+/-CI	Estimate	+/-CI	Estimate	+/-CI	Estimate	+/-CI	Estimate	+/-CI
United Kingdom																										
Balance																										
2004	+ 151	26	19	11	35	17	+ 80	13	+ 17	9	+ 105	20	+ 73	13	+ 6	3	+ 7	9	+ 4	6	+ 15	10	0~	1	+ 245	49
2005	+ 129	22	12	7	27	15	+ 67	12	+ 22	9	+ 63	18	+ 48	10	+ 1	2	+ 4	10	+ 1	5	+ 9	8	0~	0~	+ 206	49
2006	+ 155	22	10	5	21	9	95	15	29	11	+ 58	17	+ 29	10	+ 5	3	+ 7	8	+ 4	4	+ 13	10	0~	0~	+ 198	52
2007	+ 144	20	17	4	22	9	84	14	21	9	+ 55	13	+ 27	7	+ 5	5	+ 12	5	+ 5	5	+ 7	6	0~	0~	+ 233	48
2008	+ 130	17	23	6	18	9	63	11	26	8	+ 56	17	+ 33	10	+ 5	4	+ 13	8	+ 7	7	- 2	7	0~	0~	+ 163	57
2009	+ 147	15	18	4	20	7	87	11	23	6	+ 31	12	+ 26	7	+ 2	3	+ 8	7	+ 4	3	- 8	6	0~	0~	+ 198	37
2010	+ 168	14	12	4	24	7	106	10	25	6	+ 45	11	+ 17	5	+ 6	6	+ 10	6	+ 5	4	+ 7	5	0~	0~	+ 252	37
2011	+ 165	16	16	5	39	9	99	11	12	5	+ 36	11	+ 16	6	+ 3	1	+ 12	7	+ 3	3	+ 2	5	0~	0~	+ 215	35
2012	+ 103	14	12	4	35	9	45	9	11	6	+ 45	12	+ 16	6	+ 5	4	+ 13	6	+ 2	4	+ 9	6	0~	0~		
2013	+ 97	15	15	4	43	11	27	7	12	5	+ 38	11	+ 13	4	+ 12	7	+ 6	6	+ 5	4	+ 2	4	0~	0~		
2014	+ 109	19	21	5	26	13	47	12	15	6	+ 76	14	+ 19	5	+ 8	3	+ 23	8	+ 15	7	+ 11	5	0~	0~		
2015	+ 115	15	24	5	42	10	35	9	14	6	+ 61	13	+ 22	6	+ 6	2	+ 14	6	+ 7	6	+ 13	6	0~	1		
2016	+ 112	17	26	6	38	12	40	9	9	5	+ 49	14	+ 21	8	+ 5	3	+ 5	7	+ 11	7	+ 8	5	1	1		
2017	+ 155	18	18	6	56	12	64	11	17	6	+ 69	17	+ 26	7	+ 5	4	+ 15	9	+ 3	4	+ 20	10	0~	0~		
2018	+ 173	20	30	7	53	12	65	12	26	8	+ 52	16	+ 21	8	+ 7	4	+ 14	10	+ 5	5	+ 7	7	1	1		
2019	+ 239	24	31	7	74	15	108	15	26	7	+ 71	20	+ 31	9	+ 8	3	+ 20	12	+ 4	9	+ 8	9	1	1		
England and Wales																										
Inflow																										
2004	179	23	22	11	49	15	82	12	26	7	149	16	78	11	6	3	19	7	10	4	36	8	0~	0~		
2005	161	18	17	6	41	11	78	10	26	8	115	11	60	9	3	1	17	4	7	2	29	5	0~	0~		
2006	192	19	16	4	38	7	104	14	33	11	113	12	45	8	5	3	22	5	8	3	33	7	0~	0~		
2007	173	17	20	4	35	8	94	12	24	8	99	11	40	7	6	5	18	4	9	5	26	5	0~	0~		
2008	167	15	25	5	32	8	80	9	29	7	106	14	45	9	6	3	21	6	12	6	22	5	0~	0~		
2009	191	13	22	4	35	6	105	10	28	5	81	9	35	6	3	3	20	3	7	3	16	4	0~	0~		
2010	207	13	18	3	39	6	119	9	30	6	84	10	28	5	7	7	18	5	10	4	21	4	0~	0~		
2011	211	14	19	4	50	8	122	10	19	4	70	8	24	5	4	1	20	1	5	2	17	4	0~	0~		
2012	154	12	16	3	51	7	68	8	19	5	75	10	23	5	6	4	21	4	5	3	20	5	0~	0~		
2013	145	13	18	4	60	11	49	6	18	4	72	10	19	4	13	7	18	7	8	3	14	3	0~	0~		
2014	156	13	24	5	48	7	64	8	21	6	98	13	24	5	8	3	29	3	16	7	21	4	0~	0~		
2015	158	13	26	4	59	9	52	6	22	5	88	11	27	5	7	1	22	1	10	6	21	6	1	1		
2016	152	15	30	5	52	11	54	8	16	4	76	11	22	6	6	2	19	2	12	6	16	4	1	1		
2017	190	16	25	5	71	11	73	10	20	5	93	15	29	7	7	4	22	4	5	2	29	10	0~	0~		
2018	204	17	30	6	68	10	74	10	32	8	78	13	26	6	7	3	23	3	9	4	13	5	1	1		
2019	266	21	32	4	91	14	116	14	28	6	89	16	32	8	7	3	24	3	11	7	15	5	1	1		

15.7 Long-Term International Migration 2004 - 2019

United Kingdom, England and Wales

Citizenship

thousands

	Asia										Non-European Union[3] Rest of the World														All citizenships Original Estimates[1]	
	All		Middle East and Central Asia		East Asia		South Asia		South East Asia		All		Sub-Saharan Africa		North Africa		North America		Central and South America		Oceania		Stateless			
Year	Estimate	+/-CI	Estimate	+/-CI	Estimate	+/-CI	Estimate	+/-CI	Estimate	+/-CI	Estimate	+/-CI	Estimate	+/-CI	Estimate	+/-CI	Estimate	+/-CI	Estimate	+/-CI	Estimate	+/-CI	Estimate	+/-CI	Estimate	+/-CI
Outflow																										
2004	35	7	4	1	16	5	7	2	8	3	52	9	12	4	1	1	12	6	6	4	20	5	0~	0~		
2005	41	11	6	2	17	9	14	5	4	3	55	9	15	4	1	1	10	5	6	3	23	5	0~	0~		
2006	44	9	7	3	17	6	15	5	5	3	61	10	18	6	0~	0~	14	5	5	3	24	6	0~	0~		
2007	40	6	4	1	14	4	16	4	6	2	47	6	15	3	1	1	7	2	5	3	19	3	0~	0~		
2008	41	6	4	1	15	4	17	4	5	1	58	8	14	4	2	2	12	3	7	3	23	4	0~	0~		
2009	49	5	5	1	17	3	21	3	5	2	54	6	12	3	1	1	13	4	4	3	24	4	0~	0~		
2010	47	5	6	2	17	3	19	3	6	2	42	5	11	3	1	1	10	2	5	2	15	3	0~	0~		
2011	56	6	5	2	16	3	27	4	8	2	36	5	8	3	1	1	10	3	3	2	14	3	0~	0~		
2012	56	6	4	2	19	4	24	3	9	3	33	5	7	2	1	1	10	2	4	2	12	3	0~	0~		
2013	54	6	5	2	20	4	23	3	7	2	34	5	7	2	2	1	10	3	4	2	12	3	0~	0~		
2014	54	9	5	2	24	8	19	3	6	3	25	4	5	2	1	1	8	3	1	1	10	3	0~	0~		
2015	49	6	4	2	18	4	19	4	8	3	30	5	6	2	1	1	9	3	5	2	8	3	0~	0~		
2016	45	6	5	2	16	4	16	4	8	3	30	6	3	1	2	2	14	5	3	2	8	3	0~	0~		
2017	43	6	7	3	19	4	11	3	6	3	25	6	3	1	2	1	7	3	4	3	9	3	0~	0~		
2018	45	7	4	3	22	5	12	4	7	3	29	7	5	3	1	1	11	5	4	2	8	4	0~	0~		
2019	41	7	5	3	20	4	11	4	4	2	27	9	4	3	0~	0~	6	3	7	5	9	6	0~	0~		
Balance																										
2004	+143	24	+18	11	+32	16	+75	12	+18	8	+97	19	+66	12	+5	3	+7	9	+4	6	+16	10	0~	1		
2005	+120	21	+11	6	+23	14	+64	11	+21	9	+60	14	+45	10	+1	1	+7	6	+1	4	+6	7	0~	0~		
2006	+148	21	+9	5	+21	9	+89	14	+29	11	+52	16	+27	9	+5	3	+7	7	+3	4	+10	9	0~	0~		
2007	+134	18	+17	4	+20	9	+78	13	+18	9	+53	13	+25	7	+5	5	+11	5	+4	5	+7	6	0~	0~		
2008	+126	16	+21	5	+18	9	+63	10	+24	8	+48	16	+31	10	+4	4	+9	7	+5	6	-2	6	0~	0~		
2009	+142	14	+17	4	+18	7	+84	10	+23	6	+27	11	+23	6	+2	3	+7	6	+4	3	-8	6	0~	0~		
2010	+159	14	+12	4	+23	7	+100	9	+25	6	+42	11	+17	5	+6	5	+8	5	+5	4	+6	5	0~	0~		
2011	+155	15	+14	5	+34	9	+95	11	+12	5	+34	9	+16	5	+3	1	+10	5	+2	3	+4	5	0~	0~		
2012	+97	14	+11	4	+32	8	+44	8	+10	6	+41	11	+15	6	+5	4	+11	5	+1	3	+8	6	0~	0~		
2013	+90	14	+14	4	+40	11	+25	7	+11	4	+39	11	+13	4	+12	7	+8	5	+4	3	+3	4	0~	0~		
2014	+102	16	+20	5	+23	11	+44	9	+15	6	+72	13	+19	5	+7	3	+21	8	+14	7	+11	5	0~	0~		
2015	+109	14	+22	5	+41	10	+33	8	+13	6	+57	12	+21	6	+5	2	+13	6	+6	6	+12	6	0~	1		
2016	+107	16	+25	5	+36	12	+38	8	+9	5	+46	13	+19	6	+4	3	+5	7	+9	6	+8	5	1	1		
2017	+146	17	+18	5	+52	11	+62	11	+14	6	+67	16	+26	7	+5	4	+15	8	+2	4	+20	10	0~	0~		
2018	+159	19	+26	6	+46	12	+62	12	+25	8	+49	15	+21	7	+6	4	+12	9	+5	5	+5	7	1	1		
2019	+226	22	+26	5	+71	15	+105	15	+23	6	+63	19	+29	8	+7	3	+18	12	+4	9	+5	8	1	1		

557

15.7 Long-Term International Migration 2004 - 2019
United Kingdom, England and Wales

thousands

Citizenship

Year	Asia											Non-European Union[3]														All citizenships	
	All		Middle East and Central Asia		East Asia		South Asia		South East Asia		Rest of the World				North America		Central and South America		Oceania		Stateless		Original Estimates[1]		Estimate +/-CI	
											All		Sub-Saharan Africa		North Africa													
	Estimate	+/-CI	Estimate	+/-CI	Estimate	+/-CI	Estimate	+/-CI	Estimate	+/-CI	Estimate	+/-CI	Estimate	+/-CI	Estimate	+/-CI	Estimate	+/-CI	Estimate	+/-CI	Estimate	+/-CI	Estimate	+/-CI		

Source: Office for National Statistics (ONS), Home Office, Central Statistics Office (CSO) Ireland, Northern Ireland Statistics and Research Agency (NISRA)

Totals may not sum due to rounding.

"z" - Not applicable. ".." - Not available. "0~" - Rounds to zero. Please see the Notes worksheet for more information.

Long-Term International Migration estimates by citizenship using the new country groupings shown above are only available from calendar year 2004.

1 Net migration ("Balance") figures for the United Kingdom for 2001 to 2011 have been revised in light of the results of the 2011 Census. The original published estimates are shown to the right of the table. The revisions are not reflected in the remainder of the table. The sums of the disaggregated estimates will not therefore match the revised balances. Users should continue to use the estimates in the table to analyse detailed breakdowns of inflows and outflows of long-term international migrants but, in doing so, should bear in mind that the headline net migration estimates have been revised. Please see the Notes worksheet for more information.

2 European Union estimates are for the EU15 (Austria, Belgium, Denmark, Finland, France, Germany, Greece, Republic of Ireland, Italy, Luxembourg, Netherlands, Portugal, Spain and Sweden) up to 2003, the EU25 (the EU15 and the EU8 groupings plus Malta and Cyprus) from 2004 to 2006, the EU27 (the EU25 plus Bulgaria and Romania) from 2007 and the EU28 (the EU27 plus Croatia) from July 2013. Estimates are also shown separately for the EU15, the EU8 (Czech Republic, Estonia, Hungary, Latvia, Lithuania, Poland, Slovakia and Slovenia), the EU2 (Bulgaria and Romania) and EU Other (Malta, Cyprus and Croatia). British citizens are excluded from all citizenship groupings and are shown separately.

3 Excludes British and other European Union citizens as defined in footnote 2.

This table uses 95% confidence intervals (CI) to indicate the robustness of each estimate. Please see the Notes worksheet for more information.

Statistically Significant Increase	Statistically Significant Decrease

The latest estimates (2018) have been compared with the corresponding estimates for the period one year earlier (2017). Where changes have been found to be statistically significant, the relevant pair of estimates have been highlighted by setting their background colour. Please see the Notes worksheet for more information.

This table has not been adjusted in line with the latest top level migration estimates.
As part of Population and Migration Statistics Transformation programme to better meet the needs of our users, preliminary adjustments were made to the Long-Term International Migration (LTIM) estimates in the **August 2019 Migration Statistics Quarterly Report (MSQR)** (https://www.ons.gov.uk/peoplepopulationandcommunity/populationandmigration/internationalmigration/bulletins/migrationstatisticsquarterlyreport/august2019).

Currently these adjustments are only available at the highest-level due to further work being needed to develop a methodology for the more detailed data. Whilst we go through this period of development and innovation, we have sought to re-classify our migration statistics as "Experimental Statistics" in line with **Office for Statistics Regulation guidance** (https://www.statisticsauthority.gov.uk/publication/experimental-statistics-official-statistics-in-development/).

As such the preliminary adjustments have not been applied to the estimates in this table but we have continued to provide detailed breakdowns due to user demand. Please note these estimates will continue to be provisional until final adjustments are developed by Summer 2020 and will be inconsistent with the MSQR tables.

15.8 Long-Term International Migration 2004 - 2019

United Kingdom, England and Wales
Country of Last or Next Residence

thousands

Year	All countries 2011 Census Revisions[1] Estimate	+/-CI	European Union[2] Estimate	+/-CI	European Union EU15 Estimate	+/-CI	European Union EU8 Estimate	+/-CI	European Union EU2 Estimate	+/-CI	European Union Other Estimate	+/-CI	Non-European Union[3] All[3] Estimate	+/-CI	Other Europe[3] Estimate	+/-CI
United Kingdom																
Inflow																
2004	589	40	151	24	98	18	51	16	z	z	2	2	438	32	19	6
2005	567	37	185	27	105	19	77	18	z	z	3	3	381	26	22	8
2006	596	39	210	30	110	20	93	22	z	z	7	5	386	25	22	7
2007	574	40	221	31	102	20	113	24	5	4	2	2	353	24	18	8
2008	590	39	224	30	115	22	89	19	16	9	5	4	366	25	15	5
2009	567	30	199	21	115	16	67	13	11	4	6	4	367	21	14	7
2010	591	31	208	24	111	17	81	15	10	3	7	5	382	19	14	4
2011	566	28	205	20	109	15	77	12	12	4	6	5	361	19	13	4
2012	498	27	182	20	112	14	57	13	10	3	3	2	316	19	17	5
2013	526	29	220	22	125	17	70	12	21	6	4	3	306	19	19	5
2014	632	36	287	27	155	20	79	15	45	9	7	5	345	24	17	7
2015	631	33	295	25	160	17	70	11	61	14	4	3	336	21	20	5
2016	589	34	273	26	160	21	46	10	64	12	3	3	316	22	19	5
2017	644	40	261	30	144	23	51	12	57	13	9	8	384	27	23	9
2018	604	42	225	31	137	26	40	12	44	10	4	4	378	28	19	10
2019	681	45	208	26	131	22	28	8	46	11	3	2	473	36	25	9
Outflow																
2004	344	28	128	21	114	20	6	4	z	z	7	6	216	19	14	5
2005	361	31	138	23	118	21	17	9	z	z	3	2	223	21	18	6
2006	398	34	145	26	118	23	24	11	z	z	3	3	253	21	19	7
2007	341	27	131	22	98	19	25	10	z	z	5	4	209	15	15	6
2008	427	41	202	38	123	26	66	20	12	19	2	2	225	15	17	6
2009	368	22	144	18	88	14	50	11	3	1	4	2	224	12	12	3
2010	339	20	136	16	93	14	38	8	2	1	4	2	203	11	15	4
2011	351	22	125	16	80	13	36	9	4	3	4	2	226	15	18	8
2012	321	20	114	16	79	13	26	6	7	8	3	2	207	12	9	3
2013	317	19	114	15	79	13	26	7	6	4	3	1	203	12	13	4
2014	319	22	127	18	88	15	33	8	4	2	3	2	192	14	13	4
2015	299	20	125	16	89	13	25	7	7	5	4	2	174	12	11	5
2016	340	23	162	18	106	14	42	10	12	6	3	2	178	14	6	2
2017	360	26	194	22	127	18	41	10	18	7	8	4	166	14	12	4
2018	344	31	181	27	119	22	42	12	14	7	6	5	164	15	14	7
2019	368	32	201	27	117	21	47	13	31	10	6	5	167	17	8	4

15.8 Long-Term International Migration 2004 - 2019
United Kingdom, England and Wales
Country of Last or Next Residence

thousands

United Kingdom — Balance

Year	All countries 2011 Census Revisions[1] Estimate	+/-CI	European Union[2] Estimate	+/-CI	European Union EU15 Estimate	+/-CI	European Union EU8 Estimate	+/-CI	European Union EU2 Estimate	+/-CI	European Union Other Estimate	+/-CI	Non-European Union[3] All[3] Estimate	+/-CI	Non-European Union[3] Other Europe[3] Estimate	+/-CI
2004	+ 268	::	+ 23	32	- 16	27	+ 45	17	z	z	- 6	6	+ 222	37	+ 5	8
2005	+ 267	::	+ 47	35	- 13	29	+ 60	20	z	z	0~	3	+ 159	34	+ 3	10
2006	+ 265	::	+ 65	40	- 8	31	+ 69	25	z	z	+ 4	5	+ 132	33	+ 3	10
2007	+ 273	::	+ 90	38	+ 4	27	+ 88	26	+ 1	5	- 3	4	+ 143	29	+ 2	10
2008	+ 229	::	+ 22	49	- 8	34	+ 23	28	+ 4	21	+ 3	4	+ 141	29	+ 2	8
2009	+ 229	::	+ 55	28	+ 27	21	+ 18	17	+ 9	5	+ 1	4	+ 143	24	+ 3	7
2010	+ 256	::	+ 73	29	+ 18	22	+ 43	17	+ 8	3	+ 4	5	+ 179	23	+ 1	6
2011	+ 205	::	+ 80	26	+ 28	20	+ 41	15	+ 8	5	+ 2	5	+ 135	24	+ 5	8
2012	+ 177	34	+ 68	26	+ 33	19	+ 31	14	+ 4	9	- 1	3	+ 109	22	+ 8	6
2013	+ 209	35	+ 106	26	+ 46	21	+ 44	14	+ 15	7	+ 1	4	+ 103	23	+ 6	7
2014	+ 313	43	+ 160	33	+ 68	25	+ 47	17	+ 41	9	+ 4	5	+ 153	28	+ 4	8
2015	+ 332	38	+ 171	30	+ 70	22	+ 45	13	+ 55	15	0~	3	+ 162	24	+ 9	7
2016	+ 249	41	+ 110	32	+ 54	25	+ 3	14	+ 52	13	+ 1	3	+ 138	26	+ 13	6
2017	+ 285	48	+ 67	37	+ 17	29	+ 9	15	+ 39	15	+ 1	9	+ 218	30	+ 11	10
2018	+ 260	52	+ 45	41	+ 19	34	- 2	17	+ 30	12	- 2	6	+ 215	32	+ 5	12
2019	+ 313	55	+ 7	38	+ 14	31	- 18	15	+ 15	15	- 3	6	+ 306	40	+ 17	10

England and Wales — Inflow

Year	All countries 2011 Census Revisions[1] Estimate	+/-CI	European Union[2] Estimate	+/-CI	European Union EU15 Estimate	+/-CI	European Union EU8 Estimate	+/-CI	European Union EU2 Estimate	+/-CI	European Union Other Estimate	+/-CI	Non-European Union[3] All[3] Estimate	+/-CI	Non-European Union[3] Other Europe[3] Estimate	+/-CI
2004	549	38	143	24	92	17	49	16	z	z	2	2	406	30	18	6
2005	523	36	174	26	96	19	75	18	z	z	3	3	349	24	19	7
2006	549	36	190	28	104	19	79	19	z	z	7	5	359	24	20	7
2007	524	38	196	30	88	19	102	23	5	4	2	2	328	23	15	8
2008	528	36	199	28	95	19	84	19	15	8	5	4	329	23	13	5
2009	507	28	169	20	96	14	58	13	10	4	5	4	338	20	13	7
2010	532	29	178	23	95	16	69	15	8	3	7	5	353	18	12	4
2011	515	26	180	19	97	14	68	12	10	3	6	5	335	18	12	4
2012	451	26	160	18	98	13	50	11	10	3	2	2	291	18	16	5
2013	484	28	199	21	112	16	63	12	20	6	4	3	285	19	16	5
2014	583	34	261	27	139	20	73	15	43	9	6	5	322	21	15	5
2015	581	31	270	24	148	17	61	11	58	14	3	3	311	19	18	5
2016	540	33	250	25	149	20	39	8	60	12	2	2	290	21	18	5
2017	596	38	240	28	130	21	47	11	54	13	9	8	357	26	22	9
2018	558	40	209	30	127	26	36	12	42	10	4	4	349	26	18	10
2019	622	41	187	25	117	22	24	7	44	11	2	2	435	32	24	9

15.8 Long-Term International Migration 2004 - 2019

United Kingdom, England and Wales

Country of Last or Next Residence

thousands

England and Wales

Outflow

Year	All countries 2011 Census Revisions² Estimate	+/-CI	European Union² Estimate	+/-CI	EU15 Estimate	+/-CI	EU8 Estimate	+/-CI	EU2 Estimate	+/-CI	EU Other Estimate	+/-CI	Non-EU All³ Estimate	+/-CI	Other Europe³ Estimate	+/-CI
2004	311	27	119	20	107	19	6	4	z	z	6	5	192	17	13	5
2005	328	29	126	22	106	20	17	9	z	z	3	2	202	19	18	6
2006	369	33	137	26	111	23	24	11	z	z	3	3	232	20	18	7
2007	307	25	119	21	90	19	20	9	3	4	5	4	188	14	15	6
2008	393	40	186	37	111	25	62	20	12	19	2	2	207	14	16	6
2009	328	20	128	17	78	13	43	11	2	1	4	2	201	11	11	3
2010	308	19	122	16	84	13	33	8	2	1	3	2	186	10	15	4
2011	312	20	108	15	71	12	30	8	4	3	4	2	204	14	15	7
2012	286	19	101	16	71	12	20	5	6	8	3	2	186	11	9	3
2013	280	18	101	14	72	12	22	6	4	3	3	1	180	11	12	4
2014	285	21	111	17	78	14	28	8	3	2	3	2	173	13	11	4
2015	272	20	112	16	84	13	19	6	6	5	4	2	160	12	10	5
2016	309	22	149	18	97	13	39	10	11	6	3	2	160	13	6	2
2017	329	24	181	21	119	17	38	9	16	7	8	4	148	13	11	4
2018	313	30	167	26	109	22	40	12	13	7	6	5	146	14	13	7
2019	340	32	189	27	110	21	43	13	29	10	6	5	152	17	7	4

Balance

Year	All countries 2011 Census Revisions² Estimate	+/-CI	European Union² Estimate	+/-CI	EU15 Estimate	+/-CI	EU8 Estimate	+/-CI	EU2 Estimate	+/-CI	EU Other Estimate	+/-CI	Non-EU All³ Estimate	+/-CI	Other Europe³ Estimate	+/-CI
2004	+ 238	47	+ 24	31	- 14	26	+ 43	16	z	z	- 5	6	+ 214	35	+ 6	7
2005	+ 195	46	+ 48	34	- 9	27	+ 57	20	z	z	+ 0~	3	+ 147	31	+ 1	10
2006	+ 180	49	+ 53	38	- 7	30	+ 55	22	z	z	+ 5	5	+ 127	31	+ 2	10
2007	+ 217	45	+ 77	37	- 3	26	+ 82	25	+ 1	5	- 3	4	+ 140	27	+ 1	10
2008	+ 135	54	+ 13	47	- 15	31	+ 22	27	+ 3	21	+ 3	4	+ 122	27	+ 3	8
2009	+ 179	35	+ 42	26	+ 18	19	+ 14	17	+ 8	4	+ 1	4	+ 137	22	+ 3	7
2010	+ 224	35	+ 56	27	+ 10	21	+ 36	17	+ 7	3	+ 3	5	+ 168	21	+ 2	6
2011	+ 203	33	+ 72	24	+ 25	18	+ 38	15	+ 6	4	+ 2	5	+ 131	23	+ 3	8
2012	+ 165	32	+ 60	24	+ 27	18	+ 30	12	+ 4	9	- 1	3	+ 106	21	+ 7	6
2013	+ 203	33	+ 98	25	+ 41	20	+ 41	13	+ 16	7	+ 1	3	+ 105	22	+ 4	6
2014	+ 298	40	+ 149	32	+ 61	24	+ 45	17	+ 40	9	+ 3	5	+ 149	25	+ 4	6
2015	+ 309	37	+ 159	29	+ 64	21	+ 42	13	+ 52	14	+ 0~	3	+ 150	23	+ 8	7
2016	+ 231	39	+ 101	31	+ 52	24	0~	13	+ 50	13	- 1	2	+ 130	25	+ 13	6
2017	+ 267	45	+ 59	35	+ 11	27	+ 9	14	+ 38	15	+ 1	9	+ 209	29	+ 11	10
2018	+ 244	50	+ 41	40	+ 18	34	- 4	17	+ 29	12	- 2	6	+ 203	30	+ 5	12
2019	+ 281	51	- 2	37	+ 7	30	+ 19	15	+ 14	15	- 4	6	+ 283	36	+ 16	10

15.8 Long-Term International Migration 2004 - 2019

United Kingdom, England and Wales
Country of Last or Next Residence

thousands

| | Asia | | | | | | | | | | Non-European Union[3] Rest of the World | | | | | | | | | | | | All countries Original Estimates[1] | |
| | All | | Middle East and Central Asia | | East Asia | | South Asia | | South East Asia | | All | | Sub-Saharan Africa | | North Africa | | North America | | Central and South America | | Oceania | | | |
	Estimate	+/-CI	Estimate	+/-CI	Estimate	+/-CI	Estimate	+/-CI	Estimate	+/-CI	Estimate	+/-CI	Estimate	+/-CI	Estimate	+/-CI	Estimate	+/-CI	Estimate	+/-CI	Estimate	+/-CI	Estimate	+/-CI
United Kingdom																								
Inflow																								
2004	213	25	31	12	57	16	91	14	33	8	206	18	96	13	7	3	34	8	15	6	53	8		
2005	188	20	22	5	49	12	88	13	29	8	172	15	72	10	4	2	32	7	9	3	54	9		
2006	210	19	25	5	46	7	106	14	33	10	154	14	53	8	6	3	30	6	11	4	53	9		
2007	199	18	29	6	43	9	101	13	26	7	136	14	48	8	6	5	29	6	11	5	42	7		
2008	194	18	37	10	40	8	83	10	34	8	157	17	57	10	9	4	38	9	15	6	38	7		
2009	217	15	31	5	42	7	108	10	35	6	136	14	44	7	4	3	39	8	12	4	37	7		
2010	241	14	27	5	50	7	127	9	37	7	127	12	34	6	8	5	30	6	13	4	42	7		
2011	240	15	30	6	61	9	128	10	22	4	108	11	31	5	4	1	32	7	7	2	34	6		
2012	183	13	27	5	58	8	71	8	27	6	116	13	27	5	6	4	37	7	9	4	37	7		
2013	176	14	28	5	67	11	57	7	24	5	111	12	25	4	14	6	28	6	10	4	34	6		
2014	189	18	37	7	58	10	67	12	27	6	139	15	27	5	9	3	42	9	21	8	40	6		
2015	189	15	42	6	67	10	54	8	26	6	127	13	33	6	7	1	35	7	14	6	37	7		
2016	178	16	42	7	59	12	58	8	20	5	119	14	30	8	7	2	32	7	17	7	32	7		
2017	225	18	39	7	83	12	76	10	28	6	136	17	36	7	6	2	40	10	9	3	45	12		
2018	237	20	46	8	79	11	76	11	35	8	122	17	29	8	8	4	40	10	17	7	27	8		
2019	310	24	51	8	106	15	117	14	36	7	139	26	50	12	7	2	37	12	12	7	33	18		
Outflow																								
2004	63	11	12	4	25	8	10	4	16	5	139	15	17	5	2	2	36	8	10	4	74	10		
2005	61	12	13	4	22	9	16	5	9	3	144	16	21	6	2	2	36	10	11	5	74	10		
2006	72	12	17	6	26	8	17	5	12	4	162	16	23	6	6	3	40	9	7	3	89	12		
2007	65	8	12	2	20	4	19	5	15	4	129	11	18	3	3	1	26	5	8	3	75	8		
2008	74	8	22	5	22	4	18	4	12	2	134	11	16	5	4	2	34	6	12	4	68	6		
2009	80	6	17	3	26	4	24	3	13	3	133	9	15	3	2	1	38	6	7	2	71	7		
2010	81	7	17	3	28	5	22	3	14	3	107	8	16	3	2	1	34	5	6	2	49	5		
2011	95	8	18	3	27	4	31	4	18	3	114	10	11	3	2	1	32	5	6	2	62	7		
2012	91	8	15	3	30	5	28	4	18	3	107	8	14	3	1	0~	29	4	6	2	56	5		
2013	83	7	15	3	27	4	25	3	15	3	108	9	11	2	3	1	34	5	5	2	54	6		
2014	88	10	20	4	32	8	21	3	15	4	91	8	10	3	1	1	27	5	4	2	48	6		
2015	76	8	15	3	26	6	20	4	16	4	87	8	10	3	2	2	29	5	7	2	39	5		
2016	75	8	17	5	26	4	19	3	13	3	97	11	8	4	4	3	39	7	8	3	38	6		
2017	72	9	14	4	28	5	16	4	14	4	82	11	8	3	2	1	31	7	6	4	35	6		
2018	69	9	10	3	28	5	14	3	16	5	81	11	7	3	1	1	29	7	7	2	37	7		
2019	77	9	17	5	31	6	15	4	13	3	83	14	7	3	0~	0~	30	9	12	6	33	8		

15.8 Long-Term International Migration 2004 - 2019

United Kingdom, England and Wales

Country of Last or Next Residence

thousands

	Asia										Non-European Union[3] Rest of the World												All countries	
	All		Middle East and Central Asia		East Asia		South Asia		South East Asia		All		Sub-Saharan Africa		North Africa		North America		Central and South America		Oceania		Original Estimates[1]	
	Estimate	+/-CI	Estimate	+/-CI	Estimate	+/-CI	Estimate	+/-CI	Estimate	+/-CI	Estimate	+/-CI	Estimate	+/-CI	Estimate	+/-CI	Estimate	+/-CI	Estimate	+/-CI	Estimate	+/-CI	Estimate	+/-CI
United Kingdom																									
Balance																									
2004	+ 150	28	19	12	+ 33	18	+ 81	14	+ 17	10	+ 67	24	+ 79	14	+ 6	3	- 2	12	+ 5	7	- 21	13	+ 245	49
2005	+ 127	23	9	7	+ 27	15	+ 72	14	+ 20	9	+ 28	22	+ 50	12	+ 3	2	- 4	12	- 1	6	- 20	13	+ 206	49
2006	+ 138	22	8	8	+ 20	11	+ 89	15	+ 20	11	- 8	22	+ 30	10	+ 5	3	- 10	10	+ 4	5	- 36	15	+ 198	52
2007	+ 134	20	17	6	+ 24	10	+ 82	14	+ 11	8	+ 7	18	+ 30	8	+ 5	5	+ 2	8	+ 2	6	- 33	11	+ 233	48
2008	+ 120	20	15	11	+ 18	9	+ 65	11	+ 22	8	+ 23	20	+ 41	11	+ 5	5	+ 4	11	+ 3	7	- 31	9	+ 163	57
2009	+ 137	16	15	6	+ 16	8	+ 84	11	+ 21	7	+ 4	17	+ 30	8	+ 2	3	+ 1	10	+ 5	4	- 33	10	+ 198	37
2010	+ 160	16	10	6	+ 22	9	+ 105	10	+ 23	7	+ 20	15	+ 18	6	+ 6	5	- 4	7	+ 7	5	- 8	9	+ 252	37
2011	+ 146	17	11	7	+ 35	10	+ 96	11	+ 4	5	- 6	15	+ 20	6	+ 2	2	0~	8	+ 1	3	- 28	10	+ 215	35
2012	+ 92	16	12	6	+ 28	9	+ 43	9	+ 9	7	+ 9	15	+ 14	6	+ 5	5	+ 7	8	+ 2	4	- 20	9		
2013	+ 94	16	13	6	+ 40	11	+ 32	7	+ 9	6	+ 3	15	+ 15	5	+ 11	7	- 7	8	+ 4	4	- 20	9		
2014	+ 101	21	17	8	+ 25	13	+ 46	12	+ 12	7	+ 48	17	+ 18	6	+ 8	3	+ 15	10	+ 16	8	- 8	8		
2015	+ 113	17	28	7	+ 41	11	+ 34	9	+ 10	7	+ 40	15	+ 23	7	+ 5	2	+ 6	8	+ 7	7	- 2	9		
2016	+ 103	18	25	8	+ 32	12	+ 39	9	+ 7	6	+ 22	18	+ 22	9	+ 3	4	+ 7	10	+ 9	8	- 6	9		
2017	+ 153	20	25	8	+ 55	13	+ 60	11	+ 13	7	+ 54	20	+ 27	8	+ 4	2	+ 10	12	+ 3	5	+ 10	13		
2018	+ 169	21	36	9	+ 51	12	+ 62	12	+ 19	9	+ 41	20	+ 22	8	+ 7	4	+ 11	12	+ 10	8	- 10	10		
2019	+ 233	25	34	9	+ 74	16	+ 102	16	+ 23	8	+ 56	29	+ 43	12	+ 7	2	+ 7	15	0~	9	0~	19		
England and Wales																									
Inflow																									
2004	198	24	30	11	53	15	86	13	30	7	190	17	88	12	6	2	32	8	14	5	50	8		
2005	174	19	20	5	44	11	83	12	28	8	155	14	68	10	4	2	27	5	9	3	47	7		
2006	199	19	23	5	43	7	100	13	32	10	140	13	49	8	6	3	29	6	10	4	45	7		
2007	185	17	27	5	41	9	93	12	23	6	128	13	45	7	6	5	27	6	10	5	40	7		
2008	178	16	29	6	37	8	81	10	31	7	138	15	53	10	7	3	30	7	13	5	35	6		
2009	205	14	29	5	39	6	104	10	33	6	120	12	40	4	4	3	33	7	11	4	31	6		
2010	223	13	25	4	45	7	120	9	34	6	118	12	32	8	8	5	27	5	12	4	39	7		
2011	224	15	27	5	55	9	121	10	20	4	98	10	29	5	4	1	28	5	6	2	31	6		
2012	169	13	24	5	53	8	68	8	23	5	106	12	25	5	6	4	34	7	8	3	33	7		
2013	164	14	26	5	63	11	53	6	22	4	105	12	25	4	14	6	26	5	9	4	32	6		
2014	176	14	35	7	53	8	63	8	25	6	131	15	26	5	8	3	39	9	20	8	37	6		
2015	177	14	39	6	63	9	51	9	24	5	115	13	32	6	6	1	30	6	12	6	35	7		
2016	164	16	38	6	54	11	53	8	19	5	108	13	26	6	7	2	30	7	15	7	30	7		
2017	210	18	37	7	77	11	72	10	24	6	125	17	33	7	6	2	34	9	7	3	44	12		
2018	219	18	42	8	71	10	73	10	34	8	112	16	28	7	8	4	35	9	16	7	25	8		
2019	287	22	45	7	96	14	113	14	33	7	124	20	46	11	7	2	31	12	12	7	29	10		

15.8 Long-Term International Migration 2004 - 2019

United Kingdom, England and Wales

Country of Last or Next Residence

thousands

England and Wales

Outflow

	Asia										Non-European Union[3] (Rest of the World)												All countries	
	All		Middle East and Central Asia		East Asia		South Asia		South East Asia		All		Sub-Saharan Africa		North Africa		North America		Central and South America		Oceania		Original Estimates[1]	
Year	Estimate	+/-CI	Estimate	+/-CI	Estimate	+/-CI	Estimate	+/-CI	Estimate	+/-CI	Estimate	+/-CI	Estimate	+/-CI	Estimate	+/-CI	Estimate	+/-CI	Estimate	+/-CI	Estimate	+/-CI	Estimate	+/-CI
2004	53	9	9	3	22	7	10	4	12	4	126	14	16	5	2	2	32	8	10	4	67	10		
2005	57	11	12	3	22	9	14	5	9	5	127	14	21	5	2	2	29	8	9	4	68	9		
2006	67	11	16	6	23	7	16	5	11	4	147	16	22	6	2	2	35	8	7	3	81	11		
2007	59	7	12	2	19	4	16	4	12	3	115	10	17	3	1	1	23	5	8	3	65	7		
2008	66	8	20	5	19	4	16	4	10	2	124	10	15	5	3	3	29	5	12	4	65	6		
2009	72	6	15	3	23	4	22	3	12	2	118	8	14	3	2	2	32	5	6	2	64	6		
2010	73	6	16	3	24	3	20	3	13	2	99	7	15	3	2	2	31	4	6	2	45	5		
2011	86	7	17	3	24	4	29	4	16	3	103	9	10	3	2	2	29	4	6	2	56	7		
2012	80	7	12	3	26	4	26	4	15	3	97	8	13	3	1	0~	27	4	6	2	50	5		
2013	76	7	14	3	25	4	22	3	14	3	92	8	10	2	3	3	30	4	5	2	45	5		
2014	80	10	18	4	30	8	20	3	13	3	82	8	9	2	1	1	25	4	4	2	43	5		
2015	71	8	13	3	24	6	19	4	15	3	79	8	9	3	2	2	27	5	6	2	34	5		
2016	67	7	13	4	24	4	17	3	13	3	87	10	5	2	3	3	35	7	7	3	36	5		
2017	65	8	12	3	26	5	14	3	14	4	72	9	6	2	2	2	26	6	6	4	32	5		
2018	64	8	9	3	44	5	13	3	15	5	70	9	7	3	1	1	24	6	6	2	32	6		
2019	69	9	15	5	69	5	14	4	12	3	76	14	7	3	0~	0~	27	9	11	6	30	8		

Balance

	Asia										Non-European Union[3] (Rest of the World)												All countries	
	All		Middle East and Central Asia		East Asia		South Asia		South East Asia		All		Sub-Saharan Africa		North Africa		North America		Central and South America		Oceania		Original Estimates[1]	
Year	Estimate	+/-CI	Estimate	+/-CI	Estimate	+/-CI	Estimate	+/-CI	Estimate	+/-CI	Estimate	+/-CI	Estimate	+/-CI	Estimate	+/-CI	Estimate	+/-CI	Estimate	+/-CI	Estimate	+/-CI	Estimate	+/-CI
2004	+ 145	26	+ 20	12	+ 31	17	+ 76	13	+ 17	9	+ 64	22	+ 71	12	+ 5	3	- 0~	3	+ 4	7	- 17	12		
2005	+ 118	22	+ 8	6	+ 22	14	+ 69	13	+ 19	9	+ 28	19	+ 47	11	+ 2	2	- 2	2	+ 1	4	- 20	12		
2006	+ 132	22	+ 7	7	+ 20	10	+ 84	14	+ 21	11	- 8	20	+ 28	10	+ 5	5	+ 7	3	+ 2	5	- 36	14		
2007	+ 126	18	+ 16	6	+ 22	10	+ 77	13	+ 11	7	+ 13	16	+ 28	8	+ 5	5	+ 4	5	+ 2	6	- 25	10		
2008	+ 112	18	+ 9	8	+ 17	9	+ 65	10	+ 21	8	+ 14	18	+ 38	11	+ 4	4	+ 0~	4	+ 1	7	- 30	9		
2009	+ 133	15	+ 14	5	+ 16	7	+ 82	10	+ 21	6	+ 2	15	+ 26	7	+ 2	3	+ 1	3	+ 5	4	- 32	8		
2010	+ 151	15	+ 9	5	+ 20	7	+ 100	9	+ 21	7	+ 19	14	+ 17	6	+ 6	5	- 4	5	+ 6	4	- 6	8		
2011	+ 139	16	+ 11	6	+ 31	10	+ 92	11	+ 4	5	- 5	13	+ 19	6	+ 2	1	- 2	1	+ 0~	3	- 24	9		
2012	+ 89	15	+ 12	6	+ 27	9	+ 43	8	+ 8	6	+ 9	14	+ 12	6	+ 5	4	+ 7	4	+ 2	4	- 17	9		
2013	+ 88	15	+ 12	6	+ 38	11	+ 31	7	+ 8	5	+ 13	14	+ 14	5	+ 11	7	- 4	7	+ 4	4	- 13	8		
2014	+ 96	17	+ 18	7	+ 23	11	+ 44	9	+ 12	7	+ 49	16	+ 18	6	+ 7	3	+ 14	3	+ 16	8	- 6	8		
2015	+ 106	16	+ 26	7	+ 40	11	+ 32	7	+ 9	7	+ 36	15	+ 23	6	+ 5	2	+ 3	2	+ 6	6	- 0~	9		
2016	+ 97	17	+ 25	7	+ 30	12	+ 36	8	+ 7	6	+ 21	17	+ 21	6	+ 3	4	- 6	4	+ 7	7	- 5	9		
2017	+ 145	19	+ 25	8	+ 51	12	+ 58	11	+ 10	7	+ 53	19	+ 27	8	+ 4	4	+ 8	4	+ 2	5	+ 12	13		
2018	+ 155	20	+ 33	9	+ 44	12	+ 60	10	+ 19	9	+ 42	19	+ 22	8	+ 7	7	+ 10	7	+ 10	8	- 7	10		
2019	+ 219	24	+ 29	8	+ 69	15	+ 99	15	+ 21	8	+ 48	25	+ 39	12	+ 6	2	+ 4	2	+ 0~	9	- 1	12		

15.8 Long-Term International Migration 2004 - 2019

United Kingdom, England and Wales

Country of Last or Next Residence

thousands

	Asia				Non-European Union[3]									All countries
					Rest of the World									
	All	Middle East and Central Asia	East Asia	South Asia	South East Asia	All	Sub-Saharan Africa	North Africa	North America	Central and South America	Oceania			Original Estimates[1]
	Estimate +/-CI	Estimate +/-CI	Estimate +/-CI	Estimate +/-CI	Estimate +/-CI	Estimate +/-CI	Estimate +/-CI	Estimate +/-CI	Estimate +/-CI	Estimate +/-CI	Estimate +/-CI			Estimate +/-CI

Source: Office for National Statistics (ONS), Home Office, Central Statistics Office (CSO) Ireland, Northern Ireland Statistics and Research Agency (NISRA)

Totals may not sum due to rounding.

"z" - Not applicable. ":" - Not available. "0~" - Rounds to zero. Please see the Notes worksheet for more information.

Long-Term International Migration estimates by citizenship using the new country groupings shown above are only available from calendar year 2004.

1 Net migration ("Balance") figures for the United Kingdom for 2001 to 2011 have been revised in light of the results of the 2011 Census. The original published estimates are shown to the right of the table. The revisions are not reflected in the remainder of the table. The sums of the disaggregated estimates will not therefore match the revised balances. Users should continue to use the estimates in the table to analyse detailed breakdowns of inflows and outflows of long-term international migrants but, in doing so, should bear in mind that the headline net migration estimates have been revised. Please see the Notes worksheet for more information.

2 European Union estimates are for the EU15 (Austria, Belgium, Denmark, Finland, France, Germany, Greece, Republic of Ireland, Italy, Luxembourg, Netherlands, Portugal, Spain and Sweden) up to 2003, the EU25 (the EU15 and the EU8 groupings plus Malta and Cyprus) from 2004 to 2006, the EU27 (the EU25 plus Bulgaria and Romania) from 2007 and the EU28 (the EU27 plus Croatia) from July 2013. Estimates are also shown separately for the EU15, the EU8 (Czech Republic, Estonia, Hungary, Latvia, Lithuania, Poland, Slovakia and Slovenia), the EU2 (Bulgaria and Romania) and EU Other (Malta, Cyprus and Croatia). British citizens are excluded from all citizenship groupings and are shown separately.

3 Excludes British and other European Union citizens as defined in footnote 2.

This table uses 95% confidence intervals (CI) to indicate the robustness of each estimate. Please see the Notes worksheet for more information.

Statistically Significant Changes   Statistically Significant Decrease

This table has not been adjusted in line with the latest top level migration estimates.
As part of Population and Migration Statistics Transformation programme to better meet the needs of our users, preliminary adjustments were made to the Long-Term International Migration (LTIM) estimates in the **August 2019 Migration Statistics Quarterly Report (MSQR)** (https://www.ons.gov.uk/peoplepopulationandcommunity/populationandmigration/internationalmigration/bulletins/migrationstatisticsquarterlyreport/august2019).

Currently these adjustments are only available at the highest-level due to further work being needed to develop a methodology for the more detailed data. Whilst we go through this period of development and innovation, we have sought to re-classify our migration statistics as "Experimental Statistics" in line with **Office for Statistics Regulation guidance** (https://www.statisticsauthority.gov.uk/publication/experimental-statistics-official-statistics-in-development/).

As such the preliminary adjustments have not been applied to the estimates in this table but we have continued to provide detailed breakdowns due to user demand. Please note these estimates will continue to be provisional until final adjustments are developed by Summer 2020 and will be inconsistent with the MSQR tables.

15.9 Grants of settlement by country of nationality, category and in-country refusals of settlement, 2019

Year	Geographical region	Country of nationality	Total grants of settlement	Total refusals of settlement
2019	*Total	*Total	91,439	3,018
2019	Africa North	*Total Africa North	3,807	67
2019	Africa Sub-Saharan	*Total Africa Sub-Saharan	15,526	517
2019	America North	*Total America North	5,383	82
2019	America Central and South	*Total America Central and South	2,728	107
2019	Asia Central	*Total Asia Central	2,237	15
2019	Asia East	*Total Asia East	6,757	142
2019	Asia South	*Total Asia South	33,264	1,697
2019	Asia South East	*Total Asia South East	5,146	131
2019	EU 14	*Total EU 14	z	z
2019	EU 2	*Total EU 2	z	z
2019	EU 8	*Total EU 8	z	z
2019	EU Other	*Total EU Other	z	z
2019	Europe Other	*Total Europe Other	5,353	114
2019	Middle East	*Total Middle East	7,962	99
2019	Oceania	*Total Oceania	2,778	39
2019	Other	*Total Other	498	8
2019	Asia Central	Afghanistan	1,915	8
2019	Europe Other	Albania	486	11
2019	Africa North	Algeria	306	9
2019	Oceania	American Samoa	0	0
2019	Europe Other	Andorra	0	0
2019	Africa Sub-Saharan	Angola	51	0
2019	Other	Anguilla (British)	0	0
2019	America Central and South	Antigua and Barbuda	5	0
2019	America Central and South	Argentina	96	1
2019	Europe Other	Armenia	63	1
2019	America Central and South	Aruba	0	0
2019	Oceania	Australia	1,945	26
2019	EU 14	Austria	z	z
2019	Europe Other	Azerbaijan	123	5
2019	America Central and South	Bahamas, The	8	0
2019	Middle East	Bahrain	51	0
2019	Asia South	Bangladesh	3,194	475
2019	America Central and South	Barbados	45	2
2019	Europe Other	Belarus	164	2
2019	EU 14	Belgium	z	z
2019	America Central and South	Belize	5	0
2019	Africa Sub-Saharan	Benin	7	0
2019	Other	Bermuda (British)	0	0
2019	Asia South	Bhutan	10	0
2019	America Central and South	Bolivia	44	2
2019	America Central and South	Bonaire, Sint Eustatius and Saba	0	0
2019	Europe Other	Bosnia and Herzegovina	24	0
2019	Africa Sub-Saharan	Botswana	26	1
2019	America Central and South	Brazil	553	23
2019	Other	British overseas citizens	21	1
2019	Asia South East	Brunei	13	0
2019	EU 2	Bulgaria	z	z
2019	Africa Sub-Saharan	Burkina	1	0
2019	Asia South East	Burma	161	1
2019	Africa Sub-Saharan	Burundi	14	0
2019	Asia South East	Cambodia	16	0
2019	Africa Sub-Saharan	Cameroon	300	6
2019	America North	Canada	1,256	23
2019	Africa Sub-Saharan	Cape Verde	1	0
2019	Other	Cayman Islands (British)	0	0
2019	Africa Sub-Saharan	Central African Republic	6	1
2019	Africa Sub-Saharan	Chad	6	0
2019	America Central and South	Chile	50	1
2019	Asia East	China	5,102	111
2019	Oceania	Christmas Island	0	0
2019	Oceania	Cocos (Keeling) Islands	0	0
2019	America Central and South	Colombia	325	13
2019	Africa Sub-Saharan	Comoros	4	0
2019	Africa Sub-Saharan	Congo	31	0
2019	Africa Sub-Saharan	Congo (Democratic Republic)	360	3

15.9 Grants of settlement by country of nationality, category and in-country refusals of settlement, 2019

Year	Geographical region	Country of nationality	Total grants of settlement	Total refusals of settlement
2019	Oceania	Cook Islands	0	0
2019	America Central and South	Costa Rica	19	0
2019	EU Other	Croatia	0	0
2019	America Central and South	Cuba	30	1
2019	America Central and South	Curacao	0	0
2019	EU Other	Cyprus	z	z
2019	Europe Other	Cyprus (Northern part of)	3	0
2019	EU 8	Czech Republic	z	z
2019	EU 14	Denmark	z	z
2019	Africa Sub-Saharan	Djibouti	7	0
2019	America Central and South	Dominica	50	0
2019	America Central and South	Dominican Republic	23	1
2019	Asia South East	East Timor	1	0
2019	America Central and South	Ecuador	47	2
2019	Africa North	Egypt	908	21
2019	America Central and South	El Salvador	10	0
2019	Africa Sub-Saharan	Equatorial Guinea	1	0
2019	Africa Sub-Saharan	Eritrea	2,923	6
2019	EU 8	Estonia	z	z
2019	Africa Sub-Saharan	Ethiopia	317	10
2019	Other	Falkland Islands (British)	0	0
2019	Europe Other	Faroe Islands	0	0
2019	Oceania	Fiji	52	1
2019	EU 14	Finland	z	z
2019	Europe Other	Former Yugoslavia	0	0
2019	EU 14	France	z	z
2019	America Central and South	French Guiana	0	0
2019	Oceania	French Polynesia	0	0
2019	Africa Sub-Saharan	Gabon	3	0
2019	Africa Sub-Saharan	Gambia, The	516	18
2019	Europe Other	Georgia	69	4
2019	EU 14	Germany	z	z
2019	Africa Sub-Saharan	Ghana	845	42
2019	Other	Gibraltar (British)	0	0
2019	EU 14	Greece	z	z
2019	Europe Other	Greenland	0	0
2019	America Central and South	Grenada	29	0
2019	America Central and South	Guadeloupe	0	0
2019	Oceania	Guam	0	0
2019	America Central and South	Guatemala	6	1
2019	Africa Sub-Saharan	Guinea	90	1
2019	Africa Sub-Saharan	Guinea-Bissau	0	1
2019	America Central and South	Guyana	36	0
2019	America Central and South	Haiti	4	0
2019	Oceania	Heard Island and McDonald Islands	0	0
2019	America Central and South	Honduras	7	0
2019	Asia East	Hong Kong	318	12
2019	EU 8	Hungary	z	z
2019	Europe Other	Iceland	z	z
2019	Asia South	India	15,092	528
2019	Asia South East	Indonesia	160	0
2019	Middle East	Iran	2,909	31
2019	Middle East	Iraq	924	23
2019	EU 14	Ireland	z	z
2019	Middle East	Israel	262	2
2019	EU 14	Italy	z	z
2019	Africa Sub-Saharan	Ivory Coast	98	3
2019	America Central and South	Jamaica	620	38
2019	Asia East	Japan	521	7
2019	Middle East	Jordan	201	4
2019	Asia Central	Kazakhstan	161	2
2019	Africa Sub-Saharan	Kenya	497	12
2019	Oceania	Kiribati	0	0
2019	Asia East	Korea (North)	26	0
2019	Asia East	Korea (South)	489	5
2019	Europe Other	Kosovo	162	2
2019	Middle East	Kuwait	51	0
2019	Asia Central	Kyrgyzstan	37	0

15.9 Grants of settlement by country of nationality, category and in-country refusals of settlement, 2019

Year	Geographical region	Country of nationality	Total grants of settlement	Total refusals of settlement
2019	Asia South East	Laos	3	0
2019	EU 8	Latvia	z	z
2019	Middle East	Lebanon	199	2
2019	Africa Sub-Saharan	Lesotho	2	1
2019	Africa Sub-Saharan	Liberia	31	2
2019	Africa North	Libya	447	15
2019	Europe Other	Liechtenstein	z	z
2019	EU 8	Lithuania	z	z
2019	EU 14	Luxembourg	z	z
2019	Asia East	Macau	7	0
2019	Europe Other	Macedonia	29	0
2019	Africa Sub-Saharan	Madagascar	8	0
2019	Africa Sub-Saharan	Malawi	170	4
2019	Asia South East	Malaysia	757	16
2019	Asia South	Maldives	27	0
2019	Africa Sub-Saharan	Mali	13	0
2019	EU Other	Malta	z	z
2019	Oceania	Marshall Islands	0	0
2019	America Central and South	Martinique	0	0
2019	Africa North	Mauritania	1	0
2019	Africa Sub-Saharan	Mauritius	346	15
2019	Africa Sub-Saharan	Mayotte	0	0
2019	America Central and South	Mexico	226	5
2019	Oceania	Micronesia	0	0
2019	Europe Other	Moldova	17	1
2019	Europe Other	Monaco	1	0
2019	Asia East	Mongolia	31	1
2019	Europe Other	Montenegro	9	0
2019	Other	Montserrat (British)	0	0
2019	Africa North	Morocco	345	10
2019	Africa Sub-Saharan	Mozambique	4	0
2019	Africa Sub-Saharan	Namibia	20	0
2019	Oceania	Nauru	0	0
2019	Asia South	Nepal	1,619	99
2019	EU 14	Netherlands	z	z
2019	America Central and South	Netherlands Antilles	z	z
2019	Oceania	New Caledonia	0	0
2019	Oceania	New Zealand	770	11
2019	America Central and South	Nicaragua	10	0
2019	Africa Sub-Saharan	Niger	8	0
2019	Africa Sub-Saharan	Nigeria	3,915	300
2019	Oceania	Niue	0	0
2019	Oceania	Norfolk Island	0	0
2019	Oceania	Northern Mariana Islands	0	0
2019	Europe Other	Norway	z	z
2019	Middle East	Occupied Palestinian Territories	139	4
2019	Middle East	Oman	5	0
2019	Other	Other and unknown	37	0
2019	Asia South	Pakistan	10,313	476
2019	Oceania	Palau	0	0
2019	America Central and South	Panama	12	0
2019	Oceania	Papua New Guinea	6	0
2019	America Central and South	Paraguay	6	1
2019	America Central and South	Peru	77	2
2019	Asia South East	Philippines	2,464	75
2019	Other	Pitcairn Islands (British)	0	0
2019	EU 8	Poland	z	z
2019	EU 14	Portugal	z	z
2019	America North	Puerto Rico	0	0
2019	Middle East	Qatar	4	0
2019	Other	Refugee	272	7
2019	Africa Sub-Saharan	Reunion	0	0
2019	EU 2	Romania	z	z
2019	Europe Other	Russia	1,935	25
2019	Africa Sub-Saharan	Rwanda	42	1
2019	Oceania	Samoa	5	0
2019	Europe Other	San Marino	0	0
2019	Africa Sub-Saharan	Sao Tome and Principe	0	0

15.9 Grants of settlement by country of nationality, category and in-country refusals of settlement, 2019

Year	Geographical region	Country of nationality	Total grants of settlement	Total refusals of settlement
2019	Middle East	Saudi Arabia	168	9
2019	Africa Sub-Saharan	Senegal	34	2
2019	Europe Other	Serbia	137	0
2019	Europe Other	Serbia and Montenegro	z	z
2019	Africa Sub-Saharan	Seychelles	14	0
2019	Africa Sub-Saharan	Sierra Leone	161	4
2019	Asia South East	Singapore	258	8
2019	EU 8	Slovakia	z	z
2019	EU 8	Slovenia	z	z
2019	Oceania	Solomon Islands	0	0
2019	Africa Sub-Saharan	Somalia	772	5
2019	Africa Sub-Saharan	South Africa	1,837	40
2019	Other	South Georgia & South Sandwich Islands	0	0
2019	EU 14	Spain	z	z
2019	Asia South	Sri Lanka	3,009	119
2019	Other	St. Helena (British)	0	0
2019	America Central and South	St. Kitts and Nevis	35	0
2019	America Central and South	St. Lucia	36	3
2019	America Central and South	St. Maarten (Dutch Part)	0	0
2019	America Central and South	St. Martin (French Part)	0	0
2019	America Central and South	St. Pierre and Miquelon	0	0
2019	America Central and South	St. Vincent and the Grenadines	32	2
2019	Other	Stateless	168	0
2019	Africa North	Sudan	1,602	7
2019	Africa Sub-Saharan	Sudan (South)	17	0
2019	America Central and South	Surinam	0	0
2019	Europe Other	Svalbard and Jan Mayen	0	0
2019	Africa Sub-Saharan	Swaziland	18	0
2019	EU 14	Sweden	z	z
2019	Europe Other	Switzerland	z	z
2019	Middle East	Syria	2,875	20
2019	Asia East	Taiwan	263	6
2019	Asia Central	Tajikistan	6	0
2019	Africa Sub-Saharan	Tanzania	189	2
2019	Asia South East	Thailand	908	17
2019	Africa Sub-Saharan	Togo	17	0
2019	Oceania	Tokelau	0	0
2019	Oceania	Tonga	0	1
2019	America Central and South	Trinidad and Tobago	119	5
2019	Africa North	Tunisia	196	5
2019	Europe Other	Turkey	1,514	51
2019	Asia Central	Turkmenistan	23	2
2019	Other	Turks and Caicos Islands (British)	0	0
2019	Oceania	Tuvalu	0	0
2019	Africa Sub-Saharan	Uganda	498	5
2019	Europe Other	Ukraine	617	12
2019	Middle East	United Arab Emirates	4	2
2019	America North	United States	4,127	59
2019	America Central and South	Uruguay	8	1
2019	Asia Central	Uzbekistan	95	3
2019	Oceania	Vanuatu	0	0
2019	Europe Other	Vatican City	0	0
2019	America Central and South	Venezuela	155	3
2019	Asia South East	Vietnam	405	14
2019	Other	Virgin Islands (British)	0	0
2019	America North	Virgin Islands (US)	0	0
2019	Oceania	Wallis and Futuna	0	0
2019	Africa North	Western Sahara	2	0
2019	Middle East	Yemen	170	2
2019	Africa Sub-Saharan	Zambia	131	8
2019	Africa Sub-Saharan	Zimbabwe	1,175	24

z = Not applicable.

: = Not available.

Source: Home Office Immigration Statistics

Nationals of EU accession countries are included or excluded according to their accession date.

Swiss nationals are excluded from 1 June 2002.

Data from 2003 exclude dependants of EEA and Swiss nationals in confirmed relationships granted permanent residence.

Include reconsideration cases and the outcome of appeals.

May include a small number of cases in which a decision is recorded twice, where an individual has dual nationality.

15.10a Number of people granted protection, resettlement, or an alternative form of leave[1,2,3]

United Kingdom

	Date[4]										Year Ending		Change (latest year)	
	2010	2011	2012	2013	2014	2015	2016	2017	2018	2019	Mar 2019	Mar 2020	Number	%
Asylum-related grants	6,444	7,184	7,797	8,638	10,101	13,945	9,944	8,564	7,771	15,091	11,628	15,371	+3,743	+32%
Asylum	4,456	5,493	6,542	7,509	8,995	12,172	8,419	7,476	6,028	12,565	9,192	12,863	+3,671	+40%
Humanitarian Protection	142	121	133	68	107	124	209	250	950	1,241	1,192	1,482	+290	+24%
Discretionary Leave	1,842	1,568	994	612	265	362	191	138	126	158	183	125	-58	-32%
UASC Leave[5]	z	z	z	120	414	853	892	418	239	181	289	162	-127	-44%
Other Grants[6]	4	2	128	329	320	434	233	282	428	946	772	739	-33	-4%
Resettlement grants	717	461	1,053	967	786	1,865	5,212	6,212	5,806	5,612	5,796	4,968	-828	-14%
Total grants	7,161	7,645	8,850	9,605	10,887	15,810	15,156	14,776	13,577	20,703	17,424	20,339	+2,915	+17%

Source: Asy_D02 - Outcomes of asylum applications at initial decision, and refugees resettled in the UK, Home Office

Data for 2019 Q1 onwards are provisional.

z = not applicable   : = not available

Notes:

1. Includes main applicants and dependants.

or an alternative form of leave will be higher.

3. Alternative forms of leave relate to non-protection grants (such as discretionary leave, UASC leave, and other grants) following an asylum application.

4. Date relates to date of decision for 'asylum-related grants', and date at which the refugee arrived in the UK for 'resettlement grants'.

5. UASC Leave was introduced from 1st April 2013. Data for 2013 is not a complete year's worth of data and is not comparable with subsequent years.

6. Other grants include grants under: (a) family and private life rules; (b) leave outside the rules; (c) Calais leave and (d) exceptional leave to remain.

15.10b Asylum applications[1] lodged in the UK, by nationality[2]

United Kingdom

	Date of application										Year Ending		Change (latest year)	
	2010	2011	2012	2013	2014	2015	2016	2017	2018	2019	Mar 2019	Mar 2020	Number	%
Iran	1,866	2,477	2,659	2,410	2,000	3,242	4,184	2,570	3,320	4,853	3,872	4,741	+869	+22%
Albania	174	395	819	1,325	1,576	1,519	1,493	1,430	2,005	3,453	2,478	3,467	+989	+40%
Iraq	378	277	275	310	588	2,216	2,672	2,379	2,700	2,971	2,944	2,696	-248	-8%
Pakistan	1,416	2,418	3,280	3,359	2,726	2,470	2,870	2,495	2,033	1,930	1,948	1,848	-100	-5%
Eritrea	711	797	728	1,387	3,233	3,695	1,230	1,085	2,151	1,885	2,419	1,846	-573	-24%
Afghanistan	1,596	1,271	1,008	1,038	1,139	2,261	2,329	1,326	1,349	1,570	1,297	1,572	+275	+21%
India	527	553	1,087	974	703	1,014	1,498	1,327	1,321	1,570	1,375	1,563	+188	+14%
Vietnam	449	328	402	437	381	582	778	1,070	1,215	1,551	1,303	1,542	+239	+18%
Sudan	573	688	636	743	1,449	2,912	1,310	1,685	1,611	1,529	1,702	1,414	-288	-17%
China	996	778	696	739	643	487	707	861	1,020	1,332	1,055	1,345	+290	+27%
Syria	127	355	988	1,648	2,025	2,539	1,376	604	711	1,038	807	1,088	+281	+35%
Bangladesh	450	616	1,057	1,123	748	1,110	1,944	1,712	1,297	1,157	1,328	1,088	-240	-18%
Nigeria	798	732	959	931	899	917	1,158	1,043	839	932	800	930	+130	+16%
Turkey	155	170	190	250	271	233	323	366	520	830	645	781	+136	+21%
El Salvador	1	1	3	9	11	11	37	38	108	607	205	717	+512	+250%
Stateless	108	181	141	136	216	502	413	184	352	655	441	677	+236	+54%
Sri Lanka	1,357	1,756	1,744	1,811	1,292	961	845	690	500	622	513	604	+91	+18%
Namibia	19	14	16	13	23	16	27	101	265	433	260	472	+212	+82%
Libya	90	722	218	243	328	410	212	409	449	392	444	359	-85	-19%
Yemen	34	39	50	39	66	114	67	123	183	284	201	347	+146	+73%
Other[3]	6,091	5,297	4,887	4,659	4,716	5,522	5,274	5,049	5,555	5,972	5,631	6,002	+371	+7%
Total applicatio	17,916	19,865	21,843	23,584	25,033	32,733	30,747	26,547	29,504	35,566	31,668	35,099	+3,431	+11%

Data for 2019 Q1 onwards are provisional.

Source: Asy_D01 - Asylum applications raised, Home Office

z = not applicable   : = not available

Notes:

1. Includes main applicants only.

2. Top 20 nationalities claiming asylum in the most recent period.

3. Other includes applications for all nationalities not featured in the table.

Please note: The asylum data tables produced by the Home Office as part of the Immigration Statistics release have been remapped to present new collections of information. This change is reflected in the new tables 15.10a and 15.10b in this edition of AOS. The Home Office has carefully considered the benefits and risks of publishing the Immigration Statistics collection in this format. Further details can be found in the publishing detailed datasets in Immigration Statistics document (https://www.gov.uk/government/publications/publishing-detailed-datasets-in-immigration-statistics). This change is reflected in the new tables 15.10a and 15.10b in this edition of AOS.

15.11 Number of marriages by type of ceremony and denomination, 1837 to 2018

England and Wales

Year (selected years only prior to 1962[1])	All marriages	All marriages to opposite-sex couples	Civil ceremonies		Religious ceremonies				
			All	Approved Premises[2]	All	Church of England and Church in Wales	Roman Catholic	Other Christian denom-inations[3]	Other[4]
2018	234,795	227,870	179,752	162,545	48,118	35,536	4,958	5,345	2,279
2017	242,842	235,910	181,607	167,415	54,303	40,051	5,841	6,103	2,308
2016	249,793	242,774	182,766	165,466	60,008	44,392	6,513	6,616	2,487
2015	245,513	239,020	176,406	157,243	62,614	45,901	7,001	6,937	2,775
2014[5]	252,222	247,372	179,344	158,057	68,028	49,717	7,598	7,895	2,818
2013	240,854	240,854	172,254	147,875	68,600	50,226	7,550	8,035	2,789
2012	263,640	263,640	184,167	156,548	79,473	58,797	8,664	9,027	2,985
2011	249,133	249,133	174,681	143,296	74,452	54,463	8,390	8,844	2,755
2010	243,808	243,808	165,680	125,612	78,128	57,607	8,622	9,032	2,867
2009	232,443	232,443	155,950	111,313	76,493	56,236	8,426	8,973	2,858
2008	235,794	235,794	157,296	106,298	78,498	57,057	8,909	9,745	2,787
2007	235,367	235,367	156,198	101,158	79,169	57,101	8,904	10,351	2,813
2006	239,454	239,454	158,350	95,763	81,104	57,963	9,263	11,249	2,629
2005	247,805	247,805	162,169	90,239	85,636	61,155	9,599	12,315	2,567
2004	273,069	273,069	184,913	85,154	88,156	62,006	9,850	13,578	2,722
2003	270,109	270,109	183,124	73,784	86,985	60,385	9,858	14,188	2,554
2002	255,596	255,596	169,210	61,749	86,386	58,980	10,044	14,844	2,518
2001	249,227	249,227	160,238	50,149	88,989	60,878	10,518	15,210	2,383
2000	267,961	267,961	170,800	45,792	97,161	65,536	11,312	17,751	2,562
1999	263,515	263,515	162,679	37,709	100,836	67,219	12,399	18,690	2,528
1998	267,303	267,303	163,072	28,879	104,231	69,494	12,615	19,746	2,376
1997	272,536	272,536	165,516	22,052	107,020	70,310	13,125	21,211	2,374
1996	278,975	278,975	164,158	15,210	114,817	75,147	13,989	23,605	2,076
1995[2]	283,012	283,012	155,490	2,496	127,522	83,685	15,181	26,622	2,034
1994	291,069	291,069	152,113	z	138,956	90,703	16,429	29,807	2,017
1993	299,197	299,197	152,930	z	146,267	96,060	17,465	30,804	1,938
1992	311,564	311,564	156,967	z	154,597	101,883	18,795	32,006	1,913
1991	306,756	306,756	151,333	z	155,423	102,840	19,551	31,069	1,963
1990	331,150	331,150	156,875	z	174,275	115,328	22,455	34,599	1,893
1989	346,697	346,697	166,651	z	180,046	118,956	23,737	35,551	1,802
1988	348,492	348,492	168,897	z	179,595	118,423	24,372	34,975	1,825
1987	351,761	351,761	168,190	z	183,571	121,293	25,020	35,589	1,669
1986	347,924	347,924	168,255	z	179,669	117,804	24,578	35,507	1,780
1985	346,389	346,389	169,025	z	177,364	116,378	25,207	33,938	1,841
1984	349,186	349,186	170,506	z	178,680	117,506	25,609	33,866	1,699
1983	344,334	344,334	167,327	z	177,007	116,854	25,211	33,252	1,690
1982	342,166	342,166	165,089	z	177,077	116,978	24,834	33,835	1,430
1981	351,973	351,973	172,514	z	179,459	118,435	26,097	33,439	1,488
1980	370,022	370,022	183,395	z	186,627	123,400	28,553	33,164	1,510
1979	368,853	368,853	187,381	z	181,472	119,420	28,477	32,007	1,568
1978	368,258	368,258	186,239	z	182,019	119,970	28,654	31,882	1,513
1977	356,954	356,954	180,446	z	176,508	116,749	28,204	30,008	1,547
1976	358,567	358,567	179,330	z	179,237	119,569	28,714	29,462	1,492
1975	380,620	380,620	181,824	z	198,796	133,074	32,307	31,845	1,570
1974[6]	384,389	384,389	178,710	z	205,679	137,767	33,702	34,210	
1973	400,435	400,435	184,724	z	215,711	143,853	36,267	35,591	
1972	426,241	426,241	194,134	z	232,107	155,538	39,694	36,875	
1971	404,737	404,737	167,101	z	237,636	160,165	41,399	36,072	
1970	415,487	415,487	164,119	z	251,368	170,146	43,658	37,564	
1969	396,746	396,746	143,115	z	253,631	172,067	43,441	38,123	
1968	407,822	407,822	144,572	z	263,250	178,700	44,931	39,619	
1967	386,052	386,052	131,576	z	254,476	173,278	43,305	37,893	

15.11 Number of marriages by type of ceremony and denomination, 1837 to 2018

England and Wales

Year (selected years only prior to 1962[1])	All marriages	All marriages to opposite-sex couples	Marriages of opposite-sex couples						
			Civil ceremonies		Religious ceremonies				
			All	Approved Premises[2]	All	Church of England and Church in Wales	Roman Catholic	Other Christian denominations[3]	Other[4]
1966	384,497	384,497	127,502	z	256,995	175,254	43,814	37,927	
1965	371,127	371,127	118,034	z	253,093	171,848	43,192	38,053	
1964	359,307	359,307	111,053	z	248,254	167,742	42,525	37,987	
1963	351,329	351,329	107,384	z	243,945	163,837	42,272	37,836	
1962	347,732	347,732	103,102	z	244,630	164,707	42,788	37,135	
1957	346,903	346,903	97,084	z	249,819	172,010	39,960	37,849	
1952	349,308	349,308	106,777	z	242,531	173,282	33,050	36,199	
1934	342,307	342,307	97,120	z	245,187	183,123	22,323	39,741	
1929	313,316	313,316	80,475	z	232,841	176,113	18,711	38,017	
1924	296,416	296,416	70,604	z	225,812	171,480	16,286	38,046	
1919	369,411	369,411	85,330	z	284,081	220,557	19,078	44,446	
1914	294,401	294,401	70,880	z	223,521	171,700	13,729	38,092	
1913	286,583	286,583	62,328	z	224,255	172,640	13,349	38,266	
1912	283,834	283,834	58,367	z	225,467	174,357	12,715	38,395	
1911	274,943	274,943	57,435	z	217,508	167,925	12,002	37,581	
1910	267,721	267,721	54,678	z	213,043	164,945	11,312	36,786	
1909	260,544	260,544	53,505	z	207,039	159,991	10,962	36,086	
1908	264,940	264,940	54,048	z	210,892	163,086	10,940	36,866	
1907	276,421	276,421	54,026	z	222,395	172,497	11,700	38,198	
1906	270,038	270,038	50,682	z	219,356	170,579	11,455	37,322	
1905	260,742	260,742	47,768	z	212,974	165,747	10,812	36,415	
1904	257,856	257,856	46,247	z	211,609	165,519	10,450	35,640	
1903	261,103	261,103	44,520	z	216,583	170,044	10,621	35,918	
1902	261,750	261,750	42,761	z	218,989	173,011	10,606	35,372	
1901	259,400	259,400	41,067	z	218,333	172,679	10,624	35,030	
1900	257,480	257,480	39,471	z	218,009	173,060	10,267	34,682	
1899	262,334	262,334	39,403	z	222,931	177,896	10,686	34,349	
1898	255,379	255,379	37,938	z	217,441	174,826	10,164	32,451	
1897	249,145	249,145	36,626	z	212,519	170,806	10,095	31,618	
1896	242,764	242,764	35,439	z	207,325	166,871	10,042	30,412	
1895	228,204	228,204	33,749	z	194,455	156,469	9,405	28,581	
1894	226,449	226,449	33,550	z	192,899	155,352	9,453	28,094	
1893	218,689	218,689	31,379	z	187,310	151,309	9,019	26,982	
1892	227,135	227,135	31,416	z	195,719	158,632	9,133	27,954	
1891	226,526	226,526	30,809	z	195,717	158,439	9,517	27,761	
1890	223,028	223,028	30,376	z	192,652	156,371	9,596	26,685	
1889	213,865	213,865	29,779	z	184,086	149,356	8,988	25,742	
1888	203,821	203,821	27,809	z	176,012	142,863	8,632	24,517	
1887	200,518	200,518	27,335	z	173,183	140,607	8,611	23,965	
1886	196,071	196,071	25,590	z	170,481	138,571	8,220	23,690	
1885	197,745	197,745	25,851	z	171,894	139,913	8,162	23,819	
1884	204,301	204,301	26,786	z	177,515	144,344	8,783	24,388	
1883	206,384	206,384	26,547	z	179,837	147,000	8,980	23,857	
1882	204,405	204,405	25,717	z	178,688	146,102	9,235	23,351	
1881	197,290	197,290	25,055	z	172,235	140,995	8,784	22,456	
1880	191,965	191,965	24,180	z	167,785	137,661	8,210	21,914	
1879	182,082	182,082	21,769	z	160,313	131,689	7,437	21,187	
1878	190,054	190,054	22,056	z	167,998	137,969	7,980	22,049	
1877	194,352	194,352	21,269	z	173,083	142,396	8,277	22,410	

15.11 Number of marriages by type of ceremony and denomination, 1837 to 2018
England and Wales

Year (selected years only prior to 1962[1])	All marriages	All marriages to opposite-sex couples	Marriages of opposite-sex couples						
			Civil ceremonies		Religious ceremonies				
			All	Approved Premises[2]	All	Church of England and Church in Wales	Roman Catholic	Other Christian denom-inations[3]	Other[4]
1876	201,874	201,874	21,709	z	180,165	148,910	8,577	22,678	
1875	201,212	201,212	21,002	z	180,210	149,685	8,411	22,114	
1874	202,010	202,010	21,256	z	180,754	150,819	8,179	21,756	
1873	205,615	205,615	21,178	z	184,437	154,581	8,222	21,634	
1872	201,267	201,267	19,995	z	181,272	152,364	8,427	20,481	
1871	190,112	190,112	18,378	z	171,734	144,663	7,647	19,424	
1870	181,655	181,655	17,848	z	163,807	137,986	7,391	18,430	
1869	176,970	176,970	16,745	z	160,225	135,082	7,231	17,912	
1868	176,962	176,962	15,878	z	161,084	136,038	7,517	17,529	
1867	179,154	179,154	15,058	z	164,096	138,930	7,918	17,248	
1866	187,776	187,776	15,246	z	172,530	146,040	8,911	17,579	
1865	185,474	185,474	14,792	z	170,682	145,104	8,742	16,836	
1864	180,387	180,387	14,611	z	165,776	141,083	8,659	16,034	
1863	173,510	173,510	13,589	z	159,921	136,743	8,095	15,083	
1862	164,030	164,030	12,723	z	151,307	129,733	7,345	14,229	
1861	163,706	163,706	11,725	z	151,981	130,697	7,782	13,502	
1860	170,156	170,156	11,257	z	158,899	137,370	7,800	13,729	
1859	167,723	167,723	10,844	z	156,879	136,210	7,756	12,913	
1858	156,070	156,070	9,952	z	146,118	128,082	6,643	11,393	
1857	159,097	159,097	9,642	z	149,455	131,031	7,360	11,064	
1856	159,337	159,337	8,097	z	151,240	133,619	7,527	10,094	
1855	152,113	152,113	7,441	z	144,672	127,751	7,344	9,577	
1854	159,727	159,727	7,593	z	152,134	134,109	7,813	10,212	
1853	164,520	164,520	7,598	z	156,922	138,042	8,375	10,505	
1852	158,782	158,782	7,100	z	151,682	133,882	7,479	10,321	
1851	154,206	154,206	6,813	z	147,393	130,958	6,570	9,865	
1850	152,744	152,744	6,207	z	146,537	130,959	5,623	9,955	
1849	141,883	141,883	5,558	z	136,325	123,182	4,199	8,944	
1848	138,230	138,230	4,790	z	133,440	121,469	3,658	8,313	
1847	135,845	135,845	4,258	z	131,587	120,876	2,961	7,750	
1846	145,664	145,664	4,167	z	141,497	130,509	3,027	7,961	
1845	143,743	143,743	3,977	z	139,766	129,515	2,816	7,435	
1844	132,249	132,249	3,446	z	128,803	120,009	2,280	6,514	
1843	123,818	123,818	2,817	z	121,001	113,637	7,364		
1842	118,825	118,825	2,357	z	116,468	110,047	6,421		
1841	122,496	122,496	2,064	z	120,432	114,371	6,061		
1841 - YE 30 June	122,482	122,482	2,036	z	120,446	114,448	5,998		
1840 - YE 30 June	124,329	124,329	1,938	z	122,391	117,018	5,373		
1839 - YE 30 June	121,083	121,083	1,564	z	119,519	114,632	4,887		
1838 - YE 30 June	111,481	111,481	1,093	z	110,388	107,201	3,187		
1837 - 1 July 1937 to 31 December 1937	58,479	58,479	431	z	58,048	56,832	1,216		

15.11 Number of marriages by type of ceremony and denomination, 1837 to 2018

England and Wales

Year (selected years only prior to 1962[1])	All marriages	Marriages of same-sex couples					
		All marriages to same-sex couples	Male	Female	Civil ceremonies		Religious ceremonies
					All	Approved Premises[2]	
2018	234,795	**6,925**	2,966	3,959	6,862	6,169	63
2017	242,842	**6,932**	3,048	3,884	6,889	6,299	43
2016	249,793	**7,019**	3,109	3,910	6,958	6,171	61
2015	245,513	**6,493**	2,860	3,633	6,449	5,663	44
2014[5]	252,222	**4,850**	2,129	2,721	4,827	4,200	23

(prior to 2014 - data not applicable)

YE = Year ending

Source: Office for National Statistics

1 Data are not available for years not shown.

2 Approved premises are buildings such as hotels, historic buildings and stately homes licensed for civil marriages. Data on approved premises is from 1 April 1995.

3 'Other Christian denominations' include Methodist, Calvinistic Methodist, United Reform Church, Congregationalist, Baptist, Presbyterian, Society of Friends (Quakers), Salvation Army, Brethren, Mormon, Unitarian and Jehovah's Witnesses.

4 'Other' include Jews, Muslim and Sikh.

5 The first marriages of same-sex couples took place on 29 March 2014; figures on marriages of same-sex couples in 2014 therefore represent a part-year only.

6 Prior to 1975 further information on denominations was not published.

15.12 Duration of marriage at divorce by age of wife at divorce, 2011 -2019
England and Wales

Year of divorce	Age of wife at divorce[1]	All durations	Duration of marriage[2]				
			0-4 years	5-9 years	10-14 years	15 or more years	Length unknown
2011	All ages	117,558	18,347	32,989	22,126	44,096	0
	Under 20	28	28	0	0	0	0
	20-24	2,353	1,920	433	0	0	0
	25-29	11,099	5,321	5,402	376	0	0
	30-34	18,020	4,700	9,521	3,603	196	0
	35-39	20,285	2,561	7,592	6,934	3,198	0
	40-44	22,370	1,732	4,802	5,712	10,124	0
	45 and over	43,403	2,085	5,239	5,501	30,578	0
	Unknown	0	0	0	0	0	0
2012	All ages	118,140	18,528	33,027	22,356	44,229	0
	Under 20	25	25	0	0	0	0
	20-24	2,207	1,811	396	0	0	0
	25-29	10,982	5,529	5,100	352	1	0
	30-34	18,041	4,818	9,529	3,487	207	0
	35-39	19,840	2,546	7,536	6,766	2,992	0
	40-44	22,506	1,738	4,987	5,984	9,797	0
	45 and over	44,539	2,061	5,479	5,767	31,232	0
	Unknown	0	0	0	0	0	0
2013	All ages	114,720	18,190	30,996	21,652	43,882	0
	Under 20	26	26	0	0	0	0
	20-24	1,871	1,522	349	0	0	0
	25-29	10,172	5,307	4,535	330	0	0
	30-34	17,521	5,045	9,002	3,254	220	0
	35-39	18,526	2,548	6,989	6,187	2,802	0
	40-44	21,278	1,669	4,720	5,900	8,989	0
	45 and over	45,326	2,073	5,401	5,981	31,871	0
	Unknown	0	0	0	0	0	0
2014	All ages	111,169	18,001	29,085	21,709	42,374	0
	Under 20	19	19	0	0	0	0
	20-24	1,394	1,197	197	0	0	0
	25-29	8,430	4,729	3,452	249	0	0
	30-34	14,979	4,673	7,391	2,715	200	0
	35-39	15,890	2,343	5,987	5,440	2,120	0
	40-44	18,593	1,459	4,028	5,470	7,636	0
	45 and over	42,516	1,945	4,958	5,940	29,673	0
	Unknown	9,348	1,636	3,072	1,895	2,745	0
2015	All ages	101,055	15,879	25,961	20,070	39,142	3
	Under 20	3	3	0	0	0	0
	20-24	1,162	1,007	155	0	0	0
	25-29	7,269	4,074	2,961	234	0	0
	30-34	13,048	4,032	6,472	2,370	174	0
	35-39	14,423	2,126	5,469	5,005	1,823	0
	40-44	16,100	1,251	3,475	4,931	6,443	0
	45 and over	39,927	1,747	4,359	5,707	28,114	0
	Unknown	9,123	1,639	3,070	1,823	2,588	3
2016	All ages	106,959	16,120	27,862	21,575	41,401	1
	Under 20	18	18	0	0	0	0
	20-24	1,070	935	135	0	0	0
	25-29	7,488	4,257	3,050	181	0	0
	30-34	14,325	4,423	7,293	2,461	148	0
	35-39	15,949	2,211	6,245	5,553	1,940	0
	40-44	16,949	1,346	3,725	5,328	6,550	0
	45 and over	43,980	1,873	4,965	6,424	30,718	0
	Unknown	7,180	1,057	2,449	1,628	2,045	1

15.12 Duration of marriage at divorce by age of wife at divorce, 2011 -2019
England and Wales

Year of divorce	Age of wife at divorce[1]	All durations	Duration of marriage[2]				
			0-4 years	5-9 years	10-14 years	15 or more years	Length unknown
2017	All ages	101,669	14,577	26,802	20,729	39,559	2
	Under 20	8	8	0	0	0	0
	20-24	949	807	142	0	0	0
	25-29	6,689	3,696	2,840	153	0	0
	30-34	13,415	4,030	7,079	2,157	149	0
	35-39	15,609	2,060	6,293	5,359	1,897	0
	40-44	15,373	1,136	3,498	4,999	5,740	0
	45 and over	42,482	1,842	4,679	6,393	29,568	0
	Unknown	7,144	998	2,271	1,668	2,205	2
2018	All ages	90,871	11,808	23,900	18,797	36,364	2
	Under 20	2	2	0	0	0	0
	20-24	594	485	109	0	0	0
	25-29	4,744	2,586	2,061	97	0	0
	30-34	10,357	2,939	5,541	1,763	114	0
	35-39	12,907	1,632	5,340	4,392	1,543	0
	40-44	12,146	838	2,763	3,952	4,593	0
	45 and over	35,916	1,395	3,885	5,306	25,330	0
	Unknown	14,205	1,931	4,201	3,287	4,784	2
2019	All ages	107,599	13,838	28,896	22,060	42,805	0
	Under 20	1	1	0	0	0	0
	20-24	413	319	94	0	0	0
	25-29	3,470	1,753	1,652	65	0	0
	30-34	8,169	2,267	4,448	1,369	85	0
	35-39	10,571	1,234	4,339	3,582	1,416	0
	40-44	10,241	666	2,431	3,313	3,831	0
	45 and over	32,240	1,260	3,424	4,456	23,100	0
	Unknown	42,494	6,338	12,508	9,275	14,373	0

Source: Office for National Statistics (from NOMIS)

1. Previous publications of this table in Annual Abstract of Statistics calculated 'Age at Marriage'. This data has not been imputed for 2014 data onwards – not stated categories have been added to published tables instead. This is because marital status and age at marriage are also not mandatory fields in the divorce process and consequently are not always collected by the courts. For this reason from 2014 onwards 'Age at Divorce' has been imputed.

2. The duration of marriage is calculated from the date of marriage and the date of decree absolute.

3. Divorce statistics are derived from information recorded by Her Majestys Courts and Tribunal Service (HMCTS) during the divorce process.

4. Divorce statistics do not include married couples who separate, but do not divorce.

5. Divorces where the marriage took place abroad are included, provided the marriage was legally recognised in the UK and 1 of the parties had a permanent home in England and Wales.

6. This table provides statistics on divorces between opposite-sex couples which took place in England and Wales.

For more information on divorce statistics please contact Office for National Statistics (email: health.data@ons.gov.uk)

15.13 Duration of marriage at divorce by age of husband at divorce, 2011 -2019

England and Wales

Year of divorce	Age of husband at divorce[1]	All durations	Duration of marriage[2]				
			0-4 years	5-9 years	10-14 years	15 or more years	Length unknown
2011	All ages	117,558	18,347	32,989	22,126	44,096	0
	Under 20	6	6	0	0	0	0
	20-24	840	745	95	0	0	0
	25-29	6,560	3,770	2,680	110	0	0
	30-34	14,752	5,149	7,817	1,742	44	0
	35-39	19,315	3,396	8,681	5,768	1,470	0
	40-44	22,781	2,234	6,252	6,688	7,607	0
	45 and over	53,304	3,047	7,464	7,818	34,975	0
	Unknown	0	0	0	0	0	0
2012	All ages	118,140	18,528	33,027	22,356	44,229	0
	Under 20	2	2	0	0	0	0
	20-24	835	747	88	0	0	0
	25-29	6,364	3,850	2,442	72	0	0
	30-34	14,835	5,335	7,748	1,696	56	0
	35-39	18,804	3,350	8,545	5,539	1,370	0
	40-44	22,568	2,132	6,312	6,812	7,312	0
	45 and over	54,732	3,112	7,892	8,237	35,491	0
	Unknown	0	0	0	0	0	0
2013	All ages	114,720	18,190	30,996	21,652	43,882	0
	Under 20	10	10	0	0	0	0
	20-24	718	621	97	0	0	0
	25-29	5,998	3,787	2,141	70	0	0
	30-34	14,155	5,273	7,132	1,683	67	0
	35-39	17,391	3,335	7,876	4,919	1,261	0
	40-44	21,278	2,145	5,888	6,568	6,677	0
	45 and over	55,170	3,019	7,862	8,412	35,877	0
	Unknown	0	0	0	0	0	0
2014	All ages	111,169	18,001	29,085	21,709	42,374	0
	Under 20	3	3	0	0	0	0
	20-24	531	485	46	0	0	0
	25-29	4,907	3,244	1,605	58	0	0
	30-34	11,824	4,774	5,706	1,297	47	0
	35-39	14,764	3,047	6,563	4,212	942	0
	40-44	18,089	1,967	5,007	5,772	5,343	0
	45 and over	51,446	2,818	7,007	8,422	33,199	0
	Unknown	9,605	1,663	3,151	1,948	2,843	0
2015	All ages	101,055	15,879	25,961	20,070	39,142	3
	Under 20	4	4	0	0	0	0
	20-24	432	398	34	0	0	0
	25-29	4,306	2,836	1,423	47	0	0
	30-34	10,240	4,101	4,953	1,156	30	0
	35-39	13,222	2,671	5,887	3,841	823	0
	40-44	15,834	1,678	4,244	5,315	4,597	0
	45 and over	47,619	2,501	6,284	7,825	31,009	0
	Unknown	9,398	1,690	3,136	1,886	2,683	3
2016	All ages	106,959	16,120	27,862	21,575	41,401	1
	Under 20	2	2	0	0	0	0
	20-24	348	322	26	0	0	0
	25-29	4,422	2,927	1,452	43	0	0
	30-34	11,067	4,489	5,424	1,132	22	0
	35-39	14,774	2,966	6,737	4,202	869	0
	40-44	16,383	1,613	4,660	5,585	4,525	0
	45 and over	52,596	2,719	7,070	8,905	33,902	0
	Unknown	7,367	1,082	2,493	1,708	2,083	1

15.13 Duration of marriage at divorce by age of husband at divorce, 2011 -2019
England and Wales

Numbers

Year of divorce	Age of husband at divorce[1]	All durations	Duration of marriage[2]				
			0-4 years	5-9 years	10-14 years	15 or more years	Length unknown
2017	All ages	101,669	14,577	26,802	20,729	39,559	2
	Under 20	1	1	0	0	0	0
	20-24	304	278	26	0	0	0
	25-29	3,900	2,480	1,385	35	0	0
	30-34	10,584	4,106	5,417	1,022	39	0
	35-39	13,979	2,680	6,521	3,937	841	0
	40-44	14,981	1,471	4,398	5,100	4,012	0
	45 and over	50,569	2,543	6,701	8,929	32,396	0
	Unknown	7,351	1,018	2,354	1,706	2,271	2
2018	All ages	90,871	11,808	23,900	18,797	36,364	2
	Under 20	1	1	0	0	0	0
	20-24	201	188	13	0	0	0
	25-29	2,701	1,645	1,034	22	0	0
	30-34	8,130	3,020	4,236	833	41	0
	35-39	11,308	2,060	5,391	3,154	703	0
	40-44	11,689	1,019	3,501	4,121	3,048	0
	45 and over	42,500	1,922	5,515	7,346	27,717	0
	Unknown	14,341	1,953	4,210	3,321	4,855	2
2019	All ages	107,599	13,838	28,896	22,060	42,805	0
	Under 20	2	2	0	0	0	0
	20-24	129	115	14	0	0	0
	25-29	1,976	1,141	814	21	0	0
	30-34	6,284	2,158	3,454	653	19	0
	35-39	9,264	1,539	4,494	2,587	644	0
	40-44	9,671	867	2,908	3,324	2,572	0
	45 and over	37,668	1,673	4,663	6,183	25,149	0
	Unknown	42,605	6,343	12,549	9,292	14,421	0

Source: Office for National Statistics (from NOMIS)

1. Previous publications of this table in Annual Abstract of Statistics calculated 'Age at Marriage'. This data has not been imputed for 2014 data onwards – not stated categories have been added to published tables instead. This is because marital status and age at marriage are also not mandatory fields in the divorce process and consequently are not always collected by the courts. For this reason from 2014 onwards 'Age at Divorce' has been imputed.

2. The duration of marriage is calculated from the date of marriage and the date of decree absolute.

3. Divorce statistics are derived from information recorded by Her Majestys Courts and Tribunal Service (HMCTS) during the divorce process.

4. Divorce statistics do not include married couples who separate, but do not divorce.

5. Divorces where the marriage took place abroad are included, provided the marriage was legally recognised in the UK and 1 of the parties had a permanent home in England and Wales.

6. This table provides statistics on divorces between opposite-sex couples which took place in England and Wales.

For more information on divorce statistics please contact Office for National Statistics (email: health.data@ons.gov.uk)

15.14 Live births by administrative area of usual residence of mother, numbers, sex, General Fertility Rates and Total Fertility Rates, 2019

England and Wales: regions (within England), unitary authorities, counties, districts, London Boroughs
Scotland: council areas, Northern Ireland: local government districts

Area of usual residence		Numbers of live births[1]			Fertility Rate (GFR)[3]	Total Fertility Rate (TFR)[4]
		Total	Male	Female		
K02000001	UNITED KINGDOM[7]	:	:	:	:	:
K04000001, J99000001	ENGLAND, WALES AND ELSEWHERE[5]	640,370	329,107	311,263	57.5	1.65
K04000001	ENGLAND AND WALES	640,209	329,023	311,186	57.5	1.65
E92000001	ENGLAND	610,505	313,832	296,673	57.7	1.66
E12000001	NORTH EAST	25,742	13,236	12,506	53.0	1.52
E06000047	County Durham	4,766	2,428	2,338	50.7	1.47
E06000005	Darlington	1,026	526	500	54.8	1.62
E06000001	Hartlepool	938	502	436	56.5	1.64
E06000002	Middlesbrough	1,755	913	842	64.3	1.80
E06000057	Northumberland	2,519	1,290	1,229	51.1	1.54
E06000003	Redcar and Cleveland	1,346	675	671	59.2	1.72
E06000004	Stockton-on-Tees	2,090	1,086	1,004	59.7	1.77
E11000007	Tyne and Wear	11,302	5,816	5,486	51.0	1.45
E08000037	Gateshead	1,995	1,011	984	53.4	1.53
E08000021	Newcastle upon Tyne	3,096	1,586	1,510	44.2	1.37
E08000022	North Tyneside	2,133	1,129	1,004	57.6	1.67
E08000023	South Tyneside	1,470	773	697	55.3	1.58
E08000024	Sunderland	2,608	1,317	1,291	51.5	1.46
E12000002	NORTH WEST	80,020	41,046	38,974	58.9	1.69
E06000008	Blackburn with Darwen	1,955	976	979	67.9	2.01
E06000009	Blackpool	1,570	794	776	66.8	1.94
E06000049	Cheshire East	3,655	1,895	1,760	60.5	1.82
E06000050	Cheshire West and Chester	3,366	1,756	1,610	57.2	1.69
E06000006	Halton	1,394	712	682	58.9	1.73
E06000007	Warrington	2,100	1,052	1,048	57.0	1.67
E10000006	Cumbria	4,233	2,151	2,082	55.3	1.65
E07000026	Allerdale	756	378	378	51.5	1.55
E07000027	Barrow-in-Furness	701	368	333	63.1	1.82
E07000028	Carlisle	1,062	546	516	57.7	1.68
E07000029	Copeland	575	285	290	53.6	1.58
E07000030	Eden	407	226	181	56.1	1.70
E07000031	South Lakeland	732	348	384	51.1	1.60
E11000001	Greater Manchester	34,396	17,717	16,679	60.7	1.71
E08000001	Bolton	3,676	1,911	1,765	70.0	2.03
E08000002	Bury	2,228	1,197	1,031	63.8	1.82
E08000003	Manchester	7,229	3,758	3,471	51.1	1.47
E08000004	Oldham	3,138	1,557	1,581	69.7	2.03
E08000005	Rochdale	2,881	1,459	1,422	68.4	1.97
E08000006	Salford	3,532	1,826	1,706	63.3	1.73
E08000007	Stockport	3,040	1,574	1,466	58.7	1.68
E08000008	Tameside	2,796	1,468	1,328	66.7	1.90
E08000009	Trafford	2,505	1,258	1,247	58.1	1.72
E08000010	Wigan	3,371	1,709	1,662	58.1	1.68
E10000017	Lancashire	12,306	6,225	6,081	57.8	1.69
E07000117	Burnley	1,165	588	577	72.7	2.08
E07000118	Chorley	1,092	550	542	54.3	1.58
E07000119	Fylde	617	307	310	55.2	1.67
E07000120	Hyndburn	1,030	520	510	70.1	2.03
E07000121	Lancaster	1,333	680	653	46.9	1.46
E07000122	Pendle	1,186	610	576	71.7	2.10
E07000123	Preston	1,744	843	901	59.6	1.73
E07000124	Ribble Valley	481	246	235	52.9	1.65
E07000125	Rossendale	724	383	341	57.6	1.71
E07000126	South Ribble	1,020	515	505	54.4	1.59
E07000127	West Lancashire	1,001	511	490	50.0	1.59
E07000128	Wyre	913	472	441	56.4	1.65
E11000002	Merseyside	15,045	7,768	7,277	55.5	1.58
E08000011	Knowsley	1,954	984	970	67.5	1.87
E08000012	Liverpool	5,574	2,897	2,677	49.9	1.44
E08000014	Sefton	2,591	1,350	1,241	58.5	1.71
E08000013	St. Helens	1,776	931	845	56.3	1.61
E08000015	Wirral	3,150	1,606	1,544	57.9	1.71
E12000003	YORKSHIRE AND THE HUMBER	58,281	29,767	28,514	56.8	1.64
E06000011	East Riding of Yorkshire	2,671	1,428	1,243	54.3	1.70
E06000010	Kingston upon Hull, City of	3,175	1,618	1,557	60.2	1.63
E06000012	North East Lincolnshire	1,669	837	832	61.3	1.81
E06000013	North Lincolnshire	1,600	790	810	56.1	1.68

15.14 Live births by administrative area of usual residence of mother, numbers, sex, General Fertility Rates and Total Fertility Rates, 2019

England and Wales: regions (within England), unitary authorities, counties, districts, London Boroughs
Scotland: council areas, Northern Ireland: local government districts

Area of usual residence		Numbers of live births[1]			Fertility Rate (GFR)[3]	Total Fertility Rate (TFR)[4]
		Total	Male	Female		
E06000014	York	1,703	881	822	37.3	1.21
E10000023	**North Yorkshire**	**5,049**	**2,523**	**2,526**	**55.8**	**1.68**
E07000163	Craven	419	198	221	53.3	1.61
E07000164	Hambleton	645	338	307	50.2	1.52
E07000165	Harrogate	1,284	649	635	54.1	1.67
E07000166	Richmondshire	417	200	217	54.9	1.63
E07000167	Ryedale	460	213	247	58.8	1.76
E07000168	Scarborough	924	472	452	60.3	1.79
E07000169	Selby	900	453	447	59.1	1.72
E11000003	**South Yorkshire**	**14,882**	**7,710**	**7,172**	**54.8**	**1.55**
E08000016	Barnsley	2,685	1,394	1,291	61.3	1.76
E08000017	Doncaster	3,457	1,800	1,657	63.1	1.82
E08000018	Rotherham	2,817	1,449	1,368	60.2	1.75
E08000019	Sheffield	5,923	3,067	2,856	46.9	1.38
E11000006	**West Yorkshire**	**27,532**	**13,980**	**13,552**	**59.8**	**1.73**
E08000032	Bradford	7,270	3,617	3,653	69.7	2.08
E08000033	Calderdale	2,163	1,125	1,038	58.2	1.72
E08000034	Kirklees	4,899	2,507	2,392	60.2	1.78
E08000035	Leeds	9,272	4,713	4,559	53.2	1.58
E08000036	Wakefield	3,928	2,018	1,910	62.3	1.78
E12000004	**EAST MIDLANDS**	**48,986**	**25,067**	**23,919**	**55.8**	**1.63**
E06000015	Derby	3,009	1,512	1,497	59.9	1.72
E06000016	Leicester	4,622	2,389	2,233	57.0	1.67
E06000018	Nottingham	3,781	1,915	1,866	46.3	1.47
E06000017	Rutland	280	159	121	49.7	1.65
E10000007	**Derbyshire**	**7,336**	**3,738**	**3,598**	**54.7**	**1.59**
E07000032	Amber Valley	1,154	585	569	53.8	1.56
E07000033	Bolsover	813	426	387	58.5	1.68
E07000034	Chesterfield	1,009	488	521	56.0	1.61
E07000035	Derbyshire Dales	482	244	238	50.0	1.58
E07000036	Erewash	1,041	541	500	51.3	1.48
E07000037	High Peak	843	441	402	55.4	1.62
E07000038	North East Derbyshire	909	453	456	57.2	1.68
E07000039	South Derbyshire	1,085	560	525	55.2	1.60
E10000018	**Leicestershire**	**6,678**	**3,422**	**3,256**	**53.5**	**1.58**
E07000129	Blaby	1,054	541	513	58.3	1.69
E07000130	Charnwood	1,718	864	854	46.8	1.40
E07000131	Harborough	823	437	386	56.2	1.73
E07000132	Hinckley and Bosworth	1,104	574	530	57.9	1.67
E07000133	Melton	455	243	212	56.8	1.76
E07000134	North West Leicestershire	1,011	509	502	55.7	1.63
E07000135	Oadby and Wigston	513	254	259	51.0	1.58
E10000019	**Lincolnshire**	**6,767**	**3,545**	**3,222**	**54.2**	**1.61**
E07000136	Boston	734	385	349	61.1	1.84
E07000137	East Lindsey	1,081	576	505	58.1	1.76
E07000138	Lincoln	1,021	560	461	44.2	1.36
E07000139	North Kesteven	991	486	505	52.8	1.55
E07000140	South Holland	903	459	444	59.7	1.78
E07000141	South Kesteven	1,249	645	604	55.1	1.71
E07000142	West Lindsey	788	434	354	54.5	1.64
E10000021	**Northamptonshire**	**8,610**	**4,400**	**4,210**	**64.2**	**1.91**
E07000150	Corby	956	484	472	67.6	1.97
E07000151	Daventry	861	420	441	62.1	1.85
E07000152	East Northamptonshire	895	454	441	57.6	1.76
E07000153	Kettering	1,213	648	565	67.2	1.99
E07000154	Northampton	2,909	1,490	1,419	67.0	1.96
E07000155	South Northamptonshire	860	454	406	55.7	1.69
E07000156	Wellingborough	916	450	466	67.4	2.06
E10000024	**Nottinghamshire**	**7,903**	**3,987**	**3,916**	**55.6**	**1.62**
E07000170	Ashfield	1,361	678	683	58.8	1.68
E07000171	Bassetlaw	1,126	576	550	60.2	1.80
E07000172	Broxtowe	1,034	547	487	51.4	1.46
E07000173	Gedling	1,098	550	548	53.1	1.54
E07000174	Mansfield	1,182	611	571	61.3	1.75
E07000175	Newark and Sherwood	1,078	533	545	54.2	1.61
E07000176	Rushcliffe	1,024	492	532	50.5	1.50

15.14 Live births by administrative area of usual residence of mother, numbers, sex, General Fertility Rates and Total Fertility Rates, 2019

England and Wales: regions (within England), unitary authorities, counties, districts, London Boroughs
Scotland: council areas, Northern Ireland: local government districts

Area of usual residence		Numbers of live births[1]			Fertility Rate (GFR)[3]	Total Fertility Rate (TFR)[4]
		Total	Male	Female		
E12000005	**WEST MIDLANDS**	**65,982**	**34,043**	**31,939**	**59.6**	**1.72**
E06000019	Herefordshire, County of	1,645	878	767	55.3	1.62
E06000051	Shropshire	2,587	1,383	1,204	52.9	1.61
E06000021	Stoke-on-Trent	3,256	1,679	1,577	67.7	1.90
E06000020	Telford and Wrekin	2,021	1,010	1,011	61.1	1.80
E10000028	**Staffordshire**	**8,301**	**4,292**	**4,009**	**56.5**	**1.65**
E07000192	Cannock Chase	1,121	582	539	62.1	1.77
E07000193	East Staffordshire	1,363	726	637	67.2	1.98
E07000194	Lichfield	991	498	493	59.7	1.79
E07000195	Newcastle-under-Lyme	1,089	550	539	44.9	1.31
E07000196	South Staffordshire	835	437	398	50.2	1.49
E07000197	Stafford	1,293	658	635	57.9	1.69
E07000198	Staffordshire Moorlands	760	406	354	51.3	1.56
E07000199	Tamworth	849	435	414	60.9	1.78
E10000031	**Warwickshire**	**5,854**	**3,026**	**2,828**	**58.1**	**1.70**
E07000218	North Warwickshire	598	309	289	55.7	1.62
E07000219	Nuneaton and Bedworth	1,535	808	727	65.5	1.89
E07000220	Rugby	1,179	601	578	61.0	1.78
E07000221	Stratford-on-Avon	1,098	565	533	56.3	1.69
E07000222	Warwick	1,444	743	701	52.1	1.65
E11000005	**West Midlands**	**36,695**	**18,885**	**17,810**	**61.1**	**1.74**
E08000025	Birmingham	15,483	7,996	7,487	61.0	1.78
E08000026	Coventry	4,198	2,131	2,067	49.4	1.40
E08000027	Dudley	3,450	1,796	1,654	60.5	1.76
E08000028	Sandwell	4,391	2,293	2,098	68.4	1.98
E08000029	Solihull	2,221	1,135	1,086	60.1	1.78
E08000030	Walsall	3,695	1,824	1,871	68.9	1.98
E08000031	Wolverhampton	3,257	1,710	1,547	65.5	1.87
E10000034	**Worcestershire**	**5,623**	**2,890**	**2,733**	**57.2**	**1.69**
E07000234	Bromsgrove	920	459	461	57.8	1.71
E07000235	Malvern Hills	541	286	255	49.0	1.53
E07000236	Redditch	1,014	502	512	64.9	1.89
E07000237	Worcester	1,135	563	572	55.3	1.62
E07000238	Wychavon	1,121	606	515	57.6	1.74
E07000239	Wyre Forest	892	474	418	56.5	1.67
E12000006	**EAST**	**67,409**	**34,868**	**32,541**	**60.7**	**1.77**
E06000055	Bedford	2,098	1,104	994	66.2	1.97
E06000056	Central Bedfordshire	3,363	1,738	1,625	63.6	1.82
E06000032	Luton	3,256	1,668	1,588	75.7	2.18
E06000031	Peterborough	2,779	1,478	1,301	71.8	2.13
E06000033	Southend-on-Sea	2,044	1,032	1,012	62.4	1.84
E06000034	Thurrock	2,464	1,263	1,201	69.3	1.99
E10000003	**Cambridgeshire**	**6,648**	**3,443**	**3,205**	**56.2**	**1.69**
E07000008	Cambridge	1,335	715	620	45.7	1.80
E07000009	East Cambridgeshire	866	449	417	56.4	1.69
E07000010	Fenland	1,033	527	506	62.0	1.82
E07000011	Huntingdonshire	1,867	964	903	61.8	1.79
E07000012	South Cambridgeshire	1,547	788	759	57.7	1.74
E10000012	**Essex**	**15,916**	**8,212**	**7,704**	**61.0**	**1.77**
E07000066	Basildon	2,476	1,254	1,222	69.2	1.98
E07000067	Braintree	1,602	832	770	61.6	1.82
E07000068	Brentwood	832	426	406	61.3	1.79
E07000069	Castle Point	813	422	391	56.7	1.69
E07000070	Chelmsford	1,812	956	856	55.8	1.61
E07000071	Colchester	2,087	1,090	997	53.3	1.52
E07000072	Epping Forest	1,642	875	767	69.5	1.98
E07000073	Harlow	1,203	598	605	70.6	2.01
E07000074	Maldon	510	261	249	54.0	1.67
E07000075	Rochford	805	377	428	57.1	1.73
E07000076	Tendring	1,227	642	585	60.1	1.80
E07000077	Uttlesford	907	479	428	59.6	1.79
E10000015	**Hertfordshire**	**13,517**	**7,029**	**6,488**	**60.2**	**1.74**
E07000095	Broxbourne	1,140	611	529	62.8	1.80
E07000096	Dacorum	1,865	959	906	65.2	1.86
E07000242	East Hertfordshire	1,529	809	720	57.6	1.70
E07000098	Hertsmere	1,212	596	616	63.1	1.85
E07000099	North Hertfordshire	1,500	786	714	62.8	1.84

15.14 Live births by administrative area of usual residence of mother, numbers, sex, General Fertility Rates and Total Fertility Rates, 2019

England and Wales: regions (within England), unitary authorities, counties, districts, London Boroughs
Scotland: council areas, Northern Ireland: local government districts

Area of usual residence		Numbers of live births[1]			Fertility Rate (GFR)[3]	Total Fertility Rate (TFR)[4]
		Total	Male	Female		
E07000240	St Albans	1,595	837	758	59.8	1.74
E07000243	Stevenage	1,100	576	524	64.3	1.80
E07000102	Three Rivers	968	500	468	57.7	1.71
E07000103	Watford	1,344	688	656	66.2	1.84
E07000241	Welwyn Hatfield	1,264	667	597	46.6	1.41
E10000020	**Norfolk**	**8,083**	**4,208**	**3,875**	**54.1**	**1.58**
E07000143	Breckland	1,293	654	639	59.7	1.75
E07000144	Broadland	1,041	529	512	51.8	1.55
E07000145	Great Yarmouth	964	501	463	61.7	1.83
E07000146	King's Lynn and West Norfolk	1,412	742	670	62.7	1.90
E07000147	North Norfolk	682	380	302	51.8	1.55
E07000148	Norwich	1,471	766	705	43.5	1.31
E07000149	South Norfolk	1,220	636	584	54.2	1.63
E10000029	**Suffolk**	**7,241**	**3,693**	**3,548**	**59.3**	**1.75**
E07000200	Babergh	725	363	362	53.6	1.67
E07000244	East Suffolk	2,005	997	1,008	55.5	1.70
E07000202	Ipswich	1,753	900	853	66.4	1.91
E07000203	Mid Suffolk	827	432	395	52.1	1.58
E07000245	West Suffolk	1,931	1,001	930	63.8	1.80
E12000007	**LONDON**	**117,897**	**60,550**	**57,347**	**58.9**	**1.60**
E13000001	**Inner London**	**45,545**	**23,327**	**22,218**	**50.0**	**1.34**
E09000007	Camden	2,448	1,255	1,193	37.0	1.05
E09000001	City of London	78	37	41	42.0	1.56
E09000012	Hackney	4,094	2,126	1,968	54.8	1.51
E09000013	Hammersmith and Fulham	2,189	1,075	1,114	48.9	1.34
E09000014	Haringey	3,595	1,881	1,714	59.7	1.66
E09000019	Islington	2,680	1,395	1,285	39.3	1.16
E09000020	Kensington and Chelsea	1,612	830	782	50.7	1.38
E09000022	Lambeth	3,844	2,019	1,825	44.3	1.21
E09000023	Lewisham	4,393	2,233	2,160	59.8	1.60
E09000025	Newham	5,492	2,758	2,734	67.8	1.83
E09000028	Southwark	4,027	2,058	1,969	49.2	1.33
E09000030	Tower Hamlets	4,307	2,166	2,141	48.2	1.26
E09000032	Wandsworth	4,471	2,325	2,146	48.1	1.24
E09000033	Westminster	2,315	1,169	1,146	39.5	1.06
E13000002	**Outer London**	**72,352**	**37,223**	**35,129**	**66.3**	**1.87**
E09000002	Barking and Dagenham	3,574	1,862	1,712	77.5	2.23
E09000003	Barnet	4,973	2,537	2,436	61.8	1.71
E09000004	Bexley	2,954	1,558	1,396	60.2	1.70
E09000005	Brent	4,919	2,524	2,395	72.6	2.06
E09000006	Bromley	3,862	1,951	1,911	60.9	1.72
E09000008	Croydon	5,304	2,694	2,610	67.2	1.92
E09000009	Ealing	4,793	2,465	2,328	69.5	1.95
E09000010	Enfield	4,548	2,356	2,192	66.5	1.90
E09000011	Greenwich	4,125	2,029	2,096	63.9	1.74
E09000015	Harrow	3,526	1,805	1,721	73.8	2.12
E09000016	Havering	3,186	1,707	1,479	62.9	1.75
E09000017	Hillingdon	4,139	2,113	2,026	65.2	1.85
E09000018	Hounslow	3,866	1,942	1,924	68.7	1.92
E09000021	Kingston upon Thames	1,946	1,047	899	51.3	1.44
E09000024	Merton	2,924	1,502	1,422	65.5	1.77
E09000026	Redbridge	4,495	2,339	2,156	71.2	2.03
E09000027	Richmond upon Thames	2,181	1,113	1,068	58.3	1.59
E09000029	Sutton	2,555	1,326	1,229	62.3	1.80
E09000031	Waltham Forest	4,482	2,353	2,129	73.1	1.98
E12000008	**SOUTH EAST**	**93,664**	**48,110**	**45,554**	**56.9**	**1.69**
E06000036	Bracknell Forest	1,304	648	656	54.5	1.58
E06000043	Brighton and Hove	2,395	1,207	1,188	34.8	1.12
E06000046	Isle of Wight	1,036	539	497	52.7	1.60
E06000035	Medway	3,330	1,698	1,632	61.7	1.76
E06000042	Milton Keynes	3,273	1,628	1,645	62.2	1.83
E06000044	Portsmouth	2,316	1,185	1,131	50.0	1.46
E06000038	Reading	2,104	1,107	997	58.7	1.71
E06000039	Slough	2,336	1,190	1,146	74.4	2.23
E06000045	Southampton	2,899	1,458	1,441	50.0	1.48
E06000037	West Berkshire	1,521	792	729	57.3	1.77
E06000040	Windsor and Maidenhead	1,515	768	747	57.6	1.72

15.14 Live births by administrative area of usual residence of mother, numbers, sex, General Fertility Rates and Total Fertility Rates, 2019

England and Wales: regions (within England), unitary authorities, counties, districts, London Boroughs
Scotland: council areas, Northern Ireland: local government districts

Area of usual residence		Numbers of live births[1]			Fertility Rate (GFR)[3]	Total Fertility Rate (TFR)[4]
		Total	Male	Female		
E06000041	Wokingham	1,705	915	790	55.6	1.72
E06000060	**Buckinghamshire**	**5,629**	**2,894**	**2,735**	**59.7**	**1.78**
E10000011	East Sussex	4,677	2,398	2,279	55.4	1.68
E07000061	Eastbourne	915	468	447	54.0	1.64
E07000062	Hastings	1,005	520	485	62.8	1.84
E07000063	Lewes	796	423	373	50.9	1.57
E07000064	**Rother**	**721**	**358**	**363**	**58.6**	**1.78**
E07000065	Wealden	1,240	629	611	52.6	1.62
E10000014	Hampshire	13,318	6,918	6,400	57.6	1.72
E07000084	Basingstoke and Deane	1,950	1,039	911	60.6	1.78
E07000085	East Hampshire	1,079	584	495	57.0	1.79
E07000086	Eastleigh	1,429	710	719	58.9	1.71
E07000087	**Fareham**	**917**	**468**	**449**	**49.6**	**1.47**
E07000088	Gosport	812	457	355	56.0	1.64
E07000089	Hart	882	444	438	55.9	1.70
E07000090	Havant	1,241	652	589	60.2	1.76
E07000091	New Forest	1,298	647	651	51.2	1.56
E07000092	Rushmoor	1,239	657	582	67.8	1.92
E07000093	Test Valley	1,381	699	682	66.7	1.97
E07000094	Winchester	1,090	561	529	49.7	1.64
E10000016	Kent	16,537	8,520	8,017	59.4	1.76
E07000105	Ashford	1,378	695	683	60.2	1.81
E07000106	Canterbury	1,310	662	648	39.0	1.32
E07000107	Dartford	1,612	832	780	69.6	1.93
E07000108	**Dover**	**1,073**	**553**	**520**	**57.6**	**1.70**
E07000112	Folkestone and Hythe	1,027	542	485	59.2	1.77
E07000109	Gravesham	1,343	693	650	68.2	1.99
E07000110	Maidstone	1,891	996	895	61.8	1.81
E07000111	Sevenoaks	1,217	634	583	61.9	1.87
E07000113	Swale	1,717	866	851	65.1	1.94
E07000114	Thanet	1,414	752	662	61.2	1.84
E07000115	Tonbridge and Malling	1,425	732	693	60.7	1.83
E07000116	Tunbridge Wells	1,130	563	567	56.8	1.75
E10000025	Oxfordshire	7,287	3,771	3,516	56.6	1.70
E07000177	Cherwell	1,810	928	882	67.6	1.98
E07000178	Oxford	1,541	783	758	40.9	1.58
E07000179	South Oxfordshire	1,400	741	659	61.3	1.87
E07000180	**Vale of White Horse**	**1,501**	**785**	**716**	**63.8**	**1.86**
E07000181	West Oxfordshire	1,035	534	501	57.7	1.72
E10000030	Surrey	12,192	6,317	5,875	57.2	1.73
E07000207	Elmbridge	1,478	792	686	65.3	2.02
E07000208	Epsom and Ewell	824	430	394	56.1	1.71
E07000209	Guildford	1,264	683	581	40.8	1.35
E07000210	**Mole Valley**	**750**	**387**	**363**	**56.5**	**1.82**
E07000211	Reigate and Banstead	1,710	886	824	63.6	1.88
E07000212	Runnymede	895	440	455	45.9	1.42
E07000213	Spelthorne	1,230	616	614	68.3	2.00
E07000214	Surrey Heath	837	420	417	56.1	1.71
E07000215	Tandridge	894	486	408	60.6	1.77
E07000216	Waverley	1,133	582	551	57.2	1.85
E07000217	Woking	1,177	595	582	66.0	1.96
E10000032	West Sussex	8,290	4,157	4,133	58.8	1.76
E07000223	Adur	593	293	300	57.8	1.76
E07000224	Arun	1,371	695	676	58.3	1.75
E07000225	Chichester	964	467	497	54.6	1.69
E07000226	**Crawley**	**1,531**	**783**	**748**	**67.6**	**1.96**
E07000227	Horsham	1,314	673	641	57.5	1.74
E07000228	Mid Sussex	1,457	690	767	57.2	1.69
E07000229	Worthing	1,060	556	504	57.2	1.70
E12000009	SOUTH WEST	52,524	27,145	25,379	54.7	1.61
E06000022	Bath and North East Somerset	1,680	845	835	43.1	1.43
E06000058	Bournemouth, Christchurch and Poole	3,508	1,786	1,722	49.9	1.48
E06000023	Bristol, City of	5,557	2,827	2,730	49.3	1.44
E06000052, E06000053	**Cornwall and Isles of Scilly[6]**	**4,828**	**2,556**	**2,272**	**54.5**	**1.66**
E06000059	Dorset	2,748	1,450	1,298	53.8	1.68
E06000024	North Somerset	2,023	1,042	981	58.6	1.78
E06000026	Plymouth	2,683	1,333	1,350	53.0	1.55

15.14 Live births by administrative area of usual residence of mother, numbers, sex, General Fertility Rates and Total Fertility Rates, 2019

England and Wales: regions (within England), unitary authorities, counties, districts, London Boroughs
Scotland: council areas, Northern Ireland: local government districts

Area of usual residence		Numbers of live births[1]			Fertility Rate (GFR)[3]	Total Fertility Rate (TFR)[4]
		Total	Male	Female		
E06000025	South Gloucestershire	3,068	1,606	1,462	57.9	1.65
E06000030	Swindon	2,632	1,359	1,273	64.1	1.87
E06000027	Torbay	1,220	654	566	61.6	1.84
E06000054	Wiltshire	4,748	2,423	2,325	59.8	1.84
E10000008	Devon	6,550	3,373	3,177	52.0	1.56
E07000040	East Devon	1,147	605	542	58.3	1.79
E07000041	Exeter	1,170	602	568	38.2	1.25
E07000042	Mid Devon	778	391	387	60.2	1.82
E07000043	**North Devon**	**820**	**421**	**399**	**57.3**	**1.74**
E07000044	South Hams	634	322	312	54.1	1.72
E07000045	Teignbridge	1,134	586	548	57.5	1.72
E07000046	Torridge	496	249	247	52.2	1.61
E07000047	West Devon	371	197	174	49.8	1.55
E10000013	Gloucestershire	6,124	3,177	2,947	56.9	1.69
E07000078	Cheltenham	1,155	555	600	52.1	1.53
E07000079	Cotswold	764	394	370	57.6	1.80
E07000080	Forest of Dean	726	400	326	54.9	1.71
E07000081	**Gloucester**	**1,461**	**763**	**698**	**59.5**	**1.71**
E07000082	Stroud	1,003	522	481	54.2	1.66
E07000083	Tewkesbury	1,015	543	472	63.9	1.82
E10000027	Somerset	5,155	2,714	2,441	60.0	1.80
E07000187	Mendip	1,075	569	506	60.2	1.86
E07000188	Sedgemoor	1,168	629	539	61.2	1.82
E07000246	Somerset West and Taunton	1,370	701	669	57.6	1.70
E07000189	**South Somerset**	**1,542**	**815**	**727**	**61.3**	**1.85**
W92000004	WALES	29,704	15,191	14,513	53.3	1.54
W06000001	Isle of Anglesey	557	303	254	54.2	1.62
W06000002	Gwynedd	1,016	513	503	46.7	1.38
W06000003	Conwy	1,008	536	472	61.0	1.83
W06000004	**Denbighshire**	**979**	**515**	**464**	**67.7**	**2.02**
W06000005	Flintshire	1,400	706	694	53.6	1.58
W06000006	Wrexham	1,395	706	689	61.8	1.83
W06000023	Powys	1,034	508	526	56.7	1.74
W06000008	Ceredigion	521	272	249	43.5	1.49
W06000009	Pembrokeshire	1,052	545	507	56.3	1.68
W06000010	Carmarthenshire	1,656	820	836	54.9	1.64
W06000011	Swansea	2,255	1,149	1,106	48.1	1.41
W06000012	Neath Port Talbot	1,272	650	622	51.3	1.53
W06000013	Bridgend	1,371	703	668	53.5	1.56
W06000014	Vale of Glamorgan	1,201	593	608	53.4	1.60
W06000015	Cardiff	3,738	1,899	1,839	44.2	1.35
W06000016	Rhondda Cynon Taf	2,481	1,285	1,196	55.1	1.56
W06000024	Merthyr Tydfil	647	320	327	57.9	1.64
W06000018	Caerphilly	1,750	915	835	53.0	1.54
W06000019	Blaenau Gwent	740	395	345	59.3	1.67
W06000020	Torfaen	973	508	465	57.6	1.64
W06000021	Monmouthshire	683	363	320	49.4	1.51
W06000022	Newport	1,975	987	988	67.3	1.90
J99000001	Usual residence outside England and Wales	161	84	77	:	:
S92000003	SCOTLAND	49,863	25,687	24,176	48.4	1.37
S12000033	Aberdeen City	2,260	1,146	1,114	44.3	1.20
S12000034	Aberdeenshire	2,400	1,217	1,183	55.8	1.68
S12000041	**Angus**	**965**	**509**	**456**	**52.3**	**1.6**
S12000035	**Argyll and Bute**	**631**	**330**	**301**	**53.0**	**1.67**
S12000036	City of Edinburgh	4,683	2,452	2,231	36.9	1.01
S12000005	Clackmannanshire	414	208	206	47.9	1.44
S12000006	Dumfries and Galloway	1,153	605	548	51.9	1.54
S12000042	Dundee City	1,417	725	692	42.9	1.20
S12000008	East Ayrshire	1,176	595	581	55.6	1.63
S12000045	East Dunbartonshire	910	471	439	53.9	1.66
S12000010	East Lothian	973	505	468	52.9	1.58
S12000011	East Renfrewshire	808	428	380	51.0	1.63
S12000014	Falkirk	1,460	776	684	50.7	1.50
S12000015	Fife	3,325	1,726	1,599	49.8	1.46
S12000046	Glasgow City	6,553	3,340	3,213	44.0	1.18
S12000017	Highland	1,966	1,033	933	51.6	1.54
S12000018	Inverclyde	615	316	299	46.8	1.39
S12000019	Midlothian	1,057	532	525	62.2	1.77

15.14 Live births by administrative area of usual residence of mother, numbers, sex, General Fertility Rates and Total Fertility Rates, 2019

England and Wales: regions (within England), unitary authorities, counties, districts, London Boroughs
Scotland: council areas, Northern Ireland: local government districts

Area of usual residence		Numbers of live births[1]			Fertility Rate (GFR)[3]	Total Fertility Rate (TFR)[4]
		Total	Male	Female		
S12000020	Moray	816	406	410	52.0	1.54
S12000013	Na h-Eileanan Siar	200	91	109	50.9	1.66
S12000021	North Ayrshire	1,124	577	547	50.1	1.49
S12000044	North Lanarkshire	3,438	1,738	1,700	53.7	1.59
S12000023	Orkney Islands	182	101	81	52.8	1.51
S12000024	Perth and Kinross	1,197	634	563	49.6	1.47
S12000038	Renfrewshire	1,693	879	814	51.8	1.47
S12000026	Scottish Borders	916	482	434	53.5	1.65
S12000027	Shetland Islands	205	99	106	55.4	1.65
S12000028	South Ayrshire	837	426	411	47.9	1.44
S12000029	South Lanarkshire	3,109	1,583	1,526	55.1	1.62
S12000030	Stirling	737	380	357	40.3	1.25
S12000039	West Dunbartonshire	845	455	390	52.7	1.50
S12000040	West Lothian	1,798	922	876	53.0	1.58
N92000002	**NORTHERN IRELAND**[7]	:	:	:	:	:
N09000001	Antrim and Newtownabbey	:	:	:	:	:
N09000011	Ards and North Down	:	:	:	:	:
N09000002	Armagh City, Banbridge and Craigavon	:	:	:	:	:
N09000003	**Belfast**	:	:	:	:	:
N09000004	Causeway Coast and Glens	:	:	:	:	:
N09000005	Derry City and Strabane	:	:	:	:	:
N09000006	Fermanagh and Omagh	:	:	:	:	:
N09000007	Lisburn and Castlereagh	:	:	:	:	:
N09000008	Mid and East Antrim	:	:	:	:	:
N09000009	Mid Ulster	:	:	:	:	:
N09000010	Newry, Mourne and Down	:	:	:	:	:

Source: Office for National Statistics (ONS), National Records of Scotland, Northern Ireland Statistics and Research Agency

1. Figures for England and Wales are based on geography boundaries as of May 2019.
2. All rates have been calculated using the mid-2018 population estimates.
3. General Fertility Rate (GFR) - all live births per 1,000 women aged 15 to 44
4. The Total Fertility Rate (TFR) is the average number of live children that a group of women would bear if they experienced the age-specific fertility rates of the calendar year in question throughout their childbearing lifespan.
   The national TFRs have been calculated using the number of live births by single year of age.
   The sub-national TFRs have been calculated using the number of live births by five year age groups.

5 A birth to a mother whose usual residence is outside England and Wales is included in total figures for "England, Wales and elsewhere " but are excluded from any sub-divisions of England and Wales. The England and Wales and elsewhere figures correspond to figures published at the national level for England and Wales not based on area of usual residence.
6 Due to the low number of births, counts for Isles of Scilly have been combined with those for Cornwall.

15.15 Live births by age of mother and registration type[1], 1985 to 2019

England and Wales

Year	Type of Registration	All ages[2]	Age of mother at birth						
			Under 20	20 to 24	25 to 29	30 to 34	35 to 39	40 to 44	45 and over
		Number of births							
2019	All	640,370	17,720	86,756	173,944	209,905	122,409	27,228	2,390
	Within Marriage or Civil Partnership[1]	329,971	840	17,372	78,113	134,931	80,829	16,426	1,454
	Outside Marriage or Civil Partnership[1]	310,399	16,880	69,384	95,831	74,974	41,580	10,802	936
	Joint Registrations same address	208,693	6,880	41,080	67,219	54,952	30,432	7,544	581
	Joint Registrations different address	68,592	6,241	19,736	20,172	13,394	6,983	1,921	142
	Sole Registrations	33,114	3,759	8,568	8,440	6,628	4,165	1,337	213
2018	All	657,076	18,976	91,095	180,858	212,707	124,567	26,499	2,366
	Within Marriage or Civil Partnership[1]	339,267	920	17,939	82,497	137,741	82,644	16,071	1,452
	Outside Marriage or Civil Partnership[1]	317,809	18,056	73,156	98,361	74,966	41,923	10,428	914
	Joint Registrations same address	214,026	7,308	43,645	68,711	55,166	31,242	7,412	541
	Joint Registrations different address	69,719	6,747	20,548	20,725	13,114	6,646	1,772	167
	Sole Registrations	34,064	4,001	8,963	8,925	6,686	4,035	1,244	206
2017	All	679,106	20,358	97,506	190,028	216,787	125,114	26,956	2,357
	Within Marriage or Civil Partnership[1]	352,270	929	19,099	88,323	142,442	83,644	16,430	1,403
	Outside Marriage or Civil Partnership[1]	326,836	19,429	78,407	101,705	74,345	41,470	10,526	954
	Joint Registrations same address	220,095	7,907	47,493	71,173	54,665	30,819	7,451	587
	Joint Registrations different address	71,538	7,293	21,516	21,288	12,895	6,638	1,749	159
	Sole Registrations	35,203	4,229	9,398	9,244	6,785	4,013	1,326	208
2016	All	696,271	22,465	102,607	196,132	220,129	125,205	27,447	2,286
	Within Marriage or Civil Partnership[1]	364,521	1,089	20,209	94,118	146,682	84,231	16,788	1,404
	Outside Marriage or Civil Partnership[1]	331,750	21,376	82,398	102,014	73,447	40,974	10,659	882
	Joint Registrations same address	223,711	8,815	50,321	71,897	54,122	30,476	7,518	562
	Joint Registrations different address	71,917	7,969	22,445	20,650	12,542	6,352	1,832	127
	Sole Registrations	36,122	4,592	9,632	9,467	6,783	4,146	1,309	193
2015	All	697,852	23,948	108,111	198,183	217,755	120,614	27,065	2,176
	Within Marriage or Civil Partnership[1]	364,628	1,069	21,241	97,465	145,600	81,396	16,554	1,303
	Outside Marriage or Civil Partnership[1]	333,224	22,879	86,870	100,718	72,155	39,218	10,511	873
	Joint Registrations same address	224,151	9,389	53,177	71,038	53,370	29,274	7,355	548
	Joint Registrations different address	72,269	8,627	23,358	20,275	11,985	6,038	1,844	142
	Sole Registrations	36,804	4,863	10,335	9,405	6,800	3,906	1,312	183
2014	All	695,233	25,977	112,615	196,818	215,642	115,171	27,021	1,989
	Within Marriage or Civil Partnership[1]	364,998	1,165	22,873	99,642	145,277	78,293	16,561	1,187
	Outside Marriage or Civil Partnership[1]	330,235	24,812	89,742	97,176	70,365	36,878	10,460	802
	Joint Registrations same address	220,106	10,075	54,581	68,082	51,889	27,543	7,433	503
	Joint Registrations different address	72,350	9,348	24,231	19,555	11,702	5,645	1,721	148
	Sole Registrations	37,779	5,389	10,930	9,539	6,774	3,690	1,306	151
2013	All	698,512	29,136	119,719	196,693	212,306	111,500	27,148	2,010
	Within Marriage or Civil Partnership[1]	367,618	1,272	25,794	102,106	144,376	76,046	16,783	1,241
	Outside Marriage or Civil Partnership[1]	330,894	27,864	93,925	94,587	67,930	35,454	10,365	769
	Joint Registrations same address	218,049	11,220	56,805	66,103	49,922	26,234	7,282	483
	Joint Registrations different address	73,546	10,628	25,440	18,908	11,195	5,499	1,736	140
	Sole Registrations	39,299	6,016	11,680	9,576	6,813	3,721	1,347	146
2012	All	729,674	33,815	132,456	202,370	216,242	114,797	28,019	1,975
	Within Marriage or Civil Partnership[1]	383,189	1,295	29,627	106,555	148,403	78,689	17,380	1,240
	Outside Marriage or Civil Partnership[1]	346,485	32,520	102,829	95,815	67,839	36,108	10,639	735
	Joint Registrations same address	227,337	13,326	62,151	67,031	50,094	26,731	7,528	476
	Joint Registrations different address	77,269	12,327	27,867	18,759	10,872	5,529	1,809	106
	Sole Registrations	41,879	6,867	12,811	10,025	6,873	3,848	1,302	153
2011	All	723,913	36,435	134,946	200,587	207,151	115,444	27,518	1,832
	Within Marriage or Civil Partnership[1]	382,574	1,410	31,785	107,383	143,519	79,951	17,388	1,138
	Outside Marriage or Civil Partnership[1]	341,339	35,025	103,161	93,204	63,632	35,493	10,130	694
	Joint Registrations same address	226,057	14,600	63,287	66,102	47,706	26,688	7,213	461
	Joint Registrations different address	73,464	12,960	26,826	17,379	9,489	5,093	1,603	114
	Sole Registrations	41,818	7,465	13,048	9,723	6,437	3,712	1,314	119

15.15 Live births by age of mother and registration type[1], 1985 to 2019

England and Wales

Year	Type of Registration	All ages[2]	Under 20	20 to 24	25 to 29	30 to 34	35 to 39	40 to 44	45 and over
		Number of births							
2010	All	723,165	40,591	137,312	199,233	202,457	115,841	25,973	1,758
	Within Marriage or Civil Partnership[1]	384,375	1,684	33,955	108,465	141,873	80,846	16,404	1,148
	Outside Marriage or Civil Partnership[1]	338,790	38,907	103,357	90,768	60,584	34,995	9,569	610
	Joint Registrations same address	224,001	16,401	63,816	64,656	45,498	26,453	6,769	408
	Joint Registrations different address	72,297	14,352	26,184	16,393	8,838	4,903	1,525	102
	Sole Registrations	42,492	8,154	13,357	9,719	6,248	3,639	1,275	100
2009	All	706,248	43,243	136,012	194,129	191,600	114,288	25,357	1,619
	Within Marriage or Civil Partnership[1]	380,069	2,334	35,920	108,499	135,802	80,156	16,318	1,040
	Outside Marriage or Civil Partnership[1]	326,179	40,909	100,092	85,630	55,798	34,132	9,039	579
	Joint Registrations same address	214,189	17,200	61,813	60,876	41,831	25,637	6,444	388
	Joint Registrations different address	68,251	14,778	24,376	14,811	7,991	4,790	1,420	85
	Sole Registrations	43,739	8,931	13,903	9,943	5,976	3,705	1,175	106
2008	All	708,711	44,691	135,971	192,960	192,450	116,220	24,991	1,428
	Within Marriage	387,930	2,739	38,239	110,353	138,066	81,602	15,991	940
	Outside Marriage	320,781	41,952	97,732	82,607	54,384	34,618	9,000	488
	Joint Registrations same address	210,076	17,231	59,913	59,104	41,178	26,036	6,289	325
	Joint Registrations different address	65,241	15,161	23,102	13,543	7,257	4,662	1,441	75
	Sole Registrations	45,464	9,560	14,717	9,960	5,949	3,920	1,270	88
2007	All	690,013	44,805	130,784	182,570	191,124	115,380	24,041	1,309
	Within Marriage	384,463	3,087	38,859	106,603	138,157	81,399	15,484	874
	Outside Marriage	305,550	41,718	91,925	75,967	52,967	33,981	8,557	435
	Joint Registrations same address	198,470	17,036	55,904	54,040	39,783	25,383	6,050	274
	Joint Registrations different address	61,379	14,714	21,415	12,204	7,024	4,587	1,359	76
	Sole Registrations	45,701	9,968	14,606	9,723	6,160	4,011	1,148	85
2006	All	669,601	45,509	127,828	172,642	189,407	110,509	22,512	1,194
	Within Marriage	378,225	3,199	40,126	103,348	137,996	78,269	14,511	776
	Outside Marriage	291,376	42,310	87,702	69,294	51,411	32,240	8,001	418
	Joint Registrations same address	185,461	17,061	52,162	48,474	38,133	23,897	5,469	265
	Joint Registrations different address	60,460	14,870	20,755	11,651	7,159	4,578	1,375	72
	Sole Registrations	45,455	10,379	14,785	9,169	6,119	3,765	1,157	81
2005	All	645,835	44,830	122,145	164,348	188,153	104,113	21,155	1,091
	Within Marriage	369,330	3,654	40,010	99,957	137,401	73,810	13,760	738
	Outside Marriage	276,505	41,176	82,135	64,391	50,752	30,303	7,395	353
	Joint Registrations same address	175,555	16,316	48,755	45,165	37,764	22,265	5,057	233
	Joint Registrations different address	55,780	14,108	18,909	10,320	6,801	4,289	1,287	66
	Sole Registrations	45,170	10,752	14,471	8,906	6,187	3,749	1,051	54
2004	All	639,721	45,094	121,072	159,984	190,550	102,228	19,884	909
	Within Marriage	369,997	4,063	41,285	98,539	139,838	72,555	13,098	619
	Outside Marriage	269,724	41,031	79,787	61,445	50,712	29,673	6,786	290
	Joint Registrations same address	171,498	16,262	47,793	43,038	37,820	21,758	4,648	179
	Joint Registrations different address	52,854	13,608	17,628	9,620	6,713	4,133	1,096	56
	Sole Registrations	45,372	11,161	14,366	8,787	6,179	3,782	1,042	55
2003	All	621,469	44,236	116,622	156,931	187,214	97,386	18,205	875
	Within Marriage	364,244	4,338	40,887	98,694	138,002	69,595	12,113	615
	Outside Marriage	257,225	39,898	75,735	58,237	49,212	27,791	6,092	260
	Joint Registrations same address	163,374	16,000	45,225	40,867	36,630	20,335	4,151	166
	Joint Registrations different address	48,976	12,706	16,076	8,815	6,488	3,831	1,014	46
	Sole Registrations	44,875	11,192	14,434	8,555	6,094	3,625	927	48
2002	All	596,122	43,467	110,959	153,379	180,532	90,449	16,441	895
	Within Marriage	354,090	4,582	40,712	97,583	134,093	65,369	11,110	641
	Outside Marriage	242,032	38,885	70,247	55,796	46,439	25,080	5,331	254
	Joint Registrations same address	154,086	15,824	42,315	39,554	34,326	18,236	3,656	175
	Joint Registrations different address	44,817	11,832	14,333	8,109	6,164	3,471	866	42
	Sole Registrations	43,129	11,229	13,599	8,133	5,949	3,373	809	37

15.15 Live births by age of mother and registration type[1], 1985 to 2019

England and Wales

Year	Type of Registration	All ages[2]	Under 20	20 to 24	25 to 29	30 to 34	35 to 39	40 to 44	45 and over
		Number of births							
2001	All	594,634	44,189	108,844	159,926	178,920	86,495	15,499	761
	Within Marriage	356,548	4,640	40,736	103,131	133,710	63,202	10,582	547
	Outside Marriage	238,086	39,549	68,108	56,795	45,210	23,293	4,917	214
	Joint Registrations same address	150,421	16,215	40,843	39,797	33,306	16,790	3,341	129
	Joint Registrations different address	43,921	11,665	13,682	8,416	6,029	3,290	800	39
	Sole Registrations	43,744	11,669	13,583	8,582	5,875	3,213	776	46
2000	All	604,441	45,846	107,741	170,701	180,113	84,974	14,403	663
	Within Marriage	365,836	4,742	40,262	111,606	136,165	62,671	9,910	480
	Outside Marriage	238,605	41,104	67,479	59,095	43,948	22,303	4,493	183
	Joint Registrations same address	149,510	17,011	40,450	41,236	31,795	15,836	3,055	127
	Joint Registrations different address	43,322	11,634	13,110	8,646	6,037	3,158	706	31
	Sole Registrations	45,773	12,459	13,919	9,213	6,116	3,309	732	25
1999	All	621,872	48,375	110,722	181,931	185,311	81,281	13,617	635
	Within Marriage	379,983	5,333	43,190	120,716	140,330	60,470	9,466	478
	Outside Marriage	241,889	43,042	67,532	61,215	44,981	20,811	4,151	157
	Joint Registrations same address	149,584	17,833	40,190	42,126	32,152	14,455	2,725	103
	Joint Registrations different address	44,102	12,015	12,865	9,153	6,214	3,135	695	25
	Sole Registrations	48,203	13,194	14,477	9,936	6,615	3,221	731	29
1998	All	635,901	48,285	113,537	193,144	188,499	78,881	12,980	575
	Within Marriage	395,290	5,278	45,724	130,747	144,599	59,320	9,189	433
	Outside Marriage	240,611	43,007	67,813	62,397	43,900	19,561	3,791	142
	Joint Registrations same address	146,521	17,589	39,818	42,212	30,938	16,410	3,118	114
	Joint Registrations different address	44,130	11,588	13,157	9,513	6,194			
	Sole Registrations	49,960	13,830	14,838	10,672	6,768	3,151	673	28
1997	All	643,095	46,372	118,589	202,792	187,528	74,900	12,332	582
	Within Marriage	404,873	5,233	49,068	139,383	145,293	56,671	8,797	428
	Outside Marriage	238,222	41,139	69,521	63,409	42,235	18,229	3,535	154
	Joint Registrations same address	141,740	16,551	39,784	42,020	28,715	15,179	2,860	122
	Joint Registrations different address	45,900	11,365	14,147	10,374	6,523			
	Sole Registrations	50,582	13,223	15,590	11,015	6,997	3,050	675	32
1996	All	649,485	44,667	125,732	211,103	186,377	69,503	11,516	587
	Within Marriage	416,822	5,365	54,651	148,770	145,898	53,265	8,421	452
	Outside Marriage	232,663	39,302	71,081	62,333	40,479	16,238	3,095	135
	Joint Registrations same address	135,282	15,410	39,978	40,384	26,875	13,347	2,517	107
	Joint Registrations different address	46,365	10,946	14,858	10,599	6,626			
	Sole Registrations	51,016	12,946	16,245	11,350	6,978	2,891	578	28
1995	All	648,138	41,938	130,744	217,418	181,202	65,517	10,779	540
	Within Marriage	428,189	5,623	61,029	157,855	144,200	51,129	7,944	409
	Outside Marriage	219,949	36,315	69,715	59,563	37,002	14,388	2,835	131
	Joint Registrations same address	127,789	14,424	39,274	38,376	24,376	11,859	2,335	99
	Joint Registrations different address	44,244	10,011	14,815	10,323	6,141			
	Sole Registrations	47,916	11,880	15,626	10,864	6,485	2,529	500	32
1994	All	664,726	42,026	140,240	229,102	179,568	63,061	10,241	488
	Within Marriage	449,190	6,099	69,227	170,605	145,563	49,668	7,662	366
	Outside Marriage	215,536	35,927	71,013	58,497	34,005	13,393	2,579	122
	Joint Registrations same address	123,874	14,168	39,827	37,168	22,288	10,892	2,084	97
	Joint Registrations different address	42,632	9,752	14,778	9,939	5,513			
	Sole Registrations	49,030	12,007	16,408	11,390	6,204	2,501	495	25
1993	All	673,467	45,121	151,975	235,961	171,061	58,824	9,986	539
	Within Marriage	456,919	6,875	76,950	178,456	139,671	46,919	7,621	427
	Outside Marriage	216,548	38,246	75,025	57,505	31,390	11,905	2,365	112
	Joint Registrations same address	118,758	14,134	40,168	35,307	20,084	9,569	1,882	85
	Joint Registrations different address	47,548	11,577	17,381	10,780	5,339			
	Sole Registrations	50,242	12,535	17,476	11,418	5,967	2,336	483	27

15.15 Live births by age of mother and registration type[1], 1985 to 2019

England and Wales

Year	Type of Registration	All ages[2]	Under 20	20 to 24	25 to 29	30 to 34	35 to 39	40 to 44	45 and over
		Number of births							
1992	All	689,656	47,861	163,311	244,798	166,839	56,650	9,696	501
	Within Marriage	474,431	7,787	86,220	188,928	137,904	45,733	7,456	403
	Outside Marriage	215,225	40,074	77,091	55,870	28,935	10,917	2,240	98
	Joint Registrations same address	119,239	15,236	42,063	34,756	18,673	8,784	1,811	78
	Joint Registrations different address	44,514	11,381	16,658	9,693	4,620			
	Sole Registrations	51,472	13,457	18,370	11,421	5,642	2,133	429	20
1991	All	699,217	52,396	173,356	248,727	161,259	53,644	9,316	519
	Within Marriage	487,923	8,948	95,605	196,281	135,542	43,810	7,294	443
	Outside Marriage	211,294	43,448	77,751	52,446	25,717	9,834	2,022	76
	Joint Registrations same address	115,298	16,351	42,245	32,532	16,468	7,861	1,594	60
	Joint Registrations different address	41,865	11,848	15,835	8,518	3,851			
	Sole Registrations	54,131	15,249	19,671	11,396	5,398	1,973	428	16
1990	All	706,140	55,541	180,136	252,577	156,264	51,905	9,220	497
	Within Marriage	506,141	10,958	106,188	204,701	133,384	43,179	7,302	429
	Outside Marriage	199,999	44,583	73,948	47,876	22,880	8,726	1,918	68
	Joint Registrations same address	106,001	16,311	39,062	29,181	14,585	6,793	1,505	55
	Joint Registrations different address	39,167	12,081	14,751	7,555	3,289			
	Sole Registrations	54,831	16,191	20,135	11,140	5,006	1,933	413	13
1989	All	687,725	55,543	185,239	242,822	145,320	49,465	8,845	491
	Within Marriage	501,921	12,027	114,456	200,961	125,439	41,528	7,079	431
	Outside Marriage	185,804	43,516	70,783	41,861	19,881	7,937	1,766	60
	Joint Registrations same address	95,858	15,686	36,582	24,859	12,543	6,156	1,341	49
	Joint Registrations different address	36,409	11,688	14,022	6,603	2,738			
	Sole Registrations	53,537	16,142	20,179	10,399	4,600	1,781	425	11
1988	All	693,577	58,741	193,726	243,460	140,974	47,649	8,520	507
	Within Marriage	516,225	14,099	125,575	205,292	123,384	40,400	7,025	450
	Outside Marriage	177,352	44,642	68,151	38,168	17,590	7,249	1,495	57
	Joint Registrations same address	87,601	15,304	33,994	22,070	10,765	5,607	1,159	44
	Joint Registrations different address	35,807	12,240	13,807	5,913	2,505			
	Sole Registrations	53,944	17,098	20,350	10,185	4,320	1,642	336	13
1987	All	681,511	57,545	193,232	238,929	136,558	46,604	8,112	531
	Within Marriage	523,080	15,588	132,809	206,036	121,252	40,159	6,751	485
	Outside Marriage	158,431	41,957	60,423	32,893	15,306	6,445	1,361	46
	Joint Registrations same address	75,572	13,808	29,114	18,671	9,210	4,836	1,026	31
	Joint Registrations different address	32,385	11,362	12,365	5,313	2,221			
	Sole Registrations	50,474	16,787	18,944	8,909	3,875	1,609	335	15
1986	All	661,018	57,406	192,064	229,035	129,487	45,465	7,033	528
	Within Marriage	519,673	17,793	137,985	201,323	116,369	39,753	5,959	491
	Outside Marriage	141,345	39,613	54,079	27,712	13,118	5,712	1,074	37
	Joint Registrations same address	65,844	12,908	25,760	15,300	7,849	4,233	768	26
	Joint Registrations different address	27,679	10,326	10,397	4,166	1,790			
	Sole Registrations	47,822	16,379	17,922	8,246	3,479	1,479	306	11
1985	All	656,417	56,929	193,958	227,486	126,185	44,393	6,882	584
	Within Marriage	530,167	20,057	146,262	203,272	114,862	39,293	5,883	538
	Outside Marriage	126,250	36,872	47,696	24,214	11,323	5,100	999	46
	Joint Registrations	81,792	21,000	31,256	16,856	8,177	3,736	734	33
	Sole Registrations	44,458	15,872	16,440	7,358	3,146	1,364	265	13

Source: Office for National Statistics

1 Live births registered to a same sex couple in a marriage or civil partnership (1,011 in 2016) are included with marital live births while live births registered to a same sex couple outside a marriage or civil partnership (393 in 2016) are included with live births outside marriage.

2 Imputation of missing mothers ages was discontinued in March 2018. For 2018 births data onwards, the records where mother's age is missing are included in the counts for 'all ages', but excluded from any age breakdowns. This means the sum of age groups will not equal all ages. For more information please see the user guide to birth statistics (https://www.ons.gov.uk/peoplepopulationandcommunity/ birthsdeathsandmarriages/livebirths/methodologies/userguidetobirthstatistics).

15.16 Legal abortions: countries of Great Britain by
(i) age, (ii) gestation weeks, (iii) procedure, (iv) parity, (v) previous abortions, (vi) grounds and (vii) principal medical condition for abortions performed under ground E, 2019

Country of abortion

numbers and percentages

	England & Wales		Scotland		Great Britain	
All legal abortions	**209,519**	*100*	**13,583**	*100*	**223,102**	*100*
(i) Age						
Under 16	1,357	*1*	135	*1*	1,492	*1*
16-17	6,201	*3*	531	*4*	6,732	*3*
18-19	15,859	*8*	1,168	*9*	17,027	*8*
20-24	54,758	*26*	3,929	*29*	58,687	*26*
25-29	52,296	*25*	3,254	*24*	55,550	*25*
30-34	42,003	*20*	2,460	*18*	44,463	*20*
35+	37,045	*18*	2,106	*16*	39,151	*18*
(ii) Gestation weeks						
3 - 9	172,253	*82*	11,297	*83*	183,550	*82*
10 - 12	19,294	*9*	1,473	*11*	20,767	*9*
13 - 19	14,351	*7*	759	*6*	15,110	*7*
20 and over	3,621	*2*	54	*0*	3,675	*2*
(iii) Procedure						
Surgical	56,785	*27*	1,671	*12*	58,456	*26*
Medical	152,734	*73*	11,912	*88*	164,646	*74*
(iv) Parity (number of previous pregnancies resulting in live or stillbirth)						
0	93,407	*45*	6,433	*47*	99,840	*45*
1+	116,112	*55*	7,148	*53*	123,260	*55*
Not stated	0	*0*	2	*0*	2	*0*
(v) Number of previous pregnancies resulting in abortion under the Act						
0	125,507	*60*	9,003	*66*	134,510	*60*
1+	84,012	*40*	4,580	*34*	88,592	*40*
(vi) Grounds [1]						
A (alone or with B, C or D) or F or G	129	*0*	..	..	..	..
B (alone or with C or D)	54	*0*	..	..	..	..
C (alone)	204,965	*98*	13,363	*98*	218,328	*98*
D (alone or with C)	1,046	*0*	7	*0*	1,053	*0*
E (alone or with A, B, C or D)	3,325	*2*	211	*2*	3,536	*2*
(vii) Total mentions of medical conditions for abortions performed under ground E [2]						
Total Ground E	4,051	*100*	215	*100*	4,266	*100*
The nervous system (Q00 - Q07)	916	*23*	59	*27*	975	*23*
Other congenital malformations (Q10-Q89)	1,218	*30*	47	*22*	1,265	*30*
Chromosomal abnormalities (Q90 - Q99)	1,181	*29*	61	*28*	1,242	*29*
Other	736	*18*	48	*22*	784	*18*

Source: ISD Scotland, Department of Health ..

Adhering to ISD Statistical Disclosure Control Protocol.
. Not available

[1] Some notifications record more than one Statutory Ground, therefore totals may not match with the numbers released by ISD Scotland.

[2] The total mentions figures show abortions where more than one medical condition is reported. Totals therefore do not equal the number of abortions performed under Ground E. There were 14 Ground E forms where the medical condition was not given. These are currently being followed up

Percentages are rounded and may not add up to 100

15.17 Death rates[1] per 1,000 population: by age groups and sex, 2019

England and Wales

Age	Total	Male	Female
All ages	**9.23**	**10.76**	**7.97**
Aged under 1	3.90	4.26	3.52
Aged 1 to 4	0.13	0.13	0.14
Aged 5 to 9	0.07	0.07	0.07
Aged 10-14	0.09	0.10	0.07
Aged 15-19	0.22	0.27	0.16
Aged 20-24	0.37	0.51	0.21
Aged 25-29	0.45	0.62	0.28
Aged 30-34	0.62	0.81	0.44
Aged 35-39	0.90	1.14	0.67
Aged 40-44	1.31	1.60	1.03
Aged 45-49	2.09	2.55	1.64
Aged 50-54	3.11	3.80	2.44
Aged 55-59	4.64	5.63	3.67
Aged 60-64	7.29	8.80	5.84
Aged 65-69	11.47	14.08	9.02
Aged 70-74	18.09	21.78	14.71
Aged 75-79	31.24	37.38	25.92
Aged 80-84	56.17	66.16	48.29
Aged 85-89	103.03	119.15	92.33
Aged 90 and over	208.01	224.24	200.33

Source: Office for National Statistics (from NOMIS)

1. Death rates are age-standardised mortality rates per 1,000 population which are standardised to the 2013 European Standard Population. Age-standardised rates are used to allow comparison between populations which may contain different proportions of people of different ages.

15.18 Stillbirths[1,2] and infant death[3] rates: age at death, 1921 to 2019

England and Wales

Infant mortality per 1,000 live births[3] at various ages

Stillbirths[2] and infant deaths per 1,000 total births

Year	Under 1 year	Neonatal mortality Under 4 weeks	Early neonatal Under 1 week	Under 1 day	1 day & under 1 week	Late neo-natal and under 4 weeks	Postneonatal mortality 4 weeks and under 1 year	4 weeks and under 3 months	3 months and under 6 months	6 months and under 1 year	Still-births	Stillbirths plus deaths under 1 week	Stillbirths plus deaths under 4 weeks	Stillbirths plus deaths under 1 year
2019	3.7	2.8	2.2	1.6	0.6	0.6	1.0	0.5	0.2	0.2	3.9	6.1	6.7	7.6
2018	3.8	2.8	2.2	1.6	0.6	0.6	1.0	0.5	0.2	0.2	4.1	6.3	6.8	7.8
2017	3.9	2.8	2.2	1.6	0.6	0.6	1.1	0.5	0.3	0.3	4.2	6.4	7.0	8.1
2016	3.8	2.7	2.2	1.6	0.6	0.6	1.1	0.5	0.3	0.2	4.4	6.6	7.2	8.2
2015	3.7	2.6	2.1	1.5	0.6	0.6	1.1	0.5	0.3	0.3	4.5	6.5	7.1	8.2
2014	3.6	2.5	2.0	1.3	0.6	0.6	1.1	0.5	0.3	0.2	4.7	6.6	7.2	8.3
2013	3.8	2.7	2.0	1.4	0.6	0.6	1.2	0.6	0.3	0.3	4.7	6.7	7.3	8.5
2012	4.0	2.8	2.2	1.5	0.6	0.6	1.2	0.6	0.3	0.3	4.9	7.0	7.6	8.8
2011	4.2	2.9	2.3	1.5	0.7	0.7	1.2	0.6	0.3	0.3	5.2	7.5	8.2	9.4
2010	4.3	2.9	2.3	1.5	0.8	0.6	1.3	0.7	0.3	0.3	5.1	7.4	8.0	9.3
2009	4.5	3.1	2.4	1.5	0.9	0.7	1.4	0.7	0.4	0.3	5.2	7.6	8.3	9.7
2008	4.6	3.2	2.4	1.6	0.8	0.7	1.4	0.7	0.4	0.3	5.1	7.5	8.3	9.7
2007	4.7	3.3	2.5	1.6	0.9	0.7	1.5	0.7	0.4	0.4	5.2	7.7	8.4	9.9
2006	5.0	3.5	2.6	1.7	0.9	0.9	1.5	0.7	0.4	0.3	5.4	8.0	8.8	10.3
2005	5.0	3.4	2.6	1.7	1.0	0.8	1.6	0.8	0.5	0.4	5.4	8.0	8.8	10.4
2004	5.0	3.5	2.7	1.7	1.0	0.8	1.6	0.8	0.4	0.4	5.7	8.4	9.2	10.7
2003	5.3	3.6	2.8	1.8	1.0	0.8	1.7	0.8	0.4	0.4	5.8	8.6	9.4	11.1
2002	5.2	3.6	2.7	1.7	1.0	1.0	1.7	0.8	0.0	0.0	5.6	8.0	9.0	11.0
2001	5.4	3.6	2.7	1.7	1.0	0.9	1.9	0.8	0.5	0.5	5.3	8.0	8.9	10.7
2000	5.6	3.9	2.9	1.7	1.2	1.0	1.7	0.8	0.5	0.4	5.3	8.2	9.1	10.8
1999	5.8	3.9	2.9	1.7	1.2	1.0	1.9	0.9	0.6	0.5	5.3	8.2	9.2	11.1
1998	5.7	3.8	2.9	1.7	1.2	0.9	1.9	0.9	0.6	0.4	5.3	8.2	9.1	11.0
1997	5.9	3.9	3.0	1.8	1.2	0.9	2.0	0.9	0.6	0.5	5.3	8.3	9.2	11.2
1996	6.1	4.1	3.2	1.9	1.3	0.9	2.0	0.9	0.6	0.5	5.4	8.6	9.5	11.5
1995	6.1	4.2	3.2	1.8	1.5	0.9	2.0	0.9	0.6	0.5	5.5	8.7	9.7	11.6
1994	6.2	4.1	3.2	1.9	1.4	0.9	2.1	0.8	0.7	0.6	5.7	8.9	9.8	11.9
1993	6.3	4.2	3.2	1.9	1.3	0.9	2.1	0.9	0.7	0.6	5.7	8.9	9.8	12.0
1992	6.6	4.3	3.3	2.0	1.4	1.0	2.3	1.0	0.8	0.6	4.3	7.6	8.5	10.8
1991	7.4	4.4	3.4	2.0	1.4	0.9	3.0	1.2	1.0	0.7	4.6	8.0	9.0	12.0
1990	7.9	4.6	3.5	2.0	1.5	1.0	3.3	1.3	1.2	0.7	4.6	8.1	9.1	12.4
1989	8.4	4.8	3.7	2.1	1.6	1.1	3.7	1.6	1.3	0.8	4.7	8.3	9.4	13.1
1988	9.0	4.9	3.9	2.2	1.7	1.0	4.1	1.7	1.5	0.9	4.9	8.7	9.8	13.8
1987	9.2	5.1	3.9	2.3	1.6	1.1	4.1	1.8	1.5	0.9	5.0	8.9	10.0	14.2
1986	9.6	5.3	4.3	2.4	1.8	1.0	4.3	1.8	1.5	1.0	5.3	9.6	10.6	14.8
1985	9.4	5.4	4.3	2.5	1.9	1.0	4.0	1.7	1.4	0.9	5.5	9.8	10.9	14.8
1984	9.5	5.6	4.4	2.6	1.9	1.1	3.9	1.6	1.3	0.9	5.7	10.1	11.2	15.1
1983	10.1	5.9	4.7	2.6	2.1	1.2	4.3	1.9	1.5	0.9	5.7	10.4	11.6	15.8
1982	10.8	6.3	5.0	2.8	2.2	1.2	4.6	1.9	1.6	1.1	6.3	11.3	12.5	17.0
1981	11.1	6.7	5.3	2.9	2.3	1.4	4.4	1.8	1.6	1.0	6.6	11.8	13.2	17.6
1980	12.0	7.7	6.2	3.4	2.8	1.5	4.4	1.8	1.5	1.1	7.2	13.3	14.8	19.2
1979	12.8	8.2	6.8	3.7	3.0	1.5	4.6	1.9	1.7	1.0	8.0	14.7	16.1	20.7
1978	13.2	8.7	7.1	3.7	3.4	1.6	4.5	1.9	1.6	1.0	8.5	15.5	17.1	21.6
1977	13.8	9.3	7.6	4.2	3.5	1.6	4.5	1.9	1.6	1.1	9.4	17.0	18.6	23.0
1976	14.3	9.7	8.2	4.7	3.5	1.5	4.6	1.9	1.6	1.1	9.7	17.7	19.3	23.8
1975	15.7	10.7	9.1	5.0	4.1	1.7	5.0	2.2	1.7	1.1	10.3	19.3	20.9	25.9
1974	16.3	11.0	9.4	5.2	4.2	1.7	5.3	2.3	1.9	1.1	11.1	20.4	22.0	27.3
1973	16.9	11.1	9.5	5.5	4.0	1.6	5.7	2.5	1.9	1.3	11.6	21.0	22.6	28.3
1972	17.2	11.5	9.8	5.8	4.1	1.7	5.7	2.4	2.0	1.4	12.0	21.7	23.4	29.0
1971	17.5	11.6	9.9	6.0	3.9	1.7	5.9	2.6	2.0	1.3	12.5	22.3	24.0	29.8

592

15.18 Stillbirths[1,2] and infant death[3] rates: age at death, 1921 to 2019

England and Wales

	Infant mortality per 1,000 live births[3] at various ages										Stillbirths[2] and infant deaths per 1,000 total births			
	Under 1 year	Neonatal mortality					Postneonatal mortality				Still-births	Stillbirths plus deaths under 1 week	Stillbirths plus deaths under 4 weeks	Stillbirths plus deaths under 1 year
Year		Under 4 weeks	Early neonatal			Late neo-natal	4 weeks and under 1 year	4 weeks and under 3 months	3 months and under 6 months	6 months and under 1 year				
			Under 1 week	Under 1 day	1 day & under 1 week	and under 4 weeks								
1970	18.2	12.3	10.6	6.3	4.3	1.7	5.9	2.6	2.0	1.3	13.0	23.5	25.2	31.0
1969	18.0	12.0	10.3	6.0	4.3	1.7	6.0	2.5	2.1	1.5	13.2	23.4	25.1	31.0
1968	18.3	12.4	10.6	6.3	4.3	1.8	5.9	2.4	2.1	1.5	14.3	24.7	26.4	32.3
1967	18.3	12.5	10.7	6.3	4.4	1.8	5.8	2.4	2.0	1.4	14.8	25.4	27.2	32.9
1966	19.0	12.9	11.1	6.5	4.6	1.7	6.1	2.5	2.0	1.6	15.3	26.3	28.0	34.1
1965	19.0	13.0	11.3	6.6	4.7	1.7	6.0	2.4	2.1	1.6	15.8	26.9	28.6	34.5
1964	19.9	13.8	12.0	7.1	4.9	1.8	6.1	2.4	2.1	1.6	16.3	28.2	29.9	35.9
1963	21.1	14.3	12.3	7.2	5.1	2.0	6.9	2.7	2.4	1.8	17.2	29.3	31.3	38.0
1962	21.7	15.1	13.0	7.4	5.6	2.1	6.6	2.5	2.3	1.8	18.1	30.8	32.9	39.4
1961	21.4	15.3	13.3	7.6	5.7	2.1	6.1	2.4	2.0	1.7	19.0	32.0	34.1	40.0
1960	21.8	15.5	13.3	7.5	5.8	2.2	6.3	2.5	2.1	1.6	19.8	32.8	35.0	41.1
1959	22.2	15.9	13.6	7.6	6.0	2.3	6.3	2.4	2.1	1.8	20.8	34.1	36.3	42.6
1958	22.5	16.2	13.8	7.5	6.3	2.4	6.4	2.6	2.1	1.7	21.5	35.0	37.3	43.6
1957	23.1	16.5	14.1	7.6	6.5	2.4	6.7	2.6	2.1	1.9	22.5	36.2	38.5	45.1
1956	23.7	16.8	14.2	7.4	6.8	2.6	6.9	2.7	2.3	1.8	22.9	36.7	39.3	46.0
1955	24.9	17.3	14.6	7.6	7.0	2.6	7.6	2.9	2.6	2.1	23.2	37.4	40.0	47.5
1954	25.4	17.7	14.9	7.6	7.4	2.8	7.7	3.0	2.6	2.1	23.5	38.1	40.8	48.4
1953	26.8	17.7	14.8	7.4	7.4	2.9	9.1	3.4	3.0	2.7	22.4	36.9	39.7	48.6
1952	27.6	18.3	15.2	7.6	7.6	3.2	9.3	3.7	3.0	2.6	22.7	37.5	40.6	49.6
1951	29.7	18.8	15.5	7.5	8.0	3.3	10.9	4.1	3.6	3.2	23.0	38.2	41.5	52.2
1950	29.6	18.5	15.2	7.2	8.0	3.3	11.1	4.3	3.7	3.1	22.6	37.4	40.7	51.7
1949	32.4	19.3	15.6	7.6	8.0	3.7	13.0	4.8	4.4	3.8	22.7	38.0	41.5	54.6
1948	33.9	19.7	15.6	7.8	7.9	4.1	14.2	5.5	4.8	3.9	23.2	38.5	42.5	56.8
1947	41.4	22.7	16.5	7.8	8.7	6.2	18.6	6.9	6.0	5.7	24.1	40.3	46.4	65.0
1946	42.9	24.5	17.8	8.7	9.1	6.7	18.4	7.1	6.1	5.2	27.2	44.3	50.7	66.9
1945	46.0	24.8	18.0	9.0	9.0	6.8	21.3	8.2	7.0	6.1	27.6	45.2	51.8	73.4
1944	45.4	24.4	17.5	8.8	8.8	6.9	21.1	8.0	7.0	6.1	27.6	44.5	51.1	70.9
1943	49.1	25.2	18.3	9.1	9.2	6.9	23.9	8.8	7.8	7.3	30.1	47.9	54.6	77.5
1942	50.6	27.2	19.6	9.6	10.0	7.7	23.4	8.7	7.5	7.2	33.2	52.1	59.4	81.1
1941	60.0	29.0	20.7	10.1	10.6	8.3	31.1	11.3	9.7	10.1	34.8	54.7	62.7	92.4
1940	56.8	29.6	21.3	9.8	11.5	8.3	27.2	9.3	8.2	9.7	37.2	57.7	65.7	92.5
1939	50.6	28.3	21.2	10.3	10.9	7.1	22.2	7.9	7.0	7.3	38.1	58.5	65.3	86.9
1938	52.8	28.3	21.1	10.3	10.8	7.1	24.5	8.2	7.3	9.0	38.3	58.6	65.5	88.9
1937	57.7	29.7	22.0	10.8	11.2	7.8	28.0	9.4	8.3	10.3	39.0	60.2	67.6	94.4
1936	58.7	30.2	21.9	10.7	11.3	8.2	28.5	9.3	8.3	10.9	39.7	60.8	68.7	95.9
1935	57.0	30.4	22.0	10.7	11.3	8.4	26.6	9.1	7.7	9.8	40.7	61.9	69.9	95.4
1934	59.3	31.4	22.7	10.9	11.8	8.7	27.9	8.9	7.7	11.3	40.5	62.2	70.5	96.7
1933	62.7	32.1	22.9	11.0	11.8	9.3	30.6	9.8	8.6	12.2	41.4	63.4	72.3	102.5
1932	64.5	31.5	22.4	10.6	11.8	9.2	33.0	10.8	9.0	13.2	41.3	62.8	71.6	103.7
1931	65.7	31.5	22.1	10.4	11.7	9.5	34.2	10.8	9.2	14.2	40.9	62.1	71.2	104.5
1930	60.0	30.9	22.0	10.4	11.6	8.9	29.1	9.6	7.8	11.6	40.8	61.9	70.4	98.3
1929	74.4	32.8	22.3	10.4	11.9	10.6	41.5	11.6	10.7	19.3	40.0	61.4	71.6	111.4
1928	65.1	31.1	21.6	10.4	11.2	9.5	34.0	10.7	9.2	14.1	40.1	60.8	69.9	102.6
1927	69.7	32.3	22.2	10.6	11.6	10.1	37.4	10.7	9.7	16.9	38.8	59.6	69.3	105.3
1926	70.2	31.9	21.3	10.0	11.3	10.6	38.3	11.6	10.4	16.3	:	:	:	:
1925	75.0	32.3	21.2	10.1	11.1	11.1	42.7	12.6	11.3	18.8	:	:	:	:
1924	75.1	33.1	21.8	10.6	11.2	11.3	42.0	12.5	10.9	18.6	:	:	:	:
1923	69.4	31.9	21.1	10.2	10.9	10.8	37.5	11.3	10.0	16.1	:	:	:	:
1922	77.1	34.1	22.0	10.4	11.6	12.1	43.0	12.7	11.0	19.3	:	:	:	:
1921	82.8	35.3	22.4	10.8	11.6	12.9	47.5	14.8	14.0	18.6	:	:	:	:

15.18 Stillbirths[1,2] and infant death[3] rates: age at death, 1921 to 2019

Source: Office for National Statistics

1 Registration of stillbirths commenced on 1 July 1927. Annual figures for 1927 are estimated.

2 From 1927 to 30 September 1992 stillbirths relate to fetal deaths at or over 28 weeks gestation, and from 1 October 1992 at or over 24 weeks gestation.

3 Infant deaths are based on the live births occurring in the year, except in the years 1931-56 when they were based on related live births - that is, the combined live births of the associated and preceding years to which they relate.

For more information see: User guide to child and infant mortality statistics:
https://www.ons.gov.uk/peoplepopulationandcommunity/birthsdeathsandmarriages/deaths/methodologies/userguidetochildmortalitystatistics

15.19 National life tables

Period expectation of life based on data for the years 2017-2019

	United Kingdom					England and Wales			
Age	Males		Females		Age	Males		Females	
x	l_x	e_x	l_x	e_x	x	l_x	e_x	l_x	e_x
0	100000.0	79.37	100000.0	83.06	0	100000.0	79.61	100000.0	83.27
5	99516.3	74.75	99596.0	78.39	5	99511.5	75.00	99592.8	78.61
10	99479.7	69.78	99561.5	73.42	10	99474.4	70.02	99558.4	73.64
15	99428.7	64.81	99524.6	68.45	15	99423.9	65.06	99523.1	68.66
20	99273.1	59.91	99440.5	63.50	20	99274.5	60.15	99441.9	63.72
25	99017.1	55.06	99333.8	58.57	25	99030.1	55.29	99339.9	58.78
30	98698.0	50.22	99190.6	53.65	30	98732.6	50.45	99201.0	53.86
35	98271.7	45.43	98966.8	48.76	35	98333.7	45.64	98985.8	48.97
40	97665.1	40.70	98611.5	43.93	40	97766.6	40.89	98650.7	44.13
45	96778.4	36.05	98075.4	39.15	45	96932.8	36.22	98140.4	39.34
50	95472.0	31.50	97247.8	34.46	50	95681.9	31.66	97335.8	34.65
55	93625.3	27.07	96019.5	29.87	55	93884.7	27.22	96147.2	30.04
60	90911.1	22.80	94171.2	25.41	60	91221.7	22.93	94352.9	25.56
65	86782.6	18.76	91307.1	21.12	65	87168.0	18.88	91562.8	21.26
70	80643.8	14.98	87045.5	17.02	70	81118.5	15.09	87404.9	17.15
75	71820.0	11.50	80501.7	13.19	75	72406.1	11.58	80995.3	13.29
80	58739.2	8.47	69955.9	9.77	80	59458.7	8.53	70639.4	9.84
85	41259.6	5.96	54046.6	6.86	85	41996.6	5.99	54839.0	6.91
90	21665.7	4.10	32805.1	4.65	90	22194.6	4.12	33510.8	4.68
95	7190.1	2.75	13050.8	3.10	95	7392.1	2.78	13424.6	3.14
100	1110.6	1.95	2663	2.1	100	1154.9	2.04	2802.8	2.16

	Scotland					Northern Ireland			
Age	Males		Females		Age	Males		Females	
x	l_x	e_x	l_x	e_x	x	l_x	e_x	l_x	e_x
0	100000.0	77.13	100000.0	81.13	0	100000.0	78.74	100000.0	82.54
5	99583.3	72.45	99664.4	76.40	5	99503.1	74.13	99535.0	77.93
10	99555.3	67.47	99630.4	71.43	10	99460.2	69.16	99495.6	72.96
15	99500.7	62.50	99574.4	66.46	15	99406.5	64.20	99458.9	67.98
20	99284.3	57.63	99461.6	61.54	20	99222.6	59.31	99363.0	63.05
25	98940.3	52.82	99318.2	56.62	25	98857.0	54.52	99218.0	58.13
30	98461.8	48.07	99131.7	51.72	30	98314.2	49.81	99070.2	53.22
35	97771.4	43.39	98834.3	46.87	35	97775.7	45.07	98790.5	48.36
40	96766.7	38.81	98244.6	42.13	40	97034.6	40.39	98463.3	43.51
45	95294.8	34.37	97411.9	37.47	45	96132.5	35.75	97967.3	38.72
50	93388.6	30.02	96359.7	32.85	50	94838.5	31.20	97098.1	34.04
55	91070.2	25.72	94779.6	28.36	55	92911.2	26.79	95743.7	29.49
60	87879.2	21.55	92469.8	24.00	60	90182.6	22.52	93736.7	25.06
65	83067.8	17.65	88966.1	19.84	65	86061.3	18.47	90722.2	20.80
70	76078.7	14.03	83751.5	15.91	70	79987.2	14.67	86297.8	16.73
75	66233.9	10.72	75954.4	12.27	75	70825.7	11.22	79414.8	12.95
80	51959.8	7.94	63801.5	9.10	80	57551.8	8.20	68473.7	9.59
85	34448.2	5.68	47013.8	6.42	85	39834.5	5.71	52522.5	6.70
90	17001.7	3.98	26697.5	4.38	90	19866.1	3.96	31104.1	4.55
95	5362.8	2.76	9677.9	3.01	95	6178.3	2.76	11923.4	3.06
100	821.2	2.07	1861.2	2.07	100	893.4	2.33	2410.6	2.1

Source: Office for National Statistics

l_x is the number of survivors to exact age x of 100,000 live births of the same sex who are assumed to be subject throughout their lives to the mortality rates experienced in the three year period to which the National Life Table relates.

e_x is the average period expectation of life at exact age x, that is the average number of years that those aged x exact will live thereafter based on the mortality rates experienced in the three year period to which the National Life Table relates.

15.19 National life tables

Period expectation of life based on data for the years 2017-2019

Notes

National life tables, which are produced annually for the United Kingdom and its constituent countries, provide period expectation of life statistics. Period life expectancy is the average number of additional years a person can be expected to live for if he or she experiences the age-specific mortality rates of the given area and time period for the rest of his or her life.

Each life table is based on the population estimates and deaths by date of registration data for a period of 3 consecutive years. The current set of national life tables for 2017-2019 is based on the mid-year population estimates for 2017, 2018 and 2019 and corresponding data on births, infant deaths and deaths by individual age from those years (the calculation of infant mortality also requires monthly births data for 2016).

1. Population estimates for those aged 90 and over (by single year of age and sex) are calculated for England and Wales separately using the Kannisto-Thatcher (KT) methodology. (These are then constrained to the 90+ totals in the annual mid-year population estimates). Prior to 1990-1992 life tables these were calculated by apportioning 90+ KT estimates at single years of age for England and Wales combined based on the respective 90+ population sizes of England and Wales.

For more information see the Quality and Methodology Information Document for Estimates of the Very Old (including Centenarians): https://www.ons.gov.uk/peoplepopulationandcommunity/birthsdeathsandmarriages/ageing/methodologies/estimatesoftheveryoldincludingcentenariansukqmi

2. Deaths of non-residents occurring in England and Wales were all allocated to England for the calculation of national life tables. National life tables for Wales do not include deaths of non-residents.

3. Death data are based on deaths by date of registration for all the constituent countries. Prior to 2007, the 1991-93 to 2003-05 tables were based on deaths by date of occurrence for England and Wales, and by date of registration for Scotland and Northern Ireland.

4. The tables for England, Wales and England & Wales, covering the years 2000-2002 to 2008-2010 were revised in October 2013 because of the revisions to the underlying population estimates following the 2011 Census.

5. In January 2006 responsibility for the production of national life tables transferred from the Government Actuary's Department (GAD) to the Office for National Statistics (ONS).

6. The figures published in this release will show marginal differences with those published in previous years. This is because estimates of the very old (EVOs) are revised each year to improve accuracy, as new data becomes available. In previous publications these revisions have not been taken into account in historical life tables. However, since the 2016-18 life tables, ONS revises historical life tables to incorporate the latest EVOs.

For National Life Tables QMI see:
https://www.ons.gov.uk/peoplepopulationandcommunity/birthsdeathsandmarriages/lifeexpectancies/methodologies/nationallifetablesqmi

15.20a i) Children looked after who were adopted by gender, age at adoption, 2015 - 2019

Years ending 31 March 2015 to 2019
Coverage: England

	numbers					percentages				
	2015	2016	2017	2018	2019	2015	2016	2017	2018	2019
All looked after children at 31 March	69,470	70,410	72,610	75,370	78,150					
All looked after children who were adopted during the year ending 31 March	5,360	4,710	4,370	3,850	3,570	*100*	*100*	*100*	*100*	*100*
Gender	5,360	4,710	4,370	3,850	3,570	*100*	*100*	*100*	*100*	*100*
Male	2,820	2,510	2,250	2,030	1,870	*53*	*53*	*52*	*53*	*52*
Female	2,550	2,200	2,120	1,820	1,700	*47*	*47*	*48*	*47*	*48*
Age at adoption (years)	5,360	4,710	4,370	3,850	3,570	*100*	*100*	*100*	*100*	*100*
Under 1	230	230	300	310	240	*4*	*5*	*7*	*8*	*7*
1 to 4	4,070	3,390	3,090	2,690	2,650	*76*	*72*	*71*	*70*	*74*
5 to 9	1,000	1,020	920	790	620	*19*	*22*	*21*	*20*	*17*
10 to 15	60	70	60	60	50	*1*	*1*	*1*	*2*	*1*
16 and over	c	c	c	c	10	*c*	*c*	*c*	*c*	*-*
Average age (yrs : months)	3:3	3:5	3:4	3:3	3:1					

Source: SSDA 903 - Children looked after in England (including adoption),
Department for Education

1. Numbers have been rounded to the nearest 10. Percentages have been rounded to the nearest whole number. See looked after children statistics guide for more information on rounding.
2. Historical data may differ from older publications. This is mainly due to the implementation of amendments and corrections sent by some local authorities after the publication date of previous materials.
c   Figures not shown in order to protect confidentiality. See looked after children statistics guide for information on data suppression.
-   Negligible. Percentage below 0.5%

15.20a ii) Children looked after who were adopted by gender, age at adoption, 2015 - 2019

Years ending 31 March 2015 to 2019
Coverage: Wales

Year	Total	Ages				
		< 1 year	1-4 yrs	5-9 yrs	10-15 yrs	16 yrs +
Total						
2015	**385**	*	310	70	*	*
2016	**340**	5	255	80	*	*
2017	**315**	*	255	55	*	*
2018	**305**	*	245	50	*	*
2019	**310**	*	225	50	*	*
Females						
2015	**200**	*	160	35	*	*
2016	**155**	*	115	40	*	*
2017	**130**	*	110	20	*	*
2018	**145**	*	120	20	*	*
2019	**165**	*	130	30	*	*
Males						
2015	**185**	*	150	35	*	*
2016	**185**	5	140	35	*	*
2017	**185**	*	145	35	*	*
2018	**160**	*	125	30	*	*
2019	**145**	*	125	20	*	*

Source: Looked After Children Census, Welsh Government

All figures have been rounded to the nearest five. Where there are less than five children in any group, the actual number has been suppressed, and replaced by the symbol *.

15.20b Adoptions by age of child and relationship of the adopter(s), Scotland, 2019

Age and sex of child		Total	Relationship of adopter(s)				
			Both parents	Step-parent	Grandparent(s)	Other relation(s)	No relation
All ages	**P**	**472**	**1**	**153**	**6**	**11**	**301**
	M	**211**	**1**	**62**	**3**	**5**	**140**
	F	**261**	**0**	**91**	**3**	**6**	**161**
Months							
less than 6	M	2	0	2	0	0	0
	F	0	0	0	0	0	0
6-8	M	1	0	1	0	0	0
	F	2	0	2	0	0	0
9-11	M	1	1	0	0	0	0
	F	3	0	0	0	0	3
12-17	M	9	0	2	0	0	7
	F	14	0	3	0	0	11
18-23	M	23	0	1	1	0	21
	F	18	0	1	0	1	16
Years							
2	M	31	0	3	0	0	28
	F	31	0	2	0	1	28
3-4	M	45	0	5	0	1	39
	F	44	0	4	1	1	38
5-9	M	63	0	20	1	2	40
	F	90	0	32	2	3	53
10-14	M	24	0	19	1	0	4
	F	38	0	30	0	0	8
15 and over	M	12	0	9	0	2	1
	F	21	0	17	0	0	4

Source: NRS Scotland

15.20c Adoptions - Northern Ireland, 2009-2019

Persons	All ages		Under 1		1-4		5-9		10-14		15-17	
Year	Numbers	Percentage	Numbers	Percentage	Numbers	Percentage	Numbers	Percentage	Numbers	Percentage	Numbers	Percentage
2009	116	100%	1	1%	43	37%	46	40%	20	17%	6	5%
2010	116	100%	3	3%	46	40%	46	40%	17	15%	4	3%
2011	104	100%	3	3%	40	38%	40	38%	13	13%	8	8%
2012	127	100%	1	1%	66	52%	39	31%	13	10%	8	6%
2013	130	100%	0	0%	67	52%	51	39%	9	7%	3	2%
2014	104	100%	1	1%	63	61%	28	27%	9	9%	3	3%
2015	113	100%	-	-	-	-	-	-	-	-	-	-
2016	168	100%	-	-	-	-	-	-	-	-	-	-
2017	91	100%	-	-	-	-	-	-	-	-	-	-
2018	105	100%	-	-	-	-	-	-	-	-	-	-
2019	125	100%	-	-	-	-	-	-	-	-	-	-

Males	All ages		Under 1		1-4		5-9		10-14		15-17	
Year	Numbers	Percentage	Numbers	Percentage	Numbers	Percentage	Numbers	Percentage	Numbers	Percentage	Numbers	Percentage
2009	55	100%	0	0%	24	44%	20	36%	10	18%	1	2%
2010	56	100%	2	4%	26	46%	21	38%	6	11%	1	2%
2011	47	100%	0	0%	19	40%	18	38%	6	13%	4	9%
2012	68	100%	0	0%	33	49%	21	31%	10	15%	4	6%
2013	69	100%	0	0%	30	43%	32	46%	6	9%	1	1%
2014	50	100%	0	0%	27	54%	18	36%	3	6%	2	4%
2015	-	-	-	-	-	-	-	-	-	-	-	-
2016	89	100%	-	-	-	-	-	-	-	-	-	-
2017	42	100%	-	-	-	-	-	-	-	-	-	-
2018	62	100%	-	-	-	-	-	-	-	-	-	-
2019	63	100%	-	-	-	-	-	-	-	-	-	-

Females	All ages		Under 1		1-4		5-9		10-14		15-17	
Year	Numbers	Percentage	Numbers	Percentage	Numbers	Percentage	Numbers	Percentage	Numbers	Percentage	Numbers	Percentage
2009	61	100%	1	2%	19	31%	26	43%	10	16%	5	8%
2010	60	100%	1	2%	20	33%	25	42%	11	18%	3	5%
2011	57	100%	3	5%	21	37%	22	39%	7	12%	4	7%
2012	59	100%	1	2%	33	56%	18	31%	3	5%	4	7%
2013	61	100%	0	0%	37	61%	19	31%	3	5%	2	3%
2014	54	100%	1	2%	36	67%	10	19%	6	11%	1	2%
2015	-	-	-	-	-	-	-	-	-	-	-	-
2016	79	100%	-	-	-	-	-	-	-	-	-	-
2017	49	100%	-	-	-	-	-	-	-	-	-	-
2018	43	100%	-	-	-	-	-	-	-	-	-	-
2019	62	100%	-	-	-	-	-	-	-	-	-	-

Source: Annual Reports of the Registrar General for Northern Ireland/Ireland
Email: info@nisra.gov.uk

In 2019:

- 125 children (63 boys and 62 girls) were adopted, an increase of 19.0 per cent from the 2018 figure of 105.
- The average age of the adopted children was five years.
- 74 children adopted this year were aged five or under. A further 34 children were aged between six and ten, with the remaining seven children aged 11 and over.
- 721 births were re-registered, 5.8 per cent fewer than the 2018 figure of 765.
- There were six adults in Northern Ireland who re-registered their birth with a new gender in the Gender Recognition Register.

this page is intentionally blank

Health

Chapter 16

Health

NHS Workforce Statistics (16.1 - 16.5)

Information on staff directly employed is sourced from each NHS Board's human resources and payroll systems including the Electronic Staff Record (ESR). These are dynamic, operational systems and data can change over time.

Staff numbers are recorded in two ways. For the number or headcount of staff, each person counts once irrespective of the number of hours worked. In order to compare staff resources across organisations taking into account different patterns of part-time and full-time working, full-time equivalent (FTE) for each person can be used instead. The FTE for each person is based on their hours worked as a proportion of the contracted hours normally worked by a full-time employee in the post. For example, a person working standard hours each day, but only 3 days out of 5, would count as 0.6 FTE.

Deaths: analysed by cause (Table 16.6)

Since 1993, the majority (approximately 80%) of Office for National Statistics (ONS) mortality data have been coded by automatic cause coding software. Specific text terms from the death certificate are converted to International Classification of Diseases (ICD) codes, and then selection and modification rules are used to assign the underlying cause of death. Using computer algorithms to apply rules increases the consistency and improves the international and temporal comparability of mortality statistics.

International Classification of Diseases, 10th edition (ICD-10) was introduced in England and Wales in January 2001. Since then, various amendments have been authorised by the World Health Organization (WHO). Amendments may, for example, correct errors in the software supporting automatic coding, accommodate new codes in response to new conditions, such as coronavirus (COVID-19) or incorporate advances in medical knowledge of the relationship between conditions.

Further information on the impacts of changes to cause of death coding software is available at: https://www.ons.gov.uk/peoplepopulationandcommunity/birthsdeathsandmarriages/deaths/methodologies/userguidetomortalitystatisticsjuly2017

Notification of infectious diseases - NOIDs (Table 16.7)

Public Health England (PHE) aims to detect possible outbreaks of disease and epidemics as rapidly as possible. 'Notification of infectious diseases' is the term used to refer to the statutory duties for reporting notifiable diseases in the Public Health (Control of Disease) Act 1984 and the Health Protection (Notification) Regulations 2010. Registered medical practitioners (RMPs) have a statutory duty to notify their local authority or local Health Protection Team of suspected cases of certain infectious diseases. For more information on notifiable infectious diseases see: https://www.gov.uk/government/collections/notifications-of-infectious-diseases-noids

Occupational ill health (Tables 16.8 and 16.9)

There are a number of sources of data on the extent of occupational or work-related ill health in Great Britain. The Health and Occupation Research (THOR) network monitors the incidence of work-related ill-health in the UK and Ireland. It is hosted by the Centre for Occupational and Environmental Health (COEH) at the University of Manchester, and collects data on work-related ill health (WRIH) and its determinants throughout the UK and (since 2005) the Republic of Ireland (ROI). THOR is (partially) funded by the two regulators of health and safety: the Health and Safety Executive (HSE) in the UK and the Health and Safety Authority (HSA) in the ROI. The network comprises a number of health surveillance schemes that utilise voluntarily submitted, medically certified data on WRIH. The schemes first developed from SWORD (Surveillance of Work-Related and Occupational Respiratory Disease) set up for occupational and respiratory physicians in 1989, and at present, 4 schemes are in operation enabling different groups of physicians to report cases - SWORD (chest physicians), EPIDERM (dermatologists), OPRA (occupational physicians) and THOR-GP (general practitioners). For more details on the THOR network see: https://sites.manchester.ac.uk/thor/

For some potentially severe lung diseases caused by exposures which are highly unlikely to be found in a non-occupational setting, it is useful to count the number of death certificates issued each year. This is also true for mesothelioma, a cancer affecting the lining of the lungs and stomach, for which the number of cases with non-occupational causes is likely to be larger (although still a minority).

Table 16.8 presents data from THOR for the last three years. It should be noted that not all cases of occupational disease will be seen by participating specialists; for example, the number of deaths due to mesothelioma (shown in Table 16.9) is known to be greater than the number of cases reported to THOR.

Table 16.9 shows the number of deaths for mesothelioma and asbestosis (linked to exposure to asbestos), pneumoconiosis (linked to coal dust or silica), byssinosis (linked to cotton dust) and some forms of allergic alveolitis (including farmer's lung). For asbestos-related diseases the figures are derived from a special register maintained by HSE.

Most conditions which can be caused or made worse by work can also arise from other factors. The remaining sources of data on work-related ill health rely on attribution of individual cases of illness to work causes.

Injuries at work (Table 16.10)

The Reporting of Injuries, Diseases and Dangerous Occurrences Regulations 2013 (RIDDOR) places a legal duty on employers to report injuries arising from work activity to the relevant enforcing authority, namely HSE, local authorities and the Office of Rail Regulation (ORR). These include injuries to employees, self-employed people and members of the public.

From 1 October 2013, RIDDOR 2013 comes into force, which introduces significant changes to the existing reporting requirements. The main changes are to simplify the reporting requirements in the following areas:

- the classification of 'major injuries' to workers is being replaced with a shorter list of 'specified injuries';
- the previous list of 47 types of industrial disease is being replaced with eight categories of reportable work-related illness;
- fewer types of dangerous occurrence require reporting.

While the enforcing authorities are informed about almost all relevant fatal workplace injuries, it is known that non-fatal injuries are substantially under-reported. Currently, it is estimated that just over half of all such injuries to employees are actually reported, with the self-employed reporting a much smaller proportion. These results are achieved by comparing reported non-fatal injuries (major as well as over-3-day), with results from the Labour Force Survey (LFS). For further information on RIDDOR see: https://www.hse.gov.uk/riddor/

16.1a Ambulance staff & support to ambulance staff, by staff groups and level, England

Staff in Trusts and CCGs

As at Sept of each year

Full Time Equivalent (FTE)

Staff Group 1	Staff Group 2	Care Setting	Level	2011	2012	2013	2014	2015	2016	2017	2018	2019
015_Ambulance staff				**17,596**	**17,514**	**17,537**	**17,437**	**17,880**	**19,114**	**20,258**	**20,951**	**16,217**
	015_Ambulance staff			17,596	17,514	17,537	17,437	17,880	19,114	20,258	20,951	16,217
		001_Ambulance Service	001_Manager	687	646	595	612	617	713	699	632	0
			002_Emergency Care Practitioner	734	694	644	618	600	656	598	540	0
			003_Ambulance Paramedic	10,739	11,296	11,843	11,950	12,024	12,315	13,083	13,957	0
			004_Ambulance Technician	5,436	4,878	4,456	4,257	4,639	5,430	5,877	5,822	0
027_Support to ambulance staff				**12,807**	**12,107**	**12,714**	**13,406**	**14,611**	**15,014**	**14,731**	**15,430**	**21,962**
	028_Ambulance personnel & trainees			7,004	6,593	6,822	7,581	8,107	8,386	8,096	8,073	17,381
		001_Ambulance Service	001_Ambulance Personnel	5,861	5,770	6,198	6,414	6,165	6,502	6,532	6,661	0
			003_Trainee Ambulance Technician	1,143	823	624	1,167	1,942	1,884	1,564	1,412	0
		001_Emergency Care	007_Ambulance Technician / Associate Practitioner	0	0	0	0	0	0	0	0	6,296
			008_Assistant Practitioner	0	0	0	0	0	0	0	0	1,501
			009_Trainee Ambulance Technician	0	0	0	0	0	0	0	0	22
			010_Emergency / Urgent Care Support Worker	0	0	0	0	0	0	0	0	4,071
			011_Ambulance Personnel	0	0	0	0	0	0	0	0	2,294
		002_Hazardous Area Response Team	007_Ambulance Technician / Associate Practitioner	0	0	0	0	0	0	0	0	3
			008_Assistant Practitioner	0	0	0	0	0	0	0	0	0
		003_Patient Transport Service	007_Ambulance Technician / Associate Practitioner	0	0	0	0	0	0	0	0	8
			008_Assistant Practitioner	0	0	0	0	0	0	0	0	1
			010_Emergency / Urgent Care Support Worker	0	0	0	0	0	0	0	0	35
			012_Ambulance Care Assistant	0	0	0	0	0	0	0	0	2,863
		004_Education	007_Ambulance Technician / Associate Practitioner	0	0	0	0	0	0	0	0	3
		005_Call Handling	007_Ambulance Technician / Associate Practitioner	0	0	0	0	0	0	0	0	284
			010_Emergency / Urgent Care Support Worker	0	0	0	0	0	0	0	0	0
	029_Healthcare assistants & support workers			1,855	1,490	1,450	954	1,228	1,154	1,116	1,401	107
		001_Ambulance Service	004_Healthcare Assistant	889	908	857	328	595	515	469	645	5
			005_Support Worker	966	582	592	626	633	640	647	755	102
	030_Clerical & administrative			3,728	3,796	4,227	4,689	5,091	5,332	5,443	5,849	4,110
		001_Ambulance Service Support	006_Clerical & administrative	3,728	3,796	4,227	4,689	5,091	5,332	5,443	5,849	4,110
	031_Estates (maintenance & works)			219	227	215	183	184	142	76	107	364
		001_Ambulance Service Support	007_Estates (maintenance & works)	219	227	215	183	184	142	76	107	364

Source: NHS Hospital & Community Health Service (HCHS) monthly workforce statistics, NHS Digital

Notes

Full Time Equivalent (FTE) refers to the proportion of full time contracted hours that the post holder is contracted to work. 1 would indicate they work a full set of hours, 0.5 that they work half time.
These data relate to the HCHS workforce directly employed in NHS Trusts and CCGs who are paid.

From April 2019 the Ambulance Staff matrix of the NHS Occupation Code manual has undergone a significant change to identify staff in greater detail especially by Care Setting.
It is likely there will be some fluctuation in data as these staff are recoded by NHS trusts according to the new categories. Further information on these changes can be found in version 16.1 of the NHS Occupation Code Manual:
https://digital.nhs.uk/data-and-information/areas-of-interest/workforce/nhs-occupation-codes

Data quality

NHS Digital seeks to minimise inaccuracies and the effect of missing and invalid data but responsibility for data accuracy lies with the organisations providing the data. Methods are continually being updated to improve data quality. Where changes impact on figures already published, this is assessed but unless it is significant at national level figures are not changed. Impact at detailed or local level is footnoted in relevant analyses. Further details are also highlighted in the Data Quality Annex document available on the website.

16.1b Ambulance Staff by type: Wales

| | As at 30 September each year | | | | As at 31 December each year | | | | | |
| | 2016 | | 2017 | | 2018 | | 2019 | | 2020 | |
	Headcount	FTE	Headcount	FTE	Headcount	FTE	Headcount	FTE	Headcount	FTE
Wales										
Ambulance staff[1]	**2132**	**2,045.35**	**2173**	**2,084.38**	**2220**	**2,121.65**	**2566**	**2,440.41**	**2835**	**2,704.99**
Manager	44	42.50	54	52.40	62	61.20	62	60.10	53	51.89
Advanced paramedic[2]	.	.	.	.	.	.	36	34.71	66	65.26
Specialist practitioner[2]	.	.	.	.	.	.	29	28.80	35	33.01
Paramedic	971	946.12	972	950.05	954	934.37	1009	983.04	1042	1,007.77
Emergency care practitioner[3]	32	30.87	42	39.36	42	40.71	.	.	.	.
Ambulance technician / Associate practitioner	428	420.44	441	431.20	497	479.79	441	423.18	536	517.64
Emergency / urgent care support worker[2]	.	.	.	.	.	.	494	478.17	574	561.53
Ambulance care assistant[2]	.	.	.	.	.	.	495	432.41	529	467.88
Ambulance personnel[3]	657	605.42	664	611.36	665	605.58	.	.	.	.
Trainee ambulance technician[3]	.	.	.	.	.	.	.	.	.	.

Source: Workforce Services, NHS Wales Shared Services Partnership
Welsh Government
https://statswales.gov.wales

. The data item is not applicable.
Rounding applied: Full-time equivalents are rounded to 1 decimal place.

1. Changes to the ambulance section of the NHS occupation codes manual in April 2019 (https://digital.nhs.uk/data-and-information/areas-of-interest/workforce/nhs-occupation-codes)

2. Data from April 2019

3. Occupation codes closed from April 2019.

a. Closure of Occupation Code AAA 'Emergency Care Practitioner' - This is a specialist role which requires additional qualifications, but does not have any line management responsibilities and is decreasingly used by Ambulance Trusts. The code A6* 'Specialist Practitioner' and Job Role 'Emergency Care Practitioner' will enable identification of those staff who hold the additional qualifications.

b. Closure of Occupation Code AGA 'Trainee Ambulance Technician' - The current definition for this Occupation Code is for staff that are undergoing the Institute of Healthcare and Development (IHCD) accredited training to become an Ambulance Technician. The IHCD no longer exists and as such this code is no longer appropriate.

c. Closure of Occupation Code A2A 'Ambulance Personnel' - This Occupation Code is a generic all-encompassing code that has been used to identify a multitude of different roles with different training requirements covering Patient Transport Services (Band 2; 3 and 4 roles); Emergency Care Assistants (Band 3) and Emergency Care Technicians (Band 4 - not IHCD qualified). Therefore new Occupation Codes have been opened so that the various different roles can be more easily identifiable.

4. At 30 June 2020, most of the staff groups included staff on short term or fixed contracts – these included health professional students and recently retired staff brought in to help during the COVID-19 pandemic.

Definitions:

Manager: those who have overall responsibility for budgets, manpower or assets or who are held accountable for a significant area of work and who have little or no patient contact.

Advanced Paramedic: an experienced paramedic who has undertaken, or is working towards a master's degree in a subject relevant to their practice. They will have acquired and continue to demonstrate an expert knowledge base, complex decision making skills, competence and judgement in their area of advanced practice (College of Paramedics definition). These staff are registered with the Health and Care Professions Council (HCPC) and are at level 7 on the NHS career framework.

Specialist Practitioner: a paramedic who has undertaken, or is working towards a post-graduate diploma (PGDip) in a subject relevant to their practice. They will have acquired and continue to demonstrate an enhanced knowledge base, complex decision making skills, competence and judgement in their area of specialist practice (College of Paramedics definition). These Specialist Practitioners are responsible for mentoring current paramedics and taking on the supervisory and responsibility for paramedics and technicians. This Occupation Code includes Specialist Paramedics who work in the community who also have more advanced skills to that of a qualified paramedic. These staff are registered with the Health and Care Professions Council (HCPC) and are at level 6 on the NHS career framework.

Paramedic: Only staff who have successfully completed an approved qualification in paramedic science and are registered with the Health and Care Professions Council (HCPC). Note that not all paramedics are ambulance paramedics.

Ambulance technician / Associate practitioner: only staff who have completed the Institute of Healthcare and Development (IHCD) Ambulance Technician award (or equivalent) training (and no higher clinical ambulance qualification), or the AAP. These staff are at level 4 on the NHS career framework.

Emergency / urgent care support worker: staff working at level 3 in the NHS career framework who are supporting qualified staff e.g. Emergency Care Assistants and Urgent Care Assistants.

16.1c Ambulance staff by type: Scotland

As of September 2019

Whole-time equivalent (WTE)

	Total	Under 20	20 - 24	25 - 29	30 - 34	35 - 39	40 - 44	45 - 49	50 - 54	55 - 59	60 - 64	65 +
						Age						
Ambulance services	**4,120.5**	-	**122.9**	**398.8**	**406.1**	**317.5**	**532.9**	**699.2**	**710.3**	**575.0**	**263.4**	**49.3**
Ambulance care assistant	759.4	-	8.0	17.9	15.4	13.1	65.2	126.8	168.7	183.5	116.9	44.1
Auxiliary	-	-	-	-	-	-	-	-	-	-	-	-
Driver	19.6	-	-	-	-	-	*	*	*	5.3	*	5.2
EMDC / control	402.5	*	36.9	64.8	66.8	55.4	58.7	52.3	32.8	15.7	12.6	*
Paramedic[4]	1,533.1	-	*	94.0	155.9	117.8	221.5	316.4	318.1	223.1	78.7	*
Technician	1,307.8	*	78.0	222.2	168.0	124.2	163.5	182.7	175.8	127.4	55.2	*
Other	98.0	-	-	*	*	7.0	24.0	21.0	15.0	20.0	*	-
Not assimilated / not known	-	-	-	-	-	-	-	-	-	-	-	-

Source: Scottish Workforce Information Standard System (SWISS)

1. Data is at 30 September.
2. - = missing data, * = censored data
3. Age is a protected characteristic and so is no longer available to the public. For this reason, the data has been censored where wte <= 5.0
4. Paramedics are classed as an Allied Health Profession. However, they have been included in the numbers for purposes of this FOI.

16.1d Ambulance staff by type: Northern Ireland

Headcount

	2009	2010	2011	2012	2013	2014	2015	2016	2017	2018	2019
Northern Ireland											
Total Ambulance staff	1,036	1026	1045	1052	1086	1060	1092	1115	117	1128	1219
Emergency Medical Technicians and Paramedics[1]	629	598	610	618	620	600	639	648	646	652	698
Other/Patient care services	227	244	240	231	263	257	243	264	262	250	275
Control Assistants	108	106	102	107	108	108	122	116	118	125	145
Ambulance Officers	72	78	93	96	95	95	88	87	91	88	88
Helicopter Emergency Medical Service Paramedic	-	-	-	-	-	-	-	-	-	8	8
Community Resuscitation Development Officer	-	-	-	-	-	-	-	-	-	5	5

Source: Human Resources, Payroll, Travel and Subsistence System (HRPTS)
Department of Health, Social Services and Public Safety
Email: workforcestatistics@dhsspsni.gov.uk

1. Includes Rapid Response Vehicle Paramedics

16.2 Hospital and primary care services Scotland

		2010/11	2011/12	2012/13	2013/14	2014/15	2015/16	2016/17	2017/18	2018/19
Hospital and community services										
In-patients:										
Average available staffed beds (all specialities)	000's	24.8	24.1	23.5	23.1	22.9	22.3	21.9	21.3	20.8
Average occupied beds:										
All Acute Specialities	%	84.2	84.4	85.8	86.1	87.8	87.0	85.9	86.7	87.2
Mental Health	%	82	80	79	81	81	82	81	79	78.4
Learning Disability	%		83	84	87	88	87	83	83	83
Outpatients:										
New attendances	000's	1,430	1,447	1,488	1,493	1,507	1,486	1,429	1,457	1,424
Total attendances	000's	4,470	4,520	4,531	4,584	4,529	4,523	4,502	4,248	4,288
All NHSScotland staff	WTE	134,964	131,340	131,845	134,171	136,685	137,728	138,651	139,492	139,765
Medical (Hospital, community and public health services)[5,6,8]	"	10,732	11,237	11,231	11,485	12,014	12,160	12,468	12,651	12,945
Dental (Hospital, community and public health services)[8]	"	708	724	713	696	685	652	650	588	593
Medical and dental support[10]	"	1,811	1,828	1,903	1,908	1,875	1,836	1,930	1,931	1,956
Nursing and midwifery[7,13]	"	57,878	56,309	56,263	57,369	58,407	58,923	59,161	59,413	59,489
Allied health professions[7,12,13,15]	"	9,596	9,347	9,422	11,042	11,287	11,342	11,478	11,518	11,667
Other therapeutic services	"	3,407	3,424	3,529	3,683	3,858	3,914	4,060	4,301	4,465
Personal and social care[13]	"	948	925	896	909	942	1,001	1,119	1,179	1,238
Healthcare science[4]	"	5,628	5,426	5,274	5,324	5,393	5,425	5,451	5,480	5,422
Ambulance Support Services[2,12,15]	"	3,698	3,643	3,640	2,338	2,385	2,440	2,555	2,615	2,631
Administrative services[13,15]	"	25,886	24,668	24,137	24,503	24,899	25,192	25,225	25,277	25,201
Support services[4]	"	14,411	13,767	13,703	13,777	13,856	13,828	13,768	13,843	13,602
Unallocated / not known[16]	"	261	41	1,133	1,135	1,084	1,014	788	697	556
Primary Medical services										
General medical practitioners (GPs):	Headcount	**4,893**	**4,873**	**4,885**	**4,922**	**4,927**	**4,884**	**4,918**	**4,987**	**5,045**
Performer	"	3,751	3,754	3,723	3,710	3,634	3,554	3,489	3,397	3,339
Performer salaried	"	524	532	549	603	690	754	835	967	1,071
Performer registrar/ST	"	478	455	490	499	502	497	516	559	583
Performer retainee	"	145	139	132	116	110	92	91	86	72
Expenditure on Primary Medical Services	£million	741	747	756	763	771	784	800	822	876
Pharmaceutical services:										
Prescriptions dispensed	Millions	91	95	97	99	101	102	103	103	104
Payments to pharmacists (gross)	£million	1160	1177	1118	1145	1191	1272	1304	1346	1343
Average gross cost per prescription	£	11.0	10.7	9.9	9.9	10.0	10.8	11.0	11.3	11.1
General Dental Services										
Dentists on list	Headcount	2,354	2,486	2,520	2564	2663	2661	2691	2736	2801
Number of courses of treatment	000's	3,830	4,100	4,289	4,418	4,490	4,575	4,641	4,700	4,795
Dentist fees:										
Actual	£million	255	268	273	278	281	286	289	293	303
Adjusted for inflation	"	319	330	329	329	329	332	327	326	329
Average gross cost per course	£	44	46	47	47	48	49	49	49	50
General Ophthalmic Services										
Number of Eye Exams given	Numbers	1,798	1,908	1,927	2031	2040	2110	2198	2214	2343
Number of vouchers claimed to provide pairs of glasses/contact lenses	000's	486	501	482	491	463	452	448	436	440

Source: ISD Scotland, Scottish Workforce Information Standard System (SWISS); NHS National Services Scotland

Notes:

Hospital and community services - inpatients

1. All data extracted in July 2018.

2. The figures include NHS beds/patients in joint-user and contractual hospitals. A joint user hospital is a local authority institution in which accommodation is made available to NHS Boards under the terms of the National Assistance Act 1948. A contractual hospital is an institution where NHS Boards have arrangements with voluntary or private bodies for the use of beds or clinical facilities.

3. Note that the specialty groupings were changed in June 2015 and March 2017.

4. The formula used to calculate the number of average available staffed beds generates fractional numbers. As a result, numbers in the table have been rounded to the nearest whole number.

5. Annual figures are shown for the last ten financial years. It is not possible to directly compare quarterly data with annual data due to the fact that the information specifically relates to averages within different time periods.

6. The specialty grouping 'All Acute Specialties' is defined as - all specialties listed under 'Medical Grouping' and all specialties listed under 'Surgery Grouping'

Average Available Staffed Beds: The daily average number of beds which are staffed and are available for the reception of inpatients (borrowed and temporary beds are included).

% Occupancy: The percentage of available staffed beds that were occupied by inpatients during the quarter [derived as: (total occupied bed days / all available staffed beds) x 100].

Source: ISD(S)1 data

Hospital and community services - outpatients

1. Data included are provisional as NHS Boards update their current and historical data monthly. This may result in changes in the recent data shown from one publication to another. There may also be changes to older years on a much smaller scale.

2 The Accident and Emergency, Genito-urinary Medicine (GUM) and Psychotherapy (G6, G61, G62 & G63) specialties have been excluded from these data.

3 These data relate to all patients treated by the NHS in Scotland.

4 Including all specialities but excluding A & E. Outpatients are based on ISD(S)1 data.

5. Data are based on the outpatient appointment date and the financial years run from 1st April to 31st March.

16.2 Hospital and primary care services Scotland

NHS Scotland workforce statistics (as at Sept of each year)

1. A process of accelerated recruitment was undertaken to help NHSScotland to manage the COVID-19 pandemic. This involved a several thousand nursing students, from both their 2nd and 3rd year of study, and doctors in their final year of university study, being brought in to work for NHSScotland. Some NHS Boards in order to process the onboarding of these individuals quickly only added their details to the NHS Payroll system, and did not add them to eESS the NHS HR system. In order to accurately count Staff in Post statistics we take data from both systems and if individuals are not recorded on both they are excluded from our statistics. Therefore the Staff in Post numbers reported for June 2020 are likely to be an under representation.

2. Scottish Ambulance Service employed around 450 mobile testing unit staff during August and September 2020 in order to cope with the demand for COVID-19 testing.

3. Public Health Scotland is the new national public health body that launched 1 April 2020. It brings the functions of Health Protection Scotland and Information Services Division (formally within NHS National Services Scotland) together with NHS Health Scotland. As a result, from June 2020 there will be a reduction in NHS National Services Scotland staff and NHS Health Scotland will no longer have any staff.

4. From 30 December 2018, Sterile Services within Support Services job family is re-categorised to Sterile Services Life within Healthcare Sciences job family.

5. From 30 September 2018, the employment model for Doctors in Training (DiT) has changed and as such, trend information for the overall Medical figures should be interpreted with caution. Key changes to the underlying medical data are:

- (a) DiT data is reported by merging a new data source, Turas People, with the main staff in post data source, SWISS, and

- (b) Inclusion of Locum Appointment in Training and Locum Appointment in Service grades for the first time.

Furthermore, small changes to the recording of grades for some medical staff have been updated as a consequence of an on-going data quality exercise stemming from the introduction of the new DiT employment model.

6. From August 2018, NHS Education for Scotland (NES) became the lead employer for all GP, Public Health and Occupational Medicine trainees. Several Boards were 'early adopters' to this change with a number of their new and existing trainees switching over with NES reported as their employer as at 31 March 2018 and 30 June 2018. This is the reason for the increase reported in these GP trainee figures for NES. Boards involved in the early adoption (Ayrshire & Arran, Borders, Dumfries & Galloway, Forth Valley, Grampian, Highland, Lanarkshire and Tayside) may show an overall decrease in trainee doctors in several specialties as a result.

7. A recoding exercise took place in June 2016 to better reflect the work carried out by NHS Education for Scotland's Nursing, Midwifery and Allied Health Professional staff. This has resulted in an increase in these areas.

8. From the 1st April 2016 NHS Grampian's medical and dental figures include medical leadership and support roles such as GP Appraisers, GP Sub Committee Members, Clinical Leads, Medical Director, most of these have a low WTE.

9. From 31 March 2016 a coding issue was rectified which had previously excluded a small number of staff (approximately 200 WTE) on fixed term secondments within NHS Boards. This has resulted in a small decrease in reported staff numbers. The biggest impact is on NHS Tayside figures which show a decrease of 179.6 WTE.

10. From December 2015, NHS Lothian saw an increase in medical and dental support due to the correction of operating department practitioners who were previously coded as nurses.

11. NHS 24 have undergone a restructure and have reassigned staff to the correct job families. Changes can be seen from December 2014 onwards.

12. From the 1st April 2013, paramedics have been reclassified from ambulance services staff to allied health professions.

13. NHS Highland and The Highland Council are currently developing an integrated model for health and social care. Staff involved in the delivery of core integrated services transferred between the organisations in April 2012 and April 2013. Staff who transferred to Highland Council are no longer shown in this table. In April 2012, 160.4 WTE (211 HC) staff transferred to Highland Council. In April 2013, 16.8 WTE (22 HC) staff transferred. For some sub job families there will be a decrease in the number of staff in June 2012 and June 2013. These staff were in administrative services, allied health professions, nursing and midwifery and personal and social care. Staff who transferred to NHS Highland but are not yet assimilated to AfC are recorded as unallocated/not known.

14. As of the 1st November 2011, NHS Scotland has responsibility for employing healthcare staff within prisons previously employed directly by the Scottish Prison Service (SPS).

15. To allow a comparable trend with 2007 information, adjustments have been made to the following job families:
- allied health profession: play staff / specialists and rehabilitation / clinical support assistants have been excluded for the period 2001 to 2006;
- ambulance services: ambulance control officers have been included for the period 2001 to 2005 (2006 information is not available due to discrepancies with these data);
- administrative services

16. From 2007, unallocated / not known staff are those employees who through AfC have not been assigned to a staff group.

General Practice – GP workforce

1. Excludes GPs working only on a locum/sessional basis and the majority of those working only in Out of Hours services.
2. Data for 2010 - 2020 are as at 30 September
3. Please note that GPs may hold multiple posts simultaneously therefore the total number of GPs may not equal the sum of the different GP post types.
4. ST = Specialist Trainee, previously and generally known as GP Registrar.
5. These data are sourced from a dynamic administrative database. Previously published figures will be subject to change due to administrative time

Source: National Primary Care Clinician Database (NPCCD), Public Health Scotland

Pharmaceutical services

Prescription items dispensed: For prescriptions dispensed in financial year by all community pharmacists (including stock orders), dispensing doctors and appliance suppliers. Gross total excludes patient charges. General medical practitioners prescribe most of the prescriptions dispensed in the community; fewer are written by nurses, general dental practitioners and pharmacists, who may prescribe a limited range of drugs, and by hospital consultants for outpatients. Stock orders (GP10A forms) are items dispensed by pharmacists for use by GPs for the immediate treatment of their patients.

General Dental Services

1. A course of treatment is defined as at least one SDR IOS being claimed on a GP17 form.
2. For children, not all SDR IOS are claimable, e.g. examinations can only be claimed for orthodontic purposes or when necessitated by trauma. As a result, data published may undercount the 'true' level of treatment for children. Therefore caution should be taken when interpreting these figures and comparisons with figures for adults should not be made.
3. Total of continuing care fees and adult SDR IOS fees for the financial year
4. Fees adjusted for inflation have been scaled to determine what the value for the year of interest would have been in 2020/21 prices
5. From April 2006, the period in which a registration lapsed if the patient didn't attend NHS GDS was extended incrementally until the introduction of 'lifetime registration' in April 2010
6. From 1 January 2014 the salaried dental service merged with the CDS to become the Public Dental Service (PDS)
7. Adults are defined as aged 18+ years
8. Excludes a share of backdated IOS payments ranging from £410,000 to over £4.5 million each year which cannot be attributed to patient age
Source: Public Health Scotland, MIDAS.

General Ophthalmic Services

1. Figures include the following Items of Service: Primary eye examination, Primary eye examination (Over 60 no photo), Primary eye examination (over 60 with photo), Primary eye examination (Over 60), HES1 Primary, sight test (HES), sight test (inc Point of Service), HES1 Supplementary, Supplementary eye examination and Supplementary Eye Exam Enhanced.
2. General Ophthalmic Service GOS(S)3 forms are referred to as 'vouchers' and are used to provide a contribution to the cost of purchasing glasses or contact lenses.
Source: Ophthalmic payment system: 2006/07 to 2016/17 (OPTIX), 2017/18 to 2020/21 (Ophthalmic Data Warehouse).

16.3 Hospital and general health services
Northern Ireland

		2011	2012	2013	2014	2015	2016	2017	2018	2019
Hospital services[1]										
In-patients:										
Beds available[2]	Numbers	6,439	6,288	6,172	6,056	5,925	5,910	5,893	5,830	5,780
Average daily occupation of beds	Percentages	84	84	83	83	84	84	84	84	84
Discharges or deaths[3]	Thousands	295	301	304	308	306	302	298	295	292
Outpatient Activity										
- All programmes of care										
Total new & review attendances	"	..	..	1,560	1,501	1,519	1,508	1,457	1499	1,406
New attendances	"	..	..	486	475	485	485	467	482	450
General health services										
Medical services[1]										
Doctors (principals) on the list[5,6]	Numbers	1,163	1,170	1,173	1,180	1,219	1,268	1,306	1,323	1,334
Number of patients per doctor	"	1,631	1,631	1,636	1,596	1,529	1,512	1,484	..	..
GPs per 100,000 of registered population	"	..	..	..	..	..	..	66	67	67
BSO processed payments towards cost of GP Services	£ million	..	..	..	..	..	..	246	259	286
Average cost per patient	£	..	..	..	..	..	..	124	130	143
Pharmaceutical services[8]										
Prescription forms dispensed	Thousands	20,860	21,416	21,723	22,473	22,809	..	..	..	..
Number of prescription items	"	36,916	38,614	40,019	40,377	40,712	41,595	41,720	41,834	43,053
Gross Cost[9]	£ thousand	462,947	457,492	463,206	478,328	496,397	..	..	..	..
Ingredient Cost (before discount)[9]	"	..	..	412,041	425,810	441,148	439,450	436,267	421,297	444,078
Average cost per prescription item	"	..	..	11	11	11	11	11	10	10
Dental services[8,11]										
Dentists on the list[5]	Numbers	956	1,015	1,027	1,053	1,055	1,081	1,108	1,136	1,139
Number of courses of paid treatment	Thousands	1,231	1,283	1,335	1,336	1,355	..	..	..	..
Net cost of dental service[17]	£ thousand	93,700	97,700	101,700	101,600	100,400	97,800	96,700	99,500	104,900
Patient payments[17, 18]	"	18,100	19,400	20,200	20,900	22,500	23,600	24,500	25,600	26,000
Total cost of dental services[17]	"	111,800	117,100	121,900	122,500	122,900	121,400	121,200	125,100	130,900
Average gross cost per paid treatment	£	69	71	70	71	71	..	..	..	..
Ophthalmic services[8]										
Number of Ophthalmic Medical Practitioners (OMPs)	Numbers	600	620	643	663	697	737	606	615	634
Number of sight tests given[12]	Thousands	434	437	446	454	468	476	464	470	469
Number of optical appliances supplied[13]	"	198	204	206	207	207	212	206	201	198
Cost of service (gross)[14]	£ thousand	20,220	20,836	21,800	22,200	22,560	23,500	22,900	23,640	23,770
Health and social services[15,16]										
Medical and dental staff:										
Whole-time	Numbers	3,347	3,415	3,358	3,539	3,596	3,551	3,630	3,480	3,537
Part-time	"	649	677	697	810	827	827	851	896	971
Nursing and midwifery staff:										
Whole-time	"	11,171	11,426	11,722	11,970	12,342	12,614	12,985	13,067	13,359
Part-time	"	9,356	9,422	9,453	9,436	9,312	9,240	9,214	9,195	9,134
Administrative and clerical staff:										
Whole-time	"	7,795	8,106	8,201	8,237	8,093	8,119	8,065	8,057	8,285
Part-time	"	4,304	4,447	4,498	4,512	4,619	4,624	4,618	4,652	4,681
Professional and technical staff:										
Whole-time	"	4,807	5,069	5,233	5,340	5,416	5,567	5,795	6,054	6,359
Part-time	"	2,639	2,725	2,859	3,005	3,123	3,112	3,245	3,288	3,357
Social services staff(excluding casual home helps):										
Whole-time	"	4,581	4,622	4,689	4,778	4,843	4,990	5,110	5,224	5,362
Part-time	"	2,896	2,919	2,930	2,844	2,913	2,843	2,893	2,995	3,040
Ancillary and other staff:										
Whole-time	"	3,814	3,740	3,726	3,731	3,710	3,741	3,774	3,515	4,104
Part-time	"	4,582	4,598	4,636	4,338	4,290	4,181	4,137	4,188	4,391

16.3 Hospital and general health services
Northern Ireland

Sources: Business Services Organisation (BSO) Northern Ireland: 028 9053 2975;
Dept of Health Northern Ireland: 028 9052 2509;
(Figures on Hospital Services: 028 9052 2800)

1 Financial Year.

2 Average available beds in wards open overnight during the year.

3 Includes transfers to other hospitals. This figure also excludes day case admissions.

4 Data before 2015 is not directly comparable with later years. Includes consultant outpatient clinics and Accident and Emergency departments.

5 At beginning of period for Dentists. Doctors numbers at 2002 (Oct), 2003 (Nov), 2004, 2005 & 2006 (Oct).

6 From 2003 onwards (UPE's).

7 BSO Payment towards GP Services refers to the payments that BSO has processed on behalf of HSCB towards the overall cost of GP Services in Northern Ireland. This expenditure is the payments processed in a given year and not the cost of the service provided in that year.

8 From 1995 onwards figures are taken from financial year. Prior to 2017, the list of Practitioners was not periodically validated. As part of ongoing validations, dispensing opticians have been removed from the figures as these are not paid by BSO and thereofore we are unable to quality assure how many there are in Northern Ireland.

9 Gross cost is defined as net ingredient costs plus on-cost, fees and other payments and is available until 2013. After which it is replaced by Incredient costs figures which refer to the list price of the drug, excluding VAT and does not take into account any contract prices or discounts, dispensing costs or fees and will be different to the actual amount that has been reimbursed.

10 Excludes amount paid by patients for pre-payment certificates.

11 Due to changes in the Dental Contract which came into force in October 1990 dentists are paid under a combination of headings relating to Capitation and Continuing Care patients. Prior to this, payment was simply on an item of service basis.

12 Excluding sight tests given in hospitals and under the school health service and in the home.

13 Relates to the number of vouchers supplied and excludes repair/replace spectacles.

14 Figures relate to the costs of the hospital, community health and personal social services,and have been estimated from financial year data.

15 Workforce figures are headcounts at 30th September and are taken from the Human Resources Management System system. All workforce figures have been revised and now exclude Home Helps, Bank staff, staff on career breaks, Chairperson / Members of Boards and staff with a whole-time equivalent equal to or less than 0.03. The Ancillary and Other staff category includes Estate Services, Support Services and Ambulance staff for all years, and from 2008 also includes Generic staff who are multidisciplinary staff. Due to Agenda for Change, new grade codes were introduced (from 2007 onwards) which resulted in some staff moving between categories. Backward comparison of the workforce is therefore not advised due to variations in definitions. 2014 figures onwards will include Northern Ireland Medical & Dental Training Agency staff and GP trainees working in Trusts.

16. Workforce figures prior to 2016 are headcounts as at 30 September. 2016 figures are as at March 2016 and sourced from the NI HSC Workforce Census 2016.

17. Figures are based on the annual assurance information supplied by the Business Services Organisation (BSO) to the Health and Social Care Board (HSCB) for each financial year. Private earnings from dentistry are excluded. Figures are rounded to the nearest £100,000.

18. Patient payments are the costs patients have paid towards their dental health service treatments.

16.4 Workforce in General Practice and Hospital and Community Health Services in NHS Trusts and Clinical Commissioning Groups, England
Experimental Statistics

headcount and percentages

	Sep-13	Sep-14	Sep-15	Sep-16	Sep-17	Sep-18	Sep-19	Change 2018 -2019	Change 2018 -2019	Change 2013 -2019	Change 2013 -2019
HEADCOUNT											
All staff	1,111,101	1,131,680	1,151,138	1,175,668	1,193,107	1,216,720	1,260,755	44,035	3.6	149,654	11.9
Professionally qualified											
clinical staff[1]	601,645	609,995	616,766	626,821	635,751	646,245	661,135	14,890	2.3	59,490	9.0
HCHS Doctors	107,639	109,944	111,127	112,875	116,040	118,510	123,979	5,469	4.6	16,340	13.2
Public Health)	42,125	43,602	45,349	46,955	48,607	50,275	52,130	1,855	3.7	10,005	19.2
Associate Specialist	3,218	2,967	2,727	2,483	2,337	2,215	2,137	-78	-3.5	-1,081	-50.6
Specialty Doctor	6,578	6,985	7,156	7,337	7,637	7,933	8,416	483	6.1	1,838	21.8
Staff Grade	502	449	478	455	432	375	370	-5	-1.3	-132	-35.7
Specialty Registrar	30,581	31,237	30,569	30,999	31,714	31,666	32,773	1,107	3.5	2,192	6.7
Core Training	8,795	8,873	9,046	9,128	9,908	11,426	13,331	1,905	16.7	4,536	34.0
Foundation Doctor Year 2	6,491	6,648	6,626	6,593	6,558	5,560	5,682	122	2.2	-809	-14.2
Foundation Doctor Year 1	6,413	6,310	6,391	6,217	6,163	6,294	6,484	190	3.0	71	1.1
Hospital Practitioner / Clinical Assistant	1,942	1,817	1,762	1,748	1,722	1,727	1,684	-43	-2.5	-258	-15.3
Other and Local HCHS Doctor Grades	1,428	1,447	1,407	1,328	1,349	1,394	1,378	-16	-1.1	-50	-3.6
GPs total[3,4,5]	...	...	41,877	41,865	42,145	42,445	43,047	602	1.4	...	...
GPs (excluding Locums)	40,236	41,105	40,648	40,490	39,843	40,613	40,879	266	0.7	643	1.6
GPs (excluding Registrars & Locums)	35,842	36,078	35,671	35,006	34,481	34,630	34,193	-437	-1.3	-1,649	-4.8
GPs (excluding Registrars, Retainers & Locums)	35,561	35,819	35,516	34,836	34,267	34,318	33,711	-607	-1.8	-1,850	-5.5
GP Providers	26,635	26,183	24,826	23,937	22,919	22,109	20,868	-1,241	-5.6	-5,767	-27.6
Salaried/Other GPs	9,153	9,885	10,775	10,988	11,497	12,342	12,980	638	5.2	3,827	29.5
GP Registrars	4,404	5,033	4,996	5,503	5,412	5,986	6,686	700	11.7	2,282	34.1
GP Retainers	284	262	155	171	218	320	482	162	50.6	198	41.1
GP Locums [2]	...	...	1,370	1,561	2,631	2,043	2,501	458	22.4	...	...
Nurses & health visitors	308,316	312,176	314,966	318,104	317,980	320,325	328,490	8,165	2.5	20,174	6.1
Midwives	25,006	25,333	25,418	25,466	25,704	25,865	26,225	360	1.4	1,219	4.6
Ambulance staff	18,419	18,374	18,862	20,195	21,455	22,245	17,265	-4,980	-22.4	-1,154	-6.7
Scientific, therapeutic & technical staff	142,701	144,540	146,792	150,529	154,923	159,675	165,555	5,880	3.7	22,854	13.8
Support to clinical staff	330,407	340,720	350,053	360,371	365,966	371,380	393,630	22,250	6.0	63,223	16.1
Support to doctors, nurses & midwives	259,002	265,590	272,588	280,224	284,513	287,500	299,885	12,385	4.3	40,883	13.6
Support to ambulance staff	13,898	14,687	15,969	16,465	16,152	16,835	23,765	6,930	41.2	9,867	41.5
Support to ST&T staff	58,031	60,934	61,982	64,154	65,748	67,460	70,370	2,910	4.3	12,339	17.5
NHS infrastructure support	177,311	178,704	181,961	185,620	188,320	195,810	204,920	9,110	4.7	27,609	13.5
Central functions	83,060	84,738	87,228	87,662	89,376	92,970	98,240	5,270	5.7	15,180	15.5
Hotel, property & estates	66,648	64,954	63,900	66,005	65,601	67,920	70,145	2,225	3.3	3,497	5.0
Senior managers	8,672	9,243	9,733	10,117	10,786	10,860	11,445	585	5.4	2,773	24.2
Managers	19,070	19,911	21,219	21,972	22,697	24,200	25,240	1,040	4.3	6,170	24.4
Other staff or those with											
unknown classification[6]	3,896	4,240	4,291	4,653	4,798	5,045	2,850	-2,195	-43.5	-1,046	-36.7

Source: NHS Digital, NHS Hospital & Community Health Service (HCHS) workforce statistics.
Tel: 0300 303 5678   Email: enquiries@nhsdigital.nhs.uk

Notes:
Headcount totals are unlikely to equal the sum of components due to some staff working in more than one role.

[1] Includes all Doctors, Nurses and health visitors, Midwives, Ambulance staff and Scientific, therapeutic and technical staff.

[2] Following the December 2016 collection, further guidance was provided to GP Practices around the recording of GP Locums on the wMDS return. The subsequently higher GP Locum numbers reported in March 2017 are not comparable to previous figures in the time series due to indications that this additional guidance has led to more accurate reporting of GP Locum staff. Further information is available in the Data Quality Statement

[3] Each period, figures contain estimates for practices that did not provide fully valid GP data. Sep 2015 – 11.9%, Mar 2016 – 7.3%, Sep 2016 – 7.6%, Dec 2016 - 7.4%, Mar 2017 - 7.0%, Jun 2017 - 5.6%, Sep 2017 - 5.4%

[4] Figures shown do not include GPs working in Prisons, Army Bases, Educational Establishments, Specialist Care Centres including Drug Rehabilitation Centres and Walk-In Centres

[5] Differences between collections should be treated with caution due to the unknown effect of seasonality on GP workforce numbers

[6] The 'Other staff or those with an unknown classification' staff group includes information on Apprentices that do not clearly fit within the usual staff group classifications. Information on these staff may be extracted if required by making a request to NHS Digital. Please contact us if you need any clarification of this.

16.5 Staffing summary - Wales

As at 30 September each year

	Unit (a)	2013	2014	2015	2016	2017	2018	2019
Directly employed NHS staff:								
Total - All staff	**Fte**	72,390	72,470	73,971	76,301	77,971	79,054	81,044
Medical and dental staff (b):	**Fte**	6,083	6,028	6,136	6,249	6,383	6,540	6,693
of which:								
Consultants	Fte	2,324	2,316	2,345	2,409	2,507	2,547	2,598
Speciality doctor	Fte	457	492	508	517	545	564	568
Staff grade	Fte	7	6	4	5	4	3	3
Associate specialist	Fte	334	306	282	267	253	225	208
Specialist registrar (e)	Fte	1,887	1,832	1,996	2,072	2,102	2,195	2,272
Community/Public health medical staff	Fte	79	76	72	71	58	47	45
Community/Public health dental staff	Fte	123	133	135	138	145	131	132
Nursing, midwifery and health visiting staff (h)	**Fte**	31,366	31,386	31,912	32,713	32,974	32,927	33,301
All registered nursing staff	Fte	20,759	20,737	20,876	21,145	21,265	21,214	21,359
All registered midwifery staff	Fte	1,245	1,316	1,319	1,333	1,347	1,363	1,389
All nursing and midwifery support staff	Fte	9,361	9,332	9,717	10,234	10,362	10,351	10,552
Scientific, therapeutic and technical staff	Fte	11,616	11,671	11,972	12,429	12,799	13,206	13,777
Health care assistants and other support staff (h)	Fte	6,169	6,161	6,090	6,199	6,254	6,294	6,071
Administration and estates staff	Fte	15,120	15,172	15,757	16,580	17,384	17,895	18,687
Ambulance staff (c)	Fte	1,918	1,948	1,998	2,045	2,084	2,095	2,431
Other non-medical staff	Fte	118	104	106	86	92	98	86
GP Practitioners:								
General medical practitioners	Headcount	2,026	2,006	1,997	2,009	1,926	1,964	1,962
GP Registrars	Headcount	233	220	231	232	239	230	293
GP Retainers	Headcount	26	23	25	19	17	14	16
GP Locums(d)	Headcount	.	.	634	684	754	778	782
General dental practitioners (f)	Headcount	1,392	1,438	1,439	1,470	1,475	1,506	1,472
Ophthalmic medical practitioners (OMPs) (g)	Headcount	8	7	7	6	5	4	3
Optometrists (g)	Headcount	781	776	818	819	836	871	872

Source: Health Statistics and Analysis Unit, Welsh Government,
NHS Dental Services, Office for National Statistics, NHS Digital

. Not applicable

(a) Fte = whole-time equivalent.

(b) In 2015, GPs in training moved to be recorded under Velindre, resulting in an increase.

(c) Following an evaluation of staff grades by the Welsh Ambulance Services NHS Trust during 2015-16, staff previously classified as HCAs and other support staff have been re-classified as ambulance personnel; further re-classification took place during 2017 affecting numbers in 2015 and 2016. This table has been updated to reflect these changes and therefore differs from previous editions.

(d) The data is sourced from the Medical Performers List, which is provided by the NHS Wales Shared Services Partnership as at 30 September each year

(e) In 2015 GPs in training moved to be recorded under Velindre, resulting in an increase in the medical staff and total numbers. These are included in both the 'specialist registrars'.

(f) Number of dental performers who have any NHS activity recorded against them via FP17 claim forms at any time in the year ending 31 March.

(g) At 31 December of each year.

(h) Health care assistants and other support staff : During 2018 Betsi Cadwaladr and Cwm Taf Health Boards recoded many of their former Health Care Assistants (HCAs) (occupation code H1) as Nursing Assistants / Auxiliaries (N9) bringing them in line with most of the other Health Boards. To show as comparable a position as possible over time, HCAs in previous years are now included within the nursing, midwifery and health visiting group.

16.6 Deaths[1]: underlying cause, sex and age-group, Summary

ICD-10 code	Underlying cause (excludes deaths under 28 days for individual causes)		2017 Age-group All ages		2018 Age-group All ages		2019 Age-group All ages
A00-R99, U00-Y89	All causes, all ages	M	262,678	M	267,960	M	265,300
		F	270,575	F	273,629	F	265,541
	All causes, ages under 28 days	M	1,117	M	1,040	M	1,061
		F	831	F	811	F	807
A00-R99, U00-Y89	All causes, ages 28 days and over	M	261,561	M	266,920	M	264,239
		F	269,744	F	272,818	F	264,734
A00-B99	Certain infectious and parasitic diseases	M	2,528	M	2,571	M	2,425
		F	2,840	F	2,871	F	2,688
C00-D48	Neoplasms	M	80,077	M	80,306	M	80,762
		F	69,575	F	69,562	F	70,103
D50-D89	Diseases of the blood and blood-forming organs and certain disorders involving the immune mechanism	M	538	M	522	M	519
		F	561	F	582	F	552
E00-E90	Endocrine, nutritional and metabolic diseases	M	4,159	M	4,464	M	4,493
		F	4,276	F	4,287	F	4,380
F00-F99	Mental and behavioural disorders	M	18,039	M	18,073	M	17,400
		F	32,726	F	32,731	F	29,801
G00-G99	Diseases of the nervous system	M	14,267	M	15,233	M	15,737
		F	18,784	F	20,385	F	20,250
H00-H59	Diseases of the eye and adnexa	M	3	M	7	M	6
		F	4	F	5	F	5
H60-H95	Diseases of the ear and mastoid process	M	18	M	18	M	19
		F	28	F	12	F	21
I00-I99	Diseases of the circulatory system	M	69,350	M	69,741	M	68,696
		F	64,161	F	62,492	F	60,725
J00-J99	Diseases of the respiratory system	M	35,982	M	37,494	M	35,837
		F	37,473	F	39,234	F	36,603
K00-K93	Diseases of the digestive system	M	12,759	M	12,963	M	12,809
		F	12,868	F	12,736	F	12,542
L00-L99	Diseases of the skin and subcutaneous tissue	M	754	M	776	M	744
		F	1,378	F	1,273	F	1,311
M00-M99	Diseases of the musculoskeletal system and connective tissue	M	1,339	M	1,372	M	1,419
		F	2,412	F	2,449	F	2,353
N00-N99	Diseases of the genitourinary system	M	4,125	M	3,991	M	4,056
		F	4,981	F	4,855	F	4,525
O00-O99	Pregnancy, childbirth and the puerperium	F	26	F	33	F	24
P00-P96	Certain conditions originating in the perinatal period	M	118	M	91	M	77
		F	70	F	81	F	71
Q00-Q99	Congenital malformations, deformations and chromosomal abnormalities	M	732	M	737	M	730
		F	680	F	614	F	686
R00-R99	Symptoms, signs and abnormal clinical and laboratory findings, not elsewhere classified	M	3,587	M	4,078	M	4,157
		F	8,861	F	9,982	F	9,553
U509, V01-Y89	External causes of morbidity and mortality	M	13,186	M	14,483	M	14,353
		F	8,040	F	8,634	F	8,541

Source: Office for National Statistics

1. Death figures are based on deaths registered rather than deaths occurring in a calendar year. For information on registration delays for a range of causes please see: https://www.ons.gov.uk/peoplepopulationandcommunity/birthsdeathsandmarriages/deaths/methodologies/impactofregistrationdelaysonmortalitystatistics2016.

2. Deaths at home are those at the usual residence of the deceased (according to the informant), where this is not a communal establishment. Care homes includes homes for the chronic sick; nursing homes; homes for people with mental health problems and non-NHS multi function sites. Hospices include Sue Ryder Homes; Marie Curie Centres; oncology centres; voluntary hospice units; and palliative care centres.
Other Communal Establishments include schools for people with learning disabilities; holiday homes and hotels;
common lodging houses; aged persons' accommodation; assessment centres; schools; convents and monasteries; nurses' homes; university and college halls of residence; young offender institutions; secure training centres; detention centres; prisons and remand homes.
Elsewhere includes all places not covered above such as deaths on a motorway; at the beach; climbing a mountain; walking down the street; at the cinema; at a football match; while out shopping; or in someone else's home. This category also includes people who are pronounced dead on arrival at hospital.

3. Figures for England and Wales include deaths of non-residents.

16.7a Notifications of infectious diseases, 2010-2019

England and Wales

Disease	2010	2011	2012	2013	2014	2015	2016	2017	2018	2019
Acute encephalitis	16	13	9	15	11	9	5	9	9	10
Acute infectious hepatitis	475	408	253	253	865	559	505	607	385	352
Acute Meningitis	922	538	522	545	474	524	435	436	282	246
Acute poliomyelitis	.	1	.	.	1	.	.	.	.	1
Anthrax	5	.	2	1	.	.	2	.	1	.
Botulism	2	.	.	.	.	3	2	6	4	.
Brucellosis	.	3	3	1	4	3	5	1	4	9
Cholera	35	16	7	3	10	13	18	13	16	11
Diphtheria	9	2	4	9	14	9	9	13	22	10
Dysentery	267	.	.	.	.	.	.	.	.	.
Enteric fever (typhoid or paratyphoid fever)	272	224	137	127	157	128	132	94	81	117
Food poisoning	57041	24384	20680	15350	17402	15716	13064	11424	11021	8811
Haemolytic uraemic syndrome (HUS)	1	5	1	4	6	4	8	7	12	15
Infectious bloody diarrhoea	386	469	418	399	511	463	355	405	517	602
Invasive group A streptococcal disease	215	186	194	223	369	403	398	485	664	289
Legionnaires' Disease	102	73	80	82	151	139	131	205	231	181
Leprosy	1	1	8	4	8	4	5	4	7	3
Leptospirosis	5	.	.	.	.	.	.	.	.	.
Malaria	327	296	267	226	201	195	205	238	177	197
Measles	2235	2355	4211	6193	1851	1193	1641	1693	2608	2422
Meningococcal septicaemia	367	261	301	300	277	227	277	200	159	104
Mumps	10402	6888	7530	10095	8334	6114	5160	7723	6749	17307
Ophthalmia neonatorum	18	.	.	.	.	.	.	.	.	.
Other	1974	2780	4751	5017	4660	4424	4574	5727	6735	6227
Paratyphoid fever	33	.	.	.	.	.	.	.	.	.
Rabies	.	.	1	.	.	.	.	.	1	.
Rubella	631	476	756	553	425	398	343	362	284	228
SARS	.	.	.	.	.	.	.	3	1	1
Scarlet fever	2969	2719	4254	4643	15637	17696	19206	17813	31904	16128
Tetanus	6	2	7	2	4	3	2	4	6	2
Tuberculosis	8333	9227	9101	8137	7261	6599	6246	5590	5121	5141
Typhoid fever	68	.	.	.	.	.	.	.	.	.
Typhus fever	2	.	4	2	1	.	.	7	.	5
Viral haemorrhagic fever	3	3	7	6	11	10	4	5	1	5
Viral hepatitis	1043	.	.	.	.	.	.	.	.	.
Whooping cough	405	911	6557	3273	2506	3083	4553	3304	2617	3994
Yellow fever	.	.	.	.	.	.	.	.	.	2
Grand Total	88570	52241	60065	55463	61151	57920	57285	56378	69619	62420

Source: Public Healt

1. As from 6th April 2010 the following diseases are no longer notifiable but may still be reported under the Other disease category: Dysentery, Leptospirosis, Ophthalmia neonatorum, Viral hepatitis

2. As from 6th April 2010 the following diseases became notifiable: Botulism, Brucellosis, Haemolytic Uraemic Syndrome (HUS), Infectious bloody diarrhoea, Legionnaire's disease,

3. As from 6th April 2010 Typhoid and Paratyphoid fever have been grouped under Enteric fever.

4. As from week 35 of 2010 Food poisoning 'otherwise ascertained' cases are no longer collected.

5. As from 6th April 2010 the Other disease category may be used to notify any cases that may present a significant risk to human health.

6. A proportion of notified cases are shown subsequently not to be the implicated infection.

7. Any disease not mentioned on a table may be assumed Where a disease is not mentioned on a table it may be assumed that no notifications were received.

16.7b Notifications of infectious diseases, 2003 - 2014
Scotland

Notifiable Disease[1,2,3]	Confirmed notifications											
	2003	2004	2005	2006	2007	2008	2009	2010	2011	2012	2013	2014
Botulism	..	..	..	..		..	..	..	0	3	0	..	1
Anthrax	0	0	0	1	0	0	4	39	0	4	1	2
Brucellosis	..	..	..	..	..	..	..	1	1	0	1	..
Cholera	1	1	6	3	8	3	5	3	3	1	1	5
Clinical Syndrome E.coli O 157 infection	..	..	..	..	..	..	..	33	4	17	3	10
Diphtheria	0	0	0	0	1	0	0	0	0	0	1	3
Haemolytic Uraemic Syndrome (HUS)	..	..	..	..	..	..	..	5	3	1	5	4
Haemophilus influenzae type b (Hib)	..	..	..	..	..	..	..	3	6	0	..	2
Measles	181	257	186	259	168	219	172	93	82	99	162	55
Meningococcal disease	117	147	139	140	150	120	122	93	103	89	83	68
Mumps	181	3 595	5 698	2 917	2 741	720	1129	727	607	920	503	335
Necrotizing fasciitis	..	..	..	..	..	..	..	2	12	4	7	9
Paratyphoid	0	0	0	0	1	4	2	2	1	0	..	10
Pertussis (Whooping cough)	60	87	51	67	98	134	104	45	85	2068	1 134	413
Poliomyelitis	0	0	0	0	0	0	0	0	0	0	..	..
Rabies	0	0	0	0	0	0	0	0	0	0	..	..
Rubella	130	222	141	153	146	106	93	39	21	43	22	24
Tetanus	1	1	1	0	0	0	0	0	0	0	..	1
Typhoid	2	2	1	3	3	3	1	6	3	2	8	6
Viral haemorrhagic fevers	0	0	0	0	0	0	0	0	0	1	..	..

Source: Health Protection Scotland (HPS SIDSS2)
Queries to: nss.hpsenquiries@nhs.net (tel 0141 300 1100)

.. Not available

1 Figures for all years are confirmed notifications

2 The following diseases were also notifiable but there were no cases in 2012: Plague, Severe Acute Respiratory Syndrome (SARS), Smallpox, Tularemia, West Nile fever, Yellow fever

3 From 2010 the following diseases are no longer notifiable - Bacillary dysentery, Chickenpox, Erysipelas, Food poisoning, Legionellosis, Leptospirosis, Lyme disease, Malaria, Puerperal fever, Scarlet fever, Toxoplasmosis, Typhus fever and Viral hepatitis

Please note: Due to changes in processes, this data is not available for 2015 through to 2019.
This table will be updated in the next edition of AOS.

16.7c Notifications of Infectious Diseases

Northern Ireland

Disease	2014	2015	2016	2017	2018	2019
Acute Encephalitis/Meningitis Bacterial	62	44	54	57	42	52
Acute Encephalitis/Meningitis Viral	16	4	6	10	1	2
Anthrax	0	0	0	0	0	0
Chickenpox	1675	1431	1410	819	1008	690
Cholera	0	0	0	2	0	1
Diphtheria	0	0	0	0	0	0
Dysentery	24	47	27	42	34	43
Food Poisoning	1820	1891	1909	2020	1936	2056
Gastroenteritis (< 2years)	447	329	318	218	42	26
Hepatitis A	3	7	12	5	6	5
Hepatitis B	126	61	76	65	53	88
Hepatitis Unspecified	0	0	8	0	17	4
Legionnaires' Disease	7	10	4	8	6	6
Leptospirosis	0	3	1	3	2	1
Malaria	6	7	2	4	3	2
Measles	17	17	17	34	11	13
Meningococcal Septicaemia	22	19	18	16	8	12
Mumps	126	339	358	361	127	633
Paratyphoid Fever	1	0	3	1	0	0
Plague	0	0	0	0	0	0
Poliomyelitis (Acute)	0	0	0	0	0	0
Poliomyelitis (Paralytic)	0	0	0	0	0	0
Rabies	0	0	0	0	0	0
Relapsing Fever	0	0	0	0	0	0
Rubella	10	5	1	4	0	1
Scarlet Fever	625	369	456	332	480	245
Smallpox	0	0	0	0	0	0
Tetanus	0	2	0	0	0	1
Tuberculosis (Non Pulmonary)	71	36	44	32	17	24
Tuberculosis (Pulmonary)	36	43	46	48	43	45
Typhoid	0	1	2	1	1	3
Typhus	0	0	0	0	0	0
Viral Haemorraghic Fever	0	0	0	0	0	0
Whooping Cough	41	115	136	84	45	205
Yellow Fever	0	0	0	0	0	0
Total	**5135**	**4780**	**4908**	**4166**	**3882**	**4158**

Public Health Agency, Northern Ireland

Food poisoning notifications include those formally notified by clinicians and reports of Salmonella, Campylobacter, Cryptosporidium, Giardia, Listeria and E Coli O 157 informally ascertained from laboratories.

16.8a Work-related and occupational respiratory disease: estimated number of cases reported by chest physicians to SWORD 2010-2019 and by occupational physicians to OPRA 2007-2010 by sex and diagnostic category

Sex	Diagnostic category	Chest physicians (SWORD)										Occupational Physicians (OPRA) (c)			
		2010	2011	2012	2013	2014	2015	2016	2017	2018	2019p	2007	2008	2009	2010
All cases (b)	Allergic alveolitis	29	25	56	53	14	10	10	57	6	36	-	-	13	-
	Asthma	205	159	189	189	132	117	125	212	133	174	104	55	47	65
	Bronchitis/emphysema	18	52	19	26	17	17	28	17	12	24	2	12	-	-
	Infectious diseases	2	60	25	14	36	0	12	1	1	1	36	-	24	12
	Inhalation accidents	3	14	3	1	1	16	37	14	3	1	16	1	-	50
	Lung cancer	71	133	16	88	97	79	74	42	54	74	-	-	-	-
	Malignant mesothelioma	522	472	577	647	369	388	287	322	334	229	1	14	-	-
	Benign pleural disease	790	831	708	708	559	564	484	445	392	366	-	-	12	1
	Pneumoconiosis	110	224	159	276	275	212	188	184	125	236	5	-	-	-
	- Asbestosis	82	159	104	194	174	146	124	143	86	159				
	- Coal worker's pneumoconiosis	12	24	25	24	48	2	37	25	16	12				
	- Silicosis	15	29	30	18	55	51	16	12	24	27				
	- Other pneumoconiosis	13	28	3	67	15	18	15	6	15	39				
	Other	61	105	61	105	80	100	109	44	50	44	114	80	77	30
	Total diagnoses	**1811**	**2075**	**1813**	**2107**	**1580**	**1503**	**1354**	**1338**	**1110**	**1185**	**278**	**162**	**173**	**158**
	Total cases (a)	**1760**	**2009**	**1747**	**2033**	**1531**	**1463**	**1299**	**1302**	**1080**	**1077**	**278**	**161**	**172**	**157**

Source: Health and Safety Executive (HSE)

Notes:

(a) Individuals may have more than one diagnosis.

(b) May not equal males plus females because sex is not recorded for some cases.

(c) No OPRA data are available for the annual statistics after 2010.

(d) Some physicians report on a sample basis, for one month in each year. Estimated totals for these are calculated by multiplying the actual number of cases reported by 12.

(e) Pneumoconiosis sub-categories are shown in italics and identify cases where the causal agent was reported as asbestos, coal dust, silica, or other. Sub-categories may not sum to the total since some reported cases have more than one or no reported agent.

"-" means zero.

p Provisional data.

617

16.8b Work-related mental ill-health cases reported to THOR-GP by diagnosis 2016 to 2020

Mental ill-health diagnoses	Number of cases reported to THOR-GP aggregate total 2016 to 2020	% of all diagnoses
Anxiety/depression	69	35.9
Post-traumatic stress disorder (PTSD)	1	0.5
Other work-related stress	98	51.0
Alcohol & drug abuse	0	0.0
Psychotic episode	0	0.0
Other psychiatric problems	24	12.5
Total diagnoses	192	100.0
Total cases	148	

Source: The Health and Occupation Research network (THOR),
data request no: 2021-02-THOR-GP,
Centre for Occupational and Environmental Health, University of Manchester.

• Reporting and estimation methods of THOR-GP were reviewed by THOR and HSE between 2013 and 2015. As a result, from 2013 we only provide THOR-GP data as actual cases.

• Information from THOR schemes is published in HSE statistics available from their website usually towards the end of the year after the year in question. Ordinarily we advise enquirers to search or await the corresponding aggregated reports published by HSE. For reasons of ethics and confidentiality we are limited in the extent to which we can disclose disaggregated data. We have carried out a limited (but not double-checked) analysis of our database and have thus provided you with the above information. However we are not transferring any intellectual property or copyright since after further analysis we may be submitting the double-checked and validated data for peer-reviewed publication.

The Health and Occupation Research Network (THOR) is a research and information dissemination programme on the incidence and health burden of occupational disease and work-related ill-health. This programme was relaunched as THOR in 2002 but consists of a group of closely linked national occupational health surveillance schemes dating back to 1989. Data are collected from a research network of over 900 specialist physicians and specially trained General Practitioners throughout the UK. The data are collated, stored, analysed, reported upon and disseminated by the Centre for Occupational and Environmental Health at the University of Manchester. Further information about THOR is available on the website: http://coeh.manchester.ac.uk/thor

16.8c Work-related skin disease: estimated number of cases reported by dermatologists to EPIDERM 2011 - 2019 and by occupational physicians to OPRA 2006 - 2010, by diagnostic category

Sex	Diagnostic category	Dermatologists (EPIDERM)									Occupational physicians (OPRA) (c)				
		2011	2012	2013	2014	2015	2016	2017	2018	2019p	2006	2007	2008	2009	2010
All cases (b)	Contact dermatitis	1194	1149	963	1117	1257	935	951	832	875	596	488	322	373	342
	Contact urticaria	39	31	11	33	26	58	16	26	5	26	15	13	14	13
	Folliculitis /acne	1	0	0	0	0	0	0	0	2	-	-	1	-	-
	Infective skin disease	1	0	1	0	1	1	0	13	0	-	14	36	2	12
	Mechanical skin disease	14	6	26	2	2	2	24	13	0	1	-	1	12	-
	Nail conditions	0	1	13	2	24	0	24	1	13	-	-	-	-	-
	Skin neoplasia	231	314	252	229	245	207	159	67	121	-	-	-	-	-
	Other dermatoses	72	3	28	12	13	49	15	12	2	68	40	36	40	37
	Total number of diagnoses	1552	1504	1294	1395	1568	1252	1189	964	1018	691	557	409	441	404
	Total number of individuals[a]	1536	1478	1265	1379	1507	1198	1150	938	1015	679	556	409	440	392

Source: Health and Safety Executive (HSE)

Notes:
(a) Individuals may have more than one diagnosis.
(b) May not equal males plus females because sex is not recorded for some cases.
(c) No OPRA data are available for the annual statistics after 2010.
(d) Some physicians report on a sample basis, for one month in each year.

Estimated totals for these are calculated by multiplying the actual number of cases reported by 12.
"-" means zero.
p Provisional data.
r Revised

16.8d Work-related musculoskeletal cases reported to THOR-GP by diagnosis 2016 to 2020

Anatomical site	Number of cases reported to THOR-GP aggregate total 2016 to 2020	% of all diagnoses
Hand/wrist/arm	36	21.1
Elbow	22	12.9
Shoulder	20	11.7
Neck/thoracic spine	8	4.7
Lumbar spine/trunk	44	25.7
Hip/knee	15	8.8
Ankle/foot	16	9.4
Other diagnoses	10	5.8
Total diagnoses	171	100.0
Total cases	159	

Source: The Health and Occupation Research network (THOR),
data request no: 2021-02-THOR-GP,
Centre for Occupational and Environmental Health, University of Manchester.

• Reporting and estimation methods of THOR-GP were reviewed by THOR and HSE between 2013 and 2015. As a result, from 2013 we only provide THOR-GP data as actual cases.

• Information from THOR schemes is published in HSE statistics available from their website usually towards the end of the year after the year in question. Ordinarily we advise enquirers to search or await the corresponding aggregated reports published by HSE. For reasons of ethics and confidentiality we are limited in the extent to which we can disclose disaggregated data. We have carried out a limited (but not double-checked) analysis of our database and have thus provided you with the above information. However we are not transferring any intellectual property or copyright since after further analysis we may be submitting the double-checked and validated data for peer-reviewed publication.

The Health and Occupation Research Network (THOR) is a research and information dissemination programme on the incidence and health burden of occupational disease and work-related ill-health. This programme was relaunched as THOR in 2002 but consists of a group of closely linked national occupational health surveillance schemes dating back to 1989. Data are collected from a research network of over 900 specialist physicians and specially trained General Practitioners throughout the UK. The data are collated, stored, analysed, reported upon and disseminated by the Centre for Occupational and Environmental Health at the University of Manchester. Further information about THOR is available on the website: http://coeh.manchester.ac.uk/thor

16.8e Work-related mental ill-health: estimated number of cases reported by occupational physicians to OPRA and estimated rates per 100,000 workers per year, by industry 2016-2019

Industry (a)	SIC2007 Section	SIC2007 Division	Occupational physician (OPRA) Annual average estimated cases (b) 2016-2019	Occupational physician (OPRA) Rate per 100,000 workers per year (c)
Agriculture, Forestry and Fishing	A		3	1
Mining and Quarrying	B		25	19
Manufacturing	C		96	3
Pharmaceutical products and preparation manufacture		21	8	6
Electricity, gas, steam and air conditioning supply	D		13	7
Water Supply, Sewerage, Waste Management and Remediation	E		15	7
Construction	F		3	-
Wholesale and Retail Trade	G		20	-
Retail trade (not motor vehicles and motorcycles)		47	19	1
Transportation and Storage	H		91	6
Land transport and transport via pipelines		49	49	6
Warehousing and support activities for transportation		52	33	9
Accomodation and Food Service Activities	I		10	1
Information and Communication	J		20	2
Financial and Insurance Activities	K		40	3
Real Estate Activities	L		6	2
Professional, Scientific and Technical Activities	M		22	1
Administrative and Support Services Activities	N		26	2
Public Administration and Defence; Compulsory Social Security	O		268	14
Education	P		199	6
Human Health and Social Work Activities	Q		967	24
Human health activities		86	883	40
Residential care activties		87	35	4
Social work activities without accomodation		88	49	5
Arts, Entertainment and Recreation	R		16	2
Other Service Activities	S		6	1
All industries			1844	6

Source: The Health and Occupation Research network (THOR),
Centre for Occupational and Environmental Health, University of Manchester.
http://research.bmh.manchester.ac.uk/epidemiology/COEH/aboutus/

Notes:

(a) All SIC 2007 sections are shown, as are SIC 2007 divisions with 10 or more actual cases reported to OPRA over the period 2016-2019. Figures are shown in light type if they are based on fewer than 10 actual cases.

(b) Some physicians report on a sample basis, for one month in each year. Estimated totals for these are calculated by multiplying the actual number of cases reported by 12.

(c) The rates have been calculated using the average of the Office for National Statistics Labour Force Survey (LFS) denominators for the years 2016-2019. Note that the LFS denominator is not representative of the population covered by occupational physicians and these are crude incidence rates that should be interpreted with caution.

"-" can mean either zero or rounds to zero.

* Estimated cases = (cases reported on a monthly basis) + cases reported by sample reporters during a single randomly allocated month per year x 12) therefore cells based on a small number of actual cases may exhibit appreciable random fluctuation.

Please note that the 2020 data was excluded from the incidence rates because due to the COVID-19 pandemic, reporting to THOR has been affected dramatically, and case numbers are too low to accurately determine meaningful incidence rates.

16.9 Deaths due to occupationally related lung disease in Great Britain, 2005 to 2019

Numbers

	2005	2006	2007	2008	2009	2010	2011	2012	2013	2014	2015r	2016	2017	2018	2019p
Asbestosis (without Mesothelioma) [1]	263	264	264	290	356	336	370	394	417	373	409	445	442	443	435
Mesothelioma [2,3,4]	2049	2060	2176	2265	2336	2360	2312	2549	2560	2522	2547	2606	2541	2453	2369
Pneumoconiosis due to dust containing silica(a) [5,6]	10	14	7	10 (2)	18 (2)	13	16	11	18 (1)	10	11 (2)	11	8 (2)	11 (1)	12 (2)
Other non-asbestosis pneumoconiosis(b) [5,6]	184 (1)	153	142 (1)	129 (1)	131	121	136	140	147	141	130	136 (1)	118	105 (1)	102
Byssinosis(c) [5],6	3 (1)	5 (3)	2 (1)	1	2 (1)	2 (2)	1 (1)	1 (1)	1 (1)	1	2 (2)	0	2 (1)	2 (1)	0
Farmer's lung and other occupational allergic alveolitis(d) [5],6	13	10	5 (2)	7 (2)	7 (1)	8	9 (2)	10	4	7 (2)	8	5	6	10	1
Total	2522	2506	2596	2702	2850	2840	2844	3105	3147	3054	3107	3203	3117	3024	2919

Source: ONS, GRO(S), Health and Safety Executive

(p) Data is provisional.

1. Some death certificates mention asbestosis with lung cancer and/or mesothelioma. In some cases - particularly where mesothelioma is mentioned - the word "asbestosis" may have been used incorrectly to indicate the role of asbestos in causing mesothelioma and/or lung cancer.
2. Typically less than 10 adjustments are made for previous years.
3. The Office for National Statistics (ONS) discontinued medical enquiries in 1993. Therefore, for deaths registered from 1993 onwards, there is often less information available to accurately code the specific site of the mesothelioma.
4. Total for Great Britain may include a small number of persons with overseas addresses
5. The figure is the number of deaths coded to the disease as underlying cause.
6. Figures in brackets show the number of females. Where no figure is given, all cases were male.
(a) ICD9 code 502; ICD10 code J62
(b) ICD9 codes 500, 503, 505; ICD10 codes J60, J63-J64
(c) ICD9 code 504; ICD10 code J66
(d) ICD9 codes 495.0, 495.3, 495.4, 495.5, 495.6, 495.8; ICD10 codes J670, J673-J676, J678
(e) Figures for 2019 exclude a small nunber of deaths in Scotland.

16.10a Fatal injuries to workers (employees and the self-employed) in Great Britain, by detailed industry 2018/19

SIC 2007 code [1]	Industry	Number of fatal injuries			Rate of fatal injury per 100,000 workers (or employees / self-employed)		
		Workers	Of which…		Workers	Of which…	
			Employees	Self-employed		Employees	Self-employed
All (01-99)	**All industry**	**149**	**106**	**43**	**0.46**	**0.39**	**0.83**
A (01-03)	**Agriculture, forestry and fishing**	**32**	**13**	**19**	**9.21**	**7.94**	**10.34**
01	*Crop and animal production, hunting and related service activities*	*31*	*12*	*19*	*9.97*	*8.37*	*11.35*
02	*Forestry and logging*	*1*	*1*	*0*	*4.23*	*6.65*	
03	*Fishing and aquaculture (2)*	*0*	*0*	*0*			
B (05-09)	**Mining and quarrying**	**0**	**0**	**0**			
05	*Mining of coal and lignite*	*0*	*0*	*0*			
06	*Extraction of crude petroleum and natural gas*	*0*	*0*	*0*			
07	*Mining of metal ores*	*0*	*0*	*0*			
08	*Other mining and quarrying*	*0*	*0*	*0*			
09	*Mining support service activities*	*0*	*0*	*0*			
C (10-33)	**Manufacturing**	**26**	**25**	**1**	**0.92**	**0.96**	**0.42**
10	*Manufacture of food products*	*2*	*2*	*0*	*0.67*	*0.71*	
11	*Manufacture of beverages*	*0*	*0*	*0*			
12	*Manufacture of tobacco products*	*0*	*0*	*0*			
13	*Manufacture of textiles*	*0*	*0*	*0*			
14	*Manufacture of wearing apparel*	*0*	*0*	*0*			
15	*Manufacture of leather and related products*	*0*	*0*	*0*			
16	*Manufacture of wood and of products of wood and cork, except furniture; manufacture of articles of straw and plaiting materials*	*0*	*0*	*0*			
17	*Manufacture of paper and paper products*	*0*	*0*	*0*			
18	*Printing and reproduction of recorded media*	*1*	*1*	*0*	*0.99*	*1.10*	
19	*Manufacture of coke and refined petroleum products*	*0*	*0*	*0*			
20	*Manufacture of chemicals and chemical products*	*4*	*4*	*0*	*3.69*	*3.84*	
21	*Manufacture of basic pharmaceutical products and pharmaceutical preparations*	*1*	*1*	*0*	*0.85*	*0.88*	
22	*Manufacture of rubber and plastic products*	*0*	*0*	*0*			
23	*Manufacture of other non-metallic mineral products*	*3*	*3*	*0*	*3.21*	*3.66*	
24	*Manufacture of basic metals*	*0*	*0*	*0*			
25	*Manufacture of fabricated metal products, except machinery and equipment*	*7*	*6*	*1*	*3.23*	*3.05*	*4.99*
26	*Manufacture of computer, electronic and optical products*	*0*	*0*	*0*			
27	*Manufacture of electrical equipment*	*0*	*0*	*0*			
28	*Manufacture of machinery and equipment n.e.c.*	*2*	*2*	*0*	*0.73*	*0.78*	
29	*Manufacture of motor vehicles, trailers and semi-trailers*	*1*	*1*	*0*	*0.46*	*0.48*	
30	*Manufacture of other transport equipment*	*2*	*2*	*0*	*1.11*	*1.18*	
31	*Manufacture of furniture*	*0*	*0*	*0*			
32	*Other manufacturing*	*2*	*2*	*0*	*1.92*	*2.20*	
33	*Repair and installation of machinery and equipment*	*1*	*1*	*0*	*0.40*	*0.47*	
D (35)	**Electricity, gas, steam and air conditioning supply**	**0**	**0**	**0**			
35	*Electricity, gas, steam and air conditioning supply*	*0*	*0*	*0*			
E (36-39)	**Water supply; sewerage, waste management and remediation activities**	**7**	**7**	**0**	**3.12**	**3.32**	
36,37	*Water collection, treatment and supply; Sewerage*	*0*	*0*	*0*			
38	*Waste collection, treatment and disposal activities; materials recovery*	*7*	*7*	*0*	*6.05*	*6.44*	
39	*Remediation activities and other waste management services.*	*0*	*0*	*0*			
F (41-43)	**Construction**	**31**	**18**	**13**	**1.36**	**1.35**	**1.37**
41,43	*Construction of buildings; Specialised construction activities*	*29*	*16*	*13*	*1.49*	*1.54*	*1.44*
42	*Civil engineering*	*2*	*2*	*0*	*0.58*	*0.69*	

16.10a Fatal injuries to workers (employees and the self-employed) in Great Britain, by detailed industry 2018/19

SIC 2007 code [1]	Industry	Number of fatal injuries			Rate of fatal injury per 100,000 workers (or employees / self-employed)		
		Workers	Of which...		Workers	Of which...	
			Employees	Self-employed		Employees	Self-employed
G,I (45-47, 55-56)	**Wholesale and retail trade; repair of motor vehicles and motorcycles; accommodation and food service activities**	**19**	**16**	**3**	**0.32**	**0.30**	**0.52**
G (45-47)	*Wholesale and retail trade; repair of motor vehicles and motorcycles*	*18*	*15*	*3*	*0.44*	*0.41*	*0.73*
45	*Wholesale and retail trade and repair of motor vehicles and motorcycles*	*8*	*5*	*3*	*1.70*	*1.29*	*3.63*
46	*Wholesale trade, except of motor vehicles and motorcycles*	*8*	*8*	*0*	*1.06*	*1.19*	
47	*Retail trade, except of motor vehicles and motorcycles*	*2*	*2*	*0*	*0.07*	*0.08*	
I (55-56)	*Accommodation and food service activities*	*1*	*1*	*0*	*0.06*	*0.06*	
55	*Accommodation*	*1*	*1*	*0*	*0.27*	*0.32*	
56	*Food and beverage service activities*	*0*	*0*	*0*			
H (49-53)	**Transportation and storage**	**16**	**15**	**1**	**1.00**	**1.18**	**0.31**
49	*Land transport and transport via pipelines*	*11*	*11*	*0*	*1.46*	*2.20*	
50	*Water transport (3)*	*0*	*0*	*0*			
51	*Air transport*	*0*	*0*	*0*			
52	*Warehousing and support activities for transportation*	*4*	*3*	*1*	*0.98*	*0.77*	*7.00*
53	*Postal and courier activities*	*1*	*1*	*0*	*0.30*	*0.36*	
J-N (58-82)	**Information and communication; financial and insurance activities; real estate activities; professional, scientific and technical activities; administrative and support service activities**	**13**	**8**	**5**	**0.19**	**0.14**	**0.34**
J (58-63)	*Information and communication*	*1*	*1*	*0*	*0.08*	*0.09*	
58	*Publishing activities*	*0*	*0*	*0*			
59	*Motion picture, video and television programme production, sound recording and music publishing activities*	*0*	*0*	*0*			
60	*Programming and broadcasting activities*	*0*	*0*	*0*			
61	*Telecommunications*	*1*	*1*	*0*	*0.57*	*0.61*	
62	*Computer programming, consultancy and related activities*	*0*	*0*	*0*			
63	*Information service activities*	*0*	*0*	*0*			
K (64-66)	*Financial and insurance activities*	*0*	*0*	*0*			
64	*Financial service activities, except insurance & pension funding*	*0*	*0*	*0*			
65	*Insurance, reinsurance and pension funding, except compulsory social security*	*0*	*0*	*0*			
66	*Activities auxiliary to financial services & insurance activities*	*0*	*0*	*0*			
L (68)	*Real estate activities*	*0*	*0*	*0*			
68	*Real estate activities*	*0*	*0*	*0*			
M (69-75)	*Professional, scientific and technical activities*	*2*	*2*	*0*	*0.08*	*0.11*	
69	*Legal and accounting activities*	*0*	*0*	*0*			
70	*Activities of head offices; management consultancy activities*	*1*	*1*	*0*	*0.19*	*0.27*	
71	*Architectural and engineering activities; technical testing and analysis*	*0*	*0*	*0*			
72	*Scientific research and development*	*0*	*0*	*0*			
73	*Advertising and market research*	*0*	*0*	*0*			
74	*Other professional, scientific and technical activities*	*1*	*1*	*0*	*0.29*	*0.58*	
75	*Veterinary activities*	*0*	*0*	*0*			
N (77-82)	*Administrative and support service activities*	*10*	*5*	*5*	*0.62*	*0.41*	*1.32*
77	*Rental and leasing activities*	*1*	*1*	*0*	*0.77*	*0.88*	
78	*Employment activities*	*0*	*0*	*0*			
79	*Travel agency, tour operator and other reservation service and related activities*	*0*	*0*	*0*			
80	*Security and investigation activities*	*0*	*0*	*0*			
81	*Services to buildings and landscape activities*	*8*	*3*	*5*	*1.10*	*0.64*	*1.91*
82	*Office administrative, office support and other business support activities*	*1*	*1*	*0*	*0.48*	*0.57*	

16.10a Fatal injuries to workers (employees and the self-employed) in Great Britain, by detailed industry 2018/19

SIC 2007 code [1]	Industry	Number of fatal injuries			Rate of fatal injury per 100,000 workers (or employees / self-employed)		
		Workers	Of which...		Workers	Of which...	
			Employees	Self-employed		Employees	Self-employed
O-Q (84-88)	**Public administration and defence; compulsory social security; education; human health and social work activities**	**3**	**3**	**0**	**0.03**	**0.03**	
O (84)	*Public administration and defence; compulsory social security*	*0*	*0*	*0*			
84	*Public administration and defence; compulsory social security*	*0*	*0*	*0*			
P (85)	*Education*	*1*	*1*	*0*	*0.03*	*0.03*	
85	*Education*	*1*	*1*	*0*	*0.03*	*0.03*	
Q (86-88)	*Human health and social work activities*	*2*	*2*	*0*	*0.05*	*0.05*	
86	*Human health activities*	*0*	*0*	*0*			
87	*Residential care activities*	*2*	*2*	*0*	*0.20*	*0.21*	
88	*Social work activities without accommodation*	*0*	*0*	*0*			
R-U (90-99)	**Arts, entertainment and recreation; other service activities; activities of households as employers; undifferentiated goods-and services-producing activities of households for own use; activities of extraterritorial organisations and bodies**	**2**	**1**	**1**	**0.10**	**0.07**	**0.15**
R (90-93)	*Arts, entertainment and recreation*	*2*	*1*	*1*	*0.21*	*0.15*	*0.33*
90	*Creative, arts and entertainment activities*	*1*	*0*	*1*	*0.41*		*0.57*
91	*Libraries, archives, museums and other cultural activities*	*0*	*0*	*0*			
92	*Gambling and betting activities*	*0*	*0*	*0*			
93	*Sports activities and amusement and recreation activities*	*1*	*1*	*0*	*0.19*	*0.25*	
S (94-96)	*Other service activities*	*0*	*0*	*0*			
94	*Activities of membership organisations*	*0*	*0*	*0*			
95	*Repair of computers and personal and household goods*	*0*	*0*	*0*			
96	*Other personal service activities*	*0*	*0*	*0*			
T (97-98)	*Activities of households as employers; undifferentiated goods-and services-producing activities of households for own use*	*0*	*0*	*0*			
97	*Activities of households as employers of domestic personnel*	*0*	*0*	*0*			
98	*Undifferentiated goods- and services-producing activities of private households for own use*	*0*	*0*	*0*			
U (99)	*Activities of extraterritorial organisations and bodies*	*0*	*0*	*0*			
99	*Activities of extraterritorial organisations and bodies*	*0*	*0*	*0*			

Source: Reporting of Injuries, Diseases and Dangerous Occurrences Regulations (RIDDOR)

(1) Standard Industrial Classification (SIC): The current system used in UK official statistics for classifying businesses by type of activity they are engaged in.

(2) Excludes sea fishing.

(3) Injuries arising from shore-based services only. Excludes incidents reported under merchant shipping legislation.

* Employment numbers are too small to provide reliable rate estimates.

This table presents the number of reportable fatal injuries to Members of the Public in each year from 2014/15 and includes deaths as a result of an accident which has arisen out of, or in connection with, work activity though the injured person was 'not at work' themselves. It should be noted that there have been recent changes in reporting requirements that have affected the annual statistical count. As from 2015/16, the member of the public death statistics no longer include 'patient and service user' deaths in England for premises registered with Care Quality Commission (CQC) (previously these deaths were recorded under SIC section Q 'Human health and social work activities').

16.10b Non-fatal injuries to employees and the self-employed in Great Britain, by broad industry group 2018/19

Employment Status	Year	Industry	Regulations Injuries reported under [1]	Industry classif-ication [2]	Source of employ-ment data for rates [3]	Number of reported non-fatal injuries to employees / self employed — Total reported non-fatal injury [4]	Major/ Specified# injury [5]	Over-3-day injury [6]	Over 7-day injury [6]	Rate of reported non-fatal injury per 100,000 employees [7] — Total reported non-fatal injury [4]	Major/ Specified injury [5]	Over-3-day injury [6]	Over 7-day injury [6]
Employee	2017/18	All industries	(g)	(I)	(o)	70,364	18,024	-	52,340	258	66	-	192
Employee	2017/18	Agriculture, forestry and fishing [8]	(g)	(I)	(o)	849	346	-	503	518	211	-	307
Employee	2017/18	Mining and Quarrying	(g)	(I)	(o)	232	73	-	159	194	61	-	133
Employee	2017/18	Gas, electricity and water supply; sewerage, waste and recycling	(g)	(I)	(o)	2,336	623	-	1,713	600	160	-	440
Employee	2017/18	Manufacturing	(g)	(I)	(o)	12,262	2,780	-	9,482	472	107	-	365
Employee	2017/18	Construction	(g)	(I)	(o)	4,911	1,708	-	3,203	369	128	-	241
Employee	2017/18	Service industries	(g)	(I)	(o)	49,774	12,494	-	37,280	221	55	-	165
Self employed	2017/18	All industries	(g)	(I)	-	2,119	1,100	-	1,019	-	-	-	-
Self employed	2017/18	Agriculture, forestry and fishing [8]	(g)	(I)	-	72	48	-	24	-	-	-	-
Self employed	2017/18	Mining and Quarrying	(g)	(I)	-	3	-	-	3	-	-	-	-
Self employed	2017/18	Gas, electricity and water supply; sewerage, waste and recycling	(g)	(I)	-	44	24	-	20	-	-	-	-
Self employed	2017/18	Manufacturing	(g)	(I)	-	123	61	-	62	-	-	-	-
Self employed	2017/18	Construction	(g)	(I)	-	1,428	730	-	698	-	-	-	-
Self employed	2017/18	Service industries	(g)	(I)	-	449	237	-	212	-	-	-	-

Source: **Reporting of Injuries, Diseases and Dangerous Occurrences Regulations (RIDDOR) and earlier regulations**

Note: Great care needs to be taken when comparing estimates over time because this non-fatal injury series is not consistent over the entire time period.

1. Since 1974 (and earlier), there has been a requirement to report cases of workplace injury to the appropriate authority. The criteria for reporting has changed during this period as new and revised regulations have come into force. Figures in the table represent cases that have been reported. Because of changes in reporting requirements this has introduced discontinuities into the time series and care must be taken when making comparisons over time. The table below details the various regulations that reports have been made under, and the main impacts on the statistics.

2. From 1981, reports have been classified by industry using the Standard Industrial Classification (SIC), an industry coding framework used in UK official statistics. (Prior to this they were classified according to the regulations they were reported under. The SIC coding classification is periodically updated to take account of changes in the industry composition of the labour market. Since 1980 there have been 3 revisions of the Classification in 1980, 1992 and 2007. The table below shows the classification system that applies in different time periods for which the statistics are presented in these tables. This change in classification system will also have introduced discontinuities in the data series. While mostly the discontinuities at the top level industry groupings presented in these tables are small, for extractive and utility supply, these industries were classified in separate SIC sections under SIC2007. Hence no estimates for this exact industry grouping are available post 2004/05. Instead estimates are presented separately for mining and quarrying and Gas, electricity and water supply; sewerage, waste and recycling industries.

3. The estimation of injury incidence rates requires the use of employment estimates. The rate of injury is calculated by dividing the number of injury cases (the numerator) by the employment estimate (the denominator), and then multiplying by a factor of 100,000. Rate estimates use a different source of employment data prior to 2004/05, as shown in the table below. The change in employment estimates from 2004/05 means that these rates are not directly comparable with earlier periods.

4. Because of differences in reporting requirements between years then great care needs to be taken when comparing estimates of non-fatal injury over time.

5. # Includes injuries that were classified as 'major' for the period April-September 2013 and as 'specified' thereafter (many injuries previously categorised as major continue to be categorised as specified, primarily most fractures and amputations).

6. RIDDOR 2012, introduced in April 2012, changed the threshold for reporting non-fatal injuries from over 3-days absence to over 7-days absence.

7. Rates of non-fatal injury in this table are presented for employees only. Injuries to the self-employed suffer from severe under-reporting meaning that rate estimates may be misleading.

8. Excludes sea fishing.

9. Figures prior to 1996/97 also include injuries in the offshore oil and gas industry reported under offshore installations safety legislation.

- Estimate not available.

* Employment numbers are too small to provide reliable rate estimates.

(g) 2014/15 onwards - Reporting of Injuries, Diseases and Dangerous Occurrence Regulations 2013 (RIDDOR 2013): The list of non-fatal 'major' injuries was revised and re-named as 'Specified' injuries (many injuries previously categorised as major continue to be categorised as specified, primarily most fractures and amputations). The introduction of RIDDOR 2013 also removed the requirement to report suicides on railway systems (introduced under RIDDOR 1995).

(I) 2004/05 onwards - Industry Classsification: SIC 2007.

(o) 2004/05 onwards - Source of employment data for estimating rates: The Annual Population Survey (APS) is the source of employment data used as the denominator for rates of injury for estimates from 2004/05. For more information see: www.hse.gov.uk/statistics/sources.pdf

this page is intentionally blank

Prices

Chapter 17

Prices

Producer price index numbers (Tables 17.1 and 17.2)

Producer Price Indices (PPIs) are a series of economic indicators that measure the price movement of goods bought and sold by UK manufacturers. The indices are split into the Producer Price Index (PPI), Export Price Index (EPI) and Import Price Index (IPI). The goods included in the PPIs are based on the classification by product activity (CPA) 2.1, which is maintained by Eurostat. The PPIs cover products from sections A to E. The prices for goods are then weighted to reflect their relative importance within the index. Producer Prices are based on the Standard Industrial Classification 2007 (SIC 2007) which means that they are broadly comparable internationally.

PPIs were published for the first time in August 1983, replacing the former wholesale price indices. Full details of the differences between the two indices were given in an article published in British Business, 15 April 1983. The producer price indices are calculated using the same general methodology as that used by the wholesale price indices.

The high level index numbers in Tables 17.1 and 17.2 are constructed on a net sector basis. That is to say, they are intended to measure only transactions between the sector concerned and other sectors. Within-sector transactions are excluded. Index numbers for the whole of manufacturing are thus not weighted averages of sector index numbers. The index numbers for selected industries in these tables are constructed on a gross sector basis, that is, all transactions are included in deriving the weighting patterns, including sales within the same industry.

Consumer prices index (Table 17.3)

The ONS publishes several consumer-focused price indices including the Retail Prices Index (RPI) and Consumer Prices Index (CPI). They are important indicators of how the UK economy is performing. They also show the impact of inflation on family budgets and affect the value of the pound in your pocket.

The major difference between the PPIs and consumer-focused price indices is a difference in perspective. Business prices measure prices from the point of view of the manufacturer. The Consumer Price Indices (CPIs) measures how much a consumer would pay for this product when buying it from a shop (as such it would include additional margins such as transport costs). The PPIs can therefore act as early indications of inflation on the consumer price statistics, as an increase in the price wholesalers pay can translate to an increased price for consumers.

The CPI, therefore, is the main UK domestic measure of consumer price inflation for macroeconomic purposes. It forms the basis for the Government's target for inflation that the Bank of England's Monetary Policy Committee (MPC) is required to achieve. From April 2011 the CPI is also being used for the indexation of benefits, tax credits and public service pensions.

The CPI continues to be published and is widely used. In particular, it is used by the government for inflation targeting, for uprating state pensions and benefits, and it is the measure reported to Eurostat. A full description of the Consumer Price Indices and consumer price inflation see: https://www.ons.gov.uk/economy/inflationandpriceindices/methodologies/consumerpriceinflationincludesall3indicescpihcpiandrpiqmi

Retail price index (Table 17.4)

The RPI was initially developed as a compensation index, derived from an index designed as an aid to protect ordinary workers from price increases associated with the First World War. The RPI provides estimates of inflation from 1947 onwards with the first official release of consumer price inflation being produced in January 1956. Until the introduction of the UK CPI (also known at the time Harmonised Index of Consumer Prices, HICP) in 1996, the RPI and its derivatives, were the only measures of UK consumer price inflation available to users.

Following a consultation on options for improving the Retail Prices Index (RPI), the National Statistician, Jil Matheson, concluded that one of the formulae used to produce the RPI does not meet international standards and recommended that a new index be published. The Retail Prices Index (RPI) and its derivatives have been assessed against the Code of Practice for Official Statistics and found not to meet the required standard for designation as National Statistics. As of 21 March 2017, the publication of RPI-related data was scaled back, limited to the information required for critical needs of existing users to be met. Further detail can be found in Clarification of publication arrangements for the RPI and related indices (https://www.ons.gov.uk/economy/ inflationand priceindices/articles/clarificationofpublicationarrangementsfortheretailpricesindexandrelated indices/november2016).

Tax and price index (TPI) (Table 17.5)

This index has been discontinued following a consultation by ONS, The last data available is Jan 2017. The TPI measured how much the average person's gross income needed to change to purchase the basket of goods, allowing for the average amount of Income Tax and National Insurance paid on earnings. More details of this change can be found at: https://www.ons.gov.uk/economy/inflationand priceindices/articles/ clarificationofpublicationarrangementsfortheretailpricesindexandrelatedindices/november2016

Agricultural price indices (API) (Tables 17.6 and 17.7)

The API is a basic tool for the measurement of price variations in agricultural outputs and inputs for the UK. The output series reflects the price farmers receive for their products (referred to as the farm-gate price). Information is collected for all major crops and on livestock and livestock products. The input series reflects the price farmers pay for goods and services. This is split into two groups: goods and services currently consumed; and goods and services contributing to investment. Goods and services currently consumed refer to items that are used up in the production process, for example fertiliser, or seed. Goods and services contributing to investment relate to items that are required but not consumed in the production process, such as tractors or buildings.

A price index is a way of measuring relative price changes compared to a reference point or base year which is given a value of 100. The year used as the base year needs to be updated over time to reflect changing market trends. The latest data are presented with a base year of 2015 = 100.

To maintain continuity with the current API time series, the UK continues to use standardised methodology adopted across the EU. Details of this internationally recognised methodology are described in the Handbook for EU agricultural price statistics (https://ec.europa.eu/eurostat/cache/metadata/Annexes/apri_pi_esms_an1.pdf).

Harmonised Index of Consumer Prices (HICP) (Table 17.8)

This table displays the HICP for EU countries to allow international comparison of consumer price inflation. The Consumer Prices Index was first published in 1997 as the Harmonised Index of Consumer Prices (HICP) – a consistent measure of inflation across Europe. The HICP was developed across the European Union (EU) for the purpose of assessing whether prospective members of the European Monetary Union would pass the inflation convergence criteria and of acting as a measure of inflation used by the European Central Bank in assessing price stability in the EU member countries. In December 2003, the National Statistician decided the name of the UK version of the HICP would change to the CPI in all National Statistics publications.

17.1 Produce Price Index (2010=SIC2007)

			Net Sector Price Indices of Materials & Fuels purchased			
	6207000050: NSI - All Manufacturing including CCL K646	**6207000010**: NSI - All Manufacturing, materials only K644	**6207000060**: NSI - Fuel Purchased by Manufacturing Industry including CCL K647	**6207990050**: NSI - Materials & Fuels Purchased other than FBTP Industries, NSA K655	**6207998950**: NSI - All Manufacturing excl FBTP (incl CCL) - SA K658	**6207990010**: NSI - Materials Purchased other than FBTP Industries, NSA K653
2013	117.4	116.6	125.0	109.3	109.3	106.8
2014	109.7	108.3	122.4	105.3	105.0	102.4
2015	95.7	93.2	117.0	99.8	99.7	96.9
2016	97.6	96.0	110.8	102.4	102.3	100.9
2017	108.3	107.4	115.6	110.3	110.3	109.4
2018	116.2	115.0	126.4	115.5	115.6	113.7
2019	116.8	114.9	134.3	118.1	118.1	115.4
2017 JAN	108.0	106.8	119.5	109.6	108.9	108
2017 FEB	108.0	106.6	119.9	109.6	109.2	107.9
2017 MAR	107.5	106.7	113.8	109.7	109.2	109
2017 APR	106.9	106.3	111.9	108.8	109.1	108.3
2017 MAY	106.3	105.4	113.4	108.7	109.4	107.8
2017 JUN	105.9	105.3	111.6	109.4	109.9	109
2017 JUL	105.9	105.3	110.6	109.3	109.9	109.1
2017 AUG	108.0	107.5	111.8	111.1	111.3	110.9
2017 SEP	108.5	107.8	113.5	110.7	110.9	110.2
2017 OCT	109.8	109.1	116.4	111.6	111.1	110.7
2017 NOV	112.0	110.9	121.1	112.7	112	111.3
2017 DEC	112.5	111.2	123.8	112.8	112.4	111
2018 JAN	112.7	111.5	122.7	112.7	112.2	111.1
2018 FEB	112.2	110.8	124.4	113.0	112.8	111.2
2018 MAR	112.3	111.0	123.6	113.0	113.0	111.3
2018 APR	112.9	111.8	122.1	112.6	113.5	111.0
2018 MAY	116.5	115.9	121.6	114.6	115.6	113.4
2018 JUN	116.8	116.1	123.0	115.4	116.1	114.1
2018 JUL	116.8	116.4	121.2	115.7	116.3	114.8
2018 AUG	118.7	117.9	125.3	117.3	117.0	116.0
2018 SEP	120.1	118.8	131.5	118.0	117.9	115.8
2018 OCT	121.2	119.9	133.3	118.0	117.5	115.4
2018 NOV	118.1	116.5	132.5	117.4	117.0	114.9
2018 DEC	116.0	113.8	135.3	118.1	117.7	115.3
2019 JAN	115.7	113.1	138.8	117.8	117.4	114.5
2019 FEB	116.8	114.1	140.9	118.0	117.8	114.3
2019 MAR	115.8	114.1	130.7	116.3	116.5	113.9
2019 APR	118.1	116.2	135.1	117.4	118.5	114.5
2019 MAY	118.1	116.8	129.7	117.0	118.0	114.9
2019 JUN	117.1	115.7	130.1	117.8	118.4	115.7
2019 JUL	117.9	116.6	130.0	119.1	119.3	117.2
2019 AUG	117.6	116.2	129.8	120.4	119.6	118.8
2019 SEP	116.5	115.2	127.6	118.9	118.4	117.5
2019 OCT	115.2	113.2	132.8	118.1	117.7	115.6
2019 NOV	116.0	113.2	140.5	117.8	117.7	114.1
2019 DEC	117.2	114.0	145.1	117.9	117.5	113.3
2020 JAN	117.6	114.6	143.8	119.0	118.6	114.9
2020 FEB	116.6	113.8	140.8	120.1	119.5	116.6
2020 MAR	111.9	109.2	135.9	120.2	120.2	117.6
2020 APR	105.6	102.6	131.7	116.6	117.8	114.0
2020 MAY	105.9	103.8	124.1	115.7	117.1	114.2
2020 JUN	109.2	107.3	125.3	116.5	117.4	115.0

17.1 Produce Price Index (2010=SIC2007)

2010=100, SIC2007

| | Gross Sector Price Indices of Materials & Fuels purchased | | | | | |
| | 6107113140: GSI Sub-section - Inputs for Manuf of Textiles & Textile products | 6107215000: GSI (excl. CCL) - Inputs for Manuf of Leather & Related products | 6107216000: GSI (excl. CCL) - Inputs for Manuf of Wood & products of Wood/Cork | 6107117180: GSI Sub-section - Inputs for Manuf of Pulp, Paper & Paper products | 6107219000: GSI (excl. CCL) - Inputs for Manuf of Coke & Refined Petroleum prod' | 6107120000: GSI Sub-section - Inputs for Manuf of Chemicals, Chemical products |
	MC36	MC3O	MC3P	MC39	MC3R	MC3B
2013	111.2	114.0	109.9	108.2	135.5	110.3
2014	110.5	113.2	111.9	107.6	118.3	106.3
2015	108.5	110.9	110.7	105.7	73.4	100.0
2016	109.1	110.6	110.5	106.0	70.1	98.6
2017	112.8	115.1	116.6	109.2	87.5	107.0
2018	115.6	117.4	126.1	114.2	107.7	115.2
2019	117.6	118.9	129.4	116.1	103.5	114.5
2017 JAN	111.7	113.1	114.6	108.1	90.9	104
2017 FEB	112	113.3	115	108.3	90.5	105.2
2017 MAR	112.2	113.6	115.1	107.9	86.9	105.7
2017 APR	112.2	114.2	115.2	107.8	86.2	106.3
2017 MAY	112.2	115	115.2	108.3	82.3	106
2017 JUN	112.5	115.2	115.6	108.8	78.8	105.9
2017 JUL	112.7	115.4	116.8	109.1	78.9	106.3
2017 AUG	113.2	116.4	117.4	109.5	83.8	107.6
2017 SEP	113.1	116.4	117.6	109.5	87.7	108.1
2017 OCT	113.4	116.4	118.3	110.3	90.5	108.7
2017 NOV	113.8	115.9	118.9	111	96	109.9
2017 DEC	114.1	116.5	119.3	111.4	97.4	110.7
2018 JAN	113.9	116.2	121.5	111.8	100.8	111.3
2018 FEB	114.4	116.2	121.8	112.3	97.3	112.6
2018 MAR	115.0	116.7	122.7	112.9	96.8	112.9
2018 APR	114.7	116.7	123.7	113.0	101.2	113.3
2018 MAY	115.3	117.3	124.7	113.7	112.6	114.5
2018 JUN	115.4	117.7	125.4	114.1	112.5	114.9
2018 JUL	115.4	117.6	127.5	114.4	112.2	115.7
2018 AUG	116.0	117.6	128.5	114.8	113.6	116.7
2018 SEP	116.6	117.9	129.1	115.4	117.7	117.7
2018 OCT	116.7	118.1	129.5	115.9	122.9	118.1
2018 NOV	117.0	118.1	129.5	116.1	108.7	117.7
2018 DEC	117.0	118.2	129.6	116.5	95.6	116.8
2019 JAN	116.9	118.0	130.0	116.9	95.5	116.6
2019 FEB	116.9	117.8	130.2	117.0	101.0	115.8
2019 MAR	116.7	118.3	129.5	115.9	102.9	114.5
2019 APR	117.5	118.8	130.1	116.3	109.8	114.9
2019 MAY	117.6	119.7	129.9	115.9	111.9	115.0
2019 JUN	117.8	119.2	130.3	116.0	104.8	114.8
2019 JUL	118.2	119.8	129.7	116.2	105.7	114.9
2019 AUG	118.6	119.8	129.8	116.5	102.8	115.1
2019 SEP	118.1	119.3	129.2	115.9	103.0	114.0
2019 OCT	117.8	118.9	128.3	115.7	99.7	113.3
2019 NOV	117.6	118.5	128.1	115.7	100.9	112.7
2019 DEC	117.4	118.9	128.2	115.7	104.4	112.0
2020 JAN	117.5	119.4	128.1	115.6	103.0	111.9
2020 FEB	117.5	119.3	127.1	115.2	94.2	111.4
2020 MAR	117.6	119.8	126.7	115.2	70.9	110.3
2020 APR	116.8	119.0	125.9	114.4	51.2	108.6
2020 MAY	116.9	119.1	125.9	113.9	54.6	108.6
2020 JUN	117.9	119.4	126.3	113.9	68.3	108.9

17.1 Produce Price Index (2010=SIC2007)

	Gross Sector Price Indices of Materials & Fuels purchased					
	6107222000: GSI (excl. CCL) - Inputs for Manufacture of Rubber/Plastic products	6107124250: GSI Sub-section - Inputs of Manuf of Basic Metals & Fabricated prod'	6107126270: GSI Sub-section - Inputs for Manuf of Computer, Elect & Opt products	6107228000: GSI (excl. CCL) - Inputs for Manufacture of Machinery & Equipment	6107129300: GSI Sub-section - Inputs for Manufacture of Motor Vechicles	6107131330: GSI Sub-section - Inputs for Manuf of Other Manufactured Goods n.e.c
	MB4R	MC3F	MC3G	MB4U	MC3I	MC3J
2013	108.7	107.0	103.1	105.6	104.3	106.3
2014	105.9	103.6	103.0	104.4	103.1	106.4
2015	101.6	95.5	102.1	102.1	101.3	105.8
2016	101.8	97.5	104.4	104.8	103.5	108.9
2017	109.0	108.6	110.0	111.3	108.6	114.5
2018	115.0	115.4	112.5	114.7	111.5	117.4
2019	115.2	117.4	114.7	116.6	113.5	119.7
2017 JAN	105.7	106.8	108.8	109.8	107	113.5
2017 FEB	106.6	107.5	108.9	110.1	107.1	113.8
2017 MAR	107.3	107.7	109.5	110.7	107.8	114.2
2017 APR	108	107.3	109.7	110.5	107.7	114.1
2017 MAY	108.1	106.5	109.5	110.4	107.8	113.8
2017 JUN	108.4	106.3	109.8	110.7	108.4	114.1
2017 JUL	108.8	106.8	109.9	111	108.7	114.2
2017 AUG	109.7	108.7	110.6	111.8	109.3	114.9
2017 SEP	110	110.1	110.4	112.1	109.1	114.7
2017 OCT	110.6	111.2	110.7	112.5	109.6	115.2
2017 NOV	111.2	112.1	111.1	112.8	109.9	115.5
2017 DEC	113.4	112.5	111.2	113.1	110.5	115.9
2018 JAN	112.0	113.3	111.1	113.1	110.1	115.7
2018 FEB	112.9	113.2	111.2	113.4	110.3	115.7
2018 MAR	113.2	113.4	111.2	113.6	110.4	116.0
2018 APR	113.4	113.5	111.1	113.5	110.3	116.0
2018 MAY	114.4	115.2	112.1	114.2	111.2	117.3
2018 JUN	114.8	116.1	112.6	114.8	111.6	117.9
2018 JUL	115.3	115.8	112.7	114.8	111.6	117.6
2018 AUG	116.2	116.5	113.4	115.4	112.2	118.4
2018 SEP	117.0	117.1	113.6	115.7	112.3	118.5
2018 OCT	117.3	117.5	113.5	115.6	112.3	118.5
2018 NOV	117.1	116.5	113.6	115.7	112.4	118.6
2018 DEC	116.7	116.2	114.0	116.2	112.7	118.9
2019 JAN	116.5	116.1	113.9	116.0	112.5	118.7
2019 FEB	116.1	116.8	114.1	116.2	112.6	118.9
2019 MAR	114.8	117.0	113.9	116.1	112.3	118.7
2019 APR	115.3	117.9	114.2	116.5	112.8	119.2
2019 MAY	115.5	117.1	114.1	116.3	112.9	119.2
2019 JUN	115.6	116.8	114.8	116.7	113.3	119.7
2019 JUL	115.7	117.6	115.5	117.2	114.4	120.9
2019 AUG	115.8	118.1	116.1	117.9	115.0	121.4
2019 SEP	114.9	118.3	115.5	117.3	114.4	120.8
2019 OCT	114.3	118.8	115.3	117.3	114.3	120.4
2019 NOV	114.0	117.0	114.6	116.2	113.6	119.7
2019 DEC	113.5	116.9	114.2	115.9	113.4	119.3
2020 JAN	113.5	118.7	114.8	116.8	114.0	119.7
2020 FEB	113.2	119.2	115.3	117.3	114.5	120.3
2020 MAR	112.8	117.9	115.9	117.9	115.2	121.1
2020 APR	111.5	115.3	115.0	117.0	114.5	120.2
2020 MAY	111.4	115.2	115.0	117.0	114.7	120.3
2020 JUN	111.9	116.2	115.2	117.0	114.8	120.4

Further information on Produce Price Indices can be found at:

Source: Office for National Statistics

https://www.ons.gov.uk/economy/inflationandpriceindices/methodologies/producerpriceindicesqmi

Abreviations

NSI - Net Sector Input	FBTP - Food, Beverages and Tobacco Products	NSA - Not Seasonally Adjusted
SA - Seasonally Adjusted	GSI - Gross Sector Input	CCL - Climate Change Levy

17.2 Producer Price Index of Output (2010=100, SIC2007)

	Net Sector Output Price Indices of Materials & Fuels purchased		Gross Sector Output Price Indices of Materials & Fuel purchased (All Manufacturing & Selected Industries)				
	7200700000: Net Sector Output - Output of Manufactured products	7200799000: Net Sector Output - All Manufacturing excl Food, Beverages Tobacco	7111101280: Gross Sector Output - Food Products, Beverages & Tobacco incl duty	7112130000: Textiles	7112140000: Wearing Apparel	7112150000: Leather & related products	7112160000: Wood, Products of Wood & Cork, except Furniture; Articles of Straw
CDID:	JVZ7	K3BI	K65A	K37R	K37S	K37T	K37U
2012	107.0	103.9	110.9	110.6	106.1	119.0	109.0
2013	108.4	104.8	114.8	111.4	106.9	123.9	110.4
2014	108.4	105.7	113.7	112.5	110.7	124.2	113.9
2015	106.6	105.9	111.3	112.3	112.3	121.8	114.9
2016	107.1	107.0	110.5	111.9	113.4	121.3	114.3
2017	110.7	109.7	114.9	112.9	114.8	124.1	118.8
2018	113.9	112.3	117.5	114.2	116.6	125.4	127.1
2019	115.7	114.3	119.2	117.3	119.1	124.8	130.2
2016 JAN	105.5	106.0	109.9	112.6	112.3	119.9	114.1
FEB	105.6	106.1	110.1	113.4	112.3	120.5	113.4
MAR	106.1	106.2	111.0	113.3	112.6	120.5	113.9
APR	106.5	106.4	111.2	113.6	113.3	119.8	113.7
MAY	106.6	106.5	110.3	112.4	113.4	120.4	113.6
JUN	106.9	106.6	110.1	110.3	113.4	120.7	114.2
JUL	107.1	107.2	109.4	110.8	113.6	120.8	113.9
AUG	107.3	107.4	109.7	111.0	113.9	121.4	114.2
SEP	107.6	107.4	110.3	111.2	114.0	122.2	114.1
OCT	108.3	107.9	111.0	111.0	114.0	123.0	115.4
NOV	108.4	108.0	111.1	111.0	114.0	123.5	115.7
DEC	108.7	108.1	111.3	111.6	114.1	123.0	115.8
2017 JAN	109.3	108.6	111.8	112.2	114.1	122.7	116.5
FEB	109.5	108.6	112.4	112.5	114.1	123.4	116.8
MAR	110.0	109.0	113.6	112.7	114.6	123.4	117.3
APR	110.3	109.4	114.1	112.8	114.6	123.0	117.9
MAY	110.4	109.5	115.1	112.8	114.6	124.2	117.7
JUN	110.4	109.7	114.9	113.1	114.7	124.0	118.1
JUL	110.6	109.9	115.2	113.1	114.6	124.6	119.2
AUG	111.0	110.2	115.5	113.1	115.0	125.2	119.6
SEP	111.2	110.1	115.7	113.1	114.9	124.5	120.1
OCT	111.4	110.3	116.3	113.1	115.0	124.6	120.5
NOV	111.8	110.5	116.7	113.3	115.9	123.8	120.9
DEC	112.1	110.6	117.5	113.4	115.9	126.0	121.0
2018 JAN	112.4	111.0	116.9	113.4	115.8	126.2	122.9
FEB	112.4	111.3	116.8	113.7	115.6	126.2	123.4
MAR	112.7	111.4	117.2	114.7	115.6	126.2	125.0
APR	113.1	111.6	117.5	114.4	115.9	126.2	126.5
MAY	113.7	111.9	117.3	114.3	116.0	126.4	127.1
JUN	114.0	112.3	117.3	114.3	116.2	127.0	127.5
JUL	114.0	112.4	117.0	114.0	116.3	127.0	127.6
AUG	114.3	112.6	117.1	114.0	116.4	123.5	128.3
SEP	114.7	112.8	118.1	114.0	116.4	123.7	128.7
OCT	115.1	113.1	118.1	114.0	118.0	124.1	129.0
NOV	115.2	113.2	118.4	114.6	118.5	124.0	129.3
DEC	114.8	113.4	118.6	114.6	118.5	124.0	129.6
2019 JAN	114.8	113.7	118.7	114.8	118.8	125.0	129.8
FEB	115.1	113.9	118.6	115.2	118.8	125.0	130.2
MAR	115.2	113.8	119.0	116.3	118.8	126.2	130.0
APR	115.5	114.0	119.3	117.1	118.8	126.2	130.7
MAY	115.9	114.1	119.7	117.4	119.0	126.8	130.5
JUN	115.8	114.2	119.7	117.6	119.1	122.9	131.2
JUL	116.2	114.6	119.6	118.0	119.2	124.2	131.1
AUG	116.2	114.8	119.2	118.1	119.4	124.2	130.9
SEP	116.1	114.7	119.0	118.2	119.8	124.2	130.7
OCT	116.0	114.6	119.2	118.2	119.3	124.2	129.2
NOV	115.8	114.5	119.0	118.1	119.4	124.2	128.9
DEC	115.7	114.4	119.3	118.0	119.3	124.2	129.5
2020 JAN	115.9	114.5	119.6	118.2	119.4	124.2	129.4
FEB	115.7	114.5	119.9	118.4	119.4	124.2	129.9
MAR	115.6	114.7	120.6	118.7	119.8	123.3	129.2
APR	114.7	114.8	120.4	118.9	119.8	123.3	129.3
MAY	114.5	114.8	120.4	119.3	119.8	123.3	130.0
JUN	114.8	114.8	120.4	119.4	119.8	123.3	130.3

17.2 Producer Price Index of Output (2010=100, SIC2007)

Gross Sector Output Price Indices of Materials & Fuel purchased (All Manufacturing & Selected Industries)

CDID:	7112170000: Paper & Paper products	7112180000: Printing & Recording Services	7112200000: Chemicals & Chemical products	7112220000: Rubber & Plastics products	7112230000: Other Non-Metallic Mineral products	7112240000: Basic Metals	7112260000: Computer, Electronic & Optical products
	K37V	K37W	K37Z	K383	K384	K385	K387
2012	106.9	99.9	108.4	107.0	106.4	104.7	96.5
2013	106.6	99.3	106.5	108.5	107.7	102.0	96.9
2014	106.9	100.0	104.8	108.7	109.6	99.7	97.5
2015	106.3	100.2	101.6	107.9	111.7	91.4	97.9
2016	107.2	100.3	99.3	109.7	113.5	95.1	98.9
2017	107.9	102.8	105.3	111.9	115.6	109.5	101.8
2018	112.3	104.1	113.1	114.9	118.5	116.6	102.8
2019	114.3	104.8	113.4	117.0	122.2	116.6	105.4
2016 JAN	107.1	99.7	99.4	109.2	113.0	85.6	98.1
FEB	107.2	99.6	99.2	109.3	113.0	85.9	98.3
MAR	107.2	99.8	98.8	109.3	113.2	88.4	98.3
APR	107	99.7	98.8	109.5	113.3	91.0	98.3
MAY	107.3	99.8	98.7	109.5	113.6	93.8	98.2
JUN	107.4	100.1	98.5	109.5	113.4	95.3	98.5
JUL	106.8	100	98.8	109.6	113.6	96.6	98.8
AUG	106.7	99.9	98.7	109.8	113.6	99.5	99.4
SEP	106.8	100.2	98.8	109.8	113.6	98.9	99.3
OCT	107.4	101.5	100.3	110.1	113.9	100.7	99.6
NOV	107.5	101.6	100.9	110.2	113.9	101.9	99.7
DEC	107.4	101.7	101.3	110.2	113.7	103.2	99.8
2017 JAN	107	102	102.7	110.3	114.9	106.0	100.0
FEB	107.3	102	103.7	110.5	115.2	107.5	100.0
MAR	107	102	104.2	111.0	115.2	108.1	100.1
APR	107.1	102.3	105	111.3	115.1	108.4	101.7
MAY	107.4	102.4	104.7	111.9	115.5	107.3	101.7
JUN	107.7	102.6	104.6	112.1	116.0	106.6	102.0
JUL	108.2	102.9	105.1	112.0	115.9	107.7	102.5
AUG	108.2	103.2	105.7	112.2	116.1	109.4	102.6
SEP	108.2	103.3	106	112.5	115.7	111.8	102.4
OCT	108.6	104	106.4	112.7	115.7	113.3	102.6
NOV	109.1	103.6	107.2	112.9	116.2	113.9	102.7
DEC	109.3	103.6	107.7	113.1	116.2	114.1	102.7
2018 JAN	110.1	104.0	108.8	113.6	117.3	115.6	102.4
FEB	110.6	104.2	109.9	114.0	117.6	115.6	102.4
MAR	111.2	104.6	110.5	114.4	118.1	116.3	102.0
APR	111.4	104.8	112.3	114.5	118.3	115.6	102.0
MAY	112.0	104.2	112.7	114.7	118.4	116.1	102.3
JUN	112.8	103.9	112.9	114.6	118.5	117.0	102.3
JUL	113.0	103.8	113.6	115.1	118.6	117.1	102.1
AUG	112.8	103.5	114.2	115.2	118.7	117.6	103.2
SEP	112.6	103.8	115.3	115.4	118.7	117.2	103.8
OCT	113.2	103.6	115.8	115.6	119.0	116.8	103.9
NOV	113.8	104.3	115.7	115.9	119.4	116.7	103.7
DEC	113.9	104.2	115.2	116.0	119.3	117.1	103.8
2019 JAN	114.2	104.4	115.7	115.9	120.3	116.8	104.0
FEB	114.8	104.7	114.3	115.9	121.6	116.5	105.3
MAR	114.7	104.5	113.8	116.3	121.4	117.8	105.2
APR	114.9	104.9	113.8	116.5	121.8	118.5	105.4
MAY	114.7	104.8	113.7	117.2	122.6	117.4	105.4
JUN	114.1	104.4	113.5	117.3	122.6	116.8	105.3
JUL	114.4	104.7	113.3	117.5	123.1	116.8	105.6
AUG	114.1	104.5	113.3	117.6	123.0	117.0	105.6
SEP	114.3	104.9	112.9	117.5	123.1	117.1	105.7
OCT	114.0	105.0	112.4	117.2	122.7	118.6	105.8
NOV	113.7	105.6	112.2	117.3	122.5	113.4	105.7
DEC	113.5	105.7	111.9	117.3	122.1	112.2	105.4
2020 JAN	113.4	105.2	112.1	117.3	123.0	113.6	105.5
FEB	113.0	105.1	111.9	117.4	123.8	113.5	105.6
MAR	112.8	105.2	111.2	117.8	123.9	115.6	105.8
APR	113.0	105.3	111.1	117.8	125.0	117.0	105.7
MAY	113.0	105.3	111.6	117.8	124.6	118.1	105.7
JUN	112.4	105.3	111.3	118.0	124.3	117.0	106.0

17.2 Producer Price Index of Output (2010=100, SIC2007)

Gross Sector Output Price Indices of Materials & Fuel purchased (All Manufacturing & Selected Industries)

CDID:	7112270000: Electrical Equipment (NSA) K388	7112280000: Machinery & Equipment n.e.c. (NSA) K389	7112290000: Motor Vehicles, Trailers & Semi-trailers (NSA) K38A	7112300000: Other Transport Equipment (NSA) K38B	7112310000: Furniture (NSA) K38C	7112320000: Other Manufactured Goods (NSA) K38D	Output in the Construction Industry All New Work (2019=100) (NSA) MV3P	Mix-adjusted house price index of new dwellings (2015=100)
2012	102.8	105.5	101.5	102.9	105.1	104.0	71.9	88.1
2013	103	108.2	102.5	105.1	105.8	105.3	72.9	90.7
2014	103.7	109.8	102.0	107.4	107.2	107.2	81.4	98
2015	104.2	111.1	100.5	108.7	108.7	108.2	86.6	102.9
2016	103.9	113.1	102.3	111.6	110.0	110.5	91.5	112.6
2017	106.6	116.2	105.8	113.7	112.9	110.7	98.1	118.3
2018	109.2	117.8	108.0	115.1	115.6	111.4	97.6	123.3
2019	110.6	119.5	109.7	118.9	116.7	113.1	100.0	124.3
2016 JAN	104.0	112.2	101.0	109.6	109.7	108.7	75.8	107.4
FEB	104.2	112.3	101.2	109.7	109.3	108.9	83.8	109.0
MAR	103.1	112.5	101.2	109.9	109.4	109.4	92.9	110.5
APR	103.3	112.6	101.5	110.0	109.4	110.7	89.2	112.0
MAY	103.4	112.4	101.3	110.6	109.8	110.9	91.3	115.0
JUN	104.1	112.6	101.5	111.0	110.0	110.8	95.4	112.5
JUL	103.8	113.2	102.6	112.5	110.0	111.1	93.9	113.2
AUG	103.7	113.4	103.0	112.5	110.1	111.1	95.7	112.7
SEP	103.9	113.4	102.9	112.9	110.3	111.2	96.6	113.1
OCT	104.1	114.0	103.9	113.4	110.3	111.3	96.8	114.8
NOV	104.3	114.2	103.6	113.5	110.5	111.3	97.0	115.1
DEC	104.7	114.3	103.4	113.5	110.9	110.9	89.5	115.3
2017 JAN	105.1	115.5	104.0	114.1	112.4	110.9	85.1	117.3
FEB	105.5	115.5	103.9	113.8	111.7	110.3	89.4	116.3
MAR	106.0	115.9	104.8	113.9	111.9	110.7	103.5	116.3
APR	106.4	115.8	105.1	113.9	112.5	110.8	93.6	117.1
MAY	106.7	116.3	105.2	113.7	112.7	110.7	99.0	117.8
JUN	106.8	116.3	105.8	113.8	113.0	110.7	103.2	117.4
JUL	106.8	116.5	106.2	113.7	113.1	110.6	98.4	119.7
AUG	106.7	116.5	107.0	113.7	113.4	110.8	103.4	119.1
SEP	106.7	116.7	106.8	113.6	113.7	110.9	100.6	119.8
OCT	106.9	116.5	106.9	113.5	113.2	110.8	102.7	120.6
NOV	107.8	116.6	106.7	113.4	113.9	110.8	103.0	118.6
DEC	107.5	116.6	106.7	113.4	113.4	110.8	94.9	119.8
2018 JAN	108.7	117.0	107.0	113.4	113.7	110.9	87.0	122.4
FEB	109.0	117.2	107.2	113.8	114.0	111.0	90.2	126.4
MAR	109.2	117.6	107.3	113.8	114.2	111.0	97.6	121.3
APR	109.0	117.7	107.3	113.8	114.4	110.8	94.7	123.2
MAY	109.4	117.6	107.4	114.3	116.4	111.1	98.3	121.3
JUN	109.5	117.9	107.9	115.2	116.6	111.2	100.8	122.2
JUL	109.7	118.1	108.1	115.5	116.6	111.2	101.5	124.0
AUG	109.9	118.2	108.3	115.9	117.0	111.4	100.5	125.2
SEP	109.6	118.0	108.6	115.6	116.1	111.8	98.8	123.6
OCT	108.1	118.0	108.9	116.6	116.0	112.0	107.4	126.1
NOV	108.8	118.0	108.9	116.6	116.0	112.0	104.3	121.2
DEC	109.3	118.1	108.8	116.8	116.3	112.6	90.4	123.1
2019 JAN	109.3	118.6	109.6	117.1	116.4	112.5	87.5	123.5
FEB	109.1	118.9	109.4	116.3	116.4	112.6	93.1	126.7
MAR	109.3	119.2	109.4	116.2	116.5	112.5	102.5	123.8
APR	109.8	119.4	109.5	116.5	116.5	112.6	98.5	124.9
MAY	109.0	119.2	109.6	116.9	117.0	112.8	101.4	123.4
JUN	111.6	119.3	109.9	116.8	117.1	113.1	101.0	121.9
JUL	112.5	119.6	110.0	120.8	117.0	114.2	104.9	128.0
AUG	112.6	120.0	110.3	121.2	116.9	113.7	103.0	124.8
SEP	111.2	120.0	109.9	121.0	116.8	113.6	104.3	126.4
OCT	110.8	120.2	109.8	121.6	116.7	113.1	107.1	126.4
NOV	110.9	120.1	109.5	121.4	116.6	113.0	103.4	120.9
DEC	110.9	120.0	109.5	121.4	116.5	112.9	93.4	121.3
2020 JAN	111.3	120.2	109.6	121.6	116.4	113.4	90.1	128.9
FEB	111.6	120.3	109.7	121.6	116.7	113.2	91.8	123.6
MAR	111.8	120.7	109.9	122.3	116.9	113.6	96.6	127.0
APR	111.8	120.7	109.8	122.4	117.0	113.6	52.1	129.1
MAY	111.6	120.5	110.1	122.6	117.0	112.4	59.2	128.9
JUN	111.8	120.3	110.1	122.9	117.0	113.1	73.4	124.1

Further information on Produce Price Indices can be found at:
https://www.ons.gov.uk/economy/inflationandpriceindices/methodologies/producerpriceindicesqmi

Source: Office for National Statistics
Department for Communities and Local Government

Abbreviations
NSI - Net Sector Input   FBTP - Food, Beverages and Tobacco Products   NSA - Not Seasonally Adjusted
SA - Seasonally Adjusted   GSI - Gross Sector Input   CCL - Climate Change Levy

17.3 CPI: Detailed figures by division [1,2]

	Food and non-alcoholic beverages	Alcoholic beverages and tobacco	Clothing and footwear	Housing, water, electricity, gas & other fuels	Furniture, household equipment & routine maintenance	Health [3]	Trans-port	Commun-ication	Recreation and culture	Edu-cation 3	Restaur-ants and hotels	Miscell-aneous goods and services [3]	CPI (overall index)
COICOP Division	1	2	3	4	5	6	7	8	9	10	11	12	
	CHZR	CHZS	CHZT	CHZU	CHZV	CHZW	CHZX	CHZY	CHZZ	CJUU	CJUV	CJUW	CHZQ
Weights 2020													
Feb-Dec	99	40	61	131	60	27	147	21	168	29	119	98	1000
Monthly indices (2015=100)													
	D7BU	D7BV	D7BW	D7BX	D7BY	D7BZ	D7C2	D7C3	D7C4	D7C5	D7C6	D7C7	D7BT
Jul 2018	101.7	110.3	98.7	104.6	103.0	107.7	111.8	105.9	105.3	110.9	108.8	101.7	105.8
Aug	101.9	111.1	101.8	104.7	104.2	108.0	113.3	106.3	105.9	110.9	108.9	102.3	106.5
Sep	101.7	111.2	104.9	105.2	104.2	108.2	111.2	106.6	106.2	112.0	109.3	102.6	106.6
Oct	101.5	111.1	104.4	105.8	104.1	107.9	110.8	107.4	106.9	114.4	109.1	102.5	106.7
Nov	101.6	112.5	106.0	105.8	104.3	107.8	110.4	107.4	107.0	114.4	109.7	102.7	107.0
Dec	102.5	111.3	104.9	105.8	105.4	108.0	111.3	107.3	106.8	114.4	110.0	102.4	107.1
Jan	102.6	114.0	100.4	104.2	103.2	108.6	109.9	107.6	106.7	114.4	109.3	102.6	106.3
Feb	103.0	115.0	101.3	104.3	105.2	108.8	110.4	107.5	107.2	114.4	109.5	102.9	106.8
Mar	103.1	114.6	102.4	104.4	105.4	109.1	110.3	107.7	107.4	114.4	110.0	103.1	107.0
Apr	102.8	114.1	102.5	107.0	104.1	110.0	112.9	109.1	106.6	114.4	110.5	103.4	107.6
May	102.9	114.4	103.0	107.1	105.2	110.1	112.5	109.8	107.1	114.4	111.4	103.7	107.9
Jun	103.1	114.7	102.0	107.1	105.9	110.4	113.0	109.9	106.7	114.4	111.3	103.5	107.9
Jul 2019	103.1	114.5	99.1	107.1	104.1	110.5	113.4	109.9	107.8	114.4	112.2	103.4	107.9
Aug	103.7	114.7	100.9	107.2	105.0	110.6	114.9	110.2	107.1	114.4	112.0	104.1	108.4
Sep	103.5	114.5	103.9	107.2	106.2	111.0	111.9	110.9	107.7	115.6	112.8	104.4	108.5
Oct	102.8	114.9	104.9	106.1	105.0	110.6	111.7	111.0	108.1	117.5	112.5	104.4	108.3
Nov	103.7	114.7	106.0	106.2	105.5	111.0	111.4	111.0	108.6	117.5	112.3	104.7	108.5
Dec	104.3	113.1	104.0	106.2	106.9	111.0	112.1	111.9	108.4	117.5	111.8	104.7	108.5
Jan	104.1	115.7	100.6	106.3	103.5	111.7	112.0	112.1	108.3	117.5	111.7	105.0	108.2
Feb	104.3	115.8	101.5	106.2	105.3	112.1	112.4	112.4	108.7	117.5	112.3	105.4	108.6
Mar	104.5	116.2	101.2	106.2	105.4	112.6	111.8	113.1	108.9	117.5	112.4	105.6	108.6
Apr	104.2	117.0	99.5	105.7	103.7	112.4	111.8	113.6	109.3	117.5	113.2	104.7	108.5
May	104.8	117.4	99.8	105.8	104.4	110.9	110.6	114.2	109.2	117.5	113.6	104.9	108.5
Jun	104.2	117.1	99.7	105.9	105.3	112.7	111.2	114.2	109.5	117.5	113.3	104.9	108.6
Jul 2020	103.9	117.5	99.0	106.2	104.9	114.0	112.6	114.7	110.6	117.5	114.2	104.9	109.1
Percentage change on a year earlier													
	D7G8	D7G9	D7GA	D7GB	D7GC	D7GD	D7GE	D7GF	D7GG	D7GH	D7GI	D7GJ	D7G7
Jul 2018	2.3	3.5	-0.4	2.3	1.3	2.2	5.7	1.6	3.1	2.8	2.5	-1.0	2.5
Aug	2.5	4.1	0.3	2.3	0.7	2.4	6.1	0.3	3.6	2.8	2.5	-0.7	2.7
Sep	1.5	4.1	-0.4	2.7	0.5	2.6	5.6	0.9	3.0	2.9	2.5	-0.3	2.4
Oct	0.9	4.0	-1.1	2.9	0.7	2.3	5.4	1.9	3.2	3.1	2.4	-	2.4
Nov	0.5	5.8	-0.8	2.8	0.7	2.2	4.9	1.6	2.5	3.1	2.7	0.4	2.3
Dec	0.7	4.1	-0.9	2.8	0.4	2.3	3.4	2.9	2.8	3.1	3.1	0.1	2.1
Jan	0.9	4.2	-1.3	1.1	1.0	2.3	3.2	3.1	2.9	3.1	2.6	0.2	1.8
Feb	1.1	5.1	-2.0	1.2	0.3	2.4	3.1	3.6	3.1	3.1	2.6	0.2	1.9
Mar	0.8	5.2	-1.6	1.2	0.6	2.5	3.3	3.7	2.7	3.1	2.8	0.6	1.9
Apr	0.7	3.9	-1.9	3.4	0.2	2.3	4.7	4.6	1.5	3.1	2.4	0.9	2.1
May	1.0	3.3	-1.6	3.4	0.6	2.5	2.8	4.9	1.8	3.1	2.8	1.1	2.0
Jun	1.6	3.7	-0.5	2.8	0.9	2.6	2.4	4.3	1.8	3.1	2.4	1.1	2.0
Jul 2019	1.4	3.8	0.4	2.4	1.1	2.6	1.5	3.8	2.4	3.1	3.1	1.7	2.1
Aug	1.8	3.3	-0.9	2.4	0.8	2.4	1.4	3.6	1.2	3.1	2.8	1.8	1.7
Sep	1.8	3.0	-1.0	2.0	1.9	2.6	0.6	4.1	1.4	3.2	3.2	1.7	1.7
Oct	1.3	3.5	0.5	0.3	0.9	2.6	0.8	3.4	1.2	2.7	3.2	1.9	1.5
Nov	2.1	1.9	-	0.3	1.2	2.9	0.9	3.3	1.5	2.7	2.4	1.9	1.5
Dec	1.7	1.5	-0.8	0.4	1.5	2.8	0.7	4.3	1.5	2.7	1.6	2.2	1.3
Jan	1.4	1.5	0.2	2.0	0.2	2.9	1.8	4.2	1.5	2.7	2.2	2.4	1.8
Feb	1.2	0.7	0.2	1.8	0.1	3.0	1.8	4.5	1.4	2.7	2.5	2.4	1.7
Mar	1.3	1.4	-1.2	1.7	-	3.2	1.3	5.0	1.3	2.7	2.1	2.5	1.5
Apr	1.3	2.5	-2.9	-1.1	-0.4	2.2	-1.0	4.2	2.6	2.7	2.4	1.3	0.8
May	1.8	2.6	-3.1	-1.2	-0.7	0.7	-1.7	4.0	2.0	2.7	2.0	1.1	0.5
Jun	1.1	2.1	-2.2	-1.1	-0.5	2.1	-1.6	3.9	2.6	2.7	1.8	1.3	0.6
Jul 2020	0.8	2.6	-0.1	-0.9	0.8	3.2	-0.7	4.3	2.6	2.7	1.8	1.4	1.0

Key: - zero or negligible

Source: Office for National Statistics

1. For the release of January consumer price inflation data on 16 February 2016, CPIH and CPI indices have been re-referenced and published with 2015=100. Full historic series for each of the re-referenced indices are now available for users to view or download. Regular re-referencing of indices is methodological good practice as it avoids rounding issues that can arise from small index values. Please note that re-referencing does not impact on published inflation rates, although when using the indices to calculate inflation rates, it is important to use indices that are calculated in the same reference year. Re-referencing does not impact on RPI. For more information, please contact cpi@ons.gov.uk.

2. More detailed CPI data are available at http://www.ons.gov.uk

3. The coverage of these categories was extended in January 2000; further extensions to coverage came into effect in January 2001 for health and miscellaneous goods and services; the coverage of miscellaneous goods and services was further extended with effect from January 2002. (Details are given in a series of Economic Trends articles available on the National Statistics website)

17.4 Retail Prices Index[1] United Kingdom

Indices (13 January 1987=100)

	All items (RPI)	All items excluding mortgage interest payments (RPIX)	All items excluding mortgage interest payments and depreciation	Housing	All items excluding Food	All items excluding Seasonal food[2]	Food and catering	Alcohol and tobacco	Housing and household expenditure	Personal expenditure	Travel and leisure	Consumer durables[3]
Weights												
	CZGU	CZGY	DOGZ	CZGX	CZGV	CZGW	CBVV	CBVW	CBVX	CBVY	CBVZ	CBWA
2005	1000	950	901	776	890	981	159	96	387	89	269	122
2006	1000	950	906	778	895	983	155	96	392	90	267	117
2007	1000	945	895	762	895	981	152	95	408	83	262	109
2008	1000	940	885	746	889	980	158	86	417	83	256	104
2009	1000	959	909	764	882	979	168	90	416	80	246	106
2010	1000	966	911	763	888	981	159	91	403	81	266	105
2011	1000	968	914	762	882	980	165	88	408	82	257	106
2012	1000	971	915	763	886	981	161	85	412	84	258	100
2013	1000	971	913	746	884	980	163	91	419	83	244	96
2014	1000	970	912	747	886	981	161	87	424	85	243	98
2015	1000	971	898	737	891	982	156	83	432	83	246	94
2016	1000	972	892	734	898	982	149	82	436	83	250	98
2017	1000	975	891	734	898	982	150	81	433	79	257	99
2018	1000	976	893	743	898	982	152	79	420	85	264	104
Pre July 2019[1]	1000	975	891	740	900	982	149	80	428	81	262	97
July 2019 onwards	1000	975	891	742	899	982	150	82	423	82	263	96
2020	1000	976	892	734	898	982	153	84	428	79	256	93
Annual averages												
	CHAW	CHMK	CHON	CHAZ	CHAY	CHAX	CHBS	CHBT	CHBU	CHBV	CHBW	CHBY
2005	192.0	188.2	182.6	173.7	198.7	193.3	172.9	239.8	219.4	131.0	179.2	95.3
2006	198.1	193.7	187.8	178.3	205.2	199.5	176.9	247.1	231.8	131.7	181.1	94.0
2007	206.6	199.9	193.3	183.2	213.9	207.9	184.3	256.2	248.1	132.9	183.8	93.3
2008	214.8	208.5	201.9	191.3	221.2	216.0	198.5	266.7	258.6	132.4	189.0	91.6
2009	213.7	212.6	207.2	196.3	218.3	214.6	207.6	276.7	247.4	131.4	191.2	90.7
2010	223.6	222.7	217.0	206.5	228.8	224.5	214.1	289.9	253.8	138.2	207.6	94.4
2011	235.2	234.5	229.3	219.6	240.5	236.3	225.6	311.3	262.5	149.8	220.1	99.7
2012	242.7	242.0	237.0	227.4	248.2	243.9	232.9	327.1	270.9	158.2	224.1	104.1
2013	250.1	249.4	244.4	235.1	255.5	251.2	240.8	341.9	279.7	166.8	226.8	108.8
2014	256.0	255.5	249.5	240.2	262.4	257.3	242.5	354.9	288.2	175.0	228.7	113.5
2015	258.5	258.1	251.0	240.9	266.0	260.0	239.8	362.7	293.7	182.6	226.7	117.6
2016	263.1	263.0	254.6	244.0	271.9	264.8	237.7	369.8	300.3	189.4	230.5	121.3
2017	272.5	273.0	264.0	253.9	282.0	274.3	243.6	383.5	308.8	200.1	241.6	129.2
2018	281.6	282.1	272.9	262.9	291.9	283.5	248.9	397.6	318.1	208.6	251.6	134.7
2019	288.8	289.3	280.2	270.2	299.7	290.8	253.8	409.4	325.8	215.7	258.6	138.9
Monthly figures												
	CHAW	CHMK	CHON	CHAZ	CHAY	CHAX	CHBS	CHBT[4]	CHBU	CHBV	CHBW	CHBY
2019 Sep	291.0	291.5	282.4	272.3	302.3	293.1	254.4	410.8	329.4	219.1	259.7	141.4
Oct	290.4	291.0	281.7	271.6	301.7	292.6	254.0	411.9	327.5	219.8	259.8	140.9
Nov	291.0	291.5	282.3	272.1	302.0	293.0	255.7	411.9	327.9	221.7	259.4	141.8
Dec	291.9	292.4	283.2	273.1	303.0	294.0	256.4	408.5	329.5	219.9	261.5	142.3
2020 Jan	290.6	291.2	281.9	271.6	301.7	292.7	256.2	413.7	327.6	216.7	260.0	136.8
Feb	292.0	292.6	283.5	273.5	303.2	294.0	256.8	414.2	328.3	221.9	261.3	141.3
Mar	292.6	293.3	284.2	274.3	303.7	294.8	257.8	415.6	328.4	222.7	262.2	142.0
Apr	292.6	293.2	284.0	273.4	303.8	294.7	258.3	416.1	328.9	220.5	261.8	140.6
May	292.2	293.3	284.0	273.4	303.2	294.3	259.2	416.6	328.5	221.6	260.1	141.5
June	292.7	293.9	284.6	274.1	303.9	294.9	258.2	416.1	329.2	222.5	261.3	143.2
July	294.2	295.4	286.1	275.6	305.8	296.5	257.9	420.3	329.6	223.1	265.1	142.3
Aug	293.3	294.5	284.9	274.2	304.6	295.5	249.7	419.0	330.2	223.5	266.1	142.8

1. See chapter text.

Source: Office for National Statistics

2. Seasonal food is defined as items of food the prices of which show significant seasonal variations. These are fresh fruit and vegetables, fresh fish, eggs and home-killed lamb.

3. Consumer durables: Furniture, furnishings, electrical appliances and other household equipment, men's, women's and children's outerwear, footwear, audio-visual equipment, CDs and tapes, toys, photographic and sports goods.

4. The index is based on less than half of the number of price quotes used in February 2020 because of the reduced availability of products for pricing due to the coronavirus (COVID-19) pandemic.

5. The Retail Prices Index and its derivatives do not meet the required standards for designation as National Statistics. A full report can be found at: http://www.statisticsauthority.gov.uk/

17.5 Tax and Price Index[1] United Kingdom

Indices and percentagescentagescentagescentages

Tax and Price Index: (January 1987=100)

DQAB

	2005	2006	2007	2008	2009	2010	2011	2012	2013	2014	2015	2016	2017	2018	2019	2020
January	172.1	175.9	183.3	190.7	188.6	194.7	205.5	212.8	218.8	222.7	223.9	225.8	232.7	..	..	..
February	172.8	176.7	184.8	192.3	189.8	196.0	207.7	214.6	220.5	224.2	225.2	226.9	..	..	..	..
March	173.7	177.4	186.1	192.9	189.7	197.4	208.8	215.6	221.6	224.8	225.6	228.0	..	..	..	..
April	174.1	178.3	186.3	192.2	188.5	199.5	209.2	215.6	219.7	224.2	225.1	228.8	..	..	..	..
May	174.5	179.5	187.1	193.4	189.7	200.3	210.0	215.5	220.2	224.4	225.5	229.5	..	..	..	..
June	174.7	180.3	188.2	195.1	190.2	200.8	210.0	214.9	219.9	224.8	225.9	230.4	..	..	..	..
July	174.7	180.3	187.0	194.8	190.2	200.3	209.5	215.2	219.9	224.5	225.6	230.7	..	..	..	..
August	175.1	181.0	188.2	195.5	191.3	201.2	210.9	216.1	221.1	225.5	226.7	231.7	..	..	..	..
September	175.6	181.9	188.9	196.7	192.2	201.9	212.7	217.2	222.0	226.1	226.6	232.1	..	..	..	..
October	175.8	182.2	189.8	196.0	192.9	202.4	212.8	218.6	222.0	226.1	226.5	232.0	..	..	..	..
November	176.1	182.8	190.6	194.3	193.4	203.4	213.2	218.6	222.2	225.6	226.7	232.7	..	..	..	..
December	176.6	184.4	191.8	191.2	194.8	204.9	214.1	219.8	223.5	226.0	227.6	234.1	..	..	..	..

CHAW (All items RPI)

	2005	2006	2007	2008	2009	2010	2011	2012	2013	2014	2015	2016	2017	2018	2019	2020
January	188.9	193.4	201.6	209.8	210.1	217.9	229.0	238.0	245.8	252.6	255.4	258.8	265.5	276.0	283.0	290.6
February	189.6	194.2	203.1	211.4	211.4	219.2	231.3	239.9	247.6	254.2	256.7	260.0	268.4	278.1	285.0	292.0
March	190.5	195.0	204.4	212.1	211.3	220.7	232.5	240.8	248.7	254.8	257.1	261.1	269.3	278.3	285.1	292.6
April	191.6	196.5	205.4	214.0	211.5	222.8	234.4	242.5	249.5	255.7	258.0	261.4	270.6	279.7	288.2	292.6
May	192.0	197.7	206.2	215.1	212.8	223.6	235.2	242.4	250.0	255.9	258.5	262.1	271.7	280.7	289.2	292.2
June	192.2	198.5	207.3	216.8	213.4	224.1	235.2	241.8	249.7	256.3	258.9	263.1	272.3	281.5	289.6	292.7
July	192.2	198.5	206.1	216.5	213.4	223.6	234.7	242.1	249.7	256.0	258.6	263.4	272.9	281.7	289.5	294.2
August	192.6	199.2	207.3	217.2	214.4	224.5	236.1	243.0	251.0	257.0	259.8	264.4	274.7	284.2	291.7	293.3
September	193.1	200.1	208.0	218.4	215.3	225.3	237.9	244.2	251.9	257.6	259.6	264.9	275.1	284.1	291.0	..
October	193.3	200.4	208.9	217.7	216.0	225.8	238.0	245.6	251.9	257.7	259.5	264.8	275.3	284.5	290.4	..
November	193.6	201.1	209.7	216.0	216.6	226.8	238.5	245.6	252.1	257.1	259.8	265.5	275.8	284.6	291.0	..
December	194.1	202.7	210.9	212.9	218.0	228.4	239.4	246.8	253.4	257.5	260.6	267.1	278.1	285.6	291.9	..

Percentage changes on one year earlier CZVL

Tax and Price Index[1]

	2005	2006	2007	2008	2009	2010	2011	2012	2013	2014	2015	2016	2017	2018	2019	2020
January	3.1	2.2	4.2	4.0	-1.1	3.2	5.5	3.6	2.8	1.8	0.5	0.8	3.1	..	..	..
February	3.1	2.3	4.6	4.1	-1.3	3.3	6.0	3.3	2.7	1.7	0.4	0.8	..	..	..	..
March	3.1	2.1	4.9	3.7	-1.7	4.1	5.8	3.3	2.8	1.4	0.4	1.1	..	..	..	..
April	3.1	2.4	4.5	3.2	-1.9	5.8	4.9	3.1	1.9	2.0	0.4	1.6	..	..	..	..
May	2.8	2.9	4.2	3.4	-1.9	5.6	4.8	2.6	2.2	1.9	0.5	1.8	..	..	..	..
June	2.8	3.2	4.4	3.7	-2.5	5.6	4.6	2.3	2.3	2.2	0.5	2.0	..	..	..	..
July	2.8	3.2	3.7	4.2	-2.4	5.3	4.6	2.7	2.2	2.1	0.5	2.3	..	..	..	..
August	2.6	3.4	4.0	3.9	-2.1	5.2	4.8	2.5	2.3	2.0	0.5	2.2	..	..	..	..
September	2.5	3.6	3.8	4.1	-2.3	5.0	5.3	2.1	2.2	1.8	0.2	2.4	..	..	..	..
October	2.3	3.6	4.2	3.3	-1.6	4.9	5.1	2.7	1.6	1.8	0.2	2.4	..	..	..	..
November	2.3	3.8	4.3	1.9	-0.5	5.2	4.8	2.5	1.6	1.5	0.5	2.6	..	..	..	..
December	2.0	4.4	4.0	-0.3	1.9	5.2	4.5	2.7	1.7	1.1	0.7	2.9	..	..	..	..

Retail Prices Index - CZBH[2]

	2005	2006	2007	2008	2009	2010	2011	2012	2013	2014	2015	2016	2017	2018	2019	2020
January	3.2	2.4	4.2	4.1	0.1	3.7	5.1	3.9	3.3	2.8	1.1	1.3	2.6	4.0	2.5	2.7
February	3.2	2.4	4.6	4.1	-	3.7	5.5	3.7	3.2	2.7	1.0	1.3	3.2	3.6	2.5	2.5
March	3.2	2.4	4.8	3.8	-0.4	4.4	5.3	3.6	3.3	2.5	0.9	1.6	3.1	3.3	2.4	2.6
April	3.2	2.6	4.5	4.2	-1.2	5.3	5.2	3.5	2.9	2.5	0.9	1.3	3.5	3.4	3.0	1.5
May	2.9	3.0	4.3	4.3	-1.1	5.1	5.2	3.1	3.1	2.4	1.0	1.4	3.7	3.3	3.0	1.0
June	2.9	3.3	4.4	4.6	-1.6	5.0	5.0	2.8	3.3	2.6	1.0	1.6	3.5	3.4	2.9	1.1
July	2.9	3.3	3.8	5.0	-1.4	4.8	5.0	3.2	3.1	2.5	1.0	1.9	3.6	3.2	2.8	1.6
August	2.8	3.4	4.1	4.8	-1.3	4.7	5.2	2.9	3.3	2.4	1.1	1.8	3.9	3.5	2.6	0.5
September	2.7	3.6	3.9	5.0	-1.4	4.6	5.6	2.6	3.2	2.3	0.8	2.0	3.9	3.3	2.4	..
October	2.5	3.7	4.2	4.2	-0.8	4.5	5.4	3.2	2.6	2.3	0.7	2.0	4.0	3.3	2.1	..
November	2.4	3.9	4.3	3.0	0.3	4.7	5.2	3.0	2.6	2.0	1.1	2.2	3.9	3.2	2.2	..
December	2.2	4.4	4.0	0.9	2.4	4.8	4.8	3.1	2.7	1.6	1.2	2.5	4.1	2.7	2.2	..

Key: - zero or negligible   .. not available

Source: Office for National Statistics: +44 (0) 1633 456900

1. Tax and Prices Index (TPI) - Following consultation and a statement by the National Statistician, this index has been discontinued, with the last available data being for January 2017. Clarification of publication arrangements for the Retail Prices Index and related indices (https://www.ons.gov.uk/economy/inflationandpriceindices/articles/clarificationofpublicationarrangementsfortheretailpricesindexandrelatedindices/november2016) provides further information.

2. The Retail Prices Index and its derivatives do not meet the required standards for designation as National Statistics. A full report can be found at: http://www.statisticsauthority.gov.uk/

17.6 Index of Producer Prices of Agricultural Products, Total Inputs, UK (2015=100)

Agricultural Price Index of agricultural inputs in the United Kingdom; annual (a)		2010	2011	2012	2013	2014	2015	2016	2017	2018	2019
All agricultural inputs	(b)	93.6	105.1	106.9	109.5	105.0	100.0	97.4	102.5	110.9	112.6
All goods and services currently consumed in agriculture	(b)	94.2	107.3	109.9	112.7	106.3	100.0	96.9	102.7	112.1	113.9
Seeds (input)	(b)	104.7	111.8	110.1	119.2	105.6	100.0	101.5	100.0	111.6	111.1
Energy and lubricants		98.8	116.7	120.8	121.8	117.6	100.0	94.9	106.8	119.2	122.8
Electricity		78.1	85.0	88.6	95.2	100.3	100.0	99.8	106.5	115.7	124.1
Fuels for heating		78.2	85.7	92.9	99.2	103.3	100.0	97.1	100.7	107.5	111.6
Motor fuels		111.2	135.7	139.5	137.1	127.4	100.0	93.2	107.7	121.9	123.9
Fertilisers and soil improvers		98.5	128.5	123.3	111.5	105.0	100.0	82.6	89.6	100.8	103.2
Straight fertilisers		96.5	135.8	123.7	111.2	107.3	100.0	78.1	87.5	99.9	102.5
Straight fertilisers - nitrogenous		94.1	136.0	123.0	111.1	108.1	100.0	76.8	86.6	99.4	102.0
Straight fertilisers - phosphatic		105.3	138.0	126.6	102.7	94.8	100.0	89.5	90.2	104.4	104.5
Straight fertilisers - potassic		124.8	131.3	131.7	118.1	102.6	100.0	89.0	97.8	103.9	108.5
Compound fertilisers		102.4	123.3	126.5	113.9	103.0	100.0	88.1	91.7	102.0	103.8
Other fertilisers and soil improvers		87.6	87.6	89.7	92.4	95.6	100.0	100.9	102.6	103.8	107.5
Plant protection products	(b)	97.5	98.2	99.5	95.3	100.1	100.0	100.0	106.8	134.2	133.0
Fungicides		97.6	107.9	106.6	97.5	101.0	100.0	100.3	101.9	122.8	124.6
Insecticides		148.4	132.8	99.8	90.5	100.2	100.0	104.6	148.1	153.4	147.6
Herbicides	(b)	104.5	99.4	93.1	95.7	101.0	100.0	98.4	102.2	147.2	144.1
Other plant protection products		66.1	65.1	100.0	90.7	95.9	100.0	101.3	112.9	112.9	112.0
Veterinary services	(b)	92.9	94.8	96.1	98.6	99.4	100.0	100.4	100.9	109.1	115.1
Animal feedingstuffs	(c)	92.5	111.6	118.8	128.9	111.6	100.0	96.7	104.6	113.2	114.3
Straight feedingstuffs		96.5	118.6	130.9	142.4	115.9	100.0	99.3	109.3	121.1	121.0
Cereal and milling by products		94.8	143.7	145.9	153.1	117.7	100.0	98.3	121.8	137.0	130.3
Feed wheat		97.3	139.9	140.6	152.8	120.9	100.0	98.6	123.0	136.6	131.2
Feed barley		91.6	146.5	150.0	151.9	113.9	100.0	96.7	113.8	139.8	124.4
Feed oats		97.3	179.9	193.0	175.8	108.1	100.0	100.7	115.3	126.5	124.8
Oilcakes		101.5	98.1	126.1	140.9	113.7	100.0	101.9	100.5	113.4	104.8
Soya bean meal		97.8	114.7	131.5	134.3	106.0	100.0	104.0	102.6	113.3	103.2
Sunflower seed meal		107.7	105.3	135.6	152.2	121.3	100.0	93.3	78.9	88.3	96.8
Rape seed meal		91.5	83.8	103.8	120.1	96.6	100.0	94.1	96.3	119.6	108.5
Products of animal origin (incl. white fish meal)		86.4	88.1	89.5	94.0	98.2	100.0	104.2	101.1	112.8	114.4
Other straights		93.1	112.4	119.5	132.9	116.8	100.0	97.8	109.3	118.4	128.4
Field peas		91.5	115.7	128.5	156.6	132.5	100.0	78.6	92.8	108.1	123.3
Field beans		91.1	114.2	128.6	161.6	129.7	100.0	79.7	94.2	106.1	129.0
Soya beans		82.5	85.7	91.2	100.6	101.3	100.0	108.0	118.9	108.6	117.1
Compound feedingstuffs	(c)	90.0	107.3	111.4	120.6	109.0	100.0	95.5	102.4	109.6	111.2
Compound feedingstuffs for cattle and calves	(c)	87.2	102.7	109.5	118.2	108.7	100.0	97.0	101.6	109.5	112.8
Compound feedingstuffs for pigs	(c)	91.3	108.3	112.7	117.4	107.2	100.0	91.2	98.8	106.3	107.4
Compound feedingstuffs for poultry	(c)	94.2	113.7	114.1	125.1	110.1	100.0	95.4	104.4	110.5	110.2
Compound feedingstuffs for sheep	(c)	83.5	100.1	106.4	118.8	109.2	100.0	98.5	104.9	113.2	117.8
Maintenance of Materials		90.3	94.7	96.1	97.8	99.6	100.0	101.2	103.2	106.6	108.9
Maintenance of Buildings		91.8	98.6	100.7	101.1	101.8	100.0	99.4	104.5	109.6	112.1
Other goods and services	(b)	91.6	97.0	97.7	99.9	100.6	100.0	101.3	104.1	107.0	109.8
Goods and services contributing to investment	(b)	90.9	94.2	92.5	93.5	98.8	100.0	99.9	101.6	105.6	107.1
Materials	(b)	90.5	93.3	89.7	90.9	98.2	100.0	100.1	100.8	104.6	105.5
Machinery and other equipment	(b)	82.4	85.5	77.7	79.8	95.4					
Plant and machinery for cultivation		80.7	84.5	75.4	77.4	95.0	100.0	100.0	101.3	107.8	109.7
Farm machinery and installations	(b)	89.0	89.5	86.7	89.4	97.0	100.0	99.6	99.7	99.7	99.6
Transport Equipment		97.9	100.2	100.6	100.8	100.8	100.0	100.3	100.8	103.6	104.0
Tractors		95.7	99.2	100.1	100.7	100.6	100.0	100.8	101.2	104.0	104.3
Other vehicles		107.6	105.7	103.6	102.3	102.3	100.0	98.4	99.0	102.0	102.7
Buildings		93.2	98.6	100.2	100.5	101.1	100.0	99.4	103.4	107.9	110.5

(a) This table shows the API for main categories and selected primary items.
   Further detail is available.
(b) Part or all of the series is made up of annual data.
(c) Part or all of the series is made up of quarterly data.

Source: Department for Environment, Food and Rural Affairs
Enquiries Defra prices team. Tel: +44 (0) 208 565 4419
Email: prices@defra.gov.uk

17.7 Index of Producer Prices of Agricultural Products, Total Outputs, UK (2015=100)

Agricultural Price Index of agricultural outputs in the United Kingdom; annual (a)		2010	2011	2012	2013	2014	2015	2016	2017	2018	2019
All agricultural outputs	(b)	**95.3**	**108.1**	**113.2**	**119.9**	**109.3**	**100.0**	**99.8**	**110.9**	**115.0**	**113.3**
Crop products	(b)	**97.4**	**115.8**	**121.0**	**125.3**	**106.3**	**100.0**	**105.0**	**114.1**	**122.2**	**122.5**
Cereals	(b)	97.3	140.9	145.6	149.0	117.3	100.0	97.8	118.1	135.6	127.2
Wheat	(b)	98.7	139.9	142.4	149.9	119.7	100.0	96.7	118.8	132.4	128.1
Wheat - Feeding	(b)	98.8	139.3	142.0	151.1	119.4	100.0	98.8	122.8	136.5	131.5
Wheat - Breadmaking		98.1	135.6	139.0	139.2	120.1	100.0	89.5	105.9	120.6	117.7
Wheat - Other Milling		98.3	149.6	150.1	155.7	121.8	100.0	96.9	119.2	131.9	128.0
Barley	(b)	94.0	141.2	151.2	145.1	112.0	100.0	100.3	116.1	145.0	123.2
Barley - Feeding	(b)	94.0	146.2	150.4	149.1	113.0	100.0	99.3	115.0	143.4	123.0
Barley - Malting		93.8	130.3	153.1	136.2	109.9	100.0	101.3	117.1	146.7	123.5
Oats	(b)	92.3	164.1	175.5	160.3	103.9	100.0	105.2	118.1	134.3	137.5
Oats - Milling		93.2	158.8	170.8	145.3	101.1	100.0	105.7	118.8	136.0	139.5
Oats - Feeding	(b)	90.8	172.3	182.6	183.5	108.4	100.0	100.8	114.6	124.9	125.7
Potatoes		94.4	101.3	115.8	147.7	98.1	100.0	132.0	124.9	121.0	130.9
Industrial Crops	(b)	101.5	133.9	131.9	123.3	103.3	100.0	103.5	115.9	113.6	119.2
Oilseed Rape (non set aside)		105.2	150.8	146.3	133.6	104.9	100.0	110.0	127.2	118.6	124.9
Sugar Beet	(b)	90.8	90.8	94.7	96.0	99.0	100.0	95.1	92.4	101.4	97.5
Forage plants		105.8	119.2	112.4	121.4	113.7	100.0	109.1	142.0	206.6	134.3
Straw		117.0	132.8	117.6	122.0	116.3	100.0	109.1	142.0	206.6	134.3
Fresh Vegetables		94.4	87.6	102.5	104.0	97.4	100.0	110.0	106.8	118.2	124.2
Cauliflowers		100.6	96.9	119.2	102.7	106.0	100.0	129.0	103.5	132.0	140.8
Tomatoes		113.2	89.3	102.7	100.0	102.0	100.0	100.7	113.2	98.1	108.8
Cabbages		93.5	101.4	112.6	106.0	88.8	100.0	109.7	113.4	126.1	140.6
Lettuce		101.3	86.6	111.5	106.3	101.3	100.0	111.1	107.9	138.2	121.4
Carrots		88.5	95.6	109.9	110.1	79.5	100.0	106.9	95.1	130.9	122.8
Onions		107.3	101.0	73.4	104.0	101.9	100.0	114.4	116.6	130.4	161.0
Beans (Green)		93.2	83.7	123.6	115.6	96.4	100.0	145.3	121.4	144.4	138.8
Mushrooms		70.0	61.2	73.1	82.4	101.0	100.0	102.2	102.1	94.6	98.3
Fresh Fruit		98.8	97.5	102.4	103.6	96.4	100.0	107.6	115.3	119.5	130.2
Dessert Apples		95.5	102.2	112.7	111.9	99.3	100.0	102.4	115.5	123.0	125.9
Cooking Apples		96.0	99.9	126.7	151.8	104.8	100.0	113.5	121.4	147.2	159.7
Dessert Pears		100.2	101.3	117.1	129.6	102.9	100.0	110.7	127.4	131.2	143.2
Strawberries		105.2	96.6	92.0	88.4	96.2	100.0	111.8	117.6	116.5	133.4
Raspberries		95.3	97.4	92.0	91.7	84.5	100.0	91.3	101.9	101.7	110.0
Flowers and plants	(b)	93.3	100.1	101.9	103.5	102.1	100.0	100.9	105.1	105.4	106.3
Other crop products	(b)	97.2	95.0	100.0	100.0	100.0	100.0	100.0	100.0	100.0	100.0
Animals and animal products	(b)	**93.9**	**102.8**	**107.8**	**116.2**	**111.3**	**100.0**	**96.6**	**108.9**	**110.6**	**107.7**
Animals (for slaughter & export)		91.2	99.9	104.7	110.4	103.5	100.0	99.6	106.8	108.3	104.7
Cattle and calves		79.3	92.4	102.6	109.3	97.8	100.0	96.9	104.1	104.1	98.3
Cattle (clean)		77.9	89.7	100.6	108.3	97.0	100.0	97.1	103.0	103.3	97.5
Cows and Bulls		88.3	109.3	115.9	115.8	102.9	100.0	96.6	112.1	110.0	104.3
Calves		71.0	80.0	89.9	84.0	78.3	100.0	89.2	61.5	80.8	67.0
Pigs		108.5	110.8	115.4	126.6	121.2	100.0	98.3	119.8	111.5	114.1
Pigs (clean)		107.6	110.0	114.2	125.8	120.7	100.0	97.9	119.1	111.5	113.0
Sows and Boars		176.2	169.4	201.1	189.0	161.6	100.0	119.5	151.3	110.8	165.8
Sheep and lambs		101.0	112.9	107.0	105.9	108.0	100.0	106.0	108.0	117.5	109.1
Sheep and lambs (clean)		102.6	114.0	108.3	110.2	110.2	100.0	107.7	110.2	120.6	111.0
Ewes and Rams		91.0	105.8	98.8	78.1	93.9	100.0	90.9	88.1	90.4	92.1
All Poultry	(b)	95.7	98.5	100.6	106.3	101.5	100.0	100.6	102.8	107.2	105.6
Chickens	(b)	98.8	100.8	102.4	108.2	102.1	100.0	100.8	103.3	107.9	103.0
Turkeys		83.5	89.2	93.8	98.9	98.8	100.0	98.6	99.0	102.8	120.7
Animal products	(b)	98.4	107.7	113.0	126.1	124.4	100.0	91.6	112.4	114.2	112.5
Milk		100.9	111.9	114.8	129.3	128.8	100.0	92.4	117.4	119.7	118.0
Eggs	(c)	84.3	84.2	104.6	110.3	103.0	100.0	85.2	83.6	82.2	82.3
Intensive eggs	(c)	83.0	84.3	112.6	115.8	105.7	100.0	85.0	83.7	81.3	83.7
Free range eggs	(c)	85.2	84.1	99.1	106.5	101.2	100.0	85.3	83.5	82.8	81.3
Wool clip		120.0	145.9	90.6	121.2	123.5	100.0	84.7	70.6	70.6	36.5

(a) This table shows the API for main categories and selected primary items. Further detail is available.

(b) Part or all of the series is made up of annual data.

(c) Part or all of the series is made up of quarterly data.

Source: Department for Environment, Food and Rural Affairs
Enquiries Defra prices team. Tel: +44 (0) 208 565 4419
Email: prices@defra.gov.uk

17.8 Harmonnised Indices of Consumer Prices (HICPs) - International comparisons: EU countries: 2014 to 2019. Percentage change over 12 months

per cent	Austria	Belgium	Bulgaria	Cyprus	Czech Republic	Denmark	Estonia	Finland	France	Germany	Greece	Hungary	Ireland	Italy	Latvia
Annual change															
	D7SK	D7SL	GHY8	D7RO	D7RP	D7SM	D7RQ	D7SN	D7SO	D7SP	D7SQ	D7RR	D7SS	D7ST	D7RS
2014	1.5	0.5	-1.6	-0.3	0.4	0.4	0.5	1.2	0.6	0.8	-1.4	-	0.3	0.2	0.7
2015	0.8	0.6	-1.1	-1.5	0.3	0.2	0.1	-0.2	0.1	0.7	-1.1	0.1	-	0.1	0.2
2016	1.0	1.8	-1.3	-1.2	0.6	-	0.8	0.4	0.3	0.4	-	0.4	-0.2	-0.1	0.1
2017	2.2	2.2	1.2	0.7	2.4	1.1	3.7	0.8	1.2	1.7	1.1	2.4	0.3	1.3	2.9
2018	2.1	2.3	2.6	0.8	2.0	0.7	3.4	1.2	2.1	1.9	0.8	2.9	0.7	1.2	2.6
2019	1.5	1.2	2.5	0.5	2.6	0.7	2.3	1.1	1.3	1.4	0.5	3.4	0.9	0.6	2.7
Monthly															
Jul 2019	1.4	1.2	2.6	0.1	2.6	0.4	2.0	1.0	1.3	1.1	0.4	3.3	0.5	0.3	3.0
Aug	1.5	0.9	2.5	0.6	2.6	0.5	2.1	1.2	1.3	1.0	0.1	3.2	0.6	0.5	3.1
Sep	1.2	0.6	1.6	-0.5	2.6	0.4	2.2	1.0	1.1	0.9	0.2	2.9	0.6	0.2	2.3
Oct	1.0	0.2	1.6	-0.5	2.6	0.6	1.4	0.9	0.9	0.9	-0.3	3.0	0.6	0.2	2.2
Nov	1.2	0.4	2.2	0.5	3.0	0.6	1.8	0.8	1.2	1.2	0.5	3.4	0.8	0.2	2.0
Dec	1.8	0.9	3.1	0.7	3.2	0.8	1.8	1.1	1.6	1.5	1.1	4.1	1.1	0.5	2.1
Jan 2020	2.2	1.4	3.4	0.7	3.8	0.8	1.6	1.2	1.7	1.6	1.1	4.7	1.1	0.4	2.2
Feb	2.2	1.0	3.1	1.0	3.7	0.7	2.0	1.1	1.6	1.7	0.4	4.4	0.9	0.2	2.3
Mar	1.6	0.4	2.4	0.1	3.6	0.3	1.0	0.9	0.8	1.3	0.2	3.9	0.5	0.1	1.4
Apr	1.5	0.0	1.3	-1.2	3.3	-0.1	-0.9	-0.3	0.4	0.8	-0.9	2.5	-0.3	0.1	-0.1
May	0.6	-0.2	1.0	-1.4	3.1	-0.2	-1.8	-0.1	0.4	0.5	-0.7	2.2	-0.8	-0.3	-0.9
Jun	1.1	0.2	0.9	-2.2	3.4	0.2	-1.6	0.1	0.2	0.8	-1.9	2.9	-0.6	-0.4	-1.1

per cent	Lithuania	Luxem-bourg	Malta	Nether-lands	Poland	Portugal	Romania	Slovakia	Slovenia	Spain	Sweden	UK[1]	EU 27 average[2]	EU 28 average[3]	MUICP average[4]
Annual change															
	D7RT	D7SU	D7RU	D7SV	D7RV	D7SX	GHY7	D7RW	D7RX	D7SY	D7SZ	D7G7	FSL3	GJ2E	D7SR
2014	0.2	0.7	0.8	0.3	0.1	-0.2	1.4	-0.1	0.4	-0.2	0.2	1.5	0.4	0.6	0.4
2015	-0.7	0.1	1.2	0.2	-0.7	0.5	-0.4	-0.3	-0.8	-0.6	0.7	-	0.1	0.1	0.2
2016	0.7	-	0.9	0.1	-0.2	0.6	-1.1	-0.5	-0.2	-0.3	1.1	0.7	0.2	0.2	0.2
2017	3.7	2.1	1.3	1.3	1.6	1.6	1.1	1.4	1.6	2.0	1.9	2.7	1.6	1.7	1.5
2018	2.5	2.0	1.7	1.6	1.2	1.2	4.1	2.5	1.9	1.7	2.0	2.5	1.8	1.9	1.8
2019	2.2	1.6	1.5	2.7	2.1	0.3	3.9	2.8	1.7	0.8	1.7	1.8	1.4	1.5	1.2
Monthly															
Jul 2019	2.5	1.6	1.8	2.6	2.5	-0.7	4.1	3.0	2.0	0.6	1.5	2.1	1.3	1.4	1.0
Aug	2.5	1.4	1.9	3.1	2.6	-0.1	4.1	3.0	2.4	0.4	1.3	1.7	1.3	1.4	1.0
Sep	2.0	1.1	1.6	2.7	2.4	-0.3	3.5	3.0	1.7	0.2	1.3	1.7	1.1	1.2	0.8
Oct	1.5	0.8	1.4	2.8	2.3	-0.1	3.2	2.9	1.5	0.2	1.6	1.5	1.0	1.1	0.7
Nov	1.7	1.0	1.3	2.6	2.4	0.2	3.8	3.2	1.4	0.5	1.8	1.5	1.3	1.3	1.0
Dec	2.7	1.8	1.3	2.8	3.0	0.4	4.0	3.2	2.0	0.8	1.7	1.3	1.6	1.6	1.3
Jan 2020	3.0	2.5	1.4	1.7	3.8	0.8	3.9	3.2	2.3	1.1	1.5	1.8	1.7	1.7	1.4
Feb	2.8	1.8	1.1	1.3	4.1	0.5	2.9	3.1	2.0	0.9	1.3	1.7	1.6	..	1.2
Mar	1.7	0.3	1.2	1.1	3.9	0.1	2.7	2.4	0.7	0.1	0.8	1.5	1.1	..	0.7
Apr	0.9	-0.8	1.1	1.0	2.9	-0.1	2.3	2.1	-1.3	-0.7	-0.2	0.8	0.6	..	0.3
May	0.2	-1.6	0.9	1.1	3.4	-0.6	1.8	2.1	-1.4	-0.9	0.1	0.5	0.5	..	0.1
Jun	0.9	-0.4	1.0	1.7	3.8	0.2	2.2	1.8	-0.8	-0.3	0.9	0.6	0.7	..	0.3

Key: - zero or negligible .. Not available * Provisional   Source: Office for National Statistics +44 (0) 1633 456900

† Date of earliest revision ⁰ Estimated

1. Published as the CPI in the UK.

2. Aggregate for European Union with 27 Member States. Following user requests, on 10 April 2018 Eurostat began to publish in its database an aggregate for the EU with 27 Member States for around 50 of the most in-demand indicators, such as population, GDP growth rate and unemployment.

3. Data for the former EU28 aggregate. For reference periods February 2020 or later, Eurostat no longer calculates or publishes the former EU28 aggregate. This means that the final time periods for which the EU28 aggregate is published are January 2020, fourth quarter 2019 or the year 2019 depending on the frequency of the dataset. Eurostat will maintain historic data for EU28 in the database and will update as revisions are received.

4. The coverage of the Monetary Union Indices of Consumer Prices (MUICP) was extended to include Greece with effect from Jan 2001 and Slovakia from Jan 2009.

Eurostat
https://ec.europa.eu/eurostat/data/database

this page is intentionally blank

Production

Chapter 18

Production

Annual Business Survey (Table 18.1)

The Annual Business Survey (ABS), formerly known as the Annual Business Inquiry – part 2 (ABI/2), is an annual survey of businesses covering the production, construction, distribution and service industries, which represent approximately two-thirds of the UK economy, by gross value added (GVA).

Every year, ABS questionnaires are sent by the Office for National Statistics (ONS) to around 62,000 businesses in Great Britain, and by the Northern Ireland Statistics and Research Agency (NISRA) to around 11,000 businesses in Northern Ireland. It is the largest ONS business survey in terms of the combined number of respondents and variables it covers. It is the main resource for understanding the detailed structure and performance of businesses across the UK and is a large contributor of business information to the UK National Accounts.

The ABS provides a number of high-level indicators of economic activity, such as the total value of sales and work completed by businesses, the value of purchases of goods, materials and services, and total employment costs. The contribution of different industries to the overall value of economic activity can be assessed. Table 18.1 presents estimates of the production and construction industries broken down to the detailed industry class four-digit UK Standard Industrial Classification 2007: SIC 2007 level.

UK Manufacturer's Sales by Industry (Table 18.2)

The UK manufacturers' sales by product (ProdCom) presents annual statistics on the value and volume of products manufactured in the UK. The datasets provide estimates of value, volume and unit values (value per unit of volume) for each product heading (where possible). Other data available by industry include total turnover, merchanted goods, work done, sales of waste products and all other income.

The ProdCom statistics concern all manufactured products included in the EU ProdCom list. The survey sample covers UK businesses active in the mining, quarrying and manufacturing sectors (Standard Industrial Classification 2007: SIC 2007 Sections B and C). The survey does not cover recycling or energy products. Data are collected via a paper questionnaire from a sample of approximately 21,500 businesses, covering 240 subsectors of the mining, quarrying and manufacturing industry sectors and approximately 3,800 products.

 ProdCom outputs are used as part of the national accounts supply use tables, an integral part of the measurement of gross domestic product (GDP). GDP is the primary measure of the overall state of a country's economy; it is extensively reported in the media to track the UK's economic performance.

The survey is governed by the European Union Regulation 3924/91 and product definitions are standardised across the EU to enable comparisons between member states' data and the production of EU aggregates at product level.

Number of local units in manufacturing industries (Table 18.3)

The table shows the number of local units (sites) in manufacturing by employment size band. The classification breakdown is at division level (two digit) as classified to SIC (2007) held on the Inter-Departmental Business Register (IDBR). The IDBR is a comprehensive list of businesses registered for Value Added Tax (VAT) and/or Pay As You Earn (PAYE). It is the main sampling frame for business surveys carried out by the Office for National Statistics (ONS) and other government departments.

UK Business: Activity, Size and Location provides further details and contains detailed information regarding enterprises in the UK including size, classification, and local units in the UK including size, classification and location. For more details see: https://www.ons.gov.uk/businessindustryandtrade/business/activitysizeandlocation

Production of primary fuels (Table 18.4)

This table shows indigenous production of primary fuels. It includes the extraction or capture of primary commodities and the generation or manufacture of secondary commodities. Production is always gross; that is, it includes the quantities used during the extraction or manufacturing process. Primary fuels are coal, natural gas (including colliery methane), oil, primary electricity (that is, electricity generated by hydro, nuclear wind and tide stations and also electricity imported from France through the interconnector) and renewables (includes solid renewables such as wood, straw and waste and gaseous renewables such as landfill gas and sewage gas). The figures are presented on a common basis expressed in million tonnes of oil equivalent. Estimates of the gross calorific values used for converting the statistics for the various fuels to these are given in the Digest of UK Energy Statistics available on the Department for Business, Energy & Industrial Strategy website.

Total inland energy consumption (Table 18.5)

This table shows energy consumption by fuel and final energy consumption by fuel and class of consumer. Primary energy consumption covers consumption of all primary fuels (defined above) for energy purposes. This measure of energy consumption includes energy that is lost by converting primary fuels into secondary fuels (the energy lost burning coal to generate electricity or the energy used by refineries to separate crude oil into fractions) in addition to losses in distribution. The other common way of measuring energy consumption is to measure the energy content of the fuels supplied to consumers. This is called final energy consumption. It is net of fuel used by the energy industries, conversion, transmission and distribution losses. The figures are presented on a common basis, measured as energy supplied and expressed in million tonnes of oil equivalent. Estimates of the gross calorific values used for converting the statistics for the various fuels to these are given in the Digest of UK Energy Statistics available on the Department for Business, Energy & Industrial Strategy website.

So far as practicable, the user categories have been grouped on the basis of the SIC(2007) although the methods used by each of the supply industries to identify end users are slightly different. Chapter 1 of the Digest of UK Energy Statistics gives more information on these figures.

Coal (Table 18.6)

Since 1995, aggregate data on coal production have been obtained from the Coal Authority. In addition, main coal producers provide data in response to an annual Department for Business, Energy & Industrial Strategy inquiry which covers production (deep mined and opencast), trade, stocks and disposals. HM Revenue & Customs (HMRC) also provides trade data for solid fuels. Department for Business, Energy & Industrial Strategy collects information on the use of coal from the UK Iron and Steel Statistics Bureau and consumption of coal for electricity generation is covered by data provided by the electricity generators.

Gas (Table 18.7)

Production figures, covering the production of gas from the UK Continental Shelf offshore and onshore gas fields and gas obtained during the production of oil, are obtained from returns made under the Department for Business, Energy & Industrial Strategy Petroleum Production Reporting System. Additional information is used on imports and exports of gas and details from the operators of gas terminals in the UK to complete the picture.

It is no longer possible to present information on fuels input into the gas industry and gas output and sales in the same format as in previous editions of this table. As such, users are directed to Chapter 4 of the Digest of UK Energy Statistics, where more detailed information on gas production and consumption in the UK is available.

The Department for Business, Energy & Industrial Strategy carry out an annual survey of gas suppliers to obtain details of gas sales to the various categories of consumer. Estimates are included for the suppliers with the smallest market share, since the inquiry covers only the largest suppliers (that is, those known to supply more than 1,750 GWh per year).

Electricity (Tables 18.8–18.10)

Tables 18.8 to 18.10 cover all generators and suppliers of electricity in the UK. The relationship between generation, supply, availability and consumption is as follows:

Electricity generated
less electricity used on works
equals electricity supplied (gross)
less electricity used in pumping at pumped storage stations.
equals electricity supplied (net)
plus imports (net of exports) of electricity
equals electricity available
less losses and statistical differences
equals electricity consumed

Major Power Producers (MPPs) are companies whose prime purpose is the generation of electricity. They represent around 80 per cent of generation. The companies included in the MPP survey are reviewed each January. Companies that no longer meet the criteria are removed and new companies are added. The current list of MPPs (and previous years) can be found in DUKES Table 5.11. (https://www.gov.uk/government/statistics/electricity-chapter-5-digest-of-united-kingdom-energy-statistics-dukes). Major wind farm companies were added to the MPP survey in 2007 and solar companies in 2015. Prior to this, these sites were all included in the 'other generators' category.

Other Generator's refer to a category collated from a range of sources including the autogenerators survey, Combined Heat and Power scheme (CHPQA), RESTATS (the UK's Renewable Energy Statistics Database), ISSB (Iron and Steel Statistics Bureau) and the London Underground.

Note: in Table 18.10 all fuels are converted to the common unit of million tonnes of oil equivalent, that is, the amounts of oil which would be needed to produce the output of electricity generated from those fuels.

Readers may wish to note that the production and consumption of fuels are presented using commodity balances. A commodity balance shows the flows of an individual fuel through from production to final consumption, showing its use in transformation and energy industry own use.

For more information on electricity statistics see: https://www.gov.uk/government/publications/electricity-statistics-data-sources-and-methodologies

For more detailed energy statistics please see 'The Digest of United Kingdom Energy Statistics' (DUKES) which is available to view online at: https://www.gov.uk/government/statistics/digest-of-uk-energy-statistics-dukes-2020

Crude oil and oil products (Tables 18.11–18.13a)

BEIS produces these energy statistics and are published in the Energy Trends and Digest of UK Energy Statistics publications.

Data on the production of crude oil, condensates and natural gases are derived from the Petroleum Production Reporting System (PPRS) which is a monthly administrative data collection census that requires all licensees operating on the UK Continental Shelf to submit monthly details of their hydrocarbon (both oil and gas) production to the Department. PPRS is used to report flows, stocks and of crude oils and NGLs from field level through to final disposal. It is a condition of operation on the UKCS that companies submit monthly returns to government, with 100% coverage and response rate.

Downstream oil information, including information on the transformation of crude oil into petroleum products at refineries, imports and exports of petroleum products, and the delivery of these products into consumption by various users, is collected monthly through the Downstream Oil Reporting System (DORS), with 100% return rate and >95% market coverage. DORS was developed in co-operation with industry and replaced the UK Petroleum Industry Association (UKPIA) reporting system in 2005.

HMRC data are also used to supplement information obtained from PPRS and DORS to cover trade activity by non-reporting companies, and as a quality control mechanism. For more information on crude oil statistics see: https://www.gov.uk/government/publications/crude-oil-and-petroleum-products-methodology-note

Released quantities of hydrocarbons (Table 18.13b)

This table displays figures of released quantities of hydrocarbon (mineral) oils for excise duty as published in the Hydrocarbon Oils Bulletin by HM Revenue and Customs (HMRC). Duty is charged when motor and heating fuels and oils are produced, imported or used in the UK. Duty is charged at different rates. Most rates are charged per litre but a small amount are charged per kilogram.

Hydrocarbon (mineral) oils are any organic compounds consisting of hydrogen and carbon. They are the main components of petroleum and natural gas. They are also used as fuels, lubricants and raw materials for the production of plastics, fibres, rubbers, solvents, explosives and industrial chemicals.

Iron and steel (Tables 18.14–18.16) and Minerals (Table 18.18)

Theses statistics are sourced from the United Kingdom Minerals Yearbook published by British Geological Survey (BGS). This annual publication provides comprehensive statistical data on minerals production, consumption and trade, and includes an authoritative commentary on the UK's minerals industry. Multiple sources of data are used to compile this publication including from the Iron and Steel Statistics Bureau, Department for Business, Energy and Industrial Strategy; Office for National Statistics and HM Revenue and Customs. For more details see: https://www2.bgs.ac.uk/mineralsuk/statistics/UKStatistics.html

Fertilisers (Table 18.17)

This table offers statistics on the overall application rates of nitrogen (N), phosphate (P2O5) and potash (K2O) on tillage crops and grass. Overall application rates are driven by a combination of the number of fields that receive a dressing and the rate of application for that field. Maximum usage was seen in the 1980s and there has been a general downward trend since then. The long-term decline in total nitrogen over this period is mainly due to decreased use on grassland.

The British Survey of Fertiliser Practice (BSFP) produced by Defra, is the primary source of data on fertiliser use in Great Britain. Its main purpose is to estimate average application rates of nitrogen, phosphate and potash used for agricultural crops and grassland. Information is also collected on applications of sulphur fertilisers, organic manures and lime. The survey data are used by Government to monitor best practice, to assess potential environmental impacts and mitigation strategies and provide important evidence to estimate greenhouse gas emissions from agriculture to inform policy.

The BSFP is a voluntary annual survey of a sample of farmers selected from a population of agricultural holdings compiled using the June Agricultural Survey. The target sample size is 1,500 farms; this sample size has been designed to achieve a statistically representative sample at the national level. Holdings of less than 20 hectares are not included in the sample. While these smaller holdings account for a significant proportion of all holdings in terms of numbers, they cover a much smaller proportion of the total area of crops and grass.

For more information on fertiliser usage statistics see: https://www.gov.uk/government/collections/fertiliser-usage

Building materials (Table 18.19)

Table 18.19a -f shows the production and deliveries of a number of building materials, including bricks, concrete blocks, sand and gravel, slate, cement, concrete roofing tiles and ready-mixed cement. This data comes from the Monthly Bulletin of Building Materials and Components published by BEIS. These statistics support analysis of the construction materials market and business planning. They are regularly reported in the construction press and are used for a variety of purposes, including policy development and evaluation concerning the construction products industry, as well as monitoring market trends

Seasonally adjusted series for deliveries of bricks, concrete blocks, ready-mixed concrete and sales of sand & gravel are shown. The purpose of correcting the reported series is to allow for seasonal factors such as winter weather (including the reduction in hours of daylight, and frost and rain) and other seasonal events such as Christmas and Easter. Thus, seasonally adjusted figures show the underlying trend more clearly.

Construction (Tables 18.20–18.21)

The volume of construction output in Table 18.20 are sourced from the Monthly Business Survey for Construction and VAT returns, which collect value of work broken down by type of work from businesses in the construction industry within Great Britain. The index of the volume of output is measured in chained volume (i.e. removing the effect of changes in price) on a seasonally adjusted basis. In 2008, the responsibility of these statistics transferred from the Department of Business, Enterprise and Regulatory Reform (BERR), now the Department for Business, Energy and Industrial Strategy (BEIS), to the Office for National Statistics (ONS).

Table 18.21 measures the value of new orders of main contractors by type of work. The main users of these data are industry analysts of the UK construction industry, trade associations and other government departments. The data are primarily sourced from local authorities in England, Scotland and Wales by a private company called Barbour ABI. Local authorities are monitored daily to identify planning applications as soon as they are published. Projects costing less than £100,000 are not included in the new orders dataset. Only projects in Great Britain are captured in the dataset. Therefore, Northern Ireland projects are not included.

Engineering turnover and orders (Tables 18.22–18.23)

The figures in these tables are the 'turnover values' of UK-based manufacturers classified to subsections DK and DL of the SIC (2007). Figures are in current price and non-seasonally adjusted. The data is sourced from the Monthly Business Survey (MBS) which underpins the Index of Production (IoP). The MBS samples around 6,000 businesses every month and the data collected is turnover excluding VAT.

In 2018 the imputation methodology for these statistics was changed from the mean of ratios method to the ratio of means. For more details on the effect of this change see: https://www.ons.gov.uk/economy/nationalaccounts/uksectoraccounts/articles/monthlybusinesssurveyimprovingthemethodforsurveynon response/2017-09-29

Alcohol Clearances (Tables 18.24)

This table provides statistics from the four different alcohol duties administered by HM Revenue and Customs (HMRC): Wine Duty, Spirits Duty, Beer Duty and Cider Duty. Duty is payable on alcohol produced or processed in the UK, or brought into the UK. In general, duty on alcohol is calculated according to its strength (except for duty on spirits which is calculated per litre of pure alcohol). Duty is payable once the alcohol product is released for consumption onto the UK market. Figures for releases include both home-produced products and commercial imports. Production figures are also available for potable spirits distilled and beer brewed in the UK.

Receipts are affected by the period immediately preceding Christmas, and large scale events such as unseasonably warm weather and sporting events when more alcohol is cleared and bought than at other times of year. Clearances can peak in the months before the Budget and then be lower in the month (or two) thereafter. This forestalling activity can lead to volatility in receipts and clearances when analysed so care should be taken when comparing receipts from one month with the same month in the previous year.

Users should also note that as a result of forestalling behaviour, changes in the level of clearances and receipts do not relate to how much alcohol is bought or drunk by consumers. Announcements on duty rates can influence forestalling behaviour in the months around a Budget and so caution must be taken when comparing year on year.

Tobacco products (Table 18.25)

Table 18.24 provides statistics on duty from cigarettes, cigars, hand-rolling tobacco, and other types of tobacco such as pipe and chewing tobacco. Duty is payable on products manufactured in the UK or brought into the UK. Duty on cigarettes is calculated as a percentage of the retail cost plus a specific amount per thousand cigarettes. Duty on hand-rolling tobacco and other tobacco products is charged by the kilogram. Manufacturers must make a return to HMRC on any day when tobacco products are released onto the UK market. Releases of cigarettes and other tobacco products tend to peak immediately before changes to duty rates are implemented (usually at a Budget or other fiscal event). Products may then be stocked, duty-paid, before being sold. Releases are then depressed in the month(s) afterwards.

Changes to tobacco product duty are announced in the Budget each year. Clearances are usually high in months immediately preceding the Budget due to tobacco manufacturers forestalling against duty increases. This means that manufacturers can pay duty at the pre-budget rate which is typically lower than the post-budget rate. This is followed by lower than usual clearances in the month or so after the Budget. Manufacturers can also forestall against their own price rises, meaning they pay duty on a lower retail price than they would otherwise. This forestalling activity can lead to volatility in receipts and clearances when analysed so care should be taken when comparing one month with the same month in the previous year. Users should also note that as a result of forestalling behaviour, monthly changes in the level of clearances and receipts do not relate to how much tobacco is bought or smoked by consumers.

18.1 Production and Construction Industries

	Description	Year	Number of enterprises	Total turnover	Approximate gross value added at basic prices (aGVA)	Total purchases of goods, materials & services	Total employment costs
	Standard Industrial Classification (Revised 2007) Section						
			Number	£ million	£ million	£ million	£ million
B-F	Production industries and construction	2017	481,906	1,001,506	334,830	662,443	148,344
		2018	494,447	1,048,449	345,289	698,856	153,284
		2019	500,102	1,054,481	349,157	701,631	157,840
		2020	509,448	937,419	314,786	615,746	153,294
B-E	Production industries	2017	151,286	732,127	231,002	495,023	107,175
		2018	152,797	751,282	236,545	508,846	109,975
		2019	151,512	747,616	237,916	503,927	112,732
		2020	153,570	665,869	212,924	444,338	109,364
B	Mining and quarrying	2017	1,235	30,881	16,905	14,327	4,727
		2018	1,263	37,205	21,717	15,566	4,797
		2019	1,296	35,734	20,004	16,250	4,689
		2020	1,270	25,790	12,202	13,547	4,583
05	Mining of coal and lignite	2017	[c]	[c]	[c]	[c]	[c]
		2018	[c]	[c]	[c]	[c]	[c]
		2019	[c]	[c]	[c]	[c]	[c]
		2020	[c]	[c]	[c]	[c]	[c]
06	Extraction of crude petroleum and natural gas	2017	150	19,100	12,508	7,076	2,079
		2018	160	25,180	17,306	8,098	2,120
		2019	155	23,243	15,063	8,750	1,871
		2020	152	14,583	7,665	6,984	1,897
07	Mining of metal ores	2016	[c]	[c]	[c]	[c]	[c]
		2017	[c]	[c]	[c]	[c]	[c]
		2018	[c]	[c]	[c]	[c]	[c]
		2019	[c]	[c]	[c]	[c]	[c]
08	Other mining and quarrying	2017	689	6,072	1,856	4,085	879
		2018	703	6,516	2,053	4,327	906
		2019	707	6,377	2,071	4,180	948
		2020	709	6,166	2,157	3,907	939
09	Mining support service activities	2017	379	5,362	2,387	2,989	1,695
		2018	385	5,288	2,279	3,013	1,696
		2019	417	5,877	2,762	3,184	1,802
		2020	395	4,864	2,299	2,557	1,679
C	Manufacturing	2017	137,051	550,224	169,279	372,759	89,300
		2018	138,194	569,922	169,693	393,038	91,843
		2019	136,581	565,274	170,442	387,004	93,856
		2020	138,277	499,709	153,511	336,323	90,633
10	Manufacture of food products	2017	8,118	81,636	21,751	60,628	11,786
		2018	8,287	84,270	22,274	62,419	12,037
		2019	8,440	84,613	23,037	61,938	12,631
		2020	8,913	84,290	22,750	62,319	12,786
11	Manufacture of beverages	2017	2,234	[c]	[c]	10,756	2,080
		2018	2,424	21,846	7,247	11,843	2,195
		2019	2,572	22,757	7,235	12,581	2,126
		2020	2,718	19,568	5,884	11,161	2,272
12	Manufacture of tobacco products	2017	13	[c]	[c]	7	17
		2018	9	13	6	7	3
		2019	9	27	7	13	6
		2020	7	14	[c]	[c]	2
13	Manufacture of textiles	2017	4,228	5,668	2,346	3,377	1,303
		2018	4,395	5,986	2,409	3,692	1,274
		2019	4,315	6,165	2,437	3,754	1,416
		2020	4,282	5,344	2,123	3,243	1,248

18.1 Production and Construction Industries

Description		Year	Number of enterprises	Total turnover	Approximate gross value added at basic prices (aGVA)	Total purchases of goods, materials & services	Total employment costs
Standard Industrial Classification (Revised 2007) Section			Number	£ million	£ million	£ million	£ million
14	Manufacture of wearing apparel	2017	3,851	2,494	873	1,657	500
		2018	3,951	2,460	1,080	1,531	507
		2019	3,877	2,464	907	1,564	451
		2020	4,068	1,838	[c]	[c]	473
15	Manufacture of leather and	2017	627	1,136	353	780	249
	related products	2018	634	1,214	449	763	246
		2019	617	1,240	439	858	246
		2020	617	924	307	642	275
16	Manufacture of wood and of products of	2017	9,287	9,131	3,315	5,911	1,705
	wood and cork, except furniture;	2018	9,419	9,572	3,690	6,045	1,801
	manufacture of articles of straw and	2019	9,266	9,735	3,683	6,084	1,856
	plaiting materials	2020	9,586	9,647	3,476	6,224	1,858
17	Manufacture of paper and paper products	2017	1,460	11,542	3,314	8,312	1,838
		2018	1,417	12,181	3,378	8,935	1,949
		2019	1,418	12,113	3,598	8,577	1,986
		2020	1,452	11,553	3,566	8,023	1,964
18	Printing and reproduction of recorded media	2017	11,782	10,814	4,697	6,170	2,862
		2018	11,583	10,838	5,027	5,917	2,863
		2019	11,095	10,412	4,456	5,989	2,541
		2020	10,893	8,668	3,833	4,879	2,154
19	Manufacture of coke and refined petroleum	2017	116	33,024	2,398	22,838	711
	products	2018	118	38,618	2,115	27,740	727
		2019	94	38,297	2,397	27,237	701
		2020	94	25,339	[c]	[c]	738
20	Manufacture of chemicals and chemical	2017	2,915	33,307	9,686	24,063	4,363
	products	2018	2,960	35,376	10,600	25,079	4,605
		2019	2,996	34,305	10,649	23,687	4,810
		2020	3,186	32,829	11,175	21,747	4,777
21	Manufacture of basic pharmaceutical	2017	636	18,273	8,569	9,563	3,659
	products and pharmaceutical preparations	2018	646	20,483	7,876	12,448	3,697
		2019	666	22,000	8,938	13,294	3,564
		2020	693	23,873	9,390	14,542	3,874
22	Manufacture of rubber and plastic products	2017	5,874	24,270	8,936	15,635	4,754
		2018	5,693	24,457	8,476	16,199	4,934
		2019	5,598	24,047	8,226	15,902	5,037
		2020	5,576	22,229	8,250	14,044	4,819
23	Manufacture of other non-metallic mineral	2017	3,744	16,356	5,961	10,392	2,961
	products	2018	3,726	17,043	6,334	10,759	3,004
		2019	3,725	17,394	6,372	11,130	3,126
		2020	3,807	15,220	5,599	9,476	2,939
24	Manufacture basic metals	2017	1,764	16,755	4,027	12,890	2,943
		2018	1,792	17,363	3,790	13,614	2,981
		2019	1,820	16,573	3,716	12,702	2,962
		2020	1,833	13,864	3,388	10,353	2,837
25	Manufacture of fabricated metal products,	2017	28,290	36,445	16,430	20,344	9,157
	except machinery and equipment	2018	28,392	37,483	16,634	21,437	9,102
		2019	26,301	38,343	16,898	21,913	9,622
		2020	26,240	35,251	15,477	19,897	9,366
26	Manufacture of computer, electronic and	2017	6,130	22,451	9,779	13,019	5,213
	optical products	2018	6,031	23,059	9,745	13,581	5,214
		2019	5,879	23,389	9,953	13,918	5,348
		2020	5,759	20,312	8,171	12,143	5,038

18.1 Production and Construction Industries

Description		Year	Number of enterprises	Total turnover	Approximate gross value added at basic prices (aGVA)	Total purchases of goods, materials & services	Total employment costs
			Number	£ million	£ million	£ million	£ million

Standard Industrial Classification (Revised 2007) Section

27	Manufacture of electrical equipment	2017	3,043	13,310	4,562	8,943	2,899
		2018	2,997	13,261	4,711	8,731	2,725
		2019	3,018	13,610	4,627	9,211	3,041
		2020	3,110	12,891	4,325	8,491	3,151
28	Manufacture of machinery and equipment n.e.c.	2017	7,709	36,186	11,554	25,124	6,979
		2018	7,639	39,424	12,901	27,129	7,387
		2019	7,578	38,625	12,748	26,090	7,310
		2020	7,540	32,253	10,425	21,615	6,711
29	Manufacture of motor vehicles, trailers and semi-trailers	2017	3,325	77,179	15,306	61,747	7,634
		2018	3,428	78,972	15,302	63,971	8,281
		2019	3,462	74,175	13,934	60,587	8,610
		2020	3,450	58,144	11,205	46,625	7,583
30	Manufacture of other transport equipment	2017	2,394	40,527	13,363	26,860	6,975
		2018	2,357	37,208	9,953	27,763	7,601
		2019	2,287	36,603	9,898	27,374	7,516
		2020	2,233	28,366	8,464	20,416	7,093
31	Manufacture of furniture	2017	6,254	8,774	3,564	5,243	2,185
		2018	6,378	8,861	3,730	5,153	2,176
		2019	6,355	8,994	3,714	5,317	2,267
		2020	6,503	8,059	3,217	4,903	2,171
32	Other manufacturing	2017	9,551	10,885	4,411	6,697	2,423
		2018	9,742	11,513	4,861	6,908	2,493
		2019	10,058	11,809	5,167	6,953	2,628
		2020	10,307	12,761	5,017	7,754	2,416
33	Repair and installation of machinery and equipment	2017	13,706	18,790	7,084	11,801	4,105
		2018	14,176	18,420	7,105	11,372	4,040
		2019	15,135	17,584	7,407	10,332	4,057
		2020	15,410	16,471	7,108	9,392	4,088
D	Electricity, gas, steam and air conditioning supply	2017	5,385	112,512	25,215	87,291	6,843
		2018	5,552	102,889	24,643	77,627	6,677
		2019	5,746	104,874	26,647	77,657	6,859
		2020	5,840	100,837	26,559	73,562	6,950
E	Water supply, sewerage, waste management and remediation activities	2017	7,615	38,509	19,602	20,646	6,304
		2018	7,788	41,266	20,491	22,614	6,658
		2019	7,889	41,734	20,822	23,017	7,328
		2020	8,183	39,533	20,652	20,907	7,198
36	Water collection, treatment and supply	2017	120	13,096	9,073	4,850	2,010
		2018	122	14,946	9,345	6,417	2,136
		2019	110	15,216	9,348	6,809	2,292
		2020	109	14,553	9,189	6,227	2,282
37	Sewerage	2017	1,027	3,180	2,594	1,454	543
		2018	1,054	3,286	2,822	1,559	633
		2019	1,047	3,391	3,050	1,550	718
		2020	1,093	3,294	3,064	1,384	705
38	Waste collection, treatment and disposal activities; materials recovery	2017	5,506	21,249	7,543	13,753	3,529
		2018	5,611	22,030	7,823	14,134	3,689
		2019	5,683	21,979	7,837	14,099	4,038
		2020	5,827	20,609	7,782	12,814	3,936
39	Remediation activities and other waste management services	2017	962	984	391	590	222
		2018	1,001	1,004	500	504	200
		2019	1,049	1,148	587	559	280
		2020	1,154	1,079	617	481	274

18.1 Production and Construction Industries

Description		Year	Number of enterprises	Total turnover	Approximate gross value added at basic prices (aGVA)	Total purchases of goods, materials & services	Total employment costs
Standard Industrial Classification (Revised 2007) Section							
			Number	£ million	£ million	£ million	£ million
F	Construction	2017	330,620	269,379	103,828	167,420	41,169
		2018	341,650	297,166	108,744	190,010	43,309
		2019	348,590	306,865	111,242	197,705	45,109
		2020	355,878	271,550	101,862	171,408	43,929
41	Construction of buildings	2017	96,633	119,258	44,748	75,281	12,423
		2018	102,203	134,201	48,529	86,391	13,302
		2019	104,677	142,054	49,867	93,358	14,895
		2020	109,735	119,130	43,740	75,707	14,562
42	Civil engineering	2017	24,488	49,901	15,825	34,540	9,386
		2018	24,869	58,006	17,510	41,005	10,709
		2019	25,708	55,770	16,550	39,703	10,099
		2020	25,593	51,310	15,481	36,500	10,059
43	Specialised construction activities	2017	209,499	100,220	43,255	57,599	19,360
		2018	214,578	104,959	42,705	62,615	19,298
		2019	218,205	109,041	44,825	64,643	20,115
		2020	220,550	101,110	42,641	59,201	19,308

18.1 Production and Construction Industries

(continued)

Description		Year	Total net capital expenditure[2]	Total capital expenditure -acquisitions[2]	Total capital expenditure -disposals[2]	Total stocks and work in progress - value at end of year	Total stocks and work in progress - value at beginning of year	Total stocks and work in progress - increase during year
Standard Industrial Classification (Revised 2007) Section								
			£ million	£ million	£ million	£ million	£ million	£ million
B-F	Production industries and construction	2017	52,407	59,050	6,643	108,412	104,032	4,381
		2018	52,625	61,093	8,467	114,866	109,436	5,430
		2019	56,932	62,726	5,793	120,264	115,027	5,237
		2020	48,848	55,978	7,130	117,628	117,123	505
B-E	Production industries	2017	44,521	48,051	3,530	68,539	65,567	2,972
		2018	43,778	49,453	5,675	70,616	66,506	4,110
		2019	46,048	48,718	2,670	75,114	71,480	3,634
		2020	41,400	44,395	2,994	73,662	73,996	-334
B	Mining and quarrying	2017	6,179	6,252	73	1,857	1,847	10
		2018	5,468	5,654	186	1,861	1,949	-87
		2019	6,575	6,667	92	1,947	1,845	102
		2020	4,367	4,462	95	1,773	1,972	-198
05	Mining of coal and lignite	2017	[c]	[c]	[c]	[c]	[c]	[c]
		2018	[c]	[c]	[c]	[c]	[c]	[c]
		2019	[c]	[c]	[c]	[c]	[c]	[c]
		2020	[c]	[c]	[c]	[c]	[c]	[c]
06	Extraction of crude petroleum and natural gas	2017	5,249	5,256	7	1,039	1,036	3
		2018	4,681	4,731	50	1,058	1,144	-86
		2019	5,046	5,064	17	1,043	998	45
		2020	3,395	3,413	18	897	1,040	-143
07	Mining of metal ores	2017	[c]	[c]	[c]	[c]	[c]	[c]
		2018	[c]	[c]	[c]	[c]	[c]	[c]
		2019	[c]	[c]	[c]	[c]	[c]	[c]
		2020	[c]	[c]	[c]	[c]	[c]	[c]
08	Other mining and quarrying	2017	481	527	46	435	402	33
		2018	585	628	43	464	418	46
		2019	1,258	1,298	40	486	469	17
		2020	654	703	49	480	516	-35
09	Mining support service activities	2017	355	371	16	340	350	-11
		2018	202	293	91	322	357	-35
		2019	271	301	30	384	350	34
		2020	315	340	25	359	382	-24
C	Manufacturing	2017	19,094	21,017	1,923	60,711	57,698	3,013
		2018	19,782	24,351	4,569	64,221	60,230	3,992
		2019	19,719	21,269	1,550	67,279	63,959	3,320
		2020	17,537	19,651	2,113	66,221	66,337	-116
10	Manufacture of food products	2017	2,754	2,953	199	5,687	5,227	460
		2018	2,595	2,863	269	6,024	5,742	282
		2019	2,809	3,001	191	6,047	5,926	121
		2020	2,743	2,980	237	6,345	5,929	415
11	Manufacture of beverages	2017	948	[c]	[c]	8,125	7,515	610
		2018	1,091	1,118	27	8,770	8,131	639
		2019	1,227	1,307	80	9,009	8,525	484
		2020	1,261	1,312	51	9,430	9,038	392
12	Manufacture of tobacco products	2017	-14	[c]	[c]	15	16	-1
		2018	[low]	[low]	[low]	2	3	[low]
		2019	[low]	[low]	[low]	4	4	1
		2020	[low]	[low]	[low]	3	3	[low]
13	Manufacture of textiles	2017	166	240	74	749	698	52
		2018	155	196	41	904	843	61
		2019	227	244	17	832	801	32
		2020	233	245	12	789	788	1

18.1 Production and Construction Industries

(continued)

Description		Year	Total net capital expenditure[2]	Total capital expenditure -acquisitions[2]	Total capital expenditure -disposals[2]	Total stocks and work in progress - value at end of year	Total stocks and work in progress - value at beginning of year	Total stocks and work in progress - increase during year
Standard Industrial Classification (Revised 2007) Section								
			£ million	£ million	£ million	£ million	£ million	£ million
14	Manufacture of wearing apparel	2017	48	50	2	323	282	41
		2018	49	53	4	478	335	143
		2019	29	34	5	414	406	7
		2020	61	[c]	[c]	317	339	-22
15	Manufacture of leather and related products	2017	33	33	1	207	198	9
		2018	29	30	1	158	160	-2
		2019	65	65	[low]	268	217	51
		2020	31	35	4	331	299	33
16	Manufacture of wood and of products of wood and cork, except furniture; manufacture of articles of straw and plaiting materials	2017	446	471	24	725	695	30
		2018	250	325	75	857	736	121
		2019	328	352	24	860	865	-5
		2020	407	470	63	865	829	36
17	Manufacture of paper and paper products	2017	445	478	34	932	906	26
		2018	424	461	37	1,065	962	104
		2019	414	462	48	1,066	1,019	47
		2020	502	536	34	1,106	1,086	20
18	Printing and reproduction of recorded media	2017	401	538	137	484	497	-14
		2018	564	662	98	568	524	43
		2019	393	478	85	542	534	7
		2020	328	402	74	476	478	-2
19	Manufacture of coke and refined petroleum products	2017	405	[c]	[c]	2,261	1,917	344
		2018	614	615	2	1,894	1,904	-9
		2019	820	823	3	2,169	1,890	279
		2020	785	[c]	[c]	1,879	2,198	-319
20	Manufacture of chemicals and chemical products	2017	1,393	1,470	77	3,850	3,465	385
		2018	1,270	1,300	30	4,240	4,003	237
		2019	1,343	1,502	160	4,134	4,174	-40
		2020	1,112	1,288	176	3,949	3,979	-30
21	Manufacture of basic pharmaceutical products and pharmaceutical preparations	2017	1,020	1,246	226	2,513	2,729	-215
		2018	1,023	[c]	[c]	2,330	2,560	-230
		2019	761	792	32	2,826	2,736	90
		2020	494	760	266	2,792	2,756	36
22	Manufacture of rubber and plastic products	2017	880	1,014	134	2,387	2,167	220
		2018	1,057	[c]	[c]	2,486	2,294	193
		2019	894	982	87	2,544	2,512	32
		2020	774	881	107	2,447	2,475	-28
23	Manufacture of other non-metallic mineral products	2017	681	746	66	1,496	1,430	66
		2018	650	739	89	1,562	1,475	87
		2019	734	816	82	1,688	1,590	98
		2020	580	652	72	1,440	1,639	-199
24	Manufacture basic metals	2017	596	675	78	2,345	2,161	184
		2018	464	592	128	2,465	2,425	40
		2019	506	569	63	2,453	2,646	-193
		2020	390	425	34	2,199	2,331	-132
25	Manufacture of fabricated metal products, except machinery and equipment	2017	1,590	1,766	176	3,982	3,686	296
		2018	1,313	[c]	[c]	4,476	3,931	545
		2019	1,550	1,768	218	4,744	4,350	394
		2020	1,720	1,936	216	4,690	4,684	6
26	Manufacture of computer, electronic and optical products	2017	572	626	54	3,230	2,953	277
		2018	645	683	38	3,401	3,153	248
		2019	789	823	34	3,730	3,374	357
		2020	598	638	39	3,552	3,620	-68

18.1 Production and Construction Industries

(continued)

Description		Year	Total net capital expenditure[2]	Total capital expenditure -acquisitions[2]	Total capital expenditure -disposals[2]	Total stocks and work in progress - value at end of year	Total stocks and work in progress - value at beginning of year	Total stocks and work in progress - increase during year
Standard Industrial Classification (Revised 2007) Section								
			£ million	£ million	£ million	£ million	£ million	£ million
27	Manufacture of electrical equipment	2017	266	333	67	1,934	1,759	174
		2018	301	332	31	1,929	1,820	110
		2019	339	366	27	1,956	1,833	123
		2020	272	287	14	1,862	1,956	-95
28	Manufacture of machinery and equipment n.e.c.	2017	768	893	124	4,694	4,254	439
		2018	932	1,031	99	5,132	4,546	586
		2019	963	1,121	158	5,390	5,168	222
		2020	720	917	197	5,157	5,453	-296
29	Manufacture of motor vehicles, trailers and semi-trailers	2017	3,265	3,396	131	4,801	5,053	-253
		2018	3,375	3,408	33	5,046	4,904	141
		2019	2,721	2,771	50	5,255	4,989	266
		2020	1,869	2,007	138	5,000	5,290	-290
30	Manufacture of other transport equipment	2017	1,255	1,296	41	5,962	6,323	-361
		2018	1,857	1,920	63	5,673	5,231	441
		2019	1,468	1,511	44	6,607	6,053	554
		2020	1,189	1,216	26	6,912	6,479	433
31	Manufacture of furniture	2017	292	310	19	650	622	28
		2018	248	268	19	710	692	18
		2019	398	436	38	682	648	34
		2020	340	365	25	814	765	49
32	Other manufacturing	2017	432	460	27	1,384	1,245	139
		2018	485	525	40	2,100	1,919	181
		2019	459	482	24	2,296	2,046	249
		2020	855	1,026	172	2,119	2,156	-37
33	Repair and installation of machinery and equipment	2017	450	499	49	1,977	1,899	77
		2018	388	428	39	1,953	1,938	15
		2019	485	564	79	1,764	1,654	110
		2020	272	381	109	1,745	1,768	-23
D	Electricity, gas, steam and air conditioning supply	2017	12,169	13,444	1,275	5,081	5,237	-156
		2018	10,663	11,443	780	3,652	3,456	196
		2019	11,769	12,201	432	4,820	4,635	185
		2020	11,847	12,243	397	4,742	4,730	13
E	Water supply, sewerage, waste management and remediation activities	2017	7,079	7,338	259	890	785	104
		2018	7,865	8,005	140	881	871	10
		2019	7,985	8,580	595	1,069	1,041	28
		2020	7,649	8,038	389	925	958	-33
36	Water collection, treatment and supply	2017	4,793	4,829	36	191	189	2
		2018	5,221	5,254	33	218	204	15
		2019	[c]	[c]	[c]	221	213	8
		2020	4,976	5,216	239	219	214	5
37	Sewerage	2017	[c]	[c]	9	25	24	1
		2018	[c]	[c]	13	22	25	-3
		2019	[c]	[c]	[c]	36	29	7
		2020	[c]	[c]	21	59	53	5
38	Waste collection, treatment and disposal activities; materials recovery	2017	[c]	[c]	212	661	556	106
		2018	[c]	[c]	92	621	624	-3
		2019	[c]	[c]	[c]	796	780	15
		2020	[c]	[c]	127	599	646	-47
39	Remediation activities and other waste management services	2017	30	32	2	12	16	-4
		2018	79	81	2	20	18	2
		2019	49	66	16	16	19	-2
		2020	29	31	2	48	45	3

18.1 Production and Construction Industries

(continued)

Description		Year	Total net capital expenditure[2]	Total capital expenditure -acquisitions[2]	Total capital expenditure -disposals[2]	Total stocks and work in progress - value at end of year	Total stocks and work in progress - value at beginning of year	Total stocks and work in progress - increase during year
Standard Industrial Classification (Revised 2007) Section								
			£ million	£ million	£ million	£ million	£ million	£ million
F	Construction	2017	7,886	10,999	3,113	39,873	38,464	1,409
		2018	8,848	11,640	2,792	44,250	42,930	1,320
		2019	10,884	14,008	3,124	45,150	43,547	1,603
		2020	7,447	11,583	4,136	43,966	43,127	839
41	Construction of buildings	2017	2,975	5,394	2,418	33,732	32,960	772
		2018	3,735	5,608	1,873	37,260	36,656	604
		2019	4,229	6,431	2,202	38,604	37,388	1,216
		2020	2,296	5,400	3,104	37,102	36,756	346
42	Civil engineering	2017	1,936	2,112	177	2,262	2,031	231
		2018	2,378	2,661	283	3,082	2,737	346
		2019	3,424	3,688	263	2,948	2,840	108
		2020	2,409	2,681	272	2,876	2,561	316
43	Specialised construction activities	2017	2,975	3,493	518	3,880	3,474	406
		2018	2,735	3,371	636	3,908	3,538	370
		2019	3,230	3,889	659	3,598	3,319	279
		2020	2,742	3,502	760	3,988	3,811	177

Source: Annual Business Survey (ABS)

The following symbols and abbreviations are used throughout the ABS releases;

c   confidential information suppressed to avoid disclosure.

..   not available.

-   nil or less than half the level of rounding.

low = a figure less than half the level of rounding.

The sum of constituent items in tables may not always agree exactly with the totals shown due to rounding.

Notes:

1. Total employment (point in time and average during the year figures) have been removed from the 'Non-financial business economy, UK and regional (ABS) 2020' publication. For more information see: https://www.ons.gov.uk/businessindustryandtrade/business/businessservices/bulletins/nonfinancialbusinesseconomyukandregionalannualbusinesssurvey/latest

2. From 2008 to 2014 the Total net capital expenditure, Total capital expenditure - acquisitions, and Total capital expenditure - disposals published values included a small element of Not yet in production (NYIP). From 2015 onwards NYIP is not estimated for and is no longer included in the published values.

18.2 UK Manufacturer's Sales by Industry

								£ Millions
Industry		2013	2014	2015	2016	2017	2018	2019
Other mining and quarrying								
Quarrying of ornamental and building stone, limestone, gypsum, chalk and slate	08110	S	S	112	107	113	120	123
Operation of gravel and sand pits; mining of clays and kaolin	08120	S	S	1,317	1,500	1,914	1,912	1,840
Mining of chemical and fertiliser minerals	08910	S	S	S	S	S	S	S
Extraction of salt	08930	S	S	S	S	S	S	92
Other mining and quarrying n.e.c.	08990	S	88	S	S	S	S	S
Manufacture of food products								
Processing and preserving of meat	10110	6,189	6,624	6,540	6,739	8,260	8,416	8,498
Processing and preserving of poultry meat	10120	3,402	3,711	3,854	4,133	4,355	4,714	4,413
Production of meat and poultry meat products	10130	5,266	5,462	5,511	5,263	5,481	5,772	5,731
Processing and preserving of fish, crustaceans and molluscs	10200	2,108	2,335	2,315	2,290	2,562	2,799	2,724
Processing and preserving of potatoes	10310	S	1,212	S	S	1,105	S	1,178
Manufacture of fruit and vegetable juice	10320	611	639	569	598	695	768	680
Other processing and preserving of fruit and vegetables	10390	3,030	3,134	3,192	3,229	3,443	3,616	3,470
Manufacture of oils and fats	10410	1,130	1,055	1,021	1,021	1,201	1,178	1,257
Manufacture of margarine and similar edible fats	10420	466	222	213	S	S	S	S
Operation of dairies and cheese making	10510	7,068	8,153	7,532	6,698	7,521	7,931	8,125
Manufacture of ice cream	10520	634	366	358	393	394	451	436
Manufacture of grain mill products	10610	S	S	3,871	3,733	3,717	3,890	4,023
Manufacture of starches and starch products	10620	385	325	270	286	315	332	297
Manufacture of bread; manufacture of fresh pastry goods and cakes	10710	6,023	6,409	6,583	6,372	6,416	6,091	5,784
Manufacture of rusks and biscuits; manufacture of preserved pastry goods and cakes	10720	4,434	4,215	4,134	3,977	S	S	4,662
Manufacture of macaroni, noodles, couscous and similar farinaceous products	10730	S	S	S	S	S	S	S
Manufacture of sugar	10810	1,210	S	S	927	867	749	643
Manufacture of cocoa, chocolate and sugar confectionery	10820	2,620	2,616	2,701	S	2,584	2,807	2,805
Processing of tea and coffee	10830	S	S	1,371	S	S	1,515	S
Manufacture of condiments and seasonings	10840	1,936	1,741	1,786	1,774	1,829	2,020	2,077
Manufacture of prepared meals and dishes	10850	S	3,038	3,144	3,279	3,619	3,654	3,351
Manufacture of homogenised food preparations and dietetic food	10860	29	18	S	11	16	59	62
Manufacture of other food products n.e.c.	10890	3,759	3,615	3,716	3,604	4,093	4,457	4,600
Manufacture of prepared feeds for farm animals	10910	4,329	4,123	3,837	4,106	4,250	4,659	4,306
Manufacture of prepared pet foods	10920	1,666	1,664	1,718	1,899	1,430	1,683	1,770
Manufacture of beverages								
Distilling, rectifying and blending of spirits	11010	S	S	S	3,735	4,132	4,633	5,001
Manufacture of wine from grape	11020	S	S	S	S	S	S	S
Manufacture of cider and other fruit wines	11030	921	860	850	S	896	853	780
Manufacture of other non-distilled fermented beverages	11040	0	0	S	S	S	S	S
Manufacture of beer	11050	3,297	S	S	3,200	3,514	3,509	3,398
Manufacture of malt	11060	S	S	S	S	417	S	S
Manufacture of soft drinks; production of mineral waters and other bottled waters	11070	S	S	4,678	S	S	S	S
Manufacture of tobacco products								
Manufacture of tobacco products	12000	1,723	S	S	S	S	S	S
Manufacture of textiles								
Preparation and spinning of textile fibres	13100	396	392	411	436	253	345	328
Weaving of textiles	13200	619	620	602	610	630	652	637
Finishing of textiles	13300	500	537	458	309	318	361	294
Manufacture of knitted and crocheted fabrics	13910	S	S	S	S	141	165	154
Manufacture of made-up textile articles, except apparel	13920	1,094	1,170	1,183	1,325	1,245	1,238	1,235
Manufacture of carpets and rugs	13930	708	761	719	723	719	738	748
Manufacture of cordage, rope, twine and netting	13940	50	59	S	S	62	68	78
Manufacture of non-wovens and articles made from non-wovens, except apparel	13950	178	177	173	208	206	223	233
Manufacture of other technical and industrial textiles	13960	315	327	335	358	366	352	355
Manufacture of other textiles n.e.c.	13990	114	129	134	134	143	138	149
Manufacture of wearing apparel								
Manufacture of leather clothes	14110	4	S	4	S	S	S	S
Manufacture of workwear	14120	107	113	101	104	105	119	126
Manufacture of other outerwear	14130	620	752	725	736	681	665	696
Manufacture of underwear	14140	388	403	271	284	215	202	241
Manufacture of other wearing apparel and accessories	14190	258	284	312	282	287	298	299
Manufacture of articles of fur	14200	1	S	2	S	S	S	S
Manufacture of knitted and crocheted hosiery	14310	84	85	80	63	38	40	29
Manufacture of other knitted and crocheted apparel	14390	172	187	170	145	S	192	213
Manufacture of leather and related products								
Tanning and dressing of leather; dressing and dyeing of fur	15110	310	249	225	270	292	275	236
Manufacture of luggage, handbags and the like, saddlery and harness	15120	133	170	170	148	158	161	191
Manufacture of footwear	15200	284	263	294	265	291	320	298

658

18.2 UK Manufacturer's Sales by Industry

£ Millions

Industry		2013	2014	2015	2016	2017	2018	2019
Manufacture of wood and of products of wood and cork; except furniture; manufacture of articles of straw and plaiting materials								
Sawmilling and planing of wood	16100	1,037	1,154	1,055	1,076	1,059	S	1195
Manufacture of veneer sheets and wood-based panels	16210	909	960	987	972	S	1,063	1,065
Manufacture of assembled parquet floors	16220	5	4	4	5	5	S	S
Manufacture of other builders' carpentry and joinery	16230	3,317	3,638	3,532	3,435	3,859	3,873	3,767
Manufacture of wooden containers	16240	492	S	585	578	583	652	S
Manufacture of other products of wood; manufacture of articles of cork, straw and plaiting materials	16290	337	421	371	387	S	517	549
Manufacture of paper and paper products								
Manufacture of pulp	17110	S	S	S	S	S	S	S
Manufacture of paper and paperboard	17120	2,384	2,370	2,078	2,141	2,300	2,530	2,445
Manufacture of corrugated paper and paperboard and of containers of paper and paperboard	17210	3,967	4,008	4,359	4,109	4,285	4,628	4,624
Manufacture of household and sanitary goods and of toilet requisites	17220	2,067	S	S	S	S	S	S
Manufacture of paper stationery	17230	419	459	406	391	386	372	335
Manufacture of wallpaper	17240	141	123	115	114	116	102	111
Manufacture of other articles of paper and paperboard	17290	999	1,266	1,119	1,072	1,174	1,129	1,167
Printing and reproduction of recorded media								
Printing of newspapers	18110	159	S	S	S	S	S	S
Other printing	18120	7,162	7,246	7,074	6,987	7,135	S	S
Pre-press and pre-media services	18130	381	401	435	469	451	430	429
Binding and related services	18140	243	230	207	220	223	222	S
Reproduction of recorded media	18200	110	99	S	S	S	S	19
Manufacture of coke and refined petroleum products								
Manufacture of coke oven products	19100	S	S	0	0	0	0	0
Manufacture of chemicals and chemical products								
Manufacture of industrial gases	20110	692	S	S	600	542	539	578
Manufacture of dyes and pigments	20120	932	966	871	999	1,141	1,171	1,151
Manufacture of other inorganic basic chemicals	20130	955	774	760	864	909	964	1031
Manufacture of other organic basic chemicals	20140	2,792	2,705	2,443	2,432	2,909	3,207	2,660
Manufacture of fertilisers and nitrogen compounds	20150	1,647	1,479	1,148	1,033	967	1,066	1,029
Manufacture of plastics in primary forms	20160	3,543	3,554	3,468	3,571	4,544	4,657	4,043
Manufacture of synthetic rubber in primary forms	20170	303	S	S	105	S	S	S
Manufacture of pesticides and other agrochemical products	20200	622	559	533	458	550	588	641
Manufacture of paints, varnishes and similar coatings, printing ink and mastics	20300	3,068	3,210	3,150	3,191	3,221	3,260	3,490
Manufacture of soap and detergents, cleaning and polishing preparations	20410	1,754	1,405	1,334	1,454	1,426	1,496	1,595
Manufacture of perfumes and toilet preparations	20420	2,602	2,020	1,985	2,056	2,040	1,970	2,048
Manufacture of explosives	20510	S	133	136	154	S	S	S
Manufacture of glues	20520	383	423	408	418	465	497	525
Manufacture of essential oils	20530	717	648	657	777	710	794	847
Manufacture of other chemical products n.e.c.	20590	2,630	2,549	2,623	3,403	3,832	3,901	4,099
Manufacture of man-made fibres	20600	200	167	166	186	343	357	359
Manufacture of basic pharmaceutical products and pharmaceutical preparations								
Manufacture of basic pharmaceutical products	21100	777	756	794	891	1,053	1,151	1,249
Manufacture of pharmaceutical preparations	21200	11,270	10,158	10,004	11,999	10,817	12,409	12,366
Manufacture of rubber and plastic products								
Manufacture of rubber tyres and tubes; retreading and rebuilding of rubber tyres	22110	S	S	S	651	673	S	597
Manufacture of other rubber products	22190	1,571	1,601	S	1,551	1,593	S	1,569
Manufacture of plastic plates, sheets, tubes and profiles	22210	4,740	5,066	4,890	5,208	5,500	5,565	5,874
Manufacture of plastic packing goods	22220	3,255	3,488	3,482	3,355	3,411	3,567	3,477
Manufacture of builders' ware of plastic	22230	4,108	4,318	4,190	4,250	4,282	4,351	4,041
Manufacture of other plastic products	22290	4,288	4,608	4,471	4,526	4,785	4,664	4,476
Manufacture of other non-metallic mineral products								
Manufacture of flat glass	23110	177	S	177	182	192	194	207
Shaping and processing of flat glass	23120	1,116	1,140	1,240	1,255	1,321	1,477	1,486
Manufacture of hollow glass	23130	726	S	764	769	785	824	1055
Manufacture of glass fibres	23140	397	410	396	407	436	427	447
Manufacture and processing of other glass, including technical glassware	23190	S	140	159	160	180	172	171
Manufacture of refractory products	23200	246	242	236	225	225	S	266
Manufacture of ceramic tiles and flags	23310	90	S	91	94	116	S	42
Manufacture of bricks, tiles and construction products, in baked clay	23320	S	573	S	S	S	752	S
Manufacture of ceramic household and ornamental articles	23410	S	295	307	S	309	S	S
Manufacture of ceramic sanitary fixtures	23420	S	S	S	S	S	S	S
Manufacture of ceramic insulators and insulating fittings	23430	S	S	16	S	15	S	S
Manufacture of other technical ceramic products	23440	S	S	S	S	S	S	S
Manufacture of other ceramic products	23490	22	S	S	S	34	S	S

18.2 UK Manufacturer's Sales by Industry

								£ Millions
Industry		2013	2014	2015	2016	2017	2018	2019
Manufacture of cement	23510	673	S	722	816	907	784	1011
Manufacture of lime and plaster	23520	S	235	242	247	264	266	277
Manufacture of concrete products for construction purposes	23610	S	1,944	2,117	2,225	2,354	2,400	2,360
Manufacture of plaster products for construction purposes	23620	S	S	S	S	S	S	S
Manufacture of ready-mixed concrete	23630	1,180	1,306	S	S	2,017	1,943	1,841
Manufacture of mortars	23640	S	S	S	300	S	280	S
Manufacture of fibre cement	23650	70	81	S	S	S	S	S
Manufacture of other articles of concrete, plaster and cement	23690	S	S	S	245	245	247	S
Cutting, shaping and finishing of stone	23700	404	434	446	500	523	568	501
Production of abrasive products	23910	140	139	132	135	146	155	148
Manufacture of other non-metallic mineral products n.e.c.	23990	1,459	1,813	1,845	1,939	2,004	2,149	2,259
Manufacture of basic metals								
Manufacture of tubes, pipes, hollow profiles and related fittings, of steel	24200	1,317	1,158	898	705	686	727	704
Cold drawing of bars	24310	150	152	132	103	147	166	86
Cold rolling of narrow strip	24320	S	S	33	34	47	S	S
Cold forming or folding	24330	S	S	S	S	S	S	S
Cold drawing of wire	24340	153	140	S	S	131	S	S
Precious metals production	24410	371	260	174	162	104	98	93
Aluminium production	24420	1,124	1,176	1,345	1,320	1,606	S	1,454
Lead, zinc and tin production	24430	506	532	S	S	S	S	366
Copper production	24440	577	472	447	428	500	511	487
Other non-ferrous metal production	24450	970	932	858	855	907	929	877
Casting of iron	24510	411	414	382	364	382	427	414
Casting of steel	24520	351	330	273	218	202	230	222
Casting of light metals	24530	401	428	476	472	467	S	513
Casting of other non-ferrous metals	24540	188	212	144	119	126	133	130
Manufacture of fabricated metal products; except machinery and equipment								
Manufacture of metal structures and parts of structures	25110	5,407	6,193	6,284	6,308	6,631	7,110	6,648
Manufacture of doors and windows of metal	25120	1,375	1,479	1,598	1,719	1,847	2,204	2,051
Manufacture of central heating radiators and boilers	25210	870	900	968	1,028	1,305	1,555	S
Manufacture of other tanks, reservoirs and containers of metal	25290	429	412	438	394	359	384	479
Manufacture of steam generators, except central heating hot water boilers	25300	S	S	S	S	S	S	S
Manufacture of weapons and ammunition	25400	1,667	1,575	1,807	1,860	2,087	1,963	2,208
Forging, pressing, stamping and roll-forming of metal; powder metallurgy	25500	1,900	1,967	1,962	1,926	2,024	2,051	2,072
Treatment and coating of metals	25610	1,325	1,323	1,277	1,251	1,370	1,468	1,371
Machining	25620	4,825	5,030	5,607	5,339	5,372	5,252	5,370
Manufacture of cutlery	25710	22	18	20	22	24	24	25
Manufacture of locks and hinges	25720	498	542	524	537	586	602	622
Manufacture of tools	25730	867	955	868	874	937	981	953
Manufacture of steel drums and similar containers	25910	S	S	84	S	S	S	83
Manufacture of light metal packaging	25920	S	S	S	S	S	S	S
Manufacture of wire products, chain and springs	25930	800	746	746	649	741	732	722
Manufacture of fasteners and screw machine products	25940	476	512	467	444	429	414	417
Manufacture of other fabricated metal products n.e.c.	25990	1,906	1,979	1,925	2,019	1,984	1,932	1,880
Manufacture of computer; electronic and optical products								
Manufacture of electronic components	26110	1,104	833	995	1,070	1,088	1,126	1,131
Manufacture of loaded electronic boards	26120	1,017	886	766	763	733	903	769
Manufacture of computers and peripheral equipment	26200	1,403	S	1,167	1,274	1,335	1,451	1,668
Manufacture of communication equipment	26300	1,362	1,258	1,255	1,187	1,181	1,306	1,437
Manufacture of consumer electronics	26400	355	398	408	429	439	449	508
Manufacture of instruments and appliances for measuring, testing and navigation	26510	5,668	5,866	5,762	5,385	5,690	5,959	6,119
Manufacture of watches and clocks	26520	24	22	21	19	21	S	20
Manufacture of irradiation, electromedical and electrotherapeutic equipment	26600	S	S	S	S	S	1,986	2,297
Manufacture of optical instruments and photographic equipment	26700	333	355	383	807	906	868	841
Manufacture of magnetic and optical media	26800	S	13	S	S	S	S	21
Manufacture of electrical equipment								
Manufacture of electric motors, generators and transformers	27110	2,763	2,578	1,986	1,773	1,861	1,766	2,117
Manufacture of electricity distribution and control apparatus	27120	2,288	2,351	2,277	2,257	2,202	2,243	2,247
Manufacture of batteries and accumulators	27200	S	275	258	226	241	S	S
Manufacture of fibre optic cables	27310	97	102	116	306	293	303	387
Manufacture of other electronic and electric wires and cables	27320	1,206	1,219	1,097	747	836	994	952
Manufacture of wiring devices	27330	590	557	591	580	711	748	837
Manufacture of electric lighting equipment	27400	1,352	1,557	1,579	1,335	1,319	1,327	1,152
Manufacture of electric domestic appliances	27510	1,186	897	909	832	880	993	960
Manufacture of non-electric domestic appliances	27520	359	S	357	344	428	S	S
Manufacture of other electrical equipment	27900	1,208	1,171	1,117	1,604	1,858	1,874	1,840

18.2 UK Manufacturer's Sales by Industry

£ Millions

Industry		2013	2014	2015	2016	2017	2018	2019
Manufacture of machinery and equipment n.e.c.								
Manufacture of engines and turbines, except aircraft, vehicle and cycle engines	28110	3,623	3,774	3,014	2,724	3,501	3,207	2,795
Manufacture of fluid power equipment	28120	979	1,016	817	819	857	1,008	1,121
Manufacture of other pumps and compressors	28130	2,167	2,021	1,781	1,906	2,022	2,219	2,207
Manufacture of other taps and valves	28140	1,729	2,415	1,826	1,747	1,797	1,763	1,869
Manufacture of bearings, gears, gearing and driving elements	28150	993	1,045	968	917	982	1,008	1,016
Manufacture of ovens, furnaces and furnace burners	28210	220	206	186	186	202	283	255
Manufacture of lifting and handling equipment	28220	2,365	2,552	2,518	2,361	2,759	3,190	3,135
Manufacture of office machinery and equipment (except computers and peripheral equipment)	28230	S	S	675	763	731	684	627
Manufacture of power-driven hand tools	28240	166	S	S	146	S	S	S
Manufacture of non-domestic cooling and ventilation equipment	28250	2,286	2,515	S	2,425	2,586	S	S
Manufacture of other general-purpose machinery n.e.c.	28290	2,163	2,296	2,112	2,271	2,334	2,607	2,610
Manufacture of agricultural and forestry machinery	28300	1,618	1,600	1,432	1,540	1,547	1,952	1,767
Manufacture of metal forming machinery	28410	663	651	563	531	559	627	537
Manufacture of other machine tools	28490	303	318	294	316	294	328	343
Manufacture of machinery for metallurgy	28910	88	89	85	65	S	103	107
Manufacture of machinery for mining, quarrying and construction	28920	4,291	4,279	3,855	3,055	3,462	3,938	4,166
Manufacture of machinery for food, beverage and tobacco processing	28930	479	493	498	467	506	570	553
Manufacture of machinery for textile, apparel and leather production	28940	58	63	66	65	74	98	68
Manufacture of machinery for paper and paperboard production	28950	125	105	85	92	100	129	142
Manufacture of plastics and rubber machinery	28960	70	56	64	57	56	61	56
Manufacture of other special-purpose machinery n.e.c.	28990	1,051	1,200	1,182	1,500	1,520	1,861	1,781
Manufacture of motor vehicles; trailers and semi-trailers								
Manufacture of motor vehicles	29100	34,204	35,926	36,359	41,962	44,484	42,888	40,304
Manufacture of bodies (coachwork) for motor vehicles; manufacture of trailers and semi-trailers	29200	1,904	2,044	2,243	2,313	2,353	2,593	2,591
Manufacture of electrical and electronic equipment for motor vehicles	29310	S	251	262	258	251	227	224
Manufacture of other parts and accessories for motor vehicles	29320	8,618	9,160	9,561	10,306	11,316	11,030	10,075
Manufacture of other transport equipment								
Building of ships and floating structures	30110	3,775	S	4,419	4,340	3,542	3,919	4,059
Building of pleasure and sporting boats	30120	747	663	706	704	730	841	840
Manufacture of railway locomotives and rolling stock	30200	S	S	S	789	2,141	2,120	1,649
Manufacture of air and spacecraft and related machinery	30300	20,316	20,674	21,047	19,791	24,182	22,457	23,168
Manufacturer of military fighting vehicles	30400	S	S	S	S	S	S	S
Manufacture of motorcycles	30910	S	S	S	S	S	S	S
Manufacture of bicycles and invalid carriages	30920	134	147	157	S	205	209	S
Manufacture of other transport equipment n.e.c.	30990	40	S	50	57	64	73	66
Manufacture of furniture								
Manufacture of office and shop furniture	31010	1,081	1,185	1,170	1,265	1,141	1,165	1,300
Manufacture of kitchen furniture	31020	1,356	1,377	1,441	1,622	1,548	1,806	1,742
Manufacture of mattresses	31030	612	692	768	814	810	833	835
Manufacture of other furniture	31090	3,257	3,303	3,331	3,657	3,497	3,374	3,305
Other manufacturing								
Striking of coins	32110	S	S	S	S	S	S	S
Manufacture of jewellery and related articles	32120	428	398	328	295	268	276	564
Manufacture of imitation jewellery and related articles	32130	36	38	37	40	S	43	48
Manufacture of musical instruments	32200	22	21	S	S	38	40	41
Manufacture of sports goods	32300	348	347	316	346	360	389	414
Manufacture of games and toys	32400	210	299	272	405	432	467	455
Manufacture of medical and dental instruments and supplies	32500	2,597	2,721	2,787	2,793	3,014	3,133	3,152
Manufacture of brooms and brushes	32910	79	S	114	116	111	S	S
Other manufacturing n.e.c.	32990	694	643	699	712	802	787	915
Repair and installation of machinery and equipment								
Repair of fabricated metal products	33110	1,236	1,116	1,073	960	S	1,050	1,026
Repair of machinery	33120	3,150	3,129	2,925	2,743	2,969	3,596	3,187
Repair of electronic and optical equipment	33130	S	765	783	749	785	761	726
Repair of electrical equipment	33140	537	490	569	479	523	516	566
Repair and maintenance of ships and boats	33150	456	458	452	S	448	468	461
Repair and maintenance of aircraft and spacecraft	33160	3,488	3,586	3,593	S	S	S	S
Repair and maintenance of other transport equipment	33170	1,119	S	1,317	S	1,337	1,539	1,672
Repair of other equipment	33190	S	S	1	S	7	S	S
Installation of industrial machinery and equipment	33200	3,214	3,510	3,506	3,373	3,658	3,053	3,103
Total		354,721	362,545	358,143	365,726	389,316	401,439	396,625

Source: Office for National Statistics

Symbols used - Excel reference tables
S - A figure has been suppressed as disclosive
S* - A value suppressed as disclosive and aggregated within the UK Manufacturer Sales of "Other" products
N/A - Data not available
E - Data has low response, and therefore a high level of estimation, which may impact on the quality of the estimate

18.2 UK Manufacturer's Sales by Industry

<u>**PRODCOM survey information**</u>

PRODCOM stands for PRODucts of the European COMmunity and is a European Union (EU) wide survey of production mainly for the manufacturing industries. Data is provided for around 3,770 products classified to 234 industries. Businesses selected for PRODCOM provide data on the value of sales for the products they manufacture, as well as non-manufacturing income. In addition, where applicable, businesses also provide data on the volume of sales, in appropriate units.

A National Statistics Publication: National Statistics are produced to high professional standards, as set out in the UK Statistics Authority's Code of Practice for Official Statistics. They undergo regular quality reviews to ensure that they maintain this high standard while continuing to meet customer needs . All ONS statistics are produced independently from any political influence.

General Information
The PRODCOM Quality and Methodology Information report provides further details relating to this publication:
https://www.ons.gov.uk/businessindustryandtrade/manufacturingandproductionindustry/methodologies/ukmaufacturerssalesbyproductsurveyprodcomqmi
A glossary for PRODCOM is available in the Technical report:
https://www.ons.gov.uk/businessindustryandtrade/manufacturingandproductionindustry/methodologies/ukmanufacturerssalesbyproductprodcom
A user interpretation manual illustrates how the data can be used:
https://www.ons.gov.uk/businessindustryandtrade/manufacturingandproductionindustry/methodologies/ukmanufacturerssalesbyproductprodcom

The SIC(2007) totals and non-production sales are defined in the PRODCOM Glossary, but the following explanations may help interpret the tables:

Suppression of data

Statistical disclosure control methodology is applied to PRODCOM data. This ensures that information attributable to an individual or individual organisation is not identifiable in any published outputs. The Code of Practice for Official Statistics, and specifically the Principle on Confidentiality (P.C) set out practices for how ONS protects data from being disclosed. The P.C includes the statement that ONS outputs should "ensure that official statistics do not reveal the identity of an individual or organisation, or any private information relating to them, taking into account other relevant sources of information". More information can be found in National Statistician's Guidance: Confidentiality of Official Statistics, on the statistical disclosure control methodology page of the ONS website, and also in the PRODCOM technical report.
For more information on the disclosure control of PRODCOM data please refer to the PRODCOM technical report.

Previous PRODCOM codes and the incorporation of additional back data
Following user feedback for a longer time series to aid statistical analysis of trends, 2008 and 2009 back data were included to these reference tables at provisional 2014 results, in addition to the 2010 to 2014 data. However, caution should be exercised when comparing certain values, due to the continuously evolving nature of the PRODCOM question list which is set by Eurostat, the European Union's Statistical Authority, in the face of new or changing products and industries. The changes can make backwards comparability difficult, as some codes may appear or disappear in future publications. In this publication, only products included in the most recent PRODCOM list have been included. This leads to difficulties with some aggregate figures in previous years, where the parts do not sum to the whole; this is caused by some of those parts being now-defunct product codes that are not included here, so the sum of the actual values in the table may not equal the aggregate total.

Further information on the back data can be found in our previous publications, while information on the PRODCOM list and reference tables can be found in the background notes of the statistical bulletin, the Quality & Methodology Information Report, and the PRODCOM Technical Report. Please contact us if you require further information.

Contact: Daniel Robinson
Tel: (01633) 455718
Email: prodcompublications@ons.gov.uk

18.3 United Kingdom Business Entities - Number of VAT and/or PAYE based local units by 2 Digit Standard Industrial Classification (UK SIC2007) division and employment sizebands, 2019

UK SIC 2007 Divisons	Local Units							
		Employment Size Bands						
	Total	0-4	5-9	10-19	20-49	50-99	100-249	250+
Total	**3,180,595**	**2,271,005**	**415,140**	**241,865**	**157,285**	**53,975**	**28,880**	**12,445**
01 : Crop and animal production; hunting and related service activities	144,970	128,975	11,565	2,835	1,080	305	140	70
02 : Forestry and logging	4,410	3,685	460	165	80	20	0	0
03 : Fishing and aquaculture	4,345	3,865	320	130	25	5	0	0
05 : Mining of coal and lignite	30	5	5	5	5	5	5	0
06 : Extraction of crude petroleum and natural gas	190	105	20	15	10	15	10	15
07 : Mining of metal ores	5	5	0	0	0	0	0	0
08 : Other mining and quarrying	1,495	730	300	225	165	50	20	5
09 : Mining support service activities	440	280	45	25	35	25	15	15
10 : Manufacture of food products	9,790	4,430	1,735	1,265	995	535	425	405
11 : Manufacture of beverages	2,725	1,805	365	230	165	60	65	35
12 : Manufacture of tobacco products	5	0	5	0	0	0	0	0
13 : Manufacture of textiles	4,535	2,755	755	480	325	130	70	20
14 : Manufacture of wearing apparel	4,085	2,800	620	355	235	60	10	5
15 : Manufacture of leather and related products	735	430	160	65	45	20	10	5
16 : Manufacture of wood and of products of wood and cork; except furniture; manufacture of articles of straw and plaiting materials	9,810	6,935	1,360	785	485	170	60	15
17 : Manufacture of paper and paper products	1,605	655	195	210	245	145	125	30
18 : Printing and reproduction of recorded media	11,900	8,225	1,750	975	605	200	115	30
19 : Manufacture of coke and refined petroleum products	110	35	15	15	15	15	10	5
20 : Manufacture of chemicals and chemical products	3,425	1,715	470	390	380	255	155	60
21 : Manufacture of basic pharmaceutical products and pharmaceutical preparations	725	420	70	45	55	45	40	50
22 : Manufacture of rubber and plastic products	6,415	2,630	1,130	985	855	440	300	75
23 : Manufacture of other non-metallic mineral products	4,975	2,680	855	605	460	200	145	30
24 : Manufacture of basic metals	1,985	1,030	245	235	250	120	70	35
25 : Manufacture of fabricated metal products; except machinery and equipment	29,440	18,725	4,155	3,165	2,270	750	305	70
26 : Manufacture of computer; electronic and optical products	6,425	3,865	890	585	595	255	180	55
27 : Manufacture of electrical equipment	3,275	1,575	470	425	440	195	130	40
28 : Manufacture of machinery and equipment n.e.c.	8,200	4,335	1,325	905	875	410	255	95
29 : Manufacture of motor vehicles; trailers and semi-trailers	3,740	2,315	455	285	255	175	145	110
30 : Manufacture of other transport equipment	2,610	1,825	255	125	140	85	85	95
31 : Manufacture of furniture	6,625	4,035	1,070	700	495	180	105	40
32 : Other manufacturing	10,140	7,245	1,555	710	380	145	75	30
33 : Repair and installation of machinery and equipment	15,260	11,945	1,475	940	540	175	130	55
35 : Electricity; gas; steam and air conditioning supply	6,535	4,660	745	490	230	135	155	120
36 : Water collection; treatment and supply	955	375	165	125	150	65	45	30
37 : Sewerage	1,505	820	275	160	170	50	25	5
38 : Waste collection; treatment and disposal activities; materials recovery	8,190	4,160	1,470	1,035	910	380	190	45

18.3 United Kingdom Business Entities - Number of VAT and/or PAYE based local units by 2 Digit Standard Industrial Classification (UK SIC2007) division and employment sizebands, 2019

UK SIC 2007 Divisons	Local Units							
		Employment Size Bands						
	Total	0-4	5-9	10-19	20-49	50-99	100-249	250+
39 : Remediation activities and other waste management services	1,110	740	160	125	70	15	0	0
41 : Construction of buildings	108,355	93,385	8,650	3,730	1,505	590	385	110
42 : Civil engineering	26,580	20,900	2,635	1,335	915	430	250	115
43 : Specialised construction activities	218,685	184,500	20,435	8,505	3,785	1,025	350	85
45 : Wholesale and retail trade and repair of motor vehicles and motorcycles	88,005	60,245	15,595	6,285	4,220	1,265	355	40
46 : Wholesale trade; except of motor vehicles and motorcycles	122,950	75,735	21,685	13,985	7,870	2,305	1,010	360
47 : Retail trade; except of motor vehicles and motorcycles	306,655	180,260	65,215	35,460	18,290	3,690	2,525	1,215
49 : Land transport and transport via pipelines	70,780	55,945	6,265	3,885	2,675	1,010	680	320
50 : Water transport	1,525	1,075	195	130	70	30	15	10
51 : Air transport	1,465	1,045	115	85	75	40	50	55
52 : Warehousing and support activities for transportation	28,370	16,380	5,545	2,580	2,010	900	610	345
53 : Postal and courier activities	26,100	21,465	1,640	825	975	715	360	120
55 : Accommodation	23,120	9,870	3,620	3,550	3,830	1,410	700	140
56 : Food and beverage service activities	181,150	79,955	46,795	31,480	19,085	2,665	1,020	150
58 : Publishing activities	12,515	9,505	1,345	780	525	185	95	80
59 : Motion picture; video and television programme production; sound recording and music publishing activities	28,385	25,305	1,325	810	605	255	55	30
60 : Programming and broadcasting activities	2,165	1,705	155	110	110	35	30	20
61 : Telecommunications	11,920	8,235	1,445	940	700	280	165	155
62 : Computer programming; consultancy and related activities	170,670	154,225	7,125	4,500	2,960	1,070	550	240
63 : Information service activities	9,280	7,490	825	505	255	100	60	45
64 : Financial service activities; except insurance and pension funding	29,835	19,155	5,035	3,225	1,570	300	245	305
65 : Insurance; reinsurance and pension funding; except compulsory social security	7,720	6,970	215	155	115	75	65	125
66 : Activities auxiliary to financial services and insurance activities	39,660	30,125	4,595	2,280	1,355	635	415	255
68 : Real estate activities	114,290	90,415	14,655	6,340	1,830	505	385	160
69 : Legal and accounting activities	83,480	63,115	9,705	5,855	2,990	980	535	300
70 : Activities of head offices; management consultancy activities	189,830	172,590	8,545	4,395	2,500	950	525	325
71 : Architectural and engineering activities; technical testing and analysis	103,890	88,675	7,095	4,250	2,485	830	400	155
72 : Scientific research and development	6,245	4,230	655	525	400	175	145	115
73 : Advertising and market research	23,505	18,880	1,935	1,265	855	315	165	90
74 : Other professional; scientific and technical activities	79,040	70,605	5,265	2,030	870	190	65	15
75 : Veterinary activities	6,955	3,180	1,495	1,490	665	95	25	5
77 : Rental and leasing activities	21,855	14,340	3,605	2,300	1,170	285	125	30
78 : Employment activities	36,585	23,190	4,105	2,950	2,410	1,745	1,445	740
79 : Travel agency; tour operator and other reservation service and related activities	11,475	7,170	2,665	900	425	180	95	40
80 : Security and investigation activities	11,290	7,700	1,365	870	665	330	190	170
81 : Services to buildings and landscape activities	65,960	46,415	9,950	4,945	2,850	950	525	325
82 : Office administrative; office support and other business support activities	121,700	103,780	10,295	4,420	1,805	755	395	250
84 : Public administration and defence; compulsory social security	24,185	10,545	2,915	3,075	3,305	1,705	1,410	1,230

18.3 United Kingdom Business Entities - Number of VAT and/or PAYE based local units by 2 Digit Standard Industrial Classification (UK SIC2007) division and employment sizebands, 2019

UK SIC 2007 Divisons	Local Units							
		Employment Size Bands						
	Total	0-4	5-9	10-19	20-49	50-99	100-249	250+
85 : Education	74,755	28,570	8,735	8,820	14,570	8,645	4,500	915
86 : Human health activities	73,285	39,545	11,745	10,320	7,280	2,185	1,330	880
87 : Residential care activities	30,075	7,805	4,650	5,770	7,245	3,680	845	80
88 : Social work activities without accommodation	57,630	21,220	12,875	12,165	8,025	2,150	945	250
90 : Creative; arts and entertainment activities	30,265	27,250	1,600	775	345	180	95	20
91 : Libraries; archives; museums and other cultural activities	5,935	2,810	1,260	825	645	240	115	40
92 : Gambling and betting activities	10,765	4,470	5,290	435	385	95	75	15
93 : Sports activities and amusement and recreation activities	40,365	24,680	5,930	4,490	3,280	1,255	575	155
94 : Activities of membership organisations	27,055	17,855	4,775	2,385	1,300	445	215	80
95 : Repair of computers and personal and household goods	9,895	8,270	905	400	185	75	45	15
96 : Other personal service activities	81,665	59,405	15,760	4,915	1,265	185	105	30
97 : Activities of households as employers of domestic personnel	0	0	0	0	0	0	0	0
98 : Undifferentiated goods- and services-producing activities of private households for own use	5	5	0	0	0	0	0	0
99 : Activities of extraterritorial organisations and bodies	5	0	0	0	0	5	0	0

Data as at March 2019

Source: Office for National Statistics

Note: All figures are rounded to avoid disclosure. Values may be rounded down to zero and so all zeros are not necessarily true zeros. Totals across tables may differ by minor amounts due to the disclosure control methods used.

Contacts
ONS welcomes any comments or feedback on this release. Please provide any comments to the contacts named below:

Rhys Hopkins
Business Registers Strategy & Outputs
Government Buildings
Cardiff Road
Newport
NP10 8XG
Tel: +44 (0) 1633 456902
Email: rhys.hopkins@ons.gov.uk

Karen Watkins
Business Registers Strategy & Outputs
Government Buildings
Cardiff Road
Newport
NP10 8XG
Tel: +44 (0) 1633 456902
Email: karen.watkins@ons.gov.uk

18.4 Production of primary fuels

United Kingdom

Million tonnes of oil equivalent

| | Total | Coal[1] | Petroleum[2] | Natural gas[3] | Bioenergy & waste[4,5] | Primary electricity | |
						Nuclear	Wind, solar and hydro[6]
2000	288.7	19.5	138.3	108.4	2.3	19.6	0.51
2001	277.4	20.0	127.8	105.9	2.5	20.8	0.43
2002	272.9	18.8	127.0	103.7	2.8	20.1	0.52
2003	260.3	17.6	116.2	103.0	3.0	20.1	0.38
2004	238.4	15.6	104.5	96.4	3.1	18.2	0.60
2005	216.5	12.7	92.9	88.2	3.7	18.4	0.68
2006	197.2	11.4	84.0	80.0	3.9	17.1	0.75
2007	186.0	10.7	83.9	72.2	4.3	14.0	0.87
2008	177.7	11.3	78.7	69.5	5.1	11.9	1.05
2009	166.2	11.0	74.8	58.5	5.5	15.2	1.25
2010	156.6	11.4	69.0	55.3	5.8	13.9	1.17
2011	136.1	11.5	56.9	44.0	6.2	15.6	1.89
2012	121.0	10.6	48.8	37.5	6.7	15.2	2.29
2013	113.4	8.0	44.5	35.3	7.2	15.4	3.02
2014	112.0	7.3	43.7	35.8	7.9	13.8	3.61
2015	123.0	5.4	49.5	38.8	9.1	15.5	4.65
2016	124.7	2.9	52.0	39.9	10.1	15.4	4.54
2017	125.2	2.1	51.1	40.0	11.2	15.1	5.76
2018	129.3	1.9	56.0	38.8	12.0	14.1	6.45
2019	128.2	1.8	57.5	37.4	12.3	12.1	7.06

Source: Department for Business, Energy & Industrial Strategy

1. Includes an estimate of slurry.

2. Crude oil, offshore and land, plus condensates and petroleum gases derived at onshore treatment plants.

3. Includes colliery methane, excludes gas flared or re-injected.

4. Includes solid renewable sources (wood, straw and waste), a small amount of renewable primary heat sources (solar, geothermal etc), liquid biofuels and sewage gas and landfill gas.

5. Bioenergy & waste introduced as a separate category from March 2014 - see special feature article in the March 2014 edition of Energy Trends at:
www.gov.uk/government/collections/energy-trends-articles

6. Includes solar PV and natural flow hydro.

18.5 Total inland energy consumption
United Kingdom

Million tonnes of oil equivalent

	2004	2005	2006	2007	2008	2009	2010	2011	2012	2013	2014	2015	2016	2017	2018	2019
Inland energy consumption of																
primary fuels and equivalents (6)	233.6	236.3	233.1	227.5	225.6	211.6	219.5	203.7	208.1	206.8	194.0	196.5	193.9	192	192.4	189.5
Coal (1)	39.1	39.9	43.4	41.0	38.2	31.2	32.6	32.2	40.9	39.0	31.5	25.1	12.7	10.3	8.6	6.1
Petroleum (2)	75.1	78.2	77.4	76.3	74.4	70.9	70.2	67.8	67.0	65.8	66.0	67.4	68.3	69.5	68.8	68.0
Natural gas (3)	96.6	94.3	89.4	90.2	93.1	86.2	93.5	77.6	73.3	72.6	66.1	68.1	76.4	74.4	75.3	74.3
Nuclear electricity	18.2	18.4	17.1	14.0	11.9	15.2	13.9	15.6	15.2	15.4	13.9	15.5	15.4	15.1	14.1	13.3
Net electricity imports	0.6	0.7	0.6	0.4	0.9	0.2	0.2	0.5	1.0	1.2	1.8	1.8	1.5	1.3	1.6	1.8
Wind, Solar PV & Hydro electricity	0.6	0.7	0.8	0.9	1.1	1.2	1.2	1.9	2.3	3.0	3.6	4.7	4.6	5.8	6.5r	7.2
Bioenergy & waste	3.5	4.2	4.4	4.7	6.0	6.7	7.8	7.9	8.4	9.6	11.2	13.9	15.0r	15.7r	17.5r	18.9
Total consumption by final users	159.9	159.7	157.0	154.3	154.2	144.2	150.5	138.6	142.3	143.0	135.6	139.4	141.4	141.2	143.4	142.0
Final energy consumption by type of fuel																
Coal (direct use)	2.0	1.7	1.6	1.8	1.8	1.7	1.9	1.8	1.7	2.1	2.1	1.8	1.7	1.5	1.4	1.3
Coke and breeze	0.6	0.6	0.5	0.5	0.5	0.4	0.3	0.3	0.4	0.5	0.5	0.4	0.2	0.2	0.2	0.2
Other solid fuels (7)	0.4	0.4	0.4	0.4	0.4	0.2	0.2	0.2	0.2	0.2	0.2	0.2	0.2	0.2	0.2	0.1
Coke oven gas	0.1	0.1	0.1	0.1	0.1	0.0	0.1	0.1	0.0	0.1	0.1	0.1	0.1	0.1	0.1	0.1
Natural gas (8)	57.1	55.4	52.6	50.0	51.5	46.8	51.6	42.9	46.9	47.4	40.4	41.9	43.1	42.2	44.0	43.6
Electricity	29.1	30.0	29.7	29.4	29.4	27.7	28.3	27.3	27.4	27.2	26.0	26.1	26.1	25.8	25.8	25.4
Petroleum	68.6	69.5	69.8	69.5	66.5	63.4	63.2	61.5	61.1	60.2	60.9	62.3	63.2	64.3	63.9	63.0
Bioenergy & waste	0.7	0.8	1.0	1.2	2.4	2.7	3.4	3.2	3.4	4.1	4.3	5.3	5.5	5.7	6.5	6.9
Heat solid	1.3	1.3	1.2	1.3	1.5	1.2	1.3	1.2	1.2	1.2	1.2	1.2	1.2	1.3	1.3	1.2
Final energy consumption by class of consumer																
Agriculture	0.9	1.0	0.9	0.9	0.9	0.9	1.0	0.9	1.0	1.1	1.3	1.0	1.5	1.5	1.5	1.5
Iron and steel industry	1.9	1.8	1.9	1.8	1.6	1.2	1.4	1.3	1.2	1.3	1.4	1.3	1.0	0.9	0.9	0.9
Other industries	31.0	30.5	29.6	28.8	28.6	24.5	25.6	24.0	23.7	23.5	22.9	22.9	21.5	21.9	22.2	21.5
Railways	1.0	1.0	1.0	1.0	1.0	1.0	1.0	1.0	1.1	1.0	1.1	1.1	1.1	1.1	1.1	1.2
Road transport	42.2	42.6	42.7	43.2	41.9	40.7	40.4	39.8	39.5	39.3	40.0	40.5	41.5	41.5	41.3	40.9
Water transport	1.2	1.4	1.8	1.6	1.0	1.0	0.9	0.9	0.8	0.7	0.7	0.9	0.9	0.9	0.9	0.9
Air transport	12.9	13.9	14.0	13.9	13.4	12.8	12.3	12.8	12.4	12.4	12.4	12.5	12.6	13.5	13.6	13.6
Domestic	49.3	47.8	46.6	44.9	46.0	44.7	49.4	40.9	44.4	44.9	38.7	40.0	39.7	38.4	39.5	38.4
Public administration	7.2	7.1	6.6	6.3	6.5	6.0	6.2	5.5	6.0	6.1	5.5	5.7	5.8	5.6	5.5	5.4
Commercial and other services	12.2	12.7	12.0	11.8	13.1	11.6	12.2	11.5	12.3	12.6	11.7	12.5	13.1	13.2	13.3	13.3

Source: Department for Business, Energy & Industrial Strategy

r - revised

(1) Includes other solid fuels.
(2) Excludes petroleum for non-energy use and marine bunkers.
(3) Includes colliery methane, non-energy use of natural gas up to 1988.
(4) Electricity generated i.e. including own use.
(5) Excludes pumped storage. Includes generation at wind stations from 1988, and solar PV from 2015.
(6) Following the introduction of the energy balance presentation it has been possible to separately identify the
　　losses from the statistical difference for gas and electricity, bringing them onto the same basis as other fuels.
　　This has been accounted for in the total from 1994 onwards.
(7) Includes, from 1994, manufactured liquid fuels.
(8) Includes town gas prior to 1989.

18.6 Coal: Supply and demand
United Kingdom

Thousand tonnes

	2004	2005	2006	2007	2008	2009	2010	2011	2012	2013	2014	2015	2016	2017	2018	2019
SUPPLY																
Indigenous production	25,096	20,498	18,517	17,007	18,053	17,874	18,347	18,552	16,967	12,767	11,648	8,598	4,178	3,041	2,782	2,591
Deep mined	12,542	9,563	9,444	7,674	8,096	7,520	7,390	7,312	6,153	4,089	3,685	2,784	22	20	24	99
Surface mining[2]	11,993	10,445	8,635	8,866	9,509	9,854	10,426	10,580	10,134	8,584	7,962	5,814	4,156	3,021	2,758	2,492
Other sources[3]	561	490	438	467	449	500	530	660	680	95	-	-	-	-	-	-
Imports[4]	36,153	43,968	50,528	43,364	43,875	38,167	26,541	32,527	44,815	50,611	42,225	22,518	8,914	8,498	10,084	6,229
Exports[5]	622	536	443	544	599	646	715	491	488	595	425	385	443	495	634	740
Stock change[6]	-60	-2,151	-1,262	3,076	-3,110	-6,609	7,206	836	2,966	-2,641	-5,131	6,869	5,374	3,378	-147	-84
Total supply	60,567	61,780	67,340	62,903	58,219	48,785	51,378	51,424	64,259	60,143	48,316	37,600	18,022	14,422	12,086	7,996
Statistical difference	+116	-72	-254	-125	-166	+67	+54	-83	217	-62	21	149	-13	-17	28	16
Total demand	60,451	61,852	67,594	63,029	58,385	48,718	51,324	51,507	64,042	60,206	48,295	37,451	18,035	14,439	12,059	7,981
FINAL CONSUMPTION	2,805	2,455	2,370	2,590	2,672	2,525	2,736	2,557	2,541	3,011	3,040	2,676	2,567	2,321	2,277	1,973
Iron & steel	-	-	1	75	69	60	64	53	51	53	54	44	35	33	33	27
Other industries	1,837	1,781	1,755	1,821	1,871	1,682	1,894	1,745	1,776	2,269	2,388	2,029	1,928	1,699	1,668	1,409
Domestic	941	614	561	648	683	689	719	705	674	639	549	552	550	536	523	491
Other final users	28	59	54	45	49	94	58	55	40	49	49	51	55	53	52	46
Stocks at end of period																
Distributed stocks	12,598	14,527	16,427	13,420	16,392	22,641	15,368	15,115	11,883	15,114	20,142	13,546	8,121	5,014	4,784	4,399
Of which:																
Major power producers[7]	11,019	12,696	14,813	11,179	14,863	21,770	13,370	13,496	9,561	11,871	17,091	12,595	6,962	4,257	3,889	3,689
Coke ovens	1,291	1,317	946	1,479	1,065	806	1,338	1,355	831	518	795	553	594	313	447	439
Undistributed stocks	1,192	1,101	783	734	854	1,450	1,517	926	1,120	530	633	360	411	139	517	985
Total stocks[8]	13,791	15,628	17,210	14,155	17,246	24,091	16,885	16,041	13,003	15,644	20,775	13,906	8,531	5,154	5,300	5,384

Source: Department for Business, Energy & Industrial Strategy

1. Percentage change between the most recent quarter and the same quarter a year earlier.
2. The term 'surface mining' has now replaced opencast production. Opencast production is a surface mining technique.
3. Not produced since 2013 as the only mine producing slurry has ceased trading
4. For a detailed breakdown of UK imports by country and grade of coal refer to Table 2.4 Coal imports (internet table only).
5. Trade is counted as an export under three conditions, when it is recorded as an import and is subsequently exported; it enters the UK port with the intention of being imported but due
   to a change of ownership at the port it is exported without having cleared the port; and when items leave the warehouse and are exported. Trade is not classified as exports when it is
   resting at a UK port and the UK is not the intended final destination.
6. Stock change + = stock draw, _ = stock build.
7. This includes stocks held at ports.
8. For some quarters, closing stocks may not be consistent with stock changes, due to additional stock adjustments

668

18.7 Fuel input and gas output: gas consumption

United Kingdom

Giga-watt hours (GWh)

	2006	2007	2008	2009	2010	2011	2012	2013	2014	2015	2016	2017	2018	2019
Analysis of gas consumption														
Transformation sector	**333,431**	**379,518**	**402,236**	**382,061**	**400,823**	**332,012**	**239,631**	**230,170**	**243,468**	**241,208r**	**327,479r**	**313,969**	**303,334**	**301,640**
Electricity generation	311,408	355,878	376,811	359,303	377,116	309,076	216,543	205,869	217,837	212,632	298,075	286,031	273,398	272,331
Heat generation	22,023	23,640	25,426	22,758	23,707	22,936	23,089	24,302	25,631	28,576r	29,404r	27,938	29,936	29,309
Energy industry use total	**81,859**	**76,025**	**70,576**	**69,584**	**72,855**	**63,968**	**56,236**	**53,219**	**52,470**	**58,456r**	**57,608r**	**57,884**	**58,792**	**62,210**
Oil and gas extraction	69,252	64,230	61,324	61,098	61,210	53,725	48,461	46,000	45,391	51,024	50,031r	49,410	51,112	53,787
Petroleum refineries	5,161	5,206	1,934	1,601	1,785	1,757	1,522	1,151	1,201	1,012r	1,025r	2,084	2,114	2,078
Coal extraction and coke manufacture	112	91	180	217	260	223	194	60	100	79	77r	76	79	79
Blast furnaces	611	719	718	450	641	453	266	363	338	323	291	294	319	314
Other	6,723	5,779	6,420	6,218	8,959	7,809	5,793	5,645	5,440	6,018	6,184	6,020	5,167	5,952
Final consumption total	**620,035**	**591,274**	**607,178**	**551,492**	**608,551**	**504,961**	**550,672**	**557,201**	**475,601**	**492,514r**	**505,878r**	**495,408**	**506,575**	**495,914**
Iron and steel industry	8,391	7,323	7,305	5,346	6,124	5,835	5,091	5,338	5,454	5,303r	4,444r	4,264	4,313	4,193
Other industries	136,150	126,028	120,971	101,018	103,145	98,920	97,503	99,677	95,182	92,598	96,118	98,802	99,773	98,810
Domestic	366,928	352,868	359,554	345,199	389,596	308,841	343,180	344,501	283,691	297,582	305,875	295,077	305,270	294,877
Public administration	45,803	42,444	44,599	40,222	43,973	35,654	41,323	42,251	34,972	36,924r	37,471r	35,372	35,674	34,780
Commercial	34,273	33,098	47,007	41,475	46,255	38,583	45,331	47,276	40,189	43,947r	45,577r	46,189	46,374	47,633
Agriculture	2,013	1,998	1,413	1,468	1,369	1,351	1,162	1,096	1,073	983	1,010r	1,023	988	1,039
Miscellaneous	18,564	17,286	18,124	9,877	10,001	9,827	11,311	11,465	9,609	9,910r	10,275r	9,726	9,262	9,743
Non energy use	7,913	10,228	8,206	6,887	8,089	5,949	5,771	5,598	5,430	5,267	5,109	4,956	4,807	4,663
Total gas consumption	**1,047,338**	**1,058,873**	**1,087,028**	**1,013,597**	**1,094,366**	**910,206**	**854,430**	**848,064**	**778,395**	**800,505r**	**896,374r**	**872,768**	**872,956**	**863,174**

Source: Department for Business, Energy & Industrial Strategy

18.8 Electricity: generation, supply and consumption

United Kingdom

Gigawatt-hours

	2007	2008	2009	2010	2011	2012	2013	2014	2015	2016	2017	2018	2019
ELECTRICITY GENERATED													
Major power producers [1]													
Total	**361,317**	**355,239**	**342,011**	**347,607**	**332,539**	**328,291**	**324,623**	**300,822**	**295,991**	**292,943**	**287,744**	**280,950**	**269,208**
Conventional thermal [2]	146,706	128,944	106,939	111,127	111,255	147,946	141,011	114,534	95,606	50,283	42,662	39,255	30,101
Combined cycle gas turbine stations	140,011	160,109	151,454	160,518	131,886	85,647	82,533	88,259	87,732	131,276	123,763	118,878	118,049
Nuclear stations	63,028	52,486	69,098	62,140	68,980	70,405	70,607	63,748	70,345	71,726	70,336	65,064	56,184
Hydro (natural flow)	4,144	4,224	4,294	2,703	4,594	4,170r	3,609	4,635	4,907	3,951	4,179	3,800	4,190
Hydro (pumped storage)	3,859	4,089	3,685	3,150	2,906	2,966	2,904	2,883	2,739	2,959	2,872	2,498	1,756
Renewables other than hydro [3]	5,910	7,966	9,210	11,752	17,563	23,270	33,170	39,460	52,355	50,148	61,698	71,419	79,772
Other generators													
Total	**35,513**	**33,663**	**34,378**	**33,926**	**34,960**	**35,582**	**33,661**	**37,274**	**42,885**	**46,221**	**50,453**	**51,773**	**54,593**
Conventional thermal [2]	20,787	19,457	20,218	18,862	20,258	20,813	15,162	18,794	21,679	23,642	24,800	26,860	30,571
Combined cycle gas turbine stations	12,073	11,522	10,790	12,113	10,560	9,582	10,953	7,974	6,667	6,353	6,779	5,139	4,911
Hydro (natural flow)	933	921	936	888	1,098	1,140	1,092	1,253	1,391	1,419	1,703	1,643	1,656
Renewables other than hydro [3]	8,702	8,679	10,767	10,835	11,956	12,665	15,337	19,172	24,711	27,472	31,299	33,133	33,923
All generating companies													
Total	**396,830**	**388,892**	**376,718**	**382,068**	**367,982**	**363,874**	**358,283**	**338,096**	**338,875**	**339,164**	**338,197**	**332,723**	**323,801**
Conventional thermal [2]	167,493	148,401	127,157	129,989	131,513	168,758	156,173	133,328	117,285	73,925r	67,462	66,115	60,671
Combined cycle gas turbine stations	152,084	171,631	162,244	172,631	142,447	95,229	93,486	96,233	94,399	137,629r	130,542	124,018	122,959
Nuclear stations	63,028	52,486	69,098	62,140	68,980	70,405	70,607	63,748	70,345	71,726	70,336	65,064	56,184
Hydro (natural flow)	5,077	5,145	5,231	3,591	5,692	5,310	4,701	5,888	6,297	5,370	5,882	5,443	5,846
Hydro (pumped storage)	3,859	4,089	3,685	3,150	2,906	2,966	2,904	2,883	2,739	2,959	2,872	2,498	1,756
Renewables other than hydro [3]	14,612	16,675	19,977	22,587	29,520	35,935	48,507	58,632	77,067	77,620	92,997	104,552	113,695
ELECTRICITY USED ON WORKS													
Total	**17,694**	**16,341**	**16,569**	**16,122**	**16,451**	**17,983**	**17,850**	**16,480**	**16,652**	**15,268**	**15,470**	**15,414**	**14,414**
Major power producers	16,090	14,662	14,750	14,403	14,479	15,860	15,658	13,957	13,818	12,347	11,712	11,090	9,845
Other generators	1,605	1,679	1,819	1,720	1,973	2,124	2,191	2,522	2,834	2,921	3,758	4,323	4,569
ELECTRICITY SUPPLIED (GROSS)													
Major power producers [1]													
Total	**345,227**	**340,577**	**327,260**	**333,205**	**318,060**	**312,431**	**308,964**	**286,864**	**282,173**	**280,597**	**276,032**	**269,859**	**259,362**
Conventional thermal [2]	138,793	121,816	101,100	105,142	105,345	139,994	133,238	107,945	89,741	46,745	39,505	36,151	27,417
Combined cycle gas turbine stations	137,657	157,417	148,907	157,818	129,669	84,207	81,145	86,775	86,256	129,069	121,682	116,880	116,035
Nuclear stations	57,249	47,673	62,762	56,442	62,655	63,949	64,133	57,903	63,895	65,149	63,887	59,098	51,032
Hydro (natural flow)	4,114	4,209	4,279	2,694	4,578	4,168	3,596	4,606	4,889	3,937	4,164	3,787	4,175
Hydro (pumped storage)	3,846	4,075	3,672	3,139	2,895	2,956	2,894	2,873	2,730	2,949	2,862	2,490	1,750
Renewables other than hydro [3]	5,675	7,734	8,942	11,373	17,097	22,656	32,245	38,185	50,579	48,401	59,914	69,414	77,679
Other generators													
Total	**33,908**	**31,974**	**32,888**	**32,739**	**33,469**	**33,455**	**31,465**	**34,750**	**40,051**	**43,300**	**46,695**	**47,450**	**50,024**
Conventional thermal [2]	19,801	18,371	18,953	17,771	18,854	19,189	13,539	16,697	19,212	21,076	21,430	23,079	26,295
Combined cycle gas turbine stations	11,471	10,947	10,251	11,509	10,033	9,104	10,406	7,576	6,334	6,036	6,441	4,883	4,666
Hydro (natural flow)	918	905	920	872	1,077	1,118	1,071	1,226	1,357	1,382	1,654	1,357	1,608
Renewables other than hydro [3]	8,147	7,998	9,924	10,085	10,947	11,481	13,837	17,360	22,635	25,338	28,368	29,850	30,243
All generating companies													
Total	**379,135**	**372,551**	**360,148**	**365,944**	**351,530**	**345,886**	**340,429**	**321,614**	**322,224**	**323,897**	**322,727**	**317,309**	**309,387**
Conventional thermal [2]	158,594	140,185	120,053	122,914	124,200	159,183	146,777	124,642	108,952	67,820	60,935	59231	53,712
Combined cycle gas turbine stations	149,127	168,364	159,159	169,327	139,702	93,311	91,552	94,351	92,591	135,105	128,123	121762	120,701
Nuclear stations	57,249	47,673	62,762	56,442	62,655	63,949	64,133	57,903	63,895	65,149	63,887	59,098	51,032
Hydro (natural flow)	5,032	5,114	5,199	3,591	5,655	5,286	4,667	5,831	6,246	5,319	5,817	5,144	5,783
Hydro (pumped storage)	3,846	4,075	3,672	3,139	2,895	2,956	2,894	2,873	2,730	2,949	2,862	2,490	1,750
Renewables other than hydro [3]	13,822	15,732	18,866	21,458	28,044	34,138	46,081	55,545	73,213	73,739	88,282	99,265	107,922
ELECTRICITY USED IN PUMPING													
Major power producers	5,071	5,371	4,843	4,212	3,843	3,978	3,930	3,884	3,711	4,014	3,859	3,391	2,360
ELECTRICITY SUPPLIED (NET)													
Total	**374,064**	**367,180**	**355,306**	**361,734**	**347,688**	**341,912**	**336,504**	**317,732**	**318,513**	**319,882**	**318,868**	**313,918**	**307,026**
Major power producers	340,156	335,206	322,417	328,993	314,217	308,454	305,035	282,980	278,462	276,582	272,173	266,468	257,002
Other generators	33,908	31,974	32,889	32,741	33,470	33,459	31,470	34,752	40,051	43,300	46,695	47,450	50,024

18.8 Electricity: generation, supply and consumption

United Kingdom

Gigawatt-hours

	2007	2008	2009	2010	2011	2012	2013	2014	2015	2016	2017	2018	2019
Net imports	5,217	11,022	2,861	2,662	6,223	11,864	14,431	20,520	21,106	17,745	14,760	19,108	21,170
Total electricity supply	402,045	399,940	379,615	384,732	374,204	375,738	372,714	358,616	359,981r	356,909r	352,957	351,831	344,971
Losses in transmission etc	28,223	27,852	28,043	27,037r	28,140	28,917	27,667	28,514	27,297r	26,086r	26,520	26,661	26,412
Final electricity consumption	341,656	341,822	321,748	328,837	317,873	318,272r	316,271	302,786	303,480	304,033	299,649	300,444	295,989
Industry	112,800r	114,151	99,738	104,538	102,416	98,456	96,981	93,005	92,938	93,316	92,308	93,871	92,216
Transport	3,962	3,954	4,051	4,068	4,205	4,480	4,352	4,504	4,517	4,690	4,833	4,984	5,655
Other	224,895	223,718	217,959	220,232	211,252	215,336	214,938	205,277	206,025	206,027	202,508	201,589	198,118
of which:													
Domestic	123,076	119,800	118,541	118,832	111,586	114,663	113,412	108,076	107,764	108,025	105,368	105,065	103,825
Public Administration	20,087	20,355	19,442	19,100	18,397	18,903	18,802	18,502	19,371	19,708	19,746	18,248	17,874
Commercial	77,677	79,496	76,176	78,272	77,320	77,899	78,849	74,854	74,773	73,984	73,046	73,961	72,214
Agriculture	4,055	4,067	3,801	4,029	3,948	3,871	3,874	3,844	4,117	4,310	4,348	4,316	4,205

Source: Department for Business, Energy & Industrial Strategy

1. Major Power Producers (MPPs) are companies whose prime purpose is the generation of electricity. Wind and solar MPPs are required to have a minimum capacity of 50 MW.
2. Includes gas turbines, oil engines, bioenergy and stations with some CCGT capacity that mainly operate in conventional thermal mode.
3. Renewables excluding hydro include wind, solar and thermal renewable sources. Prior to 2007, non-biodegradable wastes are also included.

18.9 Electricity: Plant capacity and transmission
United Kingdom

At end of December | | | | | | | | | | | | **Megawatts (MW)**

	2007	2008	2009	2010	2011	2012	2013	2014	2015	2016	2017	2018	2019
Major power producers (1)													
Total transmission entry capacity (2) (3)	75,979	77,000	77,887	83,387	81,790	81,876	77,167	75,694	70,322r	67,965r	71,049	72,165	66,648
Coal fired	23,008	23,069	23,077	23,085	23,072	23,072	20,591	18,732	17,534	13,677r	13,341	12,315	6,796
Oil fired	4,471	4,482	4,620	4,620	4,547	3,247	2,337	2,337	1,037	1,001	938	1,129	1,170
Gas fired	25,066	27,000	27,582	32,521	30,980	33,855	33,639	32,670	29,685	30,571	32,344	32,378	31,472
Mixed or dual fired (4)	7,488	6,116	6,116	6,116	5,053	3,113	1,180	1,180	930	930r	970	969	679
Nuclear stations	10,979	10,979	10,858	10,865	10,663	9,946	9,906	9,937	9,261	9,261	9,261	9,261	9,261
Hydro (natural flow)	1,293	1,399	1,401	1,397	1,397	1,398	1,399	1,400	1,400	1,399	1,399	1,401	1,401
Pumped hydro	2,744	2,744	2,744	2,744	2,744	2,744	2,744	2,744	2,744	2,744	2,744	2,744	2,744
Onshore wind	669	780	979	1,239	1,450	1,987	2,358	2,595	2,730	3,244	3,815	4,121	4,478
Offshore wind	126	218	296	577	790	1,288	1,589	1,932	2,187	2,187r	2,989	3,513	4,169
Solar	-	-	-	-	-	-	-	-	288	400	574	615	683
Bioenergy and waste	134	213	213	223	1,092	1,226	1,424	2,166	2,526r	2,552r	2,674	3,719	3,796
Other generators (3) (5) (6)							-	-		-		-	
Total capacity of own generating plant	6,763	6,697	6,944	7,006	7,315	7,423	7,474	8,718	9,119r	10,047r	10,251	10,763	11,250
Coal fired	611	606	601	597	593	589	28	33	22	22	22	22	22
Oil fired	467	473	508	548	447	383	363	333	357	285r	268	67	40
Gas fired	3,310	3,061	2,999	3,043	3,018	3,177	3,080	3,063	2,792	2,678r	2,702	2,828	3,111
Hydro (natural flow)	126	124	127	130	153	158	163	169	186	205	219	220	220
Onshore wind	207	446	513	515	596	608	905	1,091	1,231r	1,414r	1,602	1,652	1,540
Offshore wind	39	39	113	-	-	-	-	3	3r	89r	16	5	83
Wave and tidal	0	0	1	2	2	3	3	3	4r	5r	7	8	9
Solar	3	4	5	16	170	298	499	940	1,344r	1,625r	1,595	1,605	1,565
Bioenergy and waste	1,388	1,347	1,511	1,665	1,782	1,648	1,911	2,590	2,564	3,149	3,384	3,790	4,040
Other fossil fuels	612	596	566	490	555	560	523	492	616r	574r	435	566	620
All generating companies													
Total capacity	82,741	83,697	84,831	90,393	89,105	89,300	84,641	84,412	79,540	78,110r	81,299	82,928	77,898
Coal fired	23,619	23,675	23,678	23,682	23,665	23,661	20,619	18,765	17,556r	13,699r	13,363	12,337	6,818
Oil fired	4,938	4,955	5,128	5,168	4,994	3,630	2,700	2,670	1,393	1,285	1,206	1,196	1,210
Gas fired	28,376	30,062	30,581	35,564	33,998	37,032	36,719	35,733	32,477r	33,248r	35,046	35,206	34,583
Mixed or dual fuelled	7,488	6,116	6,116	6,116	5,053	3,113	1,180	1,180	930	930	970	969	679
Nuclear stations	10,979	10,979	10,858	10,865	10,663	9,946	9,906	9,937	9,261	9,261r	9,261	9,261	9,261
Hydro (natural flow)	1,419	1,524	1,528	1,527	1,550	1,556	1,561	1,569	1,586	1,604	1,618	1,621	1,621
Pumped hydro	2,744	2,744	2,744	2,744	2,744	2,744	2,744	2,744	2,744r	2,744r	2,744	2,744	2,744
Onshore wind	876	1,225	1,493	1,754	2,046	2,595	3,262	3,686	3,961r	4,658r	5,417	5,773	6,017
Offshore wind	166	256	409	577	790	1,288	1,589	1,936	2,190r	2,276r	3,005	3,518	4,252
Wave and tidal	0	0	1	2	2	3	3	3	4r	5r	7	8	9
Solar	3	4	5	16	170	298	499	940	1,632r	2,025r	2,169	2,220	2,248
Bioenergy and waste	1,522	1,560	1,724	1,888	2,874	2,873	3,335	4,756	5,090r	5,701r	6,058	7,509	7,836
Other fossil fuels	612	596	566	490	555	560	523	492	616r	574r	435	566	620

Source: Department for Business, Energy & Industrial Strategy

Data source:
Digest of United Kingdom Energy Statistics (DUKES). Table 5.7 - Plant capacity
https://www.gov.uk/government/statistics/electricity-chapter-5-digest-of-united-kingdom-energy-statistics-dukes

(1) Major Power Producers (MPPs) are companies whose prime purpose is the generation of electricity. Wind and solar MPPs are required to have a minimum capacity of 50 MW. Table 5.11 gives a full list of MPPs and the sites they own.
(2) See section 4.10.2 of 'Electricity statistics: data sources and methodologies' for details.
(3) Small-scale hydro, wind and solar photovoltaics capacity are shown on declared net capability basis, and are de-rated to account for intermittency, by factors of 0.365, 0.43 and 0.17 respectively. See section 4.10.2 and 4.10.3 of 'Electricity statistics: data sources and methodologies' for details.
(4) Includes gas fired stations that are not Combined Cycle Gas Turbines, or have some CCGT capability but mainly operate as conventional thermal stations.
(5) Other generators refer to autogenerators, domestic generation, and smaller renewable electricity generators (e.g., small wind farms) who are not included as MPPs due to their comparatively small size. Data before 2006 are based on declared net capacity.
(6) Falls in capacity in 2007, 2010 and 2012 are due to re-classification of capacity to Major Power Producers.

18.10 Electricity: fuel used in generation

Millions of tonnes of oil equivalent

	Unit	2007	2008	2009	2010	2011	2012	2013	2014	2015	2016	2017	2018	2019
Major power producers (2)														
Coal		31.99	28.99	23.79	24.78	25.23	33.67	31.31	24.00	18.33	7.52r	5.55	4.23	1.84
Oil (3)		0.70	1.10	1.03	0.63	0.35	0.41	0.24	0.18	0.23	0.22r	0.16	0.19	0.15
Gas		27.50	29.62	28.22	29.72	23.86	15.85	15.07	16.33	15.99	23.35r	22.15	21.18	21.08
Nuclear		14.04	11.91	15.23	13.93	15.63	15.21	15.44	13.85	15.48	15.41r	15.12	14.06	12.09
Hydro (natural flow) (7)		0.36	0.36	0.37	0.23	0.40	0.36	0.31	0.40	0.42	0.34r	0.36	0.33	0.36
Wind		0.31	0.46	0.56	0.69	1.11	1.48	2.06	2.30	2.86	2.64r	3.52	4.12	4.74
Solar		-	-	-	-	-	-	-	-	0.12	0.18r	0.26	0.30	0.33
Other renewables (7)		0.63	0.80	0.74	1.01	1.26	1.77	2.22	2.97	3.82	3.84r	3.99	4.43	4.72
Other fuels (8)		-	-	-	-	-	-	0.18	0.19	0.24	0.40r	0.45	0.46	0.47
Net imports		0.45	0.95	0.25	0.23	0.54	1.02	1.24	1.76	1.81r	1.53r	1.27	1.64	1.82
Total major power producers (2)		**75.96**	**74.20**	**70.19**	**71.22**	**68.37**	**69.75**	**68.07**	**61.98**	**59.30r**	**55.42r**	**52.82**	**50.95**	**47.60**
Of which: conventional thermal and other stations (9)		35.36	31.84	26.42	27.56	28.25	37.56	36.19	29.88	25.87r	15.07r	14.21	14.03	12.52
combined cycle gas turbine stations		**25.77**	**29.14**	**27.92**	**29.28**	**23.56**	**15.60**	**14.89**	**16.09**	**15.72r**	**23.07r**	**21.86**	**20.89**	**20.81**
Other generators (2)														
Transport undertakings:														
Gas (6)		0.00	0.00	0.00	0.00	0.00	0.00	-	-	-	-	-	-	-
Undertakings in industrial and commercial sectors:														
Coal (5)		0.93	0.97	0.87	0.78	0.79	0.66	0.02	0.01	0.01	0.01	0.01	0.01	0.01
Oil (4)		0.46	0.48	0.49	0.54	0.44	0.32	0.35	0.37	0.38	0.37	0.39	0.30	0.34
Gas		3.10	2.78	2.67	2.70	2.71	2.77	2.64	2.40	2.29	2.28	2.44	2.33	2.39
Hydro (natural flow) (7)		0.08	0.08	0.08	0.08	0.09	0.10	0.09	0.11	0.12	0.12	0.15	0.14	0.14
Wind, wave and solar photovoltaics		0.15	0.15	0.24	0.20	0.28	0.35	0.55	0.80	1.13r	1.27r	1.48	1.56	1.50
Other renewables (7)		2.79	2.74	3.13	3.30	3.34	3.19	2.81	3.14	3.58r	3.83r	4.00	4.44	4.77
Other fuels (8)		1.26	1.12	0.99	0.80	1.02	1.11	1.41	1.62	1.71	1.90	1.69	1.79	1.94
Total other generators (2)		**8.77**	**8.32**	**8.47**	**8.41**	**8.68**	**8.51**	**7.88**	**8.45**	**9.23**	**9.78**	**10.16**	**10.57**	**11.10**
All generating companies														
Coal (5)		32.92	29.96	24.66	25.56	26.03	34.33	31.33	24.01	18.34r	7.53r	5.55	4.24	1.85
Oil (3)(4)		1.16	1.58	1.51	1.18	0.78	0.73	0.59	0.55	0.61r	0.58	0.54	0.49	0.50
Gas (6)		30.60	32.40	30.89	32.43	26.58	18.62	17.70	18.73	18.28r	25.63r	24.60	23.51	23.47
Nuclear		14.04	11.91	15.23	13.93	15.63	15.21	15.44	13.85	15.48r	15.41	15.12	14.06	12.09
Hydro (natural flow) (7)		0.44	0.44	0.45	0.31	0.49	0.46	0.40	0.51	0.54r	0.46	0.51	0.47	0.50
Wind, wave and solar photovoltaics		0.45	0.61	0.80	0.89	1.39	1.82	2.61	3.10	4.11r	4.09r	5.25	5.98	6.57
Other renewables (7)		3.42	3.54	3.88	4.31	4.60	4.96	5.04	6.11	7.41r	7.67r	7.99	8.87	9.50
Other fuels (8)		1.26	1.12	0.99	0.80	1.02	1.11	1.60	1.81	1.95r	2.29r	2.14	2.25	2.41
Net imports		0.45	0.95	0.25	0.23	0.54	1.02	1.24	1.76	1.81r	1.53r	1.27	1.64	1.82
Total all generating companies		**84.73**	**82.52**	**78.67**	**79.63**	**77.05**	**78.25**	**75.95**	**70.43**	**68.53r**	**65.20r**	**62.98**	**61.52**	**58.69**

Source: Department for Business, Energy & Industrial Strategy

Data source:
Digest of United Kingdom Energy Statistics (DUKES). Table 5.3 - Fuel used in generation
https://www.gov.uk/government/statistics/electricity-chapter-5-digest-of-united-kingdom-energy-statistics-dukes

(1) A monthly update of fuel used in electricity generation by Major Power Producers is given in Table 5.3 of Energy Trends, and a quarterly update of fuel used in electricity generation by all generating companies is given in Table 5.1 of Energy Trends.

(2) Major Power Producers (MPPs) are companies whose prime purpose is the generation of electricity. Wind and solar MPPs are required to have a minimum capacity of 50 MW. Table 5.11 gives a full list of MPPs and the sites they own

(3) Includes orimulsion, oil used in gas turbine and diesel plant, and oil used for lighting up coal fired boilers.

(4) Includes refinery gas.

(5) Includes coke oven coke.

(6) Includes colliery methane.

(7) More detailed information on renewables can be found in Chapter 6, with Table 6.5 showing generation, and Table 6.6 showing fuel use.

(8) For Major Power Producers, 'other fuels' only includes non-biodegradable waste. This was included in 'other renewables' prior to 2013. For 'other generators', 'other fuels' includes mainly non-biodegradable waste, coke oven gas, blast furnace gas, and waste products from chemical processes. Non-biodegradable waste was included in 'other renewables' prior to 2007.

(9) Includes gas turbines, oil engines, coal and plants producing electricity from renewable sources other than hydro. Excludes nuclear.

18.11 Indigenous production, refinery receipts, imports and exports of oil

United Kingdom

Thousand tonnes

| | Indigenous production[1] | | | | Refinery receipts | | Foreign trade[6,7] | | | | | | | | |
| | Total | Crude oil | NGLs [2,11] | Feed-stocks [12] | Total receipts[3] | Indig-enous[4] | Net imports/exports[5] | Crude oil and NGLs[8] | | Process oils[13] | | Petroleum products | | Bunkers[9] |
								Imports	Exports	Imports	Exports	Imports	Exports	
2001	**116,678**	108,387	8,292	-	**82,955**	29,403	-35,233	48,992	84,441	4,559	2,489	17,234	19,088	2,274
2002	**115,944**	107,430	8,514	-	**85,512**	28,544	-38,720	52,042	85,028	4,926	2,116	14,900	23,444	1,913
2003	**106,073**	97,835	8,238	-	**85,006**	30,829	-27,571	48,589	72,526	5,588	2,372	16,472	23,323	1,764
2004	**95,374**	87,516	7,858	-	**90,022**	27,505	-13,937	55,858	63,413	6,659	1,091	18,545	30,495	2,085
2005	**84,721**	77,179	7,543	-	**85,810**	26,925	-2,455	52,211	52,107	6,675	1,992	22,481	29,722	2,055
2006	**76,578**	69,665	6,913	-	**84,649**	25,206	+7,140	51,446	47,551	7,997	2,643	26,836	28,945	2,348
2007	**76,575**	70,357	6,218	-	**83,940**	26,584	+1,484	50,151	47,713	7,206	3,287	25,110	29,983	2,371
2008	**71,789**	65,497	6,292	-	**83,962**	23,627	+7,037	52,409	44,377	7,926	3,858	23,741	28,803	3,472
2009	**68,199**	62,820	5,379	-	**79,693**	24,691	+6,333	48,231	41,710	6,771	3,641	22,172	25,491	3,306
2010	**62,962**	58,047	4,915	-	**77,813**	22,749	+10,600	48,431	39,107	6,633	2,957	23,665	26,065	2,807
2011	**51,972**	48,571	3,401	-	**79,746**	21,653	+19,323	50,954	29,716	7,139	3,908	22,656	27,800	3,130
2012	**44,561**	42,052	2,508	-	**74,297**	13,821	+25,832	55,340	29,826	5,135	1,120	26,207	29,904	2,663
2013	**41,101**	38,456	2,190	454	**68,404**	9,438	+27,369	52,470	31,670	6,497	1,436	28,418	26,910	2,720
2014	**40,328**	37,474	2,454	400	**63,635**	9,997	+29,405	48,890	29,809	4,747	1,060	29,384	22,748	2,824
2015	**45,698**	42,826	2,462	410	**61,010**	10,411	+26,253	45,281	31,820	5,318	1,890	32,290	22,926	2,509
2016	**47,872**	44,306	3,139	427	**60,165**	11,376	+24,812	42,406	33,247	6,383	1,609	35,142	24,264	2,659
2017	**47,049**	43,185	3,446	419	**60,699**	7,408	+26,478	46,624	36,863	6,667	1,456	34,634	23,128	2,451
2018	**51,551**	47,848	3,339	363	**58,229**	5,946	+20,703	45,650	42,582	6,633	1,926	35,188	22,260	2,448
2019	**52,856**	49,344	3,144	368	**59,334**	7,845	+18,666	45,613	42,843	5,876	2,097	32,742	20,625	2,277

Source: Department for Business, Energy & Industrial Strategy

1. Includes offshore and land production.
2. Condensates and petroleum gases derived at onshore treatment plants.
3. Crude oil, natural gas liquids (NGLs) and process oils (i.e. partly refined oils) as received at the refinery. Receipts can go into stock rather than being processed that month. Refinery throughput and output can be found in ET 3.12.
4. Crude oil plus NGLs.
5. Net imports + or net exports - of oil and oil products.
6. Foreign trade recorded by the Petroleum Industry and may differ from figures published in the Overseas Trade Statistics.
7. Prior years data are subject to further revision as information on imports and exports of petroleum products become available.
8. Since October 2016 imports of NGLs include those sourced from Shale Gas.
9. International marine bunkers. Fuel consumption in International Bunkers has been revised for 2008 to 2013 using new estimates of marine fuel use. Further detail can be found in Chapter 3 of the Digest of the UK's Energy Statistics 2014 (paragraphs 3.64 and 3.65).
10. Percentage change between the most recent quarter and the same quarter a year earlier.
11. Production of NGLs in 2020 broken down by product are as follows: Propane (1,048kte), Condensate (814kte), Butane (942kte) and Ethane (523kte).
12. Volumes received as backflows at refineries from petrochemical processing plants.
13. From January 2018 Process oils includes fuels that fall under the categories additives/oxygenates and other hydrocarbons.

18.12 Refinery throughput and output of petroleum products

United Kingdom

Thousand tonnes

	Throughput of crude and process oil	Refinery use Fuel	Refinery use Losses/(gains)	Total[1,2] output of petroleum products	Gases Butane and propane	Gases Other[3] petroleum	Naphtha (LDF)	Motor spirit	Kerosene Aviation turbine fuel	Kerosene Burning oil	Gas oil	DERV oil	Fuel oil	Lubricating oils	Bitumen
2001	83,343	5,059	1,233	77,050	1,763	272	3,428	21,455	5,910	3,088	10,353	16,395	10,179	656	1,707
2002	84,784	5,677	788	78,319	2,139	538	3,154	22,944	5,365	3,506	10,948	17,396	8,506	509	1,918
2003	84,585	5,456	56	79,073	2,281	716	3,504	22,627	5,278	3,522	10,580	16,800	9,494	576	1,924
2004	89,821	5,418	-8	84,411	2,150	520	3,168	24,590	5,615	3,613	11,080	17,567	11,309	1,137	2,197
2005	86,134	5,601	387	80,145	2,184	427	3,019	22,604	5,167	3,325	9,430	19,056	10,155	936	1,912
2006	83,213	4,878	374	77,961	2,104	661	2,734	21,443	6,261	3,374	10,215	15,821	11,280	617	1,749
2007	81,477	4,676	293	76,509	2,259	517	2,561	21,313	6,176	2,968	10,165	16,138	10,433	547	1,628
2008	81,034	4,706	470	75,857	2,251	369	2,660	19,521	6,549	3,091	10,566	16,350	10,483	514	1,485
2009	75,551	4,304	723	70,523	2,113	449	2,507	19,184	6,022	2,830	9,487	15,908	8,043	530	1,338
2010	73,543	4,378	566	68,599	2,247	518	2,440	19,074	5,781	2,570	9,505	15,332	7,004	412	1,276
2011	75,080	4,586	373	70,122	2,598	434	2,526	18,823	6,411	2,377	8,683	16,800	7,432	430	1,476
2012	71,839	4,299	209	67,331	2,512	285	2,328	18,650	5,775	2,268	8,941	15,771	7,158	457	1,222
2013	65,972	3,759	575	61,638	2,326	352	2,013	17,691	4,527	2,705	8,193	14,831	6,230	387	777
2014	61,063	3,198	671	57,194	2,127	348	2,290	15,709	4,635	2,093	8,049	13,726	5,269	373	1,006
2015	61,391	3,352	462	57,577	2,208	394	2,368	16,894	4,973	2,031	7,204	13,483	4,818	350	991
2016	60,395	3,381	426	56,588	2,227	453	2,306	17,343	4,392	2,049	6,982	13,524	4,097	352	968
2017	60,257	3,389	460	56,407	2,178	424	2,280	17,416	5,031	2,047	6,878	13,425	3,685	443	817
2018	58,697	3,334	493	54,871	2,079	324	2,209	16,575	5,129	2,053	7,444	12,599	3,032	436	875
2019	59,140	3,224	413	55,502	2,214	350	2,072	16,488	5,185	2,057	7,236	13,292	2,893	293	892

Source: Department for Business, Energy & Industrial Strategy

1. Including aviation gasoline, white spirit, petroleum wax, petroleum coke and miscellaneous products.
2. Total production minus refinery use.
3. Ethane and other petroleum gases (OPG).

18.13a Deliveries of petroleum products for inland consumption[4]

Thousand tonnes

	Total[1]	Butane[2] and propane	Other[3] petroleum gases	Naphtha [LDF]	Motor Spirit[5]	Kerosene Aviation turbine fuel	Kerosene Burning Oil	Gas/diesel oil Derv fuel[5]	Gas/diesel oil Other	Fuel oil	Lubricating oils	Bitumen
2001	71,354	2,097	2,077	1,592	20,940	10,614	4,236	16,059	6,959	2,579	846	1,935
2002	70,557	2,553	2,181	1,592	20,808	10,519	3,578	16,926	6,099	1,723	829	2,002
2003	71,698	3,019	2,114	2,332	19,919	10,764	3,567	17,712	6,326	1,540	868	1,959
2004	73,642	3,115	1,918	2,029	19,484	11,637	3,948	18,514	6,023	2,064	914	1,991
2005	75,496	3,315	2,021	1,916	18,852	12,497	3,869	19,377	6,852	2,207	750	1,906
2006	74,896	3,127	1,920	2,278	18,091	12,641	4,016	20,161	6,525	2,251	713	1,610
2007	72,748	2,827	1,815	1,608	17,615	12,574	3,628	21,038	6,117	2,209	672	1,563
2008	70,264	3,320	1,698	741	16,542	12,142	3,681	20,501	5,632	1,945	510	1,741
2009	67,060	3,229	1,591	988	15,613	11,533	3,732	20,112	5,034	1,516	510	1,381
2010	66,295	3,032	1,524	1,037	14,602	11,116	4,012	20,740	5,059	1,371	580	1,370
2011	64,243	3,077	1,292	1,061	13,895	11,574	3,288	20,991	4,721	939	491	1,621
2012	63,048	2,492	1,090	1,094	13,231	11,221	3,329	21,538	5,148	706	412	1,355
2013	62,397	2,611	1,245	1,012	12,574	11,242	3,507	21,926	4,732	479	437	1,358
2014	62,852	2,655	1,293	986	12,326	11,220	3,187	22,675	4,837	555	436	1,410
2015	64,835	3,110	1,402	1,195	12,082	11,331	3,189	23,656	5,274	534	411	1,464
2016	66,194	3,194	1,649	1,295	11,951	11,339	3,448	24,649	5,265	538	408	1,327
2017	67,318	3,132	1,668	1,348	11,793	12,186	3,312	24,911	5,355	557	414	1,632
2018	66,394	3,118	1,446	1,176	11,584	12,272	3,435	24,627	5,351	450	369	1,601
2019	64,803	3,109	1,101	1,210	11,713	12,319	3,210	23,806	5,129	328	358	1,663

Source: Department for Business, Energy & Industrial Strategy

1. Includes aviation spirit, industrial white spirits, petroleum wax, petroleum coke and miscellaneous products.
2. Including amounts for use at petro-chemical plants.
3. Ethane and other petroleum gases (OPG).
4. Excluding refinery fuel.
5. Motor spirit and DERV fuel figures for June and July 2021 are estimated and should be seen as provisional.

Data source: table ET 3.13 Oil and oil products statistics - Energy Trends (quarterly)

18.13b Hydrocarbon Oils - Quantities released for consumption

Litres (millions)
Kgs (millions)

Calendar Year	Motor Spirit							Diesel					Other Selected Fuels			Road Fuel Gases (Natural Gas/LPG)
	Ultra low Sulphur Petrol	Sulphur Free Petrol	Un-leaded Petrol	Super Unleaded Petrol/LRP	Leaded Petrol	Bio-ethanol	Total Petrol	Ultra low Sulphur Diesel	Sulphur Free Diesel	Diesel	Biodiesel and Bioblended	Total Diesel	Fuel Oil	Gas Oil	Total	
2002	27,856	-	145	2	0	-	28,002	19,779	-	-14 *	3	19,767	1,324	6,572	55,552	85
2003	27,368	-	24	-1 *	2	-	27,393	20,818	-	69	19	20,906	1,047	6,416	55,665	103
2004	27,030	-	-4 *	0	-1 *	-	27,025	22,088	-	72	21	22,181	929	6,277	56,310	110
2005	25,612	-	-5 *	0	1	85	25,693	22,482	684	34	33	23,233	910	6,395	56,140	118
2006	24,568	84	-23 *	-	0 *	95	24,724	12,376	11,721	20	169	24,286	1,057	6,435	56,379	124
2007	23,792	92	-17 *	-	-1 *	153	24,019	9,903	15,216	35	347	25,501	606	5,831	55,852	117
2008	5,442	173	16,888	-	-1 *	206	22,709	1,045	5,104	18,650	886	25,686	726	5,901	54,964	122
2009	-	-	21,709	-	0	320	22,029	-	-	24,045	1,044	25,089	410	5,306	52,993	107
2010	-	-	20,019	-	0	631	20,650	-	-	24,724	1,049	25,773	269	5,366	52,259	107
2011	-	-	18,896	-	0	652	19,548	-	-	25,001	925	25,926	-191 *	5,256	50,692	98
2012	-	-	18,017	-	-	775	18,792	-	-	25,714	634	26,348	-57 *	5,094	50,336	94
2013	-	-	17,200	-	-	820	18,020	-	-	26,204	766	26,969	112	5,177	50,417	93
2014	-	-	16,859	-	0	814	17,672	-	-	27,031	954	27,985	114	5,312	51,186	89
2015	-	-	16,523	-	0	796	17,319	-	-	28,214	670	28,884	204	5,277	51,762	84
2016	-	-	16,341	-	0	758	17,100	-	-	29,393	707	30,100	156	5,226	52,709	71
2017	-	-	16,020	-	-	752	16,772	-	-	29,712	697	30,410	243	5,196	52,715	62
2018	-	-	15,837	-	-	761	16,598	-	-	29,367	1,140	30,506	176	5,233	52,627	69
2019	-	-	16,099	-	-	753	16,851	-	-	28,438	1,597	30,035	199	5,069	52,333	56

Source: Hydrocarbon Oils Bulletin, HM Revenue and Customs

* = Negative quantities: Adjustments are sometimes made to quantities in historical months, but the adjustment cannot be aligned to the correct month in which the misreporting occurred.

It is instead made to the month in which the adjustment was subsequently reported, which can lead to negative quantities being reported in that month, with corresponding negative receipts.
-0 may occur where there are small negative quantities due to rounding.

- = data not available

1. Significant changes in quantities released for consumption between different fuel categories occur where the structure of duty rates has changed.

18.14 Iron ore: summary of consumption, imports and exports

United Kingdom

Commodity	2015	2016	2017	2018	2019	2015	2016	2017	2018	2019
	Tonnes					£ thousand				
Iron ore										
Consumption	12,975,100	9,126,300	9,022,900	8,497,100	8,464,500					
Imports										
Iron ore	12,044,762	9,281,505	9,128,808	8,898,721	7,658,408	495,481	422,027	611,301	587,059	592,978
Fe content (a)	7,200,000	5,600,000	5,500,000	5,300,000	4,600,000					
Exports										
Iron ore	91,853	3,722	2,205	2,923	1,623	3,134	989	594	819	572

(a) BGS estimates

Source: United Kingdom Minerals Yearbook 2020
British Geological Survey

18.15 Iron and steel: summary of production, consumption, imports and exports

United Kingdom

Commodity	2015	2016	2017	2018	2019	2015	2016	2017	2018	2019
	Tonnes					£ thousand				
Iron and steel										
Production										
Pig iron	8 773 500	6 142 400	5 996 500	5 587 900	5 621 700					
Crude steel-										
Alloy qualities	502 300	404 500	466 100	454 200	345 100					
Other	10 404 400	7 230 400	7 025 200	6 813 500	6 873 000					
Total	10 906 700	7 634 900	7 491 300	7 267 700	7 218 100					
Consumption										
Pig iron (a)	8 737 000	6 082 000	5 920 000	5 613 000	5 618 000					
Finished steel (b)	9 587 000	9 880 000	10 118 000	9 913 000	9 344 000					
Scrap	3 699 800	2 550 800	2 691 800	2 788 500	2 685 700					
Imports										
Pig iron	40 920	32 063	42 350	37 901	43 079	16 147	7 814	14 469	12 353	14 214
Shot, powder, sponge etc	36 452	30 459	21 310	22 664	24 092	33 130	25 797	32 352	40 618	45 928
Ferro-alloys	180 427	147 268	163 971	181 157	159 385	169 833	128 084	202 586	246 329	196 933
Ingots and other primary forms	353 841	417 001	422 137	725 999	574 167	189 724	203 481	254 965	410 305	329 885
Scrap	238 363	226 250	321 663	366 533	268 277	67 137	68 287	112 448	144 746	80 363
Exports										
Pig iron	2 525	346	4 470	8 058	6 322	1 911	196	787	1 692	1 597
Shot, powder, sponge etc	36 638	59 228	44 528	36 124	42 604	47 689	48 605	57 180	65 374	69 262
Ferro-alloys	35 071	34 285	38 592	36 765	31 465	142 485	121 163	197 018	251 672	230 847
Ingots and other primary forms	2 412 446	470 280	476 459	663 715	466 558	916 498	427 734	549 308	707 814	533 873
Scrap	7 155 388	7 928 339	8 567 251	8 546 485	7 914 657	1 408 537	1 460 245	2 168 719	2 332 820	1 989 400

(a) Consumption in steel making only.
(b) Net home disposals

Source: United Kingdom Minerals Yearbook 2020
British Geological Survey

18.16 Consumption in the United Kingdom iron and steel industry

Thousand tonnes

	2010	2011	2012	2013	2014	2015	2016	2017	2018	2019
Iron ore –										
Home produced (a)	—	—	—	—	—	—	—	—	—	—
Imported (b)	10 572	9 735	10 511	14 037	14 353	12 975	9 126	9 023	8 497	8 465
Manganese ore	—	—	—	3	—	—	10	2	—	—
Iron and steel scrap (f)	3 713	3 890	3 675	4 085	4 145	3 700	2 551	2 692	2 789	2 686
Pig iron (f)	7 088	6 610	7 325	9 909	9 678	8 737	6 082	5 920	5 613	5 618
Alloy metals (c) –										
Nickel	10	12	10	...	...	...	...	...	...	...
Molybdenum	1	2	2	...	...	...	...	...	...	...
Tungsten	0	0	0	...	...	...	...	...	...	...
Vanadium	0	0	0	...	...	...	...	...	...	...
Cobalt	0	0	0	...	...	...	...	...	...	...
Chromium	34	44	42	...	...	...	...	...	...	...
Niobium	0	0	0	...	...	...	...	...	...	...
Ferro-alloys –										
Ferro-manganese	67	66	66	...	...	...	...	...	...	...
Ferro-silico-manganese	16	16	16	...	...	...	...	...	...	...
Ferro-aluminium	2	2	2	...	...	...	...	...	...	...
Ferro-chromium	(d)	(d)	(d)	...	...	...	...	...	...	...
Ferro-silico-chromium	(d)	(d)	(d)	...	...	...	...	...	...	...
Ferro-silicon	26	26	26	...	...	...	...	...	...	...
Ferro-silico-zirconium	0	0	0	...	...	...	...	...	...	...
Calcium silicide	0	0	0	...	...	...	...	...	...	...
Ferro-phosphorus	1	1	1	...	...	...	...	...	...	...
Ferro-niobium	(d)	(d)	(d)	...	...	...	...	...	...	...
Ferro-titanium	1	1	1	...	...	...	...	...	...	...
Dolomite (raw and burnt) (e)	399	344	556	759	793	790	494	451	427	492
Limestone (e)	948	932	912	1 147	1 255	1 041	680	653	638	591
Lime (e)	371	395	379	387	461	415	294	324	335	400
Zinc for galvanising	49	48	42	...	...	...	...	...	...	...
Tin for tinplating	3	2	2	...	...	...	...	...	...	...

Average Fe content: (a) 55%, (b) 62%.

(c) Metal content.

(d) Included under alloying metals.

(e) Restricted to consumption in blast furnaces, sinter plants and steel furnaces.

(f) Consumption in steel making only.

Source: Iron and Steel Statistics Bureau,
United Kingdom Minerals Yearbook 2019
British Geological Survey

18.17 Fertilisers - UK consumption

Years ending 30 June

Thousand tonnes

Nutrient Content

		2006	2007	2008	2009	2010	2011	2012	2013	2014	2015	2016	2017	2018	2019e
Nitrogen (N):	XXXX	1003	1008	1001	948	1016	1022	1000	999	1060	1049	1026	1041	1033	1038
Straight	KGRM	631	656	744	733	771									
Compounds	KGRN	372	352	292	180	245									
Phosphate (P2O5)	KGRO	235	224	215	129	184	192	188	194	201	196	197	195	188	186
Potash (K2O)	KGRP	325	317	325	208	251	283	259	267	284	272	270	276	262	267
Compounds - total product	KGRQ	2,134	2,039	1,827	1,116	1,529									

Source: British Survey of Fertiliser Practice (Defra)

Table 18.17 gives the quantity of the fertiliser nutrients nitrogen (N), phosphate (P2O5) and potash (K2O) used by UK farmers during the fertiliser year, which runs from 1st July to 30th June. The year shown in the table is the year in which the harvest takes place, at the end of each fertiliser year.

Note: Years are harvest (e.g. 2019 refers to the 2018/19 cropping year) rather than calendar years. Data for 2019 are estimates.

18.18a United Kingdom production of minerals 2012–2019

Thousand tonnes

Mineral	2012	2013	2014	2015	2016	2017	2018	2019
Coal:								
Deep-mined	6,153	4,089	3,685	2,784	22	20	24	99
Opencast	10,134	8,584	7,962	5,814	4156	3021	2556	2067
Other (a)	680	95	—	—	—	—	—	—
Natural gas and oil:								
Methane (oil equivalent)								
Colliery	52	52	34	30	38	35	33	24
Onshore	15	10	38	183	179	179	236	366
Offshore	38,850	35,268	35,690	38,633	39,659	38,685	38,442	37,381
Crude oil								
Onshore	870	1,003	1,014	962	966	836	845	832
Offshore	41,182	37,453	36,461	41,864	43,339	42,349	46,299	47,911
Condensates and other (b)								
Onshore	13	20	19	18	17	14	14	63
Offshore	2,495	2,170	2,435	2,444	3,122	3,432	3,306	3,011
Non-ferrous ores (metal content):								
Tin	—	—	—	—	0.2	0.3	0.2	—
Tungsten	—	—	—	0.2	0.9	1.4	1.2	—
Lead (e)	0.1	0.1	0.1	0.1	0.1	0.1	0.1	0.2
Gold (kg)	102	42	—	—	(d) 6	—	—	50
Silver (kg)	230	82	—	—	(d) 14	—	—	130
Clay and shale (c)	5,497	6,464	6,806	4,552	4,694	5,544	4,606	4,529
Chalk (c)	3,473	3,528	3,312					
Igneous rock (f) (g)	(l) 37,300	(l) 37,700	(l) 41,500					
Limestone (excluding dolomite)	(l) 52,300	(l) 55,400	(l) 64,200	(l) 119,901	126,201	(l) 126,839	130,898	(l) 129,300
Dolomite (excluding limestone)	4,896	3,432	3,730					
Sandstone	(l) 10,700	11,217	13,614					
Slate (h)	701	885	868	(e) 760	(e) 780	(e) 820	(e) 820	(e) 160
Sand and gravel:								
Land	41,516	43,379	46,832	51,053	51,231	50,143	52,065	(l) 48,700
Marine (i)	14,840	14,577	14,327	15,390	16,844	17,402	17,817	18,088
Ball clay (sales) (e)	748	740	733	740	753	850	867	738
Barytes	30	30	44	50	56	55	(e) 55	(e) 50
China clay (sales) (j) (e)	1,150	1,110	1,090	1,014	940	970	996	715
Fireclay (c)	96	105	129	...	...	...	...	...
Fluorspar (e)	—	16	25	17	12	11	11	12
Gypsum (natural) (e)	800	700	1,100	1,800	1,600	1,300	1,400	1,600
Peat (000 m³)	568	1,254	795	...	...	...	...	...
Potash (k)	(e) 900	(e) 540	576	594	432	216	210	—
Polyhalite	—	—	—	200	200	500	400	635
Salt	6,460	6,930	4,690	(e) 4,000	3,899	2,362	3,430	2,254
Silica sand	3,888	3,961	3,948	3,822	4,251	5,051	4,890	4,443
Talc	4	3	5	5	3	3	2	3

(a) Slurry etc. recovered from dumps, ponds, rivers etc.
(b) Including ethane, propane and butane, in addition to condensates.
(c) Excluding a small production in Northern Ireland.
(d) Production from metalurgical testwork.
(e) BGS estimate.
(f) Excluding a small production of granite in Northern Ireland.
(g) In addition, the following amounts of igneous rock were produced in Guernsey (thousand tonnes): 2013: 149; 2014: 117; 2015: 116; 2016: 88; 2017: 105; 2018: 122; 2019: 111 and Jersey: 2013: 176; 2014: 243; 2015: 275; 2016: 258; 2017: 247; 2018: 265; 2019: 275.
(h) Slate figures include waste used for constructional fill and powder and granules used in industry.
(i) Including marine-dredged landings at foreign ports (exports).
(j) Dry weight.
(k) Marketable product (KCl).
(l) Including an estimate for production in Northern Ireland.

Sources: Mineral Products Association; Office for National Statistics; Department of Business, Energy & Industrial Strategy; Department for Economy (Northern Ireland); Crown Estate Commissioners; and company data

18.18b Minerals produced in Northern Ireland, the Isle of Man, Guernsey and Jersey 2011-2019

Thousand tonnes

	2011	2012	2013	2014	2015	2016	2017	2018	2019
Northern Ireland (d)									
Gold (kg)	202	102	42	0	0	0	0	0	(c) 50
Silver (kg)	531	230	82	0	0	0	0	0	(c) 130
Lead (tonnes)	280	61	36	0	0	0	0	0	(c) 50
Limestone	...	...	...	...	1,709	2,146	2,323	3,158	...
Sand and gravel	...	...	...	...	2,481	2,354	2,606	3,175	...
Basalt and igneous rock (a)	...	...	...	...	2,587	4,216	3,227	4,164	...
Sandstone	...	...	...	...	3,946	5,043	3,722	5,339	...
Granite	...	...	...	...	...	...	...	...	...
Clay and shale	...	...	...	...	...	...	...	...	...
Others (b)	...	...	...	...	1,044	1,264	795	1,565	...
Total	...	...	...	...	**11,766**	**15,023**	**12,673**	**17,401**	...
Isle of Man									
Limestone	82	72	56	53	58	50	48	41	54
Sand and gravel	141	101	96	97	101	106	109	108	92
Igneous rock	96	94	110	98	94	89	86	86	85
Slate	29	23	17	26	33	28	39	39	38
Total	**347**	**290**	**279**	**274**	**286**	**272**	**281**	**274**	**269**
Guernsey									
Igneous rock	156	169	149	117	116	88	105	122	111
Jersey									
Igneous rock (c)	220	239	176	243	275	258	247	265	275
Sand and gravel	74	46	44	48	51	46	47	52	59

Sources: Department of the Economy (Northern Ireland), Department of Environment, Food and Agriculture (Isle of Man), Company data (Guernsey and Jersey).

(a) Excluding granite.
(b) Including rock salt, chalk, dolomite, fireclay and granite.
(c) BGS estimates.
(d) Data for Northern Ireland is based on the following numbers of quarry returns: 2015, 106; 2016, 116; 2017, 90 and 2018, 114. No extrapolation for missing returns is included in this table.

18.19a Building Materials and Components

Bricks - Production, Deliveries and Stocks

Great Britain | | | | | | | | | | | | | Millions of Bricks

Brick Type		Seasonally Adjusted Deliveries	Production	Deliveries (from)	Stocks*	Production	Deliveries (from)	Stocks*	Production	Deliveries (from)	Stocks*	Production	Deliveries (from)	Stocks*
		All Types	All Types			Commons			Facings			Engineerings		
2015		1,704	1915	1704	561	167	159	33	1548	1380	477	200	166	51
2016		1,830	1800	1830	531	170	167	35	1464	1511	430	166	151	66
2017		2,037	1877	2037	371	178	178	35	1567	1679	318	132	180	18
2018		2,052	2025	2050	346	140	128	33	1738	1770	302	147	152	11
2019		2,001 p	c	1998	424	109	108	39	1808	1743	367	c	147	19
	Q4	531	496	509	346	29	30	33	430	441	302	36	38	11
2019	Q1	510	503	457	392	21	25	29	442	398	346	40	33	17
	Q2	511	523	547	373	26	28	31	457	479	324	40	39	18
	Q3	491 p	536	517	392	34	30	34	466	449	341	37	38	16
	Q4	490 p	c	478	424	28	24	39	443	417	367	c	36	19
2020	Q1	433 p	456	395	485	26	25	40	395	346	416	35	24	29
	Q2	202 p	110	216	379	8	14	34	96	182	330	5	20	15
	Q3	434 p	427	468	338	28	27	35	363	404	289	36	37	13
2018	November	174	175	185	343	9	10	32	153	163	299	13	12	12
	December	185	133	130	346	8	7	33	116	112	302	10	11	11
2019	January	162	160	136	370	8	9	32	140	118	324	13	10	13
	February	172	162	152	380	6	9	29	140	131	333	16	12	17
	March	175	181	168	392	8	7	29	162	149	346	12	11	17
	April	170	176	175	393	7	9	27	157	155	348	13	12	18
	May	170	178	189	386	8	10	29	156	166	338	15	13	20
	June	171	168	182	373	11	9	31	144	158	324	13	14	18
	July	159	183	177	380	14	12	33	157	151	330	12	14	17
	August	161	173	163	390	10	9	34	150	143	337	14	11	19
	September	171	180	178	392	10	10	34	159	155	341	11	13	16
	October	158 p	190	181	400	12	10	36	166	157	350	12	14	14
	November	158 p	183	163	419	11	8	39	156	143	362	16	12	18
	December	173 p	c	133	424	5	6	39	121	116	367	c	11	19
2020	January	155 p	151	132	443	8	8	39	129	117	379	14	7	26
	February	155 p	166	141	468	10	9	39	145	122	401	11	9	27
	March	123 p	139	122	485	8	7	40	121	107	416	10	8	29
	April	23 p	4	23	466	c	2	39	3	18	401	c	3	26
	May	73 p	26	70	422	c	4	36	24	58	367	c	7	19
	June	106 p	80	123	379	6	8	34	69	106	330	5	10	15
	July	140 p	136	156	359	c	9	33	116	135	311	c	12	14
	August	148 p	142	147	354	c	8	35	120	126	305	c	13	14
	September	146 p	149	165	338	10	10	35	128	143	289	12	12	13
	October	151 p	157	167	327	c	9	35	136	145	281	c	13	11
	November	153 p	164	164	327	c	9	34	141	141	281	c	14	12

* Refers to stocks at end of period

Source: Department for Business, Energy & Industrial Strategy

1. From March 2015, seasonally adjusted figures for deliveries of bricks have been included in this table. In the production of these figures, brick deliveries data back to January 1983 have been seasonally adjusted. This long run data series is available on request.

2. The current unusual circumstances are affecting the seasonal adjustment of deliveries, therefore we will not be publishing revisions as normal until we can carry out further analysis.

18.19b Building Materials and Components

Concrete Blocks - Production, Deliveries and Stocks

Great Britain   Thousand square metres

	All Types	All Types			Dense			Lightweight			Aerated		
	Seasonally Adjusted Deliveries	Production	Deliveries (from)	Stocks*	Production	Deliveries (from)	Stocks*	Production	Deliveries (from)	Stocks*	Production	Deliveries (from)	Stocks*
2009	50,639	50,394	50,639	8,320	22,607	22,748	3,291	13,421	13,989	1,522	14,367	13,903	3,507
2010	51,758	53,629	51,758	10,152	22,393	21,731	3,833	14,415	13,923	2,044	16,822	16,104	4,276
2011	52,901	54,583	52,901	10,810	22,940	22,101	4,486	15,153	14,821	1,728	16,490	15,978	4,596
2012	47,364	51,693	52,021	10,700	21,551	22,323	3,808	14,383	14,103	2,024	15,759	15,595	4,868
2013	57,995	56,031	57,995	4,171	23,599	24,340	1,894	17,055	17,508	1,208	15,377	16,147	1,069
2014	56,953	57,943	56,953	5,413	25,088	24,943	2,147	17,499	17,447	1,402	15,356	14,563	1,864
2015	64,920	64,718	64,920	6,282	25,828	25,474	2,393	19,036	18,727	1,712	19,853	20,719	2,177
2016	70,893	70,537	70,893	5,838	26,987	26,995	2,315	20,453	20,820	1,329	23,096	23,078	2,195
2017	71,929	73,545	71,929	6,808	26,626	26,324	2,540	22,105	20,991	1,905	24,814	24,614	2,363
2018	71,603	70,632	71,308	6,252	26,241	25,946	2,716	21,479	21,434	2,067	22,911	23,927	1,468
2019	70,505 p	73,554	70,081	9,144	24,577	24,076	2,945	21,071	20,625	2,252	27,907	25,379	3,948
2015 Q3	17,068	17,197	18,615	5,419	6,789	6,816	2,286	4,894	4,859	1,499	5,514	6,940	1,635
Q4	16,443	16,130	15,223	6,282	5,857	5,726	2,393	4,282	4,047	1,712	5,991	5,449	2,177
2016 Q1	17,339	15,124	15,545	5,974	5,734	5,782	2,409	4,434	4,332	1,864	4,956	5,431	1,702
Q2	17,589	18,648	19,273	5,280	6,864	7,126	2,146	5,164	5,594	1,364	6,620	6,552	1,770
Q3	17,034	18,750	18,713	5,330	7,461	7,463	2,151	5,539	5,569	1,341	5,749	5,681	1,838
Q4	18,932	18,015	17,362	5,838	6,928	6,624	2,315	5,316	5,325	1,329	5,771	5,414	2,195
2017 Q1	17,984	18,427	16,673	7,667	6,419	6,247	2,554	5,434	4,872	1,898	6,575	5,555	3,215
Q2	18,174	18,984	19,294	7,295	7,129	7,263	2,365	5,369	5,562	1,686	6,487	6,469	3,243
Q3	17,948	18,533	19,372	6,467	6,880	6,902	2,450	5,749	5,583	1,791	5,904	6,888	2,227
Q4	17,823	17,601	16,589	6,808	6,199	5,913	2,540	5,554	4,973	1,905	5,848	5,703	2,363
2018 Q1	17,168	15,539	15,070	7,235	5,874	5,641	2,712	4,921	4,488	2,358	4,744	4,942	2,165
Q2	18,015	18,664	19,510	6,459	6,855	7,142	2,360	5,473	5,813	2,032	6,336	6,556	2,067
Q3	18,416	19,244	19,759	6,020	7,081	7,082	2,352	5,897	5,978	2,034	6,266	6,699	1,634
Q4	18,005	17,184	16,968	6,252	6,432	6,083	2,716	5,187	5,155	2,067	5,565	5,731	1,468
2019 Q1	18,591	18,631	16,653	7,941	6,110	5,793	2,904	5,422	5,035	2,294	7,098	5,824	2,742
Q2	17,782	18,631	18,896	7,663	6,477	6,615	2,754	5,638	5,585	2,347	6,515	6,695	2,563
Q3	17,262 p	18,604	18,887	7,199	6,527	6,559	2,673	5,569	5,587	2,244	6,508	6,741	2,282
Q4	16,869 p	17,689	15,646	9,144	5,462	5,109	2,945	4,441	4,418	2,252	7,785	6,119	3,948
2020 Q1	17,543 p	16,767	16,520	9,367	5,101	5,192	2,853	4,452	4,502	2,178	7,214	6,826	4,336
Q2	9,493 p	8,747	10,276	7,983	4,192	4,375	2,562	3,037	2,832	2,373	1,517	3,069	3,048
Q3	16,975 p	17,701	18,989	5,229	6,533	6,460	2,148	5,015	5,130	1,421	6,152	7,398	1,660
November	6,112	6,418	6,317	5,842	2,473	2,320	2,561	1,962	1,899	1,998	1,984	2,098	1,282
December	5,686	4,078	3,687	6,252	1,376	1,241	2,716	1,165	1,097	2,067	1,536	1,350	1,468
2019 January	6,678	6,330	5,521	7,024	1,999	1,897	2,778	1,926	1,668	2,329	2,405	1,956	1,917
February	5,783	5,821	5,188	7,405	1,950	1,809	2,831	1,639	1,588	2,216	2,232	1,791	2,357
March	6,130	6,480	5,944	7,941	2,161	2,088	2,904	1,856	1,779	2,294	2,462	2,077	2,742
April	6,232	5,979	6,493	7,426	2,024	2,191	2,738	1,834	1,902	2,226	2,120	2,400	2,462
May	5,931	6,618	6,627	7,417	2,231	2,371	2,598	1,942	1,910	2,258	2,445	2,346	2,561
June	5,619	6,034	5,776	7,663	2,222	2,053	2,754	1,862	1,773	2,347	1,950	1,949	2,563
July	5,767	6,588	6,824	7,419	2,396	2,361	2,781	1,953	2,022	2,278	2,239	2,441	2,360
August	5,593	5,689	5,845	7,183	2,017	2,064	2,694	1,758	1,781	2,263	1,914	2,000	2,226
September	5,902	6,327	6,218	7,199	2,114	2,134	2,673	1,858	1,784	2,244	2,356	2,300	2,282
October	5,604	6,837	6,304	7,739	2,299	2,148	2,830	1,869	1,804	2,309	2,669	2,351	2,600
November	5,649 p	5,914	5,661	7,876	1,825	1,816	2,732	1,430	1,640	2,090	2,660	2,206	3,054
December	5,616 p	4,937	3,681	9,144	1,339	1,145	2,945	1,143	974	2,252	2,456	1,562	3,948
2020 January	6,176 p	5,763	5,476	9,431	1,787	1,756	2,976	1,425	1,533	2,144	2,551	2,187	4,311
February	6,176 p	5,844	5,665	9,610	1,779	1,782	2,973	1,666	1,540	2,270	2,399	2,343	4,367
March	5,190 p	5,160	5,379	9,367	1,535	1,654	2,853	1,361	1,430	2,178	2,264	2,296	4,336
April	1,133 p	732	1,634	8,456	554	840	2,551	c	c	2,042	c	c	3,863
May	3,560 p	2,355	3,385	7,580	1,196	1,481	2,174	c	c	1,605	c	c	3,801
June	4,801 p	5,659	5,257	7,983	2,442	2,054	2,562	2,296	1,528	2,373	921	1,674	3,048
July	5,645 p	5,389	6,618	5,471	2,349	2,334	2,119	1,654	1,838	1,363	1,387	2,445	1,989
August	5,506 p	5,858	5,804	5,570	2,043	1,964	2,244	1,583	1,546	1,400	2,232	2,294	1,927
September	5,825 p	6,453	6,567	5,229	2,142	2,163	2,148	1,778	1,746	1,421	2,533	2,658	1,660
October	5,745 p	6,438	6,329	5,338	2,142	2,054	2,235	1,753	1,673	1,501	2,543	2,601	1,602
November	5,764 p	6,260	5,930	5,662	1,930	1,926	2,239	1,731	1,635	1,591	2,599	2,368	1,833

* Refers to stocks at end of period   Source: Department for Business, Energy & Industrial Strategy

Notes:

1. From March 2015, seasonally adjusted figures for deliveries of concrete blocks have been included in this table. In the production of these figures, blocks deliveries data back to January 1983 have been seasonally adjusted. This long run data series is available on request.

2. The current unusual circumstances are affecting the seasonal adjustment of deliveries, therefore we will not be publishing revisions as normal until we can carry out further analysis.

18.19c Building Materials and Components

Concrete Roofing Tiles and Ready-Mixed Concrete

		Great Britain			United Kingdom	United Kingdom
		Concrete Roofing Tiles (Th.sq.m. of roof area covered)			**Ready-Mixed Concrete #** (Th.cu.m.)	**Seasonally Adjusted Ready-Mixed Concrete** (Th.cu.m.)
		Production	Deliveries	Stocks *	Deliveries	Deliveries
2009		14,079	15,612	2,344	14,069	14,069
2010		17,817	17,146	3,023	14,038	14,038
2011		17,712	17,684	3,126	15,121	15,121
2012		17,476	17,578	3,061	13,758	13,758
2013		18,745	19,580	2,214	15,089	15,089
2014		24,086	23,058	3,275	15,348	15,348
2015		25,105	24,475	3,904	16,294	16,294
2016		24,615	25,833	2,689	17,670	17,664
2017		26,111	25,741	2,492	17,209	17,209
2018		26,931	26,109	5,903	17,060	17,071
2019		25,927	27,832	3,999	16,426	16,426 p
2011	Q3	4,210	4,901	3,316	3,908	3,740
	Q4	4,116	4,306	3,126	3,479	3,633
2012	Q1	4,673	3,928	3,872	3,463	3,551
	Q2	4,236	4,100	4,008	3,399	3,320
	Q3	4,095	5,004	3,136	3,556	3,395
	Q4	4,471	4,547	3,061	3,340	3,493
2013	Q1	4,514	4,055	3,520	3,325	3,609
	Q2	4,209	4,598	3,131	4,108	3,825
	Q3	4,550	5,468	2,214	3,972	3,793
	Q4	5,471	5,459	2,214	3,684	3,862
2014	Q1	6,151	5,414	2,932	3,475	3,571
	Q2	6,195	5,491	3,687	3,977	3,923
	Q3	5,815	6,238	3,261	4,183	3,975
	Q4	5,925	5,915	3,275	3,713	3,880
2015	Q1	6,547	5,400	4,422	4,035	4,146
	Q2	6,296	5,843	4,875	3,992	3,933
	Q3	5,697	6,420	4,152	4,225	3,996
	Q4	6,565	6,812	3,904	4,042	4,219
2016	Q1	6,323	5,837	4,391	4,045	4,417
	Q2	6,082	6,292	4,185	4,662	4,358
	Q3	5,857	6,912	3,129	4,739	4,487
	Q4	6,352	6,792	2,689	4,223	4,402
2017	Q1	7,050	6,772	2,968	4,217	4,371
	Q2	6,754	6,862	2,860	4,461	4,407
	Q3	6,546	6,665	2,740	4,517	4,260
	Q4	5,761	5,442	2,492	4,013	4,170
2018	Q1	7,817	5,742	5,143	3,652	4,031
	Q2	4,828	6,221	4,444	4,546	4,255
	Q3	6,884	7,280	5,367	4,616	4,369
	Q4	7,402	6,866	5,903	4,245	4,416
2019	Q1	6,963	6,961	5,905	4,011	4,204
	Q2	5,364	5,512	4,239	4,200	4,131
	Q3	6,000	7,844	3,914	4,381	4,117 p
	Q4	7,601	7,516	3,999	3,835	3,975 p
2020	Q1	4,024	3,637	3,647	3,540	3,602 p
	Q2	2,240	3,382	2,686	2,490	2,504 p
	Q3	3,691	3,716	1,535	:	:

* Refers to stocks at the end of the period.   Source: Department for Business, Energy & Industrial Strategy

\# In April 2012, the Mineral Products Association (who provide these figures), estimated that data understates UK deliveries by around 20-25%. Previously, they had estimated that figures understate UK deliveries by 14-18%.

Concrete roofing tiles data have included imputation for non-responders in each quarter since 2012Q1.

1. From March 2015, seasonally adjusted figures for deliveries of ready-mixed concrete have been included in this table. In the production of these figures, ready-mixed concrete deliveries data back to Q1 1983 have been seasonally adjusted. This long run data series is available on request. Data has been revised and estimates are sourced from the mpa.

2. The current unusual circumstances are affecting the seasonal adjustment of deliveries, therefore we will not be publishing revisions as normal until we can carry out further analysis.

18.19d Building Materials and Components
Slate - Production, Deliveries and Stocks

Great Britain   Tonnes

	Production			Deliveries			Stocks [1]			Deliveries
	Roofing [2]	Cladding, decorative & crude blocks	Powder & Granules	Roofing [2]	Cladding, decorative & crude blocks	Powder & Granules	Roofing [2]	Cladding, decorative & crude blocks	Powder & Granules	Fill & Other Uses
2008	c	59,644	16,915	c	58,129	18,402	c	2,749	2,253	c
2009	c	33,759	9,150	22,555	34,322	10,637	2,420	2,186	766	615,346
2010	c	28,001	c	c	27,355	c	c	3,063	c	582,111
2011	c	30,665	c	c	30,437	c	c	3,245	c	662,003
2012	c	29,634	c	c	28,083	c	c	1,351	c	607,127
2013	c	32,419	c	c	31,375	c	c	c	665	692,319
2014	19,358	30,900	15,467	18,596	31,268	15,393	2,925	1,076	739	620,887
2015	c	29,990	c	c	29,996	c	2,130	605	794	534,879
2016	14,705	28,628	13,565	14,902	28,403	13,874	1,821	814	1,109	559,713
2017	13,877	25,962	11,847	14,212	26,005	11,671	1,379	559	1,285	594,954
2018	13,518	27,922	10,661	13,965	25,578	10,616	326	998	1,330	593,769
2019	12,129	c	c	12,251	c	c	807	c	c	79,567
2012 Q3	c	6,219	c	c	6,167	c	c	1,206	c	146,152
Q4	c	5,952	c	c	3,410	c	c	1,351	c	151,916
2013 Q1	c	6,052	c	c	9,220	c	c	c	802	157,215
Q2	c	9,638	c	c	9,440	c	c	c	736	216,035
Q3	c	10,429	c	c	6,843	c	c	c	537	169,995
Q4	c	6,300	c	c	5,872	c	c	c	665	149,074
2014 Q1	4,670	5,639	4,036	4,337	5,637	4,209	2,721	1,134	492	159,818
Q2	4,693	7,413	3,946	4,299	7,428	3,657	3,085	1,049	781	179,396
Q3	5,141	8,533	3,837	4,996	8,145	4,054	3,034	988	564	152,155
Q4	4,854	9,315	3,648	4,964	10,058	3,473	2,925	1,076	739	129,518
2015 Q1	c	7,488	c	c	7,564	c	c	833	c	156,704
Q2	3,575	8,461	3,421	4,075	8,443	3,692	2,143	583	366	148,002
Q3	4,115	7,209	3,636	3,940	7,177	3,667	2,318	615	335	130,949
Q4	3,519	6,832	3,380	3,713	6,812	2,921	2,130	605	794	99,224
2016 Q1	4,276	6,533	3,341	4,046	6,541	3,618	2,360	587	517	111,123
Q2	3,538	7,062	3,419	3,865	7,120	3,419	2,033	529	517	168,008
Q3	3,655	7,996	3,465	3,786	7,836	3,870	1,902	689	112	167,602
Q4	3,236	7,037	3,340	3,205	6,906	2,967	1,821	814	1,109	112,980
2017 Q1	3,499	5,667	3,431	3,552	5,767	3,261	1,750	422	1,279	188,449
Q2	3,486	6,347	2,880	3,712	6,246	2,702	1,435	553	1,457	163,538
Q3	3,842	7,638	2,680	3,625	7,788	2,977	1,652	403	1,160	143,548
Q4	3,050	6,310	2,856	3,323	6,204	2,731	1,379	559	1,285	99,419
2018 Q1	3,441	7,908	3,321	3,428	5,893	3,095	1,392	674	1,511	112,797
Q2	3,272	7,554	3,202	3,350	7,550	3,271	1,314	678	1,442	342,237
Q3	3,691	6,839	1,452	3,802	6,537	1,426	1,203	975	1,468	129,654
Q4	3,114	5,621	2,686	3,385	5,598	2,824	326	998	1,330	9,081
2019 Q1	3,077	7,586	3,755	3,201	7,542	3,865	808	1,042	1,220	12,945
Q2	2,983	c	c	3,197	c	c	594	c	c	25,532
Q3	3,110	c	c	3,202	c	c	499	c	c	24,014
Q4	2,959	c	c	2,651	c	c	807	c	c	17,076
2020 Q1	c	7,159	c	2,219	c	c	c	c	c	c
Q2	c	4,972	c	c	5,183	c	c	c	c	9,954
Q3	c	7,779	c	c	7,750	c	c	c	c	c

Source: Department for Business, Energy & Industrial Strategy

1. Refers to stocks at the end of the period.

2. Consists of all slate tiles which could be used as roofing tiles.

Note: Response for Q1 2020 was lower than normal due to sites and/or site offices being closed due to Covid-19 restrictions, meaning that the majority of figures required suppression.

18.19e Building Materials and Components
Cement & Clinker - Production and Deliveries

Great Britain — Thousand tonnes

| | Cement | | | | | | | | Clinker |
| | Production | | Deliveries | Imports (into GB) | | Cementitious Material | | | Production |
		of which Exports (from GB)	(into GB from GB production)	by 'Manuf.	by Others*	other	total		
2003	11,215	164	11,072	576	646	2,329	14,623	10,146
2004	11,405	141	11,074	609	825	2,443	14,951	10,402
2005	11,216	110	11,004	306	971	2,385	14,666	10,074
2006	11,469	127	11,221	124	1,089	2,648	15,082	10,069
2007	11,887	74	11,638	255	1,121	2,769	15,783	10,227
2008	10,071	61	9,937	283	1,084	2,432	13,660	8,700
2009	7,623	21	7,474	99	1,085	1,680	10,338	6,421
2010	7,883	0	7,767	61	1,153	1,535	10,515	6,598
2011	8,529	0	8,318	86	1,173	1,736	11,312	7,096
2012	7,952	0	7,728	61	1,122	1,605	10,515	6,555
2013	8,203	0	8,204	117	1,322	1,892	11,535	6,712
2014	8,958	3	8,751	227	1,590	1,864	12,433	7,197
2015	9,235	0	9,526	635	1,425	2,382	13,967	7,804
2016	9,370	:	:	:	1,503	3,003	15,004	8,056
2017	9,359	:	9,063	1,114	1,932	3,160	15,269	7,824
2018	9,197	:	9,141	935	1,663	3,449	15,188	7,734
2019	9,079	:	9,078	801	1,727	3,613	15,218	7,830

Source: Department for Business, Energy & Industrial Strategy

1. Arrangements for publication of the cementitious data have been revised following discussion and agreement by the Mineral Products Association (MPA) Cement members. Data are now provided on an annual basis. For quarterly and monthly data up to September 2013, please refer to earlier editions of this publication.

2. Where the coverage is for Great Britain, the figures for imports & exports are defined accordingly and have been estimated. Cementitious material covers cement itself, fly ash to EN 450 Part 1 where used as part of the cement in concrete (previously known as pulverised fuel ash (pfa) to BS 3892 Part 1) and ground granulated blast furnace slag (ggbs) to EN 15167 Part 1 (previously BS 6699).

* Estimated

18.19f Building Materials and Components

Sales of Sand and Gravel in Great Britain

Great Britain
Thousand tonnes

	Seasonally Adjusted Sand & Gravel	Sand		Gravel	Sand & Gravel	Sand, Gravel & Hoggin	Sand & Gravel	of which
	Total	for Building	for Concreting	for Concreting & other uses	for Coating	for Fill	Total	Marine-Dredged
2009	58,482	7,270	21,582	c	c	c	58,482	9,589
2010	54,530	6,074	19,887	c	c	c	54,530	9,341
2011	57,062	6,041	23,489	c	c	c	57,062	11,169
2012	57,972	6,499	21,994	23,077	c	c	57,972	10,320
2013	52,591	5,722	19,036	18,890	c	c	52,591	10,489
2014	52,430	5,803	19,217	20,356	1,416	5,640	52,430	11,713
2015	52,721	5,814	20,529	19,315	1,412	5,650	52,721	11,737
2016	58,585	6,312	22,422	21,435	1,791	5,056	57,014	11,770
2017	60,447	6,309	24,632	24,038	1,498	3,848	60,325	13,664
2018	58,424	6,372	23,329	23,196	1,676	3,692	58,264	11,599
2019	58,493 p	7,103	23,043	23,030	1,494	3,828	58,493	11,810
2014 Q3	13,512	1,593	5,456	5,511	387	1,388	14,334	3,138
Q4	13,355	1,359	4,796	4,825	333	1,340	12,653	2,832
2015 Q1	13,269	1,352	4,722	4,643	283	1,598	12,599	2,905
Q2	13,771	1,626	5,539	5,170	413	1,617	14,364	3,150
Q3	12,513	1,465	5,140	4,841	386	1,464	13,297	3,003
Q4	13,168	1,371	5,128	4,661	330	971	12,461	2,679
2016 Q1	14,495	1,406	5,213	4,893	349	1,167	13,027	2,593
Q2	15,165	1,796	5,775	5,587	600	1,408	15,165	3,116
Q3	14,646	1,661	6,042	5,912	449	1,312	15,376	3,245
Q4	14,279	1,449	5,392	5,043	393	1,169	13,446	2,816
2017 Q1	15,430	1,478	5,978	5,867	354	1,101	14,778	2,982
Q2	15,123	1,703	6,515	6,345	390	950	15,903	4,045
Q3	14,945	1,666	6,376	6,397	413	828	15,679	3,520
Q4	14,948	1,462	5,763	5,429	341	969	13,965	3,117
2018 Q1	13,510	1,366	5,043	4,741	387	876	12,414	2,608
Q2	14,658	1,782	6,276	6,190	393	1,041	15,681	3,140
Q3	15,727	1,691	6,393	7,176	527	935	16,721	3,121
Q4	14,529	1,533	5,617	5,089	369	840	13,448	2,730
2019 Q1	14,732	1,657	5,454	5,435	371	781	13,699	2,895
Q2	14,837 p	2,043	5,863	6,252	390	1,077	15,619	3,154
Q3	14,494 p	1,910	6,224	6,118	384	1,040	15,677	3,008
Q4	14,431 p	1,493	5,502	5,225	349	930	13,498	2,753
2020 Q1	13,826 p	1,486	4,980	5,115	337	897	12,815	2,612
Q2	9,966 p	1,235	3,993	4,397	244	707	10,575	2,318
Q3	13,708 p	1,604	5,914	6,007	337	988	14,850	3,101

Source: Department for Business, Energy & Industrial Strategy

1. From Quarter 1 2019, sand and gravel data reported in this publication includes recycled material.

c   confidential
p   provisional

18.20 Volume of construction output in Great Britain by sector

Seasonally adjusted index numbers

2019=100

Period		New Housing			Other New Work				All New Work	Repair and Maintenance					All Work
					Infra-structure	Excluding Infrastructure				Housing			Non Housing R&M	All Repair and Maintenance	
		Public	Private	Total Housing		Public	Private Industrial	Private Commercial		Public	Private	Total			
		MV36	MV37	MVL7	MV38	MV39	MV3A	MV3B	MV3C	MV3D	MV3E	MV3F	MV3G	MV3H	MV3I
2014	Q1	88.8	63.1	67.0	70.5	107.8	76.1	91.5	78.3	109.2	86.6	92.6	90.6	91.6	82.9
	Q2	96.8	66.5	71.1	68.8	112.5	86.2	93.4	81.0	110.4	86.3	92.6	95.5	94.1	85.5
	Q3	99.6	69.8	74.3	70.0	112.6	84.0	93.1	82.3	112.1	87.3	93.8	96.5	95.1	86.8
	Q4	96.7	70.4	74.4	74.1	115.9	80.9	95.6	84.0	111.1	85.0	91.9	95.3	93.6	87.3
2015	Q1	92.6	72.4	75.4	83.3	110.7	89.6	95.1	86.0	112.8	85.8	92.9	94.1	93.5	88.6
	Q2	85.9	75.3	76.9	85.3	113.3	90.4	95.7	87.5	112.0	89.1	95.1	90.2	92.7	89.3
	Q3	71.6	72.4	72.3	84.4	113.0	95.6	94.6	85.4	113.0	89.7	95.9	90.0	93.0	88.0
	Q4	70.0	76.2	75.2	84.8	115.0	91.4	98.2	87.5	110.1	90.5	95.6	91.6	93.7	89.7
2016	Q1	77.4	81.9	81.2	81.6	112.2	83.8	101.1	89.4	111.8	92.0	97.2	90.7	94.0	91.0
	Q2	73.8	83.8	82.2	80.2	121.5	89.9	102.7	91.1	108.4	92.9	97.0	92.5	94.8	92.4
	Q3	74.9	83.9	82.6	85.3	118.3	83.4	104.6	92.1	102.0	94.0	96.1	91.2	93.7	92.7
	Q4	78.0	85.3	84.2	86.7	118.2	86.2	104.9	93.3	103.9	96.1	98.2	92.7	95.5	94.0
2017	Q1	87.8	88.5	88.4	92.6	119.8	81.5	112.0	97.9	103.3	98.5	99.8	95.0	97.4	97.7
	Q2	88.8	88.5	88.6	93.6	117.6	84.0	111.5	98.0	104.8	99.8	101.1	95.5	98.3	98.1
	Q3	88.4	89.4	89.3	94.4	109.7	91.7	109.8	97.6	103.8	100.2	101.2	95.6	98.4	97.9
	Q4	89.3	95.6	94.6	94.3	112.4	89.4	105.7	98.8	102.9	101.6	101.9	96.0	99.0	98.9
2018	Q1	83.8	95.1	93.4	95.7	99.9	92.7	105.9	97.7	100.1	98.3	98.8	95.9	97.3	97.6
	Q2	84.1	93.2	91.8	95.4	100.5	98.6	103.7	96.7	101.2	102.1	101.9	99.7	100.8	98.1
	Q3	87.5	96.5	95.2	97.3	104.0	95.4	99.1	97.4	100.6	100.6	100.6	101.7	101.1	98.7
	Q4	89.5	97.6	96.4	99.9	104.0	95.7	100.0	98.7	96.9	98.2	97.9	97.5	97.7	98.3
2019	Q1	96.4	101.0	100.3	101.1	102.5	100.3	98.8	100.3	96.7	101.6	100.3	102.0	101.1	100.6
	Q2	103.5	98.8	99.5	100.4	99.2	97.5	100.4	99.8	98.1	100.5	99.9	101.7	100.8	100.2
	Q3	97.7	101.9	101.3	99.9	98.5	101.7	100.5	100.6	102.6	99.6	100.4	98.7	99.5	100.2
	Q4	102.5	98.3	98.9	98.5	99.8	100.5	100.3	99.4	102.6	98.3	99.4	97.6	98.5	99.1
2020	Q1	98.4	96.2	96.5	98.6	101.7	104.2	96.3	97.7	102.9	91.5	94.5	96.7	95.6	97.0

Source: Office for National Statistics (ONS)

18.21 Value of orders for new construction obtained by main contractors in Great Britain, by sector

Seasonally Adjusted

£million

		New Housing				Other New Work						Period on period growths (%)	Period on same period one year ago growths (%)
							Excluding Infrastructure						
		Public	Private	All New Housing	Infra-structure	Public	Private Industrial	Private Com-mercial	All Other Work	All New Work			
2014		1,835	13,118	14,953	7,305	8,321	3,501	15,040	34,167	49,120	3.5%	
2015		1,416	13,133	14,549	11,119	6,522	4,416	14,681	36,738	51,287	4.4%	
2016		1,761	13,545	15,307	11,440	6,912	3,940	15,185	37,477	52,783	2.9%	
2017		1,458	14,067	15,525	15,410	5,901	4,022	13,912	39,245	54,770	3.8%	
2018		1,061	14,312	15,374	8,212	6,270	4,016	12,295	30,793	46,166	-15.7%	
2019		968	13,205	14,173	8,978	5,924	4,203	12,469	31,574	45,747	-0.9%	
2020		981	11,140	12,121	9,123	4,250	3,666	10,698	27,737	39,858	-12.9%	
2014	Q1	587	3,252	3,839	1,449	2,142	967	3,143	7,701	11,541	-6.7%	7.0%
	Q2	545	3,109	3,654	1,798	2,303	940	3,693	8,734	12,388	7.3%	-0.1%
	Q3	373	3,466	3,839	1,893	2,015	550	4,380	8,838	12,677	2.3%	6.3%
	Q4	329	3,291	3,620	2,166	1,861	1,044	3,823	8,894	12,515	-1.3%	1.2%
2015	Q1	351	3,326	3,676	2,462	1,815	1,107	3,650	9,034	12,710	1.6%	10.1%
	Q2	367	3,234	3,601	3,343	1,518	1,179	3,280	9,320	12,921	1.7%	4.3%
	Q3	256	3,057	3,313	3,084	1,691	1,126	3,500	9,401	12,714	-1.6%	0.3%
	Q4	443	3,516	3,959	2,230	1,498	1,005	4,250	8,983	12,942	1.8%	3.4%
2016	Q1	538	2,709	3,247	2,808	1,420	1,006	4,067	9,301	12,547	-3.0%	-1.3%
	Q2	453	3,704	4,157	2,495	2,114	1,005	4,247	9,861	14,018	11.7%	8.5%
	Q3	404	3,575	3,980	3,112	1,515	1,020	3,698	9,345	13,325	-4.9%	4.8%
	Q4	366	3,557	3,923	3,025	1,863	909	3,173	8,970	12,893	-3.2%	-0.4%
2017	Q1	238	3,639	3,878	2,791	1,300	994	3,908	8,993	12,871	-0.2%	2.6%
	Q2	369	3,389	3,758	2,393	1,613	1,185	3,387	8,578	12,336	-4.2%	-12.0%
	Q3	480	3,579	4,059	6,665	1,538	1,178	3,318	12,699	16,758	35.8%	25.8%
	Q4	370	3,460	3,830	3,560	1,451	666	3,299	8,976	12,806	-23.6%	-0.7%
2018	Q1	257	4,317	4,574	1,745	1,686	1,077	2,761	7,269	11,842	-7.5%	-8.0%
	Q2	385	3,331	3,717	2,184	1,333	997	3,017	7,531	11,247	-5.0%	-8.8%
	Q3	210	3,306	3,516	2,007	1,705	1,103	3,299	8,114	11,631	3.4%	-30.6%
	Q4	209	3,358	3,567	2,276	1,545	839	3,219	7,879	11,446	-1.6%	-10.6%
2019	Q1	228	3,250	3,478	2,485	2,078	993	3,653	9,209	12,686	10.8%	7.1%
	Q2	225	3,187	3,412	2,300	1,347	872	2,686	7,205	10,618	-16.3%	-5.6%
	Q3	294	3,559	3,853	2,151	1,172	947	2,727	6,997	10,850	2.2%	-6.7%
	Q4	221	3,210	3,430	2,042	1,326	1,390	3,403	8,161	11,593	6.8%	1.3%
2020	Q1	252	3,429	3,681	3,959	1,176	902	3,447	9,484	13,165	13.6%	3.8%

Source: Office for National Statistics (ONS)

18.22 Total engineering[1]

Values at current prices   £ million

		Turnover		
		Export	Home	Total
		JWO5	JWO6	JWO7
2013		41,248.8	61,547.6	102,796.4
2014		40,394.7	64,246.7	104,641.4
2015		36,561.2	61,585.5	98,146.7
2016		37,341.4	62,236.2	99,577.6
2017		42,210.3	64,624.8	106,835.1
2018		44,089.6	67,669.0	111,758.6
2019		45,334.8	67,383.9	112,718.7
2014	Q1	9,857.3	15,703.2	25,560.5
	Q2	10,127.1	16,002.1	26,129.2
	Q3	9,778.6	16,277.0	26,055.6
	Q4	10,631.7	16,264.4	26,896.1
2015	Q1	9,128.9	15,403.7	24,532.6
	Q2	9,437.4	15,423.6	24,861.0
	Q3	9,028.4	15,450.3	24,478.7
	Q4	8,966.5	15,307.9	24,274.4
2016	Q1	8,739.0	15,172.5	23,911.5
	Q2	9,147.7	15,635.4	24,783.1
	Q3	9,193.3	15,725.4	24,918.7
	Q4	10,261.4	15,702.9	25,964.3
2017	Q1	10,310.3	15,650.3	25,960.6
	Q2	10,455.5	15,651.7	26,107.2
	Q3	10,361.7	16,276.1	26,637.8
	Q4	11,082.8	17,046.7	28,129.5
2018	Q1	10,953	17,057	28,010
	Q2	11,223	16,615	27,838
	Q3	10,592	16,746	27,338
	Q4	11,321	17,251	28,572
2019	Q1	11,516	16,735	28,251
	Q2	11,407	16,793	28,200
	Q3	10,955	17,105	28,060
	Q4	11,457	16,751	28,208
2018	Jan	3,530.6	5,360.2	8,890.8
	Feb	3,418.0	5,417.6	8,835.6
	Mar	4,004.7	6,279.0	10,283.7
	Apr	3,565.6	5,420.5	8,986.1
	May	3,650.5	5,560.9	9,211.4
	June	4,006.8	5,634.0	9,640.8
	July	3,505.6	5,600.5	9,106.1
	August	3,446.5	5,514.2	8,960.7
	September	3,640.2	5,631.2	9,271.4
	October	3,902.8	6,037.9	9,940.7
	November	3,822.2	6,011.2	9,833.4
	December	3,596.1	5,201.8	8,797.9
2019	Jan	3,655.9	5,220.5	8,876.4
	Feb	3,568.5	5,367.6	8,936.1
	Mar	4,291.8	6,146.6	10,438.4
	Apr	3,632.5	5,405.5	9,038.0
	May	3,771.2	5,783.1	9,554.3
	June	4,003.5	5,604.4	9,607.9
	July	3,672.5	5,812.8	9,485.3
	August	3,369.7	5,433.3	8,803.0
	September	3,912.6	5,858.8	9,771.4
	October	4,046.1	5,957.1	10,003.2
	November	3,689.0	5,704.7	9,393.7
	December	3,721.5	5,089.5	8,811.0

Source: Office for National Statistics : 01633 646659 -

As of January 2013, New Orders data is no longer being collected

1 The data for this table is based on SIC 2007 (the Industrial Classification for 2007). The change is a result of the SIC 2003 based MPI survey (which provided figures up to the April edition of the Monthly Digest) becoming part of the SIC 2007 based Monthly Business Survey (MBS). This is part of an ONS wide project to convert all data series to the latest SIC. This means that this table is now Total engineering (SIC 07 25-28).Please note this new table does not include Orders on Hand.

18.23 Manufacture of fabricated metal products and machinery and equipment n.e.c.[1]

Values at current prices   £ million

		Turnover		
		Export	Home	Total
		JWM9	JWN2	JWN3
2013		23,644.6	43,936.4	67,581.0
2014		23,079.1	46,767.2	69,846.3
2015		21,651.8	44,430.1	66,081.9
2016		22,294.3	45,161.8	67,456.1
2017		25,743.9	46,556.3	72,300.2
2018		26,849.0	48,636.6	75,485.6
2019		27,046.8	47,628.7	74,675.5
2014	Q1	5,836.5	11,255.1	17,091.6
	Q2	5,875.0	11,827.6	17,702.6
	Q3	5,579.8	12,006.1	17,585.9
	Q4	5,787.8	11,678.4	17,466.2
2015	Q1	5,484.4	11,130.8	16,615.2
	Q2	5,667.9	11,227.1	16,895.0
	Q3	5,361.8	11,176.8	16,538.6
	Q4	5,137.7	10,895.4	16,033.1
2016	Q1	5,207.0	10,982.9	16,189.9
	Q2	5,535.6	11,472.0	17,007.6
	Q3	5,415.3	11,627.0	17,042.3
	Q4	6,136.4	11,079.9	17,216.3
2017	Q1	6,341.9	11,275.3	17,617.2
	Q2	6,426.6	11,263.5	17,690.1
	Q3	6,266.3	11,752.3	18,018.6
	Q4	6,709.1	12,265.2	18,974.3
2018	Q1	6,752.0	12,483.6	19,235.6
	Q2	6,867.7	11,981.6	18,849.3
	Q3	6,483.8	11,996.9	18,480.7
	Q4	6,745.5	12,174.5	18,920.0
2019	Q1	6,847.8	11,980.7	18,828.5
	Q2	6,901.0	11,829.9	18,730.9
	Q3	6,547.2	12,086.7	18,633.9
	Q4	6,750.8	11,731.4	18,482.2
2018	Jan	2,161.1	3,933.6	6,094.7
	Feb	2,135.5	3,986.0	6,121.5
	Mar	2,455.4	4,564.0	7,019.4
	Apr	2,193.6	3,936.3	6,129.9
	May	2,208.8	3,986.5	6,195.3
	June	2,465.3	4,058.8	6,524.1
	July	2,167.0	4,048.3	6,215.3
	August	2,078.2	3,959.5	6,037.7
	September	2,238.6	3,989.1	6,227.7
	October	2,355.5	4,325.3	6,680.8
	November	2,323.8	4,232.6	6,556.4
	December	2,066.2	3,616.6	5,682.8
2019	Jan	2,146.9	3,839.1	5,986.0
	Feb	2,122.8	3,880.7	6,003.5
	Mar	2,578.1	4,260.9	6,839.0
	Apr	2,205.2	3,814.0	6,019.2
	May	2,295.3	4,052.6	6,347.9
	June	2,400.5	3,963.3	6,363.8
	July	2,186.6	4,139.9	6,326.5
	August	1,995.5	3,886.1	5,881.6
	September	2,365.1	4,060.7	6,425.8
	October	2,349.4	4,297.4	6,646.8
	November	2,166.0	4,048.6	6,214.6
	December	2,235.4	3,385.4	5,620.8

Source: Office for National Statistics : 01633 646659

- As of Jan 2013, new orders data is no longer collected

1 The data for this table is based on SIC 2007 (the Industrial Classification for 2007). The change is a result of the SIC 2003 based MPI survey (which provided figures up to the April edition of the Monthly Digest) becoming part of the SIC 2007 based Monthly Business Survey (MBS). This is part of an ONS wide project to convert all data series to the latest SIC. Manufacture of fabricated metal products and machinery and equipment n.e.c. (SIC 07 25, 28). Please note this new table does not include Orders on Hand.

18.24 Alcoholic drink: Quantities released for consumption

Spirits

	Production and Quantities						hectolitres of pure alcohol
	Production of Potable Spirits [1]	Net Quantities of Spirits Charged with Duty					
		Home Produced Whisky					
	Total	Malt	Grain and Blended [2]	Total	Spirit Based RTDs	Imported and Other Spirits	Total
Calendar Year							
2003	4,552,539	30,674	294,041	324,715	124,391	744,279	1,193,386
2004	4,080,834	33,541	294,763	328,304	114,315	792,404	1,235,023
2005	4,364,669	32,176	276,802	308,978	84,123	821,615	1,214,716
2006	4,485,270	31,051	259,486	290,537	64,920	766,890	1,122,347
2007	5,498,490	31,698	261,612	293,311	51,797	832,200	1,177,308
2008	6,072,239	32,544	263,472	296,016	41,723	816,629	1,154,368
2009	5,756,752	28,013	234,668	262,680	31,834	801,522	1,096,035
2010	5,073,551	33,318	239,533	272,850	35,319	841,938	1,150,107
2011	5,696,986	32,172	225,123	257,294	30,384	828,489	1,116,167
2012	6,185,095	30,955	226,849	257,805	23,528	835,990	1,117,322
2013	8,433,710	30,583	214,322	244,905	21,702	820,808	1,087,415
2014	8,667,957	31,813	201,373	233,186	16,036	835,479	1,084,702
2015	8,967,478	34,486	203,349	237,834	14,345	867,252	1,119,431
2016	8,602,713	38,405	205,760	244,165	16,361	921,987	1,182,514
2017	5,830,893	40,594	200,444	241,039	15,533	975,250	1,231,822
2018	4,296,195	41,165	185,886	227,051	19,011	1,063,827	1,309,890
2019	[r]	41,250	185,930	227,180	20,216	1,061,170	1,308,565

Source: Her Majesty's Revenue and Customs

1. Data are available on a quarterly basis only.
2. From April 2011 onwards, UK produced grain whisky clearances have been added to UK produced blended whisky clearances to preserve taxpayer confidentiality
3. HMRC have temporarily removed the UK potable spirits production time series whilst the underlying data is reviewed. Removed data is indicated by [r] markings.

Beer & Cider

	UK Beer Production		Beer Clearances [1]				Cider Clearances
			Thousand hectolitres				
	Thousand hectolitres	Thousand hectolitres of alcohol (production)	UK registered premises	Ex-warehouse and imports	Total beer clearances	Thousand hectolitres of alcohol (clearances)	Cider Thousand hectolitres
Calendar Year							
2003	58,016	2,414	43,248	12,736	55,984	2,514	5,876
2004	57,461	2,433	42,480	12,742	55,221	2,502	6,139
2005	56,253	2,338	40,586	13,354	53,940	2,398	6,440
2006	53,768	2,250	39,901	12,515	52,416	2,342	7,523
2007	51,341	2,159	37,797	12,065	49,862	2,235	8,047
2008	49,611	2,062	36,123	11,828	47,950	2,133	8,414
2009	45,141	1,891	31,970	12,388	44,358	1,952	9,404
2010	44,997	1,905	30,548	12,425	42,973	1,926	9,309
2011	45,694	1,934	29,472	13,055	42,527	1,881	9,280
2012	42,047	1,752	28,938	14,024	42,962	1,790	8,737
2013	41,956	1,735	28,770	13,653	42,422	1,758	8,640
2014	41,204	1,713	29,477	14,275	43,752	1,819	7,937
2015	41,270	1,738	29,216	14,547	43,762	1,837	7,758
2016	38,084	1,611	29,234	14,497	43,731	1,840	7,214
2017	40,480	1,624	31,502	14,422	45,924	1,864	7,410
2018	40,885	1,652	31,734	16,038	47,772	1,949	6,804
2019	39,247	1,637	30,410	16,708	47,119	1,962	6,794

Source: Her Majesty's Revenue and Customs

1. There have been minor revisions back to 2015 in the clearance figures on cider; this is due to methodological improvements.

18.24 Alcoholic drink: Quantities released for consumption

Wine Of Fresh Grape[1]

	Quantities Released for Consumption						hectolitres
	Not exceeding 15% ABV			Composition by Origin above 5.5% ABV			
	Still	Sparkling	Over 15% ABV	Imported ex-ship	Ex-warehouse	UK origin	Total wine of fresh grape
Calendar Year							
2003	10,661,812	632,942	293,087	2,930,230	8,644,152	13,460	11,587,841
2004	11,762,465	667,980	294,419	3,674,387	9,036,297	14,180	12,724,863
2005	12,139,448	712,725	302,389	3,829,564	9,311,438	13,559	13,154,562
2006	11,663,074	706,419	297,984	3,790,874	8,862,064	14,538	12,667,477
2007	12,578,475	829,693	301,944	4,237,414	9,454,030	18,668	13,710,112
2008	12,426,434	748,145	319,985	4,932,155	8,544,932	17,477	13,494,563
2009	11,738,732	721,709	216,249	5,040,845	7,611,848	23,997	12,676,689
2010	11,896,447	794,491	216,078	4,783,583	8,101,095	22,338	12,907,016
2011	11,843,704	799,538	216,517	4,686,446	8,155,571	17,742	12,859,759
2012	11,705,405	872,345	223,867	4,620,328	8,161,814	19,476	12,801,618
2013	11,585,699	925,118	227,717	4,351,349	8,371,574	15,611	12,738,533
2014	11,243,599	1,117,124	201,323	4,025,953	8,516,735	19,359	12,562,046
2015	11,209,744	1,375,241	196,290	3,746,946	9,016,786	17,543	12,781,276
2016	11,181,927	1,547,326	205,651	3,396,281	9,520,899	17,723	12,934,904
2017	11,322,703	1,628,199	204,102	3,526,424	9,599,595	25,529	13,151,548
2018	11,110,242	1,606,374	185,047	3,508,704	9,374,840	23,761	12,907,305
2019	10,868,915	1,523,396	194,125	3,460,506	9,101,005	24,926	12,586,437

Source: Her Majesty's Revenue and Customs

1. Also called wine of fresh grape.
2. Ex-warehouse relates to clearances of UK produced and imported products from registered duty suspension warehouses. Ex-ship relates to other products imported into the UK.

Made Wine

	Quantities Released for Consumption							hectolitres
	Above 1.2% but not exceeding 5.5% ABV [1]	Above 5.5% ABV but not exceeding 15%		Over 15% ABV	Composition by Origin above 5.5% ABV			Total made wine
		Still[2]	Sparkling		Imported ex-ship	Ex-warehouse	UK registered premises	
Calendar year								
2003	423,702	338,263	849	[d]	24,289	314,822	[d]	762,814
2004	507,799	350,427	692	[d]	25,673	325,445	[d]	858,918
2005	598,119	334,030	364	[d]	35,974	298,420	[d]	932,513
2006	527,770	315,529	1,099	[d]	34,984	281,644	[d]	844,399
2007	720,432	342,809	6,666	[d]	52,363	297,112	[d]	1,069,907
2008	611,804	374,725	7,897	[d]	55,111	327,511	[d]	994,427
2009	596,479	390,124	2,395	[d]	37,296	355,223	[d]	988,999
2010	758,167	399,768	4,721	[d]	41,116	363,373	[d]	1,162,655
2011	827,777	440,357	6,518	[d]	31,972	414,903	[d]	1,274,651
2012	999,933	424,228	2,954	[d]	12,033	415,150	[d]	1,427,114
2013	1,394,602	421,770	5,279	[d]	12,407	414,642	[d]	1,821,651
2014	1,715,025	465,357	6,840	[d]	18,522	453,675	[d]	2,187,221
2015	1,950,431	489,496	12,505	[d]	24,512	477,489	[d]	2,452,432
2016	2,229,521	455,069	9,869	[d]	18,340	446,598	[d]	2,694,459
2017	2,335,674	505,749	3,886	[d]	16,007	493,628	[d]	2,845,308
2018	2,231,269	546,950	5,023	[d]	14,807	537,165	[d]	2,783,241
2019	2,156,387	546,291	7,134	[d]	16,480	536,945	[d]	2,709,812

Source: Her Majesty's Revenue and Customs

1. Does not include product mixed duty paid. Includes alcoholic lemonade and similar products of appropriate strength.
2. Ex-warehouse relates to clearances of UK produced and imported products from registered duty suspension warehouses. Ex-ship relates to other products imported into the UK.
3. Clearances over 15% ABV are included within still 5.5% to 15% ABV clearances and UK origin clearances over 5.5% ABV are included within ex-warehouse clearances over 5.5% ABV to preserve trader confidentiality and are marked as [d].

18.25 Tobacco products: recent receipts

£ million

	Cigarettes			Other Tobacco Products			Overall Total
	Home Produced	Imported	Cigarettes Total	Cigars	HRT	Other	
Calendar Year							
2008	7,005	579	7,585	86	473	27	8,171
2009	7,473	578	8,051	92	607	29	8,779
2010	7,590	662	8,252	86	683	29	9,051
2011	7,899	657	8,556	87	845	28	9,517
2012	7,954	637	8,591	88	991	29	9,699
2013	7,723	625	8,348	82	1,073	27	9,530
2014	7,557	668	8,225	83	1,108	27	9,442
2015 [1]	*	*	8,032	78	1,134	24	9,269
2016	*	*	7,794	73	1,204	22	9,092
2017	*	*	8,007	76	1,371	23	9,476
2018	*	*	7,339	74	1,405	25	8,844
2019	*	*	7,123	73	1,464	27	8,688

Source: Her Majesty's Revenue and Customs

1. From November 2015 onwards, the home produced and imported split of total cigarette receipts has been removed to preserve commercial confidentiality.

2. Tobacco for Heating receipts are included within Other tobacco receipts.

* = data not available

this page is intentionally blank

National accounts

Chapter 19

National accounts

The tables are based on those in The Blue Book 2019 Edition. The Blue Book presents the full set of economic accounts for the United Kingdom. The accounts are based on the European System of Accounts 2010 (ESA 2010), a system of national accounts that all European Union members have agreed to use. The structure of the ESA 2010 is consistent with the worldwide guidelines on national accounting set out in the System of National Accounts 2008 (2008 SNA).

The Blue Book contains an introduction which provides an overview of the accounts and an explanation of the underlying framework. A detailed description of the structure of the accounts and the methods used to derive the figures is provided in a separate Office for National Statistics (ONS) publication United Kingdom National Accounts: Concepts, Sources and Methods (TSO 1998). Further information on the financial accounts is given in the Financial Statistics Explanatory Handbook.

Brief definitions of some national accounting terms used in this chapter are included here. Current prices (or, more precisely, current price estimates) describe values during the period of the observation. Hence, in a time series, they will describe changes to price and to volume. Chain volume measures exclude the effects of price change. Basic prices do not include taxes and subsidies on products, whereas these are included in market prices.

Gross Domestic Product and Gross National Income (Tables 19.1, 19.2, 19.3)

Table 19.1 shows three of the most important economic aggregates: Gross Domestic Product (GDP), Gross National Income (GNI) and Gross National Disposable Income (GNDI). In all three cases 'gross' denotes that depreciation (or consumption) of fixed capital is ignored. GDP is the total value of the UK's output. GNI is GDP plus primary incomes received from the rest of the world minus primary incomes paid to the rest of the world. Primary income comprises taxes on production and imports, property income and compensation of employees. These measures are given as current price estimates and chained volume measures. GNDI equals GNI plus net current transfers to the rest of the world. Transfers are unrequited payments such as taxes, social benefits and remittances.

There are three different approaches to measuring GDP: output, income and expenditure. Table 19.2 shows the various money flows which are used in these different approaches, and those that are used to measure GNI at current prices. The output approach to measuring GDP takes the gross value added for the entire economy (that is, the value of the UK's output minus the goods and services consumed in the productive process) to give gross value added at basic prices. This figure is then adjusted to include taxes and exclude subsidies on products. This gives gross value added at market prices for the UK, which is equivalent to GDP.

The expenditure approach to GDP shows consumption expenditure by households and government, gross capital formation and expenditure on UK exports. The sum of these items overstates the amount of income generated in the UK by the value of imported goods and services. This item is therefore subtracted to produce GDP at market prices.

The income approach to GDP shows gross operating surplus, mixed income and compensation of employees (previously known as income from employment). Production taxes less subsidies are added to produce the total of the income-based components at market prices.

Table 19.2 also shows the primary incomes received from the rest of the world, which are added to GDP, and primary incomes payable to non-resident units, which are deducted from GDP, to arrive at GNI. Primary income comprises compensation of employees, taxes less subsidies on production, and property and entrepreneurial income. The data in Table 19.2 are in current prices. This means that changes between years will be driven by a combination of price effects and changes in the volume of production. The second of these components is often referred to as 'real growth'.

Table 19.3 shows the expenditure approach to the chained volume measure of GDP, that is to say the effects of price change have been removed. In chained volume series, volume measures for each year are produced in prices of the previous year. These volume measures are then 'chain-linked' together to produce a continuous time series.

Industrial analysis (Tables 19.4, 19.5)

The analysis of gross value added by industry at current prices shown in Table 19.4 reflects the estimates based on the 2007 Standard Industrial Classification (SIC2007). The table is based on current price data reconciled through the input–output process.

Table 19.5 shows chained volume measures of gross value added by industry. These indices are based on basic price measures. Chained volume measures of gross value added provides a lead economic indicator. The analysis of gross value added is estimated in terms of change and expressed in index number form.

Sector analysis – Distribution of income accounts and capital account (Tables 19.6 to 19.13)

The National Accounts accounting framework includes the sector accounts which provide, by institutional sector, a description of the different stages of the economic process, from the income generated by production and its distribution and re-distribution to different economic units, and finally, capital accumulation and financing. Tables 19.6 to 19.12 show the 'allocation of primary income account' and the 'secondary distribution of income account' for the non-financial corporations, financial corporations, government and households sectors. Additionally, Table 19.12 shows the 'use of income account' for the households sector and Table 19.13 provides a summary of the capital account. The full sequence of accounts is shown in The Blue Book.

The allocation of primary income account shows the resident units and institutional sectors as recipients rather than as producers of primary income. The balancing item of this account is the gross balance of primary income (B.5g) for each sector and, if the gross balance is aggregated across all sectors of the economy, the result is Gross National Income.

The secondary distribution of income account describes how the balance of income for each sector is allocated by redistribution; through transfers such as taxes on income, social contributions and benefits, and other current transfers. The balancing item of this account is Gross Disposable Income (GDI). For the households sector, the chained volume measure of GDI is shown as real household disposable income.

Table 19.12 shows, for the household sector, the use of disposable income where the balancing item is saving (B.8g). For the non-financial corporations sector the balancing item of the secondary distribution of income account, gross disposable income (B.6g), is equal to saving (B.8g).

The summary capital account (Table 19.13) brings together the saving and investment of the sectors of the economy. It shows saving, capital transfers, gross capital formation and net acquisition of non-financial assets for each of these.

Households' and non-profit institutions serving households' consumption expenditure at current market prices and chained volume measures (Tables 19.14 to 19.17)

Households' and non-profit institutions serving households' (NPISH) final consumption expenditure is a major component of the expenditure measure of GDP. In Table 19.2 this expenditure is given at current market prices, broken down by the type of goods or service purchased. Table 19.3 supplies the same breakdown in chain volume measures. Household final consumption expenditure includes the value of income-in-kind and imputed rent of owner-occupied dwellings. It includes expenditure on durable goods (for instance motor cars) which, from the point of view of the individual might more appropriately be treated as capital expenditure. The purchase of land and dwellings (including costs incurred in connection with the transfer of their ownership) and expenditure on major improvements by occupiers are treated as personal capital expenditure. Other goods and services purchased by the household sector (with the exception of goods and services that are to be used in self-employment) are treated as final consumption expenditure.

Change in inventories (Table 19.18)

This table gives a broad analysis by industry of the value of entries less withdrawals and losses of inventories (stocks), and analysis by asset for manufacturing industry.

Gross fixed capital formation (Table 19.19 to 19.22)

Gross fixed capital formation is the total value of the acquisition less disposal of fixed assets, and improvements to land.

19.1 UK national and domestic product
Main aggregates: Index numbers and values
Current prices and chained volume measures (reference year 2018)

			2012	2013	2014	2015	2016	2017	2018	2019
Indices (2018=100)										
Values at current prices										
Gross domestic product at market prices ("Money GDP")	YBEU	B.1*g	79.9	83.1	87.0	89.6	93.1	96.6	100.0	103.4
Gross value added at basic prices	YBEX	B.1g	80.1	83.2	87.0	89.6	93.0	96.5	100.0	103.5
Chained volume measures										
Gross domestic product at market prices	YBEZ	B.1*g	88.7	90.6	93.2	95.4	97.1	98.8	100.0	101.3
Gross national disposable income at market prices	YBFP	B.6*g	87.3	88.5	91.8	94.5	96.1	98.7	100.0	100.8
Gross value added at basic prices	CGCE	B.1g	88.7	90.7	93.4	95.4	97.0	98.7	100.0	101.4
Implied deflator										
Implied deflator of GDP at market prices	YBGB		90.1	91.7	93.3	93.9	95.9	97.8	100.0	102.1
Values at current prices (£million)										
Gross measures (before deduction of consumption of fixed capital) at current market prices										
Gross domestic product ("Money GDP")	YBHA	B.1*g	1 711 770	1 780 336	1 863 008	1 919 641	1 994 712	2 068 757	2 141 792	2 214 362
Employment, property and entrepreneurial income from rest of the world (receipts less payments)	YBGG	D.1+D.4	–17 510	–35 869	–37 357	–43 157	–47 533	–24 370	–26 746	–36 158
Subsidies (receipts) less taxes (payments) on products from/to rest of the world	QZOZ	-D.21+D.31	2 898	2 926	2 960	3 087	3 327	3 427	3 335	3 343
Other subsidies on production from/to rest of the world	IBJL	+D.29-D.39	–2 627	–2 452	–2 306	–1 956	–2 431	–2 185	–2 203	–2 188
Gross balance of primary incomes/ gross national income (GNI)	ABMX	B.5*g	1 693 989	1 743 993	1 824 997	1 875 353	1 946 283	2 043 145	2 113 914	2 177 049
Current transfers from rest of the world (receipts less payments)	YBGF	D.5,6,7	20 897	25 740	23 944	23 875	23 848	22 462	25 488	27 495
Gross national disposable income	NQCO	B.6*g	1 673 092	1 718 253	1 801 053	1 851 478	1 922 435	2 020 683	2 088 426	2 149 554
Adjustment to current basic prices										
Gross domestic product (at market prices)	YBHA	B.1*g	1 711 770	1 780 336	1 863 008	1 919 641	1 994 712	2 068 757	2 141 792	2 214 362
Adjustment to current basic prices (less taxes plus subsidies on products)	NQBU	D.21-D.31	182 105	191 541	201 775	207 569	217 346	224 747	231 545	237 266
Gross value added (at basic prices)	ABML	B.1g	1 529 665	1 588 795	1 661 233	1 712 072	1 777 366	1 844 010	1 910 247	1 977 096
Net measures (after deduction of consumption of fixed capital) at current market prices										
Consumption of fixed capital	NQAE	P.51c	250 247	257 408	265 638	274 744	287 314	302 915	315 534	327 897
Net domestic product	NHRK	B.1*n	1 461 523	1 522 928	1 597 370	1 644 897	1 707 398	1 765 842	1 826 258	1 886 465
Net national income	NSRX	B.5*n	1 443 742	1 486 585	1 559 359	1 600 609	1 658 969	1 740 230	1 798 380	1 849 152
Net national disposable income	NQCP	B.6*n	1 422 845	1 460 845	1 535 415	1 576 734	1 635 121	1 717 768	1 772 892	1 821 657
Chained volume measures (reference year 2016, £million)										
Gross measures (before deduction of consumption of fixed capital) at market prices										
Gross domestic product	ABMI	B.1*g	1 899 626	1 941 155	1 996 725	2 043 909	2 079 113	2 115 296	2 141 792	2 168 798
Terms of trade effect ("trading gain or loss")	YBGJ	TGL	–34 264	–25 747	–13 183	1 708	2 961	–3 926	–	–355
Real gross domestic income	YBGL	GDI	1 865 362	1 915 408	1 983 542	2 045 617	2 082 074	2 111 370	2 141 792	2 168 443
Real employment, property and entrepreneurial income from rest of the world (receipts less payments)	YBGI	D.1+D.4	–19 074	–38 569	–39 785	–46 009	–49 617	–24 867	–26 746	–35 413
Subsidies (receipts) less taxes (payments) on products from/to rest of the world	QZPB	-D.21+D.31	3 157	3 146	3 152	3 291	3 473	3 497	3 335	3 274
Other subsidies on production from/to rest of the world	IBJN	+D.29-D.39	–2 862	–2 637	–2 456	–2 085	–2 538	–2 230	–2 203	–2 143
Gross balance of primary incomes/ gross national income (GNI)	YBGM	B.5*g	1 845 998	1 876 329	1 943 060	1 998 402	2 031 524	2 085 236	2 113 914	2 131 899
Real current transfers from rest of the world (receipts less payments)	YBGP	D.5,6,7	22 763	27 678	25 500	25 453	24 894	22 921	25 488	26 929
Gross national disposable income	YBGO	B.6*g	1 823 236	1 848 650	1 917 561	1 972 950	2 006 630	2 062 316	2 088 426	2 104 970
Adjustment to basic prices										
Gross domestic product (at market prices)	ABMI	B.1*g	1 899 626	1 941 155	1 996 725	2 043 909	2 079 113	2 115 296	2 141 792	2 168 798
Adjustment to basic prices (less taxes plus subsidies on products)	NTAQ	-D.21+D.31	204 786	208 273	213 540	221 355	226 545	230 401	231 545	231 978
Gross value added (at basic prices)	ABMM	B.1g	1 694 891	1 732 920	1 783 227	1 822 556	1 852 573	1 884 900	1 910 247	1 936 820
Net measures (after deduction of consumption of fixed capital) at market prices										
Consumption of fixed capital	CIHA	P.51c	280 491	283 274	286 685	291 629	299 233	308 266	315 534	321 817
Net national income at market prices	YBET	B.5*n	1 564 468	1 592 258	1 655 002	1 704 596	1 730 700	1 776 592	1 798 380	1 810 082
Net national disposable income at market prices	YBEY	B.6*n	1 541 700	1 564 598	1 629 508	1 679 146	1 705 809	1 753 672	1 772 892	1 783 153

Source: Office for National Statistics, Blue Book 2020

19.2 UK gross domestic product and national income, current prices

(£ million)

Gross domestic product: production

B.1g Gross value added, at basic prices

	Output of goods and services[1] P.1	less intermediate consumption[1] P.2	Total B.1g	Value added taxes (VAT) on products D.211	Other taxes on products D.212,4	less subsidies on products D.31	Gross domestic product at market prices B.1*g
	KN26	KN25	ABML	QYRC	NSUI	NZHC	YBHA
2012	2959580	1429915	1529665	116459	72717	7071	1711770
2013	3084875	1496080	1588795	121650	76659	6768	1780336
2014	3187665	1526432	1661233	127647	81424	7296	1863008
2015	3258296	1546224	1712072	132948	83148	8527	1919641
2016	3369420	1592054	1777366	137531	89255	9440	1994712
2017	3513338	1669328	1844010	142655	92988	10896	2068757
2018	3648466	1738219	1910247	149228	94309	11992	2141792
2019			1977096	154799	95552	13085	2214362

(£ million)

Gross domestic product: expenditure

P.31 Final consumption expenditure

P.41 Actual individual consumption

	Gross domestic product at market prices B.1*g	Household final consumption expenditure P.31	Final consumption expenditure of NPISH[2] P.31	Individual govt. final consumption expenditure P.31	Total P.41	Collective govt. final consumption expenditure P.32
	YBHA	ABPB	ABNV	NNAQ	NQEP	NQEO
2012	1711770	1058472	45519	224666	1328657	131782
2013	1780336	1109534	44228	229372	1383134	129725
2014	1863008	1153351	44631	238431	1436413	131768
2015	1919641	1187215	46231	241808	1475254	132842
2016	1994712	1248091	44859	248411	1541361	133576
2017	2068757	1287278	47118	252906	1587302	134378
2018	2141792	1335216	50475	259735	1645426	138686
2019	2214362	1364462	52415	274131	1691008	148990

P.31 Total final consumption expenditure

P.31 Households and NPISH

	Households P.31	NPISH P.31	Total P.31	Central government P.31	Local government P.31	Total P.31
	ABPB	ABNV	NSSG	NMBJ	NMMT	ABKW
2012	1058472	45519	1103991	230070	126378	1460439
2013	1109534	44228	1153762	233390	125707	1512859
2014	1153351	44631	1197982	245452	124747	1568181
2015	1187215	46231	1233446	249982	124668	1608096
2016	1248091	44859	1292950	257389	124598	1674937
2017	1287278	47118	1334396	263012	124272	1721680
2018	1335216	50475	1385691	271403	127018	1784112
2019	1364462	52415	1416877	293244	129877	1839998

(£ million)

Gross domestic product: expenditure

P.5 Gross capital formation

	Gross fixed capital formation P.51g	Changes in inventories[1] P.52	Acquisitions less disposals of valuables P.53	Total P.5	Exports of goods and services P.6	less imports of goods and services P.7	External balance of goods and services B.11 Total B.11	Statistical discrepancy between expenditure components and GDP de	Gross domestic product at market prices B.1*g
	NPQX	ABMP	NPJO	NQFM	KTMW	KTMX	KTMY	RVFD	YBHA
2012	268984	4020	-483	272521	513317	534507	-21190	0	1711770
2013	284080	3509	4894	292483	531790	556796	-25006	0	1780336
2014	309788	14164	-192	323760	525324	554257	-28933	0	1863008
2015	330807	9357	-347	339817	523366	551638	-28272	0	1919641
2016	353218	2772	-102	355888	563248	599361	-36113	0	1994712
2017	372333	3478	1155	376966	622868	652757	-29889	0	2068757
2018	381249	-756	2674	383167	661601	687088	-25487	0	2141792
2019	399470	6432	-453	405449	690823	721325	-30502	-583	2214362

Gross domestic product: income

B.2g Operating surplus, gross

Non financial corporations

	Public non-financial corporations B.2g	Private non-financial corporations B.2g	Financial corporations B.2g	General government B.2g	Households B.2g	NPISH B.2g	Total B.2g	Mixed income B.3g
	NRJT	NRJK	NQNV	NMXV	HABM	HABV	ABNF	QWLT
2012	15762	297453	55483	35289	138969	12205	555161	107430
2013	16413	307105	55999	36433	140823	12936	569709	112452
2014	16509	333104	57810	37915	152580	13616	611534	119938
2015	17396	348382	48048	38983	163283	14228	630320	125939
2016	17780	354390	54557	40353	174023	14652	655755	130045
2017	16746	374140	53452	41713	173545	15270	674866	135623
2018	11065	388598	54706	42683	180758	16090	693900	141059
2019	11352	395799	53118	44363	184041	17142	705815	147822

19.2 UK gross domestic product and national income, current prices (contd.)

(£ million)

	Gross domestic product: income						D.1 Compensation of employees					D.4 Property and entrepreneurial income			Gross national income at market prices
	Compen-sation of employees D.1	Taxes on production and imports D.2	less subsidies D.3	Statistical discrepancy between income components and GDP di	Gross domestic product at market prices B.1*g	Gross domestic product at market prices B.1*g	Receipts from rest of the world D.1	less payments to rest of the world D.1	Total D.1	Subsidies (receipts) less taxes (payments) on products from/to rest of the world -D.21+D.31	Other subsidies on production from/to rest of the world +D.29-D.39	from rest of the world D.4	(receipts less payments) D.4	Total D.4	Gross balance of primary incomes/gross national income (GNI) B.5*g
	HAEA	NZGX	AAXJ	RVFC	YBHA	YBHA	KTMN	KTMO	KTMP	QZOZ	IBJL	HMBN	HMBO	HMBM	ABMX
2012	843093	217853	11767	0	1711770	1711770	1124	1272	-148	2898	-2627	171162	188524	-17362	1693989
2013	880999	228290	11114	0	1780336	1780336	1094	1420	-326	2926	-2452	157794	193337	-35543	1743993
2014	903674	239834	11972	0	1863008	1863008	1082	1551	-469	2960	-2306	142441	179329	-36888	1824997
2015	929699	247917	14234	0	1919641	1919641	1295	1384	-89	3087	-1956	132256	175324	-43068	1875353
2016	966821	259046	16955	0	1994712	1994712	1375	1735	-360	3327	-2431	134365	181538	-47173	1946283
2017	1006970	270597	19299	0	2068757	2068757	1323	1633	-310	3427	-2185	183973	208033	-24060	2043145
2018	1048243	280130	21541	0	2141792	2141792	1262	1648	-386	3335	-2203	214928	241288	-26360	2113914
2019	1096110	287683	23978	910	2214362	2214362	1336	1793	-457	3343	-2188	203973	239674	-35701	2177049

Notes

1 These series are not available for the latest year
2 Non-profit institutions serving households

Source: Office for National Statistics, Blue Book 2020

19.3 UK gross domestic product
Chained volume measures (reference year 2018)

£ million

			2012	2013	2014	2015	2016	2017	2018	2019
Gross domestic product										
Gross domestic product: expenditure approach										
Final consumption expenditure		P.3								
Actual individual consumption		P.41								
Household final consumption expenditure	ABPF	P.3	1 157 971	1 192 501	1 222 479	1 258 941	1 305 040	1 318 430	1 335 216	1 346 185
Final consumption expenditure of NPISH[1]	ABNU	P.3	49 401	46 703	45 742	47 447	45 888	47 785	50 475	51 529
Individual government final consumption expenditure	NSZK	P.31	232 598	236 019	242 816	248 954	253 942	258 428	259 735	267 851
Total	YBIO	P.41	1 440 244	1 475 343	1 511 171	1 555 452	1 604 794	1 624 628	1 645 426	1 665 565
Collective government final consumption expenditure	NSZL	P.32	144 439	138 948	139 622	140 242	139 127	137 466	138 686	146 908
Total	ABKX	P.3	1 584 557	1 614 258	1 650 768	1 695 692	1 743 923	1 762 091	1 784 112	1 812 473
Gross capital formation		P.5								
Gross fixed capital formation	NPQR	P.51g	302 815	314 073	335 949	353 830	369 569	379 787	381 249	387 085
Changes in inventories	ABMQ	P.52	5 623	6 991	14 222	11 458	8 838	13 486	−756	571
Acquisitions less disposals of valuables	NPJP	P.53	−200	7 180	907	514	1 231	1 889	2 674	−1 089
Total	NPQU	P.5	301 688	326 157	364 232	382 949	377 033	379 867	383 167	386 567
Gross national final expenditure	YBIK		1 887 227	1 941 109	2 014 611	2 077 770	2 120 959	2 141 976	2 167 279	2 199 040
Exports of goods and services	KTMZ	P.6	570 563	575 443	576 799	592 946	609 198	642 143	661 601	679 984
Gross final expenditure	ABME		2 458 361	2 517 315	2 592 296	2 671 674	2 730 956	2 784 209	2 828 880	2 879 024
less imports of goods and services	KTNB	P.7	558 266	575 444	594 717	626 901	651 643	668 897	687 088	709 637
Statistical discrepancy between expenditure components and GDP	GIXS	de	−	−	−	−	−	−	−	−589
Gross domestic product at market prices	ABMI	B.1*g	1 899 626	1 941 155	1 996 725	2 043 909	2 079 113	2 115 296	2 141 792	2 168 798
Of which: external balance of goods and services	KTNC	B.11	12 297	−1	−17 918	−33 955	−42 445	−26 754	−25 487	−29 653

1 Non-profit institutions serving households

Source: Office for National Statistics, Blue Book 2020

19.4 Output and capital formation: by industry[1,2]
Gross value added at current basic prices

£ million

			2011	2012	2013	2014	2015	2016	2017	2018
Agriculture										
Output										
Compensation of employees	KLR2	D.1	4 165	4 266	4 337	4 198	4 373	4 398	4 559	4 597
Taxes less subsidies on production other than those on products	KLR3	D.29-D.39	−2 963	−2 425	−2 242	−2 119	−1 832	−2 286	−1 998	−2 020
Operating surplus and mixed income, gross	KLR4	B.2g+B.3g	10 369	9 179	9 383	11 986	9 888	9 381	9 306	9 608
Gross value added at basic prices	KLR5	B.1g	11 571	11 020	11 478	14 065	12 429	11 493	11 867	12 185
Intermediate consumption at purchasers' prices	KLR6	P.2	16 806	16 690	17 523	16 717	17 841	18 312	19 254	20 585
Total output at basic prices	KLR7	P.1	28 377	27 710	29 001	30 782	30 270	29 805	31 121	32 770
Gross capital formation	KLR8	P.5	5 307	4 172	4 572	5 760	4 716	3 437	5 096	5 016
Production										
Output										
Compensation of employees	KLR9	D.1	120 569	122 245	130 016	130 894	131 122	132 297	136 770	141 958
Taxes less subsidies on production other than those on products	KLS4	D.29-D.39	3 990	4 228	4 562	4 617	4 549	4 569	4 156	4 173
Operating surplus and mixed income, gross	KLS3	B.2g+B.3g	100 200	104 909	107 199	108 198	108 083	106 187	115 359	118 860
Gross value added at basic prices	KLS5	B.1g	224 759	231 382	241 777	243 709	243 754	243 053	256 285	264 991
Intermediate consumption at purchasers' prices	KLS6	P.2	425 461	435 519	441 169	440 473	425 293	435 897	455 369	480 137
Total output at basic prices	KLS7	P.1	650 220	666 901	682 946	684 182	669 047	678 950	711 654	745 128
Gross capital formation	KLS8	P.5	40 399	47 495	51 798	57 530	61 640	63 808	58 672	58 690
Construction										
Output										
Compensation of employees	KLS9	D.1	41 273	41 056	43 356	43 702	46 903	48 522	51 294	54 151
Taxes less subsidies on production other than those on products	KLT3	D.29-D.39	1 174	1 397	1 203	1 208	1 458	1 242	1 262	1 235
Operating surplus and mixed income, gross	KLT2	B.2g+B.3g	43 510	46 104	50 700	56 916	61 481	63 288	66 999	67 813
Gross value added at basic prices	KLT4	B.1g	85 957	88 557	95 259	101 826	109 842	113 052	119 555	123 199
Intermediate consumption at purchasers' prices	KLT5	P.2	125 836	130 496	136 476	149 879	162 001	171 686	182 417	192 431
Total output at basic prices	KLT6	P.1	211 793	219 053	231 735	251 705	271 843	284 738	301 972	315 630
Gross capital formation	KLT7	P.5	19 052	22 498	19 348	24 472	25 317	26 337	28 034	29 833

19.4 Output and capital formation: by industry[1,2]
Gross value added at current basic prices

continued

£ million

			2011	2012	2013	2014	2015	2016	2017	2018
Distribution, transport, hotels and restaurants										
Output										
Compensation of employees	KLT8	D.1	175 505	179 838	187 284	192 083	197 460	206 819	217 904	226 443
Taxes less subsidies on production other than		D.29-D.39								
those on products	KLU2		11 987	12 545	13 252	13 598	14 008	14 264	15 149	16 186
Operating surplus and mixed income, gross	KLT9	B.2g+B.3g	70 217	71 151	72 460	81 130	83 498	84 509	88 074	90 419
Gross value added at basic prices	KLU3	B.1g	257 709	263 534	272 996	286 811	294 966	305 592	321 127	333 048
Intermediate consumption at purchasers' prices	KLU4	P.2	230 082	238 001	254 333	260 072	269 230	274 044	283 793	297 604
Total output at basic prices	KLU5	P.1	487 791	501 535	527 329	546 883	564 196	579 636	604 920	630 652
Gross capital formation	KLU6	P.5	32 436	33 609	36 413	47 660	46 960	46 851	50 229	44 374
Information and communication										
Output										
Compensation of employees	KLU7	D.1	56 965	58 251	59 908	62 174	65 099	69 282	72 724	75 973
Taxes less subsidies on production other than		D.29-D.39								
those on products	KLU9		645	641	789	705	240	−28	−200	−291
Operating surplus and mixed income, gross	KLU8	B.2g+B.3g	36 878	38 322	38 228	41 231	42 480	47 375	48 589	49 836
Gross value added at basic prices	KLV2	B.1g	94 488	97 214	98 925	104 110	107 819	116 629	121 113	125 518
Intermediate consumption at purchasers' prices	KLV3	P.2	68 314	69 685	73 754	75 949	79 479	79 839	90 045	95 933
Total output at basic prices	KLV4	P.1	162 802	166 899	172 679	180 059	187 298	196 468	211 158	221 451
Gross capital formation	KLV5	P.5	17 686	18 726	20 146	20 781	22 031	26 112	27 707	27 536
Financial and insurance										
Output										
Compensation of employees	KLV6	D.1	60 827	58 744	62 361	63 800	65 704	68 452	69 630	71 152
Taxes less subsidies on production other than										
those on products	KLV8	D.29-D.39	2 812	2 920	3 033	3 103	3 153	3 203	3 260	3 345
Operating surplus and mixed income, gross	KLV7	B.2g+B.3g	54 882	55 598	56 092	57 849	48 057	54 642	53 516	54 770
Gross value added at basic prices	KLV9	B.1g	118 521	117 262	121 486	124 752	116 914	126 297	126 406	129 267
Intermediate consumption at purchasers' prices	KLW2	P.2	131 491	129 242	138 436	138 244	139 433	150 675	154 671	154 589
Total output at basic prices	KLW3	P.1	250 012	246 504	259 922	262 996	256 347	276 972	281 077	283 856
Gross capital formation	KLW4	P.5	8 873	9 940	8 790	9 540	10 471	10 969	11 672	11 648

19.4 **Output and capital formation: by industry[1,2]**
Gross value added at current basic prices

continued

£ million

			2011	2012	2013	2014	2015	2016	2017	2018
Real estate										
Output										
Compensation of employees	KLW5	D.1	11 261	11 868	12 550	12 907	13 827	14 282	14 837	16 356
Taxes less subsidies on production other than		D.29-D.39								
those on products	KLW7		349	387	581	379	177	–94	–351	–541
Operating surplus and mixed income, gross	KLW6	B.2g+B.3g	170 909	187 418	191 282	207 254	221 640	234 062	233 434	242 076
Gross value added at basic prices	KLW8	B.1g	182 519	199 673	204 413	220 540	235 644	248 250	247 920	257 891
Intermediate consumption at purchasers' prices	KLW9	P.2	67 046	64 887	71 830	68 077	67 284	68 490	72 205	65 457
Total output at basic prices	KLX2	P.1	249 565	264 560	276 243	288 617	302 928	316 740	320 125	323 348
Gross capital formation	KLX3	P.5	–1 368	–1 121	–1 479	–2 119	–1 797	–957	154	615
Professional and support										
Output										
Compensation of employees	KLX4	D.1	103 844	108 796	121 145	127 779	133 687	139 458	147 379	154 559
Taxes less subsidies on production other than		D.29-D.39								
those on products	KLX6		2 519	2 548	2 621	2 728	2 514	2 112	3 123	2 682
Operating surplus and mixed income, gross	KLX5	B.2g+B.3g	61 825	63 716	66 889	72 315	80 629	83 807	87 135	90 282
Gross value added at basic prices	KLX7	B.1g	168 188	175 060	190 655	202 822	216 830	225 377	237 637	247 523
Intermediate consumption at purchasers' prices	KLX8	P.2	126 702	131 644	139 869	145 199	152 928	158 801	174 476	184 424
Total output at basic prices	KLX9	P.1	294 890	306 704	330 524	348 021	369 758	384 178	412 113	431 947
Gross capital formation	KLY2	P.5	22 195	20 282	20 742	21 926	26 553	27 880	29 631	29 048
Government, health and education										
Output										
Compensation of employees	KLY3	D.1	225 059	229 149	229 383	234 826	239 416	248 351	255 646	264 562
Taxes less subsidies on production other than those on products	KLY5	D.29-D.39	557	644	701	805	810	692	965	1 080
Operating surplus and mixed income, gross	KLY4	B.2g+B.3g	63 344	65 852	67 575	69 948	73 700	75 640	78 479	80 479
Gross value added at basic prices	KLY6	B.1g	288 960	295 645	297 659	305 579	313 926	324 683	335 090	346 121
Intermediate consumption at purchasers' prices	KLY7	P.2	175 113	180 390	189 435	197 991	198 575	198 608	200 916	210 557
Total output at basic prices	KLY8	P.1	464 073	476 035	487 094	503 570	512 501	523 291	536 006	556 678
Gross capital formation	KLY9	P.5	40 234	39 156	40 478	43 188	44 831	45 729	49 868	50 805

19.4 Output and capital formation: by industry[1,2]
Gross value added at current basic prices

£ million

			2011	2012	2013	2014	2015	2016	2017	2018
Other services											
Output											
Compensation of employees	KLZ2	D.1	28 230	28 880	30 659	31 311	32 108	34 960	36 227	38 493
Taxes less subsidies on production other		D.29-D.39								
than those on products	KLZ4		1 033	1 096	1 135	1 063	1 037	1 071	1 185	1 195
Operating surplus and mixed income, gross	KLZ3	B.2g+B.3g	19 939	20 342	22 353	24 645	26 803	26 909	29 598	30 816
Gross value added at basic prices	KLZ5	B.1g	49 202	50 318	54 147	57 019	59 948	62 940	67 010	70 504
Intermediate consumption at purchasers' prices	KLZ6	P.2	30 700	33 361	33 255	33 831	34 160	35 702	36 182	36 502
Total output at basic prices	KLZ7	P.1	79 902	83 679	87 402	90 850	94 108	98 642	103 192	107 006
Gross capital formation	KLZ8	P.5	5 147	5 339	6 289	6 091	6 244	6 937	8 043	8 199
Not allocated to industries											
Gross capital formation[3]	KN28	P.5	71 556	72 425	85 386	88 931	92 851	98 785	107 860	117 403
All industries											
Output											
Compensation of employees	HAEA	D.1	827 698	843 093	880 999	903 674	929 699	966 821	1 006 970	1 048 243
Taxes less subsidies on production other		D.29-D.39								
than those on products	KN22		22 103	23 981	25 635	26 087	26 114	24 745	26 551	27 044
Operating surplus, gross	ABNF	B.2g	528 796	555 161	569 709	611 534	630 320	655 755	674 866	693 900
Mixed income, gross	QWLT	B.3g	103 277	107 430	112 452	119 938	125 939	130 045	135 623	141 059
Statistical discrepancy between income and GDP	RVFC	di	–	–	–	–	–	–	–	–
Gross value added at basic prices	ABML	B.1g	1 481 874	1 529 665	1 588 795	1 661 233	1 712 072	1 777 366	1 844 010	1 910 247
Intermediate consumption at purchasers' prices	KN25	P.2	1 397 551	1 429 915	1 496 080	1 526 432	1 546 224	1 592 054	1 669 328	1 738 219
Total output at basic prices	KN26	P.1	2 879 425	2 959 580	3 084 875	3 187 665	3 258 296	3 369 420	3 513 338	3 648 466
Gross capital formation											
Gross fixed capital formation	NPQX	P.51g	258 901	268 984	284 080	309 788	330 807	353 218	372 333	381 249
Changes in inventories	ABMP	P.52	2 657	4 020	3 509	14 164	9 357	2 772	3 478	–756
Acquisitions less disposals of valuables[4]	NPJO	P.53	–41	–483	4 894	–192	–347	–102	1 155	2 674
Total gross capital formation	NQFM	P.5	261 517	272 521	292 483	323 760	339 817	355 888	376 966	383 167

1 The contribution of each industry to the gross domestic product before providing for consumption of fixed capital.
2 Components may not sum to totals due to rounding.
3 Gross fixed capital formation of dwellings and costs associated with the transfer of non-produced assets and acquisitions less disposals of valuables.
4 Acquisitions less disposals of valuables can be a volatile series but any volatility is likely to be GDP neutral as it is offset in UK trade figures.

Source: Office for National Statistics, Blue Book 2020

19.5 Gross value added at basic prices: by industry[1,2,3]
Chained volume indices

		Weight per 1000[1]		2012	2013	2014	2015	2016	2017	2018	2019
		2018									
Agriculture	A	6.4	L2KL	90.4	91.0	103.4	103.4	97.2	103.4	100.0	106.3
Production and construction	B-F										
Production	B-E										
Mining and quarrying	B	11.2	L2KR	100.6	95.1	94.4	96.5	94.3	95.0	100.0	99.2
Manufacturing	C										
Food products, beverages and tobacco	CA	15.7	KN3D	94.3	92.7	96.2	96.2	96.4	98.2	100.0	101.4
Textiles, wearing apparel and leather products	CB	3.6	KN3E	113.4	107.8	105.2	104.4	102.2	101.8	100.0	100.0
Wood, paper products and printing	CC	6.5	KN3F	97.8	100.1	101.0	101.6	100.3	101.1	100.0	100.9
Coke and refined petroleum products	CD	1.5	KN3G	113.8	112.0	102.3	104.2	103.2	104.3	100.0	102.8
Chemicals and chemical products	CE	5.9	KN3H	98.2	97.3	98.7	103.0	96.6	98.7	100.0	99.3
Basic pharmaceutical products and preparations	CF	6.7	KN3I	106.1	103.3	96.9	96.5	99.3	97.9	100.0	106.8
Rubber, plastic and other non-metallic mineral products	CG	7.1	KN3J	93.2	90.2	98.8	100.1	102.5	101.7	100.0	97.2
Basic metals and metal products	CH	10.5	KN3K	102.9	100.9	103.6	103.1	99.8	100.4	100.0	97.7
Computer, electronic and optical products	CI	7.1	KN3L	86.1	84.0	87.2	84.7	83.9	87.8	100.0	98.3
Electrical equipment	CJ	2.5	KN3M	116.2	110.6	106.9	106.9	102.3	105.3	100.0	98.8
Machinery and equipment n.e.c.	CK	8.4	KN3N	115.5	101.6	106.0	92.3	91.6	97.7	100.0	92.7
Transport equipment	CL	15.3	KN3O	80.2	86.0	89.5	93.5	97.6	100.7	100.0	94.6
Other manufacturing and repair	CM	9.5	KN3P	81.6	84.8	89.8	88.7	92.9	98.7	100.0	95.9
Total manufacturing	C	100.6	L2KX	95.2	94.2	96.8	96.4	96.6	98.9	100.0	98.3
Electricity, gas, steam and air conditioning supply	D	14.2	L2MW	102.7	102.1	97.6	99.7	103.3	101.2	100.0	101.0
Water supply, sewerage, waste mgmt and remediation	E	12.7	L2N2	86.7	90.2	90.6	93.3	99.2	101.5	100.0	99.8
Total production	B - E	138.7	L2KQ	95.6	94.6	96.0	96.3	97.3	99.1	100.0	98.8
Construction	F	64.5	L2N8	78.1	79.4	87.2	90.6	94.2	100.0	100.0	101.8
Total production and construction	B - F	203.2	L2KP	90.0	89.7	93.2	94.4	96.3	99.4	100.0	99.8

1 The weights shown are in proportion to total gross value added (GVA) in 2016 and are used to combine the industry output indices to calculate the totals. For 2015 and earlier, totals are calculated using the equivalent weights for the previous year (e.g. totals for 2009 use 2008 weights). Weights may not sum to totals due to rounding.

2 As GVA is expressed in index number form, it is inappropriate to show as a statistical adjustment any divergence from the other measures of GDP. Such an adjustment does, however, exist implicitly.

3 Because of differences in the annual and monthly production inquiries, estimates of current price output and gross value added by industry derived from the current price Input-Output Supply and Use Tables are not consistent with the equivalent measures of chained volume measures growth given in 2.3. These differences do not affect GDP totals.

19.5 Gross value added at basic prices: by industry[1,2,3]
Chained volume indices
continued

			Weight per 1000[1]		2012	2013	2014	2015	2016	2017	2018	2019
			2018									
Services	G-T											
Distribution, transport, hotels and restaurants	G-I											
Wholesale, retail, repair of motor vehicles and m/cycles	G	104.5	L2NE	80.9	85.2	88.8	91.9	95.1	97.0	100.0	102.5
Transportation and storage	H	40.4	L2NI	92.3	93.8	98.2	99.2	97.6	98.5	100.0	101.6
Accommodation and food service activities	I	29.4	L2NQ	90.8	89.3	91.3	95.9	97.1	98.6	100.0	102.4
Total distribution, transport, hotels and restaurants	G - I	174.3	L2ND	84.9	87.8	91.2	94.1	96.0	97.6	100.0	102.3
Information and communication	J										
Publishing, audiovisual and broadcasting activities	JA	16.9	L2NU	81.4	86.5	83.0	90.3	96.6	100.6	100.0	108.4
Telecommunications	JB	17.9	L2NZ	107.7	103.4	98.0	101.8	97.4	97.4	100.0	100.6
IT and other information service activities	JC	30.8	L2O3	63.8	68.6	73.5	78.0	85.7	92.0	100.0	110.5
Total information and communication	J	65.7	L2NT	78.9	81.9	82.2	87.3	91.6	95.6	100.0	107.3
Financial and insurance	K	67.7	L2O6	104.7	104.2	101.4	96.5	100.6	100.9	100.0	97.1
Real estate	L	135.0	L2OC	91.0	94.1	96.8	100.2	101.7	100.7	100.0	100.6
Professional and support	M-N										
Professional, scientific and technical activities	M										
Legal, accounting, management, architect, engineering etc	MA	52.6	L2OJ	74.6	80.8	84.9	89.6	92.4	95.8	100.0	100.8
Scientific research and development	MB	6.9	L2OQ	73.1	77.7	81.0	88.5	95.1	100.0	100.0	109.9
Other professional, scientific and technical activities	MC	17.3	L2OS	83.0	85.2	88.6	90.9	91.6	94.0	100.0	103.1
Total professional, scientific and technical activities	M	76.9	L2OI	76.1	81.4	85.3	89.7	92.4	95.8	100.0	102.1
Administrative and support service activities	N	52.7	L2OX	74.6	79.9	87.3	91.9	93.0	96.6	100.0	102.5
Total professional and support	M - N	129.6	L2OH	75.5	80.8	86.1	90.6	92.7	96.1	100.0	102.3
Government, health and education	O-Q										
Public admin, defence, compulsory social security	O	49.1	L2P8	107.3	106.0	103.3	101.4	99.3	99.3	100.0	102.0
Education	P	56.8	L2PA	97.6	98.9	99.6	100.6	99.3	99.8	100.0	103.1
Human health and social work activities	Q										
Human health activities	QA	51.5	L2PD	86.2	89.2	92.5	94.9	97.3	98.6	100.0	101.0
Residential care and social work activities	QB	23.8	L2PF	98.1	99.8	100.2	101.7	100.7	101.1	100.0	100.9
Total human health and social work activities	Q	75.3	L2PC	89.7	92.3	94.8	96.9	98.3	99.4	100.0	101.0
Total government, health and education	O - Q	181.2	L2P7	96.8	98.0	98.6	99.3	98.9	99.5	100.0	101.9
Other services	R-T										
Arts, entertainment and recreation	R	16.1	L2PJ	96.4	95.1	98.9	100.4	98.4	101.0	100.0	101.8
Other service activities	S	17.8	L2PP	88.3	90.1	99.4	103.8	97.3	97.4	100.0	99.1
Activities of households as employers, undiff. Goods	T	3.0	L2PT	78.8	82.4	79.1	80.5	95.7	95.5	100.0	101.6
Total other services	R - T	36.9	L2PI	90.8	91.4	97.3	100.2	97.7	98.8	100.0	100.5
Total service industries	G - T	790.4	L2NC	88.4	91.0	93.3	95.6	97.1	98.5	100.0	101.8
All industries	B.1g	1 000.0	CGCE	88.7	90.7	93.4	95.4	97.0	98.7	100.0	101.4

1 The weights shown are in proportion to total gross value added (GVA) in 2016 and are used to combine the industry output indices to calculate the totals. For 2015 and earlier, totals are calculated using the equivalent weights for the previous year (e.g. totals for 2009 use 2008 weights). Weights may not sum to totals due to rounding.

Source: Office for National Statistics, Blue Book 2020

2 As GVA is expressed in index number form, it is inappropriate to show as a statistical adjustment any divergence from the other measures of GDP. Such an adjustment does, however, exist implicitly.

3 Because of differences in the annual and monthly production inquiries, estimates of current price output and gross value added by industry derived from the current price Input-Output Supply and Use Tables are not consistent with the equivalent measures of chained volume measures growth given in 2.3. These differences do not affect GDP totals.

19.6 Non-financial corporations
ESA 2010 sector S.11

£ million

			2012	2013	2014	2015	2016	2017	2018	2019
Allocation of primary income account		II.1.2								
Resources										
Operating surplus, gross	NQBE	B.2g	313 215	323 518	349 613	365 778	372 170	390 886	399 663	407 151
Property income, received		D.4								
Interest		D.41								
Interest before FISIM allocation[1]	J4WQ	D.41g	8 932	9 573	9 367	8 984	9 974	15 767	13 524	14 394
plus FISIM[1]	IV89	P.119	3 585	3 118	4 872	5 566	5 753	5 213	6 559	5 539
Total	EABC	D.41	12 517	12 691	14 239	14 550	15 727	20 980	20 083	19 933
Distributed income of corporations	EABD	D.42	53 319	55 287	75 033	52 998	54 997	48 970	64 529	113 991
Reinvested earnings on foreign direct investment	WEYD	D.43	11 717	6 982	−19 005	−9 895	−10 223	18 860	16 864	−44 325
Other investment income		D.44								
Attributable to insurance policy holders	L8GM	D.441	219	280	331	153	148	134	156	129
Attributable to collective investment fund shareholders		D.443								
Dividends	L8H9	D.4431	−	4	4	4	4	4	4	4
Retained earnings	L8HG	D.4432	4	4	4	4	4	8	8	8
Total	L8H2	D.443	4	8	8	8	8	12	12	12
Total other investment income	FAOF	D.44	223	288	339	161	156	146	168	141
Rent	FAOG	D.45	131	135	140	139	141	147	154	180
Total	FAKY	D.4	77 907	75 383	70 746	57 953	60 798	89 103	101 798	89 920
Total resources	FBXJ	TR	391 122	398 901	420 359	423 731	432 968	479 989	501 461	497 071
Uses										
Property income, paid		D.4								
Interest		D.41								
Interest before FISIM allocation[1]	J4WS	D.41g	41 249	41 878	40 412	36 703	37 814	36 727	39 673	40 110
less FISIM[1]	IV88	P.119	7 968	7 980	6 355	5 938	6 749	8 188	7 998	9 482
Total	EABG	D.41	33 281	33 898	34 057	30 765	31 065	28 539	31 675	30 628
Distributed income of corporations	NVCS	D.42	160 193	171 354	179 172	207 356	187 759	202 146	226 391	218 135
Of which: PNFCs dividends[2]	NETZ	D.421	132 584	141 979	148 258	177 241	157 964	171 115	194 411	185 851
Reinvested earnings on foreign direct investment	HDVB	D.43	−5 363	5 263	−1 055	−3 583	472	−3 663	804	3 086
Rent	FBXO	D.45	1 557	1 706	1 715	1 713	1 734	1 762	1 759	1 804
Total	FBXK	D.4	189 668	212 221	213 889	236 251	221 030	228 784	260 629	253 653
Balance of primary incomes, gross	**NQBG**	**B.5g**	**201 454**	**186 680**	**206 470**	**187 480**	**211 938**	**251 205**	**240 832**	**243 418**
Total uses	FBXJ	TU	391 122	398 901	420 359	423 731	432 968	479 989	501 461	497 071
less consumption of fixed capital	DBGF	P.51c	137 794	140 667	144 158	150 048	158 255	168 518	175 278	182 694
Balance of primary incomes, net	FBXQ	B.5n	63 660	46 013	62 312	37 432	53 683	82 687	65 554	60 724

1 Financial intermediation services indirectly measured.

Source: Office for National Statistics, Blue Book 2020

19.7 Non-financial corporations
ESA 2010 sector S.11

£ million

			2012	2013	2014	2015	2016	2017	2018	2019
Secondary distribution of income account		**II.2**								
Resources										
Balance of primary incomes, gross	NQBG	**B.5g**	**201 454**	**186 680**	**206 470**	**187 480**	**211 938**	**251 205**	**240 832**	**243 418**
Net social contributions		D.61								
Employers' imputed social contributions	L8RD	D.612	3 804	4 442	4 045	3 892	4 282	3 810	4 108	5 116
Total	L8TP	D.61	3 804	4 442	4 045	3 892	4 282	3 810	4 108	5 116
Current transfers other than taxes, social contributions and benefits		D.7								
Non-life insurance claims	FCBP	D.72	3 523	6 458	5 700	4 923	5 615	5 970	6 633	6 438
Miscellaneous current transfers	CY8C	D.75	724	136	–	–	–	–	–	–
Total	NRJB	D.7	4 247	6 594	5 700	4 923	5 615	5 970	6 633	6 438
Total resources	FCBR	TR	209 505	197 716	216 215	196 295	221 835	260 985	251 573	254 972
Uses										
Current taxes on income, wealth etc.		D.5								
Taxes on income	FCBS	D.51	38 998	38 625	38 338	38 192	41 702	43 936	45 682	43 563
Social benefits other than social transfers in kind		D.62								
Other social insurance benefits	L8S3	D.622	3 804	4 442	4 045	3 892	4 282	3 810	4 108	5 116
Total	L8TD	D.62	3 804	4 442	4 045	3 892	4 282	3 810	4 108	5 116
Current transfers other than taxes, social contributions and benefits		D.7								
Net non-life insurance premiums	FCBY	D.71	3 523	6 458	5 700	4 923	5 615	5 970	6 633	6 438
Miscellaneous current transfers	CY8B	D.75	5 033	5 046	5 713	5 058	4 916	5 661	4 659	4 654
Total	FCBX	D.7	8 556	11 504	11 413	9 981	10 531	11 631	11 292	11 092
Disposable income, gross	NRJD	**B.6g**	**158 147**	**143 145**	**162 419**	**144 230**	**165 320**	**201 608**	**190 491**	**195 201**
Total uses	FCBR	TU	209 505	197 716	216 215	196 295	221 835	260 985	251 573	254 972
less consumption of fixed capital	DBGF	P.51c	137 794	140 667	144 158	150 048	158 255	168 518	175 278	182 694
Disposable income, net	FCCF	B.6n	20 353	2 478	18 261	−5 818	7 065	33 090	15 213	12 507

Source: Office for National Statistics, Blue Book 2020

19.8 Private non-financial corporations
ESA 2010 sectors S.11002 and S.11003 [1]

£ million

			2012	2013	2014	2015	2016	2017	2018	2019
Allocation of primary income account **before deduction of fixed capital consumption**		II.1.2								
Resources										
Operating surplus, gross	NRJK	B.2g	297 453	307 105	333 104	348 382	354 390	374 140	388 598	395 799
Property income, received		D.4								
Interest		D.41								
Interest before FISIM allocation[2]	I69R	D.41g	8 492	9 156	8 936	8 570	9 533	15 362	13 340	14 242
plus FISIM[2]	IV87	P.119	3 574	3 105	4 842	5 542	5 739	5 209	6 545	5 515
Total	DSZR	D.41	12 066	12 261	13 778	14 112	15 272	20 571	19 885	19 757
Distributed income of corporations	DSZS	D.42	53 188	55 105	74 721	52 609	54 624	48 641	64 434	113 897
Reinvested earnings on foreign direct investment	HDVR	D.43	11 656	6 911	−19 122	−9 958	−10 288	18 796	16 800	−44 389
Other investment income		D.44								
Attributable to insurance policy holders	KZI4	D.441	219	280	331	153	148	134	156	129
Attributable to collective investment fund shares		D.443								
Dividends	KZI6	D.4431	–	4	4	4	4	4	4	4
Retained earnings	KZI7	D.4432	4	4	4	4	4	8	8	8
Total	L5U6	D.443	4	8	8	8	8	12	12	12
Total	FCFP	D.44	223	288	339	161	156	146	168	141
Rent	FAOL	D.45	131	135	140	139	141	147	154	180
Total	FACV	D.4	77 264	74 700	69 856	57 063	59 905	88 301	101 441	89 586
Total resources	FCFQ	TR	374 717	381 805	402 960	405 445	414 295	462 441	490 039	485 385
Uses										
Property income, paid		D.4								
Interest		D.41								
Interest before FISIM allocation[2]	I6A2	D.41g	37 466	37 703	36 151	31 949	32 962	32 207	38 257	38 901
less FISIM[2]	IV86	P.119	7 944	7 967	6 347	5 931	6 732	8 172	7 985	9 477
Total	DSZV	D.41	29 522	29 736	29 804	26 018	26 230	24 035	30 272	29 424
Distributed income of corporations	NVDC	D.42	158 941	170 074	178 224	206 473	186 927	201 338	225 583	217 503
Of which: dividend payments	NETZ	D.421	132 584	141 979	148 258	177 241	157 964	171 115	194 411	185 851
Reinvested earnings on foreign direct investment	HDVB	D.43	−5 363	5 263	−1 055	−3 583	472	−3 663	804	3 086
Rent	FCFU	D.45	1 557	1 706	1 715	1 713	1 734	1 762	1 759	1 804
Total	FCFR	D.4	184 657	206 779	208 688	230 621	215 363	223 472	258 418	251 817
Balance of primary incomes, gross	NRJM	**B.5g**	**190 060**	**175 026**	**194 272**	**174 824**	**198 932**	**238 969**	**231 621**	**233 568**
Total uses	FCFQ	TU	374 717	381 805	402 960	405 445	414 295	462 441	490 039	485 385
less consumption of fixed capital	NSRK	P.51c	129 206	132 271	136 003	142 074	150 359	160 851	168 467	176 024
Balance of primary incomes, net	FCFW	B.5n	60 854	42 755	58 269	32 750	48 573	78 118	63 154	57 544

1 S.11002 National controlled and S.11003 Foreign controlled
2 Financial intermediation services indirectly measured

Source: Office for National Statistics, Blue Book 2020

19.9 Private non-financial corporations
ESA 2010 sectors S.11002 and S.11003[1]

£ million

			2012	2013	2014	2015	2016	2017	2018	2019
Secondary distribution of income account		**II.2**								
Resources										
Balance of primary incomes, gross	NRJM	**B.5g**	**190 060**	**175 026**	**194 272**	**174 824**	**198 932**	**238 969**	**231 621**	**233 568**
Net social contributions		D.61								
Employers' imputed social contributions	L8RJ	D.612	3 682	4 336	3 977	3 825	4 212	3 748	4 043	5 035
Total	L8TV	D.61	3 682	4 336	3 977	3 825	4 212	3 748	4 043	5 035
Other current transfers		D.7								
non-life insurance claims	FDBA	D.72	3 523	6 458	5 700	4 923	5 615	5 970	6 633	6 438
Total resources	FDBC	TR	197 265	185 820	203 949	183 572	208 759	248 687	242 297	245 041
Uses										
Current taxes on income, wealth etc.		D.5								
Taxes on income	FCCP	D.51	38 916	38 568	38 320	38 131	41 623	43 861	45 583	43 502
Social security benefits other than social transfers in kind		D.62								
Other social insurance benefits	L8S9	D.622	3 682	4 336	3 977	3 825	4 212	3 748	4 043	5 035
Total	L8TH	D.62	3 682	4 336	3 977	3 825	4 212	3 748	4 043	5 035
Current transfers other than taxes, social contributions and benefits		D.7								
Net non-life insurance premiums	FDBH	D.71	3 523	6 458	5 700	4 923	5 615	5 970	6 633	6 438
Miscellaneous current transfers	CY88	D.75	5 033	5 046	5 713	5 058	4 916	5 661	4 659	4 654
Total	FCCN	D.7	8 556	11 504	11 413	9 981	10 531	11 631	11 292	11 092
Disposable income, gross	NRJQ	**B.6g**	**146 111**	**131 412**	**150 239**	**131 635**	**152 393**	**189 447**	**181 379**	**185 412**
Total uses	FDBC	TU	197 265	185 820	203 949	183 572	208 759	248 687	242 297	245 041
less consumption of fixed capital	NSRK	P.51c	129 206	132 271	136 003	142 074	150 359	160 851	168 467	176 024
Disposable income, net	FDBK	B.6n	16 905	−859	14 236	−10 439	2 034	28 596	12 912	9 388

1 S.11002 National controlled and S.11003 Foreign controlled

Source: Office for National Statistics, Blue Book 2020

19.10 Households and non-profit institutions serving households
ESA 2010 sectors S.14 and S.15

£ million

			2012	2013	2014	2015	2016	2017	2018	2019
Allocation of primary income account before deduction of fixed capital consumption		II.1.2								
Resources										
Gross operating surplus and gross mixed income		B.2g+B.3g								
Operating surplus, gross	QWLS	B.2g	151 174	153 759	166 196	177 511	188 675	188 815	196 848	201 183
Mixed income, gross	QWLT	B.3g	107 430	112 452	119 938	125 939	130 045	135 623	141 059	147 822
Total	RVGJ	B.2g+B.3g	258 604	266 211	286 134	303 450	318 720	324 438	337 907	349 005
Compensation of employees		D.1								
Wages and salaries	QWLW	D.11	689 315	721 347	749 095	774 393	801 648	830 184	866 584	897 084
Employers' social contributions	QWLX	D.12	153 630	159 326	154 110	155 217	164 813	176 476	181 274	198 569
Total	QWLY	D.1	842 945	880 673	903 205	929 610	966 461	1 006 660	1 047 858	1 095 653
Property income, received	•	D.4								
Interest		D.41								
Interest before FISIM[1] allocation	J4WY	D.41g	21 948	19 698	15 875	14 573	13 442	10 537	12 141	12 904
plus FISIM	IV8W	P.119	216	−607	8 408	10 622	11 199	9 089	14 038	10 899
Total	QWLZ	D.41	22 164	19 091	24 283	25 195	24 641	19 626	26 179	23 803
Distributed income of corporations		D.42								
Dividends	CRWE	D.421	43 048	52 191	54 909	81 488	67 881	68 139	80 311	85 482
Withdrawals from the income of quasi-corporations	CRWG	D.422	27 225	29 408	31 334	30 777	36 323	36 466	39 461	41 035
Earnings on property investment	CRWI	D.423	812	817	778	751	883	911	929	846
Total	QWMA	D.42	71 085	82 416	87 021	113 016	105 087	105 516	120 701	127 363
Other investment income		D.44								
Attributable to insurance policy holders	L8GL	D.441	21 982	21 670	19 989	23 874	22 841	21 137	21 668	22 622
Payable on pension entitlements	L8GS	D.442	65 766	63 260	79 242	72 391	74 296	64 217	62 815	55 093
Attributable to collective investment fund shareholders		D.443								
Dividends	L8H8	D.4431	956	974	1 011	1 089	1 196	1 384	1 514	1 656
Retained earnings	L8HF	D.4432	1 499	1 527	1 580	1 703	1 872	2 166	2 367	2 586
Total	L8GZ	D.443	2 455	2 501	2 591	2 792	3 068	3 550	3 881	4 242
Total	QWMC	D.44	90 203	87 431	101 822	99 057	100 205	88 904	88 364	81 957
Rent	QWMD	D.45	95	121	133	146	173	182	197	200
Total	QWME	D.4	183 547	189 059	213 259	237 414	230 106	214 228	235 441	233 323
Total resources	QWMF	TR	1 285 096	1 335 943	1 402 598	1 470 474	1 515 287	1 545 326	1 621 206	1 677 981
Uses										
Property income, paid		D.4								
Interest		D.41								
Interest before FISIM allocation	J4WZ	D.41g	61 548	61 221	59 936	57 768	57 699	55 998	57 250	58 159
less FISIM	IV8X	P.119	35 930	38 583	31 758	29 558	28 912	31 966	26 533	29 704
Interest	QWMG	D.41	25 618	22 638	28 178	28 210	28 787	24 032	30 717	28 455
Rent	QWMH	D.45	19	18	17	17	32	26	23	8
Total	QWMI	D.4	25 637	22 656	28 195	28 227	28 819	24 058	30 740	28 463
Balance of primary incomes, gross	QWMJ	B.5g	1 259 459	1 313 287	1 374 403	1 442 247	1 486 468	1 521 268	1 590 466	1 649 518
Total uses	QWMF	TU	1 285 096	1 335 943	1 402 598	1 470 474	1 515 287	1 545 326	1 621 206	1 677 981
less consumption of fixed capital	QWLL	P.51c	67 695	70 558	73 648	75 479	77 891	81 125	85 431	88 097
Balance of primary incomes, net	QWMK	B.5n	1 191 764	1 242 729	1 300 755	1 366 768	1 408 577	1 440 143	1 505 035	1 561 421
Sector share of gross national income	RVGG		74.4	75.3	75.3	76.9	76.4	74.5	75.3	75.8

1 Financial intermediation services indirectly measured

Source: Office for National Statistics, Blue Book 2020

19.11 Households and non-profit institutions serving households
ESA 2010 sectors S.14 and S.15

£ million

			2012	2013	2014	2015	2016	2017	2018	2019
Secondary distribution of income account		II.2								
Resources										
Balance of primary incomes, gross	QWMJ	B.5g	1 259 459	1 313 287	1 374 403	1 442 247	1 486 468	1 521 268	1 590 466	1 649 518
Net social contributions		D.61								
Employers' imputed social contributions	L8RF	D.612	302	342	332	322	343	299	331	329
Total	L8TR	D.61	302	342	332	322	343	299	331	329
Social benefits other than social transfers in kind		D.62								
Social security benefits in cash	L8QF	D.621	89 187	91 231	93 650	96 462	98 992	100 996	103 892	105 406
Other social insurance benefits	L8QT	D.622	115 306	118 585	116 875	124 552	127 384	134 126	141 919	148 217
Social assistance benefits in cash	MT3B	D.623R	118 918	119 642	120 610	121 462	120 963	120 427	122 144	124 672
Total	QWML	D.62	323 411	329 458	331 135	342 476	347 339	355 549	367 955	378 295
Other current transfers		D.7								
Non-life insurance claims	QWMM	D.72	30 112	32 375	28 017	28 626	27 909	29 403	30 445	29 572
Miscellaneous current transfers	QWMN	D.75	52 880	49 410	48 986	48 055	47 625	47 578	48 959	49 630
Total	QWMO	D.7	82 992	81 785	77 003	76 681	75 534	76 981	79 404	79 202
Total resources	QWMP	TR	1 666 164	1 724 872	1 782 873	1 861 726	1 909 684	1 954 097	2 038 156	2 107 344
Uses										
Current taxes on income, wealth, etc		D.5								
Taxes on income	QWMQ	D.51	153 730	158 986	162 609	171 392	178 961	187 783	194 691	203 223
Of which:										
Taxes on employment	DBBO	D.511pt	128 622	131 084	136 201	141 848	145 758	150 504	157 651	162 930
Taxes on self-employment and other	ZAFG	D.511pt	20 840	24 126	22 668	24 016	26 295	29 014	29 378	31 265
Other current taxes	NVCO	D.59	34 658	35 752	36 542	37 166	38 679	40 578	43 430	45 696
Total	QWMS	D.5	188 388	194 738	199 151	208 558	217 640	228 361	238 121	248 919
Net social contributions		D.61								
Employers' actual social contributions	L8NJ	D.611	135 669	140 067	136 184	137 516	146 531	158 051	161 424	175 998
Employers' imputed social contributions	M9X2	D.612	17 961	19 259	17 926	17 701	18 282	18 425	19 850	22 571
Households' actual social contributions	L8PR	D.613	61 714	64 492	68 053	68 731	70 954	73 558	78 811	86 273
Households' social contribution supplements	L8Q7	D.614	65 766	63 260	79 242	72 391	74 296	64 217	62 815	55 093
Social insurance scheme service charge	L8LT	D.61SC	−16 464	−17 625	−18 213	−19 108	−19 983	−22 069	−23 591	−24 407
Total	QWMY	D.61	264 646	269 453	283 192	277 231	290 080	292 182	299 309	315 528
Social benefits other than social transfers in kind		D.62								
Other social insurance benefits	L8S5	D.622	302	342	332	322	343	299	331	329
Total	QWMZ	D.62	302	342	332	322	343	299	331	329
Other current transfers		D.7								
Net non-life insurance premiums	QWNA	D.71	30 112	32 375	28 017	28 626	27 909	29 403	30 445	29 572
Miscellaneous current transfers	QWNB	D.75	20 464	21 768	24 382	24 861	26 095	27 609	28 781	30 061
Total	QWNC	D.7	50 576	54 143	52 399	53 487	54 004	57 012	59 226	59 633
Disposable income, gross	QWND	B.6g	1 162 252	1 206 196	1 247 799	1 322 128	1 347 617	1 376 243	1 441 169	1 482 935
Total uses	QWMP	TU	1 666 164	1 724 872	1 782 873	1 861 726	1 909 684	1 954 097	2 038 156	2 107 344
Real households' & NPISH expenditure implied deflator (reference year 2016)	CRXB		91.4	93.1	94.5	94.4	95.7	97.7	100.0	101.4
Real households' & NPISH disposable income: (Chained volume measures)										
£ Million (reference year 2016)[1]	RVGK		1 271 089	1 295 521	1 320 959	1 400 314	1 408 046	1 409 060	1 441 169	1 462 879
Index (2016=100)	OSXR		88.2	89.9	91.7	97.2	97.7	97.8	100.0	101.5

1 Gross household disposable income deflated by the households and NPISH final consumption deflator

Source: Office for National Statistics, Blue Book 2020

19.12 Households and non-profit institutions serving households
ESA 2010 sectors S.14 and S.15

£ million

			2012	2013	2014	2015	2016	2017	2018	2019
Use of income account		II.4								
Use of disposable income account		II.4.1								
Resources										
Disposable income, gross	QWND	B.6g	1 162 252	1 206 196	1 247 799	1 322 128	1 347 617	1 376 243	1 441 169	1 482 935
Adjustment for the change in pension entitlements	NSSE	D.8	54 796	55 022	68 803	49 826	52 188	38 767	34 748	32 643
Total resources	NSSF	TR	1 217 048	1 261 218	1 316 602	1 371 954	1 399 805	1 415 010	1 475 917	1 515 578
Uses										
Final consumption expenditure		P.3								
Individual consumption expenditure	NSSG	P.31	1 103 991	1 153 762	1 197 982	1 233 446	1 292 950	1 334 396	1 385 691	1 416 877
Gross saving	NSSH	B.8g	**113 057**	**107 456**	**118 620**	**138 508**	**106 855**	**80 614**	**90 226**	**98 701**
Total uses	NSSF	TU	1 217 048	1 261 218	1 316 602	1 371 954	1 399 805	1 415 010	1 475 917	1 515 578
less consumption of fixed capital	QWLL	P.51c	67 695	70 558	73 648	75 479	77 891	81 125	85 431	88 097
Saving, net	NSSI	B.8n	45 362	36 898	44 972	63 029	28 964	−511	4 795	10 604
Use of adjusted disposable income account		II.4.2								
Resources										
Adjusted disposable income, gross	NSSD	B.7g	1 386 918	1 435 568	1 486 230	1 563 936	1 596 028	1 629 149	1 700 904	1 757 066
Adjustment for the change in pension entitlements	NSSE	D.8	54 796	55 022	68 803	49 826	52 188	38 767	34 748	32 643
Total resources	NSSJ	TR	1 441 714	1 490 590	1 555 033	1 613 762	1 648 216	1 667 916	1 735 652	1 789 709
Uses										
Actual final consumption		P.4								
Actual individual consumption	ABRE	P.41	1 328 657	1 383 134	1 436 413	1 475 254	1 541 361	1 587 302	1 645 426	1 691 008
Gross saving	NSSH	B.8g	**113 057**	**107 456**	**118 620**	**138 508**	**106 855**	**80 614**	**90 226**	**98 701**
Total uses	NSSJ	TU	1 441 714	1 490 590	1 555 033	1 613 762	1 648 216	1 667 916	1 735 652	1 789 709
Households & NPISH saving ratio (per cent)	RVGL		9.3	8.5	9.0	10.1	7.6	5.7	6.1	6.5

Source: Office for National Statistics, Blue Book 2020

19.13 The sector accounts: Key economic indicators

£ million

			2012	2013	2014	2015	2016	2017	2018	2019
Net lending(+)/borrowing(-) by:										
Non-financial corporations										
Public	CPCM		7	197	−2 305	−1 233	−2 122	−4 078	−1 006	−261
Private	DTAL		4 142	−23 222	−22 954	−51 870	−39 511	−6 307	−22 076	−31 074
Total	EABO	B.9	4 149	−23 025	−25 259	−53 103	−41 633	−10 385	−23 082	−31 335
Financial corporations	NHCQ	B.9	13 880	−11 232	−14 989	−25 791	−33 815	−15 522	−14 569	−22 548
General government										
Central	NMFJ		−131 598	−95 777	−105 029	−86 064	−58 713	−41 368	−40 935	−42 808
Local	NMOE		−7 654	−2 305	1 836	−1 607	−7 017	−8 867	−6 948	−9 304
Total	NNBK	B.9	−139 252	−98 082	−103 193	−87 671	−65 730	−50 235	−47 883	−52 112
Households and NPISH[1]										
Households	A99R		58 546	44 937	52 777	70 299	32 326	887	12 538	22 181
NPISH	AA7W		2 217	−869	−2 151	−1 929	−909	−4 274	−9 079	−13 780
Total	NSSZ	B.9	60 763	44 068	50 626	68 370	31 417	−3 387	3 459	8 401
Rest of the world	NHRB	B.9	60 457	88 270	92 815	98 195	109 761	79 529	82 075	96 101
Private non-financial corporations										
Gross trading profits										
Continental shelf profits	CAGD		25 246	23 470	16 702	10 253	9 575	11 079	17 894	12 604
Others	CAED		256 780	267 776	297 741	316 603	332 112	349 644	361 399	364 290
Rental of buildings	DTWR		18 160	18 957	19 669	18 813	18 442	19 208	19 715	20 285
less holding gains of inventories	DLRA		2 733	3 098	1 008	−2 713	5 739	5 791	10 410	1 380
Gross operating surplus	CAER	B.2g	297 453	307 105	333 104	348 382	354 390	374 140	388 598	395 799
Households sector										
Disposable income, gross	HABN	B.6g	1 107 318	1 152 816	1 195 778	1 270 370	1 295 043	1 324 194	1 389 040	1 431 678
Implied deflator of households and NPISH										
Individual consumption expenditure Index (2015=100)[2]	CRXA		91.4	93.0	94.3	94.3	95.6	97.6	100.0	101.4
Real households disposable income:										
Chained volume measures (reference year 2015)	DG2V		1 211 409	1 239 019	1 267 449	1 347 120	1 354 134	1 356 239	1 389 040	1 412 501
Index (2015=100)[2]	DG2Z		87.2	89.2	91.2	97.0	97.5	97.7	100.0	101.7
Gross saving	HADA	B.8g	103 642	98 304	111 230	132 981	99 140	75 683	88 572	99 859
Households total resources	HAYW		1 162 114	1 207 838	1 264 581	1 320 196	1 347 231	1 362 961	1 423 788	1 464 321
Saving ratio (per cent)	DG5H		8.9	8.1	8.8	10.1	7.4	5.5	6.2	6.8

1 Non-profit institutions serving households
2 Rounded to one decimal place

Source: Office for National Statistics, Blue Book 2020

**Household final consumption expenditure: classified by purpose
At current market prices**

£ million

			2012	2013	2014	2015	2016	2017	2018	2019
Final consumption expenditure of households		P.31								
Durable goods										
Furnishings, household equipment and routine maintenance of the house	LLIJ	05	21 496	21 178	22 817	24 179	24 564	26 373	27 820	27 143
Health	LLIK	06	3 104	3 656	3 630	3 632	3 582	3 852	4 297	4 267
Transport	LLIL	07	37 832	42 509	46 807	47 911	51 961	50 012	50 974	53 087
Communication	LLIM	08	959	1 062	813	1 009	1 429	1 422	1 519	1 417
Recreation and culture	LLIN	09	22 605	24 333	24 797	27 637	28 930	32 621	33 446	33 627
Miscellaneous goods and services	LLIO	12	5 585	5 435	6 492	6 870	8 592	7 194	7 556	8 232
Total durable goods	UTIA	D	91 581	98 173	105 356	111 238	119 058	121 474	125 612	127 773
Semi-durable goods										
Clothing and footwear	LLJL	03	52 982	57 264	58 433	61 352	63 607	64 802	66 095	71 725
Furnishings, household equipment and routine maintenance of the house	LLJM	05	16 054	16 995	17 176	18 574	19 912	22 602	22 306	22 172
Transport	LLJN	07	4 449	4 971	5 094	4 886	5 211	5 282	4 938	4 765
Recreation and culture	LLJO	09	26 144	26 752	27 127	28 627	30 259	33 584	36 078	38 799
Miscellaneous goods and services	LLJP	12	6 049	7 452	7 024	7 083	6 740	7 659	7 694	7 780
Total semi-durable goods	UTIQ	SD	105 678	113 434	114 854	120 522	125 729	133 929	137 111	145 241
Non-durable goods										
Food and drink	ABZV	01	89 215	92 080	93 329	91 345	96 721	101 009	104 927	107 492
Alcoholic beverages, tobacco and narcotics	ADFL	02	41 119	42 346	42 121	40 767	40 424	42 223	44 350	43 549
Housing, water, electricity, gas and other fuels	LLIX	04	38 088	40 114	36 801	37 088	37 601	36 427	39 282	39 405
Furnishings, household equipment and routine maintenance of the house	LLIY	05	3 077	2 838	3 003	3 303	3 248	3 312	3 347	3 519
Health	LLIZ	06	6 527	8 537	8 908	8 834	9 333	9 974	10 205	10 716
Transport	LLJA	07	34 888	33 809	32 605	28 511	27 923	31 203	34 786	34 635
Recreation and culture	LLJB	09	16 787	17 651	18 423	18 258	19 952	20 212	21 105	20 877
Miscellaneous goods and services	LLJC	12	13 485	13 640	14 944	16 794	16 951	18 901	19 871	21 086
Total non-durable goods	UTII	ND	243 186	251 015	250 134	244 900	252 153	263 261	277 873	281 279
Total goods	UTIE		440 445	462 622	470 344	476 660	496 940	518 664	540 596	554 293
Services										
Clothing and footwear	LLJD	03	1 076	1 070	1 137	993	1 036	1 121	1 065	1 128
Housing, water, electricity, gas and other fuels	LLJE	04	248 024	258 993	269 969	281 599	295 281	297 310	300 947	307 830
Furnishings, household equipment and routine maintenance of the house	LLJF	05	5 032	5 357	5 584	5 670	6 577	6 740	7 543	7 395
Health	LLJG	06	7 040	7 820	7 960	8 386	9 267	9 916	10 026	10 394
Transport	LLJH	07	69 576	72 839	75 083	77 824	81 377	84 629	92 219	94 125
Communication	LLJI	08	19 169	18 954	19 400	19 509	20 102	20 984	20 815	20 511
Recreation and culture	LLJJ	09	41 237	44 365	47 630	50 576	52 613	53 650	54 604	55 625
Education	ADIE	10	18 428	21 323	23 357	25 898	28 631	29 278	30 889	32 601
Restaurants and hotels	ADIF	11	100 169	105 810	110 667	114 900	119 507	126 914	129 392	133 877
Miscellaneous goods and services	LLJK	12	99 878	103 166	115 486	116 539	122 024	123 432	130 704	129 519
Total services	UTIM	S	609 629	639 697	676 273	701 894	736 415	753 974	778 204	793 005
Final consumption expenditure in the UK by resident and non-resident households (domestic concept)	ABQI	0	1 050 074	1 102 319	1 146 617	1 178 554	1 233 355	1 272 638	1 318 800	1 347 298
Final consumption expenditure outside the UK by UK resident households	ABTA	P.33	33 895	35 895	37 255	40 309	46 949	49 051	49 928	53 655
Final consumption expenditure in the UK by households resident in rest of the world	CDFD	P.34	−25 497	−28 680	−30 521	−31 648	−32 213	−34 411	−33 512	−36 491
Final consumption expenditure by UK resident households in the UK and abroad (national concept)	ABPB	P.31	1 058 472	1 109 534	1 153 351	1 187 215	1 248 091	1 287 278	1 335 216	1 364 462

1 ESA 2010 Classification of Individual Consumption by Purpose (COICOP).

Source: Office for National Statistics, Blue Book 2020

**Household final consumption expenditure: classified by purpose
Chained volume measures (reference year 2016)**

£ million

			2012	2013	2014	2015	2016	2017	2018	2019
Final consumption expenditure of households		P.31								
Durable goods										
Furnishings, household equipment and routine maintenance of the house	LLME	05	23 612	23 242	24 447	25 679	25 929	26 913	27 820	26 890
Health	LLMF	06	3 208	3 810	3 720	3 661	3 609	3 849	4 297	4 224
Transport	LLMG	07	40 828	46 481	50 537	51 810	55 009	51 806	50 974	50 856
Communication	LLMH	08	1 045	1 141	876	1 045	1 455	1 420	1 519	1 367
Recreation and culture	LLMI	09	19 967	22 439	23 535	27 169	29 579	32 411	33 446	34 152
Miscellaneous goods and services	LLMJ	12	6 167	5 840	6 978	7 413	9 159	7 318	7 556	8 255
Total durable goods	UTIC	D	94 307	102 622	109 648	116 581	124 554	123 669	125 612	125 744
Semi-durable goods										
Clothing and footwear	LLNG	03	55 368	59 337	60 493	63 318	65 601	65 264	66 095	72 325
Furnishings, household equipment and routine maintenance of the house	LLNH	05	15 989	16 896	17 141	19 508	20 713	23 136	22 306	22 118
Transport	LLNI	07	4 760	5 251	5 365	5 227	5 524	5 410	4 938	4 649
Recreation and culture	LLNJ	09	27 055	27 394	27 739	29 637	31 286	34 536	36 078	38 577
Miscellaneous goods and services	LLNK	12	6 095	7 379	6 952	7 039	6 789	7 646	7 694	7 628
Total semi-durable goods	UTIS	SD	109 263	116 261	117 672	124 755	129 908	135 994	137 111	145 297
Non-durable goods										
Food and drink	ADIP	01	89 552	91 433	94 334	93 629	101 169	103 217	104 927	105 972
Alcoholic beverages, tobacco and narcotics	ADIS	02	49 479	49 610	47 743	45 795	44 553	44 255	44 350	42 492
Housing, water, electricity, gas and other fuels	LLMS	04	42 983	42 919	38 149	39 817	41 309	38 691	39 282	38 414
Furnishings, household equipment and routine maintenance of the house	LLMT	05	2 879	2 602	2 725	3 097	3 222	3 212	3 347	3 602
Health	LLMU	06	6 815	9 102	9 367	9 250	9 670	10 173	10 205	10 427
Transport	LLMV	07	32 124	31 446	31 988	32 221	32 459	33 439	34 786	34 552
Recreation and culture	LLMW	09	19 158	19 327	19 557	19 478	21 604	21 077	21 105	20 294
Miscellaneous goods and services	LLMX	12	12 811	12 895	14 336	16 431	16 786	18 882	19 871	20 770
Total non-durable goods	UTIK	ND	254 232	257 702	257 259	259 150	270 517	272 934	277 873	276 523
Total goods	UTIG		457 762	476 639	484 538	500 417	524 906	532 614	540 596	547 564
Services										
Clothing and footwear	LLMY	03	1 217	1 190	1 239	1 058	1 080	1 147	1 065	1 100
Housing, water, electricity, gas and other fuels	LLMZ	04	273 039	280 930	288 103	295 481	303 367	300 761	300 947	304 683
Furnishings, household equipment and routine maintenance of the house	LLNA	05	5 484	5 818	5 974	6 030	6 861	6 872	7 543	7 243
Health	LLNB	06	8 457	9 055	8 934	9 152	9 882	10 113	10 026	10 074
Transport	LLNC	07	78 389	79 485	81 667	83 445	86 762	89 448	92 219	92 230
Communication	LLND	08	20 407	20 091	20 543	20 640	20 632	21 184	20 815	19 744
Recreation and culture	LLNE	09	48 418	50 286	53 119	54 932	55 111	54 947	54 604	54 320
Education	ADMJ	10	28 891	28 525	28 376	28 994	30 579	30 129	30 889	31 631
Restaurants and hotels	ADMK	11	116 770	121 304	123 044	124 714	126 861	130 570	129 392	130 529
Miscellaneous goods and services	LLNF	12	113 450	114 582	119 761	120 980	123 705	127 490	130 704	131 157
Total services	UTIO	S	694 391	711 325	730 998	745 624	765 018	772 768	778 204	782 711
Final consumption expenditure in the UK by resident and non-resident households (domestic concept)	ABQJ	0	1 151 753	1 187 981	1 215 310	1 245 989	1 289 952	1 305 386	1 318 800	1 330 275
Final consumption expenditure outside the UK by UK resident households	ABTC	P.33	36 373	36 997	40 609	46 933	48 998	48 324	49 928	51 659
Final consumption expenditure in the UK by households resident in rest of the world	CCHX		−30 090	−32 507	−33 606	−33 988	−33 864	−35 236	−33 512	−35 749
Final consumption expenditure by UK resident households in the UK and abroad (national concept)	ABPF	P.3	1 157 971	1 192 501	1 222 479	1 258 941	1 305 040	1 318 430	1 335 216	1 346 185

Source: Office for National Statistics, Blue Book 2020

19.16 Individual consumption expenditure at current market prices by households, non-profit institutions serving households and general government

Classified by function (COICOP/COPNI/COFOG)[1]

£ million

		2012	2013	2014	2015	2016	2017	2018	2019
Final consumption expenditure of households	**P.31**								
Food and non-alcoholic beverages	ABZV 01	89 215	92 080	93 329	91 345	96 721	101 009	104 927	107 492
Food	ABZW 01.1	78 657	81 728	83 196	81 156	86 245	90 085	93 296	95 508
Non-alcoholic beverages	ADFK 01.2	10 558	10 352	10 133	10 189	10 476	10 924	11 631	11 984
Alcoholic beverages, tobacco and narcotics	ADFL 02	41 119	42 346	42 121	40 767	40 424	42 223	44 350	43 549
Alcoholic beverages	ADFM 02.1	16 559	18 161	17 769	18 146	18 229	19 393	20 869	20 902
Tobacco	ADFN 02.2	18 758	18 925	19 856	19 222	19 112	19 360	19 914	19 262
Narcotics	MNC2 02.3	5 802	5 260	4 496	3 399	3 083	3 470	3 567	3 385
Clothing and footwear	ADFP 03	54 058	58 334	59 570	62 345	64 643	65 923	67 160	72 853
Clothing	ADFQ 03.1	46 076	50 013	50 653	52 789	55 388	55 981	57 096	61 506
Footwear	ADFR 03.2	7 982	8 321	8 917	9 556	9 255	9 942	10 064	11 347
Housing, water, electricity, gas and other fuels	ADFS 04	286 112	299 107	306 770	318 687	332 882	333 737	340 229	347 235
Actual rentals for housing	ADFT 04.1	65 022	69 543	73 612	77 864	80 836	81 160	82 520	85 057
Imputed rentals for housing	ADFU 04.2	177 025	183 249	190 019	197 369	207 812	209 453	211 474	215 829
Maintenance and repair of the dwelling	ADFV 04.3	2 539	2 640	2 663	2 859	3 131	3 237	3 267	2 951
Water supply and miscellaneous dwelling services	ADFW 04.4	8 606	8 858	9 356	9 371	9 512	9 536	9 901	10 134
Electricity, gas and other fuels	ADFX 04.5	32 920	34 817	31 120	31 224	31 591	30 351	33 067	33 264
Furnishings, household equipment and routine maintenance of the house	ADFY 05	45 659	46 368	48 580	51 726	54 301	59 027	61 016	60 229
Furniture, furnishings, carpets and other floor coverings	ADFZ 05.1	14 823	14 712	16 001	17 595	17 845	19 060	19 426	18 862
Household textiles	ADGG 05.2	4 575	5 101	5 274	6 211	6 662	8 491	7 521	7 642
Household appliances	ADGL 05.3	7 935	7 820	8 389	8 255	8 123	8 799	10 012	9 949
Glassware, tableware and household utensils	ADGM 05.4	6 019	6 443	6 363	6 408	7 082	7 517	8 108	8 340
Tools and equipment for house and garden	ADGN 05.5	4 734	4 610	4 502	4 834	5 434	5 846	5 921	5 311
Goods and services for routine household maintenance	ADGO 05.6	7 573	7 682	8 051	8 423	9 155	9 314	10 028	10 125
Health	ADGP 06	16 671	20 013	20 498	20 852	22 182	23 742	24 528	25 377
Medical products, appliances and equipment	ADGQ 06.1	9 631	12 193	12 538	12 466	12 915	13 826	14 502	14 983
Out-patient services	ADGR 06.2	3 975	4 758	4 676	5 016	5 901	6 505	6 726	6 853
Hospital services	ADGS 06.3	3 065	3 062	3 284	3 370	3 366	3 411	3 300	3 541
Transport	ADGT 07	146 745	154 128	159 589	159 132	166 472	171 126	182 917	186 612
Purchase of vehicles	ADGU 07.1	37 832	42 509	46 807	47 911	51 961	50 012	50 974	53 087
Operation of personal transport equipment	ADGV 07.2	66 816	66 650	66 559	63 403	64 527	70 610	76 599	76 389
Transport services	ADGW 07.3	42 097	44 969	46 223	47 818	49 984	50 504	55 344	57 136
Communication	ADGX 08	20 128	20 016	20 213	20 518	21 531	22 406	22 334	21 928
Postal services	CDEF 08.1	834	654	741	1 098	1 080	1 155	1 342	1 375
Telephone and telefax equipment	ADWO 08.2	959	1 062	813	1 009	1 429	1 422	1 519	1 417
Telephone and telefax services	ADWP 08.3	18 335	18 300	18 659	18 411	19 022	19 829	19 473	19 136
Recreation and culture	ADGY 09	106 773	113 101	117 977	125 098	131 754	140 067	145 233	148 928
Audio-visual, photographic and information processing equipment	ADGZ 09.1	21 277	21 871	20 443	22 324	23 070	24 151	26 595	27 338
Other major durables for recreation and culture	ADHL 09.2	7 794	8 951	10 667	12 374	13 399	14 992	14 817	14 526
Other recreational items and equipment; flowers, garden and pets	ADHZ 09.3	28 017	29 285	31 671	32 241	35 045	39 757	41 524	44 592
Recreational and cultural services	ADIA 09.4	38 570	41 404	44 605	47 375	48 819	49 380	50 192	50 949
Newspapers, books and stationery	ADIC 09.5	11 115	11 590	10 591	10 784	11 421	11 787	12 105	11 523
Package holidays[2]	ADID 09.6	–	–	–	–	–	–	–	–
Education	10								
Education services	ADIE 10	18 428	21 323	23 357	25 898	28 631	29 278	30 889	32 601
Restaurants and hotels	ADIF 11	100 169	105 810	110 667	114 900	119 507	126 914	129 392	133 877
Catering services	ADIG 11.1	82 569	85 880	89 696	92 496	96 438	102 202	104 895	108 454
Accommodation services	ADIH 11.2	17 600	19 930	20 971	22 404	23 069	24 712	24 497	25 423
Miscellaneous goods and services	ADII 12	124 997	129 693	143 946	147 286	154 307	157 186	165 825	166 617
Personal care	ADIJ 12.1	21 307	21 808	23 474	25 482	26 313	28 589	30 115	31 983
Prostitution	MNC8 12.2	4 678	4 804	4 950	5 110	5 394	5 609	5 813	6 056
Personal effects n.e.c.	ADIK 12.3	9 919	10 998	11 596	12 195	13 374	13 037	13 195	13 537
Social protection	ADIL 12.4	14 826	17 354	18 197	20 115	20 789	21 239	21 365	21 322
Insurance	ADIM 12.5	23 738	23 619	26 253	21 144	22 593	21 765	21 265	20 122
Financial services n.e.c.	ADIN 12.6	35 772	35 635	43 805	47 456	49 128	49 728	55 827	55 225
Other services n.e.c.	ADIO 12.7	14 757	15 475	15 671	15 784	16 716	17 219	18 245	18 372
Final consumption expenditure in the UK by resident and non-resident households(domestic concept)	0 ABQI	1 050 074	1 102 319	1 146 617	1 178 554	1 233 355	1 272 638	1 318 800	1 347 298
Final consumption expenditure outside the UK by UK resident households	P.33 ABTA	33 895	35 895	37 255	40 309	46 949	49 051	49 928	53 655
Final consumption expenditure in the UK by households resident in rest of the world	P.34 CDFD	−25 497	−28 680	−30 521	−31 648	−32 213	−34 411	−33 512	−36 491
Final consumption expenditure by UK resident households in the UK and abroad (national concept)	P.31 ABPB	1 058 472	1 109 534	1 153 351	1 187 215	1 248 091	1 287 278	1 335 216	1 364 462

Individual consumption expenditure at current market prices by households, non-profit institutions serving households and general government

Classified by function (COICOP/COPNI/COFOG)[1]

£ million

			2012	2013	2014	2015	2016	2017	2018	2019
Consumption expenditure of UK resident households		P.31								
Final consumption expenditure of UK resident households in theUK and abroad	ABPB	P.31	1 058 472	1 109 534	1 153 351	1 187 215	1 248 091	1 287 278	1 335 216	1 364 462
Final individual consumption expenditure of NPISH		13								
Final individual consumption expenditure of NPISH	ABNV	P.31	45 519	44 228	44 631	46 231	44 859	47 118	50 475	52 415
Final individual consumption expenditure of general government		14								
Health	IWX5	14.1	121 344	124 472	130 436	133 688	139 532	142 828	146 822	156 465
Recreation and culture	IWX6	14.2	6 721	6 149	6 077	5 759	5 684	5 553	5 598	5 287
Education	IWX7	14.3	62 260	63 610	66 048	66 088	66 499	67 340	68 497	72 791
Social protection	IWX8	14.4	34 341	35 141	35 870	36 273	36 696	37 185	38 818	39 588
Final individual consumption expenditure of general government	NNAQ	P.31	224 666	229 372	238 431	241 808	248 411	252 906	259 735	274 131
Total, individual consumption expenditure/ actual individual consumption	ABRE	P.31 P.41	1 328 657	1 383 134	1 436 413	1 475 254	1 541 361	1 587 302	1 645 426	1 691 008

1 "Purpose" or "function" classifications are designed to indicate the "socio-economic objectives" that institutional units aim to achieve through various kinds of outlays. COICOP is the Classification of Individual Consumption by Purpose and applies to households. COPNI is the Classification of the Purposes of Non-profit Institutions Serving Households and COFOG is the Classification of the Functions of Government.

2 Package holidays data are dispersed between components (transport etc).

Source: Office for National Statistics, Blue Book 2020

19.17 Individual consumption expenditure by households, NPISH and general government Chained volume measures (reference year 2018)

Classified by function (COICOP/COPNI/COFOG)[1]

£ million

			2012	2013	2014	2015	2016	2017	2018	2019
Final consumption expenditure of households		P.31								
Food and non-alcoholic beverages	ADIP	01	89 552	91 433	94 334	93 629	101 169	103 217	104 927	105 972
Food	ADIQ	01.1	79 593	81 180	83 726	83 227	90 261	91 864	93 296	94 357
Non-alcoholic beverages	ADIR	01.2	9 968	10 256	10 611	10 401	10 908	11 351	11 631	11 615
Alcoholic beverages, tobacco and narcotics	ADIS	02	49 479	49 610	47 743	45 795	44 553	44 255	44 350	42 492
Alcoholic beverages	ADIT	02.1	18 645	19 541	18 954	19 348	19 395	20 042	20 869	20 529
Tobacco	ADIU	02.2	27 683	26 109	25 376	23 493	22 323	20 766	19 914	18 380
Narcotics	MNC4	02.3	3 880	4 134	3 728	3 217	3 035	3 482	3 567	3 583
Clothing and footwear	ADIW	03	56 567	60 516	61 720	64 375	66 681	66 410	67 160	73 425
Clothing	ADIX	03.1	48 728	52 273	52 884	54 837	57 438	56 471	57 096	61 743
Footwear	ADIY	03.2	7 863	8 279	8 852	9 539	9 268	9 939	10 064	11 682
Housing, water, electricity, gas and other fuels	ADIZ	04	315 956	323 808	326 141	335 201	344 569	339 476	340 229	343 097
Actual rentals for housing	ADJA	04.1	71 302	74 810	77 675	80 642	82 259	82 059	82 520	84 550
Imputed rentals for housing	ADJB	04.2	195 297	199 650	204 039	208 392	214 336	211 899	211 474	213 365
Maintenance and repair of the dwelling	ADJC	04.3	2 820	2 769	2 833	3 170	3 425	3 435	3 267	2 889
Water supply and miscellaneous dwelling services	ADJD	04.4	9 187	9 108	9 337	9 437	9 645	9 669	9 901	9 859
Electricity, gas and other fuels	ADJE	04.5	37 484	37 582	32 379	33 668	35 045	32 391	33 067	32 434
Furnishings, household equipment and routine maintenance		05								
of the house	ADJF		47 881	48 494	50 190	54 306	56 718	60 125	61 016	59 853
Furniture, furnishings, carpets and other floor coverings	ADJG	05.1	16 242	16 144	16 967	18 426	18 598	19 174	19 426	18 489
Household textiles	ADJH	05.2	4 540	5 043	5 293	6 238	6 821	8 589	7 521	7 592
Household appliances	ADJI	05.3	8 665	8 502	9 148	9 025	8 778	9 236	10 012	10 088
Glassware, tableware and household utensils	ADJJ	05.4	5 795	6 081	5 993	6 758	7 247	7 602	8 108	8 360
Tools and equipment for house and garden	ADJK	05.5	4 906	4 907	4 770	5 322	5 881	6 174	5 921	5 261
Goods and services for routine household maintenance	ADJL	05.6	7 861	7 880	8 133	8 583	9 405	9 345	10 028	10 063
Health	ADJM	06	18 373	21 978	22 041	22 068	23 146	24 128	24 528	24 725
Medical products, appliances and equipment	ADJN	06.1	10 028	12 915	13 086	12 910	13 271	14 016	14 502	14 651
Out-patient services	ADJO	06.2	4 694	5 448	5 262	5 440	6 288	6 682	6 726	6 659
Hospital services	ADJP	06.3	3 783	3 609	3 678	3 717	3 593	3 429	3 300	3 415
Transport	ADJQ	07	156 611	162 943	169 709	172 813	179 916	180 164	182 917	182 287
Purchase of vehicles	ADJR	07.1	40 828	46 481	50 537	51 810	55 009	51 806	50 974	50 856
Operation of personal transport equipment	ADJS	07.2	68 687	68 375	69 570	70 314	71 548	74 312	76 599	75 266
Transport services	ADJT	07.3	46 755	47 863	49 488	50 589	53 201	54 013	55 344	56 165
Communication	ADJU	08	21 445	21 222	21 413	21 675	22 086	22 603	22 334	21 111
Postal services	CCGZ	08.1	990	746	811	1 162	1 093	1 169	1 342	1 326
Telephone and telefax equipment	ADQF	08.2	1 046	1 142	876	1 045	1 455	1 420	1 519	1 367
Telephone and telefax services	ADQG	08.3	19 426	19 330	19 721	19 478	19 539	20 015	19 473	18 418
Recreation and culture	ADJV	09	113 758	118 941	123 394	130 963	137 455	142 954	145 233	147 343
Audio-visual, photographic and information processing equipment	ADJW	09.1	17 595	19 004	18 637	21 439	23 207	23 753	26 595	28 066
Other major durables for recreation and culture	ADJX	09.2	8 864	9 943	11 670	13 366	14 370	15 534	14 817	14 208
Other recreational items and equipment; flowers, gardens and pets	ADJY	09.3	28 737	29 596	31 688	32 764	36 351	40 878	41 524	44 182
Recreational and cultural services	ADJZ	09.4	45 499	47 107	49 953	51 605	51 142	50 591	50 192	49 760
Newspapers, books and stationery	ADKM	09.5	13 835	13 850	12 094	12 166	12 532	12 318	12 105	11 127
Package holidays[2]	ADMI	09.6	–	–	–	–	–	–	–	–
Education		10								
Education services	ADMJ	10	28 891	28 525	28 376	28 994	30 579	30 129	30 889	31 631
Restaurants and hotels	ADMK	11	116 770	121 304	123 044	124 714	126 861	130 570	129 392	130 529
Catering services	ADML	11.1	96 028	97 466	99 087	100 056	102 185	105 578	104 895	105 709
Accommodation services	ADMM	11.2	20 720	23 843	23 949	24 663	24 674	24 986	24 497	24 820
Miscellaneous goods and services	ADMN	12	138 182	140 462	147 844	151 800	156 288	161 326	165 825	167 810
Personal care	ADMO	12.1	21 204	21 558	23 340	25 566	26 471	28 771	30 115	31 431
Prostitution	MND2	12.2	5 220	5 273	5 329	5 398	5 592	5 710	5 813	5 951
Personal effects n.e.c.[3]	ADMP	12.3	10 562	11 415	12 024	12 682	13 881	13 123	13 195	13 455
Social protection	ADMQ	12.4	17 564	20 192	20 467	21 978	21 811	21 763	21 365	20 663
Insurance	ADMR	12.5	25 927	23 183	25 764	22 894	22 618	22 176	21 265	20 542
Financial services n.e.c.[3]	ADMS	12.6	41 497	42 429	44 236	47 027	48 922	52 369	55 827	57 871
Other services n.e.c.[3]	ADMT	12.7	16 300	16 687	16 678	16 392	17 026	17 365	18 245	17 897
Final consumption expenditure in the UK by resident and non-resident households (domestic concept)	ABQJ	0	1 151 753	1 187 981	1 215 310	1 245 989	1 289 952	1 305 386	1 318 800	1 330 275
Final consumption expenditure outside the UK by UK resident households	ABTC	P.33	36 373	36 997	40 609	46 933	48 998	48 324	49 928	51 659
Final consumption expenditure in the UK by households resident in rest of the world	CCHX	P.34	−30 090	−32 507	−33 606	−33 988	−33 864	−35 236	−33 512	−35 749
Final consumption expenditure by UK resident households in the UK and abroad (national concept)	ABPF	P.31	1 157 971	1 192 501	1 222 479	1 258 941	1 305 040	1 318 430	1 335 216	1 346 185

19.17
continued

Individual consumption expenditure by households, NPISH and general government Chained volume measures (reference year 2018)
Classified by function (COICOP/COPNI/COFOG)[1]

£ million

			2012	2013	2014	2015	2016	2017	2018	2019
Consumption expenditure of UK resident households		P.31								
Final consumption expenditure of UK resident households in the UK and abroad	ABPF	P.31	1 157 971	1 192 501	1 222 479	1 258 941	1 305 040	1 318 430	1 335 216	1 346 185
Final individual consumption expenditure of NPISH		13								
Final individual consumption expenditure of NPISH	ABNU	P.31	49 401	46 703	45 742	47 447	45 888	47 785	50 475	51 529
Final individual consumption expenditure of general government		14								
Health	K4CP	14.1	123 930	126 344	131 512	136 744	141 390	145 719	146 822	151 367
Recreation and culture	K4CQ	14.2	7 081	6 437	6 268	5 979	5 875	5 685	5 598	5 240
Education	K4CR	14.3	65 277	66 292	67 893	68 448	68 539	68 907	68 497	71 754
Social protection	K4CS	14.4	36 480	37 098	37 247	37 847	38 175	38 117	38 818	39 490
Final individual consumption expenditure of general government	NSZK	P.31	232 598	236 019	242 816	248 954	253 942	258 428	259 735	267 851
Total, individual consumption expenditure/ actual individual consumption	YBIO	P.31 P.41	1 440 244	1 475 343	1 511 171	1 555 452	1 604 794	1 624 628	1 645 426	1 665 565

1 "Purpose" or "function" classifications are designed to indicate the "socio-economic objectives" that institutional units aim to achieve through various kinds of outlays.
COICOP is the Classification of Individual Consumption by Purpose and applies to households. COPNI is the Classification of the Purposes of Non-profit Institutions Serving Households.
COFOG is the Classification of the Functions of Government.
2 Package holidays are dispersed between components (transport etc.)
3 Not elsewhere classified

Source: Office for National Statistics, Blue Book 2020

19.18 Change in inventories at chained volume measures [1]

Reference year 2019, £ million

	Mining and quarrying	Manufacturing industries				Electricity, gas and water supply	Distributive trades		Other industries	Changes in inventories [4]
		Materials and fuel	Work in progress	Finished goods	Total		Wholesale [3]	Retail [3]		
Level of inventories held at end-December										
2019 [2]	555	28,419	19,068	21,578	69,065	354	43,107	34,887	63,662	211,630
	FADO	FBID	FBIE	FBIF	DHBH	FADP	FAJM	FBYH	DLWV	ABMQ
2015	1,097	949	-580	-259	10	758	-1,730	604	12,808	11,782
2016	-1,953	1,068	2,810	-919	2,928	-1,195	-1,220	677	8,867	8,195
2017	-319	1,062	-2,695	1,911	190	917	652	-1,133	12,903	12,690
2018	-430	1,369	2,087	-83	3,254	-2,134	928	-1,243	1,803	1,798
2019	357	5,486	-974	-1,376	3,136	1,183	1,930	440	-537	6,509
Seasonally adjusted										
	FAEA	FBNF	FBNG	FBNH	DHBM	FAEB	FAJX	FBYN	DLWX	CAFU
2015 Q1	657	89	283	1,082	1,429	1,168	-1,854	-644	4,940	5,223
2015 Q2	-161	1,191	-151	-582	439	-512	-2,057	371	-2,919	-5,145
2015 Q3	333	-314	236	-214	-323	-45	523	508	-681	-165
2015 Q4	268	-17	-948	-545	-1,535	147	1,658	369	11,468	11,869
2016 Q1	267	-610	1,083	58	546	806	320	-300	-367	616
2016 Q2	-1,120	-473	620	904	1,046	-685	271	-394	1,446	945
2016 Q3	-499	1,785	709	-465	1,998	-665	-750	228	3,301	3,812
2016 Q4	-601	366	398	-1,416	-662	-651	-1,061	1,143	4,487	2,822
2017 Q1	-136	1,760	-1,772	206	166	150	1,259	99	2,591	4,044
2017 Q2	432	-676	1,071	609	985	556	324	-128	2,296	4,266
2017 Q3	-76	-393	1,453	971	2,015	776	-1,182	-450	3,619	4,529
2017 Q4	-539	371	-3,447	125	-2,976	-565	251	-654	4,397	-149
2018 Q1	-264	24	151	-796	-652	-898	1,112	281	-1,609	-2,074
2018 Q2	-215	-375	2,384	306	2,256	-420	-697	-292	2,224	2,747
2018 Q3	-199	507	329	247	1,061	-460	897	-308	-666	212
2018 Q4	248	1,213	-777	160	589	-356	-384	-924	1,854	913
2019 Q1	165	1,952	917	1,114	3,967	680	1,501	-527	1,158	6,971
2019 Q2	-147	2,304	-1,259	-1,279	-202	-221	9	531	791	682
2019 Q3	212	451	-552	-912	-1,019	549	-267	-361	325	-518
2019 Q4	127	779	-80	-299	390	175	687	797	-2,811	-626

Source: Office for National Statistics

1. Estimates are given to the nearest £ million but cannot be regarded as accurate to this degree.
2. Estimates of level based on previously available data
3. Wholesaling and retail estimates exclude the motor trade.
4. Quarterly alignment adjustment included in this series.

19.19 Gross fixed capital formation at current purchasers' prices[1]
Analysis by broad sector and type of asset
Total economy

£ million

			2012	2013	2014	2015	2016	2017	2018	2019
Private sector		S.1PT								
New dwellings, excluding land	L5ZQ	AN.111	45 512	50 885	54 346	57 867	61 450	70 012	80 333	82 880
Other buildings and structures	EQBU	AN.112	42 451	46 999	49 965	60 755	63 952	66 131	65 686	74 377
Transport equipment	EQBV	AN.1131	10 052	10 437	15 894	19 190	24 179	24 299	19 797	20 375
ICT[2] equipment and other machinery and equipment and cultivated biological resources	EQBW	AN.1132+AN.1139+ AN.115	38 389	38 481	41 200	42 000	45 481	49 224	49 194	46 289
Intellectual property products	EQBX	AN.117	58 048	61 629	63 303	64 658	68 332	71 019	74 709	77 500
Costs associated with the transfer of ownership of non-produced assets	L5ZR	AN.116	15 228	17 383	20 052	21 075	22 978	21 654	23 572	25 138
Total	EQBZ	P.51g, S.1PT	209 678	225 814	244 760	265 546	286 373	302 340	313 289	326 561
Public non-financial corporations		S.11001								
New dwellings, excluding land	L5YQ	AN.111	7 454	7 035	8 300	8 130	8 362	8 464	4 618	4 713
Other buildings and structures	DEES	AN.112	1 499	1 408	1 673	1 567	1 919	2 137	2 091	1 915
Transport equipment	DEEP	AN.1131	619	461	400	552	196	60	60	48
ICT equipment and other machinery and equipment and cultivated biological resources	DEEQ	AN.1132+AN.1139+ AN.115	933	887	853	823	882	872	881	998
Intellectual property products	DLXJ	AN.116	2 197	2 296	2 240	2 347	2 410	2 446	2 432	2 466
Costs associated with the transfer of ownership of non-produced assets	L5ZL	N116G	447	521	655	687	725	773	759	767
Total	FCCJ	P.51g, S.11001	13 148	12 607	14 123	14 104	14 493	14 753	10 841	10 906
General government		S.13								
New dwellings, excluding land	L5ZU	AN.111	115	–	–	–	53	–	2	–
Other buildings and structures	EQCH	AN.112	27 175	26 297	29 367	29 778	30 653	32 277	34 411	36 438
Transport equipment	EQCI	AN.1131	458	436	467	478	499	533	551	571
ICT equipment, other machinery and equipment, Cultivated biological resources, weapons	EQCJ	AN.1132+AN.1139+ AN.115+AN.114	9 364	9 442	10 191	10 124	10 428	11 610	12 047	14 308
Intellectual property products	EQCK	AN.117	4 890	4 817	5 110	5 339	5 398	5 020	4 660	5 340
Costs associated with the transfer of ownership of non-produced assets	L5ZV	AN.116	4 153	4 668	5 771	5 438	5 318	5 801	5 445	5 348
Total	NNBF	P.51g, S.13	46 155	45 659	50 905	51 158	52 350	55 240	57 117	62 005
Total gross fixed capital formation	NPQX	P.51g, S.1	268 984	284 080	309 788	330 807	353 218	372 333	381 249	399 470

1 Components may not sum to totals due to rounding
2 Information Communication Technology.

Source: Office for National Statistics, Blue Book 2020

19.20 Gross fixed capital formation at current purchasers' prices[1]
Analysis by type of asset
Total economy

£ million

			2012	2013	2014	2015	2016	2017	2018	2019
Tangible fixed assets		AN.11								
New dwellings, excluding land	DFDK	AN.111	53 081	57 920	62 646	65 997	69 865	78 476	84 953	87 593
Other buildings and structures	DLWS	AN.112	71 125	74 704	81 005	92 100	96 524	100 545	102 188	112 730
Transport equipment	DLWZ	AN.1131	11 129	11 334	16 761	20 220	24 874	24 892	20 408	20 994
ICT[2] equipment, other machinery and equipment, cultivated biological resources, weapons[3]	DLXI	AN.1132+AN.1139+ AN.115+AN.114	48 685	48 809	52 244	52 947	56 791	61 705	62 119	61 594
Total	EQCQ	AN.11, S.1	184 019	192 767	212 655	231 263	248 054	265 618	269 667	282 913
Intellectual property products	DLXP	AN.117	65 135	68 741	70 654	72 343	76 140	78 487	81 800	85 307
Costs associated with the transfer of ownership of non-produced assets	DFBH	AN.116	19 827	22 571	26 477	27 201	29 023	28 228	29 776	31 252
Total gross fixed capital formation	NPQX	P.51g, S.1	268 984	284 080	309 788	330 807	353 218	372 333	381 249	399 470

1 Components may not sum to totals due to rounding
2 Information Communication Technology
3 Weapons data are central government only.

Source: Office for National Statistics, Blue Book 2020

19.21 Gross fixed capital formation[1,2]
Chained volume measures (reference year 2018)
Total economy: Analysis by broad sector and type of asset

£ million

			2012	2013	2014	2015	2016	2017	2018	2019
Private sector		S.1PT								
New dwellings, excluding land	L62K	AN.111	52 353	56 715	58 742	62 499	65 099	72 148	80 334	80 449
Other buildings and structures	EQCU	AN.112	49 052	52 756	54 345	65 417	67 617	68 789	65 689	70 984
Transport equipment	EQCV	AN.1131	10 910	11 212	17 149	20 487	25 834	25 639	19 796	20 058
ICT[3] equipment and other machinery and equipment and cultivated biological resources	EQCW	AN.1132+AN.1139+ AN.115	44 134	44 884	48 200	47 137	48 625	48 684	49 193	45 012
Intellectual property products	EQCX	AN.117	62 717	65 299	66 220	67 357	69 599	71 839	74 710	75 885
Costs associated with the transfer of ownership of non-produced assets	L62L	AN.116	17 027	19 393	21 792	22 154	23 511	21 433	23 569	24 690
Total	EQCZ	P.51g, S.1PT	235 960	249 880	266 167	284 955	300 252	308 513	313 296	317 077
Public non-financial corporations		S.11001								
New dwellings, excluding land	L62M	AN.111	8 348	7 745	8 946	8 747	8 857	8 713	4 618	4 557
Other buildings and structures	DEEX	AN.112	1 756	1 589	1 814	1 686	2 019	2 203	2 091	1 823
Transport equipment	DEEU	AN.1131	622	464	411	567	207	62	60	48
ICT equipment and other machinery and equipment and cultivated biological resources	DEEV	AN.1132+AN.1139+ AN.115	1 105	1 052	1 015	919	940	849	881	951
Intellectual property products	EQDE	AN.117	2 053	2 140	2 173	2 303	2 377	2 412	2 431	2 483
Costs associated with the transfer of ownership of non-produced assets	L62N	AN.116	479	560	692	711	742	786	759	743
Total	EQDG	P.51g, S.11001	14 267	13 490	14 959	14 873	15 069	14 962	10 840	10 606
General government		S.13								
New dwellings, excluding land costs	L62O	AN.111	106	–	–	–	53	–	2	–
Other buildings and structures	EQDI	AN.112	31 354	29 153	31 331	31 406	31 865	33 194	34 411	34 532
Transport equipment	EQDJ	AN.1131	466	446	489	498	530	566	550	573
ICT equipment, other machinery and equipment, Cultivated biological resources, weapons	EQDK	AN.1132+AN.1139+ AN.115+AN.114	10 671	10 704	11 335	10 787	10 875	11 594	12 047	13 853
Intellectual property services	EQDL	AN.117	5 462	5 186	5 385	5 550	5 422	5 034	4 660	5 257
Costs associated with the transfer of ownership of non-produced assets	L62P	AN.116	4 526	5 085	6 165	5 679	5 473	5 916	5 446	5 186
Total	EQDN	P.51g, S.13	52 572	50 583	54 719	53 953	54 253	56 312	57 116	59 403
Total gross fixed capital formation	NPQR	P.51g	302 815	314 073	335 949	353 830	369 569	379 787	381 249	387 085

1 For the years before the reference year (2016), totals differ from the sum of their components
2 Components may not sum to totals due to rounding
3 Information Communication Technology.

Source: Office for National Statistics, Blue Book 2020

19.22 Gross fixed capital formation[1,2]
Chained volume measures (reference year 2018)
Total economy: Analysis by type of asset

£ million

			2012	2013	2014	2015	2016	2017	2018	2019
Tangible fixed assets		AN.11								
New dwellings, excluding land	DFDV	AN.111	60 866	64 457	67 696	71 251	74 018	80 865	84 955	85 004
Other buildings and structures	EQDP	AN.112	82 172	83 519	87 532	98 489	101 481	104 187	102 176	107 341
Transport equipment	DLWJ	AN.1131	12 037	12 146	18 061	21 572	26 575	26 269	20 424	20 681
ICT[3] equipment, other machinery and equipment, cultivated biological resources, weapons[4]	DLWM	AN.1132+AN.1139+ AN.115, AN.114	55 910	56 649	60 555	58 839	60 424	61 130	62 119	59 816
Total	EQDS	AN.11, S.1	210 256	216 007	233 340	250 017	262 421	272 360	269 674	272 840
Intellectual property products	EQDT	AN.117	70 216	72 632	73 776	75 216	77 409	79 285	81 801	83 624
Costs associated with the transfer of ownership of non-produced assets	DFDW	AN.116	22 031	25 036	28 658	28 546	29 723	28 133	29 775	30 619
Total gross fixed capital formation	NPQR	P.51g, S.1	302 815	314 073	335 949	353 830	369 569	379 787	381 249	387 085

1 For the years before the reference year (2016), totals differ from the sum of their components
2 Components may not sum to totals due to rounding
3 Information Communication Technology
4 Weapons data are central government only.

Source: Office for National Statistics, Blue Book 2020

Education

Chapter 20

Education

Educational establishments in the UK are administered and financed in several ways.

Maintained and non-maintained schools

Most schools are controlled by and receive funding through their local authority (LA) and are referred to as 'maintained' schools. These schools are free to allocate their funds received by their local authority, but the government do hold back funds for central services. Maintained schools cannot set their own pay or working conditions, and have their performance managed by their LA.

Other schools are controlled directly by the Secretary of State for Education. Most of these are academies or free schools. These are not maintained or controlled by LAs but they are subject to a contract with the Secretary of State known as the "Funding Agreement". Much of the law and guidance for maintained schools applies to them and they are subject to the same inspections as state schools by Ofsted.

Schools that are maintained by their LA or receive government funding are termed 'state schools'. The With the exception of Academies and Free Schools, all state schools must follow the National Curriculum, although they can focus on specific subjects provided the National Curriculum requirements are met. Pupils are assessed at all key stages, and the school is regularly inspected by their country's inspection board.

Lastly, and outside of the public sector, are schools not controlled by either an LA or the Secretary of State, referred to as non-maintained schools, which are run by individuals, companies or charitable institutions and controlled by private contracts between parties. These are broadly referred to as independent (or private) schools and are classified as non-mainstream schools. They are fee-charging schools that receive no state funding, instead relying on tuition fees, gifts, and endowments. Some may also hold charity status. Pupils do not have to follow the national curriculum and the schools have much more control over staffing, spending, and the length of the school day and term etc. All independent schools must be registered with the government and are inspected regularly. Independent schools include public schools, pre-prep / prep schools and most boarding schools.

State schools

State schools fall under the following broad categories:

- community schools, which are sometimes called local authority maintained schools - they are not influenced by business or religious groups and follow the national curriculum.
- foundation schools and voluntary schools, which are funded by the local authority but have more freedom to change the way they do things - sometimes they are supported by representatives from religious groups.
- academies and free schools, which are run by not-for-profit academy trusts, are independent from the local authority - they have more freedom to change how they run things and can follow a different curriculum.
- grammar schools, which can be run by the local authority, a foundation body or an academy trust - they select their pupils based on academic ability and there is a test to get in.

Special schools

Special schools provide education for children with Special Educational Needs (SEN) (in Scotland, Record of Needs or a Coordinated Support Plan), who cannot be educated satisfactorily in an ordinary school, because, for example, they have physical or other difficulties. Maintained special schools are run by local authorities while non-maintained special schools are financed by voluntary bodies where their expenditure is met primarily from the fees charged to local authorities for pupils placed in schools. Only pupils with Educational Health and Care Plans are able to attend Special Schools. Most Special Schools provide in-house or visiting NHS therapist care, including Speech and Language Therapists, Occupational Therapists, and Physiotherapists.

Pupil Referral Units

Pupil referral units (PRUs) teach children who aren't able to attend school and may not otherwise receive suitable education. This could be because they have a short- or long-term illness, have been excluded or are a new starter waiting for a mainstream school place. They are funded by the local authority, and follow most state school guidelines. However, they don't have to follow the National Curriculum, provided they deliver a 'broad and balanced' curriculum that must include English, Maths, Science, IT, and PSHE. They also put a much larger focus on personal development, such as teaching socialisation, behaviour, and anger management skills. SEND pupils may attend Pupil Referral Units for short periods of time while waiting for a longterm solution (such as a place at a Special School). For all pupils, Pupil Referral Units are designed to be a short-term measure to address any issues and get pupils back into mainstream school as quickly as possible.

Schools in Scotland are categorised as Education Authority, Grant-aided, Opted-out/Self-governing (these three being grouped together as 'Publicly funded' schools), Independent schools and Partnership schools.

The Education and Skills Funding Agency (ESFA) brings together the former responsibilities of the Education Funding Agency (EFA) and Skills Funding Agency (SFA) to create a single agency accountable for funding education and skills for children, young people and adults. It is an executive agency, sponsored by the Department for Education.

Education is devolved in the UK and each country's government publishes statistics on its separate system (see links below).
England: https://www.gov.uk/government/organisations/department-for-education
Wales: https://statswales.gov.wales/Catalogue/Education-and-Skills
Northern Ireland: https://www.education-ni.gov.uk/topics/statistics-and-research/statistics
Scotland: https://www.gov.scot/statistics-and-research/?topics=Education

From the academic year 1994/95 onwards, the Higher Education Statistics Agency (HESA) has collected information for HE students within UK HE institutions. Since 2014, the Higher Education Funding Council for England (HEFCE), and now the Office for Students (OfS), have maintained a register of the HE institutions in England.

Education systems in the UK

Across the UK there are five stages of education: early years; primary; secondary; Further Education (FE) and Higher Education (HE). Education is compulsory for all children between the ages of 5 (4 in Northern Ireland) and 16. In England, young people must also do one of the following until they are 18: stay in full-time education; start an apprenticeship or traineeship; work or volunteer while in part-time education or training. FE is not compulsory and covers non-advanced education that can be taken at further (including tertiary) education colleges and HE institutions (HEIs). The fifth stage, HE, is study beyond A levels and their equivalent which, for most full-time students, takes place in universities and other HEIs and colleges.

Early years education

In England since 2010, all three and four year-olds are entitled to 15 hours of free nursery education for 38 weeks of the year, increasing to 30 hours from September 2017. Early Years education takes place in a variety of settings including state nursery schools, nursery classes and reception classes within primary schools, as well as settings outside the state sector such as voluntary pre-schools, privately run nurseries and childminders. The Foundation Stage was first introduced in 2000, and covered children's education from the age of 3 to the end of the reception year, when children are aged 5. The Early Years Foundation Stage (EYFS) came into force in 2008, and is a single regulatory and quality framework for the provision of learning, development and care for children in all registered early years settings between birth and the academic year in which they turn 5.

In Wales, children are entitled to a free part-time place from the term following a child's third birthday until they enter statutory education. These places can be in a maintained school or a non-maintained setting such as a voluntary playgroup, private nursery or childminder that is approved to provide education. The Foundation Phase is a holistic developmental curriculum for 3 to 7-year-olds based on the needs of the individual child to meet their stage of development. Statutory roll-out of the Foundation Phase framework started in 2008 and the process was completed in the 2011/12 school year.

In Northern Ireland, funded pre-school places are available in statutory nursery schools and units and in those voluntary and private settings participating in the Pre-School Education Programme (PSEP). Places in the voluntary/ private sector are part-time whilst, in the statutory nursery sector, both full-time and part-time places are available. Pre-school education is designed for children in the year immediately before they enter Primary 1. Taking into account the starting age for compulsory education in Northern Ireland, this means children are aged between 3 years 2 months and 4 years 2 months in the September in which they enter their final pre-school year.

In Scotland, early learning and childcare covers ages 0-5 with Curriculum for Excellence being introduced from the age of 3. Nationally funded learning provision typically starts with early learning and childcare. The Children and Young People (Scotland) Act 2014 has increased the amount of funded early learning and childcare to 600 hours a year for all 3 and 4 year-olds, and extended this provision to over a quarter of all 2 year-olds.

Primary education

The primary stage covers three age ranges: nursery (under 5), infant (5 to 7 or 8) (key stage 1) and junior (up to 11 or 12) (key stage 2). In Northern Ireland the statutory curriculum is split across 3 stages: Foundation Stage (the first two years of primary school, ages 4-6), KS1 (6 to 8) and KS2 (9 to 11). In Wales, although the types of school are the same, the Foundation Phase has brought together what was previously known as the Early Years (from 3 to 5-year-olds) and key stage 1 (from 5 to 7-year-olds) of the national curriculum to create one phase of education for children aged between three and seven. In Scotland, learning in primary schools (ages 5-11 in general) is part of the broad general education phase of Curriculum for Excellence (CfE), an integrated curriculum from 3-18.

In England, primary schools generally cater for 4-11 year-olds. Some primary schools may have a nursery or a children's centre attached to cater for younger children. Most public sector primary schools take both boys and girls in mixed classes. It is usual to transfer straight to secondary school at age 11 in England, Wales and Northern Ireland or 12 in Scotland, but in England some children make the transition via middle schools catering for various ages ranges between 8 and 14. Depending on their individual age ranges, middle schools are classified as either primary or secondary. In England, the first primary academies (publicly funded state schools that are independent of local authorities) opened in 2010. In Wales, middle schools are a separate sector as they have pupils from nursery to the end of secondary years.

The major goals of primary education are achieving basic literacy and numeracy amongst all pupils, as well as establishing foundations in science, mathematics and other subjects. In England, all schools are legally required to provide a broad and balanced curriculum, and all maintained schools must teach the national curriculum for 5-16 year-olds. Children in England and Northern Ireland are assessed at the end of key stage 1 and key stage 2. In Wales, all learners in their final year of Foundation Phase and key stage 2 must be assessed through teacher assessment and National Reading and Numeracy Tests track the progress of pupils from the end of the Foundation Phase right the way through into secondary education. In Scotland, primary features learning across 8 curriculum areas, as well as a strong focus on the development of literacy and numeracy skills and health and wellbeing across learning. Teachers will use a range of assessment methods to monitor learners' progress, including national standardised assessments at P1, P4 and P7, and to plan next steps in learning.

Secondary education

In England, public provision of secondary education in an area may consist of a combination of different types of school, the pattern reflecting historical circumstance and the policy adopted by the local authority. Comprehensive schools largely admit pupils without reference to ability or aptitude and cater for all the children in a neighbourhood, but in some areas they co-exist with other types of schools, for example grammar schools.

Academies, operating in England, are publicly funded independent schools. Academies have greater freedoms to innovate and raise standards. These include freedom from local authority control, the ability to set their own pay and conditions for staff, freedom around the delivery of the curriculum and the ability to change the lengths of terms and school days. The first academies opened in 2002 with the objective of replacing poorly performing schools.

Free schools were introduced by the Conservative-Liberal Democrat coalition as an extension of the academies programme making it possible for parents, teachers, charities and businesses to set up their new schools provided there is demand from parents for them to do so. The first free schools opened in 2011 and about a third are secondary schools.

University technical colleges are 14-19 institutions that provide a technical education alongside GCSEs. They are employer and university led and these sponsors design the curriculum and specialisms, provide mentoring and working experience opportunities to equip the students with the skills that employers demand.

Studio schools also offer academic and vocational qualifications that are taught in a practical and project-based way. Study is combined with work placements with local and national employers who are involved in the school. The distinction between studio schools and other 14-19 provision is that they have a strong emphasis on practical work and enterprise. Though studio schools may have a 'specialism', they will focus mainly on equipping students with a wide range of employability skills and a core of academic qualifications.

In Wales, secondary schools take pupils at 11 years old until the end of statutory school age and beyond. Secondary education is also provided in middle schools and some special schools, Pupil Referral Units and Independent schools. All are maintained by the local authorities with the exception of Independent schools.

In Northern Ireland, post-primary education consists of five compulsory years and two further years if students wish to remain in school to pursue post GCSE / Level 2 courses to Level 3. The statutory curriculum runs until a pupil has completed the compulsory years of education and is split across two key stages (Key Stage 3 and 4) year. In Key Stage 4, children are entitled to access to at least 21 courses, of which at least one third must be general subjects, and one third applied subjects.

In Scotland Education authority secondary schools are comprehensive in character and offer six years of secondary education, with compulsory age being 16 (S4); however, in some remote areas there are several schools which cover only some of these six years, with primary provision also sometimes offered within the same establishment. The broad general education phase of CfE is up to the end of S3, providing a strong grounding for a move to study for qualifications and awards in the senior phase (S4-S6).

At the end of secondary education, pupils are normally entered for a range of external examinations. Most frequently, these are GCSE (General Certificate of Secondary Education) in England, Wales and Northern Ireland. In Scotland, pupils can study for a wide range of National Qualifications (NQ), vocational qualifications, awards, Foundation and Modern Apprenticeships (across SCQF levels 1 to 7).

Advanced Subsidiary (AS) and Advanced (A) level qualifications are the traditional academic qualifications offered by schools and colleges in England, Wales and Northern Ireland. Many students take AS and A level qualifications in years 12 and 13 (years 13 and 14 in Northern Ireland) after completing their GCSEs, though adults can take them too. Students can choose from a wide range of academic subjects, as well as some work-related subjects. The primary purpose of A levels is to prepare students for degree-level study; over 80% of students with 2 or more A levels go on to higher education. The A level normally takes two years to complete full-time, although they are also available to study part-time. In Scotland pupils tend to study qualifications at SCQF level 6 (including Highers) in their fifth year at secondary school, and in sixth year they may study more SCQF level 6 and/or SCQF level 7 qualifications (including Advanced Highers). A wide range of qualifications and awards are available at each SCQF level, to meet the needs and aspirations of learners. Scottish universities usually express their entry requirements in terms of Highers.

Qualifications

The qualifications that pupils work towards at the end of their secondary schooling and beyond are determined by the devolved authorities in each of the four UK countries. In England, Northern Ireland and Wales all qualifications can be mapped onto the National Qualifications Framework (NQF), which has nine levels from entry level to doctorate (for example, PhD) level. In Scotland all qualifications can be mapped onto the Scottish Credit and Qualifications Framework (SCQF).

NQF Entry Level	NQF Level 1	NQF Level 2	NQF Level 3	NQF Level 4	NQF Level 5	NQF Level 6	NQF Level 7	NQF Level 8
Entry level awards, certificates or diplomas	GCSE grades D-G / 1-3	GCSE grades A*-C / 4-9	AS and A levels	Certificate of Higher Education	Diploma of Higher Education, Foundation Degree	Honours Degree	Master's degree	Doctorate

SCQF Level 1	SCQF Level 2	SCQF Level 3	SCQF Level 4	SCQF Level 5	SCQF Level 6
National 1	National 2	National 3	National 4	National 5	Higher

SCQF Level 7	SCQF Level 8	SCQF Level 9	SCQF Level 10	SCQF Level 11	SCQF Level 12
Advanced Higher, Certificate of Higher Education	Diploma of Higher Education	Bachelors, Ordinary Degree	Honours Degree, Graduate Diploma	Master's Degree	Doctorate

In England, new GCSEs in English and mathematics were taught from September 2015 with the first examinations taking place in Summer 2017. New GCSEs in other subjects were phased in for first teaching from September 2016, continuing into 2017 and a very small number from 2018. As part of these reforms, a new grading system was introduced from 2017 to replace the A* to G system with a new 9 to 1 scale.

In England, Wales and Northern Ireland, pupils commonly take GCSEs at 16 and A levels at 18. GCSEs at grades G to D (1-3 for new GCSEs in England) are equivalent to a Level 1 on the NQF, whilst GCSEs at grades C to A* (4-9 for new GCSEs in England) are equivalent to a Level 2. A levels at all grades (A* to E) are equivalent to a Level 3.

New national performance measures were introduced for England in 2015/16:

Progress 8 aims to capture the progress a pupil makes from the end of primary school to the end of secondary school. It is a type of value added measure, which means that pupils' results are compared to the actual achievements of other pupils with the same prior attainment at the end of primary school.

Attainment 8 measures the achievement of a pupil across eight 8 qualifications including English (double weighted if the combined English qualification, or both language and literature are taken), maths (double weighted), three further qualifications that count in the English Baccalaureate (EBacc) and three further qualifications that can be GCSE qualifications (including EBacc subjects) or any other non-GCSE qualifications on the DfE approved list.

Users should be cautious when comparing headline measures between 2018 and 2017 in England. In 2018, Attainment 8 had a maximum point score of 90, compared to a maximum of 87 to 2017, as a result of the phased introduction of reformed GCSEs. This difference should be taken into account when considering any change in Attainment 8 scores between 2017 and 2018.

Qualifications in Scotland are based on the Scottish Credit and Qualifications Framework (SCQF). There are 12 levels on the framework, SCQF levels 1 to 7 are covered by school education. The new National qualifications make up SCQF levels 3 to 5. For most young people in Scotland S4 is the last compulsory year of school, but the majority will choose to stay on and complete S5 and S6. Highers (SCQF level 6) are generally taken in S5/S6; Highers, sometimes along with Advanced Highers (SCQF level 7, usually taken in S6) are the qualifications required for entry to Higher Education.

Further education

Further Education in a general sense covers all courses taken after the period of compulsory education between the ages of 16 to 18. This may be at any level from basic skills training to higher vocational education.

A distinction is usually made between FE and HE. HE is education at a higher level than secondary school and is usually provided in distinct institutions such as universities. FE in the United Kingdom includes education for people over 16, usually excluding universities. It is primarily taught in FE colleges, work-based learning, and adult and community learning institutions, although some HEIs are involved in some FE provision. This includes post-16 courses similar to those taught at schools and sub-degree courses similar to those taught at HE colleges (which also teach degree-level courses) and at some universities.

Colleges in England that are regarded as part of the FE sector include general FE (GFEC) and tertiary colleges, sixth form colleges, specialist colleges (mainly colleges of agriculture and horticulture, and colleges of drama and dance), National Colleges, Institutes of Technology and adult education institutes.

In England, FE is often seen as forming one part of a wider learning and skills sector, alongside workplace education, prison education, and other types of non-school, non-university education and training. Since 2016 the sector has been overseen by Department for Education.

In Wales, there are 13 institutions that deliver a diverse range of FE courses. FE is considered part of a wider post-16 sector that includes work-based learning and adult community learning. Under the Learning and Skills (Wales) Measure 2009, learners are entitled to 30 subject choices, of which at least five must be vocational.

In Wales, there are 13 institutions that deliver a diverse range of FE courses. FE is considered part of a wider post-16 sector that includes work-based learning and adult community learning. Under the Learning and Skills (Wales) Measure 2009, learners are entitled to 30 subject choices, of which at least five must be vocational.

In Scotland, the college sector delivers around 40% of undergraduate entrants at the HE level. HNCs and HNDs make up the majority of the HE courses at college and are at SCQF level 7 and 8. Colleges run FE courses from SCQF levels 1 to 6 including most apprenticeship training programmes. School pupils are also able to study at college as part of their curriculum. Some of these pupils will study HNC qualifications that are at the HE level. In contrast to other parts of the UK, Scottish colleges deliver more HE courses alongside their FE level provision.

In Northern Ireland, FE is defined as post-statutory education that is not delivered in a school and is not HE. It therefore encompasses professional and technical education and training for full-time learners who left school at 16, apprenticeships, adult education (including part-time learners and continuing education for people in employment) and leisure courses to support lifelong learning. Learners in Northern Ireland schools post-16 are entitled to access to at least 21 courses, of which at least one third must be general subjects, and one third applied subjects; courses may be offered in the child's own school or may be accessed in another school or FE college.

Higher Education (HE)

Higher education in the UK is defined as any course that is of a standard that is higher than GCE A level, the Higher Grade of the SCE/National Qualification, GNVQ/NVQ level 3 or the Edexcel (formerly BTEC) or SQA National Certificate/Diploma.

Students normally attend HE courses at Higher Education Institutions (HEIs), but some attend at Further Education Colleges (FECs). As a result of the Further and Higher Education Act 1992, former polytechnics and some other HEIs were designated as universities in 1992/93.

There are three main levels of HE course:

a. Undergraduate courses which include first degrees (honors and ordinary), first degrees with qualified teacher status, enhanced first degrees, first degrees obtained concurrently with a diploma, and intercalated first degrees (where first degree students, usually in medicine, dentistry or veterinary medicine, interrupt their studies to complete a one-year course of advanced studies in a related topic).

b. Postgraduate courses leading to higher degrees, diplomas and certificates (including Doctorate, Masters (research and taught), Postgraduate diplomas and certificates as well as postgraduate certificates of education (PGCE) and professional qualifications) which usually require a first degree as entry qualification.

c. Other undergraduate courses that include all other HE courses, for example SVQ or NVQ: Level 5, Diploma (HNC/D level for diploma and degree holders), HND (or equivalent), HNC (or equivalent) and SVQ or NVQ: Level 4 and Diplomas in HE.

For more information on UK education and training statistics please see:
https://www.gov.uk/government/collections/statistics-education-and-training

For enquiries email the international evidence and statistics team at:
InternationalEvidence.STATISTICS@education.gov.uk

20.1 Number of schools by type of school, time series

United Kingdom **Numbers**

	2000/01	2012/13	2013/14	2014/15	2015/16	2016/17	2017/18	2018/19
UNITED KINGDOM								
Public sector mainstream								
Nursery	3,228	3,085	3,031	2,969	3,007	3,022	3,037	3,039
Primary	22,902	21,069	21,040	20,980	20,954	20,925	20,863	20,832
Middle(1)	.	4	4	6	7	10	13	19
Secondary(2)	4,352	4,077	4,116	4,158	4,169	4,168	4,190	4,188
of which Middle deemed secondary	316	189	176	154	138	125	110	104
Non-maintained mainstream	2,397	2,497	2,497	2,437	2,391	2,381	2,404	2,408
Special schools	1,498	1,269	1,264	1,263	1,261	1,256	1,258	1,257
of which state-funded	1,401	1,198	1,195	1,194	1,195	1,192	1,199	1,199
of which non-maintained	97	71	69	69	66	64	59	58
Pupil referral units	338	400	371	362	353	351	352	352
ALL SCHOOLS	34,715	32,401	32,323	32,175	32,142	32,113	32,117	32,095
ENGLAND	7.5%	2,602						
Public sector mainstream								
Maintained nursery	506	417	414	411	406	402	399	391
State-funded primary(3)	18,069	16,784	16,788	16,766	16,778	16,786	16,766	16,769
State-funded seconday(2)	3,496	3,281	3,329	3,381	3,401	3,408	3,436	3,448
of which Middle deemed secondary	316	189	176	154	138	125	110	104
Non-maintained mainstream(4)	2,190	2,414	2,412	2,357	2,311	2,297	2,320	2,319
Special schools	1,175	1,032	1,033	1,040	1,039	1,037	1,043	1,044
of which state-funded(5)	1,113	961	964	971	973	973	984	986
of which non-maintained	62	71	69	69	66	64	59	58
Pupil referral units	308	400	371	362	353	351	352	352
ALL SCHOOLS	25,744	24,328	24,347	24,317	24,288	24,281	24,316	24,323
WALES								
Public sector mainstream								
Nursery	41	20	17	13	13	11	11	9
Primary	1,631	1,374	1,357	1,330	1,310	1,287	1,261	1,238
Middle(1)	.	4	4	6	7	10	13	19
Secondary	229	216	213	207	205	200	195	187
Non-maintained mainstream	54	68	70	66	66	70	70	75
Special (maintained)	45	42	42	39	39	39	41	41
Pupil referral units	30	..	..	..	..	..	0	..
ALL SCHOOLS	2,030	1,724	1,703	1,661	1,640	1,617	1,591	1,569
SCOTLAND								
Public sector mainstream								
Nursery(6)(8)	2,586	2,551	2,504	2,449	2,492	2,514	2,532	2,544
Primary	2,278	2,064	2,056	2,048	2,039	2,031	2,019	2,012
Secondary	389	365	364	362	361	359	360	357
Non-maintained mainstream	127	..	..	..	..	..	0	..
Special schools	230	155	149	145	144	141	135	133
of which maintained	195	155	149	145	144	141	135	133
of which non-maintained	35	..	..	..	..	..	0	..
ALL SCHOOLS	5,610	5,135	5,073	5,004	5,036	5,045	5,046	5,046
NORTHERN IRELAND								
Grant aided mainstream								
Nursery(7)	95	97	96	96	96	95	95	95
Primary	924	847	839	836	827	821	817	813
Secondary	238	215	210	208	202	201	199	196
Non-maintained mainstream	26	15	15	14	14	14	14	14
Special (maintained)	48	40	40	39	39	39	39	39
ALL SCHOOLS	1,331	1,214	1,200	1,193	1,178	1,170	1,164	1,157

Source: Department for Education; Welsh Government;
Scottish Government; Northern Ireland Department of Education

1 In Wales, the Middle School for pupils of both primary and secondary school age was introduced in 2012/13.

2 In England, includes secondary sponsor-led academies, secondary converter academies and secondary free schools from 2012/13

3 In England, includes middle deemed primary schools as well as primary sponsor-led academies, primary convertor academies and primary free schools.

4 In England, includes direct grant nurseries.

5 In England, includes special converter academies. Excludes general hospital schools.

6 In Scotland, there was a change in the timing of the Pre-School Education Census in 2010/11, from January to September. September figures from 2010/11 may not be directly comparable with previously published January figures.

7 In Northern Ireland, excludes voluntary and private pre-school education centres.

8 In Scotland, figures include all providers of funded Early Learning and childcare, not only nurseries.

20.2 Full-time and part-time pupils by gender, age and school type, 2019/20

United Kingdom

	Maintained schools					Total main-tained schools	Non-maintained mainstream		All schools
	Nursery schools	Primary schools	Middle schools	Secondary schools	Special schools		Mainstream schools	Special schools	
All									
Under 2	3,150	4,171	0	41	8	7,370	3,483	4	10,857
2	21,015	58,449	173	547	230	80,414	9,214	25	89,653
3	59,353	264,483	734	2,704	1,450	328,724	19,834	40	348,598
4	61,471	672,353	823	8,286	4,954	747,887	23,704	55	771,646
5	3	732,121	797	8,256	6,744	747,921	25,144	57	773,122
6	0	751,062	809	8,154	7,745	767,770	26,811	82	794,663
7	0	769,704	855	8,558	9,063	788,180	30,520	112	818,812
8	0	769,679	884	8,254	9,704	788,521	33,318	145	821,984
9	0	745,348	820	18,670	10,356	775,194	35,322	193	810,709
10	0	732,761	870	18,819	10,798	763,248	37,648	268	801,164
11	0	63,568	2,862	677,624	14,772	758,826	46,653	356	805,835
12	0	4,890	2,634	708,585	15,039	731,148	47,111	358	778,617
13	0	8	2,463	688,618	15,737	706,826	48,156	383	755,365
14	0	0	2,466	671,494	17,118	691,078	49,448	398	740,924
15	0	1	2,306	651,747	19,485	673,539	51,312	395	725,246
16	0	1	700	279,841	7,776	288,318	41,359	324	330,001
17	0	0	524	237,326	6,411	244,261	39,279	324	283,864
18	0	0	26	19,575	4,507	24,108	6,425	236	30,769
19 and over	0	0	0	597	104	701	2,129	32	2,862
Total	144,992	5,568,599	20,746	4,017,696	162,001	9,914,034	577,478	3,787	10,495,299
of which									
England	42,110	4,714,771	n/a	3,409,277	143,542	8,309,700	576,870	3,787	8,890,357
Wales	683	271,323	20,746	171,271	5,153	469,176	:	n/a	469,176
Scotland	96,375	398,794	n/a	292,063	7,132	794,364	:	n/a	794,364
Northern Ireland	5,824	183,711	n/a	145,085	6,174	340,794	608	n/a	341,402
Females									
Under 2	1,257	2,073	0	12	4	3,346	1,672	2	5,020
2	7,249	29,088	90	276	106	36,809	4,786	13	41,608
3	14,456	130,810	385	1,363	505	147,519	10,100	19	157,638
4	216	328,721	415	4,041	1,407	334,800	12,150	18	346,968
5	0	358,748	406	4,036	1,767	364,957	12,525	18	377,500
6	0	367,768	384	4,004	2,028	374,184	13,330	24	387,538
7	0	377,402	412	4,212	2,328	384,354	15,033	27	399,414
8	0	377,533	426	4,064	2,380	384,403	16,219	37	400,659
9	0	365,903	420	9,216	2,565	378,104	17,148	44	395,296
10	0	360,497	443	9,378	2,614	372,932	18,074	68	391,074
11	0	30,967	1,389	334,731	3,926	371,013	22,637	96	393,746
12	0	1,907	1,320	349,819	4,027	357,073	22,823	94	379,990
13	0	4	1,218	339,778	4,225	345,225	23,443	115	368,783
14	0	0	1,208	331,510	4,822	337,540	23,863	107	361,510
15	0	1	1,157	321,765	5,789	328,712	24,764	103	353,579
16	0	0	397	146,987	2,663	150,047	20,132	97	170,276
17	0	0	307	128,032	2,191	130,530	19,239	96	149,865
18	0	0	13	10,075	1,634	11,722	2,940	79	14,741
19 and over	0	0	0	279	49	328	890	14	1,232
Total	23,178	2,731,422	10,390	2,003,578	45,030	4,813,598	281,768	1,071	5,096,437
of which									
England	20,007	2,312,803	n/a	1,700,083	39,639	4,072,532	281,768	1,071	4,355,371
Wales	313	132,997	10,390	85,175	1,445	230,320	:	n/a	230,320
Scotland	:	195,232	n/a	145,185	2,134	342,551	:	n/a	342,551
Northern Ireland	2,858	90,390	n/a	73,135	1,812	168,195	:	n/a	168,195

20.2 Full-time and part-time pupils by gender, age and school type, 2019/20

United Kingdom

	Maintained schools					Total main-tained schools	Non-maintained mainstream		All schools
	Nursery schools	Primary schools	Middle schools	Secondary schools	Special schools		Mainstream schools	Special schools	
Males									
Under 2	1,284	2,098	0	29	4	3,415	1,811	2	5,228
2	7,776	29,361	83	271	124	37,615	4,428	12	42,055
3	15,933	133,673	349	1,341	945	152,241	9,734	21	161,996
4	443	343,632	408	4,245	3,547	352,275	11,554	37	363,866
5	3	373,373	391	4,220	4,977	382,964	12,619	39	395,622
6	0	383,294	425	4,150	5,717	393,586	13,481	58	407,125
7	0	392,302	443	4,346	6,735	403,826	15,487	85	419,398
8	0	392,146	458	4,190	7,324	404,118	17,099	108	421,325
9	0	379,445	400	9,454	7,791	397,090	18,174	149	415,413
10	0	372,264	427	9,441	8,184	390,316	19,574	200	410,090
11	0	32,601	1,473	342,893	10,846	387,813	24,016	260	412,089
12	0	2,983	1,314	358,766	11,012	374,075	24,288	264	398,627
13	0	4	1,245	348,840	11,512	361,601	24,713	268	386,582
14	0	0	1,258	339,984	12,296	353,538	25,585	291	379,414
15	0	0	1,149	329,982	13,696	344,827	26,548	292	371,667
16	0	1	303	132,854	5,113	138,271	21,227	227	159,725
17	0	0	217	109,294	4,220	113,731	20,040	228	133,999
18	0	0	13	9,500	2,873	12,386	3,485	157	16,028
19 and over	0	0	0	318	55	373	1,239	18	1,630
Total	**25,439**	**2,837,177**	**10,356**	**2,014,118**	**116,971**	**5,004,061**	**295,102**	**2,716**	**5,301,879**
of which									
England	22,103	2,401,968	n/a	1,709,194	103,903	4,237,168	295,102	2,716	4,534,986
Wales	370	138,326	10,356	86,096	3,708	238,856	:	n/a	238,856
Scotland	:	203,562	n/a	146,878	4,998	355,438	:	n/a	355,438
Northern Ireland	2,966	93,321	n/a	71,950	4,362	172,599	:	n/a	172,599

Source: Department for Education; Welsh Government; Scottish Funding Council; Northern Ireland Department for the Economy
Publication: Education and training statistics for the UK (https://explore-education-statistics.service.gov.uk/)

(1) In England, special schools include pupil referral units.
(2) In Scotland, figures include all providers of funded Early Learning and childcare, not only nurseries.
(3) Primary and secondary figures include middle schools as deemed. Secondary schools include all-through schools.

20.3 Pupil: teacher ratios and pupil: adult ratios within schools by type of school time series

United Kingdom   Numbers

	Pupil: teacher ratio within schools(1)							Pupil: adult ratio within schools(2)						
	2000/01	2012/13	2013/14	2014/15	2015/16	2017/18	2018/19	2000/01	2012/13	2013/14	2014/15	2015/16	2017/18	2018/19
United Kingdom														
Public sector mainstream														
Nursery schools[3]	23.1	17.5	18.0	19.2	20.2	22.2	22.9	..	..	..	..	..	..	..
Primary schools[4][5]	22.3	20.5	20.5	20.7	20.8	20.6	20.5	..	..	..	..	..	..	..
Middle[6]	.	16.2	15.8	14.9	15.3	16.7	17.7	.	..	..	..	..	..	..
Secondary schools[7]	16.5	15.2	15.4	15.4	15.7	15.6	15.9	..	..	..	..	..	..	..
Non-maintained mainstream schools	9.7	8.0	8.1	7.9	7.8	7.6	7.5	..	..	..	..	..	..	..
Special schools														
Maintained[8]	6.4	5.9	5.7	6.1	6.2	6.0	6.0	..	..	..	..	..	..	..
Non-maintained	..	..	..	..	..	..	..	..	..	..	..	..	..	..
All schools	17.9	16.2	16.3	16.4	16.5	16.4	16.4	..	..	..	..	..	..	..
England[9][12]														
Public sector mainstream														
Nursery schools	17.7	16.5	17.1	18.4	19.6	22.0	22.8	6.8	4.9	4.8	4.9	5.0	5.6	5.7
State-funded primary schools[5]	22.9	20.9	21.0	21.0	21.1	20.9	20.9	15.7	11.5	11.3	11.1	11.0	11.2	11.2
State-funded secondary schools[7]	17.1	15.5	15.7	15.8	16.1	16.0	16.3	14.0	10.5	10.6	10.5	10.8	11.4	11.6
Non-maintained mainstream schools	9.7	8.0	8.1	7.9	7.8	7.6	7.5	..	..	..	..	..	..	..
Special schools														
State-funded[8]	6.7	6.2	5.9	6.4	6.5	6.3	6.1	..	..	..	..	..	2.1	2.1
Non-maintained	4.8	..	..	..	..	..	..	..	..	..	..	..	2.1	..
All schools	18.1	16.2	16.3	16.5	16.6	16.4	16.5	..	..	..	..	..	11.2	10.6
Wales														
Public sector mainstream														
Nursery schools	17.3	15.1	14.9	14.6	14.0	12.6	13.1	..	5.4	5.3	5.4	5.4	4.7	4.5
Primary schools	21.5	20.7	20.8	21.2	21.6	22.0	22.0	..	9.9	9.8	10.0	10.2	10.5	10.0
Middle[6]	.	16.2	15.8	14.9	15.3	16.7	17.7	.	10.6	10.2	9.2	9.6	9.9	9.9
Secondary schools	16.6	16.3	16.1	16.2	16.3	16.5	17.0	..	11.5	11.2	11.3	11.4	11.6	10.7
Non-maintained mainstream schools	9.6	7.9	7.9	8.2	8.0	8.1	8.4	..	..	..	5.8	5.6	4.5	1.9
Special schools (maintained)	6.8	6.7	6.5	6.6	6.5	6.7	6.7	..	..	..	1.7	1.7	1.7	1.6
All schools	18.4	17.8	17.7	18.0	18.2	18.4	18.7	..	..	..	9.8	9.9	10.0	8.9
Scotland														
Public sector mainstream														
Nursery schools[3]	28.5	..	..	..	..	..	..	..	..	..	..			
Primary schools[10]	19.0	16.3	16.5	16.7	16.7	16.4	16.1	..	11.8	11.9	12.1	12.3	11.8	11.6
Secondary schools	13.0	12.2	12.2	12.1	12.2	12.2	12.3	..	10.3	10.3	10.2	10.3	10.2	10.3
Non-maintained mainstream schools	10.1	..	..	..	..	..	..	..	..	..	..	..		
Special schools														
Maintained	4.2	3.4	3.5	3.5	3.6	3.6	3.6	..	..	..	..	..	..	..
Non-maintained	3.3	..	..	..	..	..	..	..	..	..	..	..	..	..
All schools	15.4	13.8	13.9	14.0	14.1	13.9	13.8	..	..	..	..	..	10.5	10.4
Northern Ireland[11]														
Grant-aided sector mainstream														
Nursery schools	24.4	25.6	25.5	25.4	25.6	25.5	25.8	..	..	..	..	..	..	..
Primary schools[4]	20.1	21.1	21.1	21.0	21.3	21.8	22.2	..	..	..	..	..	..	..
Secondary schools	14.5	15.3	15.4	15.2	15.1	15.4	15.7	..	..	..	..	..	..	..
Non-maintained mainstream schools	9.3	6.8	6.8	6.5	6.6	7.0	6.8	..	..	..	..	..	..	..
Special schools (maintained)	5.9	6.0	5.9	6.4	6.4	6.4	6.7	..	..	..	..	..	..	..
All schools	16.6	17.5	17.5	17.4	17.6	17.9	18.2	..	..	..	..	..	..	..

Source: Department for Education; Welsh Government; Scottish Government; Northern Ireland Department of Education

1 The Pupil:teacher ratio (PTR) within schools is calculated by dividing the total full-time equivalent (FTE) number of pupils on roll in schools by the total FTE number of qualified teachers. It excludes centrally employed teachers regularly employed in schools.
2 The Pupil: adult ratio (PAR) within schools is calculated by dividing the total FTE number of pupils on roll in schools by the total FTE number of all teachers and support staff employed in schools, excluding administrative and clerical staff.
3 Excludes pre-school education figures for Scotland as FTE pupil numbers are not available.
4 Includes figures for preparatory departments attached to grammar schools in Northern Ireland.
5 Figures for England include primary converter academies, primary sponsor-led academies and primary free schools.
6 In Wales, the Middle School for pupils of both primary and secondary school age was introduced in 2012/13.
7 Figures for England include secondary converter academies, secondary sponsor-led academies and secondary free schools.
8 Figures for England include special converter academies. Excludes general hospital schools.
9 Figures for England from 2010 are derived from the School Workforce Census and are not comparable with figures for earlier years.
10 In Scotland, 2010, 2011 and 2012 pre-school and primary school teacher FTEs and PTRs were revised to remove double counting across these two sectors.
11 Figures for Northern Ireland exclude temporary teachers i.e. teachers filling vacant posts, secondments or career breaks.
12 Figures for England include teachers without qualified teacher status (QTS) from 2016/17. For time series of PTRs in England, both including and excluding teachers without QTS, see the 'School workforce in England' publication - https://www.gov.uk/government/collections/statistics-school-workforce

20.4 All Schools [(1)] : Pupils with special educational needs by school type and type of provision [(2)(3)]

As at January each year: 2007-2019
England

	2007	2008	2009	2010	2011	2012	2013	2014	2015	2016	2017	2018	2019
ALL SCHOOLS													
Pupils on roll	8,167,715	8,121,955	8,092,280	8,098,360	8,123,865	8,178,200	8,249,810	8,331,385	8,438,145	8,559,540	8,669,080	8,735,100	8,819,765
Pupils with SEN	1,577,265	1,630,210	1,672,610	1,704,980	1,673,895	1,618,340	1,545,610	1,492,950	1,301,445	1,228,785	1,244,255	1,276,215	1,318,330
Incidence (%)	19.3	20.1	20.7	21.1	20.6	19.8	18.7	17.9	15.4	14.4	14.4	14.6	14.9
Pupils with statements or EHC plans	232,760	227,315	225,400	223,945	224,210	226,125	229,390	232,190	236,165	236,805	242,185	253,680	271,165
Incidence (%)	2.8	2.8	2.8	2.8	2.8	2.8	2.8	2.8	2.8	2.8	2.8	2.9	3.1
Pupils with SEN without statements or EHC plans	1,344,505	1,402,895	1,447,205	1,481,035	1,449,685	1,392,215	1,316,220	1,260,760	1,065,280	991,980	1,002,070	1,022,535	1,047,165
Incidence (%)	16.5	17.3	17.9	18.3	17.8	17.0	16.0	15.1	12.6	11.6	11.6	11.7	11.9
STATE-FUNDED SCHOOLS													
Maintained nursery													
Pupils on roll	37,640	37,440	37,285	37,575	38,830	39,395	38,820	39,915	41,455	43,730	43,785	42,845	42,205
Pupils with SEN	4,320	4,230	4,205	4,375	4,740	5,155	5,025	5,420	5,275	5,655	5,990	5,895	6,045
Incidence (%)	11.5	11.3	11.3	11.6	12.2	13.1	12.9	13.6	12.7	12.9	13.7	13.8	14.3
Placement (%)	0.3	0.3	0.3	0.3	0.3	0.3	0.3	0.4	0.4	0.5	0.5	0.5	0.5
Pupils with statements or EHC plans	310	265	285	265	250	305	245	265	265	315	370	350	390
Incidence (%)	0.8	0.7	0.8	0.7	0.6	0.8	0.6	0.7	0.6	0.7	0.8	0.8	0.9
Placement (%)	0	0	0	0.1	0.1	0.1	0.1	0.1	0.1	0.1	0.2	0.1	0.1
Pupils with SEN without statements or EHC plans	4,015	3,960	3,920	4,110	4,490	4,855	4,780	5,155	5,015	5,340	5,625	5,545	5,655
Incidence (%)	10.7	10.6	10.5	10.9	11.6	12.3	12.3	12.9	12.1	12.2	12.8	12.9	13.4
Placement (%)	0.3	0.3	0.3	0.3	0.3	0.3	0.4	0.4	0.5	0.5	0.6	0.5	0.5
State-funded primary													
Pupils on roll	4,110,750	4,090,400	4,077,350	4,096,580	4,137,755	4,217,000	4,309,580	4,416,710	4,510,310	4,615,170	4,689,660	4,716,245	4,727,090
Pupils with SEN	790,695	800,800	802,850	818,440	800,420	779,655	749,770	733,740	649,605	619,095	633,105	650,455	670,110
Incidence (%)	19.2	19.6	19.7	20.0	19.3	18.5	17.4	16.6	14.4	13.4	13.5	13.8	14.2
Placement (%)	50.1	49.1	48.0	48.0	47.8	48.2	48.5	49.1	49.9	50.4	50.9	51.0	50.8
Pupils with statements or EHC plans	61,800	59,695	58,505	57,850	57,855	58,535	59,710	60,830	61,970	60,445	62,390	66,790	74,405
Incidence (%)	1.5	1.5	1.4	1.4	1.4	1.4	1.4	1.4	1.4	1.3	1.3	1.4	1.6
Placement (%)	26.6	26.3	26.0	25.8	25.8	25.9	26.0	26.2	26.2	25.5	25.8	26.3	27.4
Pupils with SEN without statements or EHC plans	728,890	741,100	744,345	760,590	742,565	721,120	690,060	672,910	587,635	558,650	570,715	583,665	595,710
Incidence (%)	17.7	18.1	18.3	18.6	17.9	17.1	16.0	15.2	13.0	12.1	12.2	12.4	12.6
Placement (%)	54.2	52.8	51.4	51.4	51.2	51.8	52.4	53.4	55.2	56.3	57.0	57.1	56.9
State-funded secondary													
Pupils on roll	3,325,625	3,294,575	3,278,130	3,278,485	3,262,635	3,234,875	3,210,120	3,181,360	3,184,730	3,193,420	3,223,090	3,258,450	3,327,970
Pupils with SEN	615,045	654,935	692,255	710,525	695,135	654,620	608,405	566,120	454,140	406,430	399,005	399,800	413,790
Incidence (%)	18.5	19.9	21.1	21.7	21.3	20.2	19.0	17.8	14.3	12.7	12.4	12.3	12.4
Placement (%)	39.0	40.2	41.4	41.7	41.5	40.4	39.4	37.9	34.9	33.1	32.1	31.3	31.4
Pupils with statements or EHC plans	71,190	67,875	65,890	64,605	63,720	62,630	61,615	59,700	58,100	55,740	53,865	53,025	55,235
Incidence (%)	2.1	2.1	2.0	2.0	2.0	1.9	1.9	1.9	1.8	1.7	1.7	1.6	1.7
Placement (%)	30.6	29.9	29.2	28.8	28.4	27.7	26.9	25.7	24.6	23.5	22.2	20.9	20.4
Pupils with SEN without statements or EHC plans	543,850	587,060	626,365	645,920	631,415	591,985	546,790	506,420	396,035	350,695	345,140	346,775	358,555
Incidence (%)	16.4	17.8	19.1	19.7	19.4	18.3	17.0	15.9	12.4	11.0	10.7	10.6	10.8
Placement (%)	40.5	41.8	43.3	43.6	43.6	42.5	41.5	40.2	37.2	35.4	34.4	33.9	34.2
State-funded special													
Pupils on roll	87,010	87,135	87,615	88,690	89,860	91,590	94,350	97,395	101,250	105,365	109,855	115,315	121,740
Pupils with SEN	85,685	85,775	86,670	87,590	88,905	90,665	93,345	96,545	100,420	104,305	109,050	114,755	121,175
Incidence (%)	98.5	98.4	98.9	98.8	98.9	99.0	98.9	99.1	99.2	99.0	99.3	99.5	99.5
Placement (%)	5.4	5.3	5.2	5.1	5.3	5.6	6.0	6.5	7.7	8.5	8.8	9.0	9.2

20.4 All Schools [1] : Pupils with special educational needs by school type and type of provision [2][3]

As at January each year: 2007-2019

England

	2007	2008	2009	2010	2011	2012	2013	2014	2015	2016	2017	2018	2019
Pupils with statements or EHC plans	83,645	83,600	84,295	85,445	86,660	88,230	90,845	94,120	97,830	101,530	106,190	112,130	118,820
Incidence (%)	96.1	95.9	96.2	96.3	96.4	96.3	96.3	96.6	96.6	96.4	96.7	97.2	97.6
Placement (%)	35.9	36.8	37.4	38.2	38.7	39.0	39.6	40.5	41.4	42.9	43.8	44.2	43.8
Pupils with SEN without statements or EHC plans	2,040	2,175	2,375	2,145	2,245	2,435	2,500	2,425	2,590	2,775	2,860	2,625	2,355
Incidence (%)	2.3	2.5	2.7	2.4	2.5	2.7	2.6	2.5	2.6	2.6	2.6	2.3	1.9
Placement (%)	0.2	0.2	0.2	0.1	0.2	0.2	0.2	0.2	0.2	0.3	0.3	0.3	0.2
Pupil Referral Units [4]													
Pupils on roll	24,165	25,290	24,760	15,550	14,050	13,495	12,950	12,895	13,585	15,015	15,670	16,730	16,135
Pupils with SEN	18,610	18,945	19,585	11,580	11,095	10,805	10,545	10,215	11,090	11,515	12,085	13,315	13,070
Incidence (%)	77.0	74.9	79.1	74.5	79.0	80.1	81.4	79.2	81.6	76.7	77.1	79.6	81.0
Placement (%)	1.2	1.2	1.2	0.7	0.7	0.7	0.7	0.7	0.9	0.9	1.0	1.0	1.0
Pupils with statements or EHC plans	3,425	3,260	3,230	1,910	1,695	1,610	1,630	1,545	1,565	1,500	1,635	1,865	2,160
Incidence (%)	14.2	12.9	13.0	12.3	12.1	11.9	12.6	12.0	11.5	10.0	10.4	11.2	13.4
Placement (%)	1.5	1.4	1.4	0.9	0.8	0.7	0.7	0.7	0.7	0.6	0.7	0.7	0.8
Pupils with SEN without statements or EHC plans	15,185	15,685	16,360	9,670	9,405	9,195	8,920	8,670	9,525	10,015	10,455	11,445	10,910
Incidence (%)	62.8	62.0	66.1	62.2	66.9	68.2	68.9	67.2	70.1	66.7	66.7	68.4	67.6
Placement (%)	1.1	1.1	1.1	0.7	0.6	0.7	0.7	0.7	0.9	1.0	1.0	1.1	1.0
OTHER SCHOOLS													
Independent													
Pupils on roll	577,785	582,425	582,490	576,940	576,325	577,515	579,740	579,035	582,865	583,030	583,270	581,875	580,955
Pupils with SEN	58,250	60,925	62,500	68,040	69,285	73,205	74,360	76,870	76,975	77,995	81,275	88,370	90,485
Incidence (%)	10.1	10.5	10.7	11.8	12.0	12.7	12.8	13.3	13.2	13.4	13.9	15.2	15.6
Placement (%)	3.7	3.7	3.7	4.0	4.1	4.5	4.8	5.1	5.9	6.3	6.5	6.9	6.9
Pupils with statements or EHC plans	7,760	8,055	8,690	9,470	9,750	10,630	11,265	11,790	12,565	13,530	14,065	15,970	16,575
Incidence (%)	1.3	1.4	1.5	1.6	1.7	1.8	1.9	2.0	2.2	2.3	2.4	2.7	2.9
Placement (%)	3.3	3.5	3.9	4.2	4.3	4.7	4.9	5.1	5.3	5.7	5.8	6.3	6.1
Pupils with SEN without statements or EHC plans	50,490	52,870	53,805	58,570	59,535	62,575	63,095	65,080	64,415	64,465	67,210	72,405	73,910
Incidence (%)	8.7	9.1	9.2	10.2	10.3	10.8	10.9	11.2	11.1	11.1	11.5	12.4	12.7
Placement (%)	3.8	3.8	3.7	4.0	4.1	4.5	4.8	5.2	6.0	6.5	6.7	7.1	7.1
Non-maintained special													
Pupils on roll	4,740	4,695	4,655	4,540	4,415	4,325	4,245	4,080	3,955	3,815	3,755	3,640	3,670
Pupils with SEN	4,665	4,605	4,540	4,430	4,310	4,235	4,155	4,040	3,935	3,795	3,740	3,625	3,655
Incidence (%)	98.4	98.1	97.6	97.6	97.6	97.8	97.9	99.0	99.6	99.5	99.5	99.7	99.6
Placement (%)	0.3	0.3	0.3	0.3	0.3	0.3	0.3	0.3	0.3	0.3	0.3	0.3	0.3
Pupils with statements or EHC plans	4,630	4,565	4,500	4,400	4,280	4,185	4,085	3,945	3,870	3,745	3,670	3,550	3,585
Incidence (%)	97.7	97.3	96.7	97.0	97.0	96.7	96.1	96.7	97.9	98.2	97.7	97.6	97.6
Placement (%)	2.0	2.0	2.0	2.0	1.9	1.9	1.8	1.7	1.6	1.6	1.5	1.4	1.3
Pupils with SEN without statements or EHC plans	35	40	40	30	25	50	75	95	65	50	65	75	70
Incidence (%)	0.7	0.8	0.9	0.6	0.6	1.1	1.7	2.3	1.7	1.3	1.8	2.1	1.9
Placement (%)	0.0	0.0	0.0	0.0	0.0	0.0	0.0	0.0	0.0	0.0	0.0	0.0	0.0

Source: School Census and School Level Annual School Census

Notes:

(1) Includes all academies including free schools, state-funded and non-maintained special schools, middle schools as deemed, all-through schools, city technology colleges, university technology colleges, studio schools, direct grant nursery schools, pupil referral units and general hospital schools.

(2) Incidence of pupils - the number of pupils with statements or EHC plans expressed as a proportion of the number of pupils on roll.

(3) Placement of pupils - the number of pupils with statements or EHC plans expressed as a proportion of the number of pupils with statements in all schools.

(4) Includes pupils registered with other providers, in alternative provision academies, including free schools and in further education colleges. Prior to 2010 includes dual subsidiary registered pupils.

20.5 GCSE, A level, SQA(1) and vocational qualifications obtained by pupils and students, 2000/01 and 2011/12 - 2017/18

United Kingdom

Percentages and thousands

	2000/01	2011/12	2012/13	2013/14	2014/15	2015/16	2016/17	2017/18
All								
GCSE and vocational qualifications								
Pupils in their last year of compulsory education(2)								
England, Wales and Northern Ireland(3)								
Percentage achieving GCSE or equivalent								
5 or more grades A*-C[4]	51.0	81.2	81.5	..	..	..	..	..
5 or more grades A*-C incl English and Maths	..	59.0	58.9	..	..	..	..	..
Any Passes	..	99.4	99.6	..	..	..	..	..
England (19)(20)(21)								
Achieved 9-4 in all components English and Maths GCSE	..	..	..	..	..	..	..	59.4
Achieved 9-4 in all components English Bacculaureate GCSE	..	..	..	..	19.7	23.1	21.9	22.2
Average Attainment 8 score per pupil					47.4	48.5	44.6	44.5
Any Passes	..	..	..	..	..	..	..	96.5
Wales								
5 or more GCSEs at grade A*-C (Level 2 threshold)								
incl. a GCSE pass (A*-C) in English/Welsh and maths	..	51.1	52.7	55.4	57.9	60.3	54.6	55.1
5 or more GCSEs at grade A*-C[4] (Level 2 threshold)	49.8	72.6	77.8	82.3	84.1	84.0	67.0	67.0
5 or more GCSEs at grade A*-G (Level 1 threshold)	84.8	91.8	93.2	94.0	94.4	95.3	94.4	93.7
Northern Ireland								
5 or more grades A*-C[4]	..	77.8	79.6	81.8	82.8	83.3	84.6	86.0
5 or more grades A*-C incl English and Maths	..	60.1	60.9	65.2	67.0	67.9	70.3	71.8
5 or more grades A* - G	..	97.5	97.7	98.2	98.4	98.6	98.6	98.8
A level and equivalent vocational qualifications								
Pupils/students in education(5)(6)								
England, Wales and Northern Ireland(3)								
Percentage achieving A levels and								
equivalent(7) 2 or more passes	37.4	54.7	54.8	54.3	55.0	..	..	..
Population aged 17 (thousands)(8)	717.9	700.4	709.0	711.0	716.4	702.4	698.8	623.3
England								
Percentage of population aged 17 achieving:								
at least 2 substantial level 3 passes (7)(12)(13)(14)	..	..	..	..	..	57.5	56.9	43.0
Wales								
Percentage of population aged 17 achieving:								
2 or more A levels at grades A-E or equivalent								
(level 3 threshold) (7)(17)	..	..	..	..	..	33.0	31.2	30.9
Percentage of students aged 17 achieving:								
2 or more A levels at grades A-E or equivalent								
(level 3 threshold) (7)(17)	92.7	96.9	96.5	97.1	97.0	98.0	97.1	97.6
Northern Ireland								
Percentage of students achieving:								
3 or more A levels grades A* - C		64.8	65.2	65.0	64.9	66.3	69.0	70.2
2 or more A levels at grades A*-E		98.1	98.1	98.0	98.1	98.1	98.7	98.3
Percentage of population aged 17 achieving:								
3 or more passes at A level or equivalent (7)(18)	..	..	..	..	..	53.0	52.2	52.3
Scotland (SQA qualifications obtained by school leavers(9))								
Percentage of school leavers attaining								
1 or more qualifications at SCQF level 4 or better	..	95.8	96.3	96.3	96.2	96.3	96.3	96.2
1 or more qualifications at SCQF level 5 or better	..	81.6	82.7	84.3	85.2	85.6	86.1	85.9
1 or more qualifications at SCQF level 6 or better	..	55.8	55.8	58.1	60.2	61.7	61.2	62.2

20.5 GCSE, A level, SQA(1) and vocational qualifications obtained by pupils and students, 2000/01 and 2011/12 - 2017/18

United Kingdom | | | | | | | | Percentages and thousands

	2000/01	2011/12	2012/13	2013/14	2014/15	2015/16	2016/17	2017/18
Males								
<u>GCSE and vocational qualifications</u>								
Pupils in their last year of compulsory education(2)								
England, Wales and Northern Ireland(3)								
Percentage achieving GCSE or equivalent								
5 or more grades A*-C[4]	45.7	77.6	77.7	..	..	..	..	..
5 or more grades A*-C incl English and Maths	..	54.3	53.7	..	..	..	..	..
Any Passes	..	99.1	99.3	..	..	..	..	..
England (19)(20)(21)								
Achieved 9-4 in all components English and Maths GCSE	..	..	..	..	..	..	..	55.5
Achieved 9-4 in all components English Bacculaureate GCSE	..	..	..	..	15.7	18.1	17.1	17.3
Average Attainment 8 score per pupil					45.0	46.0	41.8	41.5
Any Passes	..	..	..	..	..	..		95.4
Wales								
5 or more GCSEs at grade A*-C (Level 2 threshold)								
incl. a GCSE pass (A*-C) in English/Welsh and maths	..	46.9	48.7	51.4	54.3	56.1	50.7	50.1
5 or more GCSEs at grade A*-C[4] (Level 2 threshold)	44.7	67.8	73.7	78.6	80.9	80.7	61.8	61.2
5 or more GCSEs at grade A*-G (Level 1 threshold)	81.7	89.8	91.6	92.5	93.2	93.9	93.1	92.1
Northern Ireland								
5 or more grades A*-C[4]	..	73.4	75.5	77.8	79.4	79.6	81.0	82.3
5 or more grades A*-C incl English and Maths	..	55.2	56.4	60.9	63.2	64.2	66.8	67.1
5 or more grades A* - G	..	96.8	97.1	97.7	98.1	98.3	98.3	98.3
<u>A level and equivalent vocational qualifications</u>								
Pupils/students in education(5)(6)								
England, Wales and Northern Ireland(3)								
Percentage achieving A levels and								
equivalent(7) 2 or more passes	33.4	49.7	50.1	49.2	49.7	..	..	..
Population aged 17 (thousands)(8)	366.6	359.9	364.1	366.8	367.5	360.4	359.1	320.5
England								
Percentage of population aged 17 achieving:								
at least 2 substantial level 3 passes (7)(12)(13)(14)	..	..	..	..	..	52.5	51.6	37.0
Wales								
Percentage of population aged 17 achieving:								
2 or more A levels at grades A-E or equivalent								
(level 3 threshold) (7)(17)	..	..	..	..	..	24.9	23.8	23.3
Percentage of students aged 17 achieving:								
2 or more A levels at grades A-E or equivalent								
(level 3 threshold) (7)(17)	90.7	95.7	95.8	96.2	95.9	97.1	96.2	96.7
Northern Ireland								
Percentage of students achieving:								
3 or more A levels grades A* - C	..	61.3	61.9	61.1	61.2	63.3	65.3	67.0
2 or more A levels at grades A*-E	..	97.5	98.0	97.6	97.6	98.1	98.4	97.9
Percentage of population aged 17 achieving:								
3 or more passes at A level or equivalent (7)(18)	..	..	..	..	..	44.9	44.2	44.3
Scotland *(SQA qualifications obtained by school leavers(9))*								
Percentage of school leavers achieving:								
1 or more qualifications at SCQF level 4 or better	..	95.1	95.8	95.7	95.7	95.9	95.9	95.6
1 or more qualifications at SCQF level 5 or better	..	79.8	81.0	82.2	83.1	83.9	84.1	83.7
1 or more qualifications at SCQF level 6 or better	..	50.6	50.6	52.9	54.7	56.3	55.5	56.0

20.5 GCSE, A level, SQA(1) and vocational qualifications obtained by pupils and students, 2000/01 and 2011/12 - 2017/18

United Kingdom · Percentages and thousands

	2000/01	2011/12	2012/13	2013/14	2014/15	2015/16	2016/17	2017/18
Females								
GCSE and vocational qualifications								
Pupils in their last year of compulsory education(2)								
England, Wales and Northern Ireland(3)								
Percentage achieving GCSE or equivalent								
5 or more grades A*-C[4]	56.5	85.0	85.4	..	..	..	..	..
5 or more grades A*-C incl English and Maths	..	63.9	64.4	..	..	..	..	..
Any Passes	..	99.8	100.0	..	..	..	..	..
England (19)(20)(21)								
Achieved 9-4 in all components English and Maths GCSE	..	..	..	..	..	..	..	63.7
Achieved 9-4 in all components English Bacculaureate GCSE	..	..	..	..	23.9	28.3	26.9	27.4
Average Attainment 8 score per pupil					49.9	51.1	47.6	47.7
Any Passes	..	..	..	..	..	..	..	97.6
Wales								
5 or more GCSEs at grade A*-C (Level 2 threshold)								
incl. a GCSE pass (A*-C) in English/Welsh and maths	..	55.5	57.0	59.7	61.8	64.7	58.8	60.5
5 or more GCSEs at grade A*-C[4] (Level 2 threshold)	55.0	77.6	82.1	86.3	87.5	87.6	72.5	73.2
5 or more GCSEs at grade A*-G (Level 1 threshold)	87.4	93.8	94.8	95.6	95.7	96.7	95.9	95.4
Northern Ireland								
5 or more grades A*-C[4]	..	82.4	83.7	85.7	86.2	87.0	88.2	89.7
5 or more grades A*-C incl English and Maths	..	65.1	65.5	69.3	70.9	71.6	73.8	76.5
5 or more grades A* - G	..	98.2	98.4	98.8	98.8	98.9	98.8	99.3
A level and equivalent vocational qualifications								
Pupils/students in education(5)(6)								
England, Wales and Northern Ireland(3)								
Percentage achieving A levels and								
equivalent(7) 2 or more passes	41.6	60.1	59.9	59.7	60.6	..	..	..
Population aged 17 (thousands)(8)	351.3	340.4	345.0	344.2	348.9	342.0	339.7	302.7
England								
Percentage of population aged 17 achieving:								
at least 2 substantial level 3 passes (7)(12)(13)(14)	..	..	..	..	..	62.7	62.6	49.3
Wales								
Percentage of population aged 17 achieving:								
2 or more A levels at grades A-E or equivalent								
(level 3 threshold) (7)(17)	..	..	..	..	..	33.0	31.2	30.9
Percentage of students aged 17 achieving:								
2 or more A levels at grades A-E or equivalent								
(level 3 threshold) (7)(17)	94.3	97.8	97.0	97.8	97.8	98.6	97.9	98.3
Northern Ireland								
Percentage of students achieving:								
3 or more A levels grades A* - C	..	67.5	67.8	68.1	67.7	68.6	71.9	72.8
2 or more A levels at grades A*-E	..	98.6	98.2	98.3	98.4	98.2	98.9	98.7
Percentage of population aged 17 achieving:								
3 or more passes at A level or equivalent (7)(18)	..	..	..	..	..	61.4	60.5	60.9
Scotland (SQA qualifications obtained by school leavers (9))								
Percentage of school leavers attaining								
1 or more qualifications at SCQF level 4 or better	..	96.5	96.8	96.9	96.7	96.8	96.7	96.8
1 or more qualifications at SCQF level 5 or better	..	83.4	84.5	86.4	87.3	87.5	88.2	88.2
1 or more qualifications at SCQF level 6 or better	..	61.1	61.1	63.4	65.9	67.3	67.2	68.6

Source: Department for Education; Welsh Government; Scottish Government; Northern Ireland Department of Education

741

20.5 GCSE, A level, SQA(1) and vocational qualifications obtained by pupils and students, 2000/01 and 2011/12 - 2017/18

United Kingdom

Footnotes (Table20.5)

1 The Scottish Qualifications Authority (SQA) is the national accreditation and awarding body in Scotland.

2 Scotland's data for 2013/14 data has been revised. Details can be found here:
http://www.gov.scot/Topics/Statistics/Browse/School-Education/leavedestla/follleavedestat/attainmentandleavers1415

3 From 2015/16, cohort based on pupils in Year 11. Up to 2014/15, cohort based on pupils aged 15 at the start of the academic year in Wales; pupils in Year S4 in Scotland. From 2004/05, pupils at the end of Key Stage 4 in England.

4 Also includes Scotland for 2009/10 and earlier.

5 The national performance measures used to hold schools to account in England no longer include the grades pupils achieved through resits. However, these are included in Wales and Northern Ireland.

6 Standard Grades 1-3/Intermediate 2 A-C/Intermediate 1 A in England for 2009/10 and earlier.

7 The number of pupils in schools and students in further education colleges in England, Wales and Northern Ireland expressed as a percentage of the 17-year-old population. Pupils and students are generally aged 16-18 at the start of the academic year in England, and aged 17 at the start of the academic year in Wales. Figures from 2002/03 for Wales and Northern Ireland relate to schools only. Figures for Wales exclude independent schools for 2016/17

8 Figures, other than for Scotland, include Vocational Certificates of Education (VCE) and, previously, Advanced level GNVQ, which is equivalent to 2 A levels or AS equivalents. From 2006/07, figures included for England cover achievements in all Level 3 qualifications approved under Section 96 of the Learning and Skills Act (2000), therefore UK aggregates are not comparable with previous years.

9 Qualifications in Scotland are based on the Scottish Credit and Qualifications Framework (SCQF). There are 12 levels on the framework, SCQF levels 1 to 7 are covered by school education. The new National qualifications, along with Standard Grades and Intermediates make up SCQF levels 3 to 5. Since 2013/14, under Curriculum for Excellence, Standard Grades are being phased out and replaced with National 3, 4 and 5 qualifications, and Intermediates will cease to exist from 2015/16. For most young people in Scotland S4 is the last compulsory year of school, but the majority will choose to stay on and complete S5 and S6. Highers (SCQF level 6) are generally taken in S5/S6; Highers, sometimes along with Advanced Highers (SCQF level 7, usually taken in S6) are the qualifications required for entry to Higher Education. School leaver data looks at a pupil's attainment throughout their school education. The leaver cohort is made up of all pupils who leave during or at the end of that year, so it contains pupils who leave at various stages of their schooling. 2 AS levels or 2 Highers/1 Advanced Higher or 1 each in Scotland, count as 1 A level pass for 2009/10 and earlier.

10 For 2015/16, based on mid-2015 based population projections. These take into account the 2011 Census. The figures for UK excluding Scotland are derived by the summation of England, Wales and Northern Ireland.

11 Qualifications in Scotland are based on the Scottish Credit and Qualifications Framework (SCQF). There are 12 levels on the framework, SCQF levels 1 to 7 are covered by school education. The new National qualifications, along with Standard Grades and Intermediates make up SCQF levels 3 to 5. Since 2013/14, under Curriculum for Excellence, Standard Grades are being phased out and replaced with National 3, 4 and 5 qualifications, and Intermediates will cease to exist from 2015/16. For most young people in Scotland S4 is the last compulsory year of school, but the majority will choose to stay on and complete S5 and S6. Highers (SCQF level 6) are generally taken in S5/S6; Highers, sometimes along with Advanced Highers (SCQF level 7, usually taken in S6) are the qualifications required for entry to Higher Education. School leaver data looks at a pupil's attainment throughout their school education. The leaver cohort is made up of all pupils who leave during or at the end of that year, so it contains pupils who leave at various stages of their schooling. Although Standard Grades were not available in 2013/14, the 2013/14 school leaver data will include Standard Grade attainment of leavers who sat these qualifications in earlier years of their schooling. New Highers were phased in in 2014/15 and run concurrently with the previous qualifications. Both sets of qualifications meet the SCQF level 6 standard and are comparable.

12 Substantial level 3 qualifications are defined as qualifications that are at least the size of an A level (180 guided learning hours per year), such as a BTEC subsidiary diploma level 3, and which count in the 16-18 performance tables. If a qualification is equal in size to 2 A levels it is counted as 2 substantial level 3 qualifications. Information on the qualifications that count in the 16-18 performance tables is available in the 16-19 technical guide:
https://www.gov.uk/government/publications/16-to-19-accountability-headline-measures-technical-guide

13 The percentage of the population achieving at least 2 substantial level 3 passes is not directly comparable to previous years since a reformed list of approved vocational level 3 qualifications has been used for 2017/18.

14 Young people generally aged 16-18 at the start of the academic year.

15 Where a candidate attempted an examination in the same subject more than once, only the highest value pass has been counted. However, some double counting may occur if a student enters for more than one subject within a subject category.

16 Pupils aged 15 at the start of the academic year.

17 Wales: For 2017/18 data this refers to the percentage of population achieving at least 2 substantial level 3 passes. This includes Vocational Certificates of Education (VCE), which is equivalent to 2 A levels or AS equivalents. It excludes Further Education colleges and Independent schools.

18 Northern Ireland: For 2017/18 data this refers to the percentage of population achieving 2 or more passes at A Level or equivalent at grades A* -E. This figure excludes Further Education Colleges.

19 As a percentage of all pupils at the end of key stage 4. In 2014/15 and earlier, where the English language and English literature option was chosen in English, exams in both must be taken and a C grade or above achieved in English language. From 2015/16, to meet the English requirement of the A*-C in English and maths attainment measure, a C in either English language or English literature counts and there is no requirement to take both. From 2017, following the introduction of the reformed 9 to 1 GCSEs in English, a grade 5 or above in either English language or English literature counts and there remains no requirement to take both in order to achieve a pass. Grades 9-4 achievement shows pupils who achieved a grade 4 or above in either English language or English literature and Mathematics and is shown alongside the headline measure for transparency and comparability.

20 As announced in July 2017, from 2018 the headline EBacc attainment measure is the EBacc average point score (EBacc APS). EBacc APS measures pupils' point scores across the five pillars of the EBacc. This ensures the attainment of all pupils is recognised, not just those at particular grade boundaries, encouraging schools to enter pupils of all abilities, and support them to achieve their full potential.

21 New GCSEs in English and maths were taught from September 2015 with the first examinations taking place in Summer 2017. New GCSEs in other subjects were phased in for first teaching from September 2016, continuing into 2017 and a very small number from 2018. To ensure all students benefit from the reformed qualifications, only the new GCSEs will be included in the secondary performance tables as they are introduced (for 2017, this included only reformed GCSEs in English and maths, and in 2018, this included a further 20 new GCSEs with a smaller number being introduced in 2019 and 2020). As part of these reforms, a new grading system has been introduced from 2017 to replace the A* to G system with a new 9 to 1 scale for new reformed GCSEs.

20.6 HE qualifications obtained by sex, subject area** and level of qualification obtained 2014/15 to 2018/19

	2014/15 All levels	2015/16 All levels	2016/17 All levels	2017/18 All levels	2018/19 Postgraduate research	Postgraduate taught	Total postgraduate	First degree	Other undergraduate	Total undergraduate	All levels
Female											
Medicine & dentistry	10880	10730	10490	10825	1470	3910	5385	5625	220	5845	11,225
Subjects allied to medicine	65035	64045	66935	68280	1280	18255	19540	37715	10695	48410	67,950
Biological sciences	37125	38400	40665	44905	2740	12410	15145	29110	3325	32435	47,580
Veterinary science	985	1020	1070	1120	55	240	295	930	15	950	1,245
Agriculture & related subjects	3695	3720	4005	3915	125	1050	1175	2115	1125	3240	4,415
Physical sciences	11010	11025	11560	12405	1375	2975	4350	7685	640	8325	12,675
Mathematical sciences	4695	4770	5015	5095	225	1155	1380	3410	250	3660	5,045
Computer science	5165	5165	5265	5705	315	2540	2855	3095	395	3490	6,345
Engineering & technology	8990	9150	9530	10095	1070	4310	5380	4810	565	5375	10,755
Architecture, building & planning	6700	6975	7270	7810	190	4125	4315	3265	585	3855	8,170
Total - Science subject areas	154280	155000	161805	170155	8850	50975	59820	97760	17820	115585	175,405
Percentage - Science subject areas	36%	36%	37%	38%	63%	30%	33%	40%	43%	40%	38%
Social studies	43210	44670	45950	47385	1170	17470	18640	28115	4830	32940	51,585
Law	18870	19135	19215	19800	280	7400	7675	12220	1080	13305	20,980
Business & administrative studies	68250	66005	67390	69325	630	37040	37670	32995	3600	36595	74,260
Mass communications & documentation	11170	11335	11565	12065	150	5415	5565	6385	485	6870	12,435
Languages	23730	23105	22775	22455	975	5315	6290	14715	1515	16230	22,520
Historical & philosophical studies	13450	13855	14260	14525	785	3485	4270	9600	790	10390	14,660
Creative arts & design	35810	36305	38030	39060	465	9795	10255	27160	3765	30925	41,180
Education	54075	52580	52055	51100	780	30645	31425	13680	6220	19900	51,325
Combined	3380	3025	3005	2910	5	35	40	1895	890	2790	2,830
Total - All subject areas	426220	425020	436055	448780	14090	167565	181660	244535	40995	285525	467,185
Male											
Medicine & dentistry	7840	7770	7735	7750	1090	2360	3450	4285	60	4350	7,800
Subjects allied to medicine	16625	16870	17960	17965	825	5840	6660	8575	2860	11440	18,100
Biological sciences	23200	24480	25165	25830	1725	5105	6830	16185	2725	18910	25,740
Veterinary science	355	345	360	320	30	125	155	235	5	240	400
Agriculture & related subjects	2330	2185	2135	2090	110	660	765	910	460	1370	2,135
Physical sciences	15950	16190	16255	16705	2315	2775	5090	10120	1105	11225	16,315
Mathematical sciences	7200	7445	7810	7980	600	1710	2305	5365	530	5890	8,200
Computer science	21600	21250	22545	24200	905	6080	6985	15520	2920	18440	25,425
Engineering & technology	41380	40940	41520	42490	2975	11385	14360	22755	4665	27425	41,785
Architecture, building & planning	11010	10790	10905	11380	225	4545	4770	5110	1375	6485	11,255
Total - Science subject areas	147490	148260	152395	156705	10795	40585	51380	89060	16715	105775	157,155
Percentage - Science subject areas	46%	47%	47%	48%	71%	38%	42%	50%	55%	50%	47%
Social studies	26280	26875	26815	27830	1040	9915	10955	16905	1880	18780	29,740
Law	12365	12375	11990	12335	285	4775	5060	6370	795	7160	12,220
Business & administrative studies	64075	62350	62200	63470	770	28970	29745	32685	4385	37070	66,815
Mass communications & documentation	6970	6850	7090	7350	95	2235	2330	4660	555	5215	7,550
Languages	10240	9730	9510	9110	580	1980	2560	5135	1035	6165	8,725
Historical & philosophical studies	11920	12140	12420	12275	945	2865	3810	7675	690	8365	12,175
Creative arts & design	20235	20430	20450	20845	370	4675	5045	14385	2185	16570	21,620
Education	16960	16620	16285	16025	340	11655	11995	1820	1655	3475	15,470
Combined	2145	1935	1840	1840	0	15	15	1035	630	1660	1,680
Total - All subject areas	318685	317570	321000	327790	15220	107680	122895	179720	30525	210245	333,145
All sexes											
Medicine & dentistry	18725	18500	18230	18590	2565	6290	8855	9915	280	10195	19,050
Subjects allied to medicine	81665	80920	84920	86290	2105	24140	26245	46310	13560	59870	86,115
Biological sciences	60325	62885	65850	70765	4465	17560	22025	45320	6055	51375	73,405
Veterinary science	1340	1365	1430	1445	85	365	450	1165	25	1190	1,645
Agriculture & related subjects	6030	5900	6140	6010	235	1715	1950	3020	1590	4610	6,560
Physical sciences	26965	27225	27830	29130	3695	5765	9460	17820	1745	19560	29,025
Mathematical sciences	11895	12220	12835	13085	825	2870	3695	8785	780	9565	13,260
Computer science	26775	26415	27820	29925	1215	8630	9850	18635	3320	21960	31,805
Engineering & technology	50375	50100	51065	52605	4050	15695	·19745	27580	5235	32815	52,560
Architecture, building & planning	17710	17770	18180	19190	415	8670	9085	8380	1965	10345	19,430
Total - Science subject areas	301795	303305	314295	327035	19650	91710	111360	186925	34555	221485	332,845
Percentage - Science subject areas	41%	41%	42%	42%	67%	33%	37%	44%	48%	45%	42%
Social studies	69500	71560	72805	75265	2215	27465	29680	45050	6715	51765	81,440
Law	31240	31510	31215	32155	560	12195	12755	18600	1880	20480	33,235
Business & administrative studies	132335	128365	129600	132815	1400	66050	67450	65695	7985	73675	141,125
Mass communications & documentation	18145	18185	18665	19435	250	7670	7920	11055	1040	12095	20,015
Languages	33975	32845	32305	31595	1555	7325	8880	19875	2545	22425	31,300
Historical & philosophical studies	25380	26020	26700	26835	1735	6385	8120	17295	1480	18775	26,895
Creative arts & design	56065	56755	58515	59980	835	14510	15350	41615	5965	47580	62,930
Education	71045	69210	68350	67145	1120	42335	43455	15500	7880	23385	66,835
Combined	5525	4960	4850	4750	5	55	60	2930	1520	4450	4,510
Total - All subject areas*	745005	742730	757300	777005	29330	275695	305025	424540	71570	496110	801,135

Source:Higher Education Statistics Agency (HESA)

In this table 0,1, 2 are rounded to 0. All other numbers are rounded up or down to the nearest multiple of 5.
Percentages are calculated on unrounded data. Percentages are rounded to the nearest whole number. Percentages calculated on populations which contain fewer than 22.5 individuals are suppressed and represented as "..".
See data intelligence.
* Students with a sex of 'other' are included in total figures but not in separate breakdowns.
** Analyses of subject information show Full-person equivalent (FPE). These are derived by splitting student instances between the different subjects that make up their course aim.

20.7 HE qualifications obtained by sex, level of qualification obtained, mode of study 2014/15 to 2018/19

	2014/15 All modes	2015/16 All modes	2016/17 All modes	2017/18 All modes	2018/19		
					Full-time	Part-time	All modes
All UK HE providers							
Female							
Postgraduate research	12505	12645	13185	13185	11560	2535	14095
Postgraduate taught	137270	137580	143735	143735	125130	48335	173465
Postgraduate Certificate in Education△	15205	14875	13735	13735	14780	665	15445
First degree	225080	231635	239955	239955	232910	15495	248410
Foundation degree	10130	8895	8340	8340	5575	2455	8035
HNC/HND	2085	4490	5280	5280	4170	565	4740
Other undergraduate	39145	35125	33755	33755	19925	12880	32805
Professional Graduate Certificate in Education	2555	1830	1530	1530	775	290	1065
Total female	**426220**	**432205**	**445785**	**445785**	**400050**	**82565**	**482610**
Male							
Postgraduate research	14130	14715	14955	14955	13010	2235	15245
Postgraduate taught	97660	97160	96705	96705	81220	30145	111365
Postgraduate Certificate in Education△	6105	5925	5710	5710	5770	260	6035
First degree	170445	174520	180990	180990	171460	11975	183435
Foundation degree	6745	6125	5360	5360	2665	1400	4060
HNC/HND	4060	6020	6460	6460	3390	1950	5340
Other undergraduate	25645	24985	24225	24225	18440	6305	24745
Professional Graduate Certificate in Education	1180	1000	740	740	385	130	510
Total male	**318685**	**324525**	**329435**	**329435**	**290565**	**54135**	**344700**
All sexes							
Postgraduate research	26640	27365	28155	28155	24585	4775	29360
Postgraduate taught	234960	234805	240555	240555	206745	78575	285320
Postgraduate Certificate in Education△	21310	20820	19460	19460	20565	930	21490
First degree	395580	406300	421095	421095	404665	27480	432145
Foundation degree	16875	15025	13705	13705	8245	3855	12100
HNC/HND	6150	10515	11745	11745	7570	2525	10095
Other undergraduate	64800	60125	58005	58005	38560	19195	57750
Professional Graduate Certificate in Education	3735	2835	2275	2275	1160	420	1575
Total all sexes*	**745005**	**756960**	**775535**	**775535**	**691530**	**136820**	**828350**

Source:Higher Education Statistics Agency

In this table 0,1, 2 are rounded to 0. All other numbers are rounded up or down to the nearest multiple of 5.

Percentages are calculated on unrounded data. Percentages are rounded to the nearest whole number. Percentages calculated on populations which contain fewer than 22.5 individuals are suppressed and represented as "..".

Please note that 'Other undergraduate' includes any qualification not listed above. 'Total other undergraduate' includes all undergraduate qualifications excluding first degrees.

See data intelligence.

* Students with a sex of 'other' are included in total figures but not in separate breakdowns.

△ Postgraduate Certificate in Education includes Professional Graduate Diploma in Education.

20.8 Further Education Students(1) in Higher Education Institutions(2) and Further Education Colleges(3), 2011/12 - 2018/19

Thousands

United Kingdom — Further education students	2011/12	2012/13	2013/14	2014/15	2015/16	2016/17	2017/18	2018/19
All								
England(4)	4,216.6	4,320.3	3,913.5	3,585.3	3,281.7	3,157.8	3,067.5	2,929.6
Wales(5)	211.3	197.5	188.8	168.1	145.9	136.2	118.3	122.0
Scotland	256.5	235.8	237.3	238.3	221.8	233.1	246.8	272.3
Northern Ireland	141.7	145.4	130.2	128.4	59.2	56.6	53.5	51.2
Males								
England(4)	1,940.9	1,985.9	1,793.2	1,629.8	1,487.0	1,433.6	1,386.8	1,304.5
Wales(5)	92.1	86.5	82.9	75.0	66.6	64.6	56.6	58.2
Scotland	121.0	113.1	115.6	116.6	109.1	118.0	120.3	134.5
Northern Ireland	71.1	73.9	66.7	65.6	29.6	28.9	27.2	26.9
Females								
England(4)	2,275.7	2,334.4	2,120.2	1,955.6	1,794.7	1,724.2	1,680.7	1,625.1
Wales(5)	119.3	111.1	105.9	93.1	79.3	71.6	61.7	63.8
Scotland	135.5	122.7	121.6	121.6	112.7	114.9	125.7	136.6
Northern Ireland	70.8	71.5	63.6	62.8	29.6	27.8	26.3	24.2

Higher education students	2011/12		2012/13		2013/14		2014/15		2015/6		2016/17		2017/18		2018/19	
	Full-time	Part-time	Full-time	Part-time	Full-time	Part-time	Full-time	Part-time	Full-time	Part-time	Full-time	Part-time	Full-time	Part-time	Full-time	Part-time
All																
Postgraduate	309.7	261.8	297.0	242.7	305.4	237.0	305.4	234.7	304.9	229.5	321.2	232.3	339.3	228.8	366.0	238.6
of which																
PhD & equivalent	69.5	25.5	71.3	25.3	74.4	25.9	74.7	25.4	75.3	24.8	76.8	24.6	77.2	24.4	79.0	24.4
Masters and Others	240.2	236.3	225.6	217.3	231.1	211.1	229.7	207.5	229.6	204.7	244.4	207.7	262.1	204.5	287.0	214.2
First Degree	1,319.8	241.3	1,319.6	229.8	1,351.8	203.6	1,358.6	187.0	1,407.5	177.7	1,449.9	170.6	1,477.8	166.7	1,530.4	179.1
Other Undergraduate	151.1	378.5	123.6	301.4	92.5	286.9	122.6	216.9	122.2	200.4	126.6	188.9	125.6	172.4	101.9	150.8
Total	1,780.6	881.6	1,740.1	773.8	1,749.7	727.5	1,786.6	638.5	1,834.6	607.7	1,897.6	591.8	1,942.7	567.9	1,998.2	568.5
Males																
Postgraduate	148.8	108.2	139.3	100.0	142.3	96.9	140.7	94.7	137.6	91.6	142.6	91.4	147.0	89.1	157.0	91.9
of which																
PhD & equivalent	38.0	12.4	39.0	12.2	40.7	12.4	40.3	12.1	40.4	11.6	40.9	11.4	40.6	11.4	41.3	11.3
Masters and Others	110.8	95.8	100.3	87.8	101.6	84.5	100.0	82.1	97.2	80.0	101.7	80.0	106.4	77.8	115.7	80.5
First Degree	601.9	100.0	599.8	95.5	610.5	86.3	608.9	80.5	626.0	76.8	641.2	74.1	650.3	72.3	671.8	78.0
Other Undergraduate	63.8	142.3	54.4	114.5	42.2	114.3	57.7	84.7	57.2	79.3	57.1	76.4	55.4	69.5	42.2	56.5
Total	814.5	350.5	793.5	310.1	795.0	297.6	807.4	260.0	820.8	247.8	840.9	241.9	852.8	230.9	871.0	226.4
Females																
Postgraduate	160.9	153.6	157.6	142.7	163.1	140.1	164.6	139.9	167.2	137.8	178.3	140.7	191.9	139.3	208.4	146.3
of which																
PhD & equivalent	31.5	13.1	32.3	13.1	33.7	13.5	34.3	13.3	34.8	13.1	35.8	13.2	36.5	13.0	37.5	13.0
Masters and Others	129.4	140.5	125.3	129.6	129.4	126.7	129.7	125.4	132.4	124.6	142.5	127.5	155.5	126.3	170.9	133.4
First Degree	717.9	141.3	719.8	134.3	741.3	117.2	749.5	106.4	781.1	100.9	808.2	96.5	826.6	94.3	857.6	101.1
Other Undergraduate	87.3	236.2	69.2	186.9	50.3	172.6	64.9	132.1	65.0	121.1	69.5	112.4	70.0	102.7	59.6	93.8
Total	966.1	531.1	946.6	463.8	954.7	429.9	979.0	378.4	1,013.4	359.8	1,056.0	349.6	1,088.6	336.3	1,125.5	341.3

Source: Department for Education; Welsh Government; Scottish Funding Council; Northern Ireland Department for the Economy

1 Includes home and overseas students.

2 Figures for Further Education Colleges (FECs) in Wales, Scotland and Northern Ireland are based on headcounts. Figures for FECs in England are based on whole year enrolments. Figures for FECs include apprenticeships. There are further education students in both Higher Education Institutions (HEIs) and FECs, mainly in FECs.

3 Figures for HEIs are based on the HESA 'standard registration' count (enrolments). They include students at The Open University. There are higher education students in both HEIs and FECs, mainly in HEIs.

4 The data field "gender" has changed to be consistent with the Managing Information across Partners (MIAP) common data definitions coding frame. Students of "indeterminate gender" are included in totals over all students. Indeterminate means unable to be classified as either male or female and is not related in any way to trans-gender.

5 Full-time mode of study includes sandwich. Part-time comprises both day and evening, including block release and open/distance learning. In Scotland, full-time covers programmes of at least 480 planned notional hours. Part-time includes short full-time, block/day release, evenings/weekends, assessment of work based learning, distance/locally based learning, college based private study, other open learning and flexible learning. In Wales, full-time learners are those with at least 450 guided contact hours in the academic year. For Northern Ireland from 2013/14 sandwich courses or short courses of less than 4 weeks full-time study are considered to be part-time rather than full-time.

20.9 Students in higher education(1) by level, mode of study(2), gender(3) and subject group, 2018/19

United Kingdom(4)(5)(6)(7)

Thousands

	Home and Overseas Students												Total higher education students	
	Postgraduate level						Undergraduate level							
	PhD & equivalent(8)		Masters and Others(9)		Total Postgraduate		First degree(10)		Other Undergraduate(11)		Total Undergraduate			
	Full-time	Part-time	Full-time	Part-time	Full-time	Part-time	Full-time	Part-time	Full-time	Part-time	Full-time	Part-time	Full-time	Part-time
All														
Medicine & Dentistry	5.7	2.1	5.1	7.4	10.8	9.5	47.3	0.1	0.2	0.2	47.6	0.2	58.4	9.6
Subjects Allied to Medicine	5.2	2.3	17.8	52.1	23.0	54.4	159.2	15.7	14.1	33.5	173.4	49.2	196.4	103.6
Biological Sciences	12.1	2.6	18.2	14.8	30.3	17.4	164.8	25.9	5.9	4.1	170.8	30.0	201.1	47.4
Vet. Science, Agriculture & related	0.9	0.2	1.7	3.4	2.6	3.6	16.8	0.7	4.7	3.6	21.5	4.3	24.1	7.8
Physical Sciences	11.6	0.7	7.0	2.2	18.6	2.9	66.2	5.4	0.7	1.2	66.9	6.6	85.5	9.6
Mathematical and Computing Sciences	6.7	0.9	15.2	6.6	21.9	7.5	111.6	17.9	4.8	2.6	116.3	20.5	138.2	28.1
Engineering & Technology	12.3	1.3	17.0	7.6	29.3	8.9	105.9	13.7	5.6	15.3	111.5	29.0	140.8	37.9
Architecture, Building & Planning	1.3	0.5	9.4	7.1	10.6	7.6	29.3	7.4	1.7	4.3	31.0	11.8	41.6	19.3
Social Sciences (inc Law)	7.1	2.7	48.2	26.7	55.3	29.4	229.5	24.4	12.2	11.1	241.6	35.5	296.9	64.9
Business & Administrative Studies	4.1	2.2	72.2	32.4	76.3	34.6	232.4	21.4	25.6	19.3	258.0	40.7	334.3	75.3
Mass Communications & Documentation	0.7	0.4	9.1	2.4	9.8	2.8	38.4	0.7	0.4	0.2	38.9	0.8	48.6	3.6
Languages	3.7	1.1	7.4	3.9	11.0	5.1	67.7	6.8	1.7	7.5	69.4	14.3	80.4	19.4
Historical and Philosophical Studies	4.0	2.0	6.5	5.2	10.5	7.2	57.3	7.3	0.7	2.4	58.0	9.7	68.5	16.9
Creative Arts & Design	1.9	1.5	18.5	6.8	20.4	8.2	155.9	7.7	11.3	2.1	167.2	9.8	187.6	18.0
Education(12)	1.8	3.9	33.7	34.3	35.5	38.2	45.5	11.7	8.4	17.0	53.9	28.7	89.4	66.9
Other subjects(13)	0.0	0.0	c	c	0.0	1.3	2.6	12.3	2.2	13.5	4.8	25.8	4.8	27.1
Unknown(14)	0.0	0.0	c	c	0.0	0.0	0.0	0.0	1.6	12.9	1.6	12.9	1.6	12.9
All subjects(15)	**79.0**	**24.4**	**287.0**	**214.2**	**366.0**	**238.6**	**1,530.4**	**179.1**	**101.9**	**150.8**	**1,632.2**	**329.9**	**1,998.2**	**568.5**
of which overseas students	38.8	4.3	158.5	19.2	197.2	23.5	252.9	4.9	8.9	10.1	261.8	15.0	459.1	38.5
Males														
Medicine & Dentistry	2.3	0.9	1.6	3.0	3.8	3.9	19.7	0.0	0.0	0.0	19.8	0.0	23.6	4.0
Subjects Allied to Medicine	2.1	0.8	4.5	12.5	6.6	13.3	30.0	4.0	2.7	5.2	32.7	9.2	39.3	22.5
Biological Sciences	4.4	1.0	5.6	4.2	9.9	5.1	60.5	7.2	3.6	1.2	64.1	8.4	74.1	13.5
Vet. Science, Agriculture & related	0.4	0.1	0.6	1.1	1.0	1.1	4.0	0.2	1.3	1.8	5.3	2.0	6.3	3.1
Physical Sciences	7.3	0.4	3.5	1.1	10.8	1.5	37.5	3.0	0.4	0.6	37.9	3.6	48.7	5.2
Mathematical and Computing Sciences	4.8	0.7	10.0	4.9	14.8	5.6	87.1	13.5	4.1	2.0	91.2	15.5	106.0	21.1
Engineering & Technology	9.1	1.0	12.2	6.0	21.3	7.1	86.6	11.9	5.0	13.9	91.6	25.8	112.8	32.9
Architecture, Building & Planning	0.7	0.3	4.7	4.4	5.4	4.7	17.7	5.9	1.1	3.5	18.7	9.4	24.1	14.1
Social Sciences (inc Law)	3.3	1.2	17.7	8.4	21.0	9.6	84.5	7.5	3.0	2.4	87.5	9.9	108.5	19.5
Business & Administrative Studies	2.1	1.3	32.4	17.1	34.5	18.4	120.1	10.9	12.0	7.4	132.1	18.4	166.6	36.8
Mass Communications & Documentation	0.3	0.2	2.6	0.7	2.9	0.9	16.8	0.4	0.3	0.1	17.1	0.4	20.0	1.3
Languages	1.3	0.4	2.1	1.1	3.4	1.5	17.8	2.0	0.8	3.0	18.6	5.0	22.0	6.5
Historical and Philosophical Studies	2.1	1.1	2.9	2.5	5.0	3.6	25.6	3.1	0.3	0.9	25.9	4.0	30.9	7.6
Creative Arts & Design	0.8	0.6	6.1	2.2	6.9	2.9	57.2	2.7	4.6	0.7	61.8	3.3	68.7	6.2
Education(12)	0.5	1.3	9.3	10.8	9.8	12.2	5.7	1.1	1.5	4.8	7.2	5.9	16.9	18.1
Other subjects(13)	0.0	0.0	c	c	0.0	0.4	0.9	4.6	1.1	5.0	2.0	9.6	2.0	10.0
Unknown(14)	0.0	0.0	c	c	0.0	0.0	0.0	0.0	0.4	3.9	0.4	3.9	0.4	3.9
All subjects(15)	**41.3**	**11.3**	**115.7**	**80.5**	**157.0**	**91.9**	**671.8**	**78.0**	**42.2**	**56.5**	**714.0**	**134.5**	**871.0**	**226.4**
of which overseas students	20.8	2.3	65.8	9.6	86.5	11.9	117.6	2.8	4.4	4.1	121.9	6.9	208.5	18.8

20.9 Students in higher education(1) by level, mode of study(2), gender(3) and subject group, 2018/19

Thousands

United Kingdom(4)(5)(6)(7)

	Home and Overseas Students												Total higher education students	
	Postgraduate level						Undergraduate level							
	PhD & equivalent(8)		Masters and Others(9)		Total Postgraduate		First degree(10)		Other Undergraduate(11)		Total Undergraduate			
	Full-time	Part-time	Full-time	Part-time	Full-time	Part-time	Full-time	Part-time	Full-time	Part-time	Full-time	Part-time	Full-time	Part-time
Females														
Medicine & Dentistry	3.4	1.2	3.5	4.3	6.9	5.5	27.6	0.1	0.2	0.1	27.8	0.1	34.7	5.6
Subjects Allied to Medicine	3.0	1.6	13.3	39.5	16.4	41.1	129.2	11.7	11.4	28.2	140.6	40.0	157.0	81.0
Biological Sciences	7.7	1.6	12.6	10.7	20.3	12.3	104.2	18.7	2.3	2.8	106.5	21.4	126.8	33.7
Vet. Science, Agriculture & related	0.5	0.1	1.1	2.4	1.6	2.5	12.8	0.5	3.4	1.8	16.2	2.2	17.7	4.7
Physical Sciences	4.3	0.3	3.5	1.0	7.8	1.4	28.6	2.4	0.4	0.6	29.0	3.0	36.8	4.4
Mathematical and Computing Sciences	1.9	0.2	5.2	1.7	7.1	1.9	24.4	4.4	0.6	0.6	25.0	5.1	32.1	7.0
Engineering & Technology	3.2	0.2	4.8	1.6	8.0	1.8	19.2	1.8	0.6	1.4	19.8	3.2	27.9	5.0
Architecture, Building & Planning	0.6	0.2	4.6	2.7	5.2	2.9	11.6	1.5	0.6	0.8	12.2	2.4	17.5	5.3
Social Sciences (inc Law)	3.7	1.5	30.5	18.2	34.2	19.7	144.8	16.9	9.1	8.7	154.0	25.6	188.2	45.3
Business & Administrative Studies	2.0	0.9	39.8	15.2	41.7	16.1	112.3	10.5	13.6	11.9	125.9	22.4	167.6	38.5
Mass Communications & Documentation	0.4	0.2	6.4	1.7	6.8	1.9	21.6	0.3	0.1	0.1	21.7	0.4	28.6	2.3
Languages	2.4	0.7	5.3	2.8	7.7	3.5	49.8	4.8	0.9	4.4	50.7	9.2	58.4	12.8
Historical and Philosophical Studies	1.9	0.9	3.6	2.7	5.5	3.6	31.6	4.2	0.4	1.3	32.0	5.6	37.5	9.2
Creative Arts & Design	1.1	0.8	12.3	4.5	13.5	5.3	98.4	5.0	6.7	1.5	105.0	6.5	118.5	11.8
Education(12)	1.3	0.0	24.4	23.4	25.7	23.4	39.8	10.6	7.0	12.2	46.7	22.8	72.4	46.2
Other subjects(13)	0.0	0.0	c	c	0.0	0.9	1.7	7.6	1.1	8.5	2.8	16.2	2.8	17.0
Unknown(14)	0.0	0.0	c	c	0.0	0.0	0.0	0.0	1.2	8.9	1.2	8.9	1.2	9.0
All subjects(15)	**37.5**	**13.0**	**170.9**	**133.4**	**208.4**	**146.3**	**857.6**	**101.1**	**59.6**	**93.8**	**917.2**	**194.9**	**1,125.5**	**341.3**
of which overseas students	17.9	2.0	92.5	9.6	110.5	11.6	135.2	2.1	4.5	6.0	139.7	8.1	250.2	19.7

Source: Department for Education; Welsh Government; Scottish Funding Council; Northern Ireland Department for the Economy
Publication: Education and training statistics for the UK (https://explore-education-statistics.service.gov.uk/)

1 Figures for Higher Education Institutions (HEIs) are Higher Education Statistics Agency 'standard registration' counts. HEIs include the Open University; all Open University enrolments are treated as being at a provider in England. Figures for Further Education Colleges are whole year enrolments at Level 4 or above. Education and Skills Funding Agency (ESFA) funded provision (e.g. Higher Apprenticeships, Trailblazer Apprenticeships) has been excluded to avoid double counting with other tables in the publication. Figures exclude the University of Buckingham.

2 Full-time mode of study includes sandwich. Part-time comprises both day and evening, including block release and open/distance learning. In Scotland, full-time covers programmes of at least 480 hours of planned notional hours. Part-time includes short full-time, block/day release, evenings/weekends, assessment of work based learning, distance/locally based learning, college based private study, other open learning and flexible learning. In Wales, full-time learners are those with at least 450 guided contact hours in the academic year. In Northern Ireland from 2013/14 sandwich courses or short courses of less than 4 weeks full-time study are considered to be part-time rather than full-time.

3 The data field "gender" has changed to be consistent with the Managing Information across Partners (MIAP) common data definitions coding frame. Students of "indeterminate gender" are included in totals over all students. Indeterminate means unable to be classified as either male or female and is not related in any way to trans-gender.

4 Figures for Further Education Colleges (FECs) in England count all students on postgraduate level courses as Masters and Others; and, all students on undergraduate other than first degree courses as part-time. Students are counted only where they are studying a prescribed higher education course. The approach adopted to select the standard registration population for learners at FECs has been revised to improve consistency with the standard registration population at HEIs. A more comprehensive method of subject classification has also been applied which allows learners to be classified across multiple subjects.

5 Figures for Further Education Colleges in Wales are counts of unique learners. As a learner may pursue more than one course, only one subject per learner has been selected (based on the most recently started course of the learner where applicable). Students have been assigned a level on the basis of learning programme type. For the purpose of this table, HE learners are those pursuing a (non-WBL) overarching HE learning programme. (It excludes learners pursuing HE level activities within an FE or WBL programme.)

6 Figures for Further Education Colleges in Scotland do not include students with under 25% attendance rate.

7 Figures for Further Education Colleges in Northern Ireland are regulated course enrolments rather than headcounts.

8 Defined as 'Doctorate' in Scotland.

9 For Scotland includes masters (research/taught) and postgraduate diploma/certificate.

10 For Scotland includes first degree honours/ordinary.

11 For Scotland includes 'SVQ or NVQ: Level 4 and Level 5,' 'Diploma (HNC/D level for diploma and degree holders),' and 'HNC/D or equivalent'.

12 Includes Initial Teacher Training (ITT) and In-Service Education and Training (INSET).

13 Includes Combined and general programmes and programmes not otherwise classified.

14 Includes data for Further Education Colleges that cannot be split by subject group.

15 The sum of Male and Female learners will not equal total learners as there are a small amount of cases where gender is unknown.

20.10 Qualified teachers by type of school and gender, 2015/16 - 2019/20

United Kingdom	Full-time equivalent number of teachers								
	2015/16	2016/17	2017/18	2018/19	2019/20 UK	*of which:* England	*Wales*	*Scotland*	*Northern Ireland*
All									
Nursery	2,585	2,481	2,408	2,251	2,213	1,197	31	793	192
Primary	262,544	265,361	264,605	265,844	264,804	219,956	11,687	25,027	8,134
Middle	345	533	714	981	1,157	n/a	1,157	n/a	n/a
Secondary	254,287	251,039	246,956	246,150	247,378	204,712	9,973	23,522	9,171
Non-maintained mainstream	74,182	74,309	75,882	77,317	76,442	76,359	:	:	83
Total maintained	550,495	550,749	545,834	547,275	548,078	453,813	23,594	52,247	18,423
Special	25,047	25,751	26,222	27,139	27,883	24,283	746	1,927	927
All schools	**624,677**	**625,058**	**621,717**	**624,592**	**624,520**	**530,172**	**23,594**	**52,247**	**18,506**
Males									
Nursery	87	87	102	c	102	65	2	35	0
Primary	39,002	39,937	40,063	40,352	40,223	34,092	2,085	2,673	1,371
Middle	118	171	226	311	352	n/a	352	n/a	n/a
Secondary	94,635	93,205	91,536	90,812	90,764	75,938	3,512	8,424	2,890
Non-maintained mainstream	27,083	26,987	27,545	28,036	27,279	27,279	:	:	:
Total maintained	142,062	141,775	140,199	140,035	139,791	117,289	6,151	11,891	4,459
Special	6,821	7,017	7,105	c	7,381	6,524	200	459	197
All schools	**169,145**	**168,762**	**167,745**	**168,072**	**167,069**	**144,568**	**6,151**	**11,891**	**4,459**
Females									
Nursery	2,497	2,395	2,305	c	2,111	1,132	30	758	192
Primary	223,499	225,379	224,504	225,401	224,534	185,816	9,601	22,354	6,762
Middle	228	362	488	671	805	n/a	805	n/a	n/a
Secondary	159,490	157,706	155,386	155,313	156,589	128,750	6,461	15,098	6,280
Non-maintained mainstream	46,999	47,222	48,246	49,187	49,080	49,080	:	:	:
Total maintained	408,225	408,799	405,561	407,121	408,174	336,411	17,444	40,356	13,964
Special	18,224	18,731	19,116	c	20,502	17,758	546	1,468	730
All schools	**455,223**	**456,022**	**453,807**	**456,308**	**457,254**	**385,491**	**17,444**	**40,356**	**13,964**

Source: Department for Education; Welsh Government; Scottish Funding Council; Northern Ireland Department for the Economy
Publication: Education and training statistics for the UK (https://explore-education-statistics.service.gov.uk/)

(1) In England and Scotland, total teachers includes centrally employed teachers.
(2) In England, special schools include pupil referral units.
(3) In Scotland, figures include all providers of funded Early Learning and childcare, not only nurseries.
(4) Primary and secondary figures include middle schools as deemed. Secondary schools include all-through schools.

Crime and Justice

Chapter 21

Crime and Justice

There are differences in the legal and judicial systems of England and Wales, Scotland and Northern Ireland which make it impossible to provide tables covering the UK as a whole in this section. These differences concern the classification of offences, the meaning of certain terms used in the statistics, the effects of the several Criminal Justice Acts and recording practices.

Police Workforce (Table 21.1)

The figures in these tables are sourced from police forces' personnel records. Forces keep records of all staff employed by the force on their HR and payroll systems.

Special constables

These are members of the public who volunteer to help the police in their duties. They have the same powers as regular officers, but do not have fixed working hours (as they may fit their time around their paid work, for example) and therefore it is inappropriate to collect figures in terms of full-time equivalent. Figures are presented in terms of headcount only. These figures can fluctuate depending on how often forces review their data and remove those who have not recently done shifts from their systems. Therefore, year on year changes in the number of special constables should be treated with some caution.

Joiners and leavers

Joiner rates are calculated by dividing the number of joiners during the financial year by the total number of workers as at the end of the year (i.e. 31st March). In other words, how many of those employed by the force at the end of the year joined during the course of the year.

Leaver rates are calculated by dividing the number of leavers during the financial year by the total number of workers at the start of the year (i.e. as at 31 March of the previous year). In other words, how many of those employed at the start of the year left during the year.

These joiner and leaver rates are good indications of staff turnover within the police. However, some workers may join and leave the force during the same year, and so would not be picked up in the joiner and leaver rates.

Prison Population (Table 21.2)

This table gives an indication of the recent trend in the prison population of EU countries between 2000 and 2020/2021. The figures include both pretrial detainees/remand prisoners and those who have been convicted and sentenced. Since about the year 2000, the total prison population has decreased by 27%. The European figure reflects large falls in prison populations in Russia (56%) and also in central and eastern Europe (49%); the prison population in Europe other than Russia has increased by 5%.

The Prison Population data sourced from the World Prison Brief (WPB) which is a unique database that provides free access to information about prison systems throughout the world. Country information is updated on a monthly basis, using data largely derived from governmental or other official sources. For more details see: World Prison Brief (www.prisonstudies.org).

Recorded crime statistics (Table 21.3)

There have been two major changes to the recording of crimes in the last two decades. In April 1998, the Home Office Counting Rules (HOCR) for recorded crime were expanded to include certain additional summary offences and counts became more victim-based (the number of victims was counted rather than the number of offences). In April 2002, the National Crime Recording Standard (NCRS) was introduced across England and Wales, (some forces adopted key elements of the standard earlier and compliance with the standard continued to improve in the years following its formal introduction). It was designed to ensure greater consistency between forces in recording crime and to take a more victim-oriented approach to crime recording, with the police being required to record any allegation of crime unless there was credible evidence to the contrary.

Both these changes resulted in an increase in the number of crimes recorded. Certain offences, such as the more minor violent crimes, were more affected by these changes than others. All of these factors need to be considered when looking at the trends in recorded crime.

Similarly, the Scottish Crime Recording Standard (SCRS) was introduced by the eight Scottish police forces with effect from 1 April 2004. This means that no corroborative evidence is required initially to record a crime-related incident as a crime if the victim perceived it as a crime. Again, the introduction of this new recording standard was expected to increase the numbers of minor crimes recorded by the police, such as minor crimes of vandalism and minor thefts and offences of petty assault and breach of the peace. However, it was expected that the SCRS would not have much impact on the figures for the more serious crimes such as serious assault, sexual assault, robbery or housebreaking.

The Sexual Offences Act 2003 introduced in May 2004 altered the definition and coverage of sexual offences. In particular, it redefined indecent exposure as a sexual offence, which is likely to account for much of the increase in sexual offences. Following this, the Sexual Offences (Scotland) Act 2009 was introduced in 1 December 2010 and provides a statutory framework for sexual offences in Scots law. The Act repealed the common law offences of rape, sodomy and clandestine injury to women and a number of statutory sexual offences in addition to creating new statutory offences relating to sexual conduct, in particular where that takes place without consent. The Act also created new "protective offences" which criminalise sexual activity with a person whose capacity to consent to sexual activity be it either entirely absent or not fully formed either because of their age or because of vulnerability.

For further information see:
Crime in England and Wales: https://www.ons.gov.uk/peoplepopulationandcommunity/crimeandjustice
Recorded Crime in Scotland: https://www.gov.scot/publications/recorded-crime-scotland-2021-2022/
Police Recorded Crime, Northern Ireland: https://www.psni.police.uk/inside-psni/Statistics/police-recorded-crime-statistics/

Court proceedings and police cautions (Tables 21.4 to 21.8, 21.12 to 21.16, 21.19 to 21.20)

The statistical basis of the tables of court proceedings is broadly similar in England and Wales, Scotland and Northern Ireland; the tables show the number of persons found guilty, recording a person under the heading of the principal offence of which they were found guilty, excluding additional findings of guilt at the same proceedings. A person found guilty at a number of separate court proceedings is included more than once.

The statistics on offenders cautioned in England and Wales cover only those who, on admission of guilt, were given a formal caution by, or on the instructions of, a senior police officer as an alternative to prosecution. Written warnings by the police for motor offences and persons paying fixed penalties for certain motoring offences are excluded. Formal cautions are not issued in Scotland. There are no statistics on cautioning available for Northern Ireland.

The Crime and Disorder Act 1998 created provisions in relation to reprimands and final warnings, new offences and orders which have been implemented nationally since 1 June 2000. They replace the system of cautioning for offenders aged under 18. Reprimands can be given to first-time offenders for minor offences. Any further offending results in either a final warning or a charge.

For persons proceeded against in Scotland, the statistics relate to the High Court of Justiciary, the sheriff courts and the district courts. The High Court deals with serious solemn (that is, jury) cases and has unlimited sentencing power. Sheriff courts are limited to imprisonment of 3 years for solemn cases, or 3 months (6 months when specified in legislation for second or subsequent offences and 12 months for certain statutory offences) for summary (that is, non-jury) cases. District courts deal only with summary cases and are limited to 60 days imprisonment and level 4 fines. Stipendiary magistrates sit in Glasgow District Court and have the summary sentencing powers of a sheriff.

In England and Wales, indictable offences are offences which are:

- triable only on indictment. These offences are the most serious breaches of the criminal law and must be tried at the Crown Court. 'Indictable-only' offences include murder, manslaughter, rape and robbery
- triable either way. These offences may be tried at the Crown Court or a magistrates' court

The Criminal Justice Act 1991 led to the following main changes in the sentences available to the courts in England and Wales:

- introduction of combination orders
- introduction of the 'unit fine scheme' at magistrates' courts
- abolishing the sentence of detention in a young offender institution for 14-year-old boys and changing the minimum and maximum sentence lengths for 15 to 17-year-olds to 10 and 12 months respectively, and
- abolishing partly suspended sentences of imprisonment and restricting the use of a fully suspended sentence

(The Criminal Justice Act 1993 abolished the 'unit fine scheme' in magistrates' courts, which had been introduced under the Criminal Justice Act 1991.

A charging standard for assault was introduced in England and Wales on 31 August 1994 with the aim of promoting consistency between the police and prosecution on the appropriate level of charge to be brought.

The Criminal Justice and Public Order Act 1994 created several new offences in England and Wales, mainly in the area of public order, but also including male rape (there is no statutory offence of male rape in Scotland, although such a crime may be charged as serious assault). The Act also:

- extended the provisions of section 53 of the Children and Young Persons Act 1993 for 10 to 13-year-olds
- increased the maximum sentence length for 15 to 17-year-olds to 2 years
- increased the upper limit from £2,000 to £5,000 for offences of criminal damage proceeded against as if triable only summarily
- introduced provisions for the reduction of sentences for early guilty pleas, and
- increased the maximum sentence length for certain firearm offences

Provisions within the Crime (Sentences) Act 1997 (as amended by the Powers of Criminal Courts Sentencing Act 2000) in England and Wales, and the Crime and Punishment (Scotland) Act 1997 in Scotland, included:

- an automatic life sentence for a second serious violent or sexual offence unless there are exceptional circumstances (this provision has not been enacted in Scotland)
- a minimum sentence of 7 years for an offender convicted for a third time of a class A drug trafficking offence unless the court considers this to be unjust in all the circumstances, and
- in England and Wales, the new section 38A of the Magistrates' Courts' Act 1980 extending the circumstances in which a magistrates' court may commit a person convicted of an offence triable-either-way to the Crown Court for sentence – it was implemented in conjunction with section 49 of the Criminal Procedure and Investigations Act 1996, which involves the magistrates' courts in asking defendants to indicate a plea before the mode of trial decision is taken and compels the court to sentence, or commit for sentence, any defendant who indicates a guilty plea.

Under the Criminal Justice and Court Service Act 2000 new terms were introduced for certain orders. Community rehabilitation order is the new name for a probation order. A community service order is now known as a community punishment order. Finally, the new term for a combination order is community punishment and rehabilitation order. In April 2000 the secure training order was replaced by the detention and training order. Section 53 of the Children and Young Persons Act 1993 was repealed on 25 August 2000 and its provisions were transferred to sections 90 to 92 of the Powers of Criminal Courts (Sentencing) Act 2000. Reparation and action plan orders were implemented nationally from 1 June 2000. The drug treatment and testing order was introduced in England, Scotland and Wales from October 2000. The referral order was introduced in England, Scotland and Wales from April 2000. Youth rehabilitation orders came into effect in November 2009 as part of the Criminal Justice and Immigration Act 2008.

Following the introduction of the Libra case management system during 2008, offenders at magistrates' courts can now be recorded as sex 'Not Stated'. In 2008 one per cent of offenders sentenced were recorded as sex 'Not Stated' as well as 'Male', 'Female', or 'Other'. Amendments to the data tables have been made to accommodate this new category.

The system of magistrates' courts and Crown courts in Northern Ireland operates in a similar way to that in England and Wales. A particularly significant statutory development, however, has been the Criminal Justice (NI) Order 1996 which introduced a new sentencing regime into Northern Ireland, largely replicating that which was introduced into England and Wales by the Criminal Justice Acts of 1991 and 1993. The order makes many changes to both community and custodial sentences, while introducing new orders such as the combination order, the custody probation order, and orders for release on licence of sexual offenders.

Types of sentence

Immediate custody: Prison sentences are given when an offence is so serious that it is the only suitable punishment. A prison sentence will also be given when the court believes the public must be protected from the offender. A custodial sentence can be suspended when given (see below), but otherwise is termed 'immediate'. There are two different categories of immediate custodial sentence: determinate sentences (those having a fixed term) and indeterminate sentences (which have only a minimum term and include life sentences).

Suspended sentence: A court may give an offender a 'suspended' prison sentence if the time they would otherwise spend in prison is under 24 months. With a suspended sentence, the offender doesn't go directly to prison but they do have to comply with conditions set out in the order made by the court. These conditions can last for up to two years. If the offender breaks these conditions, or commits another offence, they will usually have to serve the original sentence in prison.

Community sentence: When a court imposes a community sentence, the offender doesn't go to prison, but the court says there are specific things the offender can, can't and must do while serving their sentence. The magistrate or judge will decide which combination of these 'requirements' will most effectively punish the offender for their crime, while also reducing the risk of them offending again.

Fine: Fines are the most common criminal sentence, given to punish an offender financially. They are usually given for less serious crimes that don't merit a community or prison sentence. They limit the amount of money offenders have to spend, with how much someone is fined depending on how serious the crime is and the offender's ability to pay.

Absolute discharge: When the court decides someone is guilty, but decides not to punish them further at this time, they will be given a 'discharge'. Discharges are given for minor offences. An 'absolute discharge' means that no more action will be taken.

Conditional discharge: When the court decides someone is guilty, but decides not to punish them further at this time, they will be given a 'discharge'. Discharges are given for minor offences. A 'conditional discharge' means that the offender won't be punished unless they commit another offence within a set period of time (no longer than three years).

Otherwise dealt with: includes a number of orders that do not fall within any of the major sentencing categories, for example hospital orders, confiscation orders and compensation orders. Different tables in this publication show more or fewer major sentencing categories; for this reason, the set of offences counted as otherwise dealt with varies between tables.

For more information on statistics relating to the criminal justice system see the following websites:

Ministry of Justice www.gov.uk/government/organisations/ministry-of-justice
This site provides information on the organisations within the justice system, reports and data, and guidance.

The Attorney General's Office www.gov.uk/government/organisations/attorney-generals-office Provides information on the role of the department including new releases; updates; reports; reviews and links to other law officers' departments and organisations.

The Welsh Government www.gov.wales Gives information on all aspects of the Welsh Government together with details of publications and statistics.

The Scottish Government www.gov.scot Gives information on all aspects of the Scottish Government together with details of publications and statistics.

Criminal Justice System Northern Ireland
www.nidirect.gov.uk/articles/introduction-justice-system Provides information about the justice system in Northern Ireland, including what court does what and the different agencies involved in the justice system.

The Sentencing Council, www.sentencingcouncil.org.uk The Sentencing Council is an independent, non-departmental public body of the Ministry of Justice which replaced the Sentencing Guidelines Council and the Sentencing Advisory Panel. The site contains information on: sentencing guidelines; general information on sentencing; and research and analysis undertaken by the Sentencing Council.

Official Statistics publications www.gov.uk/government/statistics Lists links to published and upcoming Official Statistics products. Official Statistics are produced impartially and free from political influence by ministerial departments, other departments and public bodies.

Office for National Statistics, statistical publications on crime in England and Wales www.ons.gov.uk/peoplepopulationandcommunity/crimeandjustice/bulletins/crimeinen glandandwales/previousReleases

21.1a Police officers, by police force area, as at 31 March 2020

England and Wales   Full-time equivalents

PFA code[1]	Police force	All officers			Officers available for duty[2]		
		Male	Female	Total	Male	Female	Total
E23000013	Cleveland	964	361	1,325	932	335	1,267
E23000008	Durham	784	357	1,141	760	339	1,099
E23000007	Northumbria	2,148	1,008	3,155	2,114	955	3,069
E12000001	**North East**	**3,895**	**1,726**	**5,621**	**3,805**	**1,629**	**5,435**
E23000006	Cheshire	1,380	708	2,088	1,347	663	2,010
E23000002	Cumbria	729	492	1,221	720	464	1,183
E23000005	Greater Manchester	4,708	2,158	6,866	4,552	2,030	6,582
E23000003	Lancashire	1,990	1,010	2,999	1,929	915	2,844
E23000004	Merseyside	2,535	1,094	3,629	2,475	1,008	3,482
E12000002	**North West**	**11,341**	**5,462**	**16,803**	**11,022**	**5,080**	**16,102**
E23000012	Humberside	1,283	683	1,966	1,252	647	1,899
E23000009	North Yorkshire	966	515	1,481	943	482	1,425
E23000011	South Yorkshire	1,623	815	2,437	1,578	773	2,351
E23000010	West Yorkshire	3,480	1,862	5,342	3,407	1,786	5,194
E12000003	**Yorkshire and the Humber**	**7,351**	**3,875**	**11,226**	**7,180**	**3,689**	**10,869**
E23000018	Derbyshire	1,211	638	1,849	1,185	606	1,791
E23000021	Leicestershire	1,378	601	1,979	1,353	562	1,915
E23000020	Lincolnshire	744	323	1,067	727	298	1,025
E23000022	Northamptonshire	861	411	1,272	834	372	1,207
E23000019	Nottinghamshire	1,424	647	2,072	1,393	619	2,012
E12000004	**East Midlands**	**5,619**	**2,620**	**8,239**	**5,492**	**2,457**	**7,950**
E23000015	Staffordshire	1,172	494	1,666	1,145	467	1,613
E23000017	Warwickshire	691	344	1,035	675	318	993
E23000016	West Mercia	1,517	702	2,219	1,471	657	2,128
E23000014	West Midlands	4,458	2,059	6,516	4,349	1,915	6,264
E12000005	**West Midlands**	**7,837**	**3,599**	**11,436**	**7,640**	**3,357**	**10,997**
E23000026	Bedfordshire	809	453	1,262	798	437	1,234
E23000023	Cambridgeshire	1,068	477	1,545	1,048	446	1,494
E23000028	Essex	2,223	1,075	3,298	2,184	1,015	3,200
E23000027	Hertfordshire	1,394	692	2,086	1,378	632	2,010
E23000024	Norfolk	1,169	496	1,665	1,148	470	1,617
E23000025	Suffolk	835	384	1,219	813	355	1,168
E12000006	**Eastern**	**7,499**	**3,577**	**11,076**	**7,369**	**3,355**	**10,724**
E23000034	London, City of	587	171	759	580	162	742
E23000001	Metropolitan Police	23,221	8,978	32,199	22,660	8,238	30,898
E12000007	**London**	**23,809**	**9,149**	**32,958**	**23,241**	**8,399**	**31,640**
E23000030	Hampshire	1,827	865	2,692	1,774	797	2,570
E23000032	Kent	2,637	1,144	3,780	2,604	1,100	3,704
E23000031	Surrey	1,282	646	1,928	1,243	590	1,833
E23000033	Sussex	1,837	880	2,717	1,800	821	2,621
E23000029	Thames Valley	2,863	1,447	4,310	2,809	1,334	4,143
E12000008	**South East**	**10,447**	**4,981**	**15,428**	**10,229**	**4,642**	**14,872**
E23000036	Avon & Somerset	1,899	904	2,803	1,869	860	2,729
E23000035	Devon & Cornwall	2,139	961	3,100	2,023	878	2,901
E23000039	Dorset	874	364	1,238	849	334	1,183
E23000037	Gloucestershire	791	385	1,176	790	372	1,162
E23000038	Wiltshire	651	357	1,007	632	325	956
E12000009	**South West**	**6,354**	**2,970**	**9,324**	**6,163**	**2,767**	**8,930**
E92000001	**England**	**84,152**	**37,959**	**122,112**	**82,141**	**35,377**	**117,518**
W15000004	Dyfed-Powys	770	395	1,165	746	358	1,104
W15000002	Gwent	858	453	1,311	830	421	1,251
W15000001	North Wales	954	556	1,510	938	521	1,459
W15000003	South Wales	2,057	956	3,012	2,017	905	2,921
W92000004	**Wales**	**4,639**	**2,360**	**6,998**	**4,531**	**2,205**	**6,735**
K04000001	**England and Wales**	**88,791**	**40,319**	**129,110**	**86,671**	**37,582**	**124,253**
N/A	Central service secondments	232	86	318	..	..	..
N/A	British Transport Police	2,345	619	2,964	2,292	579	2,871
N/A	National Crime Agency[3]	2,882	1,955	4,837	..	..	..

Source: Home Office

Notes

'..' Denotes data not available

1. PFA codes and other geo codes can be found here: https://geoportal.statistics.gov.uk/datasets/police-force-areas-december-2019-names-and-codes-in-the-united-kingdom

2. Officers available for duty is the number of officers in post excluding long-term absentees.

3. Data for the National Crime Agency includes both warranted and non-warranted officers.

21.1b Special constables[1] by police force area and sex, as at 31 March 2020

Headcount[1]

PFA code[2]	Police force	Total			Black, Asian and Minority Ethnic (BAME)			Joiners[3]			Leavers[3]		
		Male	Female	Total	Male	Female	Total	Male	Female	Total	Male	Female	Total
E23000013	Cleveland	69	32	101	2	-	2	9	2	11	5	1	6
E23000008	Durham	39	13	52	-	-	-	-	-	-	17	7	24
E23000007	Northumbria	94	31	125	2	-	2	31	20	51	59	12	71
E12000001	**North East**	**202**	**76**	**278**	**4**	**-**	**4**	**40**	**22**	**62**	**81**	**20**	**101**
E23000006	Cheshire	201	80	281	5	2	7	51	27	78	72	48	120
E23000002	Cumbria	35	18	53	3	-	3	7	10	17	9	4	13
E23000005	Greater Manchester	248	77	325	25	4	29	85	39	124	111	52	163
E23000003	Lancashire	153	69	222	10	5	15	39	23	62	64	45	109
E23000004	Merseyside	120	64	184	10	2	12	27	23	50	74	38	112
E12000002	**North West**	**757**	**308**	**1,065**	**53**	**13**	**66**	**209**	**122**	**331**	**330**	**187**	**517**
E23000012	Humberside	102	41	143	-	-	-	22	17	39	29	16	45
E23000009	North Yorkshire	57	42	99	-	3	3	10	11	21	24	10	34
E23000011	South Yorkshire	93	33	126	5	3	8	21	14	35	39	22	61
E23000010	West Yorkshire	215	104	319	25	10	35	43	34	77	85	71	156
E12000003	**Yorkshire & the Humber**	**467**	**220**	**687**	**30**	**16**	**46**	**96**	**76**	**172**	**177**	**119**	**296**
E23000018	Derbyshire	104	51	155	5	2	7	14	6	20	30	28	58
E23000021	Leicestershire	138	69	207	20	7	27	26	16	42	73	33	106
E23000020	Lincolnshire	96	36	132	-	1	1	20	14	34	24	11	35
E23000022	Northamptonshire	184	70	254	6	3	9	35	26	61	45	20	65
E23000019	Nottinghamshire	107	49	156	9	3	12	22	20	42	44	41	85
E12000004	**East Midlands**	**629**	**275**	**904**	**40**	**16**	**56**	**117**	**82**	**199**	**216**	**133**	**349**
E23000015	Staffordshire	143	62	205	6	4	10	53	14	67	56	33	89
E23000017	Warwickshire	75	17	92	7	-	7	-	-	-	28	6	34
E23000016	West Mercia	88	22	110	1	-	1	-	-	-	40	18	58
E23000014	West Midlands	182	38	220	58	8	66	44	19	63	10	10	20
E12000005	**West Midlands**	**488**	**139**	**627**	**72**	**12**	**84**	**97**	**33**	**130**	**134**	**67**	**201**
E23000026	Bedfordshire	103	29	132	15	4	19	30	15	45	46	19	65
E23000023	Cambridgeshire	126	71	197	8	3	11	30	21	51	43	27	70
E23000028	Essex	354	167	521	31	5	36	96	74	170	103	58	161
E23000027	Hertfordshire	180	65	245	14	4	18	29	14	43	55	26	81
E23000024	Norfolk	140	53	193	1	1	2	26	13	39	39	21	60
E23000025	Suffolk	99	38	137	3	-	3	31	26	57	35	20	55
E12000006	**Eastern**	**1,002**	**423**	**1,425**	**72**	**17**	**89**	**242**	**163**	**405**	**321**	**171**	**492**
E23000034	London, City of	58	17	75	11	2	13	8	4	12	7	5	12
E23000001	Metropolitan Police	1,317	524	1,841	426	150	576	285	150	435	258	130	388
E12000007	**London**	**1,375**	**541**	**1,916**	**437**	**152**	**589**	**293**	**154**	**447**	**265**	**135**	**400**
E23000030	Hampshire	199	84	283	6	3	9	24	10	34	62	30	92
E23000032	Kent	227	57	284	11	3	14	62	25	87	51	19	70
E23000031	Surrey	81	35	116	2	2	4	19	13	32	38	24	62
E23000033	Sussex	81	20	101	1	1	2	4	3	7	31	7	38
E23000029	Thames Valley	253	92	345	16	13	29	74	30	104	92	58	150
E12000008	**South East**	**841**	**288**	**1,129**	**36**	**22**	**58**	**183**	**81**	**264**	**274**	**138**	**412**
E23000036	Avon & Somerset	197	92	289	11	6	17	48	36	84	36	26	62
E23000035	Devon & Cornwall	226	98	324	3	-	3	53	35	88	42	19	61
E23000039	Dorset	82	35	117	2	1	3	21	9	30	23	9	32
E23000037	Gloucestershire	96	37	133	4	2	6	5	-	5	24	14	38
E23000038	Wiltshire	139	54	193	-	-	-	17	12	29	47	22	69
E12000009	**South West**	**740**	**316**	**1,056**	**20**	**9**	**29**	**144**	**92**	**236**	**172**	**90**	**262**
E92000001	**England**	**6,501**	**2,586**	**9,087**	**764**	**257**	**1,021**	**1,421**	**825**	**2,246**	**1,970**	**1,060**	**3,030**
W15000004	Dyfed-Powys	48	39	87	-	-	-	16	13	29	16	13	29
W15000002	Gwent	51	19	70	5	-	5	29	12	41	12	3	15
W15000001	North Wales	103	67	170	-	-	-	30	10	40	33	34	67
W15000003	South Wales	117	40	157	6	2	8	54	25	79	16	11	27
W92000004	**Wales**	**319**	**165**	**484**	**11**	**2**	**13**	**129**	**60**	**189**	**77**	**61**	**138**
K04000001	**England and Wales**	**6,820**	**2,751**	**9,571**	**775**	**259**	**1,034**	**1,550**	**885**	**2,435**	**2,047**	**1,121**	**3,168**
N/A	British Transport Police	205	39	244	26	4	30	47	11	58	-	-	-
N/A	**Total**	**7,025**	**2,790**	**9,815**	**801**	**263**	**1,064**	**1,597**	**896**	**2,493**	**2,047**	**1,121**	**3,168**

Source: Home Office

Notes

'-' Denotes nil

1. Special constable figures are provided on a headcount basis.

2. PFA codes and other geo codes can be found here: https://geoportal.statistics.gov.uk/datasets/police-force-areas-december-2019-names-and-codes-in-the-united-kingdom

3. Excludes transfers to and from other territorial police forces in England and Wales.

21.1c Police forces strength[1]: by country and sex

Full Time Equivalents

			2005	2006	2007	2008	2009	2010	2011	2012	2013	2014	2015	2016	2017	2018	2019
Northern Ireland[2,3]																	
Regular police																	
Strength																	
	Men	**KERU**	6,016	5,992	5,949	5,761	5,669	5,548	5,371	5,238	5,085	4,988	4,988	4,952	4,855	4,803	4,747
	Women	**KERV**	1,547	1,534	1,600	1,653	1,735	1,837	1,922	1,907	1,877	1,882	1,882	1,932	1,910	1,909	1,937
Reserve[4]																	
Strength																	
	Men	**KERW**	1,431	1,424	1,212	1,119	930	774	597	333	313	278	278	235	201	176	161
	Women	**KERX**	410	402	400	382	345	311	283	247	222	184	184	148	126	115	111

Source: Police Service of Northern Ireland

1. All figures are full-time equivalent strength figures that have been rounded to the nearest whole.
2. Excludes personnel out on secondment and career breaks.
3. Includes Student Officers.
4. As at 31/03/12 No longer any FTR in PSNI, As at 31/03/12 Reserve figures only include Con PT (Formerly known as PTR)

21.1d Number of Police Officers (Full-time Equivalent) in Scotland[1,2] and by Local Policing Divisions, as at 31st March 2020

as at 31st March	Scotland
2020	17,431

1. All figures are expressed in terms of full-time equivalent (FTE) police officers, rounded to the nearest whole number.
2. Number of police officers in Scotland are defined in note 5 (in the Statistical Release Notes worksheet) and exclude officers on career breaks.

Note 5: Police Scotland Resource Planning & Co-ordination provide quality assurance of the HR and Duty Management System data relating to both staff and officers. Internal manuals of guidance have been developed for both staff and officers, providing instruction and process for the completion of quality assurance tasks on a weekly basis. This allows the provision of management information at an executive level of the Force and external reporting of statistics to the Scottish Government.

Police Officer Distribution

The chart below outlines the distribution of officers across each of the 13 local policing divisions together with the available regional and national resources.

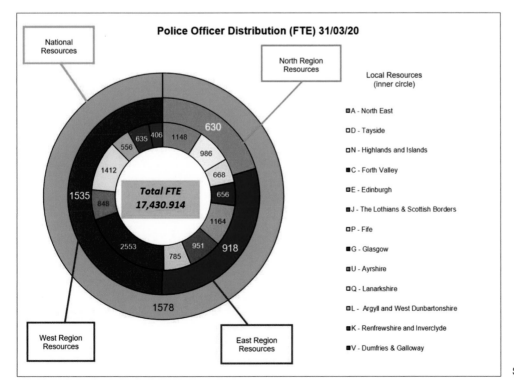

Police Officer Distribution (FTE) 31/03/20

Source: Police Scotland

21.2 Prison Population International Comparisons with other EU Countries

	Year: 2000 (or closest available year)			Year: 2021 (or latest available year)			Change		Estimated national population 2021/22[3]	Source of prison population total
	Date	Prison population total[1]	Prison population rate[2]	Date	Prison population total[1]	Prison population rate[2]	Prison population total[1]	Prison population rate[2]		
Northern Europe										
Denmark	2000	3,382	63	2020	4,085	70	703	7	5.89m	NPA
Estonia	2000	4,712	343	2020	2,450	184	-2,262	-159	1.33m	NPA
Finland	2000	2,855	55	2020	2,800	51	-55	-4	5.55m	NPA
Iceland	2000	78	28	2021	150	41	72	13	369,180	CoE
Ireland, Republic of	2000	2,948	77	2020	3,717	74	769	-3	5.08m	NPA
Latvia	2000	8,815	370	2021	3,124	165	-5,691	-205	1.89m	NPA
Lithuania	2000	14,412	410	2020	6,138	220	-8,274	-190	2.80m	NPA
Norway	2000	2,548	57	2020	2,932	54	384	-3	5.43m	NPA
Sweden	2000	5,326	60	2021	7,317	70	1,991	10	10.38m	CoE
United Kingdom								0		
England and Wales	2000	64,602	124	2020	79,514	133	14,912	9	60.33m	ONS
Northern Ireland	2000	1,068	64	2021	1,709	90	641	26	1.90m	Northern Ireland prison administration
Scotland	2000	5,869	116	2020	7,004	128	1,135	12	5.47m	Scottish prison administration
Faeroe Islands (Denmark)	2000	8	18	2019	9	18	1	0	51,600	Danish NPA
Guernsey (UK)	2000	59	94	2020	86	131	27	37	66,300	Guernsey prison administration
Isle of Man (UK)	2000	54	70	2021	109	126	55	56	86,500	Isle of Man prison administration
Jersey (UK)	2000	130	150	2020	146	135	16	-15	108,300	Jersey prison administration
Southern Europe										
Albania	2001	3,053	99	2021	4,956	176	1,903	77	2.81m	NPA
Andorra	2001	48	72	2021	61	78	13	6	78,140	CoE
Bosnia and Herzegovina, Federation	2000	1,041	45	2019	1,813	83	772	38	2.19m	Federation Ministry of Justice
Bosnia and Herzegovina, Republika Srpska	2001	849	61	2021	562	47	-287	-14	1.2m	NPA
Croatia	2000	2,027	45	2020	3,533	87	1,506	42	4.0m	NPA
Cyprus, Republic of	2000	312	45	2020	716	80	404	35	893,700	CoE
Greece	2000	7,625	70	2021	11,131	105	3,506	35	10.65m	Government of Greece
Italy	2000	53,165	93	2020	53,364	89	199	-4	58.62m	Ministry of Justice
Kosovo / Kosova	2000	227	11	2020	1,642	93	1,415	82	1.77m	NPA
Malta	1999	230	61	2021	821	159	591	98	516,300	Home Affairs Minister
Montenegro	2000	664	110	2021	836	135	172	25	620,640	CoE
North Macedonia	2000	1,178	59	2021	2,220	107	1,042	48	2.07m	CoE
Portugal	2000	12,944	126	2020	11,424	111	-1,520	-15	10.30m	NPA
San Marino	2000	-	-	2021	9	26	-	-	34,700	CoE
Serbia	2000	6,160	82	2021	10,436	153	4,276	71	6.84m	Ministry of Justice
Slovenia	2000	1,148	58	2021	1,397	66	249	8	2.13m	NPA
Spain	2000	45,309	113	2021	55,097	116	9,788	3	47.46m	NPA
Gibraltar (UK)	2000	18	67	2018	47	139	29	72	33,700	Gibraltar statistics

21.2 Prison Population International Comparisons with other EU Countries

	Year: 2000 (or closest available year)			Year: 2021 (or latest available year)			Change		Estimated national population 2021/22[3]	Source of prison population total
	Date	Prison population total[1]	Prison population rate[2]	Date	Prison population total[1]	Prison population rate[2]	Prison population total[1]	Prison population rate[2]		
Western Europe										
Austria	2000	6,862	86	2020	8,348	94	1,486	8	8.99m	Ministry of Justice
Belgium	2000	8,688	85	2021	10,379	90	1,691	5	11.57m	CoE
France	2000	48,049	82	2020	77,062	119	29,013	37	67.94m	NPA
Germany	2000	70,252	85	2021	56,069	67	-14,183	-18	83.2m	Federal Statistical Office
Liechtenstein	1999	24	74	2021	12	31	-12	-43	39,080	CoE
Luxemburg	2000	394	90	2020	548	87	154	-3	647,300	NPA
Monaco	2000	18	51	2021	13	34	-5	-17	38,370	CoE
Netherlands	2000	13,847	87	2021	11,623	66	-2,224	-21	17.48m	CoE
Switzerland	2000	5,760	80	2020	6,897	80	1,137	0	8.73m	Swiss Federal Statistical Office
Europe / Asia										
Armenia	2000	7,281	236	2021	2,113	71	-5,168	-165	2.97m	Justice Minister
Azerbaijan	2000	24,851	317	2021	21,813	216	-3,038	-101	10.12m	CoE
Georgia	2000	8,349	190	2020	9,143	245	794	55	3.66m	national statistical office
Russian Federation	2000	1,060,404	729	2020	523,928	363	-536,476	-366	144.5m	NPA
Turkey	2000	49,512	73	2020	266,831	319	217,319	246	84.19m	Ministry of Justice
Central and Eastern Europe										
Belarus	2000	56,590	566	2018	32,556	345	-24,034	-221	9.43m	Statistical Yearbook
Bulgaria	2000	10,147	124	2021	6,080	88	-4,067	-36	6.89m	NPA
Czech Republic	2000	21,538	210	2020	19,286	180	-2,252	-30	10.72m	NPA
Hungary	2000	15,539	152	2020	16,752	172	1,213	20	9.68m	NPA
Moldova, Republic of	2000	9,449	260	2020	6,716	191	-2,733	-69	3.53m	NPA
Poland	2000	70,544	184	2020	67,894	179	-2,650	-5	37.64m	NPA
Romania	2000	48,267	215	2020	21,753	113	-26,514	-102	19.00m	NPA
Slovakia	2000	6,941	129	2020	10,519	192	3,578	63	5.46m	NPA
Ukraine[4]	2000	218,800	443	2021	49,823	126	-168,977	-317	39.0m	Ukraine State Statistics Department

Source: World Prison Brief, Institute for Crime & Justice Policy Research

1. Including pre-trail detainees / remand prisoners. It should be noted that the number of pre-trial/remand prisoners fluctuates from day to day, month to month and year to year. Consequently the above figures give an indication of the trend but the picture is inevitably incomplete.

2. Prison population rate per 100,000 of national population total.

3 All national population figures are inevitably estimates but the estimates used in the World Prison Brief are based on official national figures, United Nations figures or figures from other recognised international authorities.

4. Ukraine - not including prisoners in Crimea and Sebastopol and areas of Donetsk and Luhansk that are not under the control of the Ukrainian authorities.

C of E - Council of Europe
NPA - National Prison Administration
ONS - Office for National Statistics

21.3 Police recorded crime by offence, year ending March 2010 to year ending December 2019 and percentage change between year ending December 2019 and year ending December 2020

England and Wales

Offence		Apr '09 to Mar '10	Apr '10 to Mar '11	Apr '11 to Mar '12	Apr '12 to Mar '13	Apr '13 to Mar '14	Apr '14 to Mar '15	Apr '15 to Mar '16	Apr '16 to Mar '17	Apr '17 to Mar '18	Apr '18 to Mar '19	Apr '19 to Mar '20	Jan '19 to Dec '19	Jan '20 to Dec '20	% change between years
VICTIM BASED CRIME		**3,760,387**	**3,598,145**	**3,454,955**	**3,150,551**	**3,107,866**	**3,170,794**	**3,452,961**	**3,789,770**	**4,233,000**	**4,516,404**	**4,510,344**	**4,536,387**	**3,960,675**	**-13**
1	Murder[3]	529	559	493	484	452	434	478	510	585	578	582	564	548	-3
4.1	Manslaughter[3]	88	75	56	68	73	98	86	200	118	88	122	131	64	-51
4.10	Corporate manslaughter	1	1	2	5	8	6	12	7	8	11	9	11	8	-
4.2	Infanticide	2	4	2	1	0	1	1	0	1	2	5	1	5	-
	Homicide [3,4,5,6,7,8]	**620**	**639**	**553**	**558**	**533**	**539**	**577**	**717**	**712**	**679**	**718**	**707**	**625**	**-12**
4.4	Causing death or serious injury by dangerous driving[9]	296	213	200	174	290	413	469	601	576	661	668	655	582	-11
4.6	drugs	36	25	24	14	23	12	38	29	26	24	15	20	10	-
4.8	Causing death by careless or inconsiderate driving	188	172	179	139	136	159	150	160	152	169	135	166	106	-36
4.4/6/8	Causing death by dangerous or careless driving	..	..	..	..	..	..	..	..	..	..	..	..	..	..
4.9	Causing death by driving: unlicensed or disqualified or uninsured drivers	16	6	6	10	5	1	12	15	9	8	10	7	20	-
37.1	Causing death by aggravated vehicle taking	5	14	7	8	4	8	6	11	13	15	17	12	15	-
	Death or serious injury - unlawful driving	**541**	**430**	**416**	**345**	**458**	**593**	**675**	**816**	**776**	**877**	**845**	**860**	**733**	**-15**
2	Attempted murder[5,10]	591	523	483	412	501	565	679	818	1,343	1,032	1,001	974	1,032	6
4.3	Intentional destruction of viable unborn child	3	3	3	1	4	9	6	12	17	11	11	8	13	-
5	More serious wounding or other act endangering life[11]	..	..	..	..	..	..	..	..	..	..	..	..	..	..
5A	Wounding[11,12]	22,795	19,489	17,777	..	..	..	..	..	..	..	..	..	..	..
5B	Use of substance or object to endanger life[11,12]	416	371	315	..	..	..	..	..	..	..	..	..	..	..
5C	Possession of items to endanger life[11,12]	331	329	298	..	..	..	..	..	..	..	..	..	..	..
5D	Assault with intent to cause serious harm[12]	..	..	..	17,006	17,929	20,565	23,133	25,442	29,836	34,273	33,426	33,740	31,886	-5
5E	Endangering life[12]	..	..	..	778	801	992	1,326	1,742	2,852	2,701	2,295	2,500	1,932	-23
6	Endangering railway passengers[12]	..	257	214	..	..	..	..	..	..	..	..	..	..	..
7	Endangering life at sea[12]	6	4	6	..	..	..	..	..	..	..	..	..	..	..
8F	Inflicting grievous bodily harm (GBH) without intent[13,14]	16,482	15,112	14,409	..	..	..	..	..	..	..	..	..	..	..
8H	Racially or religiously aggravated inflicting GBH without intent[13,14]	224	188	169	..	..	..	..	..	..	..	..	..	..	..
4.7	Causing or allowing death or serious physical harm of child or vulnerable person[15]	3	5	6	8	22	16	25	26	39	49	43	47	45	-
8A	Other wounding[13]	..	..	..	..	..	..	..	..	..	..	..	..	..	..
8G	Actual bodily harm (ABH) and other injury[13,14]	355,962	328,463	301,223	..	..	..	..	..	..	..	..	..	..	..
8D	Racially or religiously aggravated other wounding[13]	..	..	..	..	..	..	..	..	..	..	..	..	..	..
8J	Racially or religiously aggravated ABH or other injury[13,14]	3,521	2,985	2,688	..	..	..	..	..	..	..	..	..	..	..
8K	Poisoning or female genital mutilation[13,14]	138	118	118	..	..	..	..	..	..	..	..	..	..	..
8N	Assault with injury[14]	..	..	..	290,956	300,653	348,605	403,456	436,567	468,794	497,483	489,431	491,191	440,775	-10
8P	Racially or religiously aggravated assault with injury[14]	..	..	..	2,579	2,452	2,736	2,936	3,127	3,299	3,590	3,318	3,433	2,950	-14
8S	Assault with injury on a constable[16]	..	..	..	..	..	0	0	0	8,290	10,436	11,107	11,100	11,291	2
8T	Assault with injury on an emergency worker (other than a constable)[17]	..	..	..	..	..	..	..	..	..	..	..	..	1,623	..
	Violence with injury	**400,703**	**367,847**	**337,709**	**311,740**	**322,362**	**373,488**	**431,561**	**467,734**	**514,470**	**549,575**	**540,632**	**542,993**	**491,547**	**-9**

21.3 Police recorded crime by offence, year ending March 2010 to year ending December 2019 and percentage change between year ending December 2019 and year ending December 2020

England and Wales

Offence	Apr '09 to Mar '10	Apr '10 to Mar '11	Apr '11 to Mar '12	Apr '12 to Mar '13	Apr '13 to Mar '14	Apr '14 to Mar '15	Apr '15 to Mar '16	Apr '16 to Mar '17	Apr '17 to Mar '18	Apr '18 to Mar '19	Apr '19 to Mar '20	Jan '19 to Dec '19	Jan '20 to Dec '20	% change between years
3 Threat or conspiracy to murder [18]	..	..	..	..	..	..	..	..	..	..	..	..	..	..
3A Conspiracy to murder [18]	45	36	36	28	30	40	50	54	65	71	93	85	77	-9
3B Threats to kill [18]	9,523	9,480	7,643	7,347	8,471	12,879	17,196	21,621	26,575	33,369	37,350	36,728	40,564	10
11 Cruelty to and neglect of children [19]	6,611	6,087	6,081	..	..	..	..	..	..	..	..	..	..	..
11A Cruelty to children/young persons [19,20]	..	..	..	6,370	8,000	9,189	12,155	14,229	16,120	19,294	22,294	21,724	23,763	9
12 Abandoning a child under the age of two years [19]	9	6	12	..	..	..	..	..	..	..	..	..	..	..
13 Child abduction	560	548	532	513	565	817	1,044	1,139	1,196	1,267	1,109	1,144	990	-13
14 Procuring illegal abortion	3	5	3	5	6	7	7	9	4	4	8	8	6	-
36 Kidnapping	1,860	1,717	1,516	1,388	1,728	2,189	3,020	3,832	4,559	5,258	5,760	5,591	5,608	0
104 Assault without injury on a constable	15,781	15,510	15,873	14,527	14,456	14,369	15,512	16,649	18,161	20,497	21,286	20,795	25,156	21
105A Assault without injury [21]	203,098	205,975	202,509	198,390	211,257	272,803	343,863	409,221	509,468	586,091	628,206	618,527	588,947	-5
105B Racially or religiously aggravated assault without injury	4,328	4,062	4,071	3,898	4,103	4,917	5,610	6,060	7,436	8,074	8,516	8,445	8,004	-5
106 Modern Slavery [22]	..	..	..	..	..	..	944	2,319	3,433	5,190	8,333	7,822	8,519	9
Violence without injury	241,818	243,426	238,276	232,466	248,616	317,210	399,401	475,133	587,017	679,115	732,955	720,869	701,634	-3
8L Harassment [23,24,25,26]	52,959	51,173	48,141	54,532	61,211	81,612	153,678	209,936	124,198	213,865	230,650	229,892	219,661	-4
8M Racially or religiously aggravated harassment [23]	2,370	1,971	1,625	1,500	1,445	1,871	1,878	1,834	1,898	3,074	3,506	3,452	4,810	39
8Q Stalking [24,26,27]	..	..	..	..	..	2,885	4,285	5,407	10,346	19,887	32,690	27,156	81,955	..
8R Malicious communication [25]	..	..	..	..	..	..	..	..	159,875	207,994	227,832	223,542	261,227	17
8U Controlling and coercive behaviour [21]	..	..	..	..	..	..	..	..	..	..	..	..	21,320	..
Stalking and harassment [21,26,27]	55,329	53,144	49,766	56,032	62,656	86,368	159,841	217,177	296,317	444,820	494,678	484,042	588,973	..
TOTAL VIOLENCE AGAINST THE PERSON	699,011	665,486	626,720	601,141	634,625	778,198	992,055	1,161,577	1,399,292	1,675,066	1,769,828	1,749,471	1,783,512	2
19A Rape of a female [28,29]	..	..	..	..	..	..	..	..	..	..	..	..	..	..
19C Rape of a female aged 16 or over [28]	9,027	9,469	9,773	9,646	12,307	18,338	22,803	26,860	35,737	39,529	39,108	39,404	37,046	-6
19D Rape of a female child under 16 [28]	2,908	2,877	2,777	2,803	3,407	4,470	5,321	5,995	7,635	7,967	7,272	7,394	6,716	-9
19E Rape of a female child under 13 [28]	1,967	2,243	2,212	2,372	2,835	3,530	4,335	4,545	5,494	5,916	5,143	5,367	4,955	-8
19J Rape of a female - undefined [30]	..	..	..	..	..	..	..	..	..	..	1,252	827	1,265	..
19B Rape of a male [28,29]	..	..	..	..	..	..	..	..	..	..	..	..	..	..
19F Rape of a male aged 16 or over [28]	368	387	387	413	661	1,026	1,296	1,641	2,490	2,811	2,658	2,641	2,591	-2
19G Rape of a male child under 16 [28]	241	246	288	352	416	669	693	841	893	984	995	945	889	-6
19H Rape of a male child under 13 [28]	563	670	601	788	1,125	1,387	1,855	2,171	2,586	2,671	2,305	2,449	1,994	-19
19K Rape of a male - undefined [30]	..	..	..	..	..	..	..	..	..	..	191	141	176	..
Rape	15,074	15,892	16,038	16,374	20,751	29,420	36,303	42,053	54,835	59,878	58,924	59,168	55,632	-6

21.3 Police recorded crime by offence, year ending March 2010 to year ending December 2019 and year ending December 2020 and percentage change between year ending December 2019 and year ending December 2020

England and Wales

Offence		Apr '09 to Mar '10	Apr '10 to Mar '11	Apr '11 to Mar '12	Apr '12 to Mar '13	Apr '13 to Mar '14	Apr '14 to Mar '15	Apr '15 to Mar '16	Apr '16 to Mar '17	Apr '17 to Mar '18	Apr '18 to Mar '19	Apr '19 to Mar '20	Jan '19 to Dec '19	Jan '20 to Dec '20	% change between years
	Violence with injury [28,29]	400,703	367,847	337,709	311,740	322,362	373,488	431,561	467,734	514,470	549,575	540,632	542,993	491,547	-9
16	Buggery [28,29]	:	:	:	:	:	:	:	:	:	:	:	:	:	:
17	Indecent assault on a male [28,29]	:	:	:	:	:	:	:	:	:	:	:	:	:	:
17A	Sexual assault on a male aged 13 and over [28]	1,208	1,285	1,261	1,400	1,957	2,907	3,457	4,422	5,418	5,841	6,244	6,083	5,491	-10
17B	Sexual assault on a male child under 13 [28]	1,054	1,126	1,011	1,270	1,652	2,437	2,657	3,373	3,799	3,838	3,779	3,821	3,330	-13
18	Gross indecency between males [29,30]	:	:	:	:	:	:	:	:	:	:	:	:	:	:
20	Indecent assault on a female [28,29]	:	:	:	:	:	:	:	:	:	:	:	:	:	:
20A	Sexual assault on a female aged 13 and over [28]	15,693	16,346	15,794	15,518	17,377	23,301	27,974	30,391	37,018	39,662	39,113	38,553	33,939	-12
20B	Sexual assault on a female child under 13 [28]	4,148	4,298	3,991	4,177	5,129	6,295	7,504	8,142	9,718	10,169	9,681	9,798	9,387	-4
21	Unlawful sexual intercourse with a girl under 13 [28]	:	:	:	:	:	:	:	:	:	:	:	:	:	:
21	Sexual activity involving a child under 13 [28]	1,817	1,769	1,808	2,173	2,892	4,708	5,949	7,913	8,666	9,550	9,572	9,790	9,600	-2
22	Unlawful sexual intercourse with a girl under 16 [28,29]	:	:	:	:	:	:	:	:	:	:	:	:	:	:
22B	Sexual activity involving a child under 16 [28]	3,992	4,039	3,971	4,468	5,881	8,680	11,525	13,363	14,823	15,569	14,857	15,213	13,502	-11
22A	Causing sexual activity without consent [28,31]	130	167	203	191	274	470	591	727	791	868	876	832	831	0
23	Incest or familial sexual offences [28]	1,111	803	637	509	491	624	775	830	846	874	906	917	873	-5
25	Abduction of female [28,29]	:	:	:	:	:	:	:	:	:	:	:	:	:	:
70	Sexual activity with a person with a mental disorder [28]	124	130	101	115	134	214	239	296	265	296	272	295	227	-23
71	Abuse of children through sexual exploitation [28,32]	134	153	159	176	289	368	569	632	1,193	1,030	1,006	990	1,059	7
72	Trafficking for sexual exploitation [22,28]	58	66	59	70	123	184	9	2	1	0	0	0	0	-
73	Abuse of position of trust of a sexual nature [28]	185	146	176	192	194	213	240	273	288	275	337	317	275	-13
74	Gross indecency with a child [28,29]	:	:	:	:	:	:	:	:	:	:	:	:	:	:
88A	Sexual grooming [28,33]	393	309	371	370	459	677	962	1,157	4,473	5,795	6,287	6,211	6,513	5
88B	Other miscellaneous sexual offences [28,34,35]	:	:	:	:	:	:	:	:	:	:	:	:	:	:
88C	Other miscellaneous sexual offences [28,35]	354	198	163	160	200	212	207	295	481	405	348	341	270	-21
88D	Unnatural sexual offences [28,35]	15	12	11	16	18	19	34	44	33	32	41	37	46	-
88E	Exposure and voyeurism [28,34,35]	7,516	7,201	7,006	6,420	6,411	7,847	8,172	9,050	9,749	10,181	10,774	10,709	10,084	-6
	Other sexual offences [28]	37,932	38,048	36,722	37,225	43,481	59,156	70,864	80,910	97,562	104,385	104,093	103,907	95,427	-8
	TOTAL SEXUAL OFFENCES [28]	53,006	53,940	52,760	53,599	64,232	88,576	107,167	122,963	152,397	164,263	163,017	163,075	151,059	-7
34A	Robbery of business property	8,182	7,729	6,770	6,120	5,789	5,398	5,430	5,980	7,627	8,272	8,859	8,872	6,721	-24
34B	Robbery of personal property	66,923	68,460	67,918	59,035	52,039	44,756	45,801	53,430	69,617	77,595	81,247	82,374	61,374	-25
	TOTAL ROBBERY	75,105	76,189	74,688	65,155	57,828	50,154	51,231	59,410	77,244	85,867	90,106	91,246	68,095	-25

21.3 Police recorded crime by offence, year ending March 2010 to year ending December 2020 and percentage change between year ending December 2019 and year ending December 2020

Offence	Apr '09 to Mar '10	Apr '10 to Mar '11	Apr '11 to Mar '12	Apr '12 to Mar '13	Apr '13 to Mar '14	Apr '14 to Mar '15	Apr '15 to Mar '16	Apr '16 to Mar '17	Apr '17 to Mar '18	Apr '18 to Mar '19	Apr '19 to Mar '20	Jan '19 to Dec '19	Jan '20 to Dec '20	% change between years
28 Burglary in a dwelling	:	:	:	:	:	:	:	:	:	:	:	:	:	:
28A Burglary in a dwelling[36]	214,889	208,484	198,853	185,147	171,416	156,935	154,151	160,044	0	5	1	1	1	-
28B Attempted burglary in a dwelling[36]	44,706	42,298	40,287	37,386	36,361	35,023	35,470	39,948	0	0	0	0	0	-
28C Distraction burglary in a dwelling[36]	6,936	5,480	4,467	3,305	2,847	3,080	3,034	3,408	0	0	0	0	0	-
28D Attempted distraction burglary in a dwelling[36]	722	543	368	257	189	239	289	420	0	0	0	0	0	-
28E Burglary - Residential[36]	:	:	:	:	:	:	:	:	249,771	236,223	211,575	218,405	167,811	-23
28F Attempted burglary - Residential[36]	:	:	:	:	:	:	:	:	53,674	53,199	50,611	51,579	43,216	-16
28G Distraction burglary - Residential[36]	:	:	:	:	:	:	:	:	2,948	2,708	2,327	2,520	1,836	-27
28H Attempted distraction burglary - Residential[36]	:	:	:	:	:	:	:	:	379	320	564	475	367	-23
29 Aggravated burglary in a dwelling[36]	1,353	1,360	1,337	1,181	1,175	1,277	1,684	2,209	0	0	10	0	10	-
29A Aggravated burglary -Residential[36]	:	:	:	:	:	:	:	:	3,160	3,101	3,478	3,318	3,510	6
Domestic burglary	268,606	258,165	245,312	227,276	211,988	196,554	194,628	206,029	0	0	11	1	11	-
of which: distraction burglary	7,658	6,023	4,835	3,562	3,036	3,319	3,323	3,828	0	5	0	0	0	-
Residential burglary	:	:	:	:	:	:	:	:	309,932	295,551	268,555	276,297	216,740	-22
of which: distraction burglary	:	:	:	:	:	:	:	:	3,327	3,028	2,891	2,995	2,203	-26
30 Burglary in a building other than a dwelling	:	:	:	:	:	:	:	:	:	:	:	:	:	:
30A Burglary in a building other than a dwelling[36]	236,019	230,868	223,153	202,440	200,570	185,382	178,692	177,125	0	6	0	0	0	-
30B Attempted burglary in a building other than a dwelling[36]	35,868	33,515	32,473	29,959	30,549	28,761	28,132	28,803	0	0	0	0	0	-
30C Burglary - business and community[36]	:	:	:	:	:	:	:	:	109,523	109,047	98,820	101,764	70,175	-31
30D Attempted burglary - business and community[36]	:	:	:	:	:	:	:	:	17,977	16,819	15,785	16,215	12,573	-22
31 Aggravated burglary in a building other than a dwelling[36]	152	135	110	120	105	169	195	265	1	0	0	0	0	-
31A Aggravated burglary - business and community[36]	:	:	:	:	:	:	:	:	367	434	512	511	369	-28
Non-domestic burglary	272,039	264,518	255,736	232,519	231,224	214,312	207,019	206,193	1	6	0	0	0	-
Non-residential burglary	:	:	:	:	:	:	:	:	127,867	126,300	115,117	118,490	83,117	-30
Burglary	**540,645**	**522,683**	**501,048**	**459,795**	**443,212**	**410,866**	**401,647**	**412,222**	**437,800**	**421,862**	**383,683**	**394,788**	**299,868**	**-24**
37.2 Aggravated vehicle taking	8,000	6,954	6,253	5,652	5,255	5,424	5,824	5,816	5,846	5,608	5,600	5,582	4,829	-13
45 Theft from a vehicle[37]	339,170	313,467	300,377	285,047	276,366	235,823	239,327	258,592	280,498	283,471	285,282	286,001	217,263	-24
48 Theft or unauthorised taking of a motor vehicle	109,684	99,208	85,803	74,168	70,053	70,216	75,901	90,987	105,829	114,094	113,181	113,644	94,915	-16
126 Vehicle interference[37,38]	38,019	29,987	25,009	22,492	20,367	38,059	45,674	52,208	65,064	65,267	62,372	63,364	54,271	-14
Vehicle offences	**494,873**	**449,616**	**417,442**	**387,359**	**372,041**	**349,522**	**366,726**	**407,603**	**457,237**	**468,440**	**466,435**	**468,591**	**371,278**	**-21**
39 Theft from the person	92,247	92,902	100,588	109,757	98,282	78,434	83,270	88,615	99,525	103,892	113,667	114,753	66,429	-42
Theft from the person	**92,247**	**92,902**	**100,588**	**109,757**	**98,282**	**78,434**	**83,270**	**88,615**	**99,525**	**103,892**	**113,667**	**114,753**	**66,429**	**-42**

21.3 Police recorded crime by offence, year ending March 2010 to year ending December 2020 and percentage change between year ending December 2019 and year ending December 2020

England and Wales

Offence		Apr '09 to Mar '10	Apr '10 to Mar '11	Apr '11 to Mar '12	Apr '12 to Mar '13	Apr '13 to Mar '14	Apr '14 to Mar '15	Apr '15 to Mar '16	Apr '16 to Mar '17	Apr '17 to Mar '18	Apr '18 to Mar '19	Apr '19 to Mar '20	Jan '19 to Dec '19	Jan '20 to Dec '20	% change between years
44	Theft or unauthorised taking of a pedal cycle	109,847	108,962	115,902	97,286	97,686	93,327	86,689	94,857	100,151	98,413	88,297	90,977	81,193	-11
	Bicycle theft	**109,847**	**108,962**	**115,902**	**97,286**	**97,686**	**93,327**	**86,689**	**94,857**	**100,151**	**98,413**	**88,297**	**90,977**	**81,193**	**-11**
46	Shoplifting	307,823	305,896	308,326	300,623	321,065	326,053	337,141	370,251	382,811	375,164	359,198	367,100	258,877	-29
	Shoplifting	**307,823**	**305,896**	**308,326**	**300,623**	**321,065**	**326,053**	**337,141**	**370,251**	**382,811**	**375,164**	**359,198**	**367,100**	**258,877**	**-29**
35	Blackmail [39]	1,450	1,491	1,369	1,497	2,134	3,507	5,917	7,350	8,329	13,853	10,994	11,174	14,056	26
40	Theft in a dwelling other than from an automatic machine or meter	53,338	54,798	54,518	52,384	50,513	50,808	51,258	52,267	53,829	53,644	49,060	50,496	42,028	-17
41	Theft by an employee	13,169	12,141	11,589	10,446	10,320	10,755	10,745	10,431	10,482	9,884	8,958	9,299	6,071	-35
42	Theft of mail	3,098	2,792	2,447	2,878	2,163	1,996	2,350	2,562	2,598	3,008	2,629	2,748	3,162	15
43	Dishonest use of electricity	1,736	1,860	1,948	2,007	2,229	2,550	2,500	2,185	2,082	1,971	2,284	2,296	2,715	18
47	Theft from automatic machine or meter [40]	7,753	6,215	6,692	6,394	4,950	4,213	3,946	3,709	4,625	4,072	3,803	3,769	2,116	-44
49	Other theft	436,244	481,585	491,559	419,685	389,024	359,183	345,199	350,988	366,974	379,578	368,897	381,326	262,279	-31
49A	Making off without payment [41]	70,397	66,505	61,351	50,833	51,550	59,393	64,521	77,832	86,551	83,177	69,379	71,330	46,678	-35
	All other theft offences	**587,185**	**627,387**	**631,473**	**546,124**	**512,883**	**492,405**	**486,436**	**507,324**	**535,470**	**549,187**	**516,004**	**532,438**	**379,105**	**-29**
	TOTAL THEFT OFFENCES	**2,132,620**	**2,107,446**	**2,074,779**	**1,900,944**	**1,845,169**	**1,750,607**	**1,761,909**	**1,880,872**	**2,012,994**	**2,016,958**	**1,927,284**	**1,968,647**	**1,456,750**	**-26**
56	Arson [42]	:	:	:	:	:	:	:	:	:	:	:	:	:	:
56A	Arson endangering life [42]	3,623	3,325	3,100	2,588	2,574	2,807	3,286	3,520	4,118	4,161	4,016	4,047	4,012	-1
56B	Arson not endangering life [42]	28,957	25,791	24,119	16,717	16,008	16,772	18,749	20,639	22,775	22,551	22,128	22,339	19,888	-11
	Arson	**32,580**	**29,116**	**27,219**	**19,305**	**18,582**	**19,579**	**22,035**	**24,159**	**26,893**	**26,712**	**26,144**	**26,386**	**23,900**	**-9**
58A	Criminal damage to a dwelling	198,623	172,916	155,982	131,157	121,525	117,969	125,637	132,108	142,013	140,423	139,108	138,689	126,556	-9
58B	Criminal damage to a building other than a dwelling	88,687	75,677	67,329	57,631	52,599	50,555	52,184	53,962	53,682	48,685	46,582	46,919	37,232	-21
58C	Criminal damage to a vehicle	336,927	289,045	259,871	222,770	217,994	214,760	227,720	232,448	233,065	217,274	204,193	207,687	173,231	-17
58D	Other criminal damage	140,575	125,751	113,478	97,008	93,438	98,586	110,977	120,050	133,069	138,999	141,772	141,972	138,186	-3
58E	Racially or religiously aggravated criminal damage to a dwelling [43]	849	639	499	:	:	:	:	:	:	:	:	:	:	:
58F	Racially or religiously aggravated criminal damage to a building other than a dwelling [43]	663	534	431	:	:	:	:	:	:	:	:	:	:	:
58G	Racially or religiously aggravated criminal damage to a vehicle [43]	1,135	869	788	:	:	:	:	:	:	:	:	:	:	:
58H	Racially or religiously aggravated other criminal damage [43]	606	537	411	:	:	:	:	:	:	:	:	:	:	:
58J	Racially or religiously aggravated criminal damage [43]	:	:	:	1,841	1,874	1,810	2,046	2,221	2,351	2,157	2,310	2,295	2,154	-6
	Criminal damage	**768,065**	**665,968**	**598,789**	**510,407**	**487,430**	**483,680**	**518,564**	**540,789**	**564,180**	**547,538**	**533,965**	**537,562**	**477,359**	**-11**
	TOTAL CRIMINAL DAMAGE AND ARSON	**800,645**	**695,084**	**626,008**	**529,712**	**506,012**	**503,259**	**540,599**	**564,948**	**591,073**	**574,250**	**560,109**	**563,948**	**501,259**	**-11**

21.3 Police recorded crime by offence, year ending March 2010 to year ending December 2020 and percentage change between year ending December 2019 and year ending December 2020

England and Wales

Offence	Apr '09 to Mar '10	Apr '10 to Mar '11	Apr '11 to Mar '12	Apr '12 to Mar '13	Apr '13 to Mar '14	Apr '14 to Mar '15	Apr '15 to Mar '16	Apr '16 to Mar '17	Apr '17 to Mar '18	Apr '18 to Mar '19	Apr '19 to Mar '20	Jan '19 to Dec '19	Jan '20 to Dec '20	% change between years
OTHER CRIMES AGAINST SOCIETY	**504,649**	**480,330**	**448,626**	**402,617**	**398,679**	**403,758**	**444,439**	**534,702**	**659,315**	**754,850**	**796,866**	**789,497**	**840,434**	**6**
92A Trafficking in controlled drugs	33,223	32,336	31,316	29,746	29,348	27,368	26,056	25,946	27,093	30,461	34,409	33,709	40,815	21
Trafficking of drugs	**33,223**	**32,336**	**31,316**	**29,746**	**29,348**	**27,368**	**26,056**	**25,946**	**27,093**	**30,461**	**34,409**	**33,709**	**40,815**	**21**
92B Possession of controlled drugs [44]	:	:	:	:	:	:	:	:	:	:	:	:	:	:
92C Other drug offences	1,122	1,142	1,127	1,034	1,198	779	594	1,085	807	804	783	785	975	24
92D Possession of controlled drugs (excluding cannabis) [44]	38,439	38,711	36,453	34,596	34,066	32,245	29,397	27,423	27,814	31,151	34,366	34,124	32,332	-5
92E Possession of cannabis [44]	162,800	160,733	160,203	142,627	133,604	110,297	93,603	84,744	82,748	91,843	113,582	109,949	130,371	19
Possession of drugs	**202,361**	**200,586**	**197,783**	**178,257**	**168,868**	**143,321**	**123,594**	**113,252**	**111,369**	**123,798**	**148,731**	**144,858**	**163,678**	**13**
TOTAL DRUG OFFENCES	**235,584**	**232,922**	**229,099**	**208,003**	**198,216**	**170,689**	**149,650**	**139,198**	**138,462**	**154,259**	**183,140**	**178,567**	**204,493**	**15**
8B Possession of weapons [45]	:	:	:	:	:	:	:	:	:	:	:	:	:	:
10A Possession of firearms with intent [45]	1,587	1,385	1,151	998	1,077	1,284	1,536	2,085	2,351	2,614	2,608	2,613	2,561	-2
10B Possession of firearms offences [46]	4,070	3,650	3,402	3,052	2,929	3,051	3,283	3,534	3,816	4,165	4,073	4,126	3,736	-9
10C Possession of other weapons [45]	11,950	10,564	9,138	7,274	7,328	7,474	9,121	10,950	13,473	15,580	15,481	15,685	15,074	-4
10D Possession of article with blade or point [45]	10,885	10,474	9,762	8,425	9,050	9,889	11,612	14,429	18,444	22,286	23,009	23,388	21,056	-10
81 Other firearms offences [47]	253	254	229	160	237	191	249	290	967	1,805	2,269	2,353	3,254	38
90 Other knives offences	13	0	6	1	2	1	4	2	3	4	4	4	5	-
TOTAL POSSESSION OF WEAPONS OFFENCES	**28,758**	**26,327**	**23,688**	**19,910**	**20,623**	**21,890**	**25,805**	**31,290**	**39,054**	**46,454**	**47,444**	**48,169**	**45,686**	**-5**
9A Public fear, alarm or distress [24,26]	126,597	114,781	97,085	81,139	79,601	96,007	135,191	199,904	285,934	337,956	347,872	344,759	365,355	6
9B Racially or religiously aggravated public fear, alarm or distress [24,26]	23,226	20,967	20,188	20,420	21,685	26,318	29,384	36,002	41,374	44,285	45,519	45,051	48,658	8
62 Treason [48]	0	0	0	:	:	:	:	:	:	:	:	:	:	:
62A Violent disorder [48]	:	:	:	656	640	766	989	1,152	1,670	1,686	1,561	1,636	1,572	-4
63 Treason felony [48]	0	0	0	:	:	:	:	:	:	:	:	:	:	:
64 Riot [48]	0	2	3	:	:	:	:	:	:	:	:	:	:	:
65 Violent disorder [48]	859	751	696	:	:	:	:	:	:	:	:	:	:	:
66 Other offences against the State or public order	37,572	36,580	32,886	29,990	32,474	36,126	39,596	47,461	57,784	65,146	64,997	65,076	64,160	-1
TOTAL PUBLIC ORDER OFFENCES	**188,254**	**173,081**	**150,858**	**132,205**	**134,400**	**159,217**	**205,160**	**284,519**	**386,762**	**449,073**	**459,949**	**456,522**	**479,745**	**5**
15 Concealing an infant death close to birth	6	9	5	2	2	5	4	9	12	19	7	11	8	-
24 Exploitation of prostitution [28]	148	153	110	120	124	154	178	213	240	238	234	251	235	-6
26 Bigamy	60	44	31	39	40	46	71	58	70	84	82	86	61	-29
27 Soliciting for prostitution [28]	1,190	826	797	883	750	870	599	437	400	410	374	408	321	-21
33 Going equipped for stealing, etc.	3,647	4,129	3,765	3,473	3,472	3,044	2,663	2,643	2,726	2,967	3,156	3,171	2,734	-14
33A Making, supplying or possessing articles for use in fraud	:	:	:	:	2,927	2,448	2,638	2,282	1,854	1,831	1,771	1,736	1,452	-16
38 Profiting from or concealing proceeds of crime [49]	2,609	2,344	1,779	1,427	1,485	1,509	1,669	1,947	2,058	2,192	2,658	2,602	3,224	24

21.3 Police recorded crime by offence, year ending March 2010 to year ending December 2019 and year ending December 2020 and percentage change between year ending December 2019 and year ending December 2020

England and Wales

Code	Offence	Apr '09 to Mar '10	Apr '10 to Mar '11	Apr '11 to Mar '12	Apr '12 to Mar '13	Apr '13 to Mar '14	Apr '14 to Mar '15	Apr '15 to Mar '16	Apr '16 to Mar '17	Apr '17 to Mar '18	Apr '18 to Mar '19	Apr '19 to Mar '20	Jan '19 to Dec '19	Jan '20 to Dec '20	% change between years
53H	Making or supplying articles for use in fraud [50]	862	975	1,301	1,384	:	:	:	:	:	:	:	:	:	:
53J	Possession of articles for use in fraud [50]	1,564	1,559	1,366	1,287	:	:	:	:	:	:	:	:	:	:
54	Handling stolen goods	9,448	9,184	9,769	8,134	8,526	6,583	5,332	4,337	3,785	3,697	3,585	3,654	3,259	-11
59	Threat etc. to commit criminal damage	5,996	5,916	5,214	4,950	5,790	8,998	12,840	18,681	27,013	34,193	35,053	34,855	37,976	9
60	Forgery or use of drug prescription	343	298	361	379	416	422	396	346	377	365	255	303	194	-36
61	Other forgery	2,526	1,632	2,124	2,984	2,864	2,290	2,912	4,425	5,741	6,479	5,414	5,912	3,316	-44
61A	Possession of false documents	2,263	1,770	1,378	962	934	987	1,051	884	858	864	849	849	601	-29
67	Perjury	184	339	151	134	96	92	123	118	121	107	87	85	96	13
68	Libel [51]	0	4	:	:	:	:	:	:	:	:	:	:	:	:
69	Offender Management Act offences	533	518	583	1,024	1,113	1,535	2,719	3,949	4,477	3,931	3,728	3,809	3,088	-19
75	Betting, gaming and lotteries [51]	21	14	12	11	11	19	32	28	24	36	46	44	65	:
76	Aiding suicide	17	7	10	:	:	:	:	:	:	:	:	:	:	-
78	Immigration offences [51]	411	445	344	:	:	:	:	:	:	:	:	:	:	:
79	Perverting the course of justice	7,997	6,890	5,698	4,947	5,368	6,297	6,433	6,647	7,219	7,243	6,822	6,989	6,738	-4
80	Absconding from lawful custody	557	499	414	482	370	442	521	591	799	904	1,027	970	908	-6
82	Customs and Revenue offences [51]	10	3	5	:	:	:	:	:	:	:	:	:	:	:
83	Bail offences	4	6	3	2	3	6	195	611	106	122	111	144	141	-2
84	Trade descriptions, etc [51]	809	486	263	:	:	:	:	:	:	:	:	:	:	:
85	Health and Safety offences [51]	6	2	8	:	:	:	:	:	:	:	:	:	:	:
86	Obscene publications, etc and protected sexual material	3,215	3,342	3,335	3,506	4,618	8,053	13,042	18,855	23,197	25,167	26,862	26,174	30,969	18
87	Protection from eviction [51]	81	73	68	:	:	:	:	:	:	:	:	:	:	:
89	Adulteration of food [51]	4	9	0	:	:	:	:	:	:	:	:	:	:	:
91	Public health offences [51, 52]	488	398	289	:	:	:	:	:	:	:	:	:	:	:
94	Planning laws [51]	0	1	1	:	:	:	:	:	:	:	:	:	:	:
95	Disclosure, obstruction, false or misleading statements etc	426	348	363	294	359	308	236	247	311	285	366	364	316	-13
96	Wildlife crime [63]	:	:	:	:	:	35	90	63	80	57	71	54	214	296
99	Other indictable or triable-either-way offences [22, 51, 53, 54]	1,629	1,569	1,589	2,510	2,575	4,153	5,481	6,821	7,496	7,841	7,686	7,701	8,506	10
802	Dangerous driving	3,941	3,475	3,239	3,092	3,152	3,277	4,090	4,848	5,304	5,136	5,138	5,128	5,272	3
814	Fraud, forgery associated with vehicle driver records	1,058	733	606	473	445	389	509	655	769	896	951	939	816	-13
	TOTAL MISCELLANEOUS CRIMES AGAINST SOCIETY	52,053	48,000	44,981	42,499	45,440	51,962	63,824	79,695	95,037	105,064	106,333	106,239	110,510	4
	TOTAL RECORDED CRIME - ALL OFFENCES EXCLUDING FRAUD AND COMPUTER MISUSE [55]	4,265,036	4,078,475	3,903,581	3,553,168	3,506,545	3,574,552	3,897,400	4,324,472	4,892,315	5,271,254	5,307,210	5,325,884	4,801,109	-10

21.3 Police recorded crime by offence, year ending March 2010 to year ending December 2020 and percentage change between year ending December 2019 and year ending December 2020

England and Wales

Offence		Apr '09 to Mar '10	Apr '10 to Mar '11	Apr '11 to Mar '12	Apr '12 to Mar '13	Apr '13 to Mar '14	Apr '14 to Mar '15	Apr '15 to Mar '16	Apr '16 to Mar '17	Apr '17 to Mar '18	Apr '18 to Mar '19	Apr '19 to Mar '20	Jan '19 to Dec '19	Jan '20 to Dec '20	% change between years
FRAUD OFFENCES															
51	Fraud by company director [56]	85	207	45	103	..	..	..	..	..	..	..	..	..	..
52	False accounting	155	108	75	59	..	..	..	..	..	..	..	..	..	..
53A	Cheque and credit card fraud (pre Fraud Act 2006) [50]	..	..	..	..	..	..	..	..	..	..	..	..	..	..
53B	Preserved other fraud and repealed fraud offences (pre-Fraud Act 2006) [41, 50]	3,666	3,342	3,799	3,027	..	..	..	..	..	..	..	..	..	..
53C	Fraud by false representation: cheque, plastic card and online bank accounts [40, 50]	27,148	24,942	22,703	17,873	1	..	..	..	..	..	..	..	..	..
53D	Fraud by false representation: other frauds [50]	39,626	42,460	44,719	40,325	5	..	..	..	..	..	..	..	..	..
53E	Fraud by failing to disclose information [50]	364	339	246	163	..	..	..	..	..	..	..	..	..	..
53F	Fraud by abuse of position [50]	1,160	1,033	1,170	927	1	..	..	..	..	..	..	..	..	..
53G	Obtaining services dishonestly [50]	1,042	..	..	..	..	..	..	..	..	..	..	..	..	..
55	Bankruptcy and insolvency offences	13	10	11	12	..	..	..	..	..	..	..	..	..	..
	TOTAL FRAUD OFFENCES RECORDED BY THE POLICE [57]	73,259	72,441	72,768	62,489	7	..	..	..	..	..	..	..	..	..
	Fraud and computer misuse offences recorded by Action fraud [57, 58, 5]			46,658	117,402	211,221	230,323	220,638	261,943	277,033	311,086	338,255	337,983	377,756	12
	Fraud offences referred to NFIB by Cifas [58, 60]			235,499	217,369	214,156	257,762	298,968	306,195	276,997	313,175	334,297	334,413	299,786	-10
	Fraud offences referred to NFIB by UK Finance [58, 59, 60, 61, 62]			121,478	113,143	96,534	104,982	99,546	84,224	84,328	69,160	101,989	94,119	106,701	13
	TOTAL FRAUD AND COMPUTER MISUSE OFFENCES	73,259	72,441	476,403	510,403	521,918	593,067	619,152	652,362	638,358	693,421	774,541	766,515	784,243	2
	TOTAL RECORDED CRIME – ALL OFFENCES INCLUDING FRAUD AND COMPUTER MISUSE [55]	4,338,295	4,150,916	4,379,984	4,063,571	4,028,463	4,167,619	4,516,552	4,976,834	5,530,673	5,964,675	6,081,751	6,092,399	5,585,352	-8

Source: Home Office - Police recorded crime

Police recorded crime data are not designated as National Statistics.

NOTES TO ACCOMPANY TABLE 21.3

1   Following the implementation of a new IT system in July 2019, Greater Manchester Police have been unable to supply data for the period July to December 2019. Figures for Greater Manchester are not included in the National and Regional totals for the years ending March and December 2018 and 2019.

2   The National Crime Recording Standard (NCRS) was introduced in April 2002, although some forces adopted NCRS practices before the standard was formally introduced. Figures before and after that date are not directly comparable. The introduction of NCRS led to a rise in recording in year ending March 2003 and, particularly for violent crime, in the following years as forces continued to improve compliance with the new standard.

3   Includes the British Transport Police from year ending March 2003 onwards.

4   Data on homicide offences given in these police recorded crime data will differ from data from the Home Office Homicide Index, which are published annually by ONS, last released as part of 'Homicide in England and Wales: year ending March 2018'. Police recorded crime data on homicide represent the recording decision of the police based on the available information at the time the offence comes to their attention. Homicide Index data take account of the charging decision and court outcome in cases that have gone to trial. It is not uncommon for offences initially recorded as murder by the police to be charged or convicted as manslaughter at court.

5   The homicide figure for year ending March 2003 includes 173 homicides attributed to Harold Shipman in previous years but coming to light in the official inquiry in 2002. In previous years, this figure has been incorrectly stated as 172.

6   The homicide figure in year ending March 2006 of 764 includes 52 homicide victims of the 7 July London bombings, which also accounted for approximately one-quarter of the total of 920 attempted murders.

7   The homicide figure for year ending March 2017 includes 96 homicide victims of Hillsborough.

8   The year ending March 2018 includes 13 homicide victims of the London Bridge/Borough Market and Westminster attacks. There were 22 homicide victims of the Manchester Arena bombing in the year ending March 2018; these are not included in Table A4. See note 1 for more information.

9   The year ending December 2019 includes 39 homicide victims, whose bodies were found in a lorry in Grays, Essex in October 2019.

10   New offence of 'causing serious injury by dangerous driving' was added to this category in April 2013.

11   The year ending March 2018 'attempted murders' include the terrorist-related incident at Parsons Green Underground station in September 2017(43)

12   Offence classifications 5A, 5B and 5C were introduced from 1 April 2008 and replaced classification 5. Classification 5A was influenced by a clarification in recording rules that had the effect of significantly increasing levels of recording in some forces. Classification 5A also included some other offences of endangering life as well as GBH with intent, though GBH with intent was the major part of this category.

13   Offence classifications 5D and 5E were introduced from 1 April 2012 and replaced classification 5A offences. Offence classification 5E was also introduced and replaced the remaining classification 5A offences, 5B, 5C, 6 and 7.

14   Offence classifications 8F, 8G, 8H, 8J and 8K were introduced from 1 April 2008 and had previously been recorded as part of classifications 8A or 8D.

15   Offence classification 8N was introduced from 1 April 2012 and replaced classifications 8F, 8G and 8K. Offence classification 8P was also introduced and replaced classifications 8H and 8J.

16   New offence of 'cause or allow a child or vulnerable adult to suffer serious physical harm' was added to this category in April 2013

17   From April 2017 new classifications 8S (assault with injury on a constable) was introduced.

18   Offence classifications 3A and 3B were introduced from 1 April 2008 and had previously been recorded as classification 3.

19   Offence classification 11A was introduced from 1 April 2012 and replaced classifications 11 and 12.

20   In June 2015, as set out in the Serious Crime Act 2015, the offence of Cruelty to children/young persons was amended to include cases where suffering or injury are psychological in nature as well as physical

21   New offence of 'coercive and controlling behaviour' was added to this category in 29 December 2015

22   Modern Slavery (106) was introduced as a separate crime classification in April 2015. During April-July 2015 this classification included all of the offences that were previously recorded under category 72 (Trafficking for sexual exploitation) and some offences that were previously recorded under category 99 (Other indictable or triable-either-way offences). From 31 July 2015, a new set of Modern Slavery Act offences commenced, replacing all the offence codes previously listed under this classification. Modern slavery will be recorded in addition to the most serious additional victim based offence involving the same victim-offender relationship if any such offence is disclosed.

23   Prior to year ending March 2009, the police sent combined figures for harassment (8L, 8M) and public fear, alarm and distress (9A, 9B) offences. For the years ending March 2003 to March 2008, figures for these offence groups are estimated based upon the proportionate split between the offences in year ending March 2009.

24   Stalking (8Q) was introduced as a separate crime classification in April 2014, following the introduction of the Protection of Freedoms Act 2012 section 111. Before this, stalking offences were included within harassment offences (8L).

25   Changes in the Home Office Counting Rules (HOCR), implemented in April 2015, resulted in the recording of two additional harassment offences (Disclosure of private sexual photographs and films with the intent to cause distress or anxiety' and 'Sending letters with intent to cause distress or anxiety'; the latter includes any form of electronic communication), not previously counted as notifiable offences under the headline category of violence without injury. There is no available back-series for these additional notifiable offences. Subsequently, from April 2017 these offences were moved into a new classification 8R (malicious communications).

26   From April 2018 a change to the Home Office Counting Rules means in a course of conduct amounting to either stalking or harassment or controlling and coercive behaviour this offence will be recorded in addition to the most serious additional offence involving the same victim/offender. This is expected to cause an increase in offences recorded against harassment and stalking.

27   The Sexual Offences Act 2003, introduced in May 2004, altered the definition and coverage of sexual offences.

28   Prior to year ending March 2010, a small number of offences continued to be recorded relating to offences repealed by the Sexual Offences Act 2003. While these may have been legitimately recorded for offences committed prior to May 2004 it is also possible that some may have been recorded in these old categories in error, so any changes based on small numbers should be interpreted with caution.

29   Offence codes 19J and 19K were introduced from April 2019 to cover rape or attempted rape by multiple undefined offenders. "Undefined Offender" is only to be used in circumstances where the victim (or person representing the victim) cannot identify individual multiple offenders as being different or distinct.

30   The increase in year ending March 2006 was accounted for by a large number of offences that were dealt with by the Norfolk Constabulary.

31   In April 2015 offence classification 71 was renamed 'Abuse of children through sexual exploitation'. This offence classification was previously named 'Abuse of children through prostitution and pornography'

32   Prior to 1st April 2017 the Sexual Grooming classification was restricted to those offences where the offender intentionally met the child or either the victim or the suspect travelled with the intention of meeting. From 1st April 2017, it also includes the criminal offence of anyone aged 18 or over intentionally communicating with a child under 16, where the person acts for a sexual purpose and the communication is sexual or intended to elicit a sexual response.

33   This offence consists solely of the former offence of 'Indecent Exposure' for years prior to year ending March 2005. This became the offence of 'Exposure' and was included within 'Other miscellaneous sexual offences' from May 2004.

34   Offence classification 88B was split into 88C–E with effect from year ending March 2009. Since that time offences of exposure have been recorded as classification 88E.

35   From April 2017 a new classification of burglary offences was introduced. New sub-categories of residential and non-residential burglary have replaced domestic and non-domestic burglary respectively. The new classification of residential burglary now includes all buildings or parts of buildings that are within the boundary of, or form a part of, a dwelling. Burglary offence codes 28A, 28B, 28C, 28D and 29 have been replaced by offence codes 28E, 28F, 28G, 28H and 29A. Offence codes 30A, 30B and 31, which formed have been replaced by 30C, 30D and 31A. Some crimes may be incorrectly recorded against the expired codes. These will be noted and sent back to forces to be recorded under the correct code ready for future publications.

36   A change in the guidance within Home Office Counting Rules (HOCR) in April 2014 is likely to have led to offences that previously might have been recorded as theft from a vehicle now being recorded as vehicle interference when the motive of the offender was not clear.

37   Includes tampering with a motor vehicle.

38   The large increase in year ending March 2007 was due to the recording of threats made against shareholders of GlaxoSmithKline by animal rights activists.

39   Following a change in the implementation of the Fraud Act 2006, offences involving theft from an automatic machine using a plastic card are now regarded as false representation and recorded under classification 53C.

40   Offence classification 49A was introduced as a separate theft classification in year ending March 2014. Before this, it was recorded under the fraud offence classification 53B. Data for 49A are provided for all years following a special request to forces. In some cases, these have been estimated where forces were unable to provide data.

41   Offence classifications 56A and 56B were introduced from 1 April 2008 and had previously been recorded as classification 56.

42   Offence classifications 58E-58H were amalgamated on 1 April 2012 to form classification 58J.

43   Possession of controlled drugs offences were split with effect from April 2004 into possession of cannabis and possession of drugs other than cannabis.

44   Offence classifications 10A, 10C and 10D were introduced from 1 April 2008 and had previously been recorded as classification 8B.

45   Offence classification 10B was introduced from 1 April 2008. Possession of firearms offences are those offences where the weapon has not been used during the commission of another offence.

46   These are offences under the Firearms Act 1968 and other Firearms Acts connected with licensing and certification of firearms. Such offences are not included in the firearms offences statistics.

47   Offence classifications 62-65 were amalgamated on 1 April 2012 to form classification 62A.

48   These offences were added to the series from 1 April 2003.

49   New offences were introduced under the Fraud Act 2006, which came into force on 15 January 2007.

50   Offence classifications 68, 75, 78, 82, 84, 85, 87, 89, 91 and 94 were included with classification 99 with effect from 1 April 2012.

51   The large increase in this offence from year ending March 2009 is mainly due to the recording of fly-tipping by some forces following advice that this offence is notifiable.

52   Wildlife crime (96) was introduced as a separate crime classification in April 2014. This saw a number of offences that were previously recorded under "Other notifiable offences" (99) brought together.

53   Due to the introduction of fly-tipping as an offence under "Other notifiable offences" (99) in April 2014, percentage changes may appear high in certain publications.

54   Some forces have revised their data and totals may therefore not agree with those previously published.

55   The large increase in this offence in year ending March 2006 was due to one large-scale fraud recorded by the Cambridgeshire Constabulary. The increase in year ending March 2008 was due to a fraud recorded by North Yorkshire Police. The large increase in year ending March 2009 was due to large-scale frauds recorded by Gwent Police, Leicestershire Constabulary and the Metropolitan Police. The increase in year ending March 2011 was due to a large-scale fraud recorded by North Yorkshire Police.

56   Action Fraud have taken over the recording of fraud and computer misuse offences on behalf of individual police forces. This process began in April 2011 and was rolled out to all police forces by March 2013. Due to this change caution should be applied when comparing data over this transitional period and with earlier years. There were 7 cases in year ending March 2014 where police forces recorded a fraud or computer misuse offence after the transfer of responsibility to Action Fraud. These cases may be revised in future quarters. See the User Guide for more details including information on transfer date to Action Fraud for each force.

57   It is possible that there may be some double or triple counting between Action Fraud, Cifas and UK Finance. Experts believe this duplication to be so small as to have an insignificant effect on crime trends, but there is currently no simple cross-referencing method within NFIB to detect the scale of it. Section 5.4 of the User Guide provides more information.

58   Following the introduction of Action Fraud's new fraud and cyber-crime reporting service in October 2018, there was a technical issue whereby an increased number of reports were not allocated to a Police Force Area. As a result, an increased number of fraud and computer misuse offences with postcodes belonging to areas outside of England and Wales may have been included in the England and Wales figures in the year to December 2018 publication. This issue has now been resolved and the figures have been revised since the year to March 2019 publication.

59   In October 2018, Action Fraud launched a new fraud and cyber-crime reporting service. The transition to the new system is not yet complete and there has been a pause in the data feed from Cifas to the NFIB. Although fraud continues to be recorded by Cifas, cases from December 2018 have not yet been 'referred' to the NFIB. Therefore the Cifas figures and any NFIB totals presented in this bulletin and accompanying data tables are based on provisional data provided by Cifas. Once the issue has been resolved the NFIB will hold a full copy of the data, allowing Cifas figures to be treated as confirmed and recognised as 'referred' to the NFIB.

60   Cifas is a UK-wide fraud prevention service representing around 350 organisations from the public and private sectors. These organisations mainly share data on confirmed cases of fraud, particularly application, identity and first party frauds, via the Cifas National Fraud Database. Data supplied by Cifas to the National Fraud Intelligence Bureau (NFIB) are recorded in line with the Home Office Counting Rules (HOCR) for recorded crime.

61   Both sets of industry data from Cifas and UK Finance relate only to fraud affecting those organisations that are part of the respective membership networks. While membership of Cifas and UK Finance has remained fairly stable over the last few years, it is possible that coverage could change as new members join or previous members withdraw, which could impact on overall figures for fraud reported. Prior to year ending March 2012, fraud cases for these organisations were not sent to the NFIB.

62   The UK Finance figures and NFIB totals presented in this bulletin and accompanying data tables are supplemented by provisional data provided by UK Finance. This is as a result of a small percentage of the records supplied by UK Finance having not been successfully processed by NFIB systems. The NFIB is working to ensure that all referrals from UK Finance are successfully processed, at which point the need for provisional data will be removed.

63   UK Finance is responsible for coordinating activities on fraud prevention in the UK payments industry. UK Finance collates information relating to cheque, plastic card and online bank accounts via its Fraud Intelligence Sharing System (FISS) database, and this is in turn provided to NFIB. FISS is an intelligence tool rather than a fraud reporting tool, and its main purpose is to share actionable intelligence about the criminals or entities relating to fraud offences rather than count the numbers of victims of fraud. As a result, the number of cases presented in Table A4 is considerably less than the total number reported to UK Finance by its members. Comprehensive statistics on these fraud types are published twice yearly by UK Finance.

64   In July 2017 FFA UK integrated into UK Finance.

-     Indicates that data are not reported because the base number of offences is less than 50.

21.4 Persons[1] sentenced at all courts, by type of sentence and offence group, 2010 to 2020[2][3]

England and Wales

Persons sentenced

Year ending December	Type of sentence	Violence against the person	Sexual offences	Robbery	Theft Offences	Criminal damage & arson	Drug offences	Possession of weapons	Public order offences	Miscellaneous crimes against society	Fraud offences	All indictable offences	Summary non-motoring	Summary motoring	All summary offences	Offence not known[4]	All offences
2010	**All Sentenced**	**32,522**	**5,720**	**8,514**	**138,065**	**7,127**	**61,435**	**12,990**	**19,254**	**46,314**	**15,481**	**347,422**	**492,345**	**517,833**	**1,010,178**	**:**	**1,357,600**
	Immediate custody	11,743	3,259	4,946	30,993	1,000	9,693	2,953	5,470	10,225	2,657	82,939	14,634	3,940	18,574	:	101,513
	Suspended sentence	7,073	450	505	9,757	382	3,820	2,061	3,012	4,302	2,814	34,176	9,560	4,382	13,942	:	48,118
	Community sentence	10,460	1,641	2,768	48,645	2,981	13,418	5,779	6,488	10,296	6,031	108,507	64,723	16,103	80,826	:	189,333
	Fine[5]	952	106	4	16,848	772	23,354	999	2,161	12,434	1,807	59,437	343,650	483,234	826,884	:	886,321
	Absolute discharge	41	7	4	588	56	425	49	179	465	21	1,835	2,909	4,068	6,977	:	8,812
	Conditional discharge	1,023	127	13	24,585	1,410	8,526	864	938	3,400	1,917	42,803	44,597	3,033	47,630	:	90,433
	Compensation	562	8	196	1,769	293	3	2	58	69	100	3,060	4,703	192	4,895	:	7,955
	Otherwise dealt with[6]	668	122	78	4,880	233	2,196	283	948	5,123	134	14,665	7,569	2,881	10,450	:	25,115
	Average custodial sentence (months)[7]	20.8	49.0	34.5	8.7	18.5	30.7	13.2	7.1	8.2	13.4	16.2	2.6	3.1	2.7	:	13.7
2011	**All Sentenced**	**30,564**	**5,928**	**9,340**	**139,526**	**6,399**	**61,094**	**12,439**	**17,858**	**43,764**	**14,882**	**341,794**	**493,177**	**470,699**	**963,876**	**:**	**1,305,670**
	Immediate custody	12,135	3,413	5,588	33,796	1,036	9,788	3,196	5,498	10,110	2,946	87,507	15,210	3,453	18,663	:	106,170
	Suspended sentence	6,415	503	541	10,325	396	4,205	2,083	2,634	4,321	2,999	34,422	9,510	4,221	13,731	:	48,153
	Community sentence	8,814	1,646	2,937	47,538	2,595	12,724	5,170	5,586	9,732	5,444	102,186	60,848	14,569	75,417	:	177,603
	Fine[5]	1,140	120	4	16,995	715	23,317	920	2,149	11,338	1,580	58,278	351,829	439,729	791,558	:	849,836
	Absolute discharge	42	8	1	572	48	428	46	157	485	17	1,804	2,722	3,626	6,348	:	8,152
	Conditional discharge	990	89	12	24,139	1,161	8,345	755	877	3,161	1,683	41,212	42,356	2,731	45,087	:	86,299
	Compensation	415	10	173	1,662	225	1	4	54	72	91	2,707	3,918	155	4,073	:	6,780
	Otherwise dealt with[6]	613	139	84	4,499	223	2,286	265	903	4,544	122	13,678	6,784	2,215	8,999	:	22,677
	Average custodial sentence (months)[7]	21.8	53.5	35.4	9.1	19.9	30.7	13.1	7.3	8.8	14.9	16.8	2.6	3.1	2.7	:	14.3
2012	**All Sentenced**	**26,325**	**5,715**	**8,345**	**126,359**	**5,364**	**57,601**	**10,164**	**16,176**	**37,825**	**12,215**	**306,089**	**469,308**	**447,838**	**917,146**	**:**	**1,223,235**
	Immediate custody	11,341	3,397	5,002	32,500	889	9,011	2,651	5,001	8,638	2,629	81,059	13,973	3,012	16,985	:	98,044
	Suspended sentence	5,582	477	555	9,709	300	4,215	1,793	2,299	4,111	2,842	31,883	9,008	3,752	12,760	:	44,643
	Community sentence	6,434	1,512	2,583	39,402	2,018	11,513	4,075	4,760	8,132	4,122	84,551	53,799	12,833	66,632	:	151,183
	Fine[5]	1,305	101	4	15,911	674	21,344	783	2,243	10,131	1,171	53,667	342,437	420,724	763,161	:	816,828
	Absolute discharge	59	8	2	530	47	407	33	157	337	23	1,603	2,592	3,301	5,893	:	7,496
	Conditional discharge	929	92	17	22,263	998	8,816	576	838	2,797	1,210	38,536	38,980	2,350	41,330	:	79,866
	Compensation	203	18	74	2,466	250	4	3	42	65	122	3,247	3,721	173	3,894	:	7,141
	Otherwise dealt with[6]	472	110	108	3,578	188	2,291	250	836	3,614	96	11,543	4,798	1,693	6,491	:	18,034
	Average custodial sentence (months)[7]	23.1	54.5	35.8	9.2	23.7	28.7	13.0	7.4	9.1	14.6	17.0	2.6	3.1	2.7	:	14.5
2013	**All Sentenced**	**24,279**	**5,634**	**6,773**	**121,637**	**4,054**	**56,323**	**9,930**	**16,213**	**34,364**	**12,093**	**291,300**	**435,505**	**443,883**	**879,388**	**:**	**1,170,688**
	Immediate custody	10,384	3,360	4,301	31,718	722	9,024	2,619	4,772	8,525	2,535	77,960	12,317	2,689	15,006	:	92,966
	Suspended sentence	5,582	581	499	11,140	296	5,173	2,108	2,537	4,522	3,093	35,531	9,555	3,679	13,234	:	48,765
	Community sentence	5,312	1,354	1,839	31,978	1,412	9,388	3,557	4,292	6,680	3,961	69,773	46,081	10,681	56,762	:	126,535
	Fine[5]	1,376	125	30	16,500	503	20,712	823	2,828	9,124	1,166	53,187	320,480	419,737	740,217	:	793,404
	Absolute discharge	60	5	1	580	19	346	33	116	352	13	1,525	2,368	3,107	5,475	:	7,000
	Conditional discharge	874	91	19	21,629	783	9,396	488	963	2,377	1,089	37,709	36,191	1,943	38,134	:	75,843
	Compensation	194	19	8	3,958	181	4	2	95	73	141	4,675	4,520	127	4,647	:	9,322
	Otherwise dealt with[6]	497	99	76	4,134	138	2,280	300	610	2,711	95	10,940	3,993	1,920	5,913	:	16,853
	Average custodial sentence (months)[7]	24.6	59.1	39.6	9.2	26.7	31.2	13.3	7.5	9.6	14.9	18.0	2.6	3.1	2.7	:	15.5

771

21.4 Persons(1) sentenced at all courts, by type of sentence and offence group, 2010 to 2020(2)(3)

England and Wales

Year ending December	Type of sentence	Violence against the person	Sexual offences	Robbery	Theft Offences	Criminal damage & arson	Drug offences	Possession of weapons	Public order offences	Miscellaneous crimes against society	Fraud offences	All indictable offences	Summary non-motoring	Summary motoring	All summary offences	Offence not known (4)	All offences
2014	All Sentenced	26,502	6,233	5,582	116,158	2,469	51,297	9,987	17,058	31,709	13,335	280,330	457,412	471,462	928,874	:	1,209,204
	Immediate custody	11,131	3,687	3,686	30,067	619	8,756	2,655	4,820	8,054	2,298	75,773	12,933	2,607	15,540	:	91,313
	Suspended sentence	6,492	721	440	11,948	263	5,525	2,321	3,036	4,835	3,356	38,937	10,373	3,669	14,042	:	52,979
	Community sentence	5,296	1,497	1,319	25,413	737	7,154	3,310	4,023	5,755	4,426	58,930	44,016	9,692	53,708	:	112,638
	Fine(5)	1,662	119	3	17,637	257	19,632	833	3,079	8,275	1,496	52,993	343,978	449,970	793,948	:	846,941
	Absolute discharge	70	7	3	522	20	321	36	110	293	20	1,402	1,922	2,439	4,361	:	5,763
	Conditional discharge	963	87	13	21,231	347	8,223	482	1,054	1,806	1,459	35,665	35,327	1,440	36,767	:	72,432
	Compensation	151	5	7	2,494	71	-	-	44	46	93	2,911	3,242	76	3,318	:	6,229
	Otherwise dealt with(6)	737	110	111	6,846	155	1,686	350	892	2,645	187	13,719	5,621	1,569	7,190	:	20,909
	Average custodial sentence (months)(7)	23.4	62.0	40.8	9.0	24.8	32.1	12.9	6.7	10.2	15.9	18.3	2.6	3.0	2.6		15.6
2015	All Sentenced	29,292	6,847	4,721	103,108	2,434	46,242	10,748	17,088	30,227	12,520	263,227	474,047	501,648	975,695	:	1,238,922
	Immediate custody	11,850	4,106	3,220	27,511	657	8,618	3,077	4,834	8,169	2,320	74,362	13,238	2,748	15,986	:	90,348
	Suspended sentence	7,587	858	365	11,966	333	5,679	2,817	3,166	5,310	3,488	41,569	11,557	3,946	15,503	:	57,072
	Community sentence	5,838	1,545	981	24,392	707	6,719	3,442	4,309	5,493	3,959	57,385	46,800	10,101	56,901	:	114,286
	Fine(5)	2,012	104	3	15,138	203	16,445	706	2,993	7,106	1,331	46,041	358,382	479,598	837,980	:	884,021
	Absolute discharge	80	10	3	950	12	430	41	202	410	23	2,161	4,533	2,248	6,781	:	8,942
	Conditional discharge	1,158	81	14	18,382	321	7,255	442	1,004	1,676	1,234	31,567	33,018	1,443	34,461	:	66,028
	Compensation	107	4	4	1,823	57	-	-	41	35	77	2,148	2,980	105	3,085	:	5,233
	Otherwise dealt with(6)	660	139	131	2,946	144	1,096	223	539	2,028	88	7,994	3,539	1,459	4,998	:	12,992
	Average custodial sentence (months)(7)	22.9	61.9	43.1	9.1	23.4	34.1	13.6	6.7	10.8	18.0	19.2	2.5	3.0	2.6		16.2
2016	All Sentenced	28,966	7,475	4,058	88,411	2,255	41,831	12,007	16,565	30,488	10,458	242,514	476,321	513,611	989,932	:	1,232,446
	Immediate custody	11,903	4,423	2,829	25,531	631	8,860	3,962	4,792	8,808	2,206	73,945	12,794	3,123	15,917	:	89,862
	Suspended sentence	7,137	1,127	258	10,991	353	4,959	3,198	3,065	6,023	2,938	40,049	11,445	4,907	16,352	:	56,401
	Community sentence	5,571	1,486	854	20,298	647	5,602	3,485	3,994	4,776	3,086	49,799	42,520	10,931	53,451	:	103,250
	Fine(5)	2,289	81	-	13,089	193	15,057	697	3,073	7,070	1,013	42,562	372,507	489,663	862,170	:	904,732
	Absolute discharge	54	16	1	357	12	190	15	117	199	17	978	2,089	1,651	3,740	:	4,718
	Conditional discharge	1,183	88	7	14,546	236	5,821	401	967	1,384	1,038	25,671	28,509	1,322	29,831	:	55,502
	Compensation	96	4	2	1,479	57	-	-	30	32	60	1,760	2,846	134	2,980	:	4,740
	Otherwise dealt with(6)	733	250	107	2,120	126	1,342	249	527	2,196	100	7,750	3,611	1,880	5,491	:	13,241
	Average custodial sentence (months)(7)	22.3	60.0	44.9	9.0	27.3	34.6	13.8	6.5	10.8	19.2	19.4	2.5	2.9	2.5		16.4
2017	All Sentenced	27,971	6,875	3,982	77,596	1,954	37,221	12,716	16,764	28,482	10,156	223,717	470,319	507,404	977,723	:	1,201,440
	Immediate custody	11,723	4,077	2,779	23,645	612	8,342	4,444	4,948	8,561	2,052	71,183	12,020	3,151	15,171	:	86,354
	Suspended sentence	6,696	1,057	222	10,001	285	4,273	3,413	2,986	6,192	2,646	37,771	10,772	4,716	15,488	:	53,259
	Community sentence	5,407	1,304	884	17,450	530	4,792	3,662	3,967	4,055	3,012	45,063	38,777	11,799	50,576	:	95,639
	Fine(5)	2,216	78	1	10,885	152	13,411	702	3,185	6,516	1,152	38,298	374,936	482,215	857,151	:	895,449
	Absolute discharge	41	21	1	281	11	191	13	80	141	5	785	2,795	1,613	4,408	:	5,193
	Conditional discharge	1,049	74	7	11,901	214	4,769	300	949	1,127	1,113	21,503	25,077	1,346	26,423	:	47,926
	Compensation	98	17	-	1,656	49	-	-	22	49	72	1,963	2,828	125	2,953	:	4,916
	Otherwise dealt with(6)	741	247	88	1,777	101	1,443	182	627	1,841	104	7,151	3,114	2,439	5,553	:	12,704
	Average custodial sentence (months)(7)	23.7	59.8	47.6	9.4	30.4	35.6	13.6	6.9	12.0	18.1	20.0	2.5	2.9	2.6		16.9

Persons sentenced

21.4 Persons(1) sentenced at all courts, by type of sentence and offence group, 2010 to 2020(2)(3)

England and Wales

Persons sentenced

Year ending December	Type of sentence	Violence against the person	Sexual offences	Robbery	Theft Offences	Criminal damage & arson	Drug offences	Possession of weapons	Public order offences	Miscellaneous crimes against society	Fraud offences	All indictable offences	Summary non-motoring	Summary motoring	All summary offences	Offence not known (4)	All offences
2018	All Sentenced	26,782	5,518	3,689	65,758	1,725	34,080	13,364	15,994	24,301	7,852	199,063	463,790	532,406	996,196	158	1,195,417
	Immediate custody	11,623	3,332	2,481	20,401	533	7,766	4,817	4,742	7,600	1,681	64,976	10,726	3,062	13,788	112	78,876
	Suspended sentence	5,465	806	188	7,690	230	3,161	3,587	2,574	4,757	1,937	30,395	8,111	4,169	12,280	24	42,699
	Community sentence	5,713	1,029	911	15,694	501	4,226	3,860	4,040	3,837	2,542	42,353	35,441	13,619	49,060	9	91,422
	Fine(5)	2,162	63	-	9,339	147	12,926	542	3,064	5,278	790	34,311	379,828	506,685	886,513	1	920,825
	Absolute discharge	51	10	1	202	16	193	15	78	109	7	682	1,924	1,488	3,412	-	4,094
	Conditional discharge	880	44	4	9,198	150	4,579	264	838	967	700	17,624	21,999	1,282	23,281	-	40,905
	Compensation	105	8	4	1,536	57	-	-	48	38	72	1,868	3,037	97	3,134	-	5,002
	Otherwise dealt with(6)	783	226	100	1,698	91	1,229	279	610	1,715	123	6,854	2,724	2,004	4,728	12	11,594
	Average custodial sentence (months)(7)	23.5	61.4	48.9	9.8	30.2	36.6	12.8	6.8	12.9	20.0	20.4	2.5	2.8	2.6	73	17.3
2019	All Sentenced	34,068	4,943	4,000	57,069	1,500	38,219	14,564	15,793	22,511	7,088	199,755	449,868	529,828	979,696	745	1,180,196
	Immediate custody	12,676	2,807	2,612	18,251	448	8,899	5,368	4,774	7,125	1,664	64,624	7,807	3,093	10,900	447	75,971
	Suspended sentence	6,067	681	182	6,297	206	3,605	4,151	2,568	4,583	1,839	30,179	5,697	3,856	9,553	151	39,883
	Community sentence	8,999	1,105	1,099	13,967	436	4,474	3,932	4,161	3,634	2,154	43,961	28,263	15,026	43,289	77	87,327
	Fine(5)	3,714	57	-	7,747	121	14,457	456	2,856	4,583	703	34,694	380,941	502,789	883,730	17	918,441
	Absolute discharge	48	17	2	129	15	191	17	71	98	7	595	2,373	1,462	3,835	1	4,431
	Conditional discharge	1,414	45	11	7,655	143	5,046	280	724	866	533	16,717	19,387	1,305	20,692	8	37,417
	Compensation	341	9	4	1,463	44	-	1	44	30	63	1,999	2,518	64	2,582	1	4,582
	Otherwise dealt with(6)	809	222	90	1,560	87	1,547	359	595	1,592	125	6,986	2,882	2,233	5,115	43	12,144
	Average custodial sentence (months)(7)	23.7	58.5	51.2	10.7	32.1	39.2	12.2	7.8	11.9	23.1	21.4	2.6	2.9	2.7	45.2	18.8
2020	All Sentenced	31,912	4,033	3,394	36,680	1,276	34,226	12,318	13,373	16,093	4,331	157,636	228,589	424,633	653,222	486	811,344
	Immediate custody	12,385	2,141	2,006	12,437	382	8,388	4,340	4,294	5,276	1,203	52,852	6,335	2,399	8,734	325	61,911
	Suspended sentence	6,352	732	206	4,948	209	3,895	3,652	2,376	4,000	1,285	27,655	4,694	3,430	8,124	110	35,889
	Community sentence	7,643	900	1,109	8,006	332	3,319	3,183	3,222	2,721	1,041	31,476	18,211	11,293	29,504	25	61,005
	Fine(5)	3,188	47	-	4,901	99	12,973	502	2,317	2,474	354	26,855	182,073	404,009	586,082	13	612,950
	Absolute discharge	40	9	1	69	10	208	17	47	57	4	462	693	762	1,455	-	1,917
	Conditional discharge	1,338	29	30	4,356	117	3,992	310	597	546	284	11,599	12,851	1,211	14,062	3	25,664
	Compensation	323	6	4	959	45	-	5	48	18	53	1,461	2,052	13	2,065	-	3,526
	Otherwise dealt with(6)	643	169	38	1,004	82	1,451	309	472	1,001	107	5,276	1,680	1,516	3,196	10	8,482
	Average custodial sentence (months)(7)	19.0	55.5	47.6	12.1	25.8	39.6	11.3	7.6	12.0	23.3	21.1	2.6	2.8	2.7	42.6	18.6

Source: Ministry of Justice Court Proceedings Database

- = nil

: = Not available

(1) Excludes other offenders, i.e. companies, public bodies, etc.

(2) Data relate to persons for whom these offences were the principal offences for which they were dealt with. When a defendant has been found guilty of two or more offences it is the offence for which the heaviest penalty is imposed. Where the same disposal is imposed for two or more offences, the offence selected is the offence for which the statutory maximum penalty is the most severe.

(3) Data are given on a principal disposal basis - i.e. reporting the most severe sentence for the principal offence.

(4) Offences are classified as 'not known' if validation checks cannot identify a valid code for the record. Validation checks target apparent anomalies in the data, for example offenders sentenced to high custodial sentences for offence codes known to be commonly misused. Some outcomes for 'not known' records may therefore appear relatively severe because such records are most likely to have been reviewed and subsequently identified as 'not known'.

(5) Due to limitations in data supply, fine data from magistrates' courts has been omitted from our data since 2009 of values between £10,000 and £99,999.

(6) Including restriction orders, hospital orders, guardianship orders, police cells, and other disposals.

(7) Excludes life and other indeterminate sentences.

21.5 Number of offenders issued a Penalty Notice for Disorder aged 16 and over[1] by offence, 2010 to December 2020[2]

England and Wales   Number of offenders

	12 months ending December										
	2010	2011	2012	2013	2014	2015	2016	2017	2018	2019	2020
Higher tier offences (£90)[3]											
Wasting police time	2,852	2,810	2,586	1,973	1,539	1,063	743	552	495	449	462
Misuse of public telecommunications system	696	745	702	467	329	269	228	178	140	122	98
Giving false alarm to fire and rescue authority	59	37	39	18	11	10	7	3	2	1	2
Causing harassment, alarm or distress	32,317	25,575	17,515	12,480	8,263	5,713	4,235	2,994	2,574	2,103	1,949
Throwing fireworks	340	335	229	67	78	47	66	46	36	18	42
Drunk and disorderly	37,119	36,001	32,648	27,907	23,698	17,982	13,992	10,608	8,875	8,324	4,793
Criminal damage (under £300)[4]	6,253	4,909	3,633	2,237	1,437	930	758	477	332	285	270
Theft (retail under £100)[4]	40,170	34,688	28,363	21,287	15,683	10,910	7,845	4,893	2,752	1,814	961
Breach of fireworks curfew	23	10	10	3	1	3	4	2	3	-	2
Possession of category 4 firework	22	23	22	5	2	2	2	1	4	4	1
Possession by a person under 18 of adult firework	61	41	34	7	2	1	-	-	-	-	-
Sale of alcohol to drunken person	74	78	94	63	51	42	34	21	14	12	5
Supply of alcohol to a person under 18	59	49	58	26	13	14	5	2	2	11	-
Sale of alcohol to a person under 18	2,098	1,546	1,395	1,008	810	569	450	428	301	234	34
Purchasing alcohol for a person under 18	330	265	150	114	71	39	37	23	29	13	9
Purchasing alcohol for a person under 18 for consumption on the premises	33	35	13	11	4	2	-	-	3	1	-
Delivery of alcohol to a person under 18 or allowing such delivery	120	106	56	38	11	14	5	4	-	1	3
Possession of Cannabis[5]	13,916	16,277	15,616	13,814	11,426	8,403	6,644	5,249	5,115	6,105	6,932
Lower tier offences (£60)[3]											
Trespassing on a railway	1,454	1,331	1,093	849	693	549	424	100	105	93	6
Throwing stones at a train / railway	11	8	8	8	2	2	1	1	-	1	1
Drunk in a highway	758	669	517	364	298	195	97	58	50	28	16
Consumption of alcohol in a designated public place	1,036	1,227	619	357	332	156	94	42	17	7	9
Depositing and leaving litter	903	707	592	363	303	220	150	113	83	81	57
Consumption of alcohol by a person under 18 on relevant premises	14	26	8	3	-	-	-	-	-	-	-
Allowing consumption of alcohol by a person under 18 on relevant premises	3	2	-	1	1	-	-	1	1	-	-
Buying or attempting to buy alcohol by a person under 18	48	30	15	9	3	1	-	-	-	-	-
Depositing and leaving litter in a Royal park	-	-	1	11	3	8	9	1	3	4	1
Use pedal cycle in a Royal park	-	-	189	767	403	269	324	211	320	221	288
Failing to remove animal faeces from a Royal park	-	-	-	11	3	4	4	2	1	1	-
Possession of khat[6]	-	-	-	-	10	15	6	4	9	12	11
Total higher tier offences	136,542	123,530	103,163	81,525	63,429	46,013	35,055	25,481	20,677	19,497	15,563
Total lower tier offences	4,227	4,000	3,042	2,743	2,051	1,419	1,109	533	589	448	389
Total all offences	140,769	127,530	106,205	84,268	65,480	47,432	36,164	26,014	21,266	19,945	15,952

Source: Ministry of Justice Court Proceedings Database

- = nil

(1) Penalty notices should no longer be available for persons aged under 18 from 8 April 2013.

community resolutions and conditional cautions.

(3) Higher tier offences increased from £80 to £90 and Lower tier offences increased from £50 to £60 from 1 July 2013.

(4) Offence added with effect from 1 November 2004. Penalty notices are no longer available for theft of goods valued at over £100 and may only be used for criminal damage up to a value of £300 from July 2009 onwards.

(5) Offence added with effect from 27 January 2009.

(6) Offence added with effect from 24 December 2014.

21.6a Offenders[1][2] found guilty at all courts by offence group, 2009 to 2019

England and Wales					12 months ending December					Number of offenders	
Offence group	2009	2010	2011[3]	2012	2013	2014	2015	2016	2017	2018	2019
Indictable offences											
Violence against the person	30,711	32,732	30,791	26,522	24,523	26,859	29,579	29,355	28,465	27,116	34,724
Sexual offences	5,042	5,733	5,958	5,728	5,665	6,251	6,885	7,511	6,958	5,657	5,017
Robbery	8,645	8,499	9,335	8,340	6,769	5,573	4,723	4,063	3,989	3,706	4,004
Theft Offences	128,707	138,815	139,965	127,217	122,644	116,835	103,828	89,213	78,430	66,711	57,760
Criminal damage and arson	7,280	7,144	6,469	5,443	4,141	2,502	2,472	2,325	2,020	1,793	1,575
Drug offences	56,831	61,979	61,657	58,125	57,012	51,814	46,810	42,632	38,111	35,133	39,332
Possession of weapons	15,080	13,112	12,456	10,302	10,026	10,077	10,846	12,047	12,696	13,350	14,267
Public order offences	17,278	19,542	17,971	16,153	16,240	17,294	17,170	16,787	16,881	16,151	15,860
Miscellaneous crimes against	44,827	47,432	44,299	38,715	35,276	32,591	31,693	31,597	29,640	25,443	23,637
Fraud offences	14,770	15,651	14,974	12,378	12,279	13,521	12,648	10,621	10,313	7,986	7,181
Total indictable offenders	329,171	350,639	343,875	308,923	294,575	283,317	266,654	246,151	227,503	203,046	203,357
Summary offences											
Summary non-motoring	514,703	493,465	494,081	470,066	436,295	458,124	475,258	477,596	472,341	465,709	451,265
Summary motoring	564,563	523,371	475,624	452,574	448,537	476,233	507,206	519,473	513,336	537,910	535,453
Total summary offenders	**1,079,266**	**1,016,836**	**969,705**	**922,640**	**884,832**	**934,357**	**982,464**	**997,069**	**985,677**	**1,003,619**	**986,718**
Offence not known[4]	:	:	:	:	:	:	:	:	:	120	644
Total offenders	**1,408,437**	**1,367,475**	**1,313,580**	**1,231,563**	**1,179,407**	**1,217,674**	**1,249,118**	**1,243,220**	**1,213,180**	**1,206,785**	**1,190,719**

Source: Ministry of Justice Court Proceedings Database

- = nil

: = Not available

(1) The figures given in the table relate to defendants for whom these offences were the principal offences for which they were dealt with. When a defendant has been found guilty of two or more offences it is the offence for which the heaviest penalty is imposed. Where the same disposal is imposed for two or more offences, the offence selected is the offence for which the statutory maximum penalty is the most severe.

(2) Includes males, females, persons where sex is unknown or not stated and other offenders, i.e. companies, public bodies, etc.

(3) Excludes convictions data for Cardiff magistrates' court for April, July, and August 2008.

(4) Offences are classified as 'not known' if validation checks cannot identify a valid code for the record. Validation checks target apparent anomalies in the data, for example offenders sentenced to high custodial sentences for offence codes known to be commonly misused. Some outcomes for 'not known' records may therefore appear relatively severe because such records are most likely to have been reviewed and subsequently identified as 'not known'.

21.6b Persons[1][2] found guilty at all courts by sex and age group, 2009 to 2019

England and Wales
Number of persons

				Males							
Year	All persons [3]	All Children [4]	All Adults [4]	All ages	Aged 10-11	Aged 12-14	Aged 15-17	Aged 18-20	Aged 21 & over	Age not known (Children)	Age not known (Adults)
2009	1,399,856	81,575	1,318,281	1,048,349	411	11,199	56,254	116,057	864,428	:	:
2010	1,359,715	73,895	1,285,820	1,015,566	281	9,680	52,211	108,098	845,296	:	:
2011[5]	1,306,509	63,456	1,243,053	960,176	228	7,912	45,489	96,874	809,673	:	:
2012	1,224,979	47,576	1,177,403	879,864	159	6,040	34,201	79,191	760,273	:	:
2013	1,172,953	36,218	1,136,735	833,870	98	4,223	26,340	66,691	736,518	:	:
2014	1,211,152	31,510	1,179,642	848,179	67	4,037	22,857	63,122	758,096	:	:
2015	1,241,082	28,797	1,212,285	851,508	82	3,846	20,641	58,685	768,254	:	:
2016	1,234,675	26,310	1,208,365	844,258	68	3,597	18,940	56,674	764,979	:	:
2017	1,203,633	24,144	1,179,489	816,742	66	3,238	17,444	53,103	712,853	36	30,002
2018	1,197,684	20,315	1,177,369	799,624	32	2,628	14,720	48,381	699,314	22	34,527
2019	1,182,061	17,954	1,164,107	782,749	18	2,082	13,037	46,065	681,655	136	39,756

Number of persons

	Females							
Year	All ages	Aged 10-11	Aged 12-14	Aged 15-17	Aged 18-20	Aged 21 & over	Age not known (Children)	Age not known (Adults)
2009	314,914	25	2,883	10,187	23,339	278,480	:	:
2010	305,249	20	2,351	8,830	21,142	272,906	:	:
2011[5]	299,942	16	1,793	7,465	20,189	270,479	:	:
2012	294,456	8	1,254	5,390	17,126	270,678	:	:
2013	285,322	9	961	4,155	14,377	265,820	:	:
2014	306,516	7	751	3,433	14,638	287,687	:	:
2015	314,302	4	743	3,058	13,363	297,134	:	:
2016	309,683	3	689	2,582	12,770	293,639	:	:
2017	293,408	3	626	2,222	12,188	261,125	18	17,226
2018	289,068	3	490	1,927	11,030	254,760	15	20,843
2019	286,409	-	435	1,628	10,728	249,715	217	23,686

Number of persons

	Sex not known							
Year	All ages	Aged 10-11	Aged 12-14	Aged 15-17	Aged 18-20	Aged 21 & over	Age not known (Children)	Age not known (Adults)
2009	36,593	6	87	523	2,981	32,996	:	:
2010	38,900	2	59	461	2,581	35,797	:	:
2011[5]	46,391	2	86	465	3,403	42,435	:	:
2012	50,659	1	70	453	2,782	47,353	:	:
2013	53,761	3	52	377	2,774	50,555	:	:
2014	56,457	2	47	309	2,959	53,140	:	:
2015	75,272	-	59	364	3,244	71,605	:	:
2016	80,734	-	67	364	3,478	76,825	:	:
2017	93,483	1	65	421	3,798	60,178	4	29,016
2018	108,992	2	68	407	4,390	67,545	1	36,579
2019	112,903	-	44	353	4,244	62,840	4	45,418

Source: Ministry of Justice Court Proceedings Database

- = nil

: = Not available

(1) The figures given in the table relate to defendants for whom these offences were the principal offences for which they were dealt with. When a defendant has been found guilty of two or more offences it is the offence for which the heaviest penalty is imposed. Where the same disposal is imposed for two or more offences, the offence selected is the offence for which the statutory maximum penalty is the most severe.

(2) Excludes other offenders, i.e. companies, public bodies, etc.

(3) Includes persons where sex or age is unknown or not stated.

(4) Children includes persons aged 10-17 and adults includes persons aged 18 and over.

(5) Due to improvements in quality assurance procedures, the number of convictions in the Crown Court in 2011 will differ from previously published figures.

21.7a Overview of defendants[(1)(2)] dealt with at magistrates' courts[(3)] (MC) and Crown Courts (CC) by offence type, 2009 to 2019

England and Wales

Number of defendants

Offence Type		12 months ending December										
	2009	2010	2011[(4)]	2012	2013	2014	2015	2016	2017	2018	2019
Indictable Only											
Number of defendants proceeded against at MC	36,907	36,718	35,138	31,031	30,692	29,047	26,470	25,175	25,217	21,184	21,588
Sent for trial at CC [(6)]	31,777	31,508	29,742	26,512	27,336	26,535	24,182	22,486	22,376	18,451	18,478
Proceedings terminated early[(7)]	369	413	456	331	199	158	163	235	196	226	236
Tried at MC	4,761	4,797	4,940	4,188	3,157	2,354	2,125	2,454	2,645	2,507	2,874
Discharged at committal proceedings[(8)]	1,209	1,271	1,199	1,004	774	566	508	530	573	402	493
Dismissed (found not guilty after summary trial)	283	314	277	268	219	186	230	173	161	121	109
Found guilty at MC	3,269	3,212	3,464	2,916	2,164	1,602	1,387	1,751	1,911	1,984	2,272
Magistrates' court conviction trial rate[(9)]	68.7%	67.0%	70.1%	69.6%	68.5%	68.1%	65.3%	71.4%	72.2%	79.1%	79.1%
For trial at CC[(10)]	22,799	22,939	22,112	20,581	18,800	18,582	18,334	17,383	16,738	14,826	13,537
Not Tried	311	364	305	248	218	228	261	210	221	243	217
Tried at CC	22,488	22,575	21,807	20,333	18,582	18,354	18,073	17,173	16,517	14,583	13,320
Acquitted	5,556	6,052	5,609	5,280	4,824	5,260	5,338	5,121	4,738	4,175	2,987
Found guilty at CC[(5)]	16,932	16,523	16,198	15,053	13,758	13,094	12,735	12,052	11,779	10,408	10,333
Crown court conviction trial rate[(9)]	75.3%	73.2%	74.3%	74.0%	74.0%	71.3%	70.5%	70.2%	71.3%	71.4%	77.6%
All convictions	20,201	19,735	19,662	17,969	15,922	14,696	14,122	13,803	13,690	12,392	12,605
Conviction Ratio[(11)]	54.7%	53.7%	56.0%	57.9%	51.9%	50.6%	53.4%	54.8%	54.3%	58.5%	58.4%
Triable Either Way Offences											
Number of defendants proceeded against at MC	378,709	401,308	388,851	345,934	339,875	326,194	296,950	267,625	248,065	220,098	222,132
Sent for trial at CC [(6)]	70,480	74,892	70,268	59,372	69,908	71,774	63,697	52,016	48,792	41,181	43,797
Proceedings terminated early[(7)]	47,675	50,683	48,468	41,754	37,370	34,846	31,143	27,846	24,203	21,807	21,694
Tried at MC	260,554	275,733	270,115	244,808	232,597	219,574	202,110	187,763	175,070	157,110	156,641
Discharged at committal proceedings[(8)]	3,840	3,296	2,599	2,206	794	2	1	17	26	23	22
Dismissed (found not guilty after summary trial)	4,232	4,471	4,104	4,296	4,156	4,891	4,756	4,289	3,941	3,354	3,193
Found guilty at MC	252,482	267,966	263,412	238,306	227,647	214,681	197,353	183,457	171,103	153,733	153,426
Magistrates' court conviction trial rate[(9)]	96.9%	97.2%	97.5%	97.3%	97.9%	97.8%	97.6%	97.7%	97.7%	97.9%	97.9%
For trial at CC[(10)]	70,169	78,718	75,158	64,748	61,624	64,971	67,055	59,809	52,089	45,440	44,735
Not Tried	782	1,030	838	612	634	570	662	580	614	657	531
Tried at CC	69,387	77,688	74,320	64,136	60,990	64,401	66,393	59,229	51,475	44,783	44,204
Acquitted	12,899	14,750	13,519	11,488	9,984	10,461	11,214	10,338	8,765	7,862	6,878
Found guilty at CC[(5)]	56,488	62,938	60,801	52,648	51,006	53,940	55,179	48,891	42,710	36,921	37,326
Crown court conviction trial rate[(9)]	81.4%	81.0%	81.8%	82.1%	83.6%	83.8%	83.1%	82.5%	83.0%	82.4%	84.4%
All convictions	308,970	330,904	324,213	290,954	278,653	268,621	252,532	232,348	213,813	190,654	190,752
Conviction Ratio[(11)]	81.6%	82.5%	83.4%	84.1%	82.0%	82.4%	85.0%	86.8%	86.2%	86.6%	85.9%

21.7a Overview of defendants[1][2] dealt with at magistrates' courts[3] (MC) and Crown Courts (CC) by offence type, 2009 to 2019

England and Wales | Number of defendants

Offence Type	\ 12 months ending December										
	2009	2010	2011[4]	2012	2013	2014	2015	2016	2017	2018	2019
Summary non-motoring offences											
Number of defendants proceeded against at MC	619,154	607,056	606,473	581,877	546,064	565,883	590,811	583,440	555,955	547,590	525,714
Sent for trial at CC [6]	737	539	461	349	676	602	529	238	229	157	169
Proceedings terminated early[7]	97,179	107,015	106,275	104,922	102,215	99,368	106,461	98,357	76,668	76,104	69,776
Tried at MC	521,238	499,502	499,737	476,606	443,173	465,913	483,821	484,845	479,058	471,329	455,769
Discharged at committal proceedings[8]	-	-	-	-	-	-	-	-	1	-	-
Dismissed (found not guilty after summary trial)[8]	9,894	10,267	9,218	9,350	9,514	10,584	11,585	10,161	9,202	7,816	6,355
Found guilty at MC	511,344	489,235	490,519	467,256	433,659	455,329	472,236	474,684	469,855	463,513	449,414
Magistrates' court conviction trial rate[9]	98.1%	97.9%	98.2%	98.0%	97.9%	97.7%	97.6%	97.9%	98.1%	98.3%	98.6%
For trial at CC[10]	3,527	4,434	3,760	2,955	2,758	2,951	3,164	3,062	2,586	2,278	1,933
Not Tried	22	33	31	24	26	18	19	19	14	15	15
Tried at CC	3,505	4,401	3,729	2,931	2,732	2,933	3,145	3,043	2,572	2,263	1,918
Acquitted	146	171	167	121	96	138	123	131	86	67	67
Found guilty at CC[5]	3,359	4,230	3,562	2,810	2,636	2,795	3,022	2,912	2,486	2,196	1,851
Crown court conviction trial rate[9]	95.8%	96.1%	95.5%	95.9%	96.5%	95.3%	96.1%	95.7%	96.7%	97.0%	96.5%
All convictions	**514,703**	**493,465**	**494,081**	**470,066**	**436,295**	**458,124**	**475,258**	**477,596**	**472,341**	**465,709**	**451,265**
Conviction Ratio[11]	83.1%	81.3%	81.5%	80.8%	79.9%	81.0%	80.4%	81.9%	85.0%	85.0%	85.8%
Summary motoring offences											
Number of defendants proceeded against at MC	659,640	608,108	549,562	525,760	524,677	546,720	577,929	583,036	572,715	600,655	604,677
Sent for trial at CC [6]	71	60	43	35	109	54	45	31	46	25	36
Proceedings terminated early[7]	87,250	76,854	67,004	66,551	69,121	64,088	63,279	56,148	51,762	55,340	61,703
Tried at MC	572,319	531,194	482,515	459,174	455,447	482,578	514,605	526,857	520,907	545,290	542,938
Discharged at committal proceedings[8]	31	15	14	11	10	-	-	-	-	-	-
Dismissed (found not guilty after summary trial)[8]	8,171	8,259	7,256	6,888	7,165	6,591	7,662	7,683	7,924	7,727	7,758
Found guilty at MC	564,117	522,920	475,245	452,275	448,272	475,987	506,943	519,174	512,983	537,563	535,180
Magistrates' court conviction trial rate[9]	98.6%	98.4%	98.5%	98.5%	98.4%	98.6%	98.5%	98.5%	98.5%	98.6%	98.6%
For trial at CC[10]	458	462	390	308	272	255	268	307	360	354	277
Not Tried	-	1	-	-	1	-	1	-	-	1	-
Tried at CC	458	461	390	308	271	255	267	307	360	353	277
Acquitted	12	10	11	9	6	9	4	8	7	6	4
Found guilty at CC[5]	446	451	379	299	265	246	263	299	353	347	273
Crown court conviction trial rate[9]	97.4%	97.8%	97.2%	97.1%	97.8%	96.5%	98.5%	97.4%	98.1%	98.3%	98.6%
All convictions	**564,563**	**523,371**	**475,624**	**452,574**	**448,537**	**476,233**	**507,206**	**519,473**	**513,336**	**537,910**	**535,453**
Conviction Ratio[11]	85.6%	86.1%	86.5%	86.1%	85.5%	87.1%	87.8%	89.1%	89.6%	89.6%	88.6%

21.7a Overview of defendants[1][2] dealt with at magistrates' courts[3] (MC) and Crown Courts (CC) by offence type, 2009 to 2019

England and Wales

Number of defendants

Offence Type	2009	2010	2011[4]	2012	2013	12 months ending December 2014	2015	2016	2017	2018	2019
Offence not known											
Number of defendants proceeded against at MC	:	:	:	:	:	:	:	:	:	1	-
Sent for trial at CC [6]	:	:	:	:	:	:	:	:	:	-	-
Proceedings terminated early[7]	:	:	:	:	:	:	:	:	:	1	-
Tried at MC	:	:	:	:	:	:	:	:	:	-	-
Discharged at committal proceedings[8]	:	:	:	:	:	:	:	:	:	-	-
Dismissed (found not guilty after summary trial)	:	:	:	:	:	:	:	:	:	-	-
Found guilty at MC	:	:	:	:	:	:	:	:	:	-	-
Magistrates' court conviction trial rate[9]	:	:	:	:	:	:	:	:	:	-	-
For trial at CC[10]	:	:	:	:	:	:	:	:	:	124	752
Not Tried	:	:	:	:	:	:	:	:	:	1	5
Tried at CC	:	:	:	:	:	:	:	:	:	123	747
Acquitted	:	:	:	:	:	:	:	:	:	3	103
Found guilty at CC[5]	:	:	:	:	:	:	:	:	:	120	644
Crown court conviction trial rate[9]	:	:	:	:	:	:	:	:	:	-	-
All convictions	:	:	:	:	:	:	:	:	:	120	644
Conviction Ratio[11]	:	:	:	:	:	:	:	:	:	*	*
Sent for trial at CC [6]	103,065	106,999	100,514	86,268	98,029	98,965	88,453	74,771	71,443	59,814	62,480
Proceedings terminated early[7]	232,473	234,965	222,203	213,558	208,905	198,460	201,046	182,586	152,829	153,478	153,409
Tried at MC	1,358,872	1,311,226	1,257,307	1,184,776	1,134,374	1,170,419	1,202,661	1,201,919	1,177,680	1,176,236	1,158,222
Discharged at committal proceedings[8]	5,080	4,582	3,812	3,221	1,578	568	509	547	600	425	515
Dismissed (found not guilty after summary trial)	22,580	23,311	20,855	20,802	21,054	22,252	24,233	22,306	21,228	19,018	17,415
Found guilty at MC	1,331,212	1,283,333	1,232,640	1,160,753	1,111,742	1,147,599	1,177,919	1,179,066	1,155,852	1,156,793	1,140,292
Magistrates' court conviction trial rate[9]	98.0%	97.9%	98.0%	98.0%	98.0%	98.1%	97.9%	98.1%	98.1%	98.3%	98.5%
For trial at CC[10]	96,953	106,553	101,420	88,592	83,454	86,759	88,821	80,561	71,773	63,022	61,234
Not Tried	1,115	1,428	1,174	884	879	816	943	809	849	917	768
Tried at CC	95,838	105,125	100,246	87,708	82,575	85,943	87,878	79,752	70,924	62,105	60,466
Acquitted	18,613	20,983	19,306	16,898	14,910	15,868	16,679	15,598	13,596	12,113	10,039
Found guilty at CC[5]	77,225	84,142	80,940	70,810	67,665	70,075	71,199	64,154	57,328	49,992	50,427
Crown court conviction trial rate[9]	80.6%	80.0%	80.7%	80.7%	81.9%	81.5%	81.0%	80.4%	80.8%	80.5%	83.4%
All convictions	1,408,437	1,367,475	1,313,580	1,231,563	1,179,407	1,217,674	1,249,118	1,243,220	1,213,180	1,206,785	1,190,719
Conviction Ratio[11]	83.1%	82.7%	83.1%	83.0%	81.8%	83.0%	83.7%	85.2%	86.5%	86.8%	86.7%

Source: Ministry of Justice Court Proceedings Database

- = nil   * = Not applicable   : = Not available

(1) The figures given in the table relate to defendants for whom these offences were the principal offences for which they were dealt with. When a defendant has been found guilty of two or more offences it is the offence for which the heaviest penalty is imposed. Where the same disposal is imposed for two or more offences, the offence selected is the offence for which the statutory maximum penalty is the most severe.

(2) Includes males, females, persons where sex is unknown or not stated and other offenders, i.e. companies, public bodies, etc.

(3) Youth Courts are categorised as magistrates' courts in the data. This will impact the figures for indictable only cases at the magistrates' court which will include a high volume of juvenile cases.

(4) Due to improvements in quality assurance procedures, the number of convictions in the Crown Court in 2011 will differ from previously published figures.

(5) Committal hearings were abolished in 2013 and defendants are now sent for trial at the Crown Court.

(6) Includes proceedings discontinued under s.23(3) of the Prosecution of Offences Act 1985, charge withdrawn and cases "written off" (e.g. bench warrant unexecuted, adjourned sine die, defendant cannot be traced etc.).

(7) Under Sec. 6 of Magistrates' Court Act 1980

(8) Conviction trial rate is calculated as the number of offenders convicted as a proportion of the number tried, in a given year and court type.

(9) Excludes offenders that were committed for sentence from the magistrates' court.

(10) Conviction ratio is calculated as the number of offenders convicted as a proportion of the number prosecuted, in a given year.

(11) Offences are classified as 'not known' if validation checks cannot identify a valid code for the record. Validation checks target apparent anomalies in the data, for example offenders sentenced to high custodial sentences for offence codes known to be commonly misused. Some outcomes for 'not known' records may therefore appear relatively severe because such records are most likely to have been reviewed and subsequently identified as 'not known' offence codes.

21.7b Defendants[1][2] proceeded against at magistrates' courts by offence group, 2009 to 2019

England and Wales   12 months ending December   Number of defendants

Offence group	2009	2010	2011[3]	2012	2013	2014	2015	2016	2017	2018	2019
Indictable											
Violence against the person	49,217	50,627	44,719	36,985	36,877	39,514	39,332	38,883	38,734	36,891	46,434
Sexual offences	9,297	10,493	10,102	9,377	10,927	11,903	12,609	12,572	11,311	7,594	7,744
Robbery	13,655	13,704	14,384	12,266	10,924	9,049	7,236	6,024	5,953	5,713	6,122
Theft Offences	147,863	158,359	159,626	144,972	142,011	135,401	118,558	100,666	88,731	75,986	65,853
Criminal damage and arson	8,975	8,892	8,039	7,042	5,570	3,562	3,436	3,099	2,784	2,525	2,180
Drug offences	61,685	67,772	67,650	63,618	63,766	57,562	51,030	45,458	42,072	38,797	43,918
Possession of weapons	19,517	17,426	16,369	13,740	13,676	13,655	13,938	14,792	15,532	16,176	16,731
Public order offences	18,482	20,897	18,388	16,258	17,206	17,941	17,372	17,497	17,777	17,132	16,784
Miscellaneous crimes against society	68,169	70,178	66,060	56,845	53,132	49,374	44,627	41,542	38,218	31,418	29,897
Fraud offences	18,756	19,678	18,652	15,862	16,478	17,280	15,282	12,267	12,170	9,050	8,057
Total indictable defendants	**415,616**	**438,026**	**423,989**	**376,965**	**370,567**	**355,241**	**323,420**	**292,800**	**273,282**	**241,282**	**243,720**
Summary											
Summary non-motoring	619,154	607,056	606,473	581,877	546,064	565,883	590,811	583,440	555,955	547,590	525,714
Summary motoring	659,640	608,108	549,562	525,760	524,677	546,720	577,929	583,036	572,715	600,655	604,677
Total summary defendants	**1,278,794**	**1,215,164**	**1,156,035**	**1,107,637**	**1,070,741**	**1,112,603**	**1,168,740**	**1,166,476**	**1,128,670**	**1,148,245**	**1,130,391**
Offence not known[4]	:	:	:	:	:	:	:	:	:	1	-
Total defendants	**1,694,410**	**1,653,190**	**1,580,024**	**1,484,602**	**1,441,308**	**1,467,844**	**1,492,160**	**1,459,276**	**1,401,952**	**1,389,528**	**1,374,111**

Source: Ministry of Justice Court Proceedings Database

21.7c Offenders[1][2] found guilty at all courts by offence group, 2009 to 2019

England and Wales   12 months ending December   Number of offenders

Offence group	2009	2010	2011[3]	2012	2013	2014	2015	2016	2017	2018	2019
Indictable offences											
Violence against the person	30,711	32,732	30,791	26,522	24,523	26,859	29,579	29,355	28,465	27,116	34,724
Sexual offences	5,042	5,733	5,958	5,728	5,665	6,251	6,885	7,511	6,958	5,657	5,017
Robbery	8,645	8,499	9,335	8,340	6,769	5,573	4,723	4,063	3,989	3,706	4,004
Theft Offences	128,707	138,815	139,965	127,217	122,644	116,835	103,828	89,213	78,430	66,711	57,760
Criminal damage and arson	7,280	7,144	6,469	5,443	4,141	2,502	2,472	2,325	2,020	1,793	1,575
Drug offences	56,831	61,979	61,657	58,125	57,012	51,814	46,810	42,632	38,111	35,133	39,332
Possession of weapons	15,080	13,112	12,456	10,302	10,026	10,077	10,846	12,047	12,696	13,350	14,267
Public order offences	17,278	19,542	17,971	16,153	16,240	17,294	17,170	16,787	16,881	16,151	15,860
Miscellaneous crimes against society	44,827	47,432	44,299	38,715	35,276	32,591	31,693	31,597	29,640	25,443	23,637
Fraud offences	14,770	15,651	14,974	12,378	12,279	13,521	12,648	10,621	10,313	7,986	7,181
Total indictable offenders	329,171	350,639	343,875	308,923	294,575	283,317	266,654	246,151	227,503	203,046	203,357
Summary offences											
Summary non-motoring	514,703	493,465	494,081	470,066	436,295	458,124	475,258	477,596	472,341	465,709	451,265
Summary motoring	564,563	523,371	475,624	452,574	448,537	476,233	507,206	519,473	513,336	537,910	535,453
Total summary offenders	**1,079,266**	**1,016,836**	**969,705**	**922,640**	**884,832**	**934,357**	**982,464**	**997,069**	**985,677**	**1,003,619**	**986,718**
Offence not known[4]	:	:	:	:	:	:	:	:	:	120	644
Total offenders	**1,408,437**	**1,367,475**	**1,313,580**	**1,231,563**	**1,179,407**	**1,217,674**	**1,249,118**	**1,243,220**	**1,213,180**	**1,206,785**	**1,190,719**

Source: Ministry of Justice Court Proceedings Database

: = Not available

: = Not available

(1) The figures given in the table relate to defendants for whom these offences were the principal offences for which they were dealt with. When a defendant has been found guilty of two or more offences it is the offence for which the heaviest penalty is imposed. Where the same disposal is imposed for two or more offences, the offence selected is the offence for which the statutory maximum penalty is the most severe.

(2) Includes males, females, persons where sex is unknown or not stated and other offenders, i.e. companies, public bodies, etc.

(3) Excludes convictions data for Cardiff magistrates' court for April, July, and August 2008.

(4) Offences are classified as 'not known' if validation checks cannot identify a valid code for the record. Validation checks target apparent anomalies in the data, for example offenders sentenced to high custodial sentences for offence codes known to be commonly misused. Some outcomes for 'not known' records may therefore appear relatively severe because such records are most likely to have been reviewed and subsequently identified as 'not known'

21.8 Persons[1] sentenced at all courts to immediate custody, for all offences and for indictable offences, by length of sentence, 2009 to 2019[2][3]

England and Wales
Number of persons

Type of offence and custody length	2009	2010	2011	2012	2013	2014	2015	2016	2017	2018	2019
					12 months ending December						
All offences											
Up to and including 1 month	13,971	15,496	16,116	14,812	14,007	14,617	14,437	14,271	13,488	11,309	9,526
Over 1 month and up to and including 2 months	11,625	12,230	12,599	11,691	11,388	11,661	11,326	11,216	10,460	9,537	8,331
Over 2 months and up to and including 3 months	10,475	10,590	10,704	9,939	9,426	9,300	8,814	8,683	8,372	7,897	7,165
Over 3 months and less than 6 months	16,016	15,172	15,310	14,406	13,480	12,806	12,466	12,296	12,097	11,220	10,627
6 months	5,305	5,009	4,959	4,926	4,756	4,370	4,558	5,249	5,050	4,699	4,734
Over 6 months and up to and including 9 months	5,656	5,487	6,078	4,977	4,710	4,419	4,379	4,045	3,770	3,492	3,609
Over 9 months and less than 12 months	1,521	1,565	1,813	1,810	1,721	1,577	1,720	1,743	1,606	1,576	1,531
12 months	5,837	5,618	5,947	4,788	4,380	4,155	4,075	3,721	3,415	2,994	2,965
Over 12 months and up to and including 18 months	7,289	7,343	8,022	7,343	6,375	5,810	5,756	5,405	5,078	4,786	4,936
Over 18 months and up to and including 2 years	5,375	5,489	5,917	5,536	5,022	4,830	4,652	4,739	4,482	3,863	3,865
Over 2 years and up to and including 3 years	6,702	6,869	7,221	7,085	7,203	6,999	7,068	7,161	7,082	6,660	7,079
Over 3 years and less than 4 years	1,811	1,937	1,990	1,973	2,092	2,120	2,178	2,152	2,234	2,350	2,486
4 years	1,977	1,934	2,094	1,787	1,704	1,639	1,611	1,734	1,647	1,336	1,373
Over 4 years and up to and including 5 years	1,980	2,061	2,208	1,913	1,945	1,932	2,008	2,034	2,106	1,975	2,106
Over 5 years and up to and including 6 years	1,151	1,133	1,414	1,338	1,225	1,409	1,440	1,480	1,525	1,376	1,539
Over 6 years and up to and including 7 years	644	661	706	666	745	723	792	848	860	781	827
Over 7 years and up to and including 8 years	510	531	590	600	664	732	698	709	759	700	777
Over 8 years and up to and including 9 years	256	253	309	315	381	416	435	451	433	404	577
Over 9 years and up to and including 10 years	223	218	288	319	402	373	449	421	401	400	391
Over 10 years and up to and including 15 years	383	403	509	507	680	736	838	806	836	755	768
Over 15 years and less than life	102	111	162	154	256	247	279	291	291	334	303
Indeterminate sentence[4]	1,001	1,019	819	747	9	-	-	-	-	-	-
Life	421	384	395	412	395	442	369	407	362	432	456
Total sentenced to immediate custody	100,231	101,513	106,170	98,044	92,966	91,313	90,348	89,862	86,354	78,876	75,971
Average custodial sentence length (months)[5]	13.7	13.7	14.3	14.5	15.5	15.6	16.2	16.4	16.9	17.3	18.9
Indictable offences											
Up to and including 1 month	10,291	11,759	12,158	11,205	11,077	11,436	11,068	10,740	10,076	8,295	7,331
Over 1 month and up to and including 2 months	7,351	8,081	8,436	8,072	8,091	8,110	7,593	7,407	6,944	6,192	5,694
Over 2 months and up to and including 3 months	6,050	6,450	6,652	6,398	6,271	6,005	5,525	5,286	5,258	4,853	4,796
Over 3 months and less than 6 months	8,935	9,081	9,328	8,721	8,422	7,771	7,424	7,634	7,470	7,263	7,266
6 months	4,833	4,603	4,571	4,425	4,198	3,895	4,011	4,738	4,594	4,360	4,450
Over 6 months and up to and including 9 months	5,642	5,464	6,004	4,961	4,706	4,417	4,374	4,041	3,754	3,459	3,553
Over 9 months and less than 12 months	1,516	1,559	1,809	1,809	1,721	1,577	1,720	1,743	1,601	1,564	1,513
12 months	5,828	5,607	5,932	4,781	4,377	4,154	4,074	3,718	3,406	2,975	2,917
Over 12 months and up to and including 18 months	7,284	7,337	8,004	7,337	6,374	5,810	5,756	5,405	5,072	4,748	4,869
Over 18 months and up to and including 2 years	5,374	5,485	5,909	5,534	5,022	4,830	4,652	4,739	4,477	3,845	3,824
Over 2 years and up to and including 3 years	6,702	6,868	7,220	7,085	7,203	6,999	7,068	7,161	7,077	6,650	7,000
Over 3 years and less than 4 years	1,811	1,937	1,990	1,973	2,092	2,120	2,178	2,152	2,234	2,344	2,453
4 years	1,977	1,934	2,094	1,787	1,704	1,639	1,611	1,734	1,647	1,331	1,354
Over 4 years and up to and including 5 years	1,980	2,061	2,208	1,913	1,945	1,932	2,008	2,034	2,106	1,968	2,070
Over 5 years and up to and including 6 years	1,151	1,133	1,414	1,338	1,225	1,409	1,440	1,480	1,525	1,366	1,510
Over 6 years and up to and including 7 years	644	661	706	666	745	723	792	848	860	776	816
Over 7 years and up to and including 8 years	510	531	590	600	664	732	698	709	759	694	764
Over 8 years and up to and including 9 years	256	253	309	315	381	416	435	451	433	397	569
Over 9 years and up to and including 10 years	223	218	288	319	402	373	449	421	401	394	372
Over 10 years and up to and including 15 years	383	403	509	507	680	736	838	806	836	744	751
Over 15 years and less than life	102	111	162	154	256	247	279	291	291	326	296
Indeterminate sentence[4]	1,001	1,019	819	747	9	-	-	-	-	-	-
Life	421	384	395	412	395	442	369	407	362	432	456
Total sentenced to immediate custody	80,265	82,939	87,507	81,059	77,960	75,773	74,362	73,945	71,183	64,976	64,624
Average custodial sentence length (months)[5]	16.5	16.2	16.8	17.0	18.0	18.3	19.2	19.4	20.0	20.4	21.4

. = nil
Source: Ministry of Justice Court Proceedings Database

(1) Excludes other offenders, i.e. companies, public bodies, etc.

(2) Data relate to persons for whom these offences were the principal offences for which they were dealt with. When a defendant has been found guilty of two or more offences it is the offence for which the heaviest penalty is imposed. Where the same disposal is imposed for two or more offences, the offence selected is the offence for which the statutory maximum penalty is the most severe.

(3) Data are given on a principal disposal basis - i.e. reporting the most severe sentence for the principal offence.

(4) Sentences of imprisonment for public protection were introduced by the Criminal Justice Act 2003, and abolished by the Legal Aid, Sentencing and Punishment of Offenders Act 2012.

(5) Excludes life and other indeterminate sentences.

21.9a Persons sentenced to life imprisonment by sex and age, 2010 to 2019

England and Wales

Sex and age	2010	2011	2012	2013	2014	2015	2016	2017	2018	2019
Male										
Aged 12-14	0	0	0	2	3	2	0	0	2	0
Aged 15-17	17	13	13	11	18	11	7	10	26	29
Aged 18-20	39	30	47	33	41	35	44	38	49	62
Aged 21-24	55	54	55	47	76	49	58	54	54	45
Aged 25+ (prior to 2017)	253	274	265	273	284	255	273	0	0	0
Aged 25-29 (2017 onwards)	-	-	-	-	-	-	-	55	48	71
Aged 30-39 (2017 onwards)	-	-	-	-	-	-	-	95	105	110
Aged 40-49 (2017 onwards)	-	-	-	-	-	-	-	51	63	65
Aged 50-59 (2017 onwards)	-	-	-	-	-	-	-	28	39	39
Aged 60-69 (2017 onwards)	-	-	-	-	-	-	-	8	16	9
Aged 70+ (2017 onwards)	-	-	-	-	-	-	-	5	1	5
All ages	**364**	**371**	**380**	**366**	**422**	**352**	**382**	**344**	**403**	**435**
Female										
Aged 12-14	0	0	0	0	0	1	0	0	0	0
Aged 15-17	2	2	1	0	0	0	1	0	0	0
Aged 18-20	2	5	1		1	3		1	2	1
Aged 21-24	2	2	3	5		2	4	2	2	3
Aged 25+ (prior to 2017)	14	15	27	24	19	11	20	0	0	0
Aged 25-29 (2017 onwards)	-	-	-	-	-	-	-	3	5	3
Aged 30-39 (2017 onwards)	-	-	-	-	-	-	-	5	7	6
Aged 40-49 (2017 onwards)	-	-	-	-	-	-	-	5	8	5
Aged 50-59 (2017 onwards)	-	-	-	-	-	-	-	2	5	2
Aged 70+ (2017 onwards)	-	-	-	-	-	-	-	-	0	1
All ages	**20**	**24**	**32**	**29**	**20**	**17**	**25**	**18**	**29**	**21**
All perons										
Aged 12-14	0	0	0	2	3	3	0	0	2	0
Aged 15-17	19	15	14	11	18	11	8	10	26	29
Aged 18-20	41	35	48	33	42	38	44	39	51	63
Aged 21-24	57	56	58	52	76	51	62	56	56	48
Aged 25+ (prior to 2017)	267	289	292	297	303	266	293	0	0	0
Aged 25-29 (2017 onwards)	-	-	-	-	-	-	-	58	53	74
Aged 30-39 (2017 onwards)	-	-	-	-	-	-	-	100	112	116
Aged 40-49 (2017 onwards)	-	-	-	-	-	-	-	56	71	70
Aged 50-59 (2017 onwards)	-	-	-	-	-	-	-	30	44	41
Aged 60-69 (2017 onwards)	-	-	-	-	-	-	-	8	16	10
Aged 70+ (2017 onwards)	-	-	-	-	-	-	-	5	1	5
All ages	**384**	**395**	**412**	**395**	**442**	**369**	**407**	**362**	**432**	**456**

Source: Courts Proceeding database, Ministry of Justice

Further information on data sources and definitions can be found in the guidance document produced alongside the main report
- Guide to Criminal Justice Statistics at:

https://www.gov.uk/government/statistics/criminal-justice-system-statistics-quarterly-december-2019

21.9b persons sentenced to determinate an indeterminate custodial sentences by age group, sex and type of sentence, 2014 to 2019

England and Wales

Sex and age	Year	Determinate Sentence	Extended sentence of imprisonment - EPP	Imprisonment for public protection - IPP	Life sentence	Total Immediate Custody
Male						
Aged Under 18	2014	1,716	0	0	21	1,737
	2015	1,672	0	0	13	1,685
	2016	1,518	0	0	7	1,525
	2017	1,480	0	0	10	1,490
	2018	1,284	0	0	28	1,312
	2019	1,115	0	0	29	1,144
Aged 18-20	2014	7,445	0	0	41	7,486
	2015	6,671	0	0	35	6,706
	2016	6,445	0	0	44	6,489
	2017	5,994	0	0	38	6,032
	2018	5,340	0	0	49	5,389
	2019	4,872	0	0	62	4,934
Aged 21 and over	2014	73,760	0	0	360	74,120
	2015	73,790	0	0	304	74,094
	2016	73,696	0	0	331	74,027
	2017	70,827	0	0	296	71,123
	2018	64,735	0	0	326	65,061
	2019	63,013	0	0	344	63,357
Female						
Aged Under 18	2014	106	0	0	0	106
	2015	71	0	0	1	72
	2016	49	0	0	1	50
	2017	51	0	0	0	51
	2018	53	0	0	0	53
	2019	46	0	0	0	46
Aged 18 - 20	2014	389	0	0	1	390
	2015	308	0	0	3	311
	2016	291	0	0	0	291
	2017	230	0	0	1	231
	2018	217	0	0	2	219
	2019	214	0	0	1	215
Aged 21 and over	2014	7,010	0	0	19	7,029
	2015	6,927	0	0	13	6,940
	2016	6,950	0	0	24	6,974
	2017	6,941	0	0	17	6,958
	2018	6,219	0	0	27	6,246
	2019	5,643	0	0	20	5,663
Sex not Stated						
Aged under 18	2014	17	0	0	0	17
	2015	29	0	0	0	29
	2016	23	0	0	0	23
	2017	48	0	0	0	48
	2018	26	0	0	0	26
	2019	30	0	0	0	30
Aged 18-20	2014	33	0	0	0	33
	2015	42	0	0	0	42
	2016	36	0	0	0	36
	2017	26	0	0	0	26
	2018	33	0	0	0	33
	2019	43	0	0	0	43
Aged 21 and over	2014	395	0	0	0	395
	2015	469	0	0	0	469
	2016	447	0	0	0	447
	2017	395	0	0	0	395
	2018	537	0	0	0	537
	2019	539	0	0	0	539

21.9b persons sentenced to determinate an indeterminate custodial sentences by age group, sex and type of sentence, 2014 to 2019

England and Wales

Sex and age	Year	Determinate Sentence	Extended sentence of imprisonment - EPP	Imprisonment for public protection - IPP	Life sentence	Total Immediate Custody
All Persons						
Aged Under 18	2014	1,839	0	0	21	1,860
	2015	1,772	0	0	14	1,786
	2016	1,590	0	0	8	1,598
	2017	1,579	0	0	10	1,589
	2018	1,363	0	0	28	1,391
	2019	1,191	0	0	29	1,220
Aged 18 - 20	2014	7,867	0	0	42	7,909
	2015	7,021	0	0	38	7,059
	2016	6,772	0	0	44	6,816
	2017	6,250	0	0	39	6,289
	2018	5,590	0	0	51	5,641
	2019	5,129	0	0	63	5,192
Aged 21 and over	2014	81,165	0	0	379	81,544
	2015	81,186	0	0	317	81,503
	2016	81,093	0	0	355	81,448
	2017	78,163	0	0	313	78,476
	2018	71,491	0	0	353	71,844
	2019	69,195	0	0	364	69,559
All Ages	2014	90,871	0	0	442	91,313
	2015	89,979	0	0	369	90,348
	2016	89,455	0	0	407	89,862
	2017	85,992	0	0	362	86,354
	2018	78,444	0	0	432	78,876
	2019	75,515	0	0	456	75,971

Source: Courts Proceeding database, Ministry of Justice

1. Determinate sentence is the sum of all custodial sentence lengths excluding life sentence.

2. The Legal Aid, Sentencing and Punishment of Offenders Act 2012 (LASPO), which was largely commenced on 3 December 2012, abolished the sentence of Imprisonment for Public Protection (IPP) and Extended Sentences for Public Protection (EPPs). These were replaced by a new Extended Determinate Sentence (EDS) which is for dangerous offenders who previously would have been eligible for an IPP or an extended sentence under the 2003 Act.

3. The figures given relate to persons for whom these offences were the principal offences for which they were dealt with. When a defendant has been found guilty of two or more offences it is the offence for which the heaviest penalty is imposed. Where the same disposal is imposed for two or more offences, the offence selected is the offence for which the statutory maximum penalty is the most severe.

4. Every effort is made to ensure that the figures presented are accurate and complete. However, it is important to note that these data have been extracted from large administrative data systems generated by the courts. As a consequence, care should be taken to ensure data collection processes and their inevitable limitations are taken into account when those data are used.

21.10 First prison receptions[1] by type of first reception, sentence length and sex

	Oct-Dec 2018	Jan-Mar 2019	Apr-Jun 2019	Jul-Sep 2019	Oct-Dec 2019	Percentage change Oct-Dec 2018 to 2019
Males and Females						
First receptions	**18,219**	**17,690**	**18,370**	**18,806**	**17,306**	**-5%**
Remand first receptions	**9,699**	**9,549**	**9,970**	**10,349**	**9,878**	**2%**
Sentenced first receptions	**8,471**	**8,105**	**8,358**	**8,400**	**7,377**	**-13%**
Fine defaulter	39	37	32	26	23	**
Less than or equal to 6 months	5,423	4,922	5,328	5,404	4,816	-11%
Greater than 6 months to less than 12 months	911	1,024	858	824	765	-16%
12 months to less than 4 years	1,620	1,706	1,729	1,770	1,413	-13%
12 months to less than 2 years	*804*	*848*	*838*	*895*	*683*	*-15%*
2 years to less than 4 years	*816*	*858*	*891*	*875*	*730*	*-11%*
4 years or more (excluding indeterminate sentences)	459	402	395	358	347	-24%
4 years to less than 5 years	*162*	*146*	*143*	*104*	*129*	*-20%*
5 years to less than 7 years	*164*	*143*	*123*	*118*	*115*	*-30%*
7 years to less than 10 years	*76*	*64*	*84*	*82*	*61*	*-20%*
10 years to less than 14 years	*33*	*31*	*26*	*33*	*27*	****
14 years or more (excluding indeterminate sentences)	*19*	*16*	*15*	*17*	*13*	****
Extended determinate sentence	*5*	*2*	*4*	*4*	*2*	****
Indeterminate sentences	3	4	3	0	2	**
Sentence length not recorded	16	10	13	18	11	**
Civil non-criminal first receptions	**49**	**36**	**42**	**57**	**51**	**
Males						
First receptions	**16,379**	**15,934**	**16,619**	**16,947**	**15,622**	**-5%**
Remand first receptions	**8,950**	**8,776**	**9,165**	**9,509**	**9,060**	**1%**
Sentenced first receptions	**7,384**	**7,126**	**7,417**	**7,384**	**6,514**	**-12%**
Fine defaulter	33	35	31	23	21	**
Less than or equal to 6 months	4,620	4,221	4,666	4,652	4,172	-10%
Greater than 6 months to less than 12 months	824	907	765	726	686	-17%
12 months to less than 4 years	1,468	1,572	1,574	1,625	1,296	-12%
12 months to less than 2 years	*729*	*785*	*769*	*824*	*627*	*-14%*
2 years to less than 4 years	*739*	*787*	*805*	*801*	*669*	*-9%*
4 years or more (excluding indeterminate sentences)	425	377	368	341	327	-23%
4 years to less than 5 years	*146*	*138*	*128*	*97*	*125*	*-14%*
5 years to less than 7 years	*150*	*128*	*116*	*110*	*103*	*-31%*
7 years to less than 10 years	*74*	*64*	*80*	*80*	*58*	*-22%*
10 years to less than 14 years	*31*	*30*	*25*	*33*	*27*	****
14 years or more (excluding indeterminate sentences)	*19*	*15*	*15*	*17*	*13*	****
Extended determinate sentence	*5*	*2*	*4*	*4*	*1*	****
Indeterminate sentences	2	4	3	0	2	**
Sentence length not recorded	12	10	10	17	10	**
Civil non-criminal first receptions	**45**	**32**	**37**	**54**	**48**	**

21.10 First prison receptions[1] by type of first reception, sentence length and sex

	Oct-Dec 2018	Jan-Mar 2019	Apr-Jun 2019	Jul-Sep 2019	Oct-Dec 2019	Percentage change Oct-Dec 2018 to 2019
Females						
First receptions	**1,840**	**1,756**	**1,751**	**1,859**	**1,684**	**-8%**
Remand first receptions	**749**	**773**	**805**	**840**	**818**	**9%**
Sentenced first receptions	**1,087**	**979**	**941**	**1,016**	**863**	**-21%**
Fine defaulter	6	2	1	3	2	**
Less than or equal to 6 months	803	701	662	752	644	-20%
Greater than 6 months to less than 12 months	87	117	93	98	79	-9%
12 months to less than 4 years	152	134	155	145	117	-23%
12 months to less than 2 years	*75*	*63*	*69*	*71*	*56*	*-25%*
2 years to less than 4 years	*77*	*71*	*86*	*74*	*61*	*-21%*
4 years or more (excluding indeterminate sentences)	34	25	27	17	20	**
4 years to less than 5 years	*16*	*8*	*15*	*7*	*4*	***
5 years to less than 7 years	*14*	*15*	*7*	*8*	*12*	***
7 years to less than 10 years	*2*	*0*	*4*	*2*	*3*	***
10 years to less than 14 years	*2*	*1*	*1*	*0*	*0*	***
14 years or more (excluding indeterminate sentences)	*0*	*1*	*0*	*0*	*0*	*-*
Extended determinate sentence	*0*	*0*	*0*	*0*	*1*	***
Indeterminate sentences	1	0	0	0	0	**
Sentence length not recorded	4	0	3	1	1	**
Civil non-criminal first receptions	**4**	**4**	**5**	**3**	**3**	****

Source: Ministry of Justice

(1) A first reception is a measure which counts a prisoner's first movement into custody following a court hearing for a particular set of offences committed, and therefore gives the best indication of the number of new prisoners in the reporting period. A first reception has three categories:

i. **remand first reception:** this describes a prisoner's first movement into custody where the prisoner spends at least one day on remand.

ii. **sentenced first reception:** this describes a prisoner's first movement into custody where the prisoner has been sentenced at court, and thus spends no time on remand.

iii. **civil non-criminal first reception:** this describes a prisoner's first movement into custody where the prisoner has only been committed to custody for a civil offence (e.g. contempt of court).

21.11 Prison population under an immediate custodial sentence by offence group, age group and sex; 2009 to 2015, England and Wales

As at 30th June each year

	2009	2010	2011	2012	2013	2014	2015
Males and females	**68,461**	**70,871**	**71,835**	**73,435**	**70,781**	**71,361**	**72,552**
Violence against the person	19,762	20,247	20,431	20,437	19,473	19,596	18,537
Sexual offences	8,176	9,304	9,850	10,473	10,540	11,192	11,490
Robbery	8,738	8,834	9,141	9,279	8,873	8,507	8,246
Burglary	7,403	6,857	7,102	7,345	7,073	7,141	..
Theft and handling	3,134	3,850	4,198	4,646	4,500	4,377	..
Fraud offences	1,923	1,544	1,376	1,454	1,320	1,352	1,409
Drug offences	10,420	11,064	10,621	10,682	10,175	10,306	10,442
Motoring offences	1,050	931	841	798	723	820	906
Other offences	6,186	7,353	7,755	7,826	7,625	7,644	7,626
Offence not recorded	1,669	887	520	495	479	426	424
Adults	**60,186**	**63,063**	**64,530**	**66,589**	**65,224**	**66,472**	**68,239**
Violence against the person	17,433	17,997	18,496	18,686	18,010	18,348	18,522
Sexual offences	7,822	8,841	9,396	10,044	10,187	10,867	11,897
Robbery	6,780	7,055	7,398	7,545	7,460	7,358	7,248
Burglary	6,329	5,808	6,052	6,379	6,316	6,527	..
Theft and handling	2,738	3,454	3,797	4,216	4,168	4,111	..
Fraud and forgery	1,881	1,513	1,352	1,425	1,298	1,337	1,445
Drug offences	9,695	10,382	10,002	10,124	9,670	9,699	9,702
Motoring offences	943	842	766	743	672	762	840
Other offences	5,221	6,403	6,813	6,984	7,011	7,062	7,189
Offence not recorded	1,344	768	458	443	432	401	437
18-20 year olds	**6,669**	**6,623**	**6,155**	**5,851**	**4,876**	**4,336**	**3,787**
Violence against the person	1,947	1,934	1,696	1,526	1,298	1,128	954
Sexual offences	281	406	406	382	326	291	291
Robbery	1,521	1,491	1,450	1,431	1,190	968	801
Burglary	816	848	846	815	676	556	..
Theft and handling	268	318	315	358	288	233	..
Fraud and forgery	41	28	22	29	21	13	22
Drug offences	641	618	560	524	471	575	573
Motoring offences	93	84	67	53	50	57	58
Other offences	760	784	745	690	518	491	355
Offence not recorded	301	112	48	43	38	24	24
15-17 year olds	**1,606**	**1,185**	**1,150**	**995**	**681**	**553**	**526**
Violence against the person	382	316	239	225	165	120	132
Sexual offences	73	57	48	47	27	34	42
Robbery	437	288	293	303	223	181	125
Burglary	258	201	204	151	81	58	..
Theft and handling	128	78	86	72	44	33	..
Fraud and forgery	1	3	2	0	1	2	4
Drug offences	84	64	59	34	34	32	48
Motoring offences	14	5	8	2	1	1	8
Other offences	205	166	197	152	96	91	82
Offence not recorded	24	7	14	9	9	1	1

21.11 Prison population under an immediate custodial sentence by offence group, age group and sex; 2009 to 2015, England and Wales

As at 30th June each year

	2009	2010	2011	2012	2013	2014	2015
Males	**65,047**	**67,450**	**68,424**	**69,976**	**67,587**	**68,163**	**69,310**
Violence against the person	18,913	19,349	19,520	19,488	18,568	18,694	18,695
Sexual offences	8,116	9,221	9,767	10,390	10,463	11,100	12,124
Robbery	8,406	8,562	8,840	8,951	8,551	8,210	7,867
Burglary	7,202	6,706	6,931	7,137	6,874	6,926	..
Theft and handling	2,741	3,412	3,747	4,141	4,034	3,852	..
Fraud and forgery	1,669	1,359	1,202	1,249	1,166	1,189	1,278
Drug offences	9,561	10,235	9,899	10,108	9,704	9,866	9,903
Motoring offences	1,034	910	824	778	701	794	890
Other offences	5,797	6,895	7,219	7,284	7,090	7,142	7,141
Offence not recorded	1,608	801	475	450	436	390	415
Adults	**57,088**	**59,951**	**61,394**	**63,374**	**62,181**	**63,397**	**65,129**
Violence against the person	16,707	17,223	17,673	17,832	17,162	17,493	17,647
Sexual offences	7,765	8,765	9,321	9,967	10,112	10,775	11,794
Robbery	6,507	6,828	7,143	7,254	7,165	7,081	6,964
Burglary	6,144	5,667	5,887	6,187	6,125	6,317	..
Theft and handling	2,371	3,039	3,365	3,734	3,719	3,598	..
Fraud and forgery	1,628	1,329	1,180	1,222	1,146	1,174	1,253
Drug offences	8,882	9,593	9,315	9,570	9,209	9,266	9,299
Motoring offences	927	822	749	723	651	738	825
Other offences	4,871	5,987	6,341	6,482	6,500	6,589	6,729
Offence not recorded	1,286	698	420	403	392	366	395
18-20 year olds	**6,398**	**6,337**	**5,896**	**5,623**	**4,733**	**4,213**	**3,655**
Violence against the person	1,840	1,820	1,615	1,439	1,244	1,081	916
Sexual offences	279	399	399	376	324	291	288
Robbery	1,473	1,451	1,408	1,396	1,165	948	778
Burglary	803	838	840	800	669	551	..
Theft and handling	245	296	296	335	271	221	..
Fraud and forgery	40	27	21	27	19	13	21
Drug offences	598	579	525	506	461	568	556
Motoring offences	93	83	67	53	49	55	57
Other offences	729	746	684	652	495	462	330
Offence not recorded	298	98	41	39	36	23	19
15-17 year olds	**1,561**	**1,162**	**1,134**	**979**	**673**	**553**	**526**
Violence against the person	366	306	232	217	162	120	132
Sexual offences	72	57	47	47	27	34	42
Robbery	426	283	289	301	221	181	125
Burglary	255	201	204	150	80	58	..
Theft and handling	125	77	86	72	44	33	..
Fraud and forgery	1	3	1	0	1	2	4
Drug offences	81	63	59	32	34	32	48
Motoring offences	14	5	8	2	1	1	8
Other offences	197	162	194	150	95	91	82
Offence not recorded	24	5	14	8	8	1	1

21.11 Prison population under an immediate custodial sentence by offence group, age group and sex; 2009 to 2015, England and Wales

As at 30th June each year

	2009	2010	2011	2012	2013	2014	2015
Females	**3,414**	**3,421**	**3,411**	**3,459**	**3,194**	**3,198**	**3,242**
Violence against the person	849	898	911	949	905	902	913
Sexual offences	60	83	83	83	77	92	106
Robbery	332	272	301	328	322	297	307
Burglary	201	151	171	208	199	215	..
Theft and handling	393	438	451	505	466	525	..
Fraud and forgery	254	185	174	205	154	163	193
Drug offences	859	829	722	574	471	440	420
Motoring offences	16	21	17	20	22	26	16
Other offences	389	458	536	542	535	502	485
Offence not recorded	61	86	45	45	43	36	47
Adults	**3,098**	**3,112**	**3,136**	**3,215**	**3,043**	**3,075**	**3,110**
Violence against the person	726	774	823	854	848	855	875
Sexual offences	57	76	75	77	75	92	103
Robbery	273	227	255	291	295	277	284
Burglary	185	141	165	192	191	210	..
Theft and handling	367	415	432	482	449	513	..
Fraud and forgery	253	184	172	203	152	163	192
Drug offences	813	789	687	554	461	433	403
Motoring offences	16	20	17	20	21	24	15
Other offences	350	416	472	502	511	473	460
Offence not recorded	58	70	38	40	40	35	42
18-20 year olds	**271**	**286**	**259**	**228**	**143**	**123**	**132**
Violence against the person	107	114	81	87	54	47	38
Sexual offences	2	7	7	6	2	0	3
Robbery	48	40	42	35	25	20	23
Burglary	13	10	6	15	7	5	..
Theft and handling	23	22	19	23	17	12	..
Fraud and forgery	1	1	1	2	2	0	1
Drug offences	43	39	35	18	10	7	17
Motoring offences	0	1	0	0	1	2	1
Other offences	31	38	61	38	23	29	25
Offence not recorded	3	14	7	4	2	1	5
15-17 year olds	**45**	**23**	**16**	**16**	**8**	**0**	**0**
Violence against the person	16	10	7	8	3	0	0
Sexual offences	1	0	1	0	0	0	0
Robbery	11	5	4	2	2	0	0
Burglary	3	0	0	1	1	0	0
Theft and handling	3	1	0	0	0	0	0
Fraud and forgery	0	0	1	0	0	0	0
Drug offences	3	1	0	2	0	0	0
Motoring offences	0	0	0	0	0	0	0
Other offences	8	4	3	2	1	0	0
Offence not recorded	0	2	0	1	1	0	0

Source: Ministry of Justice

On 30 June 2015 the classifications used to report the prison population by offence group transitioned over to the offence groups that the Office for National Statistics (ONS) introduced in 2013. These annual tables retain the figures on the old offence groups so comparisons can be made. Further information on these changes can be found in the "Statistical Notice and Consultation – Part 4" document which is published here: https://www.gov.uk/government/statistics/offender-management-statistics-quarterly-january-to-march-2015

21.11 Prison population under an immediate custodial sentence by offence group, age group and sex; 2015 to 2019, England and Wales

As at 30th June each year

	2015	2016	2017	2018	2019
Males and females	**72,552**	**74,214**	**74,716**	**72,546**	**72,743**
Violence against the person	18,537	18,990	18,874	18,713	19,533
Sexual offences	11,490	12,531	13,324	13,580	13,196
Robbery	8,246	7,822	7,353	7,156	7,174
Theft offences	11,567	10,943	10,431	9,351	8,852
Criminal damage and arson	1,181	1,113	1,080	1,072	1,153
Drug offences	10,442	11,008	11,250	10,917	11,121
Possession of weapons	1,753	2,141	2,390	2,579	3,021
Public order offences	1,190	1,267	1,258	1,266	1,208
Miscellaneous crimes against society	3,225	3,538	3,617	3,221	3,000
Fraud offences	1,409	1,373	1,415	1,293	1,228
Summary non-motoring	2,707	2,760	3,009	2,763	2,630
Summary motoring	381	405	396	351	346
Offence not recorded	424	323	319	284	281
Adults	**68,239**	**70,118**	**70,706**	**68,861**	**69,142**
Violence against the person	17,618	18,073	17,978	17,810	18,568
Sexual offences	11,205	12,220	12,996	13,300	12,996
Robbery	7,312	7,051	6,643	6,528	6,570
Theft offences	10,788	10,377	9,971	8,936	8,452
Criminal damage and arson	1,126	1,072	1,050	1,033	1,124
Drug offences	9,821	10,317	10,426	10,219	10,415
Possession of weapons	1,588	1,916	2,128	2,315	2,723
Public order offences	1,099	1,163	1,172	1,186	1,127
Miscellaneous crimes against society	3,075	3,377	3,472	3,091	2,883
Fraud offences	1,385	1,360	1,405	1,283	1,224
Summary non-motoring	2,453	2,512	2,788	2,562	2,475
Summary motoring	368	383	381	334	327
Offence not recorded	401	297	296	264	258
18-20 year olds	**3,787**	**3,609**	**3,540**	**3,241**	**3,192**
Violence against the person	809	815	781	781	823
Sexual offences	251	281	298	254	185
Robbery	807	651	598	523	507
Theft offences	697	507	411	371	364
Criminal damage and arson	48	36	27	35	28
Drug offences	573	640	778	662	682
Possession of weapons	145	194	219	225	249
Public order offences	78	96	77	77	77
Miscellaneous crimes against society	132	145	137	122	108
Fraud offences	20	13	10	10	4
Summary non-motoring	192	186	170	149	129
Summary motoring	12	22	15	17	18
Offence not recorded	23	23	19	15	18
15-17 year olds	**526**	**487**	**470**	**444**	**409**
Violence against the person	110	102	115	122	142
Sexual offences	34	30	30	26	15
Robbery	127	120	112	105	97
Theft offences	82	59	49	44	36
Criminal damage and arson	7	5	3	4	1
Drug offences	48	51	46	36	24
Possession of weapons	20	31	43	39	49
Public order offences	13	8	9	3	4
Miscellaneous crimes against society	18	16	8	8	9
Fraud offences	4	0	0	0	0
Summary non-motoring	62	62	51	52	26
Summary motoring	1	0	0	0	1
Offence not recorded	0	3	4	5	5

21.11 Prison population under an immediate custodial sentence by offence group, age group and sex; 2015 to 2019, England and Wales

As at 30th June each year

	2015	2016	2017	2018	2019
Males	**69,310**	**70,920**	**71,318**	**69,307**	**69,546**
Violence against the person	17,664	18,047	17,911	17,779	18,590
Sexual offences	11,402	12,423	13,213	13,452	13,070
Robbery	7,934	7,538	7,056	6,845	6,854
Theft offences	10,825	10,273	9,730	8,731	8,293
Criminal damage and arson	1,066	1,015	990	971	1,062
Drug offences	10,013	10,564	10,799	10,476	10,675
Possession of weapons	1,697	2,080	2,305	2,502	2,904
Public order offences	1,153	1,232	1,222	1,218	1,157
Miscellaneous crimes against society	3,008	3,324	3,438	3,023	2,819
Fraud offences	1,227	1,185	1,221	1,138	1,061
Summary non-motoring	2,568	2,582	2,793	2,573	2,465
Summary motoring	374	388	381	344	338
Offence not recorded	379	269	259	255	258
Adults	**65,129**	**66,931**	**67,394**	**65,726**	**66,027**
Violence against the person	16,788	17,165	17,045	16,905	17,652
Sexual offences	11,120	12,112	12,886	13,177	12,874
Robbery	7,023	6,777	6,356	6,235	6,259
Theft offences	10,066	9,720	9,277	8,326	7,902
Criminal damage and arson	1,014	975	962	936	1,034
Drug offences	9,409	9,889	9,990	9,793	9,977
Possession of weapons	1,534	1,859	2,052	2,244	2,613
Public order offences	1,063	1,130	1,137	1,142	1,082
Miscellaneous crimes against society	2,866	3,167	3,296	2,895	2,705
Fraud offences	1,204	1,172	1,212	1,129	1,057
Summary non-motoring	2,319	2,354	2,576	2,381	2,316
Summary motoring	362	366	367	327	319
Offence not recorded	361	245	238	236	237
18-20 year olds	**3,655**	**3,502**	**3,454**	**3,137**	**3,110**
Violence against the person	766	780	751	752	796
Sexual offences	248	281	297	249	181
Robbery	784	641	588	505	498
Theft offences	677	494	404	361	355
Criminal damage and arson	45	35	25	31	27
Drug offences	556	624	763	647	674
Possession of weapons	143	190	210	219	242
Public order offences	77	94	76	73	71
Miscellaneous crimes against society	124	141	134	120	105
Fraud offences	19	13	9	9	4
Summary non-motoring	187	166	166	140	123
Summary motoring	11	22	14	17	18
Offence not recorded	18	21	17	14	16
15-17 year olds	**526**	**487**	**470**	**444**	**409**
Violence against the person	110	102	115	122	142
Sexual offences	34	30	30	26	15
Robbery	127	120	112	105	97
Theft offences	82	59	49	44	36
Criminal damage and arson	7	5	3	4	1
Drug offences	48	51	46	36	24
Possession of weapons	20	31	43	39	49
Public order offences	13	8	9	3	4
Miscellaneous crimes against society	18	16	8	8	9
Fraud offences	4	0	0	0	0
Summary non-motoring	62	62	51	52	26
Summary motoring	1	0	0	0	1
Offence not recorded	0	3	4	5	5

21.11 Prison population under an immediate custodial sentence by offence group, age group and sex; 2015 to 2019, England and Wales

As at 30th June each year

	2015	2016	2017	2018	2019
Females	**3,242**	**3,294**	**3,398**	**3,239**	**3,197**
Violence against the person	873	943	963	934	943
Sexual offences	88	108	111	128	126
Robbery	312	284	297	311	320
Theft offences	742	670	701	620	559
Criminal damage and arson	115	98	90	101	91
Drug offences	429	444	451	441	446
Possession of weapons	56	61	85	77	117
Public order offences	37	35	36	48	51
Miscellaneous crimes against society	217	214	179	198	181
Fraud offences	182	188	194	155	167
Summary non-motoring	139	178	216	190	165
Summary motoring	7	17	15	7	8
Offence not recorded	45	54	60	29	23
Adults	**3,110**	**3,187**	**3,312**	**3,135**	**3,115**
Violence against the person	830	908	933	905	916
Sexual offences	85	108	110	123	122
Robbery	289	274	287	293	311
Theft offences	722	657	694	610	550
Criminal damage and arson	112	97	88	97	90
Drug offences	412	428	436	426	438
Possession of weapons	54	57	76	71	110
Public order offences	36	33	35	44	45
Miscellaneous crimes against society	209	210	176	196	178
Fraud offences	181	188	193	154	167
Summary non-motoring	134	158	212	181	159
Summary motoring	6	17	14	7	8
Offence not recorded	40	52	58	28	21
18-20 year olds	**132**	**107**	**86**	**104**	**82**
Violence against the person	43	35	30	29	27
Sexual offences	3	0	1	5	4
Robbery	23	10	10	18	9
Theft offences	20	13	7	10	9
Criminal damage and arson	3	1	2	4	1
Drug offences	17	16	15	15	8
Possession of weapons	2	4	9	6	7
Public order offences	1	2	1	4	6
Miscellaneous crimes against society	8	4	3	2	3
Fraud offences	1	0	1	1	0
Summary non-motoring	5	20	4	9	6
Summary motoring	1	0	1	0	0
Offence not recorded	5	2	2	1	2
15-17 year olds	**0**	**0**	**0**	**0**	**0**
Violence against the person	0	0	0	0	0
Sexual offences	0	0	0	0	0
Robbery	0	0	0	0	0
Theft offences	0	0	0	0	0
Criminal damage and arson	0	0	0	0	0
Drug offences	0	0	0	0	0
Possession of weapons	0	0	0	0	0
Public order offences	0	0	0	0	0
Miscellaneous crimes against society	0	0	0	0	0
Fraud offences	0	0	0	0	0
Summary non-motoring	0	0	0	0	0
Summary motoring	0	0	0	0	0
Offence not recorded	0	0	0	0	0

Source: Ministry of Justice

(1) Due to the introduction of a new prison IT system the 2010 prison population data is now taken from a different source. The 2009 figures from both the old and new systems have been presented to aid comparison.

On 30 June 2015 the classifications used to report the prison population by offence group transitioned over to the offence groups that the Office for National Statistics (ONS) introduced in 2013. These annual tables retain the figures on the old offence groups so comparisons can be made. Further information on these changes can be found in the "Statistical Notice and Consultation – Part 4" document which is published here:

https://www.gov.uk/government/statistics/offender-management-statistics-quarterly-january-to-march-2015

21.12 Crimes recorded by the police, Scotland, 2010-11 to 2019-20

Crime group	2010-11	2011-12	2012-13	2013-14	2014-15	2015-16	2016-17	2017-18*	2018-19	2019-20	% change 18-19 to 19-20	% change 10-11 to 19-20
Total Crimes	323,247	314,188	273,053	270,397	256,350	246,243	238,921	244,504	246,480	246,516	0	-24
Non-sexual crimes of violence	11,437	9,484	7,468	6,686	6,272	6,737	7,164	7,251	8,008	9,316	16	-19
Homicide etc.3 (incl. causing death by driving)	122	121	91	106	105	81	105	98	102	121	19	-1
Attempted murder & serious assault4	5,493	4,693	3,643	3,268	3,166	4,007	4,186	4,189	4,359	4,097	-6	-25
Robbery	2,557	2,244	1,832	1,499	1,497	1,327	1,435	1,556	1,807	1,738	-4	-32
Domestic Abuse (Scotland) Act 2018	-	-	-	-	-	-	-	-	-	1,681	-	-
Other violence	3,265	2,426	1,902	1,813	1,504	1,322	1,438	1,408	1,740	1,679	-4	-49
Sexual crimes5	6,696	7,361	7,693	8,604	9,557	10,273	11,092	12,487	13,547	13,364	-1	100
Rape & attempted rape	1,131	1,274	1,462	1,808	1,901	1,809	1,878	2,255	2,426	2,343	-3	107
Sexual assault	3,220	2,908	3,008	3,405	3,727	3,963	4,281	4,826	5,123	4,936	-4	53
Crimes associated with prostitution	576	567	534	490	374	247	303	136	235	101	-57	-82
Other sexual crimes	1,769	2,612	2,689	2,901	3,555	4,254	4,630	5,270	5,763	5,984	4	238
Crimes of dishonesty	155,870	154,337	135,899	137,324	126,857	115,789	113,205	114,474	114,506	111,409	-3	-29
Housebreaking6	25,017	24,222	21,515	22,272	20,607	17,637	16,299	15,130	13,777	12,903	-6	-48
Theft by opening a lockfast place (OLP)	4,059	3,529	3,239	3,218	2,879	2,193	1,940	2,027	1,684	1,728	3	-57
Theft from a motor vehicle by OLP	9,495	8,988	6,159	6,189	5,816	4,684	3,888	3,734	3,532	2,982	-16	-69
Theft of a motor vehicle	8,716	7,060	5,731	5,976	5,423	5,028	5,216	5,024	4,950	5,002	1	-43
Shoplifting	29,660	29,758	26,449	27,693	27,364	28,424	28,650	31,321	33,523	30,688	-8	3
Other theft	64,680	66,681	58,704	58,794	53,539	46,419	45,173	44,437	42,880	41,421	-3	-36
Fraud	8,983	8,892	8,898	8,088	6,913	7,400	7,811	8,628	9,675	11,939	23	33
Other dishonesty	5,260	5,207	5,204	5,094	4,316	4,004	4,228	4,173	4,485	4,746	6	-10
Fire-raising, vandalism etc.	82,020	75,201	59,479	54,418	52,091	54,226	52,514	51,322	47,997	47,731	-1	-42
Fire-raising	3,966	3,755	3,066	2,549	2,351	2,595	2,793	2,632	2,481	2,657	7	-33
Vandalism etc.	78,054	71,446	56,413	51,869	49,740	51,631	49,721	48,690	45,516	45,074	-1	-42
Other crimes	67,224	67,805	62,514	63,365	61,573	59,218	54,946	58,970	62,422	64,589	3	-4
Crimes against public justice	26,294	26,635	23,401	23,610	21,100	20,361	18,795	18,679	18,512	19,441	5	-26
Handling offensive weapons								7,733	8,896	9,644	8	n/r
Not used in other criminal activity	6,283	5,631	4,015	3,795	3,289	3,111	3,271	3,570	4,216	4,484	6	-29
Used in other criminal activity								4,163	4,680	5,160	10	-
Drugs	34,347	35,157	34,688	35,616	36,836	35,479	32,641	32,399	34,831	35,303	1	3
Coronavirus restrictions	-	-	-	-	-	-	-	-	-	107	-	-

Source: Recorded Crime in Scotland, Scottish Government

Notes:

3. Includes Murder, and Culpable homicide (common law), which includes Causing death by dangerous driving, Causing death by careless driving while under the influence of drink or drugs, Causing death by careless driving, Illegal driver involved in fatal accident and Corporate homicide.

4. For the definition of Serious assault and the distinction between Serious assault and Common assault please see Annex 1.

5. Implementation of the Sexual Offences (Scotland) Act on 1 December 2010 affected the comparability of the breakdown of Sexual crimes over time. For further information please see the 'Data Considerations' section under Sexual crimes within Chapter 2.

6. Includes dwellings, non-dwellings and other premises. For a more detailed definition see Annex 1.

This table is part of the statistical bulletin 'Recorded Crime in Scotland, 2019-20' (https://www.gov.scot/publications/recorded-crime-scotland-2019-2020)

21.13 People convicted by main crime/offence, 2010-11 to 2019-20, Scotland

Main crime or offence	2010-11	2011-12	2012-13	2013-14	2014-15	2015-16	2016-17	2017-18	2018-19	2019-20[1]	% change 2018-19 to 2019-20	All offences proceeded, 2019-20 [2]
All crimes and offences	**115,581**	**108,424**	**101,018**	**105,658**	**106,575**	**99,954**	**92,330**	**83,177**	**78,488**	**75,251**	**-4**	**108,184**
All crimes	**42,350**	**40,725**	**37,024**	**36,275**	**36,565**	**35,790**	**32,611**	**29,742**	**28,520**	**28,033**	**-2**	**40,852**
Non-sexual crimes of violence	**2,540**	**2,461**	**2,143**	**1,804**	**1,745**	**1,776**	**1,725**	**1,829**	**1,772**	**2,142**	**21**	**2,388**
Homicide etc	117	111	115	93	81	84	78	89	81	81	-	83
Attempted murder and serious assault	1,419	1,365	1,285	1,043	1,053	1,118	1,115	1,176	1,166	1,298	11	1,396
Robbery	526	606	520	448	386	384	370	410	361	410	14	497
Domestic Abuse (Scotland) Act	-	-	-	-	-	-	-	-	-	206	-	208
Other non-sexual crimes of violence	478	379	223	220	225	190	162	154	164	147	-10	204
Sexual crimes	**818**	**838**	**911**	**1,130**	**1,213**	**1,215**	**1,080**	**1,110**	**1,224**	**1,204**	**-2**	**2,353**
Rape and attempted rape	36	49	77	91	125	105	99	106	142	130	-8	264
Sexual assault[3]	160	151	204	236	276	278	266	300	301	305	1	760
Crimes associated with prostitution	245	200	142	169	145	86	84	47	37	45	22	52
Other sexual crimes	377	438	488	634	667	746	631	657	744	724	-3	1,277
Crimes of dishonesty	**15,613**	**14,772**	**13,250**	**12,579**	**12,526**	**11,605**	**10,809**	**9,862**	**9,771**	**9,076**	**-7**	**14,008**
Housebreaking	1,540	1,498	1,365	1,037	979	858	873	812	765	796	4	1,094
Theft by opening lockfast places	284	291	247	218	212	196	184	147	161	111	-31	192
Theft from a motor vehicle	270	250	200	143	112	101	94	84	110	89	-19	142
Theft of a motor vehicle	483	450	373	272	318	302	270	249	222	200	-10	471
Shoplifting	7,853	7,267	6,500	6,532	6,942	6,596	6,248	5,661	5,928	5,395	-9	7,893
Other theft	2,871	2,961	2,720	2,577	2,341	2,093	1,796	1,634	1,487	1,460	-2	2,150
Fraud	1,070	811	624	681	602	545	545	471	411	410	-	1,064
Other dishonesty	1,242	1,244	1,221	1,119	1,020	914	799	804	687	615	-10	1,002
Fire-raising, vandalism, etc.	**3,362**	**3,016**	**2,583**	**2,504**	**2,442**	**2,233**	**1,972**	**1,827**	**1,771**	**1,693**	**-4**	**2,298**
Fire-raising	159	146	133	130	133	116	114	124	119	121	2	173
Vandalism etc.	3,203	2,870	2,450	2,374	2,309	2,117	1,858	1,703	1,652	1,572	-5	2,125
Other crimes	**20,017**	**19,638**	**18,137**	**18,258**	**18,639**	**18,961**	**17,025**	**15,114**	**13,982**	**13,918**	**-**	**19,805**
Crimes against public justice	9,822	10,170	9,767	9,672	10,013	10,177	9,033	8,108	7,298	7,652	5	11,138
Handling offensive weapons	2,445	2,265	1,709	1,684	1,586	1,489	1,436	1,476	1,579	1,735	10	2,244
Drugs	7,531	6,990	6,449	6,720	6,868	7,144	6,371	5,417	5,005	4,430	-11	6,268
Other crime	219	213	212	182	172	151	185	113	100	101	1	155
All offences	**73,231**	**67,699**	**63,994**	**69,383**	**70,010**	**64,164**	**59,719**	**53,435**	**49,968**	**47,218**	**-6**	**67,332**
Miscellaneous offences	**29,125**	**29,416**	**28,541**	**29,098**	**31,051**	**31,599**	**29,140**	**25,765**	**22,464**	**21,538**	**-4**	**33,219**
Common assault	12,600	12,762	11,648	11,213	11,762	12,080	11,240	9,901	8,727	8,301	-5	12,550
Breach of the peace etc.	12,114	12,544	12,961	13,731	15,585	16,298	15,303	13,674	11,901	11,449	-4	17,975
Drunkenness and other disorderly conduct	624	309	220	306	250	148	69	42	31	31	-	100
Urinating etc	43	20	32	41	43	29	13	14	9	2	-78	9
Other miscellaneous	3,744	3,781	3,680	3,807	3,411	3,044	2,515	2,134	1,796	1,755	-2	2,585
Motor vehicle offences	**44,106**	**38,283**	**35,453**	**40,285**	**38,959**	**32,565**	**30,579**	**27,670**	**27,504**	**25,680**	**-7**	**34,113**
Dangerous and careless driving	3,167	2,858	2,811	3,574	3,411	3,569	3,759	3,813	3,118	3,360	8	4,017
Driving under the influence	5,351	5,287	4,735	4,091	3,681	3,537	3,634	3,660	3,552	3,385	-5	4,085
Speeding	12,955	12,381	12,034	14,125	14,007	12,370	10,686	9,410	9,069	9,171	1	9,508
Unlawful use of motor vehicle	11,069	9,020	7,863	8,526	8,318	6,334	7,164	6,923	7,643	6,285	-18	10,971
Vehicle defect offences	1,723	1,504	1,243	1,611	1,580	1,537	1,335	981	1,130	1,067	-6	1,852
Seat belt offences	2,673	1,982	2,052	2,539	2,172	481	312	86	209	173	-17	258
Mobile phone offences	3,603	2,641	2,663	3,096	3,162	2,281	1,477	861	688	463	-33	499
Other motor vehicle offences	3,565	2,610	2,052	2,723	2,628	2,456	2,212	1,936	2,095	1,776	-15	2,923

1. Figures for some categories dealt with by the high court - including homicide, rape and major drug cases - may be underestimated due to late recording of disposals - see annex notes B16 to B19.
2. Number of individual offences relating to people with a charge proved, whether or not the main crime/offence involved.
3. Before the introductions of the Sexual Offences (Scotland) Act 2010, a number of sexual assaults may have been classified as common assault with a sexual aggravation.

Source: Criminal Proceedings in Scotland, Scottish Government

21.14 People convicted by type of court, 2010-11 to 2019-20, Scotland

Number

Type of court	2010-11	2011-12	2012-13	2013-14	2014-15	2015-16	2016-17	2017-18	2018-19	2019-20	% change 2018-19 to 2019-20
All court types	115,581	108,424	101,018	105,658	106,575	99,954	92,330	83,177	78,488	75,251	-4%
High court [1,2]	706	765	708	704	595	603	649	598	582	660	13%
Sheriff solemn	4,022	4,141	4,292	4,180	4,745	4,984	4,658	3,908	4,219	4,511	7%
Sheriff summary [3]	65,360	64,264	60,055	59,200	59,911	59,218	55,534	51,227	46,542	45,901	-1%
Justice of the Peace court	45,493	39,254	35,963	41,574	41,324	35,149	31,489	27,444	27,145	24,179	-11%

percent

Type of court	2010-11	2011-12	2012-13	2013-14	2014-15	2015-16	2016-17	2017-18	2018-19	2019-20
All court types	100	100	100	100	100	100	100	100	100	100
High court [1,2]	1	1	1	1	1	1	1	1	1	1
Sheriff solemn	3	4	4	4	4	5	5	5	5	6
Sheriff summary [3]	57	59	59	56	56	59	60	62	59	61
Justice of the Peace court	39	36	36	39	39	35	34	33	35	32

Index: 2010-11=100

Type of court	2010-11	2011-12	2012-13	2013-14	2014-15	2015-16	2016-17	2017-18	2018-19	2019-20
All court types	100	94	87	91	92	86	80	72	68	65
High court [1,2]	100	108	100	100	84	85	92	85	82	93
Sheriff solemn	100	103	107	104	118	124	116	97	105	112
Sheriff summary [3]	100	98	92	91	92	91	85	78	71	70
Justice of the Peace court	100	86	79	91	91	77	69	60	60	53

Source: Criminal Proceedings in Scotland, Scottish Government

1. Includes cases remitted to the High court from the Sheriff court.
2. The figures for the most recent year, and to an extent earlier years, may be underestimated due to late recording of disposals. See annex notes B16 to B18.
3. Includes any remaining cases seen in the stipendiary magistrates court in Glasgow.
This table is part of the statistical bulletin 'Criminal Proceedings in Scotland' (https://www.gov.scot/publications/criminal-proceedings-scotland-2019-20)

21.15 People convicted by main penalty, 2010-11 to 2019-20, Scotland

Main penalty	2010-11	2011-12	2012-13	2013-14	2014-15	2015-16	2016-17	2017-18	2018-19	2019-20	% change 2018-19 to 2019-20
Total	**115,581**	**108,424**	**101,018**	**105,658**	**106,575**	**99,954**	**92,330**	**83,177**	**78,488**	**75,251**	**-4**
Custody	**15,320**	**15,950**	**14,789**	**14,172**	**14,038**	**13,755**	**12,699**	**11,980**	**12,221**	**11,101**	**-9**
Prison	12,810	13,356	12,727	12,402	12,324	12,029	11,158	10,755	10,988	10,032	-9
Young offenders institution	2,082	2,105	1,606	1,244	1,155	1,184	998	763	763	583	-24
Supervised release order	230	267	265	286	325	351	316	287	269	308	14
Extended sentence	185	212	174	223	214	181	218	162	186	164	-12
Order for life-long restriction	13	10	17	17	20	10	9	13	15	14	-7
Community sentence	**15,615**	**16,937**	**17,263**	**18,272**	**18,580**	**18,952**	**18,644**	**17,301**	**15,211**	**16,296**	**7**
Community payback order	461	10,380	14,940	16,375	16,765	16,766	15,974	14,072	11,812	12,530	6
Restriction of liberty order	831	845	919	1,078	1,174	1,643	2,207	2,712	2,848	3,261	15
Drug treatment & testing order	806	642	607	589	525	474	418	497	529	493	-7
Community service order	5,306	2,642	479	141	68	40	18	6	6	3	-50
Probation and other community sentences[1]	8,211	2,428	318	89	48	29	27	14	16	9	-44
Financial penalty	**67,576**	**59,320**	**53,429**	**57,795**	**56,779**	**49,872**	**44,938**	**39,235**	**37,283**	**34,661**	**-7**
Fine	66,492	58,395	52,661	56,921	55,939	49,100	44,213	38,447	36,495	33,870	-7
Compensation order	1,084	925	768	874	840	772	725	788	788	791	0
Other sentence	**17,070**	**16,217**	**15,537**	**15,419**	**17,178**	**17,375**	**16,049**	**14,661**	**13,773**	**13,193**	**-4**
Admonition[2]	16,421	15,577	15,011	14,839	16,426	16,501	15,234	13,874	13,060	12,504	-4
Absolute discharge, no order made	460	476	361	465	660	788	687	677	607	580	-4
Remit to children's hearing	170	140	133	94	67	77	100	86	87	89	2
Insanity, hospital, guardianship order	19	24	32	21	25	9	28	24	19	20	5
Average amount of penalty											
Custody (days)[3]	277	289	284	295	287	293	316	319	326	356	
Fine (£)[4,5]	180	200	200	180	200	200	200	230	230	240	
Compensation order(£)[5,6]	190	200	200	200	200	200	250	290	250	250	

1. Includes supervised attendance orders, community reparation orders and anti-social behaviour orders. 2. Includes a small number of court cautions and dog-related disposals. 3. Excludes life long restriction orders. 4. Excludes company fines. 5. Calculated as the median. 6. As main or secondary penalty.

Percentage

Main penalty	2010-11	2011-12	2012-13	2013-14	2014-15	2015-16	2016-17	2017-18	2018-19	2019-20
Total	**100**	**100**	**100**	**100**	**100**	**100**	**100**	**100**	**100**	**100**
Custody	**13**	**15**	**15**	**13**	**13**	**14**	**14**	**14**	**16**	**15**
Prison	11	12	13	12	12	12	12	13	14	13
Young offenders institution	2	2	2	1	1	1	1	1	1	1
Supervised release order	-	-	-	-	-	-	-	-	-	-
Extended sentence	-	-	-	-	-	-	-	-	-	-
Order for life-long restriction	-	-	-	-	-	-	-	-	-	-
Community sentence	**14**	**16**	**17**	**17**	**17**	**19**	**20**	**21**	**19**	**22**
Community payback order	-	10	15	15	16	17	17	17	15	17
Restriction of liberty order	1	1	1	1	1	2	2	3	4	4
Drug treatment & testing order	1	1	1	-	-	-	-	1	1	1
Community service order	5	2	-	-	-	-	-	-	-	-
Probation and other community sentences[1]	7	2	-	-	-	-	-	-	-	-
Financial penalty	**58**	**55**	**53**	**55**	**53**	**50**	**49**	**47**	**48**	**46**
Fine	58	54	52	54	52	49	48	46	46	45
Compensation order	1	1	1	1	1	1	1	1	1	1
Other sentence	**15**	**15**	**15**	**15**	**16**	**17**	**17**	**18**	**18**	**18**
Admonition[2]	14	14	15	14	15	17	16	17	17	17
Absolute discharge, no order made	-	1	1	1	1	1	1	1	1	1
Remit to children's hearing	-	-	-	-	-	-	-	-	-	-
Insanity, hospital, guardianship order	-	-	-	-	-	-	-	-	-	-

Source: Criminal Proceedings in Scotland Scottish Government

21.16 People convicted by main penalty, gender and age, 2010-11 to 2019-20, Scotland

		2010-11	2011-12	2012-13	2013-14	2014-15	2015-16	2016-17	2017-18	2018-19	2019-20	% change 18-19 to 19-20
Total[1]		**115,581**	**108,424**	**101,018**	**105,658**	**106,575**	**99,954**	**92,330**	**83,177**	**78,488**	**75,251**	**-4**
Males[2]	Total	97,042	90,902	84,347	87,983	88,650	83,010	76,476	68,572	64,655	62,126	-4
	Under 21	15,145	13,135	10,358	9,187	8,628	8,417	7,599	6,401	5,696	5,182	-9
	21-30	35,177	32,761	30,338	30,705	30,155	28,123	25,777	22,480	20,753	19,130	-8
	31-40	23,564	22,467	21,567	22,836	23,756	22,101	20,699	19,347	18,755	18,584	-1
	41-100	23,156	22,539	22,084	25,255	26,111	24,369	22,401	20,344	19,451	19,230	-1
Females[2]	Total	18,532	17,437	16,558	17,590	17,921	16,944	15,852	14,603	13,833	13,123	-5
	Under 21	2,228	1,952	1,616	1,429	1,448	1,358	1,217	1,090	942	842	-11
	21-30	6,573	5,989	5,874	5,656	5,515	5,178	4,666	4,048	3,757	3,615	-4
	31-40	4,985	4,853	4,492	5,001	5,313	4,998	4,964	4,821	4,658	4,420	-5
	41-100	4,746	4,643	4,576	5,504	5,645	5,410	5,005	4,644	4,476	4,246	-5
Custody[1]		**15,320**	**15,950**	**14,789**	**14,172**	**14,038**	**13,755**	**12,699**	**11,980**	**12,221**	**11,101**	**-9**
Males[2]	Total	14,018	14,582	13,499	12,959	12,745	12,563	11,704	10,839	11,115	10,157	-9
	Under 21	2,014	2,050	1,588	1,238	1,137	1,190	1,007	758	771	598	-22
	21-30	6,074	6,059	5,486	5,021	4,983	4,748	4,415	3,948	3,948	3,371	-15
	31-40	3,776	4,094	3,973	4,025	3,903	3,914	3,672	3,682	3,835	3,765	-2
	41-100	2,154	2,379	2,452	2,675	2,722	2,711	2,610	2,451	2,561	2,423	-5
Females[2]	Total	1,302	1,368	1,290	1,213	1,293	1,192	995	1,141	1,106	944	-15
	Under 21	168	160	116	83	84	72	52	61	49	35	-29
	21-30	588	620	599	491	483	400	325	324	302	267	-12
	31-40	324	349	345	395	488	462	377	500	515	427	-17
	41-100	222	239	230	244	238	258	241	256	240	215	-10
Community sentence[1]		**15,615**	**16,937**	**17,263**	**18,272**	**18,580**	**18,952**	**18,644**	**17,301**	**15,211**	**16,296**	**7**
Males[2]	Total	12,977	14,090	14,395	15,245	15,503	15,866	15,623	14,444	12,777	13,751	8
	Under 21	3,446	3,292	2,743	2,635	2,522	2,497	2,359	1,988	1,648	1,595	-3
	21-30	4,696	5,249	5,590	5,674	5,763	5,768	5,755	4,929	4,349	4,619	6
	31-40	2,724	3,168	3,403	3,796	3,966	4,135	4,063	4,041	3,666	4,098	12
	41-100	2,111	2,381	2,659	3,140	3,252	3,466	3,446	3,486	3,114	3,439	10
Females[2]	Total	2,638	2,847	2,868	3,027	3,077	3,086	3,020	2,857	2,434	2,545	5
	Under 21	453	433	428	340	378	341	309	269	219	237	8
	21-30	1,020	1,014	1,063	1,030	1,014	967	903	816	689	678	-2
	31-40	661	769	735	882	862	949	952	1,012	875	947	8
	41-100	504	631	642	775	823	829	856	760	651	683	5
Financial Penalty[1]		**67,576**	**59,320**	**53,429**	**57,795**	**56,779**	**49,872**	**44,938**	**39,235**	**37,283**	**34,661**	**-7**
Males[2]	Total	57,359	50,260	45,145	48,435	47,734	42,012	37,564	32,726	30,775	28,602	-7
	Under 21	7,071	5,365	4,061	3,697	3,343	3,037	2,672	2,238	1,964	1,780	-9
	21-30	20,360	17,798	15,813	16,478	15,554	13,867	12,306	10,630	9,648	8,675	-10
	31-40	14,085	12,261	11,185	12,005	12,455	10,727	9,878	8,753	8,420	7,925	-6
	41-100	15,843	14,836	14,086	16,255	16,382	14,381	12,708	11,105	10,743	10,222	-5
Females[2]	Total	10,211	8,983	8,175	9,282	9,041	7,860	7,373	6,507	6,508	6,057	-7
	Under 21	909	746	530	519	533	444	382	347	323	291	-10
	21-30	3,382	2,907	2,706	2,772	2,604	2,311	2,121	1,828	1,698	1,636	-4
	31-40	2,844	2,463	2,192	2,551	2,557	2,177	2,169	1,913	2,010	1,804	-10
	41-100	3,076	2,867	2,747	3,440	3,347	2,928	2,701	2,419	2,477	2,326	-6
Other sentence[1]		**17,070**	**16,217**	**15,537**	**15,419**	**17,178**	**17,375**	**16,049**	**14,661**	**13,773**	**13,193**	**-4**
Males[2]	Total	12,688	11,970	11,308	11,344	12,668	12,569	11,585	10,563	9,988	9,616	-4
	Under 21	2,614	2,428	1,966	1,617	1,626	1,693	1,561	1,417	1,313	1,209	-8
	21-30	4,047	3,655	3,449	3,532	3,855	3,740	3,301	2,973	2,808	2,465	-12
	31-40	2,979	2,944	3,006	3,010	3,432	3,325	3,086	2,871	2,834	2,796	-1
	41-100	3,048	2,943	2,887	3,185	3,755	3,811	3,637	3,302	3,033	3,146	4
Females[2]	Total	4,381	4,239	4,225	4,068	4,510	4,806	4,464	4,098	3,785	3,577	-5
	Under 21	698	613	542	487	453	501	474	413	351	279	-21
	21-30	1,583	1,448	1,506	1,363	1,414	1,500	1,317	1,080	1,068	1,034	-3
	31-40	1,156	1,272	1,220	1,173	1,406	1,410	1,466	1,396	1,258	1,242	-1
	41-100	944	906	957	1,045	1,237	1,395	1,207	1,209	1,108	1,022	-8

Source: Criminal Proceedings in Scotland, Scottish Government

1. Includes a small number of cases for companies and where age and gender are unknown.
2. Gender totals exclude companies and where age and gender are unknown. The sum of gender totals may not equal disposal totals.

21.17 Average daily prison population by type of custody, gender and age in Scotland from 2008-09 to 2018-19

	2008-09	2009-10	2010-11	2011-12	2012-13	2013-14	2014-15*	2015-16*	2016-17*	2017-18*	2018-19*	% change over 2016-17 and 2017-18	% change over 2017-18 and 2018-19
Total	**7,827**	**7,964**	**7,854**	**8,179**	**8,057**	**7,894**	**7,731**	**7,676**	**7,552**	**7,464**	**7,789**	**-1**	**4**
Remand	1,679	1,522	1,474	1,601	1,469	1,474	1,525	1,495	1,370	1,361	1,525	-1	12
Untried	1,415	1,170	1,112	1,238	1,155	1,163	1,285	1,257	1,105	1,102	1,251	0	14
Convicted awaiting sentence	264	352	362	363	314	311	241	238	265	259	274	-2	6
Sentenced	6,148	6,442	6,380	6,578	6,588	6,420	6,206	6,181	6,182	6,103	6,264	-1	3
Women	**414**	**426**	**436**	**469**	**459**	**432**	**425**	**404**	**366**	**370**	**384**	**1**	**4**
Remand	133	105	105	108	107	106	105	98	88	89	93	1	4
Untried	85	63	68	67	69	70	78	76	63	62	69	-2	11
Convicted awaiting sentence	49	41	38	41	38	36	27	22	25	27	24	8	-11
Sentenced	280	321	331	361	353	326	320	306	279	281	291	1	4
Men	**7,413**	**7,538**	**7,418**	**7,710**	**7,598**	**7,462**	**7,306**	**7,272**	**7,185**	**7,094**	**7,405**	**-1**	**4**
Remand	1,545	1,417	1,369	1,493	1,362	1,368	1,420	1,396	1,282	1,273	1,432	-1	12
Untried	1,330	1,107	1,044	1,171	1,086	1,093	1,207	1,181	1,042	1,040	1,182	0	14
Convicted awaiting sentence	215	311	325	322	276	275	214	216	240	233	250	-3	7
Sentenced	5,868	6,121	6,049	6,217	6,236	6,094	5,886	5,875	5,903	5,821	5,972	-1	3
Under 21	**1,021**	**1,024**	**865**	**814**	**690**	**566**	**484**	**447**	**416**	**346**	**340**	**-17**	**-2**
Remand	334	305	262	258	198	167	170	164	135	116	121	-14	4
Untried	231	211	172	171	134	114	122	121	100	84	90	-16	7
Convicted awaiting sentence	104	94	90	88	64	54	48	43	35	32	31	-9	-3
Sentenced	687	719	604	555	492	399	314	283	282	230	219	-18	-5
21 and over	**6,806**	**6,940**	**6,989**	**7,365**	**7,368**	**7,328**	**7,247**	**7,228**	**7,136**	**7,119**	**7,449**	**0**	**5**
Remand	1,344	1,217	1,212	1,342	1,271	1,307	1,355	1,331	1,236	1,246	1,405	1	13
Untried	1,184	959	940	1,068	1,021	1,049	1,163	1,136	1,006	1,018	1,161	1	14
Convicted awaiting sentence	160	258	273	275	250	257	192	195	230	228	244	-1	7
Sentenced	5,461	5,723	5,776	6,022	6,097	6,022	5,892	5,898	5,900	5,873	6,044	0	3

Source

Scottish Government Justice Analytical Services prisons database for figures up to 2013-14. These data have been released as National Statistics and are available on the Scottish Government website at http://www.gov.scot/Topics/Statistics/Browse/Crime-Justice/PubPrisons

* Due to technical issues, data for 2014-15 onward are derived directly from the Scottish Prison Service management information system and are reported in the SPS annual reports. These are available on the Scottish Prison Service website at http://www.sps.gov.uk/Corporate/Publications/Publications.aspx

Notes

1. The data presented in this table are drawn from an administrative IT system. While the figures shown have been checked as far as practicable, they should be regarded as approximate and not necessarily accurate to the last whole number shown in the tables. The figures shown here may differ slightly from those published previously.

2. Figures in the tables have been rounded to the nearest whole number, and may not always add to the totals as these are calculated and rounded independently.

3. Figures **exclude** prisoners on home detention curfew.

4. Prisoners may be classified as unlawfully at large due to abscond (not returning from temporary release as scheduled), being subject to recall due to breach of home detention curfew conditions, or escape.

    Figures up to 2013-14 **include** unlawfully at large prisoners.

    Figures derived from SPS management information from 2014-15 onward **exclude** those classified as unlawfully at large (about 40-50).

21.18 Scottish Prison Service Statement of Comprehensive Net Expenditure for the year ended 31 March 2019

	Note	2018-19 £000	2017-18 £000
Income			
Income from sale of goods/services	2	**(7,328)**	(7,026)
Other operating income	2	**(384)**	(363)
Total operating income		**(7,712)**	(7,389)
Expenditure			
Staff costs	3	**173,521**	170,468
Other expenditure	3	**169,875**	161,050
Total operating expenditure		**343,396**	331,518
Net operating expenditure		**335,684**	324,129
Finance expense	3	**6,490**	7,096
Net expenditure for the year		**342,174**	331,225

Other comprehensive net expenditure

	2018-19 £000	2017-18 £000
Items that will not be reclassified to net operating costs:		
Net (gain) on revaluation of property, plant and equipment	**(22,809)**	(86,512)
Comprehensive net expenditure for the year	**319,365**	244,713

21.19 Recorded crime by offence, 2018-19 to 2020/21[1] - Northern Ireland

Numbers and percentages

Offence	2018/19[28]	2019/20	2020/21	change 2019/20 to 2020/21	% change 2019/20 to 2020/21
VICTIM-BASED OFFENCES					
TOTAL VIOLENCE AGAINST THE PERSON OFFENCES	**36,426**	**41,305**	**39,284**	**-2,021**	**-4.9**
Homicide[35]	29	21	22	1	-
Death or serious injury caused by unlawful driving[29]	138	164	93	-71	-43.3
Violence with injury[5,29,33,34]	14,109	13,426	11,638	-1,788	-13.3
Violence without injury[5,29]	16,876	17,638	16,172	-1,466	-8.3
Harassment[29,30]	5,274	10,056	11,359	1,303	13.0
TOTAL SEXUAL OFFENCES[10,14]	**3,535**	**3,550**	**3,335**	**-215**	**-6.1**
Rape	1,095	1,014	1,028	14	1.4
Other sexual offences[10,14]	2,440	2,536	2,307	-229	-9.0
TOTAL ROBBERY OFFENCES	**639**	**629**	**501**	**-128**	**-20.3**
34A Robbery of business property	141	118	94	-24	-20.3
34B Robbery of personal property	498	511	407	-104	-20.4
TOTAL THEFT OFFENCES (INCLUDING BURGLARY)	**30,657**	**29,147**	**20,467**	**-8,680**	**-29.8**
Total theft - burglary offences[32]	6,127	6,078	4,133	-1,945	-32.0
Total domestic burglary [32]	..	..	.. ..		..
Total non-domestic burglary [32]	..	..	.. ..		..
Total Burglary - Residential [32]	*4,572*	*4,521*	*3,188*	*-1,333*	*-29.5*
Total Burglary - Business & Community [32]	*1,555*	*1,557*	*945*	*-612*	*-39.3*
Total theft - vehicle offences	3,661	3,271	2,498	-773	-23.6
Total theft from the person	499	475	206	-269	-56.6
Total bicycle theft	833	882	731	-151	-17.1
Total theft - shoplifting	6,464	6,584	4,468	-2,116	-32.1
Total all other theft offences	13,073	11,857	8,431	-3,426	-28.9
TOTAL CRIMINAL DAMAGE OFFENCES	**17,658**	**18,698**	**17,280**	**-1,418**	**-7.6**
OTHER CRIMES AGAINST SOCIETY					
TOTAL DRUG OFFENCES	**7,048**	**7,802**	**8,165**	**363**	**4.7**
Trafficking of drugs	**888**	**916**	**1,038**	**122**	**13.3**
Possession of drugs	**6,160**	**6,886**	**7,127**	**241**	**3.5**
TOTAL POSSESSION OF WEAPONS OFFENCES	**1,062**	**1,100**	**1,094**	**-6**	**-0.5**
TOTAL PUBLIC ORDER OFFENCES	**1,002**	**1,297**	**1,282**	**-15**	**-1.2**
TOTAL MISCELLANEOUS CRIMES AGAINST SOCIETY	**2,826**	**2,964**	**2,931**	**-33**	**-1.1**
TOTAL RECORDED CRIME - ALL OFFENCES (excluding Action Fraud)	**100,853**	**106,492**	**94,339**	**-12,153**	**-11.4**
TOTAL OTHER FRAUD (police recorded)[27]	..	..	..	..	..
TOTAL Action Fraud	3,608	4,253	5,856	1,603	37.7

All footnotes can be found in Notes to accompany Table 21.19   Source: Police Service Northern Ireland

'..' in the table indicates that data are not available.
'-' indicates that for offences recorded, a percentage change is not reported because the base number of offences is less than 50.

Notes to accompany Table 21.19

1. Between 1998/99 and 2000/01 crimes were recorded through a paper-based system where a completed form was forwarded to PSNI's Statistics Branch for input onto a stand-alone system, from which crime figures were then extracted. In April 2001 PSNI introduced electronic recording through an integrated crime information system (ICIS), resulting in more low level crime being captured than would have occurred through the previous crime recording process. This system remained in place until the end of 2006/07. In April 2007, the NICHE record management system was introduced within PSNI for crime recording, a product specifically designed for police services to record and manage occurrences. Further information on administrative data sources within PSNI can be obtained from the PSNI website:
https://www.psni.police.uk/globalassets/inside-the-psni/our-statistics/official-statistics/psni-admin-data-sources-updated-may-2016.pdf

2. Number of crimes recorded using the expanded offence coverage and revised Counting Rules which came into effect on 1 April 1998.

3. The National Crime Recording Standard was introduced in April 2002, although some forces adopted NCRS practices before the standard was formally introduced. Figures before and after that date are not directly comparable. The introduction of NCRS led to a rise in recording in 2002/03 and, particularly for violent crime, in the following years as forces continued to improve compliance with the new standard. Much of the impact of introducing NCRS was experienced by PSNI in 2001/02, through the introduction of an integrated crime information system (ICIS) within PSNI which improved the capture of low level crimes.

4. The number of murders in 1998/99 includes the 29 persons killed in the Omagh bomb which occurred on 15 August 1998. This incident also accounts for approximately 90% of all wounding with intent and wounding offences recorded in 1998/99.

5. Prior to April 2003, offences where the victim received minor injuries (e.g. bruising or minor abrasions) were recorded as assault without injury. Since April 2003 assaults with minor injuries have been recorded as assault occasioning actual bodily harm (AOABH). This accounts for the large increase in AOABH offences and the large fall in assault without injury offences between 2002/03 and 2003/04. The Home Office introduced this change for England & Wales a year earlier, in April 2002.

6. Prior to 2008/09 classification 4.4 Causing death by dangerous driving was the only classification of this nature. From 2008/09 onwards these offences are split across classifications 4.4, 4.6, 4.8 and 4.9.

7. In April 2008 the Home Office issued clarification to police forces on how to record offences of wounding with intent/GBH with intent for those assaults resulting in minor or no injury to a victim, but where the intent was to cause serious injury. This revised technical guidance was issued to ensure that these offences were recorded in a consistent manner by all police forces. The effect of this clarification was that some offences that would previously have been recorded as other types of assault are now recorded as GBH with intent. While the clarification was introduced in 2008/09, PSNI continued to experience the impact of this during 2009/10. The majority of police forces in England and Wales experienced similar increases in these offences as a result of this clarification.

8. The offence of aggravated vehicle taking was introduced in Northern Ireland in 2004.

9. The offence of obstructing police was removed from the notifiable offence list in April 2003.

10. The Sexual Offences (Northern Ireland) Order 2008 was introduced in February 2009 and has altered the definition and coverage of sexual offences.

11. Up to 2003/04 the offence of rape could only be committed against a female. However the Criminal Justice (Northern Ireland) Order 2003 redefined the offence so that buggery without consent would constitute an offence of rape (i.e. rape could then be committed against a male).

12. Offences classified as 17 Indecent assault on a male, 20 Indecent assault on a female, 21 Unlawful sexual intercourse with a girl under 14, 22 Unlawful sexual intercourse with a girl under 17, 74 Gross indecency with a child, 16 Buggery and 18 Gross indecency between males relate to legislation that existed prior to that introduced in February 2009. From April 2010 offences are no longer recorded using these classifications (see 13. below).

13. Under the Home Office Counting Rules, offences which were reported to the police between February 2009 and March 2010 but which were committed prior to February 2009 were recorded under the previous legislation wherever possible. However in April 2010 this guidance was changed so that historic allegations committed under previous legislation should be recorded and detected as if committed today.

14. The classification of 106 Modern Slavery came into effect from April 2015, offences which were previously classified in Sexual offences - 72 Trafficking for sexual exploitation have moved into this category along with offences of Modern Slavery which were previously classified in 99 Other offences.

15. Offences were originally implemented through the Sexual Offences Act 2003.

16. From 1 April 2002, a change in the Home Office Counting Rules meant that most attempted thefts/unauthorised taking of motor vehicles previously recorded in Theft or unauthorised taking of a motor vehicle are now recorded as Vehicle interference.

17. This classification contains explosives and petrol bombing offences for which information prior to 2007/08 is not available to allow classification to dwelling, building other than a dwelling, vehicle or other.

18. Cannabis was classified as a Class B drug until 29 January 2004 when it was reclassified to a Class C drug. Cannabis was then reclassified back to a Class B drug on 26 January 2009. The systems from which the crime figures were extracted did not record the type of Class B or Class C drug until the first cannabis reclassification took place. Therefore it is not possible to provide a complete data series separately identifying cannabis possession offences.

19. These offences were added to the data series in 2005/06.

20. The sub-classification of 'Other' includes offences such as affray, unlawful assembly and offences relating to incitement to hatred.

21. The reclassification exercise conducted during 2010/11 identified that, within Northern Ireland, offences of soliciting for the purposes of prostitution had not been identified as notifiable offences. This omission has been rectified and these offences are included in the recorded crime figures from April 2011.

22. New offences were introduced under the Fraud Act 2006 which came into force in January 2007.

23. These offences were added to the data series from 1 April 2003.

24. While the Offender Management Act offences which are included in the notifiable offence list do not extend to Northern Ireland, offences which do extend to Northern Ireland and are similar in nature are recorded in this classification.

25. These offences were added to the series from 1 April 2002.

26. From April 2014 a change was introduced in the Home Office Counting Rules (HOCR) making it more difficult for crimes of making off without payment (MOWP) to meet the criteria allowing offences to be removed from the crime figures (ie for the crime to be cancelled). This may have contributed to the increase seen in this classification between 2013/14 and 2014/15. Such cancellations occur mainly where police intervention confirms there are no aggravating factors present (eg false registration plate) and there is no intent to avoid payment. PSNI worked with the Petrol Retailer's Association and Retail NI to introduce a pilot scheme (March 2017) where the petrol station deals with non payment of fuel through the Civil Debt Recovery process, allowing police to focus on those who are deliberately seeking to avoid paying for their fuel. Where a petrol station in the pilot area makes a report of MOWP to police this is still recorded as an offence as per HOCR guidance. Once police confirm no aggravating factors exist, there is no additional requirement for police intervention; however the strict cancellation criteria in the HOCR means that it is not possible to cancel such MOWP reports leading to an increase in the number of these offences remaining recorded. This pilot scheme was extended to all policing districts in March 2018. A recent audit of crime recording resulted in clearer guidance and a greater number of reports which may have been recorded as a Making off without Payment offence being recorded by Action Fraud. This has resulted in fewer Making off without Payment offences recorded from October 2020.

27. For offences of Fraud by false representation, counting changed from a per fraudulent transaction to a per account basis from January 2007. From 1 April 2007 these offences were reported to a single point of contact within each police force by financial institutions.

28. Revisions to previously published police recorded crime and outcome figures for 2015/16 to 2018/19: The Home Office introduced a wider outcomes framework for police recorded crime which was adopted within PSNI in April 2015; this approach means that every crime record should eventually be assigned an outcome. In a small number of cases changes to crimes, such as crime cancellation or identification of an outcome, occur after the figures have been published. To take account of such changes, revisions are made to crimes recorded since 2015/16 which have since been cancelled or which have since had a sanction outcome identified. This results in slight changes to the police recorded crime, outcome and outcome rate figures for 2015/16 to 2018/19, when compared with previous publications. Revisions of this nature are routinely applied on an annual basis.

29. Offences relating to Causing Death or Serious Injury by Unlawful Driving were previously included in the Violence with Injury classification, while offences relating to Harassment were previously included in the Violence without Injury classification. These offences are now presented in their own classifications within the Home Office Counting Rules.

30. The overall harassment classification includes malicious communications offences, the recording of which started for the first time in Northern Ireland from 1st April 2017. Also included within malicious communications offences are those relating to 'revenge porn'; new legislation on disclosing private sexual photographs and film with intent to cause distress was introduced in June 2016. A Home Office change introduced in April 2018 requires harassment to be recorded in addition to the most serious additional victim based offence. Both of these changes in recording practice, along with increasing awareness of the application of these rules in the recording process, will have contributed to the increased levels recorded in the overall harassment classification.

31. Much of the increase in classification 88A Sexual Grooming during 2017/18 can be attributed to the activity of Online Child Sexual Abuse Activist Groups (more commonly known as paedophile hunters) who engage by posing as a child under 16. This activity has had an impact on the number of attempted offences recorded within this classification; the increase in attempted sexual grooming and attempted sexual communication with a child accounts for more than two thirds of the overall increase. This did not continue into 2018/19.

32. From 1 April 2017 the classifications within burglary have been changed from domestic burglary and non-domestic burglary to burglary–residential and burglary–business & community. This reflects a revised approach within the Home Office Counting Rules. What constitutes a burglary does not change; however burglary-residential and burglary-business & community represent a new data series. For example sheds, garages, outhouses etc within the boundary of a dwelling are recorded under burglary-residential, while previously they may have been recorded as non-domestic burglary. Where such a building is used solely for business purposes, it will be recorded as burglary-business & community. The individual series for domestic burglary and burglary-residential cannot be added together to create an overall figure. The same applies to non-domestic burglary and burglary-business & community. The full definition for these classifications is provided below.

Burglary Classification Residential: The classification of residential burglary includes all buildings or parts of buildings that are within the boundary of, or form a part of, a dwelling and includes the dwelling itself, vacant dwellings, sheds, garages, outhouses, summer houses and any other structure that meets the definition of a building. It also includes other premises used for residential purposes such as houseboats, residential care homes and hostels. Where an outbuilding **within such a boundary but not forming part of the dwelling building**, such as a garage or workshop is used solely for business purposes this should be recorded as burglary – business and community. Where both a dwelling house and an outbuilding used for business purposes **(belonging to the same victim)** are subject of a burglary at the same time, then only the residential burglary is to be recorded.

Burglary Classification Business & Community: The classification of business and community burglary includes all buildings or parts of buildings that are used **solely and exclusively for business purposes** or are otherwise entirely outside the classification of residential burglary such as a place of worship. Where an outbuilding is **within the boundary of a dwelling, but not forming part of the dwelling building**, such as a garage or workshop and is used solely for business purposes this should be recorded as burglary – business and community. Where both a dwelling house and an outbuilding used for business purposes **(belonging to the same victim)** are subject of a burglary at the same time then only the residential burglary is to be recorded.

33. A new classification came into effect from April 2018 within Violence with injury to reflect assaults on police officers - 8S Assault with injury on a police constable. Previously these offences were classified in 5D Assault with intent to cause serious harm and 8N Assault with injury.

34. Prior to 2018/19 offences of Ill-treatment of patients (The Mental Health (Northern Ireland) Order 1986 were classified to 99 Other offences. In 2018/19 these offences were reclassified to 8N Assault with Injury - AOABH.

35. Homicide figures were revised in 2019/20 to take account of directions from the PPS to prosecute legacy homicides involving the security forces.

36. The offence of sexual communication with a child was introduced under the Justice Act (Northern Ireland) 2015. Similar legislation was introduced in England and Wales in 2017.

37. Offences of shining a laser light, previously classified to 5E Endangering life, were reclassified to 99 Other offenc

38. Offence of Intentionally encouraging or assisting an offender, previously classified to 66 Public Order were reclassified to 99 Other offences.

39. Revisions have been applied to 104 Assault without injury on a constable and 105A Assault without injury, offences were incorrectly classified to 105A Assault without injury for some police officers, these have been reclassified to 104 Assault without injury on a constable

'..' in the table indicates that data are not available.

'-' indicates that for offences recorded, a percentage change is not reported because the base number of offences is less than 50.

21.20 Northern Ireland Prison Receptions by Prisoner Type, Gender and Establishment

		2016/17	2017/18	2018/19	2019/20
Remand	Maghaberry	2,239	2,216	2,560	2,704
	Magilligan	0	19	26	26
	Hydebank Wood College Males	316	305	351	304
	Hydebank Wood College Females	235	246	269	276
	Total	2,790	2,786	3,206	3,310
Immediate Custody	Maghaberry	1,473	1,361	1,373	1,489
	Magilligan	0	7	11	8
	Hydebank Wood College Males	151	134	129	126
	Hydebank Wood College Females	105	117	103	111
	Total	1,729	1,619	1,616	1,734
Fine Default	Maghaberry	547	532	308	181
	Magilligan	0	1	1	2
	Hydebank Wood College Males	38	20	25	18
	Hydebank Wood College Females	68	58	37	21
	Total	653	611	371	222
Non-Criminal	Maghaberry	77	61	47	47
	Magilligan	0	6	5	5
	Hydebank Wood College Males	6	7	5	3
	Hydebank Wood College Females	2	2	2	1
	Total	85	76	59	56
Males		4,847	4,669	4,841	4,913
Females		410	423	411	409
Establishment	Maghaberry	4,336	4,170	4,288	4,421
	Magilligan	0	33	43	41
	Hydebank Wood College Males	511	466	510	451
	Hydebank Wood College Females	410	423	411	409
	Total	**5,257**	**5,092**	**5,252**	**5,322**

Source: The Northern Ireland Prison Population 2019-20

1. Receptions are counted whenever there is a entry into prison and/or a change in a prisoner's custody type from one day to the next.
2. Females includes Transgender persons.

Transport and communications

Chapter 22

Transport and communication

National Travel Survey data (Tables 22.1 , 22.10, 22.11)

The National Travel Survey (NTS) is a household survey of personal travel by residents of England travelling within Great Britain, from data collected via interviews and a one week travel diary. The NTS is part of a continuous survey that began in 1988, following ad-hoc surveys from the 1960s, which enables analysis of patterns and trends.

The NTS is designed to provide a representative sample of households in England and is based on a stratifed, clustered random sample of 12,852 private households. The NTS used to cover all households in Great Britain but since 2013 it has covered England only.

NTS coverage:

Personal travel: The subject of the National Travel Survey is personal travel. This is travel for private purposes or for work or education, provided the main reason for the trip is for the traveller himself or herself to reach the destination.

Geographical coverage: The NTS covers private households within England. Therefore, it excludes people not living in households, such as students in halls of residence and tourists. Since 2013 residents of Scotland and Wales are not sampled. Only travel within Great Britain is included. Trips to other places are included only up to the ticket control point at which the boat, plane or train using the Channel Tunnel, is boarded. Travel by road vehicle away from the public highway is excluded, but travel on public roads in parks and on cycleways is included.

Trips in course of work: Trips made in the course of work are included provided that the purpose of the trip is for the traveller to reach a destination. Travel to deliver goods, or to convey a vehicle or passengers (e.g. as a bus driver or taxi driver), is not covered.

Leisure travel: Travel for a leisure purpose is normally included. However, trips which are themselves a form of recreation are not. Examples are yachting or gliding, which are done for the pleasure of going in a boat or plane rather than to get somewhere.

Trips, stages and distance

Definition of a trip :The basic unit of travel, a trip, is defined as a one-way course of travel with a single main purpose. Outward and return halves of a return trip are treated as two separate trips.

Stages: A trip consists of one or more stages. A new stage is defined when there is a change in the form of transport or when there is a change of vehicle requiring a separate ticket.

Distance travelled: The length of any trip stage is the distance actually covered, as reported by the traveller, and not the distance 'as the crow fies'.

For more details on the NTS see: https://www.gov.uk/government/statistics/national-travel-survey-2020

Domestic Freight by mode of travel (Table 22.2)

In this table freight activity is measured in terms of the weight of goods (tonnes) carried taking no account of the distance they are carried (termed 'goods lifted'), and as 'goods moved' (tonne kilometres) which does take into account distance. 'Goods moved' for each loaded journey is the weight of the load multiplied by the distance it is carried, and therefore a better measure of the activity done by heavy goods vehicles.

Figures for rail are for each financial year. Data for goods moved and goods lifted come from diferent sources and caution should be exercised if making comparisons between the two series.

These freight statistics are part of the Transport Statistics Great Britain (TSGB) compendium published each year by the Department for Transport (DfT). For more information see: https://www.gov.uk/government/collections/transport-statistics-great-britain

Passenger transport - modal comparisons (Table 22.3)

These statistics (modal comparisons - TSGB01) are part of the Transport Statistics Great Britain (TSGB) compendium published each year by the DfT.

Buses and coaches: From 2004, data is based on the average distance travelled by bus and coach per person per year from the National Travel Survey (NTS), using population estimates from the Office for National Statistics (ONS) to gross up to total passenger kilometres. Bus and coach covers the London bus, other local bus, nin-local bus and private hire bus categories recorded in the NTS.

Cars, vans, taxis and motorcycles: Estimates for cars (which include taxis) and motorcycles (which include mopeds and scooters) are derived from the traffic series TRA0101 (vehicle miles) and average occupancy rates (persons per vehicle) from the NTS.

Rail: Figures include National Rail, London Underground, Glasgow Underground, public metro and light rail systems.

Air: Figures are revenue passenger kilometres on schedules and non-schedules domestic services on UK airlines only. Further details are available in the Notes on table AVI0201.

All modes: Figures excludes travel by water.

Road data (Tables 22.4 - 22.6)

Urban roads are defined as major and minor roads within an urban area with a population of 10,000 or more. These are based on the 2011 Census definition of urban settlements from 2017 onwards. Prior to 2017, the 2001 urban settlement definition was used. In 2017 a set of methodological changes were made that will affect comparability of road length compared to previous years. These figures are part of the road traffic statistics published annually by the DfT.

Annual estimates are currently based on around 8,000 manual counts, where trained enumerators count traffic by vehicle type over a 12 hour period. This data is combined with Automatic Traffic Counter (ATC) data and road lengths statistics to produce the number of vehicle miles travelled each year by vehicle type, road category, and region.

For major roads (motorways and 'A' roads) a rolling-Census approach is taken to manual counts, and the large number of counts enable detailed road-level traffic estimates to be produced for these road types. For minor roads ('B', 'C', and unclassified roads) a panel sample approach is taken, whereby the same roads across Great Britain are counted each year (over 4,000 locations). This enables robust national level minor road traffic estimates to be produced.

For more information on road traffic statistics see: https://www.gov.uk/guidance/road-traffic-statistics-information

Cars licensed by propulsion / fuel type (Table 22.7)

This data is part of Vehicle licensing statistics produced by the DfT and are sources from extracts of the Driver and Vehicle Licensing Agency (DVLA) vehicle database. The most common fuel types used to propel vehicles are petrol and diesel, sometimes referred to as Internal Combustion Engine (ICE) vehicles. Since about 2014, several alternatives have been growing in popularity. The term "electric vehicle" is vague and can relate to different groupings of fuel types depending on the context, but most commonly refers to just battery electric vehicles.

Main fuel types:

Petrol: Propelled by an ICE using petrol. Can include mild hybrids.

Diesel: Propelled by an ICE using diesel. Can include mild hybrids.

Hybrid electric: Propelled by an ICE or an electric motor. The battery is charged when the fuel is used to propel the vehicle. Can include mild hybrids.

Plug-in hybrid electric: Propelled by an ICE or an electric motor. The battery is charged when the fuel is used or by connecting to a mains electricity supply.

Range extended electric: Propelled by an electric motor. The battery is charged when the fuel is used or by connecting to a mains electricity supply.

Battery electric: Propelled by an electric motor only. The battery is charged by connecting to a mains electricity supply.

Fuel cell electric: Propelled by an electric motor. The battery is charged using a fuel cell. Fuel cells typically generate electricity using oxygen from the air and compressed hydrogen.

New vehicle registrations by tax class (Table 22.8)

This data is part of Vehicle licensing statistics produced by the DfT and are sources from extracts of the Driver and Vehicle Licensing Agency (DVLA) vehicle database. All vehicles registered by DVLA are allocated a tax class, reflecting the way in which the vehicle is used and, in some cases, by whom it is used. It does not always reflect the physical construction of the vehicle. In some cases, the precise tax class depends upon certain vehicle characteristics such as engine size, propulsion type, emission rates, gross weight, number of axles or, in the case of public transport vehicles, and the number of seats.

Key tax class groupings:

Private and light goods (PLG): This is the most common tax class group, covering approximately 90% of licensed vehicles. This primarily consists of cars and light goods vehicles but can include other vehicles used only for private purposes. This used to be a singular tax class, but is now made up of several classes, based on various characteristics such as engine size and CO2 emissions.

Motorcycles, scooters and mopeds:The standard tax class for motorcycles, scooters and mopeds; based on engine size. This excludes tricycles which are in "Other vehicles".

Goods vehicles: Vehicles with a gross weight over 3.5 tonnes that are used for carrying goods. The rate of Vehicle Excise Duty (VED) depends on the maximum gross weight and the axle configuration of the vehicle.

Buses: This group covers buses and coaches with more than eight seats (excluding the driver) used for commercial purposes. Vehicles not used for commercial purposes would be licensed in the PLG tax class. The rate of VED is dependent upon the number of seats in the vehicle.

Crown and Exempt: This group includes vehicles which are exempt from VED. This can be for a variety of reasons, including vehicles driven by disabled drivers, emergency and crown vehicles and historic vehicles.
Special Machines became part of the 'Crown and Exempt' taxation class with effect from January 2002.

Other vehicles: All tax classes not covered in other groups. This includes agricultural vehicles, recovery vehicles, general haulage vehicles, small island vehicles and tricycles.

Driver and rider testing statistics (Table 22.9)

This table provides statistics on the number of driving tests taken in Great Britain and their pass rates for cars, motorcycles, LGVs and PCVs. These figures are published by Department for Transport (DfT) and Driver and Vehicle Standards Agency (DVSA). The majority of practical test statistics are derived from two main sources, the Testing and Registration System (TARS) and the Road Safety Information System (RSIS). TARS is the core system for administering the booking and delivery of practical driving tests, the register of approved driving instructors (ADIs) and the register of driver trainers. The RSIS database holds a record of the data captured for each practical driving test by driving examiners using the driving test report form. Theory test data are held by the theory test provider. The information supplied to DVSA is an aggregation of individual driving test records collected on the theory test provider's database.

Households with regular use of cars (Table 22.11)

The mid-year estimates of the percentage of households with regular use of a car or van are based on data from the National Travel Survey. The method for calculating these figures was changed slightly in 2006, to incorporate weighted data from the NTS and the GHS. Figures since have also been revised to incorporate weighted data. Results by area type are based on weighted data from the NTS only.

Domestic road freight activity (Tables 22.17-18)

These figures are mainly derived from the Continuing Survey of Road Goods Transport Great Britain (CSRGT GB). This survey provides information on the domestic activity of GB-registered heavy goods vehicles over 3.5 tonnes gross vehicle weight (HGVs) working in the UK.

The activity of Northern Ireland-registered HGVs, foreign-registered HGVs and freight carrying vehicles 3.5 tonnes gross vehicle weight or less (Light Goods Vehicles) are not captured by this survey.

Goods lifted: The quantity derived by adding together the weight of all the loads carried. Measured in tonnes.

Goods moved: A measure of freight moved which takes account of the weight of the load and the distance through which it is hauled. Measured in tonne kilometres. For example, a load of 26 tonnes carried a distance of 100 kilometres represents 2,600 tonne kilometres

Commodity groupings: The standard goods classification for transport statistics, Nomenclature Statistique de Transport - abbreviated as NST (2007), is a statistical nomenclature for the goods transported by four modes of transport: road, rail, inland waterways and sea (maritime). NST 2007 considers the economic activity from which the goods originate. For further information and a breakdown of first level classifications see: http://ec.europa.eu/eurostat/statistics-explained/index.php/Glossary:NST_2007

Railways - Passenger journeys and revenue (Tables 20.19)

Annual passenger rail usage statistics are published by the Office of Rail and Road (ORR). The data presented in this release are for mainline operators in Great Britain. The data do not include Eurostar, London Underground, light rail, heritage and charter services.

Most of the data is sourced from the rail industry's LENNON (Latest Earnings Networked Nationally Over Night) ticketing and revenue system. LENNON holds information on the vast majority of national rail tickets purchased in Great Britain and is used to allocate the revenue from ticket sales between train operating companies (TOCs). LENNON contains two datasets: pre-allocation (sales) and post-allocation (earnings). Passenger usage statistics are based on the post-allocation dataset so that kilometres, journeys and revenue data can be assigned to TOCs.

Passenger journeys are estimated using ticket sales data. For the purpose of these statistics, where travel requires one or more changes of train, each train used is counted as one journey. For example, a journey from Leicester to Manchester would be classed as two journeys due to the need to change trains. This differs from the definition used in the Regional rail usage statistical release, which would class this example as one journey.

Passenger kilometres are calculated by multiplying the number of passenger journeys on a particular flow by the number of corresponding track kilometres between stations.

Passenger revenue statistics include all ticket revenue and miscellaneous charges associated with passenger travel on national railways.

Passenger train kilometres refers to the number of train kilometres (million) travelled by passenger trains.

Figures on railway infrastructure, revenue and urban systems (Glasgow and London undergrounds) are sourced from light rail & tram statistics published by the DfT. This data is compiled from responses to the Light Rail and Tram Survey, which collects information on light rail and tram system use, infrastructure and revenue. For more details see: https://www.gov.uk/government/collections/light-rail-and-tram-statistics

Northern Ireland - rail service assets and passengers (Table 22.21 - 22)

These figures are sourced from NI Transport Statistics report which is produced by the Analysis, Statistics and Research Branch (ASRB) of the Department for Infrastructure (DfI)

Aviation statistics (Tables 22.23 - 22.26)

These aviation statistics provide information on activity at UK airports, passengers, volume of freight handled,UK airlines, major international airports and airlines. Most of these statistics are collected by the Civil Aviation Authority (CAA). For more information and statistics published by CAA see: www.caa.co.uk.

Air transport movements: All scheduled movements (whether loaded or empty) and loaded charter movements. Empty positioning flights by scheduled aircraft and empty charter movements are excluded.

International services: These services are flown between the United Kingdom, Isle of Man and Channel Islands and airports in other countries.

Scheduled services: Those performed according to a published timetable, including those supplementary thereto, available for use by members of the public.

Non-scheduled services: Air transport movements other than scheduled services.

Terminal passengers: All revenue and non-revenue passengers joining or leaving an aircraft at a United Kingdom airport (a passenger who changes from one aircraft to another, carrying the same flight number, is counted as a terminal passenger both on arrival and departure). Transit passengers who arrive and depart on the same aircraft are not included.

Freight: All other property carried on an aircraft excluding mail and passengers' and crews' permitted baggage. Thus excess baggage is included, as are diplomatic bags. Freight in transit through an airport on the same aircraft is excluded

Cargo (freight and mail) uplifted are calculated by counting each tonne of revenue cargo or mail on a particular journey once only and not repeatedly on each individual stage of the flight. Cargo tonne kilometres are calculated by multiplying the number of tonnes of revenue load on each stage flight by the stage distance.

Search and rescue helicopter statistics (Table 22.27)

Tables 22.27a,b and c provide statistics on civilian search and rescue helicopter (SARH) taskings for the UK, with breakdowns by tasking type, location type (land, maritime or coast) and helicopter base. The data are derived from information recorded by the Aeronautical Rescue Coordination Centre (ARCC), who are responsible for the coordination of search and rescue helicopters. For more information see: https://www.gov.uk/government/collections/search-and-rescue-helicopter-statistics

22.1 Average number of trips (trip rates) by purpose and main mode: England, 2019

Trips per person per year

Purpose	Walk[1,4]	Bicycle	Car / van driver	Car / van passenger	Motorcycle	Other private transport[2]	Bus in London	Other local bus	Non-local bus	London Under-ground	Surface rail	Taxi / minicab	Other public transport[3]	All modes
Commuting	17	5	75	10	1	1	5	6	-	7	10	1	1	140
Business	2	-	18	2	-	-	1	-	-	1	2	-	-	28
Education / escort education	52	2	27	29	0	2	3	7	-	1	1	1	-	125
Shopping	46	2	83	34	-	1	3	7	0	-	1	1	-	181
Other escort	12	-	45	23	0	-	1	1	0	-	-	-	-	83
Personal business	20	1	38	20	-	1	2	3	-	1	1	1	-	88
Leisure[5]	40	5	93	81	1	2	4	6	-	2	6	6	1	247
Other including just walk	61	0	-	-	-	0	0	-	0	0	0	0	0	61
All purposes	250	16	380	200	2	7	18	32	-	12	21	11	3	953
Unweighted sample size: trips ('000s)	66	4	101	53	1	2	4	8	-	2	5	3	1	250

1 There is an apparent under-recording of short walks in 2002 and 2003 and short trips in 2007 and 2008 compared to other years.
2 Mostly private hire bus (including school buses).
3 Air, ferries and light rail.
4 Walk includes all travel on foot. It is also used when respondents ride in non-motorised wheelchairs, prams or pushchairs, as well as when they ride on toy bicycles, roller-skates, skateboards, non-motorised scooters, or when they jog. For example, children who accompany their parents on a visit to the shops on toy bicycles/tricycles (where the parents are walking) are coded as having walked there.
5 Visit friends at home and elsewhere, entertainment, sport, holiday and day trip.
The figures in this table are National Statistics

Source: National Travel Survey
Email: national.travelsurvey@dft.gov.uk

22.2 Domestic freight transport by mode: 2011 to 2019

	2011[R]	2012[R]	2013[R]	2014[R]	2015[R]	2016[R]	2017[R]	2018[R]	2019[R]
(a) Goods moved								Billion tonne kilometres/*percentage*	
Coke and refined petroleum products									
Road [1]	5.5	6.4	5.0	5.1	5.6	4.4	4.2	4.1	3.4
Rail [2,3]	1.3	0.9	0.0	0.0	1.0	0.7	0.6	0.5	0.6
Water	5.4	4.6	5.0	4.1	4.5	4.2	5.4	4.7	4.3
ow: coastwise	4.7	3.9	4.3	3.5	4.1	3.3	4.2	3.5	3.0
All modes	**12.2**	**11.8**	**10.0**	**9.2**	**11.1**	**9.3**	**10.1**	**9.3**	**8.3**
Coal and lignite									
Road [1]	0.7	1.0	0.8	1.0	0.8	0.5	0.7	0.5	0.4
Rail [2,3]	6.4	7.6	9.0	8.5	3.8	2.0	1.8	2.0	1.2
Water	24.5	17.8	11.6	8.7	12.5	12.5	5.3	5.7	5.7
ow: coastwise	18.2	11.9	7.8	6.9	11.1	9.4	2.5	2.0	3.1
All modes	**31.6**	**26.4**	**21.3**	**18.2**	**17.1**	**14.9**	**7.8**	**8.2**	**7.3**
Other freight									
Road [1]	134.1	135.3	125.7	121.8	136.9	143.6	142.2	147.6	150.0
Rail [2,3]	13.4	13.0	13.4	13.7	14.6	14.4	14.8	14.7	15.1
Water	13.1	13.1	12.5	14.2	14.4	13.7	14.2	13.8	14.0
All modes	**160.5**	**161.4**	**151.7**	**149.6**	**165.9**	**171.7**	**171.2**	**176.1**	**179.2**
All traffic									
Road [1]	140.4	142.6	131.5	127.9	143.3	148.5	147.0	152.2	153.8
Rail [2,3]	21.0	21.4	22.4	22.1	19.3	17.1	17.2	17.2	16.9
Water	43.0	35.5	29.1	27.0	31.4	30.4	24.9	24.2	25.2
All modes	**204.3**	**199.6**	**183.0**	**177.0**	**194.1**	**195.9**	**189.1**	**193.6**	**195.8**
Percentage of all traffic									
Road [1]	*69*	*71*	*72*	*72*	*74*	*76*	*78*	*79*	*79*
Rail [2,3]	*10*	*11*	*12*	*13*	*10*	*9*	*9*	*9*	*9*
Water	*21*	*18*	*16*	*15*	*16*	*16*	*13*	*13*	*13*
All modes	***100***	***100***	***100***	***100***	***100***	***100***	***100***	***100***	***101***
(b) Goods lifted									
Coke and refined petroleum products									
Road [1]	64	71	53	52	63	48	43	39	36
Rail [2,3]	5	7	0	0	4	4	3	3	3
Water	20	20	21	23	26	27	26	25	24
ow: coastwise	9	8	9	8	10	8	9	8	6
All modes	**89**	**98**	**74**	**75**	**93**	**78**	**73**	**68**	**63**
Coal and lignite									
Road [1]	9	10	7	12	9	3	7	3	2
Rail [2,3]	42	48	53	42	25	11	8	7	4
Water	27	22	15	13	17	16	10	10	10
ow: coastwise	20	16	11	11	15	12	6	6	8
All modes	**78**	**80**	**75**	**67**	**51**	**30**	**24**	**20**	**16**
Other freight									
Road [1]	1,384	1,346	1,256	1,257	1,373	1,382	1,347	1,363	1,402
Rail [2,3]	53	60	64	66	68	64	65	65	64
Water	57	54	55	59	55	60	61	62	58
All modes	**1,493**	**1,460**	**1,375**	**1,383**	**1,496**	**1,506**	**1,473**	**1,490**	**1,524**
All traffic									
Road [1]	1,457	1,427	1,316	1,322	1,445	1,434	1,397	1,405	1,440
Rail [2,3]	100	115	118	109	97	79	76	75	71
Water	104	96	91	95	98	102	97	98	97
All modes	**1,661**	**1,638**	**1,525**	**1,525**	**1,640**	**1,614**	**1,570**	**1,578**	**1,608**
Percentage of all traffic									
Road [1]	*88*	*87*	*86*	*87*	*88*	*89*	*89*	*89*	*90*
Rail [2]	*6*	*7*	*8*	*7*	*6*	*5*	*5*	*5*	*4*
Water [3]	*6*	*6*	*6*	*6*	*6*	*6*	*6*	*6*	*6*
All modes	***100***	***100***	***100***	***100***	***100***	***100***	***100***	***100***	***100***

1. Statistics for heavy goods vehicles only, those over 3.5 tonnes gross vehicle weight.
2. Rail data are not directly comparable with other rail figures such as in TSGB0401.
3. Rail and water data is for the United Kingdom which includes freight in both Great Britain and Northern Ireland.
R: The goods moved figures for rail and water in 2015 have been revised the table's publication in December 2016.
R: Road freight figures from 2011 onwards have been revised following a review of part of the methodology used to produce these estimates.

Sources: Road and Water - DfT
Rail - ORR/Eurostat
Last updated: December 2020
Next update: December 2021
Road: 020 7944 3095
Rail: 020 7944 2419
Water: 020 7944 4847

22.3 Passenger transport: by mode, annual from 2002

Billion passenger kilometres/*percentage*

Year	Buses and coaches	%	Cars, vans & taxis	%	Motor cycles	%	Pedal cycles	%	All Road	%	Rail[1]	%	Air (UK)[2]	%	All modes [3]	%
2002	47	6	673	86	5	1	4	1	729	93	48	6	8	1.1	786	100
2003	47	6	667	85	6	1	4	1	725	93	49	6	9	1.2	783	100
2004	41	5	672	86	5	1	4	1	723	92	50	6	10	1.2	783	100
2005	42	5	667	85	6	1	4	1	719	92	51	7	10	1.3	780	100
2006	40	5	672	85	5	1	5	1	723	92	54	7	10	1.3	787	100
2007	41	5	673	85	6	1	4	1	724	92	57	7	10	1.2	791	100
2008	43	5	667	84	5	1	5	1	720	91	60	8	9	1.1	789	100
2009	44	6	662	84	5	1	5	1	716	91	60	8	8	1.1	785	100
2010	45	6	651	84	5	1	5	1	705 r	91	63	8	8	1.0	776	100
2011	43	5	654	84	5	1	5	1	706 r	90	66	8	8	1.1	781	100
2012	42	5	661	84	5	1	5	1	713 r	90	69	9	8	1.0	791	100
2013	40	5	659	84	5	1	5	1	709 r	90	71	9	8	1.1	789	100
2014	40	5	677	84	5	1	6	1	727 r	90	74	9	8	1.1	809	100
2015	39	5	682	84	5	1	5	1	732 r	90	76	9	9	1.1	816	100
2016	34	4	697	84	5	1	5	1	742 r	90	78	9	8	1.0	828	100
2017	38	4	707	84	5	1	5	1	756 r	90	79	9	9	1.1	845	100
2018	35	4	721	84	5	1	5	1	767 r	89	81	9	9	1.1	858	100
2019	33	4	738	84	5	1	6	1	781 r	89	83	9	9	1.1	873	100

Sources: Road - DfT Traffic Estimates, National Travel Survey; Rail - ORR; Air - CAA

1. Financial years. National Rail (franchised operators only to 2008, franchised and non-franchised operators from 2009), urban metros and modern trams.

2. UK airlines, domestic passenger services on scheduled and non-scheduled flights.

3. Excluding travel by water.

r. Road estimates for the period 2010-2018 have been revised to take into account the minor road benchmarking exercise. Further details available at:
https://www.gov.uk/government/publications/road-traffic-statistics-minor-road-benchmarking

See Notes and Definitions for details of discontinuity in road passengers figures from 1993 and 1996 onwards.

Notes & definitions:
https://www.gov.uk/government/publications/road-traffic-statistics-guidance

Telephone:
Road: 020 7944 3097
Rail: 020 7944 2419
Air: 020 7944 2168

Email: publicationgeneral.enq@dft.gov.uk

The Air and London Underground figures in this table are outside the scope of National Statistics.

22.4 Motor vehicle traffic (vehicle kilometres) by road class in Great Britain, annual from 2002

Billion vehicle kilometres

	Major roads					Minor roads			
		'A' roads							
	Motorway [1]	Rural	Urban [2]	All 'A' roads	All major roads	Rural	Urban [2]	All minor roads	All roads
2002	92.6	136.4	82.2	218.6	311.2	63.9	108.6	172.5	**483.7**
2003	93.0	139.3	81.8	221.0	314.0	63.6	109.0	172.6	**486.7**
2004	96.6	141.3	82.8	224.1	320.7	64.9	108.3	173.3	**493.9**
2005	97.0	141.4	81.8	223.1	320.2	65.6	108.1	173.7	**493.9**
2006	99.5	143.6	82.5	226.1	325.5	67.9	107.6	175.5	**501.1**
2007	100.6	143.5	81.3	224.9	325.4	70.3	109.7	180.0	**505.4**
2008	100.1	142.8	80.1	222.8	323.0	70.3	107.3	177.6	**500.6**
2009	99.5	142.0	80.4	222.4	321.9	68.3	105.7	174.0	**495.8**
2010 [3]	98.2	139.8	79.7	219.5	317.7	69.4	104.9	174.4	**492.1**
2011 [3]	99.5	141.2	79.3	220.4	319.9	68.5	107.7	176.1	**496.1**
2012 [3]	100.4	140.4	78.1	218.5	319.0	67.7	110.7	178.4	**497.3**
2013 [3]	101.9	140.5	78.1	218.6	320.5	70.2	111.2	181.5	**502.0**
2014 [3]	104.3	143.5	79.4	222.9	327.2	75.2	116.1	191.4	**518.5**
2015 [3]	107.0	147.0	79.9	226.9	333.9	77.8	118.6	196.5	**530.4**
2016 [3]	108.9	152.1	81.1	233.1	342.1	81.7	120.5	202.2	**544.3**
2017 [2 3]	110.5	158.0	77.7	235.7	346.2	81.4	127.9	209.3	**555.5**
2018 [3]	111.1	160.3	78.8	239.1	350.2	82.6	129.8	212.3	**562.5**
2019	113.5	162.5	79.2	241.7	355.2	84.7	133.9	218.6	**573.8**

1 Includes trunk motorways and principal motorways
2 Urban roads: Major and minor roads within an urban area with a population
of 10,000 or more. These are based on the 2011 Census definition of urban
settlements from 2017 onwards. Prior to 2017, the 2001 urban settlement definition
was used. Further information can be found on the Notes & definitions web page (see link below)
3 Estimates for the period since 2010 have been revised to take into account the
minor road benchmarking exercise. Further details available at:
https://www.gov.uk/government/publications/road-traffic-statistics-minor-road-benchmarking

Source: DfT National Road Traffic Survey
Telephone: 020 7944 3095
Email: roadtraff.stats@dft.gov.uk

Notes & definitions:
https://www.gov.uk/government/publications/road-traffic-statistics-guidance
The figures in this table are National Statistics.

22.5 Road lengths (kilometres) by road type in Great Britain, 2001 - 2019

Kilometres

Year	Motorways			'A' roads			All major roads	Minor roads				All minor roads	All roads
	Trunk	Prin-cipal	Total	Trunk	Principal	Total		'B' road	C' road	U' road	C' and 'U' roads		
2001 [1]	3,431	45	3,476	11,369	35,285	46,654	50,130	30,196	84,742	225,901	310,643	340,838	390,969
2002	3,433	45	3,478	10,679	35,995	46,674	50,152	30,192	84,858	226,462	311,320	341,512	391,664
2003	3,432	46	3,478	9,615	37,038	46,653	50,131	30,188	84,976	227,048	312,024	342,212	392,343
2004 [2]	3,478	46	3,523	9,147	37,521	46,669	50,192	30,178	84,223	223,082	307,304	337,482	387,674
2005	3,471	48	3,518	8,708	38,019	46,727	50,246	30,189	84,459	223,183	307,642	337,830	388,076
2006 [2]	3,508	48	3,555	8,706	38,030	46,735	50,291	30,018	84,469	229,605	314,074	344,092	394,383
2007	3,518	41	3,559	8,670	38,073	46,743	50,302	30,265	84,423	229,889	314,312	344,577	394,879
2008	3,518	41	3,559	8,634	38,057	46,691	50,249	30,161	84,574	229,482	314,056	344,217	394,467
2009	3,519	41	3,560	8,596	38,173	46,770	50,329	30,141	84,813	229,145	313,958	344,099	394,428
2010	3,517	41	3,558	8,489	38,218	46,707	50,265	30,192	84,827	228,970	313,797	343,989	394,253
2011	3,529	41	3,570	8,508	38,225	46,734	50,304	30,208	84,831	228,953	313,784	343,992	394,296
2012	3,576	41	3,617	8,507	38,235	46,742	50,359	30,214	84,903	229,414	314,317	344,531	394,890
2013 [3]	3,600	41	3,641	8,505	38,245	46,749	50,391	30,217	:	:	314,853	345,070	395,461
2014 [3]	3,603	41	3,645	8,485	38,301	46,785	50,430	30,207	:	:	314,983	345,190	395,620
2015	3,612	41	3,654	8,478	38,298	46,776	50,430	30,286	84,362	230,626	314,988	345,274	395,703
2016 [3]	3,608	41	3,649	8,465	38,351	46,815	50,465	30,295	:	:	315,959	346,254	396,719
2017 [4]	3,644	44	3,688	8,481	38,416	46,896	50,584	30,324	:	:	316,131	346,455	397,039
2018	3,679	44	3,723	8,672	38,708	47,380	51,103	30,314	85,926	229,678	315,604	345,918	397,021
2019 [3]	3,694	48	3,742	8,700	38,749	47,450	51,191	30,323	:	:	316,082	346,404	397,596

Source: Department for Transport
Telephone: 020 7944 5032
Email: road.length@dft.gov.uk

Values may not sum to totals due to rounding

1. Figures for trunk and principal 'A' roads in England from 2001 onwards are affected by the detrunking programme.
2. New information from 2004 and from 2006 enabled better estimates of road lengths to be made - see Notes and definitions.
3. Minor roads figures in 2013, 2014 and 2016 have been derived differently, with 'C' and 'U' roads combined, as no R199b road length consultation with local authorities took place. See methodology note for further detail.
4. In 2017 a set of methodological changes were made that will affect comparability of road length compared to previous years.

Symbols
: Value not available
. Not applicable
The figures in this table are National Statistics

22.6 Road traffic (vehicle kilometres) by vehicle type in Great Britain, annual from 2002

Billion vehicle kilometres

	Cars and taxis	Light Commercial Vehicles [1]	Heavy Goods Vehicles [2]	Other Vehicles			All motor vehicles
				Motorcycles	Buses & Coaches	Total [3]	
2002	390.6	54.7	28.3	5.0	5.2	10.2	483.7
2003	390.0	57.4	28.4	5.6	5.3	10.9	486.7
2004	394.2	60.2	29.3	5.1	5.1	10.2	493.9
2005	392.7	61.8	28.9	5.3	5.1	10.4	493.9
2006	397.4	64.3	29.0	5.1	5.3	10.4	501.1
2007	397.9	67.4	29.3	5.5	5.4	10.9	505.4
2008	395.0	66.9	28.6	5.0	5.0	10.1	500.6
2009	394.0	65.5	26.2	5.1	5.0	10.1	495.8
2010 [5]	389.2	66.7	26.4	4.7	5.1	9.8	492.1
2011 [5]	393.2	67.6	25.7	4.7	4.7	9.5	496.1
2012 [5]	395.1	67.9	25.1	4.7	4.5	9.2	497.3
2013 [5]	396.9	70.5	25.4	4.5	4.7	9.2	502.0
2014 [5]	408.0	75.0	26.1	4.7	4.7	9.4	518.5
2015 [5]	415.4	78.7	27.1	4.7	4.5	9.2	530.4
2016 [5]	424.7	83.1	27.4	4.8	4.2	9.0	544.3
2017 [5]	432.9	86.0	27.7	4.8	4.1	8.9	555.5
2018 [5]	438.3	87.6	27.9	4.8	4.0	8.8	562.5
2019	447.8	89.4	28.0	4.8	3.9	8.7	573.8

1 Not exceeding 3,500 kgs gross vehicle weight, post 1982

2 Over 3,500 kgs gross vehicle weight, post 1982

3 Total of all other vehicles (i.e. motorcycles, buses, and coaches)

4 Data for 1993 onwards are not directly comparable with the figures for 1992 and earlier

5 Estimates for the period since 2010 have been revised to take into account the minor road benchmarking exercise. Further details available at:

https://www.gov.uk/government/publications/road-traffic-statistics-minor-road-benchmarking

Notes & definitions:

https://www.gov.uk/government/publications/road-traffic-statistics-guidance

The figures in this table are National Statistics.

Source: DfT National Road Traffic Survey

Telephone: 020 7944 3095

Email: roadtraff.stats@dft.gov.uk

22.7 Cars licensed by propulsion / fuel type, Great Britain from 1994 to 2019

As at end of year

Thousand / *Percentage*

Year	Petrol	Diesel	Hybrid Electric [1]	Plug-in Hybrid Electric [2]	Battery Electric	Range-Extended Electric [3]	Fuel Cell Electric [4]	Gas [5]	Other [6]	Total	Alternative Fuels [7]	Zero Emission [8]
Thousands												
1994	19,620.9	1,576.2	0.0	0.0	0.1	0.0	0.0	1.8	0.2	21,199.2	2.1	0.1
1995	19,499.8	1,891.3	0.0	0.0	0.1	0.0	0.0	2.9	0.1	21,394.1	3.1	0.1
1996	20,051.6	2,181.6	0.0	0.0	0.1	0.0	0.0	4.1	0.1	22,237.5	4.3	0.1
1997	20,384.7	2,440.5	0.0	0.0	0.1	0.0	0.0	6.2	0.1	22,831.7	6.5	0.1
1998	20,590.5	2,692.9	0.0	0.0	0.2	0.0	0.0	9.6	0.1	23,293.3	9.9	0.2
1999	21,031.0	2,929.9	0.0	0.0	0.2	0.0	0.0	13.8	0.1	23,974.9	14.1	0.2
2000	21,232.4	3,152.7	0.2	0.0	0.2	0.0	0.0	20.0	-	24,405.5	20.4	0.2
2001	21,640.8	3,459.5	0.8	0.0	0.3	0.0	0.0	24.4	0.1	25,125.9	25.5	0.3
2002	21,839.2	3,912.4	1.1	0.0	0.3	0.0	-	28.8	0.1	25,781.9	30.3	0.3
2003	21,805.2	4,399.6	1.5	0.0	0.4	0.0	-	33.6	0.1	26,240.4	35.6	0.4
2004	21,976.4	5,010.6	3.0	0.0	0.4	0.0	-	37.6	0.1	27,028.1	41.2	0.4
2005	21,875.7	5,596.1	8.3	0.0	0.6	0.0	-	39.5	0.1	27,520.4	48.6	0.6
2006	21,465.5	6,083.3	16.9	0.0	0.8	0.0	-	42.4	0.2	27,609.2	60.3	0.8
2007	21,264.2	6,657.4	32.1	0.0	1.2	0.0	-	45.1	0.3	28,000.3	78.7	1.2
2008	20,898.8	7,163.5	47.0	0.0	1.3	0.0	-	49.6	0.4	28,160.7	98.4	1.4
2009	20,490.9	7,641.4	61.3	0.0	1.5	0.0	-	50.9	0.4	28,246.5	114.1	1.5
2010	20,082.8	8,202.7	82.1	0.3	1.6	0.0	-	51.0	0.5	28,420.9	135.3	1.6
2011	19,548.2	8,763.5	102.0	0.5	2.6	-	-	49.9	0.4	28,467.3	155.6	2.6
2012	19,158.6	9,385.1	124.0	1.1	4.1	0.5	-	48.7	0.4	28,722.5	178.7	4.1
2013	18,870.1	10,064.2	151.3	1.7	6.2	0.9	-	46.3	0.4	29,140.9	206.7	6.2
2014	18,632.4	10,730.9	182.4	7.9	12.1	2.2	-	43.2	0.4	29,611.5	248.2	12.1
2015	18,511.5	11,428.9	221.8	23.8	20.5	3.8	-	39.7	0.4	30,250.3	310.0	20.5
2016	18,410.2	12,052.1	268.5	49.1	29.1	5.5	-	35.4	0.4	30,850.4	388.1	29.1
2017	18,348.1	12,360.2	332.7	78.5	41.2	7.7	0.1	31.3	0.4	31,200.2	491.9	41.3
2018	18,499.6	12,397.6	411.7	115.5	55.3	9.5	0.1	27.8	0.3	31,517.6	620.3	55.4
2019	18,821.9	12,286.3	510.3	144.8	89.6	9.8	0.2	25.3	0.3	31,888.4	780.2	89.8
Percentage												
1994	*92.6*	*7.4*	*0.0*	*0.0*	*-*	*0.0*	*0.0*	*-*	*-*	*100.0*	*-*	*-*
1995	*91.1*	*8.8*	*0.0*	*0.0*	*-*	*0.0*	*0.0*	*-*	*-*	*100.0*	*-*	*-*
1996	*90.2*	*9.8*	*0.0*	*0.0*	*-*	*0.0*	*0.0*	*-*	*-*	*100.0*	*-*	*-*
1997	*89.3*	*10.7*	*0.0*	*0.0*	*-*	*0.0*	*0.0*	*-*	*-*	*100.0*	*-*	*-*
1998	*88.4*	*11.6*	*0.0*	*0.0*	*-*	*0.0*	*0.0*	*-*	*-*	*100.0*	*-*	*-*
1999	*87.7*	*12.2*	*0.0*	*0.0*	*-*	*0.0*	*0.0*	*0.1*	*-*	*100.0*	*0.1*	*-*
2000	*87.0*	*12.9*	*-*	*0.0*	*-*	*0.0*	*0.0*	*0.1*	*-*	*100.0*	*0.1*	*-*
2001	*86.1*	*13.8*	*-*	*0.0*	*-*	*0.0*	*0.0*	*0.1*	*-*	*100.0*	*0.1*	*-*
2002	*84.7*	*15.2*	*-*	*0.0*	*-*	*0.0*	*-*	*0.1*	*-*	*100.0*	*0.1*	*-*
2003	*83.1*	*16.8*	*-*	*0.0*	*-*	*0.0*	*-*	*0.1*	*-*	*100.0*	*0.1*	*-*
2004	*81.3*	*18.5*	*-*	*0.0*	*-*	*0.0*	*-*	*0.1*	*-*	*100.0*	*0.2*	*-*
2005	*79.5*	*20.3*	*-*	*0.0*	*-*	*0.0*	*-*	*0.1*	*-*	*100.0*	*0.2*	*-*
2006	*77.7*	*22.0*	*0.1*	*0.0*	*-*	*0.0*	*-*	*0.2*	*-*	*100.0*	*0.2*	*-*
2007	*75.9*	*23.8*	*0.1*	*0.0*	*-*	*0.0*	*-*	*0.2*	*-*	*100.0*	*0.3*	*-*
2008	*74.2*	*25.4*	*0.2*	*0.0*	*-*	*0.0*	*-*	*0.2*	*-*	*100.0*	*0.3*	*-*
2009	*72.5*	*27.1*	*0.2*	*0.0*	*-*	*0.0*	*-*	*0.2*	*-*	*100.0*	*0.4*	*-*
2010	*70.7*	*28.9*	*0.3*	*-*	*-*	*0.0*	*-*	*0.2*	*-*	*100.0*	*0.5*	*-*
2011	*68.7*	*30.8*	*0.4*	*-*	*-*	*-*	*-*	*0.2*	*-*	*100.0*	*0.5*	*-*
2012	*66.7*	*32.7*	*0.4*	*-*	*-*	*-*	*-*	*0.2*	*-*	*100.0*	*0.6*	*-*
2013	*64.8*	*34.5*	*0.5*	*-*	*-*	*-*	*-*	*0.2*	*-*	*100.0*	*0.7*	*-*
2014	*62.9*	*36.2*	*0.6*	*-*	*-*	*-*	*-*	*0.1*	*-*	*100.0*	*0.8*	*-*
2015	*61.2*	*37.8*	*0.7*	*0.1*	*0.1*	*-*	*-*	*0.1*	*-*	*100.0*	*1.0*	*0.1*
2016	*59.7*	*39.1*	*0.9*	*0.2*	*0.1*	*-*	*-*	*0.1*	*-*	*100.0*	*1.3*	*0.1*
2017	*58.8*	*39.6*	*1.1*	*0.3*	*0.1*	*-*	*-*	*0.1*	*-*	*100.0*	*1.6*	*0.1*
2018	*58.7*	*39.3*	*1.3*	*0.4*	*0.2*	*-*	*-*	*0.1*	*-*	*100.0*	*2.0*	*0.2*
2019	*59.0*	*38.5*	*1.6*	*0.5*	*0.3*	*-*	*-*	*0.1*	*-*	*100.0*	*2.4*	*0.3*

1. A hybrid electric vehicle uses an internal combustion engine plus an electric motor.

Source: DVLA/DfT
Telephone: 020 7944 3077
Email: vehicles.stats@dft.gov.uk

22.7 Cars licensed by propulsion / fuel type, Great Britain from 1994 to 2019

As at end of year   Thousand / *Percentage*

2. A plug-in hybrid electric vehicle is a hybrid electric vehicle that can be connected to a mains electricity supply to replenish the electric supply. Plug-in hybrid electric vehicles are identified using a supplementary data source, including information on models that are eligible for the Plug-in grants at the date of latest table update. Therefore earlier data in the series may be changed retrospectively as models are added to the eligible list. For more details, see:

https://www.gov.uk/plug-in-car-van-grants/eligibility

3. A range-extended electric vehicle is a battery electric vehicle that includes an auxiliary power unit (APU), which can replenish the electric supply before recharging is required.
4. A fuel cell electric vehicle is a type of electric vehicle which uses a fuel cell, instead of a battery. Fuel cells in vehicles generate electricity to power the motor, generally using oxygen from the air and compressed hydrogen.
5. Includes gas, gas bi-fuel, petrol/gas and gas-diesel.
6. Includes new fuel technologies and steam.
7. Alternative fuels includes all vehicles powered by something other than petrol or diesel.
8. Zero Emission Vehicles (ZEVs) do not emit any CO_2 emissions from their tailpipe.

Notes & definitions (https://www.gov.uk/government/publications/vehicles-statistics-guidance)

22.8 Vehicles registered for the first time by tax class, Great Britain, annually 2000 to 2019

Great Britain   Thousand

| Year | Private and light goods [1] | | Goods vehicles | Motorcycles, scooters and mopeds | Buses [2] | Special machines [3] | Other vehicles [3,4] | Total |
	Private cars	Other PLGs						
2000	2,430.0		50.0	183.0	8.0	24.0	176.0	2,871.0
2001	2,431.8	277.9	48.6	177.1	6.8	26.8	168.7	3,137.7
2002	2,528.8	286.8	44.9	162.2	7.8	.	199.0	3,229.4
2003	2,497.1	323.5	48.4	157.3	8.4	.	197.1	3,231.9
2004	2,437.4	347.3	48.0	133.7	8.3	.	210.7	3,185.4
2005	2,266.3	337.2	51.2	132.3	8.9	.	225.5	3,021.4
2006	2,160.7	338.4	47.9	131.9	7.6	.	227.1	2,913.6
2007	2,191.5	347.8	41.1	143.0	9.0	.	264.6	2,996.9
2008	1,891.9	296.4	47.0	138.4	8.3	.	290.2	2,672.2
2009	1,765.5	193.5	27.0	111.5	7.2	.	266.3	2,371.2
2010	1,765.3	229.3	27.0	97.1	6.4	.	292.7	2,417.8
2011	1,663.8	264.8	36.9	96.2	5.8	.	314.0	2,381.5
2012	1,784.1	244.4	38.0	96.6	7.8	.	299.0	2,469.8
2013	1,988.1	276.0	48.1	94.2	7.6	.	302.1	2,716.1
2014	2,180.8	324.9	33.4	103.6	7.0	.	324.1	2,973.7
2015	2,349.7	375.6	43.1	117.7	8.2	.	317.6	3,212.0
2016	2,418.0	379.4	45.0	132.0	8.6	.	313.0	3,296.0
2017	2,266.1	365.6	44.0	107.9	7.6	.	311.7	3,102.9
2018	2,102.0	362.7	41.5	108.7	7.0	.	310.4	2,932.3
2019	2,023.1	368.1	47.0	110.6	6.0	.	346.5	2,901.3

1. Figures for 1969 to 1979 are estimated using the October 1982 tax classes. Figures for 1951 to 1969 refer to earlier classes. From 1980 onwards figures refer to the October 1990 taxation classes. Figures for 1969 and 1980 are given twice, once for the tax regime before and once for the tax regime afterwards.
2. Prior to 1995 this tax class was called 'Public Transport' and taxis and Hackney Carriages were included. Prior to 1969, tram cars were also included.
3. Special Machines became part of the 'Crown and Exempt' taxation class with effect from January 2002.
4. Includes crown and exempt vehicles, three wheelers, pedestrian controlled vehicles and showmen's goods vehicles. Excludes vehicles officially registered by the armed forces.

Source: DVLA/DfT
Telephone: 020 7944 3077
Email : vehicles.stats@dft.gov.uk

Notes & definitions (https://www.gov.uk/government/publications/vehicles-statistics-guidance)

22.9a Practical car test[1] pass rates by gender, Great Britain:2007/08 to 2019/20

Numbers / *Per cent*

| | Male tests | | | Female tests | | | Total tests [2] | | |
	Conducted	Passes	Pass rate (%)	Conducted	Passes	Pass rate (%)	Conducted	Passes	Pass rate (%)
Annually (financial years)									
2007/08	865,427	409,222	47.3	896,314	369,795	41.3	1,762,148	779,207	44.2
2008/09	849,757	413,014	48.6	888,917	374,466	42.1	1,738,992	787,618	45.3
2009/10	753,618	370,049	49.1	780,007	333,770	42.8	1,533,738	703,859	45.9
2010/11	772,551	383,417	49.6	833,040	360,639	43.3	1,605,599	744,058	46.3
2011/12	744,487	374,472	50.3	824,572	361,685	43.9	1,569,069	736,158	46.9
2012/13	682,699	345,599	50.6	753,774	331,653	44.0	1,436,481	677,255	47.1
2013/14	706,757	358,143	50.7	770,823	337,436	43.8	1,477,585	695,580	47.1
2014/15	733,161	370,343	50.5	799,341	348,367	43.6	1,532,504	718,711	46.9
2015/16	736,261	372,777	50.6	801,472	350,667	43.8	1,537,735	723,444	47.0
2016/17	826,085	417,879	50.6	904,843	397,286	43.9	1,730,936	815,168	47.1
2017/18	803,464	402,005	50.0	915,051	393,885	43.0	1,718,519	795,892	46.3
2018/19	779,980	386,889	49.6	884,238	375,082	42.4	1,664,219	761,972	45.8
2019/20	762,303	378,034	49.6	837,193	356,542	42.6	1,599,566	734,600	45.9

1. Practical test category B (cars).
2. Total tests may be higher than the sum of male and female tests, as the candidate's gender is not always recorded.

Source: DVSA/DfT
Telephone: 020 7944 3077
Email: vehicles.stats@dft.gov.uk

Notes & definitions (https://www.gov.uk/government/organisations/department-for-transport/series/driving-tests-and-instructors-statistics)

22.9b Practical motorcycle test[1] (Module 1) pass rates by gender, monthly, Great Britain: 2009/10 to 2019/20

Numbers / *Per cent*

	Male tests			Female tests			Total tests[2]		
	Conducted	Passes	Pass rate (%)	Conducted	Passes	Pass rate (%)	Conducted	Passes	Pass rate (%)
Annually (financial years)									
2009/10 [3]	44,165	28,123	63.7	6,655	2,765	41.5	50,823	30,891	60.8
2010/11	50,046	33,735	67.4	7,665	3,498	45.6	57,711	37,233	64.5
2011/12	52,726	38,325	72.7	6,868	3,706	54.0	59,594	42,031	70.5
2012/13	58,280	42,490	72.9	7,770	4,092	52.7	66,050	46,582	70.5
2013/14	41,299	29,366	71.1	4,964	2,458	49.5	46,263	31,824	68.8
2014/15	46,361	33,398	72.0	5,644	2,863	50.7	52,005	36,261	69.7
2015/16	49,784	36,744	73.8	5,986	3,043	50.8	55,770	39,787	71.3
2016/17	52,626	39,138	74.4	6,147	3,238	52.7	58,773	42,376	72.1
2017/18	50,882	37,837	74.4	6,357	3,290	51.8	57,239	41,127	71.9
2018/19	49,217	36,651	74.5	6,046	3,234	53.5	55,263	39,885	72.2
2019/20	46,263	34,392	74.3	5,658	3,040	53.7	51,921	37,432	72.1

1. Practical test categories A, A1 and A2 (motorcycles). Excludes all mopeds.
2. Total tests may be higher than the sum of male and female tests, as the candidate's gender is not always recorded.
3. Motorcycle module 1 and test 2 figures are only from 27 April 2009, and are not included in the Total test figures until 27 April 2009, as the motorcycle Module 1 and 2 tests were not introduced until 27 April 2009. Prior to April, 2009 a different motorcycle test scheme was used.

Source: DVSA/DfT
Telephone: 020 7944 3077
Email: vehicles.stats@dft.gov.uk

Notes & definition: https://www.gov.uk/government/organisations/department-for-transport/series/driving-tests-and-instructors-statistics

22.9c Practical motorcycle test[1] (Module 2) pass rates by gender, Great Britain: 2009/10 to 2019/20

Numbers / *Percent*

	Male tests			Female tests			Total tests[2]		
	Conducted	Passes	Pass rate (%)	Conducted	Passes	Pass rate (%)	Conducted	Passes	Pass rate (%)
Annually (financial years)									
2009/10 [3]	34,550	24,122	69.8	3,363	2,352	69.9	37,914	26,474	69.8
2010/11	44,991	31,236	69.4	4,654	3,249	69.8	49,645	34,485	69.5
2011/12	52,619	36,367	69.1	5,292	3,559	67.3	57,911	39,926	68.9
2012/13	59,237	40,871	69.0	5,891	4,018	68.2	65,128	44,889	68.9
2013/14	40,052	28,110	70.2	3,423	2,343	68.4	43,475	30,453	70.0
2014/15	45,211	31,847	70.4	3,983	2,709	68.0	49,194	34,556	70.2
2015/16	48,972	35,001	71.5	4,212	2,924	69.4	53,184	37,925	71.3
2016/17	52,917	37,491	70.8	4,499	3,117	69.3	57,416	40,608	70.7
2017/18	51,544	36,781	71.4	4,566	3,240	71.0	56,110	40,021	71.3
2018/19	49,747	35,320	71.0	4,517	3,117	69.0	54,264	38,437	70.8
2019/20	46,684	33,240	71.2	4,309	2,965	68.8	50,993	36,205	71.0

1. Practical test categories A, A1 and A2 (motorcycles). Excludes all mopeds.
2. Total tests may be higher than the sum of male and female tests, as the candidate's gender is not always recorded.
3. Motorcycle module 1 and test 2 figures are only from 27 April 2009, and are not included in the Total test figures until 27 April 2009, as the motorcycle Module 1 and 2 tests were not introduced until 27 April 2009. Prior to April, 2009 a different motorcycle test scheme was used.

Source: DVSA/DfT
Telephone: 020 7944 3077
Email: vehicles.stats@dft.gov.uk

Notes & definitions: https://www.gov.uk/government/organisations/department-for-transport/series/driving-tests-and-instructors-statistics

22.9d Practical large goods vehicle (LGV) test[1] rates by gender, Great Britain: 2007/08 to 2019/20

Numbers / Per cent

	Male tests			Female tests			Total tests [2]		
	Conducted	Passes	Pass rate (%)	Conducted	Passes	Pass rate (%)	Conducted	Passes	Pass rate (%)
Annually (financial years)									
2007/08	66,445	30,693	*46.2*	4,305	2,077	*48.2*	70,766	32,779	*46.3*
2008/09	61,950	30,258	*48.8*	3,892	2,035	*52.3*	65,852	32,298	*49.0*
2009/10	43,119	22,058	*51.2*	3,305	1,816	*54.9*	46,426	23,876	*51.4*
2010/11	41,011	21,122	*51.5*	2,883	1,542	*53.5*	43,894	22,664	*51.6*
2011/12	43,525	22,762	*52.3*	3,024	1,639	*54.2*	46,549	24,401	*52.4*
2012/13	42,937	22,736	*53.0*	3,309	1,762	*53.2*	46,246	24,498	*53.0*
2013/14	44,993	24,296	*54.0*	3,290	1,928	*58.6*	48,283	26,224	*54.3*
2014/15	51,314	28,310	*55.2*	3,847	2,264	*58.9*	55,161	30,574	*55.4*
2015/16	65,295	36,113	*55.3*	4,938	2,887	*58.5*	70,233	39,000	*55.5*
2016/17	72,472	40,859	*56.4*	5,765	3,487	*60.5*	78,237	44,346	*56.7*
2017/18	64,951	37,424	*57.6*	5,668	3,384	*59.7*	70,619	40,808	*57.8*
2018/19	67,521	39,114	*57.9*	6,374	3,951	*62.0*	73,895	43,065	*58.3*
2019/20	63,653	37,314	*58.6*	6,635	4,120	*62.1*	70,288	41,434	*58.9*

1. Practical test categories C1 (medium-sized vehicles), C1E (medium-sized vehicles with a trailer), C (large vehicles), CE (large vehicles with a trailer).
2. Total tests may be higher than the sum of male and female tests, as the candidate's gender is not always recorded.

Source: DVSA/DfT
Telephone: 020 7944 3077
Email: vehicles.stats@dft.gov.uk

Notes & definitions: https://www.gov.uk/government/organisations/department-for-transport/series/driving-tests-and-instructors-statistics

22.9e Practical passenger carrying vehicle (PCV) CPC test[1,2] rates by gender, annually, Great Britain: 2008/09 to 2019/20

Numbers / *Per cent*

	Male tests			Female tests			Total tests [3]		
	Conducted	Passes	Pass rate (%)	Conducted	Passes	Pass rate (%)	Conducted	Passes	Pass rate (%)
Annually (financial years)									
2008/09 [4]	1,089	763	*70.1*	123	92	*74.8*	1,212	855	*70.5*
2009/10	2,436	1,881	*77.2*	273	225	*82.4*	2,709	2,106	*77.7*
2010/11	2,280	1,892	*83.0*	265	230	*86.8*	2,545	2,122	*83.4*
2011/12	2,177	1,852	*85.1*	296	263	*88.9*	2,474	2,116	*85.5*
2012/13	2,626	2,254	*85.8*	309	259	*83.8*	2,935	2,513	*85.6*
2013/14	3,179	2,760	*86.8*	372	330	*88.7*	3,551	3,090	*87.0*
2014/15	2,720	2,364	*86.9*	325	291	*89.5*	3,046	2,656	*87.2*
2015/16	2,910	2,510	*86.3*	374	345	*92.2*	3,284	2,855	*86.9*
2016/17	3,055	2,689	*88.0*	451	414	*91.8*	3,506	3,103	*88.5*
2017/18	2,122	1,873	*88.3*	319	289	*90.6*	2,441	2,162	*88.6*
2018/19	1,394	1,250	*89.7*	234	212	*90.6*	1,628	1,462	*89.8*
2019/20	1,251	1,135	*90.7*	227	213	*93.8*	1,478	1,348	*91.2*

1. Certificate of Professional Competence (CPC) test passes are required in addition to all other Large Good Vehicles (LGVs) or Passenger Carrying Vehicles (PCVs) tests to drive professionally (i.e. as the main purpose of one's job). CPC tests are not required to obtain a license to drive LGVs or PCVs.
2. Includes all Passenger Carrying Vehicles (PCVs) Certificate of Professional Competence (CPC) module 4 tests. These statistics cover DVSA tests only. In recent years a number of practical CPC tests have been carried out by external authorised assessors and these are not included here.
3. Total tests may be higher than the sum of male and female tests, as the candidate's gender is not always recorded.
4. The Passenger Carrying Vehicle (PCV) Certificate for Professional Competence (CPC) was introduced on 10th September 2008. PCV CPC figures for 2008/09 only include tests conducted from 10 September onwards.

Source: DVSA/DfT
Telephone: 020 7944 3077
Email: vehicles.stats@dft.gov.uk

Notes & definitions (https://www.gov.uk/government/organisations/department-for-transport/series/driving-tests-and-instructors-statistics)

22.10 Full car driving licence holders by age and gender: England, 1975/76 to 2019

	All aged 17+	17-20	21-29	30-39	40-49	50-59	60-69	70+	Estimated licence holders (millions)	r	Unweighted sample size (individuals aged 17+)
				Percentage							
All adults:											
1975/76	48	28	59	67	60	50	35	15	19		17,064
1985/86	57	33	63	74	71	60	47	27	24		19,835
1989/911	64	44	74	78	79	68	55	32	24		17,466
1992/94	67	48	75	82	80	74	59	33	25		16,401
1995/972	69	44	74	82	82	76	64	39	26		16,716
1998/00	71	41	75	85	83	78	68	40	27		16,529
2002	71	32	67	83	83	81	70	45	28	r	13,839
2003	71	29	67	82	84	81	72	44	28	r	14,562
2004	70	27	65	82	83	81	73	46	28	r	14,230
2005	72	31	65	82	84	83	75	52	29	r	15,063
2006	72	35	67	82	84	82	76	51	29	r	14,819
2007	72	38	66	81	84	82	76	53	29	r	14,695
2008	73	36	64	83	84	83	78	53	30	r	14,294
2009	73	36	64	80	84	83	80	55	30	r	14,800
2010	73	33	63	81	85	83	80	57	31	r	14,131
2011	72	31	64	78	84	83	80	59	31	r	13,730
2012	73	36	64	78	85	82	80	59	31	r	14,590
2013	74	31	66	80	85	84	82	62	32	r	14,710
2014	73	29	63	79	85	83	81	62	32	r	13,981
2015	74	33	64	78	84	84	81	64	32	r	14,269
2016	73	31	66	76	83	85	81	62	32	r	13,827
2017	74	30	67	79	83	85	81	64	33	r	12,940
2018	75	37	65	76	85	87	83	67	34	r	12,540
2019	75	35	62	79	86	86	85	67	34	r	12,656
Males:											
1975/76	69	36	78	85	83	75	58	32	13		8,113
1985/86	74	37	73	86	87	81	72	51	15		9,367
1989/911	80	54	83	88	90	86	79	58	14		8,306
1992/94	82	55	83	90	89	88	82	59	15		7,652
1995/972	82	51	81	90	89	89	83	65	15		7,934
1998/00	82	44	81	90	91	89	83	66	15		7,857
2002	80	34	72	89	89	89	85	68	15	r	6,588
2003	81	34	72	87	91	91	88	69	15	r	6,952
2004	80	29	69	87	89	90	87	72	15	r	6,724
2005	81	36	68	86	90	91	88	74	16	r	7,159
2006	81	37	71	87	88	90	90	77	16	r	7,080
2007	81	41	69	86	90	90	88	77	16	r	6,980
2008	81	36	67	88	90	91	90	75	16	r	6,819
2009	80	38	67	85	89	91	91	77	16	r	7,024
2010	80	34	66	86	90	89	90	78	16	r	6,777
2011	80	31	68	81	89	90	90	79	16	r	6,525
2012	80	40	67	81	88	89	90	80	17	r	6,985
2013	81	30	67	83	90	90	91	82	17	r	7,056
2014	80	34	66	82	91	89	90	80	17	r	6,641
2015	80	33	67	81	88	90	90	81	17	r	6,806
2016	80	33	68	80	87	91	90	78	17	r	6,555
2017	80	29	69	82	87	91	87	80	17	r	6,174
2018	81	37	67	79	89	91	90	83	18	r	6,003
2019	80	34	65	83	89	89	90	81	18	r	5,996

22.10 Full car driving licence holders by age and gender: England, 1975/76 to 2019

	Percentage								Estimated licence holders (millions)	r	Unweighted sample size (individuals aged 17+)
	All aged 17+	17-20	21-29	30-39	40-49	50-59	60-69	70+			
Females:											
1975/76	29	20	43	48	37	24	15	4	6		8,951
1985/86	41	29	54	62	56	41	24	11	9		10,468
1989/911	50	35	65	68	67	50	33	15	10		9,160
1992/94	55	42	69	74	71	59	38	16	11		8,749
1995/972	58	36	68	74	74	63	46	22	11		8,781
1998/00	61	38	70	79	75	67	54	22	12		8,672
2002	61	30	62	77	77	74	55	28	12	r	7,251
2003	61	24	62	77	77	71	58	26	12	r	7,610
2004	61	24	61	77	77	71	60	28	13	r	7,506
2005	64	26	61	77	79	75	62	36	13	r	7,904
2006	64	32	62	78	80	74	64	32	13	r	7,739
2007	64	35	63	76	78	74	64	36	13	r	7,715
2008	65	35	61	78	80	76	67	37	14	r	7,475
2009	65	33	62	76	79	75	69	38	14	r	7,776
2010	66	32	60	77	80	77	70	41	14	r	7,354
2011	66	30	59	74	79	76	71	44	14	r	7,205
2012	66	31	62	75	81	75	71	43	14	r	7,605
2013	68	31	64	77	80	77	73	47	15	r	7,654
2014	67	25	61	75	80	78	73	47	15	r	7,340
2015	68	32	61	74	80	78	73	50	15	r	7,463
2016	67	29	63	72	80	79	73	50	15	r	7,272
2017	69	30	65	76	80	79	75	50	16	r	6,766
2018	70	38	62	74	81	83	77	54	16	r	6,537
2019	71	35	60	74	83	83	79	55	16	r	6,660

1 Figures prior to 1989 for Great Britain, rather than England only.

2 Figures prior to 1995 are based on unweighted data.

r Marks a revision to previously published figures in this table, due to an administrative error.

The figures in this table are National Statistics

The results presented in this table are weighted. The base (unweighted sample size) is shown in the table for information.

Weights are applied to adjust for non-response to ensure the characteristics of the achieved sample match the population of Great Britain (1995-2012) or England (2013 onwards) and for the drop off in trip recording in diary data.

The survey results are subject to sampling error.

Notes & definitions: https://www.gov.uk/government/statistics/national-travel-survey-2020

Source: National Travel Survey
Email: national.travelsurvey@dft.gov.uk

22.11a Household car availability: England, 2002 to 2019

Year	Percentage				Cars / vans per household	Cars / vans per adult (aged 17+)	Unweighted sample size (households)
	No car / van	One car / van	Two or more cars / vans	All households			
2002	26	44	30	100	1.09	0.59	7,535
2003	26	42	31	100	1.11	0.60	7,853
2004	25	44	30	100	1.11	0.59	7,692
2005	25	43	33	100	1.16	0.61	8,065
2006	24	44	32	100	1.16	0.61	7,884
2007	25	43	33	100	1.16	0.61	7,879
2008	25	43	33	100	1.15	0.61	7,665
2009	25	43	32	100	1.15	0.60	7,858
2010	25	42	33	100	1.17	0.61	7,534
2011	25	43	32	100	1.15	0.60	7,289
2012	25	44	31	100	1.14	0.60	7,724
2013	25	43	32	100	1.15	0.60	7,820
2014	24	43	32	100	1.16	0.61	7,436
2015	25	42	33	100	1.18	0.62	7,563
2016	23	43	34	100	1.20	0.63	7,328
2017	24	41	35	100	1.22	0.63	6,846
2018	24	41	35	100	1.21	0.63	6,660
2019	24	41	35	100	1.21	0.64	6,789

Source: National Travel Survey

1 Figures from 1985/86 are from the National Travel Survey. Earlier years Email: national.travelsurvey@dft.gov.uk are derived from other household surveys.

2 Figures prior to 1989 for Great Britain, rather than England only.

3 Figures prior to 1995 are based on unweighted data.

The figures in this table are National Statistics

The results presented in this table are weighted. The base (unweighted sample size) is shown in the table for information.

Weights are applied to adjust for non-response to ensure the characteristics of the achieved sample match the population of Great Britain (1995-2012) or England (2013 onwards) and for the drop off in trip recording in diary data.

The survey results are subject to sampling error.

22.11b Household car ownership by region and Rural-Urban Classification[1]: England, 2002/03 to 2018/19[2]

	No car / van		One car / van		Two or more cars / vans		Cars / vans per household		Unweighted sample size (Households)	
	Percentage									
	2002/03	2018/19	2002/03	2018/19	2002/03	2018/19	2002/03	2018/19	2002/03	2018/19
Region of residence:										
North East	37	28	44	40	20	32	0.86	1.10	847	785
North West	27	22	44	44	28	33	1.05	1.19	2,164	1,782
Yorkshire and The Humber	30	23	45	43	25	34	0.99	1.19	1,605	1,383
East Midlands	20	20	45	40	34	39	1.20	1.33	1,321	1,163
West Midlands	26	26	40	36	34	38	1.15	1.25	1,593	1,314
East of England	20	15	42	44	38	42	1.26	1.38	1,637	1,520
London	41	45	40	39	19	16	0.82	0.74	2,228	1,881
South East	18	16	43	40	39	44	1.30	1.41	2,332	2,224
South West	19	15	47	43	34	41	1.24	1.39	1,661	1,397
England excluding London	24	20	44	41	33	39	1.16	1.30	13,160	11,568
England	26	24	43	41	31	35	1.10	1.21	15,388	13,449
Rural-Urban Classification[2] of residence:										
Urban Conurbation	35	34	41	41	24	25	0.93	0.97	5,882	4,907
Urban City and Town	24	21	46	42	31	37	1.13	1.27	6,842	5,908
Rural Town and Fringe	17	14	42	43	41	43	1.32	1.43	1,440	1,329
Rural Village, Hamlet and Isolated Dwelling	7	5	39	34	53	60	1.63	1.78	1,224	1,305
All areas	26	24	43	41	31	35	1.10	1.21	15,388	13,449

1. For more information on Rural-Urban Classifications see:
https://www.gov.uk/government/collections/rural-urban-classification
2 Two survey years combined for 2002/03. 2020 is presented as a single year.
The figures in this table are National Statistics.
The results presented in this table are weighted. The base (unweighted sample size) is shown in the table for information.
The survey results are subject to sampling error.
Notes & definitions: https://www.gov.uk/government/statistics/national-travel-survey-2020

Source: National Travel Survey
Email: national.travelsurvey@dft.gov.uk

22.12: Vehicles Licensed & SORN by body type, Northern Ireland 2014-2019

As at 31 December

	Private Cars		Motorcycles		Light Goods		Heavy Goods	
	Licensed	SORN	Licensed	SORN	Licensed	SORN	Licensed	SORN
2014	901,779	61,551	24,044	23,896	98,333	10,632	22,841	4,384
2015	920,407	84,330	22,301	28,029	102,458	14,394	22,850	5,879
2016	941,819	108,331	22,142	30,303	107,697	18,021	23,506	7,234
2017	959,761	131,741	22,270	33,027	113,173	22,354	23,983	8,935
2018	975,661	150,533	22,452	35,198	117,669	26,883	24,279	10,593
2019	995,872	171,428	23,170	36,956	123,093	31,213	24,276	12,496

	Buses		Agricultural Vehicles		Other Vehicles		Total	
	Licensed	SORN	Licensed	SORN	Licensed	SORN	Licensed	SORN
2014	5,589	632	24,268	1,043	4,873	1,038	1,081,727	103,176
2015	5,524	826	24,591	1,749	4,951	1,382	1,103,082	136,589
2016	5,556	967	25,513	2,128	5,178	1,742	1,131,411	168,726
2017	5,594	1,207	28,023	2,748	5,531	2,154	1,158,335	202,166
2018	5,529	1,453	29,131	3,183	5,821	2,477	1,180,542	230,320
2019	5,493	1,654	30,148	3,682	5,691	2,855	1,207,743	260,284

Source: Department for Transport

Due to rounding conventions, some totals may not add to 100%.

22.13. Motor vehicles registered for the first time by body type, Northern Ireland, 2013/14 - 2019/20

Annual	Private Cars			Motorcycles			Light Goods			Heavy Goods		
	New	Used	Total	New	Used	Total	New	Used	Total	New	Used	Total
2013/14	55,676	35,990	91,666	1,305	837	2,142	5,343	4,948	10,291	1,082	2,017	3,099
2014/15	58,737	12,097	70,834	1,315	615	1,930	6,613	1,730	8,343	957	725	1,682
2015/16	58,133	1,124	59,257	1,591	126	1,717	6,931	358	7,289	1,117	192	1,309
2016/17	58,089	648	58,737	1,723	130	1,853	7,685	286	7,971	1,330	139	1,469
2017/18	52,069	894	52,963	1,688	133	1,821	7,155	180	7,335	1,085	86	1,171
2018/19	50,799	884	51,683	1,861	121	1,982	6,660	203	6,863	1,324	77	1,401
2019/20	45,781	772	46,553	1,699	129	1,828	5,546	159	5,705	1,201	60	1,261

Annual	Buses			Agricultural Vehicles			Other Vehicles			Total		
	New	Used	Total	New	Used	Total	New	Used	Total	New	Used	Total
2013/14	402	208	610	783	1,400	2,183	8	11	19	64,599	45,411	110,010
2014/15	439	91	530	715	878	1,593	243	50	293	69,019	16,186	85,205
2015/16	204	85	289	657	159	816	355	50	405	68,988	2,094	71,082
2016/17	181	50	231	749	209	958	424	66	490	70,181	1,528	71,709
2017/18	194	57	251	726	168	894	421	49	470	63,338	1,567	64,905
2018/19	236	14	250	937	195	1,132	487	65	552	62,304	1,559	63,863
2019/20	132	21	153	807	186	993	346	51	397	55,512	1,378	56,890

Source: Department for Transport

Due to rounding conventions, some totals may not add to 100%.

22.14 Vehicle kilometres on local bus services by metropolitan area status and country: Great Britain, annual from 2000/1 to 2019/20

Million

Year	Estimation method[1]	London	English metropolitan areas	English non-metropolitan areas	England	Scotland	Wales	Great Britain	England outside London
2000/01		371	654	1,134	2,158	369	126	2,653	1,788
2001/02		381	646	1,102	2,129	368	126	2,622	1,748
2002/03		404	630	1,088	2,122	374	123	2,619	1,718
2003/04		444	596	1,069	2,109	369	113	2,590	1,665
2004/05	Old	:	575	1,077	2,122	357	116	2,594	1,652
2004/05	New	470	592	1,061	2,122	359	129	2,611	1,652
2005/06		461	588	1,071	2,121	374	127	2,622	1,660
2006/07		465	591	1,067	2,122	385	123	2,630	1,657
2007/08		465	597	1,067	2,129	397	124	2,649	1,664
2008/09		474	589	1,077	2,139	386	125	2,650	1,665
2009/10		479	569	1,071	2,119	377	124	2,620	1,640
2010/11		481	567	1,072	2,121	346	124	2,591	1,639
2011/12		485	563	1,054	2,102	338	117	2,557	1,617
2012/13		486	553	1,048	2,087	327	116	2,529	1,600
2013/14		487	546	1,045	2,078	332	112	2,522	1,591
2014/15		485	531	1,038	2,053	336	106	2,496	1,569
2015/16		488	517	1,011	2,016	341	107	2,465	1,528
2016/17		490	495	1,008	1,992	337	98	2,428	1,502
2017/18		485	484	953	1,922	334	100	2,357	1,437
2018/19		476	484	923	1,883	332	101	2,316	1,407
2019/20		476	459	891	1,825	335	89	2,248	1,350

[1] Break in the local bus series (outside London) due to changes in the estimation methodology from 2004/05 [2] Deregulation of the bus market took place in October 1986. For more information see the technical information (link below).

Source: DfT Public Service Vehicle Survey, Transport for London
Telephone: 020 7944 3094   Email: bus.statistics@dft.gov.uk

Notes & Definitions: https://www.gov.uk/government/statistics/buses-statistics-guidance

The figures in this table are National Statistics

22.15 Local bus fares index (at current prices[2]) by metropolitan area status and country: Great Britain, annual from 2000

Index: March 2005=100

Year[1]	All items Retail Prices Index[3]	All items Consumer Prices Index (CPI)	Local bus fares index							
			London	English metropolitan areas	English non-metropolitan areas	England	Scotland	Wales	Great Britain	England outside London
2000	88.4	93.3	83.2	79.1	78.4	79.6	89.6	80.3	80.9	78.7
2001	90.4	94.1	83.9	83.3	82.7	82.9	92.2	84.7	84.1	82.9
2002	91.6	95.6	81.5	87.3	86.6	85.3	93.5	88.6	86.4	86.9
2003	94.4	97.1	81.8	90.3	90.8	88.0	96.1	91.6	89.2	90.6
2004	96.9	98.1	86.9	94.7	95.3	92.7	97.1	95.8	93.4	95.1
2005	100.0	100.0	100.0	100.0	100.0	100.0	100.0	100.0	100.0	100.0
2006	102.4	101.8	105.7	111.9	107.8	108.3	105.1	105.0	107.9	109.6
2007	107.3	104.9	116.6	113.6	102.0	110.2	111.4	111.5	110.4	106.9
2008	111.3	107.5	111.2	121.6	106.7	112.8	116.7	117.5	113.4	113.0
2009	110.9	110.6	120.0	136.5	113.9	122.5	126.5	125.3	123.1	123.2
2010	115.9	114.3	135.2	137.6	115.6	128.8	129.5	128.7	129.0	124.7
2011	122.0	119.0	144.5	146.3	119.4	135.7	132.2	130.1	135.2	130.3
2012	126.4	123.1	151.7	156.0	126.9	143.8	139.1	137.8	143.1	138.7
2013	130.6	126.6	158.1	160.9	134.0	150.3	145.1	147.2	149.6	145.1
2014	133.8	128.6	162.3	164.8	138.4	154.6	149.8	149.5	153.9	149.4
2015	135.0	128.6	166.1	170.7	143.3	159.3	153.2	155.8	158.6	154.7
2016	137.1	129.2	167.4	174.2	145.9	161.7	157.6	156.5	161.1	157.7
2017	141.4	132.2	163.7	177.9	152.5	163.8	163.6	157.2	163.6	163.3
2018	146.1	135.4	166.0	182.5	158.8	168.2	171.9	162.8	168.4	169.1
2019	149.7	138.0	167.6	188.9	166.1	173.2	175.5	168.1	173.3	176.2
2020	153.6	140.1	167.6	194.9	173.6	177.5	181.7	173.9	177.8	183.2

[1] Index as at March.
[2] Not adjusted for inflation.
[3] These figures are not National Statistics

Source: DfT Fares Survey, Office for National Statistics
Telephone: 020 7082 6602
Email: bus.statistics@dft.gov.uk

Notes & Definitions: https://www.gov.uk/government/statistics/buses-statistics-guidance

The figures in this table are National Statistics except where indicated

22.16 Reported casualties by road user type and severity, Great Britain, 2011 - 2019

Number

	2011	2012	2013	2014	2015	2016	2017	2018	2019
Pedestrians									
Killed	453	420	398	446	408	448	470	456	470
KSI (unadjusted)[1]	5,907	5,978	5,388	5,504	5,337	5,527	6,038	6,210	6,200
KSI (adjusted)[1]	8,175	8,155	7,461	7,631	7,333	6,971	6,957	7,106	6,839
All casualties	26,198	25,218	24,033	24,748	24,061	23,550	23,805	22,432	21,770
of whom children: 0 - 15 years									
Killed	*33*	*20*	*26*	*29*	*25*	*34*	*22*	*28*	*18*
KSI (unadjusted)[1]	*1,602*	*1,545*	*1,356*	*1,378*	*1,282*	*1,260*	*1,263*	*1,292*	*1,239*
KSI (adjusted)[1]	*2,242*	*2,101*	*1,864*	*1,896*	*1,771*	*1,609*	*1,511*	*1,526*	*1,414*
All casualties	*7,807*	*6,999*	*6,396*	*6,481*	*6,317*	*5,998*	*5,838*	*5,426*	*5,200*
Pedal cyclists									
Killed	107	118	109	113	100	102	101	99	100
KSI (unadjusted)[1]	3,192	3,338	3,245	3,512	3,337	3,473	3,774	3,792	3,757
KSI (adjusted)[1]	4,517	4,678	4,639	5,060	4,651	4,428	4,412	4,400	4,221
All casualties	19,215	19,091	19,438	21,287	18,844	18,477	18,321	17,550	16,884
Motorcycle users									
Killed	362	328	331	339	365	319	349	354	336
KSI (unadjusted)[1]	5,609	5,328	5,194	5,620	5,397	5,841	5,923	5,821	5,570
KSI (adjusted)[1]	7,412	7,061	6,883	7,436	7,146	6,979	6,538	6,416	6,003
All casualties	20,150	19,310	18,752	20,366	19,918	19,297	18,042	16,818	16,224
Car occupants									
Killed	883	801	785	797	754	816	787	777	736
KSI (unadjusted)[1]	9,225	9,031	8,403	8,809	8,605	9,634	9,545	9,960	10,354
KSI (adjusted)[1]	13,656	13,287	12,318	12,927	12,486	12,210	11,605	11,919	11,724
All casualties	124,924	119,708	109,787	115,530	111,707	109,046	100,082	93,979	89,331
Bus and coach occupants									
Killed	7	11	10	7	5	9	7	8	14
KSI (unadjusted)[1]	332	323	341	300	279	283	284	350	301
KSI (adjusted)[1]	548	520	528	489	458	407	367	416	339
All casualties	6,177	5,234	4,873	5,198	4,626	4,246	4,236	3,801	3,085
Goods vehicle occupants									
Killed	62	62	58	47	65	66	63	55	66
KSI (unadjusted)[1]	535	560	537	579	624	620	619	679	706
KSI (adjusted)[1]	793	815	800	856	883	790	767	812	799
All casualties	5,914	5,873	5,734	6,326	6,073	5,768	5,454	5,071	4,985
Other vehicle/Unknown vehicle occupants									
Killed	27	14	22	26	33	32	16	35	30
KSI (unadjusted)[1]	223	229	217	220	232	224	226	246	237
KSI (adjusted)[1]	323	327	289	296	297	273	273	289	262
All casualties	1,372	1,289	1,053	1,022	960	1,000	1,053	946	879
All road users									
Killed	1,901	1,754	1,713	1,775	1,730	1,792	1,793	1,784	1,752
KSI (unadjusted)[1]	25,023	24,787	23,325	24,544	23,811	25,602	26,409	27,058	27,125
KSI (adjusted)[1]	35,424	34,843	32,916	34,696	33,255	32,059	30,919	31,358	30,187
All casualties	203,950	195,723	183,670	194,477	186,189	181,384	170,993	160,597	153,158
of whom children: 0 - 15 years									
Killed	*60*	*61*	*48*	*53*	*54*	*69*	*48*	*48*	*39*
KSI (unadjusted)[1]	*2,412*	*2,272*	*1,974*	*2,077*	*1,960*	*2,062*	*2,121*	*2,112*	*2,172*
KSI (adjusted)[1]	*3,510*	*3,220*	*2,841*	*2,977*	*2,795*	*2,654*	*2,589*	*2,549*	*2,491*
All casualties	*19,474*	*17,251*	*15,756*	*16,727*	*16,103*	*15,976*	*15,721*	*14,266*	*13,574*
Casualty rates[2]									
Killed	6	6	5	5	5	5	5	5	5
KSI (unadjusted)[1]	80	79	74	75	72	75	76	77	75
KSI (adjusted)[1]	114	112	104	107	100	94	89	89	84
All casualties	655	627	583	597	559	531	491	455	425

1 Killed or seriously injured.
2 Casualties per billion vehicle miles.
Notes & Definitions: https://www.gov.uk/government/publications/road-accidents-and-safety-statistics-guidance

Source: STATS19, DfT National Road Traffic Survey
Telephone: 020 7944 6595
Email: roadacc.stats@dft.gov.uk

Figures for serious and slight injuries are shown both adjusted and unadjusted for changes in severity reporting. Since 2016, changes in severity reporting systems for a large number of police forces mean that serious injury figures, and to a lesser extent slight injuries, as reported by the police are not comparable with earlier years. Adjustments to account for the change have been produced for high level series. More information on the change and the adjustment process is available in the 2018 annual report. For analysis of trends over time, using the experimental adjusted series is recommended.
The figures in this table are National Statistics

22.17a Goods lifted[1] and goods moved[2] by mode of working[3]: annual 2000 - 2019

UK activity of GB-registered heavy goods vehicles

	Million tonnes					Billion tonne kilometres				
	Goods lifted					Goods moved				
Year	Mainly public haulage	% of total	Mainly own account	% of total	All modes	Mainly public haulage	% of total	Mainly own account	% of total	All modes
2000	1,038	65	556	35	1,593	113	75	37	25	150
2001	1,052	67	529	33	1,581	115	77	35	23	149
2002	1,019	63	608	37	1,627	111	74	39	26	150
2003	1,053	64	590	36	1,643	114	75	37	25	152
2004	1,101	63	643	37	1,744	111	73	41	27	152
2005	1,079	62	667	38	1,746	110	72	43	28	153
2006	1,104	62	671	38	1,776	110	72	43	28	152
2007	1,116	61	706	39	1,822	113	72	45	28	157
2008	948	57	720	43	1,668	99	68	47	32	146
2009	690	51	666	49	1,356	77	62	48	38	125
2010	800	54	689	46	1,489	89	64	50	36	139
2011	750	51	707	49	1,457	84	60	56	40	140
2012	788	55	639	45	1,427	93	65	50	35	143
2013	744	57	572	43	1,316	88	67	44	33	131
2014	783	59	539	41	1,322	88	69	40	31	128
2015	864	60	581	40	1,445	99	69	45	31	143
2016	845	59	589	41	1,434	101	68	47	32	148
2017	850	61	547	39	1,397	104	70	44	30	147
2018	873	62	532	38	1,405	107	71	45	29	152
2019	856	59	584	41	1,440	107	70	46	30	154

1. Goods lifted: the weight of goods carried, measured in tonnes.
2. Goods moved: the weight of goods carried multiplied by the distance hauled, measured in tonne kilometres.
3. Either public haulage operators, those who carry goods for other companies or individuals, or, own account operators, those who carry goods only for their own trade or business.

Note: discontinuities in the series (denoted by lines) are described in detail within the methodology note; comparisons across years where methodological changes have occurred should be treated with caution.

Methodology note: https://www.gov.uk/government/collections/road-freight-domestic-and-international-statistics
Notes & definitions: https://www.gov.uk/government/collections/road-freight-domestic-and-international-statistics

Source: Continuing Survey of Road Goods Transport (Great Britain)
Telephone: 020 7944 3905
Email: roadfreight.stats@dft.gov.uk

22.17b Goods moved[1] by type and weight[2] of vehicle: annual 2000 - 2019

UK activity of GB-registered heavy goods vehicles

Billion tonne kilometres

	Rigid vehicles					Articulated vehicles			
Year	Over 3.5t to 7.5t	Over 7.5t to 17t	Over 17t to 25t	Over 25t	All Rigids	Over 3.5t to 33t	Over 33t	All Artics	All vehicles
2000	5	11	5	15	36	14	100	114	150
2001	5	9	6	16	34	13	102	115	149
2002	5	7	6	17	36	10	104	114	150
2003	4	6	7	18	35	9	108	116	152
2004	4	5	7	19	36	7	109	116	152
2005	4	5	8	21	37	6	110	116	153
2006	4	3	8	20	36	6	111	117	152
2007	3	3	9	22	37	6	115	120	157
2008	3	2	8	20	33	5	108	113	146
2009	3	2	7	17	30	5	91	96	125
2010	3	2	7	18	31	4	104	108	139
2011	3	2	7	21	33	4	103	107	140
2012	2	2	7	19	30	4	108	112	143
2013	2	1	6	18	27	4	101	105	131
2014	2	1	6	17	27	3	98	101	128
2015	2	1	7	19	29	3	111	114	143
2016	2	2	6	23	33	4	112	116	148
2017	2	1	6	21	30	4	113	117	147
2018	2	1	6	22	31	3	118	121	152
2019	2	2	7	22	32	3	119	122	154

1. Goods moved: the weight of goods carried multiplied by the distance hauled, measured in tonne kilometres.
2. Gross vehicle weight: the total weight of the vehicle plus its carrying capacity, from 3.5 to 44 tonnes.

Note: discontinuities in the series (denoted by lines) are described in detail within the methodology note; comparisons across years where methodological changes have occurred should be treated with caution.

Methodology note: https://www.gov.uk/government/collections/road-freight-domestic-and-international-statistics
Notes & definitions: https://www.gov.uk/government/collections/road-freight-domestic-and-international-statistics

Source: Continuing Survey of Road Goods Transport (Great Britain)
Telephone: 020 7944 3905
Email: roadfreight.stats@dft.gov.uk

22.17c Goods moved[1] by commodity[2]: annual 2005 - 2019

UK activity of GB-registered heavy goods vehicles

Million tonne kilometres

Commodity	2005	2006	2007	2008	2009	2010	2011	2012	2013[3]	2014	2015	2016	2017	2018	2019
Agricultural products	11,886	11,466	12,252	11,730	10,073	10,730	11,497	12,536	11,023	11,871	12,231	11,047	11,397	13,239	11,784
Cereals									1,650	2,058	2,170	1,531	1,347	2,224	2,319
Potatoes									1,141	1,063	1,075	1,524	1,117	1,471	1,135
Sugar beet									203	339	255	188	211	297	683
Other fresh fruit and vegetables									1,706	1,932	2,538	1,875	1,500	1,845	1,938
Products of forestry and logging									2,056	2,463	1,596	1,890	2,780	2,365	563
Live plants and flowers									448	381	533	517	397	522	426
Other substances of vegetable origin									865	800	932	580	1,054	1,096	820
Live animals									649	896	837	787	753	867	1,182
Raw milk from bovine cattle, sheep and goats									1,759	1,400	1,571	1,372	1,528	1,511	2,241
Other raw materials of animal origin									452	254	441	469	479	956	444
Fish and other fishing products									85	226	283	316	231	85	34
Unspecified															
Coal and lignite	1,461	1,399	1,525	1,719	1,186	1,500	743	954	785	1,040	772	494	673	537	383
Coal and lignite									785	726	650	370	393	366	297
Crude petroleum															
Natural gas										302			226		
Unspecified													55		
Metal ore and other mining and quarrying	16,299	16,311	16,840	14,444	11,542	13,575	10,358	11,431	9,349	10,752	11,779	12,916	12,266	12,169	10,983
Iron ores															
Non-ferrous metal ores (except Uranium and Thorium ores)															
Chemical and natural fertilizer minerals														308	606
Salt									486	295	325	384	197	479	367
Stone, sand, gravel, clay, peat and other mining/quarrying products									8,826	10,431	11,429	12,456	12,053	11,382	10,010
Uranium and thorium ores															
Unspecified															
Food products, including beverages and tobacco	29,888	30,694	32,776	31,156	32,247	34,262	33,021	36,759	34,470	29,039	33,809	37,231	39,308	37,889	35,236
Meat, raw hides and skins and meat products									1,025	1,047	1,052	845	1,042	1,105	831
Fish and fish products, processed and preserved									389	226	353	348	230	164	508
Fruit and vegetables, processed and preserved									373	395	573	204	187	670	493
Animal and vegetable oils and fats									675	660	596	341	437	318	218
Dairy products and ice cream									2,290	1,170	1,767	2,352	2,660	1,725	1,699
Grain mill products, starches, starch products and prepared animal feeds									3,810	3,287	3,369	3,655	3,909	4,209	5,123
Beverages									5,621	4,938	6,306	4,343	4,815	5,624	5,574
Various food or tobacco products (Not in parcel service or grouped)									3,308	2,936	3,297	2,785	2,527	2,136	2,035
Various food and tobacco products in parcel service or grouped									16,980	14,120	16,496	22,357	23,502	21,939	18,755
Unspecified										260					
Textiles and textiles products, leather and leather products	1,894	2,198	2,171	1,610	2,030	1,991	1,496	1,287	2,224	1,692	1,686	1,679	2,315	1,576	1,366
Textiles									785	895	757	880	1,084	613	663
Wearing apparel and articles of fur									1,410	747	808	731	1,189	910	654
Leather and leather products									20			69		52	
Unspecified									9						
Wood products	12,572	12,832	11,840	10,640	8,967	10,285	9,155	7,869	7,941	6,518	7,629	6,745	5,390	6,374	6,621
Products of wood and cork (except furniture)									3,521	2,240	3,327	2,852	2,372	2,966	2,717
Pulp, paper and paper products									3,481	3,356	3,743	3,350	2,432	2,849	3,252
Printed matter and recorded media									939	741	559	542	586	559	652
Unspecified										181					

22.17c Goods moved[1] by commodity[2]: annual 2005 - 2019

UK activity of GB-registered heavy goods vehicles

Million tonne kilometres

Commodity	2005	2006	2007	2008	2009	2010	2011	2012	2013[3]	2014	2015	2016	2017	2018	2019
Coke and refined petroleum products	5,466	5,402	4,957	5,488	4,271	5,921	5,548	6,361	5,000	5,086	5,643	4,421	4,194	4,057	3,418
Coke oven products, briquettes, ovoids and similar solid fuels									158	149	112	227	215	94	125
Liquid refined petroleum products									4,026	4,186	4,340	3,397	2,837	2,838	2,325
Gaseous, liquefied or compressed petroleum products									708	573	1,157	698	793	881	609
Solid or waxy defined petroleum products									109		34		350	243	359
Unspecified															
Chemical products	8,773	7,132	7,723	6,868	6,134	5,877	7,653	7,467	5,510	6,344	5,845	6,155	7,129	7,699	6,729
Basic mineral chemicals products									975	796	1,008	627	1,281	1,271	1,159
Basic organic chemical products									135	217	294	116	480	320	672
Nitrogen compounds and fertilizers (except natural fertilizers)									737	620	577	1,036	1,322	1,065	319
Basic plastics and synthetic rubber in primary forms									817	955	789	931	1,002	1,507	1,139
Pharmaceuticals and parachemicals, including pesticides and other agri-chemical products									1,102	1,789	1,436	1,633	1,181	2,090	2,142
Rubber or plastic products									1,002	1,253	1,180	1,183	1,382	1,193	1,296
Nuclear fuel									742	713	562	629	481	253	
Unspecified															
Glass, cement and other non-metallic mineral products	10,992	11,490	11,525	10,789	8,241	9,082	9,752	7,849	8,783	8,951	9,729	8,745	10,668	10,325	11,190
Glass and glass products, ceramic and porcelain products									2,112	2,678	2,659	2,166	2,828	2,658	3,267
Cement, lime and plaster									2,365	1,571	2,823	2,656	2,473	2,126	2,183
Other construction materials									4,305	4,702	4,246	3,924	5,367	5,541	5,740
Unspecified															
Metal products	7,291	6,683	8,188	5,744	4,908	5,008	4,956	7,003	4,385	4,666	4,876	4,874	5,677	4,040	3,599
Basic iron, steel and ferro-alloys and first processing of iron and steel products (except tubes)									2,635	2,741	2,883	3,033	3,471	2,260	1,175
Non-ferrous metals and products									323	526	341	376	433	412	386
Tubes, pipes, hollow profiles and related fittings									160	257	295	490	538	195	143
Structural metal products									171	175	753	356	384	339	356
Boilers, hardware, weapons and other fabricated metal products									1,087	800	604	612	848	831	1,539
Unspecified										168					
Machinery and equipment	4,503	4,499	4,794	4,142	3,578	3,724	3,967	3,335	2,882	2,531	3,059	3,335	2,606	3,345	4,184
Agricultural and forestry machinery									414	111	184	240	193	200	115
Domestic appliances (white goods)									383	386	397	609	473	655	1,793
Office machinery and computers									48	163	120	131	56	34	104
Electric machinery and apparatus									322	324	536	450	567	550	283
Electronic components and emission and transmission appliances									143	501	527	234	240	170	49
Television and radio receivers, sound or video recording or reproducing apparatus (brown goods)									26	65	49	84	51	173	25
Medical, precision and optical instruments, watches and clocks									66	28	99	96	145	248	91
Other machines, machine tools and parts									1,149	675	906	1,312	881	1,314	1,723
Unspecified									331	278	241	180			
Transport equipment	4,749	4,744	4,486	4,370	3,343	3,814	3,567	4,049	2,388	3,674	3,941	5,188	4,328	4,551	3,712
Automobile industry products									2,163	3,052	3,633	4,871	4,023	4,307	3,477
Other transport equipment									226	585	309	318	305	244	235
Unspecified															
Furniture and other manufactured goods	5,922	5,831	5,804	4,272	3,363	2,882	2,407	2,301	1,555	2,115	1,908	2,074	2,188	1,970	1,688
Furniture and furnishings									1,019	1,377	1,106	1,327	1,210	1,067	1,440
Other manufactured goods									536	737	802	746	978	904	247
Unspecified															

22.17c Goods moved[1] by commodity[2]: annual 2005 - 2019
UK activity of GB-registered heavy goods vehicles

Million tonne kilometres

Commodity	2005	2006	2007	2008	2009	2010	2011	2012	2013[3]	2014	2015	2016	2017	2018	2019
Waste related products	6,429	6,407	7,375	6,267	4,646	5,554	8,470	8,310	8,099	8,213	9,855	11,323	9,495	10,620	12,546
Household and municipal waste	:	:	:	:	:	:	:	:	2,468	2,706	3,602	3,604	3,341	3,649	4,715
Other waste and secondary raw materials	:	:	:	:	:	:	:	:	5,631	5,395	6,253	7,719	6,154	6,971	7,831
Unspecified	:	:	:	:	:	:	:	:	:	111	:	:	:	:	:
Mail and parcels	4,122	4,224	3,638	3,768	2,970	3,932	5,352	3,980	2,926	3,395	4,232	5,778	5,345	8,749	6,043
Mail	:	:	:	:	:	:	:	:	1,310	1,373	1,496	1,818	1,583	4,450	2,016
Parcels and small packages	:	:	:	:	:	:	:	:	1,616	2,007	2,736	3,960	3,762	4,300	4,028
Unspecified	:	:	:	:	:	:	:	:	:	:	:	:	:	:	:
Empty containers, pallets and other packaging	3,384	3,385	3,478	3,718	3,700	3,915	3,905	4,257	2,907	2,785	4,143	4,089	4,116	3,238	2,466
Empty containers and swap bodies in service	:	:	:	:	:	:	:	:	349	357	766	791	1,094	1,047	359
Empty pallets and other packaging in service	:	:	:	:	:	:	:	:	2,558	2,426	3,370	3,299	3,023	2,183	2,107
Unspecified	:	:	:	:	:	:	:	:	:	:	:	:	:	:	:
Household and office removals and other non-market goods	185	169	139	112	41	97	902	1,571	2,340	2,505	2,497	2,459	2,573	2,058	2,981
Household removal	:	:	:	:	:	:	:	:	298	124	149	156	90	98	105
Baggage and articles accompanying travellers	:	:	:	:	:	:	:	:	:	:	:	28	:	:	:
Vehicles for repair	:	:	:	:	:	:	:	:	35	20	28	57	87	48	142
Plant equipment and scaffolding	:	:	:	:	:	:	:	:	1,576	2,127	2,046	1,994	2,058	1,640	2,491
Other non-market goods	:	:	:	:	:	:	:	:	429	234	270	224	337	270	243
Unspecified	:	:	:	:	:	:	:	:	:	:	:	:	:	:	:
Groupage	16,692	17,580	17,799	18,923	13,936	16,701	15,855	14,159	14,150	12,888	15,685	15,066	14,405	16,107	25,280
Unidentifiable goods	59	:	:	:	:	:	1,753	1,104	4,731	2,929	3,663	4,662	2,860	3,387	3,579
Unidentifiable goods in containers or swap bodies	:	:	:	:	:	:	:	:	1,346	973	1,032	824	740	1,396	1,442
Other unidentifiable goods	:	:	:	:	:	:	:	:	3,385	1,956	2,632	3,838	2,121	1,991	2,137
Other goods not elsewhere classified	:	:	:	:	:	:	:	43	45	891	311	213	116	221	:
All commodities	152,566	152,445	157,311	145,760	125,177	138,850	140,366	142,625	131,493	127,885	143,294	148,494	147,049	152,152	153,792

Source: Continuing Survey of Road Goods Transport (Great Britain)
Telephone: 020 7944 3095
Email: roadfreight.stats@dft.gov.uk

1. Goods moved: the weight of goods carried multiplied by the distance hauled, measured in tonne kilometres.
2. For mixed consignments, the commodity is recorded as the main type of good carried if it represents 75% or more of the consignment weight, otherwise it is recorded as groupage.
3. Commodity data from 2013 have been coded using a different coding frame, with classifications being retrospectively applied to earlier years. See the notes and definitions for more information.
':' = none recorded in the sample or not available due to small sample size.
'.' = not applicable. Prior to 2013, data was not collected at the commodity group level.

Notes: Sub-commodity categories may not sum to totals due to rounding and supressed data. Discontinuities in the series (denoted by lines) are described in detail within the methodology note; comparisons across years where methodological changes have occurred should be treated with caution.
Methodology note: https://www.gov.uk/government/collections/road-freight-domestic-and-international-statistics
Notes & definitions: https://www.gov.uk/government/collections/road-freight-domestic-and-international-statistics

22.18a Goods lifted[1] by type and weight[2] of vehicle: annual 2000 - 2019

UK activity of GB-registered heavy goods vehicles

Million tonnes

Year	Rigid vehicles					Articulated vehicles			All vehicles
	Over 3.5t to 7.5t	Over 7.5t to 17t	Over 17t to 25t	Over 25t	All Rigids	Over 3.5t to 33t	Over 33t	All artics	All vehicles
2000	77	152	87	424	741	107	746	852	1,593
2001	80	123	86	443	733	97	751	848	1,581
2002	77	111	90	491	768	81	778	859	1,627
2003	70	89	100	506	765	69	809	878	1,643
2004	77	87	108	540	812	59	873	932	1,744
2005	70	70	110	562	812	51	883	934	1,746
2006	64	64	118	585	831	49	896	945	1,776
2007	54	52	127	614	848	49	926	975	1,822
2008	56	44	118	513	731	44	892	937	1,668
2009	56	37	102	377	572	38	746	785	1,356
2010	54	37	103	414	607	33	848	881	1,489
2011	49	31	96	429	606	37	814	851	1,457
2012	41	23	91	383	539	33	855	888	1,427
2013	36	19	79	364	499	33	784	817	1,316
2014	34	19	81	365	500	24	798	822	1,322
2015	36	20	86	409	551	26	868	894	1,445
2016	47	27	89	395	558	31	845	876	1,434
2017	35	24	90	396	544	29	823	852	1,397
2018	36	24	85	371	517	26	863	889	1,405
2019	35	25	96	386	542	24	874	897	1,440

Source: Continuing Survey of Road Goods Transport (Great Britain)
Telephone: 020 7944 3905
Email: roadfreight.stats@dft.gov.uk

1. Goods lifted: the weight of goods carried, measured in tonnes.
2. Gross vehicle weight: the total weight of the vehicle plus
   its carrying capacity, from 3.5 to 44 tonnes.
Note: discontinuities in the series (denoted by lines) are described in detail within the
methodology note; comparisons across years where methodological changes have occurred
should be treated with caution.

Methodology note: https://www.gov.uk/government/collections/road-freight-domestic-and-international-statistics

Notes & definitions: https://www.gov.uk/government/collections/road-freight-domestic-and-international-statistics

22.18b Goods lifted[1] by commodity[2]: annual 2005 - 2019
UK activity of GB-registered heavy goods vehicles

Million tonnes

Commodity	2005	2006	2007	2008	2009	2010	2011	2012	2013[3]	2014	2015	2016	2017	2018	2019
Agricultural products	112	103	107	102	100	106	103	110	98	104	97	94	97	112	92
Cereals									20	22	20	15	16	23	23
Potatoes									8	7	8	9	7	9	8
Sugar beet									3	5	4	2	3	4	7
Other fresh fruit and vegetables									11	13	17	14	10	12	12
Products of forestry and logging									18	20	13	18	22	20	5
Live plants and flowers									3	3	4	4	3	4	3
Other substances of vegetable origin									9	6	8	7	8	9	7
Live animals									6	8	5	6	7	7	9
Raw milk from bovine cattle, sheep and goats									16	15	12	13	14	15	15
Other raw materials of animal origin									3	3	3	5	4	7	3
Fish and other fishing products									~	1	1	2	1	1	~
Unspecified															
Coal and lignite	20	17	23	21	13	12	9	10	7	12	9	3	7	3	2
Coal and lignite									7	8	8	2	5	3	2
Crude petroleum													2		
Natural gas										4			1		
Unspecified															
Metal ore and other mining and quarrying	394	390	398	335	234	270	212	208	196	198	229	196	195	182	155
Iron ores															
Non-ferrous metal ores (except Uranium and Thorium ores)															
Chemical and natural fertilizer minerals														2	5
Salt									4	2	2	4	2	4	3
Stone, sand, gravel, clay, peat and other mining/quarrying products									192	194	226	192	194	176	147
Uranium and thorium ores															
Unspecified															
Food products, including beverages and tobacco	236	257	266	261	259	285	279	290	277	235	258	272	287	282	261
Meat, raw hides and skins and meat products									7	7	6	6	7	6	5
Fish and fish products, processed and preserved									2	1	2	2	1	1	2
Fruit and vegetables, processed and preserved									2	3	3	2	1	4	3
Animal and vegetable oils and fats									3	5	5	3	4	4	1
Dairy products and ice cream									18	8	12	14	19	14	13
Grain mill products, starches, starch products and prepared animal feeds									35	31	29	32	37	38	46
Beverages									44	35	45	31	34	40	37
Other food or tobacco products (Not in parcel service or grouped)									24	23	26	20	19	15	14
Various food and tobacco products in parcel service or grouped									142	121	130	162	165	160	138
Unspecified										1					
Textiles and textiles products, leather and leather products	14	15	13	11	15	15	11	10	16	12	11	13	16	11	10
Textiles									6	7	6	7	8	5	5
Wearing apparel and articles of fur									9	5	5	6	7	6	5
Leather and leather products									~			~		~	
Unspecified									~						
Wood products	95	89	92	89	71	74	65	57	56	49	55	48	39	49	48
Products of wood and cork (except furniture)									25	17	27	21	17	24	23
Pulp, paper and paper products									24	25	24	23	17	21	21
Printed matter and recorded media									7	5	4	4	4	4	4
Unspecified										2					

22.18b Goods lifted[1] by commodity[2]: annual 2005 - 2019

UK activity of GB-registered heavy goods vehicles

Million tonnes

Commodity	2005	2006	2007	2008	2009	2010	2011	2012	2013[3]	2014	2015	2016	2017	2018	2019
Coke and refined petroleum products	69	66	69	69	53	67	64	71	53	52	63	48	43	39	36
Coke oven products, briquettes, ovoids and similar solid fuels									3	3	2	3	3	2	3
Liquid refined petroleum products									43	44	51	38	30	28	26
Gaseous, liquefied or compressed petroleum products									6	5	10	6	7	7	4
Solid or waxy defined petroleum products									1	..	~	..	2	2	2
Unspecified									..	..	..	..	..	..	..
Chemical products	64	55	56	53	46	44	60	53	38	47	41	45	51	50	49
Basic mineral chemicals products									6	9	10	5	10	8	10
Basic organic chemical products									1	1	2	2	3	3	5
Nitrogen compounds and fertilizers (except natural fertilizers)									4	4	3	8	9	8	2
Basic plastics and synthetic rubber in primary forms									7	7	5	7	7	8	7
Pharmaceuticals and parachemicals, including pesticides and other agri-chemical products									8	10	9	12	8	13	17
Rubber or plastic products									8	9	8	9	10	8	9
Nuclear fuel															
Unspecified									5	6	4	4	4	2	..
Glass, cement and other non-metallic mineral products	170	177	173	173	121	140	135	116	116	134	139	128	135	135	143
Glass and glass products, ceramic and porcelain products									17	26	23	22	22	21	25
Cement, lime and plaster									20	20	26	26	22	21	23
Other construction materials									79	88	89	80	91	94	96
Unspecified															
Metal products	61	61	65	51	44	46	39	55	37	33	37	42	45	34	28
Basic iron, steel and ferro-alloys and first processing of iron and steel products (except tubes)									23	18	23	27	29	19	9
Non-ferrous metals and products									4	4	3	3	3	3	3
Tubes, pipes, hollow profiles and related fittings									1	2	3	3	4	2	1
Structural metal products									1	2	4	3	3	3	2
Boilers, hardware, weapons and other fabricated metal products									8	5	5	6	6	7	12
Unspecified									..	1	..	..	..	..	..
Machinery and equipment	44	46	48	40	39	39	38	30	22	19	24	31	20	29	32
Agricultural and forestry machinery									3	1	2	2	1	2	1
Domestic appliances (white goods)									3	2	3	5	3	5	12
Office machinery and computers									~	2	1	1	~	~	1
Electric machinery and apparatus									3	2	4	4	4	4	2
Electronic components and emission and transmission appliances									1	3	4	3	2	1	~
Television and radio receivers, sound or video recording or reproducing apparatus (brown goods)									~	~	~	1	~	1	~
Medical, precision and optical instruments, watches and clocks									1	~	1	1	1	1	1
Other machines, machine tools and parts									8	6	7	14	7	14	14
Unspecified									2	2	2	1	..	..	..
Transport equipment	32	32	34	40	29	29	28	30	21	26	28	37	32	35	29
Automobile industry products									20	22	26	35	30	33	27
Other transport equipment									1	3	2	3	2	2	2
Unspecified															
Furniture and other manufactured goods	40	41	40	29	26	22	16	15	11	17	16	15	16	14	11
Furniture and furnishings									7	11	8	10	9	7	9
Other manufactured goods									4	6	8	5	7	7	2
Unspecified															

22.18b Goods lifted[1] by commodity[2]: annual 2005 - 2019
UK activity of GB-registered heavy goods vehicles

Million tonnes

Commodity	2005	2006	2007	2008	2009	2010	2011	2012	2013[3]	2014	2015	2016	2017	2018	2019
Waste related products	**195**	**220**	**239**	**178**	**131**	**140**	**172**	**158**	**140**	**157**	**166**	**175**	**153**	**159**	**183**
Household and municipal waste									53	57	62	71	66	64	80
Other waste and secondary raw materials									87	99	105	105	87	95	103
Unspecified										1	:	:	:	:	:
Mail and parcels	**32**	**31**	**29**	**29**	**22**	**33**	**35**	**29**	**23**	**24**	**29**	**43**	**36**	**48**	**42**
Mail									12	10	12	13	10	21	14
Parcels and small packages									11	13	17	29	26	27	27
Unspecified									:	:	:	:	:	:	:
Empty containers, pallets and other packaging	**39**	**37**	**41**	**40**	**36**	**37**	**39**	**36**	**27**	**29**	**35**	**35**	**36**	**28**	**20**
Empty containers and swap bodies in service									4	6	8	7	10	10	4
Empty pallets and other packaging in service									24	23	27	27	26	18	16
Unspecified									:	:	:	:	:	:	:
Household and office removals and other non-market goods	**2**	**1**	**1**	**1**	**1**	**1**	**12**	**19**	**32**	**33**	**36**	**33**	**37**	**30**	**43**
Household removal									3	1	2	2	1	1	2
Baggage and articles accompanying travellers									~	:	~	~	:	:	:
Vehicles for repair									~	~	~	1	1	1	2
Plant equipment and scaffolding									24	29	31	29	32	26	38
Other non-market goods									4	2	3	1	3	2	2
Unspecified									:	:	:	:	:	:	:
Groupage	**128**	**135**	**129**	**152**	**121**	**128**	**128**	**123**	**114**	**109**	**136**	**138**	**129**	**141**	**230**
Unidentifiable goods	**1**						**11**	**7**	**32**	**26**	**32**	**34**	**22**	**22**	**27**
Unidentifiable goods in containers or swap bodies									7	9	11	6	6	9	10
Other unidentifiable goods									25	17	21	29	16	12	16
Other goods not elsewhere classified								**~**	**~**	**8**	**3**	**2**	**1**	**1**	**:**
All commodities	**1,746**	**1,776**	**1,822**	**1,668**	**1,356**	**1,489**	**1,457**	**1,427**	**1,316**	**1,322**	**1,445**	**1,434**	**1,397**	**1,405**	**1,440**

Source: Continuing Survey of Road Goods Transport (Great Britain)
Telephone: 020 7944 3095
Email: roadfreight.stats@dft.gov.uk

Notes:
1. Goods lifted: the weight of goods carried, measured in tonnes.
2. For mixed consignments, the commodity is recorded as the main type of good carried if it represents 75% or more of the consignment weight, otherwise it is recorded as groupage.
3. Commodity data from 2013 have been coded using a different coding frame, with classifications being retrospectively applied to earlier years. See the notes and definitions for more information.
 : = none recorded in the sample or not available due to small sample size.
 .. = not applicable. Prior to 2013, data was not collected at the commodity group level.
~ represents values less than 1 (in units given).

Notes: Sub-commodity categories may not sum to totals due to rounding and supressed data. Discontinuities in the series (denoted by lines) are described in detail within the methodology note; comparisons across years where methodological changes have occurred should be treated with caution.
Methodology note: https://www.gov.uk/government/collections/road-freight-domestic-and-international-statistics

Notes & definitions: https://www.gov.uk/government/collections/road-freight-domestic-and-international-statistics

22.19a Passenger journeys by sector

Great Britain annual data (financial year): 2002-3 to 2019-20, Number of passenger journeys made (millions)

Financial year	Franchised long distance operators	Franchised London and South East operators	Franchised regional operators	Total franchised passenger journeys	Non franchised
2002-03	77.2	679.1	219.2	975.5	5.0
2003-04	81.5	690.0	240.2	1,011.7	5.1
2004-05	83.7	704.5	251.3	1,039.5	5.0
2005-06	89.5	719.7	267.3	1,076.5	5.3
2006-07	99.0	769.5	276.5	1,145.0	5.3
2007-08	103.9	828.4	285.8	1,218.1	5.2
2008-09	109.4	854.3	302.8	1,266.5	5.5
2009-10	111.6	842.2	304.0	1,257.9	6.3
2010-11 (r)	117.0	910.6	315.8	1,343.4	7.2
2011-12 (b) (r)	122.0	991.0	336.1	1,449.1	7.2
2012-13 (r)	123.1	1,030.0	337.2	1,490.3	7.3
2013-14 (r)	125.8	1,099.3	350.5	1,575.7	7.7
2014-15 (r)	131.8	1,144.0	366.7	1,642.5	7.9
2015-16 (r)	135.4	1,194.8	375.1	1,705.4	8.2
2016-17 (r)	140.4	1,190.5	388.0	1,719.0	8.5
2017-18 (r)	141.4	1,165.4	388.4	1,695.2	8.8
2018-19 (r)	143.5	1,209.0	391.7	1,744.3	8.7
2019-20 (r)	139.2	1,195.9	395.4	1,730.5	8.3

Symbols: (:) Data not available (r) Data revised
(p) Data are provisional (b) Break in time series

Source(s): CAPRI (Computer Analysis of Passenger Revenue Information) ticketing and revenue database, LENNON ticketing and revenue database, Train Operating Companies (TOCs)

Email: rail.stats@orr.gov.uk

Notes:

1. Data does not include Eurostar, Underground or light rail services.

2. The non-franchised figures now include Heathrow Express in addition to journeys made on Grand Central and Hull Trains. There were no non-franchised passenger operators before 1998-99 Q1.

3. Data for 1986-87 to 2002-03 sourced from CAPRI (Computer Analysis of Passenger Revenue Information), which was the rail industry's former central ticketing system, and train operating companies (1999-00 to 2002-03). Passenger journeys made using some operator-specific tickets and Passenger Transport Executive multi-modal tickets are not included in the estimates for 1986-87 to 1998-99.

4. Data for 2003-04 onwards sourced from the LENNON (Latest Earnings Networked Nationally Over Night) ticketing and revenue database and train operating companies.

(b). Data from Passenger Transport Executives was included from 1999-00 onwards, which is why a series break is indicated at the start of 1999-00. The distribution of operator provided (non-LENNON) data by sector is on an operator basis from the start of 2011-12, which is why a series break is indicated at the start of 2011-12. Before 2011-12, non-LENNON usage was distributed to the sectors at the national (GB) level.

(r). The distribution of non-LENNON data between the sectors has been improved. This affects both the annual and quarterly data from the start of 2010-11. The regional figures from the start of 2010-11 have been revised down by around 11 million journeys a year due to the overstating of Merseyrail journeys included as part of the non-LENNON component of the data.

Passenger rail usage statistical release: https://dataportal.orr.gov.uk/statistics/usage/passenger-rail-usage/
Passenger rail usage quality and methodology report: https://dataportal.orr.gov.uk/media/1234/passenger-usage-quality-report.pdf
Revisions log: http://dataportal.orr.gov.uk/footer/revisions-log/

22.19a (contd.)Passenger journeys by sector

Passenger journeys on light rail and trams by system: Great Britain

	Light Rail and Tram Systems, England										Light Rail and Tram Systems, GB	
Financial year	Docklands Light Railway	London Tramlink	Nottingham Express Transit	West Midlands Metro	Sheffield Supertram	Tyne and Wear Metro	Manchester Metrolink	Blackpool Tramway	England outside of London	England	Edin-burgh Trams	GB
2000/01	38.4	15.0	.	5.4	11.1	32.5	17.2	4.1	70.3	**123.6**	.	**123.6**
2001/02	41.3	18.2	.	4.8	11.4	33.4	18.2	4.9	72.7	**132.2**	.	**132.2**
2002/03	45.7	18.7	.	4.9	11.5	36.6	18.8	4.5	76.3	**140.7**	.	**140.7**
2003/04	48.5	19.8	0.4	5.1	12.3	37.9	18.9	3.7	78.3	**146.5**	.	**146.5**
2004/05	50.1	22.0	8.5	5.0	12.8	36.8	19.7	3.9	86.6	**158.7**	.	**158.7**
2005/06	53.5	22.5	9.8	5.1	13.1	35.8	19.9	3.6	87.3	**163.4**	.	**163.4**
2006/07	63.9	24.6	10.1	4.9	14.0	37.9	19.8	3.4	90.1	**178.6**	.	**178.6**
2007/08	66.6	27.2	10.2	4.8	14.8	39.8	20.0	2.9	92.5	**186.2**	.	**186.2**
2008/09	67.8	27.2	9.8	4.7	15.0	40.6	21.1	2.3	93.6	**188.6**	.	**188.6**
2009/10	69.4	25.8	9.0	4.7	14.7	40.8	19.6	2.2	91.0	**186.2**	.	**186.2**
2010/11	78.3	27.9	9.7	4.8	15.0	39.9	19.2	1.6	90.3	**196.5**	.	**196.5**
2011/12	86.1	28.6	9.0	4.9	15.0	37.9	22.3	1.1	90.1	**204.8**	.	**204.8**
2012/13	100.0	30.1	7.4	4.8	14.4	37.0	25.0	3.7	92.3	**222.5**	.	**222.5**
2013/14	101.6	31.2	7.9	4.7	12.6	35.7	29.2	4.3	94.4	**227.1**	.	**227.1**
2014/15	110.2	30.7	8.1	4.4	11.5	38.1	31.2	4.1	97.3	**238.2**	4.1	**242.4**
2015/16	116.9	27.0	12.2	4.8	11.6	40.3	34.3	4.9	108.1	**252.0**	5.3	**257.3**
2016/17	122.3	29.5	16.4	6.2	12.6	37.7	37.8	5.1	115.9	**267.7**	5.8	**273.5**
2017/18	119.6	29.1	17.8	5.7	12.3	36.4	41.2	5.2	118.6	**267.2**	6.8	**274.7**
2018/19	121.8	28.7	18.8	8.3	11.9	36.4	43.7	5.2	124.4	**274.8**	7.5	**282.3**
2019/20	116.8	27.2	18.7	8.0	10.5	33.1	44.3	4.8	119.4	**263.4**	7.1	**270.6**

1. For further information on these systems including network and infrastructure changes that may affect the figures, please refer to the quality report (https://www.gov.uk/government/publications/light-rail-and-tram-statistics-guidance)
2. Manchester Metrolink have revised their method for calculation of passenger boardings so the figures from 2010/11 are not directly comparable with previous years.

The figures in this table are National Statistics

Source: DfT Light Rail and Tram Survey
Telephone: 020 7082 6602
Email: bus.statistics@dft.gov.uk

22.19b Passenger revenue by sector

Great Britain annual data (financial year): 2002-03 to 2019-20. Passenger revenue by sector (£ millions).

Financial year	Franchised long distance operators	Franchised London & South East operators	Franchised regional operators	Total franchised passenger revenue	Non franchised
2002-03	1,279	1,848	535	3,663	64.0
2003-04	1,384	1,932	585	3,901	67.0
2004-05	1,465	2,059	634	4,158	69.0
2005-06	1,609	2,197	687	4,493	74.0
2006-07	1,842	2,437	733	5,012	80.0
2007-08	2,036	2,717	801	5,555	80.6
2008-09	2,168	2,963	872	6,004	103.8
2009-10	2,216	3,046	916	6,179	131.2
2010-11	2,366	3,264	990	6,620	150.9
2011-12	2,533	3,602	1,094	7,229	157.1
2012-13	2,652	3,888	1,167	7,707	167.0
2013-14	2,779	4,180	1,244	8,203	179.4
2014-15	2,975	4,486	1,342	8,803	191.8
2015-16	3,128	4,676	1,409	9,213	187.6
2016-17	3,250	4,725	1,466	9,441	195.7
2017-18	3,342	4,786	1,528	9,655	198.4
2018-19	3,527	5,120	1,595	10,241	199.5
2019-20	3,447	5,129	1,632	10,208	189.5

Symbols: (:) Data not available **(r)** Data revised
(p) Data are provisional **(b)** Break in time series

Source(s): LENNON ticketing and revenue database
Email: rail.stats@orr.gov.uk

Notes:
1. Data does not include Eurostar, Underground or light rail services.
2. The non-franchised figures now include Heathrow Express in addition to Grand Central and Hull Trains. There were no non-franchised passenger operators before 1998-99 Q1.
Passenger rail usage statistical release: https://dataportal.orr.gov.uk/statistics/usage/passenger-rail-usage/
Passenger rail usage quality and methodology report: https://dataportal.orr.gov.uk/media/1234/passenger-usage-quality-report.pdf
Revisions log: http://dataportal.orr.gov.uk/footer/revisions-log/

Passenger revenue at actual prices on light rail and trams by system: Great Britain

£ Millions

Financial year	Docklands Light Railway	London Tramlink	Nottingham Express Transit	West Midlands Metro	Sheffield Supertram	Tyne and Wear Metro	Manchester Metrolink	Blackpool Tramway	England outside of London	England	Edinburgh Trams	GB
					Light Rail and Tram Systems, England						Light Rail and Tram Systems, GB	
2000/01	28.8	12.2	.	3.1	7.1	24.1	18.1	4.3	56.7	97.7	.	97.7
2001/02	32.2	12.9	.	3.9	7.6	25.0	20.1	4.7	61.3	106.5	.	106.5
2002/03	35.6	15.0	.	5.0	10.2	28.7	21.0	4.6	69.4	120.0	.	120.0
2003/04	37.2	16.1	.	5.2	9.2	31.4	20.9	3.9	70.7	124.0	.	124.0
2004/05	40.4	18.0	5.9	5.4	11.1	32.6	22.1	4.3	81.3	139.7	.	139.7
2005/06	46.1	18.8	7.3	5.9	10.4	34.4	22.6	4.4	85.0	150.0	.	150.0
2006/07	53.9	19.0	7.5	6.3	12.4	35.2	23.6	4.5	89.5	162.3	.	162.3
2007/08	63.1	20.9	7.9	6.3	13.7	37.3	22.4	4.0	91.6	175.5	.	175.5
2008/09	64.0	18.1	8.6	6.6	15.2	41.3	22.5	3.5	97.6	179.7	.	179.7
2009/10	74.9	16.2	7.9	6.5	15.0	40.8	23.4	3.0	96.7	187.7	.	187.7
2010/11	88.8	19.1	9.0	7.0	15.3	41.6	27.4	2.5	102.8	210.6	.	210.6
2011/12	102.8	21.2	8.4	7.4	15.4	42.2	33.7	1.7	108.8	232.8	.	232.8
2012/13	122.1	22.5	8.5	7.8	14.4	43.6	42.0	5.0	121.3	265.9	.	265.9
2013/14	130.0	23.5	8.3	7.9	13.9	45.2	51.8	6.1	133.2	286.7	.	286.7
2014/15	146.2	24.4	8.8	7.7	12.6	47.9	56.8	5.6	139.4	309.9	7.0	317.0
2015/16	158.4	22.8	13.6	8.6	11.4	50.2	62.4	6.1	152.2	333.4	9.6	343.1
2016/17	166.5	25.5	17.8	10.3	13.5	50.5	67.3	6.5	165.9	357.9	11.2	369.1
2017/18	168.3	24.1	19.1	9.8	13.9	50.9	74.8	6.7	175.2	367.6	13.2	383.3
2018/19	171.6	23.5	20.6	10.7	14.0	51.9	82.1	7.0	186.3	381.5	15.7	397.1
2019/20	168.8	22.7	21.3	11.3	13.8	49.9	82.6	6.7	185.7	377.2	15.9	393.1

These figures are not adjusted for inflation.
For further information on these systems including infrastructure changes that may affect the figures, please refer to the Quality Report.
The figures for Docklands Light Railway from 2011/12 to 2018/19 have been revised.
The 2018/19 figure for Blackpool Tramway has been revised.
Quality Report: https://www.gov.uk/government/publications/light-rail-and-tram-statistics-guidance
The figures in this table are National Statistics

Source: DfT Light Rail and Tram Survey
Telephone: 020 7082 6602
Email: bus.statistics@dft.gov.uk

22.19c Passenger kilometres by sector

Great Britain annual data (financial year): from 2002-03 - Number of passenger kilometres travelled (billions)

Financial year	Franchised long distance operators	Franchised London and South East operators	Franchised regional operators	Total franchised passenger kilometres	Non franchised
2002-03	12.9	19.8	6.9	39.7	0.1
2003-04	13.3	20.1	7.5	40.9	0.1
2004-05	13.4	20.5	7.8	41.7	0.1
2005-06	14.2	20.7	8.2	43.1	0.1
2006-07	15.6	22.2	8.4	46.2	0.1
2007-08	16.5	23.5	8.9	48.9	0.1
2008-09	17.0	24.2	9.4	50.6	0.3
2009-10	17.6	23.8	9.7	51.1	0.4
2010-11 (r)	18.6	25.0	10.4	54.0	0.5
2011-12 (b) (r)	19.4	26.3	10.9	56.6	0.5
2012-13 (r)	19.5	27.1	11.1	57.7	0.6
2013-14 (r)	19.7	28.4	11.5	59.6	0.6
2014-15 (r)	20.9	29.3	12.1	62.3	0.7
2015-16 (r)	21.3	30.2	12.5	64.0	0.7
2016-17 (r)	22.0	30.4	12.9	65.3	0.8
2017-18 (r)	22.3	30.0	13.1	65.5	0.8
2018-19 (r)	22.6	31.0	13.3	66.9	0.8
2019-20 (r)	21.8	30.7	13.5	66.0	0.8

Symbols: **(:)** Data not available **(r)** Data revised
(p) Data are provisional **(b)** Break in time series

Source(s): CAPRI ticketing and revenue database, LENNON ticketing and revenue database, Train Operating Companies (TOCs)

Email: rail.stats@orr.gov.uk

Notes:

1. Data does not include Eurostar, Underground or light rail services.

2. The non-franchised figures now include Heathrow Express in addition to kilometres travelled on Grand Central and Hull Trains. There were no non-franchised passenger operators before 1998-99 Q1.

3. Data for 1986-87 to 2002-03 sourced from CAPRI (Computer Analysis of Passenger Revenue Information), which was the rail industry's former central ticketing system, and train operating companies (1999-00 to 2002-03). Passenger kilometres travelled using some operator-specific tickets and Passenger Transport Executive multi-modal tickets are not included in the estimates for 1986-87 to 1998-99.

4. Data for 2003-04 onwards sourced from the LENNON (Latest Earnings Networked Nationally Over Night) ticketing and revenue database and train operating companies.

(b). Data from Passenger Transport Executives was included from 1999-00 onwards. The distribution of operator provided (non-LENNON) data by sector is on an operator basis from the start of 2011-12, which is why a series break is indicated at the start of 2011-12. Before 2011-12, non-LENNON usage were distributed to the sectors at the national (GB) level.

(r). The distribution of non-LENNON data between the sectors has been improved. This affects both the annual and quarterly data from the start of 2010-11. The regional figures from the start of 2010-11 have been revised down by around 120 million kilometres a year due to the overstating of Merseyrail journeys included as part of the non-LENNON component of the data.

Passenger rail usage statistical release: https://dataportal.orr.gov.uk/statistics/usage/passenger-rail-usage/
Passenger rail usage quality and methodology report: https://dataportal.orr.gov.uk/media/1234/passenger-usage-quality-report.pdf
Revisions log: http://dataportal.orr.gov.uk/footer/revisions-log/

22.19c (contd.) Passenger kilometres by sector

Passenger miles on light rail and trams by system: Great Britain

Millions

	Light Rail and Tram Systems, England										Light Rail and Tram Systems, GB	
Financial year	Docklands Light Railway	London Tramlink	Nottingham Express Transit	West Midlands Metro	Sheffield Supertram	Tyne and Wear Metro	Manchester Metrolink	Blackpool Tramway	England outside of London	England	Edin-burgh Trams	GB
2000/01	124.3	59.7	.	34.7	48.1	142.4	94.6	7.8	327.7	**511.6**	.	**511.6**
2001/02	128.5	61.5	.	31.1	49.7	148.1	100.2	9.3	338.5	**528.5**	.	**528.5**
2002/03	144.2	62.1	.	31.1	50.0	170.8	103.5	8.5	364.0	**570.3**	.	**570.3**
2003/04	146.3	65.2	1.2	33.3	53.5	176.4	105.0	7.0	376.5	**588.0**	.	**588.0**
2004/05	152.5	69.7	23.0	32.5	55.7	176.0	126.8	7.4	421.4	**643.7**	.	**643.7**
2005/06	160.0	72.7	25.9	33.5	57.0	173.4	128.0	6.9	424.8	**657.4**	.	**657.4**
2006/07	186.8	79.5	26.9	31.9	60.9	183.2	129.0	6.5	438.4	**704.7**	.	**704.7**
2007/08	202.8	87.9	27.3	31.4	64.4	194.4	130.5	5.4	453.4	**744.1**	.	**744.1**
2008/09	197.5	89.2	26.1	31.0	65.2	198.5	137.1	4.4	462.3	**749.0**	.	**749.0**
2009/10	226.5	83.5	23.6	30.8	64.0	203.2	128.1	4.1	453.8	**763.8**	.	**763.8**
2010/11	257.2	90.0	25.7	31.3	60.5	195.8	124.8	3.1	441.1	**788.4**	.	**788.4**
2011/12	283.0	92.2	24.9	31.7	60.3	188.8	141.9	2.1	449.7	**824.9**	.	**824.9**
2012/13	316.8	97.2	20.5	31.3	58.0	186.0	162.6	9.9	468.3	**882.2**	.	**882.2**
2013/14	333.6	100.9	22.2	30.5	50.7	183.5	188.3	12.7	487.9	**922.4**		**922.4**
2014/15	368.9	110.8	27.0	28.6	46.3	201.8	202.5	11.3	517.5	**997.1**	20.5	**1,017.7**
2015/16	386.9	105.1	49.8	31.6	46.6	213.8	223.0	13.5	578.3	**1,070.3**	26.5	**1,096.8**
2016/17	408.1	115.0	67.2	40.8	50.8	204.9	245.6	13.8	623.1	**1,146.2**	29.0	**1,175.2**
2017/18	399.9	94.0	72.8	37.2	49.6	197.1	267.8	14.1	638.6	**1,132.5**	34.0	**1,166.5**
2018/19	406.1	92.7	77.0	54.0	48.1	198.0	284.2	14.1	675.4	**1,174.2**	37.3	**1,211.5**
2019/20	385.7	87.8	76.6	52.4	42.4	179.6	287.7	13.1	651.8	**1,125.3**	35.6	**1,161.0**

For further information on these systems including infrastructure changes that may affect the figures, please refer to the Quality Report (https://www.gov.uk/government/publications/light-rail-and-tram-statistics-guidance).
Manchester Metrolink have revised their method for calculation of passenger boardings so the figures from 2010/11 are not directly comparable with previous years.
1983/84 to 1998/99 Blackpool Tramway data are imputed. The figures use passenger journeys data and an assumed average distance.
The 2018/19 figure for Midland Metro has been revised.
Midland Metro changed operator in June 2018. For this reason, figures from 2018/19 onwards may not be directly comparable with previous years.
Edinburgh Trams figures from 2014/15 to 2019/20 have been revised.

The figures in this table are National Statistics

Source: DfT Light Rail and Tram Survey
Telephone: 020 7082 6602
Email: bus.statistics@dft.gov.uk

22.19d Infrastructure on the railways

This table shows the characteristics of the infrastructure on the rail network, Great Britain
Annual data (financial year): 2000-01 to 2019-2020

Financial year	Route open for traffic	Of which electrified	Route Open for Passenger & Freight Traffic	Route Open for Freight Traffic Only	Track kilometres	Of which electrified	New electrification projects track km (see note 2)
2000-01	16,652	5,167	15,042	1,610	30,846	:	0
2001-02	16,652	5,167	15,042	1,610	31,972	:	0
2002-03	16,670	5,167	15,042	1,610	31,766	:	0
2003-04	16,493	5,200	14,883	1,610	31,564	:	22
2004-05 (b)	16,116	5,200	14,328	1,788	31,482	:	38
2005-06	15,810	5,205	14,356	1,454	31,105	:	5
2006-07 (b)	15,795	5,250	14,353	1,442	31,063	:	0
2007-08	15,814	5,250	14,484	1,330	31,082	:	0
2008-09	15,814	5,250	14,494	1,320	31,119	:	36
2009-10	15,753	5,239	14,482	1,271	31,073	:	0
2010-11	15,777	5,262	14,506	1,271	31,108	:	106
2011-12	15,742	5,261	14,506	1,236	31,063	:	0
2012-13	15,753	5,265	14,504	1,249	31,075	12,810	10
2013-14	15,753	5,268	14,504	1,249	31,092	12,887	61
2014-15	15,760	5,272	14,506	1,254	31,120	13,034	177
2015-16	15,799	5,331	14,552	1,247	31,194	13,063	7
2016-17 (b)	15,811	5,374	14,491	1,320	31,221	13,046	0
2017-18	15,878	5,766	14,548	1,330	31,038	13,729	291
2018-19	15,847	6,010	14,634	1,214	31,091	14,074	883
2019-20 (r)	15,904	6,049	14,668	1,236	31,218	14,486	252

Symbols: (:) Data not available; (r) Data revised; (p) Data are provisional; (b) Break in time series

Source(s): Network Rail
Email: rail.stats@orr.gov.uk

Notes:

(b) Prior to 2004-05 route length data and electrification data was collected using various systems and collected on a semi-annual basis. These systems, whilst often the most accurate measures available at the time, would not have provided as accurate a measure as the GEOGIS system and there is therefore a break in the time series between 2003-04 and 2004-05.

(b) There is a break in the time series between 2006-07 and 2007-08 due to a new methodology where the route classification reference data was revamped.

(b) There is a break in the time series between 2016-17 and 2017-18 due to Network Rail replacing GEOGIS, its master database for track assets, with a new system called INM (Integrated Network Model).This means any comparison of the current route length with previous years must be treated with caution.

(b) Prior to 2012-13, data is only available for Great Britain as a whole and not split by country. However, the data for new electrification projects track km is available separately for England, Wales and Scotland going back to 1995-96. This may not equal the Great Britain total due to rounding.

(r) The total Great Britain figure does not include Isle of Wight line, which is 17.4 track km. This line is leased from Network Rail to First MTR South Western Trains Limited (operating as South Western Railway).

1. High Speed 1 is not included in these figures. This has a route length of 109km.

2. The majority of the total new electrification projects track km was in England between 1995-96 and 2011-12. In 2005-06 5km of new electrified track km was added in Scotland. In 2010-11 106km of new electrified track was added in Scotland.

Rail infrastructure and assets release: https://dataportal.orr.gov.uk/statistics/infrastructure-and-emissions/rail-infrastructure-and-assets/
Rail infrastructure and assets quality and methodology report: https://dataportal.orr.gov.uk/statistics/infrastructure-and-emissions/rail-infrastructure-and-assets/
ORR Revisions log: https://dataportal.orr.gov.uk/footer/revisions-log/

22.19d (cond.) Infrastructure on the railways

Vehicle miles on light rail and trams by system: Great Britain

Millions

Financial year	Docklands Light Railway	London Tramlink	Nottingham Express Transit	West Midlands Metro	Sheffield Supertram	Tyne and Wear Metro	Manchester Metrolink	Blackpool Tramway	England outside of London	England	Edinburgh Trams	GB
2000/01	1.8	1.3	.	1.2	1.5	2.9	2.7	0.8	9.1	12.2	.	12.2
2001/02	1.8	1.5	.	1.0	1.5	2.9	2.8	0.8	9.1	12.4	.	12.4
2002/03	2.0	1.5	.	1.1	1.6	3.9	2.9	0.7	10.1	13.7	.	13.7
2003/04	2.1	1.6	.	1.0	1.5	3.6	2.8	0.6	9.6	13.2	.	13.2
2004/05	2.0	1.5	0.6	1.0	1.5	3.5	2.8	0.5	9.9	13.5	.	13.5
2005/06	2.1	1.5	0.7	1.0	1.5	3.4	2.8	0.5	9.9	13.5	.	13.5
2006/07	2.7	1.6	0.7	1.0	1.5	3.6	2.3	0.6	9.8	14.1	.	14.1
2007/08	2.8	1.4	0.7	1.0	1.5	3.8	2.5	0.5	10.0	14.1	.	14.1
2008/09	2.5	1.4	0.7	1.0	1.5	3.5	2.4	0.5	9.7	13.5	.	13.5
2009/10	2.8	1.6	0.7	1.0	1.5	3.5	2.1	0.4	9.2	13.6	.	13.6
2010/11	2.9	1.6	0.7	1.0	1.5	3.5	2.3	0.3	9.4	13.9	.	13.9
2011/12	3.1	1.7	0.7	1.0	1.5	3.5	2.9	0.1	9.8	14.5	.	14.5
2012/13	3.6	1.8	0.7	1.0	1.5	3.4	3.6	0.5	10.8	16.1	.	16.1
2013/14	3.6	1.9	0.7	1.0	1.4	3.4	5.2	0.6	12.3	17.8	.	17.8
2014/15	3.6	2.0	0.8	1.0	1.4	3.5	5.6	0.5	12.8	18.4	0.6	19.0
2015/16	3.8	2.0	1.6	1.0	1.4	3.5	7.2	0.6	15.3	21.0	0.7	21.7
2016/17	3.8	2.0	1.9	1.2	1.5	3.5	7.2	0.6	15.9	21.6	0.7	22.4
2017/18	3.8	2.1	1.9	1.1	1.5	3.4	7.2	0.6	15.7	21.6	0.9	22.5
2018/19	3.8	2.0	1.9	1.1	1.6	3.4	8.0	0.6	16.7	22.5	0.9	23.4
2019/20	3.8	2.0	1.9	1.2	1.5	3.3	7.9	0.7	16.5	22.3	0.9	23.1

For further information on these systems including infrastructure changes that may affect the figures, please refer to the Quality Report (https://www.gov.uk/government/publications/light-rail-and-tram-Figures for Manchester Metrolink represent total mileage of each tram 'set'. Where two sets are joined to form one train, the kilometres run will therefore be counted twice. Based on information supplied by the Midland Metro changed operator in June 2018. For this reason, figures from 2018/19 onwards may not be directly comparable with previous years.

The figures in this table are National Statistics

Source: DfT Light Rail and Tram Survey
Telephone: 020 7082 6602
Email: bus.statistics@dft.gov.uk

22.19e Number of stations or stops on light rail and trams by system: Great Britain

Financial year	Docklands Light Railway	London Tramlink	Nottingham Express Transit	West Midlands Metro	Sheffield Supertram	Tyne and Wear Metro	Manchester Metrolink	Blackpool Tramway	England outside of London	England	Edinburgh Trams	GB
1995/96	28	.	.	.	45	46	26	62	179	207	.	207
1996/97	28	.	.	.	45	46	26	62	179	207	.	207
1997/98	29	.	.	.	46	46	26	62	180	209	.	209
1998/99	29	.	.	.	47	46	26	62	181	210	.	210
1999/00	34	.	.	23	47	46	36	62	214	248	.	248
2000/01	34	38	.	23	47	46	36	62	214	286	.	286
2001/02	34	38	.	23	48	58	36	62	227	299	.	299
2002/03	34	38	.	23	48	58	37	62	228	300	.	300
2003/04	34	38	23	23	48	58	37	62	251	323	.	323
2004/05	34	38	23	23	48	58	37	62	251	323	.	323
2005/06	38	39	23	23	48	59	37	62	252	329	.	329
2006/07	34	39	23	23	48	59	37	61	251	324	.	324
2007/08	39	38	23	23	48	60	37	61	252	329	.	329
2008/09	40	39	23	23	48	60	37	61	252	331	.	331
2009/10	40	39	23	23	48	60	37	59	250	329	.	329
2010/11	40	39	23	23	48	60	38	59	251	330	.	330
2011/12	45	39	23	23	48	60	42	31	227	311	.	311
2012/13	45	39	23	23	48	60	65	37	256	340	.	340
2013/14	45	39	23	23	48	60	77	37	268	352	.	352
2014/15	45	39	23	23	48	60	92	37	283	367	15	382
2015/16	45	39	50	24	48	60	92	39	313	397	15	412
2016/17	45	39	50	26	48	60	93	39	316	400	16	416
2017/18	45	39	50	26	48	60	93	39	316	400	16	416
2018/19	45	39	50	26	50	60	93	39	318	402	16	418
2019/20	45	39	50	28	50	60	99	39	326	410	16	426

For further information on these systems including infrastructure changes that may affect the figures, please refer to the Quality Report (https://www.gov.uk/government/publications/light-rail-and-tram-statistics-guidance).

Blackpool Tramway: The number of stops has been shown for one direction of the route (as is the case with the other systems). In publications prior to 2011/12 the figures shown covered both directions.

Additionally, in 2012/13 Blackpool Tramway had 37 stops on the outward journey and 36 stops on the inward journey, as Fleetwood Ferry only had one platform.

The figures in this table are National Statistics

Source: DfT Light Rail and Tram Survey
Telephone: 020 7082 6602
Email: bus.statistics@dft.gov.uk

22.19f London Underground statistics, annual

	Passenger journeys, vehicle miles and occupancy (millions)			Underground infrasturcture			Receipts (£ million)	
	All Passenger journeys	Passenger miles	Loaded train miles	Stations	Rail carriages	Route miles	Traffic receipts[1]	Traffic receipts at 2020/21 prices[2]
2000/01	970	4,642	40	274	3,954	254	1,129	1,787
2001/02	953	4,630	40	274	3,954	254	1,151	1,795
2002/03	942	4,578	41	274	3,954	254	1,138	1,736
2003/04	948	4,561	43	274	3,959	254	1,161	1,734
2004/05	976	4,726	43	274	3,959	254	1,241	1,802
2005/06	970	4,714	43	274	4,070	254	1,308	1,850
2006/07	1,040	4,938	44	273	4,070	254	1,417	1,949
2007/08	1,096	5,190	44	268	4,070	254	1,525	2,040
2008/09	1,089	5,372	44	270	4,070	254	1,615	2,104
2009/10	1,059	5,255	43	270	4,078	249	1,635	2,096
2010/11	1,107	5,515	43	270	4,134	249	1,759	2,215
2011/12	1,171	5,915	45	270	4,127	249	1,982	2,458
2012/13	1,229	6,275	47	270	4,180	249	2,126	2,583
2013/14	1,265	6,476	47	270	4,283	249	2,287	2,731
2014/15	1,305	6,740	50	270	4,281	250	2,410	2,839
2015/16	1,349	7,119	51	270	4,281	250	2,576	3,009
2016/17	1,378	7,331	52	270	4,281	250	2,670	3,043
2017/18	1,395	7,816	52	270	4,319	250	2,633	2,949
2018/19	1,384	7,536	53	270	4,319	257	2,770	3,032
2019/20	1,337	7,304	51	270	4,319	257	2,732	2,925

1. These figures are not adjusted for inflation.
2. Adjusted for inflation using the GDP market price deflator (as at 31 March 2021).
For further information on these systems including infrastructure changes that may affect the figures, please refer to the Quality Report (https://www.gov.uk/government/publications/light-rail-and-tram-statistics-guidance).

The figures in this table are outside the scope of National Statistics

Source: DfT Light Rail and Tram Survey
Telephone: 020 7082 6602
Email: bus.statistics@dft.gov.uk

22.19g Glasgow Underground statistics, annual

	Passenger journeys, vehicle miles and occupancy (millions)			Underground infrasturcture			Receipts (£ million)	
	Passenger journeys	Passenger miles	Loaded train miles [also referred to as vehicle miles] [1]	Stations or stops served	Passenger carriages	Route miles open for passenger traffic	Passenger revenue [1]	Passenger revenue at 2020/21 prices [2]
2000/01	14.4	28.6	0.6	15	41	7	10.0	15.8
2001/02	13.8	27.4	0.6	15	41	7	10.1	15.7
2002/03	13.4	26.6	0.6	15	41	7	10.2	15.5
2003/04	13.3	26.5	0.6	15	41	7	10.3	15.4
2004/05	13.3	26.5	0.6	15	41	7	10.9	15.9
2005/06	13.2	26.2	0.6	15	41	7	11.2	15.8
2006/07	13.5	26.8	0.6	15	41	7	12.4	17.1
2007/08	14.5	28.8	0.6	15	41	7	12.9	17.2
2008/09	14.1	28.1	0.7	15	41	7	14.7	19.1
2009/10	13.1	26.0	0.6	15	41	7	14.1	18.0
2010/11	13.0	25.9	0.6	15	41	7	14.2	17.9
2011/12	12.9	25.6	0.7	15	41	7	14.3	17.7
2012/13	12.6	25.0	0.7	15	41	7	14.5	17.7
2013/14	12.7	25.3	0.7	15	41	7	16.0	19.1
2014/15	13.0	25.8	0.7	15	41	7	17.8	20.9
2015/16	11.4	22.7	0.7	15	41	7	17.5	20.5
2016/17	11.1	22.1	0.7	15	41	7	16.1	18.3
2017/18	12.7	25.8	0.7	15	40	7	18.5	20.7
2018/19	13.1	26.0	0.7	15	40	7	20.1	22.0
2019/20	12.7	25.3	0.7	15	41	7	20.2	21.6

1. These figures are not adjusted for inflation.
2. Adjusted for inflation using the GDP market price deflator (as at 31 March 2021).

For further information on these systems including infrastructure changes that may affect the figures, please refer to the Quality Report (https://www.gov.uk/government/publications/light-rail-and-tram-statistics-guidance).

The figures in this table are outside the scope of National Statistics

Source: DfT Light Rail and Tram Survey
Telephone: 020 7082 6602
Email: bus.statistics@dft.gov.uk

22.20a Freight moved

Great Britain annual data (financial year): 2003-04 - amount of freight moved on the rail network (billion net tonne kilometres)

Financial year	Coal	Metals	Construction	Oil and petroleum	International	Domestic intermodal (incl. maritime)	Other	Total[1]	Infrastructure[2]
2003-04	5.82	2.41	2.68	1.19	0.48	3.53	2.77	18.87	1.23
2004-05	6.66	2.59	2.86	1.22	0.54	3.96	2.53	20.35	1.29
2005-06	8.26	2.22	2.91	1.22	0.46	4.33	2.29	21.70	1.38
2006-07	8.56	2.04	2.70	1.53	0.44	4.72	1.89	21.88	1.36
2007-08	7.73	1.83	2.79	1.58	0.37	5.15	1.73	21.18	1.70
2008-09	7.91	1.53	2.70	1.52	0.42	5.17	1.38	20.63	1.55
2009-10	6.23	1.64	2.78	1.45	0.44	5.51	1.01	19.06	1.43
2010-11	5.46	2.23	3.19	1.32	0.42	5.68	0.94	19.23	1.54
2011-12	6.41	2.24	3.45	1.20	0.45	6.31	0.99	21.06	1.86
2012-13	7.50	1.81	3.05	1.21	0.43	6.30	1.16	21.46	1.73
2013-14	8.07	1.77	3.56	1.27	0.47	6.19	1.36	22.71	1.72
2014-15	6.50	1.82	3.93	1.21	0.60	6.49	1.67	22.21	1.69
2015-16	2.32	1.53	3.98	1.17	0.48	6.42	1.86	17.76	1.71
2016-17	1.43	1.50	4.25	1.13	0.43	6.81	1.70	17.25	1.71
2017-18	1.24	1.42	4.31	1.08	0.49	6.72	1.70	16.95	1.38
2018-19	1.17	1.44	4.53	1.07	0.51	6.79	1.89	17.39	1.41
2019-20	0.37	1.38	4.64	0.99	0.49	6.76	1.94	16.58	1.33

Symbols: (:) Data not available; **(r)** Data revised; **(p)** Data are provisional
Notes
1. Infrastructure data are not included in the total
2. This series excludes some possession trains used during engineering works
3. Annual and quarterly data up to and including 1998-99 are only available to one decimal place so any discrepancies in the totals is due to rounding

Freight rail usage and performance statistical release: https://dataportal.orr.gov.uk/statistics/usage/freight-rail-usage-and-performance/

Freight rail usage and performance quality and methodology report: https://dataportal.orr.gov.uk/media/1233/freight-quality-report.pdf

Revisions log: https://dataportal.orr.gov.uk/footer/revisions-log/

Source: Network Rail
Email: rail.stats@orr.gov.uk

22.20b Freight lifted

Great Britain annual data (financial year): 2003-04 to 2016-17 - mass of freight goods carried on the rail network (million tonnes)

Financial year	Coal	Other	Total
2003-04	35.2	53.7	88.9
2004-05	44.1	56.8	100.9
2005-06	47.6	57.7	105.3
2006-07	48.7	59.5	108.2
2007-08	43.3	59.1	102.4
2008-09	46.6	56.1	102.7
2009-10	37.9	49.3	87.2
2010-11	38.8	51.8	90.7
2011-12	44.6	58.1	102.7
2012-13	52.5	62.3	114.8
2013-14	52.3	66.1	118.4
2014-15	44.0	68.3	112.3
2015-16	19.8	68.5	88.3
2016-17	12.0	69.7	81.7
2017-18	9.8	68.1	77.9
2018-19	10.5	67.4	77.9
2019-20	6.2	66.0	72.2

Symbols: (:) Data not available; **(r)** Data revised; **(p)** Data are provisional; **(b)** Break in time series.

Source(s): Freight Operators
Email: rail.stats@orr.gov.uk

Notes

1. Annual and quarterly data up to and including 1998-99 are only available to one decimal place so any discrepancies in the totals is due to rounding.

2. Data includes estimates for two operators: Devon & Cornwall Railways (from 2011-12 Q1 to 2021-22 Q1) and Colas Freight (from 2010-11 Q1 to 2019-20 Q4). Colas Freight supplied freight lifted data from 2020-21 Q1.

Freight rail usage and performance statistical release: https://dataportal.orr.gov.uk/statistics/usage/freight-rail-usage-and-performance/
Freight rail usage and performance quality and methodology report: https://dataportal.orr.gov.uk/media/1233/freight-quality-report.pdf
Revisions log: https://dataportal.orr.gov.uk/footer/revisions-log/

22.21 Railways: Rail service assets and staff, Northern Ireland

As at end of financial year

Number

	2011-12	2012-13	2013-14	2014-15	2015-16	2016-17	2017-18	2018-19	2019-20
Route miles of track	211	211	211	211	211	211	211	211	211
Rolling stock[1,2]:									
Locomotives	2[r]	2[r]	2[r]	2	2	2	2	2	2
Passenger coaches	116[r]	143[r]	143[r]	143	143	143	143	143	143
Stations	22	22	22	22	22	22	22	22	22
Staff employed	895	908	931	949	916	911	942	990	1005

Source: Translink

1. Rolling stock is any rail vehicle which is used for passenger service
2. Includes only rolling stock which are currently in service. New cars, which have been brought into service over the last few years, all come fitted with an integrated engine and carry passengers and have therefore been included in the 'passenger coaches' category. The locomotives figure only includes those used for passenger services.

r Figures for rolling stock locomotives and passenger coaches have been revised back to 2011-12. Previously the figures incorrectly included old rolling stock (i.e. 450 class) which had been removed from service. New vehicles were brought into service between 2011-12 and 2012-13.

22.22 Railways: Rail service passenger journeys and receipts, Northern Ireland [1]

As at end of financial year

Millions/£ Thousands

	2011-12	2012-13 [2]	2013-14	2014-15	2015-16	2016-17	2017-18	2018-19	2019-20
Passenger journeys (Millions)	10.7	11.5	12.5	13.4	13.5	14.2	15.0	15.8	15.1
Passenger miles (Millions)	202.9	216.1	237.2	258.7	271.2	281.6	299.7	314.6	299.9
Passenger kilometres (Millions)	326.7	347.8	381.9	416.5	436.6	453.4	482.5	506.6	482.8
Passenger receipts (£ Thousands)	32,868	35,738	41,313	43,597	44,991	46,946	49,455	54,853	51,127

Source: Translink

1. Figures for NI Rail passenger journeys and miles were revised and updated back to April 2013. The journey factors used to calculate the estimated number of journeys taken using weekly, monthly and annual rail tickets were revised down. There was also a revision and update of the commuter mileage calculations. Therefore, figures for NI Rail passenger journeys and miles from 2013-14 onwards are not directly comparable with figures for previous years which were calculated using higher journey factors.

2. 2012-13 covers a 53 week period and the 2012-13 passenger miles/ kilometres and passenger receipts data are based on this 53 week period. However, the 2012-13 passenger journeys figure has been restated for a 52 week period. All other years in the table cover 52 week periods.

22.23 Main outputs for UK registered airlines by type of service[1]: 2009 to 2019

	2009	2010	2011	2012	2013	2014	2015	2016 [2]	2017	2018	2019
(a) Aircraft kilometres flown											Million kilometres
International:											
Scheduled	1,320	1,293	1,390	1,375	1,401	1,480	1,507	..	1,711	1,856	1,735
Non-scheduled	347	330	332	308	290	271	272	..	236	240	233
Total	1,667	1,624	1,722	1,683	1,691	1,752	1,779	..	1,947	2,096	1,967
Domestic:											
Scheduled	123	115	116	113	109	105	110	..	109	105	104
Non-scheduled	7	8	7	8	8	7	9	..	7	8	7
Total	131	123	123	121	117	112	119	..	116	113	111
All services:											
Scheduled	1,444	1,409	1,506	1,488	1,511	1,586	1,616	1,746	1,820	1,961	1,839
Non-scheduled	354	338	339	316	297	278	282	236	243	248	240
Total	1,798	1,747	1,845	1,804	1,808	1,864	1,898	1,982	2,063	2,208	2,079
(b) Passengers uplifted											Millions
International:											
Scheduled	83	83	92	96	99	105	111	..	130	144	121
Non-scheduled	22	20	20	19	17	16	15	..	11	11	11
Total	105	104	112	114	116	121	126	..	141	155	133
Domestic:											
Scheduled	19.5	18.2	19.1	19.1	19	20	20	..	21	21	21
Non-scheduled	0.2	0.2	0.2	0.2	0	0	0	..	0	0	0
Total	19.7	18.4	19.3	19.3	20	20	20	..	21	21	21
All services:											
Scheduled	102	101	111	115	118	125	131	142	151	165	142
Non-scheduled	22	21	20	19	18	16	16	11	11	11	11
Total	124	122	132	134	136	141	147	154	162	176	154
(c) Passenger kilometres flown											Billion kilometres
International:											
Scheduled	222	218	234	242	251	268	275	..	314	347	335
Non-scheduled	66	63	62	58	52	48	49	..	40	41	40
Total	288	280	296	300	303	315	324	..	354	388	376
Domestic:											
Scheduled	8.3	7.7	8.2	8.2	8.4	8	9	..	9	9	9
Non-scheduled	0.1	0.1	0.1	0.1	0.1	0.1	0.2	..	0	0	0
Total	8.4	7.8	8.2	8.3	8.4	8.5	8.8	..	9	9	9
All services:											
Scheduled	231	226	242	251	259	276	284	306	323	356	345
Non-scheduled	66	63	62	58	52	48	49	39	40	41	40
Total	297	288	304	309	311	324	333	345	363	398	385

22.23 (contd.) Main outputs for UK registered airlines by type of service[1]: 2009 to 2019

	2009	2010	2011	2012	2013	2014	2015	2016[2]	2017	2018	2019
(d) Passenger seat occupancy											Percentage
International:											
Scheduled	79.5	80.6	79.9	81.8	83.1	82.9	83.4	..	84.6	84.9	0.86
Non-scheduled	88.6	89.0	89.1	90.9	91.0	90.1	91.2	..	90.6	90.4	0.90
Total	**81.4**	**82.3**	**81.6**	**83.4**	**84.4**	**83.9**	**84.5**	..	**85.2**	**85.5**	**0.86**
Domestic:											
Scheduled	66.4	65.7	68.4	69.4	69.4	73.0	72.7	..	76.9	80.1	0.80
Non-scheduled	51.1	48.2	54.2	47.1	61.4	62.8	62.5	..	50.6	55.8	0.45
Total	**66.2**	**65.5**	**68.3**	**69.0**	**69.3**	**72.8**	**72.4**	..	**76.3**	**79.5**	**0.79**
All services:											
Scheduled	78.9	80.0	79.4	81.3	82.6	82.6	83.0	83.1	84.4	84.8	0.85
Non-scheduled	88.6	88.9	89.0	90.8	90.9	90.1	91.1	91.2	90.3	90.2	0.90
Total	**80.9**	**81.8**	**81.2**	**82.9**	**83.9**	**83.6**	**84.1**	**83.9**	**85.0**	**85.3**	**0.86**
(e) Cargo uplifted (freight and mail)											Thousand tonnes
International:											
Scheduled	895	924	957	946	904	875	828	..	892	916	856
Non-scheduled	120	88	112	113	143	138	134	..	267	218	211
Total	**1,015**	**1,013**	**1,069**	**1,059**	**1,048**	**1,013**	**962**	..	**1,159**	**1,134**	**1,067**
Domestic:											
Scheduled	5	5	5	5	3	3	4	..	3	2	2
Non-scheduled	78	75	76	72	63	62	57	..	37	36	40
Total	**83**	**80**	**81**	**77**	**67**	**65**	**61**	..	**40**	**39**	**42**
All services:											
Scheduled	901	929	961	951	908	878	832	842	895	918	858
Non-scheduled	198	163	188	185	206	200	191	223	304	255	251
Total	**1,098**	**1,092**	**1,149**	**1,136**	**1,114**	**1,078**	**1,023**	**1,066**	**1,198**	**1,173**	**1,108**
(f) Cargo tonne-kilometres flown (freight and mail)											Millions
International:											
Scheduled	5,951	6,165	6,381	6,366	6,156	5,970	5,586	..	6,045	6,311	5,953
Non-scheduled	866	695	692	670	825	784	769	..	1,221	1,092	1,082
Total	**6,817**	**6,860**	**7,073**	**7,036**	**6,981**	**6,754**	**6,355**	..	**7,266**	**7,403**	**7,035**
Domestic:											
Scheduled	2	1	1	1	1	1	1	..	1	1	1
Non-scheduled	33	31	31	29	26	24	23	..	20	20	21
Total	**35**	**32**	**33**	**31**	**27**	**24**	**24**	..	**21**	**21**	**22**
All services:											
Scheduled	5,952	6,167	6,382	6,367	6,157	5,971	5,587	5,670	6,046	6,311	5,953
Non-scheduled	899	726	723	699	851	808	792	976	1,241	1,112	1,104
Total	**6,851**	**6,892**	**7,106**	**7,066**	**7,008**	**6,779**	**6,379**	**6,646**	**7,287**	**7,424**	**7,057**

1. Excludes sub-charter operations performed on behalf of UK airlines.
2. The international and domestic breakdowns are unavailable for 2016.

Source: Civil Aviation Authority
Telephone: 020 7944 4847
Email: aviation.stats@dft.gov.uk
The figures in this table are outside the scope of National Statistics

22.24 Air Passengers by Type and Nationality of Operator 2019

	Total Terminal and Transit	Scheduled Services						Charter Flights					
		UK Operators		Other EU Operators		Other Overseas Operators		UK Operators		Other EU Operators		Other Overseas Operators	
	Passengers	Terminal	Transit	Terminal	Transit	Terminal	Transit	Terminal	Transit	Terminal	Transit	Terminal	Transit
London Area Airports													
GATWICK	3,098,831	2,144,944	-	541,328	-	248,929	-	152,816	-	9,425	-	1,389	-
HEATHROW	5,482,288	2,863,403	-	850,926	-	1,766,145	-	1,184	-	630	-	-	-
LONDON CITY	365,102	239,062	-	97,479	-	28,561	-	-	-	901	-	-	-
LUTON	1,191,996	660,750	-	518,388	313	3,123	-	8,521	-	-	-	-	-
SOUTHEND	81,510	63,389	-	18,121	-	-	-	-	-	-	-	-	-
STANSTED	1,873,730	258,086	-	1,523,675	-	69,238	-	20,667	-	1,425	-	639	-
Total London Area Airports	12,093,457	6,229,634	-	3,549,917	313	2,115,996	-	183,188	-	12,381	-	2,028	-
Other UK Airports													
ABERDEEN	196,653	105,155	-	44,610	-	6,281	-	38,235	-	2,372	-	-	-
BARRA	959	959	-	-	-	-	-	-	-	-	-	-	-
BELFAST CITY (GEORGE BEST)	173,705	150,077	-	23,029	-	-	-	595	-	4	-	-	-
BELFAST INTERNATIONAL	446,116	353,951	-	80,573	-	-	-	10,291	-	1,227	-	74	-
BENBECULA	2,651	2,651	-	-	-	-	-	-	-	-	-	-	-
BIGGIN HILL	84	-	-	-	-	-	-	-	-	84	-	-	-
BIRMINGHAM	792,205	291,741	63	331,138	-	112,901	-	54,486	-	1,512	-	364	-
BLACKPOOL	1,258	-	-	-	-	-	-	1,258	-	-	-	-	-
BOURNEMOUTH	34,274	3,675	-	18,177	-	3,032	-	9,359	-	31	-	-	-
BRISTOL	523,742	337,257	348	142,414	-	197	-	37,535	-	5,728	-	263	-
CAMPBELTOWN	465	465	-	-	151	-	-	-	-	-	-	-	-
CARDIFF WALES	78,061	34,993	-	20,148	-	5,435	-	16,417	-	917	-	-	-
CITY OF DERRY (EGLINTON)	13,865	2,768	-	11,097	-	-	-	-	-	-	-	-	-
DONCASTER SHEFFIELD	68,048	12,021	-	40,866	-	91	-	14,681	-	374	-	15	-
DUNDEE	1,543	1,531	-	-	-	-	-	-	-	12	-	-	-

22.24 Air Passengers by Type and Nationality of Operator 2019

Other UK Airports

	Total Terminal and Transit	Scheduled Services						Charter Flights					
	Passengers	UK Operators Terminal	UK Operators Transit	Other EU Operators Terminal	Other EU Operators Transit	Other Overseas Operators Terminal	Other Overseas Operators Transit	UK Operators Terminal	UK Operators Transit	Other EU Operators Terminal	Other EU Operators Transit	Other Overseas Operators Terminal	Other Overseas Operators Transit
DURHAM TEES VALLEY	11,283	1,450	317	9,089	-	-	-	427	-	-	-	-	-
EAST MIDLANDS INTERNATIONAL	213,338	88,976	-	102,819	-	-	-	20,989	-	554	-	-	-
EDINBURGH	938,914	540,433	-	339,803	-	41,507	211	15,440	-	1,520	-	-	-
EXETER	61,279	50,280	-	55	-	-	-	10,849	-	95	-	-	-
GLASGOW	533,638	397,363	357	84,567	-	38,838	-	11,644	-	869	-	-	-
HUMBERSIDE	14,648	1,766	338	10,222	-	-	-	2,322	-	-	-	-	-
INVERNESS	53,606	50,071	-	3,535	-	-	-	-	-	-	-	-	-
ISLAY	1,849	1,821	28	-	-	-	-	-	-	-	-	-	-
ISLES OF SCILLY (ST.MARYS)	3,313	3,313	-	-	-	-	-	-	-	-	-	-	-
KIRKWALL	11,864	11,102	707	-	-	-	-	55	-	-	-	-	-
LANDS END (ST JUST)	2,931	2,909	22	-	-	-	-	-	-	-	-	-	-
LEEDS BRADFORD	196,953	103,391	-	93,181	-	-	-	381	-	-	-	-	-
LERWICK (TINGWALL)	197	197	-	-	-	-	-	-	-	-	-	-	-
LIVERPOOL (JOHN LENNON)	339,357	185,678	-	151,100	-	753	-	442	-	1,228	-	156	-
MANCHESTER	1,801,038	811,973	-	580,246	-	289,054	1,665	113,751	-	3,491	-	404	74
NEWCASTLE	283,488	181,855	1,176	81,589	-	18,442	-	338	19	69	380	-	-
NEWQUAY	24,307	20,114	-	4,193	-	-	-	-	-	-	-	-	-
NORWICH	30,971	10,830	-	11,087	-	-	-	8,339	-	715	-	-	-
PRESTWICK	21,262	-	-	21,184	11	-	-	67	-	-	-	-	-
SCATSTA	8,928	-	-	-	-	-	-	8,928	-	-	-	-	-
SOUTHAMPTON	123,812	113,893	-	5,630	-	3,239	-	1,050	-	-	-	-	-
STORNOWAY	9,298	9,077	221	-	-	-	-	-	-	-	-	-	-
SUMBURGH	16,591	10,305	-	-	-	-	-	6,286	-	-	-	-	-

22.24 Air Passengers by Type and Nationality of Operator 2019

| | Total Terminal and Transit | Scheduled Services | | | | | | Charter Flights | | | | | |
| | | UK Operators | | Other EU Operators | | Other Overseas Operators | | UK Operators | | Other EU Operators | | Other Overseas Operators | |
	Passengers	Terminal	Transit	Terminal	Transit	Terminal	Transit	Terminal	Transit	Terminal	Transit	Terminal	Transit
Other UK Airports													
TIREE	742	717	25	-	-	-	-	-	-	-	-	-	-
WICK JOHN O GROATS	1,079	1,029	50	-	-	-	-	-	-	-	-	-	-
Total Other UK Airports	7,038,315	3,895,787	3,652	2,210,352	162	519,770	1,876	384,165	19	20,802	380	1,276	74
Total All Reporting UK Airports	19,131,772	10,125,421	3,652	5,760,269	475	2,635,766	1,876	567,353	19	33,183	380	3,304	74
Non UK Reporting Airports													
ALDERNEY	2,923	2,923	-	-	-	-	-	-	-	-	-	-	-
GUERNSEY	53,778	51,025	2,622	-	-	-	-	129	-	2	-	-	-
ISLE OF MAN	60,851	57,926	-	2,785	-	-	-	140	-	-	-	-	-
JERSEY	99,271	96,576	1,558	-	-	-	-	278	-	859	-	-	-
Total Non UK Reporting Airports	216,823	208,450	4,180	2,785	-	-	-	547	-	861	-	-	-

Source: Civil Aviation Authority

851

22.25 Scheduled and Non-Scheduled Services: All Services 2019 (a)

	Aircraft-Km (000)	Stage Flights	A/C Hours	Number of Passengers Uplifted	Seat-Km Available (000)	Seat-Km Used (000)	As % of Avail	Cargo Uplifted Tonnes	Tonne-Km Available (000)	Total (000)	Mail (000)	Freight (000)	Passenger (000)	As % of Avail
Passenger Services														
2 EXCEL AVIATION LTD T/A THE BLADES BROADSWORD SCIMITAR SABRE AND T2	367	508	746	7 553	14 860	10 241	68.9	-	2 408	1 024	-	-	1 024	42.5
ACROPOLIS AVIATION LTD	362	126	481	1 112	6 877	3 487	50.7	-	1 267	297	-	-	297	23.4
AIRTANKER SERVICES LTD	8 869	2 120	12 040	47 950	2 779 939	2 193 744	78.9	-	361 849	188 738	-	-	188 738	52.2
AURIGNY AIR SERVICES	2 806	13 127	10 968	524 570	208 823	139 343	66.7	297	22 743	11 695	5	33	11 657	51.4
BA CITYFLYER LTD	31 394	42 406	65 331	2 827 616	2 919 964	2 181 191	74.7	1	292 093	191 832	-	1	191 831	65.7
BAE SYSTEMS (CORP AIR TVL) LTD	372	574	704	16 483	20 876	10 408	49.9	-	2 368	874	-	-	874	36.9
BLUE ISLANDS LIMITED	1 985	10 870	8 124	425 844	129 728	82 657	63.7	115	11 671	7 403	-	22	7 381	63.4
BRITISH AIRWAYS PLC	757 974	290 902	1 115 355	44 556 463	183 277 321	153 432 783	83.7	561 241	26 476 108	19 125 871	102 159	3 879 327	15 144 385	72.2
CATREUS AOC LTD	906	622	1 362	623	8 669	3 519	40.6	-	2 234	354	-	-	354	15.8
EASTERN AIRWAYS	4 844	13 894	11 084	297 621	231 015	112 960	48.9	-	23 165	11 329	-	-	11 329	48.9
EASYJET UK LTD	404 092	344 086	715 118	51 853 928	70 730 667	63 927 561	90.4	-	6 017 424	5 434 953	-	-	5 434 953	90.3
EXECUJET EUROPE	34	13	47	84	479	204	42.6	-	51	23	-	-	23	45.1
EXECUTIVE JET CHARTER LTD	512	169	634	427	6 186	1 243	20.1	-	522	124	-	-	124	23.8
FLYBE LTD	67 658	146 184	184 239	8 590 887	5 649 763	4 406 063	78.0	221	610 541	374 599	-	68	374 531	61.4
GAMA AVIATION (UK) LTD	343	278	485	905	3 875	963	24.9	-	1 064	94	-	-	94	8.8
JET2.COM LTD	181 564	82 931	278 434	14 393 162	35 260 253	32 047 435	90.9	-	3 457 303	2 724 090	-	-	2 724 090	78.8
JOTA AVIATION LTD	1 011	1 454	2 274	28 051	95 328	66 242	69.5	-	9 318	5 561	-	-	5 561	59.7
LOGANAIR LTD	17 890	53 858	53 102	947 587	727 515	394 317	54.2	760	78 342	33 752	22	196	33 534	43.1
LONDON EXECUTIVE AVIATION LTD	390	277	576	830	4 761	1 392	29.2	-	1 441	139	-	-	139	9.6
NORWEGIAN AIR UK LTD	59 772	8 505	74 971	2 146 874	20 355 103	16 964 024	83.3	27 868	3 109 562	1 914 084	-	209 258	1 704 825	61.6
RVL AVIATION LTD	76	187	165	-	457	148	32.4	-	114	18	-	3	15	15.8
RYANAIR UK LTD	1 702	1 396	2 990	-	321 670	283 281	88.1	-	34 890	23 050	-	1	23 049	66.1

(b) | (b) | Tonne-Kilometres Used

22.25 Scheduled and Non-Scheduled Services: All Services 2019 (a)

	Aircraft-Km (000)	Stage Flights	A/C Hours	Number of Passengers Uplifted (b)	Seat-Km Available (000)	Seat-Km Used (000)	As % of Avail	Cargo Uplifted Tonnes (b)	Tonne-Km Available (000)	Total (000)	Mail (000)	Freight (000)	Passenger (000)	As % of Avail
SAXONAIR CHARTER LTD	753	458	1 063	1 714	9 285	3 464	37.3	-	941	300	-	-	300	31.9
TAG AVIATION (UK) LTD	1 595	848	2 169	7 792	47 583	20 670	43.4	-	8 891	1 767	-	-	1 767	19.9
THOMAS COOK AIRLINES LTD	96 372	30 303	137 077	6 135 804	23 492 012	21 541 553	91.7	2 087	2 624 290	1 853 842	-	22 605	1 831 237	70.6
TITAN AIRWAYS LTD	12 222	5 634	18 581	212 464	2 533 357	2 041 038	80.6	12	215 308	174 264	-	37	174 226	80.9
TUI AIRWAYS LTD	179 617	60 633	254 752	11 817 783	42 142 960	39 171 206	92.9	5 780	5 199 832	3 586 969	-	40 505	3 546 464	69.0
VIRGIN ATLANTIC AIRWAYS LTD	159 258	23 093	203 429	5 601 985	48 547 303	38 694 566	79.7	177 338	8 581 991	4 896 514	-	1 259 196	3 637 318	57.1
VIRGIN ATLANTIC INTERNATIONAL	4 445	854	5 825	139 698	1 275 573	949 285	74.4	1 115	210 225	96 792	-	7 556	89 237	46.0
VOLUXIS LTD	368	274	563	65	3 309	1 416	42.8	-	304	123	-	-	123	40.5
WIZZ AIR UK LTD	33 001	17 196	51 411	3 112 182	6 926 490	6 052 394	87.4	-	674 425	589 335	-	-	589 335	87.4
Total Passenger Services	2 032 554	1 153 780	3 214 100	153 698 057	447 732 001	384 738 798	85.9	776 834	58 032 685	41 249 810	102 186	5 418 808	35 728 815	71.1
Cargo Services														
2 EXCEL AVIATION LTD T/A THE BLADES BROADSWORD SCIMITAR SABRE AND T2	15	22	39	-	-	-	-	-	14	2	-	2	-	14.3
BLUE ISLANDS LIMITED	22	95	74	-	-	-	-	-	132	51	51	-	-	38.6
BRITISH AIRWAYS PLC	6 301	3 095	10 216	-	-	-	-	49 922	314 445	222 722	35	222 635	52	70.8
CARGOLOGICAIR LTD	10 180	1 994	13 538	-	-	-	-	139 957	1 270 611	810 476	-	810 476	-	63.8
DHL AIR LTD	20 137	18 136	35 230	-	-	-	-	63 821	820 790	432 012	-	432 012	-	52.6
JOTA AVIATION LTD	196	160	373	-	-	-	-	738	2 156	951	-	951	-	44.1
LOGANAIR LTD	47	175	169	-	-	-	-	282	285	102	102	-	-	35.8
RVL AVIATION LTD	242	627	722	-	-	-	-	-	360	95	-	95	-	26.4
TITAN AIRWAYS LTD	654	1 162	1 391	-	-	-	-	6 062	9 834	4 036	3 332	704	-	41.0
WEST ATLANTIC UK LTD	8 458	14 005	18 057	-	-	-	-	70 578	166 251	65 698	21 372	44 336	(10)	39.5
Total Cargo Services	46 252	39 471	79 809	-	-	-	-	331 360	2 584 878	1 536 145	24 892	1 511 211	42	59.4
Grand Total	2 078 806	1 193 251	3 293 909	153 698 057	447 732 001	384 738 798	85.9	1 108 194	60 617 563	42 785 955	127 078	6 930 019	35 728 857	70.6

(a) Excludes small airlines transport operations (see table1.13)
(b) Excludes Passengers AND cargo uplifted ON sub - charter operations
(c) Excludes some charter operations performed by aircraft below15 MTOM

Source: Civil Aviation Authority

22.26a Aircraft Movements 2019

	Total	<------Commercial Movements------>						<------Non Commercial Movements------>				
		Air Transport Total	Of Which Air Taxi	Positioning Flights	Local Movements	Test and Training	Other Flights by Air Transport Operators	Aero Club	Private	Official	Military	Business Aviation
London Area Airports												
GATWICK	284,987	280,681	-	3,457	-	70	103	-	-	29	-	647
HEATHROW	478,059	475,957	98	1,343	-	56	33	-	312	347	11	-
LONDON CITY	84,260	83,536	4,185	450	-	274	-	-	-	-	-	-
LUTON	141,858	112,209	-	1,276	6	47	250	-	184	69	4	27,813
SOUTHEND	36,327	20,108	337	850	402	1,873	226	7,990	3,265	119	71	1,423
STANSTED	199,925	183,514	424	5,134	2	53	989	-	-	8	158	10,067
Total London Area Airports	1,225,416	1,156,005	5,044	12,510	410	2,373	1,601	7,990	3,761	572	244	39,950
METRO LONDON HELIPORT	10,200	2,640	2,640	2,293	656	-	1,249	-	2,953	26	126	257
Other UK Airports												
ABERDEEN	91,248	81,543	5,405	2,706	373	3,224	2,224	1,031	-	1	65	81
BARRA	1,389	1,266	1	9	-	26	-	-	72	-	16	-
BELFAST CITY (GEORGE BEST)	35,382	34,871	558	212	1	27	2	-	222	30	10	7
BELFAST INTERNATIONAL	59,259	47,968	669	869	848	164	2,995	388	127	595	5,092	213
BENBECULA	3,484	3,182	1,271	162	2	12	5	-	62	-	59	-
BIGGIN HILL	39,390	10,805	10,480	180	2,216	-	-	7,265	13,891	-	192	4,841
BIRMINGHAM	109,357	103,501	1,726	2,072	12	144	3,021	-	484	76	47	-
BLACKPOOL	36,289	5,084	1,070	871	-	1,867	10	20,545	6,954	-	258	700
BOURNEMOUTH	38,540	4,992	6	194	-	19,176	4,828	1,955	5,430	-	322	1,643
BRISTOL	69,434	62,644	387	875	-	127	1,800	3,939	-	16	33	-
CAMBRIDGE	16,732	-	-	-	2,623	76	-	10,433	1,717	3	232	1,648
CAMPBELTOWN	1,823	1,122	129	128	-	95	-	-	216	-	262	-
CARDIFF WALES	31,881	16,549	6	572	-	625	-	7,634	6,155	-	346	-
CARLISLE	14,421	856	240	154	4	7	16	8,990	2,698	26	563	1,107
CITY OF DERRY (EGLINTON)	7,096	3,104	56	39	386	1,320	-	667	1,124	7	158	291
COVENTRY	31,708	1	1	1	6	21,785	-	-	9,914	-	1	-
DONCASTER SHEFFIELD	23,043	11,569	2,084	472	-	1,396	568	8,561	150	85	242	-
DUNDEE	43,354	1,402	224	315	353	634	203	39,014	769	5	120	539
EAST MIDLANDS INTERNATIONAL	74,566	59,410	3,296	3,870	2	769	3,097	-	1,276	-	24	6,118
EDINBURGH	131,617	127,017	640	1,480	10	15	20	-	2,989	16	70	-

22.26a Aircraft Movements 2019

	Total	Commercial Movements				Non Commercial Movements						
		Air Transport Total	Of Which Air Taxi	Positioning Flights	Local Movements	Test and Training	Other Flights by Air Transport Operators	Aero Club	Private	Official	Military	Business Aviation
Other UK Airports												
EXETER	44,306	14,433	12	390	3,312	3,171	433	12,176	6,724	2	443	3,222
GLASGOW	91,812	80,383	2,117	1,517	18	409	3,707	5,291	-	2	114	371
GLOUCESTERSHIRE	74,523	312	312	463	1,528	9,646	339	46,605	13,681	12	318	1,619
HAWARDEN	18,103	-	-	3	1,583	658	2,154	7,412	3,782	43	960	1,508
HUMBERSIDE	18,228	6,870	135	1,398	530	6,565	1,213	-	1,038	4	408	202
INVERNESS	31,338	16,065	3,563	1,809	483	2,078	128	8,772	1,187	-	70	746
ISLAY	3,199	2,056	247	240	-	16	-	-	855	-	32	-
ISLES OF SCILLY (ST.MARYS)	12,329	10,714	117	36	-	134	-	-	1,162	283	-	-
KIRKWALL	14,247	12,291	1,563	836	38	259	354	-	443	-	12	14
LANDS END (ST JUST)	11,177	8,720	410	123	71	879	19	74	1,133	15	139	4
LEEDS BRADFORD	35,641	30,648	1,107	1,724	-	1,094	100	-	1,931	2	142	-
LERWICK (TINGWALL)	1,461	1,215	310	172	-	-	-	-	74	-	-	-
LIVERPOOL (JOHN LENNON)	58,968	35,050	602	675	-	121	29	18,956	1,863	6	224	2,044
LYDD	26,676	148	135	242	-	244	-	11,803	12,653	1,457	102	27
MANCHESTER	202,892	194,159	4	3,669	22	188	74	-	2	-	24	4,754
NEWCASTLE	50,688	39,781	104	812	90	118	27	-	6,975	2,149	616	120
NEWQUAY	46,338	11,937	3,910	379	4	13,865	717	-	8,624	-	10,067	745
NORWICH	35,187	19,536	24	3,971	3,622	991	357	2,658	4,031	-	21	-
OXFORD (KIDLINGTON)	47,026	260	260	3,902	190	30,829	24	-	8,945	-	28	2,848
PRESTWICK	24,463	4,637	18	503	-	4,897	-	8,219	1,915	-	4,292	-
SCATSTA	4,989	4,823	-	127	-	27	12	-	-	-	-	-
SHOREHAM	46,223	861	861	158	619	223	260	31,404	12,130	5	193	370
SOUTHAMPTON	36,473	31,653	142	1,639	19	39	402	-	-	1	82	2,638
STORNOWAY	9,444	7,691	2,026	309	220	774	-	-	294	-	156	-
SUMBURGH	18,056	13,815	1,195	1,139	375	721	1,903	-	58	-	45	-
SWANSEA	5,779	1	1	-	-	-	-	4,770	998	-	10	-
TEESSIDE INTERNATIONAL AIRPORT	16,746	3,578	73	52	-	505	5,562	5,647	721	5	676	-
TIREE	1,800	1,579	113	9	2	31	2	-	177	-	-	-
WICK JOHN O GROATS	4,064	1,691	402	738	4	488	200	-	891	-	52	-

22.26a Aircraft Movements 2019

	Total	<------Commercial Movements------>				<------Non Commercial Movements------>						
		Air Transport Total	Of Which Air Taxi	Positioning Flights	Local Movements	Test and Training	Other Flights by Air Transport Operators	Aero Club	Private	Official	Military	Business Aviation
Total Other UK Airports	1,852,189	1,131,793	48,012	42,216	19,566	130,459	36,805	274,209	146,537	4,846	27,338	38,420
Total All Reporting UK Airports	3,087,805	2,290,438	55,696	57,019	20,632	132,832	39,655	282,199	153,251	5,444	27,708	78,627
Non UK Reporting Airports												
ALDERNEY	8,326	4,535	126	93	841	22	18	526	2,231	58	2	-
GUERNSEY	36,397	23,190	546	1,134	2,968	121	209	4,146	3,892	32	46	659
ISLE OF MAN	21,155	14,781	1,421	566	-	208	20	1,824	2,106	-	164	1,486
JERSEY	41,296	24,964	60	443	-	90	6,265	8,807	-	559	168	-
Total Non UK Reporting Airports	107,174	67,470	2,153	2,236	3,809	441	6,512	15,303	8,229	649	380	2,145

Source: Civil Aviation Authority

Note
Business Aviation was collected under a category in its own right with effect from June 2001 data. However, currently it is not possible for all airports to report using this category

22.26b Terminal and Transit Passengers 2019 Comparison with the Previous Year

	< Terminal and Transit Passengers >			<----- Terminal Passengers ----->			<----- Transit Passengers ----->		
	2019	2018	Percentage Change	2019	2018	Percentage Change	2019	2018	Percentage Change
London Area Airports									
GATWICK	46,576,473	46,086,089	1	46,574,786	46,081,327	1	1,687	4,762	-65
HEATHROW	80,890,031	80,124,537	1	80,886,589	80,100,311	1	3,442	24,226	-86
LONDON CITY	5,122,271	4,820,403	6	5,122,271	4,820,403	6	-	-	::
LUTON	18,216,207	16,769,634	9	18,213,901	16,766,552	9	2,306	3,082	-25
SOUTHEND	2,035,535	1,480,139	38	2,035,535	1,480,139	38	-	-	::
STANSTED	28,124,292	27,996,116	-	28,124,292	27,995,121	-	-	995	::
Total London Area Airports	180,964,809	177,276,918	2	180,957,374	177,243,853	2	7,435	33,065	-78
Other UK Airports									
ABERDEEN	2,912,883	3,056,018	-5	2,912,743	3,055,995	-5	140	23	509
BARRA	14,599	14,706	-1	14,599	14,706	-1	-	-	::
BELFAST CITY (GEORGE BEST)	2,455,259	2,511,261	-2	2,455,259	2,510,294	-2	-	967	::
BELFAST INTERNATIONAL	6,278,563	6,268,960	-	6,278,374	6,268,953	-	189	7	2600
BENBECULA	34,691	35,417	-2	34,656	35,404	-2	35	13	169
BIGGIN HILL	2,262	1,674	35	2,262	1,674	35	-	-	::
BIRMINGHAM	12,650,607	12,457,051	2	12,646,456	12,454,642	2	4,151	2,409	72
BLACKPOOL	15,213	19,321	-21	15,213	19,321	-21	-	-	::
BOURNEMOUTH	803,307	674,972	19	803,127	674,972	19	180	-	::
BRISTOL	8,964,242	8,699,529	3	8,959,679	8,696,653	3	4,563	2,876	59
CAMPBELTOWN	8,086	8,532	-5	7,975	8,472	-6	111	60	85
CARDIFF WALES	1,656,085	1,581,131	5	1,654,920	1,579,204	5	1,165	1,927	-40
CITY OF DERRY (EGLINTON)	203,777	185,843	10	203,777	185,843	10	-	-	::
DONCASTER SHEFFIELD	1,407,862	1,222,347	15	1,407,862	1,222,295	15	-	52	::
DUNDEE	20,917	21,185	-1	20,917	21,185	-1	-	-	::
EAST MIDLANDS INTERNATIONAL	4,675,411	4,873,831	-4	4,674,338	4,873,757	-4	1,073	74	1350
EDINBURGH	14,737,497	14,294,305	3	14,733,966	14,291,811	3	3,531	2,494	42
EXETER	1,021,784	931,265	10	1,021,705	931,182	10	79	83	-5
GLASGOW	8,847,100	9,656,227	-8	8,843,214	9,652,516	-8	3,886	3,711	5
HUMBERSIDE	204,463	192,526	6	201,818	191,828	5	2,645	698	279
INVERNESS	938,232	894,360	5	937,728	892,971	5	504	1,389	-64
ISLAY	34,992	32,775	7	34,771	32,508	7	221	267	-17
ISLES OF SCILLY (ST.MARYS)	93,927	92,195	2	93,927	92,195	2	-	-	::
KIRKWALL	172,625	181,562	-5	161,516	169,683	-5	11,109	11,879	-6
LANDS END (ST JUST)	64,056	64,216	-	63,847	63,862	-	209	354	-41
LEEDS BRADFORD	3,992,862	4,038,889	-1	3,992,209	4,037,686	-1	653	1,203	-46

22.26b Terminal and Transit Passengers 2019 Comparison with the Previous Year

	Terminal and Transit Passengers			Terminal Passengers			Transit Passengers		
	2019	2018	Percentage Change	2019	2018	Percentage Change	2019	2018	Percentage Change
Other UK Airports									
LERWICK (TINGWALL)	3,309	3,881	-15	3,309	3,881	-15	-	-	::
LIVERPOOL (JOHN LENNON)	5,045,991	5,046,995	-	5,043,975	5,042,312	-	2,016	4,683	-57
LYDD	39	284	-86	39	284	-86	-	-	::
MANCHESTER	29,397,357	28,292,797	4	29,367,477	28,254,970	4	29,880	37,827	-21
NEWCASTLE	5,203,624	5,334,095	-2	5,198,952	5,332,238	-2	4,672	1,857	152
NEWQUAY	461,478	456,888	1	461,469	456,511	1	9	377	-98
NORWICH	530,328	536,578	-1	530,328	536,578	-1	-	-	::
OXFORD (KIDLINGTON)	-	100	::	-	100	::	-	-	::
PRESTWICK	640,055	681,715	-6	638,975	680,958	-6	1,080	757	43
SCATSTA	109,480	174,934	-37	109,480	174,934	-37	-	-	::
SOUTHAMPTON	1,781,457	1,991,014	-11	1,781,308	1,990,930	-11	149	84	77
STORNOWAY	131,441	135,700	-3	129,500	133,375	-3	1,941	2,325	-17
SUMBURGH	267,456	245,868	9	267,420	245,766	9	36	102	-65
TEESSIDE INTERNATIONAL AIRPORT	150,735	142,080	6	147,824	139,549	6	2,911	2,531	15
TIREE	12,178	12,625	-4	11,944	12,285	-3	234	340	-31
WICK JOHN O GROATS	13,149	16,775	-22	12,892	16,756	-23	257	19	1253
Total Other UK Airports	115,959,379	115,082,427	1	115,881,750	115,001,039	1	77,629	81,388	-5
Total All Reporting UK Airports	296,924,188	292,359,345	2	296,839,124	292,244,892	2	85,064	114,453	-26
Non UK Reporting Airports									
ALDERNEY	53,155	53,343	-	53,155	53,343	-	-	-	::
GUERNSEY	882,374	837,615	5	855,396	804,536	6	26,978	33,079	-18
ISLE OF MAN	854,676	836,656	2	854,676	836,656	2	-	-	::
JERSEY	1,762,949	1,664,175	6	1,728,973	1,646,423	5	33,976	17,752	91
Total Non UK Reporting Airports	3,553,154	3,391,789	5	3,492,200	3,340,958	5	60,954	50,831	20

Source: Civil Aviation Authority

22.26c Freight by Type and Nationality of Operator 2019 - Tonnes

	Total	Scheduled Services						Charter Flights					
		UK Operators		Other EU Operators		Other Overseas Operators		UK Operators		Other EU Operators		Other Overseas Operators	
		Set Down	Picked Up	Set Down	Picked Up	Set Down	Picked Up	Set Down	Picked Up	Set Down	Picked Up	Set Down	Picked Up
London Area Airports													
GATWICK	110 358	17 857	47 854	278	453	20 420	20 733	1 537	1 215	6	5	-	-
HEATHROW	1 587 486	301 773	349 468	27 053	28 610	446 812	415 706	81	56	14 902	3 026	-	-
LONDON CITY	4	1	1	1	1	-	-	-	-	-	-	-	-
LUTON	35 761	-	1	28 602	2 175	3 788	1 174	1	20	-	-	-	-
STANSTED	224 139	3 348	205	14 613	3 771	119 007	80 896	17	112	257	14	1 504	395
Total London Area Airports	1 957 749	322 979	397 529	70 546	35 009	590 027	518 509	1 636	1 404	15 165	3 045	1 504	395
Other UK Airports													
ABERDEEN	5 986	63	193	1 712	1 247	112	124	644	1 030	510	351	-	-
BARRA	12	12	-	-	-	-	-	-	-	-	-	-	-
BELFAST CITY (GEORGE BEST)	196	88	79	28	2	-	-	-	-	-	-	-	-
BELFAST INTERNATIONAL	25 095	310	53	10 965	4 649	10	98	-	18	5 938	2 927	-	126
BENBECULA	38	31	5	-	-	-	-	2	-	-	-	-	-
BIRMINGHAM	29 866	154	56	869	309	17 022	10 864	175	126	1	70	148	70
BRISTOL	11	-	-	5	-	-	-	5	9	-	-	-	-
CARDIFF WALES	1 803	-	1	-	-	1 734	61	-	7	-	-	-	-
DONCASTER SHEFFIELD	17 647	-	1	60	15	14 286	287	28	7	804	27	608	1 524
EAST MIDLANDS INTERNATIONAL	335 948	16 769	16 749	101 642	99 492	30 570	24 559	56	402	22 817	21 700	405	786
EDINBURGH	19 410	34	2	9 244	7 447	8	-	39	-	1 495	1 137	-	-
GLASGOW	12 822	64	422	75	90	2 918	9 234	7	12	-	-	1	-
HUMBERSIDE	117	-	1	-	-	-	-	-	68	-	-	-	-
ISLAY	313	146	167	-	-	-	-	-	-	-	-	-	-
ISLES OF SCILLY (ST.MARYS)	68	45	23	-	-	-	-	-	-	-	-	-	-
KIRKWALL	33	10	23	-	-	-	-	-	-	-	-	-	-
LANDS END (ST JUST)	71	19	52	-	-	-	-	-	-	-	-	-	-
LIVERPOOL (JOHN LENNON)	784	14	28	1	12	-	5	45	42	81	16	325	216
LYDD	21	-	-	-	-	-	-	-	-	7	7	4	4
MANCHESTER	108 382	3 969	7 424	1 043	509	53 573	40 325	696	792	14	-	9	27
NEWCASTLE	4 745	4	3	5	2	1 549	2 512	-	38	10	10	195	417
NEWQUAY	2	-	1	1	-	-	-	-	-	-	-	-	-
NORWICH	257	-	-	-	-	-	-	122	135	-	-	-	-
PRESTWICK	13 054	207	100	7 792	3 955	-	-	3	10	118	2	237	631

22.26c Freight by Type and Nationality of Operator 2019 - Tonnes

	Total	Scheduled Services						Charter Flights					
		UK Operators --->		Other EU <--- Operators --->		Other Overseas <--- Operators --->		UK <--- Operators --->		Other EU <--- Operators --->		Other Overseas <--- Operators --->	
		Set Down	Picked Up	Set Down	Picked Up	Set Down	Picked Up	Set Down	Picked Up	Set Down	Picked Up	Set Down	Picked Up
SCATSTA	275	-	-	-	-	-	-	128	148	-	-	-	-
SOUTHAMPTON	203	43	160	-	-	-	-	-	-	-	-	-	-
STORNOWAY	179	165	14	-	-	-	-	-	-	-	-	-	-
SUMBURGH	322	150	7	-	-	-	-	83	82	-	-	-	-
TIREE	12	11	1	-	-	-	-	-	-	-	-	-	-
Total Other UK Airports	577 673	22 308	25 564	133 441	117 730	121 783	88 072	2 080	2 917	31 795	26 247	1 933	3 802
Total All Reporting UK Airports	2 535 422	345 287	423 093	203 987	152 739	711 810	606 581	3 716	4 321	46 960	29 293	3 437	4 197
Non UK Reporting Airports													
ALDERNEY	80	60	20	-	-	-	-	-	-	-	-	-	-
GUERNSEY	979	144	79	-	-	-	-	338	55	238	126	-	-
ISLE OF MAN	120	24	16	1	1	-	-	-	-	78	-	-	-
JERSEY	785	103	63	104	50	-	-	-	-	458	6	-	-
Total Non UK Reporting Airports	1 964	331	178	105	51	-	-	338	55	775	132	-	-

Source: Civil Aviation Authority

22.26d Mail by Type and Nationality of Operator 2019 - Tonnes

		Scheduled Services						Charter Flights					
		UK Operators --->		Other EU Operators --->		Other Overseas Operators --->		UK Operators --->		Other EU Operators --->		Other Overseas Operators --->	
	Total	Set Down	Picked Up	Set Down	Picked Up	Set Down	Picked Up	Set Down	Picked Up	Set Down	Picked Up	Set Down	Picked Up
London Area Airports													
GATWICK	7 640	286	1 357	1 037	1 993	918	2 040	3	4	-	2	-	-
HEATHROW	85 423	7 584	13 889	4 339	3 436	20 214	35 961	-	-	-	-	-	-
LONDON CITY	759	-	-	118	30	33	577	-	-	-	-	-	-
LUTON	801	-	-	-	801	-	-	-	-	-	-	-	-
STANSTED	17 094	102	102	-	-	299	81	6 211	10 299	-	-	-	-
Total London Area Airports	111 716	7 972	15 347	5 493	6 260	21 465	38 660	6 214	10 303	-	2	-	-
Other UK Airports													
ABERDEEN	1 446	-	-	-	-	-	-	424	92	715	215	-	-
BELFAST INTERNATIONAL	11 538	4 265	2 340	397	102	-	-	2 581	1 799	37	18	-	-
BENBECULA	24	-	-	-	-	-	-	18	6	-	-	-	-
BIRMINGHAM	143	3	-	-	2	3	135	-	-	-	-	-	-
EAST MIDLANDS INTERNATIONAL	22 041	8 844	13 197	-	-	-	-	-	-	-	-	-	-
EDINBURGH	22 968	13 262	9 652	32	21	-	-	-	-	-	-	-	-
EXETER	3 363	-	-	-	-	-	-	1 877	1 486	-	-	-	-
GLASGOW	34	7	23	-	-	-	-	2	-	2	-	-	-
INVERNESS	628	-	-	-	-	-	-	269	196	156	8	-	-
ISLAY	90	68	22	-	-	-	-	-	-	-	-	-	-
ISLES OF SCILLY (ST.MARYS)	195	133	62	-	-	-	-	-	-	-	-	-	-
KIRKWALL	21	7	14	-	-	-	-	-	-	-	-	-	-
LANDS END (ST JUST)	201	70	131	-	-	-	-	-	-	-	-	-	-
MANCHESTER	2 364	-	39	-	-	6	2 319	-	-	-	-	-	-
NEWCASTLE	3	3	-	-	-	-	-	-	-	-	-	-	-
PRESTWICK	17	-	-	-	14	-	-	-	-	3	-	-	-
SOUTHAMPTON	37	12	25	-	-	-	-	-	-	-	-	-	-
STORNOWAY	88	-	-	-	-	-	-	68	20	-	-	-	-
TIREE	41	35	6	-	-	-	-	-	-	-	-	-	-
Total Other UK Airports	65 242	26 708	25 511	430	140	9	2 454	5 239	3 598	912	241	-	-
Total All Reporting UK Airports	176 959	34 681	40 859	5 923	6 400	21 474	41 114	11 452	13 901	912	243	-	-

22.26d Mail by Type and Nationality of Operator 2019 - Tonnes

	Total	Scheduled Services						Charter Flights					
		UK Operators		Other EU Operators		Other Overseas Operators		UK Operators		Other EU Operators		Other Overseas Operators	
		Set Down	Picked Up	Set Down	Picked Up	Set Down	Picked Up	Set Down	Picked Up	Set Down	Picked Up	Set Down	Picked Up
Non UK Reporting Airports													
ALDERNEY	96	82	14	-	-	-	-	-	-	-	-	-	-
GUERNSEY	2 767	17	79	-	-	-	-	1 147	1 524	-	-	-	-
ISLE OF MAN	1 868	-	-	-	-	-	-	-	-	1 135	733	-	-
JERSEY	2 027	1 733	294	-	-	-	-	-	-	-	-	-	-
Total Non UK Reporting Airports	6 758	1 833	386	-	-	-	-	1 147	1 524	1 135	733	-	-

Source: Civil Aviation Authority

862

22.27a UK Civilian Search and Rescue Helicopter (SARH) - Tasking summary statistics

Emergencies requiring the involvment of SAR helicopters:

By financial year	2016/17	2017/18	2018/19	2019/20	Number of taskings 2020/21
Tasking by month [1]					
April	193	183	208	233	64
May	249	216	259	204	192
June	269	253	216	215	183
July	290	312	311	258	276
August	372	313	276	295	365
September	202	235	211	211	242
October	204	200	199	175	159
November	152	154	161	163	152
December	162	169	155	169	139
January	155	170	146	157	167
February	151	220	140	146	136
March	195	211	156	154	133
Total taskings	**2594**	**2636**	**2438**	**2380**	**2208**
Type of tasking [2]					
Aborted / Not required		-	-	-	-
Pre-arranged transfer	309	306	341	347	313
Rescue / Recovery	1542	1403	1207	1249	1017
Search only	560	520	452	420	345
Support	183	407	438	364	533
Tasking by base					
Caernarfon	**344**	303	291	261	218
Humberside	282	246	222	180	193
Inverness	269	271	254	273	222
Lee On Solent	208	286	296	244	252
Lydd	221	189	214	204	220
Newquay	309	359	341	298	255
Portland	123	31	:	:	:
Prestwick	342	361	318	338	350
St Athan	246	311	228	246	231
Stornoway	123	145	131	140	139
Sumburgh	127	134	143	196	128
Tasking location					
Maritime	18%	14%	14%	16%	12%
Coast	32%	33%	36%	34%	40%
Land	50%	53%	50%	50%	48%
Total people rescued	-	1687	1606	1555	1226

The figures in this table are National Statistics.

1. April 2020 figures capture the impact on SARH taskings of national lockdown in response to COVID-19

Source: DfT Search and Rescue Helicopter Statistics
Telephone: 020 7944 4847
Email: SARH.stats@dft.gov.uk

2. Since April 2016, there has been an update to the methodology of the tasking category data including a more thorough breakdown of the type of tasking the base responded to i.e. whether the tasking was aborted, complete, stood down etc. Therefore, it will not be possible to compare the latest data to 2015/16 data.

3. Please note, taskings are recorded by financial year ie: year 2019 - 20 covers all taskings between April 2019 and March 2020

Data from April 2017 onwards has been derived from a new data source originating from the Aeronautical Rescue Coordination Centre (ARCC). Data prior to this date originated from an administrative system used by the helicopter operators. The change to the data source has minimal impact on past trends therefore comparisons can be made over time. More information on the changes of the data source can be found here:

https://assets.publishing.service.gov.uk/government/uploads/system/uploads/attachment_data/file/685911/sarh-changes-to-data-series.pdf

22.27b UK Civilian Search and Rescue Helicopter Taskings - Location type by base
Annually 2017 to 2020

Base	2017 Total[1]						2018 Total				
	Beach/ Cliff	Mountain	Other	Vessel	Total		Beach/ Cliff	Mountain	Other	Vessel	Total
Caernarfon	41	111	69	11	232		50	155	88	17	310
Humberside	34	8	102	38	182		57	15	121	60	253
Inverness	20	79	71	11	181		26	147	108	17	298
Lee On Solent	51	0	117	53	221		66	0	183	52	301
Lydd	69	1	49	34	153		101	0	77	39	217
Newquay	82	0	164	41	287		69	2	228	50	349
Portland	12	1	12	5	30		:	:	:	:	:
Prestwick	34	77	140	27	278		39	110	164	23	336
St Athan	104	25	103	25	257		95	32	100	17	244
Stornoway	21	36	38	25	120		14	36	57	24	131
Sumburgh	1	0	57	28	86		2	0	119	37	158
Total	469	338	922	298	2027		519	497	1245	336	2597

Base	2019 Total						2020 Total				
	Beach/ Cliff	Mountain	Other	Vessel	Total		Beach/ Cliff	Mountain	Other	Vessel	Total
Caernarfon	46	129	75	20	270		50	98	67	11	226
Humberside	48	9	89	41	187		75	12	66	34	187
Inverness	24	110	106	16	256		25	92	84	31	232
Lee On Solent	45	0	153	43	241		84	1	147	44	276
Lydd	87	1	61	40	189		127	0	64	42	233
Newquay	83	0	188	53	324		95	0	127	25	247
Portland	:	:	:	:	:		:	:	:	:	:
Prestwick	45	75	178	30	328		64	85	185	10	344
St Athan	108	23	88	17	236		108	17	93	13	231
Stornoway	19	41	61	17	138		11	24	81	17	133
Sumburgh	7	0	140	49	196		4	0	98	18	120
Total	512	388	1139	326	2365		643	329	1012	245	2229

Source: DfT Search and Rescue Helicopter Statistics
Telephone: 020 7944 4847
Email: SARH.stats@dft.gov.uk

1. For 2017 data - figures for 3 quarters have been collected and totalled (i.e. Apr - Jun, Jul - Sep and Oct - Dec).

: Base not operational during this period. Portland base ceased operation on 30 June 2017.

Data from April 2017 onwards has been derived from a new data source originating from the Aeronautical Rescue Coordination Centre (ARCC). Data prior to this date originated from an administrative system used by the helicopter operators. The change to the data source has minimal impact on past trends therefore comparisons can be made over time. More information on the changes of the data source can be found here:
https://assets.publishing.service.gov.uk/government/uploads/system/uploads/attachment_data/file/685911/sarh-changes-to-data-series.pdf

The figures in this table are National Statistics.

22.27c UK Civilian Search and Rescue Helicopter Taskings - Rescued and Assisted by Base

Annual 2017- 2018 and quarterly 2019 - 2020

Base	2017 Total Persons Assisted	2017 Total Persons Rescued	2018 Total Persons Assisted	2018 Total Persons Rescued	2019 Jan to Mar Persons Assisted	2019 Jan to Mar Persons Rescued	2019 Apr to Jun Persons Assisted	2019 Apr to Jun Persons Rescued	2019 Jul to Sep Persons Assisted	2019 Jul to Sep Persons Rescued	2019 Oct to Dec Persons Assisted	2019 Oct to Dec Persons Rescued	2019 Total Persons Assisted	2019 Total Persons Rescued
Caernarfon	15	156	17	229	2	17	7	56	17	77	1	29	27	179
Humberside	9	74	10	143	3	22	1	30	3	36	1	11	8	99
Inverness	81	153	14	182	1	34	11	58	3	64	1	36	16	192
Lee On Solent	26	141	18	172	3	42	5	42	3	40	10	47	21	171
Lydd	20	32	59	57	2	8	6	10	29	21	0	11	37	50
Newquay	18	196	16	289	1	55	9	77	5	70	2	49	17	251
Portland	3	20	..	..	..	..	..	..	..	..	..	..	..	..
Prestwick	20	166	28	219	5	37	10	46	8	62	3	52	26	197
St Athan	22	133	16	129	4	26	8	35	5	39	5	18	22	118
Stornoway	20	85	8	98	2	15	4	28	5	32	1	13	12	88
Sumburgh	65	149	3	190	0	30	2	38	0	55	0	105	2	228
Total	299	1305	189	1708	23	286	63	420	78	496	24	371	188	1573

Base	2020 Jan to Mar Persons Assisted	2020 Jan to Mar Persons Rescued	2020 Apr to Jun Persons Assisted	2020 Apr to Jun Persons Rescued	2020 Jul to Sep Persons Assisted	2020 Jul to Sep Persons Rescued	2020 Oct to Dec Persons Assisted	2020 Oct to Dec Persons Rescued	2020 Total Persons Assisted	2020 Total Persons Rescued
Caernarfon	2	25	3	11	14	79	2	19	21	134
Humberside	2	11	5	18	4	55	1	15	12	99
Inverness	3	36	0	10	1	69	2	27	6	142
Lee On Solent	2	38	0	33	10	42	2	36	14	149
Lydd	4	16	23	13	61	12	17	8	105	49
Newquay	1	30	2	38	9	54	3	39	15	161
Portland	..	..	..	..	..	..	..	..	..	..
Prestwick	1	39	2	22	8	84	6	48	17	193
St Athan	3	24	2	10	15	49	1	27	21	110
Stornoway	3	20	1	13	3	37	4	23	11	93
Sumburgh	0	29	5	14	1	32	0	25	6	100
Total	21	268	43	182	126	513	38	267	228	1230

The figures in this table are National Statistics.

.. : Base not operational during this period. Portland base ceased operation on 30 June 2017.

Data from April 2017 onwards has been derived from a new data source originating from the Aeronautical Rescue Coordination Centre (ARCC). Data prior to this date originated from an administrative system used by the helicopter operators. The change to the data source has minimal impact on past trends therefore comparisons can be made over time. More information on the changes of the data source can be found here:
https://assets.publishing.service.gov.uk/government/uploads/system/uploads/attachment_data/file/685911/sarh-changes-to-data-series.pdf

Source: DfT Search and Rescue Helicopter Statistics
Telephone: 020 7944 4847   Email: SARH.stats@dft.gov.uk

this page is intentionally blank

Government finance

Chapter 23

Government Finance

Public sector (Tables 23.1 to 23.3 and 23.6)

In the UK, the public sector consists of five sub-sectors: central government, local government, public non-financial corporations, Bank of England and public financial corporations (or public sector banks). All monetary values in the public sector finances (PSF) are expressed in terms of "current prices", that is, they represent the price in the period to which the expenditure or revenue relates and are not adjusted for inflation. Due to the volatility of the monthly data, the cumulative financial year-to-date borrowing figures provide a better indication of the position of the public finances than the individual months.

Table 23.1 shows the key fiscal balances. This provides details on public sector net debt which represents the amount of money the public sector owes to private sector organisations including overseas institutions, largely as a result of issuing gilts and Treasury Bills, less the amount of cash and other short-term assets it holds. While borrowing (or the deficit) represents the difference between total spending and receipts over a period of time, debt represents the total amount of money owed at a point in time. The debt has been built up by successive government administrations over many years. When the government borrows (that is, runs a deficit), this normally adds to the debt total. So, reducing the deficit is not the same as reducing the debt.

Central government - oversees the nation's finance, commerce, national defence, foreign affairs and laws. In the UK, central government consists of 25 ministerial departments (such as HM Treasury and Department for Education), 20 non-ministerial departments (such as HM Revenue and Customs and UK Statistics Authority), along with many government executive agencies (such as Driver Vehicle Licencing Agency).

Local government - is responsible for a range of public services for people and businesses in defined geographical areas. These include social care, many schools, housing and waste collection.

Public corporations - An institution is classified as a public corporation where it behaves like a commercial body but is controlled by central government, local government or other public corporations. Examples of public corporations include Channel 4 and the Civil Aviation Authority.

Net borrowing - Measures the gap between total revenue and total spending (current expenditure plus net investment). A positive value indicates borrowing while a negative value indicates a surplus. Borrowing is often referred to by commentators as "the deficit".

Net cash requirement - Represents the cash needed to be raised from the financial markets over a period to finance the government's activities. This can be close to borrowing (the deficit) for the same period; however, there are some transactions, for example, loans to the private sector, that need to be financed but do not contribute to the deficit. It is also close, but not identical, to the changes in the level of net debt between two points in time.

Net investment - Spending on capital assets, for example, infrastructure projects, property and IT equipment, both as grants and by public sector bodies themselves minus capital receipts (sale of capital assets).

Net debt - A measure of how much the government owes at a point in time to private sector organisations including overseas institutions, minus the amount of cash and other short-term assets it holds. Net debt is often referred to by commentators as "the national debt".

ESA – European System of Accounts: The system of national and regional accounts used by members of the European Union. UK National Accounts and the public sector finances are currently compiled according to ESA 2010

Table 23.2 shows the public sector transactions and fiscal balances. The table shows the component detail of the public sector key fiscal balance by economic category. The tables are consistent with the Budget.

Table 23.3 shows public sector net debt. General government gross debt (consolidated) in this table is consistent with the definition of general government gross debt reported to the European Commission under the requirements of the Maastricht Treaty.

More information on the concepts in Table 23.1, 23.2 and 23.3 can be found in a guide to monthly public sector finance statistics (https://www.ons.gov.uk/economy/governmentpublicsectorandtaxes/publicsectorfinance/methodologies/monthlystatisticsonthepublicsectorfinancesamethodologicalguide).

Table 23.6 provides a breakdown of the main taxes and social contributions payable by UK residents to both the government (central and local government) and the European Union (EU). The majority of government income is provided by taxes and social contributions.

Taxes on production are included in gross domestic product (GDP) at market prices. Other taxes on production include taxes levied on inputs to production. These include national non-domestic rates, also known as business rates, and a range of compulsory unrequited levies that producers have to pay. Taxes on products are taxes levied on the sale of goods and services; this includes Value Added Tax (VAT) and Fuel Duty. Taxes on income and wealth include Income Tax and Corporation Tax. Income Tax is the largest single source of tax revenue paid by UK residents. This category also includes a number of other charges payable by households including Council Tax, the BBC licence fee and taxes such as Vehicle Excise Duty, which, when paid by businesses, are classified as taxes on production. The totals include tax credits and reliefs recorded as expenditure in the national accounts, such as Working Tax Credit and Child Tax Credit.

Public sector finance (PSF) statistics for the UK are published jointly by the Office for National Statistics (ONS) and HM Treasury (HMT). All statistical aggregates published are defined using national accounts concepts and rules. The Office for National Statistics (ONS) produces the UK National Accounts on an internationally comparable basis, in accordance with the System of National Accounts 2008: SNA 2008 and the European System of Accounts 2010: ESA 2010. The SNA and ESA guidelines are updated periodically and since 2014 ONS have compiled PSF data with reference to the most recent guidance, ESA 2010.

Consolidated Fund and National Loans Fund (Tables 23.4, 23.5 and 23.7)

The central government embraces all bodies for whose activities a Minister of the Crown, or other responsible person, is accountable to Parliament. It includes, in addition to the ordinary government departments, a number of bodies administering public policy, but without the substantial degree of financial independence which characterises the public corporations. It also includes certain extra-budgetary funds and accounts controlled by departments.

The government's financial transactions are handled through a number of statutory funds or accounts. The most important of these is the Consolidated Fund, which is the government's main account with the Bank of England. Up to 31 March 1968 the Consolidated Fund was virtually synonymous with the term 'Exchequer', which was then the government's central cash account. From 1 April 1968 the National Loans Fund, with a separate account at the Bank of England, was set up by the National Loans Act 1968. The general effect of this Act was to remove from the Consolidated Fund most of the government's domestic lending and the whole of the government's borrowing transactions, and to provide for them to be brought to account in the National Loans Fund.

• interest payable on loans to the nationalised industries, local authorities and other bodies, whether the loans were made before or after 1 April 1968 and

• the profits of the Issue Department of the Bank of England, mainly derived from interest on government securities, which were formerly paid into the Exchange Equalisation Account.

The net cost of servicing the National Debt after applying these interest receipts and similar items is a charge on the Consolidated Fund as part of the standing services. Details of National Loans Fund loans outstanding are shown in Table 23.5. Details of borrowing and repayments of debt, other than loans from the National Loans Fund, are shown in Table 23.7.

HM Revenue Receipt (Table 23.9)

This table provides an annual record of receipts over the last 10 years from tax and duties, National Insurance contributions (NICs), and fines and penalties that HM Revenue and Customs (HMRC) are responsible for collecting. Receipts are on a cash basis and so represent when a payment for a tax liability is received by HMRC. Receipts data in the more recent years are liable to revision, mainly for Corporation Tax as the totals are gross of provisional tax credits and due to the lag in return data becoming available, are subject to change. All statistics on taxes and expenditure administered by HMRC are available on the HMRC Statistics home page on GOV.UK (https://www.gov.uk/government/organisations/hm-revenue-customs/about/statistics)

Income tax (Table 23.10, 23.11)

Following the introduction of Independent Taxation from 1990/91, the Married Couple's Allowance was introduced. It is payable in addition to the Personal Allowance and between 1990/91 and 1992/93 went to the husband unless the transfer condition was met. The condition was that the husband was unable to make full use of the allowance himself and, in that case, he could transfer only part or all of the Married Couple's Allowance to his wife. In 1993/94 all or half of the allowance could be transferred to the wife if the couple had agreed beforehand. The wife has the right to claim half the allowance. The Married Couple's Allowance, and allowances linked to it, were restricted to 20 per cent in 1994/95 and to 15 per cent from 1995/96. From 2000/01 only people born before 6 April 1935 are entitled to Married Couple's Allowance.

The age allowance replaces the single allowance, provided the taxpayer's income is below the limits shown in the table. From 1989/90, for incomes in excess of the limits, the allowance is reduced by £1 for each additional £2 of income until the ordinary limit is reached (before it was £2 for each £3 of additional income). The relief is due where the taxpayer is aged 65 or over in the year of assessment.

The additional Personal Allowance could be claimed by a single parent (or by a married man if his wife was totally incapacitated) who maintained a resident child at his or her own expense. Widow's Bereavement Allowance was due to a widow in the year of her husband's death and in the following year provided the widow had not remarried before the beginning of that year. Both the additional Personal Allowance and the Widow's Bereavement Allowance were abolished from April 2000.

The Blind Person's Allowance may be claimed by blind persons (in England and Wales, registered as blind by a local authority) and surplus Blind Person's Allowance may be transferred to a husband or wife. Relief on life assurance premiums is given by deduction from the premium payable. From 1984/85, it is confined to policies made before 14 March 1984.

From 1993/94 until 1998/99 a number of taxpayers with taxable income in excess of the lower rate limit only paid tax at the lower rate. This was because it was only their dividend income and (from 1996/97) their savings income which took their taxable income above the lower rate limit but below the basic rate limit, and such income was chargeable to tax at the lower rate and not the basic rate.

In 1999/2000 the 10 per cent starting rate replaced the lower rate and taxpayers with savings or dividend income at the basic rate of tax are taxed at 20 per cent and 10 per cent respectively. Before 1999/2000 these people would have been classified as lower rate taxpayers.

The Dividend Allowance, introduced for 2016-17, means that no tax is payable on the first £5,000 of dividend income, irrespective of the total amount of dividend and non-dividend income received. The amount was reduced to £2,000 in 2018-19.

The Personal Savings Allowance, introduced for 2016-17, provides for an amount of savings income to be received tax-free. The upper bound for the tax-free allowance depends on the top marginal tax rate on an individual's total income; the threshold for higher rate taxpayers is half that for basic rate taxpayers and is set to £0 for additional rate taxpayers.

Rateable values (Table 23.12)

Major changes to local government finance in England and Wales took effect from 1 April 1990. These included the abolition of domestic rating (replaced by the Community Charge, then replaced in 1993 by the Council Tax), the revaluation of all non-domestic properties, and the introduction of the Uniform Business Rate. Also in 1990, a new classification scheme was introduced which has resulted in differences in coverage. Further differences are caused by legislative changes which have changed the treatment of certain types of property. There was little change in the total rateable value of non-domestic properties when all these properties were re-valued in April 1995. Rateable values for offices fell and there was a rise for all other property types shown in the table.

With effect from 1 April 2000, all non-domestic properties were re-valued. Overall there was an increase in rateable values of over 25 per cent compared with the last year of the 1995 list. The largest proportionate increase was for offices and cinemas, with all property types given in the table showing rises.

The latest revaluation affecting all non-domestic properties took effect from 1 April 2010. In this revaluation the overall increase in rateable values between 1 April of the first year of the new list and the same day on the last year of the 2005 list was 21 per cent. The largest proportionate increase was for offices and educational properties, with all property types in the table showing rises.

Rateable property (also known as hereditament): a unit of property that is, or may become, liable to nondomestic rating and thus appears in a rating list.

Rateable value (RV): The legal term for the notional annual rental value of a rateable property, assessed by the valuation officers of the VOA. Every property has a rateable value that is based broadly on the annual rent for which the property could have been let on the open market at a particular date.

Local authority financing for capital expenditure (Tables 23.15 - 23.17)

Capital expenditure comprises the buying, constructing or improving physical assets, such as buildings, land, vehicles and other miscellaneous property, including streetlights and road signs. It also includes grants and advances that authorities make to other bodies for capital purposes. Because of the project-based nature of capital expenditure, there can be relatively larger variance in expenditure over time compared with revenue expenditure.

Authorities finance their capital spending in a number of ways. A breakdown of the main elements of local authority capital funding is given below:

• Prudential borrowing is borrowing freely undertaken by the local authority within the affordability limits stated by their auditors, as specified in the Local Government Act 2003. This is the largest source of financing of capital expenditure.
• Capital grants are provided by government departments and other organisations. The majority of governmental grants are not ring-fenced, giving authorities flexibility to choose how to spend this money, provided it is used for capital purposes.
• Revenue resources can be used by local authorities to support capital spend. There is no restriction on revenue funds being used in this way, although accounting convention prevents capital resources being used to cover revenue spend.
• Capital receipts are from the sale of capital assets.

Local authorities do not provide data on how service areas are funded (except for HRA), so it is not possible to directly link changes in the profile of expenditure to changes in the profile of financing.

Capital receipts – income from the sale of capital assets. Such income may only be used to repay loan debt or to finance new capital expenditure

Local Authority – A Statutory body created by Acts of Parliament, responsible for delivering services (in line with national objectives) to meet the diverse requirements of different neighbourhoods and communities.

23.1 Sector analysis of key fiscal balances[1]
United Kingdom

Not seasonally adjusted

£ million[2]

		2012	2013	2014	2015	2016	2017	2018	2019
Surplus on current budget[3]									
Central Government	ANLV	-101,395	-69,280	-72,284	-50,908	-25,202	-2,386	1,247	3,799
Local Government	NMMX	-4,312	-7,536	-4,641	-7,436	-13,487	-12,106	-11,793	-14,313
General Government	ANLW	-105,707	-76,816	-76,925	-58,344	-38,689	-14,492	-10,546	-10,514
Public Corporations	IL6M	16,966	12,022	12,148	11,199	12,933	19,089	10,679	11,396
Public Sector	ANMU	-80,520	-71,420	-60,976	-44,265	-23,791	6,827	2,148	4,684
Net investment[4]									
Central government	-ANNS	30,213	26,554	32,763	34,782	34,380	37,900	41,486	44,646
Local government	-ANNT	3,280	-5,324	-6,550	-5,897	-6,451	-3,058	-5,161	-5,504
General Government	-ANNV	33,493	21,230	26,213	28,885	27,929	34,842	36,325	39,142
Public corporations	-JSH6	3,004	2,557	5,408	5,249	6,660	7,616	1,755	2,145
Public sector	-ANNW	37,502	25,747	33,587	34,455	35,406	43,162	42,720	43,206
Net borrowing[5]									
Central government	-NMFJ	131,608	95,834	105,047	85,690	59,582	40,286	40,239	40,847
Local government	-NMOE	7,592	2,212	-1,909	1,539	7,036	9,048	6,632	8,809
General Government	-NNBK	139,200	98,046	103,138	87,229	66,618	49,334	46,871	49,656
Public corporations	-IL6E	-13,962	-9,465	-6,740	-5,950	-6,273	-11,473	-8,924	-9,251
Public sector	-ANNX	118,022	97,167	94,563	78,720	59,197	36,335	40,572	38,522
Net cash requirement									
Central government[6]	RUUX	103,586	73,275	89,042	68,788	74,971	32,945	24,848	44,369
Local government	ABEG	6,076	1,921	307	-2,438	5,257	4,387	6,057	2,931
General Government	RUUS	109,662	75,196	89,349	66,350	80,228	37,332	30,905	47,300
Public corporations	IL6F	-123,425	-94,538	-3,439	-18,156	15,805	-16,534	11,792	13,867
Public sector	RURQ	-25,624	-32,218	73,479	35,629	98,178	73,668	46,688	25,148
Public sector debt									
Public sector net debt	BKQK	2,244,384	2,264,954	1,841,452	1,871,959	1,965,231	1,992,750	2,064,964	2,109,851
Public sector net debt (£ billion)	RUTN	2,244.4	2,265.0	1,841.5	1,872.0	1,965.2	1,992.8	2,065.0	2,109.9
Excluding financial interventions Net debt	HF6W	1,329.5	1,430.3	1,529.3	1,583.3	1,665.6	1,725.3	1,773.3	1,805.9
Net debt as a % GDP	HF6X	75.7	77.7	80.3	80.3	81.0	81.0	80.0	82.3

Source: Office for National Statistics

1 Consistent with the latest Public Sector Finances data, compliant with the European System of Accounts 2010 (ESA10)
2 Unless otherwise stated.
3 Net saving *plus* capital taxes.
4 Gross capital formation *plus* payments *less* receipts of investment grants *less depreciation.*
5 Net investment *less* surplus on current budget. A version of General government net borrowing is reported to the European Commision under the requirements of the Maastricht Treaty.
6 Central government net cash requirement (own account).

23.2 Public sector transactions and fiscal balances[1]

United Kingdom

£ million

		2012	2013	2014	2015	2016	2017	2018	2019
Current receipts									
Taxes on income and wealth	ANSO	198,386	201,632	207,216	215,820	229,879	243,672	250,433	254,880
Taxes on production	NMYE	216,130	226,413	237,736	245,272	256,172	268,879	277,988	286,460
Other current taxes[2]	MJBC	37,055	39,207	40,312	41,562	42,843	44,388	47,578	50,045
Taxes on capital	HZS7	3,129	4,255	3,886	4,470	4,804	5,381	5,352	5,164
Social contributions	ANBO	104,319	106,085	109,120	114,173	121,963	130,449	135,378	143,306
Gross operating surplus	ANBP	66,094	67,181	73,872	76,172	78,550	79,201	74,776	76,162
Interest and dividends from private sector and Rest of World	ANBQ	58,561	51,854	31,848	25,830	26,805	32,421	28,891	30,123
Rent and other current transfers[3]	ANBS	1,960	2,317	3,903	3,292	2,788	3,679	2,850	3,281
Total current receipts	ANBT	685,634	698,944	707,893	726,591	763,804	808,070	823,246	849,421
Current expenditure									
Current expenditure on goods and services[4]	GZSN	357,695	360,749	371,712	375,950	383,971	389,683	400,202	425,311
Subsidies	NMRL	9,803	9,304	10,343	12,934	15,191	17,751	20,020	22,356
Social benefit	ANLY	207,352	210,685	215,181	218,330	221,152	220,873	227,026	226,001
Net current grants abroad[5]	C627	5,950	7,923	7,048	6,849	7,494	7,321	7,697	8,707
Other current grants private sector	JW3F	25,173	22,578	20,389	19,068	18,953	18,339	17,833	17,488
and Rest of World	ANLO	90,363	85,873	71,089	63,528	66,902	71,600	69,994	64,063
Total current expenditure	ANLT	719,690	722,963	720,650	721,737	737,443	749,798	769,348	791,523
Saving, gross plus capital taxes	ANSP	-34,056	-24,019	-12,757	4,854	26,361	58,272	53,898	57,898
Depreciation	-ANNZ	-46,464	-47,401	-48,219	-49,119	-50,152	-51,445	-51,750	-53,214
Surplus on current budget	ANMU	-80,520	-71,420	-60,976	-44,265	-23,791	6,827	2,148	4,684
Net investment									
Gross fixed capital formation[6]	ANSQ	61,338	60,098	67,799	65,473	67,178	72,378	70,380	72,406
Less depreciation	-ANNZ	-46,464	-47,401	-48,219	-49,119	-50,152	-51,445	-51,750	-53,214
Increase in inventories and valuables	ANSR	-34	37	23	-139	-204	-216	-128	-195
Capital grants to private sector and Rest of World	ANSS	24,039	15,871	17,939	21,382	21,157	25,160	28,585	28,055
Capital grants from private sector and Rest of World	-ANST	-1,377	-2,858	-3,955	-3,142	-2,573	-2,715	-4,367	-3,846
Total net investment	-ANNW	37,502	25,747	33,587	34,455	35,406	43,162	42,720	43,206
Net borrowing[7]	-ANNX	118,022	97,167	94,563	78,720	59,197	36,335	40,572	38,522
Financial transactions determining net cash requirement									
Net lending to private sector and Rest of World	ANSU	-47,147	-24,892	-4,759	-5,715	13,506	-6,016	11,074	15,312
Net acquisition of UK company securities	ANSV	-63,533	-62,389	-6,166	-26,584	-3,947	4,143	-29,586	18,504
Accounts receivable/payable	ANSW	-2,679	825	6,826	4,222	12,934	4,793	-1,126	-11,604
Adjustment for interest on gilts	ANSX	-5,937	2,286	-4,477	795	5,755	-6,803	-8,414	-2,743
Other financial transactions[8]	ANSY	-24,350	-45,215	-12,508	-15,809	10,733	41,216	34,168	-32,843
Public sector net cash requirement	RURQ	-25,624	-32,218	73,479	35,629	98,178	73,668	46,688	25,148

Source: Office for National Statistics

1 See chapter text.
2 Includes domestic rates, council tax, community charge, motor vehicle duty paid by household and some licence fees.
3 ESA10 transactions D44, D45, D74, D75 and D72-D71: includes rent of land, oil royalties, other property income and fine .
4 Includes non-trading capital consumption.

5 Net of current grants received from abroad.
6 Including net acquisition of land.
7 Net investment less sur plus on current budget.
8 Includes statistical discrepancy, finance leasing and similar borrowing, insurance technical reserves and some other minor adjustments.

23.3 Public Sector net debt[1]

United Kingdom

£ million

		2012	2013	2014	2015	2016	2017	2018	2019
Central government (CG) sterling gross debt:									
British government stock Conventional gilts	BKPK	858,142	938,835	964,638	983,501	1,014,539	1,048,754	1,064,625	1,060,589
Index linked gilts	BKPL	282,130	304,475	342,757	369,661	379,392	396,404	426,377	442,645
Total	BKPM	1,140,272	1,243,310	1,307,395	1,353,162	1,393,931	1,445,158	1,491,002	1,503,234
Sterling Treasury bills	BKPJ	51,101	36,610	62,554	82,339	94,863	79,933	71,032	107,204
National savings	ACUA	101,035	104,180	111,049	133,155	142,130	152,740	164,727	174,881
Tax instruments	ACRV	702	867	1,384	1,218	1,585	1,742	892	539
Other sterling debt and foreign currency debt[2]	KW6Q	42,314	32,727	43,844	39,391	48,318	58,961	60,794	57,811
Central government sterling gross debt total	BKSL	1,335,424	1,417,694	1,525,922	1,608,961	1,680,523	1,738,534	1,788,447	1,843,669
Central government foreign currency gross debt:									
US$ bonds	BKPG	0	0	0	0	0	0	0	0
ECU bonds	EYSJ	0	0	0	0	0	0	0	0
ECU/Euro Treasury notes	EYSV	0	0	0	0	0	0	0	0
Other foreign currency debt	BKPH	0	0	0	0	0	0	0	0
Central government foreign currency gross debt total	BKPI	0	0	0	0	0	0	0	0
Central government gross debt total	BKPW	1,407,272	1,482,160	1,585,927	1,646,217	1,710,002	1,763,422	1,813,927	1,868,862
Local government (LG) gross debt total	EYKP	83,947	85,184	87,037	88,617	91,633	95,915	101,483	110,078
less									
Central government holdings of local government debt	-EYKZ	-63,697	-64,202	-64,770	-65,595	-67,932	-70,530	-76,329	-85,526
Local government holdings of central government debt	-EYLA	-3,921	-4,812	-4,806	-4,465	-2,715	-2,926	-2,127	-2,725
LG/CG cross holdings of debt	KSC7	-67,618	-69,014	-69,576	-70,060	-70,647	-73,456	-78,456	-88,251
General government (GG) consolidated gross debt (Maastricht) (from PSA8A)	BKPX	1,423,601	1,498,330	1,603,388	1,664,774	1,730,988	1,785,881	1,836,954	1,890,689
Non-financial PCs (NFPCs) gross debt	EYYD	77,283	77,427	82,416	85,799	89,548	22,439	15,365	16,052
less CG/NFPCs cross holdings of debt	KSC8	-8,614	-6,660	-6,880	-6,822	-6,714	-6,573	-6,354	-5,888
less LG/NFPCs cross holdings of debt	KSC9	-3,316	-3,553	-3,956	-4,616	-5,377	-6,184	-7,250	-8,261
GG and NFPC consolidated gross debt	KSD2	1,475,574	1,551,378	1,659,319	1,721,724	1,788,241	1,772,801	1,813,368	1,867,754
Public corporations holdings of local government debt	-EYXV	553	588	510	601	568	552	626	591
Public sector (PS) consolidated gross debt[3]	BKQA	2,877,876	2,797,276	2,248,271	2,241,570	2,301,460	2,288,572	2,314,512	2,371,475
Public sector liquid assets:									
Official reserves	AIPD	64,945	65,814	69,991	88,204	102,732	113,412	133,893	136,520
Central government (CG) deposits and other short term assets									
Bank and building society deposits	BKSM	7,772	6,648	6,568	6,823	9,381	8,721	11,563	11,141
Other liquid assets	BKSN	31,841	37,641	38,285	29,332	32,636	43,550	33,690	38,737
Local government (LG) deposits and other short term assets									
Bank and building society deposits	BKSO	24,197	24,860	25,368	27,075	24,019	22,575	20,770	23,841
Other liquid assets	BKQG	6,034	4,288	5,529	7,757	9,427	8,580	10,107	10,470
Public Corporation deposits and other short term assets									
Bank and building society deposits	BKSP	6,789	7,799	8,327	9,200	9,483	3,781	2,595	2,398
Other public corporations short term assets	BKSQ	2,220	2,273	2,278	2,484	2,555	2,498	2,375	2,298
Public Sector Net Debt (PSND)									
: sector liquid assets total	BKQJ	647,765	575,349	449,877	417,322	417,238	466,122	439,585	440,119
Public sector net debt (PSND)	BKQK	2,244,384	2,264,954	1,841,452	1,871,959	1,965,231	1,992,750	2,064,964	2,109,851
as percentage of GDP[4]	RUTO	127.9	123.1	96.7	94.9	95.6	93.5	93.1	96.1

Source: Office for National Statistics

1. See chapter text.
2. Including overdraft with Bank of England, Renminbi and Sukuk.
3. Excludes gross debt of Bank of England and its schemes (such as APF)

23.4a Central government surplus on current budget and net borrowing

£ million

	Taxes on production	of which	Taxes on income and wealth				Compulsory social contribution s[4]	Total Interest and dividends	Interest and dividends, of which Bank of England Asset Purchase Facility Fund 5	Other receipts[6]	Total current receipts[7]
	Total	VAT	Total	Income and capital gains tax[1]	Other[2,3]	Other taxes					
dataset identifier code	1	2	3	4	5	6	7	8	9	10	11
	NMBY	NZGF	NMCU	LIBR	LIBP	LIQR	AIIH	LIQP	L6BD	LIQQ	ANBV
2007	180,903	93,348	206,714	157,087	49,627	13,225	93,210	7,879	0	20,303	522,234
2008	178,959	93,419	207,145	161,631	45,514	13,179	98,319	9,451	0	22,157	529,210
2009	168,109	81,262	191,382	152,553	38,829	12,666	94,445	8,301	0	24,004	498,907
2010	193,271	97,565	199,576	153,503	46,073	13,370	97,346	7,653	0	24,975	536,191
2011	209,200	113,461	204,207	159,066	45,141	15,528	101,441	7,935	0	25,987	564,298
2012	215,549	116,459	198,380	155,274	43,106	15,354	104,319	11,742	0	27,908	573,252
2013	225,882	121,650	203,277	160,693	42,584	17,542	106,085	26,479	18,609	29,465	608,730
2014	237,157	127,647	208,849	164,153	44,696	17,358	109,120	16,343	8,682	32,136	620,963
2015	244,645	132,790	216,737	172,794	43,943	18,371	114,173	16,761	8,685	32,262	642,949
2016	255,409	137,215	232,010	180,033	51,977	18,720	121,963	17,601	10,011	32,629	678,332
2017	268,050	143,636	244,977	189,372	55,605	19,156	130,449	19,596	11,677	34,314	716,542
2018	277,116	149,454	252,247	195,784	56,463	19,875	135,378	18,553	9,766	33,787	736,956
2019	285,441	155,023	256,435	203,077	53,358	20,299	143,306	18,380	7,359	35,124	758,985
2007/08	181,891	93,800	211,822	162,360	49,462	13,444	95,437	8,552	0	20,722	531,868
2008/09	172,962	89,227	200,173	158,691	41,482	12,976	96,613	9,513	0	22,749	514,986
2009/10	175,463	86,244	191,198	149,639	41,559	12,759	96,638	7,626	0	24,216	507,900
2010/11	197,949	101,286	202,862	156,847	46,015	13,418	97,747	7,813	0	25,348	545,137
2011/12	211,208	114,204	201,432	157,039	44,393	16,077	101,597	9,501	0	26,236	566,051
2012/13	216,908	117,312	199,320	156,218	43,102	15,669	104,483	16,500	6,428	28,405	581,285
2013/14	229,578	123,592	203,964	161,526	42,438	17,718	107,306	20,102	12,181	29,983	608,651
2014/15	237,943	128,316	213,988	169,178	44,810	17,636	110,260	18,720	10,739	32,182	630,729
2015/16	247,582	133,953	220,906	175,934	44,972	18,453	114,205	16,525	8,529	32,423	650,094
2016/17	257,936	139,483	239,271	185,512	53,759	18,744	125,978	17,914	10,316	33,605	693,448
2017/18	269,080	143,646	244,394	188,402	55,992	19,361	131,781	18,213	10,028	33,762	716,591
2018/19	280,582	151,803	258,638	201,696	56,942	19,967	137,680	18,644	9,686	34,159	749,670
2019/20	283,178	152,731	254,768	203,212	51,556	20,414	144,982	18,112	7,137	35,843	757,297
2012 Q1	52,654	28,618	64,453	53,660	10,793	3,867	28,266	3,708	0	6,823	159,771
2012 Q2	52,312	28,740	42,738	31,480	11,258	3,624	25,631	4,204	0	6,991	135,500
2012 Q3	54,277	28,625	49,727	38,313	11,414	4,093	25,201	1,917	0	7,037	142,252
2012 Q4	56,306	30,476	41,462	31,821	9,641	3,770	25,221	1,913	0	7,057	135,729
2013 Q1	54,013	29,471	65,393	54,604	10,789	4,182	28,430	8,466	6,428	7,320	167,804
2013 Q2	54,978	29,941	44,794	34,027	10,767	5,101	26,556	13,628	11,655	7,241	152,298
2013 Q3	58,018	30,908	49,626	38,764	10,862	4,281	25,239	2,675	526	7,323	147,162
2013 Q4	58,873	31,330	43,464	33,298	10,166	3,978	25,860	1,710	0	7,581	141,466
2014 Q1	57,709	31,413	66,080	55,437	10,643	4,358	29,651	2,089	0	7,838	167,725
2014 Q2	58,084	31,383	44,246	32,939	11,307	4,410	26,432	5,843	4,107	7,639	146,654
2014 Q3	59,706	31,476	52,464	40,890	11,574	4,551	26,279	2,632	525	7,838	153,470
2014 Q4	61,658	33,375	46,059	34,887	11,172	4,039	26,758	5,779	4,050	8,821	153,114
2015 Q1	58,495	32,082	71,219	60,462	10,757	4,636	30,791	4,466	2,057	7,884	177,491
2015 Q2	60,078	32,631	46,224	34,687	11,537	4,689	28,035	5,713	3,904	8,580	153,319
2015 Q3	62,445	33,674	53,062	41,953	11,109	4,777	27,447	2,558	411	7,822	158,111
2015 Q4	63,627	34,403	46,232	35,692	10,540	4,269	27,900	4,024	2,313	7,976	154,028
2016 Q1	61,432	33,245	75,388	63,602	11,786	4,718	30,823	4,230	1,901	8,045	184,636
2016 Q2	62,773	33,826	49,005	35,353	13,652	4,760	30,156	5,433	3,806	8,140	160,267
2016 Q3	64,344	34,281	57,976	44,087	13,889	4,804	30,222	3,166	1,148	8,164	168,676
2016 Q4	66,860	35,863	49,641	36,991	12,650	4,438	30,762	4,772	3,156	8,280	164,753
2017 Q1	63,959	35,513	82,649	69,081	13,568	4,742	34,838	4,543	2,206	9,021	199,752
2017 Q2	65,844	34,584	50,606	36,241	14,365	5,066	31,829	6,163	4,401	8,543	168,051
2017 Q3	68,444	36,375	58,676	44,736	13,940	4,869	31,426	2,700	824	8,340	174,455
2017 Q4	69,803	37,164	53,046	39,314	13,732	4,479	32,356	6,190	4,246	8,410	174,284
2018 Q1	64,989	35,523	82,066	68,111	13,955	4,947	36,170	3,160	557	8,469	199,801
2018 Q2	69,841	37,162	53,063	37,947	15,116	5,101	32,828	5,362	3,350	8,328	174,523
2018 Q3	70,256	37,646	62,291	48,115	14,176	5,195	32,796	4,616	2,587	8,487	183,641
2018 Q4	72,030	39,123	54,827	41,611	13,216	4,632	33,584	5,415	3,272	8,503	178,991
2019 Q1	68,455	37,872	88,457	74,023	14,434	5,039	38,472	3,251	477	8,841	212,515
2019 Q2	71,082	38,472	53,023	39,154	13,869	5,027	35,032	5,970	2,997	8,742	178,876
2019 Q3	72,594	39,231	63,356	49,340	14,016	5,191	34,599	3,863	468	8,672	188,275
2019 Q4	73,310	39,448	51,599	40,560	11,039	5,042	35,203	5,296	3,417	8,869	179,319
2020 Q1	66,192	35,580	86,790	74,158	12,632	5,154	40,148	2,983	255	9,560	210,827

Source: Public Sector Finances

1. Includes capital gains tax paid by households Includes income tax and capital gains tax paid by corporations.
2. Mainly comprises corporation tax and petroleum revenue tax.
3. Includes diverted profit tax
4. Mainly national insurance contributions.
5. Includes only the dividend payments to central government, changes in equity are recorded in the financial account.
6. Consists largely of gross operating surplus which equates to depreciation for government and rent receipts.
7. Relationship between columns 11=1+3+6+7+8+10

23.4a (contd.) Central government surplus on current budget and net borrowing

£ million

dataset identifier code	Current expenditure				Saving, gross plus capital taxes	Depreciation	Current budget deficit[3]	Net investment	Net borrowing[4]
	Interest[1]	Net Social Benefits	Other	Total[2]					
	12	13	14	15	16	17	18	19	20
	NMFX	GZSJ	LIQS	ANLP	ANPM	NSRN	-ANLV	-ANNS	-NMFJ
2007	31,761	143,582	340,560	515,903	6,331	18,642	12,311	25,942	38,253
2008	33,103	154,145	359,040	546,288	-17,078	20,374	37,452	38,992	76,444
2009	27,957	170,874	379,704	578,535	-79,628	22,067	101,695	45,757	147,452
2010	44,997	178,154	398,154	621,305	-85,114	22,729	107,843	37,747	145,590
2011	51,367	183,639	394,685	629,691	-65,393	23,660	89,053	31,503	120,556
2012	48,039	193,094	408,976	650,109	-76,857	24,538	101,395	30,213	131,608
2013	49,261	195,702	407,889	652,852	-44,122	25,158	69,280	26,554	95,834
2014	48,533	199,990	418,625	667,148	-46,185	26,099	72,284	32,763	105,047
2015	43,375	202,853	420,773	667,001	-24,052	26,856	50,908	34,782	85,690
2016	47,433	205,269	423,095	675,797	2,535	27,737	25,202	34,380	59,582
2017	54,791	206,895	428,688	690,374	26,168	28,554	2,386	37,900	40,286
2018	52,017	213,114	441,679	706,810	30,146	28,899	-1,247	41,486	40,239
2019	46,728	214,350	464,289	725,367	33,618	29,819	-3,799	44,646	40,847
2007/08	31,472	145,283	348,242	524,997	6,871	19,084	12,213	31,200	43,413
2008/09	31,788	159,242	362,334	553,364	-38,378	20,899	59,277	41,473	100,750
2009/10	31,820	172,791	386,978	591,589	-83,689	22,236	105,925	43,855	149,780
2010/11	46,843	178,821	398,571	624,235	-79,098	23,005	102,103	36,266	138,369
2011/12	49,911	186,176	399,933	636,020	-69,969	23,926	93,895	21,461	115,356
2012/13	49,061	194,774	404,557	648,392	-67,107	24,567	91,674	34,803	126,477
2013/14	48,859	196,140	413,261	658,260	-49,609	25,410	75,019	29,782	104,801
2014/15	45,436	201,316	417,862	664,614	-33,885	26,270	60,155	33,640	93,795
2015/16	45,211	203,682	419,856	668,749	-18,655	27,043	45,698	33,737	79,435
2016/17	48,753	204,720	424,668	678,141	15,307	28,008	12,701	34,918	47,619
2017/18	55,128	208,420	432,271	695,819	20,772	28,636	7,864	38,793	46,657
2018/19	48,899	214,737	445,810	709,446	40,224	29,098	-11,126	44,092	32,966
2019/20	48,107	215,728	474,259	738,094	19,203	29,998	10,795	44,611	55,406
2012 Q1	10,107	45,069	106,286	161,462	-1,691	6,219	7,910	4,050	11,960
2012 Q2	14,272	48,454	101,293	164,019	-28,519	6,085	34,604	15,238	49,842
2012 Q3	9,652	51,098	99,382	160,132	-17,880	6,099	23,979	5,217	29,196
2012 Q4	14,008	48,473	102,015	164,496	-28,767	6,135	34,902	5,708	40,610
2013 Q1	11,129	46,749	101,867	159,745	8,059	6,248	-1,811	8,640	6,829
2013 Q2	14,474	48,567	108,799	171,840	-19,542	6,270	25,812	5,251	31,063
2013 Q3	10,276	51,693	96,971	158,940	-11,778	6,306	18,084	6,493	24,577
2013 Q4	13,382	48,693	100,252	162,327	-20,861	6,334	27,195	6,170	33,365
2014 Q1	10,727	47,187	107,239	165,153	2,572	6,500	3,928	11,868	15,796
2014 Q2	13,955	49,693	108,213	171,861	-25,207	6,521	31,728	6,784	38,512
2014 Q3	11,026	52,950	100,421	164,397	-10,927	6,519	17,446	6,493	23,939
2014 Q4	12,825	50,160	102,752	165,737	-12,623	6,559	19,182	7,618	26,800
2015 Q1	7,630	48,513	106,476	162,619	14,872	6,671	-8,201	12,745	4,544
2015 Q2	13,450	50,401	107,234	171,085	-17,766	6,722	24,488	9,049	33,537
2015 Q3	10,519	53,388	102,710	166,617	-8,506	6,721	15,227	7,111	22,338
2015 Q4	11,776	50,551	104,353	166,680	-12,652	6,742	19,394	5,877	25,271
2016 Q1	9,466	49,342	105,559	164,367	20,269	6,858	-13,411	11,700	-1,711
2016 Q2	13,522	50,956	107,699	172,177	-11,910	6,913	18,823	9,909	28,732
2016 Q3	12,332	53,949	104,889	171,170	-2,494	6,935	9,429	7,303	16,732
2016 Q4	12,113	51,022	104,948	168,083	-3,330	7,031	10,361	5,468	15,829
2017 Q1	10,786	48,793	107,132	166,711	33,041	7,129	-25,912	12,238	-13,674
2017 Q2	16,652	51,887	111,602	180,141	-12,090	7,132	19,222	10,922	30,144
2017 Q3	12,963	54,317	104,927	172,207	2,248	7,124	4,876	7,481	12,357
2017 Q4	14,390	51,898	105,027	171,315	2,969	7,169	4,200	7,259	11,459
2018 Q1	11,123	50,318	110,715	172,156	27,645	7,211	-20,434	13,131	-7,303
2018 Q2	14,670	53,143	109,751	177,564	-3,041	7,193	10,234	10,368	20,602
2018 Q3	12,222	55,707	111,206	179,135	4,506	7,230	2,724	8,659	11,383
2018 Q4	14,002	53,946	110,007	177,955	1,036	7,265	6,229	9,328	15,557
2019 Q1	8,005	51,941	114,846	174,792	37,723	7,410	-30,313	15,737	-14,576
2019 Q2	16,845	53,514	115,403	185,762	-6,886	7,406	14,292	10,735	25,027
2019 Q3	10,613	55,623	116,544	182,780	5,495	7,452	1,957	10,772	12,729
2019 Q4	11,265	53,272	117,496	182,033	-2,714	7,551	10,265	7,402	17,667
2020 Q1	9,384	53,319	124,816	187,519	23,308	7,589	-15,719	15,702	-17

Source: Office for National Statistics

1. Includes investment income attributable to insurance policy holders.
2. Relationship between columns 15=12+13+14 ; 18=(15-11)+17 20=18+19
3. Relationship between columns 18=17-16
4. Relationship between columns 20=18+19

23.4b Central government surplus on current budget and net borrowing, UK - monthly

Not seasonally adjusted

£ million

	Current receipts										
	Taxes on production	of which	Taxes on income and wealth				Compulsory social	Total Interest and dividends	Interest and dividends, of which Bank of England Asset Purchase Facility Fund [5]	Other receipts [6]	Total current receipts [7]
				Income and capital gains		Other	contributions [4]				
	Total	VAT	Total	tax [1]	Other [2,3]	taxes		dividends			
dataset identifier	1	2	3	4	5	6	7	8	9	10	11
code	NMBY	NZGF	NMCU	LIBR	LIBP	LIQR	AIIH	LIQP	L6BD	LIQQ	ANBV
2018 Jan	0	0	0	0	0	0	0	0	0	0	0
2018 Feb	0	0	0	0	0	0	0	0	0	0	0
2018 Mar	0	0	0	0	0	0	0	0	0	0	0
2018 Apr	0	0	0	0	0	0	0	0	0	0	0
2018 May	0	0	0	0	0	0	0	0	0	0	0
2018 Jun	0	0	0	0	0	0	0	0	0	0	0
2018 Jul	0	0	0	0	0	0	0	0	0	0	0
2018 Aug	0	0	0	0	0	0	0	0	0	0	0
2018 Sep	0	0	0	0	0	0	0	0	0	0	0
2018 Oct	0	0	0	0	0	0	0	0	0	0	0
2018 Nov	0	0	0	0	0	0	0	0	0	0	0
2018 Dec	0	0	0	0	0	0	0	0	0	0	0
2019 Jan	0	0	0	0	0	0	0	0	0	0	0
2019 Feb	0	0	0	0	0	0	0	0	0	0	0
2019 Mar	0	0	0	0	0	0	0	0	0	0	0
2019 Apr	0	0	0	0	0	0	0	0	0	0	0
2019 May	0	0	0	0	0	0	0	0	0	0	0
2019 Jun	0	0	1	1	0	0	0	0	0	0	1
2019 Jul	0	0	-20	-20	0	0	0	0	0	0	-20
2019 Aug	0	0	-20	-20	0	0	0	0	0	0	-20
2019 Sep	0	0	-20	-20	0	0	0	0	0	0	-20
2019 Oct	0	0	-3	-3	0	0	0	0	0	0	-3
2019 Nov	0	0	-3	-3	0	0	0	0	0	0	-3
2019 Dec	0	0	44	-3	47	0	0	0	0	0	44
2020 Jan	0	0	13	-34	47	0	0	0	0	0	13
2020 Feb	0	0	13	-34	47	0	0	0	0	0	13
2020 Mar	0	0	12	-35	47	0	0	0	0	0	12
2020 Apr	0	0	44	0	44	0	0	0	0	0	44
2020 May	0	0	45	0	45	0	0	0	0	0	45
2020 Jun	0	0	47	0	47	0	0	0	0	0	47

1. Includes capital gains tax paid by households. Includes income tax and capital gains tax paid by corporations.

Source: Office for National Statistics

2. Mainly comprises corporation tax and petroleum revenue tax.
3. Includes diverted profit tax
4. Mainly national insurance contributions.
5. Includes only the dividend payments to central government, changes in equity are recorded in the financial account.
6. Consists largely of gross operating surplus which equates to depreciation for government and rent receipts.
7. Relationship between columns 11=1+3+6+7+8+10

23.4a *(contd.)* Central government surplus on current budget and net borrowing - monthly

£ million

	Current expenditure				Saving, gross plus capital taxes	Depreciation	Current budget deficit [3]	Net investment	Net borrowing[4]
dataset identifier code	Interest [1]	Net Social Benefits	Other	Total [2]					
	12	13	14	15	16	17	18	19	20
	NMFX	GZSJ	LIQS	ANLP	ANPM	NSRN	-ANLV	-ANNS	-NMFJ
2018 Jan	0	0	0	0	0	0	0	0	0
2018 Feb	0	0	0	0	0	0	0	0	0
2018 Mar	0	0	0	0	0	0	0	0	0
2018 Apr	0	0	0	0	0	0	0	0	0
2018 May	0	0	0	0	0	0	0	0	0
2018 Jun	0	0	0	0	0	0	0	0	0
2018 Jul	0	0	0	0	0	0	0	0	0
2018 Aug	0	0	0	0	0	0	0	0	0
2018 Sep	0	0	0	0	0	0	0	0	0
2018 Oct	0	0	0	0	0	0	0	0	0
2018 Nov	0	0	0	0	0	0	0	0	0
2018 Dec	0	0	0	0	0	0	0	0	0
2019 Jan	0	0	0	0	0	0	0	0	0
2019 Feb	0	0	0	0	0	0	0	0	0
2019 Mar	0	0	0	0	0	0	0	0	0
2019 Apr	0	0	0	0	0	0	0	0	0
2019 May	0	0	0	0	0	0	0	0	0
2019 Jun	0	0	0	0	1	0	-1	0	-1
2019 Jul	0	0	0	0	-20	0	20	0	20
2019 Aug	0	0	0	0	-20	0	20	0	20
2019 Sep	0	0	0	0	-20	0	20	0	20
2019 Oct	0	0	0	0	-3	0	3	0	3
2019 Nov	0	0	0	0	-3	0	3	0	3
2019 Dec	0	0	0	0	44	0	-44	0	-44
2020 Jan	0	0	0	0	13	0	-13	0	-13
2020 Feb	0	0	0	0	13	0	-13	0	-13
2020 Mar	0	0	0	0	12	0	-12	0	-12
2020 Apr	0	0	0	0	44	0	-44	0	-44
2020 May	0	0	0	0	45	0	-45	0	-45
2020 Jun	0	0	0	0	47	0	-47	0	-47

1. Includes investment income attributable to insurance policy holders.
2. Relationship between columns 15=12+13+14 ; 18=(15-11)+17
3. Relationship between columns 18=17-16
4. Relationship between columns 20=18+19

Source: Office for National Statistics

23.5 National Loans Fund: assets and liabilities

United Kingdom as at 31 March 2020

	Note	At 31 March 2020 £m	At 31 March 2019 £m
Assets			
Advances	6	**153,215**	162,508
Loans	7	**3,560**	3,343
Other assets	8	**93,892**	83,186
IMF Quota Subscription & Lending	9	**22,792**	22,112
Total assets		**273,459**	271,149
Liabilities			
Gilt-edged stock	10	**1,716,715**	1,680,955
National Savings and Investments products	11	**179,175**	167,570
Other debt:			
FLS Treasury Bills	12	**3,178**	23,165
Other	12	**88,079**	47,899
Liabilities to the IMF	9	**17,649**	17,211
Total liabilities		**2,004,796**	1,936,800
Net liabilities		**1,731,337**	1,665,651
Liability of the Consolidated Fund to the National Loans Fund		**1,731,337**	1,665,651

Tom Scholar
Accounting Officer
HM Treasury

23.6a Taxes paid by UK residents to general government and the European Union

Total economy sector S.1

£ million

			2012	2013	2014	2015	2016	2017	2018	2019
Generation of income										
Uses										
Taxes on production and imports		D.2								
Taxes on products and imports		D.21								
Value added tax (VAT)		D.211								
Paid to central government	NZGF		116 459	121 650	127 647	132 948	137 531	142 655	149 228	154 799
Total	QYRC	D.211	116 459	121 650	127 647	132 948	137 531	142 655	149 228	154 799
Taxes and duties on imports excluding VAT		D.212								
Paid to central government: import duties[1]	NMXZ	D.2121	–	–	–	–	–	–	–	–
Paid to EU: import duties	FJWE	D.2121	2 885	2 914	2 949	3 077	3 318	3 419	3 335	3 343
Total	QYRB	D.212	2 885	2 914	2 949	3 077	3 318	3 419	3 335	3 343
Taxes on products excluding VAT and import duties		D.214								
Paid to central government										
Customs and excise revenue										
Beer	GTAM		3 425	3 337	3 337	3 294	3 288	3 443	3 638	3 659
Wines, cider, perry and spirits	GTAN		6 775	7 063	7 246	7 385	7 578	8 151	8 355	8 457
Tobacco	GTAO		9 897	9 479	9 436	9 190	9 087	9 122	8 976	9 038
Hydrocarbon oils	GTAP		26 703	26 697	27 094	27 415	27 989	27 973	27 919	27 795
Car tax	GTAT		–	–	–	–	–	–	–	–
Betting, gaming and lottery	CJQY		1 207	1 538	1 708	2 053	2 329	2 235	2 202	2 502
Air passenger duty	CWAA		2 766	2 960	3 154	3 119	3 150	3 398	3 513	3 810
Insurance premium tax	CWAD		3 022	3 018	2 964	3 294	4 827	5 670	6 201	6 417
Landfill tax[2]	BKOF		1 094	1 191	1 143	1 028	1 024	904	820	784
Other	ACDN		–	–	–	–	–	–	–	–
Fossil fuel levy	CIQY		–	–	–	–	–	–	–	–
Gas levy	GTAZ		–	–	–	–	–	–	–	–
Stamp duties[2]	GTBC		8 918	11 542	14 069	13 791	16 025	17 101	16 486	15 962
Levies on exports (third country trade)	CUDF		–	–	–	–	–	–	–	–
Camelot payments to national lottery										
Distribution fund	LIYH		1 832	1 644	1 721	1 713	1 713	1 713	1 713	1 713
Hydro-benefit	LITN		–	–	–	–	–	–	–	–
Aggregates levy	MDUQ		264	282	342	354	405	375	366	396
Milk super levy	DFT3		–	–	–	–	–	–	–	–
Climate change levy	LSNT		624	1 098	1 506	1 752	1 881	1 878	1 911	2 091
Channel 4 funding formula	EG9G		–	–	–	–	–	–	–	–
Renewable energy obligations	EP89		1 842	2 391	2 931	3 691	4 401	5 209	5 949	6 118
Contracts for difference	CW5G		–	–	–	–	78	510	911	1 471
Rail franchise premia	LITT		1 275	1 275	1 501	1 611	1 656	1 380	1 257	1 258
Other taxes and levies	GCSP		–	–	–	–	–	–	–	–
Vehicle registration tax	MVPC		125	138	151	169	171	162	152	157
Air travel organisers' licensing protection contribution	N3DV		46	44	57	55	61	62	66	66
Soft drinks levy	CT9U		–	–	–	–	–	–	237	336
Total paid to central government[3]	NMBV		69 815	73 697	78 360	79 914	85 663	89 286	90 672	92 030
Paid to local government										
Community infrastructure levy	DMHG		4	36	104	147	265	275	302	179
Total paid to local government	CPPM		4	36	104	147	265	275	302	179
Paid to the european union										
Sugar levy	GTBA		13	12	11	10	9	8	–	–
European coal and steel community levy	GTBB		–	–	–	–	–	–	–	–
Total paid to the european union	FJWG		13	12	11	10	9	8	–	–
Total taxes on products excluding VAT and import duties[3]	QYRA	D.214	69 832	73 745	78 475	80 071	85 937	89 569	90 974	92 209
Total taxes on products and imports	NZGW	D.21	189 176	198 309	209 071	216 096	226 786	235 643	243 537	250 351
Production taxes other than on products		D.29								
Paid to central government										
Consumer credit act fees	CUDB		480	480	480	480	480	480	480	480
National non-domestic rates	CUKY		23 749	24 599	25 173	25 834	26 574	27 382	28 410	29 084
Northern Ireland non-domestic rates	NSEZ		366	373	378	397	410	420	431	448
Levies paid to central government levy-funded bodies	LITK		903	922	993	970	1 019	915	859	853
London regional transport levy	GTBE		–	–	–	–	–	–	–	–
Apprenticeship levy	CRSN		–	–	–	–	–	1 862	2 604	2 764
Immigration skills charge	CSH8		–	–	–	–	–	63	85	85
IBA levy	GTAL		–	–	–	–	–	–	–	–
Motor vehicle duties paid by businesses	EKED		1 679	1 789	1 865	2 076	1 945	2 019	2 001	2 007
Regulator fees	GCSQ		81	84	93	87	75	135	129	120
Northern Ireland driver vehicle agency	IY9N		4	4	4	4	4	4	4	4
Bank payroll tax: accrued receipts	JT2Q		–	–	–	–	–	–	–	–
Emissions trading scheme	M98G		278	339	418	493	386	335	293	274
Carbon reduction commitment	L8UA		348	607	569	659	520	440	384	298
Light dues	DPIH		87	89	86	78	73	79	78	78
Payments under police service agreement	CY6Z		125	128	133	142	145	145	145	145
Total	NMBX		28 100	29 414	30 192	31 221	31 631	34 279	35 903	36 640
Paid to local government										
Non-domestic rates[4]	DM9L		344	350	353	376	398	404	414	421
Crossrail business rates supplement	MHG4		233	217	218	224	231	271	276	271
Total	NMYH		577	567	571	600	629	675	690	692
Total production taxes other than on products	NMYD	D.29	28 677	29 981	30 763	31 821	32 260	34 954	36 593	37 332
Total taxes on production and imports, paid		D.2								
Paid to central government	NMBY		214 374	224 761	236 199	244 083	254 825	266 220	275 803	283 469
Paid to local government	DMHD		581	603	675	747	894	950	992	871
Paid to the European Union	FJWB		2 898	2 926	2 960	3 087	3 327	3 427	3 335	3 343
Total	NZGX	D.2	217 853	228 290	239 834	247 917	259 046	270 597	280 130	287 683

23.6b Taxes paid by UK residents to general government and the European Union

Total economy sector S.1

£ million

			2012	2013	2014	2015	2016	2017	2018	2019
Secondary distribution of income										
Uses										
Current taxes on income, wealth etc.		D.5								
Taxes on income		D.51								
Paid to central government										
Households income taxes	DRWH		149 445	155 194	158 852	165 840	172 021	179 509	187 022	194 185
Corporation tax	CPRO		39 439	39 899	42 835	42 385	49 667	50 931	50 698	45 761
Petroleum revenue tax	DBHA		2 106	1 296	568	−552	−768	−634	−817	−319
Windfall tax	EYNK		–	–	–	–	–	–	–	–
Other taxes on income	BMNX		7 401	6 899	6 596	9 031	11 541	14 686	15 420	17 563
Total	NMCU	D.51	198 391	203 288	208 851	216 704	232 461	244 492	252 323	257 190
Other current taxes		D.59								
Paid to central government										
Motor vehicle duty paid by households	CDDZ		4 201	4 312	4 110	3 823	4 044	4 207	4 512	4 998
Northern Ireland domestic rates	NSFA		416	409	404	384	372	362	351	334
Boat licences	NSNP		–	–	–	–	–	–	–	–
Fishing licences	NRQB		21	21	21	21	21	21	21	27
National non-domestic rates paid by Non-market sectors[4]	BMNY		1 709	1 731	1 752	1 773	1 790	1 832	1 866	1 752
Passport fees	E8A6		362	343	386	439	447	441	502	512
Television licence fee	DH7A		3 117	3 082	3 124	3 131	3 156	3 184	3 206	3 265
Northern Ireland driver vehicle agency	IY9O		12	12	12	12	12	12	12	12
Bank levy	KIH3		1 641	2 352	2 853	3 369	3 120	2 568	2 613	2 523
Total	NMCV		11 479	12 262	12 662	12 952	12 962	12 627	13 083	13 423
Paid to local government										
Domestic rates[4]	NMHK		164	170	176	195	208	218	229	246
Community charge	NMHL		–	–	–	–	–	–	–	–
Council tax	NMHM		26 045	27 061	27 946	28 777	30 018	31 690	34 120	35 939
Total	NMIS		26 209	27 231	28 122	28 972	30 226	31 908	34 349	36 185
Total	NVCM	D.59	37 688	39 493	40 784	41 924	43 188	44 535	47 432	49 608
Total current taxes on income, wealth etc		D.5								
Paid to central government	NMCP		209 870	215 550	221 513	229 656	245 423	257 119	265 406	270 613
Paid to local government	NMIS		26 209	27 231	28 122	28 972	30 226	31 908	34 349	36 185
Total	NMZL	D.5	236 079	242 781	249 635	258 628	275 649	289 027	299 755	306 798
Social contributions		D.61								
Actual social contributions										
Paid to central government										
(National insurance contributions)										
Employers' compulsory contributions	CEAN		60 600	62 019	63 892	66 491	71 539	76 591	79 240	82 507
Employees' compulsory contributions	GCSE		41 159	41 481	42 556	44 454	47 302	50 412	52 055	55 958
Self- and non-employed persons' Compulsory contributions	NMDE		2 560	2 585	2 672	3 122	3 189	3 436	3 691	4 185
Total	AIIH		104 319	106 085	109 120	114 067	122 030	130 439	134 986	142 650
Capital account		Part								
Changes in liabilities and net worth										
Other capital taxes		D.91								
Paid to central government										
Inheritance tax	GILF		3 041	3 293	3 702	4 359	4 703	5 283	5 198	5 097
Tax on other capital transfers	GILG		50	50	50	50	50	50	50	50
Tax on swiss bank accounts[6]	KW69		–	876	–	–	–	–	–	–
Development land tax and other	GCSV		–	–	–	–	–	–	–	–
Tax paid on local government equal pay settlements	C625		38	36	134	33	48	49	53	18
FSCS levies on private sector[7]	HZQ4		–	–	–	–	–	–	–	–
Total	NMGI	D.91	3 129	4 255	3 886	4 442	4 801	5 382	5 301	5 165
Total taxes and Compulsory social contributions										
Paid to central government	GCSS		531 692	550 651	570 718	592 248	627 079	659 160	681 496	701 897
Paid to local government	GCST		26 786	27 798	28 693	29 572	30 855	32 583	35 039	36 877
Paid to the European Union	FJWB		2 898	2 926	2 960	3 087	3 327	3 427	3 335	3 343
Total	GCSU		561 376	581 375	602 371	624 907	661 261	695 170	719 870	742 117

1 These taxes existed before the UKs entry into the EEC in 1973
2 Landfill Wales and Stamp Duty Wales are not included in these totals
3 Total taxes for D.214 will not necessarily equal the sum of its components
4 From 1990/1991 onwards these series only contain rates paid in Northern Ireland

5 Up until 1995/96 these payments are included in national non-domestic rates under production taxes other than on products
6 *BLANK Tax liable from banking deposits of UK residents held in Swiss ban
7 Financial Services Compensation Scheme

23.7 Central government
ESA 2010 sector S.1311

£ million

			2012	2013	2014	2015	2016	2017	2018	2019
Financial account		III.2								
Net acquisition of financial assets		F.A								
Monetary gold and special drawing rights		F.1								
Monetary gold	NARO	F.11	–	–	–	–	–	–	–	–
Special drawing rights	NARP	F.12	111	43	–14	55	–1 397	1 231	1 624	893
Total	NWXM	F.1	111	43	–14	55	–1 397	1 231	1 624	893
Currency and deposits		F.2								
Transferable deposits		F.22								
With UK monetary financial institutions	NART	F.22N1	5 222	–3 186	1 026	–6 849	–2 007	4 529	–659	3 425
Of which: foreign currency deposits with UK MFIs[1]	NARV	F.22N12	–271	901	–1 117	–850	75	2 466	–2 923	4 670
With rest of the world monetary financial institutions	NARX	F.22N9	935	142	463	2 997	2 958	2 867	15 793	–7 184
Other deposits	RYWO	F.29	–898	9 862	4 152	–7 938	826	13 324	–11 804	8 092
Total	NARQ	F.2	5 259	6 818	5 641	–11 790	1 777	20 720	3 330	4 333
Debt securities		F.3								
Short-term		F.31								
Issued by UK monetary financial institutions	NSUN	F.31N5	–		–		–	–	–	–
Money market instruments										
MMIs Issued by other UK residents[2]	NSRI	F.31N6	–3 404	1 459	–1 137	–2 348	487	–300	3 076	–2 978
MMIs Issued by rest of the world	NASM	F.31N9	–967	–2 314	363	908	2 309	–1 881	–1 671	–2 010
Long-term		F.32								
Issued by UK monetary financial institutions[3] and other UK residents	NASV	F.32N5-6	1 152	–327	–	–	–	–	–	–
Issued by rest of the world	NASW	F.32N9	5 182	–2 863	5 566	17 583	3 701	1 043	2 459	7 430
Total	NARZ	F.3	1 963	–4 045	4 792	16 143	6 497	–1 138	3 864	2 442
Loans		F.4								
Long-term		F.42								
Secured on dwellings	NATM	F.422	–6 649	–6 500	–9 030	–17 678	–5 417	–13 711	–7 688	–5 325
Other loans by UK residents[4]	NATR	F.424N1	14 337	6 317	8 106	8 206	10 256	9 207	14 115	20 817
Other loans by rest of the world	NATS	F.424N9	–	–	–	–	–	–	–	–
Total	NATB	F.4	7 688	–183	–924	–9 472	4 839	–4 504	6 427	15 492
Equity and investment fund shares/units		F.5								
Equity		F.51								
Listed UK shares[3]	NATY	F.511N1	1 832	–9 222	–5 524	–13 627	–2 163	–3 613	–4 689	–936
Unlisted UK shares[3]	NATZ	F.512N1	7	–21 957	–2 375	–758	–3	1	7	–
Other equity		F.519								
Other UK equity	NAUA	F.519N6	–	–10	–40	–1	–	–	–	–
UK shares and bonds issued by other UK residents[3]	NSOX	F.519N7	–	–	–	–	–	–	–	–
Shares and other equity issued by rest of the world	NAUD	F.519N9	178	1 497	285	93	277	364	339	443
Total	NATT	F.5	2 017	–29 692	–7 654	–14 293	–1 889	–3 248	–4 343	–493
Financial derivatives and employee stock options	MN5T	F.7	587	–11	–855	–1 219	894	1 880	1 446	1 966
Of which: financial derivatives	CFZG	F.71	587	–11	–855	–1 219	894	1 880	1 446	1 966
Other accounts receivable	NAUN	F.8	2 445	6 345	8 227	8 970	15 130	10 253	5 750	–6 635
Total net acquisition of financial assets	NARM	F.A	20 070	–20 725	9 213	–11 606	25 851	25 194	18 098	17 998

23.7 Central government
ESA 2010 sector S.1311

continued

£ million

			2012	2013	2014	2015	2016	2017	2018	2019
Financial account		III.2								
Net acquisition of financial liabilities		F.L								
Special drawing rights	M98C	F.12	–	–	–	–	–	–	–	–
Currency and deposits		F.2								
Currency	NAUV	F.21	158	30	191	168	140	–174	24	99
Other deposits	NAVC	F.29	–2 254	–7 912	17 852	10 689	17 856	16 526	1 642	10 195
Total	NAUU	F.2	–2 096	–7 882	18 043	10 857	17 996	16 352	1 666	10 294
Debt securities		F.3								
Short-term		F.31								
Issued by UK central government	NAVF	F.31N1	–18 706	–14 315	25 809	19 721	12 524	–14 930	–8 901	36 172
Long-term		F.32								
UK central government securities	NAVT	F.32N11	129 283	103 137	64 402	58 475	57 276	58 731	46 781	18 515
Other UK central government bonds	NAVU	F.32N12	4 584	2 993	193	–5 225	–1 193	–4 032	945	52
Bonds issued by UK MFIs[1] and other UK residents[3]	MNR7	F.32N5-6	–5 296	–11 682	–3 738	–14 718	–6 613	–26	–	–200
Total	NAVD	F.3	109 865	80 133	86 666	58 253	61 994	39 743	38 825	54 539
Loans		F.4								
Short-term		F.41								
By UK monetary financial institutions[5]	NAWH	F.41N1	–601	848	–1 423	3 799	–81	3 531	10 241	–1 812
By rest of the world	NAWL	F.41N9	911	–825	1 228	5 021	–2 398	3 798	11 435	–7 134
Long-term		F.42								
Finance leasing	NAWU	F.423	–	–	413	498	632	–182	158	–649
Other loans by UK residents	NAWV	F.424N1	193	194	41	–5	–8	–2	–3	–2
Other loans by rest of the world	NAWW	F.424N9	–256	293	797	449	41	67	–48	21
Total	NAWF	F.4	247	510	1 056	9 762	–1 814	7 212	21 783	–9 576
Insurance, pensions and standardised guarantee schemes		F.6								
Pension Schemes[6]	CSZ2	F.6M	803	856	855	855	374	246	243	279
Provisions for calls under standardised guarantees	MW4E	F.66	–	–	27	14	–	–6	–8	–8
Total	DM53	F.6	803	856	882	869	374	240	235	271
Other accounts payable	NAXR	F.8	42 541	511	7 390	–5 763	5 918	3 016	–3 318	4 512
Total net acquisition of financial liabilities	NAUQ	F.L	151 360	74 128	114 037	73 978	84 468	66 563	59 191	60 040
Net lending(+) / net borrowing(-)		B.9								
Total net acquisition of financial assets	NARM	F.A	20 070	–20 725	9 213	–11 606	25 851	25 194	18 098	17 998
less total net acquisition of financial liabilities	NAUQ	F.L	151 360	74 128	114 037	73 978	84 468	66 563	59 191	60 040
Net lending(+) / borrowing(-) from the financial account	NZDX	B.9f	–131 290	–94 853	–104 824	–85 584	–58 617	–41 369	–41 093	–42 042
Statistical discrepancy between the financial and non-financial accounts	NZDW	dB.9	–308	–924	–205	–480	–96	1	158	–766
Net lending (+) / borrowing (-) from non-financial accounts	NMFJ	B.9n	–131 598	–95 777	–105 029	–86 064	–58 713	–41 368	–40 935	–42 808

1 Monetary financial institutions.
2 Money market instruments
3 Prior to 1990, it is not possible to distinguish some elements of F.32N5-6, F.511N1 and F.512N1. These elements are shown combined as F.519N7
4 Other than direct investment loans, loans secured on dwellings and loans for finance leasing
5 All loans secured on dwellings and all finance leasing are treated as long-term loans
6 F.63 Pension entitlements, F.64 Claims of pension funds on pension managers F.65 Entitlements to non-pension benefits

Source: Office for National Statistics, The Blue Book 2020

23.8 Central government net cash requirement on own account (receipts and outlays on a cash basis)

£ million

	Cash receipts HM Revenue and Customs[8]									Cash outlays				
dataset identifier	Total paid over[1]	Income tax[2]	Corporation tax[8,9]	NICs[3]	V.A.T.[4]	Other[9]	Interest and dividends	Other receipts[5]	Total	Interest payments	Net acquisition of company securities[6]	Net departmental outlays[7]	Total	Own account NCR
	1	2	3	4	5		6	7	8	9	10	11	12	13
code	MIZX	RURC	N445	ABLP	EYOO	-	RUUL	RUUM	RUUN	RUUO	ABIF	RUUP	RUUQ	M98S
2007	422,465	154,346	44,528	96,656	80,301	46,634	8,251	30,082	460,798	25,537	-2,340	470,169	493,366	32,567
2008	428,380	162,758	47,288	98,504	80,709	39,121	9,354	30,556	468,290	26,033	19,714	544,720	590,467	122,177
2009	384,875	153,101	36,236	95,053	68,637	31,848	6,666	31,282	422,823	29,304	41,809	548,810	619,923	197,100
2010	411,846	153,237	42,153	95,860	80,865	39,731	5,274	34,063	451,183	34,008	0	569,599	603,607	152,424
2011	434,438	157,066	42,741	101,033	95,208	38,390	5,757	42,235	482,430	43,923	0	557,494	601,417	118,987
2012	436,196	154,430	40,081	102,232	98,619	40,834	9,842	38,399	484,437	39,934	-14,287	565,919	591,566	107,129
2013	451,668	159,730	39,211	106,702	103,726	42,299	46,577	36,652	534,897	48,025	-5,954	566,940	609,011	74,114
2014	467,588	164,107	39,794	109,238	109,408	45,041	16,854	92,517	576,959	41,777	-5,164	635,115	671,728	94,769
2015	489,449	173,361	43,403	113,130	114,060	45,495	14,882	64,357	568,687	42,255	-18,070	632,308	656,493	87,806
2016	516,568	179,093	46,146	121,118	118,301	51,910	16,908	38,405	571,881	51,034	-3,392	604,309	651,951	80,070
2017	553,087	188,588	54,081	129,598	124,692	56,128	18,287	43,347	614,721	44,536	-17,079	622,001	649,458	34,737
2018	577,436	195,985	56,850	135,379	130,146	59,076	16,619	30,392	624,446	38,537	-11,440	624,699	651,796	27,350
2019	605,833	202,399	60,297	141,915	135,898	65,324	17,829	21,707	645,369	37,420	-5,622	658,179	689,977	44,608
2008 Q1	126,971	55,652	13,108	27,550	19,850	10,811	2,646	5,997	135,614	6,472	0	118,768	125,240	-10,374
2008 Q2	97,153	35,630	8,722	23,517	20,087	9,197	2,252	8,154	107,559	6,449	0	131,441	137,890	30,331
2008 Q3	108,990	40,772	12,955	24,801	21,235	9,227	2,266	9,143	120,399	6,566	-255	150,477	156,788	36,389
2008 Q4	95,266	30,704	12,503	22,636	19,537	9,886	2,190	7,262	104,718	6,546	19,969	144,034	170,549	65,831
2009 Q1	115,103	54,185	9,749	25,930	17,580	7,659	2,016	3,449	120,568	6,386	12,536	131,608	150,530	29,962
2009 Q2	85,699	32,649	6,569	22,727	16,102	7,652	1,892	9,626	97,217	8,534	-2,021	145,058	151,571	54,354
2009 Q3	93,410	37,031	8,256	23,574	16,847	7,702	1,357	9,721	104,488	7,577	0	133,158	140,735	36,247
2009 Q4	90,663	29,236	11,662	22,822	18,108	8,835	1,401	8,486	100,550	6,807	31,294	138,986	177,087	76,537
2010 Q1	112,559	48,458	10,146	26,393	19,103	8,459	1,551	4,493	118,603	9,271	0	139,909	149,180	30,577
2010 Q2	94,699	35,719	7,404	22,870	19,886	8,820	1,049	8,868	104,616	6,956	0	147,380	154,336	49,720
2010 Q3	107,569	38,793	11,525	23,950	20,564	12,737	1,370	11,557	120,496	10,782	0	136,851	147,633	27,137
2010 Q4	97,019	30,267	13,078	22,647	21,312	9,715	1,304	9,145	107,468	6,999	0	145,459	152,458	44,990
2011 Q1	120,293	52,311	11,038	27,081	21,737	8,126	1,836	9,019	131,148	11,840	0	135,142	146,982	15,834
2011 Q2	99,487	34,458	7,426	24,283	24,084	9,236	1,229	10,614	111,330	7,392	0	145,667	153,059	41,729
2011 Q3	110,502	38,849	11,681	25,861	23,984	10,127	1,506	13,346	125,354	17,071	0	137,097	154,168	28,814
2011 Q4	104,156	31,448	12,596	23,808	25,403	10,901	1,186	9,256	114,598	7,620	0	139,588	147,208	32,610
2012 Q1	123,458	50,524	10,772	27,665	24,821	9,676	3,331	6,142	132,931	12,421	-747	135,613	147,287	14,356
2012 Q2	100,129	34,290	7,369	24,669	24,469	9,332	3,583	11,978	115,690	7,542	-11,109	147,487	143,920	28,230
2012 Q3	109,251	38,709	9,939	25,873	24,524	10,206	1,462	10,843	121,556	12,622	-1,174	136,553	148,001	26,445
2012 Q4	103,358	30,907	12,001	24,025	24,805	11,620	1,466	9,436	114,260	7,349	-1,257	146,266	152,358	38,098
2013 Q1	124,619	52,049	10,533	27,470	26,772	7,795	13,219	14,153	151,991	13,618	-733	143,648	156,533	4,542
2013 Q2	105,685	36,960	7,136	27,227	24,915	9,447	13,088	7,493	126,266	7,110	-383	148,768	155,495	29,229
2013 Q3	114,459	39,123	10,181	26,916	25,681	12,558	14,898	8,414	137,771	20,372	-3,427	135,452	152,397	14,626
2013 Q4	106,905	31,598	11,361	25,089	26,358	12,499	5,372	6,592	118,869	6,925	-1,411	139,072	144,586	25,717
2014 Q1	129,451	53,123	10,254	28,459	27,731	9,884	4,136	51,055	184,642	13,707	-4,218	186,210	195,699	11,057
2014 Q2	109,055	36,578	7,889	26,589	26,961	11,038	5,319	11,695	126,069	7,044	-85	154,377	161,336	35,267
2014 Q3	118,047	41,060	9,931	28,124	26,883	12,049	1,725	12,207	131,979	14,039	-519	140,326	153,846	21,867
2014 Q4	111,035	33,346	11,720	26,066	27,833	12,070	5,674	17,560	134,269	6,987	-342	154,202	160,847	26,578
2015 Q1	138,508	57,683	11,552	29,629	29,682	9,962	4,087	16,646	159,241	13,714	-1,736	154,996	166,974	7,733
2015 Q2	113,944	38,284	9,052	28,415	26,824	11,369	5,156	10,234	129,332	7,255	-4,950	157,963	160,268	30,936
2015 Q3	121,984	42,789	10,550	28,587	28,401	11,657	2,080	17,614	141,678	14,081	-4,898	153,689	162,872	21,194
2015 Q4	115,013	34,605	12,249	26,499	29,153	12,507	3,559	19,863	138,436	7,205	-6,486	165,660	166,379	27,943
2016 Q1	143,924	59,832	11,166	30,202	30,372	12,352	4,018	17,010	164,952	13,687	-1,651	150,340	162,376	-2,576
2016 Q2	118,923	39,575	9,209	29,949	28,045	12,145	5,390	6,735	131,048	7,144	-523	152,236	158,857	27,809
2016 Q3	129,030	44,285	11,008	31,203	29,450	13,084	2,990	9,362	141,382	23,210	-12	147,576	170,774	29,392
2016 Q4	124,691	35,401	14,763	29,764	30,434	14,329	4,510	5,298	134,499	6,993	-1,206	154,157	159,944	25,445
2017 Q1	156,035	66,365	14,319	33,552	31,664	10,135	4,252	11,754	172,041	13,437	-2,617	148,100	158,920	-13,121
2017 Q2	127,294	40,411	11,235	31,814	30,194	13,640	5,902	18,535	151,732	6,784	-12,753	169,583	163,614	11,882
2017 Q3	136,608	44,697	13,038	32,899	31,078	14,896	2,446	6,376	145,430	13,286	-1,703	146,635	158,218	12,788
2017 Q4	133,150	37,115	15,489	31,333	31,756	17,457	5,687	6,682	145,518	11,029	-6	157,683	168,706	23,188
2018 Q1	160,626	65,620	14,949	34,884	33,152	12,021	2,037	10,175	172,837	13,010	-5	149,261	162,266	-10,571
2018 Q2	132,480	42,444	11,627	33,188	30,734	14,487	5,170	9,506	147,156	6,503	-8,550	163,269	161,222	14,066
2018 Q3	146,505	47,979	13,639	34,286	33,453	17,148	4,405	4,906	155,816	12,474	-5	148,620	161,089	5,273
2018 Q4	137,825	39,942	16,635	33,021	32,807	15,420	5,007	5,805	148,637	6,550	-2,880	163,549	167,219	18,582
2019 Q1	172,870	69,856	14,399	36,355	35,316	16,944	2,395	5,120	180,385	12,256	-1,304	161,264	172,216	-8,169
2019 Q2	138,996	44,736	12,821	35,053	32,095	14,291	6,054	4,444	149,494	6,879	-4,304	165,701	168,276	18,782
2019 Q3	151,768	49,247	15,804	36,218	34,292	16,207	4,014	7,551	163,333	11,564	-9	160,479	172,034	8,701
2019 Q4	142,199	38,560	17,273	34,289	34,195	17,882	5,366	4,592	152,157	6,721	-5	170,735	177,451	25,294
2020 Q1	169,227	70,525	17,769	37,310	29,136	14,487	3,121	14,700	187,048	10,679	0	171,328	182,007	-5,041

Source: Office for National Statistics

1. Comprises payments into the Consolidated Fund and all payovers of national insurance contributions excluding those for Northern Ireland.
2. Income tax includes capital gains tax and is gross of any tax credits treated by HM Revenue and Customs as tax deductions.
3. UK receipts net of personal pension rebates; gross of Statutory Maternity Pay and Statutory Sick Pay.
4. Payments into Consolidated Fund.
5. Including some elements of expenditure not separately identified.
6. Mainly comprises privatisation proceeds.
7. Net of certain receipts, and excluding on-lending to local authorities and public corporations.
8. Gross of tax credits. Includes diverted profit tax.
9. A detailed breakdown of tax receipts are available from HM Revenue and Customs at:
https://wwwgovuk/government/statistics/hmrc-tax-and-nics-receipts-for-the-uk#history

23.9 HM Revenue and Customs receipts

Amounts: £ million

Year	Total Paid Over	Total HMRC receipts	Total Income Tax	Of which: PAYE Income Tax	Of which: SA Income Tax	Capital Gains Tax	Apprenticeship Levy	NICs	VAT	Total Corporation Tax	Of which offshore	Bank Levy	Bank Surcharge	Diverted Profits Tax	Bank payroll tax	Petroleum Revenue Tax	Hydrocarbon Oil (Fuel duties) duties	Inheritance Tax	Shares	Stamp Duty Land Tax
	MIZX	[X]	[X]	BKMR	LISB	[X]	[X]	ABLP	EYOO	[X]	[X]	[X]	[X]	[X]	JT2R	ACCJ	ACDD	ACCH	BKST	BKSU
2008-09	416,512	445,531	153,442	128,470	22,531	7,852	[X]	96,882	78,439	43,927	9,826	[X]	[X]	[X]	[X]	2,567	24,615	2,839	3,203	4,796
2009-10	382,331	414,920	144,881	122,584	21,708	2,491	[X]	95,517	70,160	36,628	4,998	[X]	[X]	[X]	[X]	923	26,197	2,384	3,017	4,886
2010-11	419,580	453,957	153,491	132,263	22,108	3,601	[X]	96,548	83,502	43,040	6,864	[X]	[X]	[X]	3,416	1,458	27,256	2,718	2,971	5,961
2011-12	437,603	472,035	150,939	132,189	20,334	4,337	[X]	101,617	98,292	42,475	8,840	1,612	[X]	[X]	-2	2,032	26,800	2,903	2,794	6,125
2012-13	437,357	473,626	152,030	132,433	20,550	3,927	[X]	102,037	104,572	39,841	4,412	1,595	[X]	[X]	0	1,737	26,571	3,105	2,234	6,907
2013-14	456,500	492,802	156,898	134,686	20,854	3,908	[X]	107,690	104,718	38,932	3,556	2,200	[X]	[X]	[X]	1,118	26,881	3,402	3,108	9,273
2014-15	476,645	514,058	163,109	139,506	23,645	5,559	[X]	110,406	111,363	41,091	2,026	2,748	[X]	[X]	[X]	77	27,156	3,804	2,926	10,738
2015-16	494,864	532,503	168,451	145,652	24,327	7,060	[X]	113,701	114,941	43,016	560	3,392	[X]	[X]	[X]	-562	27,623	4,650	3,320	10,682
2016-17	528,677	567,990	177,065	149,751	29,293	8,561	[X]	124,469	119,799	48,017	295	2,975	1,145	138	[X]	-654	27,936	4,824	3,714	11,766
2017-18	557,677	593,317	180,049	154,266	28,294	7,793	2,271	130,931	126,423	52,714	1,757	2,764	1,778	219	[X]	-569	27,877	5,205	3,519	12,906
2018-19	589,679	621,049	191,030	161,909	31,356	9,191	2,713	136,850	132,540	54,382	1,912	2,591	1,904	12	[X]	-744	27,993	5,359	3,620	11,942
2019-20	602,155	633,420	193,243	164,841	32,010	9,826	2,798	142,871	129,885	61,684	1,274	2,472	1,978	5	[X]	-408	27,573	5,122	3,619	11,601
Apr-16	48,485	51,881	16,126	15,627	-115	7	[X]	10,707	11,087	5,656	[X]	564	20	[X]	[X]	-15	2,366	417	246	1,172
May-16	37,768	40,941	11,943	12,542	-180	2	[X]	9,352	10,957	1,800	[X]	[X]	[X]	[X]	[X]	0	2,314	391	241	713
Jun-16	32,668	35,482	11,479	11,926	22	18	[X]	9,890	6,058	1,733	[X]	[X]	[X]	[X]	[X]	0	2,425	432	278	816
Jul-16	55,009	58,952	19,820	12,275	7,478	6	[X]	11,474	12,227	7,044	[X]	827	344	[X]	[X]	-259	2,339	381	380	973
Aug-16	40,721	43,540	13,567	12,033	1,770	2	[X]	10,140	10,789	1,446	[X]	[X]	[X]	[X]	[X]	-95	2,354	386	247	1,016
Sep-16	33,300	35,796	10,893	11,390	147	-2	[X]	9,589	6,486	2,174	[X]	[X]	[X]	[X]	[X]	0	2,350	402	349	927
Oct-16	48,946	51,805	11,767	11,663	30	14	[X]	10,070	12,323	8,461	-21	787	444	[X]	[X]	-4	2,361	412	557	1,024
Nov-16	38,755	42,336	11,465	11,704	40	2	[X]	9,935	10,984	2,032	[X]	[X]	[X]	[X]	[X]	-7	2,398	400	239	1,072
Dec-16	36,990	39,989	12,150	11,564	1,012		[X]	9,759	7,193	3,827	[X]	[X]	[X]	[X]	[X]	-141	2,396	368	370	1,216
Jan-17	73,160	75,728	26,557	12,694	13,691	6,094	[X]	11,985	13,334	9,612	210	796	336	[X]	[X]	-109	2,050	385	221	935
Feb-17	45,356	50,431	17,227	12,550	4,785	2,142	[X]	10,838	10,999	2,145	[X]	[X]	[X]	[X]	[X]	-23	2,426	367	267	887
Mar-17	37,519	41,111	14,071	13,785	612	275	[X]	10,729	7,364	2,087	106	[X]	[X]	138	[X]	-1	2,158	482	320	1,015
Apr-17	53,962	56,228	16,222	16,278	-106	3	[X]	11,721	13,240	6,676	[X]	711	384	[X]	[X]	-8	2,451	531	217	1,007
May-17	38,761	42,702	12,237	12,940	-190		162	9,946	10,528	2,030	[X]	[X]	[X]	[X]	[X]	-85	2,279	555	318	1,033
Jun-17	34,572	37,847	11,941	12,177	139	5	198	10,147	6,485	2,145	[X]	[X]	[X]	[X]	[X]	-200	2,391	439	334	1,090
Jul-17	58,981	62,167	20,389	12,649	8,046	5	211	12,267	12,729	7,838	[X]	707	501	[X]	[X]	-24	2,353	427	272	1,216
Aug-17	41,243	44,235	12,888	12,171	1,344	7	210	10,549	10,604	1,921	[X]	[X]	[X]	[X]	[X]	0	2,358	426	309	1,195
Sep-17	36,384	39,285	11,403	11,674	144	5	206	10,083	7,812	2,778	[X]	[X]	[X]	[X]	[X]	0	2,349	423	291	1,113
Oct-17	51,981	54,992	12,551	12,084	81	5	207	10,575	13,181	9,467	402	683	516	[X]	[X]	9	2,311	442	297	1,162
Nov-17	42,019	43,997	11,969	11,951	97	6	208	10,358	11,539	1,485	[X]	[X]	[X]	[X]	[X]	-52	2,440	444	291	1,111
Dec-17	39,149	41,895	12,573	11,677	1,108	10	176	10,400	7,098	4,021	785	[X]	[X]	[X]	[X]	-140	2,407	387	333	1,197
Jan-18	75,495	76,392	26,080	13,291	12,756	5,599	252	12,790	13,904	9,979	[X]	662	377	[X]	[X]	-67	2,126	376	259	1,014
Feb-18	46,205	51,206	16,963	12,868	4,271	1,876	218	11,151	11,701	2,253	[X]	[X]	[X]	[X]	[X]	0	2,360	372	289	851
Mar-18	38,925	42,373	14,833	14,507	605	269	223	10,943	7,602	2,121	570	[X]	[X]	219	[X]	-13	2,053	382	309	917
Apr-18	55,734	57,979	17,054	17,090	-65	5	273	12,379	12,554	7,246	[X]	512	456	[X]	[X]	0	2,404	425	415	961
May-18	40,689	45,098	13,038	13,628	-102	4	228	10,321	10,896	2,231	[X]	[X]	[X]	[X]	[X]	-67	2,302	487	236	894
Jun-18	36,057	38,720	12,338	12,585	216	5	212	10,488	7,312	1,694	[X]	[X]	[X]	[X]	[X]	-138	2,459	507	301	938
Jul-18	62,884	66,344	22,141	13,349	9,004	5	220	12,748	13,834	8,375	[X]	744	502	[X]	[X]	-62	2,338	465	288	1,121
Aug-18	44,390	47,001	13,771	12,872	1,338	8	228	10,947	11,430	2,072	[X]	[X]	[X]	[X]	[X]	-6	2,364	473	296	1,155
Sep-18	39,231	40,638	12,051	12,866	225	3	213	10,591	8,273	2,690	479	[X]	[X]	[X]	[X]	0	2,402	441	234	921
Oct-18	54,012	56,491	13,258	12,676	154	5	218	11,191	13,160	9,778	[X]	648	524	[X]	[X]	0	2,229	460	421	1,126
Nov-18	43,861	47,895	13,033	12,463	130	6	219	10,924	12,033	2,271	[X]	[X]	[X]	[X]	[X]	-324	2,518	437	406	1,061
Dec-18	39,952	42,722	13,626	12,463	1,384	14	213	10,906	7,674	4,062	812	[X]	[X]	[X]	[X]	-125	2,364	396	278	1,105
Jan-19	79,677	79,847	28,479	13,950	14,690	6,666	233	13,196	13,701	9,757	[X]	687	422	[X]	[X]		2,230	370	238	848

23.9 HM Revenue and Customs receipts

Amounts: £ million

Year	Total Paid Over	Total HMRC receipts	Total Income Tax	Of which: PAYE Income Tax	Of which: SA Income Tax	Capital Gains Tax	Apprenticeship Levy	NICs	VAT	Total Corporation Tax	Of which offshore	Bank Levy	Bank Surcharge	Diverted Profits Tax	Bank payroll tax	Petroleum Revenue Tax	Hydrocarbon Oil (Fuel duties)	Inheritance Tax	Shares	Stamp Duty Land Tax
	MIZX	[X]	[X]	BKMR	LJSB	[X]	[X]	ABLP	EYOO	[X]	[X]	[X]	[X]	[X]	JT2R	ACCJ	ACDD	ACCH	BKST	BKSU
Feb-19	49,697	54,354	17,197	13,580	3,838	2,192	226	11,570	13,373	2,026	[X]	[X]	[X]	[X]	[X]	4	2,241	372	225	881
Mar-19	43,495	43,960	15,043	14,533	543	279	230	11,589	8,297	2,182	621	[X]	[X]	12	[X]	-13	2,142	527	281	930
Apr-19	58,431	60,904	18,577	18,622	-183	5	271	13,210	13,041	7,322	[X]	560	427	[X]	[X]	0	2,380	456	276	962
May-19	41,635	45,333	13,235	13,754	-245	4	226	10,765	10,994	2,226	[X]	[X]	[X]	[X]	[X]	0	2,277	393	259	831
Jun-19	38,930	41,680	12,910	13,085	160	5	230	11,078	8,118	2,846	[X]	[X]	[X]	[X]	[X]	0	2,393	357	227	831
Jul-19	65,830	68,208	22,706	13,785	9,356	4	246	13,641	13,640	9,178	[X]	627	465	[X]	[X]	-137	2,279	438	279	1,116
Aug-19	45,349	48,763	14,129	12,851	1,697	8	226	11,379	12,446	2,166	[X]	[X]	[X]	[X]	[X]	-26	2,394	405	312	1,029
Sep-19	40,589	42,965	12,396	12,591	297	4	218	11,198	8,254	3,995	468	[X]	[X]	[X]	[X]	-7	2,356	432	231	1,004
Oct-19	53,727	55,547	12,793	12,990	117	4	234	11,619	13,569	8,537	[X]	667	413	[X]	[X]	-1	2,308	489	287	1,059
Nov-19	44,316	47,167	12,219	12,473	234	5	221	11,147	13,031	2,180	[X]	[X]	[X]	[X]	[X]	-14	2,362	404	365	941
Dec-19	44,150	46,428	13,534	12,621	1,409	6	223	11,523	7,622	6,143	424	[X]	[X]	[X]	[X]	0	2,433	478	304	1,299
Jan-20	81,573	81,602	29,327	13,981	15,295	7,048	238	13,764	14,476	8,613	[X]	617	287	[X]	[X]	-162	2,133	417	312	777
Feb-20	49,324	53,870	17,134	14,026	3,296	2,408	243	12,237	12,586	1,916	[X]	[X]	[X]	[X]	[X]	-28	2,302	407	299	824
Mar-20	38,300	40,955	14,282	14,060	576	326	222	11,309	2,107	6,562	381	[X]	386	5	[X]	-34	1,955	446	466	928
Apr-20	32,745	35,266	14,579	15,587	-765	7	210	11,034	-896	3,345	[X]	611	301	[X]	[X]	0	1,373	307	439	548

23.9 HM Revenue and Customs receipts

									Receipts (contd.)									Expenditure			
Year	Annual Tax on Enveloped Dwellings	Tobacco duties	Spirits duties	Beer duties	Wines duties	Cider duties	Betting & Gaming	Air Passenger Duty	Insurance Premium Tax	Landfill Tax	Climate Change Levy	Aggregates Levy	Soft Drinks Industry Levy	Swiss Capital Tax	Misc	Customs Duties	Penalties	Child and Working Tax Credits	Corporation Tax Credits	Child Benefit Payments	Tax-Free Child Care
	[x]	ACDE	ACDF	ACDG	ACDH	ACDI	ACDJ	ACDP	ACDO	[x]	LSNS	MDUP	[x]	[x]	[x]	ADET	[x]	[x]	JPPT [x]	[x]	[x]
2008-09	[x]	8,219	2,358	3,127	2,741	244	1,474	1,862	2,281	954	716	334	[x]	[x]	[x]	2,659	[x]	24,099	1,181	11,262	[x]
2009-10	[x]	8,813	2,570	3,182	2,949	311	1,439	1,856	2,259	842	695	275	[x]	[x]	[x]	2,646	[x]	27,601	1,147	11,824	[x]
2010-11	[x]	9,144	2,675	3,296	3,101	324	1,533	2,155	2,400	1,065	674	288	[x]	[x]	[x]	2,998	343	28,879	1,313	12,160	[x]
2011-12	[x]	9,551	2,889	3,463	3,356	329	1,633	2,607	2,941	1,090	676	290	[x]	[x]	[x]	2,912	375	29,830	1,385	12,177	[x]
2012-13	[x]	9,681	2,931	3,426	3,537	326	1,680	2,791	3,021	1,092	635	265	[x]	342	[x]	2,854	490	29,888	1,438	12,167	[x]
2013-14	100	9,531	3,056	3,346	3,713	340	2,098	3,013	3,014	1,189	1,068	285	[x]	466	[x]	2,901	551	29,710	1,156	11,438	[x]
2014-15	116	9,531	3,023	3,310	3,837	320	2,116	3,175	2,965	1,144	1,491	342	[x]	66	[x]	3,007	623	29,732	1,813	11,582	[x]
2015-16	178	9,485	3,147	3,271	3,973	296	2,666	3,077	3,293	919	1,763	356	[x]	32	[x]	3,089	685	28,539	3,273	11,681	[x]
2016-17	175	8,909	3,378	3,320	4,169	288	2,742	3,157	4,861	874	1,864	374	[x]	-1	[x]	3,359	766	27,429	4,410	11,640	[x]
2017-18	143	8,827	3,430	3,460	4,256	294	2,860	3,352	5,669	757	1,861	376	[x]	51	[x]	3,412	689	25,940	5,409	11,599	32
2018-19	139	9,290	3,779	3,661	4,392	279	2,985	3,632	6,196	683	1,922	367	240	-1	[x]	3,356	748	22,878	6,262	11,552	117
2019-20	128	8,804	3,825	3,446	4,296	270	3,019	3,641	6,415	641	2,004	397	337	0	[x]	3,287	641	18,003	7,314	11,460	236
Apr-16	88	1,074	239	286	346	26	265	224	239	144	237	40	[x]	0	[x]	252	68	2,654	[x]	1,023	[x]
May-16	51	269	235	290	301	25	308	257	883	46	253	22	[x]	0	[x]	243	45	2,453	[x]	980	[x]
Jun-16	10	625	277	320	343	29	85	262	36	9	-3	20	[x]	0	[x]	248	90	2,442	[x]	904	[x]
Jul-16	7	726	257	296	327	27	358	277	326	173	222	51	[x]	0	[x]	263	87	2,882	[x]	1,006	[x]
Aug-16	0	760	221	274	338	26	261	265	899	51	222	27	[x]	0	[x]	282	63	2,286	[x]	1,007	[x]
Sep-16	4	843	256	300	345	25	75	364	31	9	0	21	[x]	0	[x]	302	54	2,410	[x]	919	[x]
Oct-16	3	857	286	260	331	20	379	299	307	225	193	53	[x]	0	[x]	320	65	2,510	[x]	970	[x]
Nov-16	3	717	359	241	390	21	246	283	869	52	212	29	[x]	0	[x]	310	70	2,209	[x]	937	[x]
Dec-16	3	633	472	328	495	23	105	240	32	6	3	19	[x]	0	[x]	279	76	2,748	[x]	974	[x]
Jan-17	5	910	227	300	332	24	405	264	361	85	248	47	[x]	0	[x]	301	57	2,221	[x]	983	[x]
Feb-17	1	716	178	181	256	16	142	210	826	59	295	26	[x]	-1	[x]	292	46	2,263	[x]	898	[x]
Mar-17	1	780	372	244	363	25	113	213	54	16	-17	21	[x]	0	[x]	267	44	2,656	[x]	981	[x]
Apr-17	60	845	214	305	315	25	234	277	62	73	288	27	[x]	0	[x]	283	59	2,436	[x]	967	[x]
May-17	47	488	198	282	309	23	374	190	1,057	58	241	44	[x]	0	[x]	260	47	2,299	[x]	1,004	[x]
Jun-17	9	755	285	320	364	23	136	364	83	37	5	18	[x]	0	[x]	284	75	2,497	[x]	954	[x]
Jul-17	7	800	274	315	356	30	391	296	297	94	240	12	[x]	0	[x]	278	61	2,761	[x]	1,009	[x]
Aug-17	4	757	254	294	350	27	125	203	1,123	68	181	47	[x]	0	[x]	300	59	2,241	[x]	939	[x]
Sep-17	2	851	288	314	370	27	80	404	42	60	4	18	[x]	0	[x]	311	50	2,336	[x]	1,032	[x]
Oct-17	2	753	309	255	344	29	538	370	289	77	189	65	[x]	0	[x]	308	67	2,334	[x]	1,160	[x]
Nov-17	1	653	415	298	424	25	175	308	1,175	75	194	39	[x]	0	[x]	301	54	2,245	[x]	745	[x]
Dec-17	2	1,170	508	344	531	28	101	243	12	41	19	17	[x]	0	[x]	281	50	2,683	[x]	969	[x]
Jan-18	2	554	243	291	332	21	455	295	269	73	245	40	[x]	0	[x]	254	41	2,033	[x]	992	[x]
Feb-18	4	524	197	200	275	16	130	65	1,167	57	235	36	[x]	51	[x]	272	60	2,272	[x]	916	[x]
Mar-18	3	677	244	242	287	20	120	337	94	45	22	15	[x]	0	[x]	281	64	2,401	[x]	994	[x]
Apr-18	76	784	304	308	369	23	377	285	162	41	258	31	[x]	0	[x]	258	33	2,476	n/a	1,034	8
May-18	36	970	272	313	351	22	281	278	1,255	81	278	37	[x]	0	[x]	235	53	2,241	n/a	1,047	7
Jun-18	7	651	320	361	366	27	129	305	13	34	5	16	[x]	0	[x]	253	47	2,003	n/a	965	8
Jul-18	2	803	296	336	366	29	445	323	339	73	237	42	61	0	[x]	256	90	2,089	n/a	982	8
Aug-18	4	744	304	338	354	26	138	358	1,346	68	203	42	1	0	[x]	290	91	2,120	n/a	1,006	8
Sep-18	2	921	308	319	330	22	85	349	13	52	14	17	0	0	[x]	303	68	1,711	n/a	936	8
Oct-18	3	705	306	257	423	23	557	337	197	20	236	39	92	0	[x]	300	73	1,943	n/a	956	11
Nov-18	2	1,242	463	318	496	24	152	310	1,341	113	152	44	1	0	[x]	339	63	1,843	[x]	941	10
Dec-18	2	269	503	342	327	27	115	231	6	49	15	18	0	0	[x]	285	49	1,901	[x]	1,015	13
Jan-19	1	686	249	304		20	257	335	203	48	271	39	84	0	[x]	263	58	1,739	[x]	929	

23.9 HM Revenue and Customs receipts

Amounts: £ million

Year	Annual Tax on Enveloped Dwellings	Tobacco duties	Spirits duties	Beer duties	Wines duties	Cider duties	Betting & Gaming	Air Passenger Duty	Insurance Premium Tax	Landfill Tax	Climate Change Levy	Aggregates Levy	Soft Drinks Industry Levy	Swiss Capital Tax	Misc	Customs Duties	Penalties	Child and Working Tax Credits	Corporation Tax Credits	Child Benefit Payments	Tax-Free Child Care
	[x]	ACDE	ACDF	ACDG	ACDH	ACDI	ACDJ	ACDP	ACDO	[x]	LSNS	MDUP	[x]	[x]	[x]	ADET	[x]	[x]	JPPT	[x]	[x]
Feb-19	1	648	228	212	395	17	323	258	1,301	69	197	29	1	0	[x]	300	68	1,632	[x]	882	12
Mar-19	3	866	226	255	248	18	126	264	21	35	59	14	0	-1	[x]	273	56	1,636	[x]	986	14
Apr-19	76	647	313	305	347	25	361	284	322	35	299	37	77	0	[x]	261	29	1,883	[x]	932	15
May-19	26	648	286	332	343	26	283	305	1,196	71	201	36	1	0	[x]	258	110	1,778	[x]	991	17
Jun-19	3	767	326	340	370	26	88	331	20	38	28	17	0	0	[x]	270	59	1,523	[x]	958	15
Jul-19	4	724	275	306	337	22	492	353	376	87	276	56	84	0	[x]	266	67	1,804	[x]	973	19
Aug-19	3	889	305	310	372	26	128	376	1,260	38	192	35	1	0	[x]	291	69	1,498	[x]	998	17
Sep-19	1	914	320	352	343	24	111	347	46	45	15	18	0	0	[x]	301	44	1,394	[x]	914	19
Oct-19	5	669	311	274	338	23	523	344	257	71	272	41	88	0	[x]	316	38	1,477	[x]	967	22
Nov-19	2	637	442	254	483	22	195	347	1,311	56	152	41	1	0	[x]	309	55	1,333	[x]	935	21
Dec-19	0	590	489	401	484	24	142	281	43	58	37	17	1	0	[x]	263	32	1,496	[x]	952	22
Jan-20	1	1,039	257	318	344	20	436	316	247	56	295	45	83	0	[x]	238	59	1,299	[x]	977	25
Feb-20	3	473	233	211	287	17	129	278	1,297	51	193	40	1	0	[x]	276	51	1,219	[x]	908	22
Mar-20	2	805	269	43	246	15	133	78	41	34	44	15	1	0	[x]	239	29	1,299	[x]	955	22
Apr-20	68	1,538	286	69	320	12	225	30	249	38	271	33	30	0	[x]	208	30	1,506	[x]	954	7

Source: HM Revenue and Customs

Receipts Notes

Income Tax. Figures are gross of personal tax credits and includes Pay As You Earn and Self-Assessment income tax (also shown seperately in the table) as well as other smaller elements of income tax such as repayments.

Corporation Tax (CT). Receipts are gross of provisional tax credits and are subject to change, due to a lag in return data becoming available for analysis. Figures include offshore which are also shown seperately in the table. From July 2011 Bank Levy receipts are shown separately and from April 2016 Bank Surcharge receipts are shown separately.

Offshore. The majority of UK Oil & Gas companies payments are due in three instalments, (Jul, Oct and Jan), and so receipts are reported in a similar pattern following each instalment.

Diverted Profits Tax (DPT). Figures are net DPT charges. DPT encourages companies to change contrived arrangements and pay CT on their profits in line with their economic activity. DPT may be repaid where a company makes an amendment to bring its taxable diverted profits into charge to CT: these are included under CT. The full impact of DPT legislation is available in the Transfer Pricing and Diverted Profits Tax statistics published on GOV.UK.

Inheritance Tax. Excludes non-cash elements which are shown in Table 12.1 Inheritance Tax: Analysis of Receipts.

Stamp Duty Land Tax (SDLT). Excludes SDLT devolved to Scotland from April 2015, and to Wales from April 2018. Includes first time buyer's relief from November 2017, and from July 2020, the SDLT holiday announced by the Chancellor on 8 July 2020.

Landfill tax (LFT). Excludes LFT devolved to Scotland from April 2015, and to Wales from April 2019.

Climate Change Levy. From April 2013, includes receipts from Carbon Price Floor.

Penalties. Penalties relate to taxes and duties only. National Insurance Contributions (NICs) penalties are included in the NICs figures. Monthly data is only available back to April 2013, and annual data back to April 2010. Prior to April 2010, penalties were recorded in the HMRC Resource Accounts.

Expenditure Notes

Corporation Tax Credits. Monthly data unavailable due to the lag in return data becoming available. Tax credits are provisional and annual data is subject to change to incorporate new available data.

Child Benefit. From April 2011, the series has been revised to ensure consistency with HMRC Resource Accounts. HMRC recently introduced a new system to administer Child Benefit. From April 2021, figures are provisional estimates while ongoing quality assurance processes are completed. HMRC will publish confirmed figures as soon as possible.

Tax-Free Child Care. Introduced in April 2017. For further information, please see the step by step guide published on GOV.UK.

23.10 Income Tax Personal Allowances and reliefs, 1990-91 to 2020-21

| Financial years | Non-aged allowances | | | | | | Aged allowances | | | | |
	Personal	Married couple's (1)	Blind person's (2)	Dividend	Savings Basic rate	Savings Higher rate	Personal 65-74	Personal 75+	Married couple's 65-74	Married couple's 75+	Income limit (3)
1990-91	3,005	1,720	1,080	N/A	N/A	N/A	3,670	3,820	2,145	2,185	12,300
1991-92	3,295	1,720	1,080	N/A	N/A	N/A	4,020	4,180	2,355	2,395	13,500
1992-93	3,445	1,720	1,080	N/A	N/A	N/A	4,200	4,370	2,465	2,505	14,200
1993-94	3,445	1,720	1,080	N/A	N/A	N/A	4,200	4,370	2,465	2,505	14,200
1994-95	3,445	1,720 (4)	1,200	N/A	N/A	N/A	4,200	4,370	2,665 (4)	2,705 (4)	14,200
1995-96	3,525	1,720 (5)	1,200	N/A	N/A	N/A	4,630	4,800	2,995 (5)	3,035 (5)	14,600
1996-97	3,765	1,799 (5)	1,250	N/A	N/A	N/A	4,910	5,090	3,115 (5)	3,155 (5)	15,200
1997-98	4,045	1,830 (5)	1,280	N/A	N/A	N/A	5,220	5,400	3,185 (5)	3,225 (5)	15,600
1998-99	4,195	1,900 (5)	1,330	N/A	N/A	N/A	5,410	5,600	3,305 (5)	3,345 (5)	16,200
1999-00	4,335	1,970 (5)	1,380	N/A	N/A	N/A	5,720	5,980	5,125 (6)	5,195 (5)	16,800
2000-01	4,385	N/A	1,400	N/A	N/A	N/A	5,790	6,050	5,185 (6,7)	5,255 (6,7)	17,000
2001-02	4,535	N/A	1,450	N/A	N/A	N/A	5,990	6,260	5,365 (6,7)	5,435 (6,7)	17,600
2002-03	4,615	N/A	1,480	N/A	N/A	N/A	6,100	6,370	5,465 (6,7)	5,535 (6,7)	17,900
2003-04	4,615	N/A	1,510	N/A	N/A	N/A	6,610	6,720	5,565 (6,7)	5,635 (6,7)	18,300
2004-05	4,745	N/A	1,560	N/A	N/A	N/A	6,830	6,950	5,725 (6,7)	5,795 (6,7)	18,900
2005-06	4,895	N/A	1,610	N/A	N/A	N/A	7,090	7,220	5,905 (6,7)	5,975 (6,7)	19,500
2006-07	5,035	N/A	1,660	N/A	N/A	N/A	7,280	7,420	6,065 (6,7)	6,135 (6,7)	20,100
2007-08	5,225	N/A	1,730	N/A	N/A	N/A	7,550	7,690	6,285 (6,7)	6,365 (6,7)	20,900
2008-09	6,035	N/A	1,800	N/A	N/A	N/A	9,030	9,180	6,535 (6,7)	6,625 (6,7)	21,800
2009-10	6,475	N/A	1,890	N/A	N/A	N/A	9,490	9,640	N/A	6,965 (6,7)	22,900
2010-11	6,475 (8)	N/A	1,890	N/A	N/A	N/A	9,490	9,640	N/A	6,965 (6,7)	22,900
2011-12	7,475 (8)	N/A	1,980	N/A	N/A	N/A	9,940	10,090	N/A	7,295 (6,7)	24,000
2012-13	8,105 (8)	N/A	2,100	N/A	N/A	N/A	10,500	10,660	N/A	7,705 (6,7)	25,400
2013-14	9,440 (8)	N/A	2,160	N/A	N/A	N/A	10,500 (9)	10,660 (10)	N/A	7,915 (6,7)	26,100
2014-15	10,000 (8)	N/A	2,230	N/A	N/A	N/A	10,500 (9)	10,660 (10)	N/A	8,165 (6,7)	27,000
2015-16	10,600 (8)	N/A	2,290	N/A	N/A	N/A	N/A	10,660 (10)	N/A	8,355 (6,7)	27,700
2016-17	11,000 (8)	N/A	2,290	5,000 (11)	1,000 (12)	500 (12)	N/A	N/A	N/A	8,355 (6,7)	27,700
2017-18	11,500 (8)	N/A	2,320	5,000 (11)	1,000 (12)	500 (12)	N/A	N/A	N/A	8,445 (6,7)	28,000
2018-19	11,850 (8)	N/A	2,390	2,000 (11)	1,000 (12)	500 (12)	N/A	N/A	N/A	8,695 (6,7)	28,900
2019-20	12,500 (8)	N/A	2,450	2,000 (11)	1,000 (12)	500 (12)	N/A	N/A	N/A	8,915 (6,7)	29,600
2020-21	12,500 (8)	N/A	2,500	2,000 (11)	1,000 (12)	500 (12)	N/A	N/A	N/A	9,075 (6,7)	30,200

Source: HM Revenue and Customs

(1) This was given in addition to the personal allowance to married couples. The additional personal allowance and the widow's bereavement allowance had the same value as the married couple's allowance.

(2) Couples where both spouses or partners are severely sight impaired get double the single amount of Blind Person's Allowance.

(3) Where an individual's income exceeds the income limit, their Married Couple's Allowance is reduced by £1 for every £2 above the income limit, potentially down to the minimum Married Couples Allowance (£3,450 for 2019-20).

(4) Allowance available at a flat rate of 20%.

(5) Allowance available at a flat rate of 15%.

(6) Allowance available at a flat rate of 10%.

(7) At least one of the partners must have been born before 6 April 1935.

(8) The Personal Allowance reduces where an individuals income is above £100,000 - by £1 for every £2 of income above the £100,000 limit. This reduction applies irrespective of age or date of birth.

(9) Available to people born in the period 6 April 1938 to 5 April 1948.

(10) Available to people born on or before 5 April 1938.

(11) The Dividend Allowance, introduced for 2016-17, means that no tax is payable on the first £5,000 of dividend income, irrespective of the total amount of dividend and non-dividend income received. The amount was reduced to £2,000 in 2018-19.

(12) The Personal Savings Allowance, introduced for 2016-17, provides for an amount of savings income to be received tax-free. The upper bound for the tax-free allowance depends on the top marginal tax rate on an individual's total income; the threshold for higher rate taxpayers is half that for basic rate taxpayers and is set to £0 for additional rate taxpayers. The effect of the Personal Allowance, Starting Rate and Personal Savings Allowance for 2016-17 is that an individual with total taxable income of £17,000 will pay no tax on savings income.

23.11 Rates of Income Tax: 2002-03 to 2020-21

Financial Years	Rate of Income Tax									
	Lower Rate		Starting Rate		Basic Rate		Higher Rate		Additional Rate	
	Bands of taxable income, £ (1)	Rate of tax, %	Bands of taxable income, £ (1)	Rate of tax, %	Bands of taxable income, £ (1)	Rate of tax, %	Bands of taxable income, £ (1)	Rate of tax, %	Bands of taxable income, £ (1)	Rate of tax, %
2002 to 2003	N/A	N/A	1 to 1,920	10	1,921 to 29,900	22 (note 5)	Over 29,900	40 (note 6)	N/A	N/A
2003 to 2004	N/A	N/A	1 to 1,960	10	1,961 to 30,500	22 (note 5)	Over 30,500	40 (note 6)	N/A	N/A
2004 to 2005	N/A	N/A	1 to 2,020	10	2,021 to 31,400	22 (note 5)	Over 31,400	40 (note 6)	N/A	N/A
2005 to 2006	N/A	N/A	1 to 2,090	10	2,091 to 32,400	22 (note 5)	Over 32,400	40 (note 6)	N/A	N/A
2006 to 2007	N/A	N/A	1 to 2,150	10	2,151 to 33,300	22 (note 5)	Over 33,300	40 (note 6)	N/A	N/A
2007 to 2008	N/A	N/A	1 to 2,230	10	2,231 to 34,600	22 (note 5)	Over 34,600	40 (note 6)	N/A	N/A
2008 to 2009	N/A	N/A	N/A	N/A	1 to 34,800	20 (note 8)	Over 34,800	40 (note 6)	N/A	N/A
2009 to 2010	N/A	N/A	N/A	N/A	1 to 37,400	20 (note 8)	Over 37,400	40 (note 6)	N/A	N/A
2010 to 2011	N/A	N/A	N/A	N/A	1 to 37,400	20 (note 8)	37,401 to 150,000	40 (note 6)	Over 150,000	50 (note 9)
2011 to 2012	N/A	N/A	N/A	N/A	1 to 35,000	20 (note 8)	35,001 to 150,000	40 (note 6)	Over 150,000	50 (note 9)
2012 to 2013	N/A	N/A	N/A	N/A	1 to 34,370	20 (note 8)	34,371 to 150,000	40 (note 6)	Over 150,000	50 (note 9)
2013 to 2014	N/A	N/A	N/A	N/A	1 to 32,010	20 (note 8)	32,011 to 150,000	40 (note 6)	Over 150,000	45 (note 10)
2014 to 2015	N/A	N/A	N/A	N/A	1 to 31,865	20 (note 8)	31,866 to 150,000	40 (note 6)	Over 150,000	45 (note 10)
2015 to 2016	N/A	N/A	N/A	N/A	1 to 31,785	20 (note 8)	31,786 to 150,000	40 (note 6)	Over 150,000	45 (note 10)
2016 to 2017	N/A	N/A	N/A	N/A	1 to 32,000	20 (note 8)	32,001 to 150,000	40 (note 12)	Over 150,000	45 (note 13)
2017 to 2018	N/A	N/A	N/A	N/A	1 to 33,500	21 (note 11)	33,501 to 150,000	40 (note 12)	Over 150,000	45 (note 13)
2018 to 2019	N/A	N/A	N/A	N/A	1 to 34,500	22 (note 11)	34,501 to 150,000	40 (note 12)	Over 150,000	45 (note 13)
2019 to 2020	N/A	N/A	N/A	N/A	1 to 37,500	23 (note 11)	37,501 to 150,000	40 (note 12)	Over 150,000	45 (note 13)
2020 to 2021	N/A	N/A	N/A	N/A	1 to 37,500	24 (note 11)	37,501 to 150,000	40 (note 12)	Over 150,000	45 (note 13)

Source: HM Revenue and Customs

RATES OF INCOME TAX FOR SAVINGS BAND ONLY

Financial years	Band of taxable income, £ (note 1)	Rate of tax, %
2008 to 2009	2,320	10
2009 to 2010	2,440	10
2010 to 2011	2,440	10
2011 to 2012	2,560	10
2012 to 2013	2,710	10
2013 to 2014	2,790	10
2014 to 2015	2,880	10
2015 to 2016	5,000	0
2016 to 2017	5,000	0
2017 to 2018	5,000	0
2018 to 2019	5,000	0
2019 to 2020	5,000	0
2020 to 2021	5,000	0

(1) Taxable income is defined as gross income for income tax purposes less any allowances and reliefs available at the taxpayer's marginal rate.
(2) Applies to the income of discretionary and accumulation trusts. Prior to 1993-94 trusts paid tax at the basic rate, with an additional rate of 10%.
(3) The basic rate of tax on gross dividend income is 20%.
(4) The basic rate of tax on gross dividends and savings income is 20%.
(5) The basic rate of tax on gross dividends is 10% and savings income is 20%.
(6) The higher rate of tax on gross dividends is 32.5%.
(7) From 2008-09 the starting rate is abolished for all non-savings income (e.g. employment, self-employed trading profits, pensions and property income), which is the first slice of income to be charged to income tax. The starting rate and the starting rate limit for savings is shown in the table below. Where taxable non-savings income does not fully occupy the starting rate limit the remainder of the starting rate limit is available for savings income.
(8) The basic rate of tax on gross dividends is 10%.
(9) The additional rate of tax on gross dividends is 42.5%.
(10) The additional rate of tax on gross dividends is 37.5%.
(11) The basic rate of tax on net dividends is 7.5%.
(12) The higher rate of tax on net dividends is 32.5%.
(13) The additional rate of tax on net dividends is 38.1%.
(14) Rates are for England, Wales and Northern Ireland. In 2017-18 a lower starting point for the Higher Rate for earned income was introduced for Scottish taxpayers. In 2018-19 the Income Tax system for Scotland further diverges from that for the rest of the UK. Two new bands called the Starter Rate and Intermediate Rate were introduced for Scottish taxpayers earned income within the Basic Rate band for the rest of the UK. See https://www.gov.uk/scottish-income-tax

23.12 Total rateable value[1] by property description[2] and country on the Central Rating List as at 31 March 2021

Coverage: England and Wales
Value (£ millions)

Property description[2]	England & Wales	England	Wales
Total	**3,744**	**3,552**	**192**
Railways	478	459	19
Light railways	17	17	0
Communications	569	548	21
National & Regional Gas Transportation	775	740	36
Local Gas Transportation	21	20	1
Gas Meters	95	90	5
Electricity Transmission	240	212	28
Electricity Distribution	593	555	38
Electricity Meters	41	38	2
Water Supply	855	815	40
Canals	0	0	0
Pipelines	60	58	2

Source: VOA administrative data as at 31 March 2021

Total rateable values are rounded to the nearest £1million with amounts smaller than £0.5million reported as negligible and denoted by '-'.

Totals may not sum due to rounding.

[1] **Rateable value** - The legal term for the notional annual rent of a rateable property assessed by the VOA. Every property has a rateable value that is based broadly on the annual rent that the property could have been let for on the open market at a particular date (this is 1 April 2015 for the 2017 lists).

[2] **Property description** - Broad category assigned to rateable properties listed on the central rating lists.

Number of rateable properties[1] and total rateable value[2] by sector type and rateable value band in England and Wales as at 31 March 2021

Coverage: England and Wales
Properties (counts), Value (£ thousands)

	England		Wales		England and Wales	
	Rateable properties[1]	Rateable value[2]	Rateable properties[1]	Rateable value[2]	Rateable properties[1]	Rateable value[2]
All properties	**2,003,100**	**63,854,102**	**125,070**	**2,433,521**	**2,128,160**	**66,287,624**
Sector:						
Retail	489,510	16,228,514	29,670	686,969	519,170	16,915,483
Office	419,830	14,866,781	19,790	265,372	439,620	15,132,153
Industry	516,870	13,770,310	33,020	595,036	549,890	14,365,347
Other	576,890	18,988,498	42,590	886,143	619,480	19,874,641

Source: VOA administrative data as at 31 March 2021

Counts are rounded to the nearest 10.

Total rateable values are rounded to the nearest £1,000 with amounts smaller than £0.5million reported as negligible and denoted by '-'.

Totals may not sum due to rounding.

[1] **Rateable property (also known as hereditament)** - A unit of property that is, or may become, liable to non-domestic rating and thus appears in a rating list.

[2] **Rateable value** - The legal term for the notional annual rent of a rateable property assessed by the VOA. Every property has a rateable value that is based broadly on the annual rent that the property could have been let for on the open market at a particular date (this is 1 April 2015 for the 2017 lists).

23.13 Revenue expenditure of local authorities

£ million - real terms [a]

	2015-16 (outturn)	2016-17 (outturn)	2017-18 (outturn)	2018-19 (outturn)	2019-20 (outturn)	2020-21 (outturn)	2021-22 (budget)
England							
Service Expenditure							
Education [b]	38,517	36,759	34,913	34,089	33,721	33,479	35,903
Highways and transport services (excl GLA)	3,439	3,103	2,952	2,781	2,849	3,569	2,860
Highways and transport services (GLA only)	1,448	1,316	1,373	1,298	1,037	4,286	3,036
Social care	25,615	25,756	26,148	26,917	27,745	29,209	29,013
of which:							
Children's Social Care	*9,368*	*9,333*	*9,559*	*9,915*	*10,260*	*10,494*	*10,384*
Adult Social Care [c]	*16,247*	*16,423*	*16,589*	*17,002*	*17,485*	*18,715*	*18,629*
Public Health [d]	3,557	3,832	3,642	3,467	3,338	3,786	3,680
Housing (excluding Housing Revenue Account)	1,815	1,661	1,662	1,769	1,836	2,060	1,865
Cultural, environmental and planning	9,815	9,299	8,974	8,920	9,057	10,113	9,312
Police	12,335	12,167	12,081	12,083	12,622	13,083	13,520
Fire & rescue	2,238	2,160	2,134	2,120	2,233	2,194	2,310
Central services	3,409	3,479	3,317	3,184	3,362	4,019	3,174
Other Services	79	61	-21	50	44	524	953
Total Service Expenditure	**102,265**	**99,591**	**97,175**	**96,679**	**97,844**	**106,322**	**105,627**
Housing Benefits [1]	21,103	20,792	20,304	17,833	15,768	15,053	15,257
Parish Precepts	409	445	486	517	554	596	587
Levies [2]	56	58	69	83	14	41	60
Trading Account Adjustments and Other adjustments [3]	-339	-332	-458	-506	-606	-556	-510
Total Net current expenditure	**112,404**	**113,089**	**111,886**	**111,370**	**110,330**	**121,450**	**121,022**
Non-Current Expenditure and External Receipts *of which:*							
Capital Expenditure charged to Revenue Account (CERA)	1,320	1,265	1,785	1,626	2,100	1,707	2,126
Capital financing and debt servicing [4]	4,463	4,193	4,261	4,688	5,173	4,953	5,067
Revenue expenditure [5] **Financed by:**	**94,533**	**93,567**	**93,104**	**94,226**	**98,178**	**109,698**	**110,288**
Total Government Grants: [6] *of which:*	57,090	53,812	50,457	48,076	48,393	51,898	59,155
Revenue Support Grant [7]	9,509	7,184	3,868	1,443	666	1,565	1,667
Police grant	7,421	7,387	7,293	7,120	7,628	7,944	8,376
Retained income from Business Rate Retention Scheme [7]	11,855	11,735	15,162	17,973	17,216	16,498	14,418
Appropriations to (-) / from (+) revenue reserves [9]	1,834	1,885	1,444	914	1,229	442	2,708
Council tax requirement [10]	24,734	26,083	27,641	29,563	31,452	33,118	34,390
Other items [11]	459	422	473	513	350	432	-383

Source: Local Authority Revenue Expenditure and Financing, Ministry of Housing, Communities and Local Government

Service Expenditure

(a) These figures are presented in real terms. ie They have been adjusted for inflation. Budget figures in 2021-22 prices.

(b) Expenditure on education services from 2014-15 is not comparable due to those schools that changed their status to become academies, which are centrally funded rather than funded via local authorities.

(c) These figures exclude transfers from the NHS (including Winter Pressures money in 2014-15 and Better Care Fund from 2015-16 onwards).

(d) The Health and Social Care Act 2012 transferred substantial duties to local authorities from 2013-14 to protect and improve the public's health, including for ages 0-5 during 2015-16.

Government Grants

1. Includes all Mandatory and Non-Mandatory Housing Benefits

2. Includes Integrated Transport Authority Levy, Waste Disposal Authority Levy, London Pensions Fund Authority Levy and Other levies

3. Includes External Trading Accounts, Internal Trading Accounts, Capital items accounted for in External Trading Accounts, Capital items accounted for in Internal Trading Accounts, Adjustments to net current expenditure and Appropriations to/from Accumulated Asbences Account

4. Includes provision for repayment of principal, leasing payments, external interest payments and HRA item 8 interest payments and receipts.

5. Whereas the returns from the majority of local authorities in 2020-21 related to budgets as initially set in the winter, some local authorities included COVID19-related grants from March 2020. When the form for this data collection launched in February 2020, there were no prescribed places for these grants. Many local authorities included them within 'grants inside Aggregate External Finance'; this table subtracts these to show an England total for Revenue Expenditure on a consistent pre-COVID-19 basis for 2020-21.

6. Includes 'Local Services Support Grant (LSSG)', 'Revenue Support Grant', 'Police Grant' and 'Specific grants inside aggregate external finance'. Figures as reported by local authorities. These may differ from allocations amounts despite data collection forms having been pre-populated with allocations data for larger grants. Budget figures are adjusted to 2021-22 prices.

7. Revenue Support Grant was lower and Retained Business Rates were higher in 2019-20 than in 2020-21 due to business rates pilots in 2019-20.

8. Education grants include Dedicated Schools grant (DSG), Pupil Premium grant and Universal Infants Free School Meals.

9. Local authorities have reported that the timing of payment of grants including notably of business rate reliefs has led to reporting higher appropriations from reserves during 2021-22.

10. Increases can be due to changes in both tax base and bills. A small number of queries challenging differences from the CTR return were unanswered at the time of publication.

11. This comprises line 980 Council tax net collection fund deficits / surpluses from the previous year, plus line 985 other items where business rates surpluses/deficits have been recorded. This reduction is driven by business rates collection fund deficits recorded in Line '985 Other Items'.

23.13 (contd.) Revenue expenditure of local authorities

£ millions

	2014/15 outturn	2015/16 outturn	2016/17 outturn	2017/18 outturn	2018/19 outturn	2019/20 outturn	2020/21 outturn	2021/22 budget
Scotland								
Education	4612	4735	4828	4839	5054	5328	5701	5630
Culture & Related Services	643	598	576	560	575	554	577	561
Social Work	3110	3178	3207	3198	3312	3458	3587	3671
Roads & Transport	420	422	399	432	384	383	463	382
Environmental Services	666	684	679	688	678	684	736	697
Planning & Development	278	243	234	213	206	191	260	233
Central Services	439	464	389	448	346	783	646	593
Non-HRA Housing	342	288	231	258	254	261	306	276
Trading Services	-5	-17	-27	-30	-35	-37	-14	-14
Total general fund net expenditure	**10504**	**10595**	**10517**	**10605**	**10774**	**11604**	**12261**	**12031**
Wales[7]								
Education (2)	2610	2576	2615	2641	2695	2813	3091	2986
Social services (3)	1673	1667	1728	1821	1921	2032	2291	2167
Council fund housing and housing benefit (4)	1151	1152	1139	1125	1081	991	970	1029
Local environmental services (5)	418	387	392	388	395	404	456	423
Roads and transport (6)	279	271	271	265	267	271	310	287
Libraries, culture, heritage, sport and recreation (7)	253	228	218	215	211	202	249	196
Planning and economic development (8)	115	83	80	77	72	80	94	87
Law and order and protective services (9)	797	754	762	789	779	806	835	958
Council tax benefit and administration (10)	36	34	32	31	36	44	51	39
Other revenue expenditure (11)	671	692	660	647	656	661	758	838
Total Unitary Authorities	**7139.9**	**7005.3**	**7064.7**	**7139.9**	**7236.0**	**7368.4**	**8118.7**	**7952.0**
Total Police	701.7	677.8	666.0	692.0	705.3	753.5	799.8	866.7
Total Fire Authorities	146.1	147.5	151.4	155.3	156.1	166.1	166.0	172.0
Total National Park Authorities	15.6	13.7	13.4	13.4	15.0	16.2	19.4	19.5
Gross revenue expenditure	**8003.3**	**7844.3**	**7895.5**	**8000.5**	**8110.8**	**8311.6**	**8654.7**	**9009.8**
less specific and special government grants (g)	1981.1	1935.1	1904.0	1930.7	1851.4	1902.5	1897.3	1,943
Net revenue expenditure	**5959.0**	**5877.7**	**5939.0**	**6019.3**	**6259.4**	**6409.2**	**6757.4**	**7067.1**
Putting to (+) /drawing from (-) reserves (h)	-72.2	-84.5	-105.1	-103.3	-147.3	-147.7	-118.0	-144.3
Council tax reduction scheme	247.3	255.7	257.7	258.0	261.7	269.9	278.2	288.6
Budget requirement (f)	**6134.1**	**6048.9**	**6091.7**	**6174.0**	**6373.8**	**6537.4**	**6917.6**	**7211.5**
Plus discretionary non-domestic rate relief	3.5	3.6	3.5	3.6	3.7	4.8	4.9	5.0
less revenue support grant	3363.5	3303.7	3261.3	3193.3	3305.0	3319.8	3481.8	3693.9
less police grant	236.2	221.9	218.0	211.2	209.0	213.9	240.6	264.8
less re-distributed non-domestic rates income	1041.0	956.0	977.0	1059.0	1050.0	1061.0	1136.0	1101.0
Council tax requirement	**1497.0**	**1570.9**	**1638.8**	**1714.0**	**1813.6**	**1947.4**	**2064.0**	**2156.7**
of which:								
Paid by council tax reduction scheme	247.3	255.7	257.7	258.0	261.7	269.9	278.2	288.6
Paid directly by council tax payers	1249.7	1315.2	1381.0	1455.9	1551.9	1677.5	1785.8	1868.1

Sources: Provisional Outturn and Budget Estimate (POBE), Scottish Government,
Revenue outturn (RO) data collection, Welsh Government (Contact email: stats.finance@gov.wales)

1. Revenue expenditure is total local authority expenditure on all services, plus debt financing, but net of any income from sales, fees, and charges and other non-grant sources. Fire and National Park levies are excluded from Unitary Authority expenditure.
2. Expenditure covers primary, secondary and special needs schools, including staff salaries, repairs and maintenance, school catering, and adult education.
3. Expenditure covers children and families services including children's homes, fostering and adoptive services. Home care and nursing homes, care for the elderly, care for people with physical, mental or learning disabilities, asylum seekers, and substance misuse.
4. Expenditure covers registered social landlords, housing advice, advances and the homeless, housing benefit payments and administration.
5. Expenditure covers cemetery, cremation and mortuary services, environmental health, street cleansing, waste collection and disposal. Includes National Park expenditure.
6. Expenditure covers construction and structural maintenance of public roads, footways, cycle paths and other public rights of way, street lighting, road safety and public transport.
7. Expenditure covers museums, galleries and arts development, theatres and public entertainment, repairs to historic buildings, sports development and facilities including leisure centres and swimming pools, tourism and promotion of open spaces.
8. Expenditure covers building and development control, community and economic development, planning policy and environmental issues.
9. Expenditure covers police and fire operational services.
10. Expenditure covers council tax benefit and council tax benefit administation (net of council tax benefit grant), and local tax collection.
11. Expenditure covers coast protection and flood defences, emergency planning, central administration and debt financing.

23.14 Financing of revenue expenditure England and Wales

England and Wales
Years ending 31 March

£ million

	2010 /11	2011 /12	2012 /13	2013 /14	2014 /15	2015 /16	2016 /17	2017 /18	2018 /19	2019 /20	2020 /21 [1]
England											
Revenue expenditure (Cash £m)	104,256	99,278	94,148	96,419	95,942	94,533	93,567	93,104	94,226	98,178	102,389
Centrally distributed income:	79,173	75,254	69,895	64,578	61,312	57,090	53,812	50,457	48,076	48,393	51898
Government grants (Cash £m) [2]	57,657	56,237	46,765	64,578	61,312	57,090	53,812	50,457	48,076	48,393	51898
Redistributed non-domestic rates	21,517	19,017	23,129	-	-	-	-	-	-	-	-
Percentage of revenue expenditure	*75.9*	*75.8*	*74.2*	*67.0*	*63.9*	*60.4*	*57.5*	*54.2*	*51.0*	*49.3*	*50.7*
Locally retained income:	26,254	26,451	26,715	34,090	35,295	36,589	37,821	42,803	47,536	48,669	49617
Retained income from Business Rate Retention Scheme (Cash £m) [3]	-	-	-	10,719	11,331	11,855	11,740	15,162	17,973	17,216	16498
Council tax (Cash £m) [4]	26,254	26,451	26,715	23,371	23,964	24,734	26,082	27,641	29,563	31,452	33118
Percentage of revenue expenditure	*25.2*	*26.6*	*28.4*	*35.4*	*36.8*	*38.7*	*40.4*	*46.0*	*50.4*	*49.6*	*48.5*
Appropriations from Reserves [5]	-1,172	-2,427	-2,461	-2,249	-665	394	1,529	-630	-1,878	766	442
Other items [6]						459	414	474	514	513	432
Percentage of revenue expenditure	*-1.1*	*-2.4*	*-2.6*	*-2.3*	*-0.7*	*0.9*	*2.1*	*-0.2*	*-1.4*	*1.3*	*0.9*
Wales											
Gross revenue expenditure [7]	7,636	7,741	7,919	8026 [12]	8,003	7,813	7,843	7950	8111	8312	9010
General government grants [8]	3,525	3,628	3,485	3751 [12]	3,600	3,526	4,456	4464	4564	4595	4859
Specific government grants [9]	2,020	2,014	2,112	2064 [12]	2,109	1,935	1,904	1931	1851	1903	1897
Share of redistributed business rates	935	787	911	1032 [12]	1,041	956	977	1059	1050	1061	1136
Council tax income [10]	1,295	1,343	1,381	1423 [12]	1,497	1,571	1,638	1714	1814	2064	2157
Other [11]	-139	-31	29	-244 [12]	-243	-175	-105	-103	-147	-142	-118

Source: Revenue Outturn returns from England local authorities 2015-16 to 2019-20,
Revenue Account (RA) budget returns 2019-20 to 2021-22,
Local Authority Revenue Budget and Capital Forecasts, Welsh Government

1. Budget estimates.
2. Includes 'Specific grants inside AEF', 'Revenue Support Grant' and 'Police Grant'. Since 13-14 the specific grants inside AEF have included 'Public Health grant', 'Local Council Tax Support grant' and the 'Central Share of non-domestic rates'.
3. The additional business reliefs introduced in 2020-21 in response to the COVID-19 pandemic and the timing of grants paid in compensation to local authorities have had a bearing on the latest figures reported here for retained income from business rates retention scheme.
4. The increase in council tax receipts reflects the combination of increases of bills and the change in tax base (i.e. the effective number of households due to pay).
5. Local authorities have reported that the timing of payment of grants including notably of business rate reliefs has led to reporting higher appropriations from reserves during 2021-22.
6. Other items include any income from inter-authority transfers and net collection fund surpluses(+)/deficits(-) from the previous year.
7. Gross revenue expenditure is total local authority expenditure on services, plus capital charges, but net of any income from sales, fees, and charges and other non-grant sources. It includes expenditure funded by specific grants. The figures have been adjusted to account for FRS17 pension costs.
8. Includes all unhypothecated grants, namely revenue support grant, police grant, council tax reduction scheme grant, transitional grant and the adjustment to reverse the transfer.
9. Comprises specific and supplementary grants,excluding police grant.
10. This includes community council precepts, and income covered by charge/council tax benefit grant, but excludes council tax reduction scheme (201
11. Includes use of reserves and discretionary non-domestic rate relief.
12. In 2013-14, the education revenue outturn data collection was changed to be comparable with the revenue budget collection. Overall education expenditure is not comparable with previous years due to the movement of all Flying Start expenditure to Social Services. Gross revenue expenditure and income for Neath Port Talbot are not consistent with previous years due to errors in reporting.

23.15: Financing of local authority capital expenditure: England: 2016-17 to 2020-21 outturn, and 2021-22 forecast

Real terms table, all monetary figures in 2020-21 prices

£ millions

Source	2016-17 Outturn (final)	2017-18 Outturn (final)	2018-19 Outturn (revised)	2019-20 Outturn (final)	2020-21 Outturn (provisional)	2021-22 Forecast (adjusted)
Total capital grants	**11,028**	**8,629**	**9,479**	**8,389**	**8,945**	**9,633**
Grants from central government departments	8,613	6,457	7,380	6,134	6,783	7,406
Grants from European structural & investment funds	14	29	70	48	46	59
Grants from private developers & leaseholders, etc.	1,204	1,266	1,303	1,203	977	1,325
Grants from non-departmental public bodies [a]	510	286	306	454	469	482
Grants from the National Lottery	64	77	48	56	50	44
Grants from Local Enterprise Partnerships [b]	622	515	373	494	620	317
Total capital receipts	**2,520**	**2,947**	**3,287**	**2,273**	**1,927**	**2,576**
Total revenue resources	**4,328**	**4,407**	**4,106**	**4,510**	**3,859**	**5,583**
Housing Revenue Account (CERA)	822	669	637	525	502	834
Major Repairs Reserve	1,778	1,733	1,780	1,836	1,544	2,069
General Fund Revenue Account (CERA)	1,727	2,005	1,689	2,149	1,813	2,681
Total prudential borrowing [c]	**7,354**	**10,706**	**10,313**	**11,688**	**9,428**	**13,068**
Loans & other financial assistance from Local Enterprise Partnerships	:	3	35	28	155	49
Other borrowing & credit arrangements not supported by central government	7,354	10,703	10,279	11,661	9,273	13,019
Total resources used to finance capital expenditure [d]	**25,230**	**26,688**	**27,185**	**26,860**	**24,159**	**30,860**

Provisional outturn 2020-21 figures were updated on 23 July 2021 (updated from version of 17 June 2021)

Sources: COR 2019-20, CPR4 2020-21 and CER 2021-22, Ministry of Housing, Communities & Local Government

(a) Non-Departmental Public Bodies, organisations that are not government departments but which have a role in the processes of national government, such as the Sport England, English Heritage and Natural England.

(b) New category introduced for 2016-17. Grants and contributions from Local Enterprise Partnerships were previously reported under the Central government grants category.

(c) The Prudential System, which came into effect on 1 April 2004, allows local authorities to raise finance for capital expenditure - without Government consent - where they can afford to service the debt without extra Government support.

(d) From 2017-18 onwards, intra-local government transfers are being netted off both expenditure and financing. However, as grants and loans made to other local authorities as part of expenditure may not equal the use of grants and loans from other authorities to finance expenditure within a financial year, financing and expenditure may not match. Over the last three years, the amount of intra local authority payments in forecast data has been notably lower in the financing table than across the expenditure data. This results in the financing total (adjusted and excluding double counting) being higher than the corresponding total in the expenditure tables. It is likely that the amount being recorded in the categories "from other local authorities" in the financing table of the forecast data is under-reported.

23.16a Capital receipts: all services: England 2018-19

Capital Outturn Return A1 (COR A1) 2018-19: Total capital expenditure & receipts by service & category for England (excluding double counting**), 2018-19

£ thousand

Service	Total Capital Receipts				
	Sale & disposal of tangible fixed assets	Sale of intangible assets	Repayments of grants loans & financial assistance	Disposal of investments (including share or loan capital)	Total capital receipts (a)
Early Years & Primary Schools	8,388	0	9	32	8,424
Secondary Schools	27,989	0	52	0	28,041
Special Schools & Alternative Provision	3,189	0	12	0	3,201
Post-16 Provision & Other Education	3,969	0	1,330	5	5,304
Total Education	43,535	0	1,403	37	44,969
Roads, Street Lighting & Road Safety	6,649	0	5	0	6,649
Parking	11,195	0	146	0	11,341
Public Transport (Bus)	500	0	1,170	0	1,670
Public Transport (Rail & Other)	150,907	0	454,100	0	605,007
Airports	1,993	0	121	0	2,114
Ports & Piers	0	0	0	0	0
Tolled Roads, Bridges, Tunnels, Ferries & Public Transport Companies	0	0	0	0	0
Total Highways & Transport	171,244	0	455,542	0	626,781
Total Social Care	42,451	0	5,596	0	48,045
Total Public Health	55	0	0	0	55
Total Housing	1,441,680	1,067	205,842	32	1,647,768
Culture & Heritage	2,341	0	991	0	3,332
Recreation & Sport	23,441	31	1,428	0	24,900
Open Spaces	5,896	10	871	0	6,777
Tourism	0	0	0	0	0
Library Services	494	0	290	0	784
Total Culture & Related Services	32,172	41	3,580	0	35,793
Cemeteries, Cremation & Mortuary	395	0	0	0	395
Coast Protection	0	0	0	0	0
Community Safety	166	0	0	0	166
Flood Defence & Land Drainage	50	0	0	0	50
Agricultural & Fisheries Services	128,618	0	0	0	128,618
Regulatory Services (Environmental Health)	393	0	723	0	1,115
Regulatory Services (Trading Standards)	0	0	0	0	0
Street Cleaning (not chargeable to highways)	301	0	94	0	395
Waste Collection	1,533	0	1,240	0	2,773
Waste Disposal	1,656	0	0	0	1,656
Trade Waste	0	0	0	0	0
Recycling	743	0	0	0	743
Waste Minimisation	613	0	0	0	613
Climate Change Costs	30	0	0	0	30
Total Environmental & Regulatory Services	134,498	0	2,057	0	136,554
Total Planning & Development Services	240,884	0	17,020	0	257,904
Total Police	86,819	78	438	1,467	84,289
Total Fire & Rescue Services	54,390	0	5,896	2,000	62,255
Total Central Services	679,896	4,316	70,722	1,260	755,716
Commercial housing	85,381	0	26,332	0	111,713
Other real estate activities	46,903	0	63	135	47,101
Finance & insurance activity	0	0	139	0	139
Energy generation & supply	0	0	0	200	200
Water supply, sewerage & remediation	0	0	0	0	0
Hospitality & catering	0	0	0	0	0
Other commercial activity	39,328	1,118	47,302	24,804	112,552
Total Industrial & Commercial Trading	171,612	1,118	73,836	25,139	271,705
Other Trading	5,773	0	847	0	6,620
Total Trading Services	177,385	1,118	74,683	25,139	278,325
All Services Total	3,105,008	6,620	842,778	29,935	3,978,453

Source: COR 2018-19, Ministry of Housing, Communities and Local Government

(a) The Total capital receipts figure for England (excluding double counting**) will not equal the sum of its part as Total receipts, of which from other local authorities have been netted off.

** This total should avoid double counting due to any flow of grants, loans or other financial assistance or receipts between local authorities

23.16b Capital expenditure: all services: England 2018-19

Capital Outturn Return A1 (COR A1) 2018-19: Total capital expenditure & receipts by service & category for England (excluding double counting**), 2018-19

£ thousand

Service	Acquisition of land & existing buildings	New construction, conversion & renovation	Vehicles	Plant, furniture & equipment	Total capital receipts (a)	Total expenditure on fixed assets	Expenditure on grants	Expenditure on grants, of which to other local authorities	Expenditure on loans & other financial assistance	Expenditure on loans & other financial assistance, of which to other local authorities	Acquisition of share or loan capital	Total financial expenditure
Early Years & Primary Schools	6,859	1,116,825	1,632	44,618	2,671	1,172,606	132,072	0	1,409	0	0	133,481
Secondary Schools	5,173	646,461	236	10,445	537	662,852	112,966	0	451	0	0	113,417
Special Schools & Alternative Provision	2,357	253,995	493	7,892	122	264,859	11,799	0	0	0	0	11,799
Post-16 Provision & Other Education	991	31,369	311	2,891	1,261	36,823	15,756	0	11,800	0	41	27,597
Total Education	15,381	2,048,650	2,672	65,847	4,590	2,137,140	272,593	0	13,660	0	41	286,294
Roads, Street Lighting & Road Safety	28,535	3,604,432	23,561	23,460	29,169	3,709,157	26,558	0	851	0	0	27,409
Parking	12,107	109,345	728	12,999	509	135,688	1,299	0	0	0	0	1,299
Public Transport (Bus)	12,040	82,650	2,854	3,789	208	101,540	12,842	0	888	0	0	13,730
Public Transport (Rail & Other)	129,289	324,830	842	37,868	4,952	497,781	408,891	0	943,619	0	1,560,000	2,912,510
Airports	0	1,515	0	0	0	1,515	0	0	300,654	0	1,217	301,871
Ports & Piers	1,072	12,259	0	5,871	190	19,392	0	0	1,000	0	0	1,000
Tolled Roads, Bridges, Tunnels, Ferries & Public Transport Companies	832	25,969	579	1,378	0	28,758	0	0	0	0	0	0
Total Highways & Transport	183,874	4,160,999	28,565	85,365	35,028	4,493,831	449,590	0	1,247,012	0	1,561,217	3,257,819
Total Social Care	16,695	172,412	6,389	41,070	21,740	258,306	77,244	0	1,090	0	0	78,334
Total Public Health	0	9,358	0	153	0	9,511	10,346	0	0	0	0	10,346
Total Housing	858,778	3,248,839	8,797	68,164	6,847	4,191,424	827,487	0	349,607	0	18,378	1,195,472
Culture & Heritage	4,746	253,512	1,887	6,402	1,045	267,592	33,462	0	21,608	0	0	55,070
Recreation & Sport	5,026	489,882	3,104	25,480	196	523,689	23,031	0	24,277	0	0	47,308
Open Spaces	2,397	105,658	11,606	9,612	310	129,583	4,207	0	0	0	0	4,207
Tourism	535	9,115	201	1,075	632	11,558	6,968	0	973	0	0	7,941
Library Services	957	48,486	263	7,328	646	57,680	544	0	0	0	0	544
Total Culture & Related Services	13,662	906,653	17,061	49,897	2,830	990,102	68,212	0	46,858	0	0	115,070
Cemeteries, Cremation & Mortuary	678	45,391	306	3,756	0	50,130	284	0	6	0	0	290
Coast Protection	0	57,089	24	78	882	58,073	100	0	4	0	0	104
Community Safety	0	10,336	2,696	9,084	265	22,381	723	0	0	0	0	723
Flood Defence & Land Drainage	1,962	77,340	333	764	3	80,402	18,690	0	0	0	0	18,690
Agricultural & Fisheries Services	2,274	10,682	0	72	280	13,308	0	0	0	0	0	0
Regulatory Services (Environmental Health)	207	16,564	2,534	4,623	411	24,340	6,243	0	0	0	0	6,243
Regulatory Services (Trading Standards)	0	388	31	50	22	491	0	0	0	0	0	0
Street Cleaning (not chargeable to highways)	0	408	11,707	1,514	32	13,661	5	0	15	0	0	20
Waste Collection	1	14,334	107,292	25,913	542	148,082	2,621	0	5,559	0	0	8,180
Waste Disposal	41,360	41,779	8,297	11,854	42	103,332	1,985	0	2	0	0	1,987
Trade Waste	0	0	1,247	323	3	1,573	0	0	0	0	0	0
Recycling	7,304	21,088	8,248	5,418	0	42,058	17	0	0	0	0	17
Waste Minimisation	0	1,950	23	385	0	2,358	0	0	0	0	0	0
Climate Change Costs	2	3,301	90	667	0	4,060	8,053	0	85	0	0	8,138
Total Environmental & Regulatory Services	53,789	300,650	142,828	64,501	2,482	564,251	38,721	0	5,671	0	0	44,392

23.16b Capital expenditure: all services: England 2018-19

*Capital Outturn Return A1 (COR A1) 2018-19: Total capital expenditure & receipts by service & category for England (excluding double counting**), 2018-19*

£ thousand

Service	Acquisition of land & existing buildings	New construction, conversion & renovation	Vehicles	Plant, furniture & equipment	Total capital receipts (a)	Total expenditure on fixed assets	Expenditure on grants	Expenditure on grants, of which to other local authorities	Expenditure on loans & other financial assistance	Expenditure on loans & other financial assistance, of which to other local authorities	Acquisition of share or loan capital	Total financial expenditure
Total Planning & Development Services	310,595	881,428	3,576	15,812	8,947	1,220,358	262,658	0	185,639	0	12,038	460,334
Total Police	49,600	223,496	97,333	245,404	63,434	679,267	1,002	0	0	0	0	1,002
Total Fire & Rescue Services	4,746	68,532	50,115	24,306	1,743	149,443	24	0	0	0	0	24
Total Central Services	423,792	654,834	62,961	209,895	145,410	1,496,893	52,177	0	125,654	0	60,677	238,508
Commercial housing	308,592	54,161	0	78	0	362,831	28,095	0	342,766	0	18,550	389,411
Other real estate activities	717,876	80,550	166	87	483	799,163	83	0	39,404	0	4,378	43,865
Finance & insurance activity	0	0	0	0	4	4	0	0	1,525	0	3,919	5,444
Energy generation & supply	0	11,572	0	1,253	23	12,848	198	0	0	0	6,500	6,698
Water supply, sewerage & remediation	0	10	35	0	0	45	1,415	0	0	0	0	1,415
Hospitality & catering	0	14,607	0	12	0	14,619	0	0	500	0	0	500
Other commercial activity	726,383	174,516	1,620	1,372	37	903,928	7,784	0	121,442	0	68,568	197,794
Total Industrial & Commercial Trading	1,752,852	335,417	1,821	2,802	547	2,093,439	37,575	0	505,637	0	101,915	645,127
Other Trading	746,538	93,364	7,476	1,055	143	848,576	129	0	408,376	0	26,978	435,483
Total Trading Services	2,499,390	428,781	9,297	3,857	690	2,942,015	37,704	0	914,013	0	128,894	1,080,611
All Services Total	4,430,302	13,104,634	429,594	874,271	293,741	19,132,541	2,097,757	0	2,889,204	0	1,781,245	6,768,206

Source: COR 2018-19, Ministry of Housing, Communities and Local Government

(a) The Total capital receipts figure for England (excluding double counting**) will not equal the sum of its part as Total receipts, of which from other local authorities have been netted off.

** This total should avoid double counting due to any flow of grants, loans or other financial assistance or receipts between local authorities

23.17 Local authority capital expenditure by service, Wales

								£ million
	1996-97	2014-15	2015-16	2016-17	2017-18	2018-19	2019-20	2019-20 over 2018-19 percentage change
Education	57.4	245.6	335.0	374.5	429.9	331.3	246.4	-26
Social services	12.4	22.9	12.6	14.7	17.0	26.3	22.0	-16
Transport	113.2	168.1	119.7	129.3	142.4	196.0	191.8	-2
Housing	271.0	260.3	316.5	330.5	318.3	336.7	382.5	14
General administration	36.0	41.9	36.3	38.0	35.8	44.4	54.6	23
Planning and development	39.3	103.3	92.7	73.1	43.8	75.6	152.3	102
Other services	145.3	125.1	1,039.4	110.4	135.4	172.4	145.1	-16
Law, order and protective services	18.6	48.0	57.3	42.7	51.6	48.1	50.8	6
Total expenditure	693.2	1,015.2	2,009.6	1,113.2	1,174.2	1,230.7	1,245.6	1
Total expenditure excluding 15-16 HRA subsidy buyout	693.2	1,015.2	1,090.6	1,113.2	1,174.2	1,230.7	1,245.6	1

Local authority capital expenditure by service

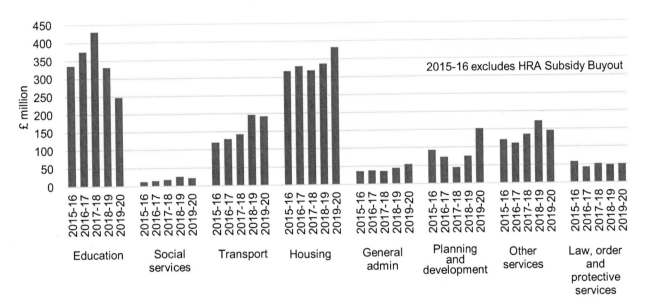

2015-16 excludes HRA Subsidy Buyout

Source: Local authority revenue and capital outturn expenditure, Welsh Government

23.18 Service Analysis of Revenue Expenditure and Income, 2019-20 Scotland

£ thousands

	Gross Service Expenditure	Gross Service Income	Net Revenue Expenditure
Education			
Pre-Primary Education	670,603	287,060	383,542
Primary Education	2,301,781	192,325	2,109,456
Secondary Education	2,269,643	182,115	2,087,529
Special Education	641,715	20,361	621,354
Community Learning	120,173	16,794	103,379
Other Non-School Funding	30,471	8,605	21,866
Total Education	**6,034,385**	**707,259**	**5,327,126**
Culture and Related Services			
Museums and Galleries	46,124	3,599	42,525
Other Cultural and Heritage	67,133	11,024	56,110
Library Service	97,567	1,928	95,639
Promotional Events	12,145	1,113	11,032
Other Tourism	14,132	3,410	10,722
Countryside Recreation and Management	24,856	3,112	21,744
Sport Facilities	185,970	37,377	148,593
Community Parks and Open Spaces	142,793	23,345	119,447
Other Recreation and Sport	57,180	9,401	47,779
Total Cultural and Related Services	**647,901**	**94,309**	**553,591**
Social Work			
Service Strategy	52,365	47,718	4,647
Children's Hearings	907	332	576
Children and Families	995,601	274,127	721,474
Adult Social Care	3,517,319	3,472,906	44,414
Criminal Justice Social Work Services	137,474	121,592	15,882
Integration Joint Boards (IJBs)	2,673,973	-	2,673,973
Total Social Work	**7,377,639**	**3,916,673**	**3,460,966**
Roads and Transport			
Roads: Construction [1]	111,999	109,146	2,853
Roads: Winter Maintenance	64,979	1,323	63,656
Roads: Other Maintenance	182,808	49,954	132,854
Roads: Lighting	62,974	5,900	57,075
Network & Traffic Management: School Crossing Patrols	12,748	15	12,733
Network & Traffic Management: Other	48,240	20,279	27,961
Parking Services	39,464	84,675	-45,211
Non-LA Public Transport: Concessionary Fares	7,541	1,163	6,378
Non-LA Public Transport: Support to Operators & Voluntary Groups	89,031	3,785	85,246
Non-LA Public Transport: Co-ordination	79,117	60,180	18,938
LA Transport Undertakings	37,606	18,759	18,847
Road Bridges	1,488	-	1,488
Total Roads and Transport	**737,995**	**355,178**	**382,817**
Environmental Services			
Cemetery, Cremation and Mortuary Services	38,554	41,299	-2,744
Coast Protection	1,433	498	935
Flood Defence and Land Drainage	9,810	401	9,409
Environmental Health	82,084	15,550	66,534
Trading Standards	36,080	3,166	32,914
Waste Management: Waste Collection	243,378	43,789	199,590
Waste Management: Waste Disposal	299,386	22,593	276,793
Waste Management: Other	105,055	4,004	101,051
Total Environmental Services	**815,781**	**131,299**	**684,481**
Planning and Development			
Planning: Building Control	36,431	41,112	-4,681
Planning: Development Control	50,048	39,851	10,197
Planning: Policy	35,966	10,188	25,778
Planning: Environmental Initiatives	23,514	12,198	11,316
Economic Development	317,382	171,778	145,604
Total Planning and Development	**463,341**	**275,127**	**188,214**

23.18 Service Analysis of Revenue Expenditure and Income, 2019-20 Scotland

£ thousands

	Gross Service Expenditure	Gross Service Income	Net Revenue Expenditure
Central Services			
Council Tax Collection	44,563	30,839	13,724
Council Tax Reduction Administration	25,502	5,556	19,946
Non-Domestic Rates Collection	8,859	2,834	6,025
Housing Benefit Administration	31,419	19,468	11,951
Registration of Births, Deaths and Marriages	12,784	8,332	4,452
Emergency Planning	3,449	227	3,222
Licensing	17,442	23,238	-5,795
Conducting Elections	11,505	8,090	3,416
Registration of Electors	10,629	1,390	9,239
Council Tax Valuation	10,935	405	10,530
Non-Domestic Lands Valuation	20,234	624	19,610
Local Land Charges	378	3	375
Non-Road Lighting	9,319	4,186	5,133
General Grants, Bequests and Donations	6,288	4,658	1,630
Corporate and Democratic Core Costs	163,567	7,267	156,299
Non-Distributed Costs	92,328	7,917	84,411
Other [2]	615,872	177,104	438,769
Total Central Services	**1,085,074**	**302,137**	**782,938**
Non-HRA Housing			
Private Sector Housing Renewal	75,442	57,890	17,552
Housing Benefits: Rent Allowances	924,181	869,539	54,642
Housing Benefits: Rent Rebate	559,107	564,756	-5,649
Homelessness	233,175	157,570	75,605
Welfare Services	12,437	1,333	11,104
Administration of Housing Advances	207	68	139
Housing Support Services (Supporting People)	80,647	18,536	62,111
Other Non-HRA housing (exc. Admin of Housing Benefits)	242,073	196,515	45,558
Total Non-HRA Housing	**2,127,269**	**1,866,207**	**261,062**
Trading Services	**65,991**	**103,020**	**-37,029**
Total General Fund (GF)	**19,355,376**	**7,751,210**	**11,604,166**
Housing Revenue Account (HRA)	**753,006**	**1,279,826**	**-526,820**
All Services (GF + HRA)	**20,108,382**	**9,031,036**	**11,077,346**

23.18 Service Analysis of Revenue Expenditure and Income, 2019-20 Scotland

£ thousands

	Gross Service Expenditure	Gross Service Income	Net Revenue Expenditure
Education			
Pre-Primary Education	670,603	287,060	383,542
Primary Education	2,301,781	192,325	2,109,456
Secondary Education	2,269,643	182,115	2,087,529
Special Education	641,715	20,361	621,354
Community Learning	120,173	16,794	103,379
Other Non-School Funding	30,471	8,605	21,866
Total Education	**6,034,385**	**707,259**	**5,327,126**
Culture and Related Services			
Museums and Galleries	46,124	3,599	42,525
Other Cultural and Heritage	67,133	11,024	56,110
Library Service	97,567	1,928	95,639
Promotional Events	12,145	1,113	11,032
Other Tourism	14,132	3,410	10,722
Countryside Recreation and Management	24,856	3,112	21,744
Sport Facilities	185,970	37,377	148,593
Community Parks and Open Spaces	142,793	23,345	119,447
Other Recreation and Sport	57,180	9,401	47,779
Total Cultural and Related Services	**647,901**	**94,309**	**553,591**
Social Work			
Service Strategy	52,365	47,718	4,647
Children's Hearings	907	332	576
Children and Families	995,601	274,127	721,474
Adult Social Care	3,517,319	3,472,906	44,414
Criminal Justice Social Work Services	137,474	121,592	15,882
Integration Joint Boards (IJBs)	2,673,973	-	2,673,973
Total Social Work	**7,377,639**	**3,916,673**	**3,460,966**
Roads and Transport			
Roads: Construction [1]	111,999	109,146	2,853
Roads: Winter Maintenance	64,979	1,323	63,656
Roads: Other Maintenance	182,808	49,954	132,854
Roads: Lighting	62,974	5,900	57,075
Network & Traffic Management: School Crossing Patrols	12,748	15	12,733
Network & Traffic Management: Other	48,240	20,279	27,961
Parking Services	39,464	84,675	-45,211
Non-LA Public Transport: Concessionary Fares	7,541	1,163	6,378
Non-LA Public Transport: Support to Operators & Voluntary Groups	89,031	3,785	85,246
Non-LA Public Transport: Co-ordination	79,117	60,180	18,938
LA Transport Undertakings	37,606	18,759	18,847
Road Bridges	1,488	-	1,488
Total Roads and Transport	**737,995**	**355,178**	**382,817**
Environmental Services			
Cemetery, Cremation and Mortuary Services	38,554	41,299	-2,744
Coast Protection	1,433	498	935
Flood Defence and Land Drainage	9,810	401	9,409
Environmental Health	82,084	15,550	66,534
Trading Standards	36,080	3,166	32,914
Waste Management: Waste Collection	243,378	43,789	199,590
Waste Management: Waste Disposal	299,386	22,593	276,793
Waste Management: Other	105,055	4,004	101,051
Total Environmental Services	**815,781**	**131,299**	**684,481**
Planning and Development			
Planning: Building Control	36,431	41,112	-4,681
Planning: Development Control	50,048	39,851	10,197
Planning: Policy	35,966	10,188	25,778
Planning: Environmental Initiatives	23,514	12,198	11,316
Economic Development	317,382	171,778	145,604
Total Planning and Development	**463,341**	**275,127**	**188,214**
Central Services			
Council Tax Collection	44,563	30,839	13,724
Council Tax Reduction Administration	25,502	5,556	19,946
Non-Domestic Rates Collection	8,859	2,834	6,025

23.18 Service Analysis of Revenue Expenditure and Income, Scotland, 2019-20

£ thousands

	Gross Service Expenditure	Gross Service Income	Net Revenue Expenditure
Housing Benefit Administration	31,419	19,468	11,951
Registration of Births, Deaths and Marriages	12,784	8,332	4,452
Emergency Planning	3,449	227	3,222
Licensing	17,442	23,238	-5,795
Conducting Elections	11,505	8,090	3,416
Registration of Electors	10,629	1,390	9,239
Council Tax Valuation	10,935	405	10,530
Non-Domestic Lands Valuation	20,234	624	19,610
Local Land Charges	378	3	375
Non-Road Lighting	9,319	4,186	5,133
General Grants, Bequests and Donations	6,288	4,658	1,630
Corporate and Democratic Core Costs	163,567	7,267	156,299
Non-Distributed Costs	92,328	7,917	84,411
Other [2]	615,872	177,104	438,769
Total Central Services	**1,085,074**	**302,137**	**782,938**
Non-HRA Housing			
Private Sector Housing Renewal	75,442	57,890	17,552
Housing Benefits: Rent Allowances	924,181	869,539	54,642
Housing Benefits: Rent Rebate	559,107	564,756	-5,649
Homelessness	233,175	157,570	75,605
Welfare Services	12,437	1,333	11,104
Administration of Housing Advances	207	68	139
Housing Support Services (Supporting People)	80,647	18,536	62,111
Other Non-HRA housing (exc. Admin of Housing Benefits)	242,073	196,515	45,558
Total Non-HRA Housing	**2,127,269**	**1,866,207**	**261,062**
Trading Services	**65,991**	**103,020**	**-37,029**
Total General Fund (GF)	**19,355,376**	**7,751,210**	**11,604,166**
Housing Revenue Account (HRA)	**753,006**	**1,279,826**	**-526,820**
All Services (GF + HRA)	**20,108,382**	**9,031,036**	**11,077,346**

Source: Scottish Government Local Financial Returns (LFR)

Notes:

[1] The significant increase between 2018-19 and 2019-20 relates to final payments made by Aberdeen City Council for the completion of the Aberdeen Western Peripheral Route.

[2] The significant increase between 2018-19 and 2019-20 relates to an equal pay settlement made by Glasgow City Council in 2019-20.

23.19a Revenue Income by Source, Scotland, 2015-16 to 2018-19

£ millions

	2015-16	2016-17	2017-18	2018-19
General Funding:	**12,003**	**11,708**	**11,753**	**11,910**
General Revenue Funding	7,147	6,839	6,799	6,885
Non-Domestic Rates Distributable Amount	2,789	2,769	2,666	2,636
Council Tax	2,055	2,091	2,278	2,376
Other Funding[1]	13	9	10	13
Service Income:	**5,226**	**5,577**	**5,780**	**6,070**
Government Grants (excl GRG)	2,036	2,138	2,206	2,380
Other Grants, Reimbursements and Contributions	768	902	1,040	1,092
Customer and Client Receipts[2]	2,423	2,537	2,537	2,597
Total Revenue Income	**17,229**	**17,285**	**17,533**	**17,980**

Source: Scottish Government - Local Financial Returns (LFR 00)

1. This includes government grants paid to joint boards and income received through NDR TIF and BRIS schemes.
2. This includes credits resulting from soft loans.

23.19b Total Capital Expenditure and Financing, Scotland, 2015-16 to 2018-19

£ thousands

	2015-16	2016-17	2017-18	2018-19
Acquisition of land, leases, existing buildings or works	58,200	233,340	362,620	168,643
New construction, conversions & enhancement to existing buildings	2,096,542	2,357,953	2,253,850	2,316,607
Vehicles, machinery & equipment	182,501	193,195	184,663	225,004
Intangible assets	6,155	9,798	4,674	4,880
Total Gross Capital Expenditure	**2,343,398**	**2,794,286**	**2,805,807**	**2,715,134**
Revenue Expenditure funded from Capital Resources	191,818	167,605	176,862	261,711
Total Expenditure to be met from Capital Resources	**2,535,216**	**2,961,891**	**2,982,669**	**2,976,845**
Scottish Government General Capital Grant	694,346	504,464	651,836	588,878
Scottish Government Specific Capital Grants	201,914	224,925	228,483	327,366
Grants from Scottish Government Agencies and NDPBs	112,017	117,836	86,305	121,384
Other Grants and Contributions	143,418	184,761	186,559	191,370
Borrowing from Loans fund (b)	831,327	1,178,810	994,376	1,127,800
Capital receipts used from asset sales/disposals	173,392	187,159	121,967	81,879
Capital Fund applied	60,374	65,282	31,342	32,800
Capital funded from current revenue	296,702	291,636	285,585	301,397
Assets acquired under credit arrangements (e.g. finance leases, PPP/PFI)	21,726	207,018	396,216	203,971
Total Financing	**2,535,216**	**2,961,891**	**2,982,669**	**2,976,845**

Source: Scottish Government - Capital Returns (CRFinal)

a. Following the Police and Fire Reform (Scotland) Act 2012 figures from 2013-14 onwards may not be comparable with previous years.

b. This includes borrowing from the loans fund used to fund grants to third party capital projects. Local authorities may have also included this within their revenue figures.

23.20 Subjective Analysis of General Fund Revenue Expenditure and Income, Scotland, 2019-20

Revenue Expenditure and Income 2019-20 by Service and Type, £ thousands - Scotland

£'000

	Education Services	Culture and Related Services	Social Work Services	Roads and Transport	Environ- mental Services	Planning and Economic Development	Central Services	Non-HRA Housing Services	Trading Services	Total General Fund	Housing Revenue Account	Total General Fund + HRA
Expenditure												
Teachers	2,704,958									2,704,958		2,704,958
Teacher pension costs	291,665									291,665		291,665
Non-Teachers	1,176,844	195,164	1,409,479	215,635	312,194	152,446	971,332	123,256	41,068	4,597,417	154,884	4,752,301
Non-Teacher pension costs	152,394	20,232	160,492	18,634	28,882	16,737	87,945	10,749	1,358	497,424	13,127	510,551
Total Employee Costs	4,325,860	215,396	1,569,971	234,269	341,076	169,183	1,059,277	134,005	42,426	8,091,464	168,011	8,259,475
Premises related costs	531,671	68,856	57,873	69,284	43,478	25,916	109,985	72,207	9,161	988,432	419,775	1,408,207
Transport related expenditure	183,156	23,196	55,827	61,596	91,400	2,800	39,105	4,681	19,757	481,517	4,035	485,552
Supplies and Services	456,647	102,176	206,700	269,957	241,274	68,614	280,103	74,272	34,578	1,734,320	85,809	1,820,129
Third Party Payments	368,313	224,301	2,477,965	233,403	160,362	88,370	73,439	184,891	3,138	3,814,181	23,738	3,837,919
Total Operating Costs	1,539,788	418,528	2,798,364	634,239	536,514	185,700	502,632	336,051	66,634	7,018,450	533,357	7,551,807
School children and students	38,676									38,676		38,676
Social Work clients			89,124							89,124		89,124
Housing Benefits								1,483,288		1,483,288		1,483,288
Transfer Payment to IJB			2,673,973							2,673,973		2,673,973
Third party capital projects funded from capital grant	564	2,238	4,061	15,144	62	51,243	1,167	182,175	0	256,654	742	257,396
Third party capital projects funded from revenue	0	0	0	18	1	222	0	688	0	929	0	929
Other transfer payments	6,344	17,762	135,035	264	2,093	33,901	9,326	30,909	0	235,633	6,711	242,344
Total Transfer Payments	45,583	20,000	2,902,193	15,426	2,156	85,366	10,493	1,697,060	0	4,778,277	7,453	4,785,730
Support Services	212,225	33,542	149,735	32,176	45,524	37,102	135,669	23,120	5,387	674,481	64,005	738,486
Recharge income from other services	78,106	39,171	27,337	131,433	77,589	12,963	585,339	62,645	48,456	1,063,038	19,630	1,082,668
Contributions from other local authorities	10,966	394	15,287	18,343	31,901	1,047	6,550	322	0	84,810	190	85,000
Requisitions from constituent councils – VJBs and RTPs only				28,339			31,108			59,447		59,447
Total Adjustments for for Intra / Inter Authority Transfers	89,072	39,565	42,624	178,115	109,490	14,010	622,997	62,967	48,456	1,207,295	19,820	1,227,115
Gross Service Expenditure	6,034,385	647,901	7,377,639	737,995	815,781	463,341	1,085,074	2,127,269	65,991	19,355,376	753,006	20,108,382

23.20 Subjective Analysis of General Fund Revenue Expenditure and Income, Scotland, 2019-20

Revenue Expenditure and Income 2019-20 by Service and Type, £ thousands - Scotland

£'000

	Education Services	Culture and Related Services	Social Work Services	Roads and Transport	Environmental Services	Planning and Economic Development	Central Services	Non-HRA Housing Services	Trading Services	Total General Fund	Housing Revenue Account	Total General Fund + HRA
Income												
Ring-Fenced Revenue Grants	406,201		100,853	10,500						517,554		517,554
General Capital Grant used to fund third party capital projects	226	2,135	800	2,226	62	9,726	1,167	25,420	0	41,762	0	41,762
Other central government capital grants used to fund third party capital	338	103	3,261	12,918	0	41,517	0	156,755	0	214,892	742	215,634
Other central government grants (excl GRG)	102,849	5,757	33,024	117,934	4,431	35,837	32,238	1,445,397	6	1,777,474	6,273	1,783,747
Total Government Grants	**509,614**	**7,995**	**137,938**	**143,578**	**4,493**	**87,080**	**33,405**	**1,627,572**	**6**	**2,551,682**	**7,015**	**2,558,697**
Contributions from NHS Boards (excluding amounts received via IJBs)			670,359							670,359		670,359
Income from IJB to commission services	2,670	224	2,634,437	0	213	419	1,347	50,393	0	2,689,703	2,096	2,691,799
All other grants, reimbursements and contributions	66,407	11,277	199,802	26,005	5,752	43,362	38,726	31,916	1,132	424,379	3,250	427,629
Total Grants, Reimbursements and Contributions	**69,077**	**11,501**	**3,504,598**	**26,005**	**5,965**	**43,781**	**40,073**	**82,309**	**1,132**	**3,784,441**	**5,346**	**3,789,787**
Income from charges to service users	68,822	51,383	236,961	115,571	60,699	51,465	92,950	55,152	46,168	779,171	15,378	794,549
Rent income	1,115	3,836	2,052	4,833	749	27,581	15,716	69,146	7,604	132,632	1,227,373	1,360,005
Other sales, fees and charges	58,630	19,594	35,124	65,191	59,394	65,219	119,992	32,028	48,110	503,283	24,714	527,997
Total Customer and Client Receipts	**128,568**	**74,813**	**274,137**	**185,596**	**120,842**	**144,265**	**228,659**	**156,326**	**101,882**	**1,415,087**	**1,267,465**	**2,682,552**
Gross Service Income	**707,259**	**94,309**	**3,916,673**	**355,178**	**131,299**	**275,127**	**302,137**	**1,866,207**	**103,020**	**7,751,210**	**1,279,826**	**9,031,036**
Net Revenue Expenditure	**5,327,126**	**553,591**	**3,460,966**	**382,817**	**684,481**	**188,214**	**782,938**	**261,062**	**-37,029**	**11,604,166**	**-526,820**	**11,077,346**

Source: Local Financial Returns (LFR00), Scottish Local Government Finance Statistics (SLGFS) 2019-20, Scottish Government

Please note the following information when using data provided in this file:

1. Figures are presented on a funding basis and so have been adjusted to remove certain accounting transactions that have been charged to services, such as depreciation and pension costs.

2. All years refer to the relevant financial year, for example 2019-20 refers to activity from 1 April 2019 to 31 March 2020.

3. Figures within tables / charts may not sum to the total exactly due to rounding.

4. Absolute zeroes are presented as a ':'; figures which round to zero are presented as '0'.

5. All figures are presented in cash terms, this means they have **not** been adjusted for inflation.

6. Expenditure and income figures are presented as positive figures, however net expenditure figures may be presented as negative where gross income has exceeded gross expenditure.

7. Roads & Transport includes figures for Road Bridges.

Local authorities are asked to complete the LFRs in line with the guidance provided to ensure returns are completed on a consistent basis to allow for a reasonable degree of comparability. However, there is the potential for inconsistent reporting between local authorities for lower level figures where local accounting practices may vary.

Net revenue expenditure can be affected by demand for services and the resources available to deliver those services, which will vary between local authorities. It can also be affected by large one-off payments in any year, for example Equal Pay back-pay settlement expenditure. It is therefore important to consider these factors when making comparisons between local authorities.

The 2019-20 SLGFS publication is available at: www.gov.scot/collections/local-government-finance-statistics/#scottishlocalgovernmentfinancialstatistics

**23.21 Local government current expenditure on services in Northern Ireland
2016-17 to 2020-21**

	National Statistics				£ million
	2016-17 outturn	2017-18 outturn	2018-19 outturn	2019-20 outturn	2020-21 plans
Northern Ireland					
4. Economic affairs	29	23	26	31	32
of which: enterprise and economic development	*29*	*23*	*26*	*31*	*32*
5. Environment protection	203	203	194	220	196
6. Housing and community amenities	124	153	180	201	252
7. Health	54	49	49	53	38
8. Recreation, culture and religion	252	208	213	212	172
Total Northern Ireland	**662**	**636**	**661**	**718**	**690**
Debt interest (1)	844	831	849	651	794
Total local government current expenditure on services	**132,399**	**130,880**	**131,511**	**133,456**	**137,124**
Accounting adjustments	23,831	24,860	27,252	28,046	56,236
Total local government current expenditure	**156,230**	**155,740**	**158,763**	**161,502**	**193,360**

Source: HM Treasury Public Expenditure Statistical Analyses (PESA)

(1) Debt interest is not allocated to individual countries, so is only included in the total UK figures. It excludes all intra-public sector debt interest payments.

this page is intentionally blank

Agriculture

Chapter 24

Agriculture

Aggregate agricultural accounts - Total income from farming (Table 24.1)

Aggregate agricultural accounts are a tool for analysing the economic situation of agriculture and are used to support policy making in the UK and EU. They include the aggregate income of the agriculture sector, known as Total Income from Farming (TIFF). This is income generated by production within the agriculture industry including direct payments and represents business profits and remuneration for work done by owners and other unpaid workers. It is the preferred measure of aggregate income for the agricultural industry in the UK and is designed to show the performance of the whole of the agricultural industry.

Total factor productivity (Table 24.2)

Total factor productivity (TFP) is a key measure of the economic performance of agriculture and an important driver of farm incomes. It represents how efficiently the agricultural industry uses the resources that are available to turn inputs into outputs. Outputs and inputs are adjusted for quality by weighting the volumes by price.

Although external factors such as weather conditions or disease outbreaks may have a short-term impact on productivity, it is developments that improve productivity over a longer period that constitute one of the main drivers of agricultural income.

TFP estimates are derived from the aggregate farm accounts data used to calculate UK Total Income from Farming (TIFF).

Agricultural censuses and surveys (Tables 24.3 and 24.5 and 24.12)

Data in these tables are sourced primarily from the June Survey of Agriculture and Horticultural activity which has a long standing tradition in England. It was first run in 1866 and since then was carried out as a full Census every year until 1995, when it decreased to a sample survey (although still surveyed around 80% of the farming population). These days, the survey samples between 30,000 and 70,000 holdings each year. A full Census is now only carried out once every ten years, 2000 and 2010 being the most recent. The survey is run by Defra to collect detailed information on arable and horticultural cropping activities, land usage, livestock populations and agricultural labour force figures. It is run on 1 June each year across England. In a full census survey year all active commercial farms in England are asked to complete the survey. The collection of the information is important and is mandatory under the Agricultural Statistics Act 1979.

The information is collected in such a way as to make is comparable with information collected by Scotland, Wales and Northern Ireland and also by other EU member states. This helps show how UK agriculture contributes to the wider EU and international markets.

For more details on the June survey see: https://www.gov.uk/guidance/structure-of-the-agricultural-industry-survey-notes-and-guidance#june-survey-of-agriculture-and-horticulture-in-england

Estimated quantity of crops and grass harvested (Table 24.4a-c)

In table 24.4a the estimated yield of sugar beet is obtained from production figures supplied by British Sugar plc in England and Wales. The data in table 24.4a is sourced from Agriculture in the United Kingdom (AUK) is an annual publication that collates statistics from a wide variety of sources to give a comprehensive overview of the UK's agriculture. In Great Britain, potato yields are estimated in consultation with the Potato Council Limited.

Tables 24.4b and c provide figures for key fruit and field vegetable production (excluding potatoes) in the UK and are sourced from the annual publication, Horticulture Statistics' published by Defra.

Marketable Production (tonnes) - the total figure for the harvested crop is derived from the planted area multiplied by harvested yield taking into account wastage figures (post harvest).

Forestry (Table 24.6)

Woodland is defined in UK forestry statistics as land under stands of trees with a canopy cover of at least 20% (25% in Northern Ireland), or having the potential to achieve this. The definition relates to land use, rather than land cover, so integral open space and felled areas that are awaiting restocking are included as woodland.

Statistics for state forestry are from Forestry Commission and Forest Service management information systems.

Certified woodland area in the UK

Certified woodland in the UK has been independently audited against the UK Woodland Assurance Standard. Forestry certification schemes are owned by international non-governmental organisations and exist to promote good forest practice. They offer product labels to demonstrate that wood or wood products come from well-managed forests. Figures for certified woodland areas are often used as an indicator of sustainable forest management. However, it should be noted that woodland that is not certified may also be managed sustainably.

Most changes to the certified woodland area figures over time are a result of new areas being certified or certificates not being renewed upon expiry. Temporary changes can also occur if there is a time lag between expiry and renewal.

Most public sector woodland is owned and managed by the Forestry Commission (FC) in England and Scotland, Natural Resources Wales (NRW) in Wales and the Forest Service (FS) in Northern Ireland. Other public sector woodland (e.g. owned by local authorities) is included with privately owned woodland as "private sector" in this release.

New planting / restocking

For private forestry in Great Britain, statistics on new planting and restocking are based on records of grant aid and estimates of planting undertaken without grant aid, and softwood production is estimated from a survey of the largest timber harvesting companies. Hardwood production is estimated from deliveries of roundwood to primary wood processors and others, based on surveys of the UK timber industry, data provided by trade associations and estimates provided by the Expert Group on Timber and Trade Statistics.

New planting is the creation of new areas of woodland by planting trees on land that was not previously woodland. The statistics presented here also include new woodland that is created by natural colonisation of trees on land near existing woodland.

Restocking is the replacement of trees on areas of woodland that have been felled; this can be done either through replanting or natural regeneration. The statistics presented here include felled areas that have been restocked by both natural regeneration and replanting. As restocking takes place on woodland that has been previously harvested and it is a condition of most felling licences that the area is restocked, restocking rates are mainly driven by harvesting levels (with a time lag, usually of around 2 years, between harvesting and restocking). Grant support in England is now provided by the Countryside Stewardship scheme, which opened for applications in early 2016.

Fishing industry (Table 24.13 -24.14)

Table 24.13 provides an overview of the UK fishing industry including fleet size / employment, landings, import/ export, household consumption, inflation and GDP for fishing. These figures are sourced from the UK Sea Fisheries Statistics published by the Marine Management Organisation.

Fishermen have a legal obligation to declare their catches. Despite this, a proportion of fishing activity remains unreported. This chiefly affects landings data and the effects on statistics on fishing effort are considered to be small. It should be noted that landings do not typically equate to total catches, as fish may be returned to the sea through a practice known as discarding. The degree of discarding varies by stock, and by the sector of the fleet involved.

The figures presented should not be interpreted as total removals from the sea. However, with the implementation of the Landing Obligation whereby discarding of fish is prohibited, the amount of discards will clearly fall. The obligation began in 2015 for pelagic species and is currently being phased in for other species in anticipation of a full discard ban in 2019 (Commission Delegated Regulations (EU) 2018/45, 2018/46, 2018/189 and 2018/190).

Imports and exports - HM Revenue & Customs (HMRC) is responsible for collecting the UK's international trade in goods data. The data are compiled from trade declarations made using commodity codes from the UN Tariff (HS Nomenclature) and its EU derivative the Intrastat Classification Nomenclature (ICN).

Household consumption and expenditure - Data on household purchases are sourced from the Living Costs and Food Survey run by the ONS. The Family Food module of the survey collects detailed quantity and expenditure information on household and eating out purchases of food and drink for use by Defra.

Inflation - The Retail Price Index (RPI) and Consumer Price Index (CPI) measures of inflation are produced by the ONS. The Landed Price Index (LPI) is produced by the MMO.

GDP for fishing - The Office for National Statistics produces data on gross value added (GVA), gross domestic product (GDP) and output indices. GVA measures the contribution to the economy of each individual producer, industry or sector in the United Kingdom. It is used in the estimation of GDP, a key indicator of the state of the whole economy.

Table 24.14 shows the number of registered and licensed fishing vessels based on information provided by the Maritime and Coastguard Agency. The number of UK fishing vessels has reduced by almost 50 per cent over the past three decades, from over 11 thousand vessels to approximately 6 thousand.

As well as the total number of vessels, the fleet can also be assessed in terms of their capacity and power. Capacity is usually measured in gross tonnage (GT) which is a volumetric measure of a vessel capacity. The power (kW) of a vessel refers to the vessel's engine power. The power (kW) of the UK fleet has also decreased by 38 per cent over the past three decades.

For more information on the UK fishing industry statistics see: https://www.gov.uk/government/collections/uk-sea-fisheries-annual-statistics

Quantity of food and drink purchased for UK households (Table 24.15)

This table provides statistics on food purchases by type of food for UK households. The data is sourced from the Family Food Module of the Living Costs and Food Survey (LCFS) run by the ONS. This module collects detailed quantity and expenditure information on food and drinks household purchases and itemised lists of food and drink eating out purchases for use by Defra.

The survey covers about 5,000 households across the United Kingdom each year. It is a voluntary sample survey of private households. The basic unit is the household. The survey is continuous, interviews being spread evenly over the year to ensure that seasonal effects are covered. Each individual aged 16 and over in the household is asked to keep diary records of daily expenditure for two weeks. Simplified diaries are kept by children aged between 7 and 15.

The 'household' category covers all food that is brought into the household. Diary entries relating to food and drink are coded into roughly 250 different categories of food and drink covering household purchases. The data collected in the survey covers food purchases not food consumption. The amount of purchases can vary substantially depending on the amount of shopping taking place in the surveyed period. It is assumed that by averaging over a large number of households the amount of food purchased in the surveyed period is a good approximation to the amount of food consumed. For more information on family food statistics see: https://www.gov.uk/government/collections/family-food-statistics

24.1 Aggregate Agricultural Accounts : Production and income accounts (at real term prices) (a)(b)

United Kingdom

£ million

											Calendar years	
	2008	2009	2010	2011	2012	2013	2014	2015	2016	2017	2018	2019
1 Output of cereals	**4,084**	**2,921**	**2,821**	**3,937**	**3,837**	**3,963**	**3,980**	**3,281**	**2,807**	**3,412**	**3,519**	**3,839**
of which: wheat	2,916	1,974	2,090	2,830	2,591	2,444	2,815	2,262	1,878	2,283	2,280	2,575
barley	1,049	852	648	986	1,103	1,328	1,043	915	823	1,004	1,096	1,134
oats	116	91	78	115	137	185	116	98	102	120	137	124
2 Output of industrial crops	**1,297**	**1,154**	**1,307**	**1,857**	**1,626**	**1,394**	**1,343**	**1,211**	**960**	**1,316**	**1,111**	**1,040**
of which: oilseed rape	810	613	839	1,353	1,182	876	792	818	609	841	706	620
protein crops	168	172	158	126	117	145	143	157	148	169	122	154
sugar beet	267	311	245	306	272	318	365	199	169	253	231	223
3 Output of forage plants	183	240	235	227	175	242	252	248	227	226	252	245
4 Output of vegetables and horticultural products	**2,451**	**2,484**	**2,815**	**2,849**	**2,874**	**2,980**	**2,740**	**2,844**	**2,998**	**3,065**	**2,986**	**3,020**
of which: fresh vegetables	1,400	1,374	1,575	1,491	1,505	1,578	1,391	1,523	1,546	1,560	1,540	1,567
plants and flowers	1,052	1,110	1,241	1,358	1,369	1,402	1,350	1,321	1,452	1,505	1,446	1,453
5 Output of potatoes (including seeds)	1,018	861	744	861	793	1,117	789	721	887	953	726	808
6 Output of fruit	687	720	728	737	687	709	720	793	788	829	851	970
7 Output of other crop products incl. seeds	430	483	546	578	771	685	750	607	563	441	791	674
Total crop output (sum 1-7)	**10,150**	**8,862**	**9,197**	**11,047**	**10,762**	**11,089**	**10,574**	**9,705**	**9,231**	**10,243**	**10,235**	**10,596**
8 Output of livestock	8,183	8,876	8,899	9,748	10,132	10,541	10,203	9,807	9,660	10,117	10,040	9,879
primarily for meat	**7,065**	**7,381**	**7,396**	**8,206**	**8,473**	**8,903**	**8,434**	**8,343**	**8,275**	**8,806**	**8,785**	**8,498**
of which: cattle	2,660	2,692	2,680	3,137	3,349	3,398	3,023	3,171	3,125	3,300	3,189	2,886
pigs	1,112	1,223	1,217	1,305	1,357	1,501	1,463	1,242	1,237	1,464	1,353	1,419
sheep	1,025	1,221	1,218	1,400	1,231	1,222	1,299	1,286	1,298	1,327	1,362	1,322
poultry	2,027	2,009	2,238	2,320	2,491	2,737	2,605	2,599	2,570	2,671	2,836	2,825
gross fixed capital formation	**1,117**	**1,495**	**1,503**	**1,542**	**1,659**	**1,638**	**1,769**	**1,464**	**1,385**	**1,311**	**1,256**	**1,381**
of which: cattle	740	947	888	769	1,026	1,080	1,110	808	754	745	731	801
pigs	8	10	10	10	10	7	6	4	6	6	5	6
sheep	160	301	368	504	380	320	382	332	328	277	209	288
poultry	208	237	237	259	243	230	271	320	298	284	311	285
9 Output of livestock products	**5,161**	**4,688**	**4,944**	**5,348**	**5,377**	**5,974**	**6,214**	**5,168**	**4,492**	**5,603**	**5,672**	**5,545**
of which: milk	4,426	3,945	4,142	4,556	4,515	5,030	5,318	4,295	3,717	4,805	4,846	4,720
eggs	668	671	698	682	794	846	786	783	679	689	693	698
Total livestock output (8+9)	**13,343**	**13,564**	**13,842**	**15,096**	**15,509**	**16,515**	**16,417**	**14,976**	**14,152**	**15,720**	**15,712**	**15,424**
10 Other agricultural activities	1,014	1,097	1,142	1,250	1,217	1,239	1,298	1,262	1,228	1,259	1,344	1,361
11 Inseparable non-agricultural activities	1,044	1,133	1,165	1,223	1,248	1,385	1,355	1,364	1,353	1,481	1,552	1,638
12 Output (at market prices) (sum 1 to 11)	25,552	24,656	25,346	28,616	28,736	30,228	29,645	27,307	25,964	28,704	28,843	29,019
13 Total subsidies (less taxes) on product	74	47	36	33	24	24	24	42	50	51	50	50
14 Gross output at basic prices (12+13)	**25,625**	**24,704**	**25,382**	**28,649**	**28,760**	**30,253**	**29,669**	**27,349**	**26,013**	**28,755**	**28,893**	**29,069**
Intermediate consumption												
15 Seeds	1,014	984	917	927	889	1,021	887	819	826	812	828	885
16 Energy	**1,497**	**1,391**	**1,513**	**1,683**	**1,713**	**1,708**	**1,595**	**1,368**	**1,275**	**1,356**	**1,474**	**1,472**
of which: electricity and fuels for heating	437	434	444	449	463	454	432	435	406	445	474	487
motor and machinery fuels	1,060	957	1,069	1,233	1,251	1,254	1,163	933	869	911	1,000	985
17 Fertilisers	1,869	1,486	1,667	1,937	1,825	1,779	1,692	1,600	1,428	1,358	1,355	1,469

24.1 Aggregate Agricultural Accounts : Production and income accounts (at real term prices) (a)(b)

United Kingdom

£ million

Calendar years

	2008	2009	2010	2011	2012	2013	2014	2015	2016	2017	2018	2019
18 Plant protection products	842	851	885	941	1,006	1,008	1,089	1,107	1,073	1,078	1,048	1,059
19 Veterinary expenses	434	460	504	489	504	527	529	532	511	513	508	486
20 Animal feed	**4,961**	**4,666**	**5,085**	**5,496**	**5,868**	**6,533**	**5,795**	**5,274**	**4,964**	**5,534**	**6,031**	**5,849**
of which: compounds	2,807	2,637	2,806	3,197	3,448	3,874	3,471	3,180	3,033	3,423	3,707	3,548
straights	1,538	1,460	1,726	1,675	1,742	1,848	1,635	1,485	1,375	1,431	1,529	1,525
feed produced & used on farm or purchased from other farms	617	569	553	625	678	811	689	608	556	680	796	776
21 Total maintenance	**1,546**	**1,617**	**1,697**	**1,760**	**1,729**	**1,768**	**1,859**	**1,840**	**1,827**	**1,831**	**1,918**	**1,893**
of which: materials	943	997	1,053	1,097	1,082	1,104	1,112	1,091	1,076	1,105	1,148	1,117
buildings	603	620	644	663	647	664	747	749	752	726	770	776
22 Agricultural services	1,014	1,097	1,142	1,250	1,217	1,239	1,298	1,262	1,228	1,259	1,344	1,361
23 FISIM	147	90	107	124	115	122	111	110	120	122	135	159
24 Other goods and services	3,364	3,432	3,492	3,673	3,738	3,698	3,664	3,634	3,520	3,589	3,706	3,741
25 Total intermediate consumption (sum 15 to 24)	**16,689**	**16,073**	**17,008**	**18,281**	**18,603**	**19,404**	**18,520**	**17,547**	**16,771**	**17,452**	**18,349**	**18,374**
26 Gross value added at market prices (12-25)	**8,863**	**8,583**	**8,338**	**10,335**	**10,132**	**10,825**	**11,125**	**9,760**	**9,192**	**11,252**	**10,494**	**10,646**
27 Gross value added at basic prices (14-25)	**8,937**	**8,630**	**8,373**	**10,368**	**10,157**	**10,849**	**11,149**	**9,802**	**9,242**	**11,303**	**10,544**	**10,696**
28 Total consumption of Fixed Capital	**4,401**	**4,448**	**4,397**	**4,726**	**4,805**	**4,694**	**4,733**	**4,562**	**4,564**	**4,555**	**4,701**	**4,819**
of which: equipment	1,644	1,722	1,791	1,871	1,930	1,971	1,989	2,021	2,040	2,092	2,183	2,207
buildings	1,355	1,240	1,170	1,195	1,203	1,153	1,120	1,115	1,112	1,119	1,128	1,131
livestock	1,402	1,486	1,436	1,660	1,672	1,570	1,624	1,426	1,413	1,344	1,390	1,481
cattle	955	924	845	964	1,043	1,010	1,054	844	781	766	812	872
pigs	9	10	9	10	9	8	6	4	5	6	5	6
sheep	241	340	362	437	360	315	336	330	313	283	286	294
poultry	197	211	219	250	259	237	228	249	314	289	287	309
29 Net value added at market prices (26-28)	**4,462**	**4,135**	**3,941**	**5,610**	**5,328**	**6,131**	**6,392**	**5,198**	**4,628**	**6,698**	**5,793**	**5,826**
30 Net value added at basic prices (27-28)	**4,536**	**4,182**	**3,977**	**5,643**	**5,352**	**6,155**	**6,416**	**5,240**	**4,678**	**6,749**	**5,843**	**5,876**
31 Other taxes on production	-132	-133	-139	-148	-145	-139	-115	-109	-105	-106	-106	-106
32 Other subsidies on production	4,157	4,567	4,381	4,271	3,945	3,933	3,409	3,151	3,629	3,586	3,403	3,339
33 Net value added at factor cost (30+31+32)	**8,561**	**8,616**	**8,219**	**9,766**	**9,152**	**9,950**	**9,709**	**8,282**	**8,202**	**10,229**	**9,139**	**9,110**
34 Compensation of employees	2,652	2,734	2,769	2,854	2,821	2,839	2,782	2,874	2,849	2,899	2,915	2,855
35 Rent	524	531	547	584	592	613	642	646	647	631	607	590
36 Interest	448	278	286	350	367	383	456	484	488	483	503	495
37 Total Income from Farming (33-34-35-36)	**4,937**	**5,073**	**4,617**	**5,978**	**5,372**	**6,115**	**5,829**	**4,278**	**4,218**	**6,215**	**5,114**	**5,169**
'Entrepreneurial Labour' (thousand Annual Work Units) (c)(d)	195	192	192	194	194	193	193	193	193	194	196	198
Total Income from Farming per unit of 'entrepreneurial labour' (£/AWU) (c)(d)	**25,294**	**26,363**	**24,060**	**30,756**	**27,626**	**31,740**	**30,237**	**22,128**	**21,901**	**31,969**	**26,030**	**26,056**

(a) All figures are expressed in 2020 prices
(b) Office of National Statistics GDP deflator series YBGB used to adjust for inflation
(c) 'Entrepreneurial labour' refers to the owners of farm businesses and any other unpaid labour
(d) Annual Work Unit (AWU) corresponds to the work performed by one person who is occupied on a full-time basis for a year

Source: Defra

Enquiries: Robin Karfoot on +44 (0)20 802 66449

24.2 Total factor productivity volume indices (2015=100)

	2008	2009	2010	2011	2012	2013	2014	2015	2016	2017	2018	2019
1 Output of cereals	**96.6**	**84.8**	**82.8**	**87.0**	**76.7**	**76.6**	**98.3**	**100.0**	**88.5**	**90.3**	**80.8**	**98.7**
wheat	103.8	85.4	91.2	95.1	80.5	69.3	100.1	100.0	88.3	88.9	79.3	96.0
rye	95.0	95.0	110.0	110.0	75.0	100.0	100.0	100.0	100.0	85.0	100.0	100.0
barley	80.5	85.8	60.8	67.3	67.6	93.6	93.2	100.0	87.6	92.3	81.1	106.2
oats and summer cereal mixtures	100.0	91.9	83.7	77.1	78.1	126.0	95.8	100.0	101.7	109.9	115.1	100.1
other cereals	86.9	134.6	112.0	111.5	104.5	118.8	117.8	100.0	87.1	106.4	135.6	155.9
2 Output of industrial crops	**85.8**	**90.9**	**91.3**	**108.0**	**96.7**	**90.1**	**101.9**	**100.0**	**76.7**	**96.7**	**83.5**	**79.6**
oil seeds	77.9	78.2	89.8	110.4	101.4	85.6	97.3	100.0	70.0	86.2	79.9	69.0
oilseed rape	77.6	76.7	87.7	108.5	100.6	83.7	96.7	100.0	69.8	85.2	79.1	68.9
other oil seeds	103.7	189.6	251.7	248.8	146.1	217.5	137.4	100.0	91.1	174.6	149.0	87.1
protein crops	74.9	94.4	80.5	61.2	44.7	55.5	65.9	100.0	91.1	100.3	58.4	78.8
sugar beet	122.9	136.0	105.0	136.8	117.3	135.6	149.7	100.0	91.5	143.4	122.2	124.8
other industrial crops	98.6	97.1	98.9	100.0	100.0	100.0	100.0	100.0	100.0	103.8	101.6	104.6
3 Output of forage plants	**85.9**	**86.8**	**82.4**	**88.3**	**89.9**	**100.0**	**100.0**	**100.0**	**100.0**	**100.0**	**100.0**	**100.0**
4 Output of vegetables and horticultural products	**99.3**	**96.3**	**99.6**	**97.0**	**94.3**	**97.2**	**99.7**	**100.0**	**100.0**	**101.3**	**96.1**	**96.9**
fresh vegetables	91.3	93.9	96.9	94.6	89.9	94.4	99.5	100.0	98.7	99.6	92.1	91.5
plants and flowers	110.1	99.0	102.7	99.8	99.3	100.3	100.0	100.0	101.6	103.1	100.5	103.1
5 Output of potatoes	**91.0**	**92.2**	**72.8**	**84.2**	**66.3**	**82.3**	**104.9**	**100.0**	**95.7**	**110.2**	**89.2**	**93.9**
6 Output of fruit	**85.8**	**90.3**	**90.6**	**91.7**	**84.3**	**90.7**	**96.8**	**100.0**	**92.1**	**97.1**	**102.9**	**100.7**
7 Output of other crop products	**78.7**	**82.4**	**79.7**	**91.1**	**101.1**	**94.8**	**106.6**	**100.0**	**92.4**	**84.8**	**103.3**	**110.4**
Total crop output (sum 1 - 7)	**93.5**	**89.7**	**88.0**	**92.8**	**84.2**	**86.2**	**99.8**	**100.0**	**91.8**	**97.4**	**89.4**	**95.8**
8 Output of livestock (meat)	**94.0**	**91.3**	**94.4**	**100.3**	**97.1**	**97.3**	**97.0**	**100.0**	**102.7**	**103.5**	**104.2**	**105.9**
cattle	97.8	95.2	99.8	111.7	101.8	97.8	96.1	100.0	104.0	102.7	100.5	100.7
pigs	82.3	79.5	83.4	88.8	90.6	93.4	96.6	100.0	104.0	102.1	103.6	107.9
sheep	101.4	98.2	90.8	96.2	91.9	93.9	98.4	100.0	96.7	98.8	95.6	102.5
poultry	91.1	88.2	95.2	94.7	97.3	100.3	97.5	100.0	103.7	107.9	114.1	113.2
other animals	103.8	103.8	103.7	103.9	103.8	103.8	103.9	100.0	100.0	100.0	100.3	100.8
9 Output of livestock products	**87.7**	**86.9**	**90.4**	**91.5**	**89.4**	**90.5**	**96.9**	**100.0**	**97.1**	**101.5**	**102.8**	**104.5**
milk	87.8	86.8	89.0	90.3	88.8	89.4	96.5	100.0	95.7	99.6	99.9	101.3
eggs	85.4	86.2	96.7	96.3	93.3	96.2	96.7	100.0	104.3	108.6	114.2	118.2
raw wool	106.5	97.9	98.8	104.1	109.2	96.3	98.7	100.0	101.1	99.9	93.7	92.3
other animal products	109.1	115.3	124.2	122.6	73.6	106.2	128.5	100.0	107.6	140.5	179.0	180.6
Total livestock output (8 + 9)	**91.3**	**89.4**	**92.7**	**96.6**	**93.9**	**94.4**	**97.0**	**100.0**	**100.6**	**102.8**	**103.7**	**105.4**
10 Inseparable non-agricultural activities	**79.4**	**87.6**	**87.2**	**88.6**	**89.9**	**100.7**	**98.7**	**100.0**	**100.6**	**109.4**	**114.4**	**121.2**
11 All outputs	**91.7**	**89.6**	**90.8**	**94.9**	**89.9**	**91.6**	**98.1**	**100.0**	**97.3**	**101.2**	**98.9**	**102.7**
12 Seeds	**89.4**	**87.6**	**94.5**	**92.2**	**96.0**	**101.1**	**101.2**	**100.0**	**101.6**	**103.2**	**95.9**	**103.5**
13 Energy	**91.6**	**104.5**	**101.9**	**98.1**	**98.1**	**98.9**	**97.7**	**100.0**	**99.7**	**96.6**	**96.5**	**95.6**
electricity and fuels for heating	113.7	121.6	120.9	114.3	113.5	105.7	97.4	100.0	96.3	101.7	102.5	101.1
motor and machinery fuels	84.4	99.0	95.7	92.8	93.1	96.5	97.8	100.0	101.4	94.2	93.7	93.0
14 Fertilisers	**96.9**	**87.7**	**99.3**	**102.5**	**97.2**	**98.5**	**99.7**	**100.0**	**112.5**	**99.0**	**89.5**	**96.5**
15 Plant protection products	**68.3**	**68.8**	**74.6**	**80.7**	**88.0**	**93.2**	**97.4**	**100.0**	**99.0**	**94.9**	**75.0**	**78.0**
16 Veterinary expenses	**90.0**	**96.5**	**94.3**	**91.6**	**94.6**	**98.2**	**99.5**	**100.0**	**97.7**	**99.6**	**93.3**	**86.4**
17 Animal feed	**89.3**	**89.4**	**96.5**	**89.8**	**91.5**	**95.5**	**97.8**	**100.0**	**100.1**	**102.2**	**105.3**	**104.4**
compounds	85.2	84.1	89.8	87.7	92.4	98.1	98.6	100.0	102.6	106.8	111.2	107.9
straights	96.9	99.8	109.8	93.7	89.5	90.1	95.9	100.0	94.8	92.7	93.0	97.0
18 Total maintenance	**88.6**	**92.1**	**93.3**	**93.1**	**92.6**	**93.7**	**99.6**	**100.0**	**101.1**	**100.0**	**103.7**	**102.6**
materials	93.1	95.8	98.4	99.7	98.6	100.6	101.3	100.0	99.5	102.3	105.3	102.5
buildings	82.3	86.8	86.1	83.8	84.2	84.1	97.3	100.0	103.4	96.6	101.4	102.8
19 FISIM	**100.0**	**100.0**	**100.0**	**100.0**	**100.0**	**100.0**	**100.0**	**100.0**	**100.0**	**100.0**	**100.0**	**100.0**
20 Other goods and services	**100.4**	**104.0**	**100.7**	**103.5**	**98.3**	**99.2**	**97.4**	**100.0**	**98.0**	**103.0**	**96.3**	**100.5**
21 Intermediate consumption (excl Agricultural services)	**91.0**	**92.4**	**96.0**	**94.6**	**94.3**	**96.9**	**98.4**	**100.0**	**100.9**	**100.8**	**97.7**	**99.2**
22 Consumption fixed capital (excluding livestock)	**91.5**	**92.4**	**91.9**	**93.9**	**95.5**	**97.3**	**98.6**	**100.0**	**100.6**	**102.3**	**103.6**	**104.7**
equipment	81.8	83.7	85.7	89.0	91.9	94.9	97.4	100.0	101.5	104.6	106.9	109.1
buildings	109.0	108.3	103.2	102.8	102.2	101.5	100.8	100.0	99.1	98.3	97.6	96.8
23 All Labour	**100.7**	**99.3**	**98.8**	**100.3**	**100.4**	**99.6**	**99.7**	**100.0**	**99.2**	**100.0**	**100.7**	**100.9**
Compensation of employees	99.9	98.7	98.0	100.3	100.4	99.7	99.7	100.0	97.9	99.1	99.1	98.0
Entrepreneurial workers (farm and specialist contractor)	101.2	99.6	99.2	100.4	100.4	99.5	99.7	100.0	99.8	100.5	101.6	102.4
24 Land	**101.0**	**101.0**	**100.5**	**100.1**	**100.2**	**100.7**	**100.5**	**100.0**	**101.2**	**101.9**	**101.2**	**102.2**
25 All Inputs and Entrepreneurial Labour	**94.5**	**95.0**	**96.6**	**96.5**	**96.6**	**98.0**	**98.9**	**100.0**	**100.4**	**100.8**	**99.5**	**100.5**
Total factor productivity (11 divided by 25)	**97.0**	**94.3**	**93.9**	**98.3**	**93.1**	**93.5**	**99.1**	**100.0**	**96.9**	**100.3**	**99.4**	**102.2**
Partial factor productivity indicators												
Productivity by intermediate consumption (11 divided by 21)	100.7	96.9	94.6	100.3	95.3	94.5	99.7	100.0	96.5	100.4	101.2	103.6
Productivity by capital consumption (11 divided by 22)	100.2	96.9	98.8	101.0	94.2	94.2	99.5	100.0	96.7	98.9	95.5	98.1
Productivity by labour (11 divided by 23)	91.0	90.2	91.9	94.5	89.6	92.0	98.3	100.0	98.1	101.1	98.2	101.8
Productivity by land (11 divided by 24)	90.8	88.7	90.3	94.7	89.7	91.0	97.6	100.0	96.1	99.3	97.7	100.4

Source: Agriculture in the UK, Department for Environment, Food and Rural Affairs

Enquiries: Alistair Murray on +44 (0) 20 8026 6121

Email: alistair.murray@defra.gov.uk

24.3 Agricultural land use (a)

Thousand hectares   At June of each year

	2007	2008	2009	2010	2011 [h]	2012	2013	2014	2015	2016	2017	2018 [g]	2019
Utilised agricultural area (UAA) (b)	17,737	17,703	17,325	17,234	17,172	17,190	17,259	17,240	17,147	17,360	17,476	17,361	17,532
UAA as a proportion of total UK area	73%	73%	71%	71%	70%	70%	71%	71%	70%	71%	72%	71%	72%
Total agricultural area	18,692	18,697	18,297	18,282	18,263	18,349	18,449	18,456	18,428	18,662	18,835	18,703	18,849
Common rough grazing	1,238	1,238	1,237	1,228	1,199	1,200	1,198	1,199	1,199	1,199	1,198	1,195	1,197
Total area on agricultural holdings	17,453	17,459	17,060	17,054	17,064	17,149	17,250	17,257	17,229	17,463	17,637	17,509	17,652
Total croppable area	6,215	6,070	6,092	6,015	6,106	6,258	6,310	6,278	6,059	6,073	6,131	6,084	6,132
Total crops	4,440	4,735	4,607	4,610	4,673	4,748	4,665	4,722	4,679	4,667	4,745	4,667	4,714
Arable crops (c)	4,271	4,565	4,437	4,441	4,497	4,576	4,502	4,559	4,505	4,505	4,577	4,502	4,551
Cereals	2,885	3,274	3,076	3,013	3,075	3,142	3,028	3,179	3,100	3,132	3,181	3,106	3,211
Oilseeds (includes linseed and borage)	687	621	600	686	742	785	752	691	670	608	590	609	547
Potatoes	140	144	144	138	146	149	139	141	129	139	145	140	144
Other crops	559	527	616	604	534	500	582	548	606	627	661	647	649
Horticultural crops	169	170	170	169	175	172	163	164	174	162	168	165	163
Uncropped arable land (d)(e)	599	194	244	174	156	153	255	160	214	262	241	265	224
Temporary grass under 5 years old	1,176	1,141	1,241	1,232	1,278	1,357	1,390	1,396	1,167	1,144	1,144	1,152	1,193
Total permanent grassland	10,284	10,395	9,996	9,980	9,858	9,725	9,742	9,755	9,880	10,079	10,138	10,072	10,193
Grass over 5 years old	5,965	6,036	5,865	5,925	5,877	5,799	5,802	5,824	6,078	6,118	6,135	6,178	6,207
Sole right rough grazing (f)	4,319	4,359	4,131	4,055	3,981	3,926	3,940	3,930	3,801	3,961	4,003	3,895	3,986
Other land on agricultural holdings	954	994	972	1,059	1,100	1,166	1,198	1,224	1,290	1,312	1,368	1,353	1,328
Woodland	663	705	726	774	786	827	865	897	961	978	1,037	1,016	1,033
Land used for outdoor pigs	..	..	..	10	9	7	9	8	9	10	10	10	10
All other non-agricultural land	291	289	246	274	305	332	324	318	320	323	321	326	284

Please note that totals may not add up to the sum of components due to rounding. Totals may not agree across tables for the same reason.

Source: June Surveys/Census of Agriculture/SAF land data Scotland.
Enquiries: Emma Howat on +44 (0) 3000 600 170
email: farming-statistics@defra.gsi.gov.uk

(a) Figures for England from 2009 onwards relate to commercial holdings only. More information on commercial holdings can be found in the introduction section of this
(b) UAA includes all arable and horticultural crops, uncropped arable land, common rough grazing, temporary and permanent grassland and land used for outdoor pigs (it excludes woodland and other non-agricultural land).
(c) Includes crops grown on previous set-aside land for England for 2007.
(d) Includes uncropped set-aside land for 2007.
(e) Includes all arable land not in production, including land managed in Good Agricultural and Environmental Condition (GAEC12), wild bird cover and game cover. In the 2009 form guidance notes for England, bird cover and game strips were for the first time explicitly stated as belonging in this category, so the 2009 figure may have captured more of this land than in previous years.
(f) Also includes mountains, hills, heathland or moorland.
(g) Results for 2018 were revised in May 2019 to take account of corrections to the English data. More information on the revisions and the scale of the changes can be found in the updated statistical release here: https://www.gov.uk/government/collections/structure-of-the-agricultural-industry
(h) The 2011 UK totals for other arable crops and glasshouse crops were revised in May 2012 to account for calculation changes in the Scotland and Northern Ireland figures. As a result some subtotals have also been revised.
- means 'nil' or 'negligible' (less than half the last digit shown).
.. means 'not available' or 'not applicable'.

24.4a Estimated quantity of crops and grass harvested

United Kingdom   Thousand tonnes

	2007	2008	2009	2010	2011	2012	2013	2014	2015	2016	2017	2018	2019 (p)
Wheat [1]	13,221	17,227	14,076	14,878	15,257	13,261	11,921	16,606	16,444	14,383	14,837	13,555	16,225
Barley [1]	5,079	6,144	6,668	5,252	5,494	5,522	7,092	6,911	7,370	6,655	7,169	6,510	8,048
Oats [1]	712	784	744	685	613	627	964	820	799	816	875	850	1,076
Sugar Beet	6,733	7,641	8,457	6,527	8,504	7,291	8,432	9,310	6,218	5,687	8,919	7,600	7,763
Potatoes [2]	5 564	6 132	6 396	6 056	6,310	4,658	5,754	5,923	5,644	5,395	6,218	5,060	5,307

Source: Agriculture in the UK, Department for Environment, Food and Rural Affairs
Enquiries: Allan Howsam on +44 (0) 02 802 66123
Email: Crops-statistics@defra.gov.uk

1. All cereal production estimates have been standardised to 14.5% moisture content
2. Following a review of methodology in 2017, figures have been revised back to 2011.
(p) provisional data

24.4b Fruit: Home Porduction marketed for the calendar year in the UK

(Thousand tonnes)

CALENDAR YEAR	2007	2008	2009	2010	2011	2012	2013	2014	2015	2016	2017	2018	2019
ORCHARD FRUIT													
Dessert Apples -													
Cox's Orange Pippin	39.2	50.8	46.5	46.4	45.9	32.0	35.1	37.8	40.9	33.4	26.3	30.5	26.6
Gala	..	..	..	..	..	..	..	..	..	63.8	70.2	83.4	93.2
Braeburn	..	..	..	..	..	..	..	..	..	23.1	12.0	27.4	29.5
Other Dessert	..	..	..	..	..	..	..	..	..	50.8	56.1	65.3	58.6
Worcester Pearmain	1.8	1.9	2.3	2.1	1.9	1.6	1.9	2.1	2.0	..	..	..	..
Discovery	2.9	2.8	2.8	3.0	2.7	2.2	2.7	3.1	3.1	..	..	..	..
Early Season	2.2	2.0	2.0	2.2	2.0	1.7	2.1	2.5	2.6	..	..	..	..
Mid Season Desserts	7.4	6.7	7.5	7.2	6.8	5.7	6.8	7.9	8.2	..	..	..	..
Late Season Desserts	52.7	54.3	60.7	63.9	68.6	73.0	82.3	94.5	103.6	..	..	..	..
Total Dessert Apples :	**106.2**	**118.4**	**121.7**	**124.9**	**127.9**	**116.2**	**130.8**	**147.9**	**160.4**	**171.1**	**164.5**	**206.7**	**207.8**
Culinary Apples -													
Bramley's Seedling	135.3	123.0	105.9	109.0	110.8	86.4	84.0	96.7	88.7	..	..	..	..
Other Culinary	1.0	1.1	1.2	1.1	1.0	0.9	1.1	1.1	1.1	..	..	..	..
Total Culinary Apples	**136.3**	**124.1**	**107.1**	**110.1**	**111.8**	**87.2**	**85.0**	**97.7**	**89.8**	**75.5**	**85.2**	**93.9**	**79.9**
Pears -													
Conference	17.7	17.2	16.6	27.1	26.9	21.1	18.2	22.0	22.6	..	..	..	..
Williams Bon Chretien	..	..	..	..	..	..	..	..	..	..	..	..	..
Comice	..	..	..	..	..	..	..	..	..	..	..	..	..
Others (b)	2.9	2.5	3.9	4.3	5.3	4.5	3.5	3.9	3.9	..	..	..	..
Total Pears :	**20.6**	**19.8**	**20.5**	**31.4**	**32.2**	**25.6**	**21.7**	**25.9**	**26.5**	**20.1**	**26.6**	**26.6**	**27.4**
Cider Apples & Perry Pears:*	..	..	..	..	..	..	..	297.2	322.6	325.8	285.6	205.0	170.0
Plums -													
Victoria	6.8	1.1	6.2	6.1	6.0	2.5	5.5	5.5	5.4	..	..	..	..
Marjorie's Seedling	..	..	..	..	..	..	..	..	..	..	..	..	..
Pershore Yellow Egg	..	..	..	..	..	..	..	..	..	..	..	..	..
Damsons	..	..	..	..	..	..	..	..	..	..	..	..	..
Other Plums	6.2	1.4	6.7	7.1	7.0	3.1	6.9	6.1	6.0	..	..	..	..
Total Plums :	**13.0**	**2.5**	**13.0**	**13.2**	**12.9**	**5.6**	**12.4**	**11.7**	**11.5**	**9.2**	**8.0**	**8.7**	**7.4**
Cherries :	**1.2**	**1.2**	**1.3**	**1.4**	**1.5**	**1.7**	**3.5**	**4.0**	**4.7**	**1.7**	**6.5**	**3.6**	**5.7**
Others & Mixed :	**2.8**	**4.0**	**4.0**	**4.3**	**4.6**	**4.0**	**4.5**	**3.8**	**4.2**	**4.7**	**4.5**	**4.2**	**4.2**
TOTAL ORCHARD FRUIT :	**411.3**	**401.1**	**398.6**	**416.4**	**422.2**	**371.4**	**389.0**	**588.1**	**619.5**	**608.1**	**581.0**	**548.5**	**502.4**
Soft Fruit													
Strawberries	83.1	94.0	98.5	95.7	101.9	94.8	93.9	104.4	115.5	120.3	127.4	140.7	143.5
Raspberries	14.8	15.5	15.6	15.9	15.5	15.6	14.6	17.8	17.2	16.1	16.5	15.8	17.3
Blackcurrants	12.3	13.7	15.8	17.7	12.1	12.0	17.0	12.7	15.2	12.2	14.1	15.1	14.0
Other Soft Fruit:	7.8	7.8	8.9	8.9	7.7	7.5	8.0	7.9	9.4	8.3	10.7	10.4	10.6
TOTAL SOFT FRUIT:	**118.1**	**130.9**	**138.9**	**138.3**	**137.1**	**130.0**	**133.4**	**142.7**	**157.3**	**157.0**	**168.7**	**182.0**	**185.5**
TOTAL FRUIT :	**529.4**	**532.1**	**537.5**	**554.6**	**559.3**	**501.4**	**522.5**	**730.8**	**776.8**	**765.1**	**749.7**	**730.6**	**687.9**

* 'England' only
". ." indicates data not available

Source: Horticultural Statistics 2020, DEFRA
Enquiries and Feedback to: Lisa Brown, Defra, Tel: (+44) (0)20 802 66340,
Email: crops-statistics@defra.gsi.gov.uk

24.4c Field Vegetables: Home Production marketed for the calendar year in the UK

(Thousand Tonnes)

CALENDAR YEAR	2006	2007	2008	2009	2010	2011	2012	2013	2014	2015	2016	2017	2018	2019
Roots and Onions														
Beetroot	57	57	55	55	57	59	62	69	72	72	..	..	..	..
Carrots	712	727	711	695	768	685	674	729	755	731	746	887	772	821
Parsnips	84	86	90	86	90	87	83	83	85	84	81	90	81	80
Turnips and Swedes	115	101	106	109	113	102	84	99	97	104	94	85	78	84
Onions, Dry Bulb	359	304	349	355	364	313	374	355	374	394	372	380	389	357
Onions, Spring	24	20	15	14	14	15	14	14	14	14	19	15	15	15
Total :	1351	1294	1327	1314	1408	1260	1291	1349	1396	1399	1311	1457	1335	1356
Brassicas														
Brussels Sprouts	50	41	43	44	43	47	43	51	50	51	51	52	37	37
Cabbage, Spring	36	35	30	28	24	24	23	23	25	24	24	27	20	23
Cabbage, Summer and Autumn	61	56	56	62	61	60	49	56	56	54	53	56	27	27
Cabbage, Winter	158	126	149	146	162	151	151	141	150	153	155	141	131	104
Cauliflower	124	122	116	108	109	102	90	91	93	91	82	87	88	90
Broccoli	72	68	73	78	79	78	65	69	68	72	69	72	58	64
Total :	500	448	468	465	479	463	421	431	441	444	435	434	362	346
Legumes														
Beans, Broad (c)	10	10	9	12	12	11	12	14	13	15	..	..	..	..
Beans, Runner and Dwarf (a)	18	17	16	15	16	15	14	15	15	14	20	20	19	21
Beans	..	..	..	..	..	..	..	..	..	..	19	..	..	..
Peas, Green for Market	6	6	6	6	6	6	6	6	6	6	..	..	..	..
Peas, Green for Processing (b,c)	124	98	153	168	156	178	124	155	155	157	157	125	119	161
Pease, Green	..	..	..	..	..	..	..	..	..	..	154	..	..	..
Peas, Harvested Dry (c)	24	33	25	40	49	57	22	44	51	72	92	..	..	..
Total :	182	163	209	241	239	268	178	234	240	263	265	145	138	182
Others														
Asparagus	3	3	3	4	4	5	5	5	6	5	6	5	5	5
Celery	36	47	50	49	51	51	51	51	53	54	53	53	54	54
Courgettes	..	..	..	..	..	..	..	..	..	..	22	27	25	23
Leeks	47	50	42	37	42	41	37	35	39	37	39	42	37	38
Lettuce	126	108	117	128	127	126	116	117	124	122	93	99	92	99
Baby Leaf*	..	..	..	..	..	..	..	..	..	..	9	12	12	12
Rhubarb (d)	17	16	16	20	21	20	22	24	30	25	17	15	12	15
Watercress	2	2	2	2	2	2	2	2	2	2	2	2	2	2
Others (f)	116	113	116	144	141	128	118	123	128	123	123	118	120	120
Total :	348	339	346	384	388	373	352	356	382	368	363	373	359	369
TOTAL FIELD VEGETABLES :	2382	2244	2349	2405	2513	2362	2242	2370	2455	2471	2333	2409	2194	2254

(a) Dwarf beans are sometimes called French beans
(b) Also known as vining peas
(c) Shelled weight
(d) Including forced rhubarb grown in sheds
(f) Includes all smaller field grown crops
". ." indicates data not available

Source: Horticultural Statistics 2017, DEFRA
Enquiries and Feedback to: Lisa Brown, Defra, Tel: (+44) (0)20 802 66340,
Email: crops-statistics@defra.gsi.gov.uk

4.5 Crop areas and livestock numbers[a]

	2008	2009	2010	2011 (h)	2012	2013	2014	2015 (g)	2016 (g)	2017 (g)	2018 (g)	2019 (g)
Crop areas (thousand hectares)												
Total area of arable crops (b)	4,565	4,437	4,441	4,497	4,576	4,502	4,559	4,505	4,505	4,577	4,502	4,551
of which: wheat	2,080	1,775	1,939	1,969	1,992	1,615	1,936	1,832	1,823	1,792	1,748	1,816
barley	1,032	1,143	921	970	1,002	1,213	1,080	1,101	1,122	1,177	1,138	1,162
oats	135	129	124	109	122	177	137	131	141	161	171	182
rye, mixed corn and triticale	27	28	29	27	26	24	26	35	45	52	49	51
oilseed rape	598	570	642	705	756	715	675	652	579	562	583	530
linseed	16	28	44	36	29	34	15	15	27	26	25	15
potatoes	144	144	138	146	149	139	141	129	139	145	140	144
sugar beet (not for stockfeeding)	120	114	118	113	120	117	116	90	86	111	114	108
peas for harvesting dry and field beans	148	228	210	155	120	147	139	213	228	233	193	178
maize	153	163	164	164	158	194	183	187	194	197	221	228
Total area of horticultural crops	170	170	169	175	172	163	164	174	162	168	165	163
of which: vegetables grown outdoors	122	125	121	129	123	116	116	123	113	117	116	115
orchard fruit (c)	24	22	24	24	24	23	23	26	25	24	24	24
soft fruit & wine grapes	10	10	10	10	9	10	9	10	10	11	11	11
outdoor plants and flowers	13	11	12	11	12	12	12	13	12	13	12	11
glasshouse crops	2	2	2	2	3	3	3	3	3	3	3	3
Livestock numbers (thousand head)												
Total cattle and calves (d)	10,163	10,082	10,170	9,988	9,952	9,844	9,837	9,919	10,033	10,004	9,891	9,739
of which: cows in the dairy herd (e)	1,892	1,838	1,830	1,796	1,796	1,782	1,841	1,895	1,897	1,891	1,883	1,871
cows in the beef herd (f)	1,678	1,633	1,668	1,687	1,666	1,611	1,569	1,576	1,596	1,589	1,558	1,527
Total sheep and lambs	33,131	31,445	31,084	31,634	32,215	32,856	33,743	33,337	33,943	34,832	33,781	33,580
of which: female breeding flock	15,616	14,636	14,740	14,868	15,229	15,561	16,026	16,024	16,304	16,669	16,286	16,035
lambs under one year old	16,574	15,892	15,431	15,990	16,229	16,381	16,936	16,528	16,840	17,340	16,621	16,672
Total pigs	4,714	4,540	4,460	4,441	4,481	4,885	4,815	4,739	4,866	4,969	5,012	5,078
of which: sows in pig and other sows for breeding	365	379	360	362	357	355	349	352	360	361	352	356
gilts in pig	55	48	67	70	69	66	57	56	55	55	58	57
Total poultry	166,200	152,753	163,867	162,551	160,061	162,609	169,684	167,579	172,697	181,811	188,960	187,072
of which: table fowl	109,859	98,754	105,309	102,461	102,558	104,576	110,374	107,056	110,729	117,612	124,384	121,590
laying flock (including pullets)	35,253	33,266	37,497	38,357	36,646	35,841	37,146	36,887	37,913	39,383	39,727	41,346
breeding flock	9,068	9,397	9,610	10,253	9,987	11,184	11,258	12,622	12,885	13,556	13,976	13,385
turkeys, ducks, geese and all other poultry	12,019	11,335	11,451	11,481	10,870	11,008	10,907	11,014	11,170	11,260	10,872	10,750

Source: June Surveys/Census of Agriculture/SAF land data Scotland.
Also Cattle Tracing System/APHIS (for cattle data).
Enquiries: Emma Howat on +44 (0) 3000 600 170
email: farming-statistics@defra.gov.uk

Please note that totals may not add up to the sum of components due to rounding.
Totals may not agree across tables for the same reason.
- means 'nil' or 'negligible' (less than half the last digit shown).
. . means 'not available' or 'not applicable'.

(a) Figures for England from 2009 onwards relate to commercial holdings only. More information on commercial holdings can be found in the introduction section of this chapter.
(b) Includes arable crops grown on set-aside land in 2007 for England only.
(c) Includes non-commercial orchards.
(d) Cattle figures in this table are based on all agricultural holdings. Therefore these figures do not match the totals in table 3.5, which are based on commercial holdings for England.
(e) Dairy cows are defined as female dairy cows over 2 years old with offspring.
(f) Beef cows are defined as female beef cows over 2 years old with offspring.
(g) Scotland have revised their poultry time series from 2015 to 2019 to reflect new information from a poultry data provider.
(h) The 2011 UK totals for other arable crops and glasshouse crops were revised in May 2012 to account for calculation changes in the Scotland and Northern Ireland figures. As a result some subtotals have also been revised.

24.6 Forestry

Certified woodland area in the UK

United Kingdom

At March of each year	2007	2008	2009	2010	2011	2012	2013	2014	2015	2016	2017	2018	2019
Woodland area (thousands of hectares)													
United Kingdom	1,325	1,310	1,332	1,347	1,324	1,366	1,364	1,377	1,375	1,350	1,388	1,375	1,402
England	364	345	352	357	335	355	355	349	356	337	337	332	325
Wales	133	130	134	133	134	138	140	141	141	141	145	145	146
Scotland	764	770	781	792	792	808	804	822	813	806	841	833	865
Northern Ireland	64	64	65	64	63	65	65	65	65	65	65	65	66
United Kingdom:													
FE/FLS/NRW/FS[3]	876	873	872	868	869	874	875	871	871	864	863	863	864
Private Sector Woodland [4]	449	437	460	479	456	491	489	506	504	486	525	512	538

Source: Forest Stewardship Council, Programme for the Endorsement of Forest Certification, Forestry England, Forestry and Land Scotland, Natural Resources Wales, Forest Service.

Note:

1. All certified woodland is certified under the Forest Stewardship Council (FSC) scheme or the Programme for the Endorsement of Forest Certification (PEFC) scheme, with many woodlands certified under both schemes.

2. The estimates are based on UK data published by FSC and PEFC, supplemented by data from individual certificates and other sources. Where possible, figures are for the woodland area certified, rather than the land area certified.

3. FE: Forestry England, FLS: Forestry and Land Scotland, NRW: Natural Resources Wales, FS: Forest Service (Northern Ireland). NRW estimates only relate to the Welsh Government Woodland Estate.

4. Private sector: all other woodland. Includes woodland managed by NRW outside the WGWE, other publicly owned woodland (e.g. owned by local authorities) and privately owned woodland.

5. All Forestry England/Forestry and Land Scotland/ Natural Resources Wales WGWE/Forest Service woodland is certified. The Forestry England/Forestry and Land Scotland/ Welsh Government Woodland Estate /Forest Service areas are the latest areas, rather than the areas shown on certificates.

24.6 Forestry *(contd.)*

New planting / restocking

Year to 31 March

	2007	2008	2009	2010	2011	2012	2013	2014	2015	2016	2017	2018	2019
New Planting - (Thousand hectares)													
United Kingdom	**10.83**	**7.52**	**6.43**	**5.44**	**9.10**	**12.76**	**10.79**	**12.89**	**10.30**	**5.61**	**6.52**	**9.05**	**13.54**
England	3.17	2.59	2.51	2.29	2.53	2.67	2.59	3.34	2.43	0.82	1.15	1.50	1.42
Wales	0.57	0.19	0.19	0.22	0.30	0.76	0.91	0.93	0.10	0.11	0.41	0.20	0.67
Scotland	6.59	4.19	3.44	2.72	6.02	9.03	7.04	8.33	7.56	4.63	4.76	7.14	11.21
Northern Ireland	0.49	0.55	0.29	0.21	0.25	0.31	0.25	0.29	0.21	0.05	0.21	0.21	0.24
United Kingdom													
Forestry England, Forestry and Land Scotland, Natural Resources Wales, Forest Service	0.24	0.16	0.94	0.74	0.84	1.32	0.85	0.62	0.40	0.71	1.08	0.87	1.06
Private Sector Woodland	10.59	7.36	5.50	4.70	8.26	11.44	9.93	12.27	9.90	4.90	5.45	8.18	12.48
Total													
Conifer	2.14	0.86	1.22	0.54	1.84	3.46	1.86	2.16	2.58	1.93	3.56	5.13	8.12
Broadleaved	8.69	6.67	5.22	4.90	7.26	9.31	8.93	10.73	7.72	3.68	2.96	3.92	5.42
Restocking - (Thousand hectares)													
United Kingdom	**18.95**	**18.91**	**16.12**	**15.10**	**14.03**	**12.29**	**13.13**	**15.81**	**17.84**	**13.71**	**17.09**	**14.30**	**15.37**
England	2.76	3.50	3.46	2.78	3.97	3.63	3.98	4.49	6.41	3.31	3.00	2.04	1.65
Wales	2.98	2.33	2.23	2.06	2.11	1.98	1.96	2.26	1.94	1.76	1.70	1.67	1.70
Scotland	12.40	12.55	9.59	9.55	6.90	5.68	6.04	7.89	8.45	7.82	11.07	9.66	11.19
Northern Ireland	0.81	0.53	0.84	0.70	1.05	1.00	1.16	1.16	1.04	0.81	1.31	0.94	0.83
United Kingdom													
Forestry England, Forestry and Land Scotland, Natural Resources Wales, Forest Service	10.97	10.42	9.18	7.12	9.96	8.94	9.31	10.91	11.20	11.06	11.74	10.23	10.72
Private Sector Woodland	7.99	8.49	6.94	7.98	4.07	3.34	3.83	4.90	6.65	2.65	5.34	4.07	4.65
Total													
Conifer	15.32	14.83	12.08	11.48	10.27	8.95	9.72	11.60	10.84	10.09	13.42	11.53	12.14
Broadleaved	3.64	4.08	4.05	3.62	3.76	3.34	3.42	4.21	7.00	3.62	3.66	2.77	3.23

Source: Forestry Commission, Forestry England, Natural Resources Wales, Welsh Government, Scottish Forestry, Forestry and Land Scotland, Forest Service, grant schemes

Notes:

New planting

1. Private sector = All other woodland, including some other publicly owned woodland.
2. Private sector figures are based on grant-supported new planting and (where possible) with estimates for areas planted without grant aid. For Northern Ireland, private sector figures are based on areas for which grants were paid during the year.
3. Figures for grant-aided planting relate to areas for which grants were paid during the year.
4. **England:** Estimates for areas planted without grant aid are believed to be under-reported and, as a result, the reported figures are likely to under-estimate the true level of planting activity. For England, woodland planting funded by sources other than the Countryside Stewardship Woodland Creation Grant include planting supported by the Woodland Trust, by the Environment Agency, by Natural England and land acquired by the National Forest Company.
   Wales: Estimates of areas planted without grant aid are also included (where possible) up to 2009-10, but no estimates are available since then. As a result, the reported figures are likely to under-estimate the true level of planting activity.
   Scotland: Estimates for areas planted without grant aid are believed to be under-reported and, as a result, the reported figures are likely to under-estimate the true level of planting activity. A small amount of new planting without grant aid was included for 2016-17 and 2019-20.
5. The planting season lies both sides of 31 March, and the weather can cause planting to be advanced or delayed.
6. Includes woodland formed by natural colonisation (where known).
7. Figures are provisional.

Restocking

1. **UK, England and Northern Ireland:** Private sector figures are based on areas for which grants were paid during the year.
   Wales and Scotland: Private sector figures are based on grant-supported new planting and (where possible) with estimates for areas planted without grant aid.
2. Estimates of areas planted without grant aid are also included (where possible) up to 2009-10, but no estimates are available since then. As a result, the reported figures are likely to under-estimate the true level of planting activity.
3. Figures for grant-aided planting relate to areas for which grants were paid during the year.
4. Estimates of areas planted without grant aid are also included (where possible) up to 2009-10, but no estimates are available since then. As a result, the reported figures are likely to under-estimate the true level of planting activity.
5. The planting season lies both sides of 31 March, and the weather can cause planting to be advanced or delayed.
6. Includes woodland restocked by natural regeneration.
7. Restocking by natural regeneration in non-clearfell areas may be under-represented.
8. Figures are provisional.

24.6 Forestry *(contd.)*

Wood production

	2007	2008	2009	2010	2011	2012	2013	2014	2015	2016	2017	2018	2019
Wood Production (volume - Thousand green tonnes)													
United Kingdom	**9,176**	**8,669**	**8,928**	**9,793**	**10,596**	**10,628**	**11,467**	**12,063**	**11,224**	**11,341**	**11,573**	**12,184**	**10,691**
Softwood total	**8,736**	**8,238**	**8,392**	**9,258**	10,056	10,095	10,936	11,527	10,659	10,745	10,836	11,349	9,822
FE/ FLS/ NRW/ FS[1] woodland	4,653	4,415	5,126	4,625	4,870	4,836	5,084	4,900	4,691	5,011	4,761	4,522	3,937
Private Sector [2]	4,083	3,823	3,266	4,633	5,186	5,259	5,852	6,627	5,968	5,734	6,075	6,827	5,884
Hardwood [3,4]	**440**	**431**	**536**	**535**	540	533	531	536	565	596	737	835	869
FE/ FLS/ NRW/ FS[1] woodland	40	43	87	70	75	55	78	71	73	68	85	88	68
Private Sector [2]	400	388	449	465	465	478	453	465	492	528	652	746	801

Source: Forestry England, Forest and Land Scotland,
Natural Resources Wales, Forest Service,
industry surveys, industry associations.

Notes:
1. FE: Forestry England, FLS: Forestry and Land Scotland, NRW: Natural Resources Wales, FS: Forest Service (Northern Ireland).
2. Private sector: removals from all other woodland (including some publicly owned woodland).
3. Most hardwood production in the UK comes from private sector woodland; the figures are estimates based on reported deliveries to wood processing industries and others.
4. The increase in hardwood removals between 2016 and 2017 is largely attributed to a revised estimate for deliveries of UK grown hardwood used for woodfuel (see Table 2.6). This new estimate should not be interpreted as an increase in a single year.
5. One green tonne is equivalent to approximately 0.98 m^3 underbark softwood or 0.88 m3 underbark hardwood, and to approximately 1.22 m3 overbark standing softwood or 1.11 m3 overbark standing hardwood.

24.7 Sales for food of agricultural produce and livestock
United Kingdom

		2007	2008	2009	2010**	2011	2012	2013	2014	2015	2016	2017	2018	2019
Milk:														
Total new supply	Million litres	13,146	12,816	12,777	13,131	13,292	13,110	13,226	14,221	14,363	13,596	14,043	14,051	14,304
of which:														
for liquid consumption	"	6,724	6,678	6,626	6,836	6,892	6,785	6,856	6,903	6,671	6,514	6,786	6,653	6,284
for manufacture	"	6,085	5,840	5,699	6,112	6,260	6,015	6,223	7,093	7,468	6,918	7,279	7,127	7,765
Hen eggs:														
UK production of eggs for human consumption	Million dozen	720	754	751	826	821	797	829	839	866	899	931	959	979
of which:														
eggs sold in shell	"	539	577	597	673	664	654	695	695	729	758	800	820	852
eggs processed	"	181	177	154	152	158	143	134	144	137	140	131	139	127
Cattle and calves:														
Calves [(1)]	Thousands	45.7	44.2	42.6	61.8	80.6	73.8	91.1	112.2	101.1	124.3	112.6	121.4	131.6
Prime Cattle	"	2167.9	2028.4	1981.4	2133.6	2114.1	1965.0	1927.1	1959.6	1929.2	1974.9	1979.6	1993.8	2009.3
Adult Cattle	"	447.6	559.2	488.9	564.1	643.3	641.8	606.9	597.4	618.8	681.0	661.4	694.9	685.5
Total	"	2,661	2,632	2,513	2,760	2,838	2,681	2,625	2,669	2,649	2,780	2,754	2,810	2,826
Sheep and lambs	"	13580.7	14352.4	13408.1	12317.8	12461.6	11899.1	12447.8	12814.5	13188.4	12844.5	13297.6	12817.1	13154.7
Ewes and rams	"	2223.1	2344.5	2192.1	1971.0	2015.8	1846.9	2068.9	1805.3	1608.7	1711.9	1574.6	1600.5	1697.4
Pigs:														
Clean pigs	"	9273.8	9191.8	8824.2	9410.8	9812.7	10034.5	10049.7	10227.2	10627.0	10733.1	10420.2	10667.1	10862.1
Sows and boars	"	209.9	235.0	206.7	(c)	(c)	264.8	252.0	242.7	244.6	256.7	236.6	258.8	244.6
Total	"	9,484	9,427	9,031	(c)	(c)	10,299	10,302	10,470	10,872	10,990	10,657	10,926	11,107
Poultry and poultry meat:														
Slaughtering	Millions	873	862	868	933	931	952	976	972	1,029	1,079	1,119	1,161	1,134

Source: Defra statistics, Slaughterhouse surveys, The Scottish Government,
DAERA (NI), Food Standards Agency (FSA)

c Data are confidential
** Denotes a 53 week statistical year

[(1)] The definition of Calves from May 2014 is "Bovines less than 1 year old". Pre-May 2014, the definition was "Bovines weighing less than 165kg". Please see Information tab for full details.

24.8 Number of livestock farmed organically [a]

Thousand heads

	2008	2009	2010	2011	2012	2013	2014	2015	2016	2017	2018	2019
United Kingdom												
Cattle	319.6	331.2	350.2	316.4	280.5	283.3	304.1	291.5	296.4	294.0	324.1	300.8
Sheep	:	884.8	981.2	1,130.0	1,132.6	999.2	954.9	844.6	840.8	887.0	826.6	782.2
Pigs	71.2	49.4	47.4	52.5	34.6	30.2	28.3	30.0	31.5	39.1	37.4	34.0
Poultry	4 362.9	3 958.7	3 870.9	2,832.9	2,451.7	2,487.6	2,398.7	2,560.2	2,821.2	3,059.9	3,380.9	3,464.1
Other livestock (b)	4.8	3.4	4.5	4.9	4.0	4.1	5.7	4.3	3.4	2.6	6.0	6.0
England												
Cattle	214.1	236.5	248.6	219.6	193.7	199.5	215.6	217.7	219.3	217.3	240.6	220.8
Sheep (a)	:	380.4	431.3	399.7	419.7	400.8	404.2	415.3	405.9	421.2	374.0	350.6
Pigs	57.1	46.5	42.1	47.8	29.4	26.5	25.8	22.2	29.4	37.2	29.2	30.6
Poultry	2 293.9	1 969.4	1 931.1	1,741.1	1,675.5	1,687.5	1,495.9	1,512.4	1,699.2	2,002.0	2,038.2	2,071.6
Other livestock (b)	2.7	1.6	2.0	1.2	3.5	3.4	3.1	3.9	2.8	2.3	4.8	5.0

Source: Department for Environment, Food and Rural Affairs
Enquiries : Sarah Thompson
sarah.thompson@defra.gsi.gov.uk

(a) Data relates to fully organic only.

(b) "Other livestock" includes goats, farmed deer, horses, camelids and any livestock not recorded elsewhere.

24.9 Total number of organic producers and processors [a]

Number

	2010	2011	2012	2013	2014	2015	2016	2017	2018	2019
United Kingdom	7 287	6 929	6 487	6 072	6 002	6 056	6 363	6 586	6 188	6 129
Wales	1 166	1 119	1 080	913	779	741	751	751	759	737
Scotland	737	679	611	551	576	539	560	578	577	559
Northern Ireland	253	234	204	189	193	197	204	220	216	206
England	5 131	4 897	4 592	4 419	4 454	4 579	4 848	5 037	4 636	4 627
North East	160	152	137	127	130	137	130	132	113	116
North West	315	301	273	253	246	277	301	308	263	274
Yorkshire & Humberside	302	278	262	240	238	257	273	275	240	246
East Midlands	408	383	366	351	346	329	371	388	350	353
West Midlands	494	476	442	426	424	438	446	514	475	460
Eastern	515	481	456	449	445	457	508	543	477	457
South East (Inc London)	984	975	950	957	1 020	1 083	1 192	1 254	1 196	1 217
South West	1 953	1 851	1 706	1 616	1 605	1 601	1 627	1 623	1 522	1 504

Source: Department for Environment, Food and Rural Affairs
Enquiries : Sarah Thompson
sarah.thompson@defra.gov.uk

(a) In 2018, work has been carried out to clarify how operators are recorded. This has resulted in a number of operators that were previously recorded as processors now being recorded in the correct categories of wholsalers/traders/retailers etc. We are unable to backdate these changes so earlier data is not directly comparable.

24.10a: Land area farmed organically

Thousand hectares

	2010	2011	2012	2013	2014	2015	2016	2017	2018	2019
In conversion land area										
North East	4.0	2.9	2.7	1.0	0.8	0.3	0.4	0.8	1.6	1.7
North West	2.4	1.4	1.1	0.9	0.6	0.3	1.1	1.0	0.6	0.5
Yorkshire & Humberside	0.9	0.7	0.6	0.5	0.6	0.5	0.6	0.8	0.6	0.7
East Midlands	1.0	0.5	0.6	0.7	0.9	0.7	0.9	0.8	1.1	1.6
West Midlands	2.1	1.8	1.4	0.8	1.2	1.0	2.0	5.1	4.4	2.0
Eastern	1.4	1.0	0.7	0.7	0.5	1.0	1.3	1.2	1.2	2.1
South East (inc. London)	4.3	3.7	3.1	3.0	1.9	0.7	1.4	1.7	2.0	2.3
South West	13.6	13.5	8.9	6.3	6.1	5.5	7.2	8.4	8.7	8.0
England	**29.8**	**25.4**	**19.2**	**14.0**	**12.5**	**10.0**	**14.7**	**19.8**	**20.3**	**19.0**
Wales	4.0	2.4	1.5	1.9	4.1	9.4	7.8	7.3	3.6	1.8
Scotland	12.6	5.1	8.0	8.4	3.0	1.0	2.3	5.1	8.5	6.8
Northern Ireland	4.4	4.0	3.6	0.1	0.2	0.3	0.3	0.4	0.5	0.5
United Kingdom	**50.8**	**36.9**	**32.2**	**24.4**	**19.7**	**20.6**	**25.2**	**32.6**	**32.9**	**28.1**
Fully organic land area										
North East	30.6	28.1	27.3	26.9	26.3	27.6	24.9	22.6	21.6	22.3
North West	20.0	16.4	15.5	14.0	13.6	13.8	11.4	13.9	11.6	11.5
Yorkshire & Humberside	13.8	12.5	9.9	10.2	10.1	10.2	10.0	10.2	9.7	10.3
East Midlands	16.3	15.2	15.5	14.1	13.7	13.5	13.6	12.6	12.6	13.7
West Midlands	35.4	28.9	30.6	30.8	29.3	28.3	28.0	27.6	28.7	30.3
Eastern	17.3	15.8	14.1	14.1	13.8	13.7	13.5	13.9	12.1	16.4
South East (inc. London)	54.1	51.4	46.5	48.1	45.6	45.0	42.4	42.5	39.4	42.8
South West	174.6	157.2	145.5	144.2	143.1	141.6	138.0	137.2	133.3	134.3
England	**362.0**	**325.6**	**304.8**	**302.4**	**295.7**	**293.7**	**281.8**	**280.5**	**269.0**	**281.6**
Wales	118.8	120.4	118.4	100.0	91.6	73.5	73.7	78.8	81.4	82.6
Scotland	176.3	164.8	143.7	140.0	132.9	125.3	119.3	117.6	83.1	85.3
Northern Ireland	10.4	8.3	6.6	9.3	8.8	8.2	8.0	7.9	7.6	7.6
United Kingdom	**667.6**	**619.1**	**573.4**	**551.7**	**529.0**	**500.8**	**482.7**	**484.8**	**441.1**	**457.1**
Total fully organic and in conversion land area										
North East	34.6	31.1	30.0	27.9	27.1	27.9	25.2	23.4	23.2	24.1
North West	22.4	17.8	16.6	14.9	14.2	14.1	12.5	14.9	12.2	12.1
Yorkshire & Humberside	14.6	13.2	10.5	10.7	10.8	10.7	10.5	11.0	10.3	11.0
East Midlands	17.3	15.7	16.1	14.8	14.6	14.3	14.5	13.4	13.7	15.2
West Midlands	37.5	30.7	31.9	31.6	30.5	29.4	30.0	32.7	33.1	32.2
Eastern	18.7	16.7	14.8	14.9	14.3	14.7	14.8	15.1	13.3	18.6
South East (inc. London)	58.4	55.1	49.6	51.1	47.5	45.7	43.8	44.2	41.4	45.1
South West	188.2	170.7	154.4	150.4	149.2	147.1	145.1	145.6	142.0	142.2
England	**391.8**	**351.0**	**323.9**	**316.4**	**308.1**	**303.7**	**296.5**	**300.3**	**289.3**	**300.6**
Wales	122.9	122.7	119.9	101.9	95.7	82.9	81.5	86.1	85.0	84.4
Scotland	188.9	169.9	151.7	148.4	135.8	126.3	121.6	122.7	91.6	92.1
Northern Ireland	14.8	12.3	10.1	9.4	9.0	8.5	8.3	8.3	8.1	8.1
United Kingdom	**718.3**	**656.0**	**605.7**	**576.0**	**548.6**	**521.4**	**507.9**	**517.4**	**474.0**	**485.2**

Source: Department for Environment, Food and Rural Affairs
Enquiries : Sarah Thompson
sarah.thompson@defra.gov.uk

24.10b: Fully organic and in conversion land use

Thousand hectares

	2010	2011	2012	2013	2014	2015	2016	2017 (b)	2018 (b)	2019
United Kingdom										
In-conversion land area										
Cereals	2.2	1.2	1.5	1.4	1.0	1.0	1.6	1.9	2.2	3.0
Other crops	0.7	0.4	0.3	0.2	0.3	0.4	0.6	0.8	0.9	0.9
Fruit & nuts	0.2	0.2	0.1	0.1	0.1	0.0	0.1	0.1	0.1	0.1
Vegetables (including potatoes)	0.5	0.3	0.3	0.2	0.1	0.1	0.5	0.4	0.8	1.1
Herbaceous & ornamentals	1.0	0.5	0.3	0.7	0.6	0.1	0.1	0.0	0.1	0.0
Temporary pasture	7.3	5.8	5.5	3.8	3.2	3.1	6.2	7.4	7.3	6.1
Permanent pasture (inc rough grazing)	35.7	24.4	22.0	16.6	13.5	15.1	15.3	17.4	20.3	15.4
Woodland	1.9	1.7	1.0	0.6	0.6	0.4	0.2	0.3	0.5	0.8
Unutilised land	1.3	2.5	1.3	0.8	0.2	0.2	0.3	0.2	0.4	0.4
Unknown [a]	na	na	na	na	0.1	0.2	0.4	4.1	0.3	0.2
Total	**50.8**	**36.9**	**32.2**	**24.4**	**19.7**	**20.6**	**25.2**	**32.6**	**32.9**	**28.1**
Fully organic area										
Cereals	54.7	51.3	46.4	42.4	41.2	38.6	36.8	35.4	34.8	36.8
Other crops	10.2	8.9	8.1	7.4	7.0	6.6	6.7	6.6	6.5	8.0
Fruit & nuts	2.0	2.0	2.0	2.0	2.0	1.9	1.9	1.7	1.6	1.9
Vegetables (including potatoes)	17.4	15.4	12.0	11.2	9.3	10.2	9.8	9.2	8.5	8.3
Herbaceous & ornamentals	5.2	5.7	5.5	6.1	7.9	6.2	5.7	5.9	6.6	0.4
Temporary pasture	117.5	110.3	100.6	95.1	90.5	89.1	85.9	84.9	54.5	89.0
Permanent pasture (inc rough grazing)	443.3	410.5	383.6	370.4	356.1	332.0	319.7	316.0	309.9	290.0
Woodland	6.2	6.6	6.4	6.9	6.4	6.6	7.1	8.6	7.1	14.4
Unutilised land	11.0	8.4	8.8	9.6	4.1	5.5	5.2	5.4	3.5	4.2
Unknown [a]	na	na	na	na	4.3	4.2	4.1	11.1	8.1	4.2
Total	**667.6**	**619.1**	**573.4**	**551.0**	**529.0**	**500.8**	**482.7**	**484.8**	**441.1**	**457.1**
Total fully organic and in conversion land use										
Cereals	56.8	52.5	47.8	43.7	42.2	39.6	38.4	37.4	37.1	39.7
Other crops	10.8	9.3	8.4	7.6	7.3	6.9	7.3	7.4	7.4	8.9
Fruit & nuts	2.3	2.2	2.1	2.1	2.1	1.9	1.9	1.8	1.7	2.0
Vegetables (including potatoes)	18.0	15.7	12.3	11.3	9.4	10.4	10.2	9.6	9.3	9.4
Herbaceous & ornamentals	6.2	6.1	5.8	6.8	8.5	6.2	5.8	5.9	6.7	0.4
Temporary pasture	124.7	116.1	106.1	98.9	93.7	92.2	92.1	92.3	61.8	95.1
Permanent pasture (inc rough grazing)	479.0	434.9	405.6	387.0	369.7	347.1	335.0	333.3	330.1	305.4
Woodland	8.1	8.3	7.4	7.6	7.0	6.9	7.4	9.0	7.6	15.2
Non cropping	12.4	10.9	10.1	10.4	4.4	5.7	5.4	5.5	4.0	4.5
Unknown [a]	na	na	na	na	4.4	4.3	4.5	15.2	8.4	4.5
Total	**718.3**	**656.0**	**605.6**	**575.3**	**548.6**	**521.4**	**507.9**	**517.4**	**474.0**	**485.2**

24.10b: Fully organic and in conversion land use

Thousand hectares

	2010	2011	2012	2013	2014	2015	2016	2017 (b)	2018 (b)	2019
England										
In-conversion area										
Cereals	1.6	1.0	1.1	1.1	0.8	0.8	1.3	1.5	1.9	2.6
Other crops	0.5	0.4	0.2	0.2	0.2	0.2	0.3	0.5	0.7	0.8
Fruit & nuts	0.2	0.2	0.1	0.1	0.1	0.0	0.0	0.1	0.1	0.1
Vegetables (including potatoes)	0.4	0.2	0.2	0.1	0.1	0.1	0.4	0.3	0.8	0.9
Herbaceous & ornamentals	0.9	0.4	0.3	0.5	0.4	0.1	0.1	0.0	0.1	0.0
Temporary pasture	6.4	5.2	5.0	3.4	2.7	2.7	4.9	6.2	6.3	5.2
Permanent pasture (inc rough grazing)	16.8	14.1	10.2	7.4	7.3	5.5	6.9	7.7	9.6	8.3
Woodland	1.6	1.6	0.8	0.6	0.5	0.4	0.2	0.3	0.3	0.6
Unutilised land	1.2	2.3	1.3	0.6	0.2	0.1	0.2	0.1	0.3	0.3
Unknown [a]	na	na	na	na	0.1	0.1	0.4	3.1	0.3	0.2
Total	**29.8**	**25.4**	**19.2**	**14.0**	**12.5**	**10.0**	**14.7**	**19.8**	**20.3**	**19.0**
Fully organic area										
Cereals	43.6	40.4	36.8	34.1	34.1	32.3	30.8	29.8	29.6	31.2
Other crops	7.2	6.6	5.7	5.4	5.1	4.9	5.1	4.9	4.9	6.1
Fruit & nuts	2.0	1.9	2.0	1.9	2.0	1.8	1.7	1.5	1.5	1.8
Vegetables (including potatoes)	13.2	11.9	9.5	9.0	7.6	8.5	8.1	7.7	6.9	6.9
Herbaceous & ornamentals	3.9	4.6	4.8	5.3	7.0	5.3	4.9	5.1	5.7	0.3
Temporary pasture	96.7	90.9	82.1	77.9	74.6	73.0	70.1	69.2	45.7	71.6
Permanent pasture (inc rough grazing)	182.6	159.0	152.9	155.9	154.4	155.4	148.6	146.2	162.6	146.6
Woodland	4.5	4.6	4.6	4.8	4.5	4.8	5.1	5.0	4.4	10.6
Unutilised land	8.3	5.6	6.3	7.3	3.0	4.3	3.8	3.9	2.4	2.7
Unknown [a]	na	na	na	na	3.5	3.3	3.4	7.0	5.3	3.9
Total	**362.0**	**325.6**	**304.8**	**301.7**	**295.7**	**293.7**	**281.8**	**280.5**	**269.0**	**281.6**
Total fully organic and in conversion land use										
Cereals	45.3	41.4	37.9	35.2	34.9	33.1	32.1	31.3	31.4	33.8
Other crops	7.8	7.0	6.0	5.6	5.3	5.1	5.4	5.4	5.5	7.0
Fruit & nuts	2.2	2.1	2.1	2.0	2.1	1.8	1.8	1.6	1.6	1.9
Vegetables (inc potatoes)	13.7	12.2	9.7	9.2	7.7	8.7	8.5	8.0	7.7	7.8
Herbaceous & ornamentals	4.8	5.0	5.1	5.8	7.4	5.4	5.0	5.2	5.8	0.3
Temporary pasture	103.1	96.1	87.1	81.2	77.3	75.7	75.0	75.5	51.9	76.8
Permanent pasture (inc rough grazing)	199.4	173.2	163.1	163.2	161.7	160.9	155.6	153.9	172.2	154.9
Woodland	6.1	6.2	5.4	5.4	5.0	5.2	5.3	5.3	4.7	11.2
Unutilised land	9.5	7.9	7.6	8.0	3.2	4.4	4.0	4.0	2.7	2.9
Unknown [a]	na	na	na	na	3.5	3.4	3.8	10.1	5.6	4.1
Total	**391.8**	**351.0**	**323.9**	**315.6**	**308.1**	**303.7**	**296.5**	**300.3**	**289.3**	**300.6**

Source: Department for Environment, Food and Rural Affairs

Enquiries : Sarah Thompson

sarah.thompson@defra.gov.uk

(a) Some land areas are provided without a crop category or land use description, therefore these are classified as unknown.

(b) In 2019 data issues have been identified with the detailed split of crops provided for 2017 and 2018. The overall totals for 2017 and 2018 remain unaffected but the breakdowns are subject to a degree of error and therefore should be treated with caution.

24.11 Wages in Agriculture: Minimum weekly rates of pay

If a worker's contract says they should work 39 hours a week (not including overtime) they must be paid the weekly rate, otherwise they must be paid the hourly rate.

1 January to 30 September, 2015-2020					
Grade 6	Grade 5	Grade 4	Grade 3	Grade 2	Grade 1
£	£	£	£	£	£
366.60	339.30	320.19	298.74	271.44	242.19

Grade 1 - Initial Grade   Grade 4 - Craft Grade   Source: Department for Environment,
Grade 2 - Standard Grade   Grade 5 - Supervisory Grade   Food and Rural Affairs
Grade 3 - Lead Worker   Grade 6 - Farm Management Grade   Data accessed on: 01 Dec 2021

Higher rates apply to Full Time and Part Time Flexible Workers.

24.12 Number of people working on commercial agricultural holdings

United Kingdom

Agricultural workforce by UK country at 1 June each year   Thousands

Agricultural workforce	2015	2016	2017	2018	2019
Total labour force (incl. farmers and spouses)	**476.5**	**466.2**	**473.9**	**477.1**	**475.7**
Farmers, business partners, directors and spouses	**293.7**	**289.9**	**293.8**	**296.4**	**299.2**
Full time	141.8	138.9	141.0	144.5	144.3
Part time (a)	152.0	151.0	152.8	151.9	154.8
Regular employees, salaried managers and casual workers (b)	**182.7**	**176.3**	**180.2**	**180.6**	**176.5**
Regular employees (c)	**115.5**	..	..	..	..
Full time	72.9	..	..	..	..
Part time (a)	42.5	..	..	..	..
Seasonal, casual or gang labour	**67.3**	..	..	..	..

.. not available   Source: Department for Environment, Food and Rural Affairs (DEFRA)

(a) Part-time is defined as working less than 39 hours per week (England & Wales), 38 hours per week (Scotland) and 30 hours per week (N. Ireland).
(b) Not all UK countries collect separate estimates for regular employees and casual labour. These figures are included in this total.
(c) Not all UK countries collect separate estimates for salaried managers. These figures are included with regular employees.
(d) Figures for 2017 for Seasonal, casual or gang labour were amended on 27 June 2019 to correct an error, the scale of change was very small , with the total only decreasing by 184 (0.04%)

24.13 Summary of UK fishing industry: 2010 to 2019

£ million (unless otherwise specified)

	2010	2011	2012	2013	2014	2015	2016	2017	2018	2019
Fleet size at end of year [a]										
(no. of vessels)	6,477	6,444	6,406	6,399	6,383	5,783	6,191	6,148	6,036	5,911
Employment										
(no. of fishermen)	12,703	12,405	12,445	12,235	11,845	12,107	11,757	11,692	11,961	12,043
Total landings by UK vessels [b]										
Quantity ('000 tonnes)	605.3	596.0	628.0	626.8	757.9	708.7	700.6	726.7	700.0	621.9
Value (£ million)	720.3	832.0	787.9	741.3	864.1	776.4	946.7	946.6	1002.8	986.8
Imports [j]										
Quantity ('000 tonnes)	703.8	720.2	754.5	739.4	721.9	680.4	729.2	704.0	674.0	726.2
Value (£ million) [c]	2254.7	2558.6	2570.0	2757.0	2737.8	2671.6	3069.3	3197.0	3192.8	3473.6
Exports [j]										
Quantity ('000 tonnes)	516.7	436.1	465.9	452.0	502.0	442.0	439.9	459.5	447.6	454.3
Value (£ million) [c]	1345.7	1463.9	1343.9	1460.0	1566.0	1336.7	1638.4	1903.8	1789.3	2013.6
Total household consumption										
of fish ('000 tonnes)	483	472	467	481	479	490	476	477.0	nd	nd
Population ('000 persons)	61,464	61,528	61,946	63,421	63,879	64,188	65,648	66,040	66,436	-
Total consumer expenditure										
on fish (£ million)	3,742	3,866	3,998	4,271	4,309	4,512	4,423	4687.0	nd	nd
on food (£ million) [d]	72,587	73,744	77,523	81,291	80,669	79,964	83,921	86542.0	nd	nd
Fish as a % of food [d]	5.2%	5.2%	5.2%	5.3%	5.3%	5.6%	5.3%	5.4%	nd	nd
Landed Price Index [e]	152.2	163.7	153.9	149.3	150.8	146.5	171.9	182.9	188.1	-
Retail Price Index [f]	138.2	151.0	157.4	163.4	168.2	163.2	159.9	173.2	176.9	-
Consumer Price Index [g] R	140.1	153.0	158.5	163.6	167.8	161.9	158.2	172.2	178.7	-
GDP for Fishing [h][i]										
Current price gross value added at basic prices (KK37)	590	685	686	644	841	584	536	639	523	459
Output index (chain volume measures) (L2KO) (2016=100)	101.5	101.9	101.7	101.0	114.3	110.5	110.5	107.2	100.0	89.3
GDP for Agriculture, Forestry and Fishing [i]										
Current price gross value added at basic prices (KKD5)	9,752	11,571	11,020	11,478	14,065	12,429	11,493	11,867	12,185	12,987
Output index (chain volume measures) (L2KL) (2016=100)	88.2	98.9	90.4	91.0	103.4	103.4	97.2	103.4	100.0	106.3
GDP at Market Prices [i]										
Current price GDP at market prices (KKP5) (£ billion)	1,446	1,482	1,530	1,589	1,661	1,712	1,777	1,844	1,910	1,972
Chain volume measures index (YBEZ) (2016=100)	86.3	87.4	88.7	90.6	93.2	95.4	97.1	98.8	100.0	101.4
Percentage contribution of GVA from fishing to GVA for agriculture, hunting, forestry and fishing										
Current prices (%)	6.1%	5.9%	6.2%	5.6%	6.0%	4.7%	4.7%	5.4%	4.3%	3.5%

Source: Fisheries Administrations in the UK, H.M. Customs and Excise, Expenditure and Food Survey, Office for National Statistics

(a) The number of vessels includes those registered in the Channel Islands and Isle of Man.

(b) The quantity of landed fish is expressed in terms of liveweight. The figures relate to landings both into the UK and abroad.

(c) Imports are valued at cost, including insurance and freight terms whereas exports are valued at free on board terms.

(d) Including non-alcoholic beverages.

(e) The landed price index has been calculated on an annual basis with 2000 = 100.

(f) The fish component of the RPI which includes canned and processed fish. The index has been re-based such that 2000 = 100.

(g) The fish component of the CPI which includes canned and processed fish. The index has been re-based such that 2000 = 100.

(h) GDP for fishing includes landings abroad, according to the KK37 index.

(i) GDP figures compiled in line with ESA2010 since September 2014. All values have been recalculated since the last publication.

(j) Excludes fish products.

24.14 UK Fishing Fleet [1]

UK Fleet as of 1st January

	2013	2014	2015	2016	2017	2018	2019
By Size Total	**6,399**	**6,383**	**6,187**	**6,191**	**6,148**	**6,036**	**5,911**
10m and under vessels	5,036	5,026	4,863	4,876	4,834	4,760	4,675
Over 10m vessels	1,363	1,357	1,324	1,315	1,314	1,276	1,236
of which:							
10 - 18m	876	877	854	852	855	831	802
18 - 24m	246	244	243	239	238	225	220
24m and over	241	236	227	224	221	220	214
By Gross tonnage (GT)[3]	**197,283**	**195,121**	**187,371**	**185,734**	**187,014**	**191,178**	**198,013**
10m and under	16,979	18,119	16,472	16,479	16,362	16190	17,686
Over 10m vessels	180,304	177,002	170,899	169,255	170,652	174,988	180,328
of which:							
10 - 18m	25,691	26,195	25,780	25,835	23,128	25,397	24,702
18 - 24m	32,112	32,106	32,008	31,905	32,904	31,390	31,444
24m and over	122,500	118,702	113,111	111,515	111,620	118,201	124,182
By Engine power (kW)	**797,661**	**789,714**	**769,532**	**765,810**	**757,899**	**752,146**	**755,343**
10m and under	275,513	275,496	270,688	272,696	270,837	267,934	264,576
Over 10m vessels	522,148	514,219	498,844	493,114	487,062	484,212	490,767
of which:							
10 - 18m	147,006	149,137	148,231	148,616	150,117	146,238	142,330
18 - 24m	87,457	87,085	86,873	86,342	87,386	83,941	83,717
24m and over	287,685	277,997	263,741	258,157	249,559	254,033	264,720
Total UK Fleet	**6,399**	**6,383**	**6,187**	**6,191**	**6,148**	**6,036**	**5,911**
Number of vessel losses from accidents	**18**	**12**	**13**	**8**	**6**	**8**	-
Total accidents	256	157	118	170	151	138	-
Fatalities[4]	4	8	7	9	5	6	-

Source: Maritime and Coastguard Agency and Fisheries Administrations in the UK,
Marine Accident Investigation Branch

1. Includes Channel Islands, the Isle of Man and vessels without an administration port. Excludes mussel dredgers.

2 An inactive vessel is defined as a registered vessel that has not undertaken fishing activity in the reference year.

3. The series for GT is on the basis of GT at the end of 2003.

4. Number of crew deaths on UK registered fishing vessels. These figures include workers on board vessels who are not crew members.

24.15 Quantity of food and drink purchased for UK households
UK

Units: average per person per week

Code		Units	2010	2011	2012	2013	2014	2015	2015/16	2016/17	2017/18	2018/19	2019/20
cat520	**Milk and milk products excluding cheese**	ml	**1,897**	**1,904**	**1,901**	**1,847**	**1,849**	**1,827**	**1,807**	**1,818**	**1,786**	**1,840**	**1,746**
4006	Liquid wholemilk, including school and welfare	ml	352	355	297	285	263	312	317	300	297	329	302
9017	Other milk and cream	ml	1,545	1,549	1,604	1,562	1,586	1,515	1,490	1,519	1,489	1,511	1,443
22023	**Cheese**	g	**118**	**118**	**114**	**118**	**111**	**112**	**115**	**124**	**125**	**123**	**129**
31041	**Carcase meat**	g	**211**	**204**	**196**	**182**	**195**	**187**	**192**	**175**	**182**	**168**	**170**
31	Beef and veal	g	114	112	104	97	101	102	103	102	99	96	97
36	Mutton and lamb	g	44	37	36	35	37	35	38	24	36	25	32
41	Pork	g	53	56	55	51	57	50	51	49	47	47	41
46095	**Non-carcase meat and meat products**	g	**805**	**794**	**793**	**766**	**760**	**742**	**745**	**778**	**775**	**794**	**779**
46	Liver	g	4	4	4	3	3	2	2	3	3	2	3
51	All offal other than liver	g	2	3	2	2	2	2	2	3	2	2	1
55	Bacon and ham, uncooked	g	70	69	68	64	62	60	59	63	57	59	54
58	Bacon and ham, cooked	g	43	43	40	39	40	39	40	41	41	38	36
59	Cooked poultry not purchased in cans	g	41	41	37	38	35	33	34	35	34	32	34
62	Corned beef, canned or sliced	g	10	8	7	7	7	7	7	7	7	7	7
66	Other cooked meat	g	12	13	14	14	14	13	13	13	12	13	11
71	Other canned meat and canned meat products	g	26	25	22	22	21	19	19	17	20	20	22
74	Chicken, uncooked - whole chicken or chicken pieces	g	181	190	192	184	186	184	184	193	186	212	209
77	Other poultry, uncooked (including frozen)	g	19	17	22	19	20	14	14	19	17	15	14
77	Other fresh, chilled and frozen meat	g	2	2	1	2	2	1	0	2	1	1	0
78	Sausages, uncooked - pork	g	62	59	62	57	55	52	52	54	57	54	52
79	Sausages, uncooked - beef and other sausages	g	4	5	4	4	4	4	4	4	5	3	4
80	Meat pies and sausage rolls, ready to eat	g	24	24	22	21	20	23	23	22	23	22	21
83	Meat pies, pasties and puddings, frozen or not frozen	g	52	48	46	43	41	42	41	46	45	39	41
84	Burgers, frozen or not frozen	g	22	21	18	18	18	18	19	18	19	22	20
85	Ready meals and convenience meat products	g	161	157	164	164	163	164	168	170	179	189	183
89	Pate and delicatessen type sausage	g	17	16	15	16	17	18	17	17	19	18	17
93	Meat pastes and spreads	g	1	1	1	1	1	1	1	1	1	0	1
95	Takeaway meats	g	52	49	49	47	50	47	47	53	47	46	49
100123	**Fish**	g	**151**	**147**	**144**	**146**	**144**	**146**	**144**	**139**	**139**	**146**	**148**
102	White fish, fresh, chilled or frozen	g	20	17	21	19	19	18	18	14	15	15	16
106	Herrings and other blue fish, fresh, chilled or frozen	g	5	4	4	4	6	4	4	3	3	3	3
107	Salmon, fresh, chilled or frozen	g	12	12	12	13	13	15	14	15	12	15	13
10801	Blue fish, dried or salted or smoked	g	6	7	6	7	7	7	7	8	7	7	6
11401	White fish, dried, salted or smoked	g	3	3	3	3	3	3	3	5	9	4	3
117	Shellfish	g	13	11	10	10	10	10	10	8	8	10	11
118	Takeaway fish	g	8	8	8	8	7	8	8	7	7	7	6
119	Salmon, tinned	g	3	3	2	2	3	2	2	2	2	2	2
120	Other tinned or bottled fish	g	25	25	25	23	24	24	25	24	23	24	27
121	Ready meals and other fish products - frozen or not frozen	g	51	54	52	54	49	52	51	50	54	57	58
123	Takeaway fish meals and fish products	g	2	3	3	3	3	3	3	2	3	3	3
129129	**Eggs**	no.	**2**	**2**	**2**	**2**	**2**	**2**	**2**	**2**	**2**	**2**	**2**
135148	**Fats**	g	**183**	**170**	**178**	**171**	**158**	**162**	**162**	**139**	**158**	**161**	**158**
135	Butter	g	40	40	41	42	40	42	44	35	35	33	33
138	Margarine	g	23	20	24	23	18	17	18	25	31	33	31
139	Lard, cooking fat	g	3	2	2	2	2	2	2	1	1	1	2
143	Vegetable and salad oils	ml	60	54	61	58	52	59	58	42	53	60	60
148	All other fats	g	57	53	50	45	46	41	41	35	37	33	33

24.15 Quantity of food and drink purchased for UK households
UK

Units: average per person per week

Code		Units	2010	2011	2012	2013	2014	2015	2015/16	2016/17	2017/18	2018/19	2019/20
150154	**Sugar and preserves**	g	**126**	**126**	**124**	**123**	**109**	**106**	**107**	**107**	**99**	**93**	**87**
150	Sugar	g	90	93	91	91	78	75	75	73	68	63	56
151	Jams and fruit curds	g	16	15	14	14	14	14	14	7	13	13	12
152	Marmalade	g	9	8	8	7	6	6	7	7	7	6	6
153	Syrup, treacle	g	4	4	4	4	3	4	3	4	4	3	4
154	Honey	g	7	6	6	7	7	7	8	9	8	8	8
cat701	**Fresh and processed potatoes**	g	**742**	**746**	**724**	**682**	**671**	**675**	**675**	**634**	**669**	**620**	**612**
155	Fresh potatoes	g	501	496	478	439	431	429	428	396	421	379	355
cat710	Processed potatoes	g	242	250	246	242	240	246	247	239	248	241	256
cat811	**Fresh and processed fruit and vegetables, excluding potatoes**	g	**2,240**	**2,240**	**2,193**	**2,216**	**2,176**	**2,195**	**2,209**	**2,267**	**2,230**	**2,245**	**2,227**
cat720	**Fresh and processed vegetables, excluding potatoes**	g	**1,107**	**1,090**	**1,086**	**1,102**	**1,080**	**1,103**	**1,117**	**1,137**	**1,134**	**1,139**	**1,147**
162171	Fresh green vegetables	g	192	189	183	179	181	181	185	180	182	173	181
172183	Other fresh vegetables	g	565	550	551	569	564	575	587	609	583	578	595
cat702	Processed vegetables excluding processed potatoes	g	350	351	352	354	334	346	345	347	369	389	372
cat810	**Fresh and processed fruit**	g	**1,133**	**1,150**	**1,107**	**1,114**	**1,096**	**1,093**	**1,092**	**1,130**	**1,097**	**1,106**	**1,080**
210231	Fresh fruit	g	755	764	744	744	766	773	780	814	784	787	767
233248	Processed fruit and fruit products	g	378	385	362	370	330	319	313	316	312	319	312
251263	**Bread**	g	**634**	**621**	**615**	**607**	**555**	**543**	**542**	**532**	**527**	**521**	**524**
cat850	White bread	g	281	259	266	247	222	221	222	199	202	198	194
cat851	Brown and wholemeal bread	g	164	175	158	156	150	143	143	150	136	137	133
264264	**Flour**	g	**58**	**71**	**73**	**57**	**52**	**61**	**63**	**55**	**75**	**48**	**54**
267270	**Cakes, buns and pastries**	g	**153**	**151**	**149**	**150**	**147**	**155**	**154**	**150**	**159**	**151**	**163**
271277	**Biscuits and crispbreads**	g	**162**	**164**	**160**	**165**	**162**	**164**	**166**	**169**	**160**	**159**	**173**
281301	**Other cereals and cereal products**	g	**556**	**547**	**542**	**549**	**560**	**566**	**565**	**562**	**582**	**589**	**607**
304313	**Beverages**	g	**56**	**53**	**53**	**52**	**52**	**53**	**53**	**54**	**49**	**52**	**56**
304	Tea	g	28	27	26	25	25	24	24	25	20	20	22
307	Coffee beans and ground coffee	g	5	4	6	5	8	8	8	9	10	11	13
308	Instant coffee	g	15	14	13	14	12	13	14	12	13	13	12
309	Coffee essences	ml	0	0	0	0	0	1	0	1	1	0	0
310	Tea and coffee from takeaway	ml	0	0	0	1	1	1	1	1	1	1	1
312	Cocoa and chocolate drinks	g	5	5	5	5	5	5	5	5	3	4	6
313	Malt drinks and chocolate versions of malted drinks	g	3	2	2	2	2	1	2	1	1	2	1
314339	**Other food and drink**	g	**706**	**726**	**776**	**778**	**787**	**815**	**829**	**855**	**884**	**1,000**	**934**
314	Mineral or spring waters	ml	245	256	305	306	341	371	379	402	439	504	426
315	Baby foods	g	8	10	10	10	10	9	9	6	7	9	7
318	Soups - canned or cartons	g	76	75	85	79	70	71	73	63	74	65	71
319	Soups - dehydrated or powdered	g	4	4	4	4	3	3	3	3	3	3	3
320	Soups - from takeaway	g	1	0	0	0	0	0	0	1	1	0	0
321	Other takeaway food brought home	g	0	0	0	0	0	0	0	0	0	0	50
322	Meals on wheels - items not specified	g	0	0	0	0	0	0	0	0	0	0	1
323	Spreads and dressings	g	42	44	45	47	44	45	47	45	43	51	41
327	Pickles and sauces	g	131	131	129	130	128	125	123	129	118	128	118
328	Stock cubes and meat and yeast extracts	g	6	6	5	5	5	6	6	5	4	5	5
329	Jelly squares or crystals	g	5	4	4	5	5	5	5	6	5	5	5
332	Ice cream tub or block	ml	97	106	103	99	88	84	86	90	84	104	52

24.15 Quantity of food and drink purchased for UK households
UK

Code		Units	Units: average per person per week										
			2010	2011	2012	2013	2014	2015	2015/16	2016/17	2017/18	2018/19	2019/20
333	Ice cream products including takeaways	ml	74	74	70	77	77	79	81	89	87	110	47
334	Salt	g	11	9	9	8	7	9	8	8	10	7	0
339	Soya and novel protein foods	g	7	7	7	6	8	8	8	9	9	9	0
303	**Soft drinks**	ml	**1,718**	**1,630**	**1,633**	**1,664**	**1,546**	**1,531**	**1,522**	**1,608**	**1,508**	**1,642**	**1,658**
350355	**Confectionery**	g	**131**	**134**	**126**	**128**	**130**	**132**	**134**	**130**	**137**	**136**	**144**
350	Chocolate bars - solid	g	32	31	33	35	36	35	35	37	40	38	43
351	Chocolate bars - filled	g	57	58	50	50	51	52	53	49	52	50	54
352	Chewing gum	g	2	2	2	1	1	1	1	2	1	2	2
353	Mints and boiled sweets	g	37	38	38	38	38	40	40	39	40	42	41
354	Fudges, toffees, caramels	g	4	3	4	3	3	4	5	4	3	4	3
355	Takeaway confectionery	g	0	0	0	0	0	0	0	0	0	0	0
380389	**Alcoholic drinks**	ml	**762**	**728**	**700**	**694**	**675**	**678**	**675**	**712**	**728**	**712**	**728**
381	Beers	ml	103	88	86	76	74	80	83	99	83	89	97
382	Lagers and continental beers	ml	274	251	240	254	249	240	244	265	252	246	261
383	Ciders and perry	ml	79	87	80	87	78	78	72	65	74	85	74
384	Wine and champagne	ml	244	246	237	226	217	226	222	229	257	239	235
385	Spirits with mixer	ml	1	1	1	1	2	2	2	2	3	4	5
386	Fortified wines	ml	9	10	8	8	8	7	8	7	7	5	7
387	Spirits	ml	34	31	34	30	33	31	31	33	37	36	39
388	Liqueurs and cocktails	ml	8	6	6	6	8	9	9	8	9	7	7
389	Alcopops	ml	9	9	8	5	6	5	5	4	5	2	2

Source: Adjusted National Food Survey data 1974 to 2000, Expenditure and Food Survey 2001-02 to 2007 and Living Costs and Food Survey 2008 onwards
Contact: Food & Trade Statistics Branch - Tel 020 8026 3006 Email: familyfood@defra.gov.uk

Family Food Survey 2019/20: Notes

It is a widely recognised characteristic of self reported diary surveys such as Family Food that survey respondents tend to under report their purchases (and any derived nutrient intakes based on purchased quantities are also likely to be underestimates). Empirical comparisons of sales and duty data for alcohol in particular suggest that reported alcohol consumption could be 40-60 per cent lower than the reality. For other food and drink, reporting is likely to be closer to actual purchases, but underreporting is likely to feature and some food types may be underreported to a greater extent than others.

Although such surveys are completely confidential, respondents may under report for a range of reasons, from self consciousness to simply forgetting to record purchases. 'Top up' and eating out purchases are probably more likely to be missed than the main household shop. There is no evidence to say whether levels of underreporting have changed over time but it is plausible that changes in household shopping and eating patterns may have contributed to increased underreporting.

Users should bear this issue in mind, when considering trends in estimated intakes and the values for individual years. For example the downward trend in energy intake estimates can appear counter-intuitive at face value given other evidence on the prevalence of obesity. Factors affecting obesity and other health issues are complex. Family Food trends are broadly consistent with other sources, such as

The National Diet and Nutrition Survey: https://www.gov.uk/government/collections/national-diet-and-nutrition-survey which also show reported energy intake in decline, although NDNS intakes are also known to be underreported.

Items of food and drink are defined as either household or eating out.

'Household' covers all food that is brought into the household.
'Eating out' covers all food that never enters the household.
Takeaway purchases for consumption within the home are classed as household purchases.

Sources:

This index of sources gives the titles of official publications or other sources containing statistics allied to those in the tables of this Annual Abstract. These publications provide more detailed analyses than are shown in the Annual Abstract. This index includes publications to which reference should be made for short–term (monthly or quarterly) series.

Table number	Government department or other organisation

Chapter 14 Defence

14.1	Defence Economics (Defence Expenditure Analysis) and Defence Resources, Ministry of Defence
14.2	Defence Statistics (Tri-Service), Ministry of Defence
14.3a	Navy Command, Ministry of Defence
14.3b	Army Org Branch, Ministry of Defence
14.3c	Navy Command; Army Org Branch; Air Command
14.4	Defence Statistics (Tri-Service), Ministry of Defence
14.5	Defence Statistics (Tri-Service), Ministry of Defence
14.6a	Defence Statistics (Tri-Service), Ministry of Defence
14.6b	Defence Statistics (Civilian), Ministry of Defence
14.6c	Defence Statistics (Civilian), Ministry of Defence
14.7a	MOD Defence Infrastructure Organisation, Ministry of Defence
14.7b	MOD Defence Infrastructure Organisation, Ministry of Defence
14.8a	Defence Statistics (Tri-Service), Ministry of Defence
14.8b	Defence Statistics (Tri-Service), Ministry of Defence
14.9a	Defence Statistics (Health), Ministry of Defence
14.9b	Defence Statistics (Health), Ministry of Defence
14.10	Joint Medical Group, Ministry of Defence

Chapter 15 Population

15.1	Office for National Statistics
15.2a	Office for National Statistics
15.2b	Office for National Statistics
15.2c	Office for National Statistics
15.2d	Office for National Statistics
15.3a	Office for National Statistics
15.3b	Office for National Statistics
15.3c	Office for National Statistics
15.3d	Office for National Statistics
15.3e	Office for National Statistics
15.3f	Office for National Statistics
15.3g	Office for National Statistics
15.3h	Office for National Statistics
15.4	Labour Force Survey, Office for National Statistics
15.5	Office for National Statistics
15.6	Annual Population Survey, Office for National Statistics
15.7	ONS; Home Office; Central Statistics Office (CSO) Ireland; Northern Ireland Statistics and Research Agency (NISRA)
15.8	ONS; Home Office; Central Statistics Office (CSO) Ireland; Northern Ireland Statistics and Research Agency (NISRA)
15.9	Immigration Statistics, Home Office
15.10	Immigration Statistics, Home Office
15.11	Office for National Statistics
15.12	Office for National Statistics
15.13	Office for National Statistics
15.14	Office for National Statistics (ONS), National Records of Scotland, Northern Ireland Statistics and Research Agency
15.15	Office for National Statistics
15.16	ISD Scotland; Department of Health
15.17	Office for National Statistics
15.18	Office for National Statistics
15.19	Office for National Statistics
15.20ai	Children Looked After in England (including adoption), Department for Education
15.20aii	Looked After Children Census, Welsh Government
15.20b	NRS-Scotland
15.20c	Annual Reports of the Registrar General for Northern Ireland

Chapter 16 Health

16.1a	NHS Hospital & Community Health Service (HCHS) monthly workforce statistics, NHS Digital
16.1b	Workforce Services, NHS Wales Shared Services Partnership, Welsh Government
16.1c	Scottish Workforce Information Standard System (SWISS)
16.1d	Human Resource, Payroll, Travel & Subsistence System (HRPTS); Department of Health, Social Services and Public Safety
16.2	ISD Scotland, Scottish Workforce Information Standard System (SWISS); NHS National Services Scotland
16.3	Business Services Organisation (BSO) Northern Ireland; Dept of Health Northern Ireland
16.4	NHS Digital, NHS Hospital & Community Health Service (HCHS) workforce statistics
16.5	Health Statistics and Analysis Unit, Welsh Government, NHS Dental Services, Office for National Statistics, NHS Digital
16.6	Office for National Statistics
16.7a	Public Health England
16.7b	Health Protection Scotland (HPS)
16.7c	Public Health Agency, Northern Ireland
16.8a	Health and Safety Executive (HSE)
16.8b	The Health and Occupation Research network (THOR), Centre for Occupational and Environmental Health, University of Manchester.
16.8c	Health and Safety Executive (HSE)
16.8d	The Health and Occupation Research network (THOR), Centre for Occupational and Environmental Health, University of Manchester.
16.8e	The Health and Occupation Research network (THOR), Centre for Occupational and Environmental Health, University of Manchester.
16.9	Office for National Statistics; Health and Safety Executive; GRO-Scotland
16.10a	RIDDOR - Reporting of Injuries, Diseases and Dangerous Occurrences Regulations, Health and Safety Executive (HSE)
16.10b	RIDDOR - Reporting of Injuries, Diseases and Dangerous Occurrences Regulations, Health and Safety Executive (HSE)

Chapter 17 Prices

17.1	Office for National Statistics
17.2	Office for National Statistics; Department for Communities and Local Government
17.3	Office for National Statistics
17.4	Office for National Statistics
17.5	Office for National Statistics
17.6	Department for Environment, Food and Rural Affairs
17.7	Department for Environment, Food and Rural Affairs
17.8	Office for National Statistics

Chapter 18 Production

18.1	Annual Business Survey (ABS), Office for National Statistics
18.2	PRODCOM , Office for National Statistics
18.3	Office for National Statistics
18.4	Department for Business, Energy & Industrial Strategy
18.5	Department for Business, Energy & Industrial Strategy
18.6	Department for Business, Energy & Industrial Strategy
18.7	Department for Business, Energy & Industrial Strategy
18.8	Department for Business, Energy & Industrial Strategy
18.9	Department for Business, Energy & Industrial Strategy
18.10	Department for Business, Energy & Industrial Strategy
18.11	Department for Business, Energy & Industrial Strategy
18.12	Department for Business, Energy & Industrial Strategy
18.13	Department for Business, Energy & Industrial Strategy; HM Revenue and Customs
18.14	United Kingdom Minerals Yearbook, British Geological Survey
18.15	United Kingdom Minerals Yearbook, British Geological Survey
18.16	International Steel Statistics Bureau
18.17	British Survey of Fertiliser Practice (Defra)
18.18a	Mineral Products Association; Office for National Statistics; Department of Business, Energy & Industrial Strategy; Department for Economy (Northern Ireland); Crown Estate Commissioners; and company data
18.18b	Department of the Economy (Northern Ireland); Department of Economic Development (Isle of Man); Company data (Guernsey and Jersey)
18.19a	Department for Business, Energy & Industrial Strategy
18.19b	Department for Business, Energy & Industrial Strategy
18.19c	Department for Business, Energy & Industrial Strategy
18.19d	Department for Business, Energy & Industrial Strategy
18.19e	Department for Business, Energy & Industrial Strategy
18.19f	Department for Business, Energy & Industrial Strategy
18.20	Office for National Statistics
18.21	Office for National Statistics
18.22	Office for National Statistics
18.23	Office for National Statistics
18.24	Her Majesty's Revenue and Customs
18.25	Her Majesty's Revenue and Customs

Table number	Government department or other organisation

Chapter 19 National Accounts

19.1	Blue Book, Office for National Statistics
19.2	Blue Book, Office for National Statistics
19.3	Blue Book, Office for National Statistics
19.4	Blue Book, Office for National Statistics
19.5	Blue Book, Office for National Statistics
19.6	Blue Book, Office for National Statistics
19.7	Blue Book, Office for National Statistics
19.8	Blue Book, Office for National Statistics
19.9	Blue Book, Office for National Statistics
19.10	Blue Book, Office for National Statistics
19.11	Blue Book, Office for National Statistics
19.12	Blue Book, Office for National Statistics
19.13	Blue Book, Office for National Statistics
19.14	Blue Book, Office for National Statistics
19.15	Blue Book, Office for National Statistics
19.16	Blue Book, Office for National Statistics
19.17	Blue Book, Office for National Statistics
19.18	Office for National Statistics
19.19	Blue Book, Office for National Statistics
19.20	Blue Book, Office for National Statistics
19.21	Blue Book, Office for National Statistics
19.22	Blue Book, Office for National Statistics

Chapter 20 Education

20.1	Department for Education; Welsh Government; Scottish Government; Northern Ireland Department of Education
20.2	Department for Education; Welsh Government; Scottish Government; Northern Ireland Department of Education
20.3	Department for Education; Welsh Government; Scottish Government; Northern Ireland Department of Education
20.4	School Census and School Level Annual School Census, Department for Education
20.5	Department for Education; Welsh Government; Scottish Government; Northern Ireland Department of Education
20.6	Higher Education Statistics Agency
20.7	Higher Education Statistics Agency
20.8	Department for Education; Welsh Government; Scottish Funding Council; Northern Ireland Department for the Economy
20.9	Department for Education; Welsh Government; Scottish Funding Council; Northern Ireland Department for the Economy
20.10	Department for Education; Welsh Government; Scottish Government; Northern Ireland Department of Education

Chapter 21 Crime and Justice

21.1a	Home Office
21.1b	Home Office
21.1c	The Police Service of Northern Ireland
21.1d	Police Scotland
21.2	World Prison Brief, Institute for Crime & Justice Policy Research
21.3	Police Recorded Crime, Home Office
21.4	Ministry of Justice Court Proceedings Database
21.5	Ministry of Justice Court Proceedings Database
21.6a	Ministry of Justice Court Proceedings Database
21.6b	Ministry of Justice Court Proceedings Database
21.7a	Ministry of Justice Court Proceedings Database
21.7b	Ministry of Justice Court Proceedings Database
21.7c	Ministry of Justice Court Proceedings Database
21.8	Ministry of Justice Court Proceedings Database
21.9a	Ministry of Justice Court Proceedings Database
21.9b	Ministry of Justice Court Proceedings Database
21.10	Ministry of Justice
21.11	Ministry of Justice
21.12	Recorded Crime in Scotland, Scottish Government
21.13	Criminal Proceedings in Scotland, Scottish Government
21.14	Criminal Proceedings in Scotland, Scottish Government
21.15	Criminal Proceedings in Scotland, Scottish Government
21.16	Criminal Proceedings in Scotland, Scottish Government
21.17	Justice Analytical Services Database, Scottish Government
21.18	Annual Report and Accounts, Scottish Prison Service
21.19	Police Service Northern Ireland
21.20	Northern Ireland Prison Population

Chapter 22 Transport

22.1	National Travel Survey, Department for Transport
22.2	Department for Transport; Office of Rail Regulation / Eurostat
22.3	Department for Transport; Office of Rail Regulation; Civil Aviation Authority
22.4	National Road Traffic Survey, Department for Transport
22.5	Department for Transport
22.6	National Road Traffic Survey, Department for Transport
22.7	Department for Transport; Driver and Vehicle Licensing Agency
22.8	Department for Transport; Driver and Vehicle Licensing Agency
22.9a	Driver & Vehicle Standards Agency DVSA; Department for Transport
22.9b	Driver & Vehicle Standards Agency DVSA; Department for Transport
22.9c	Driver & Vehicle Standards Agency DVSA; Department for Transport
22.9d	Driver & Vehicle Standards Agency DVSA; Department for Transport
22.9e	Driver & Vehicle Standards Agency DVSA; Department for Transport
22.10	National Travel Survey, Department for Transport
22.11a	National Travel Survey, Department for Transport
22.11b	National Travel Survey, Department for Transport
22.12	Department for Transport
22.13	Department for Transport
22.14	DfT Public Service Vehicle Survey, Transport for London
22.15	DfT Fares Survey; Office for National Statistics
22.16	National Travel Survey, Department for Transport
22.17a	Continuing Survey of Road Goods Transport (GB), Department for Transport
22.17b	Continuing Survey of Road Goods Transport (GB), Department for Transport
22.17c	Continuing Survey of Road Goods Transport (GB), Department for Transport
22.18a	Continuing Survey of Road Goods Transport (GB), Department for Transport
22.18b	Continuing Survey of Road Goods Transport (GB), Department for Transport
22.19a	Office of Rail and Road; LENNON Database and train operating companies; DfT Light Rail and Tram Survey
22.19b	Office of Rail and Road; LENNON Database and train operating companies; DfT Light Rail and Tram Survey
22.19c	Office of Rail and Road; LENNON Database and train operating companies; DfT Light Rail and Tram Survey
22.19d	Network Rail; DfT Light Rail and Tram Survey
22.19e	DfT Light Rail and Tram Survey
22.19f	Transport for London
22.19g	DfT Light Rail and Tram Survey
22.20a	Network Rail
22.20b	Freight operating companies
22.21	Translink, Department for Regional Development, Northern Ireland
22.22	Translink, Department for Regional Development, Northern Ireland
22.23	Civil Aviation Authority
22.24a	Civil Aviation Authority
22.24b	Civil Aviation Authority
22.25	Civil Aviation Authority
22.26a	Civil Aviation Authority
22.26b	Civil Aviation Authority
22.26c	Civil Aviation Authority
22.26d	Civil Aviation Authority
22.27a	DfT Search and Rescue Helicopter Statistics
22.27b	DfT Search and Rescue Helicopter Statistics
22.27c	DfT Search and Rescue Helicopter Statistics

Chapter 23 Government Finance

23.1	Office for National Statistics
23.2	Office for National Statistics
23.3	Office for National Statistics
23.4a	Office for National Statistics
23.4b	Office for National Statistics
23.5	HM Treasury
23.6a	Blue Book, Office for National Statistics
23.6b	Blue Book, Office for National Statistics
23.7	Blue Book, Office for National Statistics
23.8	Office for National Statistics
23.9	HM Revenue & Customs
23.10	HM Revenue & Customs
23.11	HM Revenue & Customs
23.12	Valuation Office Agency
23.13	Local Authority Revenue Expenditure and Financing, Ministry of Housing, Communities & Local Government Scottish Government; Welsh Government
23.14	Department for Communities and Local Government; Welsh Government
23.15	Ministry of Housing, Communities & Local Government
23.16a	Ministry of Housing, Communities & Local Government
23.16b	Ministry of Housing, Communities & Local Government
23.17	Local Authority Revenue and capital outturn expenditure, Welsh Government
23.18	Scottish Government, Local Financial Returns (LFR)
23.19a	Scottish Government Local Financial Returns (LFR)